THE FIRST AMENDMENT

EDITORIAL ADVISORS

Rachel E. Barkow
Segal Family Professor of Regulatory Law and Policy
Faculty Director, Center on the Administration of Criminal Law
New York University School of Law

Erwin Chemerinsky
Dean and Jesse H. Choper Distinguished Professor of Law
University of California, Berkeley School of Law

Richard A. Epstein
Laurence A. Tisch Professor of Law
New York University School of Law
Peter and Kirsten Bedford Senior Fellow
The Hoover Institution
Senior Lecturer in Law
The University of Chicago

Ronald J. Gilson
Charles J. Meyers Professor of Law and Business
Stanford University
Marc and Eva Stern Professor of Law and Business
Columbia Law School

James E. Krier
Earl Warren DeLano Professor of Law Emeritus
The University of Michigan Law School

Tracey L. Meares
Walton Hale Hamilton Professor of Law
Director, The Justice Collaboratory
Yale Law School

Richard K. Neumann, Jr.
Alexander Bickel Professor of Law
Maurice A. Deane School of Law at Hofstra University

Robert H. Sitkoff
John L. Gray Professor of Law
Harvard Law School

David Alan Sklansky
Stanley Morrison Professor of Law
Faculty Co-Director, Stanford Criminal Justice Center
Stanford Law School

ASPEN CASEBOOK SERIES

THE FIRST AMENDMENT

Second Edition

Erwin Chemerinsky
Dean and Jesse H. Choper Distinguished Professor of Law
University of California, Berkeley School of Law

Copyright © 2021 Erwin Chemerinsky.

No part of this publication may be reproduced or transmitted in any form or by any means, electronic or mechanical, including photocopy, recording, or utilized by any information storage or retrieval system, without written permission from the publisher. For information about permissions or to request permissions online, visit us at www.AspenPublishing.com.

To contact Customer Service, e-mail customer.service@aspenpublishing.com, call 1-800-950-5259, or mail correspondence to:

> Aspen Publishing
> Attn: Order Department
> PO Box 990
> Frederick, MD 21705

Printed in the United States of America.

3 4 5 6 7 8 9 0

ISBN 978-1-5438-2684-5

Library of Congress Cataloging-in-Publication Data

Names: Chemerinsky, Erwin, author.
Title: The First Amendment / Erwin Chemerinsky, Dean and Jesse H. Choper, Distinguished Professor of Law, University of California, Berkeley School of Law.
Description: Second edition. | Frederick, MD: Aspen Publishing, 2021. | Series: Aspen casebook series | Includes index. | Summary: "Casebook covering the First Amendment for use by law students enrolled in constitutional law courses"—Provided by publisher.
Identifiers: LCCN 2020048237 (print) | LCCN 2020048238 (ebook) | ISBN 9781543826845 (hardcover) | ISBN 9781543826852 (ebook)
Subjects: LCSH: United States. Constitution. 1st Amendment. | Freedom of speech—United States. | Freedom of expression—United States. | Freedom of association—United States. | Freedom of the press—United States. | Freedom of religion—United States. | LCGFT: Casebooks (Law)
Classification: LCC KF4770.C44 2021 (print) | LCC KF4770 (ebook) | DDC 342.7308/5—dc23
LC record available at https://lccn.loc.gov/2020048237
LC ebook record available at https://lccn.loc.gov/2020048238

About Aspen Publishing

Aspen Publishing is a leading provider of educational content and digital learning solutions to law schools in the U.S. and around the world. Aspen provides best-in-class solutions for legal education through authoritative textbooks, written by renowned authors, and breakthrough products such as Connected eBooks, Connected Quizzing, and PracticePerfect.

The Aspen Casebook Series (famously known among law faculty and students as the "red and black" casebooks) encompasses hundreds of highly regarded textbooks in more than eighty disciplines, from large enrollment courses, such as Torts and Contracts to emerging electives such as Sustainability and the Law of Policing. Study aids such as the *Examples & Explanations* and the *Emanuel Law Outlines* series, both highly popular collections, help law students master complex subject matter.

Major products, programs, and initiatives include:

- **Connected eBooks** are enhanced digital textbooks and study aids that come with a suite of online content and learning tools designed to maximize student success. Designed in collaboration with hundreds of faculty and students, the Connected eBook is a significant leap forward in the legal education learning tools available to students.

- **Connected Quizzing** is an easy-to-use formative assessment tool that tests law students' understanding and provides timely feedback to improve learning outcomes. Delivered through CasebookConnect.com, the learning platform already used by students to access their Aspen casebooks, Connected Quizzing is simple to implement and integrates seamlessly with law school course curricula.

- **PracticePerfect** is a visually engaging, interactive study aid to explain commonly encountered legal doctrines through easy-to-understand animated videos, illustrative examples, and numerous practice questions. Developed by a team of experts, PracticePerfect is the ideal study companion for today's law students.

- The **Aspen Learning Library** enables law schools to provide their students with access to the most popular study aids on the market across all of their courses. Available through an annual subscription, the online library consists of study aids in e-book, audio, and video formats with full text search, note-taking, and highlighting capabilities.

- Aspen's **Digital Bookshelf** is an institutional-level online education bookshelf, consolidating everything students and professors need to ensure success. This program ensures that every student has access to affordable course materials from day one.

- **Leading Edge** is a community centered on thinking differently about legal education and putting those thoughts into actionable strategies. At the core of the program is the Leading Edge Conference, an annual gathering of legal education thought leaders looking to pool ideas and identify promising directions of exploration.

This book is dedicated to my students—
past, present, and future.

SUMMARY OF CONTENTS

Contents		xi
Preface		xxi
The First Amendment		xxiii
The Constitution of the United States		xxv
Part I.	First Amendment: Freedom of Expression	1
Chapter 1.	Introduction to Freedom of Speech	3
Chapter 2.	Free Speech Methodology	13
Chapter 3.	Types of Unprotected and Less Protected Speech	139
Chapter 4.	What Places are Available for Speech?	365
Chapter 5.	Freedom of Association	441
Chapter 6.	Freedom of the Press	471
Part II.	The First Amendment: Religion	501
Chapter 7.	Introduction to the Religion Clauses	503
Chapter 8.	The Free Exercise Clause	515
Chapter 9.	The Establishment Clause	579
Table of Cases		687
Index		695

CONTENTS

Preface	xxi
The First Amendment	xxiii
The Constitution of the United States	xxv

PART I

FIRST AMENDMENT: FREEDOM OF EXPRESSION — 1

CHAPTER 1

INTRODUCTION TO FREEDOM OF SPEECH — 3

A.	Historical Background	3
B.	Why Should Freedom of Speech Be a Fundamental Right?	5
	1. Self-Governance	6
	2. Discovering Truth	7
	3. Advancing Autonomy	9
	4. Promoting Tolerance	10
	5. Conclusion	10
C.	The Issues in Free Expression Analysis	11

CHAPTER 2

FREE SPEECH METHODOLOGY — 13

A.	The Distinction Between Content-Based and Content-Neutral Laws	13
	1. The Importance of the Distinction	14
	Reed v. Town of Gilbert	14
	2. How Is It Determined Whether a Law Is Content-Based?	22
	The Requirement for Viewpoint Neutrality	22
	Matal v. Tam	22
	Subject-Matter Restrictions	29
	Williams-Yulee v. Florida Bar	30
	Content-Neutral Laws	38
	3. Problems in Applying the Distinction Between Content-Based and Content-Neutral Laws	38
	a. Permissible Purposes and Content-Neutrality	39
	City of Renton v. Playtime Theatres, Inc.	39

		b.	When the Government Must Make Content-Based Choices	43
			National Endowment for the Arts v. Finley	*43*
		c.	Government Speech	47
			Pleasant Grove City, Utah v. Summum	*47*
			Walker v. Texas Division, Sons of Confederate Veterans	*51*
B.	Vagueness and Overbreadth			57
	1.	Vagueness		57
			Coates v. City of Cincinnati	*58*
	2.	Overbreadth		59
			Schad v. Borough of Mount Ephraim	*59*
	3.	Relationship Between Vagueness and Overbreadth		64
			Board of Airport Commissioners of the City of Los Angeles v. Jews for Jesus, Inc.	*64*
C.	Prior Restraints			65
	1.	What Is a Prior Restraint?		65
	2.	Are Prior Restraints Really So Bad?		66
	3.	Types of Prior Restraints		68
		a.	Court Orders as a Prior Restraint	68
			Near v. State of Minnesota ex rel. Olson	*68*
			i. Court Orders to Protect National Security	71
			New York Times Co. v. United States	*71*
			ii. Court Orders to Protect Fair Trials	78
			Nebraska Press Association v. Stuart	*78*
			iii. Court Orders Seizing the Assets of Businesses Convicted of Obscenity Violations	83
			Alexander v. United States	*83*
		b.	Licensing as a Prior Restraint	85
			Lovell v. City of Griffin, Ga.	*85*
			Watchtower Bible & Tract Society of New York, Inc. v. Village of Stratton	*87*
			i. Important Reason for Licensing	92
			ii. Clear Standards Leaving Almost No Discretion to the Government	92
			City of Lakewood v. Plain Dealer Publishing Co.	*92*
			iii. Procedural Safeguards	94
D.	What Is an Infringement of Freedom of Speech?			95
	1.	Civil Liability and Denial of Compensation for Speech		96
	2.	Prohibitions on Compensation		97
			United States v. National Treasury Employees Union	*97*
	3.	Compelled Speech		99
			West Virginia State Board of Education v. Barnette	*99*
			National Federation of Family and Life Advocates v. Becerra	*101*
			Rumsfeld v. Forum for Academic & Institutional Rights, Inc.	*113*
			McIntyre v. Ohio Elections Commission	*118*

	4.	Unconstitutional Conditions		123
		Speiser v. Randall		123
		Rust v. Sullivan		*125*
		Legal Services Corp. v. Velazquez		*129*
	5.	Government Pressures		136

CHAPTER 3

TYPES OF UNPROTECTED AND LESS PROTECTED SPEECH — 139

A.	Incitement of Illegal Activity			140
	1.	The "Clear and Present Danger" Test		141
			Schenck v. United States	*142*
			Frohwerk v. United States	*143*
			Debs v. United States	*144*
			Abrams v. United States	*145*
	2.	The Reasonableness Approach		148
			Gitlow v. New York	*148*
			Whitney v. California	*151*
	3.	The Risk Formula Approach		155
			Dennis v. United States	*155*
	4.	The *Brandenburg* Test		160
			Brandenburg v. Ohio	*161*
			Holder v. Humanitarian Law Project	*163*
B.	Fighting Words, the Hostile Audience, and the Problem of Racist Speech			172
	1.	Fighting Words		173
			Chaplinsky v. New Hampshire	*173*
		a.	Narrowing the Fighting Words Doctrine	175
		b.	Fighting Words Laws Invalidated as Vague and Overbroad	176
			Gooding v. Wilson	*176*
		c.	Narrow Fighting Words Laws as Content-Based Restrictions	178
			R.A.V. v. City of St. Paul, Minnesota	*178*
	2.	The Hostile Audience Cases		184
	3.	The Problem of Racist Speech		187
			Virginia v. Black	*189*
C.	Sexually Oriented Speech			196
	1.	Obscenity		197
		a.	Supreme Court Decisions Finding Obscenity Unprotected	197
			Roth v. United States	*197*
			Paris Adult Theatre I v. Slaton	*199*
			Miller v. California	*202*

		b.	Should Obscenity Be a Category of Unprotected Speech?	204
		c.	Should There Be a New Exception for Pornography?	206
	2.	Child Pornography		207
			New York v. Ferber	*207*
	3.	Protected but Low-Value Sexual Speech		211
		a.	Zoning Ordinances	212
			Young v. American Mini Theatres, Inc.	*212*
		b.	Nude Dancing	215
			City of Erie v. Pap's A.M.	*216*
		c.	Should There Be Such a Category as Low-Value Sexual Speech?	220
	4.	Government Techniques for Controlling Obscenity and Child Pornography	221
			Stanley v. Georgia	*221*
			Osborne v. Ohio	*222*
	5.	Profanity and "Indecent" Speech	223
			Cohen v. California	*223*
		a.	The Broadcast Media	227
			Federal Communications Commission v. Pacifica Foundation	*227*
		b.	Telephones	230
		c.	The Internet	230
			Reno v. American Civil Liberties Union	*231*
		d.	Cable Television	234
D.	A New Exception for Violent Speech?		236
			United States v. Stevens	*237*
			Brown v. Entertainment Merchants Association	*244*
E.	Commercial Speech		251
	1.	Constitutional Protection for Commercial Speech	251
			Virginia State Board of Pharmacy v. Virginia Citizens Consumer Council, Inc.	*252*
			Overview of the Section	257
	2.	What Is Commercial Speech?	258
			Bolger v. Youngs Drug Products Corp.	*258*
			Sorrell v. IMS Health Inc.	*259*
	3.	The Test for Evaluating Regulation of Commercial Speech	266
			Central Hudson Gas & Electric Corp. v. Public Service Commission of New York	*266*
			Is Least Restrictive Alternative Analysis Applicable?	269
	4.	Advertising of Illegal Activities	271
	5.	False and Deceptive Advertising	272
	6.	Advertising That Inherently Risks Deception	272
			Restrictions on Trade Names	272
			Attorney Solicitation of Prospective Clients	273
			Solicitation by Accountants	274

	7. Regulating Commercial Speech to Achieve Other Goals		275
		a. "For Sale" Signs on Houses	276
		b. Alcohol Products	276
		44 Liquormart, Inc. v. Rhode Island	*276*
		c. Tobacco Products	278
		Lorillard Tobacco Co. v. Reilly	*278*
		d. Gambling	284
		e. Advertising by Lawyers and Other Professionals	285
F.	Reputation, Privacy, Publicity, and the First Amendment: Torts and the First Amendment		287
	1. Defamation		288
		a. Public Officials as Defamation Plaintiffs	288
		New York Times Co. v. Sullivan	*288*
		b. Public Figures as Plaintiffs	294
		Gertz v. Welch	*295*
		c. Private Figures, Matters of Public Concern	300
		d. Private Figures, Matters Not of Public Concern	301
		e. Conclusion	301
	2. Intentional Infliction of Emotional Distress		302
		Hustler Magazine v. Falwell	*302*
		Snyder v. Phelps	*304*
	3. Public Disclosure of Private Facts		309
		Cox Broadcasting Corp. v. Cohn	*309*
		Information from Nongovernment Sources	312
	4. Right of Publicity		313
G.	Conduct That Communicates		314
	1. What Is Speech?		314
	2. When Is Conduct Communicative?		314
	3. When May the Government Regulate Conduct That Communicates?		315
		a. The *O'Brien* Test	315
		United States v. O'Brien	*316*
		b. Flag Desecration	319
		Texas v. Johnson	*320*
		c. Spending Money as Political Speech	325
		Buckley v. Valeo	*325*
		Criticisms of *Buckley*	332
		The Continuing Distinction Between Contributions and Expenditures	333
		When Are Contribution Limits Too Low?	334
		Are Corporate Expenditures Protected Speech?	336
		First National Bank of Boston v. Bellotti	*336*
		Citizens United v. Federal Election Commission	*340*
		The Constitutionality of Public Financing of Elections	357
		Arizona Free Enterprise Club's Freedom Club PAC v. Bennett	*357*

CHAPTER 4

WHAT PLACES ARE AVAILABLE FOR SPEECH?   365

A. Government Properties and Speech   365
    1. Initial Rejection and Subsequent Recognition of a Right to Use Government Property for Speech   365
        Hague v. Committee for Industrial Organization   *366*
        Schneider v. New Jersey   *367*
    2. What Government Property and Under What Circumstances?   369
        a. Public Forums   371
            i. Content Neutrality   371
                Police Department of the City of Chicago v. Mosley   *371*
            ii. Time, Place, and Manner Restrictions   373
                Hill v. Colorado   *374*
                McCullen v. Coakley   *379*
            iii. Licensing and Permit Systems   389
            iv. No Requirement for Use of the Least Restrictive Alternative   391
                Ward v. Rock Against Racism   *391*
        b. Designated Public Forums   392
        c. Limited Public Forums   393
            Christian Legal Society Chapter of the University of California, Hastings College of the Law v. Martinez   *394*
        d. Nonpublic Forums   405
    3. Private Property and Speech   409
    4. Speech in Authoritarian Environments: Military, Prisons, and Schools   410
        a. Military   410
            Parker v. Levy   *410*
        b. Prisons   412
            Thornburgh v. Abbott   *413*
        c. Schools   417
            Tinker v. Des Moines Independent Community School District   *417*
            Bethel School District No. 403 v. Fraser   *421*
            Morse v. Frederick   *424*
        d. The Speech Rights of Government Employees   432
            Garcetti v. Ceballos   *434*

CHAPTER 5

FREEDOM OF ASSOCIATION   441

A. Laws Prohibiting and Punishing Membership   442
B. Laws Requiring Disclosure of Membership   443

		NAACP v. State of Alabama ex rel. Patterson	443
		Campaign Finance Disclosure	445
	C.	Compelled Association	446
		Janus v. American Federation of State, County, and Municipal Employees, Council 31	447
		Board of Regents of the University of Wisconsin System v. Southworth	457
	D.	Laws Prohibiting Discrimination	460
		Roberts v. United States Jaycees	460
		Boy Scouts of America v. Dale	466

CHAPTER 6

FREEDOM OF THE PRESS — 471

A.	Introduction: Are There Special Rights for the Press?	471
B.	Freedom of the Press as a Shield to Protect the Press from the Government	472
	1. Taxes on the Press	472
	Minneapolis Star & Tribune Co. v. Minnesota Commissioner of Revenue	473
	2. Application of General Regulatory Laws	477
	Cohen v. Cowles Media Co.	478
	3. Keeping Reporters' Sources and Secrets Confidential	480
	Branzburg v. Hayes	480
	4. Laws Requiring That the Media Make Access Available	487
C.	Freedom of the Press as a Sword: A First Amendment Right of Access to Government Places and Papers?	488
	1. Access to Judicial Proceedings	489
	Richmond Newspapers v. Virginia	489
	2. Prisons	495
	Houchins v. KQED	496

PART II

FIRST AMENDMENT: RELIGION — 501

CHAPTER 7

INTRODUCTION TO THE RELIGION CLAUSES — 503

A.	Constitutional Provisions Concerning Religion and the Tension Between Them	503
B.	History in Interpreting the Religion Clauses	505
C.	What Is Religion?	506
	The Attempt to Define Religion Under the Selective Service Act	507

	United States v. Seeger	*507*
	Requirement for Sincerely Held Beliefs	510
	United States v. Ballard	*510*
	The Relevance of Religious Dogma and Shared Beliefs	512

CHAPTER 8

THE FREE EXERCISE CLAUSE — 515

A.	Introduction: Free Exercise Clause Issues	515
B.	The Law Before Employment Division v. Smith	516
	1. Government Benefit Cases	518
	2. Compulsory Schooling	518
	3. Cases Rejecting Exemptions Based on the Free Exercise Clause	519
C.	The Current Test	521
	Employment Division, Department of Human Resources of Oregon v. Smith	*521*
D.	Supreme Court Decisions Since Employment Division v. Smith	529
	1. Animus Against Religion	529
	Masterpiece Cake Shop, Ltd. v. Colorado Civil Rights Commission	*530*
	2. Interfering with Choices as to Clergy and Teachers	540
	Our Lady of Guadalupe School v. Morrissey-Berru	*541*
	3. Denial of Funding to Religious Entities	548
	Locke v. Davey	*549*
	Trinity Lutheran Church of Columbia, Inc. v. Comer	*552*
	Espinoza v. Montana Department of Revenue	*563*
E.	Statutory Protection of Religious Freedom	576

CHAPTER 9

THE ESTABLISHMENT CLAUSE — 579

A.	Competing Theories of the Establishment Clause	579
	1. Strict Separation	579
	2. Neutrality Theory	580
	3. Accommodation	583
	4. The Theories Applied: An Example	584
	County of Allegheny v. American Civil Liberties Union, Greater Pittsburgh Chapter	*584*
B.	Government Discrimination Among Religions	589
C.	The *Lemon* Test for the Establishment Clause	590
	Lemon v. Kurtzman	*590*
	The Requirement for a Secular Purpose	592
	The Requirement for a Secular Effect	593
	The Prohibition of Excessive Entanglement	594

D.	Religious Speech and the First Amendment	595
	1. Religious Group Access to School Facilities	595
	2. Student Religious Groups' Receipt of Government Funds	597
E.	When Can Religion Become a Part of Government Activities?	598
	1. Religion as a Part of Government Activities: Schools	598
	Release Time	598
	School Prayers and Bible Reading	599
	Engel v. Vitale	*599*
	Lee v. Weisman	*602*
	Santa Fe Independent School District v. Doe	*610*
	Curricular Decisions	614
	2. Religion as a Part of Government Activities: Legislative Chaplains	615
	Town of Greece v. Galloway	*615*
	3. Religion as a Part of Government Activities: Religious Symbols on Government Property	624
	McCreary County v. American Civil Liberties Union of Kentucky	*624*
	Van Orden v. Perry	*634*
	American Legion v. American Humanist Association	*644*
F.	When Can Government Give Aid to Religion?	652
	Aid to Parochial Elementary and Secondary Schools	653
	Mitchell v. Helms	*654*
	Zelman v. Simmons-Harris	*666*
	Tax Exemptions for Religious Organizations	681
	Aid to Religious Colleges and Universities	682
	Aid to Religious Institutions Other than Schools	684

Table of Cases   687
Index   695

PREFACE

There is no standard way of teaching constitutional law in American law schools. Some schools have a year-long course covering all aspects of the Constitution. Others have a semester on structure of government and one focusing on individual liberties. At the law schools where I have spent most of my teaching career, there is a basic constitutional law course that does not cover the First Amendment and an upper-level elective on the First Amendment, focusing on both freedom of expression and the religion clauses.

My casebook, *Constitutional Law*, was written as to be able to be used in all of these different ways of teaching constitutional law. But since so many schools have the First Amendment as a separate course, it made sense to take these chapters and make them into a separate book. Over the years, many professors have asked me about doing this and I am delighted that Joe Terry at Aspen Publishing enthusiastically agreed.

This book is Chapters 9 and 10 from *Constitutional Law*, Sixth Edition. I present the material here in two parts: Part I focuses on the First Amendment's protection of expression, and Part II examines the religion clauses. The only difference is that it includes cases from the October 2019 Term. *Constitutional Law* is complete through the October 2018 Term. This is particularly important in Part II on religion, which includes two major decisions from 2020.

I will continue to prepare a new edition of *Constitutional Law* every four years (and will do a new edition of *The First Amendment* at the same time) and a Supplement each year.

I welcome comments and suggestions from professors and students who are using this book.

Erwin Chemerinsky

February 2021

THE FIRST AMENDMENT

AMENDMENT I [1791]

Congress shall make no law respecting an establishment of religion, or prohibiting the free exercise thereof; or abridging the freedom of speech, or of the press; or the right of the people peaceably to assemble, and to petition the Government for a redress of grievances.

THE CONSTITUTION OF THE UNITED STATES

We the People of the United States, in Order to form a more perfect Union, establish justice, insure domestic Tranquility, provide for the common defence, promote the general Welfare, and secure the Blessings of Liberty to ourselves and our Posterity, do ordain and establish this Constitution for the United States of America.

ARTICLE I

Section 1. All legislative Powers herein granted shall be vested in a Congress of the United States which shall consist of a Senate and House of Representatives.

Section 2. [1] The House of Representatives shall be composed of Members chosen every second Year by the People of the several States, and the Electors in each State shall have the Qualifications requisite for Electors of the most numerous Branch of the State Legislature.

[2] No Person shall be a Representative who shall not have attained to the Age of twenty five Years, and been seven Years a Citizen of the United States, and who shall not, when elected, be an Inhabitant of that State in which he shall be chosen.

[3] Representatives and direct Taxes shall be apportioned among the several States which may be included within this Union, according to their respective Numbers, which shall be determined by adding to the whole Number of free Persons, including those bound to Service for a Term of Years, and excluding Indians not taxed, three fifths of all other Persons. The actual Enumeration shall be made within three Years after the first meeting of the Congress of the United States, and within every subsequent Term of ten Years, in such Manner as they shall by Law direct. The Number of Representatives shall not exceed one for every thirty Thousand, but each State shall have at Least One Representative; and until such enumeration shall be made, the State of New Hampshire shall be entitled to chuse three, Massachusetts eight, Rhode Island and Providence Plantations one, Connecticut five, New York six, New Jersey four, Pennsylvania eight, Delaware one, Maryland six, Virginia ten, North Carolina five, South Carolina five, and Georgia three.

[4] When vacancies happen in the Representation from any State, the Executive Authority thereof shall issue Writs of Election to fill such Vacancies.

[5] The House of Representatives shall chuse their Speaker and other Officers; and shall have the sole Power of Impeachment.

Section 3. [1] The Senate of the United States shall be composed of two Senators from each State, chosen by the Legislature thereof, for six Years; and each Senator shall have one Vote.

[2] Immediately after they shall be assembled in Consequence of the first Election, they shall be divided as equally as may be into three Classes. The Seats of the Senators of the first Class shall be vacated at the Expiration of the second Year, of the second Class at the Expiration of the fourth Year, and of the third Class at the Expiration of the sixth Year, so that one third may be chosen every second Year; and if Vacancies happen by Resignation, or otherwise, during the Recess of the Legislature of any State, the Executive thereof may make temporary Appointments until the next Meeting of the Legislature, which shall then fill such Vacancies.

[3] No Person shall be a Senator who shall not have attained to the Age of thirty Years, and been nine Years a Citizen of the United States, and who shall not, when elected, be an Inhabitant of that State for which he shall be chosen.

[4] The Vice President of the United States shall be President of the Senate, but shall have no Vote, unless they be equally divided.

[5] The Senate shall chuse their other Officers, and also a President pro tempore, in the absence of the Vice President, or when he shall exercise the Office of President of the United States.

[6] The Senate shall have the sole Power to try all Impeachments. When sitting for that Purpose, they shall be on Oath or Affirmation. When the President of the United States is tried, the Chief Justice shall preside: And no Person shall be convicted without the Concurrence of two thirds of the Members present.

[7] Judgment in Cases of Impeachment shall not extend further than to removal from Office, and disqualification to hold and enjoy any Office of honor, Trust or Profit under the United States: but the Party convicted shall nevertheless be liable and subject to Indictment, Trial, judgment and Punishment, according to Law.

Section 4. [1] The Times, Places and Manner of holding Elections for Senators and Representatives, shall be prescribed in each State by the Legislature thereof; but the Congress may at any time by law make or alter such Regulations, except as to the Places of chusing Senators.

[2] The Congress shall assemble at least once in every Year, and such Meeting shall be on the first Monday in December, unless they shall by Law appoint a different Day.

Section 5. [1] Each house shall be the Judge of the Elections, Returns and Qualifications of its own members, and a Majority of each shall constitute a Quorum to do Business; but a smaller Number may adjourn from day to day, and may be authorized to compel the Attendance of absent members, in such Manner, and under such Penalties as each House may provide.

[2] Each House may determine the Rules of its Proceedings, punish its Members for disorderly Behavior, and, with the Concurrence of two thirds, expel a Member.

[3] Each House shall keep a Journal of its Proceedings, and from time to time publish the same, excepting such Parts as may in their Judgment require Secrecy; and the Yeas and Nays of the Members of either House on any question shall, at the Desire of one fifth of those Present, be entered on the Journal.

[4] Neither House, during the Session of Congress, shall, without the Consent of the other, adjourn for more than three days, nor to any other Place than that in which the two Houses shall be sitting.

Section 6. [1] The Senators and Representatives shall receive a Compensation for their Services, to be ascertained by Law, and paid out of the Treasury of the United States. They shall in all Cases, except Treason, Felony and Breach of the Peace, be privileged from Arrest during their Attendance at the Session of their respective Houses, and in going to and returning from the same; and for any Speech or Debate in either House, they shall not be questioned in any other Place.

[2] No Senator or Representative shall, during the time for which he was elected, be appointed to any civil Office under the Authority of the United States, which shall have been created, or the Emoluments whereof shall have been encreased during such time; and no Person holding any office under the United States, shall be a Member of either House during his Continuance in Office.

Section 7. [1] All Bills for raising Revenue shall originate in the House of Representatives; but the Senate may propose or concur with Amendments as on other Bills.

[2] Every Bill which shall have passed the House of Representatives and the Senate, shall, before it becomes a Law, be presented to the President of the United States; If he approve he shall sign it, but if not he shall return it, with his Objections to the House in which it shall have originated, who shall enter the Objections at large on their Journal, and proceed to reconsider it. If after such Reconsideration two thirds of that House shall agree to pass the Bill, it shall be sent, together with the Objections, to the other House, by which it shall likewise be reconsidered, and if approved by two thirds of that House, it shall become a Law. But in all such Cases the Votes of both Houses shall be determined by Yeas and Nays, and the Names of the Persons voting for and against the Bill shall be entered on the Journal of each House respectively. If any Bill shall not be returned by the President within ten Days (Sundays excepted) after it shall have been presented to him, the Same shall be a Law, in like Manner as if he had signed it, unless the Congress by their Adjournment prevents its Return, in which Case it shall not be a Law.

[3] Every Order, Resolution, or Vote to Which the Concurrence of the Senate and House of Representatives may be necessary (except on a question of Adjournment) shall be presented to the President of the United States; and before the Same shall take Effect, shall be approved by him, or being disapproved by him, shall be repassed by two thirds of the Senate and House of Representatives, according to the Rules and Limitations prescribed in the Case of a Bill.

Section 8. [1] The Congress shall have Power To lay and collect Taxes, Duties, Imposts and Excises, to pay the Debts and provide for the common Defence and general Welfare of the United States; but all Duties, Imposts and Excises shall be uniform throughout the United States;

[2] To borrow money on the credit of the United States;

[3] To regulate Commerce with foreign Nations, and among the several States, and with the Indian Tribes;

[4] To establish an uniform Rule of Naturalization, and uniform Laws on the subject of Bankruptcies throughout the United States;

[5] To coin Money, regulate the Value thereof, and of foreign Coin, and fix the Standard of Weights and Measures;

[6] To provide the Punishment of counterfeiting the Securities and current Coin of the United States;

[7] To establish Post Offices and post Roads;

[8] To promote the Progress of Science and useful Arts, by securing for limited Times to Authors and Inventors the exclusive Right to their respective Writings and Discoveries;

[9] To constitute Tribunals inferior to the supreme Court;

[10] To define and punish Piracies and Felonies committed on the high Seas, and Offenses against the Law of Nations;

[11] To declare War, grant Letters of Marque and Reprisal, and make Rules concerning Captures on Land and Water;

[12] To raise and support Armies, but no Appropriation of Money to that Use shall be a longer Term than two Years;

[13] To provide and maintain a Navy;

[14] To make Rules for the Government and Regulation of the land and naval Forces;

[15] To provide for calling forth the Militia to execute the Laws of the Union, suppress Insurrections and repel Invasions;

[16] To provide for organizing, arming, and disciplining, the Militia, and for governing such Part of them as may be employed in the Service of the United States, reserving to the States respectively, the Appointment of the Officers, and the Authority of training the Militia according to the discipline prescribed by Congress;

[17] To exercise exclusive Legislation in all Cases whatsoever, over such District (not exceeding ten Miles square) as may, by Cession of particular States, and the Acceptance of Congress, become the Seat of the Government of the United States, and to exercise like Authority over all Places purchased by the Consent of the Legislature of the State in which the Same shall be, for the Erection of Forts, Magazines, Arsenals, dock-Yards, and other needful Buildings;—And

[18] To make all Laws which shall be necessary and proper for carrying into Execution the foregoing Powers, and all other Powers vested by this Constitution in the Government of the United States, or in any Department or Officer thereof.

Section 9. [1] The Migration or Importation of such Persons as any of the States now existing shall think proper to admit, shall not be prohibited by the Congress prior to the Year one thousand eight hundred and eight, but a Tax or duty may be imposed on such Importation, not exceeding ten dollars for each Person.

[2] The privilege of the Writ of Habeas Corpus shall not be suspended, unless when in Cases of Rebellion or Invasion the public Safety may require it.

[3] No Bill of Attainder or ex post facto Law shall be passed.

[4] No Capitation, or other direct, Tax shall be laid, unless in Proportion to the Census or Enumeration herein before directed to be taken.

[5] No Tax or Duty shall be laid on articles exported from any State.

[6] No Preference shall be given by any Regulation of Commerce or Revenue to the Ports of one State over those of another: nor shall Vessels bound to, or from, one State, be obliged to enter, clear, or pay Duties in another.

[7] No Money shall be drawn from the Treasury, but in Consequence of Appropriations made by Law; and a regular Statement and Account of the Receipts and Expenditures of all public Money shall be published from time to time.

[8] No title of Nobility shall be granted by the United States: And no Person holding any Office of Profit or Trust under them, shall, without the Consent of the Congress, accept of any present, Emolument, Office, or Title, of any kind whatever, from any King, Prince, or foreign State.

Section 10. [1] No State shall enter into any Treaty, Alliance, or Confederation; grant Letters of Marque and Reprisal; coin Money; emit Bills of Credit; make any Thing but gold and silver Coin a Tender in Payment of Debts; pass any Bill of Attainder, ex post facto Law, or Law impairing the Obligation of Contracts, or grant any title of Nobility.

[2] No State shall, without the Consent of the Congress, lay any Imposts or Duties on Imports or Exports, except what may be absolutely necessary for executing its inspection Laws: and the net Produce of all Duties and Imposts, laid by any State on Imports or Exports, shall be for the Use of the Treasury of the United States; and all such Laws be subject to the Revision and Controul of the Congress.

[3] No State shall, without the Consent of Congress, lay any Duty of Tonnage, keep Troops, or Ships of War in time of Peace, enter into any Agreement or Compact with another State, or with a foreign Power, or engage in War, unless actually invaded, or in such imminent Danger as will not admit of delay.

ARTICLE II

Section 1. [1] The executive Power shall be vested in a President of the United States of America. He shall hold his Office during the Term of four Years, and, together with the Vice President, chosen for the same Term, be elected, as follows:

[2] Each State shall appoint, in such Manner as the Legislature thereof may direct, a Number of Electors, equal to the whole Number of Senators and Representatives to which the State may be entitled in the Congress: but no Senator or Representative, or Person holding an Office of Trust or Profit under the United States, shall be appointed an Elector.

[3] The Electors shall meet in their respective States, and vote by Ballot for two Persons, of whom one at least shall not be an Inhabitant of the same State with themselves. And they shall make a List of all the Persons voted for, and of the Number of Votes for each; which List they shall sign and certify, and transmit sealed to the Seat of the Government of the United States, directed to the President of the Senate. The President of the Senate shall, in the Presence of the Senate and House of Representatives, open all the Certificates, and the Votes shall then be counted. The Person having the greatest Number of Votes shall be the President, if such Number be a Majority of the whole Number of Electors appointed; and if there be more than one who have such Majority, and have an equal Number of Votes, then the House of Representatives shall immediately chuse by Ballot one of them for President; and if no Person have a Majority, then from the five highest on the List the said House shall in like Manner chuse the President. But in chusing the President, the Votes shall be taken by States, the Representation from each State having one vote; a quorum for this Purpose shall consist of a Member or Members from two thirds of the

States, and a Majority of all the States shall be necessary to a Choice. In every Case, after the Choice of the President, the Person having the Greatest Number of Votes of the Electors shall be the Vice President. But if there should remain two or more who have equal Votes, the Senate shall chuse from them by Ballot the Vice President.

[4] The Congress may determine the Time of chusing the Electors, and the Day on which they shall give their Votes; which Day shall be the same throughout the United States.

[5] No person except a natural born Citizen, or a Citizen of the United States, at the time of the Adoption of this Constitution, shall be eligible to the Office of President; neither shall any Person be eligible to that Office who shall not have attained to the Age of thirty five Years, and been fourteen Years a Resident within the United States.

[6] In case of the removal of the President from Office, or of his Death, Resignation, or Inability to discharge the Powers and Duties of the said Office, the Same shall devolve on the Vice President, and the Congress may by Law provide for the Case of Removal, Death, Resignation or Inability, both of the President and Vice President, declaring what Officer shall then act as President, and such Officer shall act accordingly, until the Disability be removed, or a President shall be elected.

[7] The President shall, at stated Times, receive for his Services, a Compensation, which shall neither be increased nor diminished during the Period for which he shall have been elected, and he shall not receive within that Period any other Emolument from the United States, or any of them.

[8] Before he enter on the Execution of his Office, he shall take the following Oath or Affirmation: "I do solemnly swear (or affirm) that I will faithfully execute the Office of President of the United States, and will to the best of my Ability, preserve, protect and defend the Constitution of the United States."

Section 2. [1] The President shall be Commander in Chief of the Army and Navy of the United States, and of the Militia of the several States, when called into the actual Service of the United States; he may require the Opinion, in writing, of the principal Officer in each of the executive Departments, upon any subject relating to the Duties of their respective Offices, and he shall have Power to grant Reprieves and Pardons for Offenses against the United States, except in Cases of Impeachment.

[2] He shall have Power, by and with the Advice and Consent of the Senate, to make Treaties, provided two thirds of the Senators present concur; and he shall nominate, and by and with the Advice and Consent of the Senate, shall appoint Ambassadors, other public Ministers and Consuls, Judges of the supreme Court, and all other Officers of the United States, whose Appointments are not herein otherwise provided for, and which shall be established by Law: but the Congress may by Law vest the Appointment of such inferior Officers, as they think proper, in the President alone, in the Courts of Law, or in the Heads of Departments.

[3] The President shall have Power to fill up all Vacancies that may happen during the Recess of the Senate by granting Commissions which shall expire at the End of their next Session.

Section 3. He shall from time to time give to the Congress Information of the State of the Union, and recommend to their Consideration such Measures as he shall judge necessary and expedient; he may, on extraordinary Occasions, convene both Houses, or either of them, and in Case of Disagreement between them, with Respect to the time of Adjournment, he may adjourn them to such

Time as he shall think proper; he shall receive Ambassadors and other public Ministers; he shall take Care that the Laws be faithfully executed, and shall Commission all the Officers of the United States.

Section 4. The President, Vice President and all civil Officers of the United States, shall be removed from Office on Impeachment for, and Conviction of, Treason, Bribery, or other high Crimes and Misdemeanors.

ARTICLE III

Section 1. The judicial Power of the United States, shall be vested in one supreme Court, and in such inferior Courts as the Congress may from time to time ordain and establish. The Judges, both of the supreme and inferior Courts, shall hold their Offices during good Behaviour, and shall, at stated Times, receive for their Services a Compensation, which shall not be diminished during their Continuance in Office.

Section 2. [1] The Judicial Power shall extend to all Cases, in Law and Equity, arising under this Constitution, the Laws of the United States, and Treaties made, or which shall be made, under their Authority;—to all Cases affecting Ambassadors, other public Ministers and Consuls;—to all Cases of admiralty and maritime Jurisdiction;—to Controversies to which the United States shall be a Party;—to Controversies between two or more States; between a State and Citizens of another State;—between Citizens of different States;—between Citizens of the same State claiming Lands under Grants of different States, and between a State, or the Citizens thereof, and foreign States, Citizens or Subjects.

[2] In all cases affecting Ambassadors, other public Ministers and Consuls, and those in which a State shall be Party, the supreme Court shall have original Jurisdiction. In all the other Cases before mentioned, the supreme Court shall have appellate Jurisdiction, both as to Law and Fact, with such Exceptions, and under such Regulations as the Congress shall make.

[3] The trial of all Crimes, except in Cases of Impeachment, shall be by Jury; and such Trial shall be held in the State where the said Crimes shall have been committed; but when not committed within any State, the Trial shall be at such Place or Places as the Congress may by Law have directed.

Section 3. [1] Treason against the United States, shall consist only in levying War against them, or in adhering to their Enemies, giving them Aid and Comfort. No person shall be convicted of Treason unless on the Testimony of two Witnesses to the same over Act, or on Confession in open Court.

[2] The Congress shall have Power to declare the Punishment of Treason, but no Attainder of Treason shall work Corruption of Blood, or Forfeiture except during the Life of the Person attainted.

ARTICLE IV

Section 1. Full Faith and Credit shall be given in each State to the public Acts, Records, and judicial Proceedings of every other State. And the Congress may by general Laws prescribe the Manner in which such Acts, Records and Proceedings shall be proved, and the Effect thereof.

Section 2. [1] The Citizens of each State shall be entitled to all Privileges and Immunities of Citizens in the several States.

[2] A Person charged in any State with Treason, Felony, or other Crime, who shall flee from Justice, and be found in another State, shall on demand of the executive Authority of the State from which he fled, be delivered up, to be removed to the State having Jurisdiction of the Crime.

[3] No Person held to Service or Labour in one State, under the Laws thereof, escaping into another, shall, in Consequence of any Law or Regulation therein, be discharged from such Service or Labour, but shall be delivered up on Claim of the Party to whom such Service or Labour may be due.

Section 3. [1] New States may be admitted by the Congress into this Union; but no new State shall be formed or erected within the Jurisdiction of any other State; nor any State be formed by the Junction of two or more States, or Parts of States, without the Consent of the Legislatures of the States concerned as well as of the Congress.

[2] The Congress shall have Power to dispose of and make all needful Rules and Regulations respecting the Territory or other Property belonging to the United States; and nothing in this Constitution shall be so construed as to Prejudice any Claims of the United States, or of any particular State.

Section 4. The United States shall guarantee to every State in this Union a Republican Form of Government, and shall protect each of them against Invasion; and on Application of the Legislature, or of the Executive (when the Legislature cannot be convened) against domestic Violence.

ARTICLE V

The Congress, whenever two thirds of both Houses shall deem it necessary, shall propose Amendments to this Constitution, or, on the Application of the Legislatures of two thirds of the several States, shall call a Convention for proposing Amendments, which, in either Case, shall be valid to all Intents and Purposes, as part of this Constitution, when ratified by the Legislatures of three fourths of the several States, or by Conventions in three fourths thereof, as the one or the other Mode of Ratification may be proposed by the Congress; Provided that no Amendment which may be made prior to the Year One thousand eight hundred and eight shall in any Manner affect the first and fourth Clauses in the Ninth Section of the first Article; and that no State, without its Consent, shall be deprived of its equal Suffrage in the Senate.

ARTICLE VI

[1] All Debts contracted and Engagements entered into, before the Adoption of this Constitution, shall be as valid against the United States under this Constitution, as under the Confederation.

[2] This Constitution, and the Laws of the United States which shall be made in Pursuance thereof; and all Treaties made, or which shall be made, under the Authority of the United States, shall be the supreme Law of the Land; and the Judges in every State shall be bound thereby, any Thing in the Constitution or Laws of any State to the Contrary notwithstanding.

[3] The Senators and Representatives before mentioned, and the Members of the several State Legislatures, and all executive and judicial Officers, both of the United States and of the several States, shall be bound by Oath or Affirmation, to support this Constitution; but no religious Test shall ever be required as a Qualification to any Office or public Trust under the United States.

ARTICLE VII

The Ratification of the Conventions of nine States shall be sufficient for the Establishment of this Constitution between the States so ratifying the Same.

Done in Convention by the Unanimous Consent of the States present the Seventeenth Day of September in the Year of our Lord one thousand seven hundred and Eighty seven and of the Independence of the United States of America the Twelfth.

ARTICLES IN ADDITION TO, AND AMENDMENT OF, THE CONSTITUTION OF THE UNITED STATES OF AMERICA, PROPOSED BY CONGRESS, AND RATIFIED BY THE LEGISLATURES OF THE SEVERAL STATES, PURSUANT TO THE FIFTH ARTICLE OF THE ORIGINAL CONSTITUTION.

AMENDMENT I [1791]

Congress shall make no law respecting an establishment of religion, or prohibiting the free exercise thereof; or abridging the freedom of speech, or of the press; or the right of the people peaceably to assemble, and to petition the Government for a redress of grievances.

AMENDMENT II [1791]

A well regulated Militia, being necessary to the security of a free State, the right of the people to keep and bear Arms, shall not be infringed.

AMENDMENT III [1791]

No Soldier shall, in time of peace be quartered in any house, without the consent of the Owner, nor in time of war, but in a manner to be prescribed by law.

AMENDMENT IV [1791]

The right of the people to be secure in their persons, houses, papers, and effects, against unreasonable searches and seizures, shall not be violated, and no Warrants shall issue, but upon probable cause, supported by Oath or affirmation, and particularly describing the place to be searched, and the persons or things to be seized.

AMENDMENT V [1791]

No person shall be held to answer for a capital, or otherwise infamous crime, unless on a presentment or indictment of a Grand Jury, except in cases arising in the land or naval forces, or in the Militia, when in actual service in time of War or public danger; nor shall any person be subject for the same offence to be twice put in jeopardy of life or limb; nor shall be compelled in any criminal case to be a witness against himself, nor be deprived of life, liberty, or property, without due process of law; nor shall private property be taken for public use, without just compensation.

AMENDMENT VI [1791]

In all criminal prosecutions, the accused shall enjoy the right to a speedy and public trial, by an impartial jury of the State and district wherein the crime shall have been committed, which district shall have been previously ascertained by law, and to be informed of the nature and cause of the accusation; to be confronted with the witnesses against him; to have compulsory process for obtaining witnesses in his favor, and to have the Assistance of Counsel for his defence.

AMENDMENT VII [1791]

In Suits at common law, where the value in controversy shall exceed twenty dollars, the right of trial by jury shall be preserved, and no fact tried by a jury, shall be otherwise reexamined in any Court of the United States, than according to the rules of the common law.

AMENDMENT VIII [1791]

Excessive bail shall not be required, nor excessive fines imposed, nor cruel and unusual punishments inflicted.

AMENDMENT IX [1791]

The enumeration in the Constitution, of certain rights, shall not be construed to deny or disparage others retained by the people.

AMENDMENT X [1791]

The powers not delegated to the United States by the Constitution, nor prohibited by it to the States, are reserved to the States respectively, or to the people.

AMENDMENT XI [1798]

The Judicial power of the United States shall not be construed to extend to any suit in law or equity, commenced or prosecuted against one of the United States by Citizens of another State, or by Citizens or Subjects of any Foreign State.

AMENDMENT XII [1804]

The Electors shall meet in their respective states and vote by ballot for President and Vice-President, one of whom, at least, shall not be an inhabitant of the same state with themselves; they shall name in their ballots the person voted for as President, and in distinct ballots the person voted for as Vice-President, and they shall make distinct lists of all persons voted for as President, and of all persons voted for as Vice-President, and of the number of votes for each, which lists they shall sign and certify, and transmit sealed to the seat of the government of the United States, directed to the President of the Senate;—The President of the Senate shall, in the presence of the Senate and House of Representatives, open all the certificates and the votes shall then be counted;—The person having the greatest number of votes for President, shall be the President, if such number be a majority of the whole number of Electors appointed; and if no person have such majority, then from the persons having the highest numbers not exceeding three on the list of those voted for as President, the House of Representatives shall choose immediately, by ballot, the President. But in choosing the President, the votes shall be taken by states, the representation from each state having one vote; a quorum for this purpose shall consist of a member or members from two-thirds of the states, and a majority of all the states shall be necessary to a choice. And if the House of Representatives shall not choose a President whenever the right of choice shall devolve upon them, before the fourth day of March next following, then the Vice-President shall act as President, as in the case of the death or other constitutional disability of the

President. — The person having the greatest number of votes as Vice-President, shall be the Vice-President, if such number be a majority of the whole number of Electors appointed, and if no person have a majority, then from the two highest numbers on the list, the Senate shall choose the Vice-President; a quorum for the purpose shall consist of two-thirds of the whole number of Senators, and a majority of the whole number shall be necessary to a choice. But no person constitutionally ineligible to the office of President shall be eligible to that of Vice-President of the United States.

AMENDMENT XIII [1865]

Section 1. Neither slavery nor involuntary servitude, except as a punishment for crime whereof the party shall have been duly convicted, shall exist within the United States, or any place subject to their jurisdiction.

Section 2. Congress shall have power to enforce this article by appropriate legislation.

AMENDMENT XIV [1868]

Section 1. All persons born or naturalized in the United States, and subject to the jurisdiction thereof, are citizens of the United States and of the State wherein they reside. No State shall make or enforce any law which shall abridge the privileges or immunities of citizens of the United States; nor shall any State deprive any person of life, liberty, or property, without due process of law; nor deny to any person within its jurisdiction the equal protection of the laws.

Section 2. Representatives shall be apportioned among the several States according to their respective numbers, counting the whole number of persons in each State, excluding Indians not taxed. But when the right to vote at any election for the choice of electors for President and Vice-President of the United States, Representatives in Congress, the Executive and Judicial officers of a State, or the members of the Legislature thereof, is denied to any of the male inhabitants of such State, being twenty-one years of age, and citizens of the United States, or in any way abridged, except for participation in rebellion, or other crime, the basis of representation therein shall be reduced in the proportion which the number of such male citizens shall bear to the whole number of male citizens twenty-one years of age in such State.

Section 3. No person shall be a Senator or Representative in Congress, or elector of President and Vice-President, or hold any office, civil or military, under the United States, or under any State, who, having previously taken an oath, as a member of Congress, or as an officer of the United States, or as a member of any State legislature, or as an executive or judicial officer of any State, to support the Constitution of the United States, shall have engaged in insurrection or rebellion against the same, or given aid or comfort to the enemies thereof. But Congress may by a vote of two-thirds of each House, remove such disability.

Section 4. The validity of the public debt of the United States, authorized by law, including debts incurred for payment of pensions and bounties for services in suppressing insurrection or rebellion, shall not be questioned. But neither the United States nor any State shall assume or pay any debt or obligation incurred in aid of insurrection or rebellion against the United States, or any claim for the loss of emancipation of any slave; but all such debts, obligations and claims shall be held illegal and void.

Section 5. The Congress shall have power to enforce, by appropriate legislation, the provisions of this article.

AMENDMENT XV [1870]

Section 1. The right of citizens of the United States to vote shall not be denied or abridged by the United States or by any State on account of race, color, or previous condition of servitude.

Section 2. The Congress shall have power to enforce this article by appropriate legislation.

AMENDMENT XVI [1913]

The Congress shall have power to lay and collect taxes on incomes, from whatever source derived, without apportionment among the several States, and without regard to any census or enumeration.

AMENDMENT XVII [1913]

[1] The Senate of the United States shall be composed of two Senators from each State, elected by the people thereof, for six years, and each Senator shall have one vote. The electors in each State shall have the qualifications requisite for electors of the most numerous branch of the State legislatures.

[2] When vacancies happen in the representation of any State in the Senate, the executive authority of such State shall issue writs of election to fill such vacancies: *Provided,* That the legislature of any State may empower the executive thereof to make temporary appointments until the people fill the vacancies by election as the legislature may direct.

[3] This amendment shall not be so construed as to affect the election or term of any Senator chosen before it becomes valid as part of the Constitution.

AMENDMENT XVIII [1919]

Section 1. After one year from the ratification of this article the manufacture, sale, or transportation of intoxicating liquors within, the importation thereof into, or the exportation thereof from the United States and all territory subject to the jurisdiction thereof for beverage purposes is hereby prohibited.

Section 2. The Congress and the several States shall have concurrent power to enforce this article by appropriate legislation.

Section 3. This article shall be inoperative unless it shall have been ratified as an amendment to the Constitution by the legislatures of the several States, as provided in the Constitution, within seven years from the date of the submission hereof to the States by the Congress.

AMENDMENT XIX [1920]

[1] The right of citizens of the United States to vote shall not be denied or abridged by the United States or by any State on account of sex.

[2] Congress shall have power to enforce this article by appropriate legislation.

AMENDMENT XX [1933]

Section 1. The terms of the President and Vice President shall end at noon on the 20th day of January, and the terms of Senators and Representatives at noon on the 3d day of January, of the years in which such terms would have ended if this article had not been ratified; and the terms of their successor shall then begin.

Section 2. The Congress shall assemble at least once in every year, and such meeting shall begin at noon on the 3d day of January, unless they shall by law appoint a different day.

Section 3. If, at the time fixed for the beginning of the term of the President, the President elect shall have died, the Vice President elect shall become President. If a President shall not have been chosen before the time fixed for the beginning of his term, or if the President elect shall have failed to qualify, then the Vice President elect shall act as President until a President shall have qualified; and the Congress may by law provide for the case wherein neither a President elect nor a Vice President elect shall have qualified, declaring who shall then act as President, or the manner in which one who is to act shall be selected, and such person shall act accordingly until a President or Vice President shall have qualified.

Section 4. The Congress may by law provide for the case of the death of any of the persons from whom the House of Representatives may choose a President whenever the right of choice shall have devolved upon them, and for the case of the death of any of the persons from whom the Senate may choose a Vice President whenever the right of choice shall have devolved upon them.

Section 5. Sections 1 and 2 shall take effect on the 15th day of October following the ratification of this article.

Section 6. This article shall be inoperative unless it shall have been ratified as an amendment to the Constitution by the legislatures of three-fourths of the several States within seven years from the date of its submission.

AMENDMENT XXI [1933]

Section 1. The eighteenth article of amendment to the Constitution of the United States is hereby repealed.

Section 2. The transportation or importation into any State, Territory, or possession of the United States for delivery or use therein of intoxicating liquors, in violation of the laws thereof, is hereby prohibited.

Section 3. This article shall be inoperative unless it shall have been ratified as an amendment to the Constitution by conventions in the several States, as provided in the Constitution, within seven years from the date of the submissions hereof to the States by the Congress.

AMENDMENT XXII [1951]

Section 1. No person shall be elected to the office of the President more than twice, and no person who has held the office of President, or acted as President, for more than two years of a term to which some other person was elected President shall be elected to the office of the President more than once. But this Article shall not apply to any person holding the office of President when this Article was proposed by the Congress, and shall not prevent any person who may be holding the office of President, or acting as President, during the term within which the Article becomes operative from holding the office of President or acting as President during the remainder of such term.

Section 2. This article shall be inoperative unless it shall have been ratified as an amendment to the Constitution by the legislatures of three-fourths of the several States within seven years from the date of its submission to the States by the Congress.

AMENDMENT XXIII [1961]

Section 1. The District constituting the seat of Government of the United States shall appoint in such manner as the Congress may direct:

A number of electors of President and Vice President equal to the whole number of Senators and Representatives in Congress to which the District would be entitled if it were a State, but in no event more than the least populous State; they shall be in addition to those appointed by the States, but they shall be considered, for the purposes of the election of President and Vice President, to be electors appointed by a State; and they shall meet in the District and perform such duties as provided by the twelfth article of amendment.

Section 2. The Congress shall have power to enforce this article by appropriate legislation.

AMENDMENT XXIV [1964]

Section 1. The right of citizens of the United States to vote in any primary or other election for President or Vice President for electors for President or Vice President, or for Senator or Representative in Congress, shall not be denied or abridged by the United States or any State by reason of failure to pay any poll tax or other tax.

Section 2. The Congress shall have power to enforce this article by appropriate legislation.

AMENDMENT XXV [1967]

Section 1. In case of the removal of the President from office or of his death or resignation, the Vice President shall become President.

Section 2. Whenever there is a vacancy in the office of the Vice President, the President shall nominate a Vice President who shall take office upon confirmation by a majority vote of both Houses of Congress.

Section 3. Whenever the President transmits to the President pro tempore of the Senate and the Speaker of the House of Representatives his written declaration that he is unable to discharge the powers and duties of his office, and until he transmits to them a written declaration to the contrary, such powers and duties shall be discharged by the Vice President as Acting President.

Section 4. Whenever the Vice President and a Majority of either the principal officers of the executive departments or of such other body as Congress may by law provide, transmit to the President pro tempore of the Senate and the Speaker of the House of Representatives their written declaration that the President is unable to discharge the powers and duties of his office, the Vice President shall immediately assume the powers and duties of the office as Acting President.

Thereafter, when the President transmits to the President pro tempore of the Senate and the Speaker of the House of Representatives his written declaration that no inability exists, he shall resume the powers and duties of his office unless the Vice President and a majority of either the principal officers of the executive department or of such other body as Congress may by law provide, transmit within four days to the President pro tempore of the Senate and the Speaker of the House of Representatives their written declaration that the President is unable to discharge the powers and duties of his office. Thereupon Congress shall decide the issue, assembling within forty-eight hours for that purpose if not in session. If the Congress, within twenty-one days after receipt of the latter written declaration, or, if Congress is not in session, within twenty-one days after Congress is required to assemble, determined by two-thirds vote of both Houses that the President is unable to discharge the powers and duties of his office, the Vice President shall continue to discharge the same as Acting President; otherwise, the President shall resume the powers and duties of his office.

AMENDMENT XXVI [1971]

Section 1. The right of citizens of the United States, who are eighteen years of age or older, to vote shall not be denied or abridged by the United States or by any State on account of age.

Section 2. The Congress shall have power to enforce this article by appropriate legislation.

AMENDMENT XXVII [1992]

Section 1. No law, varying the Compensation for the services of the Senators and Representatives, shall take effect, unless an election of Representatives shall have intervened.

THE FIRST AMENDMENT

PART I

FIRST AMENDMENT: FREEDOM OF EXPRESSION

PART

I

INSTRUMENTS THROUGH
OUR SENSES

CHAPTER 1

INTRODUCTION TO FREEDOM OF SPEECH

The First Amendment states, "Congress shall make no law respecting an establishment of religion, or prohibiting the free exercise thereof; or abridging the freedom of speech, or of the press; or the right of the people peaceably to assemble, and to petition the Government for a redress of grievances." Part II of this book considers the Religion Clauses. Part I focuses on the other provisions of the First Amendment, all of which concern aspects of freedom of expression.

A. HISTORICAL BACKGROUND

The First Amendment undoubtedly was a reaction against the suppression of speech and of the press that existed in English society. Until 1694, there was an elaborate system of licensing in England, and no publication was allowed without a government-granted license. Blackstone, in his famous commentaries on the law, remarked that "[t]he liberty of the press consists in laying no *previous* restraints upon publications, and not in freedom from censure for criminal matter when published. . . . [To] subject the press to the restrictive power of a licenser . . . is to subject all freedom of sentiment to the prejudices of one man, and make him the arbitrary and infallible judge of all controverted points in learning, religion, and government."[1] It is widely accepted that the First Amendment was meant, at the very least, to abolish such prior restraints on publication.

Speech in England also was restricted by the law of seditious libel that made criticizing the government a crime.[2] The English Court of the Star Chamber announced the principle that the king was above public criticism and that, therefore, statements critical of the government were forbidden. Chief Justice Holt, writing in 1704, explained the perceived need for the prohibition of

---

1. 4 William Blackstone, *Commentaries on the Laws of England*, 151-152 (1769) (emphasis in original).
2. A classic history of the First Amendment, which reviews this background, is Zechariah Chaffee, Jr., *Free Speech in the United States* (1941).

seditious libel: "If people should not be called to account for possessing the people with an ill opinion of the government, no government can subsist. For it is very necessary for all governments that the people should have a good opinion of it."[3] Truth was not a defense to the crime because the goal was to prevent and punish all criticism of the government; if anything, true speech was perceived as worse because it might do more to damage the image and reputation of the government. Professor Zechariah Chaffee said that "the First Amendment was . . . intended to wipe out the common law of sedition, and make further prosecutions for criticism of the government, without any incitement to lawbreaking, forever impossible in the United States of America."[4]

The record for protection of freedom of speech in the colonies was mixed. There were fewer prosecutions for seditious libel than in England during the time period, but there were other controls, formal and informal, over dissident speech. Professor Leonard Levy said that each community "tended to be a tight little island clutching its own respective orthodoxy and . . . eager to banish or extralegally punish unwelcome dissidents."[5]

Of the prosecutions that occurred for seditious libel, the most famous was the trial of John Peter Zenger in 1735 for publishing criticisms of the governor of New York. Zenger's lawyer argued that truth should be a defense to the crime of seditious libel. Although the court rejected this argument, the jury was persuaded to disregard the law and to acquit Zenger.[6]

There is thus little doubt that the First Amendment was meant to prohibit licensing of publication such as existed in England and to forbid punishment for seditious libel. Beyond this, though, there is little indication of what the framers intended. Certainly nothing in the historical record sheds light on most of the free speech issues that face society and the courts in the early twenty-first century. Professor Rodney Smolla remarked that "[o]ne can keep going round and round on the original meaning of the First Amendment, but no clear, consistent vision of what the framers meant by freedom of speech will ever emerge."[7]

In fact, ascertaining the framers' intent is made more difficult by the fact that Congress in 1798—with many of the Constitution's drafters and ratifiers participating—adopted the Alien and Sedition Acts of 1798.[8] The law prohibited the publication of "false, scandalous, and malicious writing or writings against the government of the United States, or either house of the Congress of the United States, or the President of the United States, with intent to defame . . . ; or to bring them . . . into contempt or disrepute; or to excite against them . . . hatred of the good people of the United States, or to stir up sedition within the United States, or to excite any unlawful combinations therein, for opposing or resisting any law of the United States, or any act of the President of the United States." The law did allow truth as a defense and required proof of malicious intent.

The Federalists under President John Adams aggressively used the law against their rivals, the Republicans. The Alien and Sedition Act was a major political

---

3. 14 Thomas Howell, *A Collection of State Trials* 1095, 1128 (1704).
4. Chaffee, *supra* note 2, at 21.
5. Leonard W. Levy, *The Emergence of a Free Press* 16 (1985).
6. *See* Vincent Buranelli, *The Trial of Peter Zenger* (1957).
7. Rodney A. Smolla, *Smolla and Nimmer on Freedom of Speech* at 1-18 (1996).
8. 1 Stat. 596, Act of July 14, 1798.

issue in the election of 1800, and after he was elected president, Thomas Jefferson pardoned those who had been convicted under the law. The Alien and Sedition Act was repealed, and the Supreme Court never ruled on its constitutionality. However, in New York Times v. Sullivan, in 1964, the Court declared, "Although the Sedition Act was never tested in this Court, the attack upon its validity has carried the day in the court of history."[9]

Not surprisingly, then, Supreme Court cases dealing with freedom of expression focus less on the framers' intent than do cases involving many other constitutional provisions. There is relatively little that can be discerned as to the drafters' views other than their desire to prohibit prior restraints, such as the licensing scheme, and their rejection of the crime of seditious libel.

B. WHY SHOULD FREEDOM OF SPEECH BE A FUNDAMENTAL RIGHT?

Inevitably, the courts must decide what speech is protected by the First Amendment and what can be regulated by the government. Although the First Amendment is written in absolute language that Congress shall make "no law," the Supreme Court never has accepted the view that the First Amendment prohibits all government regulation of expression. Justice Hugo Black took the absolutist view of the First Amendment,[10] but he is virtually alone among Supreme Court justices.[11] Indeed, the Court expressly declared that it "reject[ed] the view that freedom of speech and association, . . . as protected by the First and Fourteenth Amendments, are absolutes."[12]

No matter how appealing the absolute position may be to the First Amendment's staunchest supporters, it is simply untenable. Even one example of an instance where government must be able to punish speech is sufficient to refute the desirability of an absolutist approach. For example, perjury laws or laws that prohibit quid pro quo sexual harassment ("sleep with me or you are fired") both punish speech, but no one would deny that such statutes are imperative.

Line drawing is inevitable as to what speech will be protected under the First Amendment and what can be proscribed or limited. Moreover, lines must be drawn as to where and when speech will be allowed. Even an absolutist view surely would not permit spectators to yell out while a court is in session and prevent the judge from hearing the proceeding. Lines also must be drawn in defining what is speech. Justice Black attempted to make his view plausible by distinguishing between speech and conduct, allowing the government

---

9. 376 U.S. 254, 276 (1964).
10. *See, e.g.*, Hugo Black, *The Bill of Rights*, 35 N.Y.U. L. Rev. 865, 874, 879 (1960) ("The phrase 'Congress shall make no law' is composed of plain words, easily understood. The language is absolute. . . . [T]he framers themselves did this balancing when they wrote the [First Amendment]. . . . Courts have neither the right nor the power to make a different judgment.").
11. Justice William O. Douglas also took this view at times. Konigsberg v. State Bar of California, 366 U.S. 36, 56 (1961) (Black, J., dissenting, joined by Douglas, J.).
12. Konigsberg v. State Bar of California, 366 U.S. at 49.

to regulate the latter, but not the former. This distinction, too, requires line drawing as to when nonverbal communication should be regarded as speech.

Because even for originalists there is little guidance from history or the framers' intent as to the meaning of the First Amendment, the Supreme Court inescapably must make value choices as to what speech is protected, under what circumstances, and when and how the government may regulate. Such analysis is possible only with reference to the goals that freedom of speech is meant to achieve.

There thus is a voluminous literature debating why freedom of speech should be regarded as a fundamental right. The issue is important in general in understanding freedom of expression, but is also crucial in appraising specific First Amendment issues and how they have been handled by the Supreme Court.

There is not a single, universally accepted theory of the First Amendment, but rather, several different views as to why freedom of speech should be regarded as a fundamental right. To a large extent, the theories are not mutually exclusive, although the choice of a theory can influence views on many specific issues. The four major theories, reviewed below, are that freedom of speech is protected to further self-governance, to aid the discovery of truth via the marketplace of ideas, to promote autonomy, and to foster tolerance. Justice Louis Brandeis offered an eloquent explanation for why freedom of speech is protected that includes all of these rationales. He wrote:

> Those who won our independence believed that the final end of the state was to make men free to develop their faculties, and that in its government the deliberative forces should prevail over the arbitrary. They valued liberty both as an end and as a means. They believed liberty to be the secret of happiness and courage to be the secret of liberty. They believed that freedom to think as you will and to speak as you think are means indispensable to the discovery and spread of political truth; that without free speech and assembly discussion would be futile; that with them, discussion affords ordinarily adequate protection against the dissemination of noxious doctrine; that the greatest menace to freedom is an inert people; that public discussion is a political duty; and that this should be a fundamental principle of American government. They recognized the risks to which all human institutions are subject. But they knew that order cannot be secured merely through fear of punishment for its infraction; that it is hazardous to discourage thought, hope, and imagination; that fear breeds repression; that repression breeds hate; that hate menaces stable government; that the path of safety lies in the opportunity to discuss freely supposed grievances and proposed remedies; and that the fitting remedy for evil counsels is good ones.[13]

1. *Self-Governance*

Freedom of speech is crucial in a democracy: Open discussion of candidates is essential for voters to make informed selections in elections; it is through speech that people can influence their government's choice of policies; public officials are held accountable through criticisms that can pave the way for their replacement. Alexander Meiklejohn wrote that freedom of speech "is

---

13. Whitney v. California, 274 U.S. 357, 375 (1927) (Brandeis, J., concurring).

B. Why Should Freedom of Speech Be a Fundamental Right?

a deduction from the basic American agreement that public issues shall be decided by universal suffrage."[14] He argued that "[s]elf-government can exist only insofar as the voters acquire the intelligence, integrity, sensitivity, and generous devotion to the general welfare that, in theory, casting a ballot is assumed to express."[15] Professor Vincent Blasi argued that freedom of speech serves an essential "checking value" on government.[16] He wrote of the value that free speech serves in checking the abuse of power by public officials and said that through speech voters retain "a veto power to be employed when the decisions of officials pass certain bounds."[17]

There is little disagreement that political speech is at the core of that protected by the First Amendment. The Supreme Court has spoken of the ability to criticize government and government officers as "the central meaning of the First Amendment."[18] Some commentators have argued that political speech should be the *only* speech protected by the First Amendment. Robert Bork is perhaps the foremost advocate of this position and argued that the "notion that all valuable types of speech must be protected by the first amendment confuses the constitutionality of laws with their wisdom. Freedom of nonpolitical speech rests, as does freedom for other valuable forms of behavior, upon the enlightenment of society and its elected representatives."[19]

The Supreme Court never has accepted this view that the First Amendment protects only political speech. Indeed, the Court has declared that the "guarantees for speech and press are not the preserve of political expression or comment upon public affairs, essential as those are to healthy government."[20] In part, this is probably because of the difficulty of defining what is political speech. Virtually everything from comic strips to commercial advertisements to even pornography can have a political dimension. In part, too, the refusal to narrowly limit the First Amendment in this way reflects the importance of freedom of speech about other topics ranging from scientific debates to accurate commercial information in the marketplace.

2. Discovering Truth

Another classic argument for protecting freedom of speech as a fundamental right is that it is essential for the discovery of truth. Justice Oliver Wendell Holmes invoked the powerful metaphor of the "marketplace of ideas" and wrote that "the best test of truth is the power of the thought to get itself accepted in the competition of the market, and that truth is the only ground upon which their wishes safely can be carried out."[21] The argument is that truth is most likely to emerge from the clash of ideas.

---

14. Alexander Meiklejohn, *Free Speech and Its Relation to Self-Government* 27 (1948).
15. Alexander Meiklejohn, *The First Amendment Is an Absolute*, 1961 Sup. Ct. Rev. 245, 255.
16. Vincent Blasi, *The Checking Value in First Amendment Theory*, 1977 Am. B. Found. Res. J. 523.
17. *Id.* at 542.
18. New York Times v. Sullivan, 376 U.S. 254, 273 (1964).
19. Robert Bork, *Neutral Principles and Some First Amendment Problems*, 47 Ind. L.J. 1, 28 (1971).
20. Time, Inc. v. Hill, 385 U.S. 374, 388 (1967).
21. Abrams v. United States, 250 U.S. 616, 630 (1919) (Holmes, J., dissenting).

John Stuart Mill expressed this view when he wrote that the "peculiar evil of silencing the expression of an opinion is that it is robbing the human race, posterity as well as the existing generation — those who dissent from the opinion, still more than those who hold it."[22] He said that an opinion may be true and may be wrongly suppressed by those in power, or a view may be false and people are informed by its refutation. Justice Brandeis embraced this view when he said that the "fitting remedy for evil counsels is good ones" and that "[i]f there be time to expose through discussion the falsehood and fallacies, to avert the evil by the processes of education, the remedy to be applied is more speech, not enforced silence."[23]

The marketplace of ideas rationale for freedom of speech has been subjected to powerful criticism by scholars.[24] Critics argue that it is wrong to assume that all ideas will enter the marketplace of ideas and even if they do, some may drown out others because some have more resources to have their voices heard. Professor Laurence Tribe observed that "[e]specially when the wealthy have more access to the most potent media of communication than the poor, how sure can we be that 'free trade in ideas' is likely to generate truth?"[25] Professor Jerome Barron said that "if ever there were a self-operating marketplace of ideas, it has long ceased to exist."[26]

Moreover, critics of the marketplace metaphor argue that it is wrong to assume that truth necessarily will triumph over falsehood; history shows that people may be swayed by emotion more than reason. Professor Edwin Baker argued that "the belief that the marketplace leads to truth, or even to the best or most desirable decision, is implausible."[27] He said that it assumes that people will use "their rational capabilities in order to eliminate distortion caused by the form and frequency of message presentation. . . . This [assumption] cannot be accepted. . . . People consistently respond to emotional or irrational appeals."[28] Moreover, even if truth ultimately prevails, enormous harms can occur in the interim. Professor Harry Wellington powerfully made this point when he wrote: "In the long run, true ideas do tend to drive out false ones. The problem is that the short run may be very long, that one short run follows hard upon another, and that we may become overwhelmed by the inexhaustible supply of freshly minted, often very seductive, false ideas. . . . [M]ost of us do believe that the book is closed on some issues. Genocide is an example. . . . Truth may win, and in the long run it may almost always win, but millions of Jews were deliberately and systematically murdered in a very short period of time. . . . Before those murders occurred, many individuals must have come 'to have false beliefs.'"[29]

However, the response to these criticisms is to concede the problems with the marketplace of ideas, but to argue that the alternative — government determination of truth and censorship of falsehoods — is worse. The

---

22. John Stuart Mill, *On Liberty* 76 (1859).
23. Whitney v. California, 274 U.S. at 375, 377 (Brandeis, J., concurring).
24. *See, e.g.*, C. Edwin Baker, *Human Liberty and Freedom of Speech* (1989); Stanley Ingber, *The Marketplace of Ideas: A Legitimizing Myth*, 1984 Duke L.J. 1.
25. Laurence H. Tribe, *American Constitutional Law* 786 (2d ed. 1988).
26. Jerome Barron, *Access to the Press — A New First Amendment Right*, 80 Harv. L. Rev. 1641, 1641 (1967).
27. Baker, *supra* note 24, at 12.
28. *Id.*
29. Harry Wellington, *On Freedom of Expression*, 88 Yale L.J. 1105, 1130, 1132 (1979).

B. Why Should Freedom of Speech Be a Fundamental Right?

marketplace of ideas may be terribly flawed, but allowing the government to decide what is true and right and suppress all else is much worse. Inevitably, government will censor to serve its own ends, such as by silencing its critics, and even a benevolent government will make mistakes as to what is true and false. Professor Nimmer thus remarked that "[i]f acceptance of an idea in the competition of the market is not the 'best test,' [what] is the alternative? It can only be acceptance of an idea by some individual or group narrower than that of the public at large."[30]

3. Advancing Autonomy

A third major rationale often expressed for protecting freedom of speech as a fundamental right is that it is an essential aspect of personhood and autonomy. Professor Baker said that "[t]o engage voluntarily in a speech act is to engage in self-definition of expression. A Vietnam war protestor may explain that when she chants 'Stop This War Now' at a demonstration, she does so without any expectation that her speech will affect continuance of the war . . . ; rather, she participates and chants in order to *define* herself publicly in opposition to the war. This war protestor provides a dramatic illustration of the importance of this self-expressive use of speech, independent of any effective communication to others, for self-fulfillment or self-realization."[31]

Protecting speech because it aids the political process or furthers the search for truth emphasizes the instrumental values of expression. Protecting speech because it is a crucial aspect of autonomy sees expression as intrinsically important.[32] Justice Thurgood Marshall observed that "[t]he First Amendment serves not only the needs of the polity but also those of the human spirit—a spirit that demands self-expression."[33]

This view, too, has been criticized. Robert Bork, for example, argued that there is no inherent reason to find speech to be a fundamental right compared with countless other activities that might be regarded as a part of autonomy or that could advance self-fulfillment. Bork said that the self-fulfillment/autonomy rationale does "not distinguish speech from any other human activity. An individual may develop his faculties or derive pleasure from trading on the stock market, working as a barmaid, engaging in sexual activity, or in any of thousands of other endeavors. Speech can be preferred to other activities only by ranking forms of personal gratification. One cannot, on neutral grounds, choose to protect speech on this basis more than one protects any other claimed freedom."[34]

Moreover, critics of this view maintain that it ignores the ways in which protecting freedom of speech for some can undermine the autonomy and self-fulfillment of others. In recent years, some have argued for restricting hate

---

30. Melville Nimmer, *Nimmer on Freedom of Speech* 1-12 (1984).
31. C. Edwin Baker, *Scope of the First Amendment Freedom of Speech*, 25 UCLA L. Rev. 964, 994 (1978).
32. *See, e.g.*, Martin Redish, *The Value of Free Speech*, 130 U. Pa. L. Rev. 591 (1982) (arguing that self-realization should be regarded as the exclusive value of the First Amendment).
33. Procunier v. Martinez, 416 U.S. 396, 427 (1974) (Marshall, J., concurring).
34. Bork, *supra* note 19, at 25.

speech or pornography because of how such expression demeans and injures others.[35]

4. Promoting Tolerance

Another explanation for protecting freedom of speech as a fundamental right that has received substantial attention in recent years is that it is integral to tolerance, which should be a basic value in our society. Professor Lee Bollinger is a primary advocate of this view, and he argued, "[W]hile free speech theory has traditionally focused on the value of the activity protected (speech), [an alternative approach] seeks a justification by looking at the disvalue of the [frequently intolerant] response to that activity. . . . [The free speech principle] involves a special act of carving out one area of social interaction for extraordinary self-restraint, the purpose of which is to develop and demonstrate a social capacity to control feelings evoked by a host of social encounters."[36] The free speech principle is thus concerned with nothing less than helping to shape "the intellectual character of the society."[37]

The claim is that tolerance is a desirable, if not essential, value and that protecting unpopular or distasteful speech is itself an act of tolerance. Moreover, such tolerance serves as a model that encourages more tolerance throughout society. But critics question why tolerance should be regarded as a basic value.[38] For example, critics argue that society need not be tolerant of the intolerance of others, such as those who advocate great harm, even genocide. Preventing such harms is claimed to be much more important than being tolerant of those who argue for them.

5. Conclusion

These four theories are not mutually exclusive.[39] None is sufficient to explain all of the cases, and none is without problems.[40] Yet all are important in understanding why freedom of speech is protected, in considering what expression should be safeguarded and what can be regulated, and in appraising the Supreme Court's decisions in this area.

---

35. *See, e.g.,* Mari Matsuda, *Public to Racist Speech: Considering the Victim's Story,* 87 Mich. L. Rev. 2320 (1989); Richard Delgado, *Words that Wound: A Tort Action for Racial Insults, Epithets, and Name-Calling,* 17 Harv. C.R.-C.L. L. Rev. 133 (1982) (arguing for restriction of hate speech); Catharine MacKinnon, *Feminism Unmodified* 146-213 (1987) (arguing for restriction of pornography because of its harmful effects on women). Hate speech is discussed below.
36. Lee Bollinger, *The Tolerant Society: Freedom of Speech and Extremist Speech in America* 9-10 (1986).
37. *Id.* at 120.
38. *See* David Strauss, *Why Be Tolerant?,* 53 U. Chi. L. Rev. 1485 (1986).
39. *See* Rodney A. Smolla, *Free Speech in an Open Society* 14-17 (1992) (arguing for "multiple justifications" for freedom of speech); Steven Shiffrin, *The First Amendment and Economic Regulation: Away from a General Theory of the First Amendment,* 78 Nw. U. L. Rev. 1212 (1983) (many values underlie the First Amendment; no need to reduce the First Amendment to a single theory).
40. *See* Ronald Cass, *The Perils of Positive Thinking: Constitutional Interpretation and Negative First Amendment Theory,* 34 UCLA L. Rev. 1405 (1987) (criticizing the foundational theories of the First Amendment).

C. THE ISSUES IN FREE EXPRESSION ANALYSIS

In examining the First Amendment's protection of freedom of expression, analysis is divided into five chapters. First, Chapter 2 examines ways of evaluating any government action restricting freedom of speech. For example, any law can be reviewed to determine whether it is content-based or content-neutral, a distinction that the Court has said is crucial in determining whether strict scrutiny or intermediate scrutiny should be used. Also, any law regulating speech is unconstitutional if it is unduly vague or overbroad. The Court additionally has said that prior restraints of speech are strongly disfavored and thus any government action restricting speech can be challenged if it constitutes a prior restraint. Finally, there is the basic question in evaluating any law as to whether it constitutes a restriction of speech; what government actions sufficiently burden expression as to trigger First Amendment analysis?

Second, Chapter 3 focuses on types of speech that are unprotected by the First Amendment or less protected. The Supreme Court has declared that some types of expression are unprotected so that they may be prohibited and punished. There are other categories of speech that are deemed less protected so that the government has more latitude in regulating them. These categories include incitement of illegal activity, fighting words and provocation of hostile audiences, obscenity and sexually oriented speech, defamatory speech, conduct that communicates, and commercial speech.

Third, Chapter 4 considers the places that are available for speech. Many First Amendment cases involve a claim of a right of access to government-owned property for speech purposes or present a challenge to restrictions on the use of public property for expression. The Supreme Court has drawn distinctions among types of government properties and has articulated rules as to when the government may regulate speech in each.

Fourth, Chapter 5 examines freedom of association. Although association is not expressly mentioned in the First Amendment, the Supreme Court has held that it is a fundamental right because of its close relationship to speech and assembly.[41]

Finally, Chapter 6 focuses on freedom of the press. Many issues concerning press freedom are discussed throughout this book. For example, prior restraint of the press—a crucial aspect of the Constitution's protection of the media—is discussed in Chapter 2. Chapter 6 considers the extent to which the First Amendment is a shield that protects the press from government regulation, such as from being taxed or forced to disclose information or being required to allow others to use it. That chapter also considers whether and when freedom of the press creates a right for the press to have access to government papers, activities, and facilities.

Part of what makes First Amendment analysis difficult is that many of these issues can be present in the same case, and there is no prescribed order for analysis. For instance, if the government were to prohibit sexually explicit displays in public parks, the law might be challenged as vague and overbroad; it might

---

41. *See, e.g.*, NAACP v. Alabama, 357 U.S. 449 (1958).

be analyzed as to whether it is obscenity unprotected by the First Amendment; and it might be considered as to whether it is a permissible restriction of speech in a public forum. All these issues and others are presented. There is no reason why one question should inherently precede the others. Simply put, it is not possible to comprehensively flowchart the First Amendment as a defined series of questions in a required sequential order. There are many ways of approaching and evaluating government actions restricting expression.

CHAPTER 2

FREE SPEECH METHODOLOGY

This chapter considers doctrines that can be used to evaluate any government restrictions of speech. Section A describes the distinction between content-based and content-neutral laws regulating speech and the significance of this difference. Section B considers the vagueness and overbreadth doctrines: Even in regulating unprotected speech, laws are unconstitutional if they are unduly vague or overbroad. Section C examines the strong presumption against prior restraints and especially focuses on classic forms of prior restraints such as court orders suppressing speech and licensing systems. Finally, section D discusses the basic question of what constitutes an infringement of speech.

A. THE DISTINCTION BETWEEN CONTENT-BASED AND CONTENT-NEUTRAL LAWS

The Supreme Court frequently has declared that the very core of the First Amendment is that the government cannot regulate speech based on its content. The Court stated, "[A]bove all else, the First Amendment means that government has no power to restrict expression because of its message, its ideas, its subject matter or its content."[1] The Court has declared that "[c]ontent-based regulations are presumptively invalid."[2] In countless First Amendment cases, involving many of the issues discussed throughout this book, the Court has invoked the content-based/content-neutral distinction as the basis for its decisions.

The material in this part begins by discussing the importance of the distinction, including the Court's dictate that strict scrutiny is generally used for content-based restrictions, while intermediate scrutiny is used for content-neutral laws. Considered next is the question of how it is determined whether a law is content-based. Finally, problems in applying the distinction between content-based and content-neutral laws are discussed.

---

1. Police Department of Chicago v. Mosley, 408 U.S. 92, 95-96 (1972).
2. R.A.V. v. City of St. Paul, 505 U.S. 377, 382 (1992).

1. The Importance of the Distinction

In Turner Broadcasting System v. Federal Communications Commission, 512 U.S. 622 (1994), the Court explained that content-based restrictions generally must meet strict scrutiny, while content-neutral laws only need meet intermediate scrutiny. The Court said: "For these reasons, the First Amendment, subject only to narrow and well-understood exceptions, does not countenance governmental control over the content of messages expressed by private individuals. Our precedents thus apply the most exacting scrutiny to regulations that suppress, disadvantage, or impose differential burdens upon speech because of its content. Laws that compel speakers to utter or distribute speech bearing a particular message are subject to the same rigorous scrutiny. In contrast, regulations that are unrelated to the content of speech are subject to an intermediate level of scrutiny because in most cases they pose a less substantial risk of excising certain ideas or viewpoints from the public dialogue."

In Reed v. Town of Gilbert, the Court applied this distinction between content-based and content-neutral laws.

REED v. TOWN OF GILBERT
576 U.S. 155 (2015)

Justice THOMAS delivered the opinion of the Court.

The town of Gilbert, Arizona (or Town), has adopted a comprehensive code governing the manner in which people may display outdoor signs. The Sign Code identifies various categories of signs based on the type of information they convey, then subjects each category to different restrictions. One of the categories is "Temporary Directional Signs Relating to a Qualifying Event," loosely defined as signs directing the public to a meeting of a nonprofit group. The Code imposes more stringent restrictions on these signs than it does on signs conveying other messages. We hold that these provisions are content-based regulations of speech that cannot survive strict scrutiny.

I

The Sign Code prohibits the display of outdoor signs anywhere within the Town without a permit, but it then exempts 23 categories of signs from that requirement. These exemptions include everything from bazaar signs to flying banners. Three categories of exempt signs are particularly relevant here.

The first is "Ideological Sign[s]." This category includes any "sign communicating a message or ideas for noncommercial purposes that is not a Construction Sign, Directional Sign, Temporary Directional Sign Relating to a Qualifying Event, Political Sign, Garage Sale Sign, or a sign owned or required by a governmental agency." Of the three categories discussed here, the Code treats ideological signs most favorably, allowing them to be up to 20 square feet in area and to be placed in all "zoning districts" without time limits.

The second category is "Political Sign[s]." This includes any "temporary sign designed to influence the outcome of an election called by a public body." The Code treats these signs less favorably than ideological signs. The Code allows the

A. The Distinction Between Content-Based and Content-Neutral Laws

placement of political signs up to 16 square feet on residential property and up to 32 square feet on nonresidential property, undeveloped municipal property, and "rights-of-way." These signs may be displayed up to 60 days before a primary election and up to 15 days following a general election.

The third category is "Temporary Directional Signs Relating to a Qualifying Event." This includes any "Temporary Sign intended to direct pedestrians, motorists, and other passersby to a 'qualifying event.'" A "qualifying event" is defined as any "assembly, gathering, activity, or meeting sponsored, arranged, or promoted by a religious, charitable, community service, educational, or other similar non-profit organization." The Code treats temporary directional signs even less favorably than political signs. Temporary directional signs may be no larger than six square feet. They may be placed on private property or on a public right-of-way, but no more than four signs may be placed on a single property at any time. And, they may be displayed no more than 12 hours before the "qualifying event" and no more than 1 hour afterward.

Petitioners Good News Community Church (Church) and its pastor, Clyde Reed, wish to advertise the time and location of their Sunday church services. The Church is a small, cash-strapped entity that owns no building, so it holds its services at elementary schools or other locations in or near the Town. In order to inform the public about its services, which are held in a variety of different locations, the Church began placing 15 to 20 temporary signs around the Town, frequently in the public right-of-way abutting the street. The signs typically displayed the Church's name, along with the time and location of the upcoming service. Church members would post the signs early in the day on Saturday and then remove them around midday on Sunday. The display of these signs requires little money and manpower, and thus has proved to be an economical and effective way for the Church to let the community know where its services are being held each week.

This practice caught the attention of the Town's Sign Code compliance manager, who twice cited the Church for violating the Code. The first citation noted that the Church exceeded the time limits for displaying its temporary directional signs. The second citation referred to the same problem, along with the Church's failure to include the date of the event on the signs. Town officials even confiscated one of the Church's signs, which Reed had to retrieve from the municipal offices.

Reed contacted the Sign Code Compliance Department in an attempt to reach an accommodation. His efforts proved unsuccessful. The Town's Code compliance manager informed the Church that there would be "no leniency under the Code" and promised to punish any future violations. Shortly thereafter, petitioners filed a complaint in the United States District Court for the District of Arizona, arguing that the Sign Code abridged their freedom of speech in violation of the First and Fourteenth Amendments.

II

The First Amendment, applicable to the States through the Fourteenth Amendment, prohibits the enactment of laws "abridging the freedom of speech." Under that Clause, a government, including a municipal government vested with state authority, "has no power to restrict expression because of its message, its ideas, its subject matter, or its content." Content-based laws—those that target speech based on its communicative content—are presumptively unconstitutional and may be justified only if the government proves that they are narrowly tailored to serve compelling state interests.

Government regulation of speech is content based if a law applies to particular speech because of the topic discussed or the idea or message expressed. This commonsense meaning of the phrase "content based" requires a court to consider whether a regulation of speech "on its face" draws distinctions based on the message a speaker conveys. Some facial distinctions based on a message are obvious, defining regulated speech by particular subject matter, and others are more subtle, defining regulated speech by its function or purpose. Both are distinctions drawn based on the message a speaker conveys, and, therefore, are subject to strict scrutiny.

Our precedents have also recognized a separate and additional category of laws that, though facially content neutral, will be considered content-based regulations of speech: laws that cannot be "'justified without reference to the content of the regulated speech,'" or that were adopted by the government "because of disagreement with the message [the speech] conveys." Those laws, like those that are content based on their face, must also satisfy strict scrutiny.

The Town's Sign Code is content based on its face. It defines "Temporary Directional Signs" on the basis of whether a sign conveys the message of directing the public to church or some other "qualifying event." It defines "Political Signs" on the basis of whether a sign's message is "designed to influence the outcome of an election." And it defines "Ideological Signs" on the basis of whether a sign "communicat[es] a message or ideas" that do not fit within the Code's other categories. It then subjects each of these categories to different restrictions.

The restrictions in the Sign Code that apply to any given sign thus depend entirely on the communicative content of the sign. If a sign informs its reader of the time and place a book club will discuss John Locke's Two Treatises of Government, that sign will be treated differently from a sign expressing the view that one should vote for one of Locke's followers in an upcoming election, and both signs will be treated differently from a sign expressing an ideological view rooted in Locke's theory of government. More to the point, the Church's signs inviting people to attend its worship services are treated differently from signs conveying other types of ideas. On its face, the Sign Code is a content-based regulation of speech. We thus have no need to consider the government's justifications or purposes for enacting the Code to determine whether it is subject to strict scrutiny. A law that is content based on its face is subject to strict scrutiny regardless of the government's benign motive, content-neutral justification, or lack of "animus toward the ideas contained" in the regulated speech.

The First Amendment requires no less. Innocent motives do not eliminate the danger of censorship presented by a facially content-based statute, as future government officials may one day wield such statutes to suppress disfavored speech. That is why the First Amendment expressly targets the operation of the laws—*i.e.,* the "abridg[ment] of speech"—rather than merely the motives of those who enacted them. "'The vice of content-based legislation . . . is not that it is always used for invidious, thought-control purposes, but that it lends itself to use for those purposes.'"

A. The Distinction Between Content-Based and Content-Neutral Laws

III

Because the Town's Sign Code imposes content-based restrictions on speech, those provisions can stand only if they survive strict scrutiny, "'which requires the Government to prove that the restriction furthers a compelling interest and is narrowly tailored to achieve that interest.'" Thus, it is the Town's burden to demonstrate that the Code's differentiation between temporary directional signs and other types of signs, such as political signs and ideological signs, furthers a compelling governmental interest and is narrowly tailored to that end.

The Town cannot do so. It has offered only two governmental interests in support of the distinctions the Sign Code draws: preserving the Town's aesthetic appeal and traffic safety. Assuming for the sake of argument that those are compelling governmental interests, the Code's distinctions fail as hopelessly underinclusive.

Starting with the preservation of aesthetics, temporary directional signs are "no greater an eyesore," than ideological or political ones. Yet the Code allows unlimited proliferation of larger ideological signs while strictly limiting the number, size, and duration of smaller directional ones. The Town cannot claim that placing strict limits on temporary directional signs is necessary to beautify the Town while at the same time allowing unlimited numbers of other types of signs that create the same problem.

The Town similarly has not shown that limiting temporary directional signs is necessary to eliminate threats to traffic safety, but that limiting other types of signs is not. The Town has offered no reason to believe that directional signs pose a greater threat to safety than do ideological or political signs. If anything, a sharply worded ideological sign seems more likely to distract a driver than a sign directing the public to a nearby church meeting.

In light of this underinclusiveness, the Town has not met its burden to prove that its Sign Code is narrowly tailored to further a compelling government interest. Because a "'law cannot be regarded as protecting an interest of the highest order, and thus as justifying a restriction on truthful speech, when it leaves appreciable damage to that supposedly vital interest unprohibited,'" the Sign Code fails strict scrutiny.

IV

Our decision today will not prevent governments from enacting effective sign laws. The Town asserts that an "'absolutist'" content-neutrality rule would render "virtually all distinctions in sign laws . . . subject to strict scrutiny," but that is not the case. Not "all distinctions" are subject to strict scrutiny, only *content-based* ones are. Laws that are *content neutral* are instead subject to lesser scrutiny.

The Town has ample content-neutral options available to resolve problems with safety and aesthetics. For example, its current Code regulates many aspects of signs that have nothing to do with a sign's message: size, building materials, lighting, moving parts, and portability. And on public property, the Town may go a long way toward entirely forbidding the posting of signs, so long as it does so in an evenhanded, content-neutral manner.

At the same time, the presence of certain signs may be essential, both for vehicles and pedestrians, to guide traffic or to identify hazards and ensure safety.

A sign ordinance narrowly tailored to the challenges of protecting the safety of pedestrians, drivers, and passengers—such as warning signs marking hazards on private property, signs directing traffic, or street numbers associated with private houses—well might survive strict scrutiny. The signs at issue in this case, including political and ideological signs and signs for events, are far removed from those purposes. As discussed above, they are facially content based and are neither justified by traditional safety concerns nor narrowly tailored.

Justice ALITO, with whom Justice KENNEDY and Justice SOTOMAYOR join, concurring.

I join the opinion of the Court but add a few words of further explanation.

As the Court holds, what we have termed "content-based" laws must satisfy strict scrutiny. Content-based laws merit this protection because they present, albeit sometimes in a subtler form, the same dangers as laws that regulate speech based on viewpoint. Limiting speech based on its "topic" or "subject" favors those who do not want to disturb the status quo. Such regulations may interfere with democratic self-government and the search for truth.

As the Court shows, the regulations at issue in this case are replete with content-based distinctions, and as a result they must satisfy strict scrutiny. This does not mean, however, that municipalities are powerless to enact and enforce reasonable sign regulations. I will not attempt to provide anything like a comprehensive list, but here are some rules that would not be content based:

> Rules regulating the size of signs. These rules may distinguish among signs based on any content-neutral criteria, including any relevant criteria listed below.
> Rules regulating the locations in which signs may be placed. These rules may distinguish between free-standing signs and those attached to buildings.
> Rules distinguishing between lighted and unlighted signs.
> Rules distinguishing between signs with fixed messages and electronic signs with messages that change.
> Rules that distinguish between the placement of signs on private and public property.
> Rules distinguishing between the placement of signs on commercial and residential property.
> Rules distinguishing between on-premises and off-premises signs.
> Rules restricting the total number of signs allowed per mile of roadway.
> Rules imposing time restrictions on signs advertising a one-time event. Rules of this nature do not discriminate based on topic or subject and are akin to rules restricting the times within which oral speech or music is allowed.

In addition to regulating signs put up by private actors, government entities may also erect their own signs consistent with the principles that allow governmental speech. They may put up all manner of signs to promote safety, as well as directional signs and signs pointing out historic sites and scenic spots.

Properly understood, today's decision will not prevent cities from regulating signs in a way that fully protects public safety and serves legitimate esthetic objectives.

A. The Distinction Between Content-Based and Content-Neutral Laws

Justice KAGAN, with whom Justice GINSBURG and Justice BREYER join, concurring in the judgment.

Countless cities and towns across America have adopted ordinances regulating the posting of signs, while exempting certain categories of signs based on their subject matter. For example, some municipalities generally prohibit illuminated signs in residential neighborhoods, but lift that ban for signs that identify the address of a home or the name of its owner or occupant. In other municipalities, safety signs such as "Blind Pedestrian Crossing" and "Hidden Driveway" can be posted without a permit, even as other permanent signs require one. Elsewhere, historic site markers—for example, "George Washington Slept Here"—are also exempt from general regulations. And similarly, the federal Highway Beautification Act limits signs along interstate highways unless, for instance, they direct travelers to "scenic and historical attractions" or advertise free coffee.

Given the Court's analysis, many sign ordinances of that kind are now in jeopardy. And although the majority holds out hope that some sign laws with subject-matter exemptions "might survive" that stringent review, the likelihood is that most will be struck down. After all, it is the "rare case[ ] in which a speech restriction withstands strict scrutiny." To clear that high bar, the government must show that a content-based distinction "is necessary to serve a compelling state interest and is narrowly drawn to achieve that end." So on the majority's view, courts would have to determine that a town has a compelling interest in informing passersby where George Washington slept. And likewise, courts would have to find that a town has no other way to prevent hidden-driveway mishaps than by specially treating hidden-driveway signs. (Well-placed speed bumps? Lower speed limits? Or how about just a ban on hidden driveways?) The consequence—unless courts water down strict scrutiny to something unrecognizable—is that our communities will find themselves in an unenviable bind: They will have to either repeal the exemptions that allow for helpful signs on streets and sidewalks, or else lift their sign restrictions altogether and resign themselves to the resulting clutter.

Although the majority insists that applying strict scrutiny to all such ordinances is "essential" to protecting First Amendment freedoms, I find it challenging to understand why that is so. This Court's decisions articulate two important and related reasons for subjecting content-based speech regulations to the most exacting standard of review. The first is "to preserve an uninhibited marketplace of ideas in which truth will ultimately prevail." The second is to ensure that the government has not regulated speech "based on hostility—or favoritism—towards the underlying message expressed." Yet the subject-matter exemptions included in many sign ordinances do not implicate those concerns. Allowing residents, say, to install a light bulb over "name and address" signs but no others does not distort the marketplace of ideas. Nor does that different treatment give rise to an inference of impermissible government motive.

We apply strict scrutiny to facially content-based regulations of speech, in keeping with the rationales just described, when there is any "realistic possibility that official suppression of ideas is afoot." That is always the case when the regulation facially differentiates on the basis of viewpoint. It is also the case (except in non-public or limited public forums) when a law restricts "discussion of an entire topic" in public debate.

But when that is not realistically possible, we may do well to relax our guard so that "entirely reasonable" laws imperiled by strict scrutiny can survive. This point is by no means new. Our concern with content-based regulation arises from the fear that the government will skew the public's debate of ideas—so when "that risk is inconsequential, . . . strict scrutiny is unwarranted." To do its intended work, of course, the category of content-based regulation triggering strict scrutiny must sweep more broadly than the actual harm; that category exists to create a buffer zone guaranteeing that the government cannot favor or disfavor certain viewpoints. But that buffer zone need not extend forever. We can administer our content-regulation doctrine with a dose of common sense, so as to leave standing laws that in no way implicate its intended function.

The absence of any sensible basis for these and other distinctions dooms the Town's ordinance under even the intermediate scrutiny that the Court typically applies to "time, place, or manner" speech regulations. The Town of Gilbert's defense of its sign ordinance—most notably, the law's distinctions between directional signs and others—does not pass strict scrutiny, or intermediate scrutiny, or even the laugh test. Accordingly, there is no need to decide in this case whether strict scrutiny applies to every sign ordinance in every town across this country containing a subject-matter exemption.

I suspect this Court and others will regret the majority's insistence today on answering that question in the affirmative. As the years go by, courts will discover that thousands of towns have such ordinances, many of them "entirely reasonable." And as the challenges to them mount, courts will have to invalidate one after the other. (This Court may soon find itself a veritable Supreme Board of Sign Review.) And courts will strike down those democratically enacted local laws even though no one—certainly not the majority—has ever explained why the vindication of First Amendment values requires that result. Because I see no reason why such an easy case calls for us to cast a constitutional pall on reasonable regulations quite unlike the law before us, I concur only in the judgment.

Another recent example of the Court stressing the need for heightened scrutiny of content-based regulation of speech is United States v. Alvarez, 567 U.S. 709 (2012). The federal Stolen Valor Act makes it a crime for a person to falsely claim to have received military honors or decorations. Xavier Alvarez was a member of a local government water district commission and lied about having won the Congressional Medal of Honor. (Justice Kennedy begins his opinion by saying of Alvarez, "Lying was his habit.")

The Court, in a six-to-three decision, without a majority opinion, declared the Stolen Valor Act unconstitutional. Justice Kennedy wrote a plurality opinion, joined by Chief Justice Roberts and Justices Ginsburg and Sotomayor, saying that the act was a content-based restriction on speech and "[w]hen content-based speech regulation is in question, exacting scrutiny is required." Justice Kennedy said that the government failed to prove sufficient harms from people lying about military honors to justify the law and also that Congress could achieve its goals in narrower ways, such as publishing lists of those who have received military honors so that liars could be quickly exposed.

A. The Distinction Between Content-Based and Content-Neutral Laws

Justice Breyer wrote an opinion concurring in the judgment, joined by Justice Kagan, and said that "intermediate scrutiny" was the appropriate test. Justice Breyer concluded that the law failed intermediate scrutiny because the government could achieve its goal through a narrower means, such as prohibiting people from lying about military honors if they were seeking a tangible benefit.

Justice Alito wrote a dissent, joined by Justices Scalia and Thomas, and argued that the law was constitutional because of the government's crucial interest in protecting the integrity of military honors and the absence of any less restrictive alternative. He emphasized that false speech should not be protected by the First Amendment: "By holding that the First Amendment nevertheless shields these lies, the Court breaks sharply from a long line of cases recognizing that the right to free speech does not protect false factual statements that inflict real harm and serve no legitimate interest."

Some categories of speech are unprotected or less protected by the First Amendment, such as incitement of illegal activity, obscenity, and defamation. These categories, by definition, are content-based. These categories, discussed in Chapter 3, are exceptions to the usual rule of strict scrutiny for content-based regulations. It also might be said that the Supreme Court essentially has found that there is a compelling interest in excluding speech such as incitement or obscenity from First Amendment protection. But apart from these categories, content-based discrimination must meet strict scrutiny, and the Court has indicated that content-based distinctions within these categories also must pass strict scrutiny.[3]

Why is there so much concern about content neutrality? Obviously, the fear is that the government will target particular messages and attempt to control thoughts on a topic by regulating speech.[4] As the Court said in *Turner Broadcasting*, "Laws of this sort pose the inherent risk that the Government seeks not to advance a legitimate regulatory goal, but to suppress unpopular ideas or information or to manipulate the public debate through coercion rather than persuasion."[5]

A viewpoint restriction does this directly. The government could try to control dissent and advance its own interests by stopping speech that expresses criticism of government policy, while allowing praise. A subject-matter restriction on speech can accomplish the same goal. In the 1960s, a law prohibiting speech about the war in Vietnam—a subject-matter restriction—obviously would have had a far greater impact on antiwar speech. The Court has explained that "[t]o allow a government the choice of permissible subjects for public debate would be to allow the government control over the search for political truth."[6]

---

3. *See* R.A.V. v. City of St. Paul, 505 U.S. 377 (1992), discussed below in Chapter 3.
4. As the Court noted, "[such restrictions] raise the specter that the government may effectively drive certain ideas or viewpoints from the marketplace." Simon & Schuster, Inc. v. Members of the New York St. Crime Victims Board, 502 U.S. 105, 116 (1991).
5. Turner Broadcasting System v. Federal Communication Commn., 512 U.S. at 641.
6. Consolidated Edison Co. of N.Y., Inc. v. Public Service Commn., 447 U.S. 530, 538 (1980).

2. How Is It Determined Whether a Law Is Content-Based?

The requirement that the government be content-neutral in its regulation of speech means that the government must be both viewpoint-neutral and subject-matter-neutral.[7] In other words, a law will be found to be content-based and must meet strict scrutiny if it is either a viewpoint or a subject-matter restriction. Viewpoint-neutral means that the government cannot regulate speech based on the ideology of the message.[8] For example, it would be clearly unconstitutional for the government to say that pro-choice demonstrations are allowed in the park but antiabortion demonstrations are not allowed. "Subject-matter-neutral" means that the government cannot regulate speech based on the topic of the speech. Consider some examples of each.

THE REQUIREMENT FOR VIEWPOINT NEUTRALITY

In two recent cases, the Supreme Court declared unconstitutional provisions of the Lanham Act, which governs registration of trademarks, on the ground that they were viewpoint restrictions of speech.

MATAL v. TAM
137 S. Ct. 1744 (2017)

Justice ALITO announced the judgment of the Court and delivered the opinion of the Court with respect to Parts I, II, and III-A, and an opinion with respect to Parts III-B, III-C, and IV, in which THE CHIEF JUSTICE, Justice THOMAS, and Justice BREYER join.

This case concerns a dance-rock band's application for federal trademark registration of the band's name, "The Slants." "Slants" is a derogatory term for persons of Asian descent, and members of the band are Asian-Americans. But the band members believe that by taking that slur as the name of their group, they will help to "reclaim" the term and drain its denigrating force.

The Patent and Trademark Office (PTO) denied the application based on a provision of federal law prohibiting the registration of trademarks that may "disparage . . . or bring . . . into contemp[t] or disrepute" any "persons, living or dead." We now hold that this provision violates the Free Speech Clause of the First Amendment. It offends a bedrock First Amendment principle: Speech may not be banned on the ground that it expresses ideas that offend.

I

"The principle underlying trademark protection is that distinctive marks—words, names, symbols, and the like—can help distinguish a particular artisan's goods from those of others." A trademark "designate[s] the goods as the product of a particular trader" and "protect[s] his good will against the sale of another's

---

7. *See, e.g.,* Perry Education Assn. v. Perry Local Educators' Assn., 460 U.S. 37, 45 (1983).
8. *See* Amy Sabrin, *Thinking About Content: Can It Play an Appropriate Role in Government Funding of the Arts?*, 102 Yale L.J. 1209, 1220 (1993).

A. The Distinction Between Content-Based and Content-Neutral Laws

product as his." It helps consumers identify goods and services that they wish to purchase, as well as those they want to avoid.

"[F]ederal law does not create trademarks." Trademarks and their precursors have ancient origins, and trademarks were protected at common law and in equity at the time of the founding of our country. The foundation of current federal trademark law is the Lanham Act, enacted in 1946. Under the Lanham Act, trademarks that are "used in commerce" may be placed on the "principal register," that is, they may be federally registered. There are now more than two million marks that have active federal certificates of registration. This system of federal registration helps to ensure that trademarks are fully protected and supports the free flow of commerce. "[N]ational protection of trademarks is desirable," we have explained, "because trademarks foster competition and the maintenance of quality by securing to the producer the benefits of good reputation."

Without federal registration, a valid trademark may still be used in commerce. And an unregistered trademark can be enforced against would-be infringers in several ways. Most important, even if a trademark is not federally registered, it may still be enforceable under §43(a) of the Lanham Act, which creates a federal cause of action for trademark infringement. And an unregistered trademark can be enforced under state common law, or if it has been registered in a State, under that State's registration system.

Federal registration, however, "confers important legal rights and benefits on trademark owners who register their marks." Registration on the principal register (1) "serves as 'constructive notice of the registrant's claim of ownership' of the mark," (2) "is 'prima facie evidence of the validity of the registered mark and of the registration of the mark, of the owner's ownership of the mark, and of the owner's exclusive right to use the registered mark in commerce on or in connection with the goods or services specified in the certificate,'" and (3) can make a mark "'incontestable'" once a mark has been registered for five years. Registration also enables the trademark holder "to stop the importation into the United States of articles bearing an infringing mark."

The Lanham Act contains provisions that bar certain trademarks from the principal register. For example, a trademark cannot be registered if it is "merely descriptive or deceptively misdescriptive" of goods, or if it is so similar to an already registered trademark or trade name that it is "likely . . . to cause confusion, or to cause mistake, or to deceive." At issue in this case is one such provision, which we will call "the disparagement clause." This provision prohibits the registration of a trademark "which may disparage . . . persons, living or dead, institutions, beliefs, or national symbols, or bring them into contempt, or disrepute." §1052(a). This clause appeared in the original Lanham Act and has remained the same to this day.

Simon Tam is the lead singer of "The Slants." He chose this moniker in order to "reclaim" and "take ownership" of stereotypes about people of Asian ethnicity. The group "draws inspiration for its lyrics from childhood slurs and mocking nursery rhymes" and has given its albums names such as "The Yellow Album" and "Slanted Eyes, Slanted Hearts."

Tam sought federal registration of "THE SLANTS," on the principal register, but an examining attorney at the PTO rejected the request, finding that "there is . . . a substantial composite of persons who find the term in the applied-for mark offensive." The examining attorney relied in part on the fact that "numerous dictionaries define 'slants' or 'slant-eyes' as a derogatory or offensive term." The examining attorney also relied on a finding that "the band's name has been found offensive numerous times"—citing a performance that was canceled because of the band's moniker and the fact that "several bloggers and commenters to articles on the band have indicated that they find the term and the applied-for mark offensive." *Id.*, at 29-30.

Tam contested the denial of registration before the examining attorney and before the PTO's Trademark Trial and Appeal Board (TTAB) but to no avail.

II

[In Part II of the opinion the Court held that the statutory provision prohibits trademarks that are disparaging to racial groups.]

III

Because the disparagement clause applies to marks that disparage the members of a racial or ethnic group, we must decide whether the clause violates the Free Speech Clause of the First Amendment. And at the outset, we must consider three arguments that would either eliminate any First Amendment protection or result in highly permissive rational-basis review. Specifically, the Government contends (1) that trademarks are government speech, not private speech, (2) that trademarks are a form of government subsidy, and (3) that the constitutionality of the disparagement clause should be tested under a new "government-program" doctrine. We address each of these arguments below.

The First Amendment prohibits Congress and other government entities and actors from "abridging the freedom of speech"; the First Amendment does not say that Congress and other government entities must abridge their own ability to speak freely. And our cases recognize that "[t]he Free Speech Clause . . . does not regulate government speech." When a government entity embarks on a course of action, it necessarily takes a particular viewpoint and rejects others. The Free Speech Clause does not require government to maintain viewpoint neutrality when its officers and employees speak about that venture.

But while the government-speech doctrine is important—indeed, essential—it is a doctrine that is susceptible to dangerous misuse. If private speech could be passed off as government speech by simply affixing a government seal of approval, government could silence or muffle the expression of disfavored viewpoints. For this reason, we must exercise great caution before extending our government-speech precedents.

At issue here is the content of trademarks that are registered by the PTO, an arm of the Federal Government. The Federal Government does not dream up these marks, and it does not edit marks submitted for registration. Except as required by the statute involved here, an examiner may not reject a mark based on the viewpoint that it appears to express. Thus, unless that section is thought to apply, an examiner does not inquire whether any viewpoint conveyed by a mark is consistent with Government policy or whether any such viewpoint is consistent with that expressed by other marks already on the principal register. Instead, if the mark meets the Lanham Act's viewpoint-neutral requirements, registration is mandatory. And if an examiner finds that a mark is eligible for placement on the principal register, that decision is not reviewed by any higher official unless the registration is challenged.

In light of all this, it is far-fetched to suggest that the content of a registered mark is government speech. If the federal registration of a trademark makes the mark government speech, the Federal Government is babbling prodigiously and incoherently. It is saying many unseemly things. It is expressing contradictory views. It is unashamedly endorsing a vast array of commercial products and services.

None of our government speech cases even remotely supports the idea that registered trademarks are government speech.

[T]rademarks often have an expressive content. Companies spend huge amounts to create and publicize trademarks that convey a message. It is true that the necessary brevity of trademarks limits what they can say. But powerful messages can sometimes be conveyed in just a few words. Trademarks are private, not government, speech.

Our cases use the term "viewpoint" discrimination in a broad sense, and in that sense, the disparagement clause discriminates on the bases of "viewpoint." To be sure, the clause evenhandedly prohibits disparagement of all groups. It applies equally to marks that damn Democrats and Republicans, capitalists and socialists, and those arrayed on both sides of every possible issue. It denies registration to any mark that is offensive to a substantial percentage of the members of any group. But in the sense relevant here, that is viewpoint discrimination: Giving offense is a viewpoint.

We have said time and again that "the public expression of ideas may not be prohibited merely because the ideas are themselves offensive to some of their hearers." For this reason, the disparagement clause cannot be saved by analyzing it as a type of government program in which some content- and speaker-based restrictions are permitted.

It is claimed that the disparagement clause serves two interests. The first is phrased in a variety of ways in the briefs. Echoing language in one of the opinions below, the Government asserts an interest in preventing "underrepresented groups" from being "bombarded with demeaning messages in commercial advertising.'" But no matter how the point is phrased, its unmistakable thrust is this: The Government has an interest in preventing speech expressing ideas that offend. And, as we have explained, that idea strikes at the heart of the First Amendment. Speech that demeans on the basis of race, ethnicity, gender, religion, age, disability, or any other similar ground is hateful; but the proudest boast of our free speech jurisprudence is that we protect the freedom to express "the thought that we hate." United States v. Schwimmer (1929) (Holmes, J., dissenting).

The second interest asserted is protecting the orderly flow of commerce. Commerce, we are told, is disrupted by trademarks that "involv[e] disparagement of race, gender, ethnicity, national origin, religion, sexual orientation, and similar demographic classification." A simple answer to this argument is that the disparagement clause is not "narrowly drawn" to drive out trademarks that support invidious discrimination. The clause reaches any trademark that disparages *any person, group, or institution*. It applies to trademarks like the following: "Down with racists," "Down with sexists," "Down with homophobes." It is not an anti-discrimination clause; it is a happy-talk clause. In this way, it goes much further than is necessary to serve the interest asserted.

The clause is far too broad in other ways as well. The clause protects every person living or dead as well as every institution. Is it conceivable that commerce would be disrupted by a trademark saying: "James Buchanan was a disastrous president" or "Slavery is an evil institution"?

There is also a deeper problem with the argument that commercial speech may be cleansed of any expression likely to cause offense. The commercial market is well stocked with merchandise that disparages prominent figures and groups, and the line between commercial and non-commercial speech is not always clear, as this case illustrates. If affixing the commercial label permits the suppression of any speech that may lead to political or social "volatility," free speech would be endangered.

For these reasons, we hold that the disparagement clause violates the Free Speech Clause of the First Amendment.

Justice KENNEDY, with whom Justice GINSBURG, Justice SOTOMAYOR, and Justice KAGAN join, concurring in part and concurring in the judgment.

As the Court is correct to hold, §1052(a) constitutes viewpoint discrimination—a form of speech suppression so potent that it must be subject to rigorous constitutional scrutiny. The Government's action and the statute on which it is based cannot survive this scrutiny.

The Court is correct in its judgment, and I join Parts I, II, and III-A of its opinion. This separate writing explains in greater detail why the First Amendment's protections against viewpoint discrimination apply to the trademark here. It submits further that the viewpoint discrimination rationale renders unnecessary any extended treatment of other questions raised by the parties.

I

Those few categories of speech that the government can regulate or punish—for instance, fraud, defamation, or incitement—are well established within our constitutional tradition. Aside from these and a few other narrow exceptions, it is a fundamental principle of the First Amendment that the government may not punish or suppress speech based on disapproval of the ideas or perspectives the speech conveys.

The First Amendment guards against laws "targeted at specific subject matter," a form of speech suppression known as content based discrimination. This category includes a subtype of laws that go further, aimed at the suppression of "particular views . . . on a subject." A law found to discriminate based on viewpoint is an "egregious form of content discrimination," which is "presumptively unconstitutional."

At its most basic, the test for viewpoint discrimination is whether—within the relevant subject category—the government has singled out a subset of messages for disfavor based on the views expressed. In the instant case, the disparagement clause the Government now seeks to implement and enforce identifies the relevant subject as "persons, living or dead, institutions, beliefs, or national symbols." Within that category, an applicant may register a positive or benign mark but not a derogatory one. The law thus reflects the Government's disapproval of a subset of messages it finds offensive. This is the essence of viewpoint discrimination.

A. The Distinction Between Content-Based and Content-Neutral Laws

The Government disputes this conclusion. It argues, to begin with, that the law is viewpoint neutral because it applies in equal measure to any trademark that demeans or offends. This misses the point. A subject that is first defined by content and then regulated or censored by mandating only one sort of comment is not viewpoint neutral. To prohibit all sides from criticizing their opponents makes a law more viewpoint based, not less so. The logic of the Government's rule is that a law would be viewpoint neutral even if it provided that public officials could be praised but not condemned. The First Amendment's viewpoint neutrality principle protects more than the right to identify with a particular side. It protects the right to create and present arguments for particular positions in particular ways, as the speaker chooses. By mandating positivity, the law here might silence dissent and distort the marketplace of ideas.

The Government next suggests that the statute is viewpoint neutral because the disparagement clause applies to trademarks regardless of the applicant's personal views or reasons for using the mark. Instead, registration is denied based on the expected reaction of the applicant's audience. The Government may not insulate a law from charges of viewpoint discrimination by tying censorship to the reaction of the speaker's audience. The Court has suggested that viewpoint discrimination occurs when the government intends to suppress a speaker's beliefs, but viewpoint discrimination need not take that form in every instance. The danger of viewpoint discrimination is that the government is attempting to remove certain ideas or perspectives from a broader debate. That danger is all the greater if the ideas or perspectives are ones a particular audience might think offensive, at least at first hearing. An initial reaction may prompt further reflection, leading to a more reasoned, more tolerant position.

Indeed, a speech burden based on audience reactions is simply government hostility and intervention in a different guise. The speech is targeted, after all, based on the government's disapproval of the speaker's choice of message. And it is the government itself that is attempting in this case to decide whether the relevant audience would find the speech offensive. For reasons like these, the Court's cases have long prohibited the government from justifying a First Amendment burden by pointing to the offensiveness of the speech to be suppressed.

II

The parties dispute whether trademarks are commercial speech and whether trademark registration should be considered a federal subsidy. The former issue may turn on whether certain commercial concerns for the protection of trademarks might, as a general matter, be the basis for regulation. However that issue is resolved, the viewpoint based discrimination at issue here necessarily invokes heightened scrutiny. "Commercial speech is no exception," the Court has explained, to the principle that the First Amendment "requires heightened scrutiny whenever the government creates a regulation of speech because of disagreement with the message it conveys." Unlike content based discrimination, discrimination based on viewpoint, including a regulation that targets speech for its offensiveness, remains of serious concern in the commercial context.

A law that can be directed against speech found offensive to some portion of the public can be turned against minority and dissenting views to the detriment of all. The First Amendment does not entrust that power to the government's benevolence. Instead, our reliance must be on the substantial safeguards of free and open discussion in a democratic society.

Two years later, in Iancu v. Brunetti, 139 S. Ct. 2294 (2019), the Court struck down another provision of the Lanham Act, which prohibited registration of trademarks which are "scandalous" or "immoral." A clothing manufacturer wished to register as a trademark "F.U.C.T." This was denied based on the provision in the Lanham Act. The Supreme Court declared this unconstitutional. Justice Kagan, writing for the Court, stressed that this was viewpoint based:

> If the "immoral or scandalous" bar similarly discriminates on the basis of viewpoint, it must also collide with our First Amendment doctrine. So the key question becomes: Is the "immoral or scandalous" criterion in the Lanham Act viewpoint-neutral or viewpoint-based?
>
> It is viewpoint-based. The meanings of "immoral" and "scandalous" are not mysterious, but resort to some dictionaries still helps to lay bare the problem. When is expressive material "immoral"? According to a standard definition, when it is "inconsistent with rectitude, purity, or good morals"; "wicked"; or "vicious." Webster's New International Dictionary 1246 (2d ed. 1949). Or again, when it is "opposed to or violating morality"; or "morally evil." Shorter Oxford English Dictionary 961 (3d ed. 1947). So the Lanham Act permits registration of marks that champion society's sense of rectitude and morality, but not marks that denigrate those concepts. And when is such material "scandalous"? Says a typical definition, when it "giv[es] offense to the conscience or moral feelings"; "excite[s] reprobation"; or "call[s] out condemnation." Webster's New International Dictionary, at 2229. Or again, when it is "shocking to the sense of truth, decency, or propriety"; "disgraceful"; "offensive"; or "disreputable." Funk & Wagnalls New Standard Dictionary 2186 (1944). So the Lanham Act allows registration of marks when their messages accord with, but not when their messages defy, society's sense of decency or propriety.
>
> Put the pair of overlapping terms together and the statute, on its face, distinguishes between two opposed sets of ideas: those aligned with conventional moral standards and those hostile to them; those inducing societal nods of approval and those provoking offense and condemnation. The statute favors the former, and disfavors the latter. "Love rules"? "Always be good"? Registration follows. "Hate rules"? "Always be cruel"? Not according to the Lanham Act's "immoral or scandalous" bar.
>
> The facial viewpoint bias in the law results in viewpoint-discriminatory application. Recall that the PTO itself describes the "immoral or scandalous" criterion using much the same language as in the dictionary definitions recited above. The PTO, for example, asks whether the public would view the mark as "shocking to the sense of truth, decency, or propriety"; "calling out for condemnation"; "offensive"; or "disreputable." Using those guideposts, the PTO has refused to register marks communicating "immoral" or "scandalous" views

about (among other things) drug use, religion, and terrorism. But all the while, it has approved registration of marks expressing more accepted views on the same topics.

SUBJECT-MATTER RESTRICTIONS

A subject-matter restriction is where the application of the law depends on the topic of the speech. It, too, is a form of content-based restrictions that must meet strict scrutiny. Carey v. Brown, 447 U.S. 455 (1980), is illustrative. Chicago adopted an ordinance prohibiting all picketing in residential neighborhoods unless it was labor picketing connected to a place of employment. The Supreme Court held this regulation unconstitutional. The Court explained that the law allowed speech if it was about the subject of labor, but not otherwise. The Court said that whenever the government attempts to regulate speech in public places it must be subject-matter-neutral.

Simon & Schuster, Inc. v. Members of the New York State Crime Victims Board, 502 U.S. 105 (1991), is another example of a case in which the Court found a law to be a subject-matter restriction. The case concerned a state law that prevented those accused or convicted of a crime from profiting from the crime; any funds derived from description of the crime were to be placed in an escrow account used to compensate crime victims. The Court unanimously invalidated the law, finding that it was content-based. Justice O'Connor, delivering the opinion of the Court, wrote:

> The Son of Sam law is such a content-based statute. It singles out income derived from expressive activity for a burden the State places on no other income, and it is directed only at works with a specified content. Whether the First Amendment "speaker" is considered to be [the author] whose income the statute places in escrow because of the story he has told, or [the publisher] which can publish books about crime with the assistance of only those criminals willing to forgo remuneration for at least five years, the statute plainly imposes a financial disincentive only on speech of a particular content.

The Court concluded, "The State's interest in compensating victims from the fruits of crime is a compelling one, but the Son of Sam law is not narrowly tailored to advance that objective. As a result, the statute is inconsistent with the First Amendment." The Court said there were alternative ways to ensure compensation of crime victims.

The fact that a law is content-based does not mean that it is necessarily unconstitutional. Rather, it will have to meet strict scrutiny. Williams-Yulee v. Florida Bar, below, is a case where the Court found strict scrutiny to be met. In Republican Party of Minnesota v. White, 536 U.S. 765 (2002), the Court, in a 5-4 decision, declared unconstitutional a provision of a state code of judicial ethics that prohibited candidates for elective judicial office from making statements about disputed legal or political issues. Williams-Yulee, though, takes a very different approach to analyzing restrictions of speech by candidates for elective judicial office.

WILLIAMS-YULEE v. FLORIDA BAR
575 U.S. 433 (2015)

Chief Justice ROBERTS delivered the opinion of the Court, except as to Part II.

Our Founders vested authority to appoint federal judges in the President, with the advice and consent of the Senate, and entrusted those judges to hold their offices during good behavior. The Constitution permits States to make a different choice, and most of them have done so. In 39 States, voters elect trial or appellate judges at the polls. In an effort to preserve public confidence in the integrity of their judiciaries, many of those States prohibit judges and judicial candidates from personally soliciting funds for their campaigns. We must decide whether the First Amendment permits such restrictions on speech.

We hold that it does. Judges are not politicians, even when they come to the bench by way of the ballot. And a State's decision to elect its judiciary does not compel it to treat judicial candidates like campaigners for political office. A State may assure its people that judges will apply the law without fear or favor—and without having personally asked anyone for money. We affirm the judgment of the Florida Supreme Court.

I

In the early 1970s, four Florida Supreme Court justices resigned from office following corruption scandals. Florida voters responded by amending their Constitution again. Under the system now in place, appellate judges are appointed by the Governor from a list of candidates proposed by a nominating committee—a process known as "merit selection." Then, every six years, voters decide whether to retain incumbent appellate judges for another term. Trial judges are still elected by popular vote, unless the local jurisdiction opts instead for merit selection.

Canon 7C(1) governs fundraising in judicial elections. The Canon, which is based on a provision in the American Bar Association's Model Code of Judicial Conduct, provides: "A candidate, including an incumbent judge, for a judicial office that is filled by public election between competing candidates shall not personally solicit campaign funds, or solicit attorneys for publicly stated support, but may establish committees of responsible persons to secure and manage the expenditure of funds for the candidate's campaign and to obtain public statements of support for his or her candidacy. Such committees are not prohibited from soliciting campaign contributions and public support from any person or corporation authorized by law."

Like Florida, most other States prohibit judicial candidates from soliciting campaign funds personally, but allow them to raise money through committees. According to the American Bar Association, 30 of the 39 States that elect trial or appellate judges have adopted restrictions similar to Canon 7C(1).

Lanell Williams-Yulee, who refers to herself as Yulee, has practiced law in Florida since 1991. In September 2009, she decided to run for a seat on the county court for Hillsborough County, a jurisdiction of about 1.3 million people that includes the city of Tampa. Shortly after filing paperwork to enter the race, Yulee drafted a letter announcing her candidacy. The letter described her experience and desire to "bring fresh ideas and positive solutions to the

A. The Distinction Between Content-Based and Content-Neutral Laws

Judicial bench." The letter then stated: "An early contribution of $25, $50, $100, $250, or $500, made payable to 'Lanell Williams-Yulee Campaign for County Judge,' will help raise the initial funds needed to launch the campaign and get our message out to the public. I ask for your support [i]n meeting the primary election fund raiser goals. Thank you in advance for your support."

Yulee signed the letter and mailed it to local voters. She also posted the letter on her campaign Web site.

Yulee's bid for the bench did not unfold as she had hoped. She lost the primary to the incumbent judge. Then the Florida Bar filed a complaint against her. That Rule requires judicial candidates to comply with applicable provisions of Florida's Code of Judicial Conduct, including the ban on personal solicitation of campaign funds in Canon 7C(1).

Yulee admitted that she had signed and sent the fundraising letter. But she argued that the Bar could not discipline her for that conduct because the First Amendment protects a judicial candidate's right to solicit campaign funds in an election.

II

The parties agree that Canon 7C(1) restricts Yulee's speech on the basis of its content by prohibiting her from soliciting contributions to her election campaign. The parties disagree, however, about the level of scrutiny that should govern our review.

We have applied exacting scrutiny to laws restricting the solicitation of contributions to charity, upholding the speech limitations only if they are narrowly tailored to serve a compelling interest. As we have explained, noncommercial solicitation "is characteristically intertwined with informative and perhaps persuasive speech." Applying a lesser standard of scrutiny to such speech would threaten "the exercise of rights so vital to the maintenance of democratic institutions."

The principles underlying these charitable solicitation cases apply with even greater force here. Before asking for money in her fundraising letter, Yulee explained her fitness for the bench and expressed her vision for the judiciary. Her stated purpose for the solicitation was to get her "message out to the public." As we have long recognized, speech about public issues and the qualifications of candidates for elected office commands the highest level of First Amendment protection. Indeed, in our only prior case concerning speech restrictions on a candidate for judicial office, this Court and both parties assumed that strict scrutiny applied. Republican Party of Minn. v. White (2002).

In sum, we hold today what we assumed in *White*: A State may restrict the speech of a judicial candidate only if the restriction is narrowly tailored to serve a compelling interest.

III

The Florida Bar faces a demanding task in defending Canon 7C(1) against Yulee's First Amendment challenge. We have emphasized that "it is the rare case" in which a State demonstrates that a speech restriction is narrowly tailored to serve a compelling interest. But those cases do arise. Here, Canon 7C(1) advances the State's compelling interest in preserving public confidence in the integrity of the judiciary, and it does so through means narrowly tailored to avoid unnecessarily abridging speech. This is therefore one of the rare cases in which a speech restriction withstands strict scrutiny.

The Florida Supreme Court adopted Canon 7C(1) to promote the State's interests in "protecting the integrity of the judiciary" and "maintaining the public's confidence in an impartial judiciary." The way the Canon advances those interests is intuitive: Judges, charged with exercising strict neutrality and independence, cannot supplicate campaign donors without diminishing public confidence in judicial integrity. This principle dates back at least eight centuries to Magna Carta, which proclaimed, "To no one will we sell, to no one will we refuse or delay, right or justice." Simply put, Florida and most other States have concluded that the public may lack confidence in a judge's ability to administer justice without fear or favor if he comes to office by asking for favors.

The parties devote considerable attention to our cases analyzing campaign finance restrictions in political elections. But a State's interest in preserving public confidence in the integrity of its judiciary extends beyond its interest in preventing the appearance of corruption in legislative and executive elections. As we explained in *White*, States may regulate judicial elections differently than they regulate political elections, because the role of judges differs from the role of politicians. Politicians are expected to be appropriately responsive to the preferences of their supporters. Indeed, such "responsiveness is key to the very concept of self-governance through elected officials." The same is not true of judges. In deciding cases, a judge is not to follow the preferences of his supporters, or provide any special consideration to his campaign donors. A judge instead must "observe the utmost fairness," striving to be "perfectly and completely independent, with nothing to influence or controul him but God and his conscience." Address of John Marshall, in Proceedings and Debates of the Virginia State Convention of 1829-1830.

The concept of public confidence in judicial integrity does not easily reduce to precise definition, nor does it lend itself to proof by documentary record. But no one denies that it is genuine and compelling. In short, it is the regrettable but unavoidable appearance that judges who personally ask for money may diminish their integrity that prompted the Supreme Court of Florida and most other States to sever the direct link between judicial candidates and campaign contributors. Moreover, personal solicitation by a judicial candidate "inevitably places the solicited individuals in a position to fear retaliation if they fail to financially support that candidate." Potential litigants then fear that "the integrity of the judicial system has been compromised, forcing them to search for an attorney in part based upon the criteria of which attorneys have made the obligatory contributions." A State's decision to elect its judges does not require it to tolerate these risks. The Florida Bar's interest is compelling.

Yulee acknowledges the State's compelling interest in judicial integrity. She argues, however, that the Canon's failure to restrict other speech equally damaging to judicial integrity and its appearance undercuts the Bar's position. In particular, she notes that Canon 7C(1) allows a judge's campaign committee to solicit money, which arguably reduces public confidence in the integrity of the judiciary just as much as a judge's personal solicitation. Yulee also points out

A. The Distinction Between Content-Based and Content-Neutral Laws

that Florida permits judicial candidates to write thank you notes to campaign donors, which ensures that candidates know who contributes and who does not.

It is always somewhat counterintuitive to argue that a law violates the First Amendment by abridging *too little* speech. We have recognized, however, that underinclusiveness can raise "doubts about whether the government is in fact pursuing the interest it invokes, rather than disfavoring a particular speaker or viewpoint."

Although a law's underinclusivity raises a red flag, the First Amendment imposes no freestanding "underinclusiveness limitation." A State need not address all aspects of a problem in one fell swoop; policymakers may focus on their most pressing concerns. We have accordingly upheld laws—even under strict scrutiny—that conceivably could have restricted even greater amounts of speech in service of their stated interests.

Viewed in light of these principles, Canon 7C(1) raises no fatal underinclusivity concerns. The solicitation ban aims squarely at the conduct most likely to undermine public confidence in the integrity of the judiciary: personal requests for money by judges and judicial candidates. The Canon applies evenhandedly to all judges and judicial candidates, regardless of their viewpoint or chosen means of solicitation. And unlike some laws that we have found impermissibly underinclusive, Canon 7C(1) is not riddled with exceptions. Indeed, the Canon contains zero exceptions to its ban on personal solicitation.

Yulee relies heavily on the provision of Canon 7C(1) that allows solicitation by a candidate's campaign committee. But Florida, along with most other States, has reasonably concluded that solicitation by the candidate personally creates a categorically different and more severe risk of undermining public confidence than does solicitation by a campaign committee. The identity of the solicitor matters, as anyone who has encountered a Girl Scout selling cookies outside a grocery store can attest. When the judicial candidate himself asks for money, the stakes are higher for all involved. The candidate has personally invested his time and effort in the fundraising appeal; he has placed his name and reputation behind the request. The solicited individual knows that, and also knows that the solicitor might be in a position to singlehandedly make decisions of great weight: The same person who signed the fundraising letter might one day sign the judgment. This dynamic inevitably creates pressure for the recipient to comply, and it does so in a way that solicitation by a third party does not. Just as inevitably, the personal involvement of the candidate in the solicitation creates the public appearance that the candidate will remember who says yes, and who says no.

In short, personal solicitation by judicial candidates implicates a different problem than solicitation by campaign committees. However similar the two solicitations may be in substance, a State may conclude that they present markedly different appearances to the public. Florida's choice to allow solicitation by campaign committees does not undermine its decision to ban solicitation by judges.

After arguing that Canon 7C(1) violates the First Amendment because it restricts too little speech, Yulee argues that the Canon violates the First Amendment because it restricts too much. In her view, the Canon is not narrowly tailored to advance the State's compelling interest through the least restrictive means.

But in reality, Canon 7C(1) leaves judicial candidates free to discuss any issue with any person at any time. Candidates can write letters, give speeches, and put up billboards. They can contact potential supporters in person, on the phone, or online. They can promote their campaigns on radio, television, or other media. They cannot say, "Please give me money." They can, however, direct their campaign committees to do so. Whatever else may be said of the Canon, it is surely not a "wildly disproportionate restriction upon speech."

Finally, Yulee contends that Florida can accomplish its compelling interest through the less restrictive means of recusal rules and campaign contribution limits. We disagree. A rule requiring judges to recuse themselves from every case in which a lawyer or litigant made a campaign contribution would disable many jurisdictions. And a flood of postelection recusal motions could "erode public confidence in judicial impartiality" and thereby exacerbate the very appearance problem the State is trying to solve. Moreover, the rule that Yulee envisions could create a perverse incentive for litigants to make campaign contributions to judges solely as a means to trigger their later recusal—a form of peremptory strike against a judge that would enable transparent forum shopping.

In sum, because Canon 7C(1) is narrowly tailored to serve a compelling government interest, the First Amendment poses no obstacle to its enforcement in this case. As a result of our decision, Florida may continue to prohibit judicial candidates from personally soliciting campaign funds, while allowing them to raise money through committees and to otherwise communicate their electoral messages in practically any way.

The desirability of judicial elections is a question that has sparked disagreement for more than 200 years. Hamilton believed that appointing judges to positions with life tenure constituted "the best expedient which can be devised in any government to secure a steady, upright, and impartial administration of the laws." Jefferson thought that making judges "dependent on none but themselves" ran counter to the principle of "a government founded on the public will." The federal courts reflect the view of Hamilton; most States have sided with Jefferson. Both methods have given our Nation jurists of wisdom and rectitude who have devoted themselves to maintaining "the public's respect . . . and a reserve of public goodwill, without becoming subservient to public opinion."

It is not our place to resolve this enduring debate. Our limited task is to apply the Constitution to the question presented in this case. Judicial candidates have a First Amendment right to speak in support of their campaigns. States have a compelling interest in preserving public confidence in their judiciaries. When the State adopts a narrowly tailored restriction like the one at issue here, those principles do not conflict. A State's decision to elect judges does not compel it to compromise public confidence in their integrity.

Justice GINSBURG with whom Justice BREYER joins as to Part II, concurring in part and concurring in the judgment.

I write separately to reiterate the substantial latitude, in my view, States should possess to enact campaign-finance rules geared to judicial elections. "Judges," the Court rightly recognizes, "are not politicians," so "States may regulate judicial elections differently than they regulate political elections." And because "the role of judges differs from the role of politicians," this Court's "precedents applying the First Amendment to political elections [should] have little bearing" on elections to judicial office.

A. The Distinction Between Content-Based and Content-Neutral Laws

The Court's recent campaign-finance decisions, trained on political actors, should not hold sway for judicial elections. States may therefore impose different campaign-finance rules for judicial elections than for political elections. Experience illustrates why States may wish to do so. When the political campaign-finance apparatus is applied to judicial elections, the distinction of judges from politicians dims. Donors, who gain audience and influence through contributions to political campaigns, anticipate that investment in campaigns for judicial office will yield similar returns. Elected judges understand this dynamic.

In recent years, moreover, issue-oriented organizations and political action committees have spent millions of dollars opposing the reelection of judges whose decisions do not tow a party line or are alleged to be out of step with public opinion. Following the Iowa Supreme Court's 2009 invalidation of the State's same-sex marriage ban, for example, national organizations poured money into a successful campaign to remove three justices from that Court. Attack advertisements funded by issue or politically driven organizations portrayed the justices as political actors; they lambasted the Iowa Supreme Court for "usurp[ing] the will of voters."

Disproportionate spending to influence court judgments threatens both the appearance and actuality of judicial independence. Numerous studies report that the money pressure groups spend on judicial elections "can affect judicial decision-making across a broad range of cases."

How does the electorate perceive outsized spending on judicial elections? Multiple surveys over the past 13 years indicate that voters overwhelmingly believe direct contributions to judges' campaigns have at least "some influence" on judicial decisionmaking. Disquieting as well, in response to a recent poll, 87% of voters stated that advertisements purchased by interest groups during judicial elections can have either "some" or "a great deal of influence" on an elected "judge's later decisions."

"A State's decision to elect its judges does not require it to tolerate these risks." States should not be put to the polar choices of either equating judicial elections to political elections, or else abandoning public participation in the selection of judges altogether. Instead, States should have leeway to "balance the constitutional interests in judicial integrity and free expression within the unique setting of an elected judiciary."

Justice SCALIA, with whom Justice THOMAS joins, dissenting.

An ethics canon adopted by the Florida Supreme Court bans a candidate in a judicial election from asking anyone, under any circumstances, for a contribution to his campaign. Faithful application of our precedents would have made short work of this wildly disproportionate restriction upon speech. Intent upon upholding the Canon, however, the Court flattens one settled First Amendment principle after another.

I

The first axiom of the First Amendment is this: As a general rule, the state has no power to ban speech on the basis of its content. One need not equate judges with politicians to see that this principle does not grow weaker merely because the censored speech is a judicial candidate's request for a campaign contribution. Our cases hold that speech enjoys the full protection of the First Amendment unless a widespread and longstanding tradition ratifies its regulation. No such tradition looms here.

One likewise need not equate judges with politicians to see that the electoral setting calls for all the more vigilance in ensuring observance of the First Amendment. When a candidate asks someone for a campaign contribution, he tends (as the principal opinion acknowledges) also to talk about his qualifications for office and his views on public issues. This expression lies at the heart of what the First Amendment is meant to protect. In addition, banning candidates from asking for money personally "favors some candidates over others—incumbent judges (who benefit from their current status) over non-judicial candidates, the well-to-do (who may not need to raise any money at all) over lower-income candidates, and the well-connected (who have an army of potential fundraisers) over outsiders." This danger of legislated (or judicially imposed) favoritism is the very reason the First Amendment exists.

Because Canon 7C(1) restricts fully protected speech on the basis of content, it presumptively violates the First Amendment. We may uphold it only if the State meets its burden of showing that the Canon survives strict scrutiny—that is to say, only if it shows that the Canon is narrowly tailored to serve a compelling interest. I do not for a moment question the Court's conclusion that States have different compelling interests when regulating judicial elections than when regulating political ones. Unlike a legislator, a judge must be impartial—without bias for or against any party or attorney who comes before him. I accept for the sake of argument that States have a compelling interest in ensuring that its judges are *seen* to be impartial. I will likewise assume that a judicial candidate's request to a litigant or attorney presents a danger of coercion that a political candidate's request to a constituent does not.

But Canon 7C(1) does not narrowly target concerns about impartiality or its appearance; it applies even when the person asked for a financial contribution has no chance of ever appearing in the candidate's court. And Florida does not invoke concerns about coercion, presumably because the Canon bans solicitations regardless of whether their object is a lawyer, litigant, or other person vulnerable to judicial pressure. So Canon 7C(1) fails exacting scrutiny and infringes the First Amendment. This case should have been just that straightforward.

II

The Court concludes that Florida may prohibit personal solicitations by judicial candidates as a means of preserving "public confidence in the integrity of the judiciary." It purports to reach this destination by applying strict scrutiny, but it would be more accurate to say that it does so by applying the appearance of strict scrutiny.

In stark contrast to *White*, the Court today relies on Florida's invocation of an ill-defined interest in "public confidence in judicial integrity." The Court at first suggests that "judicial integrity" involves the "ability to administer justice without fear or favor." As its opinion unfolds, however, today's concept of judicial integrity turns out to be "a mere thing of wax in the hands of the judiciary, which they may twist, and shape into any form they please." 12 The Works of Thomas Jefferson 137 (P. Ford ed. 1905). When the Court explains how solicitation undermines confidence in judicial integrity, integrity starts to sound like saintliness. It involves independence from any "'*possible* temptation'" that "'*might* lead'" the judge, "even unknowingly," to favor one party. And when the Court confronts Florida's decision to prohibit mass-mailed solicitations, concern about pressure fades away. More outrageous still, the Court at times molds the interest in the perception that judges have integrity into an interest in the perception that judges do not solicit—for example when it says, "all personal solicitations by judicial candidates create a public appearance that undermines confidence in the integrity of the judiciary; banning all personal solicitations by judicial candidates is narrowly tailored to address that concern." This is not strict scrutiny; it is sleight of hand.

Neither the Court nor the State identifies the slightest evidence that banning requests for contributions will substantially improve public trust in judges. Nor does common sense make this happy forecast obvious. The concept of judicial integrity "dates back at least eight centuries," and judicial elections in America date back more than two centuries—but rules against personal solicitations date back only to 1972. The peaceful coexistence of judicial elections and personal solicitations for most of our history calls into doubt any claim that allowing personal solicitations would imperil public faith in judges. Many States allow judicial candidates to ask for contributions even today, but nobody suggests that public confidence in judges fares worse in these jurisdictions than elsewhere. And in any event, if candidates' appeals for money are "'characteristically intertwined'" with discussion of qualifications and views on public issues, how can the Court be so sure that the public will regard them as improprieties rather than as legitimate instances of campaigning? In the final analysis, Florida comes nowhere near making the convincing demonstration required by our cases that the speech restriction in this case substantially advances its objective.

Justice KENNEDY, dissenting.

This separate dissent is written to underscore the irony in the Court's having concluded that the very First Amendment protections judges must enforce should be lessened when a judicial candidate's own speech is at issue. It is written to underscore, too, the irony in the Court's having weakened the rigors of the First Amendment in a case concerning elections, a paradigmatic forum for speech and a process intended to protect freedom in so many other manifestations.

First Amendment protections are both personal and structural. Free speech begins with the right of each person to think and then to express his or her own ideas. Protecting this personal sphere of intellect and conscience, in turn, creates structural safeguards for many of the processes that define a free society. The individual speech here is political speech. The process is a fair election. These realms ought to be the last place, not the first, for the Court to allow unprecedented content-based restrictions on speech. The Court's decision in this case imperils the content neutrality essential both for individual speech and the election process.

With all due respect for the Court, it seems fair and necessary to say its decision rests on two premises, neither one correct. One premise is that in certain elections—here an election to choose the best qualified judge—the public lacks the necessary judgment to make an informed choice. Instead, the State must protect voters by altering the usual dynamics of free speech.

The other premise is that since judges should be accorded special respect and dignity, their election can be subject to certain content-based rules that would be unacceptable in other elections. In my respectful view neither premise can justify the speech restriction at issue here. Although States have a compelling interest in seeking to ensure the appearance and the reality of an impartial judiciary, it does not follow that the State may alter basic First Amendment principles in pursuing that goal.

Whether an election is the best way to choose a judge is itself the subject of fair debate. But once the people of a State choose to have elections, the First Amendment protects the candidate's right to speak and the public's ensuing right to open and robust debate. One advantage of judicial elections is the opportunity offered for the public to become more knowledgeable about their courts and their law. This might stimulate discourse over the requisite and highest ethical standards for the judiciary, including whether the people should elect a judge who personally solicits campaign funds. Yet now that teaching process is hindered by state censorship. By allowing the State's speech restriction, the Court undermines the educational process that free speech in elections should facilitate.

This law comes nowhere close to being narrowly tailored. And by saying that it survives that vital First Amendment requirement, the Court now writes what is literally a casebook guide to eviscerating strict scrutiny any time the Court encounters speech it dislikes.

CONTENT-NEUTRAL LAWS

These cases show that a law is content-based if it is either a subject-matter or a viewpoint restriction. In contrast, a law regulating speech is content-neutral if it applies to all speech regardless of the message. For example, a law prohibiting the posting of all signs on public utility poles would be content-neutral because it would apply to every sign regardless of its subject matter or viewpoint.[9] In Turner Broadcasting v. FCC, the Supreme Court found that a federal law requiring cable companies to carry local broadcast stations was content-neutral because the companies were required to include all stations, whatever their programming. A law might also be content-neutral if it regulates conduct and it has an effect on speech without regard to its content. For example, a sales tax applicable to all purchases, including purchases of reading material, might have a significant incidental effect on speech, but it is content-neutral.

3. Problems in Applying the Distinction Between Content-Based and Content-Neutral Laws

Three important problems arise in applying the distinction between content-based and content-neutral laws.

---

9. *See* Members of the City Council of Los Angeles v. Taxpayers for Vincent, 466 U.S. 789 (1984).

A. The Distinction Between Content-Based and Content-Neutral Laws

a. Permissible Purposes and Content-Neutrality

First, does a permissible purpose for a law prevent it from being deemed content-based, even if a content restriction is on the face of the law? In Turner Broadcasting v. FCC (preceding), the Court said, "Nor will the mere assertion of a content-neutral purpose be enough to save a law which, on its face, discriminates based on content." However, in other cases, the Supreme Court has indicated that a facial content-based restriction will be deemed content-neutral if it is motivated by a permissible content-neutral purpose. The Court articulated this rule in City of Renton v. Playtime Theatres, Inc.

<u>CITY OF RENTON v. PLAYTIME THEATRES, INC.</u>
475 U.S. 41 (1986)

Justice REHNQUIST delivered the opinion of the Court.

This case involves a constitutional challenge to a zoning ordinance, enacted by appellant city of Renton, Washington, that prohibits adult motion picture theaters from locating within 1,000 feet of any residential zone, single- or multiple-family dwelling, church, park, or school.

I

In May 1980, the Mayor of Renton, a city of approximately 32,000 people located just south of Seattle, suggested to the Renton City Council that it consider the advisability of enacting zoning legislation dealing with adult entertainment uses. No such uses existed in the city at that time. In April 1981, acting on the basis of the Planning and Development Committee's recommendation, the City Council enacted Ordinance No. 3526. The ordinance prohibited any "adult motion picture theater" from locating within 1,000 feet of any residential zone, single- or multiple-family dwelling, church, or park, and within one mile of any school. The term "adult motion picture theater" was defined as "[a]n enclosed building used for presenting motion picture films, video cassettes, cable television, or any other such visual media, distinguished or characteri[zed] by an emphasis on matter depicting, describing or relating to 'specified sexual activities' or 'specified anatomical areas' . . . for observation by patrons therein."

The Renton ordinance does not ban adult theaters altogether, but merely provides that such theaters may not be located within 1,000 feet of any residential zone, single- or multiple-family dwelling, church, park, or school. The ordinance is therefore properly analyzed as a form of time, place, and manner regulation. This Court has long held that regulations enacted for the purpose of restraining speech on the basis of its content presumptively violate the First Amendment. On the other hand, so-called "content-neutral" time, place, and manner regulations are acceptable so long as they are designed to serve a substantial governmental interest and do not unreasonably limit alternative avenues of communication.

At first glance, the Renton ordinance does not appear to fit neatly into either the "content-based" or the "content-neutral" category. To be sure, the ordinance treats theaters that specialize in adult films differently from other kinds of theaters. Nevertheless, as the District Court concluded, the Renton ordinance is aimed not at the content of the films shown at "adult motion picture theatres," but rather at the secondary effects of such theaters on the surrounding community. The District Court found that the City Council's "predominate concerns" were with the secondary effects of adult theaters, and not with the content of adult films themselves.

The appropriate inquiry in this case, then, is whether the Renton ordinance is designed to serve a substantial governmental interest and allows for reasonable alternative avenues of communication. It is clear that the ordinance meets such a standard. As a majority of this Court recognized in Young v. American Mini Theatres (1976), a city's "interest in attempting to preserve the quality of urban life is one that must be accorded high respect." Exactly the same vital governmental interests are at stake here.

Justice BRENNAN, with whom Justice MARSHALL joins, dissenting.

Renton's zoning ordinance selectively imposes limitations on the location of a movie theater based exclusively on the content of the films shown there. The constitutionality of the ordinance is therefore not correctly analyzed under standards applied to content-neutral time, place, and manner restrictions. But even assuming that the ordinance may fairly be characterized as content neutral, it is plainly unconstitutional under the standards established by the decisions of this Court. Although the Court's analysis is limited to cases involving "businesses that purvey sexually explicit materials," and thus does not affect our holdings in cases involving state regulation of other kinds of speech, I dissent.

"[A] constitutionally permissible time, place, or manner restriction may not be based upon either the content or subject matter of speech." Consolidated Edison Co. v. Public Service Commn. of N.Y. (1980). The Court asserts that the ordinance is "aimed not at the content of the films shown at 'adult motion picture theatres,' but rather at the secondary effects of such theaters on the surrounding community," and thus is simply a time, place, and manner regulation. This analysis is misguided.

The fact that adult movie theaters may cause harmful "secondary" land-use effects may arguably give Renton a compelling reason to regulate such establishments; it does not mean, however, that such regulations are content neutral. Because the ordinance imposes special restrictions on certain kinds of speech on the basis of content, I cannot simply accept, as the Court does, Renton's claim that the ordinance was not designed to suppress the content of adult movies.

The ordinance discriminates on its face against certain forms of speech based on content. Movie theaters specializing in "adult motion pictures" may not be located within 1,000 feet of any residential zone, single- or multiple-family dwelling, church, park, or school. Other motion picture theaters, and other forms of "adult entertainment," such as bars, massage parlors, and adult bookstores, are not subject to the same restrictions. This selective treatment strongly suggests that Renton was interested not in controlling the "secondary effects" associated with adult businesses, but in discriminating against adult theaters based on the content of the films they exhibit. The Court ignores this discriminatory treatment, declaring that Renton is free "to address the potential problems created by one particular kind of adult business," and to amend the ordinance in the future to include other adult enterprises. However, because of the First Amendment interests at stake here, this one-step-at-a-time analysis is wholly inappropriate. In this case, the city has not justified treating adult movie theaters differently from other adult entertainment businesses. The ordinance's underinclusiveness is cogent evidence that it was aimed at the content of the films shown in adult movie theaters.

Applying this standard to the facts of this case, the ordinance is patently unconstitutional. Renton has not shown that locating adult movie theaters in proximity to its churches, schools, parks, and residences will necessarily result in undesirable "secondary effects," or that these problems could not be effectively addressed by less intrusive restrictions.

Renton has been strongly criticized by commentators.[10] Critics argue that *Renton* "permits an end run around the First Amendment: The government can always point to some neutral, nonspeech justification for its actions."[11] Justice Brennan expressed his "continued disagreement with the proposition that an otherwise content-based restriction on speech can be recast as 'content-neutral' if the restriction 'aims' at 'secondary-effects' of the speech. . . . [S]uch secondary effects offer countless excuses for content-based suppression of political speech."[12]

The argument is that the *Renton* approach seems to confuse whether a law is content-based or content-neutral with the question of whether a law is justified by a sufficient purpose. The law may have been properly upheld as needed to combat crime and the secondary effects of adult theaters, but it nonetheless was clearly content-based: It applied only to theaters showing films with sexually explicit content.

The Court has been inconsistent in applying *Renton*. In some cases, the Court has distinguished *Renton* and rejected the argument that the goal of preventing secondary effects prevents a law from being deemed content-based. For example, in Boos v. Barry, 485 U.S. 312 (1988), the Court considered a District of Columbia ordinance that prohibits the display of any sign within 500 feet of a foreign embassy if that sign tends to bring that foreign government into "public odium" or "public disrepute." Challengers were three individuals who wish to carry signs critical of the governments of the Soviet Union and Nicaragua on the public sidewalks within 500 feet of the embassies of those Governments in Washington, D.C. The Court declared this unconstitutional:

> [T]he display clause operates at the core of the First Amendment by prohibiting petitioners from engaging in classically political speech. We have recognized that the First Amendment reflects a "profound national commitment" to the principle that "debate on public issues should be uninhibited, robust, and wide-open," New York Times Co. v. Sullivan (1964), and have consistently commented on the central importance of protecting speech on public issues.

---

10. For an excellent summary of these criticisms, *see* Marcy Strauss, *From Witness to Riches: The Constitutionality of Restricting Witness Speech*, 38 Ariz. L. Rev. 291 (1996).
11. *Id.* at 317.
12. Boos v. Barry, 485 U.S. at 334-335 (Brennan, J., concurring in part and concurring in the judgment).

> [The display clause] is content-based. Whether individuals may picket in front of a foreign embassy depends entirely upon whether their picket signs are critical of the foreign government or not. One category of speech has been completely prohibited within 500 feet of embassies. Other categories of speech, however, such as favorable speech about a foreign government or speech concerning a labor dispute with a foreign government, are permitted.

The government argued that the restriction of speech critical of foreign governments near their embassies was justified based on an international law obligation to shield diplomats from speech that offends their dignity. Justice O'Connor, writing for the plurality in declaring this part of the law unconstitutional, distinguished *Renton* because the ordinance restricting speech near embassies was "justified *only* by reference to the content of the speech. Respondents and the United States do not point to the 'secondary effects' of picket signs in front of embassies. They do not point to congestion, to interference with ingress or egress, to visual clutter, or to the need to protect the security of embassies. Rather, they rely on the need to protect the dignity of foreign diplomatic personnel by shielding them from speech that is critical of their governments. This justification focuses *only* on the content of the speech and the direct impact that speech has on its listeners."

The Court also distinguished *Renton* in City of Cincinnati v. Discovery Network, Inc., 507 U.S. 410 (1993), where the Court declared unconstitutional a prohibition on the use of newsracks on public property for the distribution of commercial handbills. The city argued that the ordinance was justified by concern over the secondary effects of such newsracks with regard to safety and aesthetics. The Court rejected this argument and characterized the ordinance as content-based. Justice Stevens, writing for the Court, said, "The argument is unpersuasive because the very basis for the regulation is the difference in content between ordinary newspapers and commercial speech. . . . Under the city's newsrack policy, whether any particular newsrack falls within the ban is determined by the content of the publication resting inside that newsrack. Thus, by any commonsense understanding of the term, the ban is 'content-based.'" Justice Stevens expressly distinguished *Renton* and said that the city's "reliance on *Renton* is misplaced." He said that "[i]n contrast to the speech at issue in *Renton*, there are no secondary effects attributable to . . . newsracks [containing commercial handbills] that distinguish them from the newsracks Cincinnati permits to remain on its sidewalks."[13]

In contrast, in City of Erie v. Pap's A.M., 529 U.S. 277 (2000), the Court upheld a city's public nudity law and its application to prevent nude dancing on the ground that the ordinance was content-neutral. Justice O'Connor's plurality opinion expressly applied *Renton* and concluded that the city's goal of preventing the secondary effects of nude dancing were sufficient to make the law content-neutral.

Thus, at this point, it appears that a law that on its face regulates speech based on its viewpoint or message will be presumed to be content-based, but the government can refute this by persuading a court that the regulation is justified by a content-neutral desire to avoid undesirable secondary effects of

---

13. *City of Cincinnati*, 507 U.S. at 430.

A. The Distinction Between Content-Based and Content-Neutral Laws

the speech. The content-neutral justification must be truly unrelated to the desire to suppress speech and it must be unique to the speech suppressed as compared to the speech allowed.

b. When the Government Must Make Content-Based Choices

A second problem in applying the content-based/content-neutral distinction concerns situations in which the government must make content-based choices. There are some instances when the government inescapably must make content choices. For instance, if the government is choosing to subsidize speech, there is no way that it can avoid content considerations in deciding what to finance. Many situations like this are discussed in this book, such as when the government runs a theater or a concert hall and is choosing programs, or when a public library is deciding what books to buy, or when a public university is evaluating a professor's writings for purposes of tenure and promotion. The government simply cannot ignore content in these situations. The Court indicated that in such circumstances the government must be viewpoint-neutral but otherwise can consider content. In reading this case, consider whether the Court was correct in finding the federal law to be viewpoint-neutral.

NATIONAL ENDOWMENT FOR THE ARTS v. FINLEY
524 U.S. 569 (1998)

Justice O'CONNOR delivered the opinion of the Court.

The National Foundation on the Arts and Humanities Act, as amended in 1990, requires the Chairperson of the National Endowment for the Arts (NEA) to ensure that "artistic excellence and artistic merit are the criteria by which [grant] applications are judged, taking into consideration general standards of decency and respect for the diverse beliefs and values of the American public." We conclude that [the law] is facially valid, as it neither inherently interferes with First Amendment rights nor violates constitutional vagueness principles.

I

With the establishment of the NEA in 1965, Congress embarked on a "broadly conceived national policy of support for the . . . arts in the United States," pledging federal funds to "help create and sustain not only a climate encouraging freedom of thought, imagination, and inquiry but also the material conditions facilitating the release of . . . creative talent." The enabling statute vests the NEA with substantial discretion to award grants; it identifies only the broadest funding priorities, including "artistic and cultural significance, giving emphasis to American creativity and cultural diversity," "professional excellence," and the encouragement of "public knowledge, education, understanding, and appreciation of the arts."

Applications for NEA funding are initially reviewed by advisory panels composed of experts in the relevant field of the arts. Under the 1990 Amendments to the enabling statute, those panels must reflect "diverse artistic and cultural points of view" and include "wide geographic, ethnic, and minority representation," as well as "lay individuals who are knowledgeable about the arts." The panels report to the 26-member National Council on the Arts (Council), which, in turn, advises the NEA Chairperson. The Chairperson has the ultimate authority to award grants but may not approve an application as to which the Council has made a negative recommendation.

Since 1965, the NEA has distributed over three billion dollars in grants to individuals and organizations, funding that has served as a catalyst for increased state, corporate, and foundation support for the arts. Throughout the NEA's history, only a handful of the agency's roughly 100,000 awards have generated formal complaints about misapplied funds or abuse of the public's trust. Two provocative works, however, prompted public controversy in 1989 and led to congressional revaluation of the NEA's funding priorities and efforts to increase oversight of its grant-making procedures. The Institute of Contemporary Art at the University of Pennsylvania had used $30,000 of a visual arts grant it received from the NEA to fund a 1989 retrospective of photographer Robert Mapplethorpe's work. The exhibit, entitled The Perfect Moment, included homoerotic photographs that several Members of Congress condemned as pornographic. Members also denounced artist Andres Serrano's work Piss Christ, a photograph of a crucifix immersed in urine. Serrano had been awarded a $15,000 grant from the Southeast Center for Contemporary Art, an organization that received NEA support.

Ultimately, Congress adopted [a law] which directs the Chairperson, in establishing procedures to judge the artistic merit of grant applications, to "tak[e] into consideration general standards of decency and respect for the diverse beliefs and values of the American public."

The four individual respondents in this case, Karen Finley, John Fleck, Holly Hughes, and Tim Miller, are performance artists who applied for NEA grants. An advisory panel recommended approval of respondents' projects, both initially and after receiving [NEA Chairman John] Frohnmayer's request to reconsider three of the applications. A majority of the Council subsequently recommended disapproval, and in June 1990, the NEA informed respondents that they had been denied funding. Respondents filed suit, alleging that the NEA had violated their First Amendment rights.

II

Respondents raise a facial constitutional challenge to [the law] and consequently they confront "a heavy burden" in advancing their claim. Facial invalidation "is, manifestly, strong medicine" that "has been employed by the Court sparingly and only as a last resort." To prevail, respondents must demonstrate a substantial risk that application of the provision will lead to the suppression of speech.

Respondents argue that the provision is a paradigmatic example of viewpoint discrimination because it rejects any artistic speech that either fails to respect mainstream values or offends standards of decency. The NEA, however, reads the provision as merely hortatory, and contends that it stops well short of an absolute restriction. Section 954(d)(1) adds "considerations" to the grant-making process; it does not preclude awards to projects that might be deemed "indecent" or "disrespectful," nor place conditions on grants, or even

A. The Distinction Between Content-Based and Content-Neutral Laws

specify that those factors must be given any particular weight in reviewing an application.

That §954(d)(1) admonishes the NEA merely to take "decency and respect" into consideration, and that the legislation was aimed at reforming procedures rather than precluding speech, undercut respondents' argument that the provision inevitably will be utilized as a tool for invidious viewpoint discrimination. In cases where we have struck down legislation as facially unconstitutional, the dangers were both more evident and more substantial.

Any content-based considerations that may be taken into account in the grant-making process are a consequence of the nature of arts funding. The NEA has limited resources and it must deny the majority of the grant applications that it receives, including many that propose "artistically excellent" projects. The agency may decide to fund particular projects for a wide variety of reasons, "such as the technical proficiency of the artist, the creativity of the work, the anticipated public interest in or appreciation of the work, the work's contemporary relevance, its educational value, its suitability for or appeal to special audiences (such as children or the disabled), its service to a rural or isolated community, or even simply that the work could increase public knowledge of an art form." As the dissent below noted, it would be "impossible to have a highly selective grant program without denying money to a large amount of constitutionally protected expression." The "very assumption" of the NEA is that grants will be awarded according to the "artistic worth of competing applications," and absolute neutrality is simply "inconceivable." In the context of arts funding, in contrast to many other subsidies, the Government does not indiscriminately "encourage a diversity of views from private speakers." The NEA's mandate is to make aesthetic judgments, and the inherently content-based "excellence" threshold for NEA support sets it apart [from other situations]. Respondents do not allege discrimination in any particular funding decision. Thus, we have no occasion here to address an as-applied challenge in a situation where the denial of a grant may be shown to be the product of invidious viewpoint discrimination.

If the NEA were to leverage its power to award subsidies on the basis of subjective criteria into a penalty on disfavored viewpoints, then we would confront a different case. We have stated that, even in the provision of subsidies, the Government may not "ai[m] at the suppression of dangerous ideas," and if a subsidy were "manipulated" to have a "coercive effect," then relief could be appropriate. In addition, as the NEA itself concedes, a more pressing constitutional question would arise if government funding resulted in the imposition of a disproportionate burden calculated to drive "certain ideas or viewpoints from the marketplace." Unless and until §954(d)(1) is applied in a manner that raises concern about the suppression of disfavored viewpoints, however, we uphold the constitutionality of the provision.

Finally, although the First Amendment certainly has application in the subsidy context, we note that the Government may allocate competitive funding according to criteria that would be impermissible were direct regulation of speech or a criminal penalty at stake. So long as legislation does not infringe on other constitutionally protected rights, Congress has wide latitude to set spending priorities. Congress may "selectively fund a program to encourage certain activities it believes to be in the public interest, without at the same time funding an alternative program which seeks to deal with the problem in another way." In doing so, "the Government has not discriminated on the basis of viewpoint; it has merely chosen to fund one activity to the exclusion of the other."

Justice SOUTER, dissenting.
The question here is whether this statute is unconstitutional on its face: "artistic excellence and artistic merit are the criteria by which applications [for grants from the National Endowment for the Arts] are judged, taking into consideration general standards of decency and respect for the diverse beliefs and values of the American public." The decency and respect proviso mandates viewpoint-based decisions in the disbursement of government subsidies, and the Government has wholly failed to explain why the statute should be afforded an exemption from the fundamental rule of the First Amendment that viewpoint discrimination in the exercise of public authority over expressive activity is unconstitutional. The Court's conclusions that the proviso is not viewpoint based, that it is not a regulation, and that the NEA may permissibly engage in viewpoint-based discrimination, are all patently mistaken.

"If there is a bedrock principle underlying the First Amendment, it is that the government may not prohibit the expression of an idea simply because society finds the idea itself offensive or disagreeable." Texas v. Johnson (1989). Because this principle applies not only to affirmative suppression of speech, but also to disqualification for government favors, Congress is generally not permitted to pivot discrimination against otherwise protected speech on the offensiveness or unacceptability of the views it expresses.

[A] statute disfavoring speech that fails to respect America's "diverse beliefs and values" is the very model of viewpoint discrimination; it penalizes any view disrespectful to any belief or value espoused by someone in the American populace. Boiled down to its practical essence, the limitation obviously means that art that disrespects the ideology, opinions, or convictions of a significant segment of the American public is to be disfavored, whereas art that reinforces those values is not. After all, the whole point of the proviso was to make sure that works like Serrano's ostensibly blasphemous portrayal of Jesus would not be funded, while a reverent treatment, conventionally respectful of Christian sensibilities, would not run afoul of the law. Nothing could be more viewpoint-based than that. The fact that the statute disfavors art insufficiently respectful of America's "diverse" beliefs and values alters this conclusion not one whit: the First Amendment does not validate the ambition to disqualify many disrespectful viewpoints instead of merely one.

In United States v. American Library Association, 539 U.S. 194 (2003), the Court, without a majority opinion, upheld a federal law requiring libraries receiving federal funds to install filters to block sexually explicit material. Chief Justice Rehnquist's plurality opinion stressed that libraries need not buy all materials or allow access to all materials on the Internet. Thus, it is constitutional for Congress to condition federal funds on a requirement that local libraries place filters on their computers which are available to users. Justices Kennedy and Breyer, concurring in the judgment, emphasized that under the law, patrons may request librarians to lift filters. They said that since none of the plaintiffs in the suit had been denied access to any materials, it was premature to consider the constitutional issue.

A. The Distinction Between Content-Based and Content-Neutral Laws

c. Government Speech

A third problem with applying the distinction between content-based and content-neutral regulations is the Court's holding that the First Amendment does not apply at all if the government is the speaker or even adopts private speech as its own. The question is how much this opens the door to the government circumventing the Constitution by being able to adopt private messages as government speech. Although the following case was unanimous, some of the justices in their concurring opinions raise exactly this question.

PLEASANT GROVE CITY, UTAH v. SUMMUM
555 U.S. 460 (2009)

Justice ALITO delivered the opinion of the Court.

This case presents the question whether the Free Speech Clause of the First Amendment entitles a private group to insist that a municipality permit it to place a permanent monument in a city park in which other donated monuments were previously erected. The Court of Appeals held that the municipality was required to accept the monument because a public park is a traditional public forum. We conclude, however, that although a park is a traditional public forum for speeches and other transitory expressive acts, the display of a permanent monument in a public park is not a form of expression to which forum analysis applies. Instead, the placement of a permanent monument in a public park is best viewed as a form of government speech and is therefore not subject to scrutiny under the Free Speech Clause.

I

Pioneer Park (or Park) is a 2.5 acre public park located in the Historic District of Pleasant Grove City (or City) in Utah. The Park currently contains 15 permanent displays, at least 11 of which were donated by private groups or individuals. These include an historic granary, a wishing well, the City's first fire station, a September 11 monument, and a Ten Commandments monument donated by the Fraternal Order of Eagles in 1971.

Respondent Summum is a religious organization founded in 1975 and headquartered in Salt Lake City, Utah. On two separate occasions in 2003, Summum's president wrote a letter to the City's mayor requesting permission to erect a "stone monument," which would contain "the Seven Aphorisms of SUMMUM" and be similar in size and nature to the Ten Commandments monument. The City denied the requests.

In May 2005, respondent's president again wrote to the mayor asking to erect a monument, but the letter did not describe the monument, its historical significance, or Summum's connection to the community. The city council rejected this request.

In 2005, respondent filed this action against the City and various local officials (petitioners), asserting, among other claims, that petitioners had violated the Free Speech Clause of the First Amendment by accepting the Ten Commandments monument but rejecting the proposed Seven Aphorisms monument.

II

No prior decision of this Court has addressed the application of the Free Speech Clause to a government entity's acceptance of privately donated, permanent monuments for installation in a public park, and the parties disagree sharply about the line of precedents that governs this situation. The parties' fundamental disagreement thus centers on the nature of petitioners' conduct when they permitted privately donated monuments to be erected in Pioneer Park. Were petitioners engaging in their own expressive conduct? Or were they providing a forum for private speech?

If petitioners were engaging in their own expressive conduct, then the Free Speech Clause has no application. The Free Speech Clause restricts government regulation of private speech; it does not regulate government speech. Indeed, it is not easy to imagine how government could function if it lacked this freedom. "If every citizen were to have a right to insist that no one paid by public funds express a view with which he disagreed, debate over issues of great concern to the public would be limited to those in the private sector, and the process of government as we know it radically transformed."

A government entity may exercise this same freedom to express its views when it receives assistance from private sources for the purpose of delivering a government-controlled message.

This does not mean that there are no restraints on government speech. For example, government speech must comport with the Establishment Clause. The involvement of public officials in advocacy may be limited by law, regulation, or practice. And of course, a government entity is ultimately "accountable to the electorate and the political process for its advocacy."

While government speech is not restricted by the Free Speech Clause, the government does not have a free hand to regulate private speech on government property. This Court long ago recognized that members of the public retain strong free speech rights when they venture into public streets and parks, "which 'have immemorially been held in trust for the use of the public and, time out of mind, have been used for purposes of assembly, communicating thoughts between citizens, and discussing public questions.'" In order to preserve this freedom, government entities are strictly limited in their ability to regulate private speech in such "traditional public fora." Reasonable time, place, and manner restrictions are allowed, but any restriction based on the content of the speech must satisfy strict scrutiny, that is, the restriction must be narrowly tailored to serve a compelling government interest, and restrictions based on viewpoint are prohibited.

III

There may be situations in which it is difficult to tell whether a government entity is speaking on its own behalf or is providing a forum for private speech, but this case does not present such a situation. Permanent monuments displayed on public property typically represent government speech.

Governments have long used monuments to speak to the public. Since ancient times, kings, emperors, and other rulers have erected statues of themselves to remind their subjects of their authority and power. Triumphal arches, columns, and other monuments have been built to commemorate military victories and sacrifices and other events of civic importance. A monument, by definition, is a structure that is designed as a means of expression. When a government entity arranges for the construction of a monument, it does so because it wishes to convey some thought or instill some feeling in those who see the structure. Neither the Court of Appeals nor respondent disputes the obvious proposition that a monument that is commissioned and financed by a government body for placement on public land constitutes government speech.

Just as government-commissioned and government-financed monuments speak for the government, so do privately financed and donated monuments that the government accepts and displays to the public on government land. In this context, there is little chance that observers will fail to appreciate the identity of the speaker. This is true whether the monument is located on private property or on public property, such as national, state, or city park land.

Public parks are often closely identified in the public mind with the government unit that owns the land. City parks ranging from those in small towns, like Pioneer Park in Pleasant Grove City, to those in major metropolises, like Central Park in New York City—commonly play an important role in defining the identity that a city projects to its own residents and to the outside world. Accordingly, cities and other jurisdictions take some care in accepting donated monuments. Government decisionmakers select the monuments that portray what they view as appropriate for the place in question, taking into account such content-based factors as esthetics, history, and local culture. The monuments that are accepted, therefore, are meant to convey and have the effect of conveying a government message, and they thus constitute government speech.

IV

In this case, it is clear that the monuments in Pleasant Grove's Pioneer Park represent government speech. Although many of the monuments were not designed or built by the City and were donated in completed form by private entities, the City decided to accept those donations and to display them in the Park. Respondent does not claim that the City ever opened up the Park for the placement of whatever permanent monuments might be offered by private donors. Rather, the City has "effectively controlled" the messages sent by the monuments in the Park by exercising "final approval authority" over their selection. The City has selected those monuments that it wants to display for the purpose of presenting the image of the City that it wishes to project to all who frequent the Park; it has taken ownership of most of the monuments in the Park, including the Ten Commandments monument that is the focus of respondent's concern; and the City has now expressly set forth the criteria it will use in making future selections.

Public parks can accommodate only a limited number of permanent monuments. Public parks have been used, "'time out of mind, . . . for purposes of assembly, communicating thoughts between citizens, and discussing public questions,'" but "one would be hard pressed to find a 'long tradition' of allowing people to permanently occupy public space with any manner of monuments."

Speakers, no matter how long-winded, eventually come to the end of their remarks; persons distributing leaflets and carrying signs at some point tire and go home; monuments, however, endure. They monopolize the use of the land on which they stand and interfere permanently with other uses of public space. A public park, over the years, can provide a soapbox for a very large number of orators—often, for all who want to speak—but it is hard to imagine how a public park could be opened up for the installation of permanent monuments by every person or group wishing to engage in that form of expression.

If government entities must maintain viewpoint neutrality in their selection of donated monuments, they must either "brace themselves for an influx of clutter" or face the pressure to remove longstanding and cherished monuments. Every jurisdiction that has accepted a donated war memorial may be asked to provide equal treatment for a donated monument questioning the cause for which the veterans fought. New York City, having accepted a donated statue of one heroic dog (Balto, the sled dog who brought medicine to Nome, Alaska, during a diphtheria epidemic) may be pressed to accept monuments for other dogs who are claimed to be equally worthy of commemoration. The obvious truth of the matter is that if public parks were considered to be traditional public forums for the purpose of erecting privately donated monuments, most parks would have little choice but to refuse all such donations. And where the application of forum analysis would lead almost inexorably to closing of the forum, it is obvious that forum analysis is out of place.

To be sure, there are limited circumstances in which the forum doctrine might properly be applied to a permanent monument—for example, if a town created a monument on which all of its residents (or all those meeting some other criterion) could place the name of a person to be honored or some other private message. But as a general matter, forum analysis simply does not apply to the installation of permanent monuments on public property.

V

In sum, we hold that the City's decision to accept certain privately donated monuments while rejecting respondent's is best viewed as a form of government speech. As a result, the City's decision is not subject to the Free Speech Clause.

Justice SOUTER, concurring in the judgment.

I agree with the Court that the Ten Commandments monument is government speech, that is, an expression of a government's position on the moral and religious issues raised by the subject of the monument. And although the government should lose when the character of the speech is at issue and its governmental nature has not been made clear, I also agree with the Court that the city need not satisfy the particular formality urged by Summum as a condition of recognizing that the expression here falls within the public category. I have qualms, however, about accepting the position that public monuments are government speech categorically.

Because the government speech doctrine is "recently minted," it would do well for us to go slow in setting its bounds, which will affect existing doctrine in ways not yet explored.

The case shows that it may not be easy to work out. After today's decision, whenever a government maintains a monument it will presumably be understood to be engaging in government speech. If the monument has some religious

A. The Distinction Between Content-Based and Content-Neutral Laws

character, the specter of violating the Establishment Clause will behoove it to take care to avoid the appearance of a flat-out establishment of religion, in the sense of the government's adoption of the tenets expressed or symbolized. In such an instance, there will be safety in numbers, and it will be in the interest of a careful government to accept other monuments to stand nearby, to dilute the appearance of adopting whatever particular religious position the single example alone might stand for. As mementoes and testimonials pile up, however, the chatter may well make it less intuitively obvious that the government is speaking in its own right simply by maintaining the monuments.

To avoid relying on a *per se* rule to say when speech is governmental, the best approach that occurs to me is to ask whether a reasonable and fully informed observer would understand the expression to be government speech, as distinct from private speech the government chooses to oblige by allowing the monument to be placed on public land. This reasonable observer test for governmental character is of a piece with the one for spotting forbidden governmental endorsement of religion in the Establishment Clause cases. The adoption of it would thus serve coherence within Establishment Clause law, and it would make sense of our common understanding that some monuments on public land display religious symbolism that clearly does not express a government's chosen views. Application of this observer test provides the reason I find the monument here to be government expression.

The Court applied the principle that the First Amendment's free speech clause cannot be used to challenge government speech in Walker v. Texas Division, Sons of Confederate Veterans.

WALKER v. TEXAS DIVISION, SONS OF CONFEDERATE VETERANS
576 U.S. 200 (2015)

Justice BREYER delivered the opinion of the Court.

Texas offers automobile owners a choice between ordinary and specialty license plates. Those who want the State to issue a particular specialty plate may propose a plate design, comprising a slogan, a graphic, or (most commonly) both. If the Texas Department of Motor Vehicles Board approves the design, the State will make it available for display on vehicles registered in Texas.

In this case, the Texas Division of the Sons of Confederate Veterans proposed a specialty license plate design featuring a Confederate battle flag. The Board rejected the proposal. We must decide whether that rejection violated the Constitution's free speech guarantees. We conclude that it did not.

I

Texas law requires all motor vehicles operating on the State's roads to display valid license plates. And Texas makes available several kinds of plates. Drivers may choose to display the State's general-issue license plates. In the alternative, drivers may choose from an assortment of specialty license plates. §504.008(b).

Each of these plates contains the word "Texas," a license plate number, and one of a selection of designs prepared by the State. Finally, Texas law provides for personalized plates (also known as vanity plates). Pursuant to the personalization program, a vehicle owner may request a particular alphanumeric pattern for use as a plate number, such as "BOB" or "TEXPL8."

Here we are concerned only with the second category of plates, namely specialty license plates, not with the personalization program. Texas offers vehicle owners a variety of specialty plates, generally for an annual fee. [T]he Board "may create new specialty license plates on its own initiative or on receipt of an application from a "nonprofit entity seeking to sponsor a specialty plate. A nonprofit must include in its application "a draft design of the specialty license plate." And Texas law vests in the Board authority to approve or to disapprove an application. The relevant statute says that the Board "may refuse to create a new specialty license plate" for a number of reasons, for example "if the design might be offensive to any member of the public . . . or for any other reason established by rule." Specialty plates that the Board has sanctioned through this process include plates featuring the words "The Gator Nation," together with the Florida Gators logo, and plates featuring the logo of Rotary International and the words "SERVICE ABOVE SELF."

In 2009, the Sons of Confederate Veterans, Texas Division (a nonprofit entity), applied to sponsor a specialty license plate through this last-mentioned process. SCV's application included a draft plate design. At the bottom of the proposed plate were the words "SONS OF CONFEDERATE VETERANS." At the side was the organization's logo, a square Confederate battle flag framed by the words "Sons of Confederate Veterans 1896." A faint Confederate battle flag appeared in the background on the lower portion of the plate. Additionally, in the middle of the plate was the license plate number, and at the top was the State's name and silhouette. The Board's predecessor denied this application.

In 2010, SCV renewed its application before the Board. [T]he Board voted unanimously against issuing the plate. The Board explained that it had found "it necessary to deny th[e] plate design application, specifically the confederate flag portion of the design, because public comments ha[d] shown that many members of the general public find the design offensive, and because such comments are reasonable." The Board added "that a significant portion of the public associate the confederate flag with organizations advocating expressions of hate directed toward people or groups that is demeaning to those people or groups."

In 2012, SCV and two of its officers (collectively SCV) brought this lawsuit against the chairman and members of the Board (collectively Board). SCV argued that the Board's decision violated the Free Speech Clause of the First Amendment, and it sought an injunction requiring the Board to approve the proposed plate design.

II

When government speaks, it is not barred by the Free Speech Clause from determining the content of what it says. Pleasant Grove City v. Summum (2009). That freedom in part reflects the fact that it is the democratic electoral process that first and foremost provides a check on government speech. Thus,

A. The Distinction Between Content-Based and Content-Neutral Laws

government statements (and government actions and programs that take the form of speech) do not normally trigger the First Amendment rules designed to protect the marketplace of ideas. Instead, the Free Speech Clause helps produce informed opinions among members of the public, who are then able to influence the choices of a government that, through words and deeds, will reflect its electoral mandate.

Were the Free Speech Clause interpreted otherwise, government would not work. How could a city government create a successful recycling program if officials, when writing householders asking them to recycle cans and bottles, had to include in the letter a long plea from the local trash disposal enterprise demanding the contrary? How could a state government effectively develop programs designed to encourage and provide vaccinations, if officials also had to voice the perspective of those who oppose this type of immunization? "[I]t is not easy to imagine how government could function if it lacked th[e] freedom" to select the messages it wishes to convey.

We have therefore refused "[t]o hold that the Government unconstitutionally discriminates on the basis of viewpoint when it chooses to fund a program dedicated to advance certain permissible goals, because the program in advancing those goals necessarily discourages alternative goals." We have pointed out that a contrary holding "would render numerous Government programs constitutionally suspect." And we have made clear that "the government can speak for itself."

That is not to say that a government's ability to express itself is without restriction. Constitutional and statutory provisions outside of the Free Speech Clause may limit government speech. And the Free Speech Clause itself may constrain the government's speech if, for example, the government seeks to compel private persons to convey the government's speech. But, as a general matter, when the government speaks it is entitled to promote a program, to espouse a policy, or to take a position. In doing so, it represents its citizens and it carries out its duties on their behalf.

III

In our view, specialty license plates issued pursuant to Texas's statutory scheme convey government speech. Our reasoning rests primarily on our analysis in *Summum*, a recent case that presented a similar problem. We conclude here, as we did there, that our precedents regarding government speech (and not our precedents regarding forums for private speech) provide the appropriate framework through which to approach the case.

Our analysis in *Summum* leads us to the conclusion that here, too, government speech is at issue. First, the history of license plates shows that, insofar as license plates have conveyed more than state names and vehicle identification numbers, they long have communicated messages from the state. Second, Texas license plate designs "are often closely identified in the public mind with the [State]." Each Texas license plate is a government article serving the governmental purposes of vehicle registration and identification. The governmental nature of the plates is clear from their faces: The State places the name "TEXAS" in large letters at the top of every plate. Moreover, the State requires Texas vehicle owners to display license plates, and every Texas license plate is issued by the

State. Texas also owns the designs on its license plates, including the designs that Texas adopts on the basis of proposals made by private individuals and organizations.

Texas license plates are, essentially, government IDs. And issuers of ID "typically do not permit" the placement on their IDs of "message[s] with which they do not wish to be associated." Consequently, "persons who observe" designs on IDs "routinely—and reasonably—interpret them as conveying some message on the [issuer's] behalf."

Third, Texas maintains direct control over the messages conveyed on its specialty plates. Texas law provides that the State "has sole control over the design, typeface, color, and alphanumeric pattern for all license plates." The Board must approve every specialty plate design proposal before the design can appear on a Texas plate. This final approval authority allows Texas to choose how to present itself and its constituency. Thus, Texas offers plates celebrating the many educational institutions attended by its citizens.

These considerations, taken together, convince us that the specialty plates here in question are similar enough to the monuments in *Summum* to call for the same result.

We have previously used what we have called "forum analysis" to evaluate government restrictions on purely private speech that occurs on government property. But forum analysis is misplaced here. Because the State is speaking on its own behalf, the First Amendment strictures that attend the various types of government-established forums do not apply.

The fact that private parties take part in the design and propagation of a message does not extinguish the governmental nature of the message or transform the government's role into that of a mere forum-provider. In *Summum*, private entities "financed and donated monuments that the government accept[ed] and display[ed] to the public." Here, similarly, private parties propose designs that Texas may accept and display on its license plates. In this case, as in *Summum*, the "government entity may exercise [its] freedom to express its views" even "when it receives assistance from private sources for the purpose of delivering a government-controlled message." And in this case, as in *Summum*, forum analysis is inapposite.

IV

Our determination that Texas's specialty license plate designs are government speech does not mean that the designs do not also implicate the free speech rights of private persons. We have acknowledged that drivers who display a State's selected license plate designs convey the messages communicated through those designs. See Wooley v. Maynard (1977) (observing that a vehicle "is readily associated with its operator" and that drivers displaying license plates "use their private property as a 'mobile billboard' for the State's ideological message"). And we have recognized that the First Amendment stringently limits a State's authority to compel a private party to express a view with which the private party disagrees. But here, compelled private speech is not at issue. And just as Texas cannot require SCV to convey "the State's ideological message," SCV cannot force Texas to include a Confederate battle flag on its specialty license plates.

A. The Distinction Between Content-Based and Content-Neutral Laws

For the reasons stated, we hold that Texas's specialty license plate designs constitute government speech and that Texas was consequently entitled to refuse to issue plates featuring SCV's proposed design.

Justice ALITO, with whom THE CHIEF JUSTICE, Justice SCALIA, and Justice KENNEDY join, dissenting.

The Court's decision passes off private speech as government speech and, in doing so, establishes a precedent that threatens private speech that government finds displeasing. Under our First Amendment cases, the distinction between government speech and private speech is critical. The First Amendment "does not regulate government speech," and therefore when government speaks, it is free "to select the views that it wants to express." By contrast, "[i]n the realm of private speech or expression, government regulation may not favor one speaker over another."

Unfortunately, the Court's decision categorizes private speech as government speech and thus strips it of all First Amendment protection. The Court holds that all the privately created messages on the many specialty plates issued by the State of Texas convey a government message rather than the message of the motorist displaying the plate. Can this possibly be correct?

Here is a test. Suppose you sat by the side of a Texas highway and studied the license plates on the vehicles passing by. You would see, in addition to the standard Texas plates, an impressive array of specialty plates. (There are now more than 350 varieties.) You would likely observe plates that honor numerous colleges and universities. You might see plates bearing the name of a high school, a fraternity or sorority, the Masons, the Knights of Columbus, the Daughters of the American Revolution, a realty company, a favorite soft drink, a favorite burger restaurant, and a favorite NASCAR driver.

As you sat there watching these plates speed by, would you really think that the sentiments reflected in these specialty plates are the views of the State of Texas and not those of the owners of the cars? If a car with a plate that says "Rather Be Golfing" passed by at 8:30 a.m. on a Monday morning, would you think: "This is the official policy of the State—better to golf than to work?" If you did your viewing at the start of the college football season and you saw Texas plates with the names of the University of Texas's out-of-state competitors in upcoming games—Notre Dame, Oklahoma State, the University of Oklahoma, Kansas State, Iowa State—would you assume that the State of Texas was officially (and perhaps treasonously) rooting for the Longhorns' opponents? And when a car zipped by with a plate that reads "NASCAR—24 Jeff Gordon," would you think that Gordon (born in California, raised in Indiana, resides in North Carolina) is the official favorite of the State government?

The Court says that all of these messages are government speech. It is essential that government be able to express its own viewpoint, the Court reminds us, because otherwise, how would it promote its programs, like recycling and vaccinations? So when Texas issues a "Rather Be Golfing" plate, but not a "Rather Be Playing Tennis" or "Rather Be Bowling" plate, it is furthering a state policy to promote golf but not tennis or bowling. And when Texas allows motorists to obtain a Notre Dame license plate but not a University of Southern California plate, it is taking sides in that long-time rivalry.

This capacious understanding of government speech takes a large and painful bite out of the First Amendment. Specialty plates may seem innocuous.

They make motorists happy, and they put money in a State's coffers. But the precedent this case sets is dangerous. While all license plates unquestionably contain *some* government speech (*e.g.*, the name of the State and the numbers and/or letters identifying the vehicle), the State of Texas has converted the remaining space on its specialty plates into little mobile billboards on which motorists can display their own messages. And what Texas did here was to reject one of the messages that members of a private group wanted to post on some of these little billboards because the State thought that many of its citizens would find the message offensive. That is blatant viewpoint discrimination.

If the State can do this with its little mobile billboards, could it do the same with big, stationary billboards? Suppose that a State erected electronic billboards along its highways. Suppose that the State posted some government messages on these billboards and then, to raise money, allowed private entities and individuals to purchase the right to post their own messages. And suppose that the State allowed only those messages that it liked or found not too controversial. Would that be constitutional?

What if a state college or university did the same thing with a similar billboard or a campus bulletin board or dorm list serve? What if it allowed private messages that are consistent with prevailing views on campus but banned those that disturbed some students or faculty? Can there be any doubt that these examples of viewpoint discrimination would violate the First Amendment? I hope not, but the future uses of today's precedent remain to be seen.

The Court believes that messages on privately created plates are government speech because motorists want a seal of state approval for their messages and therefore prefer plates over bumper stickers. This is dangerous reasoning. There is a big difference between government speech (that is, speech by the government in furtherance of its programs) and governmental blessing (or condemnation) of private speech. Many private speakers in a forum would welcome a sign of government approval. But in the realm of private speech, government regulation may not favor one viewpoint over another.

What Texas has done by selling space on its license plates is to create what we have called a limited public forum. It has allowed state property (*i.e.*, motor vehicle license plates) to be used by private speakers according to rules that the State prescribes. Under the First Amendment, however, those rules cannot discriminate on the basis of viewpoint. But that is exactly what Texas did here. The Board rejected Texas SCV's design, "specifically the confederate flag portion of the design, because public comments have shown that many members of the general public find the design offensive, and because such comments are reasonable." These statements indisputably demonstrate that the Board denied Texas SCV's design because of its viewpoint.

The Board's decision cannot be saved by its suggestion that the plate, if allowed, "could distract or disturb some drivers to the point of being unreasonably dangerous." This rationale cannot withstand strict scrutiny. Other States allow specialty plates with the Confederate Battle Flag, and Texas has not pointed to evidence that these plates have led to incidents of road rage or accidents. Texas does not ban bumper stickers bearing the image of the Confederate battle flag. Nor does it ban any of the many other bumper stickers that convey political messages and other messages that are capable of exciting the ire of those who loathe the ideas they express.

B. VAGUENESS AND OVERBREADTH

Messages that are proposed by private parties and placed on Texas specialty plates are private speech, not government speech. Texas cannot forbid private speech based on its viewpoint. That is what it did here.

B. VAGUENESS AND OVERBREADTH

Laws that regulate speech can be challenged as facially unconstitutional on the grounds that they are unduly vague and overbroad. A successful facial challenge usually means that the law is entirely invalidated, as opposed to being declared unconstitutional as to certain applications. Vagueness and overbreadth are thus powerful doctrines that can be used to challenge any law regulating speech, including by a person whose speech is unprotected by the First Amendment. This section looks first at vagueness, then it considers overbreadth, and finally it discusses the relationship between the two doctrines.

1. *Vagueness*

A law is unconstitutionally vague if a reasonable person cannot tell what speech is prohibited and what is permitted.[14] It is important to emphasize that unduly vague laws violate due process whether or not speech is regulated.[15] For example, in Kolender v. Lawson, the Court declared unconstitutional California's loitering law and declared that "the void-for-vagueness doctrine requires that a penal statute define the criminal offense with sufficient definiteness that ordinary people can understand what conduct is prohibited and in a manner that does not encourage arbitrary and discriminatory enforcement."[16]

In part, the vagueness doctrine is about fairness; it is unjust to punish a person without providing clear notice as to what conduct was prohibited. Vague laws also risk selective prosecution; under vague statutes and ordinances the government can choose who to prosecute based on their views or politics. Justice O'Connor said that "[t]he more important aspect of the vagueness doctrine 'is not actual notice, but the other principal element of the doctrine — the requirement that a legislature establish minimal guidelines to govern law enforcement.' Where the legislature fails to provide such minimal guidelines, a criminal statute may permit 'a standardless sweep [that] allows policemen, prosecutors, and juries to pursue their personal predilections.'"[17]

Although all laws regulating conduct can be challenged under the due process vagueness doctrine, courts are particularly troubled about vague laws restricting

---

14. *See, e.g.*, Connally v. General Construction Co., 269 U.S. 385, 391 (1926) (a law is unconstitutionally vague when people "of common intelligence must necessarily guess at its meaning").
15. *See, e.g.*, Papachristou v. Jacksonville, 405 U.S. 156 (1972) (declaring vagrancy law unconstitutional).
16. 461 U.S. 352, 357 (1983).
17. *Id.* at 358.

speech out of concern that they will chill constitutionally protected speech. The Court has observed that freedom of speech is "delicate and vulnerable, as well as supremely precious in our society . . . [and] the threat of sanctions may deter their exercise almost as potently as the actual application of sanctions."[18] Thus, the Supreme Court has declared laws regulating speech to be void on vagueness grounds when they are so ambiguous that the reasonable person cannot tell what expression is forbidden and what is allowed. Coates v. City of Cincinnati is illustrative.

COATES v. CITY OF CINCINNATI, 402 U.S. 611 (1971): Justice STEWART delivered the opinion of the Court.

A Cincinnati, Ohio, ordinance makes criminal offense for "three or more persons to assemble . . . on any of the sidewalks . . . and there conduct themselves in a manner annoying to persons passing by. . . ." The issue before us is whether this ordinance is unconstitutional on its face.

The record brought before the reviewing courts tells us no more than that the appellant Coates was a student involved in a demonstration and the other appellants were pickets involved in a labor dispute. For throughout this litigation it has been the appellants' position that the ordinance on its face violates the First and Fourteenth Amendments of the Constitution.

We are thus relegated, at best, to the words of the ordinance itself. If three or more people meet together on a sidewalk or street corner, they must conduct themselves so as not to annoy any police officer or other person who should happen to pass by. In our opinion this ordinance is unconstitutionally vague because it subjects the exercise of the right of assembly to an unascertainable standard, and unconstitutionally broad because it authorizes the punishment of constitutionally protected conduct.

Conduct that annoys some people does not annoy others. Thus, the ordinance is vague, not in the sense that it requires a person to conform his conduct to an imprecise but comprehensible normative standard, but rather in the sense that no standard of conduct is specified at all. As a result, "men of common intelligence must necessarily guess at its meaning."

It is said that the ordinance is broad enough to encompass many types of conduct clearly within the city's constitutional power to prohibit. And so, indeed, it is. The city is free to prevent people from blocking sidewalks, obstructing traffic, littering streets, committing assaults, or engaging in countless other forms of antisocial conduct. It can do so through the enactment and enforcement of ordinances directed with reasonable specificity toward the conduct to be prohibited. It cannot constitutionally do so through the enactment and enforcement of an ordinance whose violation may entirely depend upon whether or not a policeman is annoyed.

The ordinance also violates the constitutional right of free assembly and association. The First and Fourteenth Amendments do not permit a State to make criminal the exercise of the right of assembly simply because its exercise may be "annoying" to some people. If this were not the rule, the right of the people to gather in public places for social or political purposes would be

---

18. NAACP v. Button, 371 U.S. 415, 433 (1963).

continually subject to summary suspension through the good-faith enforcement of a prohibition against annoying conduct.

The ordinance before us makes a crime out of what under the Constitution cannot be a crime. It is aimed directly at activity protected by the Constitution.

Similarly, in Baggett v. Bullitt, 377 U.S. 360 (1964), the Court declared unconstitutional a state's loyalty oath that, among other things, prevented any "subversive person" from being employed in the state and required a person to swear that he or she was not such an individual or a part of any subversive organization. The Court found "the oath requirements and the statutory provisions on which they are based . . . invalid on their face because their language is unduly vague, uncertain, and broad." The Court stressed that the ambiguities inherent in the term "subversive" and in the language of the statute gave individuals little guidance as to what speech and associational activities were proscribed.

There is not and never will be a litmus test for evaluating when a law is too vague and thus offends the Constitution. Ambiguity is inherent in language and all laws will have some vagueness. But the Court has made it clear that greater precision is required when laws regulate speech, and statutes will be invalidated if a judge concludes that they provide inadequate notice as to what speech is prohibited and what is allowed. The void-for-vagueness doctrine is thus a powerful tool in First Amendment litigation because it allows facial challenges to laws even by those whose speech otherwise would be unprotected by the First Amendment.

2. Overbreadth

A law is unconstitutionally overbroad if it regulates substantially more speech than the Constitution allows to be regulated, and a person to whom the law constitutionally can be applied can argue that it would be unconstitutional as applied to others. In other words, in an area where the government can regulate speech, such as obscenity, a law that regulates much more expression than the Constitution allows to be restricted will be declared unconstitutional on overbreadth grounds. An individual whose speech is unprotected by the First Amendment and who could constitutionally be punished under a more narrow statute may argue that the law is unconstitutional because of how it might be applied to third parties not before the Court. Schad v. Borough of Mount Ephraim is illustrative.

SCHAD v. BOROUGH OF MOUNT EPHRAIM, 452 U.S. 61 (1981): Justice WHITE delivered the opinion of the Court.

In 1973, appellants began operating an adult bookstore in the commercial zone in the Borough of Mount Ephraim in Camden County, N.J. The store sold adult books, magazines, and films. Amusement licenses shortly issued permitting the store to install coin-operated devices by virtue of which a customer could sit in a booth, insert a coin, and watch an adult film. In 1976, the store introduced an additional coin-operated mechanism permitting the customer to watch a live dancer, usually nude, performing behind a glass panel.

Appellants appealed to this Court. Their principal claim is that the imposition of criminal penalties under an ordinance prohibiting all live entertainment, including nonobscene, nude dancing, violated their rights of free expression guaranteed by the First and Fourteenth Amendments of the United States Constitution. By excluding live entertainment throughout the Borough, the Mount Ephraim ordinance prohibits a wide range of expression that has long been held to be within the protections of the First and Fourteenth Amendments. Entertainment, as well as political and ideological speech, is protected; motion pictures, programs broadcast by radio and television, and live entertainment, such as musical and dramatic works fall within the First Amendment guarantee.

Whatever First Amendment protection should be extended to nude dancing, live or on film, however, the Mount Ephraim ordinance prohibits all live entertainment in the Borough: no property in the Borough may be principally used for the commercial production of plays, concerts, musicals, dance, or any other form of live entertainment. Because appellants' claims are rooted in the First Amendment, they are entitled to rely on the impact of the ordinance on the expressive activities of others as well as their own. Because overbroad laws, like vague ones, deter privileged activit[ies], our cases firmly establish appellant's standing to raise an overbreadth challenge.

There are thus two major aspects to the overbreadth doctrine. First, a law must be substantially overbroad; that is, it must restrict significantly more speech than the Constitution allows to be controlled. In Broadrick v. Oklahoma, 413 U.S. 601 (1973), the Court said that "particularly where conduct and not merely speech is involved, we believe that the overbreadth of a statute must not only be real, but substantial as well, judged in relation to the statute's plainly legitimate sweep." In *Broadrick*, the Court upheld the constitutionality of an Oklahoma law that prohibited political activities by government employees. The challengers argued that the law was overbroad because it prohibited constitutionally protected activity such as the wearing of political buttons or the displaying of bumper stickers. The Supreme Court acknowledged some overbreadth, but upheld the law because it was "not substantially overbroad and whatever overbreadth may exist should be cured through case-by-case analysis of the fact situations to which its sanctions, assertedly, may not be applied." In other words, the Court said that the law should not be declared unconstitutional on its face because it was not substantially overbroad, but that particular applications of the law could be declared unconstitutional in future cases.

In subsequent cases, the Court made it clear that the requirement for substantial overbreadth applies in all cases, whether the law regulates conduct that communicates or "pure speech."[19] The Court has declared that "[a] statute may be invalidated on its face . . . only if the overbreadth is substantial."[20] In City Council v. Taxpayers for Vincent, 466 U.S. 789 (1984), the Court upheld

---

19. *See, e.g.*, City Council of Los Angeles v. Taxpayers for Vincent, 466 U.S. 789, 800 (1984); New York v. Ferber, 458 U.S. 747, 772 (1982).
20. Board of Airport Commissioners of Los Angeles v. Jews for Jesus, Inc., 482 U.S. 569, 574 (1987).

B. Vagueness and Overbreadth

a municipal ordinance that prohibited the posting of signs on public property and emphasized that "substantial overbreadth" was required in order for a law to be invalidated.

In *Vincent*, the Court also addressed the question of what is "substantial overbreadth." The Court said that "[t]he concept of substantial overbreadth is not readily reduced to an exact definition. It is clear, however, that the mere fact that one can conceive of some impermissible applications of a statute is not sufficient to render it susceptible to an overbreadth challenge. . . . In short, there must be a realistic danger that the statute itself will significantly compromise recognized First Amendment protections of parties not before the Court for it to be facially challenged on overbreadth grounds."

It appears, then, that substantial overbreadth might be demonstrated by showing a significant number of situations where a law could be applied to prohibit constitutionally protected speech. For example, in City of Houston v. Hill, 482 U.S. 451 (1987), the Court declared unconstitutional an ordinance that made it unlawful to interrupt police officers in the performance of their duties. An individual was convicted of violating the law for shouting at police officers to divert their attention from arresting his friend. The Court declared the law unconstitutional and said that the "ordinance criminalizes a substantial amount of constitutionally protected speech, and accords the police unconstitutional discretion in enforcement. The ordinance's plain language is admittedly violated scores of times daily . . . , yet only some individuals—those chosen by the police in their unguided discretion—are arrested. Far from providing the 'breathing space' that 'First Amendment freedoms need to survive,' the ordinance is susceptible of regular application to protected expression. We conclude that the statute is substantially overbroad."

In contrast, if the Court believes that the law will apply to relatively few situations where speech is constitutionally protected, it will not be declared overbroad. For example, in New York v. Ferber, 458 U.S. 747 (1982), the Court upheld a state law prohibiting child pornography, although it acknowledged that the statute could be applied to material with serious literary, scientific, or educational value. The Court said that the law was constitutional because these applications of the statute would not "amount to more than a tiny fraction of the materials within the statute's reach." These applications thus could be dealt with on a case-by-case basis if prosecutions arose, rather than by declaring the entire law unconstitutional.

The second major aspect of the overbreadth doctrine is that a person to whom the law constitutionally may be applied can argue that it would be unconstitutional as applied to others. The usual rule of standing is "that a person to whom a statute may constitutionally be applied will not be heard to challenge that statute on the ground that it may conceivably be applied unconstitutionally to others, in other situations not before the Court."[21] But overbreadth is an exception to this general standing principle that requires people to assert only their own rights.

Secretary of State v. J.H. Munson Co., 467 U.S. 947 (1984), illustrates this aspect of the overbreadth doctrine. A Maryland statute prohibited charitable

---

21. Broadrick v. Oklahoma, 413 U.S. at 610.

organizations from soliciting funds unless at least 75 percent of their revenue was used for "charitable purposes." The law was challenged by a professional fundraiser who raised the First Amendment rights of his clients, charities who were not parties to the lawsuit. The Supreme Court permitted the fundraiser standing to argue the constitutional claims of charitable organizations. The Court said that "where the claim is that a statute is overly broad in violation of the First Amendment, the Court has allowed a party to assert the rights of another without regard to the ability of the other to assert his own claims and with no requirement that the person making the attack demonstrate that his own conduct could not be regulated by a statute drawn with the requisite narrow specificity."

The Supreme Court thus regards the overbreadth doctrine as "strong medicine"[22] because it involves the facial invalidation of a law and because it permits individuals standing to raise the claims of others not before the Court. Individuals who otherwise could be constitutionally punished are allowed to go free. The Court has justified the overbreadth doctrine because the "First Amendment needs breathing space."[23] The concerns are that overbroad laws will chill significant constitutionally protected speech and that individuals to whom the law is unconstitutional may refrain from expression rather than bring a challenge to the statute. Justice Brennan explained that the overbreadth doctrine is "necessary because persons whose expression is constitutionally protected may well refrain from exercising their rights for fear of criminal sanctions provided by a statute susceptible of application to protected expression."[24]

This rationale for the overbreadth doctrine is illustrated by the Court's holding that it does not apply in challenges to laws regulating commercial speech.[25] The Court believes that the incentive to engage in advertising is sufficiently strong as to lessen any worries that such speech will be chilled.

Because the overbreadth doctrine is perceived as "strong medicine," the Court has said that it will avoid invalidating laws by allowing courts to construe statutes narrowly and thus avoid overbreadth. In Osborne v. Ohio, 495 U.S. 103 (1990), the Court used this approach to avoid declaring a child pornography law unconstitutional on overbreadth grounds. The law prohibited private possession of child pornography and, by its terms, outlawed possession of nude photographs. The Supreme Court has long recognized that nudity, by itself, is not enough to place pictures outside the scope of the First Amendment. The Ohio Supreme Court adopted a narrowing construction of the law so that it applied only to "the possession or viewing of material or performance of a minor who is in a state of nudity, where such nudity constitutes a lewd exhibition or involves a graphic focus on the genitals, and where the person depicted is neither the child nor the ward of the person charged." The U.S. Supreme Court accepted this narrowing construction as avoiding "penalizing persons for viewing or possessing innocuous photographs of naked children." The Court thus found that the law was not impermissibly overbroad.

---

22. *Id.* at 613.
23. *Id.* at 611.
24. Gooding v. Wilson, 405 U.S. 518, 521 (1972).
25. *See, e.g.,* Village of Hoffman Estates v. Flipside, Hoffman Estates, Inc., 455 U.S. 489, 497 (1982) ("the overbreadth doctrine does not apply to commercial speech").

B. Vagueness and Overbreadth

In contrast, in Gooding v. Wilson, 405 U.S. 518 (1972), the absence of narrowing constructions by state courts led to a law prohibiting fighting words being invalidated on overbreadth grounds. A Georgia law made it a crime for "[a]ny person who shall, without provocation, use to or of another, and in his presence opprobrious words or abusive language, tending to cause a breach of the peace." The Court said that the law could be upheld under the First Amendment "only if, as authoritatively construed by the Georgia courts, it is not susceptible of application to speech, although vulgar or offensive, that is protected by the First and Fourteenth Amendments." The Court reviewed Georgia court decisions and, finding no such limiting construction, declared the law unconstitutionally overbroad.

The Court effectively invalidated a law on overbreadth grounds without using that term in Packingham v. North Carolina, 137 S. Ct. 1730 (2017). North Carolina law made it a felony for a registered sex offender "to access a commercial social networking Web site where the sex offender knows that the site permits minor children to become members or to create or maintain personal Web pages." When he was 21 years old, Lester Packingham was convicted of taking indecent liberties with a minor and as a result is a registered sex offender.

Packingham got a traffic ticket quashed by a judge and went on Facebook and posted the message, "God is Good." He then was indicted under the North Carolina law for going on a website where minors can be present. He was convicted and given a suspended sentence. In fact, thousands of individuals had been convicted under this North Carolina law.

The Court unanimously declared the North Carolina law unconstitutional. Justice Kennedy wrote the majority opinion. Justice Alito wrote an opinion concurring in the judgment, joined by two other Justices.

Justice Kennedy began by strongly emphasizing the importance of the Internet as a place for speech. He spoke of the "vast democratic forums of the Internet" in general, and of the importance of social media in particular. He said that seven in ten American adults use at least one Internet social networking service and that more people are on Facebook than the entire population of North America. The Court noted the unique importance of social media for free speech. He said "the Court must exercise extreme caution before suggesting that the First Amendment provides scant protection for access to vast networks in that medium."

The Court said that even if it assumed the North Carolina law was content-neutral, it still was unconstitutional and vastly overbroad in keeping individuals from having access not just to Facebook, but to washingtonpost.com, Amazon, and Web MD. He said that the state could have a narrower law, such as preventing registered sex offenders from having contact with minors over social media. "In sum, to foreclose access to social media altogether is to prevent the user from engaging in the legitimate exercise of First Amendment rights."

Justice Alito concurred in the judgment, but lamented the "undisciplined dicta" and "loose rhetoric" in Justice Kennedy's majority opinion. Justice Alito, too, found the North Carolina law too broad, but disliked Justice Kennedy's strong language protecting the Internet as a medium for speech and his failure to adequately recognize the need for states to regulate sexual predators on the Internet.

3. Relationship Between Vagueness and Overbreadth

The concepts of vagueness and overbreadth are closely related; laws often are challenged under both of these doctrines simultaneously. Both vagueness and overbreadth involve facial challenges to laws. But these concepts are best understood as overlapping, not identical. Sometimes a law might be overbroad but not vague. Board of Airport Commissioners of Los Angeles v. Jews for Jesus, Inc., illustrates this.

BOARD OF AIRPORT COMMISSIONERS OF THE CITY OF LOS ANGELES v. JEWS FOR JESUS, INC., 482 U.S. 569 (1987): Justice O'CONNOR delivered the opinion of the Court.

The issue presented in this case is whether a resolution banning all "First Amendment activities" at Los Angeles International Airport (LAX) violates the First Amendment. On July 13, 1983, the Board of Airport Commissioners (Board) adopted Resolution No. 13787, which provides in pertinent part:

> NOW, THEREFORE, BE IT RESOLVED by the Board of Airport Commissioners that the Central Terminal Area at Los Angeles International Airport is not open for First Amendment activities by any individual and/or entity.

Respondent Jews for Jesus, Inc., is a nonprofit religious corporation. On July 6, 1984, Alan Howard Snyder, a minister of the Gospel for Jews for Jesus, was stopped by a Department of Airports peace officer while distributing free religious literature on a pedestrian walkway in the Central Terminal Area at LAX. Snyder stopped distributing the leaflets and left the airport terminal. Jews for Jesus and Snyder then filed this action in the District Court for the Central District of California, challenging the constitutionality of the resolution.

Under the First Amendment overbreadth doctrine, an individual whose own speech or conduct may be prohibited is permitted to challenge a statute on its face "because it also threatens others not before the court—those who desire to engage in legally protected expression but who may refrain from doing so rather than risk prosecution or undertake to have the law declared partially invalid." A statute may be invalidated on its face, however, only if the overbreadth is "substantial." The requirement that the overbreadth be substantial arose from our recognition that application of the overbreadth doctrine is, "manifestly, strong medicine," and that "there must be a realistic danger that the statute itself will significantly compromise recognized First Amendment protections of parties not before the Court for it to be facially challenged on overbreadth grounds."

On its face, the resolution at issue in this case reaches the universe of expressive activity, and, by prohibiting all protected expression, purports to create a virtual "First Amendment Free Zone" at LAX. The resolution does not merely regulate expressive activity in the Central Terminal Area that might create problems such as congestion or the disruption of the activities of those who use LAX. Instead, the resolution expansively states that LAX "is not open for First Amendment activities by any individual and/or entity." The resolution therefore does not merely reach the activity of respondents at LAX; it prohibits even talking and reading, or the wearing of campaign buttons or symbolic clothing. Under such a sweeping ban, virtually every individual who enters LAX may be found to violate the resolution by engaging in some "First Amendment activit[y]." We think it obvious that such a ban cannot be justified even if LAX were a nonpublic forum because no conceivable governmental interest would justify such an absolute prohibition of speech.

Sometimes a law can be vague but not overbroad. For example, if the Los Angeles ordinance declared unconstitutional in *Board of Airport Commissioners* was rewritten to prohibit all speech not protected by the First Amendment, it would, by definition, not be overbroad. It would forbid only expression that by law could be regulated. But the law would be vague because a reasonable person could not know what was outlawed and what was permitted.

Often, however, laws that are vulnerable to vagueness challenges also can be objected to on overbreadth grounds. For instance, in Coates v. Cincinnati, above, the Court declared unconstitutional an ordinance that made it a criminal offense for "three or more persons to assemble . . . on any of the sidewalks . . . and there conduct themselves in a manner annoying to persons passing by." The Court said that the law "is unconstitutionally vague because it subjects the exercise of the right of assembly to an unascertainable standard, and unconstitutionally broad because it authorizes the punishment of constitutionally protected conduct."

C. PRIOR RESTRAINTS

1. What Is a Prior Restraint?

The Supreme Court has declared that "prior restraints on speech and publication are the most serious and least tolerable infringement on First Amendment rights."[26] The Supreme Court frequently has said that "[a]ny system of prior restraints of expression comes to this Court bearing a heavy presumption against its constitutional validity."[27] As explained above, the First Amendment was, in part, a reaction against the licensing requirements for publication that had existed in England. It was this legacy that prompted Blackstone to declare that "the liberty of the press is, indeed, essential to the nature of a free state; but this consists in laying no previous restraints upon publication, and not in freedom from censure for criminal matter when published."[28] Although it is clear that "the prohibition of laws abridging the freedom of speech is not confined to previous restraints,"[29] there is no doubt that prior restraints are regarded as a particularly undesirable way of regulating speech.

---

26. Nebraska Press Association v. Stuart, 427 U.S. 539, 559 (1976).
27. New York Times v. United States, 403 U.S. 713, 714 (1971).
28. 4 William Blackstone, *Commentaries*, 151-152 (1769).
29. Schenck v. United States, 249 U.S. 47, 51 (1919).

Yet a clear definition of "prior restraint" is elusive. It is too broad to say that a prior restraint is a government action that prevents speech from occurring. All laws outlawing speech would constitute prior restraints by this definition. Nor is the traditional distinction between censorship before speech and after-the-fact punishments sufficient. All punishment for speech—whether under prior restraints or other laws—occurs after the expression takes place. All government actions regulating speech—whether prior restraints or not—exist before the speech occurs.

The clearest definition of prior restraint is as an administrative system or a judicial order that prevents speech from occurring. For example, in Alexander v. United States, 509 U.S. 444 (1993), the Court said that "[t]he term prior restraint is used 'to describe administrative and judicial orders forbidding certain communications when issued in advance of the time that such communication are to occur.'" As Professor Rodney Smolla has observed, "[i]n practice, most prior restraints involve either an administrative rule requiring some form of license or permit before one may engage in expression, or a judicial order directing an individual not to engage in expression, on pain of contempt."[30]

While court injunctions stopping speech and licensing systems are classic forms of prior restraints, they are not the only types of government actions that constitute prior restraints.[31] For example, a prior restraint clearly would exist if the government were to seize every copy of a particular newspaper.

2. *Are Prior Restraints Really So Bad?*

The Supreme Court repeatedly has found that prior restraints are the worst form of government regulation of speech and that there is a strong presumption against prior restraints. But why are prior restraints so bad? After-the-fact punishments, if large enough, can prevent speech just as much as any prior restraint.[32] Also, prior restraints have the virtue that they are usually specific in the form of a court order stopping particular speech or the denial of a license for certain expression.[33] There usually is some due process in the form of a judicial or administrative hearing before the prior restraint.

A classic argument as to why prior restraints are the worst form of speech regulations was advanced by noted First Amendment scholar Thomas Emerson: "A system of prior restraint is in many ways more inhibiting than a system of subsequent punishment: It is likely to bring under government scrutiny a far wider range of expression; it shuts off communication before it takes place; suppression by a stroke of the pen is more likely to be applied than suppression

---

30. Rodney Smolla, *Smolla and Nimmer on Freedom of Speech*, 8-4 (1996).
31. *See, e.g.,* Bantam Books, Inc. v. Sullivan, 372 U.S. 58 (1963), finding that there was a prior restraint when the Rhode Island Commission to Encourage Morality in Youth encouraged booksellers not to sell certain materials that it deemed objectionable. Although there was no court or administrative order preventing the sale of the books, the Court found sufficient coercive pressure to constitute a prior restraint.
32. *See, e.g.,* John C. Jeffries, Jr., *Rethinking Prior Restraint*, 92 Yale L.J. 409 (1983) (questioning the usefulness and desirability of the prior restraint doctrine).
33. *See, e.g.,* William T. Mayton, *Toward a Theory of First Amendment Process: Injunctions of Speech, Subsequent Punishment, and the Costs of the Prior Restraint Doctrine*, 67 Cornell L. Rev. 245 (1982).

C. Prior Restraints

through a criminal process; the procedures do not require attention to the safeguards of the criminal process; the system allows less opportunity for public appraisal and criticism; the dynamics of the system drive toward excesses, as the history of all censorship shows."[34]

Prior restraints prevent speech from ever occurring. The Court explained that "[b]ehind the distinction is a theory deeply etched in our law: a free society prefers to punish the few who abuse rights of speech *after* they break the law than to throttle them and all others beforehand."[35] Inevitably, prior restraints could be imposed based on predictions of danger that would not actually materialize and thus would not be the basis for subsequent punishments.[36]

Perhaps the most persuasive argument as to why prior restraints are worse than other ways of regulating speech is the collateral bar rule: A person violating an unconstitutional law may not be punished, but a person violating an unconstitutional prior restraint generally may be punished. Specifically, the collateral bar rule provides that "a court order must be obeyed until it is set aside, and that persons subject to the order who disobey it may not defend against the ensuing charge of criminal contempt on the ground that the order was erroneous or even unconstitutional."[37]

For example, in Walker v. City of Birmingham, 388 U.S. 307 (1967), the Court upheld the contempt convictions of defendants, civil rights protestors, who had violated a court order preventing them from engaging in demonstrations on city streets without a permit. The Court ruled that the protestors—Dr. Martin Luther King and seven other African American ministers—were barred from challenging the constitutionality of the court order because they had violated it. The Court said, "This Court cannot hold that the petitioners were constitutionally free to ignore all the procedures of the law and carry their battle to the streets. . . . [R]espect for judicial process is a small price to pay for the civilizing hand of law, which alone can give abiding meaning to constitutional freedom." The Court indicated that the collateral bar rule precluded challenges to punishment for violating a court order, unless the injunction was "transparently invalid or had only a frivolous pretense to validity."

The collateral bar rule explains why prior restraints are worse than after-the-fact punishments. A law prohibiting expression and imposing punishments for violations always can be challenged as unconstitutional. But an unconstitutional court order cannot be challenged if it has been violated. The collateral bar rule is justified as necessary to protect respect for the judiciary and compliance with its orders. Yet it seems unjust to punish a person for constitutionally protected speech.

The Court, at times, has applied the collateral bar rule to licensing schemes as well as to court orders. In Poulos v. New Hampshire, 345 U.S. 395 (1953), the Court affirmed an individual's conviction for conducting a religious service in a public park without the required license. The Court said that the defendant could not challenge the denial of a license as arbitrary and unconstitutional when the licensing system is valid on its face and when he

---

34. Thomas Emerson, *The System of Freedom of Expression* 506 (1970).
35. Southeastern Promotions, Ltd. v. Conrad, 420 U.S. 546, 559 (1975).
36. *See, e.g.*, Vincent Blasi, *Toward a Theory of Prior Restraint: The Central Linkage*, 66 Minn. L. Rev. 11, 49-54 (1981).
37. Stephen Barnett, *The Puzzle of Prior Restraint*, 29 Stan. L. Rev. 539, 552 (1977).

proceeded without a license rather than challenge its denial. The Court said, "The valid requirements of license are for the good of the applicants and the public. . . . Delay is unfortunate but the expense and annoyance of litigation is a price citizens must pay for life in an orderly society. . . . Nor can we say that a state's requirement that redress must be sought through appropriate judicial procedure violates due process."

But in Shuttlesworth v. City of Birmingham, 394 U.S. 147 (1969), the Court overturned the convictions of civil rights protestors who violated a city's ordinance by having a demonstration without the required permit. The Court found the permit law unconstitutional because it gave city officials unfettered discretion in granting and denying permits. The Court refused to apply the collateral bar rule and prevent a challenge. In fact, the Court said that "a person faced with such an unconstitutional licensing law may ignore it and engage with impunity in the exercise of the right of free expression for which the law purports to require a license."

The difference between *Poulos* and *Shuttlesworth* is that the former involved a law that was valid on its face because it contained adequate standards and safeguards, whereas the latter case concerned a law that was facially invalid because of the absence of criteria to limit administrative discretion. *Shuttlesworth* establishes that courts will not preclude a person who failed to apply for a license from challenging a licensing law as facially unconstitutional, such as in giving too much discretion to government officials in awarding licenses. But *Poulos* likely remains good law in that a licensing law that is valid on its face must be complied with; a failure to follow the procedures or to challenge the denial of a permit through available administrative and judicial challenges will preclude later assertion that the speech was protected by the First Amendment. Yet, even here, the justification for the collateral bar rule in preserving respect for courts and in ensuring compliance with judicial orders is absent in administrative licensing systems.

3. *Types of Prior Restraints*

a. Court Orders as a Prior Restraint

One classic form of prior restraint is a court order stopping speech from occurring. This subsection begins by presenting Near v. Minnesota, a key case recognizing court orders as a prior restraint. The subsection then considers court orders in three areas: to protect national security, to safeguard a defendant's right to a fair trial, and to seize the assets of businesses convicted of obscenity law violations.

NEAR v. STATE OF MINNESOTA ex rel. OLSON
283 U.S. 697 (1931)

Chief Justice HUGHES delivered the opinion of the Court.

Chapter 285 of the Session Laws of Minnesota for the year 1925 provides for the abatement, as a public nuisance, of a "malicious, scandalous and defamatory newspaper, magazine or other periodical." [The law provides]: "Any person

C. Prior Restraints

who, as an individual, or as a member or employee of a firm, or association or organization, shall be engaged in the business of regularly or customarily producing, publishing or circulating, having in possession, selling or giving away (a) an obscene, lewd and lascivious newspaper, magazine, or other periodical, or (b) a malicious, scandalous and defamatory newspaper, magazine or other periodical[] — is guilty of a nuisance, and all persons guilty of such nuisance may be enjoined." The court is empowered, as in other cases of contempt, to punish disobedience to a temporary or permanent injunction by fine of not more than $1,000 or by imprisonment in the county jail for not more than twelve months.

Under this statute, the county attorney of Hennepin County brought this action to enjoin the publication of what was described as a "malicious, scandalous and defamatory newspaper, magazine or other periodical," known as The Saturday Press, published by the defendants in the city of Minneapolis. The complaint alleged that the defendants, on September 24, 1927, and on eight subsequent dates in October and November, 1927, published and circulated editions of that periodical which were "largely devoted to malicious, scandalous and defamatory articles." Without attempting to summarize the contents of the voluminous exhibits attached to the complaint, we deem it sufficient to say that the articles charged, in substance, that a Jewish gangster was in control of gambling, bootlegging, and racketeering in Minneapolis, and that law enforcing officers and agencies were not energetically performing their duties.

Judgment was entered adjudging that "the newspaper, magazine and periodical known as The Saturday Press," as a public nuisance, "be and is hereby abated." The judgment perpetually enjoined the defendants "from producing, editing, publishing, circulating, having in their possession, selling or giving away any publication whatsoever which is a malicious, scandalous or defamatory newspaper, as defined by law," and also "from further conducting said nuisance under the name and title of said The Saturday Press or any other name or title."

This statute, for the suppression as a public nuisance of a newspaper or periodical, is unusual, if not unique, and raises questions of grave importance transcending the local interests involved in the particular action. The object of the statute is not punishment, in the ordinary sense, but suppression of the offending newspaper or periodical. The reason for the enactment, as the state court has said, is that prosecutions to enforce penal statutes for libel do not result in "efficient repression or suppression of the evils of scandal."

The statute not only operates to suppress the offending newspaper or periodical, but to put the publisher under an effective censorship. When a newspaper or periodical is found to be "malicious, scandalous and defamatory," and is suppressed as such, resumption of publication is punishable as a contempt of court by fine or imprisonment. Thus, where a newspaper or periodical has been suppressed because of the circulation of charges against public officers of official misconduct, it would seem to be clear that the renewal of the publication of such charges would constitute a contempt, and that the judgment would lay a permanent restraint upon the publisher, to escape which he must satisfy the court as to the character of a new publication. Whether he would be permitted again to publish matter deemed to be derogatory to the same or other public officers would depend upon the court's ruling. In the present instance the judgment restrained the defendants from "publishing, circulating, having in their possession, selling or giving away any publication whatsoever which is malicious, scandalous or defamatory."

The question is whether a statute authorizing such proceedings in restraint of publication is consistent with the conception of the liberty of the press as historically conceived and guaranteed. In determining the extent of the constitutional protection, it has been generally, if not universally, considered that it is the chief purpose of the guaranty to prevent previous restraints upon publication. The struggle in England, directed against the legislative power of the licenser, resulted in renunciation of the censorship of the press. The liberty deemed to be established was thus described by Blackstone: "The liberty of the press is indeed essential to the nature of a free state; but this consists in laying no previous restraints upon publications, and not in freedom from censure for criminal matter when published."

The objection has been made that the principle as to immunity from previous restraint is stated too broadly, if every such restraint is deemed to be prohibited. That is undoubtedly true; the protection even as to previous restraint is not absolutely unlimited. But the limitation has been recognized only in exceptional cases. "When a nation is at war many things that might be said in time of peace are such a hindrance to its effort that their utterance will not be endured so long as men fight and that no Court could regard them as protected by any constitutional right." Schenck v. United States (1919). No one would question but that a government might prevent actual obstruction to its recruiting service or the publication of the sailing dates of transports or the number and location of troops. On similar grounds, the primary requirements of decency may be enforced against obscene publications. The security of the community life may be protected against incitements to acts of violence and the overthrow by force of orderly government. The constitutional guaranty of free speech does not "protect a man from an injunction against uttering words that may have all the effect of force." These limitations are not applicable here. Nor are we now concerned with questions as to the extent of authority to prevent publications in order to protect private rights according to the principles governing the exercise of the jurisdiction of courts of equity.

The statute in question cannot be justified by reason of the fact that the publisher is permitted to show, before injunction issues, that the matter published is true and is published with good motives and for justifiable ends. If such a statute, authorizing suppression and injunction on such a basis, is constitutionally valid, it would be equally permissible for the Legislature to provide that at any time the publisher of any newspaper could be brought before a court, or even an administrative officer (as the constitutional protection may not be regarded as resting on mere procedural details), and required to produce proof of the truth of his publication, or of what he intended to publish and of his motives, or stand enjoined. If this can be done, the Legislature may provide machinery for determining in the complete exercise of its discretion what are justifiable ends and restrain publication accordingly. And it would be but a step to a complete system of censorship. The recognition of authority to impose previous restraint upon publication in order to protect the community against the circulation of charges of misconduct, and especially of official misconduct, necessarily would carry with it the admission of the authority of the censor against which the constitutional barrier was erected.

C. Prior Restraints

For these reasons we hold the statute to be an infringement of the liberty of the press guaranteed by the Fourteenth Amendment.

i. Court Orders to Protect National Security

Near spoke of national security—such as to prevent publication of the details of when and where a military action would occur—as justifying prior restraints. New York Times v. United States, the Pentagon Papers case, is the primary decision thus far considering national security as the basis for a court order stopping speech. The New York Times, and then the Washington Post, published excerpts from a top secret Defense Department history of the Vietnam War. The United States government sought federal court injunctions precluding publication on national security grounds. The federal district courts refused to issue such orders. The District of Columbia Circuit affirmed, while the Second Circuit reversed and approved the injunction. The case proceeded quickly: Just 18 days elapsed from the first article in the New York Times until the decision in the Supreme Court.

NEW YORK TIMES CO. v. UNITED STATES
403 U.S. 713 (1971)

PER CURIAM.

We granted certiorari, in these cases in which the United States seeks to enjoin the New York Times and the Washington Post from publishing the contents of a classified study entitled "History of U.S. Decision-Making Process on Viet Nam Policy."

"Any system of prior restraints of expression comes to this Court bearing a heavy presumption against its constitutional validity." The Government "thus carries a heavy burden of showing justification for the imposition of such a restraint." The District Court for the Southern District of New York in the New York Times case, and the District Court for the District of Columbia and the Court of Appeals for the District of Columbia Circuit, in the Washington Post case held that the Government had not met that burden. We agree.

Justice BLACK, with whom Justice DOUGLAS joins, concurring.

I adhere to the view that the Government's case against the Washington Post should have been dismissed and that the injunction against the New York Times should have been vacated without oral argument when the cases were first presented to this Court. I believe that every moment's continuance of the injunctions against these newspapers amounts to a flagrant, indefensible, and continuing violation of the First Amendment. In my view it is unfortunate that some of my Brethren are apparently willing to hold that the publication of news may sometimes be enjoined. Such a holding would make a shambles of the First Amendment.

Our Government was launched in 1789 with the adoption of the Constitution. The Bill of Rights, including the First Amendment, followed in 1791. Now, for the first time in the 182 years since the founding of the Republic, the federal courts are asked to hold that the First Amendment does not mean what it says, but rather means that the Government can halt the publication of current news of vital importance to the people of this country.

In seeking injunctions against these newspapers and in its presentation to the Court, the Executive Branch seems to have forgotten the essential purpose and history of the First Amendment. [T]he Solicitor General argues and some members of the Court appear to agree that the general powers of the Government adopted in the original Constitution should be interpreted to limit and restrict the specific and emphatic guarantees of the Bill of Rights adopted later. I can imagine no greater perversion of history. Madison and the other framers of the First Amendment, able men that they were, wrote in language they earnestly believed could never be misunderstood: "Congress shall make no law . . . abridging the freedom . . . of the press. . . ." Both the history and language of the First Amendment support the view that the press must be left free to publish news, whatever the source, without censorship, injunctions, or prior restraints.

Justice DOUGLAS, with whom Justice BLACK joins, concurring.

It should be noted at the outset that the First Amendment provides that "Congress shall make no law . . . abridging the freedom of speech, or of the press." That leaves, in my view, no room for governmental restraint on the press. There is, moreover, no statute barring the publication by the press of the material which the Times and the Post seek to use.

The dominant purpose of the First Amendment was to prohibit the widespread practice of governmental suppression of embarrassing information. It is common knowledge that the First Amendment was adopted against the widespread use of the common law of seditious libel to punish the dissemination of material that is embarrassing to the powers-that-be. The present cases will, I think, go down in history as the most dramatic illustration of that principle. A debate of large proportions goes on in the Nation over our posture in Vietnam. That debate antedated the disclosure of the contents of the present documents. The latter are highly relevant to the debate in progress.

Secrecy in government is fundamentally anti-democratic, perpetuating bureaucratic errors. Open debate and discussion of public issues are vital to our national health. On public questions there should be "uninhibited, robust, and wide-open" debate.

The stays in these cases that have been in effect for more than a week constitute a flouting of the principles of the First Amendment as interpreted in Near v. Minnesota ex rel. Olson.

Justice BRENNAN, concurring.

The error that has pervaded these cases from the outset was the granting of any injunctive relief whatsoever, interim or otherwise. The entire thrust of the Government's claim throughout these cases has been that publication of the material sought to be enjoined "could," or "might," or "may" prejudice the national interest in various ways. But the First Amendment tolerates absolutely no prior judicial restraints of the press predicated upon surmise or conjecture that untoward consequences may result. Our cases, it is true, have indicated that there is a single, extremely narrow class of cases in which the First Amendment's ban on prior judicial restraint may be overridden. Our cases have thus far

C. Prior Restraints

indicated that such cases may arise only when the Nation "is at war," Schenck v. United States (1919), during which times "[n]o one would question but that a government might prevent actual obstruction to its recruiting service or the publication of the sailing dates of transports or the number and location of troops." Near v. Minnesota ex rel. Olson (1931).

Thus, only governmental allegation and proof that publication must inevitably, directly, and immediately cause the occurrence of an event kindred to imperiling the safety of a transport already at sea can support even the issuance of an interim restraining order. In no event may mere conclusions be sufficient: for if the Executive Branch seeks judicial aid in preventing publication, it must inevitably submit the basis upon which that aid is sought to scrutiny by the judiciary. And therefore, every restraint issued in this case, whatever its form, has violated the First Amendment—and not less so because that restraint was justified as necessary to afford the courts an opportunity to examine the claim more thoroughly. Unless and until the Government has clearly made out its case, the First Amendment commands that no injunction may issue.

Justice STEWART, with whom Justice WHITE joins, concurring.

If the Constitution gives the Executive a large degree of unshared power in the conduct of foreign affairs and the maintenance of our national defense, then under the Constitution the Executive must have the largely unshared duty to determine and preserve the degree of internal security necessary to exercise that power successfully. It is an awesome responsibility, requiring judgment and wisdom of a high order.

We are asked, quite simply, to prevent the publication by two newspapers of material that the Executive Branch insists should not, in the national interest, be published. I am convinced that the Executive is correct with respect to some of the documents involved. But I cannot say that disclosure of any of them will surely result in direct, immediate, and irreparable damage to our Nation or its people. That being so, there can under the First Amendment be but one judicial resolution of the issues before us. I join the judgments of the Court.

Justice WHITE, with whom Justice STEWART joins, concurring.

I concur in today's judgments, but only because of the concededly extraordinary protection against prior restraints enjoyed by the press under our constitutional system. I do not say that in no circumstances would the First Amendment permit an injunction against publishing information about government plans or operations. Nor, after examining the materials the Government characterizes as the most sensitive and destructive, can I deny that revelation of these documents will do substantial damage to public interests. Indeed, I am confident that their disclosure will have that result. But I nevertheless agree that the United States has not satisfied the very heavy burden that it must meet to warrant an injunction against publication in these cases, at least in the absence of express and appropriately limited congressional authorization for prior restraints in circumstances such as these.

The Government's position is simply stated: The responsibility of the Executive for the conduct of the foreign affairs and for the security of the Nation is so basic that the President is entitled to an injunction against publication of a newspaper story whenever he can convince a court that the information to be revealed threatens "grave and irreparable" injury to the public interest;

and the injunction should issue whether or not the material to be published is classified, whether or not publication would be lawful under relevant criminal statutes enacted by Congress, and regardless of the circumstances by which the newspaper came into possession of the information.

At least in the absence of legislation by Congress, based on its own investigations and findings, I am quite unable to agree that the inherent powers of the Executive and the courts reach so far as to authorize remedies having such sweeping potential for inhibiting publications by the press. Indeed, even today where we hold that the United States has not met its burden, the material remains sealed in court records and it is properly not discussed in today's opinions. Moreover, because the material poses substantial dangers to national interests and because of the hazards of criminal sanctions, a responsible press may choose never to publish the more sensitive materials. To sustain the Government in these cases would start the courts down a long and hazardous road that I am not willing to travel, at least without congressional guidance and direction.

Justice MARSHALL, concurring.

The Government contends that the only issue in these cases is whether in a suit by the United States, "the First Amendment bars a court from prohibiting a newspaper from publishing material whose disclosure would pose a 'grave and immediate danger to the security of the United States.'" With all due respect, I believe the ultimate issue in this case is even more basic than the one posed by the Solicitor General. The issue is whether this Court or the Congress has the power to make law.

The problem here is whether in these particular cases the Executive Branch has authority to invoke the equity jurisdiction of the courts to protect what it believes to be the national interest. It would be utterly inconsistent with the concept of separation of powers for this Court to use its power of contempt to prevent behavior that Congress has specifically declined to prohibit. There would be a similar damage to the basic concept of these co-equal branches of Government if when the Executive Branch has adequate authority granted by Congress to protect "national security" it can choose instead to invoke the contempt power of a court to enjoin the threatened conduct. The Constitution provides that Congress shall make laws, the President execute laws, and courts interpret laws. It did not provide for government by injunction in which the courts and the Executive Branch can "make law" without regard to the action of Congress. It may be more convenient for the Executive Branch if it need only convince a judge to prohibit conduct rather than ask the Congress to pass a law, and it may be more convenient to enforce a contempt order than to seek a criminal conviction in a jury trial. Moreover, it may be considered politically wise to get a court to share the responsibility for arresting those who the Executive Branch has probable cause to believe are violating the law. But convenience and political considerations of the moment do not justify a basic departure from the principles of our system of government.

Chief Justice BURGER, dissenting.

So clear are the constitutional limitations on prior restraint against expression, that we have had little occasion to be concerned with cases involving prior restraints against news reporting on matters of public interest. There is, therefore, little variation among the members of the Court in terms of resistance to prior

C. Prior Restraints

restraints against publication. Adherence to this basic constitutional principle, however, does not make these cases simple ones. In these cases, the imperative of a free and unfettered press comes into collision with another imperative, the effective functioning of a complex modern government and specifically the effective exercise of certain constitutional powers of the Executive. Only those who view the First Amendment as an absolute in all circumstances—a view I respect, but reject—can find such cases as these to be simple or easy.

These cases are not simple for another and more immediate reason. We do not know the facts of the cases. No District Judge knew all the facts. No Court of Appeals Judge knew all the facts. No member of this Court knows all the facts. Why are we in this posture, in which only those judges to whom the First Amendment is absolute and permits of no restraint in any circumstances or for any reason, are really in a position to act?

I suggest we are in this posture because these cases have been conducted in unseemly haste. The prompt settling of these cases reflects our universal abhorrence of prior restraint. But prompt judicial action does not mean unjudicial haste.

Here, moreover, the frenetic haste is due in large part to the manner in which the Times proceeded from the date it obtained the purloined documents. It seems reasonably clear now that the haste precluded reasonable and deliberate judicial treatment of these cases and was not warranted. The precipitate action of this Court aborting trials not yet completed is not the kind of judicial conduct that ought to attend the disposition of a great issue.

An issue of this importance should be tried and heard in a judicial atmosphere conducive to thoughtful, reflective deliberation, especially when haste, in terms of hours, is unwarranted in light of the long period the Times, by its own choice, deferred publication. It is not disputed that the Times has had unauthorized possession of the documents for three to four months, during which it has had its expert analysts studying them, presumably digesting them and preparing the material for publication. During all of this time, the Times, presumably in its capacity as trustee of the public's "right to know," has held up publication for purposes it considered proper and thus public knowledge was delayed. No doubt this was for a good reason; the analysis of 7,000 pages of complex material drawn from a vastly greater volume of material would inevitably take time and the writing of good news stories takes time. But why should the United States Government, from whom this information was illegally acquired by someone, along with all the counsel, trial judges, and appellate judges be placed under needless pressure? After these months of deferral, the alleged "right to know" has somehow and suddenly become a right that must be vindicated instanter.

Would it have been unreasonable, since the newspaper could anticipate the Government's objections to release of secret material, to give the Government an opportunity to review the entire collection and determine whether agreement could be reached on publication? Stolen or not, if security was not in fact jeopardized, much of the material could no doubt have been declassified, since it spans a period ending in 1968. With such an approach—one that great newspapers have in the past practiced and stated editorially to be the duty of an honorable press—the newspapers and Government might well have narrowed the area of disagreement as to what was and was not publishable, leaving the remainder to be resolved in orderly litigation, if necessary. To me it is hardly believable that a newspaper long regarded as a great institution in

American life would fail to perform one of the basic and simple duties of every citizen with respect to the discovery or possession of stolen property or secret government documents. That duty, I had thought—perhaps naively—was to report forthwith, to responsible public officers. This duty rests on taxi drivers, Justices, and the New York Times. The course followed by the Times, whether so calculated or not, removed any possibility of orderly litigation of the issues. If the action of the judges up to now has been correct, that result is sheer happenstance.

The consequence of all this melancholy series of events is that we literally do not know what we are acting on. As I see it, we have been forced to deal with litigation concerning rights of great magnitude without an adequate record, and surely without time for adequate treatment either in the prior proceedings or in this Court. I would affirm the Court of Appeals for the Second Circuit and allow the District Court to complete the trial aborted by our grant of certiorari, meanwhile preserving the status quo in the post case.

Justice HARLAN, with whom THE CHIEF JUSTICE and Justice BLACKMUN join, dissenting.

With all respect, I consider that the Court has been almost irresponsibly feverish in dealing with these cases. Both the Court of Appeals for the Second Circuit and the Court of Appeals for the District of Columbia Circuit rendered judgment on June 23. The New York Times' petition for certiorari, its motion for accelerated consideration thereof, and its application for interim relief were filed in this Court on June 24 at about 11 A.M. The application of the United States for interim relief in the Post case was also filed here on June 24 at about 7:15 P.M. This Court's order setting a hearing before us on June 26 at 11 A.M., a course which I joined only to avoid the possibility of even more peremptory action by the Court, was issued less than 24 hours before. The record in the Post case was filed with the Clerk shortly before 1 P.M. on June 25; the record in the Times case did not arrive until 7 or 8 o'clock that same night. The briefs of the parties were received less than two hours before argument on June 26.

This frenzied train of events took place in the name of the presumption against prior restraints created by the First Amendment. Due regard for the extraordinarily important and difficult questions involved in these litigations should have led the Court to shun such a precipitate timetable.

There are difficult questions of fact, of law, and of judgment; the potential consequences of erroneous decision are enormous. The time which has been available to us, to the lower courts, and to the parties has been wholly inadequate for giving these cases the kind of consideration they deserve. It is a reflection on the stability of the judicial process that these great issues—as important as any that have arisen during my time on the Court—should have been decided under the pressures engendered by the torrent of publicity that has attended these litigations from their inception.

Forced as I am to reach the merits of these cases, I dissent from the opinion and judgments of the Court. Pending further hearings in each case conducted under the appropriate ground rules, I would continue the restraints on publication. I cannot believe that the doctrine prohibiting prior restraints reaches to the point of preventing courts from maintaining the status quo long enough to act responsibly in matters of such national importance as those involved here.

C. Prior Restraints

Justice BLACKMUN, dissenting.

The First Amendment, after all, is only one part of an entire Constitution. Article II of the great document vests in the Executive Branch primary power over the conduct of foreign affairs and places in that branch the responsibility for the Nation's safety. Each provision of the Constitution is important, and I cannot subscribe to a doctrine of unlimited absolutism for the First Amendment at the cost of downgrading other provisions. First Amendment absolutism has never commanded a majority of this Court.

What is needed here is a weighing, upon properly developed standards, of the broad right of the press to print and of the very narrow right of the Government to prevent. Such standards are not yet developed. The parties here are in disagreement as to what those standards should be. But even the newspapers concede that there are situations where restraint is in order and is constitutional.

I strongly urge, and sincerely hope, that these two newspapers will be fully aware of their ultimate responsibilities to the United States of America. Judge Wilkey, dissenting in the District of Columbia case, after a review of only the affidavits before his court (the basic papers had not then been made available by either party), concluded that there were a number of examples of documents that, if in the possession of the Post, and if published, "could clearly result in great harm to the nation," and he defined "harm" to mean "the death of soldiers, the destruction of alliances, the greatly increased difficulty of negotiation with our enemies, the inability of our diplomats to negotiate. . . ." I, for one, have now been able to give at least some cursory study not only to the affidavits, but to the material itself. I regret to say that from this examination I fear that Judge Wilkey's statements have possible foundation. I therefore share his concern. I hope that damage has not already been done. If, however, damage has been done, and if, with the Court's action today, these newspapers proceed to publish the critical documents and there results therefrom "the death of soldiers, the destruction of alliances, the greatly increased difficulty of negotiation with our enemies, the inability of our diplomats to negotiate," to which list I might add the factors of prolongation of the war and of further delay in the freeing of United States prisoners, then the Nation's people will know where the responsibility for these sad consequences rests.

New York Times leaves two major questions open. First, what circumstances, if any, would justify a court order preventing publication so as to protect national security? Second, what difference, if any, would it make if there was a statute authorizing a prior restraint?

No Supreme Court case has dealt with these issues since the Pentagon Papers case. One case that might have presented these questions was resolved before it reached the Supreme Court. In United States v. Progressive, Inc., 467 F. Supp. 990 (W.D. Wis. 1979), a federal district court issued an injunction to keep a magazine from publishing an article on how to build a hydrogen bomb. Unlike the Pentagon Papers case, there was a provision in the Atomic Energy Act that appeared to authorize the injunction and the government claimed that preventing nuclear proliferation was a justification sufficient to warrant the prior restraint. The case, however, was dismissed while on appeal because others published the same information in other places.

ii. Court Orders to Protect Fair Trials

Another major area where the Court has considered court orders as prior restraints is in injunctions against pretrial coverage of legal proceedings so as to enhance a criminal defendant's ability to receive a fair trial. In Nebraska Press Assn. v. Stuart, the Supreme Court ruled that the strong presumption against prior restraints means that such gag orders on the press will be allowed only in the rarest of circumstances, if at all.

NEBRASKA PRESS ASSOCIATION v. STUART
427 U.S. 539 (1976)

Chief Justice BURGER delivered the opinion of the Court.

The respondent State District Judge entered an order restraining the petitioners from publishing or broadcasting accounts of confessions or admission made by the accused or facts "strongly implicative" of the accused in a widely reported murder of six persons. We granted certiorari to decide whether the entry of such an order on the showing made before the state court violated the constitutional guarantee of freedom of the press.

I

On the evening of October 18, 1975, local police found the six members of the Henry Kellie family murdered in their home in Sutherland, Neb., a town of about 850 people. Police released the description of a suspect, Erwin Charles Simants, to the reporters who had hastened to the scene of the crime. Simants was arrested and arraigned in Lincoln County Court the following morning, ending a tense night for this small rural community.

The crime immediately attracted widespread news coverage, by local, regional, and national newspapers, radio and television stations. Three days after the crime, the County Attorney and Simants' attorney joined in asking the County Court to enter a restrictive order relating to "matters that may or may not be publicly reported or disclosed to the public," because of the "mass coverage by news media" and the "reasonable likelihood of prejudicial news which would make difficult, if not impossible, the impaneling of an impartial jury and tend to prevent a fair trial." The County Court heard oral argument but took no evidence; no attorney for members of the press appeared at this stage. The County Court granted the prosecutor's motion for a restrictive order and entered it the next day, October 22. The order prohibited everyone in attendance from "releas[ing] or authoriz[ing] the release for public dissemination in any form or manner whatsoever any testimony given or evidence adduced"; the order also required members of the press to observe the Nebraska Bar-Press Guidelines.

C. Prior Restraints

Petitioners several press and broadcast associations, publishers, and individual reporters moved on October 23 for leave to intervene in the District Court, asking that the restrictive order imposed by the County Court be vacated. The judge found "because of the nature of the crimes charged in the complaint that there is a clear and present danger that pre-trial publicity could impinge upon the defendant's right to a fair trial." The order applied only until the jury was impaneled, and specifically prohibited petitioners from reporting five subjects: (1) the existence or contents of a confession Simants had made to law enforcement officers, which had been introduced in open court at arraignment; (2) the fact or nature of statements Simants had made to other persons; (3) the contents of a note he had written the night of the crime; (4) certain aspects of the medical testimony at the preliminary hearing; and (5) the identity of the victims of the alleged sexual assault and the nature of the assault. It also prohibited reporting the exact nature of the restrictive order itself.

II

The problems presented by this case are almost as old as the Republic. Neither in the Constitution nor in contemporaneous writings do we find that the conflict between these two important rights was anticipated, yet it is inconceivable that the authors of the Constitution were unaware of the potential conflicts between the right to an unbiased jury and the guarantee of freedom of the press. The Sixth Amendment in terms guarantees "trial, by an impartial jury . . ." in federal criminal prosecutions. Because "trial by jury in criminal cases is fundamental to the American scheme of justice," the Due Process Clause of the Fourteenth Amendment guarantees the same right in state criminal prosecutions.

[But] pretrial publicity even pervasive, adverse publicity does not inevitably lead to an unfair trial. The capacity of the jury eventually impaneled to decide the case fairly is influenced by the tone and extent of the publicity, which is in part, and often in large part, shaped by what attorneys, police, and other officials do to precipitate news coverage. The trial judge has a major responsibility. What the judge says about a case, in or out of the courtroom, is likely to appear in newspapers and broadcasts. More important, the measures a judge takes or fails to take to mitigate the effects of pretrial publicity may well determine whether the defendant receives a trial consistent with the requirements of due process.

The costs of failure to afford a fair trial are high. In the most extreme cases, like *Sheppard* and *Estes*, the risk of injustice was avoided when the convictions were reversed. But a reversal means that justice has been delayed for both the defendant and the State; in some cases, because of lapse of time retrial is impossible or further prosecution is gravely handicapped. Moreover, in borderline cases in which the conviction is not reversed, there is some possibility of an injustice unredressed.

III

The First Amendment provides that "Congress shall make no law . . . abridging the freedom . . . of the press," and it is "no longer open to doubt that the liberty of the press and of speech, is within the liberty safeguarded by the due process clause of the Fourteenth Amendment from invasion by state action." Near v. Minnesota ex rel. Olson (1931). The Court has interpreted these guarantees to afford special protection against orders that prohibit the publication or broadcast of particular information or commentary orders that impose a "previous" or "prior" restraint on speech.

"Any prior restraint on expression comes to this Court with a 'heavy presumption' against its constitutional validity." [P]rior restraints on speech and publication are the most serious and the least tolerable infringement on First Amendment rights. The damage can be particularly great when the prior restraint falls upon the communication of news and commentary on current events. Truthful reports of public judicial proceedings have been afforded special protection against subsequent punishment. For the same reasons the protection against prior restraint should have particular force as applied to reporting of criminal proceedings, whether the crime in question is a single isolated act or a pattern of criminal conduct.

The authors of the Bill of Rights did not undertake to assign priorities as between First Amendment and Sixth Amendment rights, ranking one as superior to the other. In this case, the petitioners would have us declare the right of an accused subordinate to their right to publish in all circumstances. But if the authors of these guarantees, fully aware of the potential conflicts between them, were unwilling or unable to resolve the issue by assigning to one priority over the other, it is not for us to rewrite the Constitution by undertaking what they declined to do. It is unnecessary, after nearly two centuries, to establish a priority applicable in all circumstances. Yet it is nonetheless clear that the barriers to prior restraint remain high unless we are to abandon what the Court has said for nearly a quarter of our national existence and implied throughout all of it.

IV

We turn now to the record in this case to determine whether, as [Chief Judge] Learned Hand put it, "the gravity of the 'evil,' discounted by its improbability, justifies such invasion of free speech as is necessary to avoid the danger." To do so, we must examine the evidence before the trial judge when the order was entered to determine (a) the nature and extent of pretrial news coverage; (b) whether other measures would be likely to mitigate the effects of unrestrained pretrial publicity; and (c) how effectively a restraining order would operate to prevent the threatened danger. The precise terms of the restraining order are also important. We must then consider whether the record supports the entry of a prior restraint on publication, one of the most extraordinary remedies known to our jurisprudence.

A

Our review of the pretrial record persuades us that the trial judge was justified in concluding that there would be intense and pervasive pretrial publicity concerning this case. He could also reasonably conclude, based on common man experience, that publicity might impair the defendant's right to a fair trial. He did not purport to say more, for he found only "a clear and present

C. Prior Restraints

danger that pre-trial publicity could impinge upon the defendant's right to a fair trial." His conclusion as to the impact of such publicity on prospective jurors was of necessity speculative, dealing as he was with factors unknown and unknowable.

B

We find little in the record that goes to another aspect of our task, determining whether measures short of an order restraining all publication would have insured the defendant a fair trial. Although the entry of the order might be read as a judicial determination that other measures would not suffice, the trial court made no express findings to that effect. [A]lternatives to prior restraint of publication in these circumstances [include]: (a) change of trial venue to a place less exposed to the intense publicity that seemed imminent in Lincoln County; (b) postponement of the trial to allow public attention to subside; (c) searching questioning of prospective jurors to screen out those with fixed opinions as to guilt or innocence; (d) the use of emphatic and clear instructions on the sworn duty of each juror to decide the issues only on evidence presented in open court. Sequestration of jurors is, of course, always available. Although that measure insulates jurors only after they are sworn, it also enhances the likelihood of dissipating the impact of pretrial publicity and emphasizes the elements of the jurors' oaths. This Court has outlined other measures short of prior restraints on publication tending to blunt the impact of pretrial publicity. Professional studies have filled out these suggestions, recommending that trial courts in appropriate cases limit what the contending lawyers, the police, and witnesses may say to anyone.

We have noted earlier that pretrial publicity, even if pervasive and concentrated, cannot be regarded as leading automatically and in every kind of criminal case to an unfair trial. The decided cases "cannot be made to stand for the proposition that juror exposure to information about a state defendant's prior convictions or to news accounts of the crime with which he is charged alone presumptively deprives the defendant of due process."

We have therefore examined this record to determine the probable efficacy of the measures short of prior restraint on the press and speech. There is no finding that alternative measures would not have protected Simants' rights, and the Nebraska Supreme Court did no more than imply that such measures might not be adequate. Moreover, the record is lacking in evidence to support such a finding.

C

We must also assess the probable efficacy of prior restraint on publication as a workable method of protecting Simants' right to a fair trial, and we cannot ignore the reality of the problems of managing and enforcing pretrial restraining orders. The territorial jurisdiction of the issuing court is limited by concepts of sovereignty. Finally, we note that the events disclosed by the record took place in a community of 850 people. It is reasonable to assume that, without any news accounts being printed or broadcast, rumors would travel swiftly by word of mouth. One can only speculate on the accuracy of such reports, given the generative propensities of rumors; they could well be more damaging than reasonably accurate news accounts. But plainly a whole community cannot be restrained from discussing a subject intimately affecting life within it. Given these practical problems, it is far from clear that prior restraint on publication would have protected Simants' rights.

Of necessity our holding is confined to the record before us. But our conclusion is not simply a result of assessing the adequacy of the showing made in this case; it results in part from the problems inherent in meeting the heavy burden of demonstrating, in advance of trial, that without prior restraint a fair trial will be denied. The practical problems of managing and enforcing restrictive orders will always be present. In this sense, the record now before us is illustrative rather than exceptional. It is significant that when this Court has reversed a state conviction, because of prejudicial publicity, it has carefully noted that some course of action short of prior restraint would have made a critical difference.

However difficult it may be, we need not rule out the possibility of showing the kind of threat to fair trial rights that would possess the requisite degree of certainty to justify restraint. This Court has frequently denied that First Amendment rights are absolute and has consistently rejected the proposition that a prior restraint can never be employed.

We hold that, with respect to the order entered in this case prohibiting reporting or commentary on judicial proceedings held in public, the barriers have not been overcome; to the extent that this order restrained publication of such material, it is clearly invalid.

The Court in *Nebraska Press* said that it was not creating an absolute ban on prior restraints to protect a defendant's right to a fair trial, but from a practical perspective, the Court did just that.[38] It is hard to imagine a case where all three requirements can be met. Even assuming that extensive pretrial publicity threatens a defendant's right to a fair trial, it is difficult to see how a court could conclude that all alternatives to a gag order would fail or that a prior restraint would be successful in keeping prospective jurors from receiving information. Indeed, as Professor Rodney Smolla observed, "[l]ower courts have treated *Nebraska Press* as tantamount to an absolute prohibition on such prior restraints, consistently refusing to permit orders limiting press coverage of judicial proceedings."[39]

Nor has the Supreme Court approved a prior restraint to protect a defendant's right to a fair trial since *Nebraska Press*. In Oklahoma Publishing Co. v. District Court, 430 U.S. 308 (1977), the Court declared unconstitutional a judge's order enjoining the news media from publishing, broadcasting, or disseminating the name or picture of an 11-year-old boy who was accused of murder. In a

---

38. It should be noted that three justices, Brennan, Stewart, and Marshall, took the position that prior restraints would never be justified to protect a defendant's right to a fair trial, and a fourth, Justice White, expressed "grave doubt" that such a prior restraint would ever be justified.

39. Smolla, *supra* note 30, at 8-41. *See id*. at n.12 (collecting cases rejecting such prior restraints). One of the few cases where a lower court imposed a prior restraint was in United States v. Noriega, 752 F. Supp. 1032 (S.D. Fla.), *aff'd*, United States v. Noriega, 917 F.2d 1543 (11th Cir.), *cert. denied*, Cable News Network, Inc. v. Noriega, 498 U.S. 976 (1990), where a federal district court enjoined CNN from broadcasting tapes of conversations between deposed Panamanian dictator Manuel Noriega and his attorneys.

C. Prior Restraints

brief *per curiam* opinion, the Court said that the media had lawfully obtained the information and thus there could be no injunction to prevent its truthful reporting.

The Supreme Court has never addressed the question of when it is permissible for courts to impose gag orders on attorneys and other trial participants. Such restrictions are increasingly common and there are lower court cases both invalidating and upholding such orders. Professor Smolla notes that the law in this area is in "significant disarray" and that "[a]ppellate courts tend to reverse such gag orders when they do not pose serious and imminent threats to the fairness of the proceedings. When the order is narrowly tailored to eliminate serious and imminent threats, however, appellate courts are inclined to sustain such orders."[40]

On the one hand, attorneys are officers of the Court, and the Supreme Court has approved greater restrictions on attorney speech than for others in society.[41] Restricting the speech of trial participants seems less restrictive than an injunction on the press. But on the other hand, a gag order on lawyers is a prior restraint and should have to overcome the same strong presumption as other prior restraints. Moreover, limiting speech by trial participants effectively restricts the media's ability to cover proceedings with complete and accurate information.

iii. *Court Orders Seizing the Assets of Businesses Convicted of Obscenity Violations*

In *Near*, *New York Times*, and *Nebraska Press*, the Supreme Court found court orders suppressing speech to be a prior restraint. In contrast, in Alexander v. United States, the Court rejected the argument that there is a prior restraint when the court seizes the assets of a business convicted of obscenity law violations.

ALEXANDER v. UNITED STATES
509 U.S. 544 (1993)

Chief Justice REHNQUIST delivered the opinion of the Court.

Petitioner was in the so-called "adult entertainment" business for more than 30 years, selling pornographic magazines and sexual paraphernalia, showing sexually explicit movies, and eventually selling and renting videotapes of a similar nature. He received shipments of these materials at a warehouse in Minneapolis, Minnesota, where they were wrapped in plastic, priced, and boxed. He then sold his products through some 13 retail stores in several different Minnesota cities, generating millions of dollars in annual revenues.

After a full criminal trial, petitioner Ferris J. Alexander, owner of more than a dozen stores and theaters dealing in sexually explicit materials, was convicted on 17 obscenity counts and 3 counts of violating the Racketeer Influenced and Corrupt Organizations Act (RICO). The obscenity convictions, based on the jury's findings that four magazines and three videotapes sold at several of

---

40. Smolla, *supra* note 30, at 8-67.
41. *See* Gentile v. State Bar of Nevada, 501 U.S. 1030 (1991).

petitioner's stores were obscene, served as the predicates for his three RICO convictions. Petitioner was sentenced to a total of six years in prison, fined $100,000, and ordered to pay the cost of prosecution, incarceration, and supervised release.

In addition to imposing a prison term and fine, the District Court ordered petitioner to forfeit certain assets that were directly related to his racketeering activity as punishment for his RICO violations. The court ultimately ordered petitioner to forfeit his wholesale and retail businesses (including all the assets of those businesses) and almost $9 million in moneys acquired through racketeering activity. Not wishing to go into the business of selling pornographic materials—regardless of whether they were legally obscene—the Government decided that it would be better to destroy the forfeited expressive materials than sell them to members of the public. Petitioner argues that this forfeiture violated the First and Eighth Amendments to the Constitution. We reject petitioner's claims under the First Amendment but remand for reconsideration of his Eighth Amendment challenge.

Petitioner first contends that the forfeiture in this case, which effectively shut down his adult entertainment business, constituted an unconstitutional prior restraint on speech, rather than a permissible criminal punishment. According to petitioner, forfeiture of expressive materials and the assets of businesses engaged in expressive activity, when predicated solely upon previous obscenity violations, operates as a prior restraint because it prohibits future presumptively protected expression in retaliation for prior unprotected speech. Practically speaking, petitioner argues, the effect of the RICO forfeiture order here was no different from the injunction prohibiting the publication of expressive material found to be a prior restraint in Near v. Minnesota ex rel. Olson (1931).

We disagree. By lumping the forfeiture imposed in this case after a full criminal trial with an injunction enjoining future speech, petitioner stretches the term "prior restraint" well beyond the limits established by our cases. To accept petitioner's argument would virtually obliterate the distinction, solidly grounded in our cases, between prior restraints and subsequent punishments.

The term prior restraint is used "to describe administrative and judicial orders forbidding certain communications when issued in advance of the time that such communications are to occur." Temporary restraining orders and permanent injunctions—i.e., court orders that actually forbid speech activities—are classic examples of prior restraints. This understanding of what constitutes a prior restraint is borne out by our cases, even those on which petitioner relies.

By contrast, the RICO forfeiture order in this case does not forbid petitioner from engaging in any expressive activities in the future, nor does it require him to obtain prior approval for any expressive activities. It only deprives him of specific assets that were found to be related to his previous racketeering violations. Assuming, of course, that he has sufficient untainted assets to open new stores, restock his inventory, and hire staff, petitioner can go back into the adult entertainment business tomorrow, and sell as many sexually explicit magazines and videotapes as he likes, without any risk of being held in contempt for violating a court order. [T]he forfeiture order in this case imposes no legal impediment to—no prior restraint on—petitioner's ability to engage in any expressive activity he chooses. He is perfectly free to open an adult bookstore or otherwise engage in the production and distribution of erotic materials; he just

C. Prior Restraints

cannot finance these enterprises with assets derived from his prior racketeering offenses.

In this case, however, the assets in question were ordered forfeited not because they were believed to be obscene, but because they were directly related to petitioner's past racketeering violations. The RICO forfeiture statute calls for the forfeiture of assets because of the financial role they play in the operation of the racketeering enterprise. The statute is oblivious to the expressive or nonexpressive nature of the assets forfeited; books, sports cars, narcotics, and cash are all forfeitable alike under RICO. Indeed, a contrary scheme would be disastrous from a policy standpoint, enabling racketeers to evade forfeiture by investing the proceeds of their crimes in businesses engaging in expressive activity. Nor were the assets in question ordered forfeited without according petitioner the requisite procedural safeguards, another recurring theme in our prior restraint cases.

Justice KENNEDY, with whom Justice BLACKMUN and Justice STEVENS join, and with whom Justice SOUTER joins, dissenting.

The Court today embraces a rule that would find no affront to the First Amendment in the Government's destruction of a book and film business and its entire inventory of legitimate expression as punishment for a single past speech offense. Until now I had thought one could browse through any book or film store in the United States without fear that the proprietor had chosen each item to avoid risk to the whole inventory and indeed to the business itself. This ominous, onerous threat undermines free speech and press principles essential to our personal freedom.

What is at work in this case is not the power to punish an individual for his past transgressions but the authority to suppress a particular class of disfavored speech. The forfeiture provisions accomplish this in a direct way by seizing speech presumed to be protected along with the instruments of its dissemination, and in an indirect way by threatening all who engage in the business of distributing adult or sexually explicit materials with the same disabling measures.

Obscenity laws would not work unless an offender could be arrested and imprisoned despite the resulting chill on his own further speech. But, at least before today, we have understood state action directed at protected books or other expressive works themselves to raise distinct constitutional concerns. [T]he destruction of books and films that were not obscene and not adjudged to be so is a remedy with no parallel in our cases. The Court's decision is a grave repudiation of First Amendment principles, and with respect I dissent.

b. Licensing as a Prior Restraint

Another form of prior restraint—in fact, the classic type of prior restraint—is where the government requires a license or permit in order for speech to occur. Lovell v. City of Griffin is an early case declaring a licensing system to be an impermissible prior restraint.

LOVELL v. CITY OF GRIFFIN, GA., 303 U.S. 444 (1938): Chief Justice HUGHES delivered the opinion of the Court.

Appellant, Alma Lovell, was convicted in the recorder's court of the City of Griffin, Ga., of the violation of a city ordinance and was sentenced to imprisonment for fifty days in default of the payment of a fine of $50. The ordinance in question is as follows:

> Section 1. That the practice of ==distributing,== either by hand or otherwise, circulars, handbooks, advertising, or ==literature of any kind==, whether said articles are being delivered free, or whether same are being sold, within the limits of the City of Griffin, without first obtaining written permission from the City Manager of the City of Griffin, such practice shall be deemed a nuisance, and punishable as an offense against the City of Griffin.
>
> Section 2. The Chief of Police of the City of Griffin and the police force of the City of Griffin are hereby required and directed to suppress the same and to abate any nuisance as is described in the first section of this ordinance.

The violation, which is not denied, consisted of the distribution without the required permission of a pamphlet and magazine in the nature of religious tracts, setting forth the gospel of the "Kingdom of Jehovah." Appellant did not apply for a permit, as she regarded herself as sent "by Jehovah to do His work" and that such an application would have been "an act of disobedience to His commandment."

The ordinance is comprehensive with respect to the method of distribution. It covers every sort of circulation "either by hand or otherwise." There is thus no restriction in its application with respect to time or place. It is not limited to ways which might be regarded as inconsistent with the maintenance of public order, or as involving disorderly conduct, the molestation of the inhabitants, or the misuse or littering of the streets. The ordinance prohibits the distribution of literature of any kind at any time, at any place, and in any manner without a permit from the city manager.

We think that the ordinance is invalid on its face. Whatever the motive which induced its adoption, ==its character is such that it strikes at the very foundation of the freedom of the press by subjecting it to license and censorship.== The struggle for the freedom of the press was primarily directed against the power of the licensor. It was against that power that John Milton directed his assault by his "Appeal for the Liberty of Unlicensed Printing." And the liberty of the press became initially a right to publish "without a license what formerly could be published only with one." While this freedom from previous restraint upon publication cannot be regarded as exhausting the guaranty of liberty, the prevention of that restraint was a leading purpose in the adoption of the constitutional provision. Legislation of the type of the ordinance in question would restore the system of license and censorship in its baldest form.

The ordinance cannot be saved because it relates to distribution and not to publication. "Liberty of circulating is as essential to that freedom as liberty of publishing; indeed, without the circulation, the publication would be of little value."

As the ordinance is void on its face, it was not necessary for appellant to seek a permit under it. She was entitled to contest its validity in answer to the charge against her.

Watchtower Bible & Tract Society of New York, Inc. v. Village of Stratton is a more recent example of the Court's invalidating a licensing system.

C. Prior Restraints

WATCHTOWER BIBLE & TRACT SOCIETY OF NEW YORK, INC. v. VILLAGE OF STRATTON
536 U.S. 150 (2002)

Justice STEVENS delivered the opinion of the Court.

Petitioners contend that a village ordinance making it a misdemeanor to engage in door-to-door advocacy without first registering with the mayor and receiving a permit violates the First Amendment. Through this facial challenge, we consider the door-to-door canvassing regulation not only as it applies to religious proselytizing, but also to anonymous political speech and the distribution of handbills.

I

Petitioner Watchtower Bible and Tract Society of New York, Inc., coordinates the preaching activities of Jehovah's Witnesses throughout the United States and publishes Bibles and religious periodicals that are widely distributed. Petitioner Wellsville, Ohio, Congregation of Jehovah's Witnesses, Inc., supervises the activities of approximately 59 members in a part of Ohio that includes the Village of Stratton (Village). Petitioners offer religious literature without cost to anyone interested in reading it. They allege that they do not solicit contributions or orders for the sale of merchandise or services, but they do accept donations.

Section 116.01 prohibits "canvassers" and others from "going in and upon" private residential property for the purpose of promoting any "cause" without first having obtained a permit pursuant to §116.03. That section provides that any canvasser who intends to go on private property to promote a cause, must obtain a "Solicitation Permit" from the office of the mayor; there is no charge for the permit, and apparently one is issued routinely after an applicant fills out a fairly detailed "Solicitor's Registration Form." The canvasser is then authorized to go upon premises that he listed on the registration form, but he must carry the permit upon his person and exhibit it whenever requested to do so by a police officer or by a resident. The ordinance sets forth grounds for the denial or revocation of a permit, but the record before us does not show that any application has been denied or that any permit has been revoked. Petitioners did not apply for a permit.

A section of the ordinance that petitioners do not challenge establishes a procedure by which a resident may prohibit solicitation even by holders of permits. If the resident files a "No Solicitation Registration Form" with the mayor, and also posts a "No Solicitation" sign on his property, no uninvited canvassers may enter his property, unless they are specifically authorized to do so in the "No Solicitation Registration Form" itself. Only 32 of the Village's 278 residents filed such forms.

II

For over 50 years, the Court has invalidated restrictions on door-to-door canvassing and pamphleteering. It is more than historical accident that most of these cases involved First Amendment challenges brought by Jehovah's

Witnesses, because door-to-door canvassing is mandated by their religion. Moreover, because they lack significant financial resources, the ability of the Witnesses to proselytize is seriously diminished by regulations that burden their efforts to canvass door-to-door.

Although our past cases involving Jehovah's Witnesses, most of which were decided shortly before and during World War II, do not directly control the question we confront today, they provide both a historical and analytical backdrop for consideration of petitioners' First Amendment claim that the breadth of the Village's ordinance offends the First Amendment. From these decisions, several themes emerge that guide our consideration of the ordinance at issue here.

The cases emphasize the value of the speech involved. For example, in Murdock v. Pennsylvania, the Court noted that "hand distribution of religious tracts is an age-old form of missionary evangelism—as old as the history of printing presses. It has been a potent force in various religious movements down through the years. . . . This form of religious activity occupies the same high estate under the First Amendment as do worship in the churches and preaching from the pulpits. It has the same claim to protection as the more orthodox and conventional exercises of religion. It also has the same claim as the others to the guarantees of freedom of speech and freedom of the press." In addition, the cases discuss extensively the historical importance of door-to-door canvassing and pamphleteering as vehicles for the dissemination of ideas.

Despite the emphasis on the important role that door-to-door canvassing and pamphleteering has played in our constitutional tradition of free and open discussion, these early cases also recognized the interests a town may have in some form of regulation, particularly when the solicitation of money is involved. Despite recognition of these interests as legitimate, our precedent is clear that there must be a balance between these interests and the effect of the regulations on First Amendment rights. We "must 'be astute to examine the effect of the challenged legislation' and must 'weigh the circumstances and . . . appraise the substantiality of the reasons advanced in support of the regulation.'"

Finally, the cases demonstrate that efforts of the Jehovah's Witnesses to resist speech regulation have not been a struggle for their rights alone. In *Martin*, after cataloging the many groups that rely extensively upon this method of communication, the Court summarized that "[d]oor to door distribution of circulars is essential to the poorly financed causes of little people."

III

The Village argues that three interests are served by its ordinance: the prevention of fraud, the prevention of crime, and the protection of residents' privacy. We have no difficulty concluding, in light of our precedent, that these are important interests that the Village may seek to safeguard through some form of regulation of solicitation activity. We must also look, however, to the amount of speech covered by the ordinance and whether there is an appropriate balance between the affected speech and the governmental interests that the ordinance purports to serve.

The text of the Village's ordinance prohibits "canvassers" from going on private property for the purpose of explaining or promoting any "cause,"

C. Prior Restraints

unless they receive a permit and the residents visited have not opted for a "no solicitation" sign. Had this provision been construed to apply only to commercial activities and the solicitation of funds, arguably the ordinance would have been tailored to the Village's interest in protecting the privacy of its residents and preventing fraud. Yet, even though the Village has explained that the ordinance was adopted to serve those interests, it has never contended that it should be so narrowly interpreted. To the contrary, the Village's administration of its ordinance unquestionably demonstrates that the provisions apply to a significant number of noncommercial "canvassers" promoting a wide variety of "causes." Indeed, on the "No Solicitation Forms" provided to the residents, the canvassers include "Camp Fire Girls," "Jehovah's Witnesses," "Political Candidates," "Trick or Treaters during Halloween Season," and "Persons Affiliated with Stratton Church." The ordinance unquestionably applies, not only to religious causes, but to political activity as well. It would seem to extend to "residents casually soliciting the votes of neighbors," or ringing doorbells to enlist support for employing a more efficient garbage collector.

The mere fact that the ordinance covers so much speech raises constitutional concerns. It is offensive—not only to the values protected by the First Amendment, but to the very notion of a free society—that in the context of everyday public discourse a citizen must first inform the government of her desire to speak to her neighbors and then obtain a permit to do so. Even if the issuance of permits by the mayor's office is a ministerial task that is performed promptly and at no cost to the applicant, a law requiring a permit to engage in such speech constitutes a dramatic departure from our national heritage and constitutional tradition.

Three obvious examples illustrate the pernicious effect of such a permit requirement. First, as our cases involving distribution of unsigned handbills demonstrate, there are a significant number of persons who support causes anonymously. "The decision to favor anonymity may be motivated by fear of economic or official retaliation, by concern about social ostracism, or merely by a desire to preserve as much of one's privacy as possible." McIntyre v. Ohio Elections Comm'n (1995). The requirement that a canvasser must be identified in a permit application filed in the mayor's office and available for public inspection necessarily results in a surrender of that anonymity.

Second, requiring a permit as a prior condition on the exercise of the right to speak imposes an objective burden on some speech of citizens holding religious or patriotic views. As our World War II–era cases dramatically demonstrate, there are a significant number of persons whose religious scruples will prevent them from applying for such a license. There are no doubt other patriotic citizens, who have such firm convictions about their constitutional right to engage in uninhibited debate in the context of door-to-door advocacy, that they would prefer silence to speech licensed by a petty official.

Third, there is a significant amount of spontaneous speech that is effectively banned by the ordinance. A person who made a decision on a holiday or a weekend to take an active part in a political campaign could not begin to pass out handbills until after he or she obtained the required permit. Even a spontaneous decision to go across the street and urge a neighbor to vote against the mayor could not lawfully be implemented without first obtaining the mayor's permission.

The Village, however, argues that the ordinance is nonetheless valid because it serves the two additional interests of protecting the privacy of the resident and the prevention of crime.

With respect to the former, it seems clear that §107 of the ordinance, which provides for the posting of "No Solicitation" signs and which is not challenged in this case, coupled with the resident's unquestioned right to refuse to engage in conversation with unwelcome visitors, provides ample protection for the unwilling listener. The annoyance caused by an uninvited knock on the front door is the same whether or not the visitor is armed with a permit.

With respect to the latter, it seems unlikely that the absence of a permit would preclude criminals from knocking on doors and engaging in conversations not covered by the ordinance. They might, for example, ask for directions or permission to use the telephone, or pose as surveyors or census takers. Or they might register under a false name with impunity because the ordinance contains no provision for verifying an applicant's identity or organizational credentials. Moreover, the Village did not assert an interest in crime prevention below, and there is an absence of any evidence of a special crime problem related to door-to-door solicitation in the record before us.

The rhetoric used in the World War II–era opinions that repeatedly saved petitioners' coreligionists from petty prosecutions reflected the Court's evaluation of the First Amendment freedoms that are implicated in this case. The value judgment that then motivated a united democratic people fighting to defend those very freedoms from totalitarian attack is unchanged. It motivates our decision today.

Chief Justice REHNQUIST, dissenting.

More than half a century ago we recognized that canvassers, "whether selling pots or distributing leaflets, may lessen the peaceful enjoyment of a home," and that "burglars frequently pose as canvassers, either in order that they may have a pretense to discover whether a house is empty and hence ripe for burglary, or for the purpose of spying out the premises in order that they may return later." Martin v. City of Struthers (1943). These problems continue to be associated with door-to-door canvassing, as are even graver ones.

A recent double murder in Hanover, New Hampshire, a town of approximately 7,500 that would appear tranquil to most Americans but would probably seem like a bustling town of Dartmouth College students to Stratton residents, illustrates these dangers. Two teenagers murdered a married couple of Dartmouth College professors, Half and Susanne Zantop, in the Zantop's home. Investigators have concluded, based on the confession of one of the teenagers, that the teenagers went door-to-door intent on stealing access numbers to bank debit cards and then killing their owners. See Dartmouth Professors Called Random Targets, Washington Post, Feb. 20, 2002, p. A2. Their modus operandi was to tell residents that they were conducting an environmental survey for school. They canvassed a few homes where no one answered. At another, the resident did not allow them in to conduct the "survey." They were allowed into the Zantop home. After conducting the phony environmental survey, they stabbed the Zantops to death.

In order to reduce these very grave risks associated with canvassing, the 278 "little people" of Stratton, who, unlike petitioners, do not have a team

C. Prior Restraints

of attorneys at their ready disposal, enacted the ordinance at issue here. The residents did not prohibit door-to-door communication, they simply required that canvassers obtain a permit before going door-to-door. And the village does not have the discretion to reject an applicant who completes the application.

The town had little reason to suspect that the negligible burden of having to obtain a permit runs afoul of the First Amendment. For over 60 years, we have categorically stated that a permit requirement for door-to-door canvassers, which gives no discretion to the issuing authority, is constitutional. The Court today, however, abruptly changes course and invalidates the ordinance.

The Stratton ordinance does not prohibit door-to-door canvassing; it merely requires that canvassers fill out a form and receive a permit. The mayor does not exercise any discretion in deciding who receives a permit; approval of the permit is automatic upon proper completion of the form. And petitioners do not contend in this Court that the ordinance is vague.

There is no support in our case law for applying anything more stringent than intermediate scrutiny to the ordinance. The ordinance is content-neutral and does not bar anyone from going door-to-door in Stratton. It merely regulates the manner in which one must canvass: A canvasser must first obtain a permit. The Stratton regulation is aimed at three significant governmental interests: the prevention of fraud, the prevention of crime, and the protection of privacy.

The ordinance prevents and detects serious crime by making it a crime not to register. Take the Hanover double murder discussed earlier. The murderers did not achieve their objective until they visited their fifth home over a period of seven months. If Hanover had a permit requirement, the teens may have been stopped before they achieved their objective. One of the residents they visited may have informed the police that there were two canvassers who lacked a permit. Such neighborly vigilance, though perhaps foreign to those residing in modern day cities, is not uncommon in small towns. Or the police on their own may have discovered that two canvassers were violating the ordinance. Apprehension for violating the permit requirement may well have frustrated the teenagers' objectives; it certainly would have assisted in solving the murders had the teenagers gone ahead with their plan.

Of course, the Stratton ordinance does not guarantee that no canvasser will ever commit a burglary or violent crime. The Court seems to think this dooms the ordinance, erecting an insurmountable hurdle that a law must provide a fool-proof method of preventing crime. In order to survive intermediate scrutiny, however, a law need not solve the crime problem, it need only further the interest in preventing crime. Some deterrence of serious criminal activity is more than enough to survive intermediate scrutiny.

The final requirement of intermediate scrutiny is that a regulation leave open ample alternatives for expression. Undoubtedly, ample alternatives exist here. Most obviously, canvassers are free to go door-to-door after filling out the permit application. And those without permits may communicate on public sidewalks, on street corners, through the mail, or through the telephone.

Ironically, however, today's decision may result in less of the door-to-door communication that the Court extols. As the Court recognizes, any homeowner may place a "No Solicitation" sign on his or her property, and it is a crime to violate that sign. In light of today's decision depriving Stratton residents of the degree of accountability and safety that the permit requirement provides, more and more residents may decide to place these signs in their yards and cut off door-to-door communication altogether.

The Supreme Court has held that licensing or permit laws are allowed only if the government has an important reason for licensing and only if there are clear criteria leaving almost no discretion to the licensing authority. In addition, there must be procedural safeguards, such as a requirement for prompt determinations as to license requests and judicial review of license denials. Each requirement is discussed in turn.

i. Important Reason for Licensing

First, there must be an important reason for licensing. For example, in Cox v. New Hampshire, 312 U.S. 569 (1941), the Court upheld an ordinance that required that those wishing to hold a parade or demonstration obtain a permit. The ordinance allowed a permit to be denied only if the area already was in use by another group. The Court emphasized that the city had an important reason for licensing: to receive notice of demonstrations to be able to "afford opportunity for proper policing" and to preserve order by ensuring only one parade at a particular place at a specific time. The Court stressed that the "licensing board was not vested with arbitrary power or an unfettered discretion."

ii. Clear Standards Leaving Almost No Discretion to the Government

Second, there must be clear standards leaving almost no discretion to the licensing authority. The Court is very concerned that discretion could be used for content-based censorship; the government could grant permits to speech that it liked but deny licenses to disfavored expression.

CITY OF LAKEWOOD v. PLAIN DEALER PUBLISHING CO., 486 U.S. 750 (1988): Justice BRENNAN delivered the opinion of the Court.

The city of Lakewood, a suburban community bordering Cleveland, Ohio, appeals a judgment of the Court of Appeals for the Sixth Circuit enjoining enforcement of its local ordinance regulating the placement of newsracks. The court's decision was based in part on its conclusion that the ordinance vests the mayor with unbridled discretion over which publishers may place newsracks on public property and where.

Prior to 1983, the city of Lakewood absolutely prohibited the private placement of any structure on public property. On the strength of that law, the city denied the Plain Dealer Publishing Company (Newspaper) permission to place its coin-operated newspaper dispensing devices on city sidewalks. The District Court adjudged the absolute prohibition unconstitutional. Although the city could have appealed the District Court's judgment, it decided instead to adopt two ordinances permitting the placement of structures on city property under certain conditions. One of those ordinances specifically concerns newsracks. That ordinance gives the mayor the authority to grant or deny applications for

C. Prior Restraints

annual newsrack permits. If the mayor denies an application, he is required to "stat[e] the reasons for such denial."

Recognizing the explicit protection accorded speech and the press in the text of the First Amendment, our cases have long held that when a licensing statute allegedly vests unbridled discretion in a government official over whether to permit or deny expressive activity, one who is subject to the law may challenge it facially without the necessity of first applying for, and being denied, a license. At the root of this long line of precedent is the time-tested knowledge that in the area of free expression a licensing statute placing unbridled discretion in the hands of a government official or agency constitutes a prior restraint and may result in censorship.

First, the mere existence of the licensor's unfettered discretion, coupled with the power of prior restraint, intimidates parties into censoring their own speech, even if the discretion and power are never actually abused. It is not difficult to visualize a newspaper that relies to a substantial degree on single issue sales feeling significant pressure to endorse the incumbent mayor in an upcoming election, or to refrain from criticizing him, in order to receive a favorable and speedy disposition on its permit application. Only standards limiting the licensor's discretion will eliminate this danger by adding an element of certainty fatal to self-censorship.

Second, the absence of express standards makes it difficult to distinguish, "as applied," between a licensor's legitimate denial of a permit and its illegitimate abuse of censorial power. Standards provide the guideposts that check the licensor and allow courts quickly and easily to determine whether the licensor is discriminating against disfavored speech. Without these guideposts, post hoc rationalizations by the licensing official and the use of shifting or illegitimate criteria are far too easy, making it difficult for courts to determine in any particular case whether the licensor is permitting favorable, and suppressing unfavorable, expression.

It is apparent that the face of the ordinance itself contains no explicit limits on the mayor's discretion. Indeed, nothing in the law as written requires the mayor to do more than make the statement "it is not in the public interest" when denying a permit application. Similarly, the mayor could grant the application, but require the newsrack to be placed in an inaccessible location without providing any explanation whatever. To allow these illusory "constraints" to constitute the standards necessary to bound a licensor's discretion renders the guarantee against censorship little more than a high-sounding ideal.

In Saia v. New York, 334 U.S. 558 (1948), the Supreme Court declared unconstitutional an ordinance that required a permit in order to use a sound amplification system on a motor vehicle. Although the Court has upheld restrictions on such sound trucks, an ordinance that gives unfettered discretion to government officials to decide who can use such vehicles violates the First Amendment. Similarly, in Kunz v. New York, 340 U.S. 290 (1951), the Court declared unconstitutional an ordinance that prohibited the holding of a religious meeting on a public street without a permit. The Court said that the government "cannot vest restraining control over the right to speak . . . in an administrative official where there are no appropriate standards to guide his action."

In Forsyth County, Georgia v. Nationalist Movement, 505 U.S. 123 (1992), the Court followed the same reasoning in declaring unconstitutional an ordinance that required a permit in order for a demonstration to occur and that vested discretion in the government to set the amount of the fee up to $1,000. The Court found that the licensing law was impermissible because "[t]here are no articulated standards either in the ordinance or in the county's established practice. The administrator is not required to rely on any objective factors. He need not provide any explanation for his decision, and that decision is unreviewable." The Court concluded that "[n]othing in the law or its application prevents the official from encouraging some views and discouraging others through the arbitrary application of the fees. The First Amendment prohibits the vesting of such unbridled discretion in a government official."

iii. Procedural Safeguards

Finally, in order for a licensing or permit system to be constitutional, there must be procedural safeguards. Any system of prior restraints must have a prompt decision made by the government as to whether the speech will be allowed;[42] there must be a full and fair hearing before speech is prevented;[43] and there must be a prompt and final judicial determination of the validity of any preclusion of speech.[44]

In Freedman v. Maryland, 380 U.S. 51 (1965), the Court unanimously declared unconstitutional a Maryland law that made it unlawful to exhibit a motion picture without having first obtained a license. The Court noted that such a licensing system presents grave dangers for freedom of speech. The Court said that such a system would be allowed "only if it takes place under procedural safeguards designed to obviate the dangers of . . . censorship." The "burden of proving that the film is unprotected expression must rest on the censor." There must be a requirement for a prompt determination by the government whether to issue or deny the license request. Also, prompt judicial review must be available for all permit denials. The Court said that "only a judicial determination in an adversary proceeding ensures the necessary sensitivity to freedom of expression."

The Court repeatedly has held that such procedural safeguards are required for government actions that operate like licensing systems, such as postal stop orders for obscene materials[45] and customs seizures of obscene materials.[46] In FW/PBS, Inc. v. City of Dallas, 493 U.S. 215 (1990), the Court declared unconstitutional a city ordinance that required licensing of "sexually oriented

---

42. *See, e.g.,* Teitel Film Corp. v. Cusack, 390 U.S. 139 (1968) (a 50-day delay before seeking an injunction, during which time the speech could not be disseminated, violated the First Amendment).

43. *See, e.g.,* Carroll v. President & Commissioners of Princess Anne County, 393 U.S. 175 (1968) (ex parte court orders are impermissible in restraining speech because of the lack of adversarial presentation).

44. *See* National Socialist Party of America v. Village of Skokie, 432 U.S. 43 (1977) (improper to leave an injuction in place pending an appeal that could take up to a year; either the injunction had to be lifted or the appeal had to be expedited).

45. Blount v. Rizzi, 400 U.S. 410 (1971).

46. United States v. Thirty-Seven Photographs, 402 U.S. 363 (1971).

businesses" because of the absence of the procedural safeguards prescribed in *Freedman*. The Court noted that the law failed to require prompt determination of license requests or to provide for judicial review of license denials.

However, in subsequent cases, the Court has not adhered to *Freedman* and has relaxed the procedural safeguards. For example, in Thomas and Windy City Hemp Development Board v. Chicago Park District, 534 U.S. 316 (2002), the Court rejected the application of some of the procedural safeguards from *Freedman* to requirements for obtaining a license in order to use a park. Specifically, the Court rejected that the "Park District, like the Board of Censors in *Freedman*, must initiate litigation every time it denies a permit and that the ordinance must specify a deadline for judicial review of a challenge to a permit denial." The Court explained that it never has "required that a content-neutral permit scheme regulating speech in a public forum must adhere to the procedural requirements set forth in *Freedman*."

In City of Littleton, Colorado v. Z.J. Gifts D-4, L.L.C., 541 U.S. 774 (2004), the Court also dealt with the application of the *Freedman* procedural requirements to a licensing system. The Court reaffirmed that a city's licensing of adult businesses must comply with the First Amendment and that this must include judicial review of license denials. However, the Court said that the ordinance itself need not specify the availability of prompt judicial review as long as timely judicial review is available.

D. WHAT IS AN INFRINGEMENT OF FREEDOM OF SPEECH?

A threshold question in many cases is whether the government has infringed freedom of speech and therefore whether First Amendment analysis is applicable. Often, it is clear that a law infringes freedom of speech and is susceptible to First Amendment challenge. For example, a statute that prohibits speech and authorizes criminal punishments obviously has to meet constitutional scrutiny. Chapter 3, below, reviews many of these laws, such as those prohibiting speech that incites illegal conduct, obscenity, and false advertising. Although these are categories of unprotected speech and regulation is allowed, there is no doubt that the laws interfere with expression and must meet First Amendment standards.

Also, there is no doubt that prior restraints, discussed above, are infringements of expression and must meet First Amendment standards. Court orders preventing speech and licensing systems precluding speech without a permit thus always are subject to review on constitutional grounds.

But what types of government actions, apart from prohibitions via laws, court orders, or licensing systems, are infringements of speech triggering First Amendment analysis? A wide variety of government actions sufficiently burden speech so as to be considered an infringement and thus be subjected to First Amendment scrutiny. A finding that a law substantially burdens or infringes speech does not, of course, mean that it is automatically unconstitutional, but it does mean that the law will have to meet heightened scrutiny unless it regulates a category of unprotected speech. As explained above, the general rule is that content-based regulations of speech must meet strict scrutiny, while content-neutral regulation must meet intermediate scrutiny.

Laws that significantly burden speech are ones that allow civil liability for expression; that prevent compensation for speech; that compel expression; that condition a benefit on a person's foregoing speech; and that pressure individuals not to speak. These are discussed, in turn, in the following subsections. Additionally, laws that regulate conduct might have an incidental effect on speech because of the communicative content of behavior. First Amendment analysis of such conduct that communicates is discussed in Chapter 3.

1. Civil Liability and Denial of Compensation for Speech

The Court repeatedly has held that civil liability for speech, even in the context of private civil litigation, is an interference with speech and therefore must meet First Amendment scrutiny. In New York Times v. Sullivan, 376 U.S. 254 (1964), the Court held that state defamation law was limited by the First Amendment. New York Times v. Sullivan, presented in detail in Chapter 3 below, involved a defamation suit brought by the Montgomery, Alabama, police commissioner against the *New York Times* and four black clergymen for an advertisement criticizing the handling of demonstrations. A jury awarded the plaintiff $500,000 under Alabama's defamation law.

The Supreme Court expressly held that the First Amendment applied. Justice Brennan, writing one of the most famous and important free speech cases in history, declared, "What a State may not constitutionally bring about by means of a criminal statute is likewise beyond the reach of its civil law of libel. The fear of damage awards under a rule such as that invoked by the Alabama courts here may be markedly more inhibiting than the fear of prosecution under a criminal statute." The Court noted that the "judgment awarded in this case—without the need for any proof of actual pecuniary loss—was one thousand times greater than the maximum fine provided by the Alabama criminal [libel law], and one hundred times greater than that provided by the Sedition Act. . . . Whether or not a newspaper can survive a succession of such judgments, the pall of fear and timidity imposed upon those who would give voice to public criticism is an atmosphere in which the First Amendment freedoms cannot survive."

The Supreme Court has followed this and held that liability for such torts as invasion of privacy,[47] false light,[48] and intentional infliction of emotional distress[49] must be consistent with the First Amendment. These torts, and the applicable First Amendment limits, are discussed in Chapter 3.

Although it is litigation between two private parties, there is clearly state action in such tort litigation. It is the state's law—whether statutory or common law—that is the basis for liability and recovery. The courts oversee the judicial proceedings and ultimately impose any judgment. In Shelley v. Kraemer, 334 U.S. 1 (1948), the Supreme Court held that judges cannot enforce racially restrictive covenants because court action is a form of state action. Similarly, court action in private civil litigation is state action and thus any civil liability must comport with First Amendment standards.

---

47. Florida Star v. B.J.F., 491 U.S. 524 (1989).
48. Time, Inc. v. Hill, 385 U.S. 374 (1967).
49. Hustler Magazine v. Falwell, 485 U.S. 46 (1988).

D. What Is an Infringement of Freedom of Speech?

2. Prohibitions on Compensation

The Supreme Court has clearly indicated that another way in which the government can infringe freedom of speech is by prohibiting individuals from being paid for their expression. In Simon & Schuster v. Members of the New York State Crime Victims Board, 502 U.S. 105 (1991), referenced above, the Court declared unconstitutional a state law that prevented an accused or convicted criminal from profiting from selling the story of his or her crime to any media. The New York law did not prohibit any speech; it only prevented individuals from keeping profits from selling the tales of their criminal activity. Nonetheless, the Supreme Court found the law to violate the First Amendment. The Court said that "[a] statute is presumptively inconsistent with the First Amendment if it imposes a financial burden on speakers because of the content of their speech."

United States v. National Treasury Employees Union reaffirms that prohibitions on compensation for speech infringe the First Amendment.

UNITED STATES v. NATIONAL TREASURY EMPLOYEES UNION
513 U.S. 454 (1995)

Justice STEVENS delivered the opinion of the Court.

In 1989 Congress enacted a law that broadly prohibits federal employees from accepting any compensation for making speeches or writing articles. The prohibition applies even when neither the subject of the speech or article nor the person or group paying for it has any connection with the employee's official duties.

Federal employees who write for publication in their spare time have made significant contributions to the marketplace of ideas. They include literary giants like Nathaniel Hawthorne and Herman Melville, who were employed by the Customs Service; Walt Whitman, who worked for the Departments of Justice and Interior; and Bret Harte, an employee of the Mint.

Even though respondents work for the Government, they have not relinquished "the First Amendment rights they would otherwise enjoy as citizens to comment on matters of public interest." They seek compensation for their expressive activities in their capacity as citizens, not as Government employees. They claim their employment status has no more bearing on the quality or market value of their literary output than it did on that of Hawthorne or Melville. With few exceptions, the content of respondents' messages has nothing to do with their jobs and does not even arguably have any adverse impact on the efficiency of the offices in which they work. They do not address audiences composed of co-workers or supervisors; instead, they write or speak for segments of the general public. Neither the character of the authors, the subject matter of their expression, the effect of the content of their expression on their official duties, nor the kind of audiences they address has any relevance to their employment.

Although [the law] neither prohibits any speech nor discriminates among speakers based on the content or viewpoint of their messages, its prohibition on compensation unquestionably imposes a significant burden on expressive activity. Publishers compensate authors because compensation provides a significant incentive toward more expression. By denying respondents that incentive, the honoraria ban induces them to curtail their expression if they wish to continue working for the Government.

The ban imposes a far more significant burden on respondents than on the relatively small group of lawmakers whose past receipt of honoraria motivated its enactment. The absorbing and time-consuming responsibilities of legislators and policymaking executives leave them little opportunity for research or creative expression on subjects unrelated to their official responsibilities. Such officials often receive invitations to appear and talk about subjects related to their work because of their official identities. In contrast, invitations to rank-and-file employees usually depend only on the market value of their messages. The honoraria ban is unlikely to reduce significantly the number of appearances by high-ranking officials as long as travel expense reimbursement for the speaker and one relative is available as an alternative form of remuneration. In contrast, the denial of compensation for lower paid, nonpolicymaking employees will inevitably diminish their expressive output.

The large-scale disincentive to Government employees' expression also imposes a significant burden on the public's right to read and hear what the employees would otherwise have written and said. We have no way to measure the true cost of that burden, but we cannot ignore the risk that it might deprive us of the work of a future Melville or Hawthorne. The honoraria ban imposes the kind of burden that abridges speech under the First Amendment.

Chief Justice REHNQUIST, with whom Justice SCALIA and Justice THOMAS join, dissenting.

I believe that the Court's opinion is seriously flawed in two respects. First, its application of the First Amendment understates the weight that should be accorded to the governmental justifications for the honoraria ban and overstates the amount of speech that actually will be deterred. Second, its discussion of the impact of the statute that it strikes down is carefully limited to only a handful of the most appealing individual situations, but when it deals with the remedy it suddenly shifts gears and strikes down the statute as applied to the entire class of Executive Branch employees below grade GS-16. I therefore dissent.

The Court concedes that in light of the abuses of honoraria by its Members, Congress could reasonably assume that "payments of honoraria to judges or high-ranking officials in the Executive Branch might generate a similar appearance of improper influence," but it concludes that Congress could not extend this presumption to federal employees below grade GS-16. The theory underlying the Court's distinction—that federal employees below grade GS-16 have negligible power to confer favors on those who might pay to hear them speak or to read their articles—is seriously flawed. Tax examiners, bank examiners, enforcement officials, or any number of federal employees have substantial power to confer favors even though their compensation level is below grade GS-16.

I believe that a proper application of the [law] to this content-neutral restriction on the receipt of compensation compels the conclusion that the honoraria ban is consistent with the First Amendment.

D. What Is an Infringement of Freedom of Speech?

3. Compelled Speech

The cases reviewed thus far concerning what constitutes an infringement of speech all have involved the government prohibiting or penalizing speech—criminally, civilly, or by withholding compensation. The government also can infringe the First Amendment by compelling speech. Just as there is a right to speak, so, it is clear, there is a right to be silent and refrain from speaking.

The classic case in this regard was West Virginia State Board of Education v. Barnette.

WEST VIRGINIA STATE BOARD OF EDUCATION v. BARNETTE
319 U.S. 624 (1943)

Justice JACKSON delivered the opinion of the Court.

The Board of Education on January 9, 1942, adopted a resolution ordering that the salute to the flag become "a regular part of the program of activities in the public schools," that all teachers and pupils "shall be required to participate in the salute honoring the Nation represented by the Flag; provided, however, that refusal to salute the Flag be regarded as an Act of insubordination, and shall be dealt with accordingly." What is now required is the "stiff-arm" salute, the saluter to keep the right hand raised with palm turned up while the following is repeated: "I pledge allegiance to the Flag of the United States of America and to the Republic for which it stands; one Nation, indivisible, with liberty and justice for all."

Failure to conform is "insubordination" dealt with by expulsion. Readmission is denied by statute until compliance. Meanwhile the expelled child is "unlawfully absent" and may be proceeded against as a delinquent. His parents or guardians are liable to prosecution, and if convicted are subject to fine not exceeding $50 and jail term not exceeding thirty days.

Appellees, citizens of the United States and of West Virginia, brought suit in the United States District Court for themselves and others similarly situated asking its injunction to restrain enforcement of these laws and regulations against Jehovah's Witnesses. The Witnesses' religious beliefs include a literal version of Exodus, Chapter 20, verses 4 and 5, which says: "Thou shalt not make unto thee any graven image, or any likeness of anything that is in heaven above, or that is in the earth beneath, or that is in the water under the earth; thou shalt not bow down thyself to them nor serve them." They consider that the flag is an "image" within this command. For this reason they refuse to salute it.

Children of this faith have been expelled from school and are threatened with exclusion for no other cause. Officials threaten to send them to reformatories maintained for criminally inclined juveniles. Parents of such children have been prosecuted and are threatened with prosecutions for causing delinquency.

There is no doubt that, in connection with the pledges, the flag salute is a form of utterance. Symbolism is a primitive but effective way of communicating ideas. The use of an emblem or flag to symbolize some system, idea, institution, or personality, is a short cut from mind to mind.

It is also to be noted that the compulsory flag salute and pledge requires affirmation of a belief and an attitude of mind. It is not clear whether the regulation contemplates that pupils forego any contrary convictions of their own and become unwilling converts to the prescribed ceremony or whether it will be acceptable if they simulate assent by words without belief and by a gesture barren of meaning. It is now a commonplace that censorship or suppression of expression of opinion is tolerated by our Constitution only when the expression presents a clear and present danger of action of a kind the State is empowered to prevent and punish. It would seem that involuntary affirmation could be commanded only on even more immediate and urgent grounds than silence. But here the power of compulsion is invoked without any allegation that remaining passive during a flag salute ritual creates a clear and present danger that would justify an effort even to muffle expression. To sustain the compulsory flag salute we are required to say that a Bill of Rights which guards the individual's right to speak his own mind, left it open to public authorities to compel him to utter what is not in his mind.

The Fourteenth Amendment, as now applied to the States, protects the citizen against the State itself and all of its creatures — Boards of Education not excepted. These have, of course, important, delicate, and highly discretionary functions, but none that they may not perform within the limits of the Bill of Rights. Such Boards are numerous and their territorial jurisdiction often small. But small and local authority may feel less sense of responsibility to the Constitution, and agencies of publicity may be less vigilant in calling it to account.

The very purpose of a Bill of Rights was to withdraw certain subjects from the vicissitudes of political controversy, to place them beyond the reach of majorities and officials and to establish them as legal principles to be applied by the courts. One's right to life, liberty, and property, to free speech, a free press, freedom of worship and assembly, and other fundamental rights may not be submitted to vote; they depend on the outcome of no elections.

The case is made difficult not because the principles of its decision are obscure but because the flag involved is our own. Nevertheless, we apply the limitations of the Constitution with no fear that freedom to be intellectually and spiritually diverse or even contrary will disintegrate the social organization. To believe that patriotism will not flourish if patriotic ceremonies are voluntary and spontaneous instead of a compulsory routine is to make an unflattering estimate of the appeal of our institutions to free minds. We can have intellectual individualism and the rich cultural diversities that we owe to exceptional minds only at the price of occasional eccentricity and abnormal attitudes. When they are so harmless to others or to the State as those we deal with here, the price is not too great. But freedom to differ is not limited to things that do not matter much. That would be a mere shadow of freedom. The test of its substance is the right to differ as to things that touch the heart of the existing order.

If there is any fixed star in our constitutional constellation, it is that no official, high or petty, can prescribe what shall be orthodox in politics, nationalism, religion, or other matters of opinion or force citizens to confess by word or act their faith therein. If there are any circumstances which permit an exception, they do not now occur to us. We think the action of the local authorities in compelling the flag salute and pledge transcends constitutional limitations on their power and invades the sphere of intellect and spirit which it is the purpose of the First Amendment to our Constitution to reserve from all official control.

D. What Is an Infringement of Freedom of Speech?

Justice FRANKFURTER, dissenting.

One who belongs to the most vilified and persecuted minority in history is not likely to be insensible to the freedoms guaranteed by our Constitution. Were my purely personal attitude relevant I should whole-heartedly associate myself with the general libertarian views in the Court's opinion, representing as they do the thought and action of a lifetime. But as judges we are neither Jew nor Gentile, neither Catholic nor agnostic. We owe equal attachment to the Constitution and are equally bound by our judicial obligations whether we derive our citizenship from the earliest or the latest immigrants to these shores. As a member of this Court I am not justified in writing my private notions of policy into the Constitution, no matter how deeply I may cherish them or how mischievous I may deem their disregard. The duty of a judge who must decide which of two claims before the Court shall prevail, that of a State to enact and enforce laws within its general competence or that of an individual to refuse obedience because of the demands of his conscience, is not that of the ordinary person.

It can never be emphasized too much that one's own opinion about the wisdom or evil of a law should be excluded altogether when one is doing one's duty on the bench. The only opinion of our own even looking in that direction that is material is our opinion whether legislators could in reason have enacted such a law. In the light of all the circumstances, including the history of this question in this Court, it would require more daring than I possess to deny that reasonable legislators could have taken the action which is before us for review.

Most unwillingly, therefore, I must differ from my brethren with regard to legislation like this. I cannot bring my mind to believe that the "liberty" secured by the Due Process Clause gives this Court authority to deny to the State of West Virginia the attainment of that which we all recognize as a legitimate legislative end, namely, the promotion of good citizenship, by employment of the means here chosen.

The Court followed this principle in other cases, such as in Wooley v. Maynard, 430 U.S. 705 (1977), where it ruled that an individual could not be punished for blocking out the portion of his automobile license plate that contained the New Hampshire state motto, "Live Free or Die." The Court said that "the right of freedom of thought protected by the First Amendment . . . includes both the right to speak freely and the right to refrain from speaking at all. The right to speak and the right to refrain from speaking are complementary components of the broader concept of 'individual freedom of mind.'"

NATIONAL FEDERATION OF FAMILY AND LIFE ADVOCATES v. BECERRA

138 S. Ct. 2361 (2018)

Justice THOMAS delivered the opinion of the Court.

The California Reproductive Freedom, Accountability, Comprehensive Care, and Transparency Act (FACT Act) requires clinics that primarily serve pregnant women to provide certain notices. Licensed clinics must notify women that

California provides free or low-cost services, including abortions, and give them a phone number to call. Unlicensed clinics must notify women that California has not licensed the clinics to provide medical services. The question in this case is whether these notice requirements violate the First Amendment.

I

The California State Legislature enacted the FACT Act to regulate crisis pregnancy centers. Crisis pregnancy centers—according to a report commissioned by the California State Assembly—are "pro-life (largely Christian belief-based) organizations that offer a limited range of free pregnancy options, counseling, and other services to individuals that visit a center." "[U]nfortunately," the author of the FACT Act stated, "there are nearly 200 licensed and unlicensed" crisis pregnancy centers in California. These centers "aim to discourage and prevent women from seeking abortions." The author of the FACT Act observed that crisis pregnancy centers "are commonly affiliated with, or run by organizations whose stated goal" is to oppose abortion—including "the National Institute of Family and Life Advocates," one of the petitioners here. To address this perceived problem, the FACT Act imposes two notice requirements on facilities that provide pregnancy-related services—one for licensed facilities and one for unlicensed facilities.

The first notice requirement applies to "licensed covered facilit[ies]." To fall under the definition of "licensed covered facility," a clinic must be a licensed primary care or specialty clinic or qualify as an intermittent clinic under California law. A licensed covered facility also must have the "primary purpose" of "providing family planning or pregnancy-related services." And it must satisfy at least two of the following six requirements:

(1) The facility offers obstetric ultrasounds, obstetric sonograms, or prenatal care to pregnant women.
(2) The facility provides, or offers counseling about, contraception or contraceptive methods.
(3) The facility offers pregnancy testing or pregnancy diagnosis.
(4) The facility advertises or solicits patrons with offers to provide prenatal sonography, pregnancy tests, or pregnancy options counseling.
(5) The facility offers abortion services.
(6) The facility has staff or volunteers who collect health information from clients."

The FACT Act exempts several categories of clinics that would otherwise qualify as licensed covered facilities. Clinics operated by the United States or a federal agency are excluded, as are clinics that are "enrolled as a Medi-Cal provider" and participate in "the Family Planning, Access, Care, and Treatment Program" (Family PACT program). To participate in the Family PACT program, a clinic must provide "the full scope of family planning . . . services specified for the program," including sterilization and emergency contraceptive pills.

If a clinic is a licensed covered facility, the FACT Act requires it to disseminate a government-drafted notice on site. The notice states that "California has public programs that provide immediate free or low-cost access to comprehensive family planning services (including all FDA-approved methods of contraception), prenatal care, and abortion for eligible women. To determine whether you qualify, contact the county social services office at [insert the telephone number]." This notice must be posted in the waiting room, printed and distributed to all clients, or provided digitally at check-in. The notice must be in English and any additional languages identified by state law. In some counties, that means the notice must be spelled out in 13 different languages.

The stated purpose of the FACT Act, including its licensed notice requirement, is to "ensure that California residents make their personal reproductive health care decisions knowing their rights and the health care services available to them." The Legislature posited that "thousands of women remain unaware of the public programs available to provide them with contraception, health education and counseling, family planning, prenatal care, abortion, or delivery." Citing the "time sensitive" nature of pregnancy-related decisions, the Legislature concluded that requiring licensed facilities to inform patients themselves would be "[t]he most effective" way to convey this information.

The second notice requirement in the FACT Act applies to "unlicensed covered facilit[ies]." To fall under the definition of "unlicensed covered facility," a facility must not be licensed by the State, not have a licensed medical provider on staff or under contract, and have the "primary purpose" of "providing pregnancy-related services." An unlicensed covered facility also must satisfy at least two of the following four requirements:

"(1) The facility offers obstetric ultrasounds, obstetric sonograms, or prenatal care to pregnant women.
(2) The facility offers pregnancy testing or pregnancy diagnosis.
(3) The facility advertises or solicits patrons with offers to provide prenatal sonography, pregnancy tests, or pregnancy options counseling.
(4) The facility has staff or volunteers who collect health information from clients."

Clinics operated by the United States and licensed primary care clinics enrolled in Medi-Cal and Family PACT are excluded. Unlicensed covered facilities must provide a government-drafted notice stating that "[t]his facility is not licensed as a medical facility by the State of California and has no licensed medical provider who provides or directly supervises the provision of services." Cal. Health & Safety Code Ann. This notice must be provided on site and in all advertising materials. Onsite, the notice must be posted "conspicuously" at the entrance of the facility and in at least one waiting area. It must be "at least 8.5 inches by 11 inches and written in no less than 48-point type." In advertisements, the notice must be in the same size or larger font than the surrounding text, or otherwise set off in a way that draws attention to it. Like the licensed notice, the unlicensed notice must be in English and any additional languages specified by state law. Its stated purpose is to ensure "that pregnant women in California know when they are getting medical care from licensed professionals."

After the Governor of California signed the FACT Act, petitioners—a licensed pregnancy center, an unlicensed pregnancy center, and an organization composed of crisis pregnancy centers—filed this suit. Petitioners alleged that the licensed and unlicensed notices abridge the freedom of speech protected by the First Amendment. The District Court denied their motion for a preliminary injunction. The Court of Appeals for the Ninth Circuit affirmed. We reverse with respect to both notice requirements.

II

We first address the licensed notice. The First Amendment, applicable to the States through the Fourteenth Amendment, prohibits laws that abridge the freedom of speech. When enforcing this prohibition, our precedents distinguish between content-based and content-neutral regulations of speech. Content-based regulations "target speech based on its communicative content." As a general matter, such laws "are presumptively unconstitutional and may be justified only if the government proves that they are narrowly tailored to serve compelling state interests." This stringent standard reflects the fundamental principle that governments have "'no power to restrict expression because of its message, its ideas, its subject matter, or its content.'"

The licensed notice is a content-based regulation of speech. By compelling individuals to speak a particular message, such notices "alte[r] the content of [their] speech." Here, for example, licensed clinics must provide a government-drafted script about the availability of state-sponsored services, as well as contact information for how to obtain them. One of those services is abortion — the very practice that petitioners are devoted to opposing. By requiring petitioners to inform women how they can obtain state-subsidized abortions — at the same time petitioners try to dissuade women from choosing that option — the licensed notice plainly "alters the content" of petitioners' speech.

Although the licensed notice is content based, the Ninth Circuit did not apply strict scrutiny because it concluded that the notice regulates "professional speech." Some Courts of Appeals have recognized "professional speech" as a separate category of speech that is subject to different rules. These courts define "professionals" as individuals who provide personalized services to clients and who are subject to "a generally applicable licensing and regulatory regime." "Professional speech" is then defined as any speech by these individuals that is based on "[their] expert knowledge and judgment," or that is "within the confines of [the] professional relationship." So defined, these courts except professional speech from the rule that content-based regulations of speech are subject to strict scrutiny.

But this Court has not recognized "professional speech" as a separate category of speech. Speech is not unprotected merely because it is uttered by "professionals." This Court has "been reluctant to mark off new categories of speech for diminished constitutional protection." And it has been especially reluctant to "exemp[t] a category of speech from the normal prohibition on content-based restrictions." This Court's precedents do not permit governments to impose content-based restrictions on speech without "'persuasive evidence . . . of a long (if heretofore unrecognized) tradition'" to that effect.

This Court's precedents do not recognize such a tradition for a category called "professional speech." This Court has afforded less protection for professional speech in two circumstances — neither of which turned on the fact that professionals were speaking. First, our precedents have applied more deferential review to some laws that require professionals to disclose factual, noncontroversial information in their "commercial speech." Second, under our

D. What Is an Infringement of Freedom of Speech?

precedents, States may regulate professional conduct, even though that conduct incidentally involves speech. But neither line of precedents is implicated here.

This Court's precedents have applied a lower level of scrutiny to laws that compel disclosures in certain contexts. Most obviously, the licensed notice is not limited to "purely factual and uncontroversial information about the terms under which . . . services will be available."

In addition, this Court has upheld regulations of professional conduct that incidentally burden speech. In Planned Parenthood of Southeastern Pa. v. Casey, for example, this Court upheld a law requiring physicians to obtain informed consent before they could perform an abortion. Pennsylvania law required physicians to inform their patients of "the nature of the procedure, the health risks of the abortion and childbirth, and the 'probable gestational age of the unborn child.'" The joint opinion in *Casey* rejected a free-speech challenge to this informed-consent requirement. It described the Pennsylvania law as "a requirement that a doctor give a woman certain information as part of obtaining her consent to an abortion," which "for constitutional purposes, [was] no different from a requirement that a doctor give certain specific information about any medical procedure." The joint opinion explained that the law regulated speech only "as part of the *practice* of medicine, subject to reasonable licensing and regulation by the State." Indeed, the requirement that a doctor obtain informed consent to perform an operation is "firmly entrenched in American tort law."

The licensed notice at issue here is not an informed-consent requirement or any other regulation of professional conduct. The notice does not facilitate informed consent to a medical procedure. In fact, it is not tied to a procedure at all. It applies to all interactions between a covered facility and its clients, regardless of whether a medical procedure is ever sought, offered, or performed. If a covered facility does provide medical procedures, the notice provides no information about the risks or benefits of those procedures.

The dangers associated with content-based regulations of speech are also present in the context of professional speech. As with other kinds of speech, regulating the content of professionals' speech "pose[s] the inherent risk that the Government seeks not to advance a legitimate regulatory goal, but to suppress unpopular ideas or information." Take medicine, for example. "Doctors help patients make deeply personal decisions, and their candor is crucial." Throughout history, governments have "manipulat[ed] the content of doctor-patient discourse" to increase state power and suppress minorities. Further, when the government polices the content of professional speech, it can fail to "'preserve an uninhibited marketplace of ideas in which truth will ultimately prevail.'"

"Professional speech" is also a difficult category to define with precision. As defined by the courts of appeals, the professional-speech doctrine would cover a wide array of individuals—doctors, lawyers, nurses, physical therapists, truck drivers, bartenders, barbers, and many others. One court of appeals has even applied it to fortune tellers. All that is required to make something a "profession," according to these courts, is that it involves personalized services and requires a professional license from the State. But that gives the States unfettered power to reduce a group's First Amendment rights by simply imposing a licensing requirement. States cannot choose the protection that speech receives under the First Amendment, as that would give them a powerful tool to impose "invidious discrimination of disfavored subjects."

In sum, neither California nor the Ninth Circuit has identified a persuasive reason for treating professional speech as a unique category that is exempt from ordinary First Amendment principles. We do not foreclose the possibility that some such reason exists. We need not do so because the licensed notice cannot survive even intermediate scrutiny. California asserts a single interest to justify the licensed notice: providing low-income women with information about state-sponsored services. Assuming that this is a substantial state interest, the licensed notice is not sufficiently drawn to achieve it.

If California's goal is to educate low-income women about the services it provides, then the licensed notice is "wildly underinclusive." The notice applies only to clinics that have a "primary purpose" of "providing family planning or pregnancy-related services" and that provide two of six categories of specific services. Other clinics that have another primary purpose, or that provide only one category of those services, also serve low-income women and could educate them about the State's services. According to the legislative record, California has "nearly 1,000 community clinics"—including "federally designated community health centers, migrant health centers, rural health centers, and frontier health centers"—that "serv[e] more than 5.6 million patients . . . annually through over 17 million patient encounters." But most of those clinics are excluded from the licensed notice requirement without explanation. Such "[u]nderinclusiveness raises serious doubts about whether the government is in fact pursuing the interest it invokes, rather than disfavoring a particular speaker or viewpoint." The FACT Act also excludes, without explanation, federal clinics and Family PACT providers from the licensed-notice requirement.

The FACT Act's exemption for these clinics, which serve many women who are pregnant or could become pregnant in the future, demonstrates the disconnect between its stated purpose and its actual scope. Yet "[p]recision . . . must be the touchstone" when it comes to regulations of speech, which "so closely touc[h] our most precious freedoms."

Further, California could inform low-income women about its services "without burdening a speaker with unwanted speech." Most obviously, it could inform the women itself with a public-information campaign. California could even post the information on public property near crisis pregnancy centers. California argues that it has already tried an advertising campaign, and that many women who are eligible for publicly-funded healthcare have not enrolled. But California has identified no evidence to that effect. And regardless, a "tepid response" does not prove that an advertising campaign is not a sufficient alternative. California cannot co-opt the licensed facilities to deliver its message for it. "[T]he First Amendment does not permit the State to sacrifice speech for efficiency."

In short, petitioners are likely to succeed on the merits of their challenge to the licensed notice. Contrary to the suggestion in the dissent, we do not question the legality of health and safety warnings long considered permissible, or purely factual and uncontroversial disclosures about commercial products.

III

We need not decide what type of state interest is sufficient to sustain a disclosure requirement like the unlicensed notice. California has not demonstrated any

D. What Is an Infringement of Freedom of Speech?

justification for the unlicensed notice that is more than "purely hypothetical." The only justification that the California Legislature put forward was ensuring that "pregnant women in California know when they are getting medical care from licensed professionals." At oral argument, however, California denied that the justification for the FACT Act was that women "go into [crisis pregnancy centers] and they don't realize what they are." Indeed, California points to nothing suggesting that pregnant women do not already know that the covered facilities are staffed by unlicensed medical professionals. The services that trigger the unlicensed notice—such as having "volunteers who collect health information from clients," "advertis[ing] . . . pregnancy options counseling," and offering over-the-counter "pregnancy testing,"—do not require a medical license. And California already makes it a crime for individuals without a medical license to practice medicine. At this preliminary stage of the litigation, we agree that petitioners are likely to prevail on the question whether California has proved a justification for the unlicensed notice.

Even if California had presented a nonhypothetical justification for the unlicensed notice, the FACT Act unduly burdens protected speech. The unlicensed notice imposes a government-scripted, speaker-based disclosure requirement that is wholly disconnected from California's informational interest. It requires covered facilities to post California's precise notice, no matter what the facilities say on site or in their advertisements. And it covers a curiously narrow subset of speakers. While the licensed notice applies to facilities that provide "family planning" services and "contraception or contraceptive methods," the California Legislature dropped these triggering conditions for the unlicensed notice. The unlicensed notice applies only to facilities that primarily provide "pregnancy-related" services. Thus, a facility that advertises and provides pregnancy tests is covered by the unlicensed notice, but a facility across the street that advertises and provides nonprescription contraceptives is excluded—even though the latter is no less likely to make women think it is licensed. This Court's precedents are deeply skeptical of laws that "distinguis[h] among different speakers, allowing speech by some but not others." Speaker-based laws run the risk that "the State has left unburdened those speakers whose messages are in accord with its own views."

The application of the unlicensed notice to advertisements demonstrates just how burdensome it is. The notice applies to all "print and digital advertising materials" by an unlicensed covered facility. These materials must include a government-drafted statement that "[t]his facility is not licensed as a medical facility by the State of California and has no licensed medical provider who provides or directly supervises the provision of services." An unlicensed facility must call attention to the notice, instead of its own message, by some method such as larger text or contrasting type or color. This scripted language must be posted in English and as many other languages as California chooses to require. As California conceded at oral argument, a billboard for an unlicensed facility that says "Choose Life" would have to surround that two-word statement with a 29-word statement from the government, in as many as 13 different languages. In this way, the unlicensed notice drowns out the facility's own message. More likely, the "detail required" by the unlicensed notice "effectively rules out" the possibility of having such a billboard in the first place. We express no view on the legality of a similar disclosure requirement that is better supported or less burdensome.

We hold that petitioners are likely to succeed on the merits of their claim that the FACT Act violates the First Amendment.

Justice KENNEDY, with whom THE CHIEF JUSTICE, Justice ALITO, and Justice GORSUCH join, concurring.

I join the Court's opinion in all respects. This separate writing seeks to underscore that the apparent viewpoint discrimination here is a matter of serious constitutional concern. The Court, in my view, is correct not to reach this question. It was not sufficiently developed, and the rationale for the Court's decision today suffices to resolve the case.

It does appear that viewpoint discrimination is inherent in the design and structure of this Act. This law is a paradigmatic example of the serious threat presented when government seeks to impose its own message in the place of individual speech, thought, and expression. For here the State requires primarily pro-life pregnancy centers to promote the State's own preferred message advertising abortions. This compels individuals to contradict their most deeply held beliefs, beliefs grounded in basic philosophical, ethical, or religious precepts, or all of these. And the history of the Act's passage and its underinclusive application suggest a real possibility that these individuals were targeted because of their beliefs.

The California Legislature included in its official history the congratulatory statement that the Act was part of California's legacy of "forward thinking." But it is not forward thinking to force individuals to "be an instrument for fostering public adherence to an ideological point of view [they] fin[d] unacceptable." It is forward thinking to begin by reading the First Amendment as ratified in 1791; to understand the history of authoritarian government as the Founders then knew it; to confirm that history since then shows how relentless authoritarian regimes are in their attempts to stifle free speech; and to carry those lessons onward as we seek to preserve and teach the necessity of freedom of speech for the generations to come. Governments must not be allowed to force persons to express a message contrary to their deepest convictions. Freedom of speech secures freedom of thought and belief. This law imperils those liberties.

Justice BREYER, with whom Justice GINSBURG, Justice SOTOMAYOR, and Justice KAGAN joins, dissenting.

The petitioners ask us to consider whether two sections of a California statute violate the First Amendment. The first section requires licensed medical facilities (that provide women with assistance involving pregnancy or family planning) to tell those women where they might obtain help, including financial help, with comprehensive family planning services, prenatal care, and abortion. The second requires *un*licensed facilities offering somewhat similar services to make clear that they are unlicensed. In my view both statutory sections are likely constitutional, and I dissent from the Court's contrary conclusions.

I

Before turning to the specific law before us, I focus upon the general interpretation of the First Amendment that the majority says it applies. It applies heightened scrutiny to the Act because the Act, in its view, is "content based."

D. What Is an Infringement of Freedom of Speech?

"As a general matter," the majority concludes, such laws are "presumptively unconstitutional" and are subject to "stringent" review.

This constitutional approach threatens to create serious problems. Because much, perhaps most, human behavior takes place through speech and because much, perhaps most, law regulates that speech in terms of its content, the majority's approach at the least threatens considerable litigation over the constitutional validity of much, perhaps most, government regulation. Virtually every disclosure law could be considered "content based," for virtually every disclosure law requires individuals "to speak a particular message." Thus, the majority's view, if taken literally, could radically change prior law, perhaps placing much securities law or consumer protection law at constitutional risk, depending on how broadly its exceptions are interpreted.

The majority, at the end of Part II of its opinion, perhaps recognizing this problem, adds a general disclaimer. It says that it does not "question the legality of health and safety warnings long considered permissible, or purely factual and uncontroversial disclosures about commercial products." But this generally phrased disclaimer would seem more likely to invite litigation than to provide needed limitation and clarification. The majority, for example, does not explain why the Act here, which is justified in part by health and safety considerations, does not fall within its "health" category. Nor does the majority opinion offer any reasoned basis that might help apply its disclaimer for distinguishing lawful from unlawful disclosures. In the absence of a reasoned explanation of the disclaimer's meaning and rationale, the disclaimer is unlikely to withdraw the invitation to litigation that the majority's general broad "content-based" test issues. That test invites courts around the Nation to apply an unpredictable First Amendment to ordinary social and economic regulation, striking down disclosure laws that judges may disfavor, while upholding others, all without grounding their decisions in reasoned principle.

Precedent does not require a test such as the majority's. Rather, in saying the Act is not a longstanding health and safety law, the Court substitutes its own approach—without a defining standard—for an approach that was reasonably clear. Historically, the Court has been wary of claims that regulation of business activity, particularly health-related activity, violates the Constitution. Ever since this Court departed from the approach it set forth in Lochner v. New York (1905), ordinary economic and social legislation has been thought to raise little constitutional concern.

I, too, value this role that the First Amendment plays—in an appropriate case. But here, the majority enunciates a general test that reaches far beyond the area where this Court has examined laws closely in the service of those goals. And, in suggesting that heightened scrutiny applies to much economic and social legislation, the majority pays those First Amendment goals a serious disservice through dilution. Using the First Amendment to strike down economic and social laws that legislatures long would have thought themselves free to enact will, for the American public, obscure, not clarify, the true value of protecting freedom of speech.

Still, what about this specific case? The disclosure at issue here concerns speech related to abortion. It involves health, differing moral values, and differing points of view. Thus, rather than set forth broad, new, First Amendment principles, I believe that we should focus more directly upon precedent more closely related to the case at hand. This Court has more than once considered disclosure laws relating to reproductive health. Though those rules or holdings have changed over time, they should govern our disposition of this case.

In Planned Parenthood of Southeastern Pa. v. Casey (1992), the Court again considered a state law that required doctors to provide information to a woman deciding whether to proceed with an abortion. That law required the doctor to tell the woman about the nature of the abortion procedure, the health risks of abortion and of childbirth, the " 'probable gestational age of the unborn child,' " and the availability of printed materials describing the fetus, medical assistance for childbirth, potential child support, and the agencies that would provide adoption services (or other alternatives to abortion). This time a joint opinion of the Court, in judging whether the State could impose these informational requirements, asked whether doing so imposed an "undue burden" upon women seeking an abortion. It held that it did not. Hence the statute was constitutional. The joint opinion stated that the statutory requirements amounted to "reasonable measure[s] to ensure an informed choice, one which might cause the woman to choose childbirth over abortion."

The joint opinion specifically discussed the First Amendment, the constitutional provision now directly before us. It concluded that the statute did not violate the First Amendment. It wrote: "All that is left of petitioners' argument is an asserted First Amendment right of a physician not to provide information about the risks of abortion, and childbirth, in a manner mandated by the State. To be sure, the physician's First Amendment rights not to speak are implicated, but only as part of the practice of medicine, subject to reasonable licensing and regulation by the State. We see no constitutional infirmity in the requirement that the physician provide the information mandated by the State here."

Thus, the Court considered the State's statutory requirements, including the requirement that the doctor must inform his patient about where she could learn how to have the newborn child adopted (if carried to term) and how she could find related financial assistance. To repeat the point, the Court then held that the State's requirements did *not* violate either the Constitution's protection of free speech or its protection of a woman's right to choose to have an abortion.

If a State can lawfully require a doctor to tell a woman seeking an abortion about adoption services, why should it not be able, as here, to require a medical counselor to tell a woman seeking prenatal care or other reproductive healthcare about childbirth and abortion services? As the question suggests, there is no convincing reason to distinguish between information about adoption and information about abortion in this context. After all, the rule of law embodies evenhandedness, and "what is sauce for the goose is normally sauce for the gander."

The majority also finds it "[t]ellin[g]" that general practice clinics—*i.e.,* paid clinics—are not required to provide the licensed notice. But the lack-of-information problem that the statute seeks to ameliorate is a problem that the State explains is commonly found among low-income women. That those with low income might lack the time to become fully informed and that this circumstance might prove disproportionately correlated with income is not intuitively surprising. Nor is it surprising that those with low income, whatever they choose in respect to pregnancy, might find information about financial assistance particularly useful. There is "nothing inherently suspect" about this distinction, which is not "based on the content of [the advocacy] each group

D. What Is an Infringement of Freedom of Speech?

offers," but upon the patients the group generally serves and the needs of that population.

Accordingly, the majority's reliance on cases that prohibit rather than require speech is misplaced. I agree that "'in the fields of medicine and public heath, . . . information can save lives,'" but the licensed disclosure *serves* that informational interest by requiring clinics to notify patients of the availability of state resources for family planning services, prenatal care, and abortion, which—unlike the majority's examples of normative statements—is truthful and nonmisleading information. Abortion is a controversial topic and a source of normative debate, but the availability of state resources is not a normative statement or a fact of debatable truth. The disclosure includes information about resources available should a woman seek to continue her pregnancy or terminate it, and it expresses no official preference for one choice over the other. Similarly, the majority highlights an interest that often underlies our decisions in respect to speech prohibitions—the marketplace of ideas. But that marketplace is fostered, not hindered, by providing information to patients to enable them to make fully informed medical decisions in respect to their pregnancies.

Of course, one might take the majority's decision to mean that speech about abortion is special, that it involves in this case not only professional medical matters, but also views based on deeply held religious and moral beliefs about the nature of the practice. But assuming that is so, the law's insistence upon treating like cases alike should lead us to reject the petitioners' arguments that I have discussed. This insistence, the need for evenhandedness, should prove particularly weighty in a case involving abortion rights. That is because Americans hold strong, and differing, views about the matter. Some Americans believe that abortion involves the death of a live and innocent human being. Others believe that the ability to choose an abortion is "central to personal dignity and autonomy," and note that the failure to allow women to choose an abortion involves the deaths of innocent women. We have previously noted that we cannot try to adjudicate who is right and who is wrong in this moral debate. But we can do our best to interpret American constitutional law so that it applies fairly within a Nation whose citizens strongly hold these different points of view. That is one reason why it is particularly important to interpret the First Amendment so that it applies evenhandedly as between those who disagree so strongly. For this reason too a Constitution that allows States to insist that medical providers tell women about the possibility of adoption should also allow States similarly to insist that medical providers tell women about the possibility of abortion.

II

The second statutory provision covers pregnancy-related facilities that provide women with certain medical-type services (such as obstetric ultrasounds or sonograms, pregnancy diagnosis, counseling about pregnancy options, or prenatal care), are not licensed as medical facilities by the State, and do not have a licensed medical provider on site. The statute says that such a facility must disclose that it is not "licensed as a medical facility." And it must make this disclosure in a posted notice and in advertising.

The majority does not question that the State's interest (ensuring that "pregnant women in California know when they are getting medical care from licensed professionals") is the type of informational interest that [prior decisions encompass]. There is no basis for finding the State's interest "hypothetical." The legislature heard that information-related delays in qualified healthcare negatively affect women seeking to terminate their pregnancies as well as women carrying their pregnancies to term, with delays in qualified prenatal care causing life-long health problems for infants. Even without such testimony, it is "self-evident" that patients might think they are receiving qualified medical care when they enter facilities that collect health information, perform obstetric ultrasounds or sonograms, diagnose pregnancy, and provide counseling about pregnancy options or other prenatal care. The State's conclusion to that effect is certainly reasonable.

Relatedly, the majority suggests that the Act is suspect because it covers some speakers but not others. There is no cause for such concern here. The Act does not, on its face, distinguish between facilities that favor pro-life and those that favor pro-choice points of view. Nor is there any convincing evidence before us or in the courts below that discrimination was the purpose or the effect of the statute. Notably, California does not single out pregnancy-related facilities for this type of disclosure requirement. And it is unremarkable that the State excluded the provision of family planning and contraceptive services as triggering conditions. After all, the State was seeking to ensure that "pregnant women in California know when they are getting medical care from licensed professionals," and pregnant women generally do not need contraceptive services.

Finally, the majority concludes that the Act is overly burdensome. But these and similar claims are claims that the statute could be applied unconstitutionally, not that it is unconstitutional on its face. As I understand the Act, it would require disclosure in no more than two languages—English and Spanish—in the vast majority of California's 58 counties. The exception is Los Angeles County, where, given the large number of different-language speaking groups, expression in many languages may prove necessary to communicate the message to those whom that message will help. Whether the requirement of 13 different languages goes too far and is unnecessarily burdensome in light of the need to secure the statutory objectives is a matter that concerns Los Angeles County alone, and it is a proper subject for a Los Angeles-based as applied challenge in light of whatever facts a plaintiff finds relevant. At most, such facts might show a need for fewer languages, not invalidation of the statute.

In Janus v. American Federation, 138 S. Ct. 2448 (2018), the Court overruled precedent and held that public employees who are non-union members cannot be required to pay the share of the union dues that go to support the collective bargaining activities of the union. The Court said that this requirement is impermissible compelled speech and association. *Janus* is presented below, in Chapter 5, as part of the discussion of freedom of association.

But in other cases, the Court has been more willing to allow compelled speech. In Johannes v. Livestock Marketing Assn., 544 U.S. 550 (2005), the Court upheld a $1 per head assessment on livestock to fund a generic ad campaign

D. What Is an Infringement of Freedom of Speech?

encouraging beef consumption. The Court stressed that the government may impose taxes, including on specific items, to engage in speech. The Court noted that livestock producers were not themselves forced to engage in any speech.

More dramatically, in Rumsfeld v. Forum for Academic & Institutional Rights, the Court upheld a provision of federal law that requires that law schools allow the military to recruit on their premises.

RUMSFELD v. FORUM FOR ACADEMIC & INSTITUTIONAL RIGHTS, INC.
547 U.S. 47 (2006)

Chief Justice ROBERTS delivered the opinion of the Court.

When law schools began restricting the access of military recruiters to their students because of disagreement with the Government's policy on homosexuals in the military, Congress responded by enacting the Solomon Amendment. *See* 10 U.S.C.A. §983. That provision specifies that if any part of an institution of higher education denies military recruiters access equal to that provided other recruiters, the entire institution would lose certain federal funds. The law schools responded by suing, alleging that the Solomon Amendment infringed their First Amendment freedoms of speech and association. The District Court disagreed but was reversed by a divided panel of the Court of Appeals for the Third Circuit, which ordered the District Court to enter a preliminary injunction against enforcement of the Solomon Amendment.

I

Respondent Forum for Academic and Institutional Rights, Inc. (FAIR), is an association of law schools and law faculties. They would like to restrict military recruiting on their campuses because they object to the policy Congress has adopted with respect to homosexuals in the military. *See* 10 U.S.C. §654.[50] The Solomon Amendment, however, forces institutions to choose between enforcing their nondiscrimination policy against military recruiters in this way and continuing to receive specified federal funding.

II

The Solomon Amendment denies federal funding to an institution of higher education that "has a policy or practice . . . that either prohibits, or in effect prevents" the military "from gaining access to campuses, or access to students . . . on campuses, for purposes of military recruiting in a manner that is at least equal in quality and scope to the access to campuses and to students that is provided to any other employer." 10 U.S.C.A. §983(b). The statute provides

---

50. Under this policy, a person generally may not serve in the Armed Forces if he has engaged in homosexual acts, stated that he is a homosexual, or married a person of the same sex. Respondents do not challenge that policy in this litigation. [Footnote by the Court.]

an exception for an institution with "a longstanding policy of pacifism based on historical religious affiliation." The Government and FAIR agree on what this statute requires: In order for a law school and its university to receive federal funding, the law school must offer military recruiters the same access to its campus and students that it provides to the nonmilitary recruiter receiving the most favorable access.

III

The Constitution grants Congress the power to "provide for the common Defence," "[t]o raise and support Armies," and "[t]o provide and maintain a Navy." Art. I, §8, cls. 1, 12-13. Congress' power in this area "is broad and sweeping," and there is no dispute in this case that it includes the authority to require campus access for military recruiters. That is, of course, unless Congress exceeds constitutional limitations on its power in enacting such legislation. But the fact that legislation that raises armies is subject to First Amendment constraints does not mean that we ignore the purpose of this legislation when determining its constitutionality; as we [have] recognized "judicial deference . . . is at its apogee" when Congress legislates under its authority to raise and support armies.

Although Congress has broad authority to legislate on matters of military recruiting, it nonetheless chose to secure campus access for military recruiters indirectly, through its Spending Clause power. The Solomon Amendment gives universities a choice: Either allow military recruiters the same access to students afforded any other recruiter or forgo certain federal funds. Congress' decision to proceed indirectly does not reduce the deference given to Congress in the area of military affairs. Congress' choice to promote its goal by creating a funding condition deserves at least as deferential treatment as if Congress had imposed a mandate on universities. Because the First Amendment would not prevent Congress from directly imposing the Solomon Amendment's access requirement, the statute does not place an unconstitutional condition on the receipt of federal funds.

A

The Solomon Amendment neither limits what law schools may say nor requires them to say anything. Law schools remain free under the statute to express whatever views they may have on the military's congressionally mandated employment policy, all the while retaining eligibility for federal funds. As a general matter, the Solomon Amendment regulates conduct, not speech. It affects what law schools must do — afford equal access to military recruiters — not what they may or may not say.

Nevertheless, the Third Circuit concluded that the Solomon Amendment violates law schools' freedom of speech in a number of ways. First, in assisting military recruiters, law schools provide some services, such as sending e-mails and distributing flyers, that clearly involve speech. The Court of Appeals held that in supplying these services law schools are unconstitutionally compelled to speak the Government's message. Second, military recruiters are, to some extent, speaking while they are on campus. The Court of Appeals held that, by forcing law schools to permit the military on campus to express its message, the Solomon Amendment unconstitutionally requires law schools to host or

D. What Is an Infringement of Freedom of Speech?

accommodate the military's speech. Third, although the Court of Appeals thought that the Solomon Amendment regulated speech, it held in the alternative that, if the statute regulates conduct, this conduct is expressive and regulating it unconstitutionally infringes law schools' right to engage in expressive conduct. We consider each issue in turn.

1

Some of this Court's leading First Amendment precedents have established the principle that freedom of speech prohibits the government from telling people what they must say. In West Virginia Bd. of Ed. v. Barnette (1943), we held unconstitutional a state law requiring schoolchildren to recite the Pledge of Allegiance and to salute the flag. And in Wooley v. Maynard (1977), we held unconstitutional another that required New Hampshire motorists to display the state motto — "Live Free or Die" — on their license plates.

The Solomon Amendment does not require any similar expression by law schools. Nonetheless, recruiting assistance provided by the schools often includes elements of speech. For example, schools may send e-mails or post notices on bulletin boards on an employer's behalf. Law schools offering such services to other recruiters must also send e-mails and post notices on behalf of the military to comply with the Solomon Amendment. As FAIR points out, these compelled statements of fact ("The U.S. Army recruiter will meet interested students in Room 123 at 11 A.M."), like compelled statements of opinion, are subject to First Amendment scrutiny.

This sort of recruiting assistance, however, is a far cry from the compelled speech in *Barnette* and *Wooley*. The Solomon Amendment, unlike the laws at issue in those cases, does not dictate the content of the speech at all, which is only "compelled" if, and to the extent, the school provides such speech for other recruiters. There is nothing in this case approaching a government-mandated pledge or motto that the school must endorse.

The compelled speech to which the law schools point is plainly incidental to the Solomon Amendment's regulation of conduct, and "it has never been deemed an abridgment of freedom of speech or press to make a course of conduct illegal merely because the conduct was in part initiated, evidenced, or carried out by means of language, either spoken, written, or printed." Congress, for example, can prohibit employers from discriminating in hiring on the basis of race. The fact that this will require an employer to take down a sign reading "White Applicants Only" hardly means that the law should be analyzed as one regulating the employer's speech rather than conduct. Compelling a law school that sends scheduling e-mails for other recruiters to send one for a military recruiter is simply not the same as forcing a student to pledge allegiance, or forcing a Jehovah's Witness to display the motto "Live Free or Die," and it trivializes the freedom protected in *Barnette* and *Wooley* to suggest that it is.

2

Our compelled-speech cases are not limited to the situation in which an individual must personally speak the government's message. We have also in a number of instances limited the government's ability to force one speaker to host or accommodate another speaker's message. See Hurley v. Irish-American Gay, Lesbian and Bisexual Group of Boston, Inc. (1995) (state law cannot require a parade to include a group whose message the parade's organizer does not wish to send); Pacific Gas & Elec. Co. v. Public Util. Comm'n of Cal. (1986) (state agency cannot require a utility company to include a third-party newsletter in its billing envelope); Miami Herald Publishing Co. v. Tornillo (right-of-reply statute violates editors' right to determine the content of their newspapers). Relying on these precedents, the Third Circuit concluded that the Solomon Amendment unconstitutionally compels law schools to accommodate the military's message "[b]y requiring schools to include military recruiters in the interviews and recruiting receptions the schools arrange."

The compelled-speech violation in each of our prior cases, however, resulted from the fact that the complaining speaker's own message was affected by the speech it was forced to accommodate. The expressive nature of a parade was central to our holding in *Hurley*. We concluded that because "every participating unit affects the message conveyed by the [parade's] private organizers," a law dictating that a particular group must be included in the parade "alter[s] the expressive content of th[e] parade." As a result, we held that the State's public accommodation law, as applied to a private parade, "violates the fundamental rule of protection under the First Amendment, that a speaker has the autonomy to choose the content of his own message."

In this case, accommodating the military's message does not affect the law schools' speech, because the schools are not speaking when they host interviews and recruiting receptions. Unlike a parade organizer's choice of parade contingents, a law school's decision to allow recruiters on campus is not inherently expressive. Law schools facilitate recruiting to assist their students in obtaining jobs. A law school's recruiting services lack the expressive quality of a parade, a newsletter, or the editorial page of a newspaper; its accommodation of a military recruiter's message is not compelled speech because the accommodation does not sufficiently interfere with any message of the school.

The schools respond that if they treat military and nonmilitary recruiters alike in order to comply with the Solomon Amendment, they could be viewed as sending the message that they see nothing wrong with the military's policies, when they do. We rejected a similar argument in PruneYard Shopping Center v. Robins (1980). In that case, we upheld a state law requiring a shopping center owner to allow certain expressive activities by others on its property. We explained that there was little likelihood that the views of those engaging in the expressive activities would be identified with the owner, who remained free to disassociate himself from those views and who was "not . . . being compelled to affirm [a] belief in any governmentally prescribed position or view."

The same is true here. Nothing about recruiting suggests that law schools agree with any speech by recruiters, and nothing in the Solomon Amendment restricts what the law schools may say about the military's policies.

3

Having rejected the view that the Solomon Amendment impermissibly regulates speech, we must still consider whether the expressive nature of the conduct regulated by the statute brings that conduct within the First Amendment's protection. [W]e have extended First Amendment protection only to conduct that is inherently expressive. In Texas v. Johnson (1989), for example, we held that burning the American flag was sufficiently expressive to warrant First Amendment protection.

Unlike flag burning, the conduct regulated by the Solomon Amendment is not inherently expressive. Prior to the adoption of the Solomon Amendment's equal-access requirement, law schools "expressed" their disagreement with the military by treating military recruiters differently from other recruiters. But these actions were expressive only because the law schools accompanied their conduct with speech explaining it. For example, the point of requiring military interviews to be conducted on the undergraduate campus is not "overwhelmingly apparent." An observer who sees military recruiters interviewing away from the law school has no way of knowing whether the law school is expressing its disapproval of the military, all the law school's interview rooms are full, or the military recruiters decided for reasons of their own that they would rather interview someplace else. The expressive component of a law school's actions is not created by the conduct itself but by the speech that accompanies it. The fact that such explanatory speech is necessary is strong evidence that the conduct at issue here is not so inherently expressive that it warrants protection. If combining speech and conduct were enough to create expressive conduct, a regulated party could always transform conduct into "speech" simply by talking about it.

B

FAIR argues that the Solomon Amendment violates law schools' freedom of expressive association. According to FAIR, law schools' ability to express their message that discrimination on the basis of sexual orientation is wrong is significantly affected by the presence of military recruiters on campus and the schools' obligation to assist them.

The Solomon Amendment, however, does not similarly affect a law school's associational rights. To comply with the statute, law schools must allow military recruiters on campus and assist them in whatever way the school chooses to assist other employers. Law schools therefore "associate" with military recruiters in the sense that they interact with them. But recruiters are not part of the law school. Recruiters are, by definition, outsiders who come onto campus for the limited purpose of trying to hire students—not to become members of the school's expressive association. This distinction is critical. The Solomon Amendment does not force a law school "to accept members it does not desire." The law schools say that allowing military recruiters equal access impairs their own expression by requiring them to associate with the recruiters, but just as saying conduct is undertaken for expressive purposes cannot make it symbolic speech, so too a speaker cannot "erect a shield" against laws requiring access "simply by asserting" that mere association "would impair its message."

The Solomon Amendment has no similar effect on a law school's associational rights. Students and faculty are free to associate to voice their disapproval of the military's message; nothing about the statute affects the composition of the group by making group membership less desirable. The Solomon Amendment therefore does not violate a law school's First Amendment rights. A military recruiter's mere presence on campus does not violate a law school's right to associate, regardless of how repugnant the law school considers the recruiter's message.

The right to not speak includes a right to not disclose one's identity when speaking. In Talley v. California, 362 U.S. 60 (1960), the Supreme Court declared unconstitutional a ban on anonymous handbills. The Court observed that the "obnoxious press licensing law of England, which was also enforced on the Colonies was due in part to the knowledge that exposure of the names of printers, writers and distributors would lessen the circulation of literature critical of the government." Justice Black, writing for the Court, said that "[p]ersecuted groups and sects from time to time throughout history have been able to criticize oppressive practices and laws either anonymously or not at all."

In McIntyre v. Ohio Elections Commn., the Court declared unconstitutional a law that prohibited the distribution of anonymous campaign literature.

McINTYRE v. OHIO ELECTIONS COMMISSION
514 U.S. 334 (1995)

Justice STEVENS delivered the opinion of the Court.

The question presented is whether an Ohio statute that prohibits the distribution of anonymous campaign literature is a "law . . . abridging the freedom of speech" within the meaning of the First Amendment.

I

On April 27, 1988, Margaret McIntyre distributed leaflets to persons attending a public meeting at the Blendon Middle School in Westerville, Ohio. At this meeting, the superintendent of schools planned to discuss an imminent referendum on a proposed school tax levy. The leaflets expressed Mrs. McIntyre's opposition to the levy. There is no suggestion that the text of her message was false, misleading, or libelous. She had composed and printed it on her home computer and had paid a professional printer to make additional copies. Some of the handbills identified her as the author; others merely purported to express the views of "CONCERNED PARENTS AND TAX PAYERS." Except for the help provided by her son and a friend, who placed some of the leaflets on car windshields in the school parking lot, Mrs. McIntyre acted independently. While Mrs. McIntyre distributed her handbills, an official of the school district, who supported the tax proposal, advised her that the unsigned leaflets did not conform to the Ohio election laws. Undeterred, Mrs. McIntyre appeared at another meeting on the next evening and handed out more of the handbills.

[T]he same school official filed a complaint with the Ohio Elections Commission charging that Mrs. McIntyre's distribution of unsigned leaflets violated the Ohio Code [which prohibits the distribution of anonymous material in connection with any election]. The commission agreed and imposed a fine of $100. [The Ohio law] provides: "No person shall write, print, post, or distribute, or cause to be written, printed, posted, or distributed, a notice, placard, dodger, advertisement, sample ballot, or any other form of general publication which is designed to promote the nomination or election or defeat of a candidate, or to promote the adoption or defeat of any issue, or to influence the voters in any election . . . unless there appears on such form of publication in a conspicuous

D. What Is an Infringement of Freedom of Speech?

place or is contained within said statement the name and residence or business address of the chairman, treasurer, or secretary of the organization issuing the same, or the person who issues, makes, or is responsible therefor."

II

"Anonymous pamphlets, leaflets, brochures and even books have played an important role in the progress of mankind." Talley v. California. Great works of literature have frequently been produced by authors writing under assumed names.[51] Despite readers' curiosity and the public's interest in identifying the creator of a work of art, an author generally is free to decide whether or not to disclose his or her true identity. The decision in favor of anonymity may be motivated by fear of economic or official retaliation, by concern about social ostracism, or merely by a desire to preserve as much of one's privacy as possible. Whatever the motivation may be, at least in the field of literary endeavor, the interest in having anonymous works enter the marketplace of ideas unquestionably outweighs any public interest in requiring disclosure as a condition of entry. Accordingly, an author's decision to remain anonymous, like other decisions concerning omissions or additions to the content of a publication, is an aspect of the freedom of speech protected by the First Amendment.

The freedom to publish anonymously extends beyond the literary realm. On occasion, quite apart from any threat of persecution, an advocate may believe her ideas will be more persuasive if her readers are unaware of her identity. Anonymity thereby provides a way for a writer who may be personally unpopular to ensure that readers will not prejudge her message simply because they do not like its proponent. Thus, even in the field of political rhetoric, where "the identity of the speaker is an important component of many attempts to persuade," the most effective advocates have sometimes opted for anonymity.

Indeed, the speech in which Mrs. McIntyre engaged—handing out leaflets in the advocacy of a politically controversial viewpoint—is the essence of First Amendment expression. That this advocacy occurred in the heat of a controversial referendum vote only strengthens the protection afforded to Mrs. McIntyre's expression: Urgent, important, and effective speech can be no less protected than impotent speech, lest the right to speak be relegated to those instances when it is least needed. No form of speech is entitled to greater constitutional protection than Mrs. McIntyre's.

When a law burdens core political speech, we apply "exacting scrutiny," and we uphold the restriction only if it is narrowly tailored to serve an overriding state interest.

---

51. American names such as Mark Twain (Samuel Langhorne Clemens) and O. Henry (William Sydney Porter) come readily to mind. Benjamin Franklin employed numerous different pseudonyms. Distinguished French authors such as Voltaire (Francois Marie Arouet) and George Sand (Amandine Aurore Lucie Dupin), and British authors such as George Eliot (Mary Ann Evans), Charles Lamb (sometimes wrote as "Elia"), and Charles Dickens (sometimes wrote as "Boz"), also published under assumed names. Indeed, some believe the works of Shakespeare were actually written by the Earl of Oxford rather than by William Shakespeare of Stratford-on-Avon. [Footnote by the Court.]

IV

Nevertheless, the State argues that, even under the strictest standard of review, the disclosure requirement is justified by two important and legitimate state interests. Ohio judges its interest in preventing fraudulent and libelous statements and its interest in providing the electorate with relevant information to be sufficiently compelling to justify the anonymous speech ban. These two interests necessarily overlap to some extent, but it is useful to discuss them separately.

Insofar as the interest in informing the electorate means nothing more than the provision of additional information that may either buttress or undermine the argument in a document, we think the identity of the speaker is no different from other components of the document's content that the author is free to include or exclude.

The state interest in preventing fraud and libel stands on a different footing. We agree with Ohio's submission that this interest carries special weight during election campaigns when false statements, if credited, may have serious adverse consequences for the public at large.

Ohio's prohibition of anonymous leaflets plainly is not its principal weapon against fraud. Rather, it serves as an aid to enforcement of the specific prohibitions and as a deterrent to the making of false statements by unscrupulous prevaricators. As this case demonstrates, the prohibition encompasses documents that are not even arguably false or misleading. It applies not only to the activities of candidates and their organized supporters, but also to individuals acting independently and using only their own modest resources. It applies not only to elections of public officers, but also to ballot issues that present neither a substantial risk of libel nor any potential appearance of corrupt advantage. It applies not only to leaflets distributed on the eve of an election, when the opportunity for reply is limited, but also to those distributed months in advance. It applies no matter what the character or strength of the author's interest in anonymity. Moreover, as this case also demonstrates, the absence of the author's name on a document does not necessarily protect either that person or a distributor of a forbidden document from being held responsible for compliance with the Election Code. Nor has the State explained why it can more easily enforce the direct bans on disseminating false documents against anonymous authors and distributors than against wrongdoers who might use false names and addresses in an attempt to avoid detection. We recognize that a State's enforcement interest might justify a more limited identification requirement, but Ohio has shown scant cause for inhibiting the leafletting at issue here.

VI

Under our Constitution, anonymous pamphleteering is not a pernicious, fraudulent practice, but an honorable tradition of advocacy and of dissent. Anonymity is a shield from the tyranny of the majority. It thus exemplifies the purpose behind the Bill of Rights, and of the First Amendment in particular: to protect unpopular individuals from retaliation—and their ideas from suppression—at the hand of an intolerant society. The right to remain anonymous may be abused when it shields fraudulent conduct. But political

D. What Is an Infringement of Freedom of Speech?

speech by its nature will sometimes have unpalatable consequences, and, in general, our society accords greater weight to the value of free speech than to the dangers of its misuse.

Justice THOMAS, concurring in the judgment.

I agree with the majority's conclusion that Ohio's election law is inconsistent with the First Amendment. I would apply, however, a different methodology to this case. Instead of asking whether "an honorable tradition" of anonymous speech has existed throughout American history, or what the "value" of anonymous speech might be, we should determine whether the phrase "freedom of speech, or of the press," as originally understood, protected anonymous political leafletting. I believe that it did.

When interpreting the Free Speech and Press Clauses, we must be guided by their original meaning, for "[t]he Constitution is a written instrument. As such its meaning does not alter. That which it meant when adopted, it means now." South Carolina v. United States (1905). We have long recognized that the meaning of the Constitution "must necessarily depend on the words of the constitution [and] the meaning and intention of the convention which framed and proposed it for adoption and ratification to the conventions . . . in the several states." Rhode Island v. Massachusetts (1838). We should seek the original understanding when we interpret the Speech and Press Clauses. When the framers did not discuss the precise question at issue, we have turned to "what history reveals was the contemporaneous understanding of [the Establishment Clause's] guarantees."

Unfortunately, we have no record of discussions of anonymous political expression either in the First Congress, which drafted the Bill of Rights, or in the state ratifying conventions. Thus, our analysis must focus on the practices and beliefs held by the Founders concerning anonymous political articles and pamphlets. There is little doubt that the framers engaged in anonymous political writing. The essays in the Federalist Papers, published under the pseudonym of "Publius," are only the most famous example of the outpouring of anonymous political writing that occurred during the ratification of the Constitution.

[T]he historical evidence indicates that Founding-era Americans opposed attempts to require that anonymous authors reveal their identities on the ground that forced disclosure violated the "freedom of the press." For example, the earliest and most famous American experience with freedom of the press, the 1735 Zenger trial, centered around anonymous political pamphlets. The case involved a printer, John Peter Zenger, who refused to reveal the anonymous authors of published attacks on the Crown Governor of New York. When the Governor and his council could not discover the identity of the authors, they prosecuted Zenger himself for seditious libel.

This evidence leads me to agree with the majority's result, but not its reasoning. The majority fails to seek the original understanding of the First Amendment. I cannot join the majority's analysis because it deviates from our settled approach to interpreting the Constitution and because it superimposes its modern theories concerning expression upon the constitutional text.

Justice SCALIA, with whom THE CHIEF JUSTICE joins, dissenting.

At a time when both political branches of Government and both political parties reflect a popular desire to leave more decisionmaking authority to the States, today's decision moves in the opposite direction, adding to the legacy of inflexible central mandates (irrevocable even by Congress) imposed by this Court's constitutional jurisprudence. [T]he Court invalidates a species of protection for the election process that exists, in a variety of forms, in every State except California, and that has a pedigree dating back to the end of the 19th century. Preferring the views of the English utilitarian philosopher John Stuart Mill to the considered judgment of the American people's elected representatives from coast to coast, the Court discovers a hitherto unknown right-to-be-unknown while engaging in electoral politics. I dissent from this imposition of free-speech imperatives that are demonstrably not those of the American people today, and that there is inadequate reason to believe were those of the society that begat the First Amendment or the Fourteenth.

I do not know where the Court derives its perception that "anonymous pamphleteering is not a pernicious, fraudulent practice, but an honorable tradition of advocacy and of dissent." I can imagine no reason why an anonymous leaflet is any more honorable, as a general matter, than an anonymous phone call or an anonymous letter. It facilitates wrong by eliminating accountability, which is ordinarily the very purpose of the anonymity. There are of course exceptions, and where anonymity is needed to avoid "threats, harassment, or reprisals" the First Amendment will require an exemption from the Ohio law. But to strike down the Ohio law in its general application — and similar laws of 49 other States and the Federal Government — on the ground that all anonymous communication is in our society traditionally sacrosanct, seems to me a distortion of the past that will lead to a coarsening of the future.

Similarly, in Buckley v. American Constitutional Law Foundation, Inc., 525 U.S. 182 (1999), the Court invalidated a law that regulated those gathering signatures for ballot initiatives in Colorado and imposed (1) the requirement that they wear an identification badge bearing the circulator's name and (2) the requirement that proponents of an initiative report the names and addresses of all paid circulators and the amount paid to each circulator.

The Court said that "the restraint on speech in this case is more severe than was the restraint in *McIntyre*. Petition circulation is the less fleeting encounter, for the circulator must endeavor to persuade electors to sign the petition. The injury to speech is heightened for the petition circulator because the badge requirement compels personal name identification at the precise moment when the circulator's interest in anonymity is greatest."

But in a more recent case, John Doe No. 1 v. Reed, 561 U.S. 186 (2010), the Court held that it does not inherently violate the First Amendment for a state to disclose who signed petitions in support of a referendum. The Washington state legislature adopted a law expanding benefits for domestic partners. The process of qualifying a referendum for the ballot requires gathering a specified number of signatures, and individuals must disclose their names and addresses. A request was made under the Washington Public Records Act for the names and addresses of those who signed the petitions.

The Supreme Court focused solely on whether disclosure inherently would violate the First Amendment. The Court, in an opinion by Chief Justice Roberts,

D. What Is an Infringement of Freedom of Speech?

recognized that disclosure burdens freedom of speech and said, "We have a series of precedents considering First Amendment challenges to disclosure requirements in the electoral context. These precedents have reviewed such challenges under what has been termed 'exacting scrutiny.' That standard 'requires a "substantial relation" between the disclosure requirement and a "sufficiently important" governmental interest.' To withstand this scrutiny, 'the strength of the governmental interest must reflect the seriousness of the actual burden on First Amendment rights.'"

The Court found that the government's interest in "(1) preserving the integrity of the electoral process by combating fraud, detecting invalid signatures, and fostering government transparency and accountability" was sufficient to "to justify the burdens of compelled disclosure under the PRA on First Amendment rights." The Court explained, "Public disclosure thus helps ensure that the only signatures counted are those that should be, and that the only referenda placed on the ballot are those that garner enough valid signatures. Public disclosure also promotes transparency and accountability in the electoral process to an extent other measures cannot. In light of the foregoing, we reject plaintiffs' argument and conclude that public disclosure of referendum petitions in general is substantially related to the important interest of preserving the integrity of the electoral process." The Court left open the possibility that there could be a challenge in a particular case, including this one, that disclosure would so burden speech (i.e., signing petitions) as to violate the First Amendment, but it concluded that in general disclosing the signers of petitions does not infringe freedom of speech.

4. *Unconstitutional Conditions*

The unconstitutional condition doctrine is the principle that the government cannot condition a benefit on the requirement that a person forgo a constitutional right. The corollary is that the "government may not deny a benefit to a person because he exercises a constitutional right."[52] Unfortunately, the Supreme Court's decisions in this area appear quite inconsistent in the application of the doctrine. In reading the cases that have applied and that have refused to apply the unconstitutional condition doctrine, it is important to consider whether there is a consistent principle being followed.

Speiser v. Randall is a classic example of the application of the unconstitutional condition doctrine.

SPEISER v. RANDALL, 357 U.S. 513 (1958): Justice BRENNAN delivered the opinion of the Court.

The appellants are honorably discharged veterans of World War II who claimed the veterans' property-tax exemption provided by the California Constitution. Under California law applicants for such exemption must annually complete a standard form of application and file it with the local assessor. The form was revised in 1954 to add an oath by the applicant: "I do not advocate the overthrow

---

52. Regan v. Taxation with Representation of Washington, 461 U.S. 540, 545 (1983), quoting Perry v. Sindermann, 408 U.S. 593, 597 (1972).

of the Government of the United States or of the State of California by force or violence or other unlawful means, nor advocate the support of a foreign Government against the United States in event of hostilities." Each refused to subscribe [to] the oath and struck it from the form which he executed and filed for the tax year 1954-1955. Each contended that the exaction of the oath as a condition of obtaining a tax exemption was forbidden by the Federal Constitution. The respective assessors denied the exemption solely for the refusal to execute the oath.

To deny an exemption to claimants who engage in certain forms of speech is in effect to penalize them for such speech. Its deterrent effect is the same as if the State were to fine them for this speech. The appellees are plainly mistaken in their argument that, because a tax exemption is a "privilege" or "bounty," its denial may not infringe speech. So here, the denial of a tax exemption for engaging in certain speech necessarily will have the effect of coercing the claimants to refrain from the proscribed speech.

The doctrine was followed in Federal Communications Commn. v. League of Women Voters of California, 468 U.S. 364 (1984). The Supreme Court declared unconstitutional a federal statute that prohibited any noncommercial educational broadcasting station that received a grant from the Corporation for Public Broadcasting from engaging in editorializing. The Court said that the government could not condition funds on a requirement that the stations relinquish their right to editorialize.

Yet other cases have allowed the government to condition a benefit on individuals' forgoing their First Amendment rights. In Regan v. Taxation with Representation of Washington, 461 U.S. 540 (1983), the Court upheld a provision of the federal tax law that conditioned tax-exempt status on the requirement that the organization not participate in lobbying or partisan political activities. The Court said, "Congress has not infringed any First Amendment rights or regulated any First Amendment activity. Congress has simply chosen not to pay for TWR's lobbying." The Court said that it found "no indication that the statute was intended to suppress any ideas or any demonstration that it has had that effect." The *Regan* Court concluded, "We have held in several contexts that a legislature's decision not to subsidize the exercise of a fundamental right does not infringe the right, and thus is not subject to strict scrutiny." In other words, the Court rejected the unconstitutional conditions argument even though the government was conditioning a very valuable tax benefit on the requirement that the recipient forgo engaging in First Amendment protected speech.

Two cases applied the unconstitutional conditions doctrine and came to opposite conclusions. In Rust v. Sullivan, the Court upheld a federal law restricting recipients of federal funds from engaging in abortion-related activities. In Legal Services Corp. v. Velazquez, the Court invalidated a restriction on federal legal services funds recipients challenge of welfare laws. In reading these cases, consider whether there is a meaningful distinction between them.

D. What Is an Infringement of Freedom of Speech?

RUST v. SULLIVAN
500 U.S. 173 (1991)

Chief Justice REHNQUIST delivered the opinion of the Court.

These cases concern a facial challenge to Department of Health and Human Services (HHS) regulations which limit the ability of Title X fund recipients to engage in abortion-related activities.

I

In 1970, Congress enacted Title X of the Public Health Service Act (Act), which provides federal funding for family-planning services. The Act authorizes the Secretary to "make grants to and enter into contracts with public or nonprofit private entities to assist in the establishment and operation of voluntary family planning projects which shall offer a broad range of acceptable and effective family planning methods and services." Grants and contracts under Title X must "be made in accordance with such regulations as the Secretary may promulgate." Section 1008 of the Act, however, provides that "[n]one of the funds appropriated under this subchapter shall be used in programs where abortion is a method of family planning." That restriction was intended to ensure that Title X funds would "be used only to support preventive family planning services, population research, infertility services, and other related medical, informational, and educational activities."

In 1988, the Secretary promulgated new regulations designed to provide "'clear and operational guidance' to grantees about how to preserve the distinction between Title X programs and abortion as a method of family planning." The regulations attach three principal conditions on the grant of federal funds for Title X projects. First, the regulations specify that a "Title X project may not provide counseling concerning the use of abortion as a method of family planning or provide referral for abortion as a method of family planning." The Title X project is expressly prohibited from referring a pregnant woman to an abortion provider, even upon specific request. One permissible response to such an inquiry is that "the project does not consider abortion an appropriate method of family planning and therefore does not counsel or refer for abortion."

Second, the regulations broadly prohibit a Title X project from engaging in activities that "encourage, promote or advocate abortion as a method of family planning." Forbidden activities include lobbying for legislation that would increase the availability of abortion as a method of family planning, developing or disseminating materials advocating abortion as a method of family planning, providing speakers to promote abortion as a method of family planning, using legal action to make abortion available in any way as a method of family planning, and paying dues to any group that advocates abortion as a method of family planning as a substantial part of its activities.

Third, the regulations require that Title X projects be organized so that they are "physically and financially separate" from prohibited abortion activities. To be deemed physically and financially separate, "a Title X project must have an objective integrity and independence from prohibited activities. Mere bookkeeping separation of Title X funds from other monies is not sufficient."

II

Petitioners contend that the regulations violate the First Amendment by impermissibly discriminating based on viewpoint because they prohibit "all discussion about abortion as a lawful option—including counseling, referral, and the provision of neutral and accurate information about ending a pregnancy—while compelling the clinic or counselor to provide information that promotes continuing a pregnancy to term." They assert that the regulations violate the "free speech rights of private health care organizations that receive Title X funds, of their staff, and of their patients" by impermissibly imposing "viewpoint-discriminatory conditions on government subsidies" and thus "penaliz[e] speech funded with non-Title X monies." Because "Title X continues to fund speech ancillary to pregnancy testing in a manner that is not evenhanded with respect to views and information about abortion, it invidiously discriminates on the basis of viewpoint."

There is no question but that the statutory prohibition is constitutional. In Maher v. Roe (1977), we upheld a state welfare regulation under which Medicaid recipients received payments for services related to childbirth, but not for nontherapeutic abortions. The Court rejected the claim that this unequal subsidization worked a violation of the Constitution. We held that the government may "make a value judgment favoring childbirth over abortion, and . . . implement that judgment by the allocation of public funds."

The Government can, without violating the Constitution, selectively fund a program to encourage certain activities it believes to be in the public interest, without at the same time funding an alternative program which seeks to deal with the problem in another way. In so doing, the Government has not discriminated on the basis of viewpoint; it has merely chosen to fund one activity to the exclusion of the other. "[A] legislature's decision not to subsidize the exercise of a fundamental right does not infringe the right." A refusal to fund protected activity, without more, cannot be equated with the imposition of a "penalty" on that activity. "There is a basic difference between direct state interference with a protected activity and state encouragement of an alternative activity consonant with legislative policy."

The challenged regulations implement the statutory prohibition by prohibiting counseling, referral, and the provision of information regarding abortion as a method of family planning. They are designed to ensure that the limits of the federal program are observed. The Title X program is designed not for prenatal care, but to encourage family planning. A doctor who wished to offer prenatal care to a project patient who became pregnant could properly be prohibited from doing so because such service is outside the scope of the federally funded program. The regulations prohibiting abortion counseling and referral are of the same ilk; "no funds appropriated for the project may be used in programs where abortion is a method of family planning," and a doctor employed by the project may be prohibited in the course of his project duties from counseling abortion or referring for abortion. This is not a case of the Government "suppressing a dangerous idea," but of a prohibition on

D. What Is an Infringement of Freedom of Speech?

a project grantee or its employees from engaging in activities outside of the project's scope.

To hold that the Government unconstitutionally discriminates on the basis of viewpoint when it chooses to fund a program dedicated to advance certain permissible goals, because the program in advancing those goals necessarily discourages alternative goals, would render numerous Government programs constitutionally suspect. When Congress established a National Endowment for Democracy to encourage other countries to adopt democratic principles, it was not constitutionally required to fund a program to encourage competing lines of political philosophy such as communism and fascism. Petitioners' assertions ultimately boil down to the position that if the government chooses to subsidize one protected right, it must subsidize analogous counterpart rights. But the Court has soundly rejected that proposition. Within far broader limits than petitioners are willing to concede, when the Government appropriates public funds to establish a program it is entitled to define the limits of that program.

Petitioners also contend that the restrictions on the subsidization of abortion-related speech contained in the regulations are impermissible because they condition the receipt of a benefit, in these cases Title X funding, on the relinquishment of a constitutional right, the right to engage in abortion advocacy and counseling. Petitioners' reliance on these cases is unavailing, however, because here the Government is not denying a benefit to anyone, but is instead simply insisting that public funds be spent for the purposes for which they were authorized. The Secretary's regulations do not force the Title X grantee to give up abortion-related speech; they merely require that the grantee keep such activities separate and distinct from Title X activities. The grantee receives Title X funds, however, for the specific and limited purpose of establishing and operating a Title X project. The regulations govern the scope of the Title X project's activities, and leave the grantee unfettered in its other activities. The Title X grantee can continue to perform abortions, provide abortion-related services, and engage in abortion advocacy; it simply is required to conduct those activities through programs that are separate and independent from the project that receives Title X funds.

In contrast, our "unconstitutional conditions" cases involve situations in which the Government has placed a condition on the recipient of the subsidy rather than on a particular program or service, thus effectively prohibiting the recipient from engaging in the protected conduct outside the scope of the federally funded program.

The condition that federal funds will be used only to further the purposes of a grant does not violate constitutional rights. "Congress could, for example, grant funds to an organization dedicated to combating teenage drug abuse, but condition the grant by providing that none of the money received from Congress should be used to lobby state legislatures." By requiring that the Title X grantee engage in abortion-related activity separately from activity receiving federal funding, Congress has, consistent with our teachings in *League of Women Voters* and *Regan*, not denied it the right to engage in abortion-related activities. Congress has merely refused to fund such activities out of the public fisc, and the Secretary has simply required a certain degree of separation from the Title X project in order to ensure the integrity of the federally funded program.

The same principles apply to petitioners' claim that the regulations abridge the free speech rights of the grantee's staff. Individuals who are voluntarily employed for a Title X project must perform their duties in accordance with the regulation's restrictions on abortion counseling and referral. The employees remain free, however, to pursue abortion-related activities when they are not acting under the auspices of the Title X project. The regulations, which govern solely the scope of the Title X project's activities, do not in any way restrict the activities of those persons acting as private individuals. The employees' freedom of expression is limited during the time that they actually work for the project; but this limitation is a consequence of their decision to accept employment in a project, the scope of which is permissibly restricted by the funding authority.

Justice BLACKMUN, with whom Justice MARSHALL and Justice STEVENS join, dissenting.

[T]he Court, for the first time, upholds viewpoint-based suppression of speech solely because it is imposed on those dependent upon the Government for economic support. Under essentially the same rationale, the majority upholds direct regulation of dialogue between a pregnant woman and her physician when that regulation has both the purpose and the effect of manipulating her decision as to the continuance of her pregnancy. I conclude that the Secretary's regulation of referral, advocacy, and counseling activities exceeds his statutory authority, and, also, that the regulations violate the First and Fifth Amendments of our Constitution.

Until today, the Court never has upheld viewpoint-based suppression of speech simply because that suppression was a condition upon the acceptance of public funds. Whatever may be the Government's power to condition the receipt of its largess upon the relinquishment of constitutional rights, it surely does not extend to a condition that suppresses the recipient's cherished freedom of speech based solely upon the content or viewpoint of that speech.

It cannot seriously be disputed that the counseling and referral provisions at issue in the present cases constitute content-based regulation of speech. Title X grantees may provide counseling and referral regarding any of a wide range of family planning and other topics, save abortion. The regulations are also clearly viewpoint based. While suppressing speech favorable to abortion with one hand, the Secretary compels antiabortion speech with the other. For example, the Department of Health and Human Services' own description of the regulations makes plain that "Title X projects are required to facilitate access to prenatal care and social services, including adoption services, that might be needed by the pregnant client to promote her well-being and that of her child, while making it abundantly clear that the project is not permitted to promote abortion by facilitating access to abortion through the referral process." 53 Fed. Reg. 2927 (1988). The regulations pertaining to "advocacy" are even more explicitly viewpoint based. These provide: "A Title X project may not encourage, promote or advocate abortion as a method of family planning."

Remarkably, the majority concludes that "the Government has not discriminated on the basis of viewpoint; it has merely chosen to fund one activity to the exclusion of the other." But the majority's claim that the regulations merely limit a Title X project's speech to preventive or preconceptional services, rings hollow in light of the broad range of nonpreventive services that the regulations authorize Title X projects to provide. By refusing to fund those family-planning projects that advocate abortion because they advocate abortion, the Government plainly has targeted a particular viewpoint. The majority's reliance on the fact that the regulations pertain solely to funding decisions simply begs the question. Clearly, there are some bases upon which government may not rest its decision to fund or not to fund. For example, the Members of the majority surely would agree that government may not base its decision to support an activity upon considerations of race. As demonstrated above, our cases make clear that ideological viewpoint is a similarly repugnant ground upon which to base funding decisions.

LEGAL SERVICES CORP. v. VELAZQUEZ
531 U.S. 533 (2001)

Justice KENNEDY delivered the opinion of the Court.

In 1974, Congress enacted the Legal Services Corporation Act. The Act establishes the Legal Services Corporation (LSC) as a District of Columbia nonprofit corporation. LSC's mission is to distribute funds appropriated by Congress to eligible local grantee organizations "for the purpose of providing financial support for legal assistance in noncriminal proceedings or matters to persons financially unable to afford legal assistance."

LSC grantees consist of hundreds of local organizations governed, in the typical case, by local boards of directors. In many instances the grantees are funded by a combination of LSC funds and other public or private sources. The grantee organizations hire and supervise lawyers to provide free legal assistance to indigent clients. Each year LSC appropriates funds to grantees or recipients that hire and supervise lawyers for various professional activities, including representation of indigent clients seeking welfare benefits.

This suit requires us to decide whether one of the conditions imposed by Congress on the use of LSC funds violates the First Amendment rights of LSC grantees and their clients. For purposes of our decision, the restriction, to be quoted in further detail, prohibits legal representation funded by recipients of LSC moneys if the representation involves an effort to amend or otherwise challenge existing welfare law. As interpreted by the LSC and by the Government, the restriction prevents an attorney from arguing to a court that a state statute conflicts with a federal statute or that either a state or federal statute by its terms or in its application is violative of the United States Constitution.

I

From the inception of the LSC, Congress has placed restrictions on its use of funds. For instance, the LSC Act prohibits recipients from making available LSC funds, program personnel, or equipment to any political party, to any political campaign, or for use in "advocating or opposing any ballot measures." The Act further proscribes use of funds in most criminal proceedings and in litigation involving nontherapeutic abortions, secondary school desegregation, military desertion, or violations of the Selective Service statute. Fund recipients are barred from bringing class-action suits unless express approval is obtained from LSC.

The relevant portion of §504(a)(16) prohibits funding of any organization "that initiates legal representation or participates in any other way, in litigation, lobbying, or rulemaking, involving an effort to reform a Federal or State welfare system, except that this paragraph shall not be construed to preclude a recipient from representing an individual eligible client who is seeking specific relief from a welfare agency if such relief does not involve an effort to amend or otherwise challenge existing law in effect on the date of the initiation of the representation."

The prohibitions apply to all of the activities of an LSC grantee, including those paid for by non-LSC funds. We are concerned with the statutory provision which excludes LSC representation in cases which "involve an effort to amend or otherwise challenge existing law in effect on the date of the initiation of the representation."

In 1997, LSC adopted final regulations clarifying §504(a)(16). LSC interpreted the statutory provision to allow indigent clients to challenge welfare agency determinations of benefit ineligibility under interpretations of existing law. For example, an LSC grantee could represent a welfare claimant who argued that an agency made an erroneous factual determination or that an agency misread or misapplied a term contained in an existing welfare statute. According to LSC, a grantee in that position could argue as well that an agency policy violated existing law. Under LSC's interpretation, however, grantees could not accept representations designed to change welfare laws, much less argue against the constitutionality or statutory validity of those laws. Even in cases where constitutional or statutory challenges became apparent after representation was well under way, LSC advised that its attorneys must withdraw.

II

The United States and LSC rely on Rust v. Sullivan (1991) as support for the LSC program restrictions. In *Rust*, Congress established program clinics to provide subsidies for doctors to advise patients on a variety of family planning topics. Congress did not consider abortion to be within its family planning objectives, however, and it forbade doctors employed by the program from discussing abortion with their patients. Recipients of funds under Title X of the Public Health Service Act, challenged the Act's restriction that provided that none of the Title X funds appropriated for family planning services could "be used in programs where abortion is a method of family planning." The recipients argued that the regulations constituted impermissible viewpoint discrimination favoring an antiabortion position over a proabortion approach in the sphere of family planning. They asserted as well that Congress had imposed an unconstitutional condition on recipients of federal funds by requiring them to relinquish their right to engage in abortion advocacy and counseling in exchange for the subsidy.

We upheld the law, reasoning that Congress had not discriminated against viewpoints on abortion, but had "merely chosen to fund one activity to the exclusion of the other." The restrictions were considered necessary "to ensure that the limits of the federal program [were] observed." Title X did not single out a particular idea for suppression because it was dangerous or disfavored; rather, Congress prohibited Title X doctors from counseling that was outside the scope of the project.

The Court in *Rust* did not place explicit reliance on the rationale that the counseling activities of the doctors under Title X amounted to governmental

D. What Is an Infringement of Freedom of Speech?

speech; when interpreting the holding in later cases, however, we have explained *Rust* on this understanding. We have said that viewpoint-based funding decisions can be sustained in instances in which the government is itself the speaker, see Board of Regents of Univ. of Wis. System v. Southworth (2000), or instances, like *Rust*, in which the government "used private speakers to transmit information pertaining to its own program." Rosenberger v. Rector and Visitors of Univ. of Va. (1995). As we said in *Rosenberger*, "[w]hen the government disburses public funds to private entities to convey a governmental message, it may take legitimate and appropriate steps to ensure that its message is neither garbled nor distorted by the grantee." The latitude which may exist for restrictions on speech where the government's own message is being delivered flows in part from our observation that, "[w]hen the government speaks, for instance to promote its own policies or to advance a particular idea, it is, in the end, accountable to the electorate and the political process for its advocacy. If the citizenry objects, newly elected officials later could espouse some different or contrary position."

Neither the latitude for government speech nor its rationale applies to subsidies for private speech in every instance, however. As we have pointed out, "[i]t does not follow . . . that viewpoint-based restrictions are proper when the [government] does not itself speak or subsidize transmittal of a message it favors but instead expends funds to encourage a diversity of views from private speakers."

Although the LSC program differs from the program at issue in *Rosenberger* in that its purpose is not to "encourage a diversity of views," the salient point is that, like the program in *Rosenberger*, the LSC program was designed to facilitate private speech, not to promote a governmental message. Congress funded LSC grantees to provide attorneys to represent the interests of indigent clients. In the specific context of §504(a)(16) suits for benefits, an LSC-funded attorney speaks on the behalf of the client in a claim against the government for welfare benefits. The lawyer is not the government's speaker. The attorney defending the decision to deny benefits will deliver the government's message in the litigation. The LSC lawyer, however, speaks on the behalf of his or her private, indigent client.

The Government has designed this program to use the legal profession and the established Judiciary of the States and the Federal Government to accomplish its end of assisting welfare claimants in determination or receipt of their benefits. The advice from the attorney to the client and the advocacy by the attorney to the courts cannot be classified as governmental speech even under a generous understanding of the concept. In this vital respect this suit is distinguishable from *Rust*.

The private nature of the speech involved here, and the extent of LSC's regulation of private expression, are indicated further by the circumstance that the Government seeks to use an existing medium of expression and to control it, in a class of cases, in ways which distort its usual functioning. Where the government uses or attempts to regulate a particular medium, we have been informed by its accepted usage in determining whether a particular restriction on speech is necessary for the program's purposes and limitations.

When the government creates a limited forum for speech, certain restrictions may be necessary to define the limits and purposes of the program. The same is true when the government establishes a subsidy for specified ends. Here the program presumes that private, nongovernmental speech is necessary, and a substantial restriction is placed upon that speech. At oral argument and in its briefs the LSC advised us that lawyers funded in the Government program may not undertake representation in suits for benefits if they must advise clients respecting the questionable validity of a statute which defines benefit eligibility and the payment structure. The limitation forecloses advice or legal assistance to question the validity of statutes under the Constitution of the United States. It extends further, it must be noted, so that state statutes inconsistent with federal law under the Supremacy Clause may be neither challenged nor questioned.

By providing subsidies to LSC, the Government seeks to facilitate suits for benefits by using the State and Federal courts and the independent bar on which those courts depend for the proper performance of their duties and responsibilities. Restricting LSC attorneys in advising their clients and in presenting arguments and analyses to the courts distorts the legal system by altering the traditional role of the attorneys in much the same way broadcast systems or student publication networks were changed in the limited forum cases we have cited. Just as government in those cases could not elect to use a broadcasting network or a college publication structure in a regime which prohibits speech necessary to the proper functioning of those systems, it may not design a subsidy to effect this serious and fundamental restriction on advocacy of attorneys and the functioning of the judiciary.

LSC has advised us, furthermore, that upon determining a question of statutory validity is present in any anticipated or pending case or controversy, the LSC-funded attorney must cease the representation at once. This is true whether the validity issue becomes apparent during initial attorney-client consultations or in the midst of litigation proceedings.

Interpretation of the law and the Constitution is the primary mission of the judiciary when it acts within the sphere of its authority to resolve a case or controversy. Marbury v. Madison (1803). An informed, independent judiciary presumes an informed, independent bar. Under §504(a)(16), however, cases would be presented by LSC attorneys who could not advise the courts of serious questions of statutory validity. The disability is inconsistent with the proposition that attorneys should present all the reasonable and well-grounded arguments necessary for proper resolution of the case. By seeking to prohibit the analysis of certain legal issues and to truncate presentation to the courts, the enactment under review prohibits speech and expression upon which courts must depend for the proper exercise of the judicial power. Congress cannot wrest the law from the Constitution which is its source.

The restriction imposed by the statute here threatens severe impairment of the judicial function. Section 504(a)(16) sifts out cases presenting constitutional challenges in order to insulate the Government's laws from judicial inquiry. If the restriction on speech and legal advice were to stand, the result would be two tiers of cases. In cases where LSC counsel were attorneys of record, there would be lingering doubt whether the truncated representation had resulted in complete analysis of the case, full advice to the client, and proper presentation to the court. The courts and the public would come to question the adequacy and fairness of professional representations when the attorney, either consciously to comply with this statute or unconsciously to continue the representation despite the statute, avoided all reference to questions of statutory validity and

D. What Is an Infringement of Freedom of Speech?

constitutional authority. A scheme so inconsistent with accepted separation-of-powers principles is an insufficient basis to sustain or uphold the restriction on speech.

It is no answer to say the restriction on speech is harmless because, under LSC's interpretation of the Act, its attorneys can withdraw. This misses the point. The statute is an attempt to draw lines around the LSC program to exclude from litigation those arguments and theories Congress finds unacceptable but which by their nature are within the province of the courts to consider.

The restriction on speech is even more problematic because in cases where the attorney withdraws from a representation, the client is unlikely to find other counsel. The explicit premise for providing LSC attorneys is the necessity to make available representation "to persons financially unable to afford legal assistance." There often will be no alternative source for the client to receive vital information respecting constitutional and statutory rights bearing upon claimed benefits. Thus, with respect to the litigation services Congress has funded, there is no alternative channel for expression of the advocacy Congress seeks to restrict. This is in stark contrast to *Rust*. There, a patient could receive the approved Title X family planning counseling funded by the Government and later could consult an affiliate or independent organization to receive abortion counseling. Unlike indigent clients who seek LSC representation, the patient in *Rust* was not required to forfeit the Government-funded advice when she also received abortion counseling through alternative channels. Because LSC attorneys must withdraw whenever a question of a welfare statute's validity arises, an individual could not obtain joint representation so that the constitutional challenge would be presented by a non-LSC attorney, and other, permitted, arguments advanced by LSC counsel.

Congress was not required to fund an LSC attorney to represent indigent clients; and when it did so, it was not required to fund the whole range of legal representations or relationships. The LSC and the United States, however, in effect ask us to permit Congress to define the scope of the litigation it funds to exclude certain vital theories and ideas. The attempted restriction is designed to insulate the Government's interpretation of the Constitution from judicial challenge. The Constitution does not permit the Government to confine litigants and their attorneys in this manner. We must be vigilant when Congress imposes rules and conditions which in effect insulate its own laws from legitimate judicial challenge. Where private speech is involved, even Congress' antecedent funding decision cannot be aimed at the suppression of ideas thought inimical to the Government's own interest. For the reasons we have set forth, the funding condition is invalid.

Justice SCALIA, with whom THE CHIEF JUSTICE, Justice O'CONNOR, and Justice THOMAS join, dissenting.

Section 504(a)(16) of the Omnibus Consolidated Rescissions and Appropriations Act of 1996 (Appropriations Act) defines the scope of a federal spending program. It does not directly regulate speech, and it neither establishes a public forum nor discriminates on the basis of viewpoint. The Court agrees with all this, yet applies a novel and unsupportable interpretation of our public-forum precedents to declare §504(a)(16) facially unconstitutional. This holding not only has no foundation in our jurisprudence; it is flatly contradicted by a recent decision that is on all fours with the present case.

The LSC Act is a federal subsidy program, not a federal regulatory program, and "[t]here is a basic difference between [the two]." Maher v. Roe (1977). Regulations directly restrict speech; subsidies do not. Subsidies, it is true, may indirectly abridge speech, but only if the funding scheme is "'manipulated' to have a 'coercive effect'" on those who do not hold the subsidized position. National Endowment for Arts v. Finley (1998). Proving unconstitutional coercion is difficult enough when the spending program has universal coverage and excludes only certain speech—such as a tax exemption scheme excluding lobbying expenses. The Court has found such programs unconstitutional only when the exclusion was "aimed at the suppression of dangerous ideas." Speiser v. Randall (1958). Proving the requisite coercion is harder still when a spending program is not universal but limited, providing benefits to a restricted number of recipients, see Rust v. Sullivan (1991). The Court has found such selective spending unconstitutionally coercive only once, when the government created a public forum with the spending program but then discriminated in distributing funding within the forum on the basis of viewpoint. See Rosenberger v. Rector and Visitors of Univ. of Va. (1995). When the limited spending program does not create a public forum, proving coercion is virtually impossible, because simply denying a subsidy "does not 'coerce' belief," and because the criterion of unconstitutionality is whether denial of the subsidy threatens "to drive certain ideas or viewpoints from the marketplace." Absent such a threat, "the Government may allocate . . . funding according to criteria that would be impermissible were direct regulation of speech or a criminal penalty at stake."

In Rust v. Sullivan, the Court applied these principles to a statutory scheme that is in all relevant respects indistinguishable from §504(a)(16). The statute in *Rust* authorized grants for the provision of family planning services, but provided that "[n]one of the funds . . . shall be used in programs where abortion is a method of family planning." Valid regulations implementing the statute required funding recipients to refer pregnant clients "for appropriate prenatal . . . services by furnishing a list of available providers that promote the welfare of mother and unborn child," but forbade them to refer a pregnant woman specifically to an abortion provider, even upon request. We rejected a First Amendment free-speech challenge to the funding scheme, explaining that "[t]he Government can, without violating the Constitution, selectively fund a program to encourage certain activities it believes to be in the public interest, without at the same time funding an alternative program which seeks to deal with the problem another way." This was not, we said, the type of "discriminate[ion] on the basis of viewpoint" that triggers strict scrutiny, because the "decision not to subsidize the exercise of a fundamental right does not infringe the right."

The same is true here. The LSC Act, like the scheme in *Rust*, does not create a public forum. Far from encouraging a diversity of views, it has always, as the Court accurately states, "placed restrictions on its use of funds." Nor does §504(a)(16) discriminate on the basis of viewpoint, since it funds neither challenges to nor defenses of existing welfare law. The provision simply declines to subsidize a certain class of litigation, and under *Rust* that decision "does not infringe the right" to bring such litigation. The Court's repeated claims that §504(a)(16) "restricts" and "prohibits" speech, and "insulates" laws from judicial review, are simply baseless. No litigant who, in the absence of LSC funding, would bring a suit challenging existing welfare law is deterred from doing so by §504(a)(16).

D. What Is an Infringement of Freedom of Speech?

Rust thus controls these cases and compels the conclusion that §504(a)(16) is constitutional.

The Court contends that *Rust* is different because the program at issue subsidized government speech, while the LSC funds private speech. This is so unpersuasive it hardly needs response. If the private doctors' confidential advice to their patients at issue in *Rust* constituted "government speech," it is hard to imagine what subsidized speech would not be government speech. Moreover, the majority's contention that the subsidized speech in these cases is not government speech because the lawyers have a professional obligation to represent the interests of their clients founders on the reality that the doctors in *Rust* had a professional obligation to serve the interests of their patients, which at the time of *Rust* we had held to be highly relevant to the permissible scope of federal regulation. Even respondents agree that "the true speaker in *Rust* was not the government, but a doctor."

The Court further asserts that these cases are different from *Rust* because the welfare funding restriction "seeks to use an existing medium of expression and to control it . . . in ways which distort its usual functioning." This is wrong on both the facts and the law. It is wrong on the law because there is utterly no precedent for the novel and facially implausible proposition that the First Amendment has anything to do with government funding that—though it does not actually abridge anyone's speech—"distorts an existing medium of expression." None of the three cases cited by the Court mentions such an odd principle.

Finally, the Court is troubled "because in cases where the attorney withdraws from a representation, the client is unlikely to find other counsel." That is surely irrelevant, since it leaves the welfare recipient in no worse condition than he would have been in had the LSC program never been enacted. Respondents properly concede that even if welfare claimants cannot obtain a lawyer anywhere else, the Government is not required to provide one. It is hard to see how providing free legal services to some welfare claimants (those whose claims do not challenge the applicable statutes) while not providing it to others is beyond the range of legitimate legislative choice. *Rust* rejected a similar argument.

This has been a very long discussion to make a point that is embarrassingly simple: The LSC subsidy neither prevents anyone from speaking nor coerces anyone to change speech, and is indistinguishable in all relevant respects from the subsidy upheld in Rust v. Sullivan. There is no legitimate basis for declaring §504(a)(16) facially unconstitutional.

In Agency for International Development v. Alliance for Open Society International, Inc., 570 U.S. 2005 (2013), the Court held that it violated the First Amendment for the government to require as a condition of federal funding that organizations adopt a policy expressing opposition to prostitution and human trafficking. The United States Leadership Against HIV/AIDS, Tuberculosis, and Malaria Act of 2003 (Leadership Act), authorized the appropriation of billions of dollars to fund efforts by nongovernmental organizations to assist in the fight. One of the conditions for receipt of federal money was that "no funds may be used by an organization 'that does not have a policy explicitly opposing prostitution and sex trafficking.'" The Court found that this requirement that organizations adopt a policy as a condition for federal funds violated the

First Amendment. The Court explained: "The Policy Requirement compels as a condition of federal funding the affirmation of a belief that by its nature cannot be confined within the scope of the Government program. In so doing, it violates the First Amendment and cannot be sustained."

But in Agency for International Development v. Alliance for Open Society International, 140 S. Ct. 2082 (2020), the Court held that this did not violate the First Amendment when applied to the foreign affiliates of American entities. Justice Kavanaugh, writing for the Court in a 5-3 decision (Justice Kagan was recused), declared: "[I]t is long settled as a matter of American constitutional law that foreign citizens outside U.S. territory do not possess rights under the U.S. Constitution." Because the foreign affiliates were separately incorporated entities and because they were foreign, the Court concluded that the First Amendment did not apply.

5. *Government Pressures*

Is it an infringement of speech if the government places pressure on individuals or entities to refrain from First Amendment behavior without actually prohibiting or in any way penalizing speech? The cases are mixed in dealing with this issue. In Bantam Books, Inc. v. Sullivan, 372 U.S. 58 (1963), the Court held that it was unconstitutional for the Rhode Island Commission to Encourage Morality in Youth to identify "objectionable" books because they were unsuitable for children and to write to sellers urging them to stop having them available. The letter also informed the recipient that the Commission recommended obscenity prosecutions to prosecutors and turned its list of distributors of objectionable books over to local police. In fact, a police officer often followed up and visited the recipient of a letter to see what actions had been taken. The Supreme Court found that such pressure constituted an unconstitutional prior restraint of speech, even though no books were actually banned and no prosecutions were undertaken.

However, other cases point in the opposite direction. In Meese v. Keene, 481 U.S. 465 (1987), the Court held that the government could label a film without violating the First Amendment. Pursuant to the Foreign Agents Registration Act, the federal government identified some Canadian films as political propaganda. One, titled *If You Love This Planet*, won the Academy Award for Best Short Documentary in 1982 and depicted an anti-nuclear weapons speech given by the president of the U.S.-based group Physicians for Social Responsibility. A second film, *Acid Rain: Requiem or Recovery?*, also produced by the National Film Board of Canada, focused on the harms from acid rain.

By labeling the films as propaganda under the Foreign Agents Registration Act, the exhibitors of the movies were required to place the words "political propaganda" at the beginning of the films. Additionally, the producer, the National Film Board of Canada, was required to provide the government with a list of all major distributors of the films and all the groups that had requested the films for viewing.

The government's actions, as in *Bantam Books*, did not prohibit any speech but created obvious pressure against showing such movies. However, the Court found no violation of the First Amendment. The Court emphasized that "[t]he statute itself neither prohibits nor censors the dissemination of

D. What Is an Infringement of Freedom of Speech?

advocacy materials by agents of foreign principles. . . . The term 'political propaganda' does nothing to place regulated expressive material 'beyond the pale of legitimate discourse.' . . . To the contrary, Congress simply required the disseminators of such material to make additional disclosures that would better enable the public to evaluate the import of the propaganda."

The underlying issue in these cases concerns when the government's own speech should be regarded as impermissible pressure and thus an infringement of the First Amendment. Would a government-imposed rating system for records or television programs simply be, in the words of *Meese*, "additional disclosures that would better enable the public to evaluate" the speech? Or would it be a form of pressure to self-censorship as in *Bantam Books*? Are letters from government agencies or commissions pressuring stores not to sell certain adult-oriented magazines simply the government expressing its views or is it an infringement of the First Amendment because of the government's prosecutorial powers?[53] Are speeches by high-level political officials condemning certain speech, such as rap lyrics, an exercise of the officials' expressive rights, or are they impermissible pressure in light of *Bantam Books*? Cases such as *Bantam Books* and *Meese* point in opposite directions. Ultimately, the task for courts is to evaluate the degree of pressure against speech. If the pressure is more than minimal, cases such as *Bantam Books* suggest that First Amendment scrutiny is required. Meese v. Keene might be distinguished on the ground that the Court saw little adverse effect on speech by the government labeling material as political propaganda. Also, subsequent to these cases, the Court has held—as discussed earlier in this chapter—that government speech cannot be challenged as violating the free speech clause of the First Amendment. This doctrine seemingly would preclude a challenge to speech by government and government officials that would be the source of pressure.

---

53. Penthouse International, Ltd. v. Meese, 939 F.2d 1011 (D.C. Cir. 1991) (finding that letters sent from a government commission to stores accusing them of selling obscene materials did not violate the First Amendment).

CHAPTER 3

TYPES OF UNPROTECTED AND LESS PROTECTED SPEECH

The Supreme Court has identified some categories of unprotected speech that the government can prohibit and punish. Incitement of illegal activity, fighting words, and obscenity are examples of such categories of unprotected speech. Additionally, there are categories of less-protected speech where the government has more latitude to regulate than usual under the First Amendment. For instance, government generally can regulate commercial speech if intermediate scrutiny is met. Also, the Court has indicated that some types of sexually oriented speech, although protected by the First Amendment, are deemed to be of "low value" and thus are more susceptible to government regulation.

These categories are defined based on the subject matter of the speech and thus represent an exception to the usual rule that content-based regulation must meet strict scrutiny. It was traditionally thought that the government had broad latitude to prohibit and regulate speech within the categories of unprotected expression. The conventional view was that laws in these areas would be upheld as long as they met the rational basis test that all government actions must satisfy. However, in R.A.V. v. City of St. Paul, 505 U.S. 377 (1992), discussed below, the Court indicated that generally content-based distinctions within categories of unprotected speech must meet strict scrutiny. In *R.A.V.*, the Court declared unconstitutional a city's ordinance that prohibited hate speech based on race, color, religion, or gender that was likely to "anger, alarm, or cause resentment." The Court said that even though fighting words are a category of unprotected speech, the law impermissibly drew content-based distinctions among fighting words, such as prohibiting expression of hate based on race, but not based on political affiliation. It is unclear after *R.A.V.* how much its reasoning will limit the ability of government to regulate within the categories of unprotected speech.

The categories of unprotected and less protected speech reflect value judgments by the Supreme Court that the justifications for regulating such speech outweigh the value of the expression. For each of the categories discussed below, the Court's judgment can be questioned. For example, is the Court correct that obscenity is "utterly without redeeming social importance" and therefore is unprotected by the First Amendment?[1] Is the Court right that

---

1. Roth v. United States, 354 U.S. 476, 484 (1957).

commercial speech is less important than other types of speech and therefore worthy only of intermediate scrutiny? Also, it is important to consider whether other categories of unprotected speech should be recognized because of the harms of such speech relative to its benefits.

Moreover, the categorical approach requires careful attention to how the types of unprotected speech are defined. For instance, the definitions of "incitement" or "obscenity" are enormously important because they determine whether the government can punish the speech or whether the expression is safeguarded by the First Amendment. A recurring theme throughout this chapter is whether the Court's definitions of the categories are sufficiently specific and a desirable way of separating protected from unprotected speech.

Also, there is the question of whether new categories of unprotected speech should be recognized. After the presentation below of the categories of unprotected speech—incitement, fighting words, obscenity—there is the question recently addressed by the Supreme Court of whether violent speech should be recognized as a new category of unprotected speech.

A. INCITEMENT OF ILLEGAL ACTIVITY

The topic of incitement is important for many reasons. It was the first area that produced a large body of Supreme Court cases. Thus, the doctrines articulated in this area—such as the clear and present danger test—have been carried over to many other areas of First Amendment law.

The issue of incitement also is important because it poses a basic value question: How should society balance its need for social order against its desire to protect freedom of speech? When, if at all, may speech that advocates criminal activity or the overthrow of the government be stopped to promote order and security?

Some commentators have argued that all such advocacy of illegal conduct should be deemed unprotected by the First Amendment. Robert Bork, for example, contended that "[a]dvocacy of law violation is a call to set aside the results that political speech has produced. The process of the 'discovery and spread of political truth' is damaged or destroyed if the outcome is defeated by a minority that makes law enforcement, and hence the putting of political truth into practice, impossible or less effective. There should, therefore, be no constitutional protection for any speech advocating violation of law."[2]

The Supreme Court never has taken this view. Justice Brandeis explained that "even advocacy of [law] violation, however reprehensible morally, is not a justification for denying free speech where the advocacy falls short of incitement and there is nothing to indicate that the advocacy would be immediately acted on."[3] The strong presumption in favor of protecting speech is viewed as justifying safeguarding even advocacy of illegality unless there is a substantial likelihood of imminent harm. Also, advocacy of law violation, or even civil disobedience,

---

2. Robert Bork, *Neutral Principles and Some First Amendment Problems*, 47 Ind. L.J. 1, 31 (1971).
3. Whitney v. California, 274 U.S. 357, 376 (1927) (Brandeis, J., concurring).

A. Incitement of Illegal Activity

is seen as a powerful way of expressing a message. But the Court also never has taken the position that such speech is completely protected by the First Amendment, and the government is limited to punishing the criminal acts themselves.

Thus, the Court has been confronted with the task of defining when advocacy of illegality constitutes unprotected incitement and when it is safeguarded by the First Amendment. Over the course of this century, the Supreme Court has used at least four major different approaches in this area. Interestingly, often the later tests have replaced earlier ones without overruling them or even acknowledging their differences.

During World War I and the years immediately following it, the Supreme Court articulated and applied the "clear and present danger test." During the 1920s and 1930s, the Court did not often use this formulation, but instead used a "reasonableness test" that allowed the government to punish advocacy of illegality as long as it was reasonable to do so. The reasonableness test is the one approach that has been expressly repudiated by later Court decisions. In the 1950s, during the McCarthy era, the Court reformulated the clear and present danger test as a risk formula; whether speech was protected depended on the gravity of the evil compared with its likelihood. Most recently, since the late 1960s, the Court has narrowly defined incitement to maximize protection of speech. Under this approach, advocacy can be punished only if there is a likelihood of imminent illegal conduct and the speech is directed to causing imminent illegality. These four approaches are discussed in turn. In reading the cases from each era, it is important to consider whether the Court was creating a new test or using an old one and also, most important, whether the Court struck an appropriate balance between protecting freedom of speech and society's need for law and order.

1. The "Clear and Present Danger" Test

There was substantial criticism within the country of American involvement in World War I.[4] There was significant opposition to the draft, and it is estimated that there were more than 350,000 draft evaders or delinquents during the war.[5] At about the same time, the success of the Bolshevik revolution in Russia led to fears of a leftist uprising in this country.

In response to all of this, two months after America's entry into World War I, Congress enacted the Espionage Act of 1917. The law, in part, made it a crime when the nation was at war for any person willfully to "make or convey false reports or false statements with intent to interfere" with the military success or "to promote the success of its enemies."[6] The law also made it a crime to willfully "obstruct the recruiting or enlistment service of the United States." Convictions could be punished by sentences of up to 20 years of imprisonment and fines of up to $10,000.

---

4. *See* David Rabban, *The First Amendment in Its Forgotten Years*, 90 Yale L.J. 514, 581-582; Zechariah Chaffee, *Free Speech in the United States* 108-111 (1941).
5. Robert J. Goldstein, *Political Repression in Modern America from 1870 to the Present* 105 (1978).
6. Act of June 15, 1917, ch. 30, tit. I, §3, 40 Stat. 219.

In 1918, Congress adopted a law even more restrictive of speech. The Sedition Act of 1918 prohibited individuals from saying anything with the intent to obstruct the sale of war bonds; to "utter, print, write, or publish any disloyal, profane, scurrilous, or abusive language" intended to cause contempt or scorn for the form of the government of the United States, the Constitution, or the flag; to urge the curtailment of production of war materials with the intent of hindering the war effort; or to utter any words supporting the cause of any country at war with the United States or opposing the cause of the United States.[7]

In a series of cases, the Supreme Court upheld the constitutionality of both the laws and their application to speech that, in hindsight, was mild and ineffectual.[8]

The Court articulated the clear and present danger test and found it was met in the cases before it. The first cases—Schenck v. United States, Frohwerk v. United States, and Debs v. United States—involved the 1917 Act. In each of these cases, the Court upheld convictions.

SCHENCK v. UNITED STATES
249 U.S. 47 (1919)

Justice HOLMES delivered the opinion of the Court.

This is an indictment [that] charges a conspiracy to violate the Espionage Act of June 15, 1917, by causing and attempting to cause insubordination in the military and naval forces of the United States, and to obstruct the recruiting and enlistment service of the United States, when the United States was at war with the German Empire, to-wit, that the defendant wilfully conspired to have printed and circulated to men who had been called and accepted for military service a document set forth and alleged to be calculated to cause such insubordination and obstruction. The count alleges overt acts in pursuance of the conspiracy, ending in the distribution of the document set forth. The defendants were found guilty.

The document in question upon its first printed side recited the first section of the Thirteenth Amendment, said that the idea embodied in it was violated by the conscription act and that a conscript is little better than a convict. In impassioned language it intimated that conscription was despotism in its worst form and a monstrous wrong against humanity in the interest of Wall Street's chosen few. It said, "Do not submit to intimidation," but in form at least confined itself to peaceful measures such as a petition for the repeal of the act. The other and later printed side of the sheet was headed "Assert Your Rights." It stated

---

7. Act of May 16, 1918, 40 Stat. 553.

8. In additional to Supreme Court rulings, there were notable decisions by lower federal courts concerning the acts. For example, in Masses Publishing Co. v. Patten, 244 F. 535 (S.D.N.Y. 1917), *rev'd*, 246 F. 24 (2d Cir. 1917), Judge Learned Hand attempted to draw a clear distinction between incitement and discussion. He wrote that one "may not counsel or advise others to violate the law as it stands. Words are not only the keys of persuasion, but the triggers of action." Criticism of the law is constitutionally protected; advocacy of its violation is not.

In Shaffer v. United States, 255 F. 886 (9th Cir. 1919), the court upheld the application of the Espionage Act of 1917 against a book critical of American involvement in World War I. The court said that the test is "whether the natural and probable tendency and effect of [the publication] are such as are calculated to produce the result condemned by statute."

reasons for alleging that any one violated the Constitution when he refused to recognize "your right to assert your opposition to the draft," and went on, "If you do not assert and support your rights, you are helping to deny or disparage rights which it is the solemn duty of all citizens and residents of the United States to retain." It described the arguments on the other side as coming from cunning politicians and a mercenary capitalist press, and even silent consent to the conscription law as helping to support an infamous conspiracy. It denied the power to send our citizens away to foreign shores to shoot up the people of other lands, and added that words could not express the condemnation such cold-blooded ruthlessness deserves, winding up, "You must do your share to maintain, support and uphold the rights of the people of this country." Of course the document would not have been sent unless it had been intended to have some effect, and we do not see what effect it could be expected to have upon persons subject to the draft except to influence them to obstruct the carrying of it out.

But it is said, suppose that that was the tendency of this circular, it is protected by the First Amendment to the Constitution. It well may be that the prohibition of laws abridging the freedom of speech is not confined to previous restraints, although to prevent them may have been the main purpose. We admit that in many places and in ordinary times the defendants in saying all that was said in the circular would have been within their constitutional rights. But the character of every act depends upon the circumstances in which it is done. The most stringent protection of free speech would not protect a man in falsely shouting fire in a theatre and causing a panic.

The question in every case is whether the words used are used in such circumstances and are of such a nature as to create a clear and present danger that they will bring about the substantive evils that Congress has a right to prevent. It is a question of proximity and degree. When a nation is at war many things that might be said in time of peace are such a hindrance to its effort that their utterance will not be endured so long as men fight and that no Court could regard them as protected by any constitutional right. It seems to be admitted that if an actual obstruction of the recruiting service were proved, liability for words that produced that effect might be enforced. The statute of 1917 in section 4 punishes conspiracies to obstruct as well as actual obstruction. If the act (speaking, or circulating a paper), its tendency, and the intent with which it is done are the same, we perceive no ground for saying that success alone warrants making the act a crime.

FROHWERK v. UNITED STATES
249 U.S. 204 (1919)

Justice HOLMES delivered the opinion of the Court.

This is an indictment in thirteen counts. The [indictment alleges] a conspiracy between the plaintiff in error and one Carl Gleeser, they then being engaged in the preparation and publication of a newspaper, the Missouri Staats Zeitung, to violate the Espionage Act of June 15, 1917. It alleges as overt acts the preparation and circulation of twelve articles in the said newspaper at different dates from July 6, 1917, to December 7 of the same year. The other counts allege attempts to cause disloyalty, mutiny and refusal of duty in the military and naval forces of the United States, by the same publications, each count being confined to the publication of a single date. There was a trial and Frohwerk was found guilty on all the counts except the seventh, which needs no further mention. He was sentenced to a fine and to ten years imprisonment on each count, the imprisonment on the later counts to run concurrently with that on the first.

The first [article] begins by declaring it a monumental and inexcusable mistake to send our soldiers to France, says that it comes no doubt from the great trusts, and later that it appears to be outright murder without serving anything practical; speaks of the unconquerable spirit and undiminished strength of the German nation, and characterizes its own discourse as words of warning to the American people. Later, on August 3, came discussion of the causes of the war, laying it to the administration and saying "that a few men and corporations might amass unprecedented fortunes we sold our honor, our very soul" with the usual repetition that we went to war to protect the loans of Wall Street. Later, after more similar discourse, comes "We say therefore, cease firing."

It may be that all this might be said or written even in time of war in circumstances that would not make it a crime. We do not lose our right to condemn either measures or men because the country is at war. It does not appear that there was any special effort to reach men who were subject to the draft.

But we must take the case on the record as it is, and on that record it is impossible to say that it might not have been found that the circulation of the paper was in quarters where a little breath would be enough to kindle a flame and that the fact was known and relied upon by those who sent the paper out. Small compensation would not exonerate the defendant if it were found that he expected the result, even if pay were his chief desire. When we consider that we do not know how strong the Government's evidence may have been we find ourselves unable to say that the articles could not furnish a basis for a conviction upon the first count at least.

DEBS v. UNITED STATES
249 U.S. 211 (1919)

Justice HOLMES delivered the opinion of the Court.

This is an indictment under the Espionage Act of June 15, 1917. It has been cut down to two counts, originally the third and fourth. The former of these alleges that on or about June 16, 1918, at Canton, Ohio, the defendant caused and incited and attempted to cause and incite insubordination, disloyalty, mutiny and refusal of duty in the military and naval forces of the United States and with intent so to do delivered, to an assembly of people, a public speech, set forth. The fourth count alleges that he obstructed and attempted to obstruct the recruiting and enlistment service of the United States and to that end and with that intent delivered the same speech, again set forth. The defendant was found guilty and was sentenced to ten years' imprisonment on each of the two counts, the punishment to run concurrently on both.

The main theme of the speech was Socialism, its growth, and a prophecy of its ultimate success. With that we have nothing to do, but if a part or the manifest intent of the more general utterances was to encourage those present to obstruct the recruiting service and if in passages such encouragement was directly given, the immunity of the general theme may not be enough to protect the speech. The speaker began by saying that he had just returned from a visit to the workhouse in the neighborhood where three of their most loyal comrades were paying the penalty for their devotion to the working class—these being Wagenknecht, Baker and Ruthenberg, who had been convicted of aiding and abetting another in failing to register for the draft. He said that he had to be prudent and might not be able to say all that he thought, thus intimating to his hearers that they might infer that he meant more, but he did say that those persons were paying the penalty for standing erect and for seeking to pave the way to better conditions for all mankind. Later he added further eulogies and said that he was proud of them. He then expressed opposition to Prussian militarism in a way that naturally might have been thought to be intended to include the mode of proceeding in the United States. There followed personal experiences and illustrations of the growth of Socialism, a glorification of minorities, and a prophecy of the success of the international Socialist crusade, with the interjection that "you need to know that you are fit for something better than slavery and cannon fodder."

Without going into further particulars we are of opinion that the verdict on the fourth count, for obstructing and attempting to obstruct the recruiting service of the United States, must be sustained. Therefore it is less important to consider whether that upon the third count, for causing and attempting to cause insubordination in the military and naval forces, is equally impregnable. The jury were instructed that for the purposes of the statute the persons designated by the Act of May 18, 1917, registered and enrolled under it, and thus subject to be called into the active service, were a part of the military forces of the United States. The Government presents a strong argument from the history of the statutes that the instruction was correct and in accordance with established legislative usage. We see no sufficient reason for differing from the conclusion but think it unnecessary to discuss the question in detail.

Interestingly, later in the year in which these cases were decided, Justice Holmes, joined by Justice Brandeis, dissented in the case of Abrams v. United States, in which the Supreme Court upheld convictions for violating the 1918 Act.[9] In reading *Abrams*, consider whether there is a meaningful distinction between it and the earlier cases, *Schenck*, *Debs*, and *Frohwerk*, in which Holmes wrote the majority opinions. Notice Justice Holmes's eloquent dissent in *Abrams* in which he articulated the marketplace of ideas metaphor for the First Amendment.

ABRAMS v. UNITED STATES
250 U.S. 616 (1919)

Justice CLARKE delivered the opinion of the Court.

On a single indictment, containing four counts, the five plaintiffs in error, hereinafter designated the defendants, were convicted of conspiring to violate

---

9. For an excellent account of why Justice Holmes shifted his position, *see* Thomas Healy, *The Great Dissent: How Oliver Wendell Holmes Changed His Mind and Changed the History of Free Speech in America* (2013).

provisions of the Espionage Act of Congress of 1917 as amended by Act of 1918. Each of the first three counts charged the defendants with conspiring, when the United States was at war with the Imperial Government of Germany, to unlawfully utter, print, write and publish: In the first count, "disloyal, scurrilous and abusive language about the form of government of the United States;" in the second count, language "intended to bring the form of government of the United States into contempt, scorn, contumely, and disrepute;" and in the third count, language "intended to incite, provoke and encourage resistance to the United States in said war." The charge in the fourth count was that the defendants conspired "when the United States was at war with the Imperial German Government, . . . unlawfully and willfully, by utterance, writing, printing and publication to urge, incite and advocate curtailment of production of things and products, to wit, ordnance and ammunition, necessary and essential to the prosecution of the war."

It was charged in each count of the indictment that it was a part of the conspiracy that the defendants would attempt to accomplish their unlawful purpose by printing, writing and distributing in the city of New York many copies of a leaflet or circular, printed in the English language, and of another printed in the Yiddish language, copies of which, properly identified, were attached to the indictment. All of the five defendants were born in Russia. They were intelligent, had considerable schooling, and at the time they were arrested they had lived in the United States terms varying from five to ten years, but none of them had applied for naturalization. Four of them testified as witnesses in their own behalf, and of these three frankly avowed that they were "rebels," "revolutionists," "anarchists," that they did not believe in government in any form, and they declared that they had no interest whatever in the government of the United States.

It was admitted on the trial that the defendants had united to print and distribute the described circulars and that 5,000 of them had been printed and distributed about the 22d day of August, 1918. The circulars were distributed, some by throwing them from a window of a building where one of the defendants was employed and others secretly, in New York City.

On the record thus described it is argued, somewhat faintly, that the acts charged against the defendants were not unlawful because within the protection of that freedom of speech and of the press which is guaranteed by the First Amendment to the Constitution of the United States, and that the entire Espionage Act is unconstitutional because in conflict with that amendment. This contention is sufficiently discussed and is definitely negatived in Schenck v. United States and in Frohwerk v. United States.

Justice HOLMES, dissenting.

This indictment is founded wholly upon the publication of two leaflets. The first of these leaflets says that the President's cowardly silence about the intervention in Russia reveals the hypocrisy of the plutocratic gang in Washington. It intimates that "German militarism combined with allied capitalism to crush the Russian revolution"—goes on that the tyrants of the world fight each other until they see a common enemy—working class enlightenment, when they combine to crush it; and that now militarism and capitalism combined, though not openly, to crush the Russian revolution. It says that there is only one enemy of the workers of the world and that is capitalism; that it is a crime for workers

A. Incitement of Illegal Activity

of America, etc., to fight the workers' republic of Russia, and ends "Awake! Awake, you workers of the world! Revolutionists." A note adds "It is absurd to call us pro-German. We hate and despise German militarism more than do you hypocritical tyrants. We have more reason for denouncing German militarism than has the coward of the White House."

The other leaflet, headed "Workers—Wake Up," with abusive language says that America together with the Allies will march for Russia to help the Czecko-Slovaks in their struggle against the Bolsheviki, and that this time the hypocrites shall not fool the Russian emigrants and friends of Russia in America. It tells the Russian emigrants that they now must spit in the face of the false military propaganda by which their sympathy and help to the prosecution of the war have been called forth and says that with the money they have lent or are going to lend "they will make bullets not only for the Germans but also for the Workers Soviets of Russia," and further, "Workers in the ammunition factories, you are producing bullets, bayonets, cannon to murder not only the Germans, but also your dearest, best, who are in Russia fighting for freedom."

No argument seems to be necessary to show that these pronunciamentos in no way attack the form of government of the United States. [I]t seems too plain to be denied that the suggestion to workers in the ammunition factories that they are producing bullets to murder their dearest, and the further advocacy of a general strike, both in the second leaflet, do urge curtailment of production of things necessary to the prosecution of the war within the meaning of the Act of May 16, 1918. But to make the conduct criminal that statute requires that it should be "with intent by such curtailment to cripple or hinder the United States in the prosecution of the war." It seems to me that no such intent is proved.

I never have seen any reason to doubt that the questions of law that alone were before this Court in the Cases of *Schenck*, *Frohwerk*, and *Debs* were rightly decided. I do not doubt for a moment that by the same reasoning that would justify punishing persuasion to murder, the United States constitutionally may punish speech that produces or is intended to produce a clear and imminent danger that it will bring about forthwith certain substantive evils that the United States constitutionally may seek to prevent. The power undoubtedly is greater in time of war than in time of peace because war opens dangers that do not exist at other times.

But as against dangers peculiar to war, as against others, the principle of the right to free speech is always the same. It is only the present danger of immediate evil or an intent to bring it about that warrants Congress in setting a limit to the expression of opinion where private rights are not concerned. Congress certainly cannot forbid all effort to change the mind of the country. Now nobody can suppose that the surreptitious publishing of a silly leaflet by an unknown man, without more, would present any immediate danger that its opinions would hinder the success of the government arms or have any appreciable tendency to do so. Publishing those opinions for the very purpose of obstructing, however, might indicate a greater danger and at any rate would have the quality of an attempt.

I do not see how anyone can find the intent required by the statute in any of the defendant's words. [I]t is evident from the beginning to the end that the only object of the paper is to help Russia and stop American intervention there against the popular government—not to impede the United States in the war that it was carrying on. In this case sentences of twenty years imprisonment have been imposed for the publishing of two leaflets that I believe the defendants had as much right to publish as the Government has to publish the Constitution of the United States now vainly invoked by them.

Persecution for the expression of opinions seems to me perfectly logical. If you have no doubt of your premises or your power and want a certain result with all your heart you naturally express your wishes in law and sweep away all opposition. To allow opposition by speech seems to indicate that you think the speech impotent, as when a man says that he has squared the circle, or that you do not care whole heartedly for the result, or that you doubt either your power or your premises. But when men have realized that time has upset many fighting faiths, they may come to believe even more than they believe the very foundations of their own conduct that the ultimate good desired is better reached by free trade in ideas — that the best test of truth is the power of the thought to get itself accepted in the competition of the market, and that truth is the only ground upon which their wishes safely can be carried out. That at any rate is the theory of our Constitution. It is an experiment, as all life is an experiment. Every year if not every day we have to wager our salvation upon some prophecy based upon imperfect knowledge. While that experiment is part of our system I think that we should be eternally vigilant against attempts to check the expression of opinions that we loathe and believe to be fraught with death, unless they so imminently threaten immediate interference with the lawful and pressing purposes of the law that an immediate check is required to save the country.

2. The Reasonableness Approach

During the 1920s and the 1930s, the Court decided a series of cases involving criminal syndicalism laws, statutes that made it a crime to advocate the overthrow of the U.S. government or industrial organization by force or violence. The Court decided these cases without invoking the clear and present danger test. Rather, the Court appeared to use a reasonableness approach; it upheld the laws and their applications as long as the government's law and prosecution were reasonable.

Gitlow v. New York, the first case that indicated that the First Amendment applied to the states through its incorporation into the Due Process Clause of the Fourteenth Amendment, upheld a conviction under the New York criminal anarchy statute.

GITLOW v. NEW YORK
268 U.S. 652 (1925)

Justice SANFORD delivered the opinion of the Court.

Benjamin Gitlow was indicted in the Supreme Court of New York, with three others, for the statutory crime of criminal anarchy. Its material provisions are: "Sec. 160. Criminal Anarchy Defined. Criminal anarchy is the doctrine that organized government should be overthrown by force or violence, or by assassination of the executive head or of any of the executive officials of government, or by any unlawful means. The advocacy of such doctrine either

A. Incitement of Illegal Activity

by word of mouth or writing is a felony." He was separately tried, convicted, and sentenced to imprisonment.

The following facts were established on the trial by undisputed evidence and admissions: The defendant is a member of the Left Wing Section of the Socialist Party, a dissenting branch or faction of that party formed in opposition to its dominant policy of "moderate Socialism." Membership in both is open to aliens as well as citizens. The Left Wing Section was organized nationally at a conference in New York City in June, 1919, attended by ninety delegates from twenty different States. The conference elected a National Council, of which the defendant was a member, and left to it the adoption of a "Manifesto." This was published in The Revolutionary Age, the official organ of the Left Wing. The defendant was on the board of managers of the paper and was its business manager. He arranged for the printing of the paper and took to the printer the manuscript of the first issue which contained the Left Wing Manifesto, and also a Communist Program and a Program of the Left Wing that had been adopted by the conference. Coupled with a review of the rise of Socialism, it condemned the dominant "moderate Socialism" for its recognition of the necessity of the democratic parliamentary state; repudiated its policy of introducing Socialism by legislative measures; and advocated, in plain and unequivocal language, the necessity of accomplishing the "Communist Revolution" by a militant and "revolutionary Socialism," based on "the class struggle" and mobilizing the "power of the proletariat in action," through mass industrial revolts developing into mass political strikes and "revolutionary mass action," for the purpose of conquering and destroying the parliamentary state and establishing in its place, through a "revolutionary dictatorship of the proletariat," the system of Communist Socialism. Sixteen thousand copies were printed, which were delivered at the premises in New York City used as the office of the Revolutionary Age and the head quarters of the Left Wing, and occupied by the defendant and other officials.

The precise question presented is whether the statute, as construed and applied in this case, by the State courts, deprived the defendant of his liberty of expression in violation of the due process clause of the Fourteenth Amendment. For present purposes we may and do assume that freedom of speech and of the press—which are protected by the First Amendment from abridgment by Congress—are among the fundamental personal rights and "liberties" protected by the due process clause of the Fourteenth Amendment from impairment by the States.

The statute does not penalize the utterance or publication of abstract "doctrine" or academic discussion having no quality of incitement to any concrete action. It is not aimed against mere historical or philosophical essays. It does not restrain the advocacy of changes in the form of government by constitutional and lawful means. What it prohibits is language advocating, advising or teaching the overthrow of organized government by unlawful means. These words imply urging to action.

It is a fundamental principle, long established, that the freedom of speech and of the press which is secured by the Constitution, does not confer an absolute right to speak or publish, without responsibility, whatever one may choose, or an unrestricted and unbridled license that gives immunity for every possible use of language and prevents the punishment of those who abuse this freedom. That a State in the exercise of its police power may punish those who abuse this freedom by utterances inimical to the public welfare, tending to corrupt public morals, incite to crime, or disturb the public peace, is not open to question. In short this freedom does not deprive a State of the primary and essential right of self preservation; which, so long as human governments endure, they cannot be denied.

By enacting the present statute the State has determined, through its legislative body, that utterances advocating the overthrow of organized government by force, violence and unlawful means, are so inimical to the general welfare and involve such danger of substantive evil that they may be penalized in the exercise of its police power. That determination must be given great weight. Every presumption is to be indulged in favor of the validity of the statute. And the case is to be considered "in the light of the principle that the State is primarily the judge of regulations required in the interest of public safety and welfare"; and that its police "statutes may only be declared unconstitutional where they are arbitrary or unreasonable attempts to exercise authority vested in the State in the public interest."

That utterances inciting to the overthrow of organized government by unlawful means, present a sufficient danger of substantive evil to bring their punishment within the range of legislative discretion, is clear. Such utterances, by their very nature, involve danger to the public peace and to the security of the State. They threaten breaches of the peace and ultimate revolution. And the immediate danger is none the less real and substantial, because the effect of a given utterance cannot be accurately foreseen. The State cannot reasonably be required to measure the danger from every such utterance in the nice balance of a jeweler's scale. A single revolutionary spark may kindle a fire that, smoldering for a time, may burst into a sweeping and destructive conflagration. It cannot be said that the State is acting arbitrarily or unreasonably when in the exercise of its judgment as to the measures necessary to protect the public peace and safety, it seeks to extinguish the spark without waiting until it has enkindled the flame or blazed into the conflagration. It cannot reasonably be required to defer the adoption of measures for its own peace and safety until the revolutionary utterances lead to actual disturbances of the public peace or imminent and immediate danger of its own destruction; but it may, in the exercise of its judgment, suppress the threatened danger in its incipiency.

We cannot hold that the present statute is an arbitrary or unreasonable exercise of the police power of the State unwarrantably infringing the freedom of speech or press; and we must and do sustain its constitutionality.

Justice HOLMES, dissenting.

Justice Brandeis and I are of opinion that this judgment should be reversed. If I am right then I think that the criterion sanctioned by the full Court in Schenck v. United States applies: "The question in every case is whether the words used are used in such circumstances and are of such a nature as to create a clear and present danger that they will bring about the substantive evils that [the State] has a right to prevent."

If what I think the correct test is applied it is manifest that there was no present danger of an attempt to overthrow the government by force on the part of the admittedly small minority who shared the defendant's views. It is said that this manifesto was more than a theory, that it was an incitement. Every idea is an incitement. It offers itself for belief and if believed it is acted on unless

A. Incitement of Illegal Activity

some other belief outweighs it or some failure of energy stifles the movement at its birth. The only difference between the expression of an opinion and an incitement in the narrower sense is the speaker's enthusiasm for the result. Eloquence may set fire to reason. But whatever may be thought of the redundant discourse before us it had no chance of starting a present conflagration. If in the long run the beliefs expressed in proletarian dictatorship are destined to be accepted by the dominant forces of the community, the only meaning of free speech is that they should be given their chance and have their way.

Similarly, the Court used a reasonableness approach to uphold a conviction for criminal syndicalism in Whitney v. California. *Whitney* is perhaps most famous for Justice Brandeis's eloquent opinion defending the importance of freedom of speech. Ironically, Brandeis's opinion is a concurrence to a majority opinion upholding the conviction.

WHITNEY v. CALIFORNIA
274 U.S. 357 (1927)

Justice SANFORD delivered the opinion of the Court.

By a criminal information filed in the Superior Court of Alameda County, California, the plaintiff in error was charged, in five counts, with violations of the Criminal Syndicalism Act of that State. The pertinent provisions of the Criminal Syndicalism Act are: "Section 1. The term 'criminal syndicalism' as used in this act is hereby defined as any doctrine or precept advocating, teaching or aiding and abetting the commission of crime, sabotage (which word is hereby defined as meaning willful and malicious physical damage or injury to physical property), or unlawful acts of force and violence or unlawful methods of terrorism as a means of accomplishing a change in industrial ownership or control or effecting any political change." She was tried, convicted on the first count, and sentenced to imprisonment.

The following facts, among many others, were established on the trial by undisputed evidence: The defendant, a resident of Oakland, in Alameda County, California, had been a member of the Local Oakland branch of the Socialist Party. This Local sent delegates to the national convention of the Socialist Party held in Chicago in 1919, which resulted in a split between the "radical" group and the old-wing Socialists. The "radicals"—to whom the Oakland delegates adhered—being ejected, went to another hall, and formed the Communist Labor Party of America. Shortly thereafter the Local Oakland withdrew from the Socialist Party, and sent accredited delegates, including the defendant, to a convention held in Oakland in November 1919, for the purpose of organizing a California branch of the Communist Labor Party. The defendant, after taking out a temporary membership in the Communist Labor Party, attended this convention as a delegate and took an active part in its proceedings. She also testified that it was not her intention that the Communist Labor Party of California should be an instrument of terrorism or violence, and that it was not her purpose or that of the Convention to violate any known law.

That the freedom of speech which is secured by the Constitution does not confer an absolute right to speak, without responsibility, whatever one may choose, or an unrestricted and unbridled license giving immunity for every possible use of language and preventing the punishment of those who abuse this freedom; and that a State in the exercise of its police power may punish those who abuse this freedom by utterances inimical to the public welfare, tending to incite to crime, disturb the public peace, or endanger the foundations of organized government and threaten its overthrow by unlawful means, is not open to question.

By enacting the provisions of the Syndicalism Act the State has declared, through its legislative body, that to knowingly be or become a member of or assist in organizing an association to advocate, teach or aid and abet the commission of crimes or unlawful acts of force, violence or terrorism as a means of accomplishing industrial or political changes, involves such danger to the public peace and the security of the State, that these acts should be penalized in the exercise of its police power. That determination must be given great weight. Every presumption is to be indulged in favor of the validity of the statute, and it may not be declared unconstitutional unless it is an arbitrary or unreasonable attempt to exercise the authority vested in the State in the public interest.

The essence of the offense denounced by the Act is the combining with others in an association for the accomplishment of the desired ends through the advocacy and use of criminal and unlawful methods. It partakes of the nature of a criminal conspiracy. That such united and joint action involves even greater danger to the public peace and security than the isolated utterances and acts of individuals is clear. We cannot hold that, as here applied, the Act is an unreasonable or arbitrary exercise of the police power of the State, unwarrantably infringing any right of free speech, assembly or association, or that those persons are protected from punishment by the due process clause who abuse such rights by joining and furthering an organization thus menacing the peace and welfare of the State.

Justice BRANDEIS, concurring.

The right of free speech, the right to teach and the right of assembly are, of course, fundamental rights. These may not be denied or abridged. But, although the rights of free speech and assembly are fundamental, they are not in their nature absolute. Their exercise is subject to restriction, if the particular restriction proposed is required in order to protect the state from destruction or from serious injury, political, economic or moral. That the necessity which is essential to a valid restriction does not exist unless speech would produce, or is intended to produce, a clear and imminent danger of some substantive evil which the state constitutionally may seek to prevent has been settled.

This court has not yet fixed the standard by which to determine when a danger shall be deemed clear; how remote the danger may be and yet be deemed present; and what degree of evil shall be deemed sufficiently substantial to justify resort to abridgment of free speech and assembly as the means of protection.

Those who won our independence believed that the final end of the state was to make men free to develop their faculties, and that in its government the deliberative forces should prevail over the arbitrary. They valued liberty both as an end and as a means. They believed liberty to [be] the secret of happiness and courage to be the secret of liberty. They believed that freedom to think as you will and to speak as you think are means indispensable to the discovery and spread of political truth; that without free speech and assembly discussion would be futile; that with them, discussion affords ordinarily adequate protection against the dissemination of noxious doctrine; that the greatest menace to freedom is an inert people; that public discussion is a political duty; and that this should be a fundamental principle of the American government. They recognized the risks to which all human institutions are subject. But they knew that order cannot be secured merely through fear of punishment for its infraction; that it is hazardous to discourage thought, hope and imagination; that fear breeds repression; that repression breeds hate; that hate menaces stable government; that the path of safety lies in the opportunity to discuss freely supposed grievances and proposed remedies; and that the fitting remedy for evil counsels is good ones. Believing in the power of reason as applied through public discussion, they eschewed silence coerced by law—the argument of force in its worst form. Recognizing the occasional tyrannies of governing majorities, they amended the Constitution so that free speech and assembly should be guaranteed.

Fear of serious injury cannot alone justify suppression of free speech and assembly. Men feared witches and burnt women. It is the function of speech to free men from the bondage of irrational fears. To justify suppression of free speech there must be reasonable ground to fear that serious evil will result if free speech is practiced. There must be reasonable ground to believe that the danger apprehended is imminent. There must be reasonable ground to believe that the evil to be prevented is a serious one. Every denunciation of existing law tends in some measure to increase the probability that there will be violation of it. Condonation of a breach enhances the probability. Expressions of approval add to the probability. Propagation of the criminal state of mind by teaching syndicalism increases it. Advocacy of lawbreaking heightens it still further. But even advocacy of violation, however reprehensible morally, is not a justification for denying free speech where the advocacy falls short of incitement and there is nothing to indicate that the advocacy would be immediately acted on. The wide difference between advocacy and incitement, between preparation and attempt, between assembling and conspiracy, must be borne in mind. In order to support a finding of clear and present danger it must be shown either that immediate serious violence was to be expected or was advocated, or that the past conduct furnished reason to believe that such advocacy was then contemplated.

Those who won our independence by revolution were not cowards. They did not fear political change. They did not exalt order at the cost of liberty. To courageous, self-reliant men, with confidence in the power of free and fearless reasoning applied through the processes of popular government, no danger flowing from speech can be deemed clear and present, unless the incidence of the evil apprehended is so imminent that it may befall before there is opportunity for full discussion. If there be time to expose through discussion the falsehood and fallacies, to avert the evil by the processes of education, the remedy to be applied is more speech, not enforced silence. Only an emergency can justify repression. Such must be the rule if authority is to be reconciled with freedom. Such, in my opinion, is the command of the Constitution. It is therefore always open to Americans to challenge a law abridging free speech and assembly by showing that there was no emergency justifying it.

Moreover, even imminent danger cannot justify resort to prohibition of these functions essential to effective democracy, unless the evil apprehended is relatively serious. Prohibition of free speech and assembly is a measure so stringent that it would be inappropriate as the means for averting a relatively trivial harm to society. A police measure may be unconstitutional merely because the remedy, although effective as means of protection, is unduly harsh or oppressive. The fact that speech is likely to result in some violence or in destruction of property is not enough to justify its suppression. There must be the probability of serious injury to the State. Among free men, the deterrents ordinarily to be applied to prevent crime are education and punishment for violations of the law, not abridgment of the rights of free speech and assembly.

I am unable to assent to the suggestion in the opinion of the court that assembling with a political party, formed to advocate the desirability of a proletarian revolution by mass action at some date necessarily far in the future, is not a right within the protection of the Fourteenth Amendment. In the present case, however, there was other testimony which tended to establish the existence of a conspiracy, on the part of members of the International Workers of the World, to commit present serious crimes, and likewise to show that such a conspiracy would be furthered by the activity of the society of which Miss Whitney was a member. Under these circumstances the judgment of the State court cannot be disturbed.

In several cases after *Gitlow* and *Whitney*, the Supreme Court overturned convictions under criminal syndicalism laws. In each, the Court still did not use the clear and present danger test, but rather, found the convictions unreasonable. In Fiske v. Kansas, 274 U.S. 380 (1927), the Supreme Court for the first time overturned a state court conviction as violating the First Amendment as applied to the states through the Fourteenth Amendment. In *Fiske*, the Court concluded that there was no evidence of criminal syndicalism because there were no declarations by the defendant, or his organization, urging unlawful acts. The Court said that the conviction was "an arbitrary and unreasonable exercise of the police power of the State."

Similarly, in DeJonge v. Oregon, 299 U.S. 353 (1937), the Court overturned a conviction for holding a meeting of the Communist Party. Again, the Court emphasized that no one at the meeting advocated illegal acts or the overthrow of the government. The Court said that "peaceable assembly for lawful discussion cannot be made a crime. The holding of meetings for peaceable political action cannot be proscribed."

The majority in all of these cases used an approach that now would be termed rational basis review. None applied the clear and present danger test or anything akin to heightened scrutiny.[10] Thus, the reasonableness approach is inconsistent with the now firmly established heightened scrutiny for fundamental rights. Indeed, the Supreme Court has declared that "*Whitney* has been thoroughly discredited by later decisions."[11]

---

10. Interestingly, in other areas, not involving advocacy of illegal activity, the Court during the 1930s and 1940s expressly used the clear and present danger test. *See, e.g.*, Bridges v. California, 314 U.S. 252 (1941) (speech critical of courts could be held in contempt only if there was a clear and present danger); Cantwell v. Connecticut, 310 U.S. 296 (1940) (speech that provokes a hostile audience can be punished only if there is a clear and present danger).

11. Brandenburg v. Ohio, 395 U.S. 444, 447 (1969).

A. Incitement of Illegal Activity

3. The Risk Formula Approach

During the late 1940s and early 1950s, Senator Joseph McCarthy led a crusade to identify and exclude communists in government. It was the age of suspicion, a time when merely being suspected of being part of a communist or radical group was enough to cause a person to lose a job or appear on a blacklist.

Amid this, in 1951, the Supreme Court decided Dennis v. United States.

DENNIS v. UNITED STATES
341 U.S. 494 (1951)

Chief Justice VINSON announced the judgment of the Court and an opinion in which Mr. Justice REED, Mr. Justice BURTON, and Mr. Justice MINTON join.

Petitioners were indicted in July, 1948, for violation of the conspiracy provisions of the Smith Act during the period of April, 1945, to July, 1948. Sections 2 and 3 of the Smith Act, provide as follows: "Sec. 2. (a) It shall be unlawful for any person — (1) to knowingly or willfully advocate, abet, advise, or teach the duty, necessity, desirability, or propriety of overthrowing or destroying any government in the United States by force or violence, or by the assassination of any officer of any such government; (2) with intent to cause the overthrow or destruction of any government in the United States, to print, publish, edit, issue, circulate, sell, distribute, or publicly display any written or printed matter advocating, advising, or teaching the duty, necessity, desirability, or propriety of overthrowing or destroying any government in the United States by force or violence; (3) to organize or help to organize any society, group, or assembly of persons who teach, advocate, or encourage the overthrow or destruction of any government in the United States by force or violence; or to be or become a member of, or affiliate with, any such society, group, or assembly of persons, knowing the purposes thereof. Sec. 3. It shall be unlawful for any person to attempt to commit, or to conspire to commit, any of the acts prohibited by the provisions of . . . this title."

The indictment charged the petitioners with wilfully and knowingly conspiring (1) to organize as the Communist Party of the United States of America a society, group and assembly of persons who teach and advocate the overthrow and destruction of the Government of the United States by force and violence, and (2) knowingly and wilfully to advocate and teach the duty and necessity of overthrowing and destroying the Government of the United States by force and violence.

The obvious purpose of the statute is to protect existing Government, not from change by peaceable, lawful and constitutional means, but from change by violence, revolution and terrorism. That it is within the power of the Congress to protect the Government of the United States from armed rebellion is a proposition which requires little discussion. Whatever theoretical merit there may be to the argument that there is a "right" to rebellion against dictatorial governments is without force where the existing structure of the government provides for peaceful and orderly change. We reject any principle of governmental helplessness in the face of preparation for revolution, which principle, carried to its logical conclusion, must lead to anarchy. No one could conceive that it is not within the power of Congress to prohibit acts intended to overthrow the Government by force and violence.

In this case we are squarely presented with the application of the "clear and present danger" test, and must decide what that phrase imports. Overthrow of the Government by force and violence is certainly a substantial enough interest for the Government to limit speech. Indeed, this is the ultimate value of any society, for if a society cannot protect its very structure from armed internal attack, it must follow that no subordinate value can be protected. If, then, this interest may be protected, the literal problem which is presented is what has been meant by the use of the phrase "clear and present danger" of the utterances bringing about the evil within the power of Congress to punish.

Obviously, the words cannot mean that before the Government may act, it must wait until the putsch is about to be executed, the plans have been laid and the signal is awaited. If Government is aware that a group aiming at its overthrow is attempting to indoctrinate its members and to commit them to a course whereby they will strike when the leaders feel the circumstances permit, action by the Government is required. The argument that there is no need for Government to concern itself, for Government is strong, it possesses ample powers to put down a rebellion, it may defeat the revolution with ease needs no answer. For that is not the question. Certainly an attempt to overthrow the Government by force, even though doomed from the outset because of inadequate numbers or power of the revolutionists, is a sufficient evil for Congress to prevent. The damage which such attempts create both physically and politically to a nation makes it impossible to measure the validity in terms of the probability of success, or the immediacy of a successful attempt. In the instant case the trial judge charged the jury that they could not convict unless they found that petitioners intended to overthrow the Government as speedily as circumstances would permit. This does not mean, and could not properly mean, that they would not strike until there was certainty of success. What was meant was that the revolutionists would strike when they thought the time was ripe. We must therefore reject the contention that success or probability of success is the criterion.

Chief Judge Learned Hand, writing for the majority below, interpreted the phrase as follows: "In each case [courts] must ask whether the gravity of the 'evil,' discounted by its improbability, justifies such invasion of free speech as is necessary to avoid the danger." We adopt this statement of the rule. As articulated by Chief Judge Hand, it is as succinct and inclusive as any other we might devise at this time. It takes into consideration those factors which we deem relevant, and relates their significances. More we cannot expect from words. The mere fact that from the period 1945 to 1948 petitioners' activities did not result in an attempt to overthrow the Government by force and violence is of course no answer to the fact that there was a group that was ready to make the attempt. The formation by petitioners of such a highly organized conspiracy, with rigidly disciplined members subject to call when the leaders, these petitioners, felt that the time had come for action, coupled with the inflammable nature of world conditions, similar uprisings in other countries, and the touch-and-go nature of our relations with countries with whom petitioners were in the very least ideologically attuned, convince us that their convictions were justified on this score. And this analysis disposes of the contention that a conspiracy to advocate, as distinguished from the advocacy itself, cannot be constitutionally restrained, because it comprises only the preparation. It is the existence of the conspiracy which creates the danger. If the ingredients of the reaction are present, we cannot bind the Government to wait until the catalyst is added.

We hold that the Smith Act [does] not inherently, or as construed or applied in the instant case, violate the First Amendment and other provisions of the Bill of Rights, or the First and Fifth Amendments because of indefiniteness. Petitioners intended to overthrow the Government of the United States as speedily as the circumstances would permit. Their conspiracy to organize the Communist Party and to teach and advocate the overthrow of the Government of the United States by force and violence created a "clear and present danger" of an attempt to overthrow the Government by force and violence. They were properly and constitutionally convicted for violation of the Smith Act. The judgments of conviction are affirmed.

> Justice FRANKFURTER, concurring in affirmance of the judgment.

In enacting a statute which makes it a crime for the defendants to conspire to do what they have been found to have conspired to do, did Congress exceed its constitutional power? Few questions of comparable import have come before this Court in recent years. The appellants maintain that they have a right to advocate a political theory, so long, at least, as their advocacy does not create an immediate danger of obvious magnitude to the very existence of our present scheme of society. On the other hand, the Government asserts the right to safeguard the security of the Nation by such a measure as the Smith Act. Our judgment is thus solicited on a conflict of interests of the utmost concern to the well-being of the country.

But how are competing interests to be assessed? Since they are not subject to quantitative ascertainment, the issue necessarily resolves itself into asking, who is to make the adjustment?—who is to balance the relevant factors and ascertain which interest is in the circumstances to prevail? Full responsibility for the choice cannot be given to the courts. Courts are not representative bodies. They are not designed to be a good reflex of a democratic society. Their judgment is best informed, and therefore most dependable, within narrow limits. Their essential quality is detachment, founded on independence. History teaches that the independence of the judiciary is jeopardized when courts become embroiled in the passions of the day and assume primary responsibility in choosing between competing political, economic and social pressures.

Primary responsibility for adjusting the interests which compete in the situation before us of necessity belongs to the Congress. The nature of the power to be exercised by this Court has been delineated in decisions not charged with the emotional appeal of situations such as that now before us. We are to set aside the judgment of those whose duty it is to legislate only if there is no reasonable basis for it. We are to determine whether a statute is sufficiently definite to meet the constitutional requirements of due process, and whether it respects the safeguards against undue concentration of authority secured by separation of power. Above all we must remember that this Court's power of judicial review is not "an exercise of the powers of a super-Legislature."

Civil liberties draw at best only limited strength from legal guaranties. Preoccupation by our people with the constitutionality, instead of with the wisdom, of legislation or of executive action is preoccupation with a false value. Even those who would most freely use the judicial brake on the democratic process by invalidating legislation that goes deeply against their grain, acknowledge, at least by paying lip service, that constitutionality does not exact a sense of proportion or the sanity of humor or an absence of fear. Focusing attention on constitutionality tends to make constitutionality synonymous with wisdom. When legislation touches freedom of thought and freedom of speech, such a tendency is a formidable enemy of the free spirit. Much that should be rejected as illiberal, because repressive and envenoming, may well be not unconstitutional. The ultimate reliance for the deepest needs of civilization must be found outside their vindication in courts of law.

Justice BLACK, dissenting.

At the outset I want to emphasize what the crime involved in this case is, and what it is not. These petitioners were not charged with an attempt to overthrow the Government. They were not charged with overt acts of any kind designed to overthrow the Government. They were not even charged with saying anything or writing anything designed to overthrow the Government. The charge was that they agreed to assemble and to talk and publish certain ideas at a later date: The indictment is that they conspired to organize the Communist Party and to use speech or newspapers and other publications in the future to teach and advocate the forcible overthrow of the Government. No matter how it is worded, this is a virulent form of prior censorship of speech and press, which I believe the First Amendment forbids.

But let us assume, contrary to all constitutional ideas of fair criminal procedure, that petitioners although not indicted for the crime of actual advocacy, maybe punished for it. Even on this radical assumption, the other opinions in this case show that the only way to affirm these convictions is to repudiate directly or indirectly the established "clear and present danger" rule. This the Court does in a way which greatly restricts the protections afforded by the First Amendment. The opinions for affirmance indicate that the chief reason for jettisoning the rule is the expressed fear that advocacy of Communist doctrine endangers the safety of the Republic. Undoubtedly, a governmental policy of unfettered communication of ideas does entail dangers. To the Founders of this Nation, however, the benefits derived from free expression were worth the risk. I have always believed that the First Amendment is the keystone of our Government, that the freedoms it guarantees provide the best insurance against destruction of all freedom. At least as to speech in the realm of public matters, I believe that the "clear and present danger" test does not "mark the furthermost constitutional boundaries of protected expression" but does "no more than recognize a minimum compulsion of the Bill of Rights."

So long as this Court exercises the power of judicial review of legislation, I cannot agree that the First Amendment permits us to sustain laws suppressing freedom of speech and press on the basis of Congress' or our own notions of mere "reasonableness." Such a doctrine waters down the First Amendment so that it amounts to little more than an admonition to Congress. The Amendment as so construed is not likely to protect any but those "safe" or orthodox views which rarely need its protection.

Justice DOUGLAS, dissenting.

If this were a case where those who claimed protection under the First Amendment were teaching the techniques of sabotage, the assassination of the

A. Incitement of Illegal Activity

President, the filching of documents from public files, the planting of bombs, the art of street warfare, and the like, I would have no doubts. The freedom to speak is not absolute; the teaching of methods of terror and other seditious conduct should be beyond the pale along with obscenity and immorality. This case was argued as if those were the facts.

The argument imported much seditious conduct into the record. That is easy and it has popular appeal, for the activities of Communists in plotting and scheming against the free world are common knowledge. But the fact is that no such evidence was introduced at the trial. There is a statute which makes a seditious conspiracy unlawful. Petitioners, however, were not charged with a "conspiracy to overthrow" the Government. They were charged with a conspiracy to form a party and groups and assemblies of people who teach and advocate the overthrow of our Government by force or violence and with a conspiracy to advocate and teach its overthrow by force and violence. It may well be that indoctrination in the techniques of terror to destroy the Government would be indictable under either statute. But the teaching which is condemned here is of a different character.

So far as the present record is concerned, what petitioners did was to organize people to teach and themselves teach the Marxist-Leninist doctrine contained chiefly in four books: Foundations of Leninism by Stalin (1924); The Communist Manifesto by Marx and Engels (1848); State and Revolution by Lenin (1917); History of the Communist Party of the Soviet Union (B.) (1939).

Those books are to Soviet Communism what Mein Kampf was to Nazism. If they are understood, the ugliness of Communism is revealed, its deceit and cunning are exposed, the nature of its activities becomes apparent, and the chances of its success less likely.

The opinion of the Court does not outlaw these texts nor condemn them to the fire, as the Communists do literature offensive to their creed. But if the books themselves are not outlawed, if they can lawfully remain on library shelves, by what reasoning does their use in a classroom become a crime?

If we are to take judicial notice of the threat of Communists within the nation, it should not be difficult to conclude that as a political party they are of little consequence. Communists in this country have never made a respectable or serious showing in any election. I would doubt that there is a village, let alone a city or county or state, which the Communists could carry. Communism in the world scene is no bogey-man; but Communism as a political faction or party in this country plainly is. Communism has been so thoroughly exposed in this country that it has been crippled as a political force. Free speech has destroyed it as an effective political party. [T]he people know Soviet Communism; the doctrine of Soviet revolution is exposed in all of its ugliness and the American people want none of it.

How it can be said that there is a clear and present danger that this advocacy will succeed is, therefore, a mystery. Some nations less resilient than the United States, where illiteracy is high and where democratic traditions are only budding, might have to take drastic steps and jail these men for merely speaking their creed. But in America they are miserable merchants of unwanted ideas; their wares remain unsold. The fact that their ideas are abhorrent does not make them powerful.

Neither prejudice nor hate nor senseless fear should be the basis of this solemn act. Free speech—the glory of our system of government—should not be sacrificed on anything less than plain and objective proof of danger that the evil advocated is imminent. On this record no one can say that petitioners and their converts are in such a strategic position as to have even the slightest chance of achieving their aims.

In the years following *Dennis*, the Supreme Court decided several cases under the Smith Act. In Yates v. United States, 354 U.S. 298 (1957), the Court overturned the convictions of several individuals for conspiracy to violate the Smith Act. The Court emphasized that there was a crucial "distinction between advocacy of abstract doctrine and advocacy directed at promoting unlawful action." The Court did not overrule *Dennis*, but distinguished it. Justice Harlan, writing for the Court, said that *Dennis* held that "the indoctrination of a group in preparation for future violent action, as well as exhortation to immediate action . . . is not constitutionally protected when the group is of sufficient size and cohesiveness, is sufficiently oriented towards action, and other circumstances are such as reasonably to justify the apprehension that action will occur." But the Court said that was not present in *Yates*. Justice Harlan explained that the "essential distinction is that those to whom the advocacy is addressed must be urged to *do* something, now or in the future, rather than merely to *believe* in something."

The problem, of course, is deciding whether speech is advocacy of doctrine or advocacy to action. In many instances, this is likely to be an ephemeral distinction based entirely on how a judge chooses to characterize the speech. As Justice Holmes said, "Every idea is an incitement."[12]

Yates did not mark the end of the Court's willingness to uphold convictions under the Smith Act. For example, in Scales v. United States, 367 U.S. 203 (1961), the Court upheld a conviction for being a member of an organization that advocates the overthrow of the government. The Court stressed that for the government to punish such association there must be proof that an individual actively affiliated with a group, knowing of its illegal objectives and with the specific intent of furthering those goals. The Court concluded that there was sufficient evidence in the record "to make a case for the jury on the issue of illegal Party advocacy." In contrast, in Noto v. United States, 367 U.S. 290 (1961), the Court reversed a conviction under the Smith Act for conspiracy because of inadequate evidence to meet these requirements.

4. The Brandenburg Test

By the mid-1960s, the Court appeared to be much more protective of speech. In Bond v. Floyd, 385 U.S. 116 (1966), the Court held that the Georgia General Assembly could not refuse to seat Representative Julian Bond because of his support for a statement strongly critical of the Vietnam War and the draft. The Court invoked Yates v. United States (1957) and concluded that Bond's statements were advocacy of ideas protected by the First Amendment.

---

12. Gitlow v. New York, 268 U.S., at 673.

A. Incitement of Illegal Activity

Also, in Watts v. United States, 394 U.S. 705 (1969), the Court reversed the conviction of an individual for violating the law that made it a crime to "knowingly and willfully . . . [threaten] to take the life of or to inflict bodily harm upon the President." An individual was convicted under this law for saying, "If they ever make me carry a rifle the first man I want to get in my sights is L.B.J. They are not going to make me kill my black brothers." The Court said that Watts's statement was "political hyperbole," not a real threat, and thus was protected by the First Amendment.

The key case defining when the government may punish advocacy of illegality is Brandenburg v. Ohio.

BRANDENBURG v. OHIO
395 U.S. 444 (1969)

PER CURIAM.

The appellant, a leader of a Ku Klux Klan group, was convicted under the Ohio Criminal Syndicalism statute for "advocat[ing] . . . the duty, necessity, or propriety of crime, sabotage, violence, or unlawful methods of terrorism as a means of accomplishing industrial or political reform" and for "voluntarily assembl[ing] with any society, group, or assemblage of persons formed to teach or advocate the doctrines of criminal syndicalism." He was fined $1,000 and sentenced to one to 10 years' imprisonment.

The record shows that a man, identified at trial as the appellant, telephoned an announcer-reporter on the staff of a Cincinnati television station and invited him to come to a Ku Klux Klan "rally" to be held at a farm in Hamilton County. With the cooperation of the organizers, the reporter and a cameraman attended the meeting and filmed the events. The prosecution's case rested on the films and on testimony identifying the appellant as the person who communicated with the reporter and who spoke at the rally. The State also introduced into evidence several articles appearing in the film, including a pistol, a rifle, a shotgun, ammunition, a Bible, and a red hood worn by the speaker in the films.

One film showed 12 hooded figures, some of whom carried firearms. They were gathered around a large wooden cross, which they burned. No one was present other than the participants and the newsmen who made the film. Most of the words uttered during the scene were incomprehensible when the film was projected, but scattered phrases could be understood that were derogatory of Negroes and, in one instance, of Jews. Another scene on the same film showed the appellant, in Klan regalia, making a speech.

The second film showed six hooded figures one of whom, later identified as the appellant, repeated a speech very similar to that recorded on the first film. The reference to the possibility of "revengeance" was omitted, and one sentence was added: "Personally, I believe the nigger should be returned to Africa, the Jew returned to Israel." Though some of the figures in the films carried weapons, the speaker did not.

The Ohio Criminal Syndicalism Statute was enacted in 1919. From 1917 to 1920, identical or quite similar laws were adopted by 20 States and two territories. In 1927, this Court sustained the constitutionality of California's Criminal Syndicalism Act, the text of which is quite similar to that of the laws of Ohio. Whitney v. California (1927). But *Whitney* has been thoroughly discredited by later decisions. See Dennis v. United States (1951). These later decisions have fashioned the principle that the constitutional guarantees of free speech and free press do not permit a State to forbid or proscribe advocacy of the use of force or of law violation except where such advocacy is directed to inciting or producing imminent lawless action and is likely to incite or produce such action.

As we said in Noto v. United States (1961), "the mere abstract teaching . . . of the moral propriety or even moral necessity for a resort to force and violence, is not the same as preparing a group for violent action and steeling it to such action." A statute which fails to draw this distinction impermissibly intrudes upon the freedoms guaranteed by the First and Fourteenth Amendments. It sweeps within its condemnation speech which our Constitution has immunized from governmental control.

Measured by this test, Ohio's Criminal Syndicalism Act cannot be sustained. The Act punishes persons who "advocate or teach the duty, necessity, or propriety" of violence "as a means of accomplishing industrial or political reform"; or who publish or circulate or display any book or paper containing such advocacy; or who "justify" the commission of violent acts "with intent to exemplify, spread or advocate the propriety of the doctrines of criminal syndicalism"; or who "voluntarily assemble" with a group formed "to teach or advocate the doctrines of criminal syndicalism." Neither the indictment nor the trial judge's instructions to the jury in any way refined the statute's bald definition of the crime in terms of mere advocacy not distinguished from incitement to imminent lawless action.

Accordingly, we are here confronted with a statute which, by its own words and as applied, purports to punish mere advocacy and to forbid, on pain of criminal punishment, assembly with others merely to advocate the described type of action. Such a statute falls within the condemnation of the First and Fourteenth Amendments. The contrary teaching of Whitney v. California, cannot be supported, and that decision is therefore overruled.

Brandenburg is the Supreme Court's most speech-protective formulation of an incitement test. A conviction for incitement under *Brandenburg* is constitutional only if several requirements are met: imminent harm, a likelihood of producing illegal action, and an intent to cause imminent illegality. None of the earlier tests had contained an intent requirement. Also, none ever had so clearly stated a requirement for a likelihood of imminent harm.

Therefore, on a doctrinal level, it is puzzling that the Court presented the *Brandenburg* test as if it followed from the *Dennis* formulation, rather than as a substantial expansion in the protection of speech. In *Dennis*, the Court expressly denied that there was a requirement for proof of an imminent danger of likely harm.

Brandenburg does not answer, however, how imminence and likelihood are to be appraised. Are these requirements to be assessed relative to the harms to be prevented, so that the more serious the danger, the less in the way of imminence or likelihood that will be required? Or is some showing of imminence and likelihood necessary no matter how great the harm? If imminence and likelihood are judged relative to the nature of the danger, then *Brandenburg* in essence creates a risk formula like the *Dennis* test, even though one is not expressly stated in the *Brandenburg* formulation. Nor does the Court in *Brandenburg* elaborate as to the intent requirement and what must be proven to satisfy it.

A. Incitement of Illegal Activity

There have been few Supreme Court cases in the decades since *Brandenburg* applying or explaining its standard. Hess v. Indiana, 414 U.S. 105 (1973), involved an individual who was convicted of disorderly conduct for declaring, "We'll take the fucking street later," after the police had cleared a demonstration from the street. The Court said that the speech was protected by the First Amendment. The Court explained that "at best . . . , the statement could be taken as counsel for present moderation; at worst, it amounted to nothing more than advocacy of illegal action at some indefinite future time." The Court said that this was insufficient to meet the *Brandenburg* test because there was "no evidence . . . that his words were intended to produce, and likely to produce, *imminent* disorder."

In NAACP v. Claiborne Hardware Co., 458 U.S. 886 (1982), the Court overturned a judgment against the NAACP for a boycott of white-owned businesses that it alleged engaged in racial discrimination. In part, the trial court had based the liability of the NAACP for damages from the boycott on a speech by an NAACP official that included the statement, "If we catch any of you going in any of them racist stores, we're gonna break your damn neck." The Court held that this speech was protected by the First Amendment under the *Brandenburg* test and thus could not be the basis for liability. The Court explained, "In the passionate atmosphere in which the speeches were delivered, they might have been understood as inviting an unlawful form of discipline or, at least, intending to create a fear of violence whether or not improper discipline was specifically intended. . . . This Court has made clear, however, that mere *advocacy* of the use of force or violence does not remove speech from the protection of the First Amendment. . . . The emotionally charged rhetoric of Charles Evers' speeches did not transcend the bounds of protected speech set forth in *Brandenburg*."

Brandenburg, *Hess*, and *NAACP* indicate that the Court has redefined the test for incitement in much more speech-protective terms. Under this law, an individual can be convicted for incitement only if it is proven that there was a likelihood of imminent illegal conduct and if the speech was directed at causing imminent illegal conduct. Yet perhaps the major difference between these cases and such earlier decisions as *Schenck*, *Gitlow*, *Whitney*, and *Dennis* is the social climate. The prior cases all were issued in tense times where there were strong pressures to suppress speech. Only in the unfortunate event that such times occur again will it be possible to know if the *Brandenburg* test better succeeds in protecting dissent in times of crisis.

In a more recent case, the Supreme Court held that the government could punish speech that materially assists a terrorist organization. It is notable that the majority upheld the law without reference to *Brandenburg* or any of the cases in this area. Justice Breyer's dissent, however, argues that *Brandenburg* should have been applied and was not met here.

HOLDER v. HUMANITARIAN LAW PROJECT
561 U.S. 1 (2010)

Chief Justice ROBERTS delivered the opinion of the Court.

Congress has prohibited the provision of "material support or resources" to certain foreign organizations that engage in terrorist activity. 18 U.S.C. §2339B(a)(1). That prohibition is based on a finding that the specified organizations "are so tainted by their criminal conduct that any contribution to such an organization facilitates that conduct." The plaintiffs in this litigation seek to provide support to two such organizations. Plaintiffs claim that they seek to facilitate only the lawful, nonviolent purposes of those groups, and that applying the material-support law to prevent them from doing so violates the Constitution. In particular, they claim that the statute is too vague, in violation of the Fifth Amendment, and that it infringes their rights to freedom of speech and association, in violation of the First Amendment. We conclude that the material-support statute is constitutional as applied to the particular activities plaintiffs have told us they wish to pursue. We do not, however, address the resolution of more difficult cases that may arise under the statute in the future.

I

This litigation concerns 18 U.S.C. §2339B, which makes it a federal crime to "knowingly provid[e] material support or resources to a foreign terrorist organization." Congress has amended the definition of "material support or resources" periodically, but at present it is defined as follows: "[T]he term 'material support or resources' means any property, tangible or intangible, or service, including currency or monetary instruments or financial securities, financial services, lodging, training, expert advice or assistance, safehouses, false documentation or identification, communications equipment, facilities, weapons, lethal substances, explosives, personnel (1 or more individuals who may be or include oneself), and transportation, except medicine or religious materials."

The authority to designate an entity a "foreign terrorist organization" rests with the Secretary of State. She may, in consultation with the Secretary of the Treasury and the Attorney General, so designate an organization upon finding that it is foreign, engages in "terrorist activity" or "terrorism," and thereby "threatens the security of United States nationals or the national security of the United States." "'[N]ational security' means the national defense, foreign relations, or economic interests of the United States." §1189(d)(2). An entity designated a foreign terrorist organization may seek review of that designation before the D.C. Circuit within 30 days of that designation.

In 1997, the Secretary of State designated 30 groups as foreign terrorist organizations. Two of those groups are the Kurdistan Workers' Party (also known as the Partiya Karkeran Kurdistan, or PKK) and the Liberation Tigers of Tamil Eelam (LTTE). The PKK is an organization founded in 1974 with the aim of establishing an independent Kurdish state in southeastern Turkey. The LTTE is an organization founded in 1976 for the purpose of creating an independent Tamil state in Sri Lanka. The District Court in this action found that the PKK and the LTTE engage in political and humanitarian activities. The Government has presented evidence that both groups have also committed numerous terrorist attacks, some of which have harmed American citizens. The LTTE sought judicial review of its designation as a foreign terrorist organization; the D.C. Circuit upheld that designation. The PKK did not challenge its designation.

Plaintiffs in this litigation are two U.S. citizens and six domestic organizations.

II

Given the complicated 12-year history of this litigation, we pause to clarify the questions before us. Plaintiffs challenge §2339B's prohibition on four types of material support—"training," "expert advice or assistance," "service," and "personnel."

Plaintiffs do not challenge the above statutory terms in all their applications. Rather, plaintiffs claim that §2339B is invalid to the extent it prohibits them from engaging in certain specified activities. With respect to the HLP, those activities are: (1) "train[ing] members of [the] PKK on how to use humanitarian and international law to peacefully resolve disputes"; (2) "engag[ing] in political advocacy on behalf of Kurds who live in Turkey"; and (3) "teach[ing] PKK members how to petition various representative bodies such as the United Nations for relief." With respect to the other plaintiffs, those activities are: (1) "train[ing] members of [the] LTTE to present claims for tsunami-related aid to mediators and international bodies"; (2) "offer[ing] their legal expertise in negotiating peace agreements between the LTTE and the Sri Lankan government"; and (3) "engag[ing] in political advocacy on behalf of Tamils who live in Sri Lanka."

[III]

A

We next consider whether the material-support statute, as applied to plaintiffs, violates the freedom of speech guaranteed by the First Amendment.[13] Both plaintiffs and the Government take extreme positions on this question. Plaintiffs claim that Congress has banned their "pure political speech." It has not. Under the material-support statute, plaintiffs may say anything they wish on any topic. They may speak and write freely about the PKK and LTTE, the governments of Turkey and Sri Lanka, human rights, and international law. They may advocate before the United Nations. As the Government states: "The statute does not prohibit independent advocacy or expression of any kind." Section 2339B also "does not prevent [plaintiffs] from becoming members of the PKK and LTTE or impose any sanction on them for doing so." Congress has not, therefore, sought to suppress ideas or opinions in the form of "pure political speech." Rather, Congress has prohibited "material support," which most often does not take the form of speech at all. And when it does, the statute is carefully drawn to cover only a narrow category of speech to, under the direction of, or in coordination with foreign groups that the speaker knows to be terrorist organizations.

For its part, the Government takes the foregoing too far, claiming that the only thing truly at issue in this litigation is conduct, not speech. Section 2339B is directed at the fact of plaintiffs' interaction with the PKK and LTTE, the

---

13. The Court also rejected the argument that the terms of the statute "training," "expert advice or assistance," "service," and "personnel" were so vague as to violate the First Amendment. [Footnote by casebook author.]

Government contends, and only incidentally burdens their expression. The Government is wrong that the only thing actually at issue in this litigation is conduct, and therefore wrong to argue that [intermediate scrutiny is] the correct standard of review. §2339B regulates speech on the basis of its content. Plaintiffs want to speak to the PKK and the LTTE, and whether they may do so under §2339B depends on what they say. If plaintiffs' speech to those groups imparts a "specific skill" or communicates advice derived from "specialized knowledge"—for example, training on the use of international law or advice on petitioning the United Nations—then it is barred. On the other hand, plaintiffs' speech is not barred if it imparts only general or unspecialized knowledge.

B

The First Amendment issue before us is more refined than either plaintiffs or the Government would have it. It is not whether the Government may prohibit pure political speech, or may prohibit material support in the form of conduct. It is instead whether the Government may prohibit what plaintiffs want to do—provide material support to the PKK and LTTE in the form of speech.

Everyone agrees that the Government's interest in combating terrorism is an urgent objective of the highest order. The objective of combating terrorism does not justify prohibiting their speech, plaintiffs argue, because their support will advance only the legitimate activities of the designated terrorist organizations, not their terrorism.

Whether foreign terrorist organizations meaningfully segregate support of their legitimate activities from support of terrorism is an empirical question. When it enacted §2339B in 1996, Congress made specific findings regarding the serious threat posed by international terrorism. One of those findings explicitly rejects plaintiffs' contention that their support would not further the terrorist activities of the PKK and LTTE: "[F]oreign organizations that engage in terrorist activity are so tainted by their criminal conduct that *any contribution to such an organization* facilitates that conduct."

Plaintiffs argue that the reference to "any contribution" in this finding meant only monetary support. There is no reason to read the finding to be so limited, particularly because Congress expressly prohibited so much more than monetary support in §2339B. Congress's use of the term "contribution" is best read to reflect a determination that any form of material support furnished "to" a foreign terrorist organization should be barred, which is precisely what the material-support statute does.

The PKK and the LTTE are deadly groups. "The PKK's insurgency has claimed more than 22,000 lives." The LTTE has engaged in extensive suicide bombings and political assassinations, including killings of the Sri Lankan President, Security Minister, and Deputy Defense Minister. "On January 31, 1996, the LTTE exploded a truck bomb filled with an estimated 1,000 pounds of explosives at the Central Bank in Colombo, killing 100 people and injuring more than 1,400. This bombing was the most deadly terrorist incident in the world in 1996." It is not difficult to conclude as Congress did that the "tain[t]" of such violent activities is so great that working in coordination with or at the command of the PKK and LTTE serves to legitimize and further their terrorist means.

Material support meant to "promot[e] peaceable, lawful conduct," can further terrorism by foreign groups in multiple ways. "Material support" is a valuable resource by definition. Such support frees up other resources

A. Incitement of Illegal Activity

within the organization that may be put to violent ends. It also importantly helps lend legitimacy to foreign terrorist groups—legitimacy that makes it easier for those groups to persist, to recruit members, and to raise funds—all of which facilitate more terrorist attacks. "Terrorist organizations do not maintain *organizational* 'fire-walls' that would prevent or deter . . . sharing and commingling of support and benefits." "[I]nvestigators have revealed how terrorist groups systematically conceal their activities behind charitable, social, and political fronts." "Indeed, some designated foreign terrorist organizations use social and political components to recruit personnel to carry out terrorist operations, and to provide support to criminal terrorists and their families in aid of such operations."

Money is fungible, and "[w]hen foreign terrorist organizations that have a dual structure raise funds, they highlight the civilian and humanitarian ends to which such moneys could be put." But "there is reason to believe that foreign terrorist organizations do not maintain legitimate *financial* firewalls between those funds raised for civil, nonviolent activities, and those ultimately used to support violent, terrorist operations." Thus, "[f]unds raised ostensibly for charitable purposes have in the past been redirected by some terrorist groups to fund the purchase of arms and explosives."

The dissent argues that there is "no natural stopping place" for the proposition that aiding a foreign terrorist organization's lawful activity promotes the terrorist organization as a whole. But Congress has settled on just such a natural stopping place: The statute reaches only material support coordinated with or under the direction of a designated foreign terrorist organization. Independent advocacy that might be viewed as promoting the group's legitimacy is not covered.

Providing foreign terrorist groups with material support in any form also furthers terrorism by straining the United States' relationships with its allies and undermining cooperative efforts between nations to prevent terrorist attacks. We see no reason to question Congress's finding that "international cooperation is required for an effective response to terrorism, as demonstrated by the numerous multilateral conventions in force providing universal prosecutive jurisdiction over persons involved in a variety of terrorist acts, including hostage taking, murder of an internationally protected person, and aircraft piracy and sabotage." The material-support statute furthers this international effort by prohibiting aid for foreign terrorist groups that harm the United States' partners abroad.

C

In analyzing whether it is possible in practice to distinguish material support for a foreign terrorist group's violent activities and its nonviolent activities, we do not rely exclusively on our own inferences drawn from the record evidence. We have before us an affidavit stating the Executive Branch's conclusion on that question. The State Department informs us that "[t]he experience and analysis of the U.S. government agencies charged with combating terrorism strongly suppor[t]" Congress's finding that all contributions to foreign terrorist organizations further their terrorism.

That evaluation of the facts by the Executive, like Congress's assessment, is entitled to deference. This litigation implicates sensitive and weighty interests of national security and foreign affairs. The PKK and the LTTE have committed terrorist acts against American citizens abroad, and the material-support statute addresses acute foreign policy concerns involving relationships with our Nation's allies.

Our precedents, old and new, make clear that concerns of national security and foreign relations do not warrant abdication of the judicial role. We do not defer to the Government's reading of the First Amendment, even when such interests are at stake. But when it comes to collecting evidence and drawing factual inferences in this area, "the lack of competence on the part of the courts is marked," and respect for the Government's conclusions is appropriate.

At bottom, plaintiffs simply disagree with the considered judgment of Congress and the Executive that providing material support to a designated foreign terrorist organization—even seemingly benign support—bolsters the terrorist activities of that organization. That judgment, however, is entitled to significant weight, and we have persuasive evidence before us to sustain it. Given the sensitive interests in national security and foreign affairs at stake, the political branches have adequately substantiated their determination that, to serve the Government's interest in preventing terrorism, it was necessary to prohibit providing material support in the form of training, expert advice, personnel, and services to foreign terrorist groups, even if the supporters meant to promote only the groups' nonviolent ends.

We turn to the particular speech plaintiffs propose to undertake. First, plaintiffs propose to "train members of [the] PKK on how to use humanitarian and international law to peacefully resolve disputes." Congress can, consistent with the First Amendment, prohibit this direct training. It is wholly foreseeable that the PKK could use the "specific skill[s]" that plaintiffs propose to impart, as part of a broader strategy to promote terrorism. The PKK could, for example, pursue peaceful negotiation as a means of buying time to recover from short-term setbacks, lulling opponents into complacency, and ultimately preparing for renewed attacks. A foreign terrorist organization introduced to the structures of the international legal system might use the information to threaten, manipulate, and disrupt. This possibility is real, not remote.

Second, plaintiffs propose to "teach PKK members how to petition various representative bodies such as the United Nations for relief." The Government acts within First Amendment strictures in banning this proposed speech because it teaches the organization how to acquire "relief," which plaintiffs never define with any specificity, and which could readily include monetary aid. Indeed, earlier in this litigation, plaintiffs sought to teach the LTTE "to present claims for tsunami-related aid to mediators and international bodies," which naturally included monetary relief. Money is fungible and Congress logically concluded that money a terrorist group such as the PKK obtains using the techniques plaintiffs propose to teach could be redirected to funding the group's violent activities.

Finally, plaintiffs propose to "engage in political advocacy on behalf of Kurds who live in Turkey," and "engage in political advocacy on behalf of Tamils who live in Sri Lanka." As explained above, plaintiffs do not specify their expected level of coordination with the PKK or LTTE or suggest what exactly their "advocacy" would consist of. Plaintiffs' proposals are phrased at such a high level of generality that they cannot prevail in this preenforcement challenge.

All this is not to say that any future applications of the material-support statute to speech or advocacy will survive First Amendment scrutiny. It is also not to say that any other statute relating to speech and terrorism would satisfy

A. Incitement of Illegal Activity

the First Amendment. In particular, we in no way suggest that a regulation of independent speech would pass constitutional muster, even if the Government were to show that such speech benefits foreign terrorist organizations. We also do not suggest that Congress could extend the same prohibition on material support at issue here to domestic organizations. We simply hold that, in prohibiting the particular forms of support that plaintiffs seek to provide to foreign terrorist groups, §2339B does not violate the freedom of speech.

Justice BREYER, with whom Justices GINSBURG and SOTOMAYOR join, dissenting.

Like the Court, and substantially for the reasons it gives, I do not think this statute is unconstitutionally vague. But I cannot agree with the Court's conclusion that the Constitution permits the Government to prosecute the plaintiffs criminally for engaging in coordinated teaching and advocacy furthering the designated organizations' lawful political objectives. In my view, the Government has not met its burden of showing that an interpretation of the statute that would prohibit this speech- and association-related activity serves the Government's compelling interest in combating terrorism. And I would interpret the statute as normally placing activity of this kind outside its scope.

The plaintiffs, all United States citizens or associations, now seek an injunction and declaration providing that, without violating the statute, they can (1) "train members of [the] PKK on how to use humanitarian and international law to peacefully resolve disputes"; (2) "engage in political advocacy on behalf of Kurds who live in Turkey"; (3) "teach PKK members how to petition various representative bodies such as the United Nations for relief"; and (4) "engage in political advocacy on behalf of Tamils who live in Sri Lanka." All these activities are of a kind that the First Amendment ordinarily protects.

In my view, the Government has not made the strong showing necessary to justify under the First Amendment the criminal prosecution of those who engage in these activities. All the activities involve the communication and advocacy of political ideas and lawful means of achieving political ends. Even the subjects the plaintiffs wish to teach—using international law to resolve disputes peacefully or petitioning the United Nations, for instance—concern political speech. We cannot avoid the constitutional significance of these facts on the basis that some of this speech takes place outside the United States and is directed at foreign governments, for the activities also involve advocacy in *this* country directed to *our* government and *its* policies. The plaintiffs, for example, wish to write and distribute publications and to speak before the United States Congress.

That this speech and association for political purposes is the *kind* of activity to which the First Amendment ordinarily offers its strongest protection is elementary. Although in the Court's view the statute applies only where the PKK helps to coordinate a defendant's activities, the simple fact of "coordination" alone cannot readily remove protection that the First Amendment would otherwise grant. That amendment, after all, also protects the freedom of association. "Coordination" with a political group, like membership, involves association.

"Coordination" with a group that engages in unlawful activity also does not deprive the plaintiffs of the First Amendment's protection under any traditional "categorical" exception to its protection. The plaintiffs do not propose to solicit a crime. They will not engage in fraud or defamation or circulate obscenity.

And the First Amendment protects advocacy even of *unlawful* action so long as that advocacy is not "directed to inciting or producing *imminent lawless action* and . . . *likely to incite or produce* such action." Here the plaintiffs seek to advocate peaceful, *lawful* action to secure *political* ends; and they seek to teach others how to do the same. No one contends that the plaintiffs' speech to these organizations can be prohibited as incitement. Moreover, the Court has previously held that a person who associates with a group that uses unlawful means to achieve its ends does not thereby necessarily forfeit the First Amendment's protection for freedom of association.

Not even the "serious and deadly problem" of international terrorism can require *automatic* forfeiture of First Amendment rights. After all, this Court has recognized that not "[e]ven the war power . . . remove[s] constitutional limitations safeguarding essential liberties." Thus, there is no general First Amendment exception that applies here. If the statute is constitutional in this context, it would have to come with a strong justification attached.

The Government does identify a compelling countervailing interest, namely, the interest in protecting the security of the United States and its nationals from the threats that foreign terrorist organizations pose by denying those organizations financial and other fungible resources. I do not dispute the importance of this interest. But I do dispute whether the interest can justify the statute's criminal prohibition. To put the matter more specifically, precisely how does application of the statute to the protected activities before us *help achieve* that important security-related end?

The Government makes two efforts to answer this question. *First*, the Government says that the plaintiffs' support for these organizations is "fungible" in the same sense as other forms of banned support. Being fungible, the plaintiffs' support could, for example, free up other resources, which the organization might put to terrorist ends. The proposition that the two very different kinds of "support" are "fungible," however, is not *obviously* true. There is no *obvious* way in which undertaking advocacy for political change through peaceful means or teaching the PKK and LTTE, say, how to petition the United Nations for political change is fungible with other resources that might be put to more sinister ends in the way that donations of money, food, or computer training are fungible. It is far from obvious that these advocacy activities can themselves be redirected, or will free other resources that can be directed, towards terrorist ends.

Second, the Government says that the plaintiffs' proposed activities will "bolste[r] a terrorist organization's efficacy and strength in a community" and "undermin[e] this nation's efforts to *delegitimize and weaken* those groups." In the Court's view, too, the Constitution permits application of the statute to activities of the kind at issue in part because those activities could provide a group that engages in terrorism with "legitimacy." The Court suggests that, armed with this greater "legitimacy," these organizations will more readily be able to obtain material support of the kinds Congress plainly intended to ban—money, arms, lodging, and the like.

Yet the Government does not claim that the statute forbids *any* speech "legitimating" a terrorist group. Rather, it reads the statute as permitting (1) membership in terrorist organizations, (2) "peaceably assembling with members of the PKK and LTTE for lawful discussion," or (3) "independent advocacy" on behalf of these organizations. The Court, too, emphasizes that activities not "*coordinated with* the terrorist groups are not banned."

A. Incitement of Illegal Activity 171

But this "legitimacy" justification cannot by itself warrant suppression of political speech, advocacy, and association. Speech, association, and related activities on behalf of a group will often, perhaps always, help to legitimate that group. Thus, were the law to accept a "legitimating" effect, in and of itself and without qualification, as providing sufficient grounds for imposing such a ban, the First Amendment battle would be lost in untold instances where it should be won. Once one accepts this argument, there is no natural stopping place.

Nor can the Government overcome these considerations simply by narrowing the covered activities to those that involve *coordinated*, rather than *independent*, advocacy. Conversations, discussions, or logistical arrangements might well prove necessary to carry out the speech-related activities here at issue (just as conversations and discussions are a necessary part of *membership* in any organization). The Government does not distinguish this kind of "coordination" from any other. I am not aware of any form of words that might be used to describe "coordination" that would not, at a minimum, seriously chill not only the kind of activities the plaintiffs raise before us, but also the "independent advocacy" the Government purports to permit. And, as for the Government's willingness to distinguish *independent* advocacy from *coordinated* advocacy, the former is *more* likely, not *less* likely, to confer legitimacy than the latter. Thus, other things being equal, the distinction "coordination" makes is arbitrary in respect to furthering the statute's purposes. And a rule of law that finds the "legitimacy" argument adequate in respect to the latter would have a hard time distinguishing a statute that sought to attack the former.

Throughout, the majority emphasizes that it would defer strongly to Congress' "informed judgment." But here, there is no evidence that Congress has made such a judgment regarding the specific activities at issue in these cases. I concede that the Government's expertise in foreign affairs may warrant deference in respect to many matters, *e.g.*, our relations with Turkey. But it remains for this Court to decide whether the Government has shown that such an interest justifies criminalizing speech activity otherwise protected by the First Amendment. And the fact that other nations may like us less for granting that protection cannot in and of itself carry the day.

For the reasons I have set forth, I believe application of the statute as the Government interprets it would gravely and without adequate justification injure interests of the kind the First Amendment protects. Thus, there is "a serious doubt" as to the statute's constitutionality. And where that is so, we must "ascertain whether a construction of the statute is fairly possible by which the question may be avoided."

I believe that a construction that would avoid the constitutional problem is "fairly possible." In particular, I would read the statute as criminalizing First-Amendment-protected pure speech and association only when the defendant knows or intends that those activities will assist the organization's unlawful terrorist actions. Under this reading, the Government would have to show, at a minimum, that such defendants provided support that they knew was significantly likely to help the organization pursue its unlawful terrorist aims.

This reading of the statute protects those who engage in pure speech and association ordinarily protected by the First Amendment. But it does not protect that activity where a defendant purposefully intends it to help terrorism or where a defendant knows (or willfully blinds himself to the fact) that the activity is significantly likely to assist terrorism. Where the activity fits into these categories of purposefully or knowingly supporting terrorist ends, the act of providing material support to a known terrorist organization bears a close enough relation to terrorist acts that, in my view, it likely can be prohibited notwithstanding any First Amendment interest. At the same time, this reading does not require the Government to undertake the difficult task of proving which, as between peaceful and nonpeaceful purposes, a defendant specifically preferred; knowledge is enough. This reading is consistent with the statute's text. The statute prohibits "*knowingly* provid[ing] *material* support or resources to a foreign terrorist organization."

Having interpreted the statute to impose the *mens rea* requirement just described, I would remand the cases so that the lower courts could consider more specifically the precise activities in which the plaintiffs still wish to engage and determine whether and to what extent a grant of declaratory and injunctive relief were warranted.

In sum, these cases require us to consider how to apply the First Amendment where national security interests are at stake. When deciding such cases, courts are aware and must respect the fact that the Constitution entrusts to the Executive and Legislative Branches the power to provide for the national defense, and that it grants particular authority to the President in matters of foreign affairs. Nonetheless, this Court has also made clear that authority and expertise in these matters do not automatically trump the Court's own obligation to secure the protection that the Constitution grants to individuals. In these cases, for the reasons I have stated, I believe the Court has failed to examine the Government's justifications with sufficient care. It has failed to insist upon specific evidence, rather than general assertion. It has failed to require tailoring of means to fit compelling ends. And ultimately it deprives the individuals before us of the protection that the First Amendment demands.

B. FIGHTING WORDS, THE HOSTILE AUDIENCE, AND THE PROBLEM OF RACIST SPEECH

The preceding section focuses on when speech can be punished because it advocates illegal acts or the overthrow of the government. This section considers a related, though distinct, question: When may speech be punished because of the risk that it may provoke an audience into using illegal force against the speaker? In other words, the former cases involve concern that an audience may follow the speaker into lawlessness; these cases concern the danger that the audience may be lawless in its reaction against the speaker.

The Court has formulated two doctrines that deal with this issue. One is the Court's holding that "fighting words"—speech that is directed at another and likely to provoke a violent response—are unprotected by the First Amendment. The other is a series of cases concerning when a speaker may be punished because of the reaction of the audience. These doctrines are discussed in turn below in subsections 1 and 2.

Closely related to these topics, but again distinct, is the question of whether and when the government may prohibit and punish expression of hate. This

B. **Fighting Words, the Hostile Audience, and the Problem of Racist Speech**

topic, which has attracted a great deal of attention over the last couple of decades because of the development of hate speech codes at campuses across the country, is discussed in subsection 3.

1. Fighting Words

In Chaplinsky v. New Hampshire, in 1942, the Supreme Court expressly held that "fighting words" are a category of speech unprotected by the First Amendment.

<u>CHAPLINSKY v. NEW HAMPSHIRE</u>
315 U.S. 568 (1942)

Appellant, a member of the sect known as Jehovah's Witnesses, was convicted in the municipal court of Rochester, New Hampshire, for violation of the Public Laws of New Hampshire: "No person shall address any offensive, derisive or annoying word to any other person who is lawfully in any street or other public place, nor call him by any offensive or derisive name, nor make any noise or exclamation in his presence and hearing with intent to deride, offend or annoy him, or to prevent him from pursuing his lawful business or occupation."

The complaint charged that appellant "with force and arms, in a certain public place in said city of Rochester, to wit, on the public sidewalk on the easterly side of Wakefield Street, near unto the entrance of the City Hall, did unlawfully repeat, the words following, addressed to the complainant, that is to say, 'You are a God damned racketeer' and 'a damned Fascist and the whole government of Rochester are Fascists or agents of Fascists' the same being offensive, derisive and annoying words and names."

There is no substantial dispute over the facts. Chaplinsky was distributing the literature of his sect on the streets of Rochester on a busy Saturday afternoon. Members of the local citizenry complained to the City Marshal, Bowering, that Chaplinsky was denouncing all religion as a "racket." Bowering told them that Chaplinsky was lawfully engaged, and then warned Chaplinsky that the crowd was getting restless. Some time later a disturbance occurred and the traffic officer on duty at the busy intersection started with Chaplinsky for the police station, but did not inform him that he was under arrest or that he was going to be arrested. On the way they encountered Marshal Bowering who had been advised that a riot was under way and was therefore hurrying to the scene. Bowering repeated his earlier warning to Chaplinsky who then addressed to Bowering the words set forth in the complaint.

Chaplinsky's version of the affair was slightly different. He testified that when he met Bowering, he asked him to arrest the ones responsible for the disturbance. In reply Bowering cursed him and told him to come along. Appellant admitted that he said the words charged in the complaint with the exception of the name of the Deity.

Allowing the broadest scope to the language and purpose of the Fourteenth Amendment, it is well understood that the right of free speech is not absolute at all times and under all circumstances. There are certain well-defined and narrowly limited classes of speech, the prevention and punishment of which has never been thought to raise any Constitutional problem. These include the lewd and obscene, the profane, the libelous, and the insulting or "fighting" words—those which by their very utterance inflict injury or tend to incite an immediate breach of the peace. It has been well observed that such utterances are no essential part of any exposition of ideas, and are of such slight social value as a step to truth that any benefit that may be derived from them is clearly outweighed by the social interest in order and morality. "Resort to epithets or personal abuse is not in any proper sense communication of information or opinion safeguarded by the Constitution, and its punishment as a criminal act would raise no question under that instrument."

On the authority of its earlier decisions, the state court declared that the statute's purpose was to preserve the public peace, no words being "forbidden except such as have a direct tendency to cause acts of violence by the person to whom, individually, the remark is addressed." The statute, as construed, does no more than prohibit the face-to-face words plainly likely to cause a breach of the peace by the addressee, words whose speaking constitute a breach of the peace by the speaker—including "classical fighting words," words in current use less "classical" but equally likely to cause violence, and other disorderly words, including profanity, obscenity and threats.

We are unable to say that the limited scope of the statute as thus construed contravenes the constitutional right of free expression. It is a statute narrowly drawn and limited to define and punish specific conduct lying within the domain of state power, the use in a public place of words likely to cause a breach of the peace.

Nor can we say that the application of the statute to the facts disclosed by the record substantially or unreasonably impinges upon the privilege of free speech. Argument is unnecessary to demonstrate that the appellations "damn racketeer" and "damn Fascist" are epithets likely to provoke the average person to retaliation, and thereby cause a breach of the peace.

Chaplinsky appears to recognize two situations where speech constitutes fighting words: Where it is likely to cause a violent response against the speaker and where it is an insult likely to inflict immediate emotional harm. Each aspect raises questions about whether such speech should be outside the protection of the First Amendment. As to the former, the danger that the listener will be provoked to fight, the issue is whether the appropriate response is to punish the speaker or rather to punish the person who actually resorts to violence. As to the latter, speech that inflicts an emotional injury, the question—which is key in the discussion of hate speech considered below—is whether speech should be punished because it is upsetting or deeply offensive to an audience.

The Supreme Court never has overturned *Chaplinsky*; fighting words remains a category of speech unprotected by the First Amendment. But in the more than 70 years since *Chaplinsky*, the Court has never again upheld a fighting words conviction. Every time the Court has reviewed a case involving fighting words, the Court has reversed the conviction, but without overruling *Chaplinsky*.

B. Fighting Words, the Hostile Audience, and the Problem of Racist Speech

The Court has used three techniques in overturning these convictions. First, the Court has narrowed the scope of the fighting words doctrine by ruling that it applies only to speech directed at another person that is likely to produce a violent response. Second, the Court frequently has found laws prohibiting fighting words to be unconstitutionally vague or overbroad. Third, the Court has found laws that prohibit some fighting words — such as expression of hate based on race or gender — to be impermissible content-based restrictions of speech.

Each of these techniques is discussed below. The cumulative impact of these decisions is to make it unlikely that a fighting words law could survive. If the law is narrow, then it likely would be deemed an impermissible content-based restriction because it outlaws some fighting words, but not others, based on the content of the speech. If the law is broad, then it probably would be invalidated on vagueness or overbreadth grounds.

a. Narrowing the Fighting Words Doctrine

In Street v. New York, 394 U.S. 576 (1969), the Supreme Court said that there is a "small class of 'fighting words' which are 'likely to provoke the average person to retaliation, and thereby cause a breach of the peace.'" In *Street*, the Court reversed the conviction of an individual who had burned an American flag after learning that James Meredith had been shot. He declared, "We don't need no damn flag. . . . If they let that happen to Meredith we don't need an American flag." The Court said that while some may have found the speech inherently inflammatory, it was not fighting words unprotected by the First Amendment.

This was further clarified in Cohen v. California, 403 U.S. 15 (1971), presented below in the discussion of symbolic speech, where the Court held that unprotected fighting words occur only if the speech is directed to a specific person and likely to provoke violent response. Cohen was convicted for disturbing the peace for having in a courthouse a jacket that had on its back the words, "Fuck the Draft." The state argued, in part, that the inscription on the jacket constituted fighting words because of the possible violent response from people who saw and were angered by the message. The Court, in an opinion by Justice Harlan, rejected this and stated: "While the four-letter word displayed by Cohen in relation to the draft is not uncommonly employed in a personally provocative fashion, in this instance it was clearly not directed to the person of the hearer. No individual actually or likely to be present could reasonably have regarded the words on appellant's jacket as a direct personal insult."

The Court applied this requirement in Texas v. Johnson, 491 U.S. 397 (1989), presented in detail below, where it held that flag burning was a form of speech protected by the First Amendment. As in *Street*, one argument made by the government was that the flag destruction was likely to provoke a violent response from the audience and thus was a form of fighting words. The Court rejected this contention for the reason given in *Cohen*: The speech was not directed at a particular person. Justice Brennan, writing for the Court, said, "[N]o reasonable onlooker would have regarded [the] generalized expression of dissatisfaction with the policies of the Federal Government as a direct personal insult or an invitation to exchange fisticuffs."

b. Fighting Words Laws Invalidated as Vague and Overbroad

In most cases since *Chaplinsky* involving fighting words, the Court has reversed the convictions by declaring the laws to be unconstitutionally vague and overbroad. Gooding v. Wilson is illustrative.

GOODING v. WILSON
405 U.S. 518 (1972)

Justice BRENNAN delivered the opinion of the Court.

Appellee was convicted in Superior Court, Fulton County, Georgia, on two counts of using opprobrious words and abusive language in violation of Georgia Code, §26-6303, which provides: "Any person who shall, without provocation, use to or of another, and in his presence . . . opprobrious words or abusive language, tending to cause a breach of the peace . . . shall be guilty of a misdemeanor."

Count 3 of the indictment alleged that the accused "did without provocation use to and of M.G. Redding and in his presence, the following abusive language and opprobrious words, tending to cause a breach of the peace: 'White son of a bitch, I'll kill you.' 'You son of a bitch, I'll choke you to death.'" Count 4 alleged that the defendant "did without provocation use to and of T.L. Raborn, and in his presence, the following abusive language and opprobrious words, tending to cause a breach of the peace: 'You son of a bitch, if you ever put your hands on me again, I'll cut you all to pieces.'"

Section 26-6303 punishes only spoken words. It can therefore withstand appellee's attack upon its facial constitutionality only if, as authoritatively construed by the Georgia courts, it is not susceptible of application to speech, although vulgar or offensive, that is protected by the First and Fourteenth Amendments. It matters not that the words appellee used might have been constitutionally prohibited under a narrowly and precisely drawn statute.

The constitutional guarantees of freedom of speech forbid the States to punish the use of words or language not within "narrowly limited classes of speech." Chaplinsky v. New Hampshire (1942). Even as to such a class, however, because "the line between speech unconditionally guaranteed and speech which may legitimately be regulated, suppressed, or punished is finely drawn," "[i]n every case the power to regulate must be so exercised as not, in attaining a permissible end, unduly to infringe the protected freedom." In other words, the statute must be carefully drawn or be authoritatively construed to punish only unprotected speech and not be susceptible of application to protected expression. "Because First Amendment freedoms need breathing space to survive, government may regulate in the area only with narrow specificity." Appellant does not challenge these principles but contends that the Georgia statute is narrowly drawn to apply only to a constitutionally unprotected class of words—"fighting" words—"those which by their very utterance inflict injury or tend to incite an immediate breach of the peace." Chaplinsky v. New Hampshire. Appellant argues that the Georgia appellate courts have by construction limited the proscription of §26-6303 to "fighting" words, as the New Hampshire Supreme Court limited the New Hampshire statute.

The dictionary definitions of "opprobrious" and "abusive" give them greater reach than "fighting" words. Webster's Third New International Dictionary

B. Fighting Words, the Hostile Audience, and the Problem of Racist Speech

(1961) defined "opprobrious" as "conveying or intended to convey disgrace," and "abusive" as including "harsh insulting language." Georgia appellate decisions have construed §26-6303 to apply to utterances that, although within these definitions, are not "fighting" words as *Chaplinsky* defines them. In Lyons v. State, 94 Ga. App. 570 (1956), a conviction under the statute was sustained for awakening 10 women scout leaders on a camp-out by shouting, "Boys, this is where we are going to spend the night." "Get the G— d— bed rolls out . . . let's see how close we can come to the G— d— tents." Again, in Fish v. State, 124 Ga. 416 (1905), the Georgia Supreme Court held that a jury question was presented by the remark, "You swore a lie." Georgia appellate decisions construing the reach of "tending to cause a breach of the peace" underscore that §26-6303 is not limited, as appellant argues, to words that "naturally tend to provoke violent resentment." Unlike the construction of the New Hampshire statute by the New Hampshire Supreme Court, the Georgia appellate courts have not construed §26-6303 "so as to avoid all constitutional difficulties."

Justice BLACKMUN, with whom THE CHIEF JUSTICE joins, dissenting.

It seems strange, indeed, that in this day a man may say to a police officer, who is attempting to restore access to a public building, "White son of a bitch, I'll kill you" and "You son of a bitch, I'll choke you to death," and say to an accompanying officer, "You son of a bitch, if you ever put your hands on me again, I'll cut you all to pieces," and yet constitutionally cannot be prosecuted and convicted under a state statute that makes it a misdemeanor to "use to or of another, and in his presence . . . opprobrious words or abusive language, tending to cause a breach of the peace. . . ." This, however, is precisely what the Court pronounces as the law today.

The Supreme Court of Georgia, when the conviction was appealed, unanimously held the other way. Surely any adult who can read—and I do not exclude this appellee-defendant from that category—should reasonably expect no other conclusion. The words of Georgia Code §26-6303 are clear. They are also concise. They are not, in my view, overbroad or incapable of being understood. Except perhaps for the "big" word "opprobrious"—and no point is made of its bigness—any Georgia schoolboy would expect that this defendant's fighting and provocative words to the officers were covered by §26-6303. Common sense permits no other conclusion. This is demonstrated by the fact that the appellee, and this Court, attack the statute, not as it applies to the appellee, but as it conceivably might apply to others who might utter other words.

In three other cases also decided in 1972—Rosenfeld v. New Jersey, 408 U.S. 901 (1972), Lewis v. City of New Orleans, 408 U.S. 913 (1972), and Brown v. Oklahoma, 408 U.S. 914 (1972)—the Court overturned fighting words laws by finding them to be impermissibly vague and overbroad. *Rosenfeld*, *Lewis*, and *Brown* all involved the angry use of profanity in a manner likely to provoke an audience. In each case, the Court overturned a fighting words conviction and vacated in light of Gooding v. Wilson. In *Rosenfeld*, the defendant, speaking at a school board meeting, repeatedly used the word "motherfucker" in describing teachers and school board members. In *Lewis*, a woman called the police, who were arresting her son, "goddamn motherfucker police." In *Brown*, an individual in a speech referred to police officers as "motherfucking fascist pig cops" and spoke of one particular officer as a "black motherfucking pig." In each of the instances, the Court reversed the convictions, making it clear that speech is protected even if it uttered in anger, filled with profanities, and likely to anger the audience.

In City of Houston v. Hill, 482 U.S. 451 (1987), the Court overturned a city ordinance that made it a crime for a person to "oppose, molest, abuse, or interrupt any policeman in the execution of his duty." The Court explained that the "ordinance's plain language is admittedly violated scores of times daily. . . . It is not limited to fighting words nor even to obscene or opprobrious language, but prohibits speech that 'in any manner . . . interrupt[s] an officer.' The Constitution does not allow such speech to be made a crime."

These cases indicate that a fighting words law will be upheld only if it is specific and narrowly tailored to apply just to speech that is not protected by the First Amendment. Otherwise, the statute or ordinance will be deemed void on vagueness grounds or invalidated as being impermissibly overbroad.

c. Narrow Fighting Words Laws as Content-Based Restrictions

However, a very narrow fighting words law likely will be declared unconstitutional as impermissibly drawing content-based distinctions as to what speech is prohibited and what is allowed. This was the result in R.A.V. v. City of St. Paul, the Supreme Court's most recent fighting words decision.

R.A.V. v. CITY OF ST. PAUL, MINNESOTA
_505 U.S. 377 (1992)_

Justice SCALIA delivered the opinion of the Court.

In the predawn hours of June 21, 1990, petitioner and several other teenagers allegedly assembled a crudely made cross by taping together broken chair legs. They then allegedly burned the cross inside the fenced yard of a black family that lived across the street from the house where petitioner was staying. Although this conduct could have been punished under any of a number of laws, one of the two provisions under which respondent city of St. Paul chose to charge petitioner (then a juvenile) was the St. Paul Bias-Motivated Crime Ordinance, St. Paul, Minn., Legis. Code §292.02 (1990), which provides: "Whoever places on public or private property a symbol, object, appellation, characterization or graffiti, including, but not limited to, a burning cross or Nazi swastika, which one knows or has reasonable grounds to know arouses anger, alarm or resentment in others on the basis of race, color, creed, religion or gender commits disorderly conduct and shall be guilty of a misdemeanor."

Petitioner moved to dismiss this count on the ground that the St. Paul ordinance was substantially overbroad and impermissibly content based and therefore facially invalid under the First Amendment. The trial court granted this motion, but the Minnesota Supreme Court reversed. That court rejected petitioner's overbreadth claim because, as construed in prior Minnesota cases, the modifying phrase "arouses anger, alarm or resentment in others" limited the reach of the ordinance to conduct that amounts to "fighting words," i.e., "conduct that itself inflicts injury or tends to incite immediate violence . . . ," and

B. Fighting Words, the Hostile Audience, and the Problem of Racist Speech

therefore the ordinance reached only expression "that the first amendment does not protect." The court also concluded that the ordinance was not impermissibly content based because, in its view, "the ordinance is a narrowly tailored means toward accomplishing the compelling governmental interest in protecting the community against bias-motivated threats to public safety and order."

I

In construing the St. Paul ordinance, we are bound by the construction given to it by the Minnesota court. Accordingly, we accept the Minnesota Supreme Court's authoritative statement that the ordinance reaches only those expressions that constitute "fighting words" within the meaning of *Chaplinsky*. Petitioner and his amici urge us to modify the scope of the *Chaplinsky* formulation, thereby invalidating the ordinance as "substantially overbroad." We find it unnecessary to consider this issue. Assuming, arguendo, that all of the expression reached by the ordinance is proscribable under the "fighting words" doctrine, we nonetheless conclude that the ordinance is facially unconstitutional in that it prohibits otherwise permitted speech solely on the basis of the subjects the speech addresses.

The First Amendment generally prevents government from proscribing speech, because of disapproval of the ideas expressed. Content-based regulations are presumptively invalid. From 1791 to the present, however, our society, like other free but civilized societies, has permitted restrictions upon the content of speech in a few limited areas, which are "of such slight social value as a step to truth that any benefit that may be derived from them is clearly outweighed by the social interest in order and morality."

We have sometimes said that these categories of expression are "not within the area of constitutionally protected speech," or that the "protection of the First Amendment does not extend" to them. Such statements must be taken in context, however, and are no more literally true than is the occasionally repeated shorthand characterizing obscenity "as not being speech at all." What they mean is that these areas of speech can, consistently with the First Amendment, be regulated because of their constitutionally proscribable content (obscenity, defamation, etc.) — not that they are categories of speech entirely invisible to the Constitution, so that they may be made the vehicles for content discrimination unrelated to their distinctively proscribable content. Thus, the government may proscribe libel; but it may not make the further content discrimination of proscribing only libel critical of the government.

Our cases surely do not establish the proposition that the First Amendment imposes no obstacle whatsoever to regulation of particular instances of such proscribable expression, so that the government "may regulate [them] freely." That would mean that a city council could enact an ordinance prohibiting only those legally obscene works that contain criticism of the city government or, indeed, that do not include endorsement of the city government. Such a simplistic, all-or-nothing-at-all approach to First Amendment protection is at odds with common sense and with our jurisprudence as well. It is not true that "fighting words" have at most a "de minimis" expressive content, or that their content is in all respects "worthless and undeserving of constitutional protection," sometimes they are quite expressive indeed. We have not said that they constitute "no part of the expression of ideas," but only that they constitute "no essential part of any exposition of ideas." Chaplinsky v. New Hampshire.

The proposition that a particular instance of speech can be proscribable on the basis of one feature (e.g., obscenity) but not on the basis of another (e.g., opposition to the city government) is commonplace and has found application in many contexts. We have long held, for example, that nonverbal expressive activity can be banned because of the action it entails, but not because of the ideas it expresses—so that burning a flag in violation of an ordinance against outdoor fires could be punishable, whereas burning a flag in violation of an ordinance against dishonoring the flag is not.

And just as the power to proscribe particular speech on the basis of a noncontent element (e.g., noise) does not entail the power to proscribe the same speech on the basis of a content element; so also, the power to proscribe it on the basis of one content element (e.g., obscenity) does not entail the power to proscribe it on the basis of other content elements.

In other words, the exclusion of "fighting words" from the scope of the First Amendment simply means that, for purposes of that Amendment, the unprotected features of the words are, despite their verbal character, essentially a "nonspeech" element of communication. Fighting words are thus analogous to a noisy sound truck: Each is, as Justice Frankfurter recognized, a "mode of speech," both can be used to convey an idea; but neither has, in and of itself, a claim upon the First Amendment. As with the sound truck, however, so also with fighting words: The government may not regulate use based on hostility—or favoritism—towards the underlying message expressed.

When the basis for the content discrimination consists entirely of the very reason the entire class of speech at issue is proscribable, no significant danger of idea or viewpoint discrimination exists. Such a reason, having been adjudged neutral enough to support exclusion of the entire class of speech from First Amendment protection, is also neutral enough to form the basis of distinction within the class. To illustrate: A State might choose to prohibit only that obscenity which is the most patently offensive in its prurience—i.e., that which involves the most lascivious displays of sexual activity. But it may not prohibit, for example, only that obscenity which includes offensive political messages. And the Federal Government can criminalize only those threats of violence that are directed against the President, see 18 U.S.C. §871—since the reasons why threats of violence are outside the First Amendment (protecting individuals from the fear of violence, from the disruption that fear engenders, and from the possibility that the threatened violence will occur) have special force when applied to the person of the President.

Another valid basis for according differential treatment to even a content-defined subclass of proscribable speech is that the subclass happens to be associated with particular "secondary effects" of the speech, so that the regulation is "justified without reference to the content of the . . . speech," Renton v. Playtime Theatres, Inc. (1986). A State could, for example, permit all obscene live performances except those involving minors. Moreover, since words can in some circumstances violate laws directed not against speech but against conduct (a law against treason, for example, is violated by telling the enemy the Nation's defense secrets), a particular content-based subcategory of a proscribable class of speech can be swept up incidentally within the reach of a statute directed at conduct rather than speech. Thus, for example, sexually

B. Fighting Words, the Hostile Audience, and the Problem of Racist Speech

derogatory "fighting words," among other words, may produce a violation of Title VII's general prohibition against sexual discrimination in employment practices. Where the government does not target conduct on the basis of its expressive content, acts are not shielded from regulation merely because they express a discriminatory idea or philosophy.

These bases for distinction refute the proposition that the selectivity of the restriction is "even arguably conditioned upon the sovereign's agreement with what a speaker may intend to say." There may be other such bases as well. Indeed, to validate such selectivity (where totally proscribable speech is at issue) it may not even be necessary to identify any particular "neutral" basis, so long as the nature of the content discrimination is such that there is no realistic possibility that official suppression of ideas is afoot. (We cannot think of any First Amendment interest that would stand in the way of a State's prohibiting only those obscene motion pictures with blue-eyed actresses.) Save for that limitation, the regulation of "fighting words," like the regulation of noisy speech, may address some offensive instances and leave other, equally offensive, instances alone.

II

Applying these principles to the St. Paul ordinance, we conclude that, even as narrowly construed by the Minnesota Supreme Court, the ordinance is facially unconstitutional. Although the phrase in the ordinance, "arouses anger, alarm or resentment in others," has been limited by the Minnesota Supreme Court's construction to reach only those symbols or displays that amount to "fighting words," the remaining, unmodified terms make clear that the ordinance applies only to "fighting words" that insult, or provoke violence, "on the basis of race, color, creed, religion or gender." Displays containing abusive invective, no matter how vicious or severe, are permissible unless they are addressed to one of the specified disfavored topics. Those who wish to use "fighting words" in connection with other ideas—to express hostility, for example, on the basis of political affiliation, union membership, or homosexuality—are not covered. The First Amendment does not permit St. Paul to impose special prohibitions on those speakers who express views on disfavored subjects.

In its practical operation, moreover, the ordinance goes even beyond mere content discrimination, to actual viewpoint discrimination. Displays containing some words—odious racial epithets, for example—would be prohibited to proponents of all views. But "fighting words" that do not themselves invoke race, color, creed, religion, or gender—aspersions upon a person's mother, for example—would seemingly be usable ad libitum in the placards of those arguing in favor of racial, color, etc., tolerance and equality, but could not be used by those speakers' opponents. One could hold up a sign saying, for example, that all "anti-Catholic bigots" are misbegotten; but not that all "papists" are, for that would insult and provoke violence "on the basis of religion." St. Paul has no such authority to license one side of a debate to fight freestyle, while requiring the other to follow Marquis of Queensberry rules.

The content-based discrimination reflected in the St. Paul ordinance comes within neither any of the specific exceptions to the First Amendment prohibition we discussed earlier nor a more general exception for content discrimination that does not threaten censorship of ideas. It assuredly does not fall within the exception for content discrimination based on the very reasons why the particular class of speech at issue (here, fighting words) is proscribable.

Let there be no mistake about our belief that burning a cross in someone's front yard is reprehensible. But St. Paul has sufficient means at its disposal to prevent such behavior without adding the First Amendment to the fire.

Justice WHITE, with whom Justice BLACKMUN and Justice O'CONNOR join, and with whom Justice STEVENS joins concurring in the judgment.

I agree with the majority that the judgment of the Minnesota Supreme Court should be reversed. However, our agreement ends there. This case could easily be decided within the contours of established First Amendment law by holding, as petitioner argues, that the St. Paul ordinance is fatally overbroad because it criminalizes not only unprotected expression but expression protected by the First Amendment.

This Court's decisions have plainly stated that expression falling within certain limited categories so lacks the values the First Amendment was designed to protect that the Constitution affords no protection to that expression. Chaplinsky v. New Hampshire (1942). For instance, the Court has held that the individual who falsely shouts "fire" in a crowded theater may not claim the protection of the First Amendment. Schenck v. United States (1919). The Court has concluded that neither child pornography nor obscenity is protected by the First Amendment. New York v. Ferber (1982); Miller v. California (1973). And the Court has observed that, "[l]eaving aside the special considerations when public officials [and public figures] are the target, a libelous publication is not protected by the Constitution."

All of these categories are content based. But the Court has held that the First Amendment does not apply to them because their expressive content is worthless or of de minimis value to society. This categorical approach has provided a principled and narrowly focused means for distinguishing between expression that the government may regulate freely and that which it may regulate on the basis of content only upon a showing of compelling need.

Today, however, the Court announces that earlier Courts did not mean their repeated statements that certain categories of expression are "not within the area of constitutionally protected speech." The present Court submits that such clear statements "must be taken in context" and are not "literally true." To the contrary, those statements meant precisely what they said: The categorical approach is a firmly entrenched part of our First Amendment jurisprudence.

Nevertheless, the majority holds that the First Amendment protects those narrow categories of expression long held to be undeserving of First Amendment protection—at least to the extent that lawmakers may not regulate some fighting words more strictly than others because of their content. The Court announces that such content-based distinctions violate the First Amendment because "[t]he government may not regulate use based on hostility—or favoritism—towards the underlying message expressed." Should the government want to criminalize certain fighting words, the Court now requires it to criminalize all fighting words.

To borrow a phrase: "Such a simplistic, all-or-nothing-at-all approach to First Amendment protection is at odds with common sense and with our jurisprudence as well." It is inconsistent to hold that the government may proscribe an entire category of speech because the content of that speech is evil, but that the government may not treat a subset of that category differently without violating the First Amendment; the content of the subset is by definition worthless and undeserving of constitutional protection.

In a second break with precedent, the Court refuses to sustain the ordinance even though it would survive under the strict scrutiny applicable to other protected expression. Assuming, arguendo, that the St. Paul ordinance is a content-based regulation of protected expression, it nevertheless would pass First Amendment review under settled law upon a showing that the regulation "is necessary to serve a compelling state interest and is narrowly drawn to achieve that end."

St. Paul has urged that its ordinance, in the words of the majority, "helps to ensure the basic human rights of members of groups that have historically been subjected to discrimination. . . ." The Court expressly concedes that this interest is compelling and is promoted by the ordinance. Nevertheless, the Court treats strict scrutiny analysis as irrelevant to the constitutionality of the legislation. Under the majority's view, a narrowly drawn, content-based ordinance could never pass constitutional muster if the object of that legislation could be accomplished by banning a wider category of speech. This appears to be a general renunciation of strict scrutiny review, a fundamental tool of First Amendment analysis.

Although I disagree with the Court's analysis, I do agree with its conclusion: The St. Paul ordinance is unconstitutional. However, I would decide the case on overbreadth grounds. Although the ordinance as construed reaches categories of speech that are constitutionally unprotected, it also criminalizes a substantial amount of expression that—however repugnant—is shielded by the First Amendment.

Justice BLACKMUN, concurring in the judgment.

I regret what the Court has done in this case. The majority opinion signals one of two possibilities: It will serve as precedent for future cases, or it will not. Either result is disheartening.

In the first instance, by deciding that a State cannot regulate speech that causes great harm unless it also regulates speech that does not (setting law and logic on their heads), the Court seems to abandon the categorical approach, and inevitably to relax the level of scrutiny applicable to content-based laws. This weakens the traditional protections of speech. If all expressive activity must be accorded the same protection, that protection will be scant. The simple reality is that the Court will never provide child pornography or cigarette advertising the level of protection customarily granted political speech. If we are forbidden to categorize, as the Court has done here, we shall reduce protection across the board. It is sad that in its effort to reach a satisfying result in this case, the Court is willing to weaken First Amendment protections.

In the second instance is the possibility that this case will not significantly alter First Amendment jurisprudence but, instead, will be regarded as an aberration—a case where the Court manipulated doctrine to strike down an ordinance whose premise it opposed, namely, that racial threats and verbal assaults are of greater harm than other fighting words. I fear that the Court has been distracted from its proper mission by the temptation to decide the issue over "politically correct speech" and "cultural diversity," neither of which is presented here. If this is the meaning of today's opinion, it is perhaps even more regrettable.

I see no First Amendment values that are compromised by a law that prohibits hoodlums from driving minorities out of their homes by burning crosses on their lawns, but I see great harm in preventing the people of Saint Paul from specifically punishing the race-based fighting words that so prejudice their community.

I concur in the judgment, however, because I agree with Justice White that this particular ordinance reaches beyond fighting words to speech protected by the First Amendment.

R.A.V. can be appraised on many levels. First, it can be analyzed in terms of what it means for the fighting words doctrine. *R.A.V.* means that a fighting words law will be upheld only if does not draw content-based distinctions among types of speech, such as by prohibiting fighting words based on race, but not based on political affiliation. The problem, though, is that it will be extremely difficult for legislation to meet this requirement without being so broad that the law will be invalidated on vagueness or overbreadth grounds.

Second, *R.A.V.* can be analyzed in terms of the Court's holding that there is a strong presumption against content-based discrimination within categories of unprotected speech. This was the issue that most divided the justices in the majority from those concurring in the judgment. On the one hand, Justice Scalia makes a powerful argument that the government should not be able to prohibit only obscenity or fighting words that contain messages critical of the government. But on the other hand, the concurring justices make a persuasive point that inevitably in regulating categories of unprotected speech, the government will not forbid all such speech but draw lines. Such lines are vulnerable after *R.A.V.* Justice Blackmun's prophecy has proven true in that the Court as not applied this aspect of *R.A.V.*

Finally, in examining *R.A.V.*, there is the question of whether the case should have been found to meet the exceptions that Justice Scalia recognized where content-based discrimination is allowed. Justice Scalia's majority opinion indicated two circumstances where content-based distinctions within categories of unprotected speech would be allowed. One instance where Justice Scalia would allow content discrimination is where the distinction advances the reason why the category is unprotected. Yet there is a strong argument that this was true with regard to the St. Paul ordinance; the law seemingly was based on a judgment that fighting words based on race, religion, or gender are most likely to cause the harms that the fighting words doctrine means to prevent.

The other exception is where the restriction of speech is meant to prevent secondary effects. The St. Paul ordinance is written specifically in terms of secondary effects; it proscribes speech that would "anger, alarm, or cause resentment." The problem is in deciding whether these are "secondary effects" or a content-based justification for regulating speech.

2. The Hostile Audience Cases

In some cases, especially in the 1940s and the 1950s, the Supreme Court applied the clear and present danger test in dealing with the issue of when the

B. Fighting Words, the Hostile Audience, and the Problem of Racist Speech

government may punish individuals for speech that provokes a hostile audience reaction. For example, in Terminiello v. Chicago, 337 U.S. 1 (1949), the Court overturned a conviction for disturbing the peace because it was not shown that the speech posed a clear and present danger of lawlessness. Terminiello was convicted for disturbing the peace because of a speech that he gave in which he attacked his opponents as "slimy scum," "snakes," and "bedbugs." Despite the presence of many police officers, disturbances broke out. The trial court's instructions to the jury said that the defendant could be convicted for speech that "stirs the public to anger, invites dispute, brings about a condition of unrest, or creates a disturbance."

The Court overturned the conviction and found that the jury instruction was not sufficiently protective of speech. The Court declared: "A function of free speech under our system is to invite dispute. It may indeed best serve its high purpose when it induces a condition of unrest, creates dissatisfaction with conditions as they are, or even stirs people to anger. [That] is why freedom of speech, though not absolute, [is] nevertheless protected against censorship or punishment, *unless shown likely to produce a clear and present danger of a serious substantive evil that rises far above public inconvenience, annoyance or unrest.*"

Similarly, in Cantwell v. Connecticut, 310 U.S. 296 (1940), the Supreme Court overturned a conviction for disturbing the peace because of the absence of proof of a clear and present danger. Jesse Cantwell, a Jehovah's Witness, was prosecuted for playing a phonograph record on a street corner that attacked the Roman Catholic religion. The Court said that "[w]hen clear and present danger of riot, disorder, interference with traffic upon the public streets, or other immediate threat to public safety, peace, or order, appears, the power of the State to prevent or punish is obvious. Equally obvious is it that a State may not unduly suppress free communication of views, religious or otherwise, under the guise of conserving desirable conditions." The Court overturned the conviction because the speech posed "no such clear and present menace to public peace and order."

Although in *Terminiello* and *Cantwell* the Court applied the clear and present danger test to protect speech, in Feiner v. New York, 340 U.S. 315 (1951), the test was used to uphold a conviction.

In *Feiner*, an individual was convicted for a speech that he gave that sharply criticized the president and local political officials for their inadequate record on civil rights. Some members of the crowd seemed angered by the speech, and the police asked the speaker to leave. After the speaker refused, the police arrested him. The Supreme Court upheld the conviction for disturbing the peace. The Court quoted *Cantwell* to state that the government may prevent or punish speech that poses a clear and present danger. The Court concluded: "It is one thing to say that the police cannot be used as an instrument for the suppression of unpopular views, and another to say that, when as here the speaker passes the bounds of argument or persuasion and undertakes incitement to riot, they are powerless to prevent a breach of the peace."

The problem with the clear and present danger test in this context is that it allows an audience reaction, if hostile enough, to be a basis for suppressing a speaker. A speaker who is acting completely lawfully can be silenced because of illegal behavior — threats of violence and use of force — by members of the audience. Indeed, Justice Black, dissenting in *Feiner*, said that the appropriate response of the police should have been to control the crowd, and only if that was impossible and a threat to breach the peace imminent could the police arrest the speaker. Justice Black argued: "I reject the implication of the Court's opinion that the police had no obligation to protect petitioner's constitutional right to talk. The police of course have power to prevent breaches of the peace. But if, in the name of preserving order, they ever can interfere with a lawful public speaker, they first must make all reasonable efforts to protect him. Here the policemen did not even pretend to try to protect petitioner."

In later cases, the Supreme Court appeared to follow the approach articulated in Justice Black's dissent in *Feiner*, although the Court never has overruled *Feiner* or the earlier cases using the clear and present danger test. For example, in Edwards v. South Carolina, 372 U.S. 229 (1963), the Court overturned a conviction for civil rights protestors who had staged a march to the South Carolina capitol. A significant hostile crowd gathered, although there was no violence or threat of violence. The speakers were arrested after they ignored a police order to disperse. The Court emphasized that "police protection at the scene was at all times sufficient to meet any foreseeable possibility of disorder." The Court distinguished *Feiner* based on the absence of any violence or threat of violence in the march to the state capitol.

In Cox v. Louisiana, 379 U.S. 536 (1965), an individual was convicted for giving a speech objecting to the racial segregation of lunch counters and urging a sit-in. Some members of the audience found the speech inflammatory and the speaker was arrested a day after the demonstration. The Court overturned the conviction and again emphasized the ability of the police to control the crowd. The Court stated, "It is virtually undisputed, however, that the students themselves were not violent and threatened no violence. The fear of violence seems to have been based upon the reaction of the groups of white citizens looking on from across the street. . . . There is no indication, however, that any member of the white group threatened violence. . . . [A police officer testified that] they could have handled the crowd."

Similarly, in Gregory v. City of Chicago, 394 U.S. 111 (1969), the Court unanimously overturned convictions for disturbing the peace for a group of civil rights demonstrators who had been arrested when an angry group threatened the marchers. The civil rights protestors were marching to the mayor's house when some members of an opposing group reacted angrily, made threats against the demonstrators, and threw rocks at them. The Court overturned the conviction because the law did not limit convictions to instances where there was a threat of imminent violence, where the police made all reasonable efforts to protect the demonstrators, and where the police requested that the demonstration be stopped.

Perhaps these cases can be read as applications of the clear and present danger test with the Court concluding that there was not sufficient evidence under the circumstances to justify a conclusion of imminent threat to a breach of the peace. But an alternative way of reading the cases is as being more speech-protective than the clear and present danger test; that is, as being much closer to Justice Black's approach in *Feiner* than to its majority opinion. From this perspective, the First Amendment requires that the police try to control the audience that is threatening violence and stop the speaker only if crowd control is impossible and a threat to breach of the peace is imminent.

3. The Problem of Racist Speech

Over the past few decades, there has been an important debate among scholars as to whether, and when, the government may punish racist speech.[14] Over 360 colleges and universities adopted hate speech codes of various types. Additionally, many governments have adopted laws prohibiting racist speech.

Those who favor restrictions on hate speech emphasize how racist hate speech undermines the constitutional value of equality. For example, in the context of colleges and universities, hate speech makes traditionally underrepresented minorities feel unwelcome and perpetuates their exclusion. Moreover, it is argued that hate speech is a form of verbal assault that the law should punish.

But those who oppose such hate speech restrictions maintain that it is wrong to stop speech because it is distasteful and offensive. Additionally, opponents argue that it is impossible to formulate a definition of racist speech that is not unconstitutionally vague and overbroad. Furthermore, opponents of hate speech codes argue that practical experience indicates that they are most likely to be used against minorities. The opponents maintain that unless the speech meets the traditional definition of an assault, racist speech, however vile, is protected by the First Amendment.

In Beauharnais v. Illinois, 343 U.S. 250 (1952), the Supreme Court upheld a state law that prohibited any publication that portrayed "depravity, criminality, unchastity, or lack of virtue of a class of citizens, of any race, color, creed, or religion [which exposes such citizens] to contempt, derision, or obloquy or which is productive of breach of the peace or riots." The Court, in an opinion by Justice Frankfurter, affirmed the conviction of individuals who urged the mayor and city council of Chicago to protect white neighborhoods from "encroachment, harassment, and invasion . . . by the Negro" and called for "one million self respecting white people in Chicago to unite."

The Court said that just as a state could punish defamation, so may a state "punish the same utterance directed at a defined group." The Court stressed the strife caused by expressions of hate based on race and religion. Justice Frankfurter's opinion concluded that the government did not need to meet the clear and present danger test because "[l]ibelous utterances not being within the area of constitutionally protected speech, it is unnecessary, neither for us or for the State courts, to consider the issues behind the phrase 'clear and present danger.'"

Beauharnais is the strongest authority for the government to regulate racist speech, and it never has been overruled. Yet for many reasons it is questionable whether *Beauharnais* is still good law.[15] *Beauharnais* is based on the assumption that

---

14. *See, e.g.,* Charles R. Lawrence, III, *If He Hollers Let Him Go: Regulating Racist Speech on Campus*, 1990 Duke L.J. 431; Mari Matsuda, *Public Response to Racist Speech: Considering the Victim's Story*, 87 Mich. L. Rev. 2320 (1989); Richard Delgado, *Words That Wound: A Tort Action for Racial Insults, Epithets, and Name-Calling*, 17 Harv. Civ. Rts.-Civ. Lib. L. Rev. 133 (1982) (all favoring restrictions on hate speech); *see also* Nadine Strossen, Hate: Why We Should Resist it with Free Speech, Not Censorship (2018); Erwin Chemerinsky & Howard Gillman, Free Speech on Campus (2017).

15. Indeed, the United States Court of Appeals for the Seventh Circuit has expressly said that it does not believe that *Beauharnais* survives and is any longer good law. American Booksellers Assn. v. Hudnut, 771 F.2d 323 (7th Cir. 1985); Collin v. Smith, 578 F.2d 1197, 1204-1205 (7th Cir. 1978).

defamation liability is unlimited by the First Amendment—a premise expressly rejected by the Supreme Court a decade later in New York Times v. Sullivan. The speech that led to the conviction in *Beauharnais*, however vile, was political speech, and it is doubtful that the Court would allow punishment of individuals for expressing opinions about racial groups or calling for government actions. The Court's decision in R.A.V. v. City of St. Paul, described above, strongly indicates that expression of hate is not a category of speech entirely outside First Amendment protection.[16] Moreover, the Illinois statute upheld in *Beauharnais* almost certainly would be declared unconstitutional today based on vagueness and overbreadth grounds.

A reflection of the unwillingness of courts to follow *Beauharnais* is found in the protection of the ability of Nazis to stage a march in the predominantly Jewish suburb of Skokie, Illinois. In 1977, the leaders of the National Socialist Party of America announced that it planned to hold a peaceful demonstration in Skokie, a town where there were many survivors of Nazi concentration camps.

A trial court issued an injunction preventing the marchers from wearing Nazi uniforms, displaying swastikas, or expressing hatred against Jewish people. The court relied in part on testimony concerning a large counterdemonstration and the fear of a violent confrontation between the two groups. Although the state appellate courts upheld this injunction, the United States Supreme Court granted certiorari and summarily reversed the state courts.[17] The Court emphasized that appellate review of the trial court's injunction could take a year or more to complete and said that a stay was required unless there was immediate appellate review.

On remand, the Illinois Court of Appeals modified the injunction so that it only prohibited display of the swastika. The Illinois Supreme Court reversed and vacated the entire injunction as violating the First Amendment.[18]

Meanwhile, Skokie adopted several ordinances that were intended to prevent the Nazis from speaking there. For example, the laws required applicants for parade permits to purchase a substantial amount of insurance, prohibited dissemination of material that "promotes and incites hatred" based on race or religion, and outlawed wearing military-style uniforms in demonstrations. The United States Court of Appeals for the Seventh Circuit declared these ordinances unconstitutional and expressly said that it no longer regarded *Beauharnais* as good law.[19] After winning in the courts, the Nazi party canceled its rally in Skokie and held a small protest march in Chicago.

The Skokie controversy reflects many basic First Amendment principles. Expression of hate is protected speech, and the government may not outlaw symbols of hate such as swastikas. Moreover, the government cannot suppress a speaker because of the reaction of the audience. Skokie was not allowed to prevent the Nazis from marching because their demonstration would deeply offend and upset Holocaust survivors or even might provoke a violent response.

---

16. *See also* Dawson v. Delaware, 503 U.S. 159 (1992) (holding that it was reversible error for a jury to be instructed that a defendant was a member of the Aryan Brotherhood, which was stipulated to be a "white racist gang," because it was irrelevant and violated the First Amendment).
17. National Socialist Party of Am. v. Village of Skokie, 432 U.S. 43, 44 (1977).
18. 69 Ill. 2d 605, 373 N.E.2d 21 (1978).
19. Collin v. Smith, 578 F.2d 1197 (7th Cir. 1978). The Supreme Court denied a stay of this decision. Smith v. Collin, 436 U.S. 953 (1978).

B. Fighting Words, the Hostile Audience, and the Problem of Racist Speech

The Supreme Court subsequently addressed the issue of racist speech in Virginia v. Black, where it considered the constitutionality of a law criminally prohibiting cross burning.

VIRGINIA v. BLACK
538 U.S. 343 (2003)

Justice O'CONNOR announced the judgment of the Court and delivered the opinion of the Court with respect to Parts I, II, and III, and an opinion with respect to Parts IV and V, in which THE CHIEF JUSTICE, Justice STEVENS, and Justice BREYER join.

In this case we consider whether the Commonwealth of Virginia's statute banning cross burning with "an intent to intimidate a person or group of persons" violates the First Amendment. We conclude that while a State, consistent with the First Amendment, may ban cross burning carried out with the intent to intimidate, the provision in the Virginia statute treating any cross burning as prima facie evidence of intent to intimidate renders the statute unconstitutional in its current form.

I

Respondents Barry Black, Richard Elliott, and Jonathan O'Mara were convicted separately of violating Virginia's cross-burning statute. That statute provides: "It shall be unlawful for any person or persons, with the intent of intimidating any person or group of persons, to burn, or cause to be burned, a cross on the property of another, a highway or other public place. Any person who shall violate any provision of this section shall be guilty of a Class 6 felony." "Any such burning of a cross shall be prima facie evidence of an intent to intimidate a person or group of persons."

On August 22, 1998, Barry Black led a Ku Klux Klan rally in Carroll County, Virginia. Twenty-five to thirty people attended this gathering, which occurred on private property with the permission of the owner, who was in attendance. The property was located on an open field just off Brushy Fork Road (State Highway 690) in Cana, Virginia. When the sheriff of Carroll County learned that a Klan rally was occurring in his county, he went to observe it from the side of the road. During the approximately one hour that the sheriff was present, about 40 to 50 cars passed the site, a "few" of which stopped to ask the sheriff what was happening on the property. Eight to ten houses were located in the vicinity of the rally. Rebecca Sechrist, who was related to the owner of the property where the rally took place, "sat and watched to see wha[t was] going on" from the lawn of her in-laws' house. She looked on as the Klan prepared for the gathering and subsequently conducted the rally itself.

During the rally, Sechrist heard Klan members speak about "what they were" and "what they believed in." The speakers "talked real bad about the blacks and the Mexicans." One speaker told the assembled gathering that "he would love to take a .30/.30 and just random[ly] shoot the blacks." The speakers also talked about "President Clinton and Hillary Clinton," and about how their tax money "goes to . . . the black people." Sechrist testified that this language made her "very . . . scared."

At the conclusion of the rally, the crowd circled around a 25- to 30-foot cross. The cross was between 300 and 350 yards away from the road. According to the sheriff, the cross "then all of a sudden . . . went up in a flame." As the cross burned, the Klan played Amazing Grace over the loudspeakers. Sechrist stated that the cross burning made her feel "awful" and "terrible."

When the sheriff observed the cross burning, he informed his deputy that they needed to "find out who's responsible and explain to them that they cannot do this in the State of Virginia." The sheriff then went down the driveway, entered the rally, and asked "who was responsible for burning the cross." Black responded, "I guess I am because I'm the head of the rally." The sheriff then told Black, "[T]here's a law in the State of Virginia that you cannot burn a cross and I'll have to place you under arrest for this."

Black was charged with burning a cross with the intent of intimidating a person or group of persons, in violation of §18.2-423. At his trial, the jury was instructed that "intent to intimidate means the motivation to intentionally put a person or a group of persons in fear of bodily harm. Such fear must arise from the willful conduct of the accused rather than from some mere temperamental timidity of the victim." The trial court also instructed the jury that "the burning of a cross by itself is sufficient evidence from which you may infer the required intent."

On May 2, 1998, respondents Richard Elliott and Jonathan O'Mara, as well as a third individual, attempted to burn a cross on the yard of James Jubilee. Jubilee, an African-American, was Elliott's next-door neighbor in Virginia Beach, Virginia. Four months prior to the incident, Jubilee and his family had moved from California to Virginia Beach. Before the cross burning, Jubilee spoke to Elliott's mother to inquire about shots being fired from behind the Elliott home. Elliott's mother explained to Jubilee that her son shot firearms as a hobby, and that he used the backyard as a firing range. On the night of May 2, respondents drove a truck onto Jubilee's property, planted a cross, and set it on fire. Their apparent motive was to "get back" at Jubilee for complaining about the shooting in the backyard. Respondents were not affiliated with the Klan. The next morning, as Jubilee was pulling his car out of the driveway, he noticed the partially burned cross approximately 20 feet from his house. Elliott and O'Mara were charged with attempted cross burning and conspiracy to commit cross burning. O'Mara pleaded guilty to both counts, reserving the right to challenge the constitutionality of the cross-burning statute. The judge sentenced O'Mara to 90 days in jail and fined him $2,500. The judge also suspended 45 days of the sentence and $1,000 of the fine.

The jury found Elliott guilty of attempted cross burning and acquitted him of conspiracy to commit cross burning. It sentenced Elliott to 90 days in jail and a $2,500 fine.

II

Cross burning originated in the 14th century as a means for Scottish tribes to signal each other. Sir Walter Scott used cross burnings for dramatic effect in The Lady of the Lake, where the burning cross signified both a summons and a call to arms. Cross burning in this country, however, long ago became unmoored

B. Fighting Words, the Hostile Audience, and the Problem of Racist Speech

from its Scottish ancestry. Burning a cross in the United States is inextricably intertwined with the history of the Ku Klux Klan.

The first Ku Klux Klan began in Pulaski, Tennessee, in the spring of 1866. Although the Ku Klux Klan started as a social club, it soon changed into something far different. The Klan fought Reconstruction and the corresponding drive to allow freed blacks to participate in the political process. Soon the Klan imposed "a veritable reign of terror" throughout the South. The Klan employed tactics such as whipping, threatening to burn people at the stake, and murder. The Klan's victims included blacks, southern whites who disagreed with the Klan, and "carpetbagger" northern whites.

From [early in the 20th century], cross burnings have been used to communicate both threats of violence and messages of shared ideology. The first initiation ceremony occurred on Stone Mountain near Atlanta, Georgia. While a 40-foot cross burned on the mountain, the Klan members took their oaths of loyalty. This cross burning was the second recorded instance in the United States. The first known cross burning in the country had occurred a little over one month before the Klan initiation, when a Georgia mob celebrated the lynching of Leo Frank by burning a "gigantic cross" on Stone Mountain that was "visible throughout" Atlanta.

Throughout the history of the Klan, cross burnings have also remained potent symbols of shared group identity and ideology. The burning cross became a symbol of the Klan itself and a central feature of Klan gatherings. According to the Klan constitution (called the kloran), the "fiery cross" was the "emblem of that sincere, unselfish devotedness of all klansmen to the sacred purpose and principles we have espoused." And the Klan has often published its newsletters and magazines under the name The Fiery Cross. At Klan gatherings across the country, cross burning became the climax of the rally or the initiation. Posters advertising an upcoming Klan rally often featured a Klan member holding a cross.

In short, a burning cross has remained a symbol of Klan ideology and of Klan unity. To this day, regardless of whether the message is a political one or whether the message is also meant to intimidate, the burning of a cross is a "symbol of hate." And while cross burning sometimes carries no intimidating message, at other times the intimidating message is the only message conveyed. For example, when a cross burning is directed at a particular person not affiliated with the Klan, the burning cross often serves as a message of intimidation, designed to inspire in the victim a fear of bodily harm. Moreover, the history of violence associated with the Klan shows that the possibility of injury or death is not just hypothetical. The person who burns a cross directed at a particular person often is making a serious threat, meant to coerce the victim to comply with the Klan's wishes unless the victim is willing to risk the wrath of the Klan. Indeed, as the cases of respondents Elliott and O'Mara indicate, individuals without Klan affiliation who wish to threaten or menace another person sometimes use cross burning because of this association between a burning cross and violence.

In sum, while a burning cross does not inevitably convey a message of intimidation, often the cross burner intends that the recipients of the message fear for their lives. And when a cross burning is used to intimidate, few if any messages are more powerful.

III

A

The hallmark of the protection of free speech is to allow "free trade in ideas"—even ideas that the overwhelming majority of people might find distasteful or discomforting. Thus, the First Amendment "ordinarily" denies a State "the power to prohibit dissemination of social, economic and political doctrine which a vast majority of its citizens believes to be false and fraught with evil consequence." The protections afforded by the First Amendment, however, are not absolute, and we have long recognized that the government may regulate certain categories of expression consistent with the Constitution. The First Amendment permits "restrictions upon the content of speech in a few limited areas, which are 'of such slight social value as a step to truth that any benefit that may be derived from them is clearly outweighed by the social interest in order and morality.'"

Thus, for example, a State may punish those words "which by their very utterance inflict injury or tend to incite an immediate breach of the peace." We have consequently held that fighting words—"those personally abusive epithets which, when addressed to the ordinary citizen, are, as a matter of common knowledge, inherently likely to provoke violent reaction"—are generally proscribable under the First Amendment. Furthermore, "the constitutional guarantees of free speech and free press do not permit a State to forbid or proscribe advocacy of the use of force or of law violation except where such advocacy is directed to inciting or producing imminent lawless action and is likely to incite or produce such action." Brandenburg v. Ohio (1969). And the First Amendment also permits a State to ban a "true threat." Watts v. United States (1969).

"True threats" encompass those statements where the speaker means to communicate a serious expression of an intent to commit an act of unlawful violence to a particular individual or group of individuals. The speaker need not actually intend to carry out the threat. Rather, a prohibition on true threats "protect[s] individuals from the fear of violence" and "from the disruption that fear engenders," in addition to protecting people "from the possibility that the threatened violence will occur." Intimidation in the constitutionally proscribable sense of the word is a type of true threat, where a speaker directs a threat to a person or group of persons with the intent of placing the victim in fear of bodily harm or death. Respondents do not contest that some cross burnings fit within this meaning of intimidating speech, and rightly so. As noted in Part II, supra, the history of cross burning in this country shows that cross burning is often intimidating, intended to create a pervasive fear in victims that they are a target of violence.

B

It is true, as the Supreme Court of Virginia held, that the burning of a cross is symbolic expression. The reason why the Klan burns a cross at its rallies, or individuals place a burning cross on someone else's lawn, is that the burning cross represents the message that the speaker wishes to communicate. Individuals burn crosses as opposed to other because cross burning carries a message in an effective and dramatic manner.[20]

---

20. Justice Thomas argues in dissent that cross burning is "conduct, not expression." While it is of course true that burning a cross is conduct, it is equally true that the First Amendment protects symbolic conduct as well as pure speech. As Justice Thomas has previously recognized, a burning cross is a "symbol of hate," and "a symbol of white supremacy." [Footnote by the Court.]

B. Fighting Words, the Hostile Audience, and the Problem of Racist Speech

The fact that cross burning is symbolic expression, however, does not resolve the constitutional question. In R.A.V. v. St. Paul (1992), we held that a local ordinance that banned certain symbolic conduct, including cross burning, when done with the knowledge that such conduct would "arouse anger, alarm or resentment in others on the basis of race, color, creed, religion or gender" was unconstitutional. We held that the ordinance did not pass constitutional muster because it discriminated on the basis of content by targeting only those individuals who "provoke violence" on a basis specified in the law. The ordinance did not cover "[t]hose who wish to use 'fighting words' in connection with other ideas—to express hostility, for example, on the basis of political affiliation, union membership, or homosexuality." This content-based discrimination was unconstitutional because it allowed the city "to impose special prohibitions on those speakers who express views on disfavored subjects."

We did not hold in *R.A.V.* that the First Amendment prohibits all forms of content-based discrimination within a proscribable area of speech. Rather, we specifically stated that some types of content discrimination did not violate the First Amendment. Indeed, we noted that it would be constitutional to ban only a particular type of threat: "[T]he Federal Government can criminalize only those threats of violence that are directed against the President . . . since the reasons why threats of violence are outside the First Amendment . . . have special force when applied to the person of the President." And a State may "choose to prohibit only that obscenity which is the most patently offensive in its prurience—i.e., that which involves the most lascivious displays of sexual activity." Unlike the statute at issue in *R.A.V.*, the Virginia statute does not single out for opprobrium only that speech directed toward "one of the specified disfavored topics." It does not matter whether an individual burns a cross with intent to intimidate because of the victim's race, gender, or religion, or because of the victim's "political affiliation, union membership, or homosexuality." Moreover, as a factual matter it is not true that cross burners direct their intimidating conduct solely to racial or religious minorities.

The First Amendment permits Virginia to outlaw cross burnings done with the intent to intimidate because burning a cross is a particularly virulent form of intimidation. Instead of prohibiting all intimidating messages, Virginia may choose to regulate this subset of intimidating messages in light of cross burning's long and pernicious history as a signal of impending violence. Thus, just as a State may regulate only that obscenity which is the most obscene due to its prurient content, so too may a State choose to prohibit only those forms of intimidation that are most likely to inspire fear of bodily harm. A ban on cross burning carried out with the intent to intimidate is fully consistent with our holding in *R.A.V.* and is proscribable under the First Amendment.

IV

The Supreme Court of Virginia ruled in the alternative that Virginia's cross-burning statute was unconstitutionally overbroad due to its provision stating that "[a]ny such burning of a cross shall be prima facie evidence of an intent to intimidate a person or group of persons." The Commonwealth added the prima facie provision to the statute in 1968. The court below did not reach whether this provision is severable from the rest of the cross-burning statute under Virginia law. The Supreme Court of Virginia has not ruled on the meaning of the prima facie evidence provision. It has, however, stated that "the act of burning a cross alone, with no evidence of intent to intimidate, will nonetheless suffice for arrest and prosecution and will insulate the Commonwealth from a motion to strike the evidence at the end of its case-in-chief."

The prima facie evidence provision, as interpreted by the jury instruction, renders the statute unconstitutional. As construed by the jury instruction, the prima facie provision strips away the very reason why a State may ban cross burning with the intent to intimidate. The prima facie evidence provision permits a jury to convict in every cross-burning case in which defendants exercise their constitutional right not to put on a defense. And even where a defendant like Black presents a defense, the prima facie evidence provision makes it more likely that the jury will find an intent to intimidate regardless of the particular facts of the case. The provision permits the Commonwealth to arrest, prosecute, and convict a person based solely on the fact of cross burning itself.

It is apparent that the provision as so interpreted "would create an unacceptable risk of the suppression of ideas." The act of burning a cross may mean that a person is engaging in constitutionally proscribable intimidation. But that same act may mean only that the person is engaged in core political speech. The prima facie evidence provision in this statute blurs the line between these two meanings of a burning cross. As interpreted by the jury instruction, the provision chills constitutionally protected political speech because of the possibility that a State will prosecute—and potentially convict—somebody engaging only in lawful political speech at the core of what the First Amendment is designed to protect.

As the history of cross burning indicates, a burning cross is not always intended to intimidate. Rather, sometimes the cross burning is a statement of ideology, a symbol of group solidarity. It is a ritual used at Klan gatherings, and it is used to represent the Klan itself. Thus, "[b]urning a cross at a political rally would almost certainly be protected expression." Indeed, occasionally a person who burns a cross does not intend to express either a statement of ideology or intimidation. Cross burnings have appeared in movies such as Mississippi Burning, and in plays such as the stage adaptation of Sir Walter Scott's The Lady of the Lake.

The prima facie provision makes no effort to distinguish among these different types of cross burnings. It does not distinguish between a cross burning done with the purpose of creating anger or resentment and a cross burning done with the purpose of threatening or intimidating a victim. It does not distinguish between a cross burning at a public rally or a cross burning on a neighbor's lawn. It does not treat the cross burning directed at an individual differently from the cross burning directed at a group of like-minded believers. It allows a jury to treat a cross burning on the property of another with the owner's acquiescence in the same manner as a cross burning on the property of another without the owner's permission.

It may be true that a cross burning, even at a political rally, arouses a sense of anger or hatred among the vast majority of citizens who see a burning cross. But this sense of anger or hatred is not sufficient to ban all cross burnings. The prima facie evidence provision in this case ignores all of the contextual factors that are necessary to decide whether a particular cross burning is intended to intimidate. The First Amendment does not permit such a shortcut.

B. Fighting Words, the Hostile Audience, and the Problem of Racist Speech

For these reasons, the prima facie evidence provision, as interpreted through the jury instruction and as applied in Barry Black's case, is unconstitutional on its face.

V

With respect to Barry Black, we agree with the Supreme Court of Virginia that his conviction cannot stand, and we affirm the judgment of the Supreme Court of Virginia. With respect to Elliott and O'Mara, we vacate the judgment of the Supreme Court of Virginia, and remand the case for further proceedings.

Justice THOMAS, dissenting.

In every culture, certain things acquire meaning well beyond what outsiders can comprehend. That goes for both the sacred, and the profane. I believe that cross burning is the paradigmatic example of the latter.

I

Although I agree with the majority's conclusion that it is constitutionally permissible to "ban . . . cross burning carried out with intent to intimidate," I believe that the majority errs in imputing an expressive component to the activity in question. In my view, whatever expressive value cross burning has, the legislature simply wrote it out by banning only intimidating conduct undertaken by a particular means. A conclusion that the statute prohibiting cross burning with intent to intimidate sweeps beyond a prohibition on certain conduct into the zone of expression overlooks not only the words of the statute but also reality.

"In holding [the ban on cross burning with intent to intimidate] unconstitutional, the Court ignores Justice Holmes' familiar aphorism that 'a page of history is worth a volume of logic.'" "The world's oldest, most persistent terrorist organization is not European or even Middle Eastern in origin. Fifty years before the Irish Republican Army was organized, a century before Al Fatah declared its holy war on Israel, the Ku Klux Klan was actively harassing, torturing and murdering in the United States. Today . . . its members remain fanatically committed to a course of violent opposition to social progress and racial equality in the United States." M. Newton & J. Newton, The Ku Klux Klan: An Encyclopedia vii (1991).

To me, the majority's brief history of the Ku Klux Klan only reinforces this common understanding of the Klan as a terrorist organization, which, in its endeavor to intimidate, or even eliminate those it dislikes, uses the most brutal of methods. Such methods typically include cross burning—"a tool for the intimidation and harassment of racial minorities, Catholics, Jews, Communists, and any other groups hated by the Klan." For those not easily frightened, cross burning has been followed by more extreme measures, such as beatings and murder. As the Solicitor General points out, the association between acts of intimidating cross burning and violence is well documented in recent American history. In our culture, cross burning has almost invariably meant lawlessness and understandably instills in its victims well-grounded fear of physical violence.

Virginia's experience has been no exception. In Virginia, though facing widespread opposition in the 1920s, the KKK developed localized strength in the southeastern part of the State, where there were reports of scattered raids and floggings. Although the KKK was disbanded at the national level in 1944, a series of cross burnings in Virginia took place between 1949 and 1952.

It strains credulity to suggest that a state legislature that adopted a litany of segregationist laws self-contradictorily intended to squelch the segregationist message. Even for segregationists, violent and terroristic conduct, the Siamese twin of cross burning, was intolerable. The ban on cross burning with intent to intimidate demonstrates that even segregationists understood the difference between intimidating and terroristic conduct and racist expression. It is simply beyond belief that, in passing the statute now under review, the Virginia legislature was concerned with anything but penalizing conduct it must have viewed as particularly vicious.

Accordingly, this statute prohibits only conduct, not expression. And, just as one cannot burn down someone's house to make a political point and then seek refuge in the First Amendment, those who hate cannot terrorize and intimidate to make their point. In light of my conclusion that the statute here addresses only conduct, there is no need to analyze it under any of our First Amendment tests.

II

Even assuming that the statute implicates the First Amendment, in my view, the fact that the statute permits a jury to draw an inference of intent to intimidate from the cross burning itself presents no constitutional problems. Therein lies my primary disagreement with the plurality.

The plurality is troubled by the presumption because this is a First Amendment case. The plurality laments the fate of an innocent cross-burner who burns a cross, but does so without an intent to intimidate. The plurality fears the chill on expression because, according to the plurality, the inference permits "the Commonwealth to arrest, prosecute and convict a person based solely on the fact of cross burning itself." First, it is, at the very least, unclear that the inference comes into play during arrest and initiation of a prosecution, that is, prior to the instructions stage of an actual trial. Second, the inference is rebuttable and, as the jury instructions given in this case demonstrate, Virginia law still requires the jury to find the existence of each element, including intent to intimidate, beyond a reasonable doubt.

C. SEXUALLY ORIENTED SPEECH

A major topic in First Amendment law is the ability of the government to regulate sexually oriented speech. First, the Supreme Court has held that obscenity is a category of speech unprotected by the First Amendment and has struggled to define what is "obscene." These cases are discussed in subsection 1. This section also considers whether obscenity should be a category of unprotected speech and the proposals that some have advanced that pornography should be banned as a form of discrimination against women.

C. Sexually Oriented Speech

Second, the Court has indicated that child pornography is not protected by the First Amendment, even if it does not fit within the definition of obscenity. This is considered in subsection 2.

Third, the Court has indicated the government has more latitude to regulate sexually oriented speech, even if it is not obscenity or child pornography that is unprotected by the First Amendment. For example, the Court has allowed the use of zoning ordinances to limit the locations of adult bookstores and movie theaters and permitted the government to ban nude dancing. These cases are discussed in subsection 3.

Subsection 4 examines the techniques that the government may and may not use in regulating sexually oriented materials. Governments have tried many techniques ranging from licensing schemes to prohibition of private possession to seizing assets of businesses convicted of violating obscenity laws.

Finally, subsection 5 considers the related question of the constitutional protection for profane language and indecent speech. The Supreme Court generally has held that profane and indecent speech are protected by the First Amendment, although there are exceptions where limits are allowed, notably over the broadcast media and in schools.

1. Obscenity

a. Supreme Court Decisions Finding Obscenity Unprotected

In Roth v. United States, the Supreme Court held that obscenity is a category of speech unprotected by the First Amendment.

<u>ROTH v. UNITED STATES</u>
354 U.S. 476 (1957)

Justice BRENNAN delivered the opinion of the Court.

The constitutionality of a criminal obscenity statute is the question. In *Roth*, the primary constitutional question is whether the federal obscenity statute violates the provision of the First Amendment. The federal obscenity statute prohibited the mailing of: "Every obscene, lewd, lascivious, or filthy book, pamphlet, picture, paper, letter, writing, print, or other publication of an indecent character."

The dispositive question is whether obscenity is utterance within the area of protected speech and press. Although this is the first time the question has been squarely presented to this Court, either under the First Amendment or under the Fourteenth Amendment, expressions found in numerous opinions indicate that this Court has always assumed that obscenity is not protected by the freedoms of speech and press.

The guaranties of freedom of expression in effect in 10 of the 14 States which by 1792 had ratified the Constitution, gave no absolute protection for every utterance. Thirteen of the 14 States provided for the prosecution of libel, and all of those States made either blasphemy or profanity, or both, statutory crimes. As early as 1712, Massachusetts made it criminal to publish "any filthy, obscene, or profane song, pamphlet, libel or mock sermon" in imitation or mimicking of religious services.

In light of this history, it is apparent that the unconditional phrasing of the First Amendment was not intended to protect every utterance. At the time of the adoption of the First Amendment, obscenity law was not as fully developed as libel law, but there is sufficiently contemporaneous evidence to show that obscenity, too, was outside the protection intended for speech and press.

The protection given speech and press was fashioned to assure unfettered interchange of ideas for the bringing about of political and social changes desired by the people. All ideas having even the slightest redeeming social importance—unorthodox ideas, controversial ideas, even ideas hateful to the prevailing climate of opinion—have the full protection of the guaranties, unless excludable because they encroach upon the limited area of more important interests. But implicit in the history of the First Amendment is the rejection of obscenity as utterly without redeeming social importance. This rejection for that reason is mirrored in the universal judgment that obscenity should be restrained, reflected in the international agreement of over 50 nations, in the obscenity laws of all of the 48 States, and in the 20 obscenity laws enacted by the Congress from 1842 to 1856.

However, sex and obscenity are not synonymous. Obscene material is material which deals with sex in a manner appealing to prurient interest.[21] The portrayal of sex, e.g., in art, literature and scientific works, is not itself sufficient reason to deny material the constitutional protection of freedom of speech and press. Sex, a great and mysterious motive force in human life, has indisputably been a subject of absorbing interest to mankind through the ages; it is one of the vital problems of human interest and public concern. Many decisions have recognized that these terms of obscenity statutes are not precise. This Court, however, has consistently held that lack of precision is not itself offensive to the requirements of due process.

In summary, then, we hold that these statutes, applied according to the proper standard for judging obscenity, do not offend constitutional safeguards against convictions based upon protected material, or fail to give mean in acting adequate notice of what is prohibited.

Justice Douglas, with whom Mr. Justice Black concurs, dissenting.

When we sustain these convictions, we make the legality of a publication turn on the purity of thought which a book or tract instills in the mind of the reader. I do not think we can approve that standard and be faithful to the command of the First Amendment, which by its terms is a restraint on Congress and which by the Fourteenth is a restraint on the States.

In the *Roth* case the trial judge charged the jury that the statutory words "obscene, lewd and lascivious", describe "that form of immorality which has

---

21. [That is], material having a tendency to excite lustful thoughts. Webster's New International Dictionary (Unabridged, 2d ed., 1949) defines prurient, in pertinent part, as follows: ". . . Itching; longing; uneasy with desire or longing; of persons, having itching, morbid, or lascivious longings; of desire, curiosity, or propensity, lewd. . . ." Pruriency is defined, in pertinent part, as follows: ". . . Quality of being prurient; lascivious desire or thought." We perceive no significant difference between the meaning of obscenity developed in the case law and the definition of the A.L.I., Model Penal Code, ". . . A thing is obscene if, considered as a whole, its predominant appeal is to prurient interest, i.e., a shameful or morbid interest in nudity, sex, or excretion, and if it goes substantially beyond customary limits of candor in description or representation of such matters." [Footnote by the Court.]

C. Sexually Oriented Speech

relation to sexual impurity and has a tendency to excite lustful thoughts." By these standards punishment is inflicted for thoughts provoked, not for overt acts nor antisocial conduct. This test cannot be squared with our decisions under the First Amendment.

The tests by which these convictions were obtained require only the arousing of sexual thoughts. Yet the arousing of sexual thoughts and desires happens every day in normal life in dozens of ways. The test of obscenity the Court endorses today gives the censor free range over a vast domain. To allow the State to step in and punish mere speech or publication that the judge or the jury thinks has an undesirable impact on thoughts but that is not shown to be a part of unlawful action is drastically to curtail the First Amendment.

In the years after *Roth*, the Court struggled to formulate a definition of obscenity.[22] The difficulty of these efforts was expressed by Justice Potter Stewart when he declared in Jacobellis v. Ohio, 378 U.S. 184 (1964) (Stewart, J., concurring): "I shall not today attempt further to define the kinds of material I understand to be embraced within that shorthand description; and perhaps I could never succeed in intelligibly doing so. But I know it when I see it, and the motion picture involved in this case is not that." Beginning in 1967, in Redrup v. New York, 386 U.S. 767 (1967), the Court overturned obscenity convictions in *per curiam* decisions without an opinion, something that the Court did more than 30 times in obscenity cases in the next six years.

In two five-to-four decisions in 1973, Paris Adult Theatre v. Slaton and Miller v. California, the Court reaffirmed that obscene "material is not protected by the First Amendment" and formulated the test for obscenity that continues to be used. The opinion in *Paris Adult Theatre* focuses primarily on justifying the continued exclusion of obscenity from First Amendment protection. Miller v. California articulated the definition of obscenity used to this day.

PARIS ADULT THEATRE I v. SLATON
413 U.S. 49 (1973)

Chief Justice BURGER delivered the opinion of the Court.

Petitioners are two Atlanta, Georgia, movie theaters and their owners and managers, operating in the style of "adult" theaters. On December 28, 1970, respondents, the local state district attorney and the solicitor for the local state trial court, filed civil complaints in that court alleging that petitioners were exhibiting to the public for paid admission two allegedly obscene films, contrary to Georgia Code Ann. The two films in question, "Magic Mirror" and "It All Comes Out in the End," depict sexual conduct characterized by the Georgia Supreme Court as "hard core pornography" leaving "little to the imagination." Paris Adult Theatre I and Paris Adult Theatre II [had] a conventional, inoffensive theater entrance, without any pictures, but with signs indicating that

---

22. *See, e.g.*, Mishkin v. New York, 383 U.S. 502 (1966); Ginzburg v. United States, 383 U.S. 463 (1966); Memoirs v. Massachusetts, 383 U.S. 413 (1966).

the theaters exhibit "Atlanta's Finest Mature Feature Films." On the door itself is a sign saying: "Adult Theatre—You must be 21 and able to prove it. If viewing the nude body offends you, Please Do Not Enter."

I

It should be clear from the outset that we do not undertake to tell the States what they must do, but rather to define the area in which they may chart their own course in dealing with obscene material. This Court has consistently held that obscene material is not protected by the First Amendment as a limitation on the state police power by virtue of the Fourteenth Amendment.

We categorically disapprove the theory, apparently adopted by the trial judge, that obscene, pornographic films acquire constitutional immunity from state regulation simply because they are exhibited for consenting adults only. This holding was properly rejected by the Georgia Supreme Court. Although we have often pointedly recognized the high importance of the state interest in regulating the exposure of obscene materials to juveniles and unconsenting adults, this Court has never declared these to be the only legitimate state interests permitting regulation of obscene material. The States have a long-recognized legitimate interest in regulating the use of obscene material in local commerce and in all places of public accommodation, as long as these regulations do not run afoul of specific constitutional prohibitions. "In an unbroken series of cases extending over a long stretch of this Court's history it has been accepted as a postulate that 'the primary requirements of decency may be enforced against obscene publications.'"

In particular, we hold that there are legitimate state interests at stake in stemming the tide of commercialized obscenity, even assuming it is feasible to enforce effective safeguards against exposure to juveniles and to passersby. These include the interest of the public in the quality of life and the total community environment, the tone of commerce in the great city centers, and, possibly, the public safety itself. The Hill-Link Minority Report of the Commission on Obscenity and Pornography indicates that there is at least an arguable correlation between obscene material and crime. As Chief Justice Warren stated, there is a "right of the Nation and of the States to maintain a decent society."

If we accept the unprovable assumption that a complete education requires the reading of certain books, and the well nigh universal belief that good books, plays, and art lift the spirit, improve the mind, enrich the human personality, and develop character, can we then say that a state legislature may not act on the corollary assumption that commerce in obscene books, or public exhibitions focused on obscene conduct, have a tendency to exert a corrupting and debasing impact leading to antisocial behavior? "Many of these effects may be intangible and indistinct, but they are nonetheless real."

To summarize, we have today reaffirmed the basic holding of Roth v. United States that obscene material has no protection under the First Amendment. We have directed our holdings, not at thoughts or speech, but at depiction and description of specifically defined sexual conduct that States may regulate within limits designed to prevent infringement of First Amendment rights. We have also reaffirmed that commerce in obscene material is unprotected

C. Sexually Oriented Speech

by any constitutional doctrine of privacy. In this case we hold that the States have a legitimate interest in regulating commerce in obscene material and in regulating exhibition of obscene material in places of public accommodation, including so-called "adult" theaters from which minors are excluded. In light of these holdings, nothing precludes the State of Georgia from the regulation of the allegedly obscene material exhibited in Paris Adult Theatre I or II, provided that the applicable Georgia law, as written or authoritatively interpreted by the Georgia courts, meets the First Amendment standards set forth in Miller v. California.

Justice BRENNAN, with whom Justice STEWART and Justice MARSHALL join, dissenting.

This case requires the Court to confront once again the vexing problem of reconciling state efforts to suppress sexually oriented expression with the protections of the First Amendment, as applied to the States through the Fourteenth Amendment. No other aspect of the First Amendment has, in recent years, demanded so substantial a commitment of our time, generated such disharmony of views, and remained so resistant to the formulation of stable and manageable standards. I am convinced that the approach initiated 16 years ago in Roth v. United States (1957), and culminating in the Court's decision today, cannot bring stability to this area of the law without jeopardizing fundamental First Amendment values, and I have concluded that the time has come to make a significant departure from that approach.

In Roth v. United States, the Court held that obscenity, although expression, falls outside the area of speech or press constitutionally protected under the First and Fourteenth Amendments against state or federal infringement. Yet our efforts to implement that approach demonstrate that agreement on the existence of something called "obscenity" is still a long and painful step from agreement on a workable definition of the term. The essence of our problem in the obscenity area is that we have been unable to provide "sensitive tools" to separate obscenity from other sexually oriented but constitutionally protected speech, so that efforts to suppress the former do not spill over into the suppression of the latter.

Of course, the vagueness problem would be largely of our own creation if it stemmed primarily from our failure to reach a consensus on any one standard. But after 16 years of experimentation and debate I am reluctantly forced to the conclusion that none of the available formulas, including the one announced today, can reduce the vagueness to a tolerable level while at the same time striking an acceptable balance between the protections of the First and Fourteenth Amendments, on the one hand, and on the other the asserted state interest in regulating the dissemination of certain sexually oriented materials. Any effort to draw a constitutionally acceptable boundary on state power must resort to such indefinite concepts as "prurient interest," "patent offensiveness," "serious literary value," and the like. The meaning of these concepts necessarily varies with the experience, outlook, and even idiosyncrasies of the person defining them. Although we have assumed that obscenity does exist and that we "know it when [we] see it," Jacobellis v. Ohio (Stewart, J., concurring), we are manifestly unable to describe it in advance except by reference to concepts so elusive that they fail to distinguish clearly between protected and unprotected speech.

Our experience since *Roth* requires us not only to abandon the effort to pick out obscene material on a case-by-case basis, but also to reconsider a fundamental postulate of *Roth*: that there exists a definable class of sexually oriented expression that may be totally suppressed by the Federal and State Governments. Assuming that such a class of expression does in fact exist, I am forced to conclude that the concept of "obscenity" cannot be defined with sufficient specificity and clarity to provide fair notice to persons who create and distribute sexually oriented materials, to prevent substantial erosion of protected speech as a byproduct of the attempt to suppress unprotected speech, and to avoid very costly institutional harms.

Like the proscription of abortions, the effort to suppress obscenity is predicated on unprovable, although strongly held, assumptions about human behavior, morality, sex, and religion. The existence of these assumptions cannot validate a statute that substantially undermines the guarantees of the First Amendment, any more than the existence of similar assumptions on the issue of abortion can validate a statute that infringes the constitutionally protected privacy interests of a pregnant woman.

In short, while I cannot say that the interests of the State—apart from the question of juveniles and unconsenting adults—are trivial or nonexistent, I am compelled to conclude that these interests cannot justify the substantial damage to constitutional rights and to this Nation's judicial machinery that inevitably results from state efforts to bar the distribution even of unprotected material to consenting adults.

MILLER v. CALIFORNIA
413 U.S. 15 (1973)

Chief Justice BURGER delivered the opinion of the Court.

This is one of a group of "obscenity-pornography" cases being reviewed by the Court in a re-examination of standards enunciated in earlier cases involving what Mr. Justice Harlan called "the intractable obscenity problem." Appellant conducted a mass mailing campaign to advertise the sale of illustrated books, euphemistically called "adult" material. After a jury trial, he was convicted of violating California Penal Code, a misdemeanor, by knowingly distributing obscene matter.

This case involves the application of a State's criminal obscenity statute to a situation in which sexually explicit materials have been thrust by aggressive sales action upon unwilling recipients who had in no way indicated any desire to receive such materials. This Court has recognized that the States have a legitimate interest in prohibiting dissemination or exhibition of obscene material when the mode of dissemination carries with it a significant danger of offending the sensibilities of unwilling recipients or of exposure to juveniles.

It is in this context that we are called on to define the standards which must be used to identify obscene material that a State may regulate without infringing on the First Amendment as applicable to the States through the Fourteenth Amendment. Apart from the initial formulation in the *Roth* case, no majority of the Court has at any given time been able to agree on a standard to determine what constitutes obscene, pornographic material subject to regulation under the States' police power.

C. Sexually Oriented Speech

This much has been categorically settled by the Court, that obscene material is unprotected by the First Amendment. We acknowledge, however, the inherent dangers of undertaking to regulate any form of expression. State statutes designed to regulate obscene materials must be carefully limited. As a result, we now confine the permissible scope of such regulation to works which depict or describe sexual conduct. That conduct must be specifically defined by the applicable state law, as written or authoritatively construed. A state offense must also be limited to works which, taken as a whole, appeal to the prurient interest in sex, which portray sexual conduct in a patently offensive way, and which, taken as a whole, do not have serious literary, artistic, political, or scientific value.

The basic guidelines for the trier of fact must be: (a) whether "the average person, applying contemporary community standards" would find that the work, taken as a whole, appeals to the prurient interest; (b) whether the work depicts or describes, in a patently offensive way, sexual conduct specifically defined by the applicable state law; and (c) whether the work, taken as a whole, lacks serious literary, artistic, political, or scientific value. We do not adopt as a constitutional standard the "utterly without redeeming social value" test of Memoirs v. Massachusetts; that concept has never commanded the adherence of more than three Justices at one time.

We emphasize that it is not our function to propose regulatory schemes for the States. That must await their concrete legislative efforts. It is possible, however, to give a few plain examples of what a state statute could define for regulation under part (b) of the standard announced in this opinion; (a) Patently offensive representations or descriptions of ultimate sexual acts, normal or perverted, actual or simulated; (b) Patently offensive representation or descriptions of masturbation, excretory functions, and lewd exhibition of the genitals.

Sex and nudity may not be exploited without limit by films or pictures exhibited or sold in places of public accommodation any more than live sex and nudity can be exhibited or sold without limit in such public places. At a minimum, prurient, patently offensive depiction or description of sexual conduct must have serious literary, artistic, political, or scientific value to merit First Amendment protection. Under the holdings announced today, no one will be subject to prosecution for the sale or exposure of obscene materials unless these materials depict or describe patently offensive "hard core" sexual conduct specifically defined by the regulating state law, as written or construed. We are satisfied that these specific prerequisites will provide fair notice to a dealer in such materials that his public and commercial activities may bring prosecution.

Since *Miller*, the Court has adhered to the test articulated in that case. First, the Court has followed *Miller*'s holding that the material must appeal to prurient interest and that is to be decided by a community standard. For example, the Court has ruled that juries applying federal obscenity laws define prurient interest from a community perspective. The Court said that "[t]he fact that distributors of allegedly obscene materials may be subjected to varying community standards in the various federal judicial districts does not render a federal statute unconstitutional because of the failure of application of uniform national standards of obscenity."[23]

Second, in order for material to be obscene it must be patently offensive under the law prohibiting obscenity. In Ward v. Illinois, 431 U.S. 767 (1977), the Supreme Court held that the law did not need to provide an "exhaustive list of the sexual conduct" that would be patently offensive. The Court said that it was sufficient that a law included the examples included in *Miller*.

However, in Jenkins v. Georgia, 418 U.S. 153 (1974), the Court ruled that there are limits on what a state may deem to be patently offensive. In *Jenkins*, the Court concluded that the mainstream movie "Carnal Knowledge," with actors including Jack Nicholson and Ann-Margret, could not be found obscene because "[t]here is no exhibition whatever of the actors' genitals, lewd or otherwise. . . . There are occasional scenes of nudity, but nudity alone is not enough to make material legally obscene under the *Miller* standards." The Court stated that "the film could not, as a matter of constitutional law, be found to depict sexual content in a patently offensive way, and is therefore not outside the protection of the First and Fourteenth Amendments because it is obscene."

Finally, in order for material to be obscene, it must, taken as a whole, lack serious redeeming artistic, literary, political, or scientific value. In Pope v. Illinois, 481 U.S. 497 (1987), the Court held that social value is to be determined by a national standard—how the work would be appraised across the country—and not a community standard. The Court said that "the value of [a] work [does not] vary from community to community. . . . The proper inquiry [is] whether a reasonable person would find such value in the material."

b. Should Obscenity Be a Category of Unprotected Speech?

Many disagree with the Court that obscenity should be deemed a category of unprotected speech.[24] They argue that the very definition of obscenity used in *Roth* focuses on controlling thoughts, something that should be beyond the reach of the government.

Those who favor allowing the government to prohibit obscenity make several arguments. One is that a community should be able to determine its moral environment. In Paris Adult Theatre I v. Slaton, the Court accepted this justification for regulating obscenity and spoke of "the interest of the public in the quality of life and the total community environment [and] the tone of commerce in the great city centers." Henry Clor argued that the "ethical convictions of social man do not simply rest upon his explicit opinions. They rest also upon a delicate network of moral and aesthetic feelings, sensibilities, tastes. These 'finer feelings' could be blunted and eroded by a steady stream of impressions which assault them. Men whose sensibilities are frequently assaulted

---

23. Hamling v. United States, 418 U.S. 87, 106 (1974).
24. *See, e.g.*, David Cole, *Playing by Pornography's Rules: The Regulation of Sexual Expression*, 143 U. Pa. L. Rev. 111 (1994); David A.J. Richards, *Free Speech and Obscenity Law: Toward a Moral Theory of the First Amendment*, 123 U. Pa. L. Rev. 45 (1974).

C. Sexually Oriented Speech

by prurient and lurid impressions may become desensitized.... This is what is meant by 'an erosion of the moral fabric.' "[25]

However, those who oppose a First Amendment exception for obscenity argue that the government should not be able to decide what is moral and suppress speech that does not advance that conception. In fact, the Supreme Court has held in other contexts that the government may not prohibit speech simply because it advances ideas that the government deems immoral. For example, in Kingsley International Pictures Corp. v. Regents, 360 U.S. 684 (1959), the Court held that a state could not prohibit the film *Lady Chatterley's Lover*, because it shows adultery and thus "portrays acts of sexual immorality [as] desirable, acceptable or proper patterns of behavior." The Court said that what the state "has done, [is] to prevent the exhibition of a motion picture because that picture advocates an idea—that adultery under certain circumstances may be proper behavior. Yet the First Amendment's basic guarantee is of freedom to advocate ideas. The State, quite simply, has thus struck at the very heart of constitutionally protected liberty." It is not for the government to stop speech to advance any particular idea of what is moral.

A second major argument for excluding obscenity from First Amendment protection is that it causes antisocial behavior, particularly violence against women. In Paris Adult Theatre I v. Slaton, Chief Justice Burger, writing for the Court, said that obscenity "possibly [endangers] the public safety itself. The Hill-Link Minority Report of the Commission on Obscenity and Pornography indicates that there is at least an arguable correlation between obscene material and crime." Professor Catharine MacKinnon, who advocates creating a new categorical exception for pornography as a form of discrimination against women, argued that "[r]ecent experimental research on pornography shows that . . . exposure to [it] increases normal men's immediately subsequent willingness to aggress against women under laboratory conditions. . . . It also significantly increases attitudinal measures known to correlate with rape."[26] The Meese Commission on Pornography believed that experimental studies found that exposure to violent pornography increased a willingness to be violent in laboratory experiments.[27]

But others challenge these studies and whether they establish that obscenity increases the likelihood of antisocial behavior. The Report of the Commission on Obscenity and Pornography, a commission appointed by President Richard Nixon, reviewed the empirical literature and concluded that there was no evidence that "exposure to explicit sexual materials plays a significant role in the causation of delinquent or criminal behavior."[28] Moreover, it is questioned whether the laboratory experiments that measure aggression in laboratory settings or conduct on mock juries indicates anything about whether obscenity causes antisocial behavior in society. Also, it is argued that these studies show, at most, that depictions of violence—whether erotic or not—correlate with more

---

25. Henry Clor, *Obsenity and Public Morality* at 170-171 (1969).
26. Catharine R. MacKinnon, *Pornography, Civil Rights, and Speech*, 20 Harv. C.R.-C.L. L. Rev. 1, 52, 54 (1985); *see also* Catharine R. MacKinnon, *Only Words* (1994).
27. Report of the Attorney General's Commission on Pornography (1986).
28. Report of the Commission on Obscenity and Pornography 26-27 (1970).

violence in laboratory experiments; they maintain that there is no evidence that nonviolent sexual depictions increase aggressive or violent behavior.[29]

A third argument made for excluding obscenity from First Amendment protection is that it should be regarded as a sex aid, not as speech. Professor Fred Schauer argued that "hardcore pornography is designed to produce a purely physical effect. [It is] essentially a physical rather than a mental stimulus. . . . The pornographic item is in a real sense a sexual surrogate. . . . Consider further rubber, plastic, or leather sex aids. It is hard to find any free speech aspects in their sale or use. . . . The mere fact that in pornography the stimulating experience is initiated by visual rather than tactile means is irrelevant. Neither means constitutes communication in the cognitive sense."[30]

Yet in response it is argued that other forms of speech produce physical reactions. A movie or book is not deprived of First Amendment protection because it provokes tears. A beautiful symphony is not unprotected because of the physical reactions it evokes. Moreover, it is argued that sexual material does have a cognitive dimension. Professor David Cole observed that the argument that sexual speech is "noncognitive" because it is designed to produce a physical effect is predicated on an impoverished view of sexuality. He wrote, "[Sexual] expression, like human sexuality itself, cannot be 'purely physical.' Rather, it is deeply and inextricably interwoven with our identities, our upbringing, our emotions, our relationships to other human beings, and the ever-changing narratives and images that our community finds stimulating."[31]

c. Should There Be a New Exception for Pornography?

Some commentators, most notably Catharine MacKinnon and Andrea Dworkin, have argued that a new exception should be created to the First Amendment that excludes pornography as a form of sex discrimination against women. They argue that pornography is "the graphic sexually explicit subordination of women through pictures and/or words."[32] They propose an ordinance that would outlaw such depictions if, for example, "[w]omen are presented as sexual objects who enjoy pain or humiliation; or . . . [w]omen are presented as sexual objects who experience sexual pleasure in being raped; or . . . women are presented as sexual objects for domination, conquest, violation, exploitation, possession, or use, or through postures or positions of servility or submission or display."[33]

MacKinnon argues that pornography causes harmful attitudes and actions toward women in society.[34] She maintains that restrictions on pornography are justified to advance equality for women. She argues furthermore that women are

---

29. *See* Deana Pollard, *Regulating Violent Pornography*, 43 Vand. L. Rev. 125, 128-129 (1990) (reviewing social science studies on the effects of pornography).

30. Frederick Schauer, *Speech and "Speech"—Obscenity and "Obscenity": An Exercise in the Interpretation of Constitutional Language*, 67 Geo. L.J. 899, 922-923 (1979).

31. Cole, *supra* note 24, at 127.

32. *See* American Booksellers Assn., Inc. v. Hudnut, 771 F.2d 323 (7th Cir. 1985) (describing Indianapolis ordinance based on MacKinnon-Dworkin proposal).

33. *Id.* at 324.

34. *See, e.g.*, Catharine MacKinnon, *Only Words* (1994); Catharine MacKinnon, *Feminism Unmodified* (1987); Catharine MacKinnon, *Pornography, Civil Rights and Speech*, 20 Harv. C.R.-C.L. L. Rev. 1, 18-20 (1985).

coerced into the making of pornography and that the prohibition of pornography is necessary to provide protection. She contends that obscenity is inadequate as an approach to sexually oriented material because it requires that the work be looked at as a whole and because of its focus on the prurient interest.[35]

Critics of the MacKinnon approach argue that it is vague and extremely broad in terms of what it would deem to be pornography unprotected by the First Amendment. Professor Thomas Emerson argued that "[t]he sweep of the [MacKinnon] ordinance is breathtaking. It would subject to governmental ban virtually all depictions of rape, verbal or pictoral, and a substantial proportion of other sexual encounters. More specifically, it would outlaw such works of literature as the *Arabian Nights,* Henry Miller's *Tropic of Cancer,* John Cleland's *Fanny Hill,* William Faulkner's *Sanctuary,* and Norman Mailer's *Ancient Evenings,* to name a few."[36]

The U.S. Court of Appeals for the Seventh Circuit, in American Booksellers Assn. v. Hudnut, 771 F.2d 323 (7th Cir. 1985), declared unconstitutional a version of the MacKinnon ordinance that had been enacted in Indianapolis. The court found that the ordinance was impermissible viewpoint discrimination because it attempted to outlaw depictions of certain images of women. The court said: "The ordinance discriminates on the ground of the content of the speech. Speech treating women in the approved way . . . is lawful no matter how sexually explicit. Speech treating women in the disapproved way—as submissive in matters sexual or as enjoying humiliation—is unlawful no matter how significant the literary, artistic, or political qualities of the work taken as a whole. The state may not ordain preferred viewpoints in this way."

The debate over pornography raises basic questions about the First Amendment. May the government restrict some speech in an attempt to advance equality by controlling how a group is treated or portrayed? How much proof of harm from speech such as pornography must there be in order to justify regulation?

2. Child Pornography

In New York v. Ferber, the Supreme Court held that the government may prohibit the exhibition, sale, or distribution of child pornography even if it does not meet the test for obscenity. However, in Ashcroft v. Free Speech Coalition, the Court made it clear that for material to be considered child pornography, children must be used in its production.

NEW YORK v. FERBER
458 U.S. 747 (1982)

Justice WHITE delivered the opinion of the Court.

At issue in this case is the constitutionality of a New York criminal statute which prohibits persons from knowingly promoting sexual performances by children under the age of 16 by distributing material which depicts such performances.

---

35. MacKinnon, *Feminism Unmodified* at 152-158.
36. Thomas Emerson, *Pornography and the First Amendment: A Reply to Professor MacKinnon,* 3 Yale L. & Pol. Rev. 130, 131-132 (1985).

I

In recent years, the exploitive use of children in the production of pornography has become a serious national problem. The Federal Government and 47 States have sought to combat the problem with statutes specifically directed at the production of child pornography. At least half of such statutes do not require that the materials produced be legally obscene. Thirty-five States and the United States Congress have also passed legislation prohibiting the distribution of such materials; 20 States prohibit the distribution of material depicting children engaged in sexual conduct without requiring that the material be legally obscene.

Like obscenity statutes, laws directed at the dissemination of child pornography run the risk of suppressing protected expression by allowing the hand of the censor to become unduly heavy. For the following reasons, however, we are persuaded that the States are entitled to greater leeway in the regulation of pornographic depictions of children.

First. It is evident beyond the need for elaboration that a State's interest in "safeguarding the physical and psychological well-being of a minor" is "compelling." "A democratic society rests, for its continuance, upon the healthy, well-rounded growth of young people into full maturity as citizens." Prince v. Massachusetts (1944). Accordingly, we have sustained legislation aimed at protecting the physical and emotional well-being of youth even when the laws have operated in the sensitive area of constitutionally protected rights. The prevention of sexual exploitation and abuse of children constitutes a government objective of surpassing importance. The legislative findings accompanying passage of the New York laws reflect this concern. The legislative judgment, as well as the judgment found in the relevant literature, is that the use of children as subjects of pornographic materials is harmful to the physiological, emotional, and mental health of the child. That judgment, we think, easily passes muster under the First Amendment.

Second. The distribution of photographs and films depicting sexual activity by juveniles is intrinsically related to the sexual abuse of children in at least two ways. First, the materials produced are a permanent record of the children's participation and the harm to the child is exacerbated by their circulation. Second, the distribution network for child pornography must be closed if the production of material which requires the sexual exploitation of children is to be effectively controlled. Indeed, there is no serious contention that the legislature was unjustified in believing that it is difficult, if not impossible, to halt the exploitation of children by pursuing only those who produce the photographs and movies. While the production of pornographic materials is a low-profile, clandestine industry, the need to market the resulting products requires a visible apparatus of distribution. The most expeditious if not the only practical method of law enforcement may be to dry up the market for this material by imposing severe criminal penalties on persons selling, advertising, or otherwise promoting the product. Thirty-five States and Congress have concluded that restraints on the distribution of pornographic materials are required in order to effectively combat the problem, and there is a body of literature and testimony to support these legislative conclusions.

The *Miller* standard, like all general definitions of what may be banned as obscene, does not reflect the State's particular and more compelling interest

C. Sexually Oriented Speech

in prosecuting those who promote the sexual exploitation of children. Thus, the question under the *Miller* test of whether a work, taken as a whole, appeals to the prurient interest of the average person bears no connection to the issue of whether a child has been physically or psychologically harmed in the production of the work. Similarly, a sexually explicit depiction need not be "patently offensive" in order to have required the sexual exploitation of a child for its production. In addition, a work which, taken on the whole, contains serious literary, artistic, political, or scientific value may nevertheless embody the hardest core of child pornography. "It is irrelevant to the child [who has been abused] whether or not the material . . . has a literary, artistic, political or social value." We therefore cannot conclude that the *Miller* standard is a satisfactory solution to the child pornography problem.

Third. The advertising and selling of child pornography provide an economic motive for and are thus an integral part of the production of such materials, an activity illegal throughout the Nation. "It rarely has been suggested that the constitutional freedom for speech and press extends its immunity to speech or writing used as an integral part of conduct in violation of a valid criminal statute." We note that were the statutes outlawing the employment of children in these films and photographs fully effective, and the constitutionality of these laws has not been questioned, the First Amendment implications would be no greater than that presented by laws against distribution: enforceable production laws would leave no child pornography to be marketed.

Fourth. The value of permitting live performances and photographic reproductions of children engaged in lewd sexual conduct is exceedingly modest, if not de minimis. We consider it unlikely that visual depictions of children performing sexual acts or lewdly exhibiting their genitals would often constitute an important and necessary part of a literary performance or scientific or educational work. As a state judge in this case observed, if it were necessary for literary or artistic value, a person over the statutory age who perhaps looked younger could be utilized. Simulation outside of the prohibition of the statute could provide another alternative. Nor is there any question here of censoring a particular literary theme or portrayal of sexual activity.

Fifth. Recognizing and classifying child pornography as a category of material outside the protection of the First Amendment is not incompatible with our earlier decisions. Thus, it is not rare that a content-based classification of speech has been accepted because it may be appropriately generalized that within the confines of the given classification, the evil to be restricted so overwhelmingly outweighs the expressive interests, if any, at stake, that no process of case-by-case adjudication is required. When a definable class of material, such as that covered by §263.15, bears so heavily and pervasively on the welfare of children engaged in its production, we think the balance of competing interests is clearly struck and that it is permissible to consider these materials as without the protection of the First Amendment.

There are, of course, limits on the category of child pornography which, like obscenity, is unprotected by the First Amendment. As with all legislation in this sensitive area, the conduct to be prohibited must be adequately defined by the applicable state law, as written or authoritatively construed. Here the nature of the harm to be combated requires that the state offense be limited to works that visually depict sexual conduct by children below a specified age. The category of "sexual conduct" proscribed must also be suitably limited and described.

The test for child pornography is separate from the obscenity standard enunciated in *Miller*, but may be compared to it for the purpose of clarity. The *Miller* formulation is adjusted in the following respects: A trier of fact need not find that the material appeals to the prurient interest of the average person; it is not required that sexual conduct portrayed be done so in a patently offensive manner; and the material at issue need not be considered as a whole. We note that the distribution of descriptions or other depictions of sexual conduct, not otherwise obscene, which do not involve live performance or photographic or other visual reproduction of live performances, retains First Amendment protection. As with obscenity laws, criminal responsibility may not be imposed without some element of scienter on the part of the defendant.

Justice BRENNAN, with whom Justice MARSHALL joins, concurring in the judgment.

I agree with much of what is said in the Court's opinion. [T]he State has a special interest in protecting the well-being of its youth. This special and compelling interest, and the particular vulnerability of children, afford the State the leeway to regulate pornographic material, the promotion of which is harmful to children, even though the State does not have such leeway when it seeks only to protect consenting adults from exposure to such material.

But in my view application of §263.15 or any similar statute to depictions of children that in themselves do have serious literary, artistic, scientific, or medical value, would violate the First Amendment. As the Court recognizes, the limited classes of speech, the suppression of which does not raise serious First Amendment concerns, have two attributes. They are of exceedingly "slight social value," and the State has a compelling interest in their regulation. The First Amendment value of depictions of children that are in themselves serious contributions to art, literature, or science, is, by definition, simply not "de minimis." At the same time, the State's interest in suppression of such materials is likely to be far less compelling. In short, it is inconceivable how a depiction of a child that is itself a serious contribution to the world of art or literature or science can be deemed "material outside the protection of the First Amendment." With this understanding, I concur in the Court's judgment in this case.

Since *Ferber*, the Court has been clear that in order to be considered child pornography, the material must use children in its production. In Ashcroft v. Free Speech Coalition, 535 U.S. 234 (2002), the Court declared unconstitutional the Child Pornography Prevention Act of 1996, which prohibits child pornography whether it is based on actual pictures of children or computer-generated images. The law prohibited "visual depiction" that "appeared to be" or "conveyed the impression" of a minor engaging in sexually explicit conduct. The Act thus banned material that included adults who are childlike in appearance, as well as computer-generated images.

The Court, in an opinion by Justice Kennedy, stressed that the material prohibited by the Act did "not involve, let alone harm, any children." The Court explained that the government's interest in banning child pornography is in safeguarding children. The Court expressed concern that many works dealing with teenage sexuality might be found to violate the law. The Court found that there was insufficient evidence to support the government's contention that enforcement of child pornography laws would be impeded without a ban of the sort in the Act.

Thus, Ashcroft v. Free Speech Coalition is an important clarification of *Ferber*. The government cannot ban child pornography based on its condemnation of the material. Rather, the government's interest is limited to protecting children from being used in the making of the material.

Congress responded to Ashcroft v. Free Speech Coalition by enacting the Prosecutorial Remedies and Other Tools to End the Exploitation of Children Today Act of 2003. The Act more narrowly defines child pornography and it prohibits offers to provide and requests to obtain child pornography. The law was challenged on overbreadth grounds in that it applies even if the material provided or requested is not actually child pornography, but instead is speech protected by the First Amendment. In United States v. Williams, 553 U.S. 285 (2008), the Court upheld the Act and concluded that "offers to provide or requests to obtain child pornography are categorically excluded from the First Amendment," even if the material involved is not child pornography and is speech protected under the First Amendment.

Justice Scalia's majority opinion emphasizes that the criminal law can punish attempts and thus argues that the government may punish the attempt to purchase or request child pornography even if it is not actually present. Justice Scalia illustrates this by noting that a drug dealer who sells baking powder believing it is cocaine can be punished for an attempted drug transaction. The analogy is powerful because selling baking powder is no more a crime than selling computer-generated images of children in sexual situations.

The problem with this argument, as Justice Souter explains in his dissent, is that there is no constitutional right to sell baking powder, but there is a First Amendment right to request or sell computer-generated images of children in sexual situations. When the government punishes the sale of baking powder, it is not compromising any constitutional rights. But when the government punishes speech safeguarded by the First Amendment, a fundamental right is sacrificed.

There is a tension between *Williams* and *Free Speech Coalition*. *Free Speech Coalition* unequivocally held that people cannot be punished for possessing, selling, distributing, or requesting nonobscene sexually explicit material unless it actually used children in its production. But the effect of *Williams* is exactly that: The government can punish people for offering or requesting this material if they have the mistaken belief that it is child pornography. On the other hand, the cases can be distinguished in that *Williams* follows basic criminal law principles in holding that a person can be punished for attempting to engage in illegal activity even if the material involved turns out not to actually be contraband.

3. Protected but Low-Value Sexual Speech

The Supreme Court has indicated there is a category of sexual speech that does not meet the test for obscenity and thus is protected by the First Amendment, but is deemed to be speech of low value, and thus the government has latitude to regulate such expression. The Court never has defined the contours of this category, but it clearly involves sexually explicit material.

a. Zoning Ordinances

The Court has upheld the ability of local governments to use zoning ordinances to regulate the location of adult bookstores and movie theaters. In Young v. American Mini Theatres, Inc., the Supreme Court upheld a city's ordinance that limited the number of adult theaters that could be on any block and prevented such enterprises from operating in residential areas.

<u>YOUNG v. AMERICAN MINI THEATRES, INC.</u>
427 U.S. 50 (1976)

Justice STEVENS delivered the opinion of the Court.

Zoning ordinances adopted by the city of Detroit differentiate between motion picture theaters which exhibit sexually explicit "adult" movies and those which do not. The principal question presented by this case is whether that statutory classification is unconstitutional because it is based on the content of communication protected by the First Amendment.

Effective November 2, 1972, Detroit adopted the ordinances challenged in this litigation. Instead of concentrating "adult" theaters in limited zones, these ordinances require that such theaters be dispersed. Specifically, an adult theater may not be located within 1,000 feet of any two other "regulated uses" or within 500 feet of a residential area. The term "regulated uses" includes 10 different kinds of establishments in addition to adult theaters.

The classification of a theater as "adult" is expressly predicated on the character of the motion pictures which it exhibits. If the theater is used to present "material distinguished or characterized by an emphasis on matter depicting, describing or relating to 'Specified Sexual Activities' or 'Specified Anatomical Areas,'" it is an adult establishment. These terms are defined as follows: "For the purpose of this Section, 'Specified Sexual Activities' is defined as: 1. Human Genitals in a state of sexual stimulation or arousal; 2. Acts of human masturbation, sexual intercourse or sodomy; 3. Fondling or other erotic touching of human genitals, pubic region, buttock or female breast." And "Specified Anatomical Areas" is defined as: "1. Less than completely and opaquely covered: (a) human genitals, pubic region, (b) buttock, and (c) female breast below a point immediately above the top of the areola; and 2. Human male genitals in a discernibly turgid state, even if completely and opaquely covered."

We are not persuaded that the Detroit zoning ordinances will have a significant deterrent effect on the exhibition of films protected by the First Amendment. [T]he only vagueness in the ordinances relates to the amount of sexually explicit activity that may be portrayed before the material can be said to "characterized by an emphasis" on such matter. For most films the question will be readily answerable; to the extent that an area of doubt exists, we see no reason why the ordinances are not "readily subject to a narrowing construction by the state courts." [T]here is surely a less vital interest in the uninhibited exhibition of material that is on the borderline between pornography and

C. Sexually Oriented Speech

artistic expression than in the free dissemination of ideas of social and political significance.

The ordinances are not challenged on the ground that they impose a limit on the total number of adult theaters which may operate in the city of Detroit. There is no claim that distributors or exhibitors of adult films are denied access to the market or, conversely, that the viewing public is unable to satisfy its appetite for sexually explicit fare. Viewed as an entity, the market for this commodity is essentially unrestrained.

It is true, however, that adult films may only be exhibited commercially in licensed theaters. But that is also true of all motion pictures. The city's general zoning laws require all motion picture theaters to satisfy certain locational as well as other requirements; we have no doubt that the municipality may control the location of theaters as well as the location of other commercial establishments, either by confining them to certain specified commercial zones or by requiring that they be dispersed throughout the city.

Putting to one side for the moment the fact that adult motion picture theaters must satisfy a locational restriction not applicable to other theaters, we are also persuaded that the 1,000-foot restriction does not, in itself, create an impermissible restraint on protected communication. The city's interest in planning and regulating the use of property for commercial purposes is clearly adequate to support that kind of restriction applicable to all theaters within the city limits.

The question whether speech is, or is not, protected by the First Amendment often depends on the content of the speech. Thus, the line between permissible advocacy and impermissible incitation to crime or violence depends, not merely on the setting in which the speech occurs, but also on exactly what the speaker had to say. Similarly, it is the content of the utterance that determines whether it is a protected epithet or an unprotected "fighting comment."

Even within the area of protected speech, a difference in content may require a different governmental response. Moreover, even though we recognize that the First Amendment will not tolerate the total suppression of erotic materials that have some arguably artistic value, it is manifest that society's interest in protecting this type of expression is of a wholly different, and lesser, magnitude than the interest in untrammeled political debate that inspired Voltaire's immortal comment. Whether political oratory or philosophical discussion moves us to applaud or to despise what is said, every schoolchild can understand why our duty to defend the right to speak remains the same. But few of us would march our sons and daughters off to war to preserve the citizen's right to see "Specified Sexual Activities" exhibited in the theaters of our choice. Even though the First Amendment protects communication in this area from total suppression, we hold that the State may legitimately use the content of these materials as the basis for placing them in a different classification from other motion pictures.

The remaining question is whether the line drawn by these ordinances is justified by the city's interest in preserving the character of its neighborhoods. The record disclosed a factual basis for the Common Council's conclusion that this kind of restriction will have the desired effect. It is not our function to appraise the wisdom of its decision to require adult theaters to be separated rather than concentrated in the same areas. In either event, the city's interest in attempting to preserve the quality of urban life is one that must be accorded high respect. Moreover, the city must be allowed a reasonable opportunity to experiment with solutions to admittedly serious problems.

Since what is ultimately at stake is nothing more than a limitation on the place where adult films may be exhibited, even though the determination of whether a particular film fits that characterization turns on the nature of its content, we conclude that the city's interest in the present and future character of its neighborhoods adequately supports its classification of motion pictures.

Justice STEWART, with whom Justice BRENNAN, Justice MARSHALL, and Justice BLACKMUN join, dissenting.

The Court today holds that the First and Fourteenth Amendments do not prevent the city of Detroit from using a system of prior restraints and criminal sanctions to enforce content-based restrictions on the geographic location of motion picture theaters that exhibit nonobscene but sexually oriented films. I dissent from this drastic departure from established principles of First Amendment law.

This case does not involve a simple zoning ordinance, or a content-neutral time, place, and manner restriction, or a regulation of obscene expression or other speech that is entitled to less than the full protection of the First Amendment. The kind of expression at issue here is no doubt objectionable to some, but that fact does not diminish its protected status.

What this case does involve is the constitutional permissibility of selective interference with protected speech whose content is thought to produce distasteful effects. It is elementary that a prime function of the First Amendment is to guard against just such interference. By refusing to invalidate Detroit's ordinance the Court rides roughshod over cardinal principles of First Amendment law, which require that time, place, and manner regulations that affect protected expression be content neutral except in the limited context of a captive or juvenile audience. In place of these principles the Court invokes a concept wholly alien to the First Amendment. Since "few of us would march our sons and daughters off to war to preserve the citizen's right to see 'Specified Sexual Activities' exhibited in the theaters of our choice," the Court implies that these films are not entitled to the full protection of the Constitution. This stands "Voltaire's immortal comment[]" on its head. For if the guarantees of the First Amendment were reserved for expression that more than a "few of us" would take up arms to defend, then the right of free expression would be defined and circumscribed by current popular opinion. The guarantees of the Bill of Rights were designed to protect against precisely such majoritarian limitations on individual liberty.

I can only interpret today's decision as an aberration. The Court is undoubtedly sympathetic, as am I, to the well-intentioned efforts of Detroit to "clean up" its streets and prevent the proliferation of "skid rows." But it is in those instances where protected speech grates most unpleasantly against the sensibilities that judicial vigilance must be at its height.

Likewise, in City of Renton v. Playtime Theatres, Inc., presented above in Chapter 2, the Supreme Court relied on *Young* to uphold a zoning ordinance that excluded adult motion picture theaters from operating within 1,000 feet

C. Sexually Oriented Speech

of any residential zone, church, park, or school. The effect was to exclude such theaters from about 95 percent of the land in the city. Of the remaining land, a substantial part was occupied by a sewage disposal and treatment plant, a horse racing track, a warehouse and manufacturing facility, an oil tank farm, and a shopping center. Nonetheless, the Supreme Court upheld the ordinance, saying that the result was "largely dictated by our decision in *Young*."

However, unlike *Young*, in which the Court acknowledged the regulation as content-based, the Court in *Renton* described the ordinance as being content-neutral because the "City Council's '*predominate* concerns' were with the secondary effects of adult theaters, and not with the content of adult films themselves." The Court said that the ordinance was designed to "prevent crime, protect the city's retail trade, maintain property values, and generally protect and preserve the quality of the city's neighborhoods, commercial districts, and the quality of urban life, not to suppress the expression of unpopular views." In other words, the Court defined content neutrality not by the terms of the law, but rather, by the legislature's predominant purpose.

Subsequently, in City of Los Angeles v. Alameda Books, Inc., 535 U.S. 425 (2002), the Supreme Court upheld a Los Angeles ordinance that prohibits "the establishment or maintenance of more than one adult entertainment business in the same building, structure, or portion thereof." The Court said that the city could rely on a study from 1977 showing that a concentration of adult business increases crime.

b. Nude Dancing

Another example of the Court's treatment of sexually oriented speech as being of "low value" is its willingness to allow the government to prohibit nude dancing.

In Barnes v. Glen Theatre, Inc., 501 U.S. 560 (1991), the Supreme Court held that the government may completely ban nude dancing. Specifically, the Court ruled that an Indiana statute prohibiting public nudity could be used to require that female dancers must, at a minimum, wear pasties and a G-string when they dance. There was no majority opinion for the Court in its five-to-four decision. Chief Justice Rehnquist wrote the plurality opinion joined by Justices O'Connor and Kennedy and initially noted that "nude dancing of the kind sought to be performed here is expressive conduct within the outer perimeters of the First Amendment, though we view it as only marginally so."

The plurality saw nude dancing as a form of conduct that communicates and applied the test used for regulating symbolic speech: "[A] government regulation is sufficiently justified if it is within the constitutional power of the Government; if it furthers an important or substantial governmental interest; if the governmental interest is unrelated to the suppression of free expression; and if the incidental restriction on alleged First Amendment freedoms is no greater than is essential to the furtherance of that interest."[37] The plurality upheld the

---

37. The topic of symbolic speech is discussed in detail below.

prohibition of nude dancing because it served the goal of "protecting societal order and morality."[38]

Justice Scalia, concurring in the judgment, took a different approach. He argued, "[T]he challenged regulation must be upheld, not because it survives some lower level of First Amendment scrutiny, but because as a general law regulating conduct and not specifically directed at expression, it is not subject to First Amendment scrutiny at all." In other cases, as well, Justice Scalia has advanced the view that the First Amendment's protections of speech and religion are not violated by neutral laws of general applicability that burden these rights.[39] Justice Scalia also expressly rejected the dissent's argument that public nudity laws exist only to protect unwilling viewers from offense. He wrote, "The purpose of Indiana's nudity law would be violated, I think, if 60,000 fully consenting adults crowded into the Hoosier Dome to display their genitals to one another, even if there were not an offended innocent in the crowd. Our society prohibits, and all human societies have prohibited, certain activities not because they harm others, but because they are considered, in the traditional phrase, . . . immoral."

Justice Souter also concurred in the judgment and focused on the secondary effects of nude dancing. He said "that legislation seeking to combat the secondary effects of adult entertainment need not await localized proof of those effects [and that] the State of Indiana could reasonably conclude that forbidding nude entertainment of the type offered at the Kitty Kat Lounge [furthers] its interest in preventing prostitution, sexual assault, and associated crimes."

Justice White wrote a dissenting opinion joined by Justices Brennan, Marshall, and Blackmun and emphasized that stopping nude dancing was suppressing a message. Justice White said, "[T]he nudity of the dancer is an integral part of the emotions and thoughts that a nude dancing performance evokes. The sight of a fully clothed, or even a partially clothed, dancer generally will have a far different impact on a spectator than that of a nude dancer, even if the same dance is performed. The nudity itself is an expressive component of the dance, not merely incidental 'conduct.'"

In 2000, in City of Erie v. Pap's A.M., the Court reaffirmed *Barnes*. Justice O'Connor's plurality opinion also reaffirmed *Renton*'s holding that the government's interest in preventing secondary effects is sufficient to make the law content-neutral and to uphold the closing of nude dancing establishments.

CITY OF ERIE v. PAP'S A.M.

529 U.S. 277 (2000)

Justice O'Connor announced the judgment of the Court and delivered an opinion in which The Chief Justice, Justice Kennedy, and Justice Breyer join.

The city of Erie, Pennsylvania, enacted an ordinance banning public nudity. Respondent Pap's A.M. (hereinafter Pap's), which operated a nude dancing establishment in Erie, challenged the constitutionality of the ordinance and

---

38. *Barnes*, 501 U.S. at 568.
39. *See, e.g.*, Cohen v. Cowles Media Co., 501 U.S. 663 (1991); Employment Division v. Smith, 494 U.S. 872 (1990).

sought a permanent injunction against its enforcement. The Pennsylvania Supreme Court, although noting that this Court in Barnes v. Glen Theatre, Inc. (1991), had upheld an Indiana ordinance that was "strikingly similar" to Erie's, found that the public nudity sections of the ordinance violated respondent's right to freedom of expression under the United States Constitution. This case raises the question whether the Pennsylvania Supreme Court properly evaluated the ordinance's constitutionality under the First Amendment. We hold that Erie's ordinance is a content-neutral regulation that satisfies the [First Amendment].

I

On September 28, 1994, the city council for the city of Erie, Pennsylvania, enacted a public indecency ordinance that makes it a summary offense to knowingly or intentionally appear in public in a "state of nudity." Respondent Pap's, a Pennsylvania corporation, operated an establishment in Erie known as "Kandyland" that featured totally nude erotic dancing performed by women. To comply with the ordinance, these dancers must wear, at a minimum, "pasties" and a "G-string." On October 14, 1994, two days after the ordinance went into effect, Pap's filed a complaint against the city of Erie, the mayor of the city, and members of the city council, seeking declaratory relief and a permanent injunction against the enforcement of the ordinance.

[II]

Being "in a state of nudity" is not an inherently expressive condition. As we explained in *Barnes*, however, nude dancing of the type at issue here is expressive conduct, although we think that it falls only within the outer ambit of the First Amendment's protection.

To determine what level of scrutiny applies to the ordinance at issue here, we must decide "whether the State's regulation is related to the suppression of expression." If the governmental purpose in enacting the regulation is unrelated to the suppression of expression, then the regulation need only satisfy the "less stringent" standard. If the government interest is related to the content of the expression, however, then the regulation must be justified under a more demanding standard.

The ordinance here, like the statute in *Barnes*, is on its face a general prohibition on public nudity. By its terms, the ordinance regulates conduct alone. It does not target nudity that contains an erotic message; rather, it bans all public nudity, regardless of whether that nudity is accompanied by expressive activity.

Respondent and Justice Stevens contend nonetheless that the ordinance is related to the suppression of expression because language in the ordinance's preamble suggests that its actual purpose is to prohibit erotic dancing of the type performed at Kandyland. That is not how the Pennsylvania Supreme Court interpreted that language, however. The Pennsylvania Supreme Court construed [the legislative history] to mean that one purpose of the ordinance was "to combat negative secondary effects."

As Justice Souter noted in *Barnes*, "on its face, the governmental interest in combating prostitution and other criminal activity is not at all inherently related to expression." So too here, the ordinance prohibiting public nudity is aimed at combating crime and other negative secondary effects caused by the presence of adult entertainment establishments like Kandyland and not at suppressing the erotic message conveyed by this type of nude dancing. Put another way, the ordinance does not attempt to regulate the primary effects of the expression, i.e., the effect on the audience of watching nude erotic dancing, but rather the secondary effects, such as the impacts on public health, safety, and welfare, which we have previously recognized are "caused by the presence of even one such" establishment. Renton v. Playtime Theatres, Inc. (1986).

[E]ven if Erie's public nudity ban has some minimal effect on the erotic message by muting that portion of the expression that occurs when the last stitch is dropped, the dancers at Kandyland and other such establishments are free to perform wearing pasties and G-strings. Any effect on the overall expression is de minimis. And as Justice Stevens eloquently stated for the plurality in Young v. American Mini Theatres, Inc. (1976), "even though we recognize that the First Amendment will not tolerate the total suppression of erotic materials that have some arguably artistic value, it is manifest that society's interest in protecting this type of expression is of a wholly different, and lesser, magnitude than the interest in untrammeled political debate," and "few of us would march our sons or daughters off to war to preserve the citizen's right to see" specified anatomical areas exhibited at establishments like Kandyland. If States are to be able to regulate secondary effects, then de minimis intrusions on expression such as those at issue here cannot be sufficient to render the ordinance content based.

We conclude that Erie's asserted interest in combating the negative secondary effects associated with adult entertainment establishments like Kandyland is unrelated to the suppression of the erotic message conveyed by nude dancing. The asserted interests of regulating conduct through a public nudity ban and of combating the harmful secondary effects associated with nude dancing are undeniably important. And in terms of demonstrating that such secondary effects pose a threat, the city need not "conduct new studies or produce evidence independent of that already generated by other cities" to demonstrate the problem of secondary effects, "so long as whatever evidence the city relies upon is reasonably believed to be relevant to the problem that the city addresses." Renton v. Playtime Theatres, Inc. Because the nude dancing at Kandyland is of the same character as the adult entertainment at issue in *Renton* and Young v. American Mini Theatres, Inc. (1976), it was reasonable for Erie to conclude that such nude dancing was likely to produce the same secondary effects. In any event, Erie also relied on its own findings. The city council members, familiar with commercial downtown Erie, are the individuals who would likely have had first-hand knowledge of what took place at and around nude dancing establishments in Erie, and can make particularized, expert judgments about the resulting harmful secondary effects. We hold, therefore, that Erie's ordinance is a content-neutral regulation that is valid under *O'Brien*.

Justice SCALIA, with whom Justice THOMAS joins, concurring in the judgment.

[E]ven were I to conclude that the city of Erie had specifically singled out the activity of nude dancing, I still would not find that this regulation violated the First Amendment unless I could be persuaded (as on this record I cannot)

C. Sexually Oriented Speech

that it was the communicative character of nude dancing that prompted the ban. When conduct other than speech itself is regulated, it is my view that the First Amendment is violated only "[w]here the government prohibits conduct precisely because of its Communicative attributes." Here, even if one hypothesizes that the city's object was to suppress only nude dancing, that would not establish an intent to suppress what (if anything) nude dancing communicates. I do not feel the need, as the Court does, to identify some "secondary effects" associated with nude dancing that the city could properly seek to eliminate. (I am highly skeptical, to tell the truth, that the addition of pasties and G-strings will at all reduce the tendency of establishments such as Kandyland to attract crime and prostitution, and hence to foster sexually transmitted disease.) The traditional power of government to foster good morals, and the acceptability of the traditional judgment (if Erie wishes to endorse it) that nude public dancing itself is immoral, have not been repealed by the First Amendment.

Justice SOUTER, dissenting in part.

I do not believe, however, that the current record allows us to say that the city has made a sufficient evidentiary showing to sustain its regulation, and I would therefore vacate the decision of the Pennsylvania Supreme Court and remand the case for further proceedings.

[T]he record before us today is deficient in its failure to reveal any evidence on which Erie may have relied, either for the seriousness of the threatened harm or for the efficacy of its chosen remedy. The plurality does the best it can with the materials to hand, but the pickings are slim. [T]he recitation does not get beyond conclusions on a subject usually fraught with some emotionalism. Nor does the invocation of Barnes v. Glen Theatre, Inc. (1991), in one paragraph of the preamble to Erie's ordinance suffice. The plurality opinion in *Barnes* made no mention of evidentiary showings at all, and though my separate opinion did make a pass at the issue, I did not demand reliance on germane evidentiary demonstrations, whether specific to the statute in question or developed elsewhere. To invoke *Barnes*, therefore, does not indicate that the issue of evidence has been addressed.

The proposition that the presence of nude dancing establishments increases the incidence of prostitution and violence is amenable to empirical treatment, and the city councilors who enacted Erie's ordinance are in a position to look to the facts of their own community's experience as well as to experiences elsewhere. Their failure to do so is made all the clearer by one of the amicus briefs, largely devoted to the argument that scientifically sound studies show no such correlation. See Brief for First Amendment Lawyers Association as Amicus Curiae.

The record before us now does not permit the conclusion that Erie's ordinance is reasonably designed to mitigate real harms. This does not mean that the required showing cannot be made, only that, on this record, Erie has not made it. I would remand to give it the opportunity to do so.

Justice STEVENS, with whom Justice GINSBURG joins, dissenting.

Far more important than the question whether nude dancing is entitled to the protection of the First Amendment are the dramatic changes in legal doctrine that the Court endorses today. Until now, the "secondary effects" of commercial enterprises featuring indecent entertainment have justified only the regulation of their location. For the first time, the Court has now held that such effects may justify the total suppression of protected speech.

The Court relies on the so-called "secondary effects" test to defend the ordinance. The present use of that rationale, however, finds no support whatsoever in our precedents. Never before have we approved the use of that doctrine to justify a total ban on protected First Amendment expression. On the contrary, we have been quite clear that the doctrine would not support that end.

[T]he city of Erie has not in fact pointed to any study by anyone suggesting that the adverse secondary effects of commercial enterprises featuring erotic dancing depends in the slightest on the precise costume worn by the performers—it merely assumes it to be so. If the city is permitted simply to assume that a slight addition to the dancers' costumes will sufficiently decrease secondary effects, then presumably the city can require more and more clothing as long as any danger of adverse effects remains.

The reason we have limited our secondary effects cases to zoning and declined to extend their reasoning to total bans is clear and straightforward: A dispersal that simply limits the places where speech may occur is a minimal imposition whereas a total ban is the most exacting of restrictions. The State's interest in fighting presumed secondary effects is sufficiently strong to justify the former, but far too weak to support the latter, more severe burden. Yet it is perfectly clear that in the present case the city of Erie has totally silenced a message the dancers at Kandyland want to convey. The fact that this censorship may have a laudable ulterior purpose cannot mean that censorship is not censorship. The Court's use of the secondary effects rationale to permit a total ban has grave implications for basic free speech principles.

c. Should There Be Such a Category as Low-Value Sexual Speech?

Ultimately, cases like *Young*, *Renton*, *Barnes*, and *Erie* raise the question of whether there should be a category of minimally protected sexually oriented speech. Answering this inquiry turns on the general question of whether there should be a hierarchy of protected speech, and on the specific question of whether sexually oriented speech that is not obscene should be regarded as low in value. The cases above do not specify the level of scrutiny used, but it obviously is far less than strict scrutiny and appears to be little more than rational basis review. But in two subsequent cases presented below, Ashcroft v. ACLU and United States v. Playboy Entertainment Group, the Court used strict scrutiny for content-based regulation of sexual speech. There is an obvious tension in the earlier cases using little more than rational basis review.

There is also the crucial issue of what justifications are sufficient to warrant regulation of this speech. *Young*, *Renton*, and especially Justice O'Connor's plurality opinion in *Erie* all focus on the need to regulate speech to stop secondary effects. But almost all speech has some secondary effects; parades and demonstrations, for example, cause litter. These cases also raise the question of whether a state's interest in advancing a certain moral vision is sufficient to warrant restriction of the speech.

Finally, it must be noted that the Court has never defined the content of this category of low-value sexually oriented speech. The Court has made it clear that nudity, alone, is not enough to place speech in this category. In Erznoznik

C. Sexually Oriented Speech

v. City of Jacksonville, 422 U.S. 205 (1975), the Court declared unconstitutional an ordinance that declared it a public nuisance for any drive-in movie theater to exhibit any motion picture "in which the human male or female bare buttocks, human female bare breasts, or human bare pubic areas are shown, if such motion picture [is] visible from any public street or public place." The Court noted that the law "sweepingly forbids display of all films containing *any* uncovered buttocks or breasts, irrespective of context or pervasiveness. . . . [A]ll nudity cannot be deemed obscene even as to minors." Nudity alone, therefore, is not enough to make speech less protected. The contours of the category of less protected sexual speech never have been defined.

4. Government Techniques for Controlling Obscenity and Child Pornography

The Supreme Court has made it clear that the government can prohibit the sale, distribution, and exhibition of obscene materials even to willing recipients. In Paris Adult Theatre I v. Slaton, presented above, the Court said that "[t]he States have the power to make a morally neutral judgment that public exhibition of obscene material, or commerce in such material, has a tendency to injure the community as a whole, to endanger the public safety, or to jeopardize . . . the States' 'right to maintain a decent society.'"

However, the Court also has held that the government cannot prohibit or punish the private possession of obscene material, although it may outlaw the private possession of child pornography.

STANLEY v. GEORGIA
394 U.S. 557 (1969)

Justice MARSHALL delivered the opinion of the Court.

An investigation of appellant's alleged bookmaking activities led to the issuance of a search warrant for appellant's home. Under authority of this warrant, federal and state agents secured entrance. They found very little evidence of bookmaking activity, but while looking through a desk drawer in an upstairs bedroom, one of the federal agents, accompanied by a state officer, found three reels of eight-millimeter film. Using a projector and screen found in an upstairs living room, they viewed the films. The state officer concluded that they were obscene and seized them. Since a further examination of the bedroom indicated that appellant occupied it, he was charged with possession of obscene matter and placed under arrest. He was later [convicted] for "knowingly hav[ing] possession of . . . obscene matter" in violation of Georgia law.

Appellant argues that the Georgia obscenity statute, insofar as it punishes mere private possession of obscene matter, violates the First Amendment, as made applicable to the States by the Fourteenth Amendment. [W]e agree that the mere private possession of obscene matter cannot constitutionally be made a crime.

[W]e do not believe that this case can be decided simply by citing *Roth*. *Roth* and its progeny certainly do mean that the First and Fourteenth Amendments recognize a valid governmental interest in dealing with the problem of obscenity. But the assertion of that interest cannot, in every context, be insulated from all constitutional protections. Neither *Roth* nor any other decision of this Court reaches that far.

It is now well established that the Constitution protects the right to receive information and ideas. This right to receive information and ideas, regardless of their social worth, is fundamental to our free society. Moreover, in the context of this case a prosecution for mere possession of printed or filmed matter in the privacy of a person's own home that right takes on an added dimension. For also fundamental is the right to be free, except in very limited circumstances, from unwanted governmental intrusions into one's privacy.

These are the rights that appellant is asserting in the case before us. He is asserting the right to read or observe what he pleases—the right to satisfy his intellectual and emotional needs in the privacy of his own home. He is asserting the right to be free from state inquiry into the contents of his library. Whatever may be the justifications for other statutes regulating obscenity, we do not think they reach into the privacy of one's own home. If the First Amendment means anything, it means that a State has no business telling a man, sitting alone in his own house, what books he may read or what films he may watch. Our whole constitutional heritage rebels at the thought of giving government the power to control men's minds.

Perhaps recognizing this, Georgia asserts that exposure to obscene materials may lead to deviant sexual behavior or crimes of sexual violence. There appears to be little empirical basis for that assertion. Given the present state of knowledge, the State may no more prohibit mere possession of obscene matter on the ground that it may lead to antisocial conduct than it may prohibit possession of chemistry books on the ground that they may lead to the manufacture of homemade spirits. We hold that the First and Fourteenth Amendments prohibit making mere private possession of obscene material a crime.

Although *Stanley* never has been overruled, the Court has been consistently unwilling to extend it. For example, in United States v. Reidel, 402 U.S. 351 (1971), the Court held that *Stanley* did not protect a right to receive obscene materials. A federal law prohibits the shipment of obscene materials in the mail. The defendant argued that the right to possess such material as recognized in *Stanley* means that there must be a right to receive it. The Supreme Court disagreed and held that the government may prohibit shipment of such materials. The Court expressly distinguished *Stanley* and said that the defendant was "in a wholly different position . . . [because he] has no complaints about governmental violations of his private thoughts or fantasies, but stands squarely on a claimed First Amendment right to do business in obscenity and use the mails in the process. . . . *Stanley* did not overrule *Roth* and we decline to do so now."

Even more significantly, the Court in Osborne v. Ohio held that the government may prohibit and punish the private possession of child pornography.

OSBORNE v. OHIO, 495 U.S. 103 (1990): JUSTICE WHITE delivered the opinion of the Court.

Petitioner, Clyde Osborne, was convicted and sentenced to six months in prison, after the Columbus, Ohio, police, pursuant to a valid search, found four photographs in Osborne's home. Each photograph depicts a nude male adolescent posed in a sexually explicit position.

C. Sexually Oriented Speech

The threshold question in this case is whether Ohio may constitutionally proscribe the possession and viewing of child pornography or whether, as Osborne argues, our decision in Stanley v. Georgia (1969), compels the contrary result. *Stanley* should not be read too broadly. We have previously noted that *Stanley* was a narrow holding, and, since the decision in that case, the value of permitting child pornography has been characterized as "exceedingly modest, if not de minimis." New York v. Ferber (1982).

But assuming, for the sake of argument, that Osborne has a First Amendment interest in viewing and possessing child pornography, we nonetheless find this case distinct from *Stanley* because the interests underlying child pornography prohibitions far exceed the interests justifying the Georgia law at issue in *Stanley*. Every court to address the issue has so concluded. The difference here is obvious: The State does not rely on a paternalistic interest in regulating Osborne's mind. Rather, Ohio has enacted [its law] in order to protect the victims of child pornography; it hopes to destroy a market for the exploitative use of children. It is also surely reasonable for the State to conclude that it will decrease the production of child pornography if it penalizes those who possess and view the product, thereby decreasing demand.

Given the importance of the State's interest in protecting the victims of child pornography, we cannot fault Ohio for attempting to stamp out this vice at all levels in the distribution chain. According to the State, since the time of our decision in *Ferber*, much of the child pornography market has been driven underground; as a result, it is now difficult, if not impossible, to solve the child pornography problem by only attacking production and distribution. Indeed, 19 States have found it necessary to proscribe the possession of this material. Given the gravity of the State's interests in this context, we find that Ohio may constitutionally proscribe the possession and viewing of child pornography.

5. *Profanity and "Indecent" Speech*

Although profanity and "indecent" speech are not obscene, government often has tried to punish them. The Supreme Court has held that such language is generally protected by the First Amendment, but there are notable exceptions. This subsection begins by presenting Cohen v. California, which is the strongest declaration of First Amendment protection for such speech. The subsection then considers how the Court has treated government regulation of indecent speech over various media. The Court has expressly adopted a medium-by-medium approach, considering indecent speech over the broadcast media (television and radio), over telephones, over the Internet, and over cable television. Each of these areas is considered below.

COHEN v. CALIFORNIA
403 U.S. 15 (1971)

Justice HARLAN delivered the opinion of the Court.

This case may seem at first blush too inconsequential to find its way into our books, but the issue it presents is of no small constitutional significance. Appellant Paul Robert Cohen was convicted in the Los Angeles Municipal Court of violating that part of California Penal Code which prohibits "maliciously and willfully disturb[ing] the peace or quiet of any neighborhood or person . . . by . . . offensive conduct. . . ." He was given 30 days' imprisonment.

On April 26, 1968, the defendant was observed in the Los Angeles County Court house in the corridor of the municipal court wearing a jacket bearing the words "Fuck the Draft" which were plainly visible. There were women and children present in the corridor. The defendant was arrested. The defendant testified that he wore the jacket knowing that the words were on the jacket as a means of informing the public of the depth of his feelings against the Vietnam War and the draft.

The defendant did not engage in, nor threaten to engage in, nor did anyone as the result of his conduct in fact commit or threaten to commit any act of violence. The defendant did not make any loud or unusual noise, nor was there any evidence that he uttered any sound prior to his arrest.

I

In order to lay hands on the precise issue which this case involves, it is useful first to canvass various matters which this record does not present. The conviction quite clearly rests upon the asserted offensiveness of the words Cohen used to convey his message to the public. The only "conduct" which the State sought to punish is the fact of communication. Thus, we deal here with a conviction resting solely upon "speech."

[T]his case cannot be said to fall within those relatively few categories of instances where prior decisions have established the power of government to deal more comprehensively with certain forms of individual expression simply upon a showing that such a form was employed. This is not, for example, an obscenity case. Whatever else may be necessary to give rise to the States' broader power to prohibit obscene expression, such expression must be, in some significant way, erotic. It cannot plausibly be maintained that this vulgar allusion to the Selective Service System would conjure up such psychic stimulation in anyone likely to be confronted with Cohen's crudely defaced jacket.

This Court has also held that the States are free to ban the simple use, without a demonstration of additional justifying circumstances, of so-called "fighting words," those personally abusive epithets which, when addressed to the ordinary citizen, are, as a matter of common knowledge, inherently likely to provoke violent reaction. While the four-letter word displayed by Cohen in relation to the draft is not uncommonly employed in a personally provocative fashion, in this instance it was clearly not "directed to the person of the hearer." No individual actually or likely to be present could reasonably have regarded the words on appellant's jacket as a direct personal insult. Nor do we have here an instance of the exercise of the State's police power to prevent a speaker from intentionally provoking a given group to hostile reaction. There is, as noted above, no showing that anyone who saw Cohen was in fact violently aroused or that appellant intended such a result.

Finally, in arguments before this Court much has been made of the claim that Cohen's distasteful mode of expression was thrust upon unwilling or unsuspecting viewers, and that the State might therefore legitimately act as it did in order to protect the sensitive from otherwise unavoidable exposure to appellant's crude form of protest. Of course, the mere presumed presence of unwitting listeners or viewers does not serve automatically to justify curtailing all speech capable of giving offense. While this Court has recognized that government may properly act in many situations to prohibit intrusion into the privacy of the home of unwelcome views and ideas which cannot be totally banned from the public dialogue, we have at the same time consistently stressed that "we are often 'captives' outside the sanctuary of the home and subject to objectionable speech." The ability of government, consonant with the Constitution, to shut off discourse solely to protect others from hearing it is, in other words, dependent upon a showing that substantial privacy interests are being invaded in an essentially intolerable manner. Any broader view of this authority would effectively empower a majority to silence dissidents simply as a matter of personal predilections.

In this regard, persons confronted with Cohen's jacket were in a quite different posture than, say, those subjected to the raucous emissions of sound trucks blaring outside their residences. Those in the Los Angeles courthouse could effectively avoid further bombardment of their sensibilities simply by averting their eyes. And, while it may be that one has a more substantial claim to a recognizable privacy interest when walking through a courthouse corridor than, for example, strolling through Central Park, surely it is nothing like the interest in being free from unwanted expression in the confines of one's own home. Given the subtlety and complexity of the factors involved, if Cohen's "speech" was otherwise entitled to constitutional protection, we do not think the fact that some unwilling "listeners" in a public building may have been briefly exposed to it can serve to justify this breach of the peace conviction where, as here, there was no evidence that persons powerless to avoid appellant's conduct did in fact object to it.

II

Against this background, the issue flushed by this case stands out in bold relief. It is whether California can excise, as "offensive conduct," one particular scurrilous epithet from the public discourse.

The constitutional right of free expression is powerful medicine in a society as diverse and populous as ours. It is designed and intended to remove governmental restraints from the arena of public discussion, putting the decision as to what views shall be voiced largely into the hands of each of us, in the hope that use of such freedom will ultimately produce a more capable citizenry and more perfect polity and in the belief that no other approach would comport with the premise of individual dignity and choice upon which our political system rests. To many, the immediate consequence of this freedom may often appear to be only verbal tumult, discord, and even offensive utterance. These are, however, within established limits, in truth necessary side effects of the broader enduring values which the process of open debate permits us to achieve. That the air may at times seem filled with verbal cacophony is, in this sense not a sign of weakness but of strength. We cannot lose sight of the fact that, in what otherwise might seem a trifling and annoying instance of individual distasteful abuse of a privilege, these fundamental societal values are truly implicated.

Against this perception of the constitutional policies involved, we discern certain more particularized considerations that peculiarly call for reversal of this conviction. First, the principle contended for by the State seems inherently boundless. How is one to distinguish this from any other offensive word? Surely the State has no right to cleanse public debate to the point where it is grammatically palatable to the most squeamish among us. Yet no readily ascertainable general principle exists for stopping short of that result were we to affirm the judgment below. For, while the particular four-letter word being litigated here is perhaps more distasteful than most others of its genre, it is nevertheless often true that one man's vulgarity is another's lyric. Indeed, we think it is largely because governmental officials cannot make principled distinctions in this area that the Constitution leaves matters of taste and style so largely to the individual.

Additionally, we cannot overlook the fact, because it is well illustrated by the episode involved here, that much linguistic expression serves a dual communicative function: it conveys not only ideas capable of relatively precise, detached explication, but otherwise inexpressible emotions as well. In fact, words are often chosen as much for their emotive as their cognitive force. We cannot sanction the view that the Constitution, while solicitous of the cognitive content of individual speech has little or no regard for that emotive function which practically speaking, may often be the more important element of the overall message sought to be communicated.

Finally, and in the same vein, we cannot indulge the facile assumption that one can forbid particular words without also running a substantial risk of suppressing ideas in the process. Indeed, governments might soon seize upon the censorship of particular words as a convenient guise for banning the expression of unpopular views. We have been able, as noted above, to discern little social benefit that might result from running the risk of opening the door to such grave results.

It is, in sum, our judgment that, absent a more particularized and compelling reason for its actions, the State may not, consistently with the First and Fourteenth Amendments, make the simple public display here involved of this single four-letter expletive a criminal offense.

Justice BLACKMUN, with whom THE CHIEF JUSTICE and Justice BLACK join.

I dissent. Cohen's absurd and immature antic, in my view, was mainly conduct and little speech. Further, the case appears to me to be well within the sphere of Chaplinsky v. New Hampshire (1942), where Justice Murphy, a known champion of First Amendment freedoms, wrote for a unanimous bench. As a consequence, this Court's agonizing over First Amendment values seem misplaced and unnecessary.

Since *Cohen*, the Court has considered government regulation of indecent speech in a variety of media—the broadcast media (television and radio), telephones, the Internet, and cable television. Indeed, at times, in the cases below, the Court has expressly said that it has followed a medium-by-medium approach. In reading these cases, it is important to consider whether there is a meaningful distinction among them. For instance, the Court has upheld regulation of indecent speech over the broadcast medium, but not over the telephone or the Internet. Also, it is important to consider the desirability

C. Sexually Oriented Speech

of the medium-by-medium approach. As increasingly all of these media, and even newspapers, are likely to be received through a single cable or internet connection, does the different treatment of separate media still make sense?

a. The Broadcast Media

Cohen's strong declaration that profane and indecent language are protected by the First Amendment can be contrasted with its decision in FCC v. Pacifica Foundation, which upheld the prohibition of indecent speech over television and radio.

FEDERAL COMMUNICATIONS COMMISSION v.
PACIFICA FOUNDATION

438 U.S. 726 (1978)

Justice STEVENS delivered the opinion of the Court and an opinion in which THE CHIEF JUSTICE and Mr. Justice REHNQUIST joined (Parts IV-A and IV-B).

This case requires that we decide whether the Federal Communications Commission has any power to regulate a radio broadcast that is indecent but not obscene.

A satiric humorist named George Carlin recorded a 12-minute monologue entitled "Filthy Words" before a live audience in a California theater. He began by referring to his thoughts about "the words you couldn't say on the public, ah, airwaves, um, the ones you definitely wouldn't say, ever." He proceeded to list those words and repeat them over and over again in a variety of colloquialisms. The transcript of the recording, which is appended to this opinion, indicates frequent laughter from the audience.

At about 2 o'clock in the afternoon on Tuesday, October 30, 1973, a New York radio station, owned by respondent Pacifica Foundation, broadcast the "Filthy Words" monologue. A few weeks later a man, who stated that he had heard the broadcast while driving with his young son, wrote a letter complaining to the Commission.

The complaint was forwarded to the station for comment. In its response, Pacifica explained that the monologue had been played during a program about contemporary society's attitude toward language and that, immediately before its broadcast, listeners had been advised that it included "sensitive language which might be regarded as offensive to some." Pacifica characterized George Carlin as "a significant social satirist" who "like Twain and Sahl before him, examines the language of ordinary people. . . . Carlin is not mouthing obscenities, he is merely using words to satirize as harmless and essentially silly our attitudes towards those words." Pacifica stated that it was not aware of any other complaints about the broadcast.

On February 21, 1975, the Commission issued a declaratory order granting the complaint and holding that Pacifica "could have been the subject of administrative sanctions." The Commission did not impose formal sanctions, but it did state that the order would be "associated with the station's license file, and in the event that subsequent complaints are received, the Commission will then decide whether it should utilize any of the available sanctions it has been granted by Congress." [T]he Commission found a power to regulate indecent broadcasting in two statutes: 18 U.S.C. §1464, which forbids the use of "any obscene, indecent, or profane language by means of radio communications," and 47 U.S.C. §303(g), which requires the Commission to "encourage the larger and more effective use of radio in the public interest."

IV

Pacifica makes two constitutional attacks on the Commission's order. First, it argues that the Commission's construction of the statutory language broadly encompasses so much constitutionally protected speech that reversal is required even if Pacifica's broadcast of the "Filthy Words" monologue is not itself protected by the First Amendment. Second, Pacifica argues that inasmuch as the recording is not obscene, the Constitution forbids any abridgment of the right to broadcast it on the radio.

A

The first argument fails because our review is limited to the question whether the Commission has the authority to proscribe this particular broadcast. As the Commission itself emphasized, its order was "issued in a specific factual context."

It is true that the Commission's order may lead some broadcasters to censor themselves. At most, however, the Commission's definition of indecency will deter only the broadcasting of patently offensive references to excretory and sexual organs and activities. While some of these references may be protected, they surely lie at the periphery of First Amendment concern.

B

When the issue is narrowed to the facts of this case, the question is whether the First Amendment denies government any power to restrict the public broadcast of indecent language in any circumstances. For if the government has any such power, this was an appropriate occasion for its exercise.

The question in this case is whether a broadcast of patently offensive words dealing with sex and excretion may be regulated because of its content. Obscene materials have been denied the protection of the First Amendment because their content is so offensive to contemporary moral standards. But the fact that society may find speech offensive is not a sufficient reason for suppressing it. Indeed, if it is the speaker's opinion that gives offense, that consequence is a reason for according it constitutional protection. For it is a central tenet of the First Amendment that the government must remain neutral in the marketplace of ideas. If there were any reason to believe that the Commission's characterization of the Carlin monologue as offensive could be traced to its political content—or even to the fact that it satirized contemporary attitudes about four-letter words—First Amendment protection might be required. But that is simply not this case. These words offend for the same reasons that obscenity offends. Their place in the hierarchy of First Amendment values was aptly sketched by Mr. Justice Murphy when he said: "Such utterances are no essential part of any exposition of ideas, and are of such slight social value as a

C. Sexually Oriented Speech

step to truth that any benefit that may be derived from them is clearly outweighed by the social interest in order and morality." Chaplinsky v. New Hampshire.

Although these words ordinarily lack literary, political, or scientific value, they are not entirely outside the protection of the First Amendment. Some uses of even the most offensive words are unquestionably protected. Indeed, we may assume, arguendo, that this monologue would be protected in other contexts. Nonetheless, the constitutional protection accorded to a communication containing such patently offensive sexual and excretory language need not be the same in every context. It is a characteristic of speech such as this that both its capacity to offend and its "social value," to use Mr. Justice Murphy's term, vary with the circumstances. Words that are commonplace in one setting are shocking in another. To paraphrase Justice Harlan, one occasion's lyric is another's vulgarity.

In this case it is undisputed that the content of Pacifica's broadcast was "vulgar," "offensive," and "shocking." We have long recognized that each medium of expression presents special First Amendment problems. And of all forms of communication, it is broadcasting that has received the most limited First Amendment protection. First, the broadcast media have established a uniquely pervasive presence in the lives of all Americans. Patently offensive, indecent material presented over the airwaves confronts the citizen, not only in public, but also in the privacy of the home, where the individual's right to be left alone plainly outweighs the First Amendment rights of an intruder. Because the broadcast audience is constantly tuning in and out, prior warnings cannot completely protect the listener or viewer from unexpected program content. To say that one may avoid further offense by turning off the radio when he hears indecent language is like saying that the remedy for an assault is to run away after the first blow. One may hang up on an indecent phone call, but that option does not give the caller a constitutional immunity or avoid a harm that has already taken place.

Second, broadcasting is uniquely accessible to children, even those too young to read. Although Cohen's written message might have been incomprehensible to a first grader, Pacifica's broadcast could have enlarged a child's vocabulary in an instant. Other forms of offensive expression may be withheld from the young without restricting the expression at its source. Bookstores and motion picture theaters, for example, may be prohibited from making indecent material available to children.

It is appropriate, in conclusion, to emphasize the narrowness of our holding. This case does not involve a two-way radio conversation between a cab driver and a dispatcher, or a telecast of an Elizabethan comedy. We have not decided that an occasional expletive in either setting would justify any sanction or, indeed, that this broadcast would justify a criminal prosecution. The Commission's decision rested entirely on a nuisance rationale under which context is all-important. The concept requires consideration of a host of variables. The time of day was emphasized by the Commission. The content of the program in which the language is used will also affect the composition of the audience, and differences between radio, television, and perhaps closed-circuit transmissions, may also be relevant. As Justice Sutherland wrote a "nuisance may be merely a right thing in the wrong place,—like a pig in the parlor instead of the barnyard." Euclid v. Ambler Realty Co. We simply hold that when the Commission finds that a pig has entered the parlor, the exercise of its regulatory power does not depend on proof that the pig is obscene.

After *Pacifica*, the FCC adopted a policy that it would not punish a "fleeting expletive," a single use of a profanity primarily as an adjective. In a few instances in 2002 and 2003, primarily at music awards shows, profanities were used, and the FCC found that even though these were "fleeting expletives," they could be punished. In FCC v. Fox Television Stations, Inc., 567 U.S. 239 (2012), the Court found that such punishment violated due process because the television stations did not have advance warning, "fair notice" that fleeting profanities or fleeting nudity could be punished. The Court stressed that because it "resolves these cases on fair notice grounds under the Due Process Clause, it need not address the First Amendment implications of the Commission's indecency policy." The issue remains open as to whether it violates the First Amendment for the government to punish a fleeting expletive.

b. Telephones

In Sable Communications v. FCC, 492 U.S. 115 (1989), the Court declared unconstitutional a federal statute designed to eliminate the "dial-a-porn" industry; the law prohibited obscene or indecent telephone conversations. The Supreme Court drew a distinction between the "obscene" and the "indecent." The Court said that while the law was constitutional in prohibiting obscene speech, it was unconstitutional in prohibiting indecent speech.

The Court emphasized that the government could not ban speech simply because it was "indecent." The Court noted that there is no "captive audience" problem here; callers will generally not be unwilling listeners. Moreover, the Court said that Congress's goal of protecting children could be achieved through means less restrictive of speech. Justice White, writing for the Court, said that the "Congressional record contains no legislative findings that would justify us in concluding that there is no constitutionally acceptable less restrictive means, short of a total ban, to achieve the Government's interest in protecting minors."

Thus, the Supreme Court in *Sable Communications* drew a distinction between the "obscene" and the "indecent." The difficulty, of course, is how to draw this distinction. It would seem exceedingly difficult for an attorney for a company like Sable Communications to advise it as to what its employees could say (the "indecent"), as opposed to what they must not say (the "obscene").

c. The Internet

The Supreme Court's first major decision concerning the Internet, Reno v. American Civil Liberties Union, involved the same distinction between obscene and indecent speech in a federal law regulating the Internet. The Court declared unconstitutional the regulation of indecent speech over the Internet.

C. Sexually Oriented Speech

RENO v. AMERICAN CIVIL LIBERTIES UNION
521 U.S. 844 (1997)

Justice STEVENS delivered the opinion of the Court.

At issue is the constitutionality of two statutory provisions enacted to protect minors from "indecent" and "patently offensive" communications on the Internet. Notwithstanding the legitimacy and importance of the congressional goal of protecting children from harmful materials, we agree with the three-judge District Court that the statute abridges "the freedom of speech" protected by the First Amendment.

I

The District Court made extensive findings of fact, most of which were based on a detailed stipulation prepared by the parties. The findings describe the character and the dimensions of the Internet, the availability of sexually explicit material in that medium, and the problems confronting age verification for recipients of Internet communications. Because those findings provide the underpinnings for the legal issues, we begin with a summary of the undisputed facts.

THE INTERNET

The Internet is an international network of interconnected computers. It is the outgrowth of what began in 1969 as a military program called "ARPANET," which was designed to enable computers operated by the military, defense contractors, and universities conducting defense-related research to communicate with one another by redundant channels even if some portions of the network were damaged in a war. While the ARPANET no longer exists, it provided an example for the development of a number of civilian networks that, eventually linking with each other, now enable tens of millions of people to communicate with one another and to access vast amounts of information from around the world. The Internet is "a unique and wholly new medium of worldwide human communication."

The Internet has experienced "extraordinary growth." The number of "host" computers—those that store information and relay communications—increased from about 300 in 1981 to approximately 9,400,000 by the time of the trial in 1996. Roughly 60% of these hosts are located in the United States. About 40 million people used the Internet at the time of trial, a number that is expected to mushroom to 200 million by 1999.

II

The Telecommunications Act of 1996 was an unusually important legislative enactment. As stated on the first of its 103 pages, its primary purpose was to reduce regulation and encourage "the rapid deployment of new telecommunications technologies." The major components of the statute have nothing to do with the Internet; they were designed to promote competition in the local telephone service market, the multichannel video market, and the market for over-the-air broadcasting. The Act includes seven Titles, six of which are the product of extensive committee hearings and the subject of discussion in Reports prepared by Committees of the Senate and the House of Representatives. By contrast, Title V—known as the "Communications Decency Act of 1996" (CDA)—contains provisions that were either added in executive committee after the hearings were concluded or as amendments offered during floor debate on the legislation. An amendment offered in the Senate was the source of the two statutory provisions challenged in this case. They are informally described as the "indecent transmission" provision and the "patently offensive display" provision.

The first, §223(a), prohibits the knowing transmission of obscene or indecent messages to any recipient under 18 years of age. The second provision, §223(d), prohibits the knowing sending or displaying of patently offensive messages in a manner that is available to a person under 18 years of age. The breadth of these prohibitions is qualified by two affirmative defenses. One covers those who take "good faith, reasonable, effective, and appropriate actions" to restrict access by minors to the prohibited communications. The other covers those who restrict access to covered material by requiring certain designated forms of age proof, such as a verified credit card or an adult identification number or code.

III

[T]here are significant differences between the order upheld in FCC v. Pacifica Foundation and the CDA. First, the order in *Pacifica*, issued by an agency that had been regulating radio stations for decades, targeted a specific broadcast that represented a rather dramatic departure from traditional program content in order to designate when—rather than whether—it would be permissible to air such a program in that particular medium. The CDA's broad categorical prohibitions are not limited to particular times and are not dependent on any evaluation by an agency familiar with the unique characteristics of the Internet. Second, unlike the CDA, the Commission's declaratory order was not punitive; we expressly refused to decide whether the indecent broadcast "would justify a criminal prosecution." Finally, the Commission's order applied to a medium which as a matter of history had "received the most limited First Amendment protection," in large part because warnings could not adequately protect the listener from unexpected program content. The Internet, however, has no comparable history. Moreover, the District Court found that the risk of encountering indecent material by accident is remote because a series of affirmative steps is required to access specific material.

According to the Government, the CDA is constitutional because it constitutes a sort of "cyberzoning" on the Internet. But the CDA applies broadly to the entire universe of cyberspace. And the purpose of the CDA is to protect children from the primary effects of "indecent" and "patently offensive" speech, rather than any "secondary" effect of such speech. Thus, the CDA is a content-based blanket restriction on speech, and, as such, cannot be "properly analyzed as a form of time, place, and manner regulation."

[IV]

In Southeastern Promotions, Ltd. v. Conrad (1975), we observed that "[e]ach medium of expression . . . may present its own problems." Thus, some of our cases have recognized special justifications for regulation of the broadcast media that are not applicable to other speakers. Those factors are not present in cyberspace. Neither before nor after the enactment of the CDA have the vast democratic forums of the Internet been subject to the type of government supervision and regulation that has attended the broadcast industry. Moreover, the Internet is not as "invasive" as radio or television. The District Court specifically found that "[c]ommunications over the Internet do not 'invade' an individual's home or appear on one's computer screen unbidden. Users seldom encounter content 'by accident.'" It also found that "[a]lmost all sexually explicit images are preceded by warnings as to the content," and cited testimony that "'odds are slim' that a user would come across a sexually explicit sight by accident."

[V]

Regardless of whether the CDA is so vague that it violates the Fifth Amendment, the many ambiguities concerning the scope of its coverage render it problematic for purposes of the First Amendment. For instance, each of the two parts of the CDA uses a different linguistic form. The first uses the word "indecent," while the second speaks of material that "in context, depicts or describes, in terms patently offensive as measured by contemporary community standards, sexual or excretory activities or organs." Given the absence of a definition of either term, this difference in language will provoke uncertainty among speakers about how the two standards relate to each other and just what they mean. Could a speaker confidently assume that a serious discussion about birth control practices, homosexuality, or the consequences of prison rape would not violate the CDA? This uncertainty undermines the likelihood that the CDA has been carefully tailored to the congressional goal of protecting minors from potentially harmful materials.

The vagueness of the CDA is a matter of special concern for two reasons. First, the CDA is a content-based regulation of speech. The vagueness of such a regulation raises special First Amendment concerns because of its obvious chilling effect on free speech. Second, the CDA is a criminal statute. In addition to the opprobrium and stigma of a criminal conviction, the CDA threatens violators with penalties including up to two years in prison for each act of violation. The severity of criminal sanctions may well cause speakers to remain silent rather than communicate even arguably unlawful words, ideas, and images.

[VI]

We are persuaded that the CDA lacks the precision that the First Amendment requires when a statute regulates the content of speech. In order to deny minors access to potentially harmful speech, the CDA effectively suppresses a large amount of speech that adults have a constitutional right to receive and to address to one another. That burden on adult speech is unacceptable if less restrictive alternatives would be at least as effective in achieving the legitimate purpose that the Statute was enacted to serve.

In evaluating the free speech rights of adults, we have made it perfectly clear that "[s]exual expression which is indecent but not obscene is protected by the First Amendment." It is true that we have repeatedly recognized the governmental interest in protecting children from harmful materials. But that interest does not justify an unnecessarily broad suppression of speech addressed to adults. As we have explained, the Government may not "reduc[e] the adult population . . . to . . . only what is fit for children."

The breadth of the CDA's coverage is wholly unprecedented. Unlike the regulations upheld in *Ginsberg* and *Pacifica*, the scope of the CDA is not limited to commercial speech or commercial entities. Its open-ended prohibitions embrace all nonprofit entities and individuals posting indecent messages or displaying them on their own computers in the presence of minors. The general, undefined terms "indecent" and "patently offensive" cover large amounts of nonpornographic material with serious educational or other value.

The Court followed the same reasoning in its subsequent decision in Ashcroft v. American Civil Liberties Union, 542 U.S. 656 (2004). The case involved the constitutionality of the Child On-Line Protection Act, a federal law that regulated sexually oriented commercial websites. The statute applied only to commercial websites that included material that appealed to the prurient interest and would be offensive to contemporary community standards. The law required that such websites verify users' ages and provided several ways in which they could do so.

A federal district court issued a preliminary injunction, and the U.S. Court of Appeals for the Third Circuit affirmed. The Supreme Court also upheld the preliminary injunction. The majority opinion was written by Justice Anthony Kennedy and joined by Justices Stevens, Souter, Ginsburg, and Thomas.

Justice Kennedy's opinion said that the law is a content-based restriction of speech, applying only to sexual speech, and that it therefore must meet strict scrutiny. The Court said that the preliminary injunction was upheld because there was a substantial likelihood that the plaintiffs would prevail in their argument that the law does not meet strict scrutiny. Justice Kennedy explained that filtering devices, which are installed on individual computers, likely are a less restrictive alternative for protecting children from exposure to sexually explicit material. The Court remanded the case to the federal district court for a determination of whether such filtering devices are a less restrictive alternative. On remand, the Third Circuit declared the law unconstitutional and issued a permanent injunction.

d. Cable Television

A final medium considered by the Court is cable television. There have been two decisions concerning federal laws regulating sexual speech over this medium. The first was Denver Area Educational Telecommunications Consortium, Inc. v. FCC, 518 U.S. 727 (1996). The case involved First Amendment challenges to three provisions of the Cable Television Consumer Protection and Competition Act of 1992 that regulate the broadcasting of "patently offensive" sexually oriented material on cable television. One provision permits a cable system operator to prohibit the broadcasting of programming that "depicts sexual

C. Sexually Oriented Speech

or excretory activities or organs in a patently offensive manner." A second challenged section requires that cable systems allowing such material segregate it on a single channel and block the channel from viewer access unless the viewer requests it in writing. The final provision allows cable systems to prohibit sexually oriented material on "public, educational, or governmental channels."

Without a majority opinion, the Court upheld the first provision but invalidated the latter two sections. As to the first clause, which allowed cable systems to refuse to carry sexually explicit broadcasting, Justice Breyer wrote a plurality opinion that was joined by Justices Stevens, O'Connor, and Souter. Justice Breyer explicitly eschewed choosing or applying a level of scrutiny, saying it was "unwise and unnecessary" to do so. Nonetheless, the plurality said that the first provision is constitutional because it serves "an extremely important justification, one that this Court has often found compelling—the need to protect children from exposure to patently offensive sex-related material." The plurality opinion expressly analogized to *Pacifica* and said that the Cable Act was even less restrictive of speech than what the Court had upheld in the earlier case; the Cable Act permits but does not require cable systems to prohibit sexually explicit material. The plurality also rejected the argument that the law was impermissibly vague.

Justice Thomas, in an opinion joined by Chief Justice Rehnquist and Justice Scalia, concurred in the judgment and said that cable system operators have the First Amendment right to decide what programming to broadcast. Accordingly, the First Amendment is not violated by allowing cable companies to refuse to carry sexually explicit material.

Justice Kennedy, joined by Justice Ginsburg, dissented as to this part of the opinion. Justice Kennedy criticized the plurality's refusal to adopt a level of scrutiny and argued that strict scrutiny was the appropriate test: "When the government identifies certain speech on the basis of its content as vulnerable to exclusion from a common carrier or public forum, strict scrutiny applies. These laws cannot survive that exacting review."

As to the second part of the act, Justice Breyer wrote a majority opinion—joined by Justices Stevens, O'Connor, Kennedy, Souter, and Ginsburg—declaring unconstitutional the requirement that sexual material be segregated and available only on request. Justice Breyer explained that this part of the act was mandatory on cable companies carrying sexual material and imposed substantial restrictions on access. For example, there could be a 30-day delay before receiving such material and "the written notice requirement will further restrict viewing by subscribers who fear for their reputations should the operator, advertently or inadvertently, disclose the list of those who wish to watch the 'patently offensive' channel." Moreover, the Court said that less restrictive alternatives could protect children, such as a system where parents could request blocking by telephone or employ lockboxes.

Justice Thomas, joined again by Justices Rehnquist and Scalia, dissented on the ground that the provision was "narrowly tailored to achieve [a] well-established compelling interest. . . . [G]overnment may support parental authority to direct the moral upbringing of their children by imposing a blocking requirement as a default position."

Finally, as to the third provision, Justice Breyer wrote a plurality opinion, joined by Justices Stevens and Souter, finding unconstitutional the provision of the Cable Act that permitted cable systems to prohibit sexually explicit material over public access channels. The plurality distinguished leased channels, where the authority to prohibit such material was upheld, from public access channels, where it was declared unconstitutional. The plurality found that there was not proof of "a compelling need, nationally, to protect children from significantly harmful material" on these channels. Justice Kennedy, again joined by Justice Ginsburg, concurred in the judgment and argued that the public access channels are public forums and that the content-based restriction on speech failed strict scrutiny. Justice Thomas, once more joined by Chief Justice Rehnquist and Justice Scalia, dissented on the ground that cable system operators have a First Amendment right to decide what programming to include or exclude.

In light of the fragmented Court,[40] it is difficult to draw generalizations from the *Denver Area* decision. The plurality's express refusal to adopt a level of scrutiny makes it even harder to assess the impact of the case. The Court's second and more recent decision concerning cable television did produce a majority opinion choosing a level of scrutiny, albeit by a five-to-four margin.

The Court returned to the issue of government regulation of sexual speech over cable television in United States v. Playboy Entertainment Group, 529 U.S. 803 (2000), in which the Court considered a challenge to §505 of the Telecommunications Act of 1996. Section 505 requires cable television operators who provide channels "primarily dedicated to sexually-oriented programming" either to "fully scramble or otherwise fully block" those channels or to limit their transmission to hours when children are unlikely to be viewing, set by administrative regulation as the hours between 10 P.M. and 6 A.M.

To comply with the statute, the majority of cable operators adopted the second, or "time channeling," approach. The effect of the widespread adoption of time channeling was to eliminate altogether the transmission of the targeted programming outside the safe harbor period in affected cable service areas.

The Supreme Court, in an opinion by Justice Kennedy, declared this unconstitutional. The Court stressed that strict scrutiny was to be used because the law was content-based; it applied to sexual content, but not to other material. The Court concluded that the law failed strict scrutiny because less restrictive alternatives existed: Individuals who did not want such channels could have them blocked.

D. A NEW EXCEPTION FOR VIOLENT SPEECH?

In two recent cases, in very different contexts, the Court considered whether there should be a new exception for violent speech. In both, the Court rejected such an exception and made clear its reluctance to create new categories of unprotected speech.

---

40. Justices Stevens, Souter, and O'Connor also wrote separate opinions.

UNITED STATES v. STEVENS
559 U.S. 460 (2010)

Chief Justice ROBERTS delivered the opinion of the Court.

Congress enacted 18 U.S.C. §48 to criminalize the commercial creation, sale, or possession of certain depictions of animal cruelty. The statute does not address underlying acts harmful to animals, but only portrayals of such conduct. The question presented is whether the prohibition in the statute is consistent with the freedom of speech guaranteed by the First Amendment.

I

Section 48 establishes a criminal penalty of up to five years in prison for anyone who knowingly "creates, sells, or possesses a depiction of animal cruelty," if done "for commercial gain" in interstate or foreign commerce. A depiction of "animal cruelty" is defined as one "in which a living animal is intentionally maimed, mutilated, tortured, wounded, or killed," if that conduct violates federal or state law where "the creation, sale, or possession takes place." In what is referred to as the "exceptions clause," the law exempts from prohibition any depiction "that has serious religious, political, scientific, educational, journalistic, historical, or artistic value."

The legislative background of §48 focused primarily on the interstate market for "crush videos." According to the House Committee Report on the bill, such videos feature the intentional torture and killing of helpless animals, including cats, dogs, monkeys, mice, and hamsters. Crush videos often depict women slowly crushing animals to death "with their bare feet or while wearing high heeled shoes," sometimes while "talking to the animals in a kind of dominatrix patter" over "[t]he cries and squeals of the animals, obviously in great pain." Apparently these depictions "appeal to persons with a very specific sexual fetish who find them sexually arousing or otherwise exciting." The acts depicted in crush videos are typically prohibited by the animal cruelty laws enacted by all 50 States and the District of Columbia. But crush videos rarely disclose the participants' identities, inhibiting prosecution of the underlying conduct.

This case, however, involves an application of §48 to depictions of animal fighting. Dogfighting, for example, is unlawful in all 50 States and the District of Columbia, and has been restricted by federal law since 1976. Respondent Robert J. Stevens ran a business, "Dogs of Velvet and Steel," and an associated Web site, through which he sold videos of pit bulls engaging in dogfights and attacking other animals.

Stevens moved to dismiss the indictment, arguing that §48 is facially invalid under the First Amendment. The District Court denied the motion. It held that the depictions subject to §48, like obscenity or child pornography, are categorically unprotected by the First Amendment. The jury convicted Stevens on all counts, and the District Court sentenced him to three concurrent sentences of 37 months' imprisonment, followed by three years of supervised release. The en banc Third Circuit, over a three-judge dissent, declared §48 facially unconstitutional and vacated Stevens's conviction.

II

The Government's primary submission is that §48 necessarily complies with the Constitution because the banned depictions of animal cruelty, as a class, are categorically unprotected by the First Amendment. We disagree.

"[A]s a general matter, the First Amendment means that government has no power to restrict expression because of its message, its ideas, its subject matter, or its content." Section 48 explicitly regulates expression based on content: The statute restricts "visual [and] auditory depiction[s]," such as photographs, videos, or sound recordings, depending on whether they depict conduct in which a living animal is intentionally harmed. As such, §48 is "'presumptively invalid,' and the Government bears the burden to rebut that presumption."

"From 1791 to the present," however, the First Amendment has "permitted restrictions upon the content of speech in a few limited areas," and has never "include[d] a freedom to disregard these traditional limitations." These "historic and traditional categories long familiar to the bar," including obscenity, defamation, fraud, incitement, and speech integral to criminal conduct, are "well-defined and narrowly limited classes of speech, the prevention and punishment of which have never been thought to raise any Constitutional problem."

The Government argues that "depictions of animal cruelty" should be added to the list. It contends that depictions of "illegal acts of animal cruelty" that are "made, sold, or possessed for commercial gain" necessarily "lack expressive value," and may accordingly "be regulated as *unprotected* speech." The claim is not just that Congress may regulate depictions of animal cruelty subject to the First Amendment, but that these depictions are outside the reach of that Amendment altogether-that they fall into a "'First Amendment Free Zone.'"

As the Government notes, the prohibition of animal cruelty itself has a long history in American law, starting with the early settlement of the Colonies. But we are unaware of any similar tradition excluding *depictions* of animal cruelty from "the freedom of speech" codified in the First Amendment, and the Government points us to none.

The Government contends that "historical evidence" about the reach of the First Amendment is not "a necessary prerequisite for regulation today," and that categories of speech may be exempted from the First Amendment's protection without any long-settled tradition of subjecting that speech to regulation. Instead, the Government points to Congress's "'legislative judgment that . . . depictions of animals being intentionally tortured and killed [are] of such minimal redeeming value as to render [them] unworthy of First Amendment protection,'" and asks the Court to uphold the ban on the same basis. The Government thus proposes that a claim of categorical exclusion should be considered under a simple balancing test: "Whether a given category of speech enjoys First Amendment protection depends upon a categorical balancing of the value of the speech against its societal costs."

As a free-floating test for First Amendment coverage, that sentence is startling and dangerous. The First Amendment's guarantee of free speech does not extend only to categories of speech that survive an ad hoc balancing of relative social costs and benefits. The First Amendment itself reflects a judgment by the American people that the benefits of its restrictions on the Government

D. A New Exception for Violent Speech?

outweigh the costs. Our Constitution forecloses any attempt to revise that judgment simply on the basis that some speech is not worth it.

When we have identified categories of speech as fully outside the protection of the First Amendment, it has not been on the basis of a simple cost-benefit analysis. In [New York v.] Ferber, for example, we classified child pornography as such a category. We noted that the State of New York had a compelling interest in protecting children from abuse, and that the value of using children in these works (as opposed to simulated conduct or adult actors) was *de minimis*. But our decision did not rest on this "balance of competing interests" alone. We made clear that *Ferber* presented a special case: The market for child pornography was "intrinsically related" to the underlying abuse, and was therefore "an integral part of the production of such materials, an activity illegal throughout the Nation." *Ferber* thus grounded its analysis in a previously recognized, long-established category of unprotected speech, and our subsequent decisions have shared this understanding.

Our decisions in *Ferber* and other cases cannot be taken as establishing a freewheeling authority to declare new categories of speech outside the scope of the First Amendment. Maybe there are some categories of speech that have been historically unprotected, but have not yet been specifically identified or discussed as such in our case law. But if so, there is no evidence that "depictions of animal cruelty" is among them. We need not foreclose the future recognition of such additional categories to reject the Government's highly manipulable balancing test as a means of identifying them.

III

Because we decline to carve out from the First Amendment any novel exception for §48, we review Stevens's First Amendment challenge under our existing doctrine.

Stevens challenged §48 on its face, arguing that any conviction secured under the statute would be unconstitutional. The court below decided the case on that basis.

To succeed in a typical facial attack, Stevens would have to establish "that no set of circumstances exists under which [§48] would be valid," or that the statute lacks any "plainly legitimate sweep." In the First Amendment context, however, this Court recognizes "a second type of facial challenge," whereby a law may be invalidated as overbroad if "a substantial number of its applications are unconstitutional, judged in relation to the statute's plainly legitimate sweep." Stevens argues that §48 applies to common depictions of ordinary and lawful activities, and that these depictions constitute the vast majority of materials subject to the statute. The Government makes no effort to defend such a broad ban as constitutional. Instead, the Government's entire defense of §48 rests on interpreting the statute as narrowly limited to specific types of "extreme" material. As the parties have presented the issue, therefore, the constitutionality of §48 hinges on how broadly it is construed. It is to that question that we now turn.

As we explained two Terms ago, "[t]he first step in overbreadth analysis is to construe the challenged statute; it is impossible to determine whether a statute reaches too far without first knowing what the statute covers." We read §48 to create a criminal prohibition of alarming breadth. To begin with, the text of the statute's ban on a "depiction of animal cruelty" nowhere requires that the depicted conduct be cruel. That text applies to "any . . . depiction" in which "a living animal is intentionally maimed, mutilated, tortured, wounded, or killed." "[M]aimed, mutilated, [and] tortured" convey cruelty, but "wounded" or "killed" do not suggest any such limitation.

The Government contends that the terms in the definition should be read to require the additional element of "accompanying acts of cruelty." But the phrase "wounded . . . or killed" at issue here contains little ambiguity. We agree that "wounded" and "killed" should be read according to their ordinary meaning. Nothing about that meaning requires cruelty.

While not requiring cruelty, §48 does require that the depicted conduct be "illegal." But this requirement does not limit §48 along the lines the Government suggests. There are myriad federal and state laws concerning the proper treatment of animals, but many of them are not designed to guard against animal cruelty.

What is more, the application of §48 to depictions of illegal conduct extends to conduct that is illegal in only a single jurisdiction. Under subsection (c)(1), the depicted conduct need only be illegal in "the State in which the creation, sale, or possession takes place, regardless of whether the . . . wounding . . . or killing took place in [that] State." A depiction of entirely lawful conduct runs afoul of the ban if that depiction later finds its way into another State where the same conduct is unlawful. This provision greatly expands the scope of §48, because although there may be "a broad societal consensus" against cruelty to animals, there is substantial disagreement on what types of conduct are properly regarded as cruel. Both views about cruelty to animals and regulations having no connection to cruelty vary widely from place to place.

In the District of Columbia, for example, all hunting is unlawful. Other jurisdictions permit or encourage hunting, and there is an enormous national market for hunting-related depictions in which a living animal is intentionally killed. Hunting periodicals have circulations in the hundreds of thousands or millions, and hunting television programs, videos, and Web sites are equally popular. The demand for hunting depictions exceeds the estimated demand for crush videos or animal fighting depictions by several orders of magnitude.

Those seeking to comply with the law thus face a bewildering maze of regulations from at least 56 separate jurisdictions. Some States permit hunting with crossbows, while others forbid it, or restrict it only to the disabled. Missouri allows the "canned" hunting of ungulates held in captivity, but Montana restricts such hunting to certain bird species. The sharp-tailed grouse may be hunted in Idaho, but not in Washington. The disagreements among the States—and the "commonwealth[s], territor[ies], or possession[s] of the United States"—extend well beyond hunting. State agricultural regulations permit different methods of livestock slaughter in different places or as applied to different animals.

The only thing standing between defendants who sell such depictions and five years in federal prison—other than the mercy of a prosecutor—is the statute's exceptions clause. Subsection (b) exempts from prohibition "any depiction that has serious religious, political, scientific, educational, journalistic, historical, or artistic value."

The Government's attempt to narrow the statutory ban, however, requires an unrealistically broad reading of the exceptions clause. But the text says "serious"

D. A New Exception for Violent Speech?

value, and "serious" should be taken seriously. We decline the Government's invitation—advanced for the first time in this Court—to regard as "serious" anything that is not "scant."

Quite apart from the requirement of "serious" value in §48(b), the excepted speech must also fall within one of the enumerated categories. Much speech does not. Most hunting videos, for example, are not obviously instructional in nature, except in the sense that all life is a lesson.

The Government explains that the language of §48(b) was largely drawn from our opinion in Miller v. California (1973), which excepted from its definition of obscenity any material with "serious literary, artistic, political, or scientific value." According to the Government, this incorporation of the *Miller* standard into §48 is therefore surely enough to answer any First Amendment objection.

We did not, however, determine that serious value could be used as a general precondition to protecting *other* types of speech in the first place. *Most* of what we say to one another lacks "religious, political, scientific, educational, journalistic, historical, or artistic value" (let alone serious value), but it is still sheltered from government regulation. Even "'[w]holly neutral futilities . . . come under the protection of free speech as fully as do Keats' poems or Donne's sermons.'" Thus, the protection of the First Amendment presumptively extends to many forms of speech that do not qualify for the serious-value exception of §48(b), but nonetheless fall within the broad reach of §48(c).

Not to worry, the Government says: The Executive Branch construes §48 to reach only "extreme" cruelty, and it "neither has brought nor will bring a prosecution for anything less." The Government hits this theme hard, invoking its prosecutorial discretion several times. But the First Amendment protects against the Government; it does not leave us at the mercy of *noblesse oblige*. We would not uphold an unconstitutional statute merely because the Government promised to use it responsibly.

Nor does the Government seriously contest that the presumptively impermissible applications of §48 (properly construed) far outnumber any permissible ones. However "growing" and "lucrative" the markets for crush videos and dogfighting depictions might be, they are dwarfed by the market for other depictions, such as hunting magazines and videos, that we have determined to be within the scope of §48. We therefore need not and do not decide whether a statute limited to crush videos or other depictions of extreme animal cruelty would be constitutional. We hold only that §48 is not so limited but is instead substantially overbroad, and therefore invalid under the First Amendment.

Justice ALITO, dissenting.

The Court strikes down in its entirety a valuable statute, 18 U.S.C. §48, that was enacted not to suppress speech, but to prevent horrific acts of animal cruelty—in particular, the creation and commercial exploitation of "crush videos," a form of depraved entertainment that has no social value. The Court's approach, which has the practical effect of legalizing the sale of such videos and is thus likely to spur a resumption of their production, is unwarranted. Respondent was convicted under §48 for selling videos depicting dogfights. On appeal, he argued, among other things, that §48 is unconstitutional as applied to the facts of this case, and he highlighted features of those videos that might distinguish them from other dogfight videos brought to our attention.

In determining whether a statute's overbreadth is substantial, we consider a statute's application to real-world conduct, not fanciful hypotheticals. Accordingly, we have repeatedly emphasized that an over-breadth claimant bears the burden of demonstrating, "from the text of [the law] *and from actual fact*," that substantial overbreadth exists. Similarly, "there must be a *realistic danger* that the statute itself will significantly compromise recognized First Amendment protections of parties not before the Court for it to be facially challenged on over-breadth grounds."

In holding that §48 violates the overbreadth rule, the Court declines to decide whether, as the Government maintains, §48 is constitutional as applied to two broad categories of depictions that exist in the real world: crush videos and depictions of deadly animal fights. Instead, the Court tacitly assumes for the sake of argument that §48 is valid as applied to these depictions, but the Court concludes that §48 reaches too much protected speech to survive. The Court relies primarily on depictions of hunters killing or wounding game and depictions of animals being slaughtered for food.

The Court's interpretation is seriously flawed. "When a federal court is dealing with a federal statute challenged as overbroad, it should, of course, construe the statute to avoid constitutional problems, if the statute is subject to such a limiting construction." Applying this canon, I would hold that §48 does not apply to depictions of hunting. First, because §48 targets depictions of "animal cruelty," I would interpret that term to apply only to depictions involving acts of animal cruelty as defined by applicable state or federal law, not to depictions of acts that happen to be illegal for reasons having nothing to do with the prevention of animal cruelty.

Second, even if the hunting of wild animals were otherwise covered by §48(a), I would hold that hunting depictions fall within the exception in §48(b) for depictions that have "serious" (i.e., not "trifling") "scientific," "educational," or "historical" value. While there are certainly those who find hunting objectionable, the predominant view in this country has long been that hunting serves many important values, and it is clear that Congress shares that view. I do not have the slightest doubt that Congress, in enacting §48, had no intention of restricting the creation, sale, or possession of depictions of hunting. Proponents of the law made this point clearly.

In sum, we have a duty to interpret §48 so as to avoid serious constitutional concerns, and §48 may reasonably be construed not to reach almost all, if not all, of the depictions that the Court finds constitutionally protected. Thus, §48 does not appear to have a large number of unconstitutional applications. Invalidation for overbreadth is appropriate only if the challenged statute suffers from *substantial* overbreadth—judged not just in absolute terms, but in relation to the statute's "plainly legitimate sweep."

IV

It is undisputed that the *conduct* depicted in crush videos may constitutionally be prohibited. All 50 States and the District of Columbia have enacted statutes prohibiting animal cruelty. But before the enactment of §48, the underlying conduct depicted in crush videos was nearly impossible to prosecute. These videos, which "often appeal to persons with a very specific sexual fetish," were made in secret, generally without a live audience, and "the faces of the women

D. A New Exception for Violent Speech?

inflicting the torture in the material often were not shown, nor could the location of the place where the cruelty was being inflicted or the date of the activity be ascertained from the depiction." Thus, law enforcement authorities often were not able to identify the parties responsible for the torture.

In light of the practical problems thwarting the prosecution of the creators of crush videos under state animal cruelty laws, Congress concluded that the only effective way of stopping the underlying criminal conduct was to prohibit the commercial exploitation of the videos of that conduct. And Congress' strategy appears to have been vindicated. We are told that "[b]y 2007, sponsors of §48 declared the crush video industry dead. Even overseas Websites shut down in the wake of §48. Now, after the Third Circuit's decision [facially invalidating the statute], crush videos are already back online."

The First Amendment protects freedom of speech, but it most certainly does not protect violent criminal conduct, even if engaged in for expressive purposes. Crush videos present a highly unusual free speech issue because they are so closely linked with violent criminal conduct. The videos record the commission of violent criminal acts, and it appears that these crimes are committed for the sole purpose of creating the videos. In addition, as noted above, Congress was presented with compelling evidence that the only way of preventing these crimes was to target the sale of the videos. Under these circumstances, I cannot believe that the First Amendment commands Congress to step aside and allow the underlying crimes to continue.

The most relevant of our prior decisions is Ferber v. New York (1982), which concerned child pornography. The Court there held that child pornography is not protected speech, and I believe that *Ferber*'s reasoning dictates a similar conclusion here.

It must be acknowledged that §48 differs from a child pornography law in an important respect: preventing the abuse of children is certainly much more important than preventing the torture of the animals used in crush videos. But while protecting children is unquestionably *more* important than protecting animals, the Government also has a compelling interest in preventing the torture depicted in crush videos.

The animals used in crush videos are living creatures that experience excruciating pain. Our society has long banned such cruelty, which is illegal throughout the country. In *Ferber*, the Court noted that "virtually all of the States and the United States have passed legislation proscribing the production of or otherwise combating 'child pornography,'" and the Court declined to "second-guess [that] legislative judgment."

In sum, §48 may validly be applied to at least two broad real-world categories of expression covered by the statute: crush videos and dogfighting videos. Thus, the statute has a substantial core of constitutionally permissible applications. Moreover, for the reasons set forth above, the record does not show that §48, properly interpreted, bans a substantial amount of protected speech in absolute terms. *A fortiori*, respondent has not met his burden of demonstrating that any impermissible applications of the statute are "substantial" in relation to its "plainly legitimate sweep." Accordingly, I would reject respondent's claim that §48 is facially unconstitutional under the overbreadth doctrine.[41]

---

41. After the Court's decision in *Stevens*, Congress enacted a new version of §48, which is much narrower and focuses just on "crush videos." [Footnote by casebook author.]

BROWN v. ENTERTAINMENT MERCHANTS ASSOCIATION
564 U.S. 786 (2011)

Justice SCALIA delivered the opinion of the Court.

We consider whether a California law imposing restrictions on violent video games comports with the First Amendment.

I

California Assembly Bill 1179 (2005) prohibits the sale or rental of "violent video games" to minors, and requires their packaging to be labeled "18." The Act covers games "in which the range of options available to a player includes killing, maiming, dismembering, or sexually assaulting an image of a human being, if those acts are depicted" in a manner that "[a] reasonable person, considering the game as a whole, would find appeals to a deviant or morbid interest of minors," that is "patently offensive to prevailing standards in the community as to what is suitable for minors," and that "causes the game, as a whole, to lack serious literary, artistic, political, or scientific value for minors." Violation of the Act is punishable by a civil fine of up to $1,000.

II

California correctly acknowledges that video games qualify for First Amendment protection. The Free Speech Clause exists principally to protect discourse on public matters, but we have long recognized that it is difficult to distinguish politics from entertainment, and dangerous to try. "Everyone is familiar with instances of propaganda through fiction. What is one man's amusement, teaches another's doctrine." Like the protected books, plays, and movies that preceded them, video games communicate ideas—and even social messages—through many familiar literary devices (such as characters, dialogue, plot, and music) and through features distinctive to the medium (such as the player's interaction with the virtual world). That suffices to confer First Amendment protection. Under our Constitution, "esthetic and moral judgments about art and literature . . . are for the individual to make, not for the Government to decree, even with the mandate or approval of a majority." And whatever the challenges of applying the Constitution to ever-advancing technology, "the basic principles of freedom of speech and the press, like the First Amendment's command, do not vary" when a new and different medium for communication appears.

The most basic of those principles is this: "[A]s a general matter, . . . government has no power to restrict expression because of its message, its ideas, its subject matter, or its content." There are of course exceptions.

Last Term, in [United States v.] Stevens, we held that new categories of unprotected speech may not be added to the list by a legislature that concludes certain speech is too harmful to be tolerated. As in *Stevens*, California has tried to make violent-speech regulation look like obscenity regulation by appending a saving clause required for the latter. That does not suffice. Our cases have been clear that the obscenity exception to the First Amendment does not cover whatever a legislature finds shocking, but only depictions of "sexual conduct."

D. A New Exception for Violent Speech?

Because speech about violence is not obscene, it is of no consequence that California's statute mimics the New York statute regulating obscenity-for-minors that we upheld in Ginsberg v. New York (1968). That case approved a prohibition on the sale to minors of *sexual* material that would be obscene from the perspective of a child.

The California Act is something else entirely. It does not adjust the boundaries of an existing category of unprotected speech to ensure that a definition designed for adults is not uncritically applied to children. California does not argue that it is empowered to prohibit selling offensively violent works *to adults*—and it is wise not to, since that is but a hair's breadth from the argument rejected in *Stevens*. Instead, it wishes to create a wholly new category of content-based regulation that is permissible only for speech directed at children.

That is unprecedented and mistaken. "[M]inors are entitled to a significant measure of First Amendment protection, and only in relatively narrow and well-defined circumstances may government bar public dissemination of protected materials to them." No doubt a State possesses legitimate power to protect children from harm, but that does not include a free-floating power to restrict the ideas to which children may be exposed. "Speech that is neither obscene as to youths nor subject to some other legitimate proscription cannot be suppressed solely to protect the young from ideas or images that a legislative body thinks unsuitable for them."

California's argument would fare better if there were a longstanding tradition in this country of specially restricting children's access to depictions of violence, but there is none. Certainly the *books* we give children to read—or read to them when they are younger—contain no shortage of gore. Grimm's Fairy Tales, for example, are grim indeed. As her just deserts for trying to poison Snow White, the wicked queen is made to dance in red hot slippers "till she fell dead on the floor, a sad example of envy and jealousy." Cinderella's evil stepsisters have their eyes pecked out by doves. And Hansel and Gretel (children!) kill their captor by baking her in an oven.

California claims that video games present special problems because they are "interactive," in that the player participates in the violent action on screen and determines its outcome. The latter feature is nothing new: Since at least the publication of *The Adventures of You: Sugarcane Island* in 1969, young readers of choose-your-own-adventure stories have been able to make decisions that determine the plot by following instructions about which page to turn to. As for the argument that video games enable participation in the violent action, that seems to us more a matter of degree than of kind. As Judge Posner has observed, all literature is interactive. "[T]he better it is, the more interactive. Literature when it is successful draws the reader into the story, makes him identify with the characters, invites him to judge them and quarrel with them, to experience their joys and sufferings as the reader's own."

III

Because the Act imposes a restriction on the content of protected speech, it is invalid unless California can demonstrate that it passes strict scrutiny—that is, unless it is justified by a compelling government interest and is narrowly drawn to serve that interest. "It is rare that a regulation restricting speech because of its content will ever be permissible."

California cannot meet that standard. At the outset, it acknowledges that it cannot show a direct causal link between violent video games and harm to minors. The State's evidence is not compelling. California relies primarily on the research of Dr. Craig Anderson and a few other research psychologists whose studies purport to show a connection between exposure to violent video games and harmful effects on children. These studies have been rejected by every court to consider them, and with good reason: They do not prove that violent video games *cause* minors to *act* aggressively (which would at least be a beginning). Instead, "[n]early all of the research is based on correlation, not evidence of causation, and most of the studies suffer from significant, admitted flaws in methodology." They show at best some correlation between exposure to violent entertainment and minuscule real-world effects, such as children's feeling more aggressive or making louder noises in the few minutes after playing a violent game than after playing a nonviolent game.

Even taking for granted Dr. Anderson's conclusions that violent video games produce some effect on children's feelings of aggression, those effects are both small and indistinguishable from effects produced by other media. And he admits that the *same* effects have been found when children watch cartoons starring Bugs Bunny or the Road Runner, *id.*, at 1304, or when they play video games like Sonic the Hedgehog that are rated "E" (appropriate for all ages), or even when they "vie[w] a picture of a gun."

Of course, California has (wisely) declined to restrict Saturday morning cartoons, the sale of games rated for young children, or the distribution of pictures of guns. The consequence is that its regulation is wildly underinclusive when judged against its asserted justification, which in our view is alone enough to defeat it. Underinclusiveness raises serious doubts about whether the government is in fact pursuing the interest it invokes, rather than disfavoring a particular speaker or viewpoint. Here, California has singled out the purveyors of video games for disfavored treatment—at least when compared to booksellers, cartoonists, and movie producers—and has given no persuasive reason why.

The Act is also seriously underinclusive in another respect—and a respect that renders irrelevant the contentions of the concurrence and the dissents that video games are qualitatively different from other portrayals of violence. The California Legislature is perfectly willing to leave this dangerous, mind-altering material in the hands of children so long as one parent (or even an aunt or uncle) says it's OK. And there are not even any requirements as to how this parental or avuncular relationship is to be verified; apparently the child's or putative parent's, aunt's, or uncle's say-so suffices. That is not how one addresses a serious social problem.

California claims that the Act is justified in aid of parental authority: By requiring that the purchase of violent video games can be made only by adults, the Act ensures that parents can decide what games are appropriate. At the outset, we note our doubts that punishing third parties for conveying protected speech to children *just in case* their parents disapprove of that speech is a proper governmental means of aiding parental authority.

But leaving that aside, California cannot show that the Act's restrictions meet a substantial need of parents who wish to restrict their children's access to violent video games but cannot do so. The video-game industry has in place

D. A New Exception for Violent Speech?

a voluntary rating system designed to inform consumers about the content of games. The system, implemented by the Entertainment Software Rating Board (ESRB), assigns age-specific ratings to each video game submitted: EC (Early Childhood); E (Everyone); E10+ (Everyone 10 and older); T (Teens); M (17 and older); and AO (Adults Only—18 and older).

And finally, the Act's purported aid to parental authority is vastly overinclusive. Not all of the children who are forbidden to purchase violent video games on their own have parents who *care* whether they purchase violent video games. While some of the legislation's effect may indeed be in support of what some parents of the restricted children actually want, its entire effect is only in support of what the State thinks parents *ought* to want. This is not the narrow tailoring to "assisting parents" that restriction of First Amendment rights requires.

California's legislation straddles the fence between (1) addressing a serious social problem and (2) helping concerned parents control their children. Both ends are legitimate, but when they affect First Amendment rights they must be pursued by means that are neither seriously underinclusive nor seriously overinclusive. As a means of protecting children from portrayals of violence, the legislation is seriously under-inclusive, not only because it excludes portrayals other than video games, but also because it permits a parental or avuncular veto. And as a means of assisting concerned parents it is seriously overinclusive because it abridges the First Amendment rights of young people whose parents (and aunts and uncles) think violent video games are a harmless pastime. And the overbreadth in achieving one goal is not cured by the underbreadth in achieving the other. Legislation such as this, which is neither fish nor fowl, cannot survive strict scrutiny.

Justice ALITO, with whom THE CHIEF JUSTICE joins, concurring in the judgment.

The California statute that is before us in this case represents a pioneering effort to address what the state legislature and others regard as a potentially serious social problem: the effect of exceptionally violent video games on impressionable minors, who often spend countless hours immersed in the alternative worlds that these games create. Although the California statute is well intentioned, its terms are not framed with the precision that the Constitution demands, and I therefore agree with the Court that this particular law cannot be sustained.

I disagree, however, with the approach taken in the Court's opinion. In considering the application of unchanging constitutional principles to new and rapidly evolving technology, this Court should proceed with caution. We should make every effort to understand the new technology.

We should take into account the possibility that developing technology may have important societal implications that will become apparent only with time. We should not jump to the conclusion that new technology is fundamentally the same as some older thing with which we are familiar. And we should not hastily dismiss the judgment of legislators, who may be in a better position than we are to assess the implications of new technology. The opinion of the Court exhibits none of this caution.

In the view of the Court, all those concerned about the effects of violent video games—federal and state legislators, educators, social scientists, and parents—are unduly fearful, for violent video games really present no serious problem. Spending hour upon hour controlling the actions of a character who guns down scores of innocent victims is not different in "kind" from reading a description of violence in a work of literature.

The Court is sure of this; I am not. There are reasons to suspect that the experience of playing violent video games just might be very different from reading a book, listening to the radio, or watching a movie or a television show.

Here, the California law does not define "violent video games" with the "narrow specificity" that the Constitution demands. I conclude that the California violent video game law fails to provide the fair notice that the Constitution requires. And I would go no further. I would not express any view on whether a properly drawn statute would or would not survive First Amendment scrutiny. We should address that question only if and when it is necessary to do so.

Justice THOMAS, dissenting.

The Court's decision today does not comport with the original public understanding of the First Amendment. The majority strikes down, as facially unconstitutional, a state law that prohibits the direct sale or rental of certain video games to minors because the law "abridg[es] the freedom of speech." But I do not think the First Amendment stretches that far. The practices and beliefs of the founding generation establish that "the freedom of speech," as originally understood, does not include a right to speak to minors (or a right of minors to access speech) without going through the minors' parents or guardians. I would hold that the law at issue is not facially unconstitutional under the First Amendment, and reverse and remand for further proceedings.

When interpreting a constitutional provision, "the goal is to discern the most likely public understanding of [that] provision at the time it was adopted." Because the Constitution is a written instrument, "its meaning does not alter." "That which it meant when adopted, it means now."

In my view, the "practices and beliefs held by the Founders" reveal another category of excluded speech: speech to minor children bypassing their parents. The historical evidence shows that the founding generation believed parents had absolute authority over their minor children and expected parents to use that authority to direct the proper development of their children. It would be absurd to suggest that such a society understood "the freedom of speech" to include a right to speak to minors (or a corresponding right of minors to access speech) without going through the minors' parents. The founding generation would not have considered it an abridgment of "the freedom of speech" to support parental authority by restricting speech that bypasses minors' parents.

"The freedom of speech," as originally understood, does not include a right to speak to minors without going through the minors' parents or guardians. Therefore, I cannot agree that the statute at issue is facially unconstitutional under the First Amendment.

Justice BREYER, dissenting.

Applying traditional First Amendment analysis, I would uphold the statute as constitutional on its face and would consequently reject the industries' facial challenge.

In determining whether the statute is unconstitutional, I would apply both this Court's "vagueness" precedents and a strict form of First Amendment scrutiny. In doing so, the special First Amendment category I find relevant is not (as the Court claims) the category of "depictions of violence," but rather

D. A New Exception for Violent Speech?

the category of "protection of children." This Court has held that the "power of the state to control the conduct of children reaches beyond the scope of its authority over adults." And the "'regulatio[n] of communication addressed to [children] need not conform to the requirements of the [F]irst [A]mendment in the same way as those applicable to adults.'" Ginsberg v. New York (1968).

Comparing the language of California's statute with the language of New York's statute, it is difficult to find any vagueness-related difference. Why are the words "kill," "maim," and "dismember" any more difficult to understand than the word "nudity?" All that is required for vagueness purposes is that the terms "kill," "maim," and "dismember" give fair notice as to what they cover, which they do.

The remainder of California's definition copies, almost word for word, the language this Court used in Miller v. California (1973), in permitting a *total ban* on material that satisfied its definition (one enforced with *criminal* penalties).

What, then, is the difference between *Ginsberg* and *Miller* on the one hand and the California law on the other? It will often be easy to pick out cases at which California's statute directly aims, involving, say, a character who shoots out a police officer's knee, douses him with gasoline, lights him on fire, urinates on his burning body, and finally kills him with a gunshot to the head. (Footage of one such game sequence has been submitted in the record.) As in *Miller* and *Ginsberg*, the California law clearly *protects* even the most violent games that possess serious literary, artistic, political, or scientific value. And it is easier here than in *Miller* or *Ginsberg* to separate the sheep from the goats at the statute's border. That is because here the industry itself has promulgated standards and created a review process, in which adults who "typically have experience with children" assess what games are inappropriate for minors.

There is, of course, one obvious difference: The *Ginsberg* statute concerned depictions of "nudity," while California's statute concerns extremely violent video games. But for purposes of vagueness, why should that matter?

Thus, I can find no meaningful vagueness-related differences between California's law and the New York law upheld in *Ginsberg*. And if there remain any vagueness problems, the state courts can cure them through interpretation.

California's law imposes no more than a modest restriction on expression. The statute prevents no one from playing a video game, it prevents no adult from buying a video game, and it prevents no child or adolescent from obtaining a game provided a parent is willing to help. All it prevents is a child or adolescent from buying, without a parent's assistance, a gruesomely violent video game of a kind that the industry *itself* tells us it wants to keep out of the hands of those under the age of 17.

Nor is the statute, if upheld, likely to create a precedent that would adversely affect other media, say films, or videos, or books. A typical video game involves a significant amount of physical activity. And pushing buttons that achieve an interactive, virtual form of target practice (using images of human beings as targets), while containing an expressive component, is not just like watching a typical movie.

The interest that California advances in support of the statute is compelling. As this Court has previously described that interest, it consists of both (1) the "basic" parental claim "to authority in their own household to direct the rearing of their children," which makes it proper to enact "laws designed to aid discharge of [parental] responsibility," and (2) the State's "independent interest in the well-being of its youth." And where these interests work in tandem, it is not fatally "under-inclusive" for a State to advance its interests in protecting children against the special harms present in an interactive video game medium through a default rule that still allows parents to provide their children with what their parents wish.

At the same time, there is considerable evidence that California's statute significantly furthers this compelling interest. That is, in part, because video games are excellent teaching tools.

In particular, extremely violent games can harm children by rewarding them for being violently aggressive in play, and thereby often teaching them to be violently aggressive in life. And video games can cause more harm in this respect than can typically passive media, such as books or films or television programs.

There are many scientific studies that support California's views. Social scientists, for example, have found *causal* evidence that playing these games results in harm. Longitudinal studies, which measure changes over time, have found that increased exposure to violent video games causes an increase in aggression over the same period. Experimental studies in laboratories have found that subjects randomly assigned to play a violent video game subsequently displayed more characteristics of aggression than those who played nonviolent games. Surveys of 8th and 9th grade students have found a correlation between playing violent video games and aggression. Cutting-edge neuroscience has shown that "virtual violence in video game playing results in those neural patterns that are considered characteristic for aggressive cognition and behavior." And "meta-analyses," *i.e.*, studies of all the studies, have concluded that exposure to violent video games "was positively associated with aggressive behavior, aggressive cognition, and aggressive affect," and that "playing violent video games is a *causal* risk factor for long-term harmful outcomes."

Experts debate the conclusions of all these studies. Like many, perhaps most, studies of human behavior, each study has its critics, and some of those critics have produced studies of their own in which they reach different conclusions. (I list both sets of research in the appendixes.) I, like most judges, lack the social science expertise to say definitively who is right. But associations of public health professionals who do possess that expertise have reviewed many of these studies and found a significant risk that violent video games, when compared with more passive media, are particularly likely to cause children harm.

I can find no "less restrictive" alternative to California's law that would be "at least as effective." The majority points to a voluntary alternative: The industry tries to prevent those under 17 from buying extremely violent games by labeling those games with an "M" (Mature) and encouraging retailers to restrict their sales to those 17 and older. But this voluntary system has serious enforcement gaps. When California enacted its law, a Federal Trade Commission (FTC) study had found that nearly 70% of unaccompanied 13- to 16-year-olds were able to buy M-rated video games. Subsequently the voluntary program has become more effective. But as of the FTC's most recent update to Congress, 20% of those under 17 are still able to buy M-rated video games, and, breaking down sales by store, one finds that this number rises to nearly 50% in the case of one large national chain.

The upshot is that California's statute, as applied to its heartland of applications (*i.e.*, buyers under 17; extremely violent, realistic video games), imposes a restriction on speech that is modest at most. That restriction is justified by a compelling interest (supplementing parents' efforts to prevent their children from purchasing potentially harmful violent, interactive material). And there is no equally effective, less restrictive alternative. California's statute is consequently constitutional on its face—though litigants remain free to challenge the statute as applied in particular instances, including any effort by the State to apply it to minors aged 17.

I add that the majority's different conclusion creates a serious anomaly in First Amendment law. *Ginsberg* makes clear that a State can prohibit the sale to minors of depictions of nudity; today the Court makes clear that a State cannot prohibit the sale to minors of the most violent interactive video games. But what sense does it make to forbid selling to a 13-year-old boy a magazine with an image of a nude woman, while protecting a sale to that 13-year-old of an interactive video game in which he actively, but virtually, binds and gags the woman, then tortures and kills her? What kind of First Amendment would permit the government to protect children by restricting sales of that extremely violent video game *only* when the woman—bound, gagged, tortured, and killed—is also topless?

This anomaly is not compelled by the First Amendment. It disappears once one recognizes that extreme violence, where interactive, and *without literary, artistic, or similar justification,* can prove at least as, if not more, harmful to children as photographs of nudity. And the record here is more than adequate to support such a view. That is why I believe that *Ginsberg* controls the outcome here *a fortiori*. And it is why I believe California's law is constitutional on its face.

This case is ultimately less about censorship than it is about education. Our Constitution cannot succeed in securing the liberties it seeks to protect unless we can raise future generations committed cooperatively to making our system of government work. Education, however, is about choices. Sometimes, children need to learn by making choices for themselves. Other times, choices are made for children—by their parents, by their teachers, and by the people acting democratically through their governments. In my view, the First Amendment does not disable government from helping parents make such a choice here—a choice not to have their children buy extremely violent, interactive video games, which they more than reasonably fear pose only the risk of harm to those children.

E. COMMERCIAL SPEECH

1. *Constitutional Protection for Commercial Speech*

In 1942 in Valentine v. Christensen, 316 U.S. 52 (1942), the Supreme Court held that commercial speech was not protected by the First Amendment. A city's ordinance prohibited the distribution of any "handbill [or] other advertising matter [in] or upon any street." An individual was prosecuted for circulating an advertisement to visit a submarine that was being exhibited. Without analysis or explanation, the Supreme Court stated, "We are equally clear that the Constitution imposes no restraint on government as respects purely commercial advertising."

Commercial speech remained unprotected by the First Amendment until 1975 when the Court decided Bigelow v. Virginia, 421 U.S. 809 (1975). The Court in *Bigelow* declared unconstitutional a state law that made it a crime to encourage or prompt the provision of abortion services; specifically, the Court held that advertisements for abortion services in newspapers are protected by the First Amendment. The Court said that "speech is not stripped of First Amendment protection merely because it appears" as a commercial advertisement. The Court said that "[t]he fact that the particular advertisement in appellant's newspaper had commercial aspects or reflected the advertiser's commercial interests did not negate all First Amendment guarantees." The Court expressly said that the state court had erred in its conclusion "that advertising, as such, was entitled to no First Amendment protection."

A year later, in Virginia State Board of Pharmacy v. Virginia Citizens Consumer Council, Inc., the Court made it even clearer that commercial speech is protected by the First Amendment and that Valentine v. Christensen no longer was the law.

VIRGINIA STATE BOARD OF PHARMACY v. VIRGINIA CITIZENS CONSUMER COUNCIL, INC.
425 U.S. 748 (1976)

Justice BLACKMUN delivered the opinion of the Court.

The plaintiff-appellees in this case attack, as violative of the First and Fourteenth Amendments, that portion of [Virginia law] which provides that a pharmacist licensed in Virginia is guilty of unprofessional conduct if he "publishes, advertises or promotes, directly or indirectly, in any manner whatsoever, any amount price, fee, premium, discount, rebate or credit terms . . . for any drugs which may be dispensed only by prescription."

Inasmuch as only a licensed pharmacist may dispense prescription drugs in Virginia, advertising or other affirmative dissemination of prescription drug price information is effectively forbidden in the State. Some pharmacies refuse even to quote prescription drug prices over the telephone. Certainly that information may be of value. Drug prices in Virginia, for both prescription and nonprescription items, strikingly vary from outlet to outlet even within the same locality. It is stipulated, for example, that in Richmond "the cost of 40 Achromycin tablets ranges from $2.59 to $6.00, a difference of 140% [sic]," and that in the Newport News-Hampton area the cost of tetracycline ranges from $1.20 to $9.00, a difference of 650%.

The appellants contend that the advertisement of prescription drug prices is outside the protection of the First Amendment because it is "commercial speech." There can be no question that in past decisions the Court has given some indication that commercial speech is unprotected. In Valentine v. Christensen, [t]he Court concluded that, although the First Amendment would forbid the banning of all communication by handbill in the public thoroughfares, it imposed "no such restraint on government as respects purely commercial advertising."

Last Term, in Bigelow v. Virginia, the notion of unprotected "commercial speech" all but passed from the scene. We reversed a conviction for violation of a Virginia statute that made the circulation of any publication to encourage or

E. Commercial Speech

promote the processing of an abortion in Virginia a misdemeanor. We rejected the contention that the publication was unprotected because it was commercial. Some fragment of hope for the continuing validity of a "commercial speech" exception arguably might have persisted because of the subject matter of the advertisement in *Bigelow*. We noted that in announcing the availability of legal abortions in New York, the advertisement "did more than simply propose a commercial transaction. It contained factual material of clear 'public interest.'" And, of course, the advertisement related to activity with which, at least in some respects, the State could not interfere.

Here, in contrast, the question whether there is a First Amendment exception for "commercial speech" is squarely before us. Our pharmacist does not wish to editorialize on any subject, cultural, philosophical, or political. He does not wish to report any particularly newsworthy fact, or to make generalized observations even about commercial matters. The "idea" he wishes to communicate is simply this: "I will sell you the X prescription drug at the Y price." Our question, then, is whether this communication is wholly outside the protection of the First Amendment.

We begin with several propositions that already are settled or beyond serious dispute. It is clear, for example, that speech does not lose its First Amendment protection because money is spent to project it, as in a paid advertisement of one form or another. If there is a kind of commercial speech that lacks all First Amendment protection, therefore, it must be distinguished by its content. Yet the speech whose content deprives it of protection cannot simply be speech on a commercial subject. No one would contend that our pharmacist may be prevented from being heard on the subject of whether, in general, pharmaceutical prices should be regulated, or their advertisement forbidden. Nor can it be dispositive that a commercial advertisement is noneditorial, and merely reports a fact. Purely factual matter of public interest may claim protection.

Focusing first on the individual parties to the transaction that is proposed in the commercial advertisement, we may assume that the advertiser's interest is a purely economic one. That hardly disqualifies him from protection under the First Amendment. The interests of the contestants in a labor dispute are primarily economic, but it has long been settled that both the employee and the employer are protected by the First Amendment when they express themselves on the merits of the dispute in order to influence its outcome.

As to the particular consumer's interest in the free flow of commercial information, that interest may be as keen, if not keener by far, than his interest in the day's most urgent political debate. Those whom the suppression of prescription drug price information hits the hardest are the poor, the sick, and particularly the aged. A disproportionate amount of their income tends to be spent on prescription drugs; yet they are the least able to learn, by shopping from pharmacist to pharmacist, where their scarce dollars are best spent. When drug prices vary as strikingly they do, information as to who is charging what becomes more than a convenience. It could mean the alleviation of physical pain or the enjoyment of basic necessities.

Generalizing, society also may have a strong interest in the free flow of commercial information. Even an individual advertisement, though entirely "commercial," may be of general public interest. The facts of decided cases furnish illustrations: advertisements stating that referral services for legal abortions are available; that a manufacturer of artificial furs promotes his product as an alternative to the extinction by his competitors of fur-bearing mammals; and that a domestic producer advertises his product as an alternative to imports that tend to deprive American residents of their jobs. Obviously, not all commercial messages contain the same or even a very great public interest element. There are few to which such an element, however, could not be added. Our pharmacist, for example, could cast himself as a commentator on store-to-store disparities in drug prices, giving his own and those of a competitor as proof. We see little point in requiring him to do so, and little difference if he does not.

Moreover, there is another consideration that suggests that no line between publicly "interesting" or "important" commercial advertising and the opposite kind could ever be drawn. Advertising, however tasteless and excessive it sometimes may seem, is nonetheless dissemination of information as to who is producing and selling what product, for what reason, and at what price. So long as we preserve a predominantly free enterprise economy, the allocation of our resources in large measure will be made through numerous private economic decisions. It is a matter of public interest that those decisions, in the aggregate, be intelligent and well informed. To this end, the free flow of commercial information is indispensable. And if it is indispensable to the proper allocation of resources in a free enterprise system, it is also indispensable to the formation of intelligent opinions as to how that system ought to be regulated or altered. Therefore, even if the First Amendment were thought to be primarily an instrument to enlighten public decisionmaking in a democracy, we could not say that the free flow of information does not serve that goal.

Arrayed against these substantial individual and societal interests are a number of justifications for the advertising ban. These have to do principally with maintaining a high degree of professionalism on the part of licensed pharmacists. Indisputably, the State has a strong interest in maintaining that professionalism. Price advertising, it is argued, will place in jeopardy the pharmacist's expertise and, with it, the customer's health. It is claimed that the aggressive price competition that will result from unlimited advertising will make it impossible for the pharmacist to supply professional services in the compounding, handling, and dispensing of prescription drugs.

The strength of these proffered justifications is greatly undermined by the fact that high professional standards, to a substantial extent, are guaranteed by the close regulation to which pharmacists in Virginia are subject. And this case concerns the retail sale by the pharmacist more than it does his professional standards. Surely, any pharmacist guilty of professional dereliction that actually endangers his customer will promptly lose his license.

The advertising ban does not directly affect professional standards one way or the other. It affects them only through the reactions it is assumed people will have to the free flow of drug price information. There is no claim that the advertising ban in any way prevents the cutting of corners by the pharmacist who is so inclined. That pharmacist is likely to cut corners in any event. The only effect the advertising ban has on him is to insulate him from price competition and to open the way for him to make a substantial, and perhaps even excessive, profit in addition to providing an inferior service. The more painstaking pharmacist is also protected but, again, it is a protection based in large part on public ignorance.

E. Commercial Speech

In concluding that commercial speech, like other varieties, is protected, we of course do not hold that it can never be regulated in any way. Some forms of commercial speech regulation are surely permissible. We mention a few only to make clear that they are not before us and therefore are not foreclosed by this case. There is no claim that prescription drug price advertisements are forbidden because they are false or misleading in any way. Untruthful speech, commercial or otherwise, has never been protected for its own sake. Obviously, much commercial speech is not provably false, or even wholly false, but only deceptive or misleading. We foresee no obstacle to a State's dealing effectively with this problem. The First Amendment, as we construe it today does not prohibit the State from insuring that the stream of commercial information flow cleanly as well as freely. Also, there is no claim that the transactions proposed in the forbidden advertisements are themselves illegal in any way.

What is at issue is whether a State may completely suppress the dissemination of concededly truthful information about entirely lawful activity, fearful of that information's effect upon its disseminators and its recipients. Reserving other questions, we conclude that the answer to this one is in the negative.

Justice REHNQUIST, dissenting.

The logical consequences of the Court's decision in this case, a decision which elevates commercial intercourse between a seller hawking his wares and a buyer seeking to strike a bargain to the same plane as has been previously reserved for the free marketplace of ideas, are far reaching indeed. Under the Court's opinion the way will be open not only for dissemination of price information but for active promotion of prescription drugs, liquor, cigarettes, and other products the use of which it has previously been thought desirable to discourage. Now, however, such promotion is protected by the First Amendment so long as it is not misleading or does not promote an illegal product or enterprise. In coming to this conclusion, the Court has overruled a legislative determination that such advertising should not be allowed and has done so on behalf of a consumer group which is not directly disadvantaged by the statute in question.

The Court insists that the rule it lays down is consistent even with the view that the First Amendment is "primarily an instrument to enlighten public decisionmaking in a democracy." I had understood this view to relate to public decisionmaking as to political, social, and other public issues, rather than the decision of a particular individual as to whether to purchase one or another kind of shampoo. It is undoubtedly arguable that many people in the country regard the choice of shampoo as just as important as who may be elected to local, state, or national political office, but that does not automatically bring information about competing shampoos within the protection of the First Amendment. It is one thing to say that the line between strictly ideological and political commentaries and other kinds of commentary is difficult to draw, and that the mere fact that the former may have in it an element of commercialism does not strip it of First Amendment protection.

In the case of "our" hypothetical pharmacist, he may now presumably advertise not only the prices of prescription drugs, but may attempt to energetically promote their sale so long as he does so truthfully. Quite consistently with Virginia law requiring prescription drugs to be available only through a physician, "our" pharmacist might run any of the following representative advertisements in a local newspaper:

> "Pain getting you down? Insist that your physician prescribe Demerol. You pay a little more than for aspirin, but you get a lot more relief."
>
> "Can't shake the flu? Get a prescription for Tetracycline from your doctor today."
>
> "Don't spend another sleepless night. Ask your doctor to prescribe Seconal without delay."

Unless the State can show that these advertisements are either actually untruthful or misleading, it presumably is not free to restrict in any way commercial efforts on the part of those who profit from the sale of prescription drugs to put them in the widest possible circulation. But such a line simply makes no allowance whatever for what appears to have been a considered legislative judgment in most States that while prescription drugs are a necessary and vital part of medical care and treatment, there are sufficient dangers attending their widespread use that they simply may not be promoted in the same manner as hair creams, deodorants, and toothpaste. The very real dangers that general advertising for such drugs might create in terms of encouraging, even though not sanctioning, illicit use of them by individuals for whom they have not been prescribed, or by generating patient pressure upon physicians to prescribe them, are simply not dealt with in the Court's opinion. If prescription drugs may be advertised, they may be advertised on television during family viewing time. Nothing we know about the acquisitive instincts of those who inhabit every business and profession to a greater or lesser extent gives any reason to think that such persons will not do everything they can to generate demand for these products in much the same manner and to much the same degree as demand for other commodities has been generated. I do not believe that the First Amendment mandates the Court's "open door policy" toward such commercial advertising.

Since 1976, the Supreme Court has decided a large number of cases involving commercial speech. The Court, however, has never wavered from the basic holding of *Virginia State Board of Pharmacy*: Commercial speech is protected by the First Amendment. The issue thus arises as to whether such speech should be safeguarded.

Critics of the protection of commercial speech argue, in part, that the expression is not worthy of protection because it does not directly concern the political process and self-government.[42] Moreover, critics argue that the deference to government economic regulation since 1937 should include deference to government restrictions of commercial speech. Professors

---

42. *See* Vincent Blasi, *The Pathological Perspective and the First Amendment*, 85 Colum. L. Rev. 449, 486 (1985); Edwin P. Baker, *Commercial Speech: A Problem, in the Theory of Freedom*, 62 Iowa L. Rev. 1 (1976).

E. Commercial Speech

Thomas Jackson and John Jeffries argue that "in terms of relevance to political decisionmaking, advertising is neither more nor less significant than a host of other market activities that legislatures concededly may regulate. . . . The decisive point is the absence of any principled distinction between commercial soliciting and other aspects of economic activity. . . . [E]conomic due process is resurrected, clothed in the ill-fitting garb of the first amendment."[43]

But defenders of the constitutional protection of commercial speech argue that the First Amendment is not limited to protecting speech about the political process.[44] Moreover, it is argued that, as Justice Blackmun concluded, commercial speech is important to individuals and thus worthy of First Amendment protection. Professor Martin Redish, for example, argued that "[i]f the individual is to achieve the maximum degree of material satisfaction permitted by his resources, he must be presented with as much information as possible concerning the relative merits of competing products."[45]

OVERVIEW OF THE SECTION

Once the Court decided that commercial speech is protected by the First Amendment, the issue inevitably arises as to what is "commercial speech." This is discussed in subsection 2. Beginning with Central Hudson Gas v. Public Service Commn. of New York (1980), the Court has formulated and refined a test for when the government can regulate commercial speech. This test, which is essentially a form of intermediate scrutiny, is reviewed in subsection 3.

Under the *Central Hudson* test, four types of government regulations of commercial speech can be identified. First are laws that outlaw advertising of illegal activities. The Court consistently has held that such advertising is not protected by the First Amendment. Second is the prohibition of false and deceptive advertising. The Court also has always held that such ads are not protected by the First Amendment. Third, the Court has indicated that the government may prohibit true advertising that inherently risks becoming false or deceptive. For example, as discussed below, the government can prohibit professionals from advertising and practicing under trade names and can forbid attorneys from engaging in in-person solicitation of clients for profit. In both instances the Court stressed the inherent danger of deception in such speech. Fourth are laws that limit commercial advertising to achieve other goals, such as enhancing the image of lawyers, decreasing consumption of alcohol or tobacco products, preventing panic selling of houses in neighborhoods, or decreasing gambling. The largest number of cases fit into this category and do not follow a consistent path. These four types of government regulation of commercial speech are discussed in subsection 4.

---

43. Thomas H. Jackson & John C. Jeffries, Jr., *Commercial Speech: Economic Due Process and the First Amendment*, 65 Va. L. Rev. 1, 18, 30 (1979).
44. *See* Sylvia A. Law, *Addiction, Autonomy, and Advertising*, 77 Iowa L. Rev. 909, 932 (1992).
45. Martin H. Redish, *The First Amendment in the Marketplace: Commercial Speech and the Values of Free Expression*, 39 Geo. Wash. L. Rev. 429, 433 (1971).

2. What Is Commercial Speech?

In *Virginia State Board of Pharmacy*, the Court said that commercial speech was expression that "propose[s] a commercial transaction." No one, of course, would disagree that advertising of prices for products is a form of commercial speech. The issue arises, though, as to what other speech, besides price advertising, should be regarded as commercial speech. Defining commercial speech as advertising is both overinclusive and underinclusive. Advertising can be pure political speech, such as in the advertisement that was the basis for New York Times v. Sullivan, 376 U.S. 254 (1964), presented below, which criticized the government's handling of civil rights demonstrations. But defining commercial speech as advertising is also underinclusive because the commercial speech may take forms other than advertising, such as in attorneys' direct solicitations of prospective clients.

In Central Hudson Gas & Electric Corp. v. Public Service Commn., presented below, the Court said that commercial speech was "expression related solely to the economic interests of the speaker and its audience." But this definition, too, is difficult to apply. A book publisher or a broadcast station may be motivated solely by economic interests in deciding what to publish or broadcast. Yet those decisions, even if related solely to economic considerations, are obviously protected by the First Amendment.

Bolger v. Youngs Drug Products Corp. is the major Supreme Court case to address directly the question of what is commercial speech.

BOLGER v. YOUNGS DRUG PRODUCTS CORP.
463 U.S. 60 (1983)

Justice MARSHALL delivered the opinion of the Court.

Title 39 U.S.C. §3001(e)(2) prohibits the mailing of unsolicited advertisements for contraceptives. Appellee Youngs Drug Products Corporation (Youngs) is engaged in the manufacture, sale and distribution of contraceptives. Youngs markets its products primarily through sales to chain warehouses and wholesale distributors, who in turn sell contraceptives to retail pharmacists, who then sell those products to individual customers. Appellee publicizes the availability and desirability of its products by various methods. This litigation resulted from Youngs' decision to undertake a campaign of unsolicited mass mailings to members of the public. In conjunction with its wholesalers and retailers, Youngs seeks to mail to the public on an unsolicited basis three types of materials:

- multi-page, multi-item flyers promoting a large variety of products available at a drug store, including prophylactics;
- flyers exclusively or substantially devoted to promoting prophylactics;
- informational pamphlets discussing the desirability and availability of prophylactics in general or Youngs' products in particular.

Because the degree of protection afforded by the First Amendment depends on whether the activity sought to be regulated constitutes commercial or noncommercial speech, we must first determine the proper classification of the mailings at issue here. Most of appellee's mailings fall within the core

E. Commercial Speech

notion of commercial speech—"speech which does 'no more than propose a commercial transaction.'" Youngs' informational pamphlets, however, cannot be characterized merely as proposals to engage in commercial transactions. Their proper classification as commercial or non-commercial speech thus presents a closer question. The mere fact that these pamphlets are conceded to be advertisements clearly does not compel the conclusion that they are commercial speech. Similarly, the reference to a specific product does not by itself render the pamphlets commercial speech. Finally, the fact that Youngs has an economic motivation for mailing the pamphlets would clearly be insufficient by itself to turn the materials into commercial speech.

The combination of all these characteristics, however, provides strong support for the District Court's conclusion that the informational pamphlets are properly characterized as commercial speech. The mailings constitute commercial speech notwithstanding the fact that they contain discussions of important public issues such as venereal disease and family planning. We have made clear that advertising which "links a product to a current public debate" is not thereby entitled to the constitutional protection afforded noncommercial speech. A company has the full panoply of protections available to its direct comments on public issues, so there is no reason for providing similar constitutional protection when such statements are made in the context of commercial transactions. Advertisers should not be permitted to immunize false or misleading product information from government regulation simply by including references to public issues.

We conclude, therefore, that all of the mailings in this case are entitled to the qualified but nonetheless substantial protection accorded to commercial speech. [After reviewing the government's argument for the law, the Court concluded:] We thus conclude that the justifications offered by the Government are insufficient to warrant the sweeping prohibition on the mailing of unsolicited contraceptive advertisements.

The definition of commercial speech in *Bolger*, while seemingly specific, leaves many questions unanswered. For example, are "image advertisements" meant to enhance the public's perception of a business or a particular product a form of commercial speech? If tobacco companies produce advertisements that discuss scientific studies about the harms of smoking, is that commercial speech? More recently, the Court confronted this in considering whether the regulation of commercial transactions is a regulation of commercial speech.

SORRELL v. IMS HEALTH INC.
564 U.S. 552 (2011)

Justice KENNEDY delivered the opinion of the Court.

Vermont law restricts the sale, disclosure, and use of pharmacy records that reveal the prescribing practices of individual doctors. Subject to certain exceptions, the information may not be sold, disclosed by pharmacies for marketing purposes, or used for marketing by pharmaceutical manufacturers. Vermont argues that its prohibitions safeguard medical privacy and diminish the likelihood that marketing will lead to prescription decisions not in the best interests of patients or the State. It can be assumed that these interests are significant. Speech in aid of pharmaceutical marketing, however, is a form of expression protected by the Free Speech Clause of the First Amendment. As a consequence, Vermont's statute must be subjected to heightened judicial scrutiny. The law cannot satisfy that standard.

I

A

Pharmaceutical manufacturers promote their drugs to doctors through a process called "detailing." This often involves a scheduled visit to a doctor's office to persuade the doctor to prescribe a particular pharmaceutical. Detailers bring drug samples as well as medical studies that explain the "details" and potential advantages of various prescription drugs. Interested physicians listen, ask questions, and receive followup data. Salespersons can be more effective when they know the background and purchasing preferences of their clientele, and pharmaceutical salespersons are no exception. Knowledge of a physician's prescription practices—called "prescriber-identifying information"—enables a detailer better to ascertain which doctors are likely to be interested in a particular drug and how best to present a particular sales message. Detailing is an expensive undertaking, so pharmaceutical companies most often use it to promote high-profit brand-name drugs protected by patent. Once a brand-name drug's patent expires, less expensive bioequivalent generic alternatives are manufactured and sold. Pharmacies, as a matter of business routine and federal law, receive prescriber-identifying information when processing prescriptions. Many pharmacies sell this information to "data miners," firms that analyze prescriber-identifying information and produce reports on prescriber behavior. Data miners lease these reports to pharmaceutical manufacturers subject to nondisclosure agreements. Detailers, who represent the manufacturers, then use the reports to refine their marketing tactics and increase sales.

In 2007, Vermont enacted the Prescription Confidentiality Law. The measure is also referred to as Act 80. It has several components. The central provision of the present case is §4631(d). "A health insurer, a self-insured employer, an electronic transmission intermediary, a pharmacy, or other similar entity shall not sell, license, or exchange for value regulated records containing prescriber-identifiable information, nor permit the use of regulated records containing prescriber-identifiable information for marketing or promoting a prescription drug, unless the prescriber consents. . . . Pharmaceutical manufacturers and pharmaceutical marketers shall not use prescriber-identifiable information for marketing or promoting a prescription drug unless the prescriber consents. . . ."

The quoted provision has three component parts. The provision begins by prohibiting pharmacies, health insurers, and similar entities from selling prescriber-identifying information, absent the prescriber's consent. The provision then goes on to prohibit pharmacies, health insurers, and similar entities from allowing prescriber-identifying information to be used for marketing, unless the prescriber consents. This prohibition in effect bars pharmacies from disclosing the information for marketing purposes. Finally, the provision's second sentence bars pharmaceutical manufacturers and pharmaceutical marketers from using prescriber-identifying information for marketing, again absent the prescriber's consent. The Vermont attorney general may pursue civil remedies against violators. §4631(f).

Separate statutory provisions elaborate the scope of the prohibitions set out in §4631(d). "Marketing" is defined to include "advertising, promotion, or any activity" that is "used to influence sales or the market share of a prescription drug." §4631(b)(5). Section 4631(c)(1) further provides that Vermont's Department of Health must allow "a prescriber to give consent for his or her identifying information to be used for the purposes" identified in §4631(d). Finally, the Act's prohibitions on sale, disclosure, and use are subject to a list of exceptions. For example, prescriber-identifying information may be disseminated or used for "health care research"; to enforce "compliance" with health insurance formularies, or preferred drug lists; for "care management educational communications provided to" patients on such matters as "treatment options"; for law enforcement operations; and for purposes "otherwise provided by law." §4631(e).

The present case involves two consolidated suits. One was brought by three Vermont data miners, the other by an association of pharmaceutical manufacturers that produce brand-name drugs. These entities are the respondents here. Contending that §4631(d) violates their First Amendment rights as incorporated by the Fourteenth Amendment, the respondents sought declaratory and injunctive relief against the petitioners, the Attorney General and other officials of the State of Vermont.

II

[Section] 4631(d) cannot be sustained even under the interpretation the State now adopts. As a consequence this Court can assume that the opening clause of §4631(d) prohibits pharmacies, health insurers, and similar entities from selling prescriber-identifying information, subject to the statutory exceptions set out at §4631(e). Under that reading, pharmacies may sell the information to private or academic researchers, see §4631(e)(1), but not, for example, to pharmaceutical marketers. There is no dispute as to the remainder of §4631(d). It prohibits pharmacies, health insurers, and similar entities from disclosing or otherwise allowing prescriber-identifying information to be used for marketing. And it bars pharmaceutical manufacturers and detailers from using the information for marketing. The questions now are whether §4631(d) must be tested by heightened judicial scrutiny and, if so, whether the State can justify the law.

A

On its face, Vermont's law enacts content- and speaker-based restrictions on the sale, disclosure, and use of prescriber-identifying information. The provision first forbids sale subject to exceptions based in large part on the content of a purchaser's speech. For example, those who wish to engage in certain "educational communications," §4631(e)(4), may purchase the information. The measure then bars any disclosure when recipient speakers will use the information for marketing. Finally, the provision's second sentence prohibits pharmaceutical manufacturers from using the information for marketing. The statute thus disfavors marketing, that is, speech with a particular content.

More than that, the statute disfavors specific speakers, namely pharmaceutical manufacturers. As a result of these content- and speaker-based rules, detailers cannot obtain prescriber-identifying information, even though the information may be purchased or acquired by other speakers with diverse purposes and viewpoints. Detailers are likewise barred from using the information for marketing, even though the information may be used by a wide range of other speakers. For example, it appears that Vermont could supply academic organizations with prescriber-identifying information to use in countering the messages of brand-name pharmaceutical manufacturers and in promoting the prescription of generic drugs. But §4631(d) leaves detailers no means of purchasing, acquiring, or using prescriber-identifying information. The law on its face burdens disfavored speech by disfavored speakers.

Any doubt that §4631(d) imposes an aimed, content-based burden on detailers is dispelled by the record and by formal legislative findings. Vermont's law thus has the effect of preventing detailers—and only detailers—from communicating with physicians in an effective and informative manner. Here, the Vermont Legislature explained that detailers, in particular those who promote brand-name drugs, convey messages that "are often in conflict with the goals of the state." The legislature designed §4631(d) to target those speakers and their messages for disfavored treatment. "In its practical operation," Vermont's law "goes even beyond mere content discrimination, to actual viewpoint discrimination." Given the legislature's expressed statement of purpose, it is apparent that §4631(d) imposes burdens that are based on the content of speech and that are aimed at a particular viewpoint.

Act 80 is designed to impose a specific, content-based burden on protected expression. It follows that heightened judicial scrutiny is warranted. The First Amendment requires heightened scrutiny whenever the government creates "a regulation of speech because of disagreement with the message it conveys." A "consumer's concern for the free flow of commercial speech often may be far keener than his concern for urgent political dialogue." That reality has great relevance in the fields of medicine and public health, where information can save lives.

The State argues that heightened judicial scrutiny is unwarranted because its law is a mere commercial regulation. It is true that restrictions on protected expression are distinct from restrictions on economic activity or, more generally, on nonexpressive conduct. It is also true that the First Amendment does not prevent restrictions directed at commerce or conduct from imposing incidental burdens on speech. That is why a ban on race-based hiring may require employers to remove "'White Applicants Only'" signs; why "an ordinance against outdoor fires" might forbid "burning a flag"; and why antitrust laws can prohibit "agreements in restraint of trade."

But §4631(d) imposes more than an incidental burden on protected expression. Both on its face and in its practical operation, Vermont's law imposes a burden based on the content of speech and the identity of the speaker. While the burdened speech results from an economic motive, so too does a great deal of vital expression. Vermont's law does not simply have an effect on speech, but is directed at certain content and is aimed at particular speakers.

This Court has held that the creation and dissemination of information are speech within the meaning of the First Amendment. Facts, after all, are the beginning point for much of the speech that is most essential to advance human

E. Commercial Speech

knowledge and to conduct human affairs. There is thus a strong argument that prescriber-identifying information is speech for First Amendment purposes.

B

In the ordinary case it is all but dispositive to conclude that a law is content-based and, in practice, viewpoint-discriminatory. The State argues that a different analysis applies here because, assuming §4631(d) burdens speech at all, it at most burdens only commercial speech. As in previous cases, however, the outcome is the same whether a special commercial speech inquiry or a stricter form of judicial scrutiny is applied. For the same reason there is no need to determine whether all speech hampered by §4631(d) is commercial, as our cases have used that term.

Under a commercial speech inquiry, it is the State's burden to justify its content-based law as consistent with the First Amendment. To sustain the targeted, content-based burden §4631(d) imposes on protected expression, the State must show at least that the statute directly advances a substantial governmental interest and that the measure is drawn to achieve that interest. There must be a "fit between the legislature's ends and the means chosen to accomplish those ends." As in other contexts, these standards ensure not only that the State's interests are proportional to the resulting burdens placed on speech but also that the law does not seek to suppress a disfavored message.

The State's asserted justifications for §4631(d) come under two general headings. First, the State contends that its law is necessary to protect medical privacy, including physician confidentiality, avoidance of harassment, and the integrity of the doctor-patient relationship. Second, the State argues that §4631(d) is integral to the achievement of policy objectives—namely, improved public health and reduced healthcare costs. Neither justification withstands scrutiny.

Vermont argues that its physicians have a "reasonable expectation" that their prescriber-identifying information "will not be used for purposes other than . . . filling and processing" prescriptions. But §4631(d) is not drawn to serve that interest. Under Vermont's law, pharmacies may share prescriber-identifying information with anyone for any reason save one: They must not allow the information to be used for marketing. Exceptions further allow pharmacies to sell prescriber-identifying information for certain purposes, including "health care research." §4631(e). And the measure permits insurers, researchers, journalists, the State itself, and others to use the information. Perhaps the State could have addressed physician confidentiality through "a more coherent policy."

The State also contends that §4631(d) protects doctors from "harassing sales behaviors." [T]he State offers no explanation why remedies other than content-based rules would be inadequate. Physicians can, and often do, simply decline to meet with detailers, including detailers who use prescriber-identifying information. Doctors who wish to forgo detailing altogether are free to give "No Solicitation" or "No Detailing" instructions to their office managers or to receptionists at their places of work.

The capacity of technology to find and publish personal information, including records required by the government, presents serious and unresolved issues with respect to personal privacy and the dignity it seeks to secure. In considering how to protect those interests, however, the State cannot engage in content-based discrimination to advance its own side of a debate. The State has burdened a form of protected expression that it found too persuasive. At the same time, the State has left unburdened those speakers whose messages are in accord with its own views. This the State cannot do.

Justice BREYER, with whom Justice GINSBURG and Justice KAGAN join, dissenting.

The Vermont statute before us adversely affects expression in one, and only one, way. It deprives pharmaceutical and data-mining companies of data, collected pursuant to the government's regulatory mandate, that could help pharmaceutical companies create better sales messages. In my view, this effect on expression is inextricably related to a lawful governmental effort to regulate a commercial enterprise. The First Amendment does not require courts to apply a special "heightened" standard of review when reviewing such an effort. And, in any event, the statute meets the First Amendment standard this Court has previously applied when the government seeks to regulate commercial speech. For any or all of these reasons, the Court should uphold the statute as constitutional.

[I]

In this case I would ask whether Vermont's regulatory provisions work harm to First Amendment interests that is disproportionate to their furtherance of legitimate regulatory objectives.

To apply a strict First Amendment standard virtually as a matter of course when a court reviews ordinary economic regulatory programs (even if that program has a modest impact upon a firm's ability to shape a commercial message) would work at cross-purposes with this more basic constitutional approach. Since ordinary regulatory programs can affect speech, particularly commercial speech, in myriad ways, to apply a "heightened" First Amendment standard of review whenever such a program burdens speech would transfer from legislatures to judges the primary power to weigh ends and to choose means, threatening to distort or undermine legitimate legislative objectives. To apply a "heightened" standard of review in such cases as a matter of course would risk what then-Justice Rehnquist, dissenting in *Central Hudson*, described as a "retur[n] to the bygone era of Lochner v. New York (1905), in which it was common practice for this Court to strike down economic regulations adopted by a State based on the Court's own notions of the most appropriate means for the State to implement its considered policies."

There are several reasons why the Court should review Vermont's law "under the standard appropriate for the review of economic regulation," not "under a heightened standard appropriate for the review of First Amendment issues." For one thing, Vermont's statute neither forbids nor requires anyone to say anything, to engage in any form of symbolic speech, or to endorse any particular point of view, whether ideological or related to the sale of a product.

For another thing, the same First Amendment standards that apply to Vermont here would apply to similar regulatory actions taken by other States or by the Federal Government acting, for example, through Food and Drug Administration (FDA) regulation. (And the Federal Government's ability to preempt state laws that interfere with existing or contemplated federal forms of regulation is here irrelevant.)

E. Commercial Speech

Further, the statute's requirements form part of a traditional, comprehensive regulatory regime. The pharmaceutical drug industry has been heavily regulated at least since 1906. Finally, Vermont's statute is directed toward information that exists only by virtue of government regulation. Under federal law, certain drugs can be dispensed only by a pharmacist operating under the orders of a medical practitioner. Vermont regulates the qualifications, the fitness, and the practices of pharmacists themselves, and requires pharmacies to maintain a "patient record system" that, among other things, tracks who prescribed which drugs. But for these regulations, pharmacies would have no way to know who had told customers to buy which drugs (as is the case when a doctor tells a patient to take a daily dose of aspirin).

Thus, it is not surprising that, until today, this Court has *never* found that the First Amendment prohibits the government from restricting the use of information gathered pursuant to a regulatory mandate—whether the information rests in government files or has remained in the hands of the private firms that gathered it. Nor has this Court ever previously applied any form of "heightened" scrutiny in any even roughly similar case.

The Court (suggesting a standard yet stricter than *Central Hudson*) says that we must give *content-based* restrictions that burden speech "heightened" scrutiny. It adds that "[c]ommercial speech is no exception." Ante, at 2664. And the Court then emphasizes that this is a case involving both "content-based" and "speaker-based" restrictions.

But neither of these categories—"content-based" nor "speaker-based"—has ever before justified greater scrutiny when regulatory activity affects commercial speech. Regulatory programs necessarily draw distinctions on the basis of content. Electricity regulators, for example, oversee company statements, pronouncements, and proposals, but only about electricity. The Federal Reserve Board regulates the content of statements, advertising, loan proposals, and interest rate disclosures, but only when made by financial institutions. And the FDA oversees the form and content of labeling, advertising, and sales proposals of drugs, but not of furniture. Given the ubiquity of content-based regulatory categories, why should the "content-based" nature of typical regulation require courts (other things being equal) to grant legislators and regulators less deference?

Nor, in the context of a regulatory program, is it unusual for particular rules to be "speaker-based," affecting only a class of entities, namely, the regulated firms. An energy regulator, for example, might require the manufacturers of home appliances to publicize ways to reduce energy consumption, while exempting producers of industrial equipment. Or a trade regulator might forbid a particular firm to make the true claim that its cosmetic product contains "cleansing grains that scrub away dirt and excess oil" unless it substantiates that claim with detailed backup testing, even though opponents of cosmetics use need not substantiate their claims.

If the Court means to create constitutional barriers to regulatory rules that might affect the *content* of a commercial message, it has embarked upon an unprecedented task—a task that threatens significant judicial interference with widely accepted regulatory activity. Nor would it ease the task to limit its "heightened" scrutiny to regulations that only affect certain speakers. As the examples that I have set forth illustrate, many regulations affect only messages sent by a small class of regulated speakers, for example, electricity generators or natural gas pipelines.

Moreover, given the sheer quantity of regulatory initiatives that touch upon commercial messages, the Court's vision of its reviewing task threatens to return us to a happily bygone era when judges scrutinized legislation for its interference with economic liberty. History shows that the power was much abused and resulted in the constitutionalization of economic theories preferred by individual jurists. See Lochner v. New York (1905) (Holmes, J., dissenting). By inviting courts to scrutinize whether a State's legitimate regulatory interests can be achieved in less restrictive ways whenever they touch (even indirectly) upon commercial speech, today's majority risks repeating the mistakes of the past in a manner not anticipated by our precedents.

Nothing in Vermont's statute undermines the ability of persons opposing the State's policies to speak their mind or to pursue a different set of policy objectives through the democratic process. Whether Vermont's regulatory statute "targets" drug companies (as opposed to affecting them unintentionally) must be beside the First Amendment point.

The Court reaches its conclusion through the use of important First Amendment categories—"content-based," "speaker-based," and "neutral"—but without taking full account of the regulatory context, the nature of the speech effects, the values these First Amendment categories seek to promote, and prior precedent. At best the Court opens a Pandora's Box of First Amendment challenges to many ordinary regulatory practices that may only incidentally affect a commercial message. At worst, it reawakens *Lochner*'s pre-New Deal threat of substituting judicial for democratic decisionmaking where ordinary economic regulation is at issue. Regardless, whether we apply an ordinary commercial speech standard or a less demanding standard, I believe Vermont's law is consistent with the First Amendment. And with respect, I dissent.

3. *The Test for Evaluating Regulation of Commercial Speech*

In Central Hudson Gas v. Public Service Commn., the Supreme Court articulated a test, often invoked in subsequent cases, for when the government may regulate commercial speech.

CENTRAL HUDSON GAS & ELECTRIC CORP. v. PUBLIC SERVICE COMMISSION OF NEW YORK
447 U.S. 557 (1980)

Justice POWELL delivered the opinion of the Court.

This case presents the question whether a regulation of the Public Service Commission of the State of New York violates the First and Fourteenth Amendments because it completely bans promotional advertising by an electrical utility.

I

In December 1973, the Commission, appellee here, ordered electric utilities in New York State to cease all advertising that "promot[es] the use of electricity."

E. Commercial Speech

The order was based on the Commission's finding that "the interconnected utility system in New York State does not have sufficient fuel stocks or sources of supply to continue furnishing all customer demands for the 1973-1974 winter." Three years later, when the fuel shortage had eased, the Commission requested comments from the public on its proposal to continue the ban on promotional advertising. Central Hudson Gas & Electric Corp., the appellant in this case, opposed the ban on First Amendment grounds. After reviewing the public comments, the Commission extended the prohibition in a Policy Statement issued on February 25, 1977.

II

The Commission's order restricts only commercial speech, that is, expression related solely to the economic interests of the speaker and its audience. The First Amendment, as applied to the States through the Fourteenth Amendment, protects commercial speech from unwarranted governmental regulation. Commercial expression not only serves the economic interest of the speaker, but also assists consumers and furthers the societal interest in the fullest possible dissemination of information. In applying the First Amendment to this area, we have rejected the "highly paternalistic" view that government has complete power to suppress or regulate commercial speech. "[P]eople will perceive their own best interests if only they are well enough informed, and . . . the best means to that end is to open the channels of communication rather than to close them. . . ." Even when advertising communicates only an incomplete version of the relevant facts, the First Amendment presumes that some accurate information is better than no information at all.

Nevertheless, our decisions have recognized "the 'commonsense' distinction between speech proposing a commercial transaction, which occurs in an area traditionally subject to government regulation, and other varieties of speech." The Constitution therefore accords a lesser protection to commercial speech than to other constitutionally guaranteed expression. The protection available for particular commercial expression turns on the nature both of the expression and of the governmental interests served by its regulation.

The First Amendment's concern for commercial speech is based on the informational function of advertising. Consequently, there can be no constitutional objection to the suppression of commercial messages that do not accurately inform the public about lawful activity. The government may ban forms of communication more likely to deceive the public than to inform it. If the communication is neither misleading nor related to unlawful activity, the government's power is more circumscribed. The State must assert a substantial interest to be achieved by restrictions on commercial speech. Moreover, the regulatory technique must be in proportion to that interest. The limitation on expression must be designed carefully to achieve the State's goal. Compliance with this requirement may be measured by two criteria. First, the restriction must directly advance the state interest involved; the regulation may not be sustained if it provides only ineffective or remote support for the government's purpose. Second, if the governmental interest could be served as well by a more limited restriction on commercial speech, the excessive restrictions cannot survive.

Under the first criterion, the Court has declined to uphold regulations that only indirectly advance the state interest involved. In both Bates v. Arizona State Bar and *Virginia Pharmacy Board*, the Court concluded that an advertising ban could not be imposed to protect the ethical or performance standards of a profession. The second criterion recognizes that the First Amendment mandates that speech restrictions be "narrowly drawn." The regulatory technique may extend only as far as the interest it serves. The State cannot regulate speech that poses no danger to the asserted state interest, nor can it completely suppress information when narrower restrictions on expression would serve its interest as well.

In commercial speech cases, then, a four-part analysis has developed. At the outset, we must determine whether the expression is protected by the First Amendment. For commercial speech to come within that provision, it at least must concern lawful activity and not be misleading. Next, we ask whether the asserted governmental interest is substantial. If both inquiries yield positive answers, we must determine whether the regulation directly advances the governmental interest asserted, and whether it is not more extensive than is necessary to serve that interest.

III

We now apply this four-step analysis for commercial speech to the Commission's arguments in support of its ban on promotional advertising. The Commission does not claim that the expression at issue either is inaccurate or relates to unlawful activity. Even in monopoly markets, the suppression of advertising reduces the information available for consumer decisions and thereby defeats the purpose of the First Amendment. Most businesses—even regulated monopolies—are unlikely to underwrite promotional advertising that is of no interest or use to consumers. Indeed, a monopoly enterprise legitimately may wish to inform the public that it has developed new services or terms of doing business. A consumer may need information to aid his decision whether or not to use the monopoly service at all, or how much of the service he should purchase.

The Commission offers as [a] justification for the ban on promotional advertising energy conservation. Any increase in demand for electricity—during peak or off-peak periods—means greater consumption of energy. In view of our country's dependence on energy resources beyond our control, no one can doubt the importance of energy conservation. Plainly, therefore, the state interest asserted is substantial. [T]he State's interest in energy conservation is directly advanced by the Commission order at issue here. There is an immediate connection between advertising and demand for electricity.

We come finally to the critical inquiry in this case: whether the Commission's complete suppression of speech ordinarily protected by the First Amendment is no more extensive than necessary to further the State's interest in energy conservation. The Commission's order reaches all promotional advertising, regardless of the impact of the touted service on overall energy use. But the energy conservation rationale, as important as it is, cannot justify suppressing information about electric devices or services that would cause no net increase in total energy use. In addition, no showing has been made that a more limited

E. Commercial Speech

restriction on the content of promotional advertising would not serve adequately the State's interests.

Thus, the *Central Hudson* test for commercial speech is: (1) Does the speech advertise illegal activities or constitute false or deceptive advertising that is unprotected by the First Amendment? (2) Is the government's restriction justified by a substantial government interest? (3) Does the law directly advance the government's interest? (4) Is the regulation of speech no more extensive than necessary to achieve the government's interest?

Hence, the test is similar, if not identical, to intermediate scrutiny in evaluating government regulation of truthful advertising for legal activities. In fact, the Court has expressly said that "we engage in 'intermediate' scrutiny of restrictions on commercial speech."[46]

The Court has ruled that the government has the burden of proof to demonstrate that the *Central Hudson* test is met in order to justify a restriction on commercial speech. The Court repeatedly has said that "[t]he party seeking to uphold a restriction on commercial speech carries the burden of justifying it."[47]

IS LEAST RESTRICTIVE ALTERNATIVE ANALYSIS APPLICABLE?

The Court has consistently invoked and applied the *Central Hudson* test in dealing with commercial speech issues. However, the Court has modified the fourth part of the test, the requirement that the regulation be no more extensive than necessary to achieve the government's purpose. In Board of Trustees of the State University of New York v. Fox, 492 U.S. 469 (1989), the Court held that government regulation of commercial speech need not use the least restrictive alternative. *Fox* concerned a state regulation that prohibited commercial solicitations on state university campuses.

The Court, in an opinion by Justice Scalia, expressly rejected the least restrictive alternative test for commercial speech. The Court said, "Our jurisprudence has emphasized that commercial speech enjoys a limited measure of protection, commensurate with its subordinate position in the scale of First Amendment values, and is subject to modes of regulation that might be impermissible in the realm of noncommercial expression. The ample scope of regulatory authority suggested by such statements would be illusory if it were subject to a least-restrictive-means requirement, which imposes a heavy burden on the State." The Court said that while the government need not use the least restrictive alternative, it must use "a means narrowly tailored to achieve the desired objective."

Although *Fox* expressly rejected least restrictive alternative analysis for commercial speech cases, in Rubin v. Coors Brewing Co., 514 U.S. 476 (1995), the Court comes close to reinstituting it. *Rubin* involved a challenge

---

46. Florida Bar v. Went for It, Inc., 515 U.S. 618, 623 (1995).
47. Bolger v. Youngs Drug Products Corp., 463 U.S. at 71; Edenfield v. Fane, 507 U.S. 761, 770 (1993).

to a provision of the Federal Alcohol Administration Act that prohibited the statement of alcohol content on beer labels. Interestingly, both sides in the case and the Court accepted that this constituted commercial speech. It, of course, is different from usual commercial speech, which is advertising for a particular product or service. Statements on labels about the alcohol content of beer are commercial speech in the sense that they may affect purchasers in deciding whether to buy a particular product.

The Court said that government regulation of commercial speech must advance the government's interest "in a direct and material way," and "[t]hat burden 'is not satisfied by mere speculation or conjecture; rather, a governmental body seeking to sustain a restriction on commercial speech must demonstrate that the harms it recites are real and that its restriction will in fact alleviate them to a material degree.'" The Court found that the government failed to meet this burden because of the "irrationality" of the regulatory scheme; the government did not prohibit listing of the alcohol content in advertisements for products, just on labels. The Court also found that there were a number of alternative ways of preventing strength wars and that these options "could advance the Government's asserted interest in a manner less intrusive to respondent's First Amendment rights." The Court said that this indicates that the law "is more extensive than necessary." Indeed, the Court concluded its opinion by emphasizing "the availability of alternatives that would prove less intrusive to the First Amendment's protections for commercial speech."

It is very difficult, if not impossible, to reconcile the language in *Rubin* with *Fox*. Where *Fox* says that government regulation of commercial speech need not use the least restrictive alternative, the *Rubin* Court says that a regulation of commercial speech is unconstitutional because less intrusive alternatives would suffice. Even more troubling is that Justice Thomas's opinion for the Court does not even cite *Fox*, let alone attempt to reconcile this inconsistency.[48]

Nor did the Court's decision in 44 Liquormart, Inc. v. Rhode Island, 517 U.S. 484 (1996), clarify this confusion. In *44 Liquormart*, the Supreme Court declared unconstitutional a state law that prohibited advertisement of liquor prices. The plurality opinion, written by Justice Stevens and joined by Justices Kennedy, Souter, and Ginsburg, said: "The State also cannot satisfy the requirement that its restriction on speech be no more extensive than necessary. It is perfectly obvious that alternative forms of regulation that would not involve any restriction on speech would be more likely to achieve the State's goal of promoting temperance." This is clearly the language of least restrictive alternative analysis. In the next paragraph, Justice Stevens invoked *Fox* and said that "even under the less than strict standard that generally applies in commercial speech cases, the State has failed to establish a 'reasonable fit' between its abridgement of speech and its temperance goal."

Nor do the other opinions in *44 Liquormart* clarify this confusion. Justice Thomas's opinion concurring in the judgment argued that the government should not be able to regulate truthful commercial speech based on the premise that people will be better off with less information. Justice Scalia wrote a short

---

48. The result in *Rubin* was unanimous. Justice Stevens concurred in the judgment and challenged the premise that commercial speech is entitled to less protection than other types of expression.

opinion expressing doubts about the *Central Hudson* test and agreeing with Justice Thomas's analysis. Justice O'Connor wrote an opinion concurring in the judgment, joined by Chief Justice Rehnquist and Justices Souter and Breyer, that expressly invoked *Fox* and said that "[w]hile the State need not employ the least restrictive means to accomplish its goal, the fit between means and ends must be 'narrowly tailored.'" Justice O'Connor concluded that the Rhode Island law failed this test.

The Court's last commercial speech case to address this issue, Greater New Orleans Broadcasting Association v. United States, 527 U.S. 173 (1999), declared unconstitutional a federal law that prohibited advertising by casinos. The Court expressly relied on the *Central Hudson* test, declaring that "*Central Hudson*, as applied in our more recent commercial speech cases, provides an adequate basis for decision." The Court said that "[t]he fourth part of the test complements the direct-advancement inquiry of the third, asking whether the speech restriction is not more extensive than necessary to serve the interests that support it. The Government is not required to employ the least restrictive means conceivable, but it must demonstrate narrow tailoring of the challenged regulation to the asserted interest—'a fit that is not necessarily perfect, but reasonable; that represents not necessarily the single best disposition but one whose scope is in proportion to the interest served.'" The Court cited *Fox* as establishing this proposition. The Court then concluded that the federal law prohibiting casino advertising was not substantially related to achieving the objective of decreasing gambling because of the many exceptions in the law, such as in allowing advertising by Native American tribes and by state-run lotteries.

Thus, *Fox*, as reaffirmed in *Greater New Orleans Broadcasting*, rejects the use of least restrictive alternative analysis, but requires that any government regulation of commercial speech be narrowly tailored to achieving its objective.

4. Advertising of Illegal Activities

The Court consistently has held that advertising of illegality is not protected by the First Amendment.[49] The Court always has stated this as an axiom and offered little explanation. In some ways, it is a curious proposition. One would think that the government would welcome advertising of illegal activity; such ads, if they occurred, could help law enforcement. Moreover, speech that advocates illegal conduct is protected by the First Amendment unless it meets the test for incitement. Yet advertising of illegality is unprotected by the First Amendment without any need to meet the test for incitement.

The only Supreme Court case to consider advertising of illegality, Pittsburgh Press Co. v. Pittsburgh Commn. on Human Relations, 413 U.S. 376 (1973), was actually decided before the Supreme Court held that commercial speech is protected by the First Amendment. The Court upheld a decision by the Pittsburgh Commission on Human Relations that a newspaper violated the city's Human Relations Ordinance by placing help-wanted advertisements in columns captioned "Jobs-Male Interest," "Jobs-Female Interest," and "Male-Female."

---

49. *See, e.g.*, Central Hudson Gas v. Public Service Commn., 447 U.S. at 563-564.

The Court emphasized that "[d]iscrimination in employment is not only commercial activity, it is *illegal* commercial activity under the Ordinance. We have no doubt that a newspaper constitutionally could be forbidden to publish a want ad proposing a sale of narcotics or soliciting prostitutes. . . . The illegality in this case may be less overt, but we see no difference in principle here."

Pittsburgh Press is constantly cited with approval as establishing that advertising of illegal activities is not protected by the First Amendment. Thus, such advertisements can be prohibited, punished, and the basis for civil liability.

5. *False and Deceptive Advertising*

It also is clearly established that false and deceptive advertisements are unprotected by the First Amendment. The Court frequently has declared that only truthful commercial speech is constitutionally protected.[50] The Supreme Court, however, has never decided a First Amendment case concerning false and deceptive ads.

False and deceptive advertisements do not contribute to the marketplace of ideas or the commercial marketplace in any useful way. In fact, false and deceptive advertisements distort those markets and thus are undeserving of First Amendment protection. Yet in contexts outside the commercial speech realm, it is clear that false speech is often protected. In New York Times v. Sullivan, 376 U.S. 254 (1964), the Court said that "erroneous statement is inevitable in free debate, [and] it must be protected if the freedoms of expression are to have the breathing space that they need to survive." The absence of protection for false commercial speech seems based on a judgment that such speech is more harmful, less likely to be chilled because of the profit motive, and more easily verified than most other types of expression.

6. *Advertising That Inherently Risks Deception*

The Supreme Court has held that even true advertisements that inherently risk deception are unprotected by the First Amendment. The Court has considered this in two areas: laws that prohibit professionals from advertising or practicing under trade names, and restrictions on the ability of professionals to solicit prospective clients.

RESTRICTIONS ON TRADE NAMES

In *Friedman v. Rogers*, 440 U.S. 1 (1979), the Supreme Court upheld a state law that prohibited optometrists from advertising and practicing under trade names. The Court said that the use of trade names "is a form of commercial speech and nothing more." Although there was no evidence that the optometrists bringing the challenge had engaged in any deception, the Court concluded that the

---

50. *See, e.g.*, Central Hudson Gas v. Public Service Commn., 447 U.S. at 566.

E. Commercial Speech

state could prohibit trade names because of their inherent risk of deception. Bad optometrists could keep changing their trade names and thereby deceive the public as to their identity. A good optometrist could go out of business and a bad one could assume that name and fool the public. The Court concluded that "there is a significant possibility that trade names will be used to mislead the public."

Friedman v. Rogers is important because it recognizes that even truthful advertising can be restricted if it is of a type that inherently risks becoming false and deceptive. Interestingly, the Court did not consider whether there would be ways of prohibiting the false and deceptive practices without prohibiting the truthful advertisements.

ATTORNEY SOLICITATION OF PROSPECTIVE CLIENTS

The Supreme Court has ruled that the government may not prohibit attorneys from engaging in truthful, nondeceptive advertising of their services.[51] However, the Supreme Court has held that the government may prohibit attorney in-person solicitation of prospective clients for profit. The underlying rationale is that such speech inherently risks becoming deceptive and thus even truthful solicitations can be forbidden when they are conducted in person and where the attorney would profit from the representation.

This rule emerged from a series of Supreme Court cases. In Ohralik v. Ohio State Bar Assn., 436 U.S. 447 (1978), the Court found no violation of the First Amendment when a lawyer was punished for impermissible solicitation for approaching an automobile accident victim in her hospital room and offering to represent her on a contingency fee basis. The Court noted that the government has a "compelling interest in preventing those aspects of solicitation that involve fraud, undue influence, intimidation, overreaching, and other forms of vexatious conduct." The Court stressed that face-to-face solicitation inherently risks deception and pressure because no one is there to monitor the communications. Because of this inherent danger, the Court said that it is not "violative of the Constitution for a State to respond with what in effect is a prophylactic rule."

However, in another case decided the same day, In re Primus, 436 U.S. 412 (1978), the Supreme Court held that solicitations are protected by the First Amendment when the lawyer offers to represent a client without charge. An attorney affiliated with the American Civil Liberties Union in South Carolina was disciplined for impermissible solicitation for offering to represent women for free after the welfare department told the women that they had to be sterilized in order to continue to receive public medical assistance. The Supreme Court, however, held that the lawyer's speech was protected by the First Amendment.

The Court noted that "[t]he ACLU engages in litigation as a vehicle for effective political expression and association, as well as a means of communicating useful information to the public." Thus, the Court said that South Carolina's action punishing the lawyer for offering free representation "must withstand the exacting scrutiny applicable to limitations on core First Amendment rights."

---

51. *See* Bates v. State Bar of Arizona, 433 U.S. 350 (1977).

The Court expressly distinguished *Ohralik* on the ground that the attorney in *Primus* was not seeking to profit directly from the client. This was important for the Court both in enhancing the importance of the speech as a form of political activity and in lessening the likelihood of deceptive practices by the attorney. The Court said that it was irrelevant that the ACLU attorney would seek attorney's fees from the state if the plaintiff prevailed in the case.

In Shapero v. Kentucky Bar Assn., 486 U.S. 466 (1988), the Court declared unconstitutional a state law that prohibited targeted direct-mail solicitation by lawyers for pecuniary gain. The Court explained that letter solicitation does not have the same risk of abuse as face-to-face solicitation. There is less risk of deception because there is a written record of the communication compared to face-to-face solicitation where no one is present to monitor the conversations. There is less risk of pressure or undue influence because people are accustomed to throwing away mail that is not of interest. The Court explained that "[l]ike print advertising, . . . letter[s] — and targeted, direct-mail solicitation generally — pose[] much less risk of overreaching or undue influence than does in-person solicitation."

Thus, *Ohralik, Primus,* and *Shapero* taken together establish the proposition that states may prohibit attorney in-person solicitation of clients for profit. Conversely, solicitation where the attorney would not profit directly from the client or solicitation by mail is generally protected by the First Amendment.

The Court, however, has carved one exception where mail solicitation by lawyers can be regulated. In Florida Bar v. Went for It, Inc., 515 U.S. 618 (1995), the Supreme Court upheld a Florida law that prohibited attorneys from soliciting personal injury or wrongful death clients for 30 days after an accident. The Court said that the "purpose of the 30-day targeted direct-mail ban is to forestall the outrage and irritation with the state-licensed legal profession that the practice of direct solicitation only days after accidents has engendered." The Court, in its 5-4 decision, concluded that the regulation was justified to protect accident victims and their estates from "invasive conduct by lawyers and in preventing the erosion of confidence in the profession that such repeated invasions have engendered."

Justice Kennedy wrote a dissenting opinion, joined by Justices Stevens, Souter, and Ginsburg. The dissent questioned whether letter solicitations are invasive and explained that they are important in informing people of their right to sue. The state did not limit the ability of claims adjusters or insurance companies to settle claims during this 30-day period; restricting such communications from plaintiffs' attorneys could harm accident victims and their estates by denying them needed information. Moreover, the Court consistently had rejected the argument that attorney advertising could be restricted because of its negative impact on the image of the profession.

SOLICITATION BY ACCOUNTANTS

The Supreme Court has held that the government may not prohibit accountants from engaging in in-person solicitation of clients for profit. In Edenfield v. Fane, 507 U.S. 761 (1993), the Court declared unconstitutional a state law that prohibited certified public accountants from engaging in in-person solicitations. The Court said that there was no evidence that accountants

E. Commercial Speech

were engaged in abusive solicitations. The Court expressly distinguished *Ohralik*, which had upheld an identical rule for lawyers. Justice Kennedy, writing for the Court, said, "The solicitation here poses none of the same dangers. Unlike a lawyer, a CPA is not a professional trained in the art of persuasion. A CPA's training emphasizes independence and objectivity, not advocacy. The typical client of a CPA is far less susceptible to manipulation than the young accident victim in *Ohralik*."

This distinction between attorneys and accountants seems questionable. Attorneys and accountants obviously are both capable of trying to pressure prospective clients. The Court in *Ohralik* upheld all prohibitions on in-person solicitation of clients, regardless of their sophistication; the Court in *Edenfield* invalidated all prohibitions of in-person solicitation by accountants, regardless of the client's lack of sophistication. As Justice O'Connor said in dissent, "[t]he attorney's rhetorical power derives not only from his specific training in the art of persuasion, but more generally from his professional expertise." Nonetheless, the current law is that the government may prohibit attorney in-person solicitation for profit, but it may not prohibit accountants from engaging in such solicitation.

7. *Regulating Commercial Speech to Achieve Other Goals*

Perhaps the most difficult issue in the area of commercial speech concerns the ability of the government to regulate truthful, nondeceptive advertising of legal activities to achieve other goals. For example, may the government regulate commercial advertising to reduce sales of houses to preserve the racial balance in a neighborhood, to decrease consumption of alcohol or tobacco products, to lessen gambling, or to enhance the image of attorneys? In all of these areas, the restriction on commercial speech is based on a premise that seems at odds with the very core of the First Amendment: that people will be better off with less information. Justice Thomas, in a recent concurring opinion, rejected the notion that the government should be able to restrict commercial speech based on the assumption that people will be better off if they are kept in the dark about particular information.[52]

For the most part, the Supreme Court's commercial speech cases are consistent with this view as the Court generally has rejected state laws limiting commercial speech based on the belief that people will be better off with less information. The primary exception has been in the area of gambling advertisements where the Court has allowed restrictions of commercial speech to achieve the goal of decreasing gambling.[53]

This section reviews these cases, focusing in turn on the Court's treatment of the regulation of commercial speech concerning the sales of houses, alcohol products, gambling, and lawyers' and other professionals' services. In all of these cases, the issue is when the government may regulate truthful advertising of legal activities so as to achieve other objectives.

---

52. 44 Liquormart, Inc. v. Rhode Island, 517 U.S. at 525-526.
53. United States v. Edge Broadcasting Co., 509 U.S. 418 (1993); Posadas de Puerto Rico Associates v. Tourism Co. of P.R., 478 U.S. 328 (1986).

a. "For Sale" Signs on Houses

In Linmark Associates, Inc. v. Township of Willingboro, 431 U.S. 85 (1977), the Supreme Court declared unconstitutional an ordinance that outlawed the display of "For Sale" or "Sold" signs. The city prohibited such signs "to prevent the flight of white home-owners from a racially integrated community." The city's concern was that the pervasive presence of "for sale" signs would encourage panic selling and white flight from the city.

The Court accepted that the ordinance served a "vital goal . . . [in] promoting stable, racially integrated housing." But the Court, in an opinion by Justice Thurgood Marshall, declared the ordinance unconstitutional because "the First Amendment disable[s] the State from achieving its goal by restricting the free flow of truthful information." The Court questioned whether there was sufficient evidence of likely panic selling or that prohibiting "for sale" signs would prevent this from occurring. But the Court said that the primary infirmity of the law was that the government suppressed truthful information based on the belief that people would be better off with less speech and knowledge. The Court unanimously held that this was unacceptable under the First Amendment.

b. Alcohol Products

The Court has refused to allow the government to limit the advertising of alcohol products based on its goal of decreasing consumption. For example, in Rubin v. Coors Brewing Co., 514 U.S. 476 (1995), the Court declared unconstitutional a federal law that prohibited stating on beer labels the alcohol content of the product. The Court accepted that the government had a substantial interest in preventing strength wars among malt beverage products. The Court said that the government has a "significant interest in protecting the health, safety, and welfare of its citizens by preventing brewers from competing on the basis of alcohol strength, which could lead to greater alcoholism and its attendant social costs."

However, the Court declared the federal law unconstitutional because the government could achieve this goal "in a manner less intrusive to respondent's First Amendment rights." The Court identified "several alternatives, such as directly limiting the alcohol content of beers, prohibiting marketing efforts emphasizing high alcohol strength (which is apparently the policy in some other western nations), or limiting the labeling ban only to malt liquors, which is the segment of the market that allegedly is threatened with a strength war."

Subsequently, in 44 Liquormart, Inc. v. Rhode Island, the Supreme Court declared unconstitutional a state law that prohibited price advertising of alcoholic beverages.

44 LIQUORMART, INC. v. RHODE ISLAND
517 U.S. 484 (1996)

Justice STEVENS announced the judgment of the Court.

Last Term we held that a federal law abridging a brewer's right to provide the public with accurate information about the alcoholic content of malt beverages is unconstitutional. Rubin v. Coors Brewing Co. (1995). We now

E. Commercial Speech

hold that Rhode Island's statutory prohibition against advertisements that provide the public with accurate information about retail prices of alcoholic beverages is also invalid. Our holding rests on the conclusion that such an advertising ban is an abridgment of speech protected by the First Amendment and that it is not shielded from constitutional scrutiny by the Twenty-first Amendment.

In 1956, the Rhode Island Legislature enacted two separate prohibitions against advertising the retail price of alcoholic beverages. The first applies to vendors licensed in Rhode Island as well as to out-of-state manufacturers, wholesalers, and shippers. The second statute applies to the Rhode Island news media. It contains a categorical prohibition against the publication or broadcast of any advertisements—even those referring to sales in other States—that "make reference to the price of any alcoholic beverages."

It is the State's interest in protecting consumers from "commercial harms" that provides "the typical reason why commercial speech can be subject to greater governmental regulation than noncommercial speech." Yet bans that target truthful, nonmisleading commercial messages rarely protect consumers from such harms. Instead, such bans often serve only to obscure an "underlying governmental policy" that could be implemented without regulating speech. In this way, these commercial speech bans not only hinder consumer choice, but also impede debate over central issues of public policy.

Precisely because bans against truthful, nonmisleading commercial speech rarely seek to protect consumers from either deception or overreaching, they usually rest solely on the offensive assumption that the public will respond "irrationally" to the truth. The First Amendment directs us to be especially skeptical of regulations that seek to keep people in the dark for what the government perceives to be their own good. That teaching applies equally to state attempts to deprive consumers of accurate information about their chosen products.

In this case, there is no question that Rhode Island's price advertising ban constitutes a blanket prohibition against truthful, nonmisleading speech about a lawful product. There is also no question that the ban serves an end unrelated to consumer protection. Accordingly, we must review the price advertising ban with "special care," mindful that speech prohibitions of this type rarely survive constitutional review.

The State argues that the price advertising prohibition should nevertheless be upheld because it directly advances the State's substantial interest in promoting temperance, and because it is no more extensive than necessary. Although there is some confusion as to what Rhode Island means by temperance, we assume that the State asserts an interest in reducing alcohol consumption.

In evaluating the ban's effectiveness in advancing the State's interest, we note that a commercial speech regulation "may not be sustained if it provides only ineffective or remote support for the government's purpose." For that reason, the State bears the burden of showing not merely that its regulation will advance its interest, but also that it will do so "to a material degree." The need for the State to make such a showing is particularly great given the drastic nature of its chosen means—the wholesale suppression of truthful, nonmisleading information. Accordingly, we must determine whether the State has shown that the price advertising ban will significantly reduce alcohol consumption.

Although the record suggests that the price advertising ban may have some impact on the purchasing patterns of temperate drinkers of modest means, the State has presented no evidence to suggest that its speech prohibition will significantly reduce marketwide consumption. Indeed, the District Court's considered and uncontradicted finding on this point is directly to the contrary. The State also cannot satisfy the requirement that its restriction on speech be no more extensive than necessary. It is perfectly obvious that alternative forms of regulation that would not involve any restriction on speech would be more likely to achieve the State's goal of promoting temperance. As the State's own expert conceded, higher prices can be maintained either by direct regulation or by increased taxation.

As a result, even under the less than strict standard that generally applies in commercial speech cases, the State has failed to establish a "reasonable fit" between its abridgment of speech and its temperance goal. Board of Trustees of State Univ. of N.Y. v. Fox (1989).

Justice THOMAS, concurring in the judgment.

In cases such as this, in which the government's asserted interest is to keep legal users of a product or service ignorant in order to manipulate their choices in the marketplace, the balancing test adopted in Central Hudson Gas & Elec. Corp. v. Public Serv. Comm'n of N.Y. (1980) should not be applied, in my view. Rather, such an "interest" is per se illegitimate and can no more justify regulation of "commercial" speech than it can justify regulation of "noncommercial" speech. I do not join the principal opinion's application of the *Central Hudson* balancing test because I do not believe that such a test should be applied to a restriction of "commercial" speech, at least when, as here, the asserted interest is one that is to be achieved through keeping would-be recipients of the speech in the dark.

c. Tobacco Products

In Lorillard Tobacco Co. v. Reilly, the Supreme Court considered the constitutionality of Massachusetts's regulation of tobacco advertising. The most significant aspects of the regulations prevented advertising of tobacco products within 1,000 feet of a school or playground and required that places selling tobacco products place ads for these items at least five feet off the ground to avoid being at eye level for children. The Supreme Court declared these regulations of cigarette advertising to be preempted by federal law. The federal law, however, only concerns cigarettes and not cigars or smokeless tobacco. Therefore, the Court considered whether the restrictions on advertising of these products violated the First Amendment.

The case seems particularly important in reaffirming that *Central Hudson*'s four-part test is used in evaluating government regulation of commercial speech. The decision also is significant in limiting the ability of the government to regulate advertising so as to discourage harmful behavior.

LORILLARD TOBACCO CO. v. REILLY
533 U.S. 525 (2001)

O'CONNOR, J., delivered the opinion of the Court, Parts III-A, III-C, and III-D of which were joined by REHNQUIST, C.J., and SCALIA, KENNEDY, SOUTER, and

E. Commercial Speech

THOMAS, JJ.; Part III-B-1 of which was joined by REHNQUIST, C.J., and STEVENS, SOUTER, GINSBURG, and BREYER, JJ.; and Parts III-B-2 of which was joined by REHNQUIST, C.J., and SCALIA, KENNEDY, and THOMAS, JJ.

[I]

By its terms, the FCLAA's pre-emption provision only applies to cigarettes. Accordingly, we must evaluate the smokeless tobacco and cigar petitioners' First Amendment challenges to the State's outdoor and point-of-sale advertising regulations.

A

For over 25 years, the Court has recognized that commercial speech does not fall outside the purview of the First Amendment. Instead, the Court has afforded commercial speech a measure of First Amendment protection "commensurate" with its position in relation to other constitutionally guaranteed expression. In recognition of the "distinction between speech proposing a commercial transaction, which occurs in an area traditionally subject to government regulation, and other varieties of speech," we developed a framework for analyzing regulations of commercial speech that is "substantially similar" to the test for time, place, and manner restrictions. The analysis contains four elements:

> At the outset, we must determine whether the expression is protected by the First Amendment. For commercial speech to come within that provision, it at least must concern lawful activity and not be misleading. Next, we ask whether the asserted governmental interest is substantial. If both inquiries yield positive answers, we must determine whether the regulation directly advances the governmental interest asserted, and whether it is not more extensive than is necessary to serve that interest. Central Hudson Gas & Electric Corp. v. Public Service Commission of New York (1980).

Petitioners urge us to reject the *Central Hudson* analysis and apply strict scrutiny. They are not the first litigants to do so. Admittedly, several Members of the Court have expressed doubts about the *Central Hudson* analysis and whether it should apply in particular cases. But we see "no need to break new ground. *Central Hudson*, as applied in our more recent commercial speech cases, provides an adequate basis for decision."

Only the last two steps of *Central Hudson*'s four-part analysis are at issue here. The Attorney General has assumed for purposes of summary judgment that petitioners' speech is entitled to First Amendment protection. With respect to the second step, none of the petitioners contests the importance of the State's interest in preventing the use of tobacco products by minors.

The third step of *Central Hudson* concerns the relationship between the harm that underlies the State's interest and the means identified by the State to advance that interest. It requires that "the speech restriction directly and materially advanc[e] the asserted governmental interest. 'This burden is not satisfied by mere speculation or conjecture; rather, a governmental body seeking to sustain a restriction on commercial speech must demonstrate that the harms it recites are real and that its restriction will in fact alleviate them to a material degree.'"

We do not, however, require that "empirical data come . . . accompanied by a surfeit of background information. . . . [W]e have permitted litigants to justify speech restrictions by reference to studies and anecdotes pertaining to different locales altogether, or even, in a case applying strict scrutiny, to justify restrictions based solely on history, consensus, and 'simple common sense.'" Florida Bar v. Went For It, Inc. (1995).

The last step of the *Central Hudson* analysis "complements" the third step, "asking whether the speech restriction is not more extensive than necessary to serve the interests that support it." We have made it clear that "the least restrictive means" is not the standard; instead, the case law requires a reasonable "fit between the legislature's ends and the means chosen to accomplish those ends, . . . a means narrowly tailored to achieve the desired objective." Focusing on the third and fourth steps of the *Central Hudson* analysis, we first address the outdoor advertising and point-of-sale advertising regulations for smokeless tobacco and cigars. We then address the sales practices regulations for all tobacco products.

B

The outdoor advertising regulations prohibit smokeless tobacco or cigar advertising within a 1,000-foot radius of a school or playground. The District Court and Court of Appeals concluded that the Attorney General had identified a real problem with underage use of tobacco products, that limiting youth exposure to advertising would combat that problem, and that the regulations burdened no more speech than necessary to accomplish the State's goal. The smokeless tobacco and cigar petitioners take issue with all of these conclusions.

1

The smokeless tobacco and cigar petitioners contend that the Attorney General's regulations do not satisfy *Central Hudson*'s third step. Our review of the record reveals that the Attorney General has provided ample documentation of the problem with underage use of smokeless tobacco and cigars. In addition, we disagree with petitioners' claim that there is no evidence that preventing targeted campaigns and limiting youth exposure to advertising will decrease underage use of smokeless tobacco and cigars. On this record and in the posture of summary judgment, we are unable to conclude that the Attorney General's decision to regulate advertising of smokeless tobacco and cigars in an effort to combat the use of tobacco products by minors was based on mere "speculation [and] conjecture."

2

Whatever the strength of the Attorney General's evidence to justify the outdoor advertising regulations, however, we conclude that the regulations do not satisfy the fourth step of the *Central Hudson* analysis. The final step of the *Central Hudson* analysis, the "critical inquiry in this case," requires a reasonable fit between the means and ends of the regulatory scheme. The Attorney General's regulations do not meet this standard. The broad sweep of the regulations indicates that the Attorney General did not "carefully calcula[te] the costs and benefits associated with the burden on speech imposed" by the regulations.

The outdoor advertising regulations prohibit any smokeless tobacco or cigar advertising within 1,000 feet of schools or playgrounds. In the District

E. Commercial Speech

Court, petitioners maintained that this prohibition would prevent advertising in 87% to 91% of Boston, Worcester, and Springfield, Massachusetts. The 87% to 91% figure appears to include not only the effect of the regulations, but also the limitations imposed by other generally applicable zoning restrictions. The Attorney General disputed petitioners' figures but "concede[d] that the reach of the regulations is substantial." Thus, the Court of Appeals concluded that the regulations prohibit advertising in a substantial portion of the major metropolitan areas of Massachusetts.

The substantial geographical reach of the Attorney General's outdoor advertising regulations is compounded by other factors. "Outdoor" advertising includes not only advertising located outside an establishment, but also advertising inside a store if that advertising is visible from outside the store. The regulations restrict advertisements of any size and the term advertisement also includes oral statements.

In some geographical areas, these regulations would constitute nearly a complete ban on the communication of truthful information about smokeless tobacco and cigars to adult consumers. The breadth and scope of the regulations, and the process by which the Attorney General adopted the regulations, do not demonstrate a careful calculation of the speech interests involved.

The State's interest in preventing underage tobacco use is substantial, and ever compelling, but it is no less true that the sale and use of tobacco products by adults is a legal activity. We must consider that tobacco retailers and manufacturers have an interest in conveying truthful information about their products to adults, and adults have a corresponding interest in receiving truthful information about tobacco products. In a case involving indecent speech on the Internet we explained that "the governmental interest in protecting children from harmful materials . . . does not justify an unnecessarily broad suppression of speech addressed to adults." Reno v. American Civil Liberties Union (1997).

We conclude that the Attorney General has failed to show that the outdoor advertising regulations for smokeless tobacco and cigars are not more extensive than necessary to advance the State's substantial interest in preventing underage tobacco use.

C

Massachusetts has also restricted indoor, point-of-sale advertising for smokeless tobacco and cigars. Advertising cannot be "placed lower than five feet from the floor of any retail establishment which is located within a one thousand foot radius of" any school or playground. We conclude that the point-of-sale advertising regulations fail both the third and fourth steps of the *Central Hudson* analysis. A regulation cannot be sustained if it "provides only ineffective or remote support for the government's purpose," or if there is "little chance" that the restriction will advance the State's goal. As outlined above, the State's goal is to prevent minors from using tobacco products and to curb demand for that activity by limiting youth exposure to advertising. The 5-foot rule does not seem to advance that goal. Not all children are less than 5 feet tall, and those who are certainly have the ability to look up and take in their surroundings.

Massachusetts may wish to target tobacco advertisements and displays that entice children, much like floor-level candy displays in a convenience store, but the blanket height restriction does not constitute a reasonable fit with that goal. The Court of Appeals recognized that the efficacy of the regulation was questionable, but decided that "[i]n any event, the burden on speech imposed by the provision is very limited." There is no de minimis exception for a speech restriction that lacks sufficient tailoring or justification. We conclude that the restriction on the height of indoor advertising is invalid under *Central Hudson*'s third and fourth prongs.

Justice THOMAS, concurring in part and concurring in the judgment.

I join the opinion of the court, [but] I continue to believe that when the government seeks to restrict truthful speech in order to suppress the ideas it conveys, strict scrutiny is appropriate, whether or not the speech in question may be characterized as "commercial." I would subject all of the advertising restrictions to strict scrutiny and would hold that they violate the First Amendment.

Whatever power the State may have to regulate commercial speech, it may not use that power to limit the content of commercial speech, as it has done here, "for reasons unrelated to the preservation of a fair bargaining process." Such content-discriminatory regulation—like all other content-based regulation of speech—must be subjected to strict scrutiny.

Underlying many of the arguments of respondents and their amici is the idea that tobacco is in some sense sui generis—that it is so special, so unlike any other object of regulation, that application of normal First Amendment principles should be suspended. Smoking poses serious health risks, and advertising may induce children (who lack the judgment to make an intelligent decision about whether to smoke) to begin smoking, which can lead to addiction. The State's assessment of the urgency of the problem posed by tobacco is a policy judgment, and it is not this Court's place to second-guess it. Nevertheless, it seems appropriate to point out that to uphold the Massachusetts tobacco regulations would be to accept a line of reasoning that would permit restrictions on advertising for a host of other products.

Tobacco use is, we are told, "the single leading cause of preventable death in the United States." The second largest contributor to mortality rates in the United States is obesity. It is associated with increased incidence of diabetes, hypertension, and coronary artery disease, and it represents a public health problem that is rapidly growing worse. Although the growth of obesity over the last few decades has had many causes, a significant factor has been the increased availability of large quantities of high-calorie, high-fat foods. Such foods, of course, have been aggressively marketed and promoted by fast food companies.

Respondents say that tobacco companies are covertly targeting children in their advertising. Fast food companies do so openly. Moreover, there is considerable evidence that they have been successful in changing children's eating behavior. The effect of advertising on children's eating habits is significant for two reasons. First, childhood obesity is a serious health problem in its own right. Second, eating preferences formed in childhood tend to persist in adulthood. So even though fast food is not addictive in the same way tobacco is, children's exposure to fast food advertising can have deleterious consequences that are difficult to reverse.

To take another example, the third largest cause of preventable deaths in the United States is alcohol. Alcohol use is associated with tens of thousands of deaths each year from cancers and digestive diseases. And the victims of alcohol use are not limited to those who drink alcohol. In 1996, over 17,000 people were killed, and over 321,000 people were injured, in alcohol-related car accidents. Each year, alcohol is involved in several million violent crimes, including almost 200,000 sexual assaults.

Although every State prohibits the sale of alcohol to those under age 21, much alcohol advertising is viewed by children. Not surprisingly, there is considerable evidence that exposure to alcohol advertising is associated with underage drinking. Like underage tobacco use, underage drinking has effects that cannot be undone later in life. Those who begin drinking early are much more likely to become dependent on alcohol. Indeed, the probability of lifetime alcohol dependence decreases approximately 14 percent with each additional year of age at which alcohol is first used. And obviously the effects of underage drinking are irreversible for the nearly 1,700 Americans killed each year by teenage drunk drivers.

Respondents have identified no principle of law or logic that would preclude the imposition of restrictions on fast food and alcohol advertising similar to those they seek to impose on tobacco advertising. In effect, they seek a "vice" exception to the First Amendment. No such exception exists. If it did, it would have almost no limit, for "any product that poses some threat to public health or public morals might reasonably be characterized by a state legislature as relating to 'vice activity.'" That is why "a 'vice' label that is unaccompanied by a corresponding prohibition against the commercial behavior at issue fails to provide a principled justification for the regulation of commercial speech about that activity."

No legislature has ever sought to restrict speech about an activity it regarded as harmless and inoffensive. Calls for limits on expression always are made when the specter of some threatened harm is looming. The identity of the harm may vary. People will be inspired by totalitarian dogmas and subvert the Republic. They will be inflamed by racial demagoguery and embrace hatred and bigotry. Or they will be enticed by cigarette advertisements and choose to smoke, risking disease. It is therefore no answer for the State to say that the makers of cigarettes are doing harm: perhaps they are. But in that respect they are no different from the purveyors of other harmful products, or the advocates of harmful ideas. When the State seeks to silence them, they are all entitled to the protection of the First Amendment.

Justice STEVENS, concurring in part and dissenting in part, joined by Justices GINSBURG and BREYER.

I would, however, reach different dispositions as to the 1,000-foot rule and the height restrictions for indoor advertising, and my evaluation of the sales practice restrictions differs from the Court's.

THE 1,000-FOOT RULE

I am in complete accord with the Court's analysis of the importance of the interests served by the advertising restrictions. As the Court lucidly explains, few interests are more "compelling[]" than ensuring that minors do not become addicted to a dangerous drug before they are able to make a mature and informed decision as to the health risks associated with that substance. Unlike other products sold for human consumption, tobacco products are addictive and ultimately lethal for many long-term users. When that interest is combined with the State's concomitant concern for the effective enforcement of its laws regarding the sale of tobacco to minors, it becomes clear that Massachusetts' regulations serve interests of the highest order and are, therefore, immune from any ends-based challenge, whatever level of scrutiny one chooses to employ.

Nevertheless, noble ends do not save a speech-restricting statute whose means are poorly tailored. Such statutes may be invalid for two different reasons. First, the means chosen may be insufficiently related to the ends they purportedly serve. Alternatively, the statute may be so broadly drawn that, while effectively achieving its ends, it unduly restricts communications that are unrelated to its policy aims. The second difficulty is most frequently encountered when government adopts measures for the protection of children that impose substantial restrictions on the ability of adults to communicate with one another.

To my mind, the 1,000-foot rule does not present a tailoring problem of the first type. For reasons cogently explained in our prior opinions and in the opinion of the Court, we may fairly assume that advertising stimulates consumption and, therefore, that regulations limiting advertising will facilitate efforts to stem consumption.

However, I share the majority's concern as to whether the 1,000-foot rule unduly restricts the ability of cigarette manufacturers to convey lawful information to adult consumers. This, of course, is a question of line-drawing. While a ban on all communications about a given subject would be the most effective way to prevent children from exposure to such material, the state cannot by fiat reduce the level of discourse to that which is "fit for children."

Finding the appropriate balance is no easy matter. Though many factors plausibly enter the equation when calculating whether a child-directed location restriction goes too far in regulating adult speech, one crucial question is whether the regulatory scheme leaves available sufficient "alternative avenues of communication." Because I do not think the record contains sufficient information to enable us to answer that question, I would vacate the award of summary judgment upholding the 1,000-foot rule and remand for trial on that issue.

d. Gambling

In sharp contrast to the Court's unwillingness to allow the government to regulate advertisements for alcohol products based on the desire to decrease consumption, the Court has permitted the government to prohibit gambling advertisements in order to attempt to reduce gambling. In Posadas de Puerto Rico Associates v. Tourism Co., 478 U.S. 328 (1986), the Supreme Court upheld a Puerto Rico law that prohibited advertising by casino gambling establishments. The Court accepted Puerto Rico's argument that the government has an important interest in discouraging gambling and said that it had "no difficulty in concluding that the Puerto Rico Legislature's interest in the health, safety, and welfare of its citizens constitutes a 'substantial' governmental interest."

The Court said that prohibiting casino advertising was sufficiently narrowly tailored to achieve this goal so as to meet the requirements of the First Amendment. The Court said that the law was not unconstitutional because it targeted advertising for casino gambling, but left advertising for other forms of gambling unregulated. The Court said that the "legislature felt that for Puerto

Ricans the risks associated with casino gambling were significantly greater than those associated with the more traditional kinds of gambling in Puerto Rico."

The Court also noted that the government could have banned all casino gambling. It concluded that it therefore could take the lesser step of only prohibiting advertisements. The Court said, "Here, on the other hand, the Puerto Rico legislature surely could have prohibited casino gambling by the residents of Puerto Rico altogether. In our view, the greater power to completely ban casino gambling necessarily includes the lesser power to ban advertising of casino gambling."

The Court followed the *Posadas* case in United States v. Edge Broadcasting Co., 509 U.S. 418 (1993), where it upheld a federal law that prohibited lottery advertising by radio stations located in states that did not operate lotteries. A radio station in North Carolina wished to broadcast advertisements for the Virginia lottery. Evidence demonstrated that over 92 percent of the broadcast station's audience resided in Virginia, where lotteries were legal. However, the federal law prohibited the radio station from broadcasting such advertisements because the station was located in North Carolina, which did not have a lottery. Again, the Court upheld the law based on the government's substantial interest in discouraging gambling by limiting advertisements for it. The Court also stressed that the federal law served to effectuate the desires of each state by permitting advertising where states choose to have lotteries and prohibiting it where they do not.

But in its most recent commercial speech case, Greater New Orleans Broadcasting Association, Inc. v. United States, 527 U.S. 173 (1999), the Supreme Court invalidated a federal law that prohibited advertising by casinos. The Court invoked the *Central Hudson* test and held that the many exceptions permitted in the federal law—such as allowing advertising on Native American reservations and by state-run lotteries—meant that the law could not be deemed narrowly tailored to achieving its goal of discouraging gambling.

e. Advertising by Lawyers and Other Professionals

One of the most frequent topics of commercial speech before the Supreme Court has been state attempts to restrict advertising by lawyers and other professionals. The ability of states to regulate solicitation by attorneys and accountants is discussed above. Additionally, states have attempted to prohibit attorneys and other professionals from advertising and to restrict the content of the ads that are produced. The Supreme Court repeatedly has made it clear that such advertisements are protected by the First Amendment as long as they are truthful and not deceptive.

The Court initially ruled that states cannot prohibit lawyers from advertising in Bates v. State Bar of Arizona, 433 U.S. 350 (1977). A lawyer had been disciplined by the bar for an advertisement that stated prices for routine legal services such as uncontested divorces, name changes, and simple nonbusiness bankruptcies. The state presented a number of justifications for prohibiting and punishing the advertisement. It argued, for example, that such advertisements cause a negative public impression of attorneys; that they foment litigation; and that they are inherently deceptive because inevitably legal services involve complications that cannot be foreseen. The Court rejected all of these justifications for prohibiting lawyer advertisements. The Court explained that it was far too tenuous and speculative to believe that lawyer advertising would have any of these ill effects.

As in *Virginia Board of Pharmacy*, the Court stressed the value to consumers of receiving truthful information about prices and availability of services. Justice Blackmun, writing for the Court, said that the state's justifications were impermissibly "based on the benefits of public ignorance." Justice Blackmun explained that the First Amendment precludes the state from acting on the premise that "the public is best kept in ignorance than trusted with correct but incomplete information."

Repeatedly since *Bates* the Supreme Court has reiterated that truthful, nondeceptive advertisements by professionals are protected by the First Amendment. Many of these cases involved other efforts by states to restrict lawyer advertisements. For example, in In re R.M.J., 455 U.S. 191 (1982), a lawyer was disciplined for not following state rules regulating lawyer advertising. The attorney, for instance, listed his specialty as "real estate" and not "property" as prescribed in the rule. He also sent announcement cards to persons other than "lawyers, clients, former clients, personal friends and relatives." The Court held that the lawyer's speech and activities were protected by the First Amendment because the expression was true and not deceptive. The Court emphasized that the state could achieve all of its goals through means less restrictive of speech. In a unanimous decision, the Court said that "although the States may regulate commercial speech, the First and Fourteenth Amendments require that they do so with care and in a manner no more extensive than reasonably necessary to further substantial state interests."

In Zauderer v. Office of Disciplinary Counsel of the Supreme Court of Ohio, 471 U.S. 626 (1985), the Supreme Court again held that truthful advertisements are protected by the First Amendment, but the government can punish deception including that which occurs through omission. An attorney published advertisements offering to represent women who were injured by the Dalkon Shield intrauterine device (a contraceptive device). The lawyer was punished for three reasons. First, he was disciplined for violating a rule that prohibited advertisements containing advice or information about a specific legal problem. Second, he was punished because his advertisement included an illustration, a drawing of a Dalkon Shield. Third, he was disciplined for deception; the advertisement stated that he would provide representation on a contingency fee basis and that the client would not have to pay any fee if the case was not won. The ad did not disclose that the clients were liable for litigation costs.

The Supreme Court rejected the first two grounds for discipline, but accepted the third. The Court said that a state could not prohibit advertisements that targeted a particular audience or a group of clients with a specific legal problem. The Court emphasized the difference from in-person solicitations, in that "[p]rint advertising . . . lack[s] the coercive force of the personal presence of a trained advocate." Moreover, the Court said that illustrations were allowed in ads unless there was proof in a specific case that they were deceptive or misleading.

But the Court said that the omission of a statement about the client's liability for litigation costs could be the basis for discipline because its absence was deceptive. The Court rejected any claim that the lawyer had a First Amendment right to not include the information. The Court said, "Because the extension of First Amendment protection to commercial speech is justified principally by the value to consumers of the information such speech provides, appellant's constitutionally protected interest in *not* providing any particular factual information in his advertising is minimal."

In Peel v. Attorney Registration and Disciplinary Commission of Illinois, 496 U.S. 91 (1990), the Court invalidated a state law that limited the ability of attorneys to advertise specialties. A lawyer had been disciplined for advertising himself as a trial specialist, as this was prohibited by a state bar rule. The plurality opinion by Justice Stevens emphasized that the statement on the attorney's letterhead about the receipt of a certificate of specialty was accurate and truthful. The plurality said that the state failed to meet its "heavy burden of justifying a categorical prohibition against the dissemination of accurate factual information to the public."

The Court followed the same reasoning in Ibanez v. Florida Department of Business and Professional Regulation, 512 U.S. 136 (1994). An attorney was disciplined for an advertisement listing that she also is a certified public accountant and a certified financial planner. The Court held that the information was accurate and thus could not be the basis for discipline.

Thus, the case law in this area is clear: Truthful, nondeceptive advertisements by lawyers are protected by the First Amendment. The Court refuses to allow the government to regulate attorney advertisements to improve the public's image of the bar, or out of fear that advertisements will foment litigation, or out of unsupported fear that the public will not understand their content and will thereby be deceived.

F. REPUTATION, PRIVACY, PUBLICITY, AND THE FIRST AMENDMENT: TORTS AND THE FIRST AMENDMENT

Many tort claims seek to impose liability for speech. For example, the tort of defamation—libel and slander—is liability for speech injurious to reputation. Similarly, the "false light" tort is liability for speech that creates a false impression about a person and his or her activities. Speech can be the basis for a claim for the intentional infliction of emotional distress. Also, speech that discloses private information or exploits the commercial likeness of another may be the basis for a tort for invasion of privacy or for violating the right of publicity. This section considers in turn each of these torts and the First Amendment limits upon them.

In New York Times v. Sullivan, below, the Supreme Court expressly held that the First Amendment limits the ability of the government to impose tort liability. Although tort litigation is generally between two private parties, there is state action in that it is the state's law, whether statutory or common law, that allows recovery. Besides, it is a branch of the government, the judiciary, that is imposing liability for the speech. The Court in New York Times v. Sullivan declared that "[w]hat a State may not constitutionally bring about by means of a criminal statute is likewise beyond the reach of its civil law. . . . The fear of damage awards . . . may be markedly more inhibiting than the fear of prosecution under a criminal statute."

1. Defamation

In New York Times v. Sullivan, the Court held that recovery for defamation—libel and slander—is limited by the First Amendment. The challenge for the Court in this area is to balance the need to protect reputation, the obvious central concern of defamation law, with the desire to safeguard expression, which can be chilled and limited by tort liability.

Since *New York Times*, the Supreme Court has attempted to strike this balance by developing a complex series of rules that depend on the identity of the plaintiff and the nature of the subject matter. As described below, there are four major categories of situations: where the plaintiff is a public official or running for public office; where the plaintiff is a public figure; where the plaintiff is a private figure and the matter is of public concern; and where the plaintiff is a private figure and the matter is not of public concern.

a. Public Officials as Defamation Plaintiffs

If the plaintiff is a public official or running for public office, the plaintiff can recover for defamation only by proving with clear and convincing evidence the falsity of the statements and actual malice. Actual malice means that the defendant knew that the statement was false or acted with reckless disregard of the truth. New York Times Co. v. Sullivan is the seminal case in this area.

NEW YORK TIMES CO. v. SULLIVAN
376 U.S. 254 (1964)

Justice BRENNAN delivered the opinion of the Court.

We are required in this case to determine for the first time the extent to which the constitutional protections for speech and press limit a State's power to award damages in a libel action brought by a public official against critics of his official conduct.

Respondent L. B. Sullivan is one of the three elected Commissioners of the City of Montgomery, Alabama. He testified that he was "Commissioner of Public Affairs and the duties are supervision of the Police Department, Fire Department, Department of Cemetery and Department of Scales." He brought this civil libel action against the four individual petitioners, who are Negroes and Alabama clergymen, and against petitioner the New York Times Company, a New York corporation which publishes the New York Times, a daily newspaper. A jury in the Circuit Court of Montgomery County awarded him damages of $500,000, the full amount claimed, against all the petitioners, and the Supreme Court of Alabama affirmed.

Respondent's complaint alleged that he had been libeled by statements in a full-page advertisement that was carried in the New York Times on March 29, 1960. Entitled "Heed Their Rising Voices," the advertisement began by stating that "As the whole world knows by now, thousands of Southern Negro students are engaged in widespread non-violent demonstrations in positive affirmation of the right to live in human dignity as guaranteed by the U.S. Constitution and

F. Reputation, Privacy, Publicity, and the First Amendment

the Bill of Rights." It went on to charge that "in their efforts to uphold these guarantees, they are being met by an unprecedented wave of terror by those who would deny and negate that document which the whole world looks upon as setting the pattern for modern freedom." Succeeding paragraphs purported to illustrate the "wave of terror" by describing certain alleged events. The text concluded with an appeal for funds.

Of the 10 paragraphs of text in the advertisement, the third and a portion of the sixth were the basis of respondent's claim of libel. They read as follows: Third paragraph: "In Montgomery, Alabama, after students sang 'My Country, 'Tis of Thee' on the State Capitol steps, their leaders were expelled from school, and truckloads of police armed with shotguns and tear-gas ringed the Alabama State College Campus. When the entire student body protested to state authorities by refusing to re-register, their dining hall was padlocked in an attempt to starve them into submission." Sixth paragraph: "Again and again the Southern violators have answered Dr. King's peaceful protests with intimidation and violence. They have bombed his home almost killing his wife and child. They have assaulted his person. They have arrested him seven times—for 'speeding,' 'loitering' and similar 'offenses.'"

It is uncontroverted that some of the statements contained in the two paragraphs were not accurate descriptions of events which occurred in Montgomery. Although Negro students staged a demonstration on the State Capitol steps, they sang the National Anthem and not "My Country, 'Tis of Thee." Although nine students were expelled by the State Board of Education, this was not for leading the demonstration at the Capitol, but for demanding service at a lunch counter in the Montgomery County Courthouse on another day. Not the entire student body, but most of it, had protested the expulsion, not by refusing to register, but by boycotting classes on a single day; virtually all the students did register for the ensuing semester. The campus dining hall was not padlocked on any occasion, and the only students who may have been barred from eating there were the few who had neither signed a preregistration application nor requested temporary meal tickets. Although the police were deployed near the campus in large numbers on three occasions, they did not at any time "ring" the campus, and they were not called to the campus in connection with the demonstration on the State Capitol steps, as the third paragraph implied. Dr. King had not been arrested seven times, but only four; and although he claimed to have been assaulted some years earlier in connection with his arrest for loitering outside a courtroom, one of the officers who made the arrest denied that there was such an assault.

The trial judge submitted the case to the jury under instructions that the statements in the advertisement were "libelous per se" and were not privileged, so that petitioners might be held liable if the jury found that they had published the advertisement and that the statements were made "of and concerning" respondent. The jury was instructed that, because the statements were libelous per se, "the law . . . implies legal injury from the bare fact of publication itself," "falsity and malice are presumed," "general damages need not be alleged or proved but are presumed," and "punitive damages may be awarded by the jury even though the amount of actual damages is neither found nor shown." In affirming the judgment, the Supreme Court of Alabama sustained the trial judge's rulings and instructions in all respects.

We hold that the rule of law applied by the Alabama courts is constitutionally deficient for failure to provide the safeguards for freedom of speech and of the press that are required by the First and Fourteenth Amendments in a libel action brought by a public official against critics of his official conduct. We further hold that under the proper safeguards the evidence presented in this case is constitutionally insufficient to support the judgment for respondent.

The question before us is whether this rule of liability, as applied to an action brought by a public official against critics of his official conduct, abridges the freedom of speech and of the press that is guaranteed by the First and Fourteenth Amendments. The general proposition that freedom of expression upon public questions is secured by the First Amendment has long been settled by our decisions. The constitutional safeguard, we have said, "was fashioned to assure unfettered interchange of ideas for the bringing about of political and social changes desired by the people." Thus we consider this case against the background of a profound national commitment to the principle that debate on public issues should be uninhibited, robust, and wide-open, and that it may well include vehement, caustic, and sometimes unpleasantly sharp attacks on government and public officials. The present advertisement, as an expression of grievance and protest on one of the major public issues of our time, would seem clearly to qualify for the constitutional protection. The question is whether it forfeits that protection by the falsity of some of its factual statements and by its alleged defamation of respondent.

Authoritative interpretations of the First Amendment guarantees have consistently refused to recognize an exception for any test of truth—whether administered by judges, juries, or administrative officials—and especially one that puts the burden of proving truth on the speaker. The constitutional protection does not turn upon "the truth, popularity, or social utility of the ideas and beliefs which are offered." As Madison said, "Some degree of abuse is inseparable from the proper use of every thing; and in no instance is this more true than in that of the press." [E]rroneous statement is inevitable in free debate, and that it must be protected if the freedoms of expression are to have the "breathing space" that they "need . . . to survive." Criticism of their official conduct does not lose its constitutional protection merely because it is effective criticism and hence diminishes their official reputations.

If neither factual error nor defamatory content suffices to remove the constitutional shield from criticism of official conduct, the combination of the two elements is no less inadequate. This is the lesson to be drawn from the great controversy over the Sedition Act of 1798, which first crystallized a national awareness of the central meaning of the First Amendment. That statute made it a crime, punishable by a $5,000 fine and five years in prison, "if any person shall write, print, utter or publish . . . any false, scandalous and malicious writing or writings against the government of the United States, or either house of the Congress . . . , or the President . . . , with intent to defame . . . or to bring them, or either of them, into contempt or disrepute; or to excite against them, or either or any of them, the hatred of the good people of the United States." The Act allowed the defendant the defense of truth, and provided that the jury were to be judges both of the law and the facts. Despite these qualifications, the Act was vigorously condemned as unconstitutional in an attack joined in by Jefferson and Madison.

Although the Sedition Act was never tested in this Court, the attack upon its validity has carried the day in the court of history. Fines levied in its prosecution

F. Reputation, Privacy, Publicity, and the First Amendment

were repaid by Act of Congress on the ground that it was unconstitutional. Calhoun, reporting to the Senate on February 4, 1836, assumed that its invalidity was a matter "which no one now doubts." Jefferson, as President, pardoned those who had been convicted and sentenced under the Act and remitted their fines.

The state rule of law is not saved by its allowance of the defense of truth. A rule compelling the critic of official conduct to guarantee the truth of all his factual assertions—and to do so on pain of libel judgments virtually unlimited in amount—leads to a comparable "self-censorship." Allowance of the defense of truth, with the burden of proving it on the defendant, does not mean that only false speech will be deterred. Under such a rule, would-be critics of official conduct may be deterred from voicing their criticism, even though it is believed to be true and even though it is in fact true, because of doubt whether it can be proved in court or fear of the expense of having to do so. They tend to make only statements which "steer far wider of the unlawful zone." The rule thus dampens the vigor and limits the variety of public debate. It is inconsistent with the First and Fourteenth Amendments.

The constitutional guarantees require, we think, a federal rule that prohibits a public official from recovering damages for a defamatory falsehood relating to his official conduct unless he proves that the statement was made with "actual malice"—that is, with knowledge that it was false or with reckless disregard of whether it was false or not.

Applying these standards, we consider that the proof presented to show actual malice lacks the convincing clarity which the constitutional standard demands, and hence that it would not constitutionally sustain the judgment for respondent under the proper rule of law. The case of the individual petitioners requires little discussion. Even assuming that they could constitutionally be found to have authorized the use of their names on the advertisement, there was no evidence whatever that they were aware of any erroneous statements or were in any way reckless in that regard. The judgment against them is thus without constitutional support. As to the Times, we similarly conclude that the facts do not support a finding of actual malice.

Under *New York Times*, there are four requirements in this category: (1) The plaintiff must be a public official or running for public office; (2) the plaintiff must prove his or her case with clear and convincing evidence; (3) the plaintiff must prove falsity of the statement; and (4) the plaintiff must prove actual malice—that the defendant knew the statement was false or acted with reckless disregard of the truth. Each is discussed in turn.

First, the plaintiff must be a public official or running for public office for the case to fit within this category. Although *New York Times* involved a plaintiff who was a government official, the Court extended this to those running for public office.[54] For example, the Court has said that *New York Times* applies to "anything which might touch on an official's fitness for office."[55]

---

54. *See* Monitor Patriot Co. v. Roy, 401 U.S. 265 (1971) (defamation of a candidate for public office covered by the *New York Times* standard).
55. Garrison v. Louisiana, 379 U.S. 64, 77 (1964).

The Supreme Court never has held that all government employees are to be considered public officials under *New York Times*, but nor has the Court formulated a precise test for determining which public employees are public officials. In *New York Times*, in a footnote, the Court said that it had "no occasion here to determine how far down into the lower ranks of government employees the 'public official' designation would extend."

The primary Supreme Court decision clarifying who is a "public official" was Rosenblatt v. Baer, 383 U.S. 75 (1966). In *Rosenblatt*, the plaintiff was a fired supervisor of a county-owned ski resort. The Court said that "public officials" are "at the very least . . . those among the hierarchy of government employees who have, or appear to the public to have, substantial responsibility for or control over the conduct of governmental affairs." The Court said that public officials are those who hold positions of such "apparent importance that the public has an independent interest in the qualifications and performance of the person who holds it."

It is certainly possible to imagine government employees who do not fit this definition. Yet, for any government employee, even at the lowest rung of the hierarchy, it is possible that issues could arise concerning their performance on the job and thus be of importance to the public. Thus, no clear definition exists as to who is a public official for purposes of the *New York Times* test.[56]

Second, the plaintiff in this category must prove his or her case with clear and convincing evidence; preponderance of the evidence, the usual standard in civil cases, is not enough. In New York Times v. Sullivan, the Court said that the plaintiff had the burden of proving falsity of the statement and actual malice with "convincing clarity." The Court subsequently equated this standard with a requirement for "clear and convincing evidence."[57]

To ensure that this requirement is met, appellate courts are required to conduct an independent review to ensure that there is clear and convincing evidence that defendant uttered false statements with actual malice. In Bose Corp. v. Consumers Union of United States, Inc., 466 U.S. 485 (1984), the Court said that under the "actual malice" standard of *New York Times*, "[a]ppellate judges in such a case must exercise independent judgment and determine whether the record establishes actual malice with convincing clarity."

Third, the plaintiff must prove the falsity of the statements. At the very least, this means that the defendant in this category cannot be forced to prove truth of the statements. A difficult issue arises here in drawing a distinction between expression of opinion and false statements of fact. In Gertz v. Welch, below, the Court observed that "[u]nder the First Amendment there is no such thing as a false idea. However pernicious an opinion may seem, we depend for its correction not on the conscience of judges and juries but on the competition of other ideas. But there is no constitutional value in false statements of fact."

However, separating opinion from fact is inherently difficult. Is calling a public official "stupid" a statement of fact, because IQ can be measured, or

---

56. Generally, lower courts have found government officials of all sorts to be public officials. *See, e.g.*, Crane v. Arizona Republic, 972 F.2d 1511 (9th Cir. 1992) (prosecutor is a public official); Stevens v. Tillman, 855 F.2d 394 (7th Cir. 1988) (elementary school principal is a public official); McKinley v. Baden, 777 F.2d 1017 (5th Cir. 1985) (police officer is a public official).

57. Gertz v. Welch, 418 U.S. 323, 331-332 (1974).

F. Reputation, Privacy, Publicity, and the First Amendment

of opinion? Is calling a person a "crook" fact or opinion? The Supreme Court addressed the fact/opinion distinction in Milkovich v. Lorain Journal Co., 497 U.S. 1 (1990). Michael Milkovich was the wrestling coach at a public high school and prevailed in a lawsuit overturning sanctions that had been imposed on him and the school because of an altercation that occurred at a match. A column in a local newspaper said that the school had prevailed with "the big lie," implying that Milkovich had lied under oath.

The Court in *Milkovich* said that the language in *Gertz*, quoted above, was not "intended to create a wholesale defamation exemption for anything that might be labeled 'opinion.'" However, the Court also made it clear that only false statements of fact could be the basis for defamation liability. Chief Justice Rehnquist, writing for the Court, said "a statement on matters of public concern must be provable as false before there can be liability under state defamation law.... [A] statement of opinion relating to matters of public concern which does not contain a provably false factual connotation will receive full constitutional protection."

Therefore, the focus is not on whether a statement is opinion, but whether it contains, directly or by clear implication, factual statements. False statements of fact are a prerequisite for defamation liability. Yet, this still leaves unresolved the key question: When are statements "rhetorical hyperbole" protected by the First Amendment and when are they factual statements that can be the basis for defamation actions? All *Milkovich* holds is that labeling a statement as opinion is not sufficient, by itself, to preclude defamation liability.

Fourth and finally in this category, there must be proof of actual malice; that is, the defendant knew that the statement was false or acted with reckless disregard of the truth. The Court has explained that this requires proof that the statements were made with "the high degree of awareness of their probable falsity."[58] The Court has said that actual malice is a "term of art denoting deliberate or reckless falsification."[59]

In St. Amant v. Thompson, 390 U.S. 727 (1968), the Supreme Court said that actual malice requires that the defendant "in fact entertained serious doubts as to the truth of his publication." In *St. Amant*, a candidate for public office made highly critical statements about the conduct of the sheriff. The Supreme Court overturned defamation liability and emphasized that actual malice could not be proven by showing that the defendant failed to verify the accuracy of facts or even that the defendant acted recklessly. Actual malice requires that the defendant have a subjective awareness of probable falsity; there must be proof that the defendant had serious doubts about the accuracy of the statements before making them.

The Court has held that even the intentional fabrication of quotations is not enough, by itself, to prove actual malice if the statements were substantially accurate in reflecting what was said. Masson v. New Yorker, 501 U.S. 496 (1991), concerned a defamation suit brought by Jeffrey Masson, a psychoanalyst, against Janet Malcolm, a writer for *New Yorker* magazine. Although the case did not involve a public official, it did involve a plaintiff who was a public figure, and as described below, this meant that the *New York Times* test applied. The article was

---

58. Garrison v. Louisiana, 379 U.S. 64, 74 (1964).
59. Masson v. New Yorker Magazine, Inc., 501 U.S. 496, 499 (1991).

based on more than 40 hours of interviews and contained many quotations; none of the quotes, however, was an actual statement made during the interviews.

The Court, in an opinion by Justice Kennedy, said that quotation marks do not convey that what is within them is a word-for-word transcription of an actual statement. Rather, the Court said that a quotation implies a substantially accurate representation of a person's statement. The issue, therefore, is not whether the quotation published is a verbatim reflection of what was said, but whether it is substantially accurate. Falsely attributing a statement to a person can be the basis for defamation liability, but there has to be proof that the statements substantially changed the meaning of what was said.

Thus, actual malice is a difficult standard to meet. It is a subjective standard that requires that the plaintiff prove that defendant knew that the statement was false or acted with serious doubts about its truth.

b. Public Figures as Plaintiffs

The Supreme Court has held that the same rules apply in defamation suits brought by public figures. The Court initially applied the *New York Times* test to public figures in Curtis Publishing Co. v. Butts, 388 U.S. 130 (1967), and Associated Press v. Walker, 388 U.S. 130 (1967). Both of these cases involved plaintiffs who did not hold public office, but were very prominent in their communities. *Butts* involved game-fixing allegations directed at a football coach at a state university who actually was employed by a private corporation that administered the school's athletic programs. *Walker* involved a former army general accused of leading an angry crowd that obstructed federal marshals who were facilitating the enrollment of James Meredith, an African-American student, and the desegregation of the University of Mississippi.

There was not a majority opinion in either case. Justice Harlan, writing for the plurality, said that although the plaintiffs were not public officials, "the public interest in the circulation of the materials here involved, and the publisher's interest in circulating them, is not less than that involved in *New York Times*." While the plurality would have allowed public figures to recover with less than proof of actual malice, a majority of the Justices rejected that view. Chief Justice Warren said that "differentiation between 'public figures' and 'public officials' and adoption of separate standards of proof for each have no basis in law, logic, or First Amendment policy." Justices Brennan and White agreed that actual malice should be required when public figures are defamation plaintiffs, and Justices Black and Douglas took an absolutist position that would have barred any defamation liability. Thus, five justices said that public figures cannot recover for defamation with less than proof of actual malice.

In Rosenbloom v. Metromedia, Inc., 403 U.S. 29 (1971), a plurality of the Court went even further and held that the actual malice test should be used as long as the matter is of public concern, even if the plaintiff was neither a public official nor a public figure. Justice Brennan, writing for the plurality, said that "[i]f a matter is a subject of public or general interest, it cannot suddenly become less so merely because a private individual is involved, or because in some sense the individual did not 'voluntarily' choose to become involved."

However, a majority of the Court never accepted this view, and in fact, it was expressly rejected in Gertz v. Welch, where the Court expressly drew the distinction between public and private figures. *Gertz* remains a key case in establishing that the *New York Times* standard applies to defamation suits by public figures and also with regard to the standard for recovery by private figures.

<u>GERTZ v. WELCH</u>
418 U.S. 323 (1974)

Justice POWELL delivered the opinion of the Court.

This Court has struggled for nearly a decade to define the proper accommodation between the law of defamation and the freedoms of speech and press protected by the First Amendment. We granted certiorari to reconsider the extent of a publisher's constitutional privilege against liability for defamation of a private citizen.

I

In 1968 a Chicago policeman named Nuccio shot and killed a youth named Nelson. The state authorities prosecuted Nuccio for the homicide and ultimately obtained a conviction for murder in the second degree. The Nelson family retained petitioner Elmer Gertz, a reputable attorney, to represent them in civil litigation against Nuccio.

Respondent publishes American Opinion, a monthly outlet for the views of the John Birch Society. Early in the 1960s the magazine began to warn of a nationwide conspiracy to discredit local law enforcement agencies and create in their stead a national police force capable of supporting a Communist dictatorship. In March 1969 respondent published the resulting article under the title "FRAME-UP: Richard Nuccio and the War on Police." The article purports to demonstrate that the testimony against Nuccio at his criminal trial was false and that his prosecution was part of the Communist campaign against the police.

In his capacity as counsel for the Nelson family in the civil litigation, petitioner attended the coroner's inquest into the boy's death and initiated actions for damages, but he neither discussed Officer Nuccio with the press nor played any part in the criminal proceeding. Notwithstanding petitioner's remote connection with the prosecution of Nuccio, respondent's magazine portrayed him as an architect of the "frame-up." The article stated that petitioner had been an official of the "Marxist League for Industrial Democracy, originally known as the Intercollegiate Socialist Society, which has advocated the violent seizure of our government." It labeled Gertz a "Leninist" and a "Communist-fronter." It also stated that Gertz had been an officer of the National Lawyers Guild, described as a Communist organization that "probably did more than any other outfit to plan the Communist attack on the Chicago police during the 1968 Democratic Convention."

These statements contained serious inaccuracies. The implication that petitioner had a criminal record was false. Petitioner had been a member and officer of the National Lawyers Guild some 15 years earlier, but there was no evidence that he or that organization had taken any part in planning the 1968 demonstrations in Chicago. There was also no basis for the charge that petitioner was a "Leninist" or a "Communist-fronter." And he had never been a member of the "Marxist League for Industrial Democracy" or the "Intercollegiate Socialist Society." The managing editor of American Opinion made no effort to verify or substantiate the charges against petitioner.

II

The principal issue in this case is whether a newspaper or broadcaster that publishes defamatory falsehoods about an individual who is neither a public official nor a public figure may claim a constitutional privilege against liability for the injury inflicted by those statements.

We begin with the common ground. Under the First Amendment there is no such thing as a false idea. However pernicious an opinion may seem, we depend for its correction not on the conscience of judges and juries but on the competition of other ideas. But there is no constitutional value in false statements of fact. Neither the intentional lie nor the careless error materially advances society's interest in "uninhibited, robust, and wide-open" debate on public issues. They belong to that category of utterances which "are no essential part of any exposition of ideas, and are of such slight social value as a step to truth that any benefit that may be derived from them is clearly outweighed by the social interest in order and morality."

Although the erroneous statement of fact is not worthy of constitutional protection, it is nevertheless inevitable in free debate. And punishment of error runs the risk of inducing a cautious and restrictive exercise of the constitutionally guaranteed freedoms of speech and press. Our decisions recognize that a rule of strict liability that compels a publisher or broadcaster to guarantee the accuracy of his factual assertions may lead to intolerable self-censorship.

The need to avoid self-censorship by the news media is, however, not the only societal value at issue. If it were, this Court would have embraced long ago the view that publishers and broadcasters enjoy an unconditional and indefeasible immunity from liability for defamation. The legitimate state interest underlying the law of libel is the compensation of individuals for the harm inflicted on them by defamatory falsehood. We would not lightly require the State to abandon this purpose. [T]he individual's right to the protection of his own good name "reflects no more than our basic concept of the essential dignity and worth of every human being—a concept at the root of any decent system of ordered liberty."

Some tension necessarily exists between the need for a vigorous and uninhibited press and the legitimate interest in redressing wrongful injury. In our continuing effort to define the proper accommodation between these competing concerns, we have been especially anxious to assure to the freedoms of speech and press that "breathing space" essential to their fruitful exercise. To that end this Court has extended a measure of strategic protection to defamatory falsehood.

The *New York Times* standard defines the level of constitutional protection appropriate to the context of defamation of a public person. Those who, by reason of the notoriety of their achievements or the vigor and success with which they seek the public's attention, are properly classed as public figures

F. Reputation, Privacy, Publicity, and the First Amendment

and those who hold governmental office may recover for injury to reputation only on clear and convincing proof that the defamatory falsehood was made with knowledge of its falsity or with reckless disregard for the truth.

This standard administers an extremely powerful antidote to the inducement to media self-censorship of the common-law rule of strict liability for libel and slander. And it exacts a correspondingly high price from the victims of defamatory falsehood. Plainly many deserving plaintiffs, including some intentionally subjected to injury, will be unable to surmount the barrier of the *New York Times* test. Despite this substantial abridgment of the state law right to compensation for wrongful hurt to one's reputation, the Court has concluded that the protection of the *New York Times* privilege should be available to publishers and broadcasters of defamatory falsehood concerning public officials and public figures.

[W]e have no difficulty in distinguishing among defamation plaintiffs. The first remedy of any victim of defamation is self-help—using available opportunities to contradict the lie or correct the error and thereby to minimize its adverse impact on reputation. Public officials and public figures usually enjoy significantly greater access to the channels of effective communication and hence have a more realistic opportunity to counteract false statements than private individuals normally enjoy. Private individuals are therefore more vulnerable to injury, and the state interest in protecting them is correspondingly greater.

More important than the likelihood that private individuals will lack effective opportunities for rebuttal, there is a compelling normative consideration underlying the distinction between public and private defamation plaintiffs. An individual who decides to seek governmental office must accept certain necessary consequences of that involvement in public affairs. He runs the risk of closer public scrutiny than might otherwise be the case.

Those classed as public figures stand in a similar position. Hypothetically, it may be possible for someone to become a public figure through no purposeful action of his own, but the instances of truly involuntary public figures must be exceedingly rare. For the most part those who attain this status have assumed roles of especial prominence in the affairs of society. Some occupy positions of such persuasive power and influence that they are deemed public figures for all purposes. More commonly, those classed as public figures have thrust themselves to the forefront of particular public controversies in order to influence the resolution of the issues involved. In either event, they invite attention and comment.

Even if the foregoing generalities do not obtain in every instance, the communications media are entitled to act on the assumption that public officials and public figures have voluntarily exposed themselves to increased risk of injury from defamatory falsehood concerning them. No such assumption is justified with respect to a private individual. He has not accepted public office or assumed an "influential role in ordering society." He has relinquished no part of his interest in the protection of his own good name, and consequently he has a more compelling call on the courts for redress of injury inflicted by defamatory falsehood. Thus, private individuals are not only more vulnerable to injury than public officials and public figures; they are also more deserving of recovery.

For these reasons we conclude that the States should retain substantial latitude in their efforts to enforce a legal remedy for defamatory falsehood injurious to the reputation of a private individual. The extension of the *New York Times* test proposed by the *Rosenbloom* plurality would abridge this legitimate state interest to a degree that we find unacceptable. And it would occasion the additional difficulty of forcing state and federal judges to decide on an ad hoc basis which publications address issues of "general or public interest" and which do not. We doubt the wisdom of committing this task to the conscience of judges.

We hold that, so long as they do not impose liability without fault, the States may define for themselves the appropriate standard of liability for a publisher or broadcaster of defamatory falsehood injurious to a private individual. This approach provides a more equitable boundary between the competing concerns involved here. It recognizes the strength of the legitimate state interest in compensating private individuals for wrongful injury to reputation, yet shields the press and broadcast media from the rigors of strict liability for defamation.

Our accommodation of the competing values at stake in defamation suits by private individuals allows the States to impose liability on the publisher or broadcaster of defamatory falsehood on a less demanding showing than that required by *New York Times*. But this countervailing state interest extends no further than compensation for actual injury. For the reasons stated below, we hold that the States may not permit recovery of presumed or punitive damages, at least when liability is not based on a showing of knowledge of falsity or reckless disregard for the truth.

Respondent's characterization of petitioner as a public figure raises a different question. Petitioner has long been active in community and professional affairs. He has served as an officer of local civic groups and of various professional organizations, and he has published several books and articles on legal subjects. Although petitioner was consequently well known in some circles, he had achieved no general fame or notoriety in the community. None of the prospective jurors called at the trial had ever heard of petitioner prior to this litigation, and respondent offered no proof that this response was atypical of the local population. In this context it is plain that petitioner was not a public figure. He plainly did not thrust himself into the vortex of this public issue, nor did he engage the public's attention in an attempt to influence its outcome.

Justice BRENNAN, dissenting.

I cannot agree, however, that free and robust debate—so essential to the proper functioning of our system of government—is permitted adequate "breathing space," when, as the Court holds, the States may impose all but strict liability for defamation if the defamed party is a private person and "the substance of the defamatory statement" makes substantial danger to reputation apparent." I adhere to my view expressed in Rosenbloom v. Metromedia, Inc., that we strike the proper accommodation between avoidance of media self-censorship and protection of individual reputations only when we require States to apply the New York Times Co. v. Sullivan (1964), knowing-or-reckless-falsity standard in civil libel actions concerning media reports of the involvement of private individuals in events of public or general interest.

Justice WHITE, dissenting.

For some 200 years—from the very founding of the Nation—the law of defamation and right of the ordinary citizen to recover for false publication injurious to his reputation have been almost exclusively the business of state

F. Reputation, Privacy, Publicity, and the First Amendment

courts and legislatures. Under typical state defamation law, the defamed private citizen had to prove only a false publication that would subject him to hatred, contempt, or ridicule. Given such publication, general damage to reputation was presumed, while punitive damages required proof of additional facts. The law governing the defamation of private citizens remained untouched by the First Amendment because until relatively recently, the consistent view of the Court was that libelous words constitute a class of speech wholly unprotected by the First Amendment, subject only to limited exceptions carved out since 1964.

But now, using that Amendment as the chosen instrument, the Court, in a few printed pages, has federalized major aspects of libel law by declaring unconstitutional in important respects the prevailing defamation law in all or most of the 50 States. That result is accomplished by requiring the plaintiff in each and every defamation action to prove not only the defendant's culpability beyond his act of publishing defamatory material but also actual damage to reputation resulting from the publication. Moreover, punitive damages may not be recovered by showing malice in the traditional sense of ill will; knowing falsehood or reckless disregard of the truth will now be required.

I assume these sweeping changes will be popular with the press, but this is not the road to salvation for a court of law. As I see it, there are wholly insufficient grounds for scuttling the libel laws of the States in such wholesale fashion, to say nothing of deprecating the reputation interest of ordinary citizens and rendering them powerless to protect themselves. I do not suggest that the decision is illegitimate or beyond the bounds of judicial review, but it is an ill-considered exercise of the power entrusted to this Court, particularly when the Court has not had the benefit of briefs and argument addressed to most of the major issues which the Court now decides. I respectfully dissent.

No subsequent Supreme Court case has formulated a precise definition of who is a public figure. The later cases all indicate, however, that in order to be a public figure a person must voluntarily, affirmatively thrust himself or herself into the limelight. For example, in Time v. Firestone, 424 U.S. 448 (1976), the Court held that Mary Alice Firestone, the wife of a member of the wealthy Firestone family, was a private figure. Firestone was prominent in social circles and often in the newspapers; she even hired a clipping service to keep track of publicity about her. *Time* magazine wrongly reported that her divorce was granted on grounds of adultery and was sued for defamation. The Court held that Firestone was a private figure because she "did not assume any role of especial prominence in the affairs of society, other than perhaps Palm Beach society, and she did not thrust herself to the forefront of any particular public controversy in order to influence the resolution of the issues involved in it."

Similarly, in Wolston v. Reader's Digest Association, 443 U.S. 157 (1979), the Court found that an individual was a private figure even though he had been convicted of contempt for his refusal to appear before a grand jury investigating espionage by the Soviet Union. An article, published 16 years after the conviction, described Wolston as a Soviet agent. The Supreme Court said that Wolston was neither a general public figure nor even a limited public figure even though there had been extensive publicity about his refusal to testify before the grand jury. The Court said that the plaintiff had not "engaged the attention of the public in an attempt to influence the resolution of the issues involved." As in Time v. Firestone, the Court stressed that the plaintiff did not "voluntarily thrust" or "inject . . . himself into the forefront."

In Hutchinson v. Proxmire, 443 U.S. 111 (1979), the Court ruled that an individual who received a "Golden Fleece of the Month Award" from Senator William Proxmire was a private figure. Ronald Hutchinson received substantial federal funding for research into aggressive monkey behavior. Senator Proxmire ridiculed the grant with his "Golden Fleece Award." The Court said that Hutchinson could sue Senator Proxmire for defamation because the statement was not protected by the "Speech or Debate Clause." The Court also ruled that Hutchinson was a private figure because he "at no time assumed any role of public prominence." The Court said that "[n]either his applications for federal grants nor his publications in professional journals can be said to have invited that degree of public attention and comment on his receipt of federal grants essential to meet the public figure level."

These cases do not offer a clear definition of who is a public figure. They do indicate a restrictive view of who is a public figure, as they require that a person take voluntary, affirmative steps to thrust himself or herself into the limelight. At the very least, they make it difficult for anyone to be found an involuntary public figure.

c. Private Figures, Matters of Public Concern

In Gertz v. Welch, above, the Court articulated the standard for defamation recovery by private figures. If the plaintiff is a private figure and the matter is of public concern, a state can allow a plaintiff to recover compensatory damages if there is proof that the statements were false and of negligence by the defendant. However, proof of presumed or punitive damages requires proof of actual malice. "Private figures" are obviously plaintiffs who are not public officials or public figures. "Matter of public concern" has never been defined, but generally it refers to issues in which the public has a legitimate interest.

In Dun & Bradstreet, Inc. v. Greenmoss Builders, Inc., 472 U.S. 749 (1985), the Supreme Court said that a distinction must be drawn in suits against private figures between speech that involves matters of public concern and that which does not. *Dun & Bradstreet* involved a confidential report prepared by a credit reporting agency for subscribers that falsely said that a company had filed a petition for bankruptcy. In a plurality opinion by Justice Powell, the Court said that "not all speech is of equal First Amendment importance. It is speech on 'matters of public concern' that is 'at the heart of the First Amendment's protection.' . . . In contrast, speech on matters of purely private concern is of less First Amendment concern." The plurality thus said that the *Gertz* requirement that presumed or punitive damages require proof of actual malice only applies in suits involving private figures and matters of public concern.

Dun & Bradstreet thus brings back into defamation law the "matters of public concern" standard that *Rosenbloom* had introduced and that was seemingly rejected in *Gertz*. Defining matters of public concern is inherently difficult. If "public concern" is defined in terms of the public's actual interest, the media's judgment to publish is likely strong, if not conclusive, evidence of people's interest in the material. But if "public concern" is defined from a more objective viewpoint, then courts are in the position of deciding what people, in their enlightened best interest, should want to know about. Such judgments are obviously troubling under the First Amendment.

Thus, it is established that if the plaintiff is a private figure and the matter is of public concern, a state can allow recovery of compensatory damages if the plaintiff proves falsity of the statement and negligence by the speaker. But presumed or punitive damages require proof of actual malice. The Court has expressly ruled that the plaintiff must bear the burden of proof in this category, just as when the plaintiff is a public official or a public figure. In Philadelphia Newspapers, Inc. v. Hepps, 475 U.S. 767 (1986), the Court held that the First Amendment requires that the plaintiff prove falsity of the statement. A newspaper ran a series of articles linking the owner of a chain of stores to organized crime. The state court had ruled that the defendant had the burden of proving truth of the statements because the plaintiff was neither a public official nor a public figure. The Court said that "[t]o ensure that true speech on matters of public concern is not deterred, we hold that the common-law presumption that defamatory speech is false cannot stand when a plaintiff seeks damages against a media defendant for speech of public concern."

Philadelphia Newspapers, Inc. v. Hepps articulates a rule for when there is a media defendant. The Court has never elaborated on the distinction between media and nonmedia defendants. On the one hand, the media obviously play a crucial role in informing the public and can claim special protection as the "press" under the First Amendment. On the other hand, defining the "media" is likely to be extremely difficult; nonmedia individuals and entities also can play an important role in informing the public. As discussed below, the Court generally has been reluctant to provide any special rights for the institutional press. In Dun & Bradstreet v. Greenmoss Builders, five justices—though in separate opinions—expressly rejected any distinction between media and nonmedia defendants for purposes of defamation liability. Justice White, in an opinion concurring in the judgment, said that he agreed with the four dissenters "that the First Amendment gives no more protection to the press in defamation suits than it does to others exercising their freedom of speech."

d. Private Figures, Matters Not of Public Concern

There only has been one case, Dun & Bradstreet v. Greenmoss Builders, above, that thus far has considered the category of private figures and speech that is not of public concern. In *Dun & Bradstreet*, the Court ruled that in this category presumed and punitive damages do not require proof of actual malice.

The Supreme Court never has considered what should be the standard of liability or even who must bear the burden of proof when a private figure is the plaintiff and the matter is not of public concern. The Court only has ruled that in this category presumed or punitive damages do not require proof of actual malice.

e. Conclusion

This law of defamation has been criticized on many grounds. The categories at times seem arbitrary and ill-defined; a great deal depends on whether a plaintiff is classified as a public figure or whether a matter is deemed a matter of public concern. Some argue that the Court's approach has provided too much protection for speech and not enough for reputation.[60] Others argue that the approach does not provide enough protection for speech and that the current law chills speech and, indeed, "perpetuates a system of censorship by libel lawyers—a system in which the relevant question is not whether a story is libelous, but whether the subject is likely to sue, and if so, how much it will cost to defend."[61]

But the current approach also can be defended as drawing sensible compromises between the important values of speech and reputation. The categories obviously try to strike a balance: They give more weight to speech that is relevant to the political process and of public interest; they give more weight to reputation when a person has not voluntarily entered the public domain and when the matter is not of public concern.

2. *Intentional Infliction of Emotional Distress*

In Hustler Magazine v. Falwell, the Supreme Court held that recovery for the tort of intentional infliction of emotional distress had to meet the *New York Times* standards. In Snyder v. Phelps, the Court went further and held that there cannot be liability for intentional infliction of emotional distress for speech that is otherwise protected by the First Amendment.

HUSTLER MAGAZINE v. FALWELL
485 U.S. 46 (1988)

Chief Justice REHNQUIST delivered the opinion of the Court.

Petitioner Hustler Magazine, Inc., is a magazine of nationwide circulation. Respondent Jerry Falwell, a nationally known minister who has been active as a commentator on politics and public affairs, sued petitioner and its publisher, petitioner Larry Flynt, to recover damages for invasion of privacy, libel, and intentional infliction of emotional distress.

The inside front cover of the November 1983 issue of Hustler Magazine featured a "parody" of an advertisement for Campari Liqueur that contained the name and picture of respondent and was entitled "Jerry Falwell talks about his first time." This parody was modeled after actual Campari ads that included interviews with various celebrities about their "first times." Although it was apparent by the end of each interview that this meant the first time they sampled Campari, the ads clearly played on the sexual double entendre of the general subject of "first times." Copying the form and layout of these Campari ads, Hustler's editors chose respondent as the featured celebrity and drafted

---

60. *See* Dun & Bradstreet v. Greenmoss Builders, 472 U.S. at 771 (White, J., concurring in the judgment).

61. David Anderson, *Libel and Press Self-Censorship*, 53 Tex. L. Rev. 422, 424-425 (1975); *see also* Rodney A. Smolla, *Let the Author Beware: The Rejuvenation of the American Law of Libel*, 132 U. Pa. L. Rev. 1 (1983).

F. Reputation, Privacy, Publicity, and the First Amendment

an alleged "interview" with him in which he states that his "first time" was during a drunken incestuous rendezvous with his mother in an outhouse. The Hustler parody portrays respondent and his mother as drunk and immoral, and suggests that respondent is a hypocrite who preaches only when he is drunk. In small print at the bottom of the page, the ad contains the disclaimer, "ad parody—not to be taken seriously." The magazine's table of contents also lists the ad as "Fiction; Ad and Personality Parody."

Soon after the November issue of Hustler became available to the public, respondent brought this diversity action. Respondent stated in his complaint that publication of the ad parody in Hustler entitled him to recover damages for libel, invasion of privacy, and intentional infliction of emotional distress. The case proceeded to trial. The jury then found against respondent on the libel claim, specifically finding that the ad parody could not "reasonably be understood as describing actual facts about [respondent] or actual events in which [he] participated." The jury ruled for respondent on the intentional infliction of emotional distress claim, however, and stated that he should be awarded $100,000 in compensatory damages, as well as $50,000 each in punitive damages from petitioners.

This case presents us with a novel question involving First Amendment limitations upon a State's authority to protect its citizens from the intentional infliction of emotional distress. We must decide whether a public figure may recover damages for emotional harm caused by the publication of an ad parody offensive to him, and doubtless gross and repugnant in the eyes of most. Respondent would have us find that a State's interest in protecting public figures from emotional distress is sufficient to deny First Amendment protection to speech that is patently offensive and is intended to inflict emotional injury, even when that speech could not reasonably have been interpreted as stating actual facts about the public figure involved. This we decline to do.

One of the prerogatives of American citizenship is the right to criticize public men and measures. Such criticism, inevitably, will not always be reasoned or moderate; public figures as well as public officials will be subject to "vehement, caustic, and sometimes unpleasantly sharp attacks."

Generally speaking the law does not regard the intent to inflict emotional distress as one which should receive much solicitude, and it is quite understandable that most if not all jurisdictions have chosen to make it civilly culpable where the conduct in question is sufficiently "outrageous." But in the world of debate about public affairs, many things done with motives that are less than admirable are protected by the First Amendment.

Thus while such a bad motive may be deemed controlling for purposes of tort liability in other areas of the law, we think the First Amendment prohibits such a result in the area of public debate about public figures. Were we to hold otherwise, there can be little doubt that political cartoonists and satirists would be subjected to damages awards without any showing that their work falsely defamed its subject. Webster's defines a caricature as "the deliberately distorted picturing or imitating of a person, literary style, etc. by exaggerating features or mannerisms for satirical effect." The appeal of the political cartoon or caricature is often based on exploitation of unfortunate physical traits or politically embarrassing events—an exploitation often calculated to injure the feelings of the subject of the portrayal. The art of the cartoonist is often not reasoned or evenhanded, but slashing and one-sided. One cartoonist expressed the nature of the art in these words: "The political cartoon is a weapon of attack, of scorn and ridicule and satire; it is least effective when it tries to pat some politician on the back. It is usually as welcome as a bee sting and is always controversial in some quarters." Long, The Political Cartoon: Journalism's Strongest Weapon, The Quill 56, 57 (Nov. 1962).

Respondent contends, however, that the caricature in question here was so "outrageous" as to distinguish it from more traditional political cartoons. There is no doubt that the caricature of respondent and his mother published in Hustler is at best a distant cousin of the political cartoons described above, and a rather poor relation at that. If it were possible by laying down a principled standard to separate the one from the other, public discourse would probably suffer little or no harm. But we doubt that there is any such standard, and we are quite sure that the pejorative description "outrageous" does not supply one. "Outrageousness" in the area of political and social discourse has an inherent subjectiveness about it which would allow a jury to impose liability on the basis of the jurors' tastes or views, or perhaps on the basis of their dislike of a particular expression. An "outrageousness" standard thus runs afoul of our longstanding refusal to allow damages to be awarded because the speech in question may have an adverse emotional impact on the audience.

We conclude that public figures and public officials may not recover for the tort of intentional infliction of emotional distress by reason of publications such as the one here at issue without showing in addition that the publication contains a false statement of fact which was made with "actual malice," i.e., with knowledge that the statement was false or with reckless disregard as to whether or not it was true. This is not merely a "blind application" of the *New York Times* standard, it reflects our considered judgment that such a standard is necessary to give adequate "breathing space" to the freedoms protected by the First Amendment.

SNYDER v. PHELPS
562 U.S. 443 (2011)

Chief Justice ROBERTS delivered the opinion of the Court.

A jury held members of the Westboro Baptist Church liable for millions of dollars in damages for picketing near a soldier's funeral service. The picket signs reflected the church's view that the United States is overly tolerant of sin and that God kills American soldiers as punishment. The question presented is whether the First Amendment shields the church members from tort liability for their speech in this case.

I

Fred Phelps founded the Westboro Baptist Church in Topeka, Kansas, in 1955. The church's congregation believes that God hates and punishes the United States for its tolerance of homosexuality, particularly in America's military. The church frequently communicates its views by picketing, often at military funerals. In the more than 20 years that the members of Westboro Baptist have publicized their message, they have picketed nearly 600 funerals.

Marine Lance Corporal Matthew Snyder was killed in Iraq in the line of duty. Lance Corporal Snyder's father selected the Catholic church in the Snyders' hometown of Westminster, Maryland, as the site for his son's funeral. Local newspapers provided notice of the time and location of the service.

Phelps became aware of Matthew Snyder's funeral and decided to travel to Maryland with six other Westboro Baptist parishioners (two of his daughters and four of his grandchildren) to picket. On the day of the memorial service, the Westboro congregation members picketed on public land adjacent to public streets near the Maryland State House, the United States Naval Academy, and Matthew Snyder's funeral. The Westboro picketers carried signs that were largely the same at all three locations. They stated, for instance: "God Hates the USA/Thank God for 9/11," "America is Doomed," "Don't Pray for the USA," "Thank God for IEDs," "Thank God for Dead Soldiers," "Pope in Hell," "Priests Rape Boys," "God Hates Fags," "You're Going to Hell," and "God Hates You."

The church had notified the authorities in advance of its intent to picket at the time of the funeral, and the picketers complied with police instructions in staging their demonstration. The picketing took place within a 10-by-25-foot plot of public land adjacent to a public street, behind a temporary fence. That plot was approximately 1,000 feet from the church where the funeral was held. Several buildings separated the picket site from the church. The Westboro picketers displayed their signs for about 30 minutes before the funeral began and sang hymns and recited Bible verses. None of the picketers entered church property or went to the cemetery. They did not yell or use profanity, and there was no violence associated with the picketing.

The funeral procession passed within 200 to 300 feet of the picket site. Although Snyder testified that he could see the tops of the picket signs as he drove to the funeral, he did not see what was written on the signs until later that night, while watching a news broadcast covering the event.

Snyder filed suit against Phelps, Phelps's daughters, and the Westboro Baptist Church (collectively Westboro or the church). A jury found for Snyder on the intentional infliction of emotional distress, intrusion upon seclusion, and civil conspiracy claims, and held Westboro liable for $2.9 million in compensatory damages and $8 million in punitive damages. The District Court remitted the punitive damages award to $2.1 million, but left the jury verdict otherwise intact.

Whether the First Amendment prohibits holding Westboro liable for its speech in this case turns largely on whether that speech is of public or private concern, as determined by all the circumstances of the case. "[S]peech on 'matters of public concern' . . . is 'at the heart of the First Amendment's protection.'" The First Amendment reflects "a profound national commitment to the principle that debate on public issues should be uninhibited, robust, and wide-open." New York Times Co. v. Sullivan (1964). That is because "speech concerning public affairs is more than self-expression; it is the essence of self-government." Accordingly, "speech on public issues occupies the highest rung of the hierarchy of First Amendment values, and is entitled to special protection."

"[N]ot all speech is of equal First Amendment importance," however, and where matters of purely private significance are at issue, First Amendment protections are often less rigorous. That is because restricting speech on purely private matters does not implicate the same constitutional concerns as limiting speech on matters of public interest: "[T]here is no threat to the free and robust debate of public issues; there is no potential interference with a meaningful dialogue of ideas"; and the "threat of liability" does not pose the risk of "a reaction of self-censorship" on matters of public import.

We noted a short time ago, in considering whether public employee speech addressed a matter of public concern, that "the boundaries of the public concern test are not well defined." Although that remains true today, we have articulated some guiding principles, principles that accord broad protection to speech to ensure that courts themselves do not become inadvertent censors.

Speech deals with matters of public concern when it can "be fairly considered as relating to any matter of political, social, or other concern to the community," or when it "is a subject of legitimate news interest; that is, a subject of general interest and of value and concern to the public."

The "content" of Westboro's signs plainly relates to broad issues of interest to society at large, rather than matters of "purely private concern." The placards read "God Hates the USA/Thank God for 9/11," "America is Doomed," "Don't Pray for the USA," "Thank God for IEDs," "Fag Troops," "Semper Fi Fags," "God Hates Fags," "Maryland Taliban," "Fags Doom Nations," "Not Blessed Just Cursed," "Thank God for Dead Soldiers," "Pope in Hell," "Priests Rape Boys," "You're Going to Hell," and "God Hates You." While these messages may fall short of refined social or political commentary, the issues they highlight—the political and moral conduct of the United States and its citizens, the fate of our Nation, homosexuality in the military, and scandals involving the Catholic clergy—are matters of public import. The signs certainly convey Westboro's position on those issues, in a manner designed to reach as broad a public audience as possible.

Apart from the content of Westboro's signs, Snyder contends that the "context" of the speech—its connection with his son's funeral—makes the speech a matter of private rather than public concern. The fact that Westboro spoke in connection with a funeral, however, cannot by itself transform the nature of Westboro's speech. Westboro's signs, displayed on public land next to a public street, reflect the fact that the church finds much to condemn in modern society. Its speech is "fairly characterized as constituting speech on a matter of public concern" and the funeral setting does not alter that conclusion.

Westboro's choice to convey its views in conjunction with Matthew Snyder's funeral made the expression of those views particularly hurtful to many, especially to Matthew's father. The record makes clear that the applicable legal term—"emotional distress"—fails to capture fully the anguish Westboro's choice added to Mr. Snyder's already incalculable grief. But Westboro conducted its picketing peacefully on matters of public concern at a public place adjacent to a public street. Such space occupies a "special position in terms of First Amendment protection." "[W]e have repeatedly referred to public streets as the archetype of a traditional public forum," noting that "'[t]ime out of mind' public streets and sidewalks have been used for public assembly and debate."

That said, "[e]ven protected speech is not equally permissible in all places and at all times." Westboro's choice of where and when to conduct its picketing is not beyond the Government's regulatory reach—it is "subject to reasonable time, place, or manner restrictions" that are consistent with the standards announced in this Court's precedents. Maryland now has a law imposing restrictions on funeral picketing. To the extent these laws are content neutral, they raise very different questions from the tort verdict at issue in this case. Maryland's law, however, was not in effect at the time of the events at issue here, so we have

F. Reputation, Privacy, Publicity, and the First Amendment

no occasion to consider how it might apply to facts such as those before us, or whether it or other similar regulations are constitutional.

Simply put, the church members had the right to be where they were. Westboro alerted local authorities to its funeral protest and fully complied with police guidance on where the picketing could be staged. The picketing was conducted under police supervision some 1,000 feet from the church, out of the sight of those at the church. The protest was not unruly; there was no shouting, profanity, or violence.

The record confirms that any distress occasioned by Westboro's picketing turned on the content and viewpoint of the message conveyed, rather than any interference with the funeral itself. A group of parishioners standing at the very spot where Westboro stood, holding signs that said "God Bless America" and "God Loves You," would not have been subjected to liability. It was what Westboro said that exposed it to tort damages.

Given that Westboro's speech was at a public place on a matter of public concern, that speech is entitled to "special protection" under the First Amendment. Such speech cannot be restricted simply because it is upsetting or arouses contempt. "If there is a bedrock principle underlying the First Amendment, it is that the government may not prohibit the expression of an idea simply because society finds the idea itself offensive or disagreeable." Indeed, "the point of all speech protection . . . is to shield just those choices of content that in someone's eyes are misguided, or even hurtful."

The jury here was instructed that it could hold Westboro liable for intentional infliction of emotional distress based on a finding that Westboro's picketing was "outrageous." "Outrageousness," however, is a highly malleable standard with "an inherent subjectiveness about it which would allow a jury to impose liability on the basis of the jurors' tastes or views, or perhaps on the basis of their dislike of a particular expression." In a case such as this, a jury is "unlikely to be neutral with respect to the content of [the] speech," posing "a real danger of becoming an instrument for the suppression of . . . 'vehement, caustic, and sometimes unpleasan[t]'" expression. Such a risk is unacceptable; "in public debate [we] must tolerate insulting, and even outrageous, speech in order to provide adequate 'breathing space' to the freedoms protected by the First Amendment." What Westboro said, in the whole context of how and where it chose to say it, is entitled to "special protection" under the First Amendment, and that protection cannot be overcome by a jury finding that the picketing was outrageous.

For all these reasons, the jury verdict imposing tort liability on Westboro for intentional infliction of emotional distress must be set aside.

Our holding today is narrow. We are required in First Amendment cases to carefully review the record, and the reach of our opinion here is limited by the particular facts before us. Westboro believes that America is morally flawed; many Americans might feel the same about Westboro. Westboro's funeral picketing is certainly hurtful and its contribution to public discourse may be negligible. But Westboro addressed matters of public import on public property, in a peaceful manner, in full compliance with the guidance of local officials. The speech was indeed planned to coincide with Matthew Snyder's funeral, but did not itself disrupt that funeral, and Westboro's choice to conduct its picketing at that time and place did not alter the nature of its speech.

Speech is powerful. It can stir people to action, move them to tears of both joy and sorrow, and—as it did here—inflict great pain. On the facts before us, we cannot react to that pain by punishing the speaker. As a Nation we have chosen a different course—to protect even hurtful speech on public issues to ensure that we do not stifle public debate. That choice requires that we shield Westboro from tort liability for its picketing in this case.

Justice ALITO, dissenting.

Our profound national commitment to free and open debate is not a license for the vicious verbal assault that occurred in this case.

Petitioner Albert Snyder is not a public figure. He is simply a parent whose son, Marine Lance Corporal Matthew Snyder, was killed in Iraq. Mr. Snyder wanted what is surely the right of any parent who experiences such an incalculable loss: to bury his son in peace. But respondents, members of the Westboro Baptist Church, deprived him of that elementary right. They first issued a press release and thus turned Matthew's funeral into a tumultuous media event. They then appeared at the church, approached as closely as they could without trespassing, and launched a malevolent verbal attack on Matthew and his family at a time of acute emotional vulnerability. As a result, Albert Snyder suffered severe and lasting emotional injury. The Court now holds that the First Amendment protected respondents' right to brutalize Mr. Snyder. I cannot agree.

Respondents and other members of their church have strong opinions on certain moral, religious, and political issues, and the First Amendment ensures that they have almost limitless opportunities to express their views. They may write and distribute books, articles, and other texts; they may create and disseminate video and audio recordings; they may circulate petitions; they may speak to individuals and groups in public forums and in any private venue that wishes to accommodate them; they may picket peacefully in countless locations; they may appear on television and speak on the radio; they may post messages on the Internet and send out e-mails. And they may express their views in terms that are "uninhibited," "vehement," and "caustic."

It does not follow, however, that they may intentionally inflict severe emotional injury on private persons at a time of intense emotional sensitivity by launching vicious verbal attacks that make no contribution to public debate. To protect against such injury, "most if not all jurisdictions" permit recovery in tort for the intentional infliction of emotional distress (or IIED). This is a very narrow tort with requirements that "are rigorous, and difficult to satisfy."

This Court has recognized that words may "by their very utterance inflict injury" and that the First Amendment does not shield utterances that form "no essential part of any exposition of ideas, and are of such slight social value as a step to truth that any benefit that may be derived from them is clearly outweighed by the social interest in order and morality." When grave injury is intentionally inflicted by means of an attack like the one at issue here, the First Amendment should not interfere with recovery.

In this case, respondents brutally attacked Matthew Snyder, and this attack, which was almost certain to inflict injury, was central to respondents' well-practiced strategy for attracting public attention.

On the morning of Matthew Snyder's funeral, respondents could have chosen to stage their protest at countless locations. They could have picketed the United States Capitol, the White House, the Supreme Court, the Pentagon, or any of the more than 5,600 military recruiting stations in this country. They

F. Reputation, Privacy, Publicity, and the First Amendment

could have returned to the Maryland State House or the United States Naval Academy, where they had been the day before. They could have selected any public road where pedestrians are allowed. They could have staged their protest in a public park. They could have chosen any Catholic church where no funeral was taking place. But of course, a small group picketing at any of these locations would have probably gone unnoticed.

Respondents' outrageous conduct caused petitioner great injury, and the Court now compounds that injury by depriving petitioner of a judgment that acknowledges the wrong he suffered.

In order to have a society in which public issues can be openly and vigorously debated, it is not necessary to allow the brutalization of innocent victims like petitioner. I therefore respectfully dissent.

3. *Public Disclosure of Private Facts*

The tort of public disclosure of private facts, a tort for invasion of privacy, exists if there is publication of nonpublic information that is not "of legitimate concern to the public" and that the reasonable person would find offensive to have published.[62] Unlike defamation where the information is false and a retraction conceivably could lessen the harm to reputation, the tort of public disclosure of private facts involves the publication of true information, and the harm is done once publication occurs.

The Supreme Court has held that the First Amendment prevents liability for public disclosure of private facts if the information was lawfully obtained from public records and is truthfully reported.

COX BROADCASTING CORP. v. COHN
420 U.S. 469 (1975)

Justice WHITE delivered the opinion of the Court.

The issue before us in this case is whether, consistently with the First and Fourteenth Amendments, a State may extend a cause of action for damages for invasion of privacy caused by the publication of the name of a deceased rape victim which was publicly revealed in connection with the prosecution of the crime.

I

In August 1971, appellee's 17-year-old daughter was the victim of a rape and did not survive the incident. Six youths were soon indicted for murder and rape. Although there was substantial press coverage of the crime and of subsequent developments, the identity of the victim was not disclosed pending trial, perhaps because of Ga. Code Ann. §26-9901 which makes it a misdemeanor to publish or broadcast the name or identity of a rape victim. In April 1972, some eight

---

62. Restatement (Second) of Torts §652(D) (1977).

months later, the six defendants appeared in court. Five pleaded guilty to rape or attempted rape, the charge of murder having been dropped. The guilty pleas were accepted by the court, and the trial of the defendant pleading not guilty was set for a later date.

In the course of the proceedings that day, appellant Wasell, a reporter covering the incident for his employer, learned the name of the victim from an examination of the indictments which were made available for his inspection in the courtroom. That the name of the victim appears in the indictments and that the indictments were public records available for inspection are not disputed. Later that day, Wassell broadcast over the facilities of station WSB-TV, a television station owned by appellant Cox Broadcasting Corp., a news report concerning the court proceedings. The report named the victim of the crime and was repeated the following day. In May 1972, appellee brought an action for money damages against appellants, relying on §26-9901 and claiming that his right to privacy had been invaded by the television broadcasts giving the name of his deceased daughter.

II

Georgia stoutly defends both §26-9901 and the State's common-law privacy action challenged here. Its claims are not without force, for powerful arguments can be made, and have been made, that however it may be ultimately defined, there is a zone of privacy surrounding every individual, a zone within which the State may protect him from intrusion by the press, with all its attendant publicity. Indeed, the central thesis of the root article by Warren and Brandeis, The Right to Privacy, 4 Harv. L. Rev. 193 (1890), was that the press was overstepping its prerogatives by publishing essentially private information and that there should be a remedy for the alleged abuses.

In this sphere of collision between claims of privacy and those of the free press, the interests on both sides are plainly rooted in the traditions and significant concerns of our society. Rather than address the broader question whether truthful publications may ever be subjected to civil or criminal liability consistently with the First and Fourteenth Amendments, or to put it another way, whether the State may ever define and protect an area of privacy free from unwanted publicity in the press, it is appropriate to focus on the narrower interface between press and privacy that this case presents, namely, whether the State may impose sanctions on the accurate publication of the name of a rape victim obtained from public records—more specifically, from judicial records which are maintained in connection with a public prosecution and which themselves are open to public inspection. We are convinced that the State may not do so. In the first place, in a society in which each individual has but limited time and resources with which to observe at first hand the operations of his government, he relies necessarily upon the press to bring to him in convenient form the facts of those operations. Great responsibility is accordingly placed upon the news media to report fully and accurately the proceedings of government, and official records and documents open to the public are the basic data of governmental operations. Without the information provided by the press most of us and many of our representatives would be unable to vote intelligently or to register opinions on the administration of

F. Reputation, Privacy, Publicity, and the First Amendment

government generally. With respect to judicial proceedings in particular, the function of the press serves to guarantee the fairness of trials and to bring to bear the beneficial effects of public scrutiny upon the administration of justice.

The special protected nature of accurate reports of judicial proceedings has repeatedly been recognized. This Court, in an opinion written by Justice Douglas, has said: "A trial is a public event. What transpires in the court room is public property. There is no special perquisite of the judiciary which enables it, as distinguished from other institutions of democratic government, to suppress, edit, or censor events which transpire in proceedings before it."

By placing the information in the public domain on official court records, the State must be presumed to have concluded that the public interest was thereby being served. Public records by their very nature are of interest to those concerned with the administration of government, and a public benefit is performed by the reporting of the true contents of the records by the media. The freedom of the press to publish that information appears to us to be of critical importance to our type of government in which the citizenry is the final judge of the proper conduct of public business. In preserving that form of government the First and Fourteenth Amendments command nothing less than that the States may not impose sanctions on the publication of truthful information contained in official court records open to public inspection.

We are reluctant to embark on a course that would make public records generally available to the media but forbid their publication if offensive to the sensibilities of the supposed reasonable man. Such a rule would make it very difficult for the media to inform citizens about the public business and yet stay within the law. The rule would invite timidity and self-censorship and very likely lead to the suppression of many items that would otherwise be published and that should be made available to the public. At the very least, the First and Fourteenth Amendments will not allow exposing the press to liability for truthfully publishing information released to the public in official court records. Once true information is disclosed in public court documents open to public inspection, the press cannot be sanctioned for publishing it. In this instance as in others reliance must rest upon the judgment of those who decide what to publish or broadcast.

In Florida Star v. B.J.F., 491 U.S. 524 (1989), the Court applied *Cox Broadcasting* and Smith v. Daily Mail Publ'g Co., 443 U.S. 97 (1979), to hold that there cannot be liability for invasion of privacy when there is the truthful reporting of information lawfully obtained from public records, at least unless there is a state interest of the highest order justifying liability. A newspaper reporter obtained a rape victim's name from publicly released police records. The name was published in the newspaper, even though Florida law prohibited the publication of the name of a victim of a sexual offense. A jury awarded the victim $75,000 in compensatory damages and $25,000 in punitive damages.

The Supreme Court overturned this liability. The Court began by refusing to hold that "truthful publication may never be punished consistent with the First Amendment." But the Court said that liability for the truthful reporting of information lawfully obtained from public records and concerning a matter of public significance would be allowed only if there was an interest of the highest order. The Court explained that the rape victim's name was lawfully obtained from police records and was truthfully communicated. The Court rejected the claim that protecting the privacy of rape victims was a sufficient interest to justify liability. The Court emphasized the failings of the Florida law that created liability for publishing a rape victim's identity, including that it allowed liability where the information was released by the government, that it permitted liability without any scienter requirement, and that it applied only to actions of the mass media.

The Court stressed that its "holding . . . is limited." The Court said, "We do not hold that truthful publication is automatically constitutionally protected, or that there is no zone of personal privacy within which the State may protect the individual from intrusion by the press, or even that a State may never punish publication of the name of a victim of a sexual offense. We hold only that where a newspaper publishes truthful information which it has lawfully obtained, punishment may lawfully be imposed, if at all, only when narrowly tailored to a state interest of the highest order."

The principle protecting publication of material gained from public records has been followed in other cases as well. In Landmark Communications, Inc. v. Virginia, 435 U.S. 829 (1978), the Supreme Court held unconstitutional a state statute that created criminal liability for divulging or publishing truthful information regarding confidential proceedings of a judicial inquiry board. A newspaper was convicted for violating this statute for accurately reporting that the Virginia Judicial Inquiry and Review Commission was initiating an investigation of a state court judge. The Court said that "the publication Virginia seeks to punish under its statute lies near the core of the First Amendment, and the Commonwealth's interests advanced by the imposition of criminal sanctions are insufficient to justify the actual and potential encroachments on freedom of speech and of the press which follow therefrom." The Court said that the "Commonwealth has offered little more than assertion and conjecture to support its claim that without criminal sanctions the objectives of the statutory scheme would be seriously undermined."

INFORMATION FROM NONGOVERNMENT SOURCES

All of these cases involve the truthful publication of information gained from the government. In Bartnicki v. Vopper, 532 U.S. 514 (2001), the Court considered privacy claims when the information was illegally obtained from nongovernment sources.

Gloria Bartnicki worked for the Pennsylvania Educators' Association and helped local teachers' unions as they negotiated new contracts with school boards. She was in Wyoming, Pennsylvania, and while on her cellular telephone had a conversation with the president of the local teachers' union. They clearly thought that they were having a private conversation, but unknown to them, it was illegally intercepted and recorded. A tape of the phone conversation was given to the president of a local taxpayers' union that was opposing a pay raise for the teachers. The tape was given to a local radio talk show host, Fred Vopper, who played it twice on his program. Bartnicki sued the radio station and Vopper on various state and federal claims.

F. Reputation, Privacy, Publicity, and the First Amendment

The Supreme Court, in a six-to-three decision, with Justice Stevens writing the majority, concluded that allowing liability in these circumstances would violate the First Amendment. Justice Stevens repeatedly emphasized the narrowness of the Court's holding. He said that the press was protected here because it did not participate in the illegal interception and recording and because the tape concerned a matter of public importance. Justice Stevens concluded, "In this case, privacy concerns give way when balanced against the interest in publishing matters of public importance. . . . One of the costs associated with participation in public affairs is an attendant loss of privacy. We think it clear that a stranger's illegal conduct does not suffice to remove the First Amendment shield from speech about a matter of public concern."

Justice Breyer wrote a concurring opinion, joined by Justice O'Connor, to stress the narrowness of the Court's holding. He said, "I join the Court's opinion because I agree with its 'narrow' holding, limited to the special circumstances present here: (1) the radio broadcasters acted lawfully (up to the time of final public disclosure); and (2) the information publicized involved a matter of unusual public concern, namely a threat of potential physical harm to others." The latter refers to a statement made during the conversation by the president of the local teachers' union that if the school board did not agree to their demands, they would have to go "blow away the porch" of the school board president's house. Although this clearly seems to be hyperbole in a private conversation, it was given great weight by Justice Breyer.

Chief Justice Rehnquist wrote a dissenting opinion, joined by Justices Scalia and Thomas, in which he stressed the chilling effect that the ruling would have on speech. He said that people would be less likely to use cell phones for communication once they learned that illegally intercepted calls could be broadcast as long as the media did not participate in the interception or recording.

Although both the majority and concurring opinions repeatedly emphasize the narrowness of the decision, it seems broader in its significance than they acknowledge. This is the first time that the Court has considered a privacy claim when the information comes from nongovernment sources. Also, it is the first time that the Court has dealt with information that was illegally obtained. Nonetheless, the Court found that freedom of speech and press outweigh the privacy interests involved.

4. *Right of Publicity*

The right of publicity protects the ability of a person to control the commercial value of his or her name, likeness, or performance. In Zacchini v. Scripps-Howard Broadcasting Co., 433 U.S. 562 (1977), the Court held that a state may allow liability for invasion of this right when a television station broadcast a tape of an entire performance without the performer's authorization. A television station broadcast a 15-second tape of a circus act featuring a "human cannonball" shot from a cannon into a net. The Supreme Court held that the broadcast station could be held liable because it broadcast the entire performance without authorization. The Court noted, however, that the plaintiff would have to prove damages and noted that it was quite possible that "respondent's news broadcast increased the value of petitioner's performance by stimulating the public's interest in seeing the act live." The *Zacchini* Court emphasized that "the State's interest is closely analogous to the goals of patent and copyright law, focusing on the right of the individual to reap the reward of his endeavors."

G. CONDUCT THAT COMMUNICATES

1. What Is Speech?

People often communicate through symbols other than words. Marches, picketing, armbands, and peace signs are just a few examples of obviously expressive conduct. To deny First Amendment protection for such forms of communication would mean a loss of some of the most effective means of communicating messages. Also, words are obviously symbols and there is no reason why the First Amendment should be limited to protecting just these symbols to the exclusion of all others.

Thus, the Supreme Court long has protected conduct that communicates under the First Amendment. For example, in Stromberg v. California, 283 U.S. 359 (1931), the Court declared unconstitutional a state law that prohibited the display of a "red flag." In West Virginia State Board of Education v. Barnette, above in Chapter 2, the Supreme Court invalidated a law that required that students salute the flag. The Court found that the state statute impermissibly compelled expression and emphasized that saluting, or not saluting, a flag is a form of speech. The Court explained that "[s]ymbolism is a primitive but effective way of communicating ideas. The use of an emblem or flag to symbolize some system, idea, institution, or personality, is a shortcut from mind to mind."

Conduct of all sorts can convey a message. Yet, if taken to the extreme, it would mean that virtually every criminal law would have to meet strict scrutiny because any criminal defendant could argue that his or her conduct was meant to communicate a message. Two interrelated questions thus emerge: When should conduct be analyzed under the First Amendment? And what should be the test for analyzing whether conduct that communicates is protected by the First Amendment?

2. When Is Conduct Communicative?

The Supreme Court observed that "[i]t is possible to find some kernel of expression in almost every activity a person undertakes—for example, walking down the street or meeting one's friends at a shopping mall—but such a kernel is not sufficient to bring the activity within the protection of the First Amendment."[63] In Spence v. Washington, 418 U.S. 405 (1974), the Court considered the issue of when conduct should be regarded as communicative.

---

63. City of Dallas v. Stanglin, 490 U.S. 19, 25 (1989).

G. Conduct That Communicates

An individual who taped a peace sign on an American flag after the killing of students at Kent State was convicted of violating a state law prohibiting flag desecration. The Supreme Court, in a *per curiam* opinion, reversed the conviction and found that the act was speech protected by the First Amendment. The Court said that "this was not an act of mindless nihilism. Rather, it was a pointed expression of anguish by appellant about the then-current domestic and foreign affairs of his government." The Court emphasized two factors in concluding that the conduct was communicative: "An intent to convey a particularized message was present, and in the surrounding circumstances the likelihood was great that the message would be understood by those who viewed it."

In other words, under this approach, conduct is analyzed as speech under the First Amendment if, first, there is the intent to convey a specific message, and second, there is a substantial likelihood that the message would be understood by those receiving it. Problems in applying this test are inevitable. How is it to be decided whether a person intended an act to communicate a message? Is it subjective, in which case a person always can claim such an intent in a hope to avoid punishment, or is it objective from the perspective of the reasonable listener, in which case it collapses the first part of the test into the second? How is it to be decided whether the message is sufficiently understood by the audience? Moreover, why should protection of speech depend on the sophistication and perceptiveness of the audience? For example, there may be great works of art whose message people fail to comprehend.

There are many examples of conduct that the Supreme Court has properly recognized as communicative.[64] For example, in Tinker v. Des Moines Independent Community School District, 393 U.S. 503 (1969), presented below in Chapter 4, the Court held that wearing a black armband to protest the Vietnam War was speech protected by the First Amendment. The Court explained that "the wearing of an armband for the purpose of expressing certain views is the type of symbolic act that is within the First Amendment. . . . It [is] closely akin to 'pure speech.'" In terms of the *Spence* test, there is little doubt that the armband was worn to communicate a message and that those seeing it, in the context of the times, would understand it as a symbol of protest against the Vietnam War.

3. When May the Government Regulate Conduct That Communicates?

a. The *O'Brien* Test

Finding that conduct communicates does not mean that it is immune from government regulation. The question then arises as to whether the government has sufficient justification for regulating the conduct. In United States v. O'Brien, the Court formulated a test for evaluating the constitutional protection for conduct that communicates.

---

64. *See also* Schacht v. United States, 398 U.S. 58 (1970), declaring unconstitutional a federal law that allowed wearing a military uniform only "if the portrayal does not tend to discredit" the armed forces. This law obviously was content-based: The symbol of the uniform could be used to express a pro-military view, but not an antimilitary sentiment.

UNITED STATES v. O'BRIEN
391 U.S. 367 (1968)

Chief Justice WARREN delivered the opinion of the Court.

On the morning of March 31, 1966, David Paul O'Brien and three companions burned their Selective Service registration certificates on the steps of the South Boston Courthouse. A sizable crowd, including several agents of the Federal Bureau of Investigation, witnessed the event. For this act, O'Brien was indicted, tried, convicted, and sentenced in the United States District Court for the District of Massachusetts.

The indictment upon which he was tried charged that he "willfully and knowingly did mutilate, destroy, and change by burning . . . [his] Registration Certificate (Selective Service System Form No. 2); in violation of Title 50, App., United States Code, Section 462(b)." Section 462(b) is part of the Universal Military Training and Service Act of 1948. Section 462(b)(3) was amended by Congress in 1965, so that at the time O'Brien burned his certificate an offense was committed by any person, "who forges, alters, knowingly destroys, knowingly mutilates, or in any manner changes any such certificate. . . ." We hold that the 1965 Amendment is constitutional both as enacted and as applied.

I

When a male reaches the age of 18, he is required by the Universal Military Training and Service Act to register with a local draft board. He is assigned a Selective Service number, and within five days he is issued a registration certificate (SSS Form No. 2). Subsequently, and based on a questionnaire completed by the registrant, he is assigned a classification denoting his eligibility for induction, and "[a]s soon as practicable" thereafter he is issued a Notice of Classification (SSS Form No. 110).

Both the registration and classification certificates are small white cards, approximately 2 by 3 inches. The registration certificate specifies the name of the registrant, the date of registration, and the number and address of the local board with which he is registered. Also inscribed upon it are the date and place of the registrant's birth, his residence at registration, his physical description, his signature, and his Selective Service number.

The classification certificate shows the registrant's name, Selective Service number, signature, and eligibility classification. It specifies whether he was so classified by his local board, an appeal board, or the President. It contains the address of his local board and the date the certificate was mailed.

Both the registration and classification certificates bear notices that the registrant must notify his local board in writing of every change in address, physical condition, and occupational, marital, family, dependency, and military status, and of any other fact which might change his classification. Both also contain a notice that the registrant's Selective Service number should appear on all communications to his local board.

By the 1965 Amendment, Congress added to §12(b)(3) of the 1948 Act the provision here at issue, subjecting to criminal liability not only one who "forges, alters, or in any manner changes" but also one who "knowingly destroys

G. Conduct That Communicates

[or] knowingly mutilates" a certificate. We note at the outset that the 1965 Amendment plainly does not abridge free speech on its face, and we do not understand O'Brien to argue otherwise. Amended §12(b)(3) on its face deals with conduct having no connection with speech. It prohibits the knowing destruction of certificates issued by the Selective Service System, and there is nothing necessarily expressive about such conduct.

O'Brien nonetheless argues that the 1965 Amendment is unconstitutional in its application to him, and is unconstitutional as enacted because what he calls the "purpose" of Congress was "to suppress freedom of speech." We consider these arguments separately.

II

O'Brien first argues that the 1965 Amendment is unconstitutional as applied to him because his act of burning his registration certificate was protected "symbolic speech" within the First Amendment. His argument is that the freedom of expression which the First Amendment guarantees includes all modes of "communication of ideas by conduct," and that his conduct is within this definition because he did it in "demonstration against the war and against the draft."

We cannot accept the view that an apparently limitless variety of conduct can be labeled "speech" whenever the person engaging in the conduct intends thereby to express an idea. However, even on the assumption that the alleged communicative element in O'Brien's conduct is sufficient to bring into play the First Amendment, it does not necessarily follow that the destruction of a registration certificate is constitutionally protected activity. This Court has held that when "speech" and "nonspeech" elements are combined in the same course of conduct, a sufficiently important governmental interest in regulating the nonspeech element can justify incidental limitations on First Amendment freedoms.

[W]e think it clear that a government regulation is sufficiently justified if it is within the constitutional power of the Government; if it furthers an important or substantial governmental interest; if the governmental interest is unrelated to the suppression of free expression; and if the incidental restriction on alleged First Amendment freedoms is no greater than is essential to the furtherance of that interest. We find that the 1965 Amendment to the Universal Military Training and Service Act meets all of these requirements, and consequently that O'Brien can be constitutionally convicted for violating it.

The power of Congress to classify and conscript manpower for military service is "beyond question." The issuance of certificates indicating the registration and eligibility classification of individuals is a legitimate and substantial administrative aid in the functioning of this system. And legislation to insure the continuing availability of issued certificates serves a legitimate and substantial purpose in the system's administration.

Many of these purposes would be defeated by the certificates' destruction or mutilation. Among these are:

1. The registration certificate serves as proof that the individual described thereon has registered for the draft. The classification certificate shows the

eligibility classification of a named but undescribed individual. Voluntarily displaying the two certificates is an easy and painless way for a young man to dispel a question as to whether he might be delinquent in his Selective Service obligations. Further, since both certificates are in the nature of "receipts" attesting that the registrant has done what the law requires, it is in the interest of the just and efficient administration of the system that they be continually available, in the event, for example, of a mix-up in the registrant's file. Additionally, in a time of national crisis, reasonable availability to each registrant of the two small cards assures a rapid and uncomplicated means for determining his fitness for immediate induction, no matter how distant in our mobile society he may be from his local board.

2. The information supplied on the certificates facilitates communication between registrants and local boards, simplifying the system and benefiting all concerned. To begin with, each certificate bears the address of the registrant's local board, an item unlikely to be committed to memory. Further, each card bears the registrant's Selective Service number, and a registrant who has his number readily available so that he can communicate it to his local board when he supplies or requests information can make simpler the board's task in locating his file. Finally, a registrant's inquiry, particularly through a local board other than his own, concerning his eligibility status is frequently answerable simply on the basis of his classification certificate; whereas, if the certificate were not reasonably available and the registrant were uncertain of his classification, the task of answering his questions would be considerably complicated.

3. Both certificates carry continual reminders that the registrant must notify his local board of any change of address, and other specified changes in his status. The smooth functioning of the system requires that local boards be continually aware of the status and whereabouts of registrants, and the destruction of certificates deprives the system of a potentially useful notice device.

4. The regulatory scheme involving Selective Service certificates includes clearly valid prohibitions against the alteration, forgery, or similar deceptive misuse of certificates. The destruction or mutilation of certificates obviously increases the difficulty of detecting and tracing abuses such as these. Further, a mutilated certificate might itself be used for deceptive purposes.

The many functions performed by Selective Service certificates establish beyond doubt that Congress has a legitimate and substantial interest in preventing their wanton and unrestrained destruction and assuring their continuing availability by punishing people who knowingly and wilfully destroy or mutilate them.

In conclusion, we find that because of the Government's substantial interest in assuring the continuing availability of issued Selective Service certificates, because amended §462(b) is an appropriately narrow means of protecting this interest and condemns only the independent noncommunicative impact of conduct within its reach, and because the noncommunicative impact of O'Brien's act of burning his registration certificate frustrated the Government's interest, a sufficient governmental interest has been shown to justify O'Brien's conviction.

G. Conduct That Communicates

III

O'Brien finally argues that the 1965 Amendment is unconstitutional as enacted because what he calls the "purpose" of Congress was "to suppress freedom of speech." We reject this argument because under settled principles the purpose of Congress, as O'Brien uses that term, is not a basis for declaring this legislation unconstitutional.

It is a familiar principle of constitutional law that this Court will not strike down an otherwise constitutional statute on the basis of an alleged illicit legislative motive. Inquiries into congressional motives or purposes are a hazardous matter. When the issue is simply the interpretation of legislation, the Court will look to statements by legislators for guidance as to the purpose of the legislature, because the benefit to sound decision-making in this circumstance is thought sufficient to risk the possibility of misreading Congress' purpose. It is entirely a different matter when we are asked to void a statute that is, under well-settled criteria, constitutional on its face, on the basis of what fewer than a handful of Congressmen said about it. What motivates one legislator to make a speech about a statute is not necessarily what motivates scores of others to enact it, and the stakes are sufficiently high for us to eschew guesswork. We decline to void essentially on the ground that it is unwise legislation which Congress had the undoubted power to enact and which could be reenacted in its exact form if the same or another legislator made a "wiser" speech about it.

b. Flag Desecration

A major area where the Supreme Court has applied the *O'Brien* test is with regard to flag burning and flag desecration laws. After initial cases that protected flag desecration on narrow grounds, but without resolving the issue, the Court in 1989 and again in 1990 made it clear that flag burning is a constitutionally protected form of speech.

In Street v. New York, 394 U.S. 576 (1969), the Court overturned a conviction of an individual who burned a flag in anger after learning that James Meredith had been shot. The individual exclaimed, "We don't need no damn flag. [If] they let that happen to Meredith we don't need an American flag." The Court said that the law was unconstitutional because it allowed the individual to be punished solely for speaking contemptuously about the flag; indeed, it was impossible to tell in *Street* whether the punishment was for the speech about the flag or for its destruction.

In Smith v. Goguen, 415 U.S. 566 (1974), the Court declared unconstitutional on vagueness grounds a state law that made it a crime when any individual "publicly mutilates, tramples upon, defaces or treats contemptuously the flag of the United States." An individual was convicted for sewing to the seat of his pants a small cloth replica of the flag. The Court found that the state law was void on vagueness grounds because of the inherent ambiguity in deciding what is "contemptuous" treatment of the flag.

In Spence v. Washington, described above, the Court found that the First Amendment protected the right of an individual to tape a peace symbol to a flag. The Court emphasized that the protestor's "message was direct, likely to be understood, and within the contours of the First Amendment."

The Court went even further in 1989 in Texas v. Johnson.

TEXAS v. JOHNSON
491 U.S. 397 (1989)

Justice BRENNAN delivered the opinion of the Court.

After publicly burning an American flag as a means of political protest, Gregory Lee Johnson was convicted of desecrating a flag in violation of Texas law. This case presents the question whether his conviction is consistent with the First Amendment. We hold that it is not.

I

While the Republican National Convention was taking place in Dallas in 1984, respondent Johnson participated in a political demonstration dubbed the "Republican War Chest Tour." As explained in literature distributed by the demonstrators and in speeches made by them, the purpose of this event was to protest the policies of the Reagan administration and of certain Dallas-based corporations. The demonstrators marched through the Dallas streets, chanting political slogans and stopping at several corporate locations to stage "die-ins" intended to dramatize the consequences of nuclear war. On several occasions they spray-painted the walls of buildings and overturned potted plants, but Johnson himself took no part in such activities. He did, however, accept an American flag handed to him by a fellow protestor who had taken it from a flagpole outside one of the targeted buildings.

The demonstration ended in front of Dallas City Hall, where Johnson unfurled the American flag, doused it with kerosene, and set it on fire. While the flag burned, the protestors chanted: "America, the red, white, and blue, we spit on you." After the demonstrators dispersed, a witness to the flag burning collected the flag's remains and buried them in his backyard. No one was physically injured or threatened with injury, though several witnesses testified that they had been seriously offended by the flag burning.

Of the approximately 100 demonstrators, Johnson alone was charged with a crime. The only criminal offense with which he was charged was the desecration of a venerated object in violation of Tex. Penal Code Ann. §42.09(a)(3). After a trial, he was convicted, sentenced to one year in prison, and fined $2,000.

II

Johnson was convicted of flag desecration for burning the flag rather than for uttering insulting words. This fact somewhat complicates our consideration of his conviction under the First Amendment. We must first determine whether Johnson's burning of the flag constituted expressive conduct, permitting him to invoke the First Amendment in challenging his conviction. See, e.g., Spence v. Washington (1974). If his conduct was expressive, we next decide whether the State's regulation is related to the suppression of free expression. See, e.g., United States v. O'Brien (1968). If the State's regulation is not related to expression, then the less stringent standard we announced in United States v. O'Brien for regulations of noncommunicative conduct controls. If it is, then we are outside of *O'Brien*'s test, and we must ask whether this interest justifies Johnson's conviction under a more demanding standard.

In order to decide whether *O'Brien*'s test applies here, therefore, we must decide whether Texas has asserted an interest in support of Johnson's conviction that is unrelated to the suppression of expression. The State offers two separate interests to justify this conviction: preventing breaches of the peace and preserving the flag as a symbol of nationhood and national unity. We hold that the first interest is not implicated on this record and that the second is related to the suppression of expression.

A

Texas claims that its interest in preventing breaches of the peace justifies Johnson's conviction for flag desecration. However, no disturbance of the peace actually occurred or threatened to occur because of Johnson's burning of the flag. Although the State stresses the disruptive behavior of the protestors during their march toward City Hall, it admits that "no actual breach of the peace occurred at the time of the flagburning or in response to the flagburning." The State's emphasis on the protestors' disorderly actions prior to arriving at City Hall is not only somewhat surprising given that no charges were brought on the basis of this conduct, but it also fails to show that a disturbance of the peace was a likely reaction to Johnson's conduct.

B

The State also asserts an interest in preserving the flag as a symbol of nationhood and national unity. We are persuaded that this interest is related to expression in the case of Johnson's burning of the flag. The State, apparently, is concerned that such conduct will lead people to believe either that the flag does not stand for nationhood and national unity, but instead reflects other, less positive concepts, or that the concepts reflected in the flag do not in fact exist, that is, that we do not enjoy unity as a Nation. These concerns blossom only when a person's treatment of the flag communicates some message, and thus are related "to the suppression of free expression" within the meaning of *O'Brien*. We are thus outside of *O'Brien*'s test altogether.

IV

It remains to consider whether the State's interest in preserving the flag as a symbol of nationhood and national unity justifies Johnson's conviction. Johnson was not, we add, prosecuted for the expression of just any idea; he was prosecuted for his expression of dissatisfaction with the policies of this country, expression situated at the core of our First Amendment values. If he had burned the flag as a means of disposing of it because it was dirty or torn, he would not have been convicted of flag desecration under this Texas law. The Texas law is thus not aimed at protecting the physical integrity of the flag in all circumstances, but is designed instead to protect it only against impairments that would cause serious offense to others. Whether Johnson's treatment of the flag violated Texas law thus depended on the likely communicative impact of his expressive conduct. Johnson's political expression was restricted because of the content of the message he conveyed. We must therefore subject the State's asserted interest in preserving the special symbolic character of the flag to "the most exacting scrutiny."

Texas argues that its interest in preserving the flag as a symbol of nationhood and national unity survives this close analysis. If there is a bedrock principle underlying the First Amendment, it is that the government may not prohibit the expression of an idea simply because society finds the idea itself offensive or disagreeable. We have not recognized an exception to this principle even where our flag has been involved. In short, nothing in our precedents suggests that a State may foster its own view of the flag by prohibiting expressive conduct relating to it.

Texas' focus on the precise nature of Johnson's expression, moreover, misses the point of our prior decisions: their enduring lesson, that the government may not prohibit expression simply because it disagrees with its message, is not dependent on the particular mode in which one chooses to express an idea. If we were to hold that a State may forbid flag burning wherever it is likely to endanger the flag's symbolic role, but allow it wherever burning a flag promotes that role—as where, for example, a person ceremoniously burns a dirty flag—we would be saying that when it comes to impairing the flag's physical integrity, the flag itself may be used as a symbol—as a substitute for the written or spoken word or a "short cut from mind to mind"—only in one direction. We would be permitting a State to "prescribe what shall be orthodox" by saying that one may burn the flag to convey one's attitude toward it and its referents only if one does not endanger the flag's representation of nationhood and national unity. We never before have held that the Government may ensure that a symbol be used to express only one view of that symbol or its referents.

To conclude that the government may permit designated symbols to be used to communicate only a limited set of messages would be to enter territory having no discernible or defensible boundaries. Could the government, on this theory, prohibit the burning of state flags? Of copies of the Presidential seal? Of the Constitution? In evaluating these choices under the First Amendment, how would we decide which symbols were sufficiently special to warrant this unique status? To do so, we would be forced to consult our own political preferences, and impose them on the citizenry, in the very way that the First Amendment forbids us to do.

We are fortified in today's conclusion by our conviction that forbidding criminal punishment for conduct such as Johnson's will not endanger the special role played by our flag or the feelings it inspires. To paraphrase Justice Holmes, we submit that nobody can suppose that this one gesture of an unknown man will change our Nation's attitude towards its flag. We are tempted to say, in fact, that the flag's deservedly cherished place in our community will be strengthened, not weakened, by our holding today. Our decision is a reaffirmation of the principles of freedom and inclusiveness that the flag best reflects, and of the conviction that our toleration of criticism such as Johnson's is a sign and source of our strength.

The way to preserve the flag's special role is not to punish those who feel differently about these matters. It is to persuade them that they are wrong. We can imagine no more appropriate response to burning a flag than waving one's own, no better way to counter a flag burner's message than by saluting the flag that burns, no surer means of preserving the dignity even of the flag that burned than by—as one witness here did—according its remains a respectful burial. We do not consecrate the flag by punishing its desecration, for in doing so we dilute the freedom that this cherished emblem represents.

Chief Justice REHNQUIST, with whom Justice WHITE and Justice O'CONNOR join, dissenting.

For more than 200 years, the American flag has occupied a unique position as the symbol of our Nation, a uniqueness that justifies a governmental prohibition against flag burning in the way respondent Johnson did here. The flag symbolizes the Nation in peace as well as in war. It signifies our national presence on battleships, airplanes, military installations, and public buildings from the United States Capitol to the thousands of county courthouses and city halls throughout the country. Two flags are prominently placed in our courtroom.

No other American symbol has been as universally honored as the flag. In 1931, Congress declared "The Star-Spangled Banner" to be our national anthem. In 1949, Congress declared June 14th to be Flag Day. In 1987, John Philip Sousa's "The Stars and Stripes Forever" was designated as the national march. Congress has also established "The Pledge of Allegiance to the Flag" and the manner of its deliverance.

The American flag, then, throughout more than 200 years of our history, has come to be the visible symbol embodying our Nation. It does not represent the views of any particular political party, and it does not represent any particular political philosophy. The flag is not simply another "idea" or "point of view" competing for recognition in the marketplace of ideas. Millions and millions of Americans regard it with an almost mystical reverence regardless of what sort of social, political, or philosophical beliefs they may have. I cannot agree that the First Amendment invalidates the Act of Congress, and the laws of 48 of the 50 States, which make criminal the public burning of the flag.

Here it may be said that the public burning of the American flag by Johnson was no essential part of any exposition of ideas, and at the same time it had a tendency to incite a breach of the peace. Johnson was free to make any verbal denunciation of the flag that he wished; indeed, he was free to burn the flag in private. He could publicly burn other symbols of the Government or effigies of political leaders. The result of the Texas statute is obviously to deny one in Johnson's frame of mind one of many means of "symbolic speech." Far from being a case of "one picture being worth a thousand words," flag burning is the equivalent of an inarticulate grunt or roar that, it seems fair to say, is most likely to be indulged in not to express any particular idea, but to antagonize others.

The Texas statute deprived Johnson of only one rather inarticulate symbolic form of protest—a form of protest that was profoundly offensive to many—and left him with a full panoply of other symbols and every conceivable form of verbal expression to express his deep disapproval of national policy. Thus, in no way can it be said that Texas is punishing him because his hearers—or any other group of people—were profoundly opposed to the message that he sought to convey. Such opposition is no proper basis for restricting speech or expression under the First Amendment. It was Johnson's use of this particular symbol, and not the idea that he sought to convey by it or by his many other expressions, for which he was punished.

Justice STEVENS, dissenting.

As the Court analyzes this case, it presents the question whether the State of Texas, or indeed the Federal Government, has the power to prohibit the public desecration of the American flag. The question is unique. In my judgment rules that apply to a host of other symbols, such as state flags, armbands, or various privately promoted emblems of political or commercial identity, are not necessarily controlling. Even if flag burning could be considered just another species of symbolic speech under the logical application of the rules that the Court has developed in its interpretation of the First Amendment in other contexts, this case has an intangible dimension that makes those rules inapplicable.

A country's flag is a symbol of more than "nationhood and national unity." It also signifies the ideas that characterize the society that has chosen that emblem as well as the special history that has animated the growth and power of those ideas. The message conveyed by some flags—the swastika, for example—may survive long after it has outlived its usefulness as a symbol of regimented unity in a particular nation.

So it is with the American flag. It is more than a proud symbol of the courage, the determination, and the gifts of nature that transformed 13 fledgling Colonies into a world power. It is a symbol of freedom, of equal opportunity, of religious tolerance, and of good will for other peoples who share our aspirations. The symbol carries its message to dissidents both at home and abroad who may have no interest at all in our national unity or survival.

The value of the flag as a symbol cannot be measured. Even so, I have no doubt that the interest in preserving that value for the future is both significant and legitimate. Conceivably that value will be enhanced by the Court's conclusion that our national commitment to free expression is so strong that even the United States as ultimate guarantor of that freedom is without power to prohibit the desecration of its unique symbol. But I am unpersuaded. The creation of a federal right to post bulletin boards and graffiti on the Washington Monument might enlarge the market for free expression, but at a cost I would not pay. Similarly, in my considered judgment, sanctioning the public desecration of the flag will tarnish its value—both for those who cherish the ideas for which it waves and for those who desire to don the robes of martyrdom by burning it. That tarnish is not justified by the trivial burden on free expression occasioned by requiring that an available, alternative mode of expression—including uttering words critical of the flag—be employed.

The ideas of liberty and equality have been an irresistible force in motivating leaders like Patrick Henry, Susan B. Anthony, and Abraham Lincoln, schoolteachers like Nathan Hale and Booker T. Washington, the Philippine Scouts who fought at Bataan, and the soldiers who scaled the bluff at Omaha Beach. If those ideas are worth fighting for—and our history demonstrates that they are—it cannot be true that the flag that uniquely symbolizes their power is not itself worthy of protection from unnecessary desecration. I respectfully dissent.

Texas v. Johnson produced an enormous amount of controversy and proposals to amend the Constitution to prohibit flag burning. In an effort to avoid such an amendment, Congress adopted the Flag Protection Act of 1989 that made it a crime for any person to knowingly mutilate, deface, defile, burn, or trample upon the flag. Unlike the Texas law, the reach of the Flag Protection Act was not limited to situations where the conduct would offend another. In United States v. Eichman, 496 U.S. 310 (1990), the Supreme Court declared this law unconstitutional. The Court's split was identical to that in Texas v. Johnson: Brennan, Marshall, Blackmun, Scalia, and Kennedy were in the majority; Rehnquist, White, Stevens, and O'Connor dissented. Justice Brennan again wrote the opinion for the Court and said that the statute had the "same fundamental flaw" as the Texas law that had been invalidated a year earlier. The law's primary purpose was to keep the flag from being used to communicate protest or dissent. The Court said that this was a purpose directly focused on the message and that strict scrutiny was therefore the appropriate test.

c. Spending Money as Political Speech

One of the most important areas in which the Court has considered conduct that communicates is in evaluating government laws regulating the spending of money in political campaigns. The seminal case addressing this issue was Buckley v. Valeo.

<u>BUCKLEY v. VALEO</u>
424 U.S. 1 (1976)

PER CURIAM.

These appeals present constitutional challenges to the key provisions of the Federal Election Campaign Act of 1971 (Act), as amended in 1974. The statutes at issue summarized in broad terms, contain the following provisions: (a) individual political contributions are limited to $1,000 to any single candidate per election, with an overall annual limitation of $25,000 by any contributor; independent expenditures by individuals and groups "relative to a clearly identified candidate" are limited to $1,000 a year; campaign spending by candidates for various federal offices and spending for national conventions by political parties are subject to prescribed limits; (b) contributions and expenditures above certain threshold levels must be reported and publicly disclosed; (c) a system for public funding of Presidential campaign activities is established by Subtitle H of the Internal Revenue Code; and (d) a Federal Election Commission is established to administer and enforce the legislation.

I. CONTRIBUTION AND EXPENDITURE LIMITATIONS

The intricate statutory scheme adopted by Congress to regulate federal election campaigns includes restrictions on political contributions and expenditures that apply broadly to all phases of and all participants in the election process. The major contribution and expenditure limitations in the Act prohibit individuals from contributing more than $25,000 in a single year or more than $1,000 to any single candidate for an election campaign and from spending more than $1,000 a year "relative to a clearly identified candidate." Other provisions restrict a candidate's use of personal and family resources in his campaign and limit the overall amount that can be spent by a candidate in campaigning for federal office.

A. GENERAL PRINCIPLES

The Act's contribution and expenditure limitations operate in an area of the most fundamental First Amendment activities. Discussion of public issues and debate on the qualifications of candidates are integral to the operation of the system of government established by our Constitution. The First Amendment affords the broadest protection to such political expression in order "to assure [the] unfettered interchange of ideas for the bringing about of political and social changes desired by the people." The First Amendment protects political association as well as political expression.

It is with these principles in mind that we consider the primary contentions of the parties with respect to the Act's limitations upon the giving and spending of money in political campaigns. Those conflicting contentions could not more sharply define the basic issues before us. Appellees contend that what the Act regulates is conduct, and that its effect on speech and association is incidental at most. Appellants respond that contributions and expenditures are at the very core of political speech, and that the Act's limitations thus constitute restraints on First Amendment liberty that are both gross and direct.

In upholding the constitutional validity of the Act's contribution and expenditure provisions on the ground that those provisions should be viewed as regulating conduct, not speech, the Court of Appeals relied upon United States v. O'Brien (1968). We cannot share the view that the present Act's contribution and expenditure limitations are comparable to the restrictions on conduct upheld in *O'Brien*. The expenditure of money simply cannot be equated with such conduct as destruction of a draft card. Some forms of communication made possible by the giving and spending of money involve speech alone, some involve conduct primarily, and some involve a combination of the two. Yet this Court has never suggested that the dependence of a communication on the expenditure of money operates itself to introduce a nonspeech element or to reduce the exacting scrutiny required by the First Amendment.

Even if the categorization of the expenditure of money as conduct were accepted, the limitations challenged here would not meet the *O'Brien* test because the governmental interests advanced in support of the Act involve "suppressing communication." The interests served by the Act include restricting the voices of people and interest groups who have money to spend and reducing the overall scope of federal election campaigns. Although the Act does not focus on the ideas expressed by persons or groups subject to its regulations, it is aimed in part at equalizing the relative ability of all voters to affect electoral outcomes by placing a ceiling on expenditures for political expression by citizens and groups. Unlike *O'Brien*, where the Selective Service System's administrative interest in the preservation of draft cards was wholly unrelated to their use as a means of communication, it is beyond dispute that the interest in regulating the alleged "conduct" of giving or spending money "arises in some measure

G. Conduct That Communicates

because the communication allegedly integral to the conduct is itself thought to be harmful."

A restriction on the amount of money a person or group can spend on political communication during a campaign necessarily reduces the quantity of expression by restricting the number of issues discussed, the depth of their exploration, and the size of the audience reached. This is because virtually every means of communicating ideas in today's mass society requires the expenditure of money. The distribution of the humblest handbill or leaflet entails printing, paper, and circulation costs. Speeches and rallies generally necessitate hiring a hall and publicizing the event. The electorate's increasing dependence on television, radio, and other mass media for news and information has made these expensive modes of communication indispensable instruments of effective political speech.

The expenditure limitations contained in the Act represent substantial rather than merely theoretical restraints on the quantity and diversity of political speech. The $1,000 ceiling on spending "relative to a clearly identified candidate," would appear to exclude all citizens and groups except candidates, political parties, and the institutional press from any significant use of the most effective modes of communication. Although the Act's limitations on expenditures by campaign organizations and political parties provide substantially greater room for discussion and debate, they would have required restrictions in the scope of a number of past congressional and Presidential campaigns and would operate to constrain campaigning by candidates who raise sums in excess of the spending ceiling.

By contrast with a limitation upon expenditures for political expression, a limitation upon the amount that any one person or group may contribute to a candidate or political committee entails only a marginal restriction upon the contributor's ability to engage in free communication. A contribution serves as a general expression of support for the candidate and his views, but does not communicate the underlying basis for the support. The quantity of communication by the contributor does not increase perceptibly with the size of his contribution, since the expression rests solely on the undifferentiated, symbolic act of contributing. At most, the size of the contribution provides a very rough index of the intensity of the contributor's support for the candidate. A limitation on the amount of money a person may give to a candidate or campaign organization thus involves little direct restraint on his political communication, for it permits the symbolic expression of support evidenced by a contribution but does not in any way infringe the contributor's freedom to discuss candidates and issues. While contributions may result in political expression if spent by a candidate or an association to present views to the voters, the transformation of contributions into political debate involves speech by someone other than the contributor.

Given the important role of contributions in financing political campaigns, contribution restrictions could have a severe impact on political dialogue if the limitations prevented candidates and political committees from amassing the resources necessary for effective advocacy. There is no indication, however, that the contribution limitations imposed by the Act would have any dramatic adverse effect on the funding of campaigns and political associations. The overall effect of the Act's contribution ceilings is merely to require candidates and political committees to raise funds from a greater number of persons and to compel people who would otherwise contribute amounts greater than the statutory limits to expend such funds on direct political expression, rather than to reduce the total amount of money potentially available to promote political expression.

In sum, although the Act's contribution and expenditure limitations both implicate fundamental First Amendment interests, its expenditure ceilings impose significantly more severe restrictions on protected freedoms of political expression and association than do its limitations on financial contributions.

B. CONTRIBUTION LIMITATIONS

Section 608(b) provides, with certain limited exceptions, that "no person shall make contributions to any candidate with respect to any election for Federal office which, in the aggregate, exceed $1,000." According to the parties and amici, the primary interest served by the limitations and, indeed, by the Act as a whole, is the prevention of corruption and the appearance of corruption spawned by the real or imagined coercive influence of large financial contributions on candidates' positions and on their actions if elected to office. Two "ancillary" interests underlying the Act are also allegedly furthered by the $1,000 limits on contributions. First, the limits serve to mute the voices of affluent persons and groups in the election process and thereby to equalize the relative ability of all citizens to affect the outcome of elections. Second, it is argued, the ceilings may to some extent act as a brake on the skyrocketing cost of political campaigns and thereby serve to open the political system more widely to candidates without access to sources of large amounts of money.

It is unnecessary to look beyond the Act's primary purpose to limit the actuality and appearance of corruption resulting from large individual financial contributions in order to find a constitutionally sufficient justification for the $1,000 contribution limitation. To the extent that large contributions are given to secure a political quid pro quo from current and potential office holders, the integrity of our system of representative democracy is undermined. Although the scope of such pernicious practices can never be reliably ascertained, the deeply disturbing examples surfacing after the 1972 election demonstrate that the problem is not an illusory one. Of almost equal concern as the danger of actual quid pro quo arrangements is the impact of the appearance of corruption stemming from public awareness of the opportunities for abuse inherent in a regime of large individual financial contributions.

The Act's $1,000 contribution limitation focuses precisely on the problem of large campaign contributions[—]the narrow aspect of political association where the actuality and potential for corruption have been identified while leaving persons free to engage in independent political expression, to associate actively through volunteering their services, and to assist to a limited but nonetheless substantial extent in supporting candidates and committees with financial resources. Significantly, the Act's contribution limitations in themselves do not undermine to any material degree the potential for robust and effective discussion of candidates and campaign issues by individual citizens, associations, the institutional press, candidates, and political parties.

We find that, under the rigorous standard of review established by our prior decisions, the weighty interests served by restricting the size of financial contributions to political candidates are sufficient to justify the limited effect upon First Amendment freedoms caused by the $1,000 contribution ceiling.

C. EXPENDITURE LIMITATIONS

The Act's expenditure ceilings impose direct and substantial restraints on the quantity of political speech. The most drastic of the limitations restricts individuals and groups, including political parties that fail to place a candidate on the ballot, to an expenditure of $1,000 "relative to a clearly identified candidate during a calendar year." Other expenditure ceilings limit spending by candidates, their campaigns, and political parties in connection with election campaigns. It is clear that a primary effect of these expenditure limitations is to restrict the quantity of campaign speech by individuals, groups, and candidates. The restrictions, while neutral as to the ideas expressed, limit political expression "at the core of our electoral process and of the First Amendment freedoms."

1. The $1,000 Limitation on Expenditures "Relative to a Clearly Identified Candidate"

Section 608(e)(1) provides that "[n]o person may make any expenditure . . . relative to a clearly identified candidate during a calendar year which, when added to all other expenditures made by such person during the year advocating the election or defeat of such candidate, exceeds $1,000." The plain effect is to prohibit all individuals, who are neither candidates nor owners of institutional press facilities, and all groups, except political parties and campaign organizations, from voicing their views "relative to a clearly identified candidate" through means that entail aggregate expenditures of more than $1,000 during a calendar year. The provision, for example, would make it a federal criminal offense for a person or association to place a single one-quarter page advertisement "relative to a clearly identified candidate" in a major metropolitan newspaper.

We find that the governmental interest in preventing corruption and the appearance of corruption is inadequate to justify §608(e)(1)'s ceiling on independent expenditures. First, assuming, arguendo, that large independent expenditures pose the same dangers of actual or apparent quid pro quo arrangements as do large contributions, §608(e)(1) does not provide an answer that sufficiently relates to the elimination of those dangers. Unlike the contribution limitations' total ban on the giving of large amounts of money to candidates, §608(e)(1) prevents only some large expenditures. So long as persons and groups eschew expenditures that in express terms advocate the election or defeat of a clearly identified candidate, they are free to spend as much as they want to promote the candidate and his views. The exacting interpretation of the statutory language necessary to avoid unconstitutional vagueness thus undermines the limitation's effectiveness as a loophole-closing provision by facilitating circumvention by those seeking to exert improper influence upon a candidate or office-holder. It would naively underestimate the ingenuity and resourcefulness of persons and groups desiring to buy influence to believe that they would have much difficulty devising expenditures that skirted the restriction on express advocacy of election or defeat but nevertheless benefited the candidate's campaign. Yet no substantial societal interest would be served by a loophole-closing provision designed to check corruption that permitted unscrupulous persons and organizations to expend unlimited sums of money in order to obtain improper influence over candidates for elective office.

Second, quite apart from the shortcomings of §608(e)(1) in preventing any abuses generated by large independent expenditures, the independent advocacy restricted by the provision does not presently appear to pose dangers of real or apparent corruption comparable to those identified with large campaign contributions. The parties defending §608(e)(1) contend that it is necessary to prevent would-be contributors from avoiding the contribution limitations by the simple expedient of paying directly for media advertisements or for other portions of the candidate's campaign activities. They argue that expenditures controlled by or coordinated with the candidate and his campaign might well have virtually the same value to the candidate as a contribution and would pose similar dangers of abuse. Yet such controlled or coordinated expenditures are treated as contributions rather than expenditures under the Act. Section 608(b)'s contribution ceilings rather than §608(e)(1)'s independent expenditure limitation prevent attempts to circumvent the Act through prearranged or coordinated expenditures amounting to disguised contributions. By contrast, §608(e)(1) limits expenditures for express advocacy of candidates made totally independently of the candidate and his campaign. Unlike contributions, such independent expenditures may well provide little assistance to the candidate's campaign and indeed may prove counterproductive. The absence of prearrangement and coordination of an expenditure with the candidate or his agent not only undermines the value of the expenditure to the candidate, but also alleviates the danger that expenditures will be given as a quid pro quo for improper commitments from the candidate. Rather than preventing circumvention of the contribution limitations, §608(e)(1) severely restricts all independent advocacy despite its substantially diminished potential for abuse.

While the independent expenditure ceiling thus fails to serve any substantial governmental interest in stemming the reality or appearance of corruption in the electoral process, it heavily burdens core First Amendment expression. For the First Amendment right to "speak one's mind . . . on all public institutions" includes the right to engage in "'vigorous advocacy' no less than 'abstract discussion.'" Advocacy of the election or defeat of candidates for federal office is no less entitled to protection under the First Amendment than the discussion of political policy generally or advocacy of the passage or defeat of legislation.

It is argued, however, that the ancillary governmental interest in equalizing the relative ability of individuals and groups to influence the outcome of elections serves to justify the limitation on express advocacy of the election or defeat of candidates imposed by §608(e)(1)'s expenditure ceiling. But the concept that government may restrict the speech of some elements of our society in order to enhance the relative voice of others is wholly foreign to the First Amendment, which was designed "to secure 'the widest possible dissemination of information from diverse and antagonistic sources,'" and "to assure unfettered interchange of ideas for the bringing about of political and social changes desired by the people."

2. Limitation on Expenditures by Candidates from Personal or Family Resources

The Act also sets limits on expenditures by a candidate "from his personal funds, or the personal funds of his immediate family, in connection with his campaigns during any calendar year." §608(a)(1). These ceilings vary from $50,000 for Presidential or Vice Presidential candidates to $35,000 for senatorial candidates, and $25,000 for most candidates for the House of Representatives.

The ceiling on personal expenditures by candidates on their own behalf, like the limitations on independent expenditures contained in §608(e)(1), imposes a substantial restraint on the ability of persons to engage in protected First Amendment expression. The candidate, no less than any other person, has a First Amendment right to engage in the discussion of public issues and vigorously and tirelessly to advocate his own election and the election of other candidates. Indeed, it is of particular importance that candidates have the unfettered opportunity to make their views known so that the electorate may intelligently evaluate the candidates' personal qualities and their positions on vital public issues before choosing among them on election day. Section 608(a)'s ceiling on personal expenditures by a candidate in furtherance of his own candidacy thus clearly and directly interferes with constitutionally protected freedoms.

The primary governmental interest served by the Act the prevention of actual and apparent corruption of the political process does not support the limitation on the candidate's expenditure of his own personal funds. Indeed, the use of personal funds reduces the candidate's dependence on outside contributions and thereby counteracts the coercive pressures and attendant risks of abuse to which the Act's contribution limitations are directed.

The ancillary interest in equalizing the relative financial resources of candidates competing for elective office, therefore, provides the sole relevant rationale for §608(a)'s expenditure ceiling. That interest is clearly not sufficient to justify the provision's infringement of fundamental First Amendment rights.

[T]he First Amendment simply cannot tolerate §608(a)'s restriction upon the freedom of a candidate to speak without legislative limit on behalf of his own candidacy. We therefore hold that §608(a)'s restriction on a candidate's personal expenditures is unconstitutional.

3. Limitations on Campaign Expenditures

Section 608(c) places limitations on overall campaign expenditures by candidates seeking nomination for election and election to federal office. Presidential candidates may spend $10,000,000 in seeking nomination for office and an additional $20,000,000 in the general election campaign. The ceiling on senatorial campaigns is pegged to the size of the voting-age population of the State with minimum dollar amounts applicable to campaigns in States with small populations. The Act imposes blanket $70,000 limitations on both primary campaigns and general election campaigns for the House of Representatives with the exception that the senatorial ceiling applies to campaigns in States entitled to only one Representative.

No governmental interest that has been suggested is sufficient to justify the restriction on the quantity of political expression imposed by §608(c)'s campaign expenditure limitations. The major evil associated with rapidly increasing campaign expenditures is the danger of candidate dependence on large contributions. The interest in alleviating the corrupting influence of large contributions is served by the Act's contribution limitations and disclosure provisions rather than by §608(c)'s campaign expenditure ceilings.

The campaign expenditure ceilings appear to be designed primarily to serve the governmental interests in reducing the allegedly skyrocketing costs of political campaigns. [T]he mere growth in the cost of federal election campaigns in and of itself provides no basis for governmental restrictions on the quantity of campaign spending and the resulting limitation on the scope of federal campaigns. The First Amendment denies government the power to determine that spending to promote one's political views is wasteful, excessive, or unwise.

In the free society ordained by our Constitution it is not the government, but the people individually as citizens and candidates and collectively as associations and political committees who must retain control over the quantity and range of debate on public issues in a political campaign.

In sum, the provisions of the Act that impose a $1,000 limitation on contributions to a single candidate, a $5,000 limitation on contributions by a political committee to a single candidate, and a $25,000 limitation on total contributions by an individual during any calendar year, are constitutionally valid. These limitations, along with the disclosure provisions, constitute the Act's primary weapons against the reality or appearance of improper influence stemming from the dependence of candidates on large campaign contributions. The contribution ceilings thus serve the basic governmental interest in safeguarding the integrity of the electoral process without directly impinging upon the rights of individual citizens and candidates to engage in political debate and discussion. By contrast, the First Amendment requires the invalidation of the Act's independent expenditure ceiling, its limitation on a candidate's expenditures from his own personal funds, and its ceilings on overall campaign expenditures. These provisions place substantial and direct restrictions on the ability of candidates, citizens, and associations to engage in protected political expression, restrictions that the First Amendment cannot tolerate.

Buckley also upheld the disclosure requirements imposed by the law because they provide important information to the electorate about candidates, they "deter actual corruption and avoid the appearance of corruption," and they provide crucial information for enforcing the contribution limits in the law. The Court noted, however, that there may be instances involving minor or dissident parties "where the threat to the exercise of First Amendment rights is so serious and the state interest furthered by disclosure so insubstantial that the Act's requirements cannot be constitutionally applied." The Court said that there was no proof of such an impact in the case before it.

Finally, the Court upheld the provision of the law that provided for public funding of presidential elections. The Court said that such government financing does not restrict speech, but rather increases expression in connection with election campaigns. The Court said that the provision is a "congressional effort, not to abridge, restrict, or censor speech, but rather to use public money to facilitate and enlarge public discussion and participation in the electoral process, goals vital to a self-governing people." The Court said that expenditure limits were permissible as a condition for receipt of such federal money because "acceptance of federal funding entails voluntary acceptance of an expenditure ceiling."

CRITICISMS OF BUCKLEY

Buckley v. Valeo had an enormous practical impact on the nature of political campaigns. The Court's invalidation of expenditure limits led to the proliferation of political action committees and the continued skyrocketing of the costs of election campaigns. There is widespread criticism that this leads to enormous inequalities in political influence and directly affects who can run for office and who can get elected.

Buckley has been criticized on many levels. First, the Court's treatment of spending money as speech, rather than as conduct that communicates, has been questioned.[65] Spending money may facilitate speech and it is a way of expressing support for a candidate, but it is arguably distinguishable from "pure" speech. The argument is that the less protective *O'Brien* test should have been applied instead of the strict scrutiny test used by the Court.

Second, the Court's distinction between expenditure and contribution limits has been questioned.[66] Elected officials can be influenced by who spends money on their behalf, just as they can be influenced by who directly contributes money to them. The perception of corruption may be generated by large expenditures for a candidate, just as it can be caused by large contributions.

Third, many have criticized the Court for giving inadequate weight to the value of equality of influence in political campaigns.[67] Allowing unlimited expenditures allows the wealthy to drown out the voices of those with less money. It thus permits those with money to have much more influence in election campaigns and ultimately with elected officials. Critics argue that equality is a compelling interest that justified the limits on expenditures that the Court invalidated.

THE CONTINUING DISTINCTION BETWEEN CONTRIBUTIONS AND EXPENDITURES

Since *Buckley*, the Court has adhered to the distinction between contributions and expenditures. For example, in California Medical Assn. v. FEC, 453 U.S. 182 (1981), the Supreme Court upheld a provision of the Federal Election Campaign Act that limited the amount that individuals and associations could contribute to a political action committee. The Court followed the same reasoning as in *Buckley*, concluding that restricting the amount of contributions does not significantly limit speech. The Court said that the speech value of contributions to political action committees is even less than when the money is given to candidates; the money is used for political expression only when spent by the political action committee.

In contrast, in FEC v. National Conservative PAC, 470 U.S. 480 (1985), the Court declared unconstitutional expenditure limits imposed on political action committees by the Presidential Election Campaign Fund Act. The law said that a political action committee could not spend more than $1,000 on behalf of a presidential candidate who accepted public financing. As in *Buckley*, the Court stressed that restrictions on expenditures limited speech; the ability of political action committees to speak in campaigns was restricted by the laws. The Court

---

65. *See, e.g.*, J. Skelly Wright, *Politics and the Constitution: Is Money Speech?*, 85 Yale L.J., 1001 (1976).
66. *See, e.g.*, Lillian R. BeVier, *Money and Politics: A Perspective on the First Amendment and Campaign Finance Reform*, 73 Cal. L. Rev. 1045 (1985).
67. *See, e.g.*, Marlene Arnold Nicholson, *Buckley v. Valeo: The Constitutionality of the Federal Election Campaign Act Amendments of 1974*, 1977 Wis. L. Rev. 323, 336.

noted that political action committees allow people to pool their resources to express themselves. The Court concluded, as in *Buckley*, that the expenditure limits violated the First Amendment.

WHEN ARE CONTRIBUTION LIMITS TOO LOW?

An issue concerning contribution limits is when they are so low as to violate the First Amendment. In Nixon v. Shrink Missouri Government PAC, the Court considered a Missouri law that set contribution limits for candidates to state government office. The statute set limits ranging from $1,075 for candidates to statewide office, such as the governor or attorney general, to $275 for candidates for state representative or for any office for which there are fewer than 100,000 people represented.

The Supreme Court, by a six-to-three margin, upheld the Missouri law. Justice Souter wrote the opinion for the Court and said that the Missouri contribution limits were constitutional for the same reasons that the contribution limits were upheld in *Buckley*; large contributions risk corruption and the appearance of corruption. The Court acknowledged that there may be laws where the judiciary will need to examine whether there is sufficient evidence of a problem to justify the restrictions, but the Court said that "this case does not present a close call requiring further definition of whatever the State evidentiary obligation may be."

Nor was the Court willing to consider whether inflation since *Buckley* makes contribution limits of the sort approved there too low now. Although the challengers pressed this argument, the Court understandably was reluctant to try and calibrate what specific contribution limits are appropriate for particular states or times.

However, in Randall v. Sorrell, 548 U.S. 230 (2006), the Court found Vermont's limits on contributions to be so restrictive as to violate the First Amendment. Vermont imposed both expenditure limits and contribution limits with regard to state elections. The Court, relying on *Buckley*, found the expenditure limits to be unconstitutional and stated: "Over the last 30 years, in considering the constitutionality of a host of different campaign finance statutes, this Court has repeatedly adhered to *Buckley*'s constraints, including those on expenditure limits."

The Court also found the contribution limits in the Vermont law to be unconstitutional. Vermont law limited contributions so that the amount that any single individual can contribute to the campaign of a candidate for state office during a "two-year general election cycle" is limited to $400 for governor, lieutenant governor, and other statewide offices; $300 for state senator; and $200 for state representative. The Court, in a 6-3 decision, found this to be so restrictive as to violate the First Amendment. Justice Breyer, writing for the Court, explained: "[W]e must recognize the existence of some lower bound. At some point the constitutional risks to the democratic electoral process become too great." The Court noted that the contribution limits in the Vermont law were lower than those upheld in *Buckley* or in any other Supreme Court decision, that they were the lowest in the country, and that they were not indexed to keep pace with inflation. The Court concluded: "[The] contribution limits are not narrowly tailored. Rather, the Act burdens First Amendment interests by

G. Conduct That Communicates

threatening to inhibit effective advocacy by those who seek election, particularly challengers; its contribution limits mute the voice of political parties; they hamper participation in campaigns through volunteer activities; and they are not indexed for inflation."

The Court looked at a number of factors in coming to this conclusion and did not prescribe a bright-line test for determining when contribution limits are too small. This opens the door to challenges to other contribution limits—in local, state, or federal laws—as being unduly restrictive.

More recently, in McCutcheon v. Federal Election Commission, 572 U.S. 185 (2014), the Court declared unconstitutional the aggregate contribution limits found in the Bipartisan Campaign Finance Reform Act. Specifically, *McCutcheon* is a challenge to a part of the Act that provides that an individual contributor cannot give more than $46,200 to candidates or their authorized agents or more than $70,800 to anyone else in a two-year election cycle. Within the $70,800 limit, a person cannot contribute more than $30,800 per calendar year to a national party committee.

Chief Justice Roberts wrote a plurality opinion, joined by Justices Scalia, Kennedy, and Alito, finding that these provisions violate the First Amendment. Chief Justice Roberts explained that limits on contributions are allowed only to prevent corruption and the appearance of corruption, and that this is limited to stopping quid pro quo corruption. He declared: "Moreover, while preventing corruption or its appearance is a legitimate objective, Congress may target only a specific type of corruption—'*quid pro quo*' corruption." He concluded that the aggregate contribution limits do not sufficiently further these goals and are thus unconstitutional. He wrote: "Spending large sums of money in connection with elections, but not in connection with an effort to control the exercise of an officeholder's official duties, does not give rise to such *quid pro quo* corruption. Nor does the possibility that an individual who spends large sums may garner influence over or access to elected officials or political parties. And because the Government's interest in preventing the appearance of corruption is equally confined to the appearance of *quid pro quo* corruption, the Government may not seek to limit the appearance of mere influence or access."

Justice Thomas concurred in the judgment, arguing that all contribution limits should be deemed to violate the First Amendment and urging the Court to overrule Buckley v. Valeo. He declared: "I adhere to the view that this Court's decision in Buckley v. Valeo denigrates core First Amendment speech and should be overruled."

Justice Breyer wrote for the dissenters and lamented that the Court has "eviscerated" federal campaign finance law and has too narrowly defined the government's interests in regulating contributions. He wrote: "The Court's legal analysis is faulty: It misconstrues the nature of the competing constitutional interests at stake. It understates the importance of protecting the political integrity of our governmental institutions. It creates a loophole that will allow a single individual to contribute millions of dollars to a political party or to a candidate's campaign. Taken together with Citizens United v. Federal Election Commission, today's decision eviscerates our Nation's campaign finance laws, leaving a remnant incapable of dealing with the grave problems of democratic legitimacy that those laws were intended to resolve."

McCutcheon will be important in challenges to local, state, and federal limits on contributions. It makes clear that restrictions are allowed only to prevent corruption or the appearance of corruption, that this is limited to quid pro quo corruption, and that any limits must be narrowly tailed to preventing this.

ARE CORPORATE EXPENDITURES PROTECTED SPEECH?

In First National Bank v. Bellotti, the Supreme Court for the first time held that corporate spending is speech protected by the First Amendment. The Court declared unconstitutional a Massachusetts law that prohibited banks or businesses from making contributions or expenditures in connection with ballot initiatives and referenda.

FIRST NATIONAL BANK OF BOSTON v. BELLOTTI
435 U.S. 765 (1978)

Justice POWELL delivered the opinion of the Court.

In sustaining a state criminal statute that forbids certain expenditures by banks and business corporations for the purpose of influencing the vote on referendum proposals, the Massachusetts Supreme Judicial Court held that the First Amendment rights of a corporation are limited to issues that materially affect its business, property, or assets. The court rejected appellants' claim that the statute abridges freedom of speech in violation of the First and Fourteenth Amendments. The issue presented in this context is one of first impression in this Court. We now reverse.

I

The statute at issue, prohibits appellants, two national banking associations and three business corporations, from making contributions or expenditures "for the purpose of . . . influencing or affecting the vote on any question submitted to the voters, other than one materially affecting any of the property, business or assets of the corporation." The statute further specifies that "[n]o question submitted to the voters solely concerning the taxation of the income, property or transactions of individuals shall be deemed materially to affect the property, business or assets of the corporation." A corporation that violates [this law] may receive a maximum fine of $50,000; a corporate officer, director, or agent who violates the section may receive a maximum fine of $10,000 or imprisonment for up to one year, or both.

Appellants wanted to spend money to publicize their views on a proposed constitutional amendment that was to be submitted to the voters as a ballot question at a general election on November 2, 1976. The amendment would have permitted the legislature to impose a graduated tax on the income of individuals.

II

The court below framed the principal question in this case as whether and to what extent corporations have First Amendment rights. We believe that the court

G. Conduct That Communicates

posed the wrong question. The Constitution often protects interests broader than those of the party seeking their vindication. The First Amendment, in particular, serves significant societal interests. The proper question therefore is not whether corporations "have" First Amendment rights and, if so, whether they are coextensive with those of natural persons. Instead, the question must be whether [this law] abridges expression that the First Amendment was meant to protect. We hold that it does.

The speech proposed by appellants is at the heart of the First Amendment's protection. As the Court said in Mills v. Alabama (1966), "there is practically universal agreement that a major purpose of [the First] Amendment was to protect the free discussion of governmental affairs." If the speakers here were not corporations, no one would suggest that the State could silence their proposed speech. It is the type of speech indispensable to decisionmaking in a democracy, and this is no less true because the speech comes from a corporation rather than an individual. The inherent worth of the speech in terms of its capacity for informing the public does not depend upon the identity of its source, whether corporation, association, union, or individual.

The court below nevertheless held that corporate speech is protected by the First Amendment only when it pertains directly to the corporation's business interests. The question in this case, simply put, is whether the corporate identity of the speaker deprives this proposed speech of what otherwise would be its clear entitlement to protection.

We find no support in the First or Fourteenth Amendment, or in the decisions of this Court, for the proposition that speech that otherwise would be within the protection of the First Amendment loses that protection simply because its source is a corporation that cannot prove, to the satisfaction of a court, a material effect on its business or property. The "materially affecting" requirement is not an identification of the boundaries of corporate speech etched by the Constitution itself. Rather, it amounts to an impermissible legislative prohibition of speech based on the identity of the interests that spokesmen may represent in public debate over controversial issues and a requirement that the speaker have a sufficiently great interest in the subject to justify communication.

[The law] permits a corporation to communicate to the public its views on certain referendum subjects—those materially affecting its business—but not others. In the realm of protected speech, the legislature is constitutionally disqualified from dictating the subjects about which persons may speak and the speakers who may address a public issue.

Appellee advances a number of arguments in support of his view that these interests are endangered by corporate participation in discussion of a referendum issue. They hinge upon the assumption that such participation would exert an undue influence on the outcome of a referendum vote, and—in the end—destroy the confidence of the people in the democratic process and the integrity of government. According to appellee, corporations are wealthy and powerful and their views may drown out other points of view. If appellee's arguments were supported by record or legislative findings that corporate advocacy threatened imminently to undermine democratic processes, thereby denigrating rather than serving First Amendment interests, these arguments would merit our consideration. But there has been no showing that the relative voice of corporations has been overwhelming or even significant in influencing referenda in Massachusetts, or that there has been any threat to the confidence of the citizenry in government.

Nor are appellee's arguments inherently persuasive or supported by the precedents of this Court. Referenda are held on issues, not candidates for public office. The risk of corruption perceived in cases involving candidate elections, simply is not present in a popular vote on a public issue. To be sure, corporate advertising may influence the outcome of the vote; this would be its purpose. But the fact that advocacy may persuade the electorate is hardly a reason to suppress it: The Constitution "protects expression which is eloquent no less than that which is unconvincing."

Finally, appellee argues that [the law] protects corporate shareholders, an interest that is both legitimate and traditionally within the province of state law. The statute is said to serve this interest by preventing the use of corporate resources in furtherance of views with which some shareholders may disagree. This purpose is belied, however, by the provisions of the statute, which are both underinclusive and overinclusive.

The underinclusiveness of the statute is self-evident. Corporate expenditures with respect to a referendum are prohibited, while corporate activity with respect to the passage or defeat of legislation is permitted, even though corporations may engage in lobbying more often than they take positions on ballot questions submitted to the voters. Nor does [the law] prohibit a corporation from expressing its views, by the expenditure of corporate funds, on any public issue until it becomes the subject of a referendum, though the displeasure of disapproving shareholders is unlikely to be any less.

The overinclusiveness of the statute is demonstrated by the fact that [the law] would prohibit a corporation from supporting or opposing a referendum proposal even if its shareholders unanimously authorized the contribution or expenditure. Ultimately shareholders may decide, through the procedures of corporate democracy, whether their corporation should engage in debate on public issues. Acting through their power to elect the board of directors or to insist upon protective provisions in the corporation's charter, shareholders normally are presumed competent to protect their own interests. In addition to intracorporate remedies, minority shareholders generally have access to the judicial remedy of a derivative suit to challenge corporate disbursements alleged to have been made for improper corporate purposes or merely to further the personal interests of management.

Justice WHITE, with whom Justice BRENNAN and Justice MARSHALL join, dissenting.

The Court invalidates the Massachusetts statute and holds that the First Amendment guarantees corporate managers the right to use not only their personal funds, but also those of the corporation, to circulate fact and opinion irrelevant to the business placed in their charge and necessarily representing their own personal or collective views about political and social questions. I do not suggest for a moment that the First Amendment requires a State to forbid such use of corporate funds, but I do strongly disagree that the First Amendment forbids state interference with managerial decisions of this kind.

By holding that Massachusetts may not prohibit corporate expenditures or contributions made in connection with referenda involving issues having no material connection with the corporate business, the Court not only invalidates a statute which has been on the books in one form or another for many years,

G. Conduct That Communicates

but also casts considerable doubt upon the constitutionality of legislation passed by some 31 States restricting corporate political activity, as well as upon the Federal Corrupt Practices Act.

The Court's fundamental error is its failure to realize that the state regulatory interests in terms of which the alleged curtailment of First Amendment rights accomplished by the statute must be evaluated are themselves derived from the First Amendment. The question posed by this case, as approached by the Court, is whether the State has struck the best possible balance, i.e., the one which it would have chosen, between competing First Amendment interests. Although in my view the choice made by the State would survive even the most exacting scrutiny, perhaps a rational argument might be made to the contrary. What is inexplicable, is for the Court to substitute its judgment as to the proper balance for that of Massachusetts where the State has passed legislation reasonably designed to further First Amendment interests in the context of the political arena where the expertise of legislators is at its peak and that of judges is at its very lowest. Moreover, the result reached today in critical respects marks a drastic departure from the Court's prior decisions which have protected against governmental infringement the very First Amendment interests which the Court now deems inadequate to justify the Massachusetts statute.

Bellotti has been sharply criticized by many commentators. The primary objection is that the Court gave inadequate weight to the value of equality and how corporate speech can distort the marketplace of ideas because of corporate wealth and resources.[68] Professor Mark Tushnet, for example, declared, "The first amendment has replaced the due process clause as the primary guarantor of the privileged. Indeed, it protects the privileged more perniciously than the due process clause ever did. . . . Today, the First Amendment stands as a general obstruction to all progressive legislative efforts. . . . Under *Buckley* and *Bellotti*, their investments in politics—or politicians—cannot be regulated significantly."[69]

In subsequent cases, the Court upheld the constitutionality of restrictions on corporate expenditures in election campaigns. In Austin v. Michigan State Chamber of Commerce, 494 U.S. 652 (1990), the Court upheld a restriction on corporate contributions or expenditures and spoke of the ability of the state to limit corporate speech so as to limit the distortions caused by corporate wealth. A Michigan law prohibited corporations from using their revenues to contribute to candidates or to make expenditures for or against candidates. The corporations, however, could create a separate fund to solicit contributions and could spend money from this segregated fund. Justice Marshall said that the Michigan law was directed at "the corrosive and distorting effects of immense aggregations of wealth that are accumulated with the help of the corporate form and that have little or no correlation to the public's support for the corporation's political ideas. The Act does not attempt to equalize the

---

68. *See* Daniel H. Lowenstein, *Campaign Spending and Ballot Propositions: Recent Experience, Public Choice Theory and the First Amendment*, 29 UCLA L. Rev. 505 (1982).
69. Mark Tushnet, *An Essay on Rights*, 62 Tex. L. Rev. 1363, 1387 (1984).

relative influence of speakers on elections; rather, it ensures that expenditures reflect actual public support for the political ideas espoused by corporations." The Court was explicit in accepting the argument that "[c]orporate wealth can unfairly influence elections."

In McConnell v. Federal Election Commission, 540 U.S. 93 (2003), the Court followed this reasoning and upheld a provision of the Bipartisan Campaign Finance Reform Act, which prohibited corporate expenditures for electronic advertising on behalf of an identifiable candidate 30 days before a primary election and 60 days before a general election.

Austin and *McConnell*, though, were overruled in Citizens United v. Federal Election Commission.

CITIZENS UNITED v. FEDERAL ELECTION COMMISSION
558 U.S. 310 (2010)

Justice KENNEDY delivered the opinion of the Court.

Federal law prohibits corporations and unions from using their general treasury funds to make independent expenditures for speech defined as an "electioneering communication" or for speech expressly advocating the election or defeat of a candidate. Limits on electioneering communications were upheld in McConnell v. Federal Election Comm'n (2003). The holding of *McConnell* rested to a large extent on an earlier case, Austin v. Michigan Chamber of Commerce (1990). *Austin* had held that political speech may be banned based on the speaker's corporate identity.

In this case we are asked to reconsider *Austin* and, in effect, *McConnell*. It has been noted that "*Austin* was a significant departure from ancient First Amendment principles." We agree with that conclusion and hold that *stare decisis* does not compel the continued acceptance of *Austin*. The Government may regulate corporate political speech through disclaimer and disclosure requirements, but it may not suppress that speech altogether. We turn to the case now before us.

I

Citizens United is a nonprofit corporation. Citizens United has an annual budget of about $12 million. Most of its funds are from donations by individuals; but, in addition, it accepts a small portion of its funds from for-profit corporations.

In January 2008, Citizens United released a film entitled *Hillary: The Movie.* It is a 90-minute documentary about then-Senator Hillary Clinton, who was a candidate in the Democratic Party's 2008 Presidential primary elections. *Hillary* mentions Senator Clinton by name and depicts interviews with political commentators and other persons, most of them quite critical of Senator Clinton. *Hillary* was released in theaters and on DVD, but Citizens United wanted to increase distribution by making it available through video-on-demand.

Video-on-demand allows digital cable subscribers to select programming from various menus, including movies, television shows, sports, news, and music. The viewer can watch the program at any time and can elect to rewind or pause the program. In December 2007, a cable company offered, for a payment of

G. Conduct That Communicates

$1.2 million, to make *Hillary* available on a video-on-demand channel called "Elections '08." Some video-on-demand services require viewers to pay a small fee to view a selected program, but here the proposal was to make *Hillary* available to viewers free of charge.

To implement the proposal, Citizens United was prepared to pay for the video-on-demand; and to promote the film, it produced two 10-second ads and one 30-second ad for *Hillary*. Each ad includes a short (and, in our view, pejorative) statement about Senator Clinton, followed by the name of the movie and the movie's Website address. Citizens United desired to promote the video-on-demand offering by running advertisements on broadcast and cable television.

Before the Bipartisan Campaign Reform Act of 2002 (BCRA), federal law prohibited—and still does prohibit—corporations and unions from using general treasury funds to make direct contributions to candidates or independent expenditures that expressly advocate the election or defeat of a candidate, through any form of media, in connection with certain qualified federal elections. BCRA §203 amended §441b to prohibit any "electioneering communication" as well. An electioneering communication is defined as "any broadcast, cable, or satellite communication" that "refers to a clearly identified candidate for Federal office" and is made within 30 days of a primary or 60 days of a general election. The Federal Election Commission's (FEC) regulations further define an electioneering communication as a communication that is "publicly distributed." Corporations and unions are barred from using their general treasury funds for express advocacy or electioneering communications. They may establish, however, a "separate segregated fund" (known as a political action committee, or PAC) for these purposes. The moneys received by the segregated fund are limited to donations from stockholders and employees of the corporation or, in the case of unions, members of the union.

In December 2007, Citizens United sought declaratory and injunctive relief against the FEC.

[II]

The law before us is an outright ban, backed by criminal sanctions. Section 441b makes it a felony for all corporations—including nonprofit advocacy corporations—either to expressly advocate the election or defeat of candidates or to broadcast electioneering communications within 30 days of a primary election and 60 days of a general election. Thus, the following acts would all be felonies under §441b: The Sierra Club runs an ad, within the crucial phase of 60 days before the general election, that exhorts the public to disapprove of a Congressman who favors logging in national forests; the National Rifle Association publishes a book urging the public to vote for the challenger because the incumbent U.S. Senator supports a handgun ban; and the American Civil Liberties Union creates a Web site telling the public to vote for a Presidential candidate in light of that candidate's defense of free speech. These prohibitions are classic examples of censorship.

Section 441b is a ban on corporate speech notwithstanding the fact that a PAC created by a corporation can still speak. A PAC is a separate association from the corporation. Even if a PAC could somehow allow a corporation to speak—and it does not—the option to form PACs does not alleviate the First

Amendment problems with §441b. PACs are burdensome alternatives; they are expensive to administer and subject to extensive regulations.

Section 441b's prohibition on corporate independent expenditures is thus a ban on speech. As a "restriction on the amount of money a person or group can spend on political communication during a campaign," that statute "necessarily reduces the quantity of expression by restricting the number of issues discussed, the depth of their exploration, and the size of the audience reached." Buckley v. Valeo (1976) (*per curiam*). Were the Court to uphold these restrictions, the Government could repress speech by silencing certain voices at any of the various points in the speech process. If §441b applied to individuals, no one would believe that it is merely a time, place, or manner restriction on speech. Its purpose and effect are to silence entities whose voices the Government deems to be suspect.

Speech is an essential mechanism of democracy, for it is the means to hold officials accountable to the people. The right of citizens to inquire, to hear, to speak, and to use information to reach consensus is a precondition to enlightened self-government and a necessary means to protect it. The First Amendment "'has its fullest and most urgent application' to speech uttered during a campaign for political office."

For these reasons, political speech must prevail against laws that would suppress it, whether by design or inadvertence. Laws that burden political speech are "subject to strict scrutiny," which requires the Government to prove that the restriction "furthers a compelling interest and is narrowly tailored to achieve that interest."

Premised on mistrust of governmental power, the First Amendment stands against attempts to disfavor certain subjects or viewpoints. Prohibited, too, are restrictions distinguishing among different speakers, allowing speech by some but not others. As instruments to censor, these categories are interrelated: Speech restrictions based on the identity of the speaker are all too often simply a means to control content.

Quite apart from the purpose or effect of regulating content, moreover, the Government may commit a constitutional wrong when by law it identifies certain preferred speakers. By taking the right to speak from some and giving it to others, the Government deprives the disadvantaged person or class of the right to use speech to strive to establish worth, standing, and respect for the speaker's voice. The Government may not by these means deprive the public of the right and privilege to determine for itself what speech and speakers are worthy of consideration. The First Amendment protects speech and speaker, and the ideas that flow from each.

We find no basis for the proposition that, in the context of political speech, the Government may impose restrictions on certain disfavored speakers. Both history and logic lead us to this conclusion.

A

The Court has recognized that First Amendment protection extends to corporations. This protection has been extended by explicit holdings to the context of political speech. Under the rationale of these precedents, political speech does not lose First Amendment protection "simply because its source is a corporation." The Court has thus rejected the argument that political speech of corporations or other associations should be treated differently

G. Conduct That Communicates

under the First Amendment simply because such associations are not "natural persons."

Thus the law stood until *Austin*. *Austin* "uph[eld] a direct restriction on the independent expenditure of funds for political speech for the first time in [this Court's] history." There, the Michigan Chamber of Commerce sought to use general treasury funds to run a newspaper ad supporting a specific candidate. Michigan law, however, prohibited corporate independent expenditures that supported or opposed any candidate for state office. A violation of the law was punishable as a felony. The Court sustained the speech prohibition.

To bypass *Buckley* and *Bellotti*, the *Austin* Court identified a new governmental interest in limiting political speech: an antidistortion interest. *Austin* found a compelling governmental interest in preventing "the corrosive and distorting effects of immense aggregations of wealth that are accumulated with the help of the corporate form and that have little or no correlation to the public's support for the corporation's political ideas."

B

The Court is thus confronted with conflicting lines of precedent: a pre-*Austin* line that forbids restrictions on political speech based on the speaker's corporate identity and a post-*Austin* line that permits them. No case before *Austin* had held that Congress could prohibit independent expenditures for political speech based on the speaker's corporate identity. Before *Austin* Congress had enacted legislation for this purpose, and the Government urged the same proposition before this Court.

As for *Austin*'s antidistortion rationale, the Government does little to defend it. And with good reason, for the rationale cannot support §441b. If the First Amendment has any force, it prohibits Congress from fining or jailing citizens, or associations of citizens, for simply engaging in political speech. If the antidistortion rationale were to be accepted, however, it would permit Government to ban political speech simply because the speaker is an association that has taken on the corporate form. The Government contends that *Austin* permits it to ban corporate expenditures for almost all forms of communication stemming from a corporation. If *Austin* were correct, the Government could prohibit a corporation from expressing political views in media beyond those presented here, such as by printing books. The Government responds "that the FEC has never applied this statute to a book," and if it did, "there would be quite [a] good as-applied challenge." This troubling assertion of brooding governmental power cannot be reconciled with the confidence and stability in civic discourse that the First Amendment must secure.

Political speech is "indispensable to decisionmaking in a democracy, and this is no less true because the speech comes from a corporation rather than an individual." This protection for speech is inconsistent with *Austin*'s antidistortion rationale. *Austin* sought to defend the antidistortion rationale as a means to prevent corporations from obtaining "'an unfair advantage in the political marketplace'" by using "'resources amassed in the economic marketplace.'"

Either as support for its antidistortion rationale or as a further argument, the *Austin* majority undertook to distinguish wealthy individuals from corporations on the ground that "[s]tate law grants corporations special advantages—such as limited liability, perpetual life, and favorable treatment of the accumulation and distribution of assets." This does not suffice, however, to allow laws prohibiting speech. "It is rudimentary that the State cannot exact as the price of those special advantages the forfeiture of First Amendment rights."

It is irrelevant for purposes of the First Amendment that corporate funds may "have little or no correlation to the public's support for the corporation's political ideas." All speakers, including individuals and the media, use money amassed from the economic marketplace to fund their speech. The First Amendment protects the resulting speech, even if it was enabled by economic transactions with persons or entities who disagree with the speaker's ideas.

Austin's antidistortion rationale would produce the dangerous, and unacceptable, consequence that Congress could ban political speech of media corporations. Media corporations are now exempt from §441b's ban on corporate expenditures. Yet media corporations accumulate wealth with the help of the corporate form, the largest media corporations have "immense aggregations of wealth," and the views expressed by media corporations often "have little or no correlation to the public's support" for those views. Thus, under the Government's reasoning, wealthy media corporations could have their voices diminished to put them on par with other media entities. There is no precedent for permitting this under the First Amendment.

The media exemption discloses further difficulties with the law now under consideration. There is no precedent supporting laws that attempt to distinguish between corporations which are deemed to be exempt as media corporations and those which are not. "We have consistently rejected the proposition that the institutional press has any constitutional privilege beyond that of other speakers." With the advent of the Internet and the decline of print and broadcast media, moreover, the line between the media and others who wish to comment on political and social issues becomes far more blurred.

The law's exception for media corporations is, on its own terms, all but an admission of the invalidity of the antidistortion rationale. And the exemption results in a further, separate reason for finding this law invalid: Again by its own terms, the law exempts some corporations but covers others, even though both have the need or the motive to communicate their views. The exemption applies to media corporations owned or controlled by corporations that have diverse and substantial investments and participate in endeavors other than news. So even assuming the most doubtful proposition that a news organization has a right to speak when others do not, the exemption would allow a conglomerate that owns both a media business and an unrelated business to influence or control the media in order to advance its overall business interest. At the same time, some other corporation, with an identical business interest but no media outlet in its ownership structure, would be forbidden to speak or inform the public about the same issue. This differential treatment cannot be squared with the First Amendment.

There is simply no support for the view that the First Amendment, as originally understood, would permit the suppression of political speech by media corporations. The Framers may not have anticipated modern business and media corporations. Yet television networks and major newspapers owned by media corporations have become the most important means of mass communication in modern times. The First Amendment was certainly not understood to condone the suppression of political speech in society's most salient media. It was understood as a response to the repression of speech and the press that had existed in England and the heavy taxes on the press that were imposed in the colonies.

G. Conduct That Communicates

Austin interferes with the "open marketplace" of ideas protected by the First Amendment. It permits the Government to ban the political speech of millions of associations of citizens.

The censorship we now confront is vast in its reach. The Government has "muffle[d] the voices that best represent the most significant segments of the economy." And "the electorate [has been] deprived of information, knowledge and opinion vital to its function." By suppressing the speech of manifold corporations, both for-profit and nonprofit, the Government prevents their voices and viewpoints from reaching the public and advising voters on which persons or entities are hostile to their interests.

The purpose and effect of this law is to prevent corporations, including small and nonprofit corporations, from presenting both facts and opinions to the public. When Government seeks to use its full power, including the criminal law, to command where a person may get his or her information or what distrusted source he or she may not hear, it uses censorship to control thought. This is unlawful. The First Amendment confirms the freedom to think for ourselves.

What we have said also shows the invalidity of other arguments made by the Government. For the most part relinquishing the antidistortion rationale, the Government falls back on the argument that corporate political speech can be banned in order to prevent corruption or its appearance. In *Buckley*, the Court found this interest "sufficiently important" to allow limits on contributions but did not extend that reasoning to expenditure limits. When *Buckley* examined an expenditure ban, it found "that the governmental interest in preventing corruption and the appearance of corruption [was] inadequate to justify [the ban] on independent expenditures."

A single footnote in *Bellotti* purported to leave open the possibility that corporate independent expenditures could be shown to cause corruption. For the reasons explained above, we now conclude that independent expenditures, including those made by corporations, do not give rise to corruption or the appearance of corruption.

When *Buckley* identified a sufficiently important governmental interest in preventing corruption or the appearance of corruption, that interest was limited to *quid pro quo* corruption. The fact that speakers may have influence over or access to elected officials does not mean that these officials are corrupt. The appearance of influence or access, furthermore, will not cause the electorate to lose faith in our democracy. By definition, an independent expenditure is political speech presented to the electorate that is not coordinated with a candidate. The fact that a corporation, or any other speaker, is willing to spend money to try to persuade voters presupposes that the people have the ultimate influence over elected officials.

The Government contends further that corporate independent expenditures can be limited because of its interest in protecting dissenting shareholders from being compelled to fund corporate political speech. This asserted interest, like *Austin*'s antidistortion rationale, would allow the Government to ban the political speech even of media corporations. Assume, for example, that a shareholder of a corporation that owns a newspaper disagrees with the political views the newspaper expresses. Under the Government's view, that potential disagreement could give the Government the authority to restrict the media corporation's political speech. The First Amendment does not allow that power.

There is, furthermore, little evidence of abuse that cannot be corrected by shareholders "through the procedures of corporate democracy."

We need not reach the question whether the Government has a compelling interest in preventing foreign individuals or associations from influencing our Nation's political process. Section 441b is not limited to corporations or associations that were created in foreign countries or funded predominately by foreign shareholders.

C

Our precedent is to be respected unless the most convincing of reasons demonstrates that adherence to it puts us on a course that is sure error. For the reasons above, it must be concluded that *Austin* was not well reasoned. The Government defends *Austin*, relying almost entirely on "the quid pro quo interest, the corruption interest or the shareholder interest," and not *Austin*'s expressed antidistortion rationale. When neither party defends the reasoning of a precedent, the principle of adhering to that precedent through *stare decisis* is diminished.

Austin is undermined by experience since its announcement. Political speech is so ingrained in our culture that speakers find ways to circumvent campaign finance laws. Our Nation's speech dynamic is changing, and informative voices should not have to circumvent onerous restrictions to exercise their First Amendment rights. Speakers have become adept at presenting citizens with sound bites, talking points, and scripted messages that dominate the 24-hour news cycle. Corporations, like individuals, do not have monolithic views. On certain topics corporations may possess valuable expertise, leaving them the best equipped to point out errors or fallacies in speech of all sorts, including the speech of candidates and elected officials.

Due consideration leads to this conclusion: *Austin* should be and now is overruled. We return to the principle established in *Buckley* and *Bellotti* that the Government may not suppress political speech on the basis of the speaker's corporate identity. No sufficient governmental interest justifies limits on the political speech of nonprofit or for-profit corporations.

Given our conclusion we are further required to overrule the part of *McConnell* that upheld BCRA §203's extension of §441b's restrictions on corporate independent expenditures. The *McConnell* Court relied on the antidistortion interest recognized in *Austin* to uphold a greater restriction on speech than the restriction upheld in *Austin* and we have found this interest unconvincing and insufficient. This part of *McConnell* is now overruled.

[IV]

When word concerning the plot of the movie *Mr. Smith Goes to Washington* reached the circles of Government, some officials sought, by persuasion, to discourage its distribution. Under *Austin*, though, officials could have done more than discourage its distribution—they could have banned the film. After all, it, like *Hillary*, was speech funded by a corporation that was critical of Members of Congress. *Mr. Smith Goes to Washington* may be fiction and caricature; but fiction and caricature can be a powerful force.

G. Conduct That Communicates

Some members of the public might consider *Hillary* to be insightful and instructive; some might find it to be neither high art nor a fair discussion on how to set the Nation's course; still others simply might suspend judgment on these points but decide to think more about issues and candidates. Those choices and assessments, however, are not for the Government to make. "The First Amendment underwrites the freedom to experiment and to create in the realm of thought and speech. Citizens must be free to use new forms, and new forums, for the expression of ideas. The civic discourse belongs to the people, and the Government may not prescribe the means used to conduct it."

Justice SCALIA, with whom Justice ALITO joins, and with whom Justice THOMAS joins in part, concurring.

I join the opinion of the Court. I write separately to address Justice Stevens' discussion of "*Original Understandings.*" This section of the dissent purports to show that today's decision is not supported by the original understanding of the First Amendment. The dissent attempts this demonstration, however, in splendid isolation from the text of the First Amendment. It never shows why "the freedom of speech" that was the right of Englishmen did not include the freedom to speak in association with other individuals, including association in the corporate form. To be sure, in 1791 (as now) corporations could pursue only the objectives set forth in their charters; but the dissent provides no evidence that their speech in the pursuit of those objectives could be censored.

Instead of taking this straightforward approach to determining the Amendment's meaning, the dissent embarks on a detailed exploration of the Framers' views about the "role of corporations in society." The Framers didn't like corporations, the dissent concludes, and therefore it follows (as night the day) that corporations had no rights of free speech. Of course the Framers' personal affection or disaffection for corporations is relevant only insofar as it can be thought to be reflected in the understood meaning of the text they enacted—not, as the dissent suggests, as a freestanding substitute for that text. But the dissent's distortion of proper analysis is even worse than that. Though faced with a constitutional text that makes no distinction between types of speakers, the dissent feels no necessity to provide even an isolated statement from the founding era to the effect that corporations are *not* covered, but places the burden on petitioners to bring forward statements showing that they *are*.

Despite the corporation-hating quotations the dissent has dredged up, it is far from clear that by the end of the 18th century corporations were despised. If so, how came there to be so many of them? The dissent's statement that there were few business corporations during the eighteenth century—"only a few hundred during all of the 18th century"—is misleading. There were approximately 335 charters issued to business corporations in the United States by the end of the 18th century.

Even if we thought it proper to apply the dissent's approach of excluding from First Amendment coverage what the Founders disliked, and even if we agreed that the Founders disliked founding-era corporations; modern corporations might not qualify for exclusion. Most of the Founders' resentment towards corporations was directed at the state-granted monopoly privileges that individually chartered corporations enjoyed. Modern corporations do not have such privileges, and would probably have been favored by most of our enterprising Founders—excluding, perhaps, Thomas Jefferson and others favoring perpetuation of an agrarian society. Moreover, if the Founders' specific intent with respect to corporations is what matters, why does the dissent ignore the Founders' views about other legal entities that have more in common with modern business corporations than the founding-era corporations? At the time of the founding, religious, educational, and literary corporations were incorporated under general incorporation statutes, much as business corporations are today. Were all of these silently excluded from the protections of the First Amendment?

The lack of a textual exception for speech by corporations cannot be explained on the ground that such organizations did not exist or did not speak. To the contrary, colleges, towns and cities, religious institutions, and guilds had long been organized as corporations at common law and under the King's charter, and as I have discussed, the practice of incorporation only expanded in the United States. Both corporations and voluntary associations actively petitioned the Government and expressed their views in newspapers and pamphlets.

The dissent says that when the Framers "constitutionalized the right to free speech in the First Amendment, it was the free speech of individual Americans that they had in mind." That is no doubt true. All the provisions of the Bill of Rights set forth the rights of individual men and women—not, for example, of trees or polar bears. But the individual person's right to speak includes the right to speak *in association with other individual persons.* Surely the dissent does not believe that speech by the Republican Party or the Democratic Party can be censored because it is not the speech of "an individual American." It is the speech of many individual Americans, who have associated in a common cause, giving the leadership of the party the right to speak on their behalf. The association of individuals in a business corporation is no different—or at least it cannot be denied the right to speak on the simplistic ground that it is not "an individual American."

But to return to, and summarize, my principal point, which is the conformity of today's opinion with the original meaning of the First Amendment. The Amendment is written in terms of "speech," not speakers. Its text offers no foothold for excluding any category of speaker, from single individuals to partnerships of individuals, to unincorporated associations of individuals, to incorporated associations of individuals—and the dissent offers no evidence about the original meaning of the text to support any such exclusion. We are therefore simply left with the question whether the speech at issue in this case is "speech" covered by the First Amendment. No one says otherwise. A documentary film critical of a potential Presidential candidate is core political speech, and its nature as such does not change simply because it was funded by a corporation. Nor does the character of that funding produce any reduction whatever in the "inherent worth of the speech" and "its capacity for informing the public," First Nat. Bank of Boston v. Bellotti (1978). Indeed, to exclude or impede corporate speech is to muzzle the principal agents of the modern free economy. We should celebrate rather than condemn the addition of this speech to the public debate.

Justice STEVENS, with whom Justice GINSBURG, Justice BREYER, and Justice SOTOMAYOR join, concurring in part and dissenting in part.

The real issue in this case concerns how, not if, the appellant may finance its electioneering. Citizens United is a wealthy nonprofit corporation that runs a political action committee (PAC) with millions of dollars in assets. Under the Bipartisan Campaign Reform Act of 2002 (BCRA), it could have used those assets to televise and promote *Hillary: The Movie* wherever and whenever it wanted to. It also could have spent unrestricted sums to broadcast *Hillary* at any time other than the 30 days before the last primary election. Neither Citizens United's nor any other corporation's speech has been "banned." All that the parties dispute is whether Citizens United had a right to use the funds in its general treasury to pay for broadcasts during the 30-day period. The notion that the First Amendment dictates an affirmative answer to that question is, in my judgment, profoundly misguided. Even more misguided is the notion that the Court must rewrite the law relating to campaign expenditures by *for-profit* corporations and unions to decide this case.

The basic premise underlying the Court's ruling is its iteration, and constant reiteration, of the proposition that the First Amendment bars regulatory distinctions based on a speaker's identity, including its "identity" as a corporation. While that glittering generality has rhetorical appeal, it is not a correct statement of the law. Nor does it tell us when a corporation may engage in electioneering that some of its shareholders oppose. It does not even resolve the specific question whether Citizens United may be required to finance some of its messages with the money in its PAC. The conceit that corporations must be treated identically to natural persons in the political sphere is not only inaccurate but also inadequate to justify the Court's disposition of this case.

In the context of election to public office, the distinction between corporate and human speakers is significant. Although they make enormous contributions to our society, corporations are not actually members of it. They cannot vote or run for office. Because they may be managed and controlled by nonresidents, their interests may conflict in fundamental respects with the interests of eligible voters. The financial resources, legal structure, and instrumental orientation of corporations raise legitimate concerns about their role in the electoral process. Our lawmakers have a compelling constitutional basis, if not also a democratic duty, to take measures designed to guard against the potentially deleterious effects of corporate spending in local and national races.

The majority's approach to corporate electioneering marks a dramatic break from our past. Congress has placed special limitations on campaign spending by corporations ever since the passage of the Tillman Act in 1907. We have unanimously concluded that this "reflects a permissible assessment of the dangers posed by those entities to the electoral process," FEC v. National Right to Work Comm. (1982) (*NRWC*), and have accepted the "legislative judgment that the special characteristics of the corporate structure require particularly careful regulation." The Court today rejects a century of history when it treats the distinction between corporate and individual campaign spending as an invidious novelty born of Austin v. Michigan Chamber of Commerce (1990). Relying largely on individual dissenting opinions, the majority blazes through our precedents, overruling or disavowing a body of case law.

Although I concur in the Court's decision to sustain BCRA's disclosure provisions and join Part IV of its opinion, I emphatically dissent from its principal holding.

I

The Court's ruling threatens to undermine the integrity of elected institutions across the Nation. The path it has taken to reach its outcome will, I fear, do damage to this institution. Before turning to the question whether to overrule *Austin* and part of *McConnell*, it is important to explain why the Court should not be deciding that question. [Justice Stevens then argued that the case should have been decided as an "as applied" rather than a facial challenge and also that it should have been decided on narrower grounds.]

II

The final principle of judicial process that the majority violates is the most transparent: *stare decisis*. I am not an absolutist when it comes to *stare decisis*, in the campaign finance area or in any other. No one is. But if this principle is to do any meaningful work in supporting the rule of law, it must at least demand a significant justification, beyond the preferences of five Justices, for overturning settled doctrine. "[A] decision to overrule should rest on some special reason over and above the belief that a prior case was wrongly decided." Planned Parenthood of Southeastern Pa. v. Casey (1992). No such justification exists in this case, and to the contrary there are powerful prudential reasons to keep faith with our precedents.

The Court's central argument for why *stare decisis* ought to be trumped is that it does not like *Austin*. The opinion "was not well reasoned," our colleagues assert, and it conflicts with First Amendment principles. This, of course, is the Court's merits argument, the many defects in which we will soon consider. I am perfectly willing to concede that if one of our precedents were dead wrong in its reasoning or irreconcilable with the rest of our doctrine, there would be a compelling basis for revisiting it. But neither is true of *Austin*, and restating a merits argument with additional vigor does not give it extra weight in the *stare decisis* calculus.

We have recognized that "[s]*tare decisis* has special force when legislators or citizens 'have acted in reliance on a previous decision, for in this instance overruling the decision would dislodge settled rights and expectations or require an extensive legislative response.'" *Stare decisis* protects not only personal rights involving property or contract but also the ability of the elected branches to shape their laws in an effective and coherent fashion. Today's decision takes away a power that we have long permitted these branches to exercise. State legislatures have relied on their authority to regulate corporate electioneering, confirmed in *Austin*, for more than a century. The Federal Congress has relied on this authority for a comparable stretch of time, and it specifically relied on *Austin* throughout the years it spent developing and debating BCRA. The total record it compiled was *100,000 pages* long. Pulling out the rug beneath Congress after affirming the constitutionality of §203 six years ago shows great disrespect for a coequal branch.

In the end, the Court's rejection of *Austin* and *McConnell* comes down to nothing more than its disagreement with their results. Virtually every one of its arguments was made and rejected in those cases, and the majority opinion is essentially an amalgamation of resuscitated dissents. The only relevant thing that

G. Conduct That Communicates

has changed since *Austin* and *McConnell* is the composition of this Court. Today's ruling thus strikes at the vitals of *stare decisis*, "the means by which we ensure that the law will not merely change erratically, but will develop in a principled and intelligible fashion" that "permits society to presume that bedrock principles are founded in the law rather than in the proclivities of individuals."

III

The novelty of the Court's procedural dereliction and its approach to *stare decisis* is matched by the novelty of its ruling on the merits. The ruling rests on several premises. First, the Court claims that *Austin* and *McConnell* have "banned" corporate speech. Second, it claims that the First Amendment precludes regulatory distinctions based on speaker identity, including the speaker's identity as a corporation. Third, it claims that *Austin* and *McConnell* were radical outliers in our First Amendment tradition and our campaign finance jurisprudence. Each of these claims is wrong.

THE SO-CALLED "BAN"
Pervading the Court's analysis is the ominous image of a "categorical ba[n]" on corporate speech. Indeed, the majority invokes the specter of a "ban" on nearly every page of its opinion. This characterization is highly misleading, and needs to be corrected.

In fact it already has been. Our cases have repeatedly pointed out that, "[c]ontrary to the [majority's] critical assumptions," the statutes upheld in *Austin* and *McConnell* do "not impose an *absolute* ban on all forms of corporate political spending." For starters, both statutes provide exemptions for PACs, separate segregated funds established by a corporation for political purposes. "The ability to form and administer separate segregated funds," we observed in *McConnell*, "has provided corporations and unions with a constitutionally sufficient opportunity to engage in express advocacy. That has been this Court's unanimous view."

Under BCRA, any corporation's "stockholders and their families and its executive or administrative personnel and their families" can pool their resources to finance electioneering communications. A significant and growing number of corporations avail themselves of this option; during the most recent election cycle, corporate and union PACs raised nearly a billion dollars. Administering a PAC entails some administrative burden, but so does complying with the disclaimer, disclosure, and reporting requirements that the Court today upholds, and no one has suggested that the burden is severe for a sophisticated for-profit corporation. To the extent the majority is worried about this issue, it is important to keep in mind that we have no record to show how substantial the burden really is, just the majority's own unsupported factfinding. Like all other natural persons, every shareholder of every corporation remains entirely free under *Austin* and *McConnell* to do however much electioneering she pleases outside of the corporate form. The owners of a "mom & pop" store can simply place ads in their own names, rather than the store's.

So let us be clear: Neither *Austin* nor *McConnell* held or implied that corporations may be silenced; the FEC is not a "censor"; and in the years since these cases were decided, corporations have continued to play a major role in the national dialogue. Laws such as §203 target a class of communications that is especially likely to corrupt the political process, that is at least one degree removed from the views of individual citizens, and that may not even reflect the views of those who pay for it. Such laws burden political speech, and that is always a serious matter, demanding careful scrutiny. But the majority's incessant talk of a "ban" aims at a straw man.

IDENTITY-BASED DISTINCTIONS

The second pillar of the Court's opinion is its assertion that "the Government cannot restrict political speech based on the speaker's . . . identity." The case on which it relies for this proposition is First Nat. Bank of Boston v. Bellotti (1978). As I shall explain, the holding in that case was far narrower than the Court implies.

[I]n a variety of contexts, we have held that speech can be regulated differentially on account of the speaker's identity, when identity is understood in categorical or institutional terms. The Government routinely places special restrictions on the speech rights of students, prisoners, members of the Armed Forces, foreigners, and its own employees. When such restrictions are justified by a legitimate governmental interest, they do not necessarily raise constitutional problems. In contrast to the blanket rule that the majority espouses, our cases recognize that the Government's interests may be more or less compelling with respect to different classes of speakers, and that the constitutional rights of certain categories of speakers, in certain contexts, "are not automatically coextensive with the rights" that are normally accorded to members of our society.

The election context is distinctive in many ways, and the Court, of course, is right that the First Amendment closely guards political speech. But in this context, too, the authority of legislatures to enact viewpoint-neutral regulations based on content and identity is well settled. We have, for example, allowed state-run broadcasters to exclude independent candidates from televised debates. Arkansas Ed. Television Comm'n v. Forbes (1998). We have upheld statutes that prohibit the distribution or display of campaign materials near a polling place. Burson v. Freeman (1992). Although we have not reviewed them directly, we have never cast doubt on laws that place special restrictions on campaign spending by foreign nationals. And we have consistently approved laws that bar Government employees, but not others, from contributing to or participating in political activities.

The same logic applies to this case with additional force because it is the identity of corporations, rather than individuals, that the Legislature has taken into account. As we have unanimously observed, legislatures are entitled to decide "that the special characteristics of the corporate structure require particularly careful regulation" in an electoral context. Not only has the distinctive potential of corporations to corrupt the electoral process long been recognized, but within the area of campaign finance, corporate spending is also "furthest from the core of political expression, since corporations' First Amendment speech and association interests are derived largely from those of their members and of the public in receiving information." Campaign finance distinctions based on corporate identity tend to be less worrisome, in other words, because the "speakers" are not natural persons, much less members of our political community, and the governmental interests are of the highest

G. Conduct That Communicates

order. Furthermore, when corporations, as a class, are distinguished from noncorporations, as a class, there is a lesser risk that regulatory distinctions will reflect invidious discrimination or political favoritism.

If taken seriously, our colleagues' assumption that the identity of a speaker has *no* relevance to the Government's ability to regulate political speech would lead to some remarkable conclusions. Such an assumption would have accorded the propaganda broadcasts to our troops by "Tokyo Rose" during World War II the same protection as speech by Allied commanders. More pertinently, it would appear to afford the same protection to multinational corporations controlled by foreigners as to individual Americans. Under the majority's view, I suppose it may be a First Amendment problem that corporations are not permitted to vote, given that voting is, among other things, a form of speech.

OUR FIRST AMENDMENT TRADITION

A third fulcrum of the Court's opinion is the idea that *Austin* and *McConnell* are radical outliers, "aberration[s]," in our First Amendment tradition. The Court has it exactly backwards. It is today's holding that is the radical departure from what had been settled First Amendment law. To see why, it is useful to take a long view.

Let us start from the beginning. The Court invokes "ancient First Amendment principles," and original understandings, to defend today's ruling, yet it makes only a perfunctory attempt to ground its analysis in the principles or understandings of those who drafted and ratified the Amendment. Perhaps this is because there is not a scintilla of evidence to support the notion that anyone believed it would preclude regulatory distinctions based on the corporate form. To the extent that the Framers' views are discernible and relevant to the disposition of this case, they would appear to cut strongly against the majority's position.

This is not only because the Framers and their contemporaries conceived of speech more narrowly than we now think of it, but also because they held very different views about the nature of the First Amendment right and the role of corporations in society. Those few corporations that existed at the founding were authorized by grant of a special legislative charter. The individualized charter mode of incorporation reflected the "cloud of disfavor under which corporations labored" in the early years of this Nation.

The Framers thus took it as a given that corporations could be comprehensively regulated in the service of the public welfare. Unlike our colleagues, they had little trouble distinguishing corporations from human beings, and when they constitutionalized the right to free speech in the First Amendment, it was the free speech of individual Americans that they had in mind. While individuals might join together to exercise their speech rights, business corporations, at least, were plainly not seen as facilitating such associational or expressive ends. In light of these background practices and understandings, it seems to me implausible that the Framers believed "the freedom of speech" would extend equally to all corporate speakers, much less that it would preclude legislatures from taking limited measures to guard against corporate capture of elections.

A century of more recent history puts to rest any notion that today's ruling is faithful to our First Amendment tradition. At the federal level, the express distinction between corporate and individual political spending on elections stretches back to 1907, when Congress passed the Tillman Act, banning all corporate contributions to candidates.

In sum, over the course of the past century Congress has demonstrated a recurrent need to regulate corporate participation in candidate elections to "[p]reserv[e] the integrity of the electoral process, preven[t] corruption, . . . sustai[n] the active, alert responsibility of the individual citizen," protect the expressive interests of shareholders, and "[p]reserv[e] . . . the individual citizen's confidence in government." Time and again, we have recognized these realities in approving measures that Congress and the States have taken. None of the cases the majority cites is to the contrary. The only thing new about *Austin* was the dissent, with its stunning failure to appreciate the legitimacy of interests recognized in the name of democratic integrity since the days of the Progressives.

IV

Having explained why this is not an appropriate case in which to revisit *Austin* and *McConnell* and why these decisions sit perfectly well with "First Amendment principles," I come at last to the interests that are at stake. The majority recognizes that *Austin* and *McConnell* may be defended on anticorruption, antidistortion, and shareholder protection rationales. It badly errs both in explaining the nature of these rationales, which overlap and complement each other, and in applying them to the case at hand.

THE ANTICORRUPTION INTEREST

Undergirding the majority's approach to the merits is the claim that the only "sufficiently important governmental interest in preventing corruption or the appearance of corruption" is one that is "limited to *quid pro quo* corruption." While it is true that we have not always spoken about corruption in a clear or consistent voice, the approach taken by the majority cannot be right, in my judgment. It disregards our constitutional history and the fundamental demands of a democratic society.

On numerous occasions we have recognized Congress' legitimate interest in preventing the money that is spent on elections from exerting an "undue influence on an officeholder's judgment" and from creating "the appearance of such influence," beyond the sphere of *quid pro quo* relationships. Corruption can take many forms. Bribery may be the paradigm case. But the difference between selling a vote and selling access is a matter of degree, not kind. And selling access is not qualitatively different from giving special preference to those who spent money on one's behalf. Corruption operates along a spectrum, and the majority's apparent belief that *quid pro quo* arrangements can be neatly demarcated from other improper influences does not accord with the theory or reality of politics. It certainly does not accord with the record Congress developed in passing BCRA, a record that stands as a remarkable testament to the energy and ingenuity with which corporations, unions, lobbyists, and politicians may go about scratching each other's backs—and which amply supported Congress' determination to target a limited set of especially destructive practices.

The cluster of interrelated interests threatened by such undue influence and its appearance has been well captured under the rubric of "democratic

G. Conduct That Communicates

integrity." This value has underlined a century of state and federal efforts to regulate the role of corporations in the electoral process.

ANTIDISTORTION

The fact that corporations are different from human beings might seem to need no elaboration, except that the majority opinion almost completely elides it. *Austin* set forth some of the basic differences. Unlike natural persons, corporations have "limited liability" for their owners and managers, "perpetual life," separation of ownership and control, "and favorable treatment of the accumulation and distribution of assets . . . that enhance their ability to attract capital and to deploy their resources in ways that maximize the return on their shareholders' investments." Unlike voters in U.S. elections, corporations may be foreign controlled. Unlike other interest groups, business corporations have been "effectively delegated responsibility for ensuring society's economic welfare"; they inescapably structure the life of every citizen. "[T]he resources in the treasury of a business corporation," furthermore, "are not an indication of popular support for the corporation's political ideas." "They reflect instead the economically motivated decisions of investors and customers. The availability of these resources may make a corporation a formidable political presence, even though the power of the corporation may be no reflection of the power of its ideas."

It might also be added that corporations have no consciences, no beliefs, no feelings, no thoughts, no desires. Corporations help structure and facilitate the activities of human beings, to be sure, and their "personhood" often serves as a useful legal fiction. But they are not themselves members of "We the People" by whom and for whom our Constitution was established.

These basic points help explain why corporate electioneering is not only more likely to impair compelling governmental interests, but also why restrictions on that electioneering are less likely to encroach upon First Amendment freedoms. One fundamental concern of the First Amendment is to "protec[t] the individual's interest in self-expression." Freedom of speech helps "make men free to develop their faculties," it respects their "dignity and choice," and it facilitates the value of "individual self-realization." Corporate speech, however, is derivative speech, speech by proxy. A regulation such as BCRA §203 may affect the way in which individuals disseminate certain messages through the corporate form, but it does not prevent anyone from speaking in his or her own voice. "Within the realm of [campaign spending] generally," corporate spending is "furthest from the core of political expression."

None of this is to suggest that corporations can or should be denied an opportunity to participate in election campaigns or in any other public forum (much less that a work of art such as *Mr. Smith Goes to Washington* may be banned), or to deny that some corporate speech may contribute significantly to public debate. What it shows, however, is that *Austin*'s "concern about corporate domination of the political process," reflects more than a concern to protect governmental interests outside of the First Amendment. It also reflects a concern to *facilitate* First Amendment values by preserving some breathing room around the electoral "marketplace" of ideas, the marketplace in which the actual people of this Nation determine how they will govern themselves. The majority seems oblivious to the simple truth that laws such as §203 do not merely pit the anticorruption interest against the First Amendment, but also pit competing First Amendment values against each other. There are, to be sure, serious concerns with any effort to balance the First Amendment rights of speakers against the First Amendment rights of listeners. But when the speakers in question are not real people and when the appeal to "First Amendment principles" depends almost entirely on the listeners' perspective, it becomes necessary to consider how listeners will actually be affected.

In critiquing *Austin*'s antidistortion rationale and campaign finance regulation more generally, our colleagues place tremendous weight on the example of media corporations. Yet it is not at all clear that *Austin* would permit §203 to be applied to them. The press plays a unique role not only in the text, history, and structure of the First Amendment but also in facilitating public discourse; as the *Austin* Court explained, "media corporations differ significantly from other corporations in that their resources are devoted to the collection of information and its dissemination to the public." Our colleagues have raised some interesting and difficult questions about Congress' authority to regulate electioneering by the press, and about how to define what constitutes the press. *But that is not the case before us.* Section 203 does not apply to media corporations, and even if it did, Citizens United is not a media corporation. There would be absolutely no reason to consider the issue of media corporations if the majority did not, first, transform Citizens United's as-applied challenge into a facial challenge and, second, invent the theory that legislatures must eschew all "identity"-based distinctions and treat a local nonprofit news outlet exactly the same as General Motors.

SHAREHOLDER PROTECTION

There is yet another way in which laws such as §203 can serve First Amendment values. Interwoven with *Austin*'s concern to protect the integrity of the electoral process is a concern to protect the rights of shareholders from a kind of coerced speech: electioneering expenditures that do not "reflec[t] [their] support." When corporations use general treasury funds to praise or attack a particular candidate for office, it is the shareholders, as the residual claimants, who are effectively footing the bill. Those shareholders who disagree with the corporation's electoral message may find their financial investments being used to undermine their political convictions.

The PAC mechanism, by contrast, helps assure that those who pay for an electioneering communication actually support its content and that managers do not use general treasuries to advance personal agendas. It "allows corporate political participation without the temptation to use corporate funds for political influence, quite possibly at odds with the sentiments of some shareholders or members."

V

In a democratic society, the longstanding consensus on the need to limit corporate campaign spending should outweigh the wooden application of judge-made rules. The majority's rejection of this principle "elevate[s] corporations to a level of deference which has not been seen at least since the days when substantive due process was regularly used to invalidate regulatory legislation thought to unfairly impinge upon established economic interests."

G. Conduct That Communicates

At bottom, the Court's opinion is thus a rejection of the common sense of the American people, who have recognized a need to prevent corporations from undermining self-government since the founding, and who have fought against the distinctive corrupting potential of corporate electioneering since the days of Theodore Roosevelt. It is a strange time to repudiate that common sense. While American democracy is imperfect, few outside the majority of this Court would have thought its flaws included a dearth of corporate money in politics.

THE CONSTITUTIONALITY OF PUBLIC FINANCING OF ELECTIONS

One frequently discussed approach to decreasing the undesirable effects of large campaign expenditures has been to have public financing of elections. Buckley v. Valeo holds that it is to limit a candidate's expenditures as a condition for receiving public funding for a campaign, though no candidate can be required to accept public funds. In Arizona Free Enterprise Club's Freedom Club PAC v. Bennett, the Court declared unconstitutional a public funding system that increased the contribution and spending limits for those not taking public money based on the amount spent by opponents.

ARIZONA FREE ENTERPRISE CLUB'S FREEDOM CLUB PAC v. BENNETT
564 U.S. 721 (2011)

Chief Justice ROBERTS delivered the opinion of the Court.

Under Arizona law, candidates for state office who accept public financing can receive additional money from the State in direct response to the campaign activities of privately financed candidates and independent expenditure groups. Once a set spending limit is exceeded, a publicly financed candidate receives roughly one dollar for every dollar spent by an opposing privately financed candidate. The publicly financed candidate also receives roughly one dollar for every dollar spent by independent expenditure groups to support the privately financed candidate, or to oppose the publicly financed candidate. We hold that Arizona's matching funds scheme substantially burdens protected political speech without serving a compelling state interest and therefore violates the First Amendment.

I

The Arizona Citizens Clean Elections Act, passed by initiative in 1998, created a voluntary public financing system to fund the primary and general election campaigns of candidates for state office. All eligible candidates for Governor, secretary of state, attorney general, treasurer, superintendent of public instruction, the corporation commission, mine inspector, and the state legislature (both the House and Senate) may opt to receive public funding. Eligibility is contingent on the collection of a specified number of five-dollar contributions from Arizona voters, and the acceptance of certain campaign restrictions and obligations. Publicly funded candidates must agree, among other things, to limit their expenditure of personal funds to $500; participate in at least one public debate; adhere to an overall expenditure cap; and return all unspent public moneys to the State.

In exchange for accepting these conditions, participating candidates are granted public funds to conduct their campaigns. In many cases, this initial allotment may be the whole of the State's financial backing of a publicly funded candidate. But when certain conditions are met, publicly funded candidates are granted additional "equalizing" or matching funds.

Matching funds are available in both primary and general elections. In a primary, matching funds are triggered when a privately financed candidate's expenditures, combined with the expenditures of independent groups made in support of the privately financed candidate or in opposition to a publicly financed candidate, exceed the primary election allotment of state funds to the publicly financed candidate. During the general election, matching funds are triggered when the amount of money a privately financed candidate receives in contributions, combined with the expenditures of independent groups made in support of the privately financed candidate or in opposition to a publicly financed candidate, exceed the general election allotment of state funds to the publicly financed candidate. A privately financed candidate's expenditures of his personal funds are counted as contributions for purposes of calculating matching funds during a general election. Once matching funds are triggered, each additional dollar that a privately financed candidate spends during the primary results in one dollar in additional state funding to his publicly financed opponent (less a 6% reduction meant to account for fundraising expenses). During a general election, every dollar that a candidate receives in contributions—which includes any money of his own that a candidate spends on his campaign—results in roughly one dollar in additional state funding to his publicly financed opponent. In an election where a privately funded candidate faces multiple publicly financed candidates, one dollar raised or spent by the privately financed candidate results in an almost one dollar increase in public funding to each of the publicly financed candidates.

Once the public financing cap is exceeded, additional expenditures by independent groups can result in dollar-for-dollar matching funds as well. Spending by independent groups on behalf of a privately funded candidate, or in opposition to a publicly funded candidate, results in matching funds. Independent expenditures made in support of a publicly financed candidate can result in matching funds for other publicly financed candidates in a race. The matching funds provision is not activated, however, when independent expenditures are made in opposition to a privately financed candidate. Matching funds top out at two times the initial authorized grant of public funding to the publicly financed candidate.

Under Arizona law, a privately financed candidate may raise and spend unlimited funds, subject to state-imposed contribution limits and disclosure requirements. Contributions to candidates for statewide office are limited to $840 per contributor per election cycle and contributions to legislative candidates are limited to $410 per contributor per election cycle.

G. Conduct That Communicates

II

"Discussion of public issues and debate on the qualifications of candidates are integral to the operation" of our system of government. As a result, the First Amendment "'has its fullest and most urgent application' to speech uttered during a campaign for political office." "Laws that burden political speech are" accordingly "subject to strict scrutiny, which requires the Government to prove that the restriction furthers a compelling interest and is narrowly tailored to achieve that interest."

Although the speech of the candidates and independent expenditure groups that brought this suit is not directly capped by Arizona's matching funds provision, those parties contend that their political speech is substantially burdened by the state law in the same way that speech was burdened by the law we recently found invalid in Davis v. Federal Election Comm'n (2008). In *Davis*, we considered a First Amendment challenge to the so-called "Millionaire's Amendment" of the Bipartisan Campaign Reform Act of 2002. Under that Amendment, if a candidate for the United States House of Representatives spent more than $350,000 of his personal funds, "a new, asymmetrical regulatory scheme [came] into play." The opponent of the candidate who exceeded that limit was permitted to collect individual contributions up to $6,900 per contributor—three times the normal contribution limit of $2,300. The candidate who spent more than the personal funds limit remained subject to the original contribution cap. Davis argued that this scheme "burden[ed] his exercise of his First Amendment right to make unlimited expenditures of his personal funds because" doing so had "the effect of enabling his opponent to raise more money and to use that money to finance speech that counteract[ed] and thus diminishe[d] the effectiveness of Davis' own speech."

The logic of *Davis* largely controls our approach to this case. Much like the burden placed on speech in *Davis*, the matching funds provision "imposes an unprecedented penalty on any candidate who robustly exercises [his] First Amendment right[s]." Under that provision, "the vigorous exercise of the right to use personal funds to finance campaign speech" leads to "advantages for opponents in the competitive context of electoral politics."

Once a privately financed candidate has raised or spent more than the State's initial grant to a publicly financed candidate, each personal dollar spent by the privately financed candidate results in an award of almost one additional dollar to his opponent. That plainly forces the privately financed candidate to "shoulder a special and potentially significant burden" when choosing to exercise his First Amendment right to spend funds on behalf of his candidacy. If the law at issue in *Davis* imposed a burden on candidate speech, the Arizona law unquestionably does so as well.

The burdens that this regime places on independent expenditure groups are akin to those imposed on the privately financed candidates themselves. Just as with the candidate the independent group supports, the more money spent on that candidate's behalf or in opposition to a publicly funded candidate, the more money the publicly funded candidate receives from the State. And just as with the privately financed candidate, the effect of a dollar spent on election speech is a guaranteed financial payout to the publicly funded candidate the group opposes. Moreover, spending one dollar can result in the flow of dollars to multiple candidates the group disapproves of, dollars directly controlled by the publicly funded candidate or candidates.

In some ways, the burden the Arizona law imposes on independent expenditure groups is worse than the burden it imposes on privately financed candidates, and thus substantially worse than the burden we found constitutionally impermissible in *Davis*. If a candidate contemplating an electoral run in Arizona surveys the campaign landscape and decides that the burdens imposed by the matching funds regime make a privately funded campaign unattractive, he at least has the option of taking public financing. Independent expenditure groups, of course, do not.

Once the spending cap is reached, an independent expenditure group that wants to support a particular candidate—because of that candidate's stand on an issue of concern to the group—can only avoid triggering matching funds in one of two ways. The group can either opt to change its message from one addressing the merits of the candidates to one addressing the merits of an issue, or refrain from speaking altogether. Presenting independent expenditure groups with such a choice makes the matching funds provision particularly burdensome to those groups. And forcing that choice—trigger matching funds, change your message, or do not speak—certainly contravenes "the fundamental rule of protection under the First Amendment, that a speaker has the autonomy to choose the content of his own message."

The State argues that the matching funds provision actually results in more speech by "increas[ing] debate about issues of public concern" in Arizona elections and "promot[ing] the free and open debate that the First Amendment was intended to foster." In the State's view, this promotion of First Amendment ideals offsets any burden the law might impose on some speakers.

Not so. Any increase in speech resulting from the Arizona law is of one kind and one kind only—that of publicly financed candidates. The burden imposed on privately financed candidates and independent expenditure groups reduces their speech; "restriction[s] on the amount of money a person or group can spend on political communication during a campaign necessarily reduces the quantity of expression." Thus, even if the matching funds provision did result in more speech by publicly financed candidates and more speech in general, it would do so at the expense of impermissibly burdening (and thus reducing) the speech of privately financed candidates and independent expenditure groups. This sort of "beggar thy neighbor" approach to free speech—"restrict[ing] the speech of some elements of our society in order to enhance the relative voice of others"—is "wholly foreign to the First Amendment."

Arizona asserts that no "candidate or independent expenditure group is 'obliged personally to express a message he disagrees with'" or "required by the government to subsidize a message he disagrees with." True enough. But that does not mean that the matching funds provision does not burden speech. The direct result of the speech of privately financed candidates and independent expenditure groups is a state-provided monetary subsidy to a political rival. That cash subsidy, conferred in response to political speech, penalizes speech to a greater extent and more directly than the Millionaire's Amendment in *Davis*. The fact that this may result in more speech by the other candidates is no more adequate a justification here than it was in *Davis*.

G. Conduct That Communicates

Because the Arizona matching funds provision imposes a substantial burden on the speech of privately financed candidates and independent expenditure groups, "that provision cannot stand unless it is 'justified by a compelling state interest.'"

There is a debate between the parties in this case as to what state interest is served by the matching funds provision. The privately financed candidates and independent expenditure groups contend that the provision works to "level[] electoral opportunities" by equalizing candidate "resources and influence." The State and the Clean Elections Institute counter that the provision "furthers Arizona's interest in preventing corruption and the appearance of corruption."

There is ample support for the argument that the matching funds provision seeks to "level the playing field" in terms of candidate resources. We have repeatedly rejected the argument that the government has a compelling state interest in "leveling the playing field" that can justify undue burdens on political speech. "Leveling electoral opportunities means making and implementing judgments about which strengths should be permitted to contribute to the outcome of an election,"—a dangerous enterprise and one that cannot justify burdening protected speech. The dissent essentially dismisses this concern, but it needs to be taken seriously; we have, as noted, held that it is not legitimate for the government to attempt to equalize electoral opportunities in this manner. And such basic intrusion by the government into the debate over who should govern goes to the heart of First Amendment values.

"Leveling the playing field" can sound like a good thing. But in a democracy, campaigning for office is not a game. It is a critically important form of speech. The First Amendment embodies our choice as a Nation that, when it comes to such speech, the guiding principle is freedom—the "unfettered interchange of ideas"—not whatever the State may view as fair.

As already noted, the State and the Clean Elections Institute disavow any interest in "leveling the playing field." They instead assert that the "Equal funding of candidates" provision, serves the State's compelling interest in combating corruption and the appearance of corruption. But even if the ultimate objective of the matching funds provision is to combat corruption—and not "level the playing field"—the burdens that the matching funds provision imposes on protected political speech are not justified.

Burdening a candidate's expenditure of his own funds on his own campaign does not further the State's anticorruption interest. Indeed, we have said that "reliance on personal funds *reduces* the threat of corruption" and that "discouraging [the] use of personal funds[ ] disserves the anticorruption interest." That is because "the use of personal funds reduces the candidate's dependence on outside contributions and thereby counteracts the coercive pressures and attendant risks of abuse" of money in politics. The matching funds provision counts a candidate's expenditures of his own money on his own campaign as contributions, and to that extent cannot be supported by any anticorruption interest.

We have also held that "independent expenditures . . . do not give rise to corruption or the appearance of corruption." "By definition, an independent expenditure is political speech presented to the electorate that is not coordinated with a candidate." The candidate-funding circuit is broken. The separation between candidates and independent expenditure groups negates the possibility that independent expenditures will result in the sort of *quid pro quo* corruption with which our case law is concerned.

"[T]here is practically universal agreement that a major purpose of" the First Amendment "was to protect the free discussion of governmental affairs," "includ[ing] discussions of candidates." That agreement "reflects our 'profound national commitment to the principle that debate on public issues should be uninhibited, robust, and wide-open.'" True when we said it and true today. Laws like Arizona's matching funds provision that inhibit robust and wide-open political debate without sufficient justification cannot stand.

Justice KAGAN, with whom Justice GINSBURG, Justice BREYER, and Justice SOTOMAYOR join, dissenting.

Imagine two States, each plagued by a corrupt political system. In both States, candidates for public office accept large campaign contributions in exchange for the promise that, after assuming office, they will rank the donors' interests ahead of all others. As a result of these bargains, politicians ignore the public interest, sound public policy languishes, and the citizens lose confidence in their government.

Recognizing the cancerous effect of this corruption, voters of the first State, acting through referendum, enact several campaign finance measures previously approved by this Court. They cap campaign contributions; require disclosure of substantial donations; and create an optional public financing program that gives candidates a fixed public subsidy if they refrain from private fundraising. But these measures do not work. Individuals who "bundle" campaign contributions become indispensable to candidates in need of money. Simple disclosure fails to prevent shady dealing. And candidates choose not to participate in the public financing system because the sums provided do not make them competitive with their privately financed opponents. So the State remains afflicted with corruption.

Voters of the second State, having witnessed this failure, take an ever-so-slightly different tack to cleaning up their political system. They too enact contribution limits and disclosure requirements. But they believe that the greatest hope of eliminating corruption lies in creating an effective public financing program, which will break candidates' dependence on large donors and bundlers. These voters realize, based on the first State's experience, that such a program will not work unless candidates agree to participate in it. And candidates will participate only if they know that they will receive sufficient funding to run competitive races. So the voters enact a program that carefully adjusts the money given to would-be officeholders, through the use of a matching funds mechanism, in order to provide this assurance. The program does not discriminate against any candidate or point of view, and it does not restrict any person's ability to speak. In fact, by providing resources to many candidates, the program creates more speech and thereby broadens public debate. And just as the voters had hoped, the program accomplishes its mission of restoring integrity to the political system. The second State rids itself of corruption.

A person familiar with our country's core values—our devotion to democratic self-governance, as well as to "uninhibited, robust, and wide-open" debate—might expect this Court to celebrate, or at least not to interfere with, the second State's success. But today, the majority holds that the second State's system—the system that produces honest government, working on behalf of all the people—clashes with our Constitution. The First Amendment, the majority insists, requires us all to rely on the measures employed in the first State, even when they have failed to break the stranglehold of special interests on elected officials.

I disagree. The First Amendment's core purpose is to foster a healthy, vibrant political system full of robust discussion and debate. Nothing in Arizona's anti-corruption statute, the Arizona Citizens Clean Elections Act, violates this constitutional protection. To the contrary, the Act promotes the values underlying both the First Amendment and our entire Constitution by enhancing the "opportunity for free political discussion to the end that government may be responsive to the will of the people." I therefore respectfully dissent.

I

Public financing of elections has emerged as a potentially potent mechanism to preserve elected officials' independence. By supplanting private cash in elections, public financing eliminates the source of political corruption. For this reason, public financing systems today dot the national landscape. Almost one-third of the States have adopted some form of public financing, and so too has the Federal Government for presidential elections.

But [the] model which distributes a lump-sum grant at the beginning of an election cycle has a significant weakness: It lacks a mechanism for setting the subsidy at a level that will give candidates sufficient incentive to participate, while also conserving public resources. Public financing can achieve its goals only if a meaningful number of candidates receive the state subsidy, rather than raise private funds. And candidates will choose to sign up only if the subsidy provided enables them to run competitive races.

The difficulty, then, is in finding the Goldilocks solution—not too large, not too small, but just right. And this in a world of countless variables—where the amount of money needed to run a viable campaign against a privately funded candidate depends on, among other things, the district, the office, and the election cycle.

II

Arizona's statute does not impose a "restriction," or "substantia[l] burde[n]," on expression. The law has quite the opposite effect: It subsidizes and so produces *more* political speech. We recognized in *Buckley* that, for this reason, public financing of elections "facilitate[s] and enlarge[s] public discussion," in support of First Amendment values. And what we said then is just as true today. Except in a world gone topsy-turvy, additional campaign speech and electoral competition is not a First Amendment injury.

At every turn, the majority tries to convey the impression that Arizona's matching fund statute is of a piece with laws prohibiting electoral speech. The majority invokes the language of "limits," "bar[s]," and "restraints." It equates the law to a "acilitate[n] on the amount of money a person or group can spend on political communication during a campaign." It insists that the statute "restrict[s] the speech of some elements of our society" to enhance the speech of others. And it concludes by reminding us that the point of the First Amendment is to protect "against unjustified government restrictions on speech."

There is just one problem. Arizona's matching funds provision does not restrict, but instead subsidizes, speech. The law "impose[s] no ceiling on [speech] and do[es] not prevent anyone from speaking." The statute does not tell candidates or their supporters how much money they can spend to convey their message, when they can spend it, or what they can spend it on. Rather, the Arizona law, like the public financing statute in *Buckley*, provides funding for political speech, thus "facilitat[ing] communication by candidates with the electorate." By enabling participating candidates to respond to their opponents' expression, the statute expands public debate, in adherence to "our tradition that more speech, not less, is the governing rule." What the law does—all the law does—is fund more speech.

This case arose because Arizonans wanted their government to work on behalf of all the State's people. On the heels of a political scandal involving the near-routine purchase of legislators' votes, Arizonans passed a law designed to sever political candidates' dependence on large contributors. They wished, as many of their fellow Americans wish, to stop corrupt dealing—to ensure that their representatives serve the public, and not just the wealthy donors who helped put them in office. The legislation that Arizona's voters enacted was the product of deep thought and care. It put into effect a public financing system that attracted large numbers of candidates at a sustainable cost to the State's taxpayers. The system discriminated against no ideas and prevented no speech. Indeed, by increasing electoral competition and enabling a wide range of candidates to express their views, the system "further[ed] . . . First Amendment values." Less corruption, more speech. Robust campaigns leading to the election of representatives not beholden to the few, but accountable to the many. The people of Arizona might have expected a decent respect for those objectives.

Today, they do not get it. No precedent compels the Court to take this step; to the contrary, today's decision is in tension with broad swaths of our First Amendment doctrine. No fundamental principle of our Constitution backs the Court's ruling; to the contrary, it is the law struck down today that fostered both the vigorous competition of ideas and its ultimate object—a government responsive to the will of the people. Arizonans deserve better. Like citizens across this country, Arizonans deserve a government that represents and serves them all. And no less, Arizonans deserve the chance to reform their electoral system so as to attain that most American of goals.

Truly, democracy is not a game. I respectfully dissent.

CHAPTER 4

WHAT PLACES ARE AVAILABLE FOR SPEECH?

Speech often requires a place for it to occur. Most people lack access to the mass media—television, radio, newspapers—to express their message. They need to have a place to distribute leaflets or a corner to place a soapbox. Moreover, some types of expression require a larger area than a private person is likely to own. A protest rally or demonstration is an important way of attracting public attention and communicating that a large group shares a sentiment. Indeed, such activity is a form of "assembly" expressly protected by the First Amendment.

Thus, the issue arises as to what property is available for speech. Most of these cases involve claims of a right to use government property for speech purposes. The Court has dealt with this issue by identifying different types of government property—public forums, designated public forus, limited public forums, and nonpublic forums—and by articulating different rules as to when the government can regulate each. These cases are discussed in section A.

There have been claims of a right to use private property for speech, especially privately owned shopping centers. After an initial decision in the other direction, it is now clearly established that there generally is no right to use private property for speech purposes. Because such property is privately owned, there is no state action, and the Constitution does not apply. These cases are briefly reviewed in section B below.

Finally, the identity of the places is sometimes relevant in another sense. The Supreme Court has treated speech in some government places differently based on the need for greater government control. These are authoritarian environments such as the military, prisons, and schools. Although the juxtaposition of these three places may seem odd, in each the Court has expressed a need for great deference to the government based on a need for deference to authority. These cases are discussed in section C.

A. GOVERNMENT PROPERTIES AND SPEECH

1. Initial Rejection and Subsequent Recognition of a Right to Use Government Property for Speech

Initially, the courts rejected any claim of a right to use government property for speech purposes. In Davis v. Massachusetts, 167 U.S. 43 (1897), the Supreme

Court upheld a Boston ordinance that prohibited "any public address" on publicly owned property "except in accordance with a permit from the mayor." The Supreme Court affirmed a decision of the Massachusetts Supreme Judicial Court that found the ordinance constitutional. Oliver Wendell Holmes, then a justice on the Massachusetts Court, concluded that the law was permissible because the government has the right to control the use of its property. Holmes wrote that for "the Legislature absolutely or conditionally to forbid public speaking in a highway or public park is no more an infringement of the rights of a member of the public than for the owner of a private house to forbid it in his house."

The U.S. Supreme Court affirmed and also spoke broadly of the government's ability to restrict the use of its property. The Court explained that the government's "right to exclude all right to use, necessarily includes the authority to determine under what circumstances such use may be availed of, as the greater power contains the lesser." The Court refused to recognize any First Amendment right to use government property for speech purposes.

Although occasionally the Supreme Court still speaks in terms of the government's ability to control its property however it wishes, including by prohibiting speech,[1] for the last half century the Court has recognized a right to use at least some government property under some circumstances for speech. Hague v. CIO and Schneider v. State, both decided in 1939, were crucial in recognizing this right.

HAGUE v. COMMITTEE FOR INDUSTRIAL ORGANIZATION
307 U.S. 496 (1939)

Justice ROBERTS delivered an opinion.

After trial upon the merits the District Court entered findings of fact and conclusions of law and a decree in favor of respondents. In brief, the court found that the purposes of respondents, were the organization of unorganized workers into labor unions, causing such unions to exercise the normal and legal functions of labor organizations, such as collective bargaining with respect to the betterment of wages, hours of work and other terms and conditions of employment, and that these purposes were lawful; that the petitioners, acting in their official capacities, have adopted and enforced the deliberate policy of excluding and removing from Jersey City the agents of the respondents; have interfered with their right of passage upon the streets and access to the parks of the city; that these ends have been accomplished by force and violence despite the fact that the persons affected were acting in an orderly and peaceful manner; that exclusion, removal, personal restraint and interference, by force and violence, is accomplished without authority of law and without promptly bringing the persons taken into custody before a judicial officer for hearing.

The court further found that the petitioners, as officials, acting in reliance on the ordinance dealing with the subject, have adopted and enforced a deliberate policy of preventing the respondents, and their associates, from distributing

---

1. *See, e.g.*, Adderley v. Florida, 385 U.S. 39 (1966) ("The State, no less than a private owner of property, has power to preserve the property under its control for the use to which it is lawfully dedicated.").

circulars, leaflets, or handbills in Jersey City; that this has been done by policemen acting forcibly and violently; that the petitioners propose to continue to enforce the policy of such prevention; that the circulars and handbills, distribution of which has been prevented, were not offensive to public morals, and did not advocate unlawful conduct, but were germane to the purposes alleged in the bill, and that their distribution was being carried out in a way consistent with public order and without molestation of individuals or misuse or littering of the streets. Similar findings were made with respect to the prevention of the distribution of placards.

We have no occasion to determine whether, on the facts disclosed, Davis v. Massachusetts was rightly decided, but we cannot agree that it rules the instant case. Wherever the title of streets and parks may rest, they have immemorially been held in trust for the use of the public and, time out of mind, have been used for purposes of assembly, communicating thoughts between citizens, and discussing public questions. Such use of the streets and public places has, from ancient times, been a part of the privileges, immunities, rights, and liberties of citizens. The privilege of a citizen of the United States to use the streets and parks for communication of views on national questions may be regulated in the interest of all; it is not absolute, but relative, and must be exercised in subordination to the general comfort and convenience, and in consonance with peace and good order; but it must not, in the guise of regulation, be abridged or denied.

We think the court below was right in holding the ordinance void upon its face. It does not make comfort or convenience in the use of streets or parks the standard of official action. It enables the Director of Safety to refuse a permit on his mere opinion that such refusal will prevent "riots, disturbances or disorderly assemblage." It can thus, as the record discloses, be made the instrument of arbitrary suppression of free expression of views on national affairs for the prohibition of all speaking will undoubtedly "prevent" such eventualities. But uncontrolled official suppression of the privilege cannot be made a substitute for the duty to maintain order in connection with the exercise of the right.

SCHNEIDER v. NEW JERSEY
308 U.S. 147 (1939)

Justice ROBERTS delivered the opinion of the Court.

The Municipal Code of the City of Los Angeles, 1936, provides: "Sec. 28.00. 'Hand-Bill' shall mean any hand-bill, dodger, commercial advertising circular, folder, booklet, letter, card, pamphlet, sheet, poster, sticker, banner, notice or other written, printed or painted matter calculated to attract attention of the public." "Sec. 2801. No person shall distribute any hand-bill to or among pedestrians along or upon any street, sidewalk or park, or to passengers on any street car, or, or throw, place or attach any hand-bill in, to or upon any automobile or other vehicle." The handbill which the appellant was distributing bore a notice of a meeting to be held under the auspices of "Friends Lincoln Brigade" at which speakers would discuss the war in Spain.

An ordinance of the City of Milwaukee, Wisconsin, provides: "It is hereby made unlawful for any person . . . to . . . throw . . . paper . . . or to circulate or distribute any circular, hand-bills, cards, posters, dodgers, or other printed or advertising matter . . . in or upon any sidewalk, street, alley, wharf, boat landing, dock or other public place, park or ground within the City of Milwaukee." The petitioner, who was acting as a picket, stood in the street in front of a meat market and distributed to passing pedestrians hand-bills which pertained to a labor dispute with the meat market, set forth the position of organized labor with respect to the market, and asked citizens to refrain from patronizing it. Some of the bills were thrown in the street by the persons to whom they were given and it resulted that many of the papers lay in the gutter and in the street. The police officers who arrested the petitioner and charged him with a violation of the ordinance did not arrest any of those who received the bills and threw them away.

An ordinance of the Town of Irvington, New Jersey, provides: "No person except as in this ordinance provided shall canvass, solicit, distribute circulars, or other matter, or call from house to house in the Town of Irvington without first having reported to and received a written permit from the Chief of Police or the officer in charge of Police Headquarters." The petitioner was arrested and charged with canvassing without a permit. The proofs show that she is a member of the Watch Tower Bible and Tract Society and, as such, certified by the society to be one of "Jehovah's Witnesses." In this capacity she called from house to house in the town at all hours of the day and night and showed to the occupants a so called testimony and identification card signed by the society. The petitioner was convicted in the Recorder's Court.

Although a municipality may enact regulations in the interest of the public safety, health, welfare or convenience, these may not abridge the individual liberties secured by the Constitution to those who wish to speak, write, print or circulate information or opinion. Municipal authorities, as trustees for the public, have the duty to keep their communities' streets open and available for movement of people and property, the primary purpose to which the streets are dedicated. So long as legislation to this end does not abridge the constitutional liberty of one rightfully upon the street to impart information through speech or the distribution of literature, it may lawfully regulate the conduct of those using the streets. For example, a person could not exercise this liberty by taking his stand in the middle of a crowded street, contrary to traffic regulations, and maintain his position to the stoppage of all traffic; a group of distributors could not insist upon a constitutional right to form a cordon across the street and to allow no pedestrian to pass who did not accept a tendered leaflet; nor does the guarantee of freedom of speech or of the press deprive a municipality of power to enact regulations against throwing literature broadcast in the streets. Prohibition of such conduct would not abridge the constitutional liberty since such activity bears no necessary relationship to the freedom to speak, write, print or distribute information or opinion.

This court has characterized the freedom of speech and that of the press as fundamental personal rights and liberties. The phrase is not an empty one and was not lightly used. It reflects the belief of the framers of the Constitution that exercise of the rights lies at the foundation of free government by free men. It stresses, as do many opinions of this court, the importance of preventing the restriction of enjoyment of these liberties.

The motive of the legislation under attack is held by the courts below to be the prevention of littering of the streets and, although the alleged offenders were not charged with themselves scattering paper in the streets, their convictions were sustained upon the theory that distribution by them encouraged or resulted in such littering. We are of opinion that the purpose to keep the streets clean and of good appearance is insufficient to justify an ordinance which prohibits a person rightfully on a public street from handing literature to one willing to receive it. Any burden imposed upon the city authorities in cleaning and caring for the streets as an indirect consequence of such distribution results from the constitutional protection of the freedom of speech and press. This constitutional protection does not deprive a city of all power to prevent street littering. There are obvious methods of preventing littering. Amongst these is the punishment of those who actually throw papers on the streets.

We are not to be taken as holding that commercial soliciting and canvassing may not be subjected to such regulation as the ordinance requires. Nor do we hold that the town may not fix reasonable hours when canvassing may be done by persons having such objects as the petitioner. Doubtless there are other features of such activities which may be regulated in the public interest without prior licensing or other invasion of constitutional liberty. We do hold, however, that the ordinance in question, as applied to the petitioner's conduct, is void.

2. What Government Property and Under What Circumstances?

Once a right to use government property for speech is recognized, the issue inevitably arises: What publicly owned property must be made available for speech and under what circumstances? For example, while *Hague* and *Schneider* recognize a presumptive right to use the sidewalks and the parks for speech purposes, there obviously would be problems with allowing speech in the middle of a courtroom during a trial or on the runways of a publicly owned airport or in the middle of a highway during rush hour.

The Court has dealt with this issue by classifying different types of government property and articulating varying rules for when speech in each can be regulated. A clear statement of these categories and the rules applied for each is in Perry Education Association v. Perry Local Educators' Association, 460 U.S. 37 (1983). The issue was whether it was permissible for a school to give the teachers' collective bargaining representative exclusive use of an interschool mail system in the district. A rival union wished to use the mail system and pointed to the fact that it was available to community groups, teachers, and the administration. The Court upheld the exclusion of the rival union from using the postal system and in doing so identified types of government property:

> The existence of a right of access to public property and the standard by which limitations upon such a right must be evaluated differ depending on the character of the property at issue.... In places which by long tradition or by government fiat have been devoted to assembly and debate, the rights of the state to limit expressive activity are sharply circumscribed ... [such as] streets and parks.... In these quintessential public forums, the government may not prohibit all communicative activity. For the state to enforce a content-based exclusion it must show that its regulation is necessary to serve a compelling state interest and is narrowly drawn to achieve that end.... A second category consists of public property which the state has voluntarily opened for use by the public as a place for expressive activity.... Although a state is not required to indefinitely retain the open character of the facility, as long as it does so it is bound by the same

standards as apply in a traditional public forum. . . . Public property which is not by tradition or designation a forum for public communication is governed by different standards. . . . [T]he state may reserve the forum for its intended purposes, communicative or otherwise, as long as the regulation on speech is reasonable and not an effort to suppress expression merely because public officials oppose the speakers' views.[2]

Thus, under *Perry* the constitutionality of a regulation of speech depends on the place and the nature of the government's action. In Christian Legal Society v. Martinez, 561 U.S. 661 (2010), the Court also defined these categories. In a footnote, Justice Ginsburg, writing for the Court, stated:

In conducting forum analysis, our decisions have sorted government property into three categories. First, in traditional public forums, such as public streets and parks, "any restriction based on the content of . . . speech must satisfy strict scrutiny, that is, the restriction must be narrowly tailored to serve a compelling government interest." Second, governmental entities create designated public forums when "government property that has not traditionally been regarded as a public forum is intentionally opened up for that purpose"; speech restrictions in such a forum "are subject to the same strict scrutiny as restrictions in a traditional public forum." Third, governmental entities establish limited public forums by opening property "limited to use by certain groups or dedicated solely to the discussion of certain subjects." As noted in text, "[i]n such a forum, a governmental entity may impose restrictions on speech that are reasonable and viewpoint-neutral."

Interestingly, although prior cases speak of "nonpublic forums," government properties that the government can and does close to speech, this formulation does not mention them. In its most recent decision, Minnesota Voters Alliance v. Mansky, 138 S. Ct. 1876 (2018), the Court identified three types of government properties: public forums, designated public forums, and nonpublic forums. The Court stated:

[O]ur cases recognize three types of government-controlled spaces: traditional public forums, designated public forums, and nonpublic forums. In a traditional public forum—parks, streets, sidewalks, and the like—the government may impose reasonable time, place, and manner restrictions on private speech, but restrictions based on content must satisfy strict scrutiny, and those based on viewpoint are prohibited. The same standards apply in designated public forums—spaces that have "not traditionally been regarded as a public forum" but which the government has "intentionally opened up for that purpose." In a nonpublic forum, on the other hand—a space that "is not by tradition or designation a forum for public communication"—the government has much more flexibility to craft rules limiting speech. The government may reserve such a forum "for its intended purposes, communicative or otherwise, as long as the regulation on speech is reasonable and not an effort to suppress expression merely because public officials oppose the speaker's view."

Thus, it is clear that nonpublic forums are a category of government property, though *Mansky* does not mention limited public forums.

---

2. The Court found that the school mail system was a nonpublic forum and that the regulation was constitutional because it was reasonable and viewpoint neutral.

A. Government Properties and Speech

The presentation below focuses on the four types of government properties identified in these decisions: public forums, designated public forums, and limited public forums—and assumes that nonpublic forums remain a category as well. The constitutionality of a regulation of speech depends on the place and the nature of the government's action. The law concerning each of these types of forums is reviewed in turn below.

a. Public Forums

Public forums are government property that the government is constitutionally obligated to make available for speech. Sidewalks and parks are paradigm examples of the public forum. The government may regulate speech in public forums only if certain requirements are met. First, the regulation must be content-neutral unless the government can justify a content-based restriction by meeting strict scrutiny. Second, it must be a reasonable time, place, or manner restriction that serves an important government interest and leaves open adequate alternative places for speech. Third, a licensing or permit system for the use of public forums must serve an important purpose, give clear criteria to the licensing authority that leaves almost no discretion, and provide procedural safeguards such as a requirement for prompt determination of license requests and judicial review of license denials. Finally, the Court has ruled that government regulation of speech in public forums need not use the least restrictive alternative, although they must be narrowly tailored to achieve the government's purpose. Each of these requirements is discussed in turn.

i. *Content Neutrality*

The general requirement that the government be content-neutral when regulating speech is discussed above in Chapter 2. The Court has specifically ruled, as in *Perry* quoted above, that government regulation of speech in public forums must be content-neutral. At a minimum, this means that the government cannot regulate speech based on its viewpoint or its subject matter unless strict scrutiny is met.[3]

POLICE DEPARTMENT OF THE CITY OF CHICAGO v. MOSLEY
408 U.S. 92 (1972)

Justice MARSHALL delivered the opinion of the Court.

The city of Chicago exempts peaceful labor picketing from its general prohibition on picketing next to a school. The question we consider here is whether this selective exclusion from a public place is permitted. Our answer is "No."

The suit was brought by Earl Mosley, a federal postal employee, who for seven months prior to the enactment of the ordinance had frequently picketed

---

3. *See, e.g.*, Niemotko v. Maryland, 340 U.S. 268 (1951) (declaring it unconstitutional for a city to deny Jehovah's Witnesses a permit to use a city park when other religious and political groups were able to do so).

Jones Commercial High School in Chicago. During school hours and usually by himself, Mosley would walk the public sidewalk adjoining the school, carrying a sign that read: "Jones High School practices black discrimination. Jones High School has a black quota." His lonely crusade was always peaceful, orderly, and quiet, and was conceded to be so by the city of Chicago.

Because Chicago treats some picketing differently from others, we analyze this ordinance in terms of the Equal Protection Clause of the Fourteenth Amendment. Of course, the equal protection claim in this case is closely intertwined with First Amendment interests; the Chicago ordinance affects picketing, which is expressive conduct; moreover, it does so by classifications formulated in terms of the subject of the picketing.

The central problem with Chicago's ordinance is that it describes permissible picketing in terms of its subject matter. Peaceful picketing on the subject of a school's labor-management dispute is permitted, but all other peaceful picketing is prohibited. The operative distinction is the message on a picket sign. But, above all else, the First Amendment means that government has no power to restrict expression because of its message, its ideas, its subject matter, or its content.

To permit the continued building of our politics and culture, and to assure self-fulfillment for each individual, our people are guaranteed the right to express any thought, free from government censorship. The essence of this forbidden censorship is content control. Any restriction on expressive activity because of its content would completely undercut the "profound national commitment to the principle that debate on public issues should be uninhibited, robust, and wide-open."

Necessarily, then, under the Equal Protection Clause, not to mention the First Amendment itself, government may not grant the use of a forum to people whose views it finds acceptable, but deny use to those wishing to express less favored or more controversial views. And it may not select which issues are worth discussing or debating in public facilities. Once a forum is opened up to assembly or speaking by some groups, government may not prohibit others from assembling or speaking on the basis of what they intend to say. Selective exclusions from a public forum may not be based on content alone, and may not be justified by reference to content alone.

This is not to say that all picketing must always be allowed. We have continually recognized that reasonable "time, place and manner" regulations of picketing may be necessary to further significant governmental interests. Similarly, under an equal protection analysis, there may be sufficient regulatory interests justifying selective exclusions or distinctions among pickets. Conflicting demands on the same place may compel the State to make choices among potential users and uses. And the State may have a legitimate interest in prohibiting some picketing to protect public order. But these justifications for selective exclusions from a public forum must be carefully scrutinized. Because picketing plainly involves expressive conduct within the protection of the First Amendment, discriminations among pickets must be tailored to serve a substantial governmental interest.

In this case, the ordinance itself describes impermissible picketing not in terms of time, place, and manner, but in terms of subject matter. The regulation "thus slip[s] from the neutrality of time, place, and circumstance into a concern about content." This is never permitted.

Similarly, in Carey v. Brown, 447 U.S. 455 (1980), the Supreme Court declared unconstitutional an Illinois statute that prohibited picketing or demonstrations in or around a person's residence unless the dwelling is used as a place of business or is a place of employment involved in a labor dispute. In other words, under the law, picketing in residential neighborhoods was allowed if it was a labor dispute connected to a place of employment, but otherwise generally speech was prohibited. The Court again applied equal protection and found the law unconstitutional. The Court applied *Mosley* and concluded, "[The] Act accords preferential treatment to the expression of views on one particular subject; information about labor disputes may be freely disseminated, but discussion of all other issues is restricted. When government discriminates among speech-related activities in a public forum, the Equal Protection Clause mandates that the legislation be finely tailored to serve substantial interests, and the justifications offered for and distinctions its draws must be carefully scrutinized."

In contrast, the Court has upheld ordinances that prohibited focused picketing at persons' homes when the laws are completely subject-matter-neutral. In Frisby v. Schultz, 487 U.S. 474 (1988), the Court upheld an ordinance that prohibited picketing "before or about" any residence. Although the law was adopted in response to targeted picketing by anti-abortion protestors of a doctor's home, the Court concluded that the law was permissible because it was content-neutral and it was narrowly tailored to protect people's tranquility and repose in their homes. The Court stressed that the ordinance allowed picketing in the area and even on the street, but just not targeted at one person's home. Justice O'Connor, writing for the Court, said that "[t]he First Amendment permits the government to prohibit offensive speech as intrusive when the 'captive' audience cannot avoid the objectionable speech. The target of the focused picketing banned by the . . . ordinance is just such a 'captive.' The resident is figuratively, and perhaps literally, trapped within the home."

Whether the analysis is under equal protection or solely under the First Amendment does not matter. The government cannot regulate speech in a public forum based on the viewpoint or subject matter of the speech unless it meets strict scrutiny. Although history shows that strict scrutiny is rarely met, occasionally the Court finds that the test is satisfied. For example, in Burson v. Freeman, 504 U.S. 191 (1992), the Court found that there was a content-based regulation, used strict scrutiny, and upheld a federal law that prohibited distribution of campaign literature within 100 feet of the entrance of a polling place. The Court said that the history of campaign workers intimidating voters around polling places created a compelling interest sufficient to justify content-based restrictions of speech.[4]

ii. *Time, Place, and Manner Restrictions*

The concept of "time, place, and manner restrictions" is often uttered in connection with the First Amendment. It refers to the ability of the government

---

4. But in Minnesota Voters Alliance v. Mansky, 138 S. Ct. 1876 (2018), discussed above, the Court struck down a state law that prohibited wearing political apparel in polling places on the grounds that the law is unduly vague and thus not reasonable.

to regulate speech in a public forum in a manner that minimizes disruption of a public place while still protecting freedom of speech. In Heffron v. International Society for Krishna Consciousness, 452 U.S. 640 (1981), the Court said that it had often approved reasonable time, place, and manner restrictions "provided that they are justified without regard to the content of the regulated speech, that they serve a significant government interest, and that they leave open ample alternative channels for communication of the information."

In *Heffron*, the Supreme Court upheld a regulation of speech at the Minnesota State Fair that prohibited the distribution of literature or the soliciting of funds except at booths. Booths were available on a first-come, first-served basis. The Court said that the regulation was content-neutral because it applied to all literature and solicitations regardless of the speaker, viewpoint, or subject matter. The Court accepted the state's argument that the regulation was justified by an important interest: regulating the flow of pedestrian traffic through the state fair grounds. The Court said the need for crowd control was "sufficient to satisfy the requirement that a place or manner restriction must serve a substantial state interest." The Court also observed that the Krishna had other ways of reaching the audience, both off the fair grounds and at booths within the grounds.

Two important cases—Hill v. Colorado and McCullen v. Coakley—have considered time, place, and manner restrictions in the context of laws designed to limit protests around reproductive health care facilities. The former upheld a law; the latter struck it down. In each there are sharp disagreements as to whether the law involved is content-neutral.

HILL v. COLORADO
530 U.S. 703 (2000)

Justice STEVENS delivered the opinion of the Court.

At issue is the constitutionality of a 1993 Colorado statute that regulates speech-related conduct within 100 feet of the entrance to any health care facility. The specific section of the statute that is challenged, makes it unlawful within the regulated areas for any person to "knowingly approach" within eight feet of another person, without that person's consent, "for the purpose of passing a leaflet or handbill to, displaying a sign to, or engaging in oral protest, education, or counseling with such other person. . . ." Although the statute prohibits speakers from approaching unwilling listeners, it does not require a standing speaker to move away from anyone passing by. Nor does it place any restriction on the content of any message that anyone may wish to communicate to anyone else, either inside or outside the regulated areas. It does, however, make it more difficult to give unwanted advice, particularly in the form of a handbill or leaflet, to persons entering or leaving medical facilities.

The question is whether the First Amendment rights of the speaker are abridged by the protection the statute provides for the unwilling listener.

I

Five months after the statute was enacted, petitioners filed a complaint in the District Court for Jefferson County, Colorado, praying for a declaration that §18-9-122(3) was facially invalid and seeking an injunction against its enforcement. They stated that prior to the enactment of the statute, they had engaged in "sidewalk counseling" on the public ways and sidewalks within 100 feet of the entrances to facilities where human abortion is practiced or where medical personnel refer women to other facilities for abortions. "Sidewalk counseling" consists of efforts "to educate, counsel, persuade, or inform passersby about abortion and abortion alternatives by means of verbal or written speech, including conversation and/or display of signs and/or distribution of literature." They further alleged that such activities frequently entail being within eight feet of other persons and that their fear of prosecution under the new statute caused them "to be chilled in the exercise of fundamental constitutional rights."

II

Before confronting the question whether the Colorado statute reflects an acceptable balance between the constitutionally protected rights of law-abiding speakers and the interests of unwilling listeners, it is appropriate to examine the competing interests at stake.

The First Amendment interests of petitioners are clear and undisputed. [T]hey correctly state that their leafletting, sign displays, and oral communications are protected by the First Amendment. The fact that the messages conveyed by those communications may be offensive to their recipients does not deprive them of constitutional protection. [T]he public sidewalks, streets, and ways affected by the statute are "quintessential" public forums for free speech. [A]lthough there is debate about the magnitude of the statutory impediment to their ability to communicate effectively with persons in the regulated zones, that ability, particularly the ability to distribute leaflets, is unquestionably lessened by this statute.

On the other hand, petitioners do not challenge the legitimacy of the state interests that the statute is intended to serve. It is a traditional exercise of the States' "police powers to protect the health and safety of their citizens." That interest may justify a special focus on unimpeded access to health care facilities and the avoidance of potential trauma to patients associated with confrontational protests. See Madsen v. Women's Health Center, Inc. (1994). It is also important when conducting this interest analysis to recognize the significant difference between state restrictions on a speaker's right to address a willing audience and those that protect listeners from unwanted communication. This statute deals only with the latter. The right to free speech, of course, includes the right to attempt to persuade others to change their views, and may not be curtailed simply because the speaker's message may be offensive to his audience. But the protection afforded to offensive messages does not always embrace offensive speech that is so intrusive that the unwilling audience cannot avoid it. Frisby v. Schultz (1988). The unwilling listener's interest in avoiding unwanted communication has been repeatedly identified in our cases. It is an aspect of the broader "right to be let alone" that one of our wisest Justices characterized as "the most comprehensive of rights and the right most valued by civilized men." Olmstead v. United States (1928) (Brandeis, J., dissenting).

III

All four of the state court opinions upholding the validity of this statute concluded that it is a content-neutral time, place, and manner regulation. It is therefore appropriate to comment on the "content neutrality" of the statute. The Colorado statute passes that test for three independent reasons. First, it is not a "regulation of speech." Rather, it is a regulation of the places where some speech may occur. Second, it was not adopted "because of disagreement with the message it conveys." This conclusion is supported not just by the Colorado courts' interpretation of legislative history, but more importantly by the State Supreme Court's unequivocal holding that the statute's "restrictions apply equally to all demonstrators, regardless of viewpoint, and the statutory language makes no reference to the content of the speech." Third, the State's interests in protecting access and privacy, and providing the police with clear guidelines, are unrelated to the content of the demonstrators' speech. As we have repeatedly explained, government regulation of expressive activity is "content neutral" if it is justified without reference to the content of regulated speech.

The Colorado statute's regulation of the location of protests, education, and counseling places no restrictions on—and clearly does not prohibit—either a particular viewpoint or any subject matter that may be discussed by a speaker. Rather, it simply establishes a minor place restriction on an extremely broad category of communications with unwilling listeners. Instead of drawing distinctions based on the subject that the approaching speaker may wish to address, the statute applies equally to used car salesmen, animal rights activists, fundraisers, environmentalists, and missionaries. Each can attempt to educate unwilling listeners on any subject, but without consent may not approach within eight feet to do so.

We also agree with the state courts' conclusion that [the law] is a valid time, place, and manner regulation. The three types of communication regulated by §18-9-122(3) are the display of signs, leafletting, and oral speech. The 8-foot separation between the speaker and the audience should not have any adverse impact on the readers' ability to read signs displayed by demonstrators. In fact, the separation might actually aid the pedestrians' ability to see the signs by preventing others from surrounding them and impeding their view. Furthermore, the statute places no limitations on the number, size, text, or images of the placards.

With respect to oral statements, the distance certainly can make it more difficult for a speaker to be heard, particularly if the level of background noise is high and other speakers are competing for the pedestrian's attention. Notably, the statute places no limitation on the number of speakers or the noise level, including the use of amplification equipment, although we have upheld such restrictions in past cases. [T]his 8-foot zone allows the speaker to communicate at a "normal conversational distance." Additionally, the statute allows the speaker to remain in one place, and other individuals can pass within eight feet of the protester without causing the protester to violate the statute. Finally, here there is a "knowing" requirement that protects speakers "who thought they were keeping pace with the targeted individual" at the proscribed distance from inadvertently violating the statute.

The burden on the ability to distribute handbills is more serious because it seems possible that an 8-foot interval could hinder the ability of a leafletter to

A. Government Properties and Speech

deliver handbills to some unwilling recipients. The statute does not, however, prevent a leafletter from simply standing near the path of oncoming pedestrians and proffering his or her material, which the pedestrians can easily accept. And, as in all leafletting situations, pedestrians continue to be free to decline the tender.

Finally, in determining whether a statute is narrowly tailored, we have noted that "[w]e must, of course, take account of the place to which the regulations apply in determining whether these restrictions burden more speech than necessary." States and municipalities plainly have a substantial interest in controlling the activity around certain public and private places. For example, we have recognized the special governmental interests surrounding schools, courthouses, polling places, and private homes. Additionally, we previously have noted the unique concerns that surround health care facilities. Persons who are attempting to enter health care facilities—for any purpose—are often in particularly vulnerable physical and emotional conditions. The State of Colorado has responded to its substantial and legitimate interest in protecting these persons from unwanted encounters, confrontations, and even assaults by enacting an exceedingly modest restriction on the speakers' ability to approach. This restriction is thus reasonable and narrowly tailored.

Justice SCALIA, with whom Justice THOMAS joins, dissenting.

What is before us is a speech regulation directed against the opponents of abortion, and it therefore enjoys the benefit of the "ad hoc nullification machine" that the Court has set in motion to push aside whatever doctrines of constitutional law stand in the way of that highly favored practice. Having deprived abortion opponents of the political right to persuade the electorate that abortion should be restricted by law, the Court today continues and expands its assault upon their individual right to persuade women contemplating abortion that what they are doing is wrong. Because, like the rest of our abortion jurisprudence, today's decision is in stark contradiction of the constitutional principles we apply in all other contexts, I dissent.

I have no doubt that this regulation would be deemed content-based in an instant if the case before us involved antiwar protesters, or union members seeking to "educate" the public about the reasons for their strike. "[I]t is," we would say, "the content of the speech that determines whether it is within or without the statute's blunt prohibition," Carey v. Brown (1980). But the jurisprudence of this Court has a way of changing when abortion is involved.

The Court asserts that this statute is not content-based for purposes of our First Amendment analysis because it neither (1) discriminates among viewpoints nor (2) places restrictions on "any subject matter that may be discussed by a speaker." But we have never held that the universe of content-based regulations is limited to those two categories, and such a holding would be absurd. Imagine, for instance, special place-and-manner restrictions on all speech except that which "conveys a sense of contentment or happiness." This "happy speech" limitation would not be "viewpoint-based"—citizens would be able to express their joy in equal measure at either the rise or fall of the NASDAQ, at either the success or the failure of the Republican Party—and would not discriminate on the basis of subject matter, since gratification could be expressed about anything at all. Or consider a law restricting the writing or recitation of poetry—neither viewpoint-based nor limited to any particular subject matter. Surely this Court would consider such regulations to be "content-based" and deserving of the most exacting scrutiny.

A restriction that operates only on speech that communicates a message of protest, education, or counseling presents exactly this risk. When applied, as it is here, at the entrance to medical facilities, it is a means of impeding speech against abortion. The Court's confident assurance that the statute poses no special threat to First Amendment freedoms because it applies alike to "used car salesmen, animal rights activists, fundraisers, environmentalists, and missionaries," is a wonderful replication (except for its lack of sarcasm) of Anatole France's observation that "[t]he law, in its majestic equality, forbids the rich as well as the poor to sleep under bridges. . . ." This Colorado law is no more targeted at used car salesmen, animal rights activists, fund raisers, environmentalists, and missionaries than French vagrancy law was targeted at the rich. We know what the Colorado legislators, by their careful selection of content ("protest, education, and counseling"), were taking aim at, for they set it forth in the statute itself: the "right to protest or counsel against certain medical procedures" on the sidewalks and streets surrounding health care facilities.

In sum, it blinks reality to regard this statute, in its application to oral communications, as anything other than a content-based restriction upon speech in the public forum. As such, it must survive that stringent mode of constitutional analysis our cases refer to as "strict scrutiny," which requires that the restriction be narrowly tailored to serve a compelling state interest. Since the Court does not even attempt to support the regulation under this standard, I shall discuss it only briefly. Suffice it to say that if protecting people from unwelcome communications (the governmental interest the Court posits) is a compelling state interest, the First Amendment is a dead letter. And if forbidding peaceful, nonthreatening, but uninvited speech from a distance closer than eight feet is a "narrowly tailored" means of preventing the obstruction of entrance to medical facilities (the governmental interest the State asserts) narrow tailoring must refer not to the standards of Versace, but to those of Omar the tentmaker. In the last analysis all of this does not matter, however, since as I proceed to discuss neither the restrictions upon oral communications nor those upon handbilling can withstand a proper application of even the less demanding scrutiny we apply to truly content-neutral regulations of speech in a traditional public forum.

Does the deck seem stacked? You bet. As I have suggested throughout this opinion, today's decision is not an isolated distortion of our traditional constitutional principles, but is one of many aggressively proabortion novelties announced by the Court in recent years. Today's distortions, however, are particularly blatant. Restrictive views of the First Amendment that have been in dissent since the 1930's suddenly find themselves in the majority. "Uninhibited, robust, and wide open" debate is replaced by the power of the state to protect an unheard-of "right to be let alone" on the public streets. I dissent.

Justice KENNEDY, dissenting.

The Court's holding contradicts more than a half century of well-established First Amendment principles. For the first time, the Court approves a law which bars a private citizen from passing a message, in a peaceful manner and on a profound moral issue, to a fellow citizen on a public sidewalk. If from this time forward the Court repeats its grave errors of analysis, we shall have no longer the proud tradition of free and open discourse in a public forum.

The statute is content based: It restricts speech on particular topics. Of course, the enactment restricts "oral protest, education, or counselling" on any subject; but a statute of broad application is not content neutral if its terms control the substance of a speaker's message. If oral protest, education, or counseling on every subject within an 8-foot zone present a danger to the public, the statute should apply to every building entrance in the State. It does not. It applies only to a special class of locations: entrances to buildings with health care facilities. We would close our eyes to reality were we to deny that "oral protest, education, or counseling" outside the entrances to medical facilities concern a narrow range of topics—indeed, one topic in particular. By confining the law's application to the specific locations where the prohibited discourse occurs, the State has made a content-based determination. The Court ought to so acknowledge. Clever content-based restrictions are no less offensive than censoring on the basis of content. If, just a few decades ago, a State with a history of enforcing racial discrimination had enacted a statute like this one, regulating "oral protest, education, or counseling" within 100 feet of the entrance to any lunch counter, our predecessors would not have hesitated to hold it was content based or viewpoint based. It should be a profound disappointment to defenders of the First Amendment that the Court today refuses to apply the same structural analysis when the speech involved is less palatable to it.

McCULLEN v. COAKLEY
573 U.S. 464 (2014)

Chief Justice ROBERTS delivered the opinion of the Court.

A Massachusetts statute makes it a crime to knowingly stand on a "public way or sidewalk" within 35 feet of an entrance or driveway to any place, other than a hospital, where abortions are performed. Petitioners are individuals who approach and talk to women outside such facilities, attempting to dissuade them from having abortions. The statute prevents petitioners from doing so near the facilities' entrances. The question presented is whether the statute violates the First Amendment.

I

In 2000, the Massachusetts Legislature enacted the Massachusetts Reproductive Health Care Facilities Act. The law was designed to address clashes between abortion opponents and advocates of abortion rights that were occurring outside clinics where abortions were performed. The Act established a defined area with an 18-foot radius around the entrances and driveways of such facilities. Anyone could enter that area, but once within it, no one (other than certain exempt individuals) could knowingly approach within six feet of another person—unless that person consented—"for the purpose of passing a leaflet or handbill to, displaying a sign to, or engaging in oral protest, education, or counseling with such other person." A separate provision subjected to criminal punishment anyone who "knowingly obstructs, detains, hinders, impedes or blocks another person's entry to or exit from a reproductive health care facility." The statute was modeled on a similar Colorado law that this Court had upheld in Hill v. Colorado (2000).

By 2007, some Massachusetts legislators and law enforcement officials had come to regard the 2000 statute as inadequate. At legislative hearings, multiple witnesses recounted apparent violations of the law. Massachusetts Attorney General Martha Coakley, for example, testified that protestors violated the statute "on a routine basis." To address these concerns, the Massachusetts Legislature amended the statute in 2007, replacing the six-foot no-approach zones (within the 18-foot area) with a 35-foot fixed buffer zone from which individuals are categorically excluded. The statute now provides:

> No person shall knowingly enter or remain on a public way or sidewalk adjacent to a reproductive health care facility within a radius of 35 feet of any portion of an entrance, exit or driveway of a reproductive health care facility or within the area within a rectangle created by extending the outside boundaries of any entrance, exit or driveway of a reproductive health care facility in straight lines to the point where such lines intersect the sideline of the street in front of such entrance, exit or driveway.

A "reproductive health care facility," in turn, is defined as "a place, other than within or upon the grounds of a hospital, where abortions are offered or performed." The 35-foot buffer zone applies only "during a facility's business hours," and the area must be "clearly marked and posted." In practice, facilities typically mark the zones with painted arcs and posted signs on adjacent sidewalks and streets.

The Act exempts four classes of individuals: (1) "persons entering or leaving such facility"; (2) "employees or agents of such facility acting within the scope of their employment"; (3) "law enforcement, ambulance, firefighting, construction, utilities, public works and other municipal agents acting within the scope of their employment"; and (4) "persons using the public sidewalk or street right-of-way adjacent to such facility solely for the purpose of reaching a destination other than such facility."

Some of the individuals who stand outside Massachusetts abortion clinics are fairly described as protestors, who express their moral or religious opposition to abortion through signs and chants or, in some cases, more aggressive methods such as face-to-face confrontation. Petitioners take a different tack. They attempt to engage women approaching the clinics in what they call "sidewalk counseling," which involves offering information about alternatives to abortion and help pursuing those options. In unrefuted testimony, petitioners say they have collectively persuaded hundreds of women to forgo abortions. The buffer zones have displaced petitioners from their previous positions outside the clinics.

II

By its very terms, the Massachusetts Act regulates access to "public way[s]" and "sidewalk[s]." Such areas occupy a "special position in terms of First

A. Government Properties and Speech

Amendment protection" because of their historic role as sites for discussion and debate. These places—which we have labeled "traditional public fora"—"have immemorially been held in trust for the use of the public and, time out of mind, have been used for purposes of assembly, communicating thoughts between citizens, and discussing public questions."

It is no accident that public streets and sidewalks have developed as venues for the exchange of ideas. Even today, they remain one of the few places where a speaker can be confident that he is not simply preaching to the choir. With respect to other means of communication, an individual confronted with an uncomfortable message can always turn the page, change the channel, or leave the Web site. Not so on public streets and sidewalks. There, a listener often encounters speech he might otherwise tune out. In light of the First Amendment's purpose "to preserve an uninhibited marketplace of ideas in which truth will ultimately prevail," this aspect of traditional public fora is a virtue, not a vice.

In short, traditional public fora are areas that have historically been open to the public for speech activities. Thus, even though the Act says nothing about speech on its face, there is no doubt—and respondents do not dispute—that it restricts access to traditional public fora and is therefore subject to First Amendment scrutiny.

Consistent with the traditionally open character of public streets and sidewalks, we have held that the government's ability to restrict speech in such locations is "very limited." In particular, the guiding First Amendment principle that the "government has no power to restrict expression because of its message, its ideas, its subject matter, or its content" applies with full force in a traditional public forum. As a general rule, in such a forum the government may not "selectively . . . shield the public from some kinds of speech on the ground that they are more offensive than others."

We have, however, afforded the government somewhat wider leeway to regulate features of speech unrelated to its content. "[E]ven in a public forum the government may impose reasonable restrictions on the time, place, or manner of protected speech, provided the restrictions are justified without reference to the content of the regulated speech, that they are narrowly tailored to serve a significant governmental interest, and that they leave open ample alternative channels for communication of the information."

While the parties agree that this test supplies the proper framework for assessing the constitutionality of the Massachusetts Act, they disagree about whether the Act satisfies the test's three requirements.

III

Petitioners contend that the Act is not content neutral for two independent reasons: First, they argue that it discriminates against abortion-related speech because it establishes buffer zones only at clinics that perform abortions. Second, petitioners contend that the Act, by exempting clinic employees and agents, favors one viewpoint about abortion over the other. If either of these arguments is correct, then the Act must satisfy strict scrutiny—that is, it must be the least restrictive means of achieving a compelling state interest.

The Act applies only at a "reproductive health care facility," defined as "a place, other than within or upon the grounds of a hospital, where abortions are offered or performed." Given this definition, petitioners argue, "virtually all speech affected by the Act is speech concerning abortion," thus rendering the Act content based.

We disagree. To begin, the Act does not draw content-based distinctions on its face. The Act would be content based if it required "enforcement authorities" to "examine the content of the message that is conveyed to determine whether" a violation has occurred. But it does not. Whether petitioners violate the Act "depends" not "on what they say," but simply on where they say it. Indeed, petitioners can violate the Act merely by standing in a buffer zone, without displaying a sign or uttering a word.

It is true, of course, that by limiting the buffer zones to abortion clinics, the Act has the "inevitable effect" of restricting abortion-related speech more than speech on other subjects. But a facially neutral law does not become content based simply because it may disproportionately affect speech on certain topics. On the contrary, "[a] regulation that serves purposes unrelated to the content of expression is deemed neutral, even if it has an incidental effect on some speakers or messages but not others." The question in such a case is whether the law is "justified without reference to the content of the regulated speech."

The Massachusetts Act is. Its stated purpose is to "increase forthwith public safety at reproductive health care facilities." Respondents have articulated similar purposes before this Court—namely, "public safety, patient access to healthcare, and the unobstructed use of public sidewalks and roadways." We have previously deemed the foregoing concerns to be content neutral.

Petitioners also argue that the Act is content based because it exempts four classes of individuals. This exemption, petitioners say, favors one side in the abortion debate and thus constitutes viewpoint discrimination-an "egregious form of content discrimination," In particular, petitioners argue that the exemption allows clinic employees and agents—including the volunteers who "escort" patients arriving at the Boston clinic—to speak inside the buffer zones.

It is of course true that "an exemption from an otherwise permissible regulation of speech may represent a governmental attempt to give one side of a debatable public question an advantage in expressing its views to the people." At least on the record before us, however, the statutory exemption for clinic employees and agents acting within the scope of their employment does not appear to be such an attempt.

There is nothing inherently suspect about providing some kind of exemption to allow individuals who work at the clinics to enter or remain within the buffer zones. In particular, the exemption cannot be regarded as simply a carve-out for the clinic escorts; it also covers employees such as the maintenance worker shoveling a snowy sidewalk or the security guard patrolling a clinic entrance. Given the need for an exemption for clinic employees, the "scope of their employment" qualification simply ensures that the exemption is limited to its purpose of allowing the employees to do their jobs.

It would be a very different question if it turned out that a clinic authorized escorts to speak about abortion inside the buffer zones. In that case, the escorts would not seem to be violating the Act because the speech would be within the scope of their employment. The Act's exemption for clinic employees would then facilitate speech on only one side of the abortion debate—a clear form of viewpoint discrimination that would support an as-applied challenge to the buffer zone at that clinic. But the record before us contains insufficient evidence

A. Government Properties and Speech 383

to show that the exemption operates in this way at any of the clinics, perhaps because the clinics do not want to doom the Act by allowing their employees to speak about abortion within the buffer zones.

We thus conclude that the Act is neither content nor view point based and therefore need not be analyzed under strict scrutiny.

IV

Even though the Act is content neutral, it still must be "narrowly tailored to serve a significant governmental interest." The tailoring requirement does not simply guard against an impermissible desire to censor. The government may attempt to suppress speech not only because it disagrees with the message being expressed, but also for mere convenience. Where certain speech is associated with particular problems, silencing the speech is sometimes the path of least resistance. But by demanding a close fit between ends and means, the tailoring requirement prevents the government from too readily "sacrific[ing] speech for efficiency."

For a content-neutral time, place, or manner regulation to be narrowly tailored, it must not "burden substantially more speech than is necessary to further the government's legitimate interests." Such a regulation, unlike a content-based restriction of speech, "need not be the least restrictive or least intrusive means of" serving the government's interests. But the government still "may not regulate expression in such a manner that a substantial portion of the burden on speech does not serve to advance its goals."

A

As noted, respondents claim that the Act promotes "public safety, patient access to healthcare, and the unobstructed use of public sidewalks and roadways." Petitioners do not dispute the significance of these interests.

At the same time, the buffer zones impose serious burdens on petitioners' speech. At each of the three Planned Parenthood clinics where petitioners attempt to counsel patients, the zones carve out a significant portion of the adjacent public sidewalks, pushing petitioners well back from the clinics' entrances and driveways. The zones thereby compromise petitioners' ability to initiate the close, personal conversations that they view as essential to "sidewalk counseling."

These burdens on petitioners' speech have clearly taken their toll. Although McCullen claims that she has persuaded about 80 women not to terminate their pregnancies since the 2007 amendment, she also says that she reaches "far fewer people" than she did before the amendment. Zarrella reports an even more precipitous decline in her success rate: She estimated having about 100 successful interactions over the years before the 2007 amendment, but not a single one since.

The buffer zones have also made it substantially more difficult for petitioners to distribute literature to arriving patients. In the context of petition campaigns, we have observed that "one-on-one communication" is "the most effective, fundamental, and perhaps economical avenue of political discourse."

Respondents also emphasize that the Act does not prevent petitioners from engaging in various forms of "protest"—such as chanting slogans and displaying signs—outside the buffer zones. That misses the point. Petitioners are not protestors. They seek not merely to express their opposition to abortion, but to inform women of various alternatives and to provide help in pursuing them. Petitioners believe that they can accomplish this objective only through personal, caring, consensual conversations. And for good reason: It is easier to ignore a strained voice or a waving hand than a direct greeting or an outstretched arm. If all that the women can see and hear are vociferous opponents of abortion, then the buffer zones have effectively stifled petitioners' message.

B

The buffer zones burden substantially more speech than necessary to achieve the Commonwealth's asserted interests. At the outset, we note that the Act is truly exceptional: Respondents and their *amici* identify no other State with a law that creates fixed buffer zones around abortion clinics. That of course does not mean that the law is invalid. It does, however, raise concern that the Commonwealth has too readily forgone options that could serve its interests just as well, without substantially burdening the kind of speech in which petitioners wish to engage.

That is the case here. The Commonwealth's interests include ensuring public safety outside abortion clinics, preventing harassment and intimidation of patients and clinic staff, and combating deliberate obstruction of clinic entrances. The Act itself contains a separate provision, subsection (e)—unchallenged by petitioners—that prohibits much of this conduct. That provision subjects to criminal punishment "[a]ny person who knowingly obstructs, detains, hinders, impedes or blocks another person's entry to or exit from a reproductive health care facility." If Massachusetts determines that broader prohibitions along the same lines are necessary, it could enact legislation similar to the federal Freedom of Access to Clinic Entrances Act of 1994 (FACE Act), which subjects to both criminal and civil penalties anyone who "by force or threat of force or by physical obstruction, intentionally injures, intimidates or interferes with or attempts to injure, intimidate or interfere with any person because that person is or has been, or in order to intimidate such person or any other person or any class of persons from, obtaining or providing reproductive health services." Some dozen other States have done so. If the Commonwealth is particularly concerned about harassment, it could also consider an ordinance such as the one adopted in New York City that not only prohibits obstructing access to a clinic, but also makes it a crime "to follow and harass another person within 15 feet of the premises of a reproductive health care facility."

All of the foregoing measures are, of course, in addition to available generic criminal statutes forbidding assault, breach of the peace, trespass, vandalism, and the like.

The point is not that Massachusetts must enact all or even any of the proposed measures discussed above. The point is instead that the Commonwealth has available to it a variety of approaches that appear capable of serving its interests, without excluding individuals from areas historically open for speech and debate.

Respondents have but one reply: "We have tried other approaches, but they do not work." Respondents emphasize the history in Massachusetts of obstruction at abortion clinics, and the Commonwealth's allegedly failed attempts to combat such obstruction with injunctions and individual prosecutions.

A. Government Properties and Speech

We cannot accept that contention. Although respondents claim that Massachusetts "tried other laws already on the books," they identify not a single prosecution brought under those laws within at least the last 17 years. And while they also claim that the Commonwealth "tried injunctions," the last injunctions they cite date to the 1990s. In short, the Commonwealth has not shown that it seriously undertook to address the problem with less intrusive tools readily available to it. Nor has it shown that it considered different methods that other jurisdictions have found effective.

Given the vital First Amendment interests at stake, it is not enough for Massachusetts simply to say that other approaches have not worked.

Petitioners wish to converse with their fellow citizens about an important subject on the public streets and sidewalks—sites that have hosted discussions about the issues of the day throughout history. Respondents assert undeniably significant interests in maintaining public safety on those same streets and sidewalks, as well as in preserving access to adjacent healthcare facilities. But here the Commonwealth has pursued those interests by the extreme step of closing a substantial portion of a traditional public forum to all speakers. It has done so without seriously addressing the problem through alternatives that leave the forum open for its time-honored purposes. The Commonwealth may not do that consistent with the First Amendment.

Justice SCALIA, with whom Justice KENNEDY and Justice THOMAS join, concurring in the judgment.

Today's opinion carries forward this Court's practice of giving abortion-rights advocates a pass when it comes to suppressing the free-speech rights of their opponents. There is an entirely separate, abridged edition of the First Amendment applicable to speech against abortion. *See, e.g.,* Hill v. Colorado (2000); Madsen v. Women's Health Center, Inc. (1994).

The second half of the Court's analysis today, invalidating the law at issue because of inadequate "tailoring," is certainly attractive to those of us who oppose an abortion-speech edition of the First Amendment. But think again. This is an opinion that has Something for Everyone, and the more significant portion continues the onward march of abortion-speech-only jurisprudence. That is the first half of the Court's analysis, which concludes that a statute of this sort is not content based and hence not subject to so-called strict scrutiny. The Court reaches out to decide that question unnecessarily—or at least unnecessarily insofar as legal analysis is concerned.

Having eagerly volunteered to take on the level-of-scrutiny question, the Court provides the wrong answer. Petitioners argue for two reasons that subsection (b) articulates a content-based speech restriction—and that we must therefore evaluate it through the lens of strict scrutiny.

A. APPLICATION TO ABORTION CLINICS ONLY

First, petitioners maintain that the Act targets abortion-related—for practical purposes, abortion-opposing—speech because it applies outside abortion clinics only (rather than outside other buildings as well).

It blinks reality to say, as the majority does, that a blanket prohibition on the use of streets and sidewalks where speech on only one politically controversial topic is likely to occur—and where that speech can most effectively be communicated—is not content based. Would the Court exempt from strict scrutiny a law banning access to the streets and sidewalks surrounding the site of the Republican National Convention? Or those used annually to commemorate the 1965 Selma-to-Montgomery civil rights marches? Or those outside the Internal Revenue Service? Surely not.

The majority says, correctly enough, that a facially neutral speech restriction escapes strict scrutiny, even when it "may disproportionately affect speech on certain topics," so long as it is "justified without reference to the content of the regulated speech." But the cases in which the Court has previously found that standard satisfied—in particular, both of which the majority cites—are a far cry from what confronts us here.

Renton upheld a zoning ordinance prohibiting adult motion-picture theaters within 1,000 feet of residential neighborhoods, churches, parks, and schools. The ordinance was content neutral, the Court held, because its purpose was not to suppress pornographic speech *qua* speech but, rather, to mitigate the "secondary effects" of adult theaters—including by "prevent[ing] crime, protect[ing] the city's retail trade, [and] maintain[ing] property values." *Ward*, in turn, involved a New York City regulation requiring the use of the city's own sound equipment and technician for events at a bandshell in Central Park. The Court held the regulation content neutral because its "principal justification [was] the city's desire to control noise levels," a justification that "'ha[d] nothing to do with [the] content'" of respondent's rock concerts or of music more generally. The regulation "ha[d] no material impact on any performer's ability to exercise complete artistic control over sound quality."

Compare these cases' reasons for concluding that the regulations in question were "justified without reference to the content of the regulated speech" with the feeble reasons for the majority's adoption of that conclusion in the present case. The majority points only to the statute's stated purpose of increasing "public safety" at abortion clinics, and to the additional aims articulated by respondents before this Court—namely, protecting "patient access to healthcare . . . and the unobstructed use of public sidewalks and roadways." Really? Does a statute become "justified without reference to the content of the regulated speech" simply because the statute itself and those defending it in court *say* that it is? Every objective indication shows that the provision's primary purpose is to restrict speech that opposes abortion.

I begin, as suggested above, with the fact that the Act burdens only the public spaces outside abortion clinics. One might have expected the majority to defend the statute's peculiar targeting by arguing that those locations regularly face the safety and access problems that it says the Act was designed to solve. But the majority does not make that argument because it would be untrue. As the Court belatedly discovers in Part IV of its opinion, although the statute applies to all abortion clinics in Massachusetts, only one is known to have been beset by the problems that the statute supposedly addresses. The Court uses this striking fact (a smoking gun, so to speak) as a basis for concluding that the law is insufficiently "tailored" to safety and access concerns (Part IV) rather than as a basis for concluding that it is not *directed* to those concerns at all, but to the suppression of antiabortion speech. That is rather like invoking the eight missed human targets of a shooter who has killed one victim to prove, not that he is guilty of attempted mass murder, but that *he has bad aim.*

A. Government Properties and Speech

Whether the statute "restrict[s] more speech than necessary" in light of the problems that it allegedly addresses, is, to be sure, relevant to the tailoring component of the First Amendment analysis (the shooter doubtless did have bad aim), but it is also relevant—powerfully relevant—to whether the law is really directed to safety and access concerns or rather to the suppression of a particular type of speech. Showing that a law that suppresses speech on a specific subject is so far-reaching that it applies even when the asserted non-speech-related problems are not present is persuasive evidence that the law is content based. In its zeal to treat abortion-related speech as a special category, the majority distorts not only the First Amendment but also the ordinary logic of probative inferences.

B. EXEMPTION FOR ABORTION-CLINIC EMPLOYEES OR AGENTS

Petitioners contend that the Act targets speech opposing abortion (and thus constitutes a presumptively invalid viewpoint-discriminatory restriction) for another reason as well: It exempts "employees or agents" of an abortion clinic "acting within the scope of their employment."

It goes without saying that "[g]ranting waivers to favored speakers (or . . . denying them to disfavored speakers) would of course be unconstitutional." Is there any serious doubt that *abortion-clinic employees or agents* "acting within the scope of their employment" near clinic entrances may—indeed, often will—speak in favor of abortion ("You are doing the right thing")? Or speak in opposition to the message of abortion opponents—saying, for example, that "this is a safe facility" to rebut the statement that it is not? The Court's contrary assumption is simply incredible.

Going from bad to worse, the majority's opinion contends that "the record before us contains insufficient evidence to show" that abortion-facility escorts have actually spoken in favor of abortion (or, presumably, hindered antiabortion speech) while acting within the scope of their employment. Here is a brave new First Amendment test: Speech restrictions favoring one viewpoint over another are not content based unless it can be shown that the favored viewpoint has actually been expressed. A city ordinance closing a park adjoining the Republican National Convention to all speakers except those whose remarks have been approved by the Republican National Committee is thus not subject to strict scrutiny unless it can be shown that someone has given committee-endorsed remarks. For this Court to suggest such a test is astonishing.

C. CONCLUSION

In sum, the Act should be reviewed under the strict-scrutiny standard applicable to content-based legislation. That standard requires that a regulation represent "the least restrictive means" of furthering "a compelling Government interest."

The obvious purpose of the challenged portion of the Massachusetts Reproductive Health Care Facilities Act is to "protect" prospective clients of abortion clinics from having to hear abortion-opposing speech on public streets and sidewalks. The provision is thus unconstitutional root and branch and cannot be saved, as the majority suggests, by limiting its application to the single facility that has experienced the safety and access problems to which it is quite obviously not addressed. I concur only in the judgment that the statute is unconstitutional under the First Amendment.

Justice ALITO, concurring in the judgment.

Consider this entirely realistic situation. A woman enters a buffer zone and heads haltingly toward the entrance. A sidewalk counselor, such as petitioners, enters the buffer zone, approaches the woman and says, "If you have doubts about an abortion, let me try to answer any questions you may have. The clinic will not give you good information." At the same time, a clinic employee, as instructed by the management, approaches the same woman and says, "Come inside and we will give you honest answers to all your questions." The sidewalk counselor and the clinic employee expressed opposing viewpoints, but only the first violated the statute.

Or suppose that the issue is not abortion but the safety of a particular facility. Suppose that there was a recent report of a botched abortion at the clinic. A nonemployee may not enter the buffer zone to warn about the clinic's health record, but an employee may enter and tell prospective clients that the clinic is safe.

It is clear on the face of the Massachusetts law that it discriminates based on viewpoint. Speech in favor of the clinic and its work by employees and agents is permitted; speech criticizing the clinic and its work is a crime. This is blatant viewpoint discrimination.

In many other cases, the Court upheld government restrictions of speech in public forums as permissible time, place, and manner restrictions. In Kovacs v. Cooper, 336 U.S. 77 (1949), the Court upheld a restriction on the use of sound amplification devices, such as loudspeakers on trucks. The Court emphasized that the law did not prohibit all such devices, but rather was a reasonable time, place, and manner restriction. In Grayned v. Rockford, 408 U.S. 104 (1972), the Court upheld a city's ordinance that prohibited any "person, while on public or private grounds adjacent to any building in which a school or any class thereof is in session, to make any noise or diversion which disturbs or tends to disturb the peace or good order of such school." The Court found that the restriction was a reasonable time, place, and manner restriction and affirmed a conviction for violating it. The Court said that the "crucial question is whether the manner of expression is basically incompatible with the normal activity of a particular place at a particular time." The Court said that the ordinance was constitutional because it prohibited speech disruptive of schools and that was permissible based on the city's important interest in ensuring order sufficient for schooling.

In Clark v. Community for Creative Non-Violence, 468 U.S. 288 (1984), the Court upheld a federal regulation and Park Service decision to keep a group protesting the plight of the homeless from sleeping in the park. The National Park Service allowed the Community for Creative Non-Violence to erect a tent city in Lafayette Park and the Mall in Washington, D.C., as a symbolic protest, but refused to allow the demonstrators to sleep in the tents because of a regulation prohibiting camping in these parks. The Supreme Court accepted arguendo the contention that overnight sleeping as a part of this protest was a form of expressive conduct, but the Court upheld the regulation as a reasonable time, place, and manner restriction. The Court emphasized that the restriction was content-neutral, that it served the important purpose of preserving the attractiveness of the parks, and that it left adequate alternative ways of expressing the message. For example, the demonstrators could "feign" sleep in the tents, just not actually sleep there.

While in *Heffron, Hill, Kovacs, Grayned,* and *Clark* the Court upheld the regulations as permissible time, place, and manner restrictions, in other cases the Court has ruled against the government using this test. For instance, in Brown v. Louisiana, 383 U.S. 131 (1966), the Court reversed the conviction of a group of African Americans who had conducted a silent sit-in as a protest at a racially segregated public library. The plurality opinion stressed that it was a silent protest that did not interfere with the operation of the library. The plurality also was undoubtedly influenced by the importance of the protest. The plurality said that the First Amendment protected "the right in a peaceful and orderly manner to protest by silent and reproachful presence, in a place where the protestant has every right to be, the unconstitutional segregation of public facilities."

In United States v. Grace, 461 U.S. 171 (1983), the Court declared unconstitutional a broad restriction of speech on the public sidewalks surrounding the Supreme Court's building. In part, the regulation prohibited the display of "any flag, banner, or device designed to bring into public notice any party, organization, or movement." The Court found that the rule was not a reasonable time, place, and manner restriction because a total ban on all speech was unnecessary to preserve order and prevent disruption of Supreme Court proceedings. Silent protests never would interfere with the Court, and the Court rejected the argument that protests could be prohibited to prevent the public from inferring that decisions were influenced by the demonstrators.

Looked at together, all of these cases indicate that the determination of whether a regulation is a reasonable time, place, and manner restriction is entirely contextual. In each instance, the Court has to assess whether it serves an important interest and whether it leaves open adequate alternative places for expression.

iii. *Licensing and Permit Systems*

As described in Chapter 2 above, a licensing or permit system is a classic form of prior restraint. The Court has made it clear that the government can require a license for speech in public forums only if there is an important reason for licensing, there are clear criteria leaving almost no discretion to the licensing authority, and there are procedural safeguards such as a requirement for prompt determination of license requests and judicial review of license denials.

A permit system that meets all of these requirements will be allowed. For instance, in Cox v. New Hampshire, 312 U.S. 569 (1941), the Court upheld an ordinance that required that those wishing to hold a parade or demonstration obtain a permit and that allowed a permit to be denied only if the area already was in use by another group. The Court found that the government had an important interest in requiring a permit for speech so as to make sure that there was only one demonstration in a place at a time. Professor Harry Kalven referred to this as "Robert's Rules of Order" for use of the public forum.[5] The

---

5. Harry Kalven, *The Concept of the Public Forum: Cox v. Louisiana,* 1965 S. Ct. Rev. 1, 26, 28-29.

Court emphasized that the "licensing board was not vested with arbitrary power or unfettered discretion."

In contrast, permit systems that leave significant discretion to the licensing authority are declared unconstitutional because they risk the government's granting permits to favored speech and denying them to unpopular expression. In Lovell v. Griffin, 303 U.S. 444 (1938), presented above, the Court declared unconstitutional a city's ordinance that prohibited the distribution of leaflets, literature, or advertising without the written permission of the city manager. The Court explained that the regulation was a prior restraint that "strikes at the very foundation of the freedom of the press by subjecting it to license and censorship. The struggle for freedom of the press was primarily directed against the power of the licensor." The Court said that "[l]egislation of the type of the ordinance in question would restore the system of license and censorship in its baldest form."

Likewise, the Court has held that the government cannot require a permit fee for demonstrations if government officials have discretion in setting the amount of the charge. In Forsyth County, Georgia v. Nationalist Movement, 505 U.S. 123 (1992), the Court declared unconstitutional an ordinance that required a permit in order for a demonstration to occur and that allowed government officials to charge a permit fee of up to $1,000. The Court found that the licensing law was impermissible because "[t]here are no articulated standards either in the ordinance or in the county's established practice. The administrator is not required to rely on any objective factors. He need not provide any explanation for his decision, and that decision is unreviewable." The Court concluded that "nothing in the law or its application prevents the official from encouraging some views and discouraging others through the arbitrary application of the fees. The First Amendment prohibits the vesting of such unbridled discretion in a government official."

Nationalist Movement did not declare unconstitutional all permit fee requirements; it simply held that such charges are unconstitutional if government officials have discretion as to the amount. In Cox v. New Hampshire, described above, the Court upheld a licensing system that allowed the government to charge a permit fee of up to $300. Although the discretion under this ordinance likely would make it unconstitutional under *Nationalist Movement*, the Court never has overruled its conclusion that the government can charge "a nominal fee imposed . . . to defray the expenses of policing the activities in question." But nor has the Court ever clarified what fees are permissible under what circumstances.

On the one hand, there is a strong argument that all charges for the use of public property for speech should be declared unconstitutional.[6] Any fee might keep some from speaking, and the loss is not just to the speaker's First Amendment rights, but to the rights of all who are denied hearing the message. If the government can charge demonstrators for use of public property or for police protection, that often will have the same effect as a complete ban on the speech. On the other hand, the government is almost never required to subsidize the exercise of constitutional rights. A prohibition of all permit fees

---

6. For an excellent development of this argument, *see* David Goldberger, *A Reconsideration of Cox v. New Hampshire: Can Demonstrators Be Required to Pay the Costs of Using America's Public Forums?*, 62 Tex. L. Rev. 403 (1983).

A. Government Properties and Speech

would be forcing the government to subsidize the use of the public forum for speech purposes. The issue has become particularly important in the context of how much college campuses must spend for safety before they can say that they will not allow particular speakers because they cannot afford security costs.

iv. No Requirement for Use of the Least Restrictive Alternative

Finally, in Ward v. Rock Against Racism, the Court has held that when the government regulates speech in the public forum, it need not use the least restrictive alternative, although any regulation must be narrowly tailored.

WARD v. ROCK AGAINST RACISM
491 U.S. 781 (1989)

Justice KENNEDY delivered the opinion of the Court.

In the southeast portion of New York City's Central Park, about 10 blocks upward from the park's beginning point at 59th Street, there is an amphitheater and stage structure known as the Naumberg Acoustic Bandshell. The bandshell faces west across the remaining width of the park. In close proximity to the bandshell, and lying within the directional path of its sound, is a grassy open area called the Sheep Meadow. The city has designated the Sheep Meadow as a quiet area for passive recreations like reclining, walking, and reading. Just beyond the park, and also within the potential sound range of the bandshell, are the apartments and residences of Central Park West.

This case arises from the city's attempt to regulate the volume of amplified music at the bandshell so the performances are satisfactory to the audience without intruding upon those who use the Sheep Meadow or live on Central Park West and in its vicinity. The city's regulation requires bandshell performers to use sound-amplification equipment and a sound technician provided by the city. The challenge to this volume control technique comes from the sponsor of a rock concert.

Music is one of the oldest forms of human expression. From Plato's discourse in the Republic to the totalitarian state in our own times, rulers have known its capacity to appeal to the intellect and to the emotions, and have censored musical compositions to serve the needs of the state.

The principal justification for the sound-amplification guideline is the city's desire to control noise levels at bandshell events, in order to retain the character of the Sheep Meadow and its more sedate activities, and to avoid undue intrusion into residential areas and other areas of the park. This justification for the guideline "ha[s] nothing to do with content," and it satisfies the requirement that time, place, or manner regulations be content neutral.

The city's regulation is also "narrowly tailored to serve a significant governmental interest." Despite respondent's protestations to the contrary, it can no longer be doubted that government "ha[s] a substantial interest in protecting its citizens from unwelcome noise." Lest any confusion on the point remain, we reaffirm today that a regulation of the time, place, or manner of protected speech must be narrowly tailored to serve the government's legitimate, content-neutral interests but that it need not be the least restrictive or least intrusive means of doing so. Rather, the requirement of narrow tailoring is satisfied "so long as the . . . regulation promotes a substantial government interest that would be achieved less effectively absent the regulation."

To be sure, this standard does not mean that a time, place, or manner regulation may burden substantially more speech than is necessary to further the government's legitimate interests. Government may not regulate expression in such a manner that a substantial portion of the burden on speech does not serve to advance its goals. So long as the means chosen are not substantially broader than necessary to achieve the government's interest, however, the regulation will not be invalid simply because a court concludes that the government's interest could be adequately served by some less-speech-restrictive alternative. While time, place, or manner regulations must also be "narrowly tailored" in order to survive First Amendment challenge, we have never applied strict scrutiny in this context. As a result, the same degree of tailoring is not required of these regulations, and least-restrictive-alternative analysis is wholly out of place.

It is undeniable that the city's substantial interest in limiting sound volume is served in a direct and effective way by the requirement that the city's sound technician control the mixing board during performances. Absent this requirement, the city's interest would have been served less well, as is evidenced by the complaints about excessive volume generated by respondent's past concerts.

The final requirement, that the guideline leave open ample alternative channels of communication, is easily met. Indeed, in this respect the guideline is far less restrictive than regulations we have upheld in other cases, for it does not attempt to ban any particular manner or type of expression at a given place or time. Rather, the guideline continues to permit expressive activity in the bandshell, and has no effect on the quantity or content of that expression beyond regulating the extent of amplification.

Justice MARSHALL, with whom Justice BRENNAN and Justice STEVENS join, dissenting.

No one can doubt that government has a substantial interest in regulating the barrage of excessive sound that can plague urban life. Unfortunately, the majority plays to our shared impatience with loud noise to obscure the damage that it does to our First Amendment rights. Until today, a key safeguard of free speech has been government's obligation to adopt the least intrusive restriction necessary to achieve its goals. By abandoning the requirement that time, place, and manner regulations must be narrowly tailored, the majority replaces constitutional scrutiny with mandatory deference. The majority's willingness to give government officials a free hand in achieving their policy ends extends so far as to permit, in this case, government control of speech in advance of its dissemination. Because New York City's Use Guidelines (Guidelines) are not narrowly tailored to serve its interest in regulating loud noise, and because they constitute an impermissible prior restraint, I dissent.

b. *Designated Public Forums*

In Christian Legal Society v. Martinez, quoted above, the Supreme Court said that "designated public forums [exist] when 'government property that has not traditionally been regarded as a public forum is intentionally opened up for that purpose'; speech restrictions in such a forum 'are subject to the same strict scrutiny as restrictions in a traditional public forum.'"

A. Government Properties and Speech

For example, the Court has held that if the public schools and universities open their property for use by student and community groups, they cannot exclude religious groups. In Widmar v. Vincent, 454 U.S. 263 (1981), the Court ruled that a university that allowed student groups to use school buildings could not exclude religious student groups from access. Similarly, in Lamb's Chapel v. Center Moriches Union Free School Dist., 508 U.S. 384 (1993), the Court held that once a school district allowed community groups to use facilities during evenings and weekends, religious groups could not be excluded. It is very unlikely that these school facilities would be considered a public forum; the government likely could exclude all use by student or community groups. But once the government chose to open these places to speech, it had to comply with all of the same rules as in public forums, including refraining from content-based discrimination.

In Good News Club v. Milford Central School, 533 U.S. 98 (2001), the Court considered the constitutionality of an elementary school's exclusion of a group's using school property after school for religious activities including prayer and Bible study, but the Court labeled this a "limited public forum."

There were two parts to the Court's holding. First, the Court ruled that excluding the group violated the Speech Clause of the First Amendment. The Court said that the parties in the case had accepted that by opening its facilities the school had created a "limited public forum." The Court said that "[w]hen the State establishes a limited public forum, the State is not required to and does not allow persons to engage in every type of speech. The State may be justified 'in reserving [its forum] for certain groups or for the discussion of certain topics.' The State's power to restrict speech, however, is not without limits. The restriction must not discriminate against speech on the basis of viewpoint, and the restriction must be 'reasonable in light of the purpose served by the forum.'" The Court found that excluding the religious speech was impermissible viewpoint discrimination. Second, the Court concluded that allowing the religious group to use the property on the same terms as other community groups would not violate the Establishment Clause of the First Amendment. The latter aspect of the case is discussed in Chapter 9.

c. Limited Public Forums

In Christian Legal Society v. Martinez, quoted above, the Supreme Court said that "governmental entities establish limited public forums by opening property 'limited to use by certain groups or dedicated solely to the discussion of certain subjects.' In such a forum, a governmental entity may impose restrictions on speech that are reasonable and viewpoint-neutral."[7] The Court, however, did not clarify how it is to be determined whether the government has created a "designated public forum," where subject-matter restrictions are not allowed, or a "limited public forum," where subject-matter restrictions are permitted.

---

7. An example of this from an earlier case would be Lehman v. Shaker Heights, 418 U.S. 298 (1974). A city allowed commercial but not political advertisements on city buses, and the Supreme Court upheld this as constitutional. Under current tests, the Court essentially said that this was a limited public forum—a place being opened just to some topics—and it was allowed because the regulation was reasonable and viewpoint-neutral.

In Christian Legal Society v. Martinez, the Court upheld the constitutionality of a law school at a public university requiring student groups to accept all members and denying recognition to student groups that discriminated based on religion and sexual orientation. The majority opinion, by Justice Ginsburg, found that the university had created a limited public forum and that the regulation was allowed because it was reasonable and viewpoint neutral.

CHRISTIAN LEGAL SOCIETY CHAPTER OF THE UNIVERSITY OF CALIFORNIA, HASTINGS COLLEGE OF THE LAW v. MARTINEZ
561 U.S. 661 (2010)

Justice GINSBURG delivered the opinion of the Court.

In a series of decisions, this Court has emphasized that the First Amendment generally precludes public universities from denying student organizations access to student activities at public universities. May a public law school condition its official recognition of a student group—and the attendant use of school funds and facilities—on the organization's agreement to open eligibility for membership and leadership to all students?

In the view of petitioner Christian Legal Society (CLS), an accept-all-comers policy impairs its First Amendment rights to free speech, expressive association, and free exercise of religion by prompting it, on pain of relinquishing the advantages of recognition, to accept members who do not share the organization's core beliefs about religion and sexual orientation. From the perspective of respondent Hastings College of the Law (Hastings or the Law School), CLS seeks special dispensation from an across-the-board open-access requirement designed to further the reasonable educational purposes underpinning the school's student-organization program.

In accord with the District Court and the Court of Appeals, we reject CLS's First Amendment challenge. Compliance with Hastings' all-comers policy, we conclude, is a reasonable, viewpoint-neutral condition on access to the student-organization forum. In requiring CLS—in common with all other student organizations—to choose between welcoming all students and forgoing the benefits of official recognition, we hold, Hastings did not transgress constitutional limitations. CLS, it bears emphasis, seeks not parity with other organizations, but a preferential exemption from Hastings' policy. The First Amendment shields CLS against state prohibition of the organization's expressive activity, however exclusionary that activity may be. But CLS enjoys no constitutional right to state subvention of its selectivity.

I

Through its "Registered Student Organization" (RSO) program, Hastings extends official recognition to student groups. Several benefits attend this school-approved status. RSOs are eligible to seek financial assistance from the Law School, which subsidizes their events using funds from a mandatory student-activity fee imposed on all students. RSOs may also use Law-School channels to communicate with students: They may place announcements in a weekly Office-of-Student-Services newsletter, advertise events on designated bulletin

A. Government Properties and Speech

boards, send e-mails using a Hastings-organization address, and participate in an annual Student Organizations Fair designed to advance recruitment efforts. In addition, RSOs may apply for permission to use the Law School's facilities for meetings and office space. Finally, Hastings allows officially recognized groups to use its name and logo.

In exchange for these benefits, RSOs must abide by certain conditions. Only a "non-commercial organization whose membership is limited to Hastings students may become [an RSO]." A prospective RSO must submit its bylaws to Hastings for approval, and if it intends to use the Law School's name or logo, it must sign a license agreement. Critical here, all RSOs must undertake to comply with Hastings' "Policies and Regulations Applying to College Activities, Organizations and Students."

The Law School's Policy on Nondiscrimination (Nondiscrimination Policy), which binds RSOs, states:

> [Hastings] is committed to a policy against legally impermissible, arbitrary or unreasonable discriminatory practices. All groups, including administration, faculty, student governments, [Hastings]-owned student residence facilities and programs sponsored by [Hastings], are governed by this policy of nondiscrimination. [Hasting's] policy on nondiscrimination is to comply fully with applicable law.
>
> [Hastings] shall not discriminate unlawfully on the basis of race, color, religion, national origin, ancestry, disability, age, sex or sexual orientation. This nondiscrimination policy covers admission, access and treatment in Hastings-sponsored programs and activities.

Hastings interprets the Nondiscrimination Policy, as it relates to the RSO program, to mandate acceptance of all comers: School-approved groups must "allow any student to participate, become a member, or seek leadership positions in the organization, regardless of [her] status or beliefs." Other law schools have adopted similar all-comers policies. From Hastings' adoption of its Nondiscrimination Policy in 1990 until the events stirring this litigation, "no student organization at Hastings . . . ever sought an exemption from the Policy." In 2004, CLS became the first student group to do so. At the beginning of the academic year, the leaders of a predecessor Christian organization—which had been an RSO at Hastings for a decade—formed CLS by affiliating with the national Christian Legal Society (CLS-National). CLS-National, an association of Christian lawyers and law students, charters student chapters at law schools throughout the country. CLS chapters must adopt bylaws that require members and officers to sign a "Statement of Faith" and to conduct their lives in accord with prescribed principles. Among those tenets is the belief that sexual activity should not occur outside of marriage between a man and a woman; CLS thus interprets its bylaws to exclude from affiliation anyone who engages in "unrepentant homosexual conduct." CLS also excludes students who hold religious convictions different from those in the Statement of Faith.

On September 17, 2004, CLS submitted to Hastings an application for RSO status, accompanied by all required documents, including the set of bylaws mandated by CLS-National. Several days later, the Law School rejected the application; CLS's bylaws, Hastings explained, did not comply with the Nondiscrimination Policy because CLS barred students based on religion and sexual orientation.

CLS formally requested an exemption from the Nondiscrimination Policy, but Hastings declined to grant one. "[T]o be one of our student-recognized organizations," Hastings reiterated, "CLS must open its membership to all students irrespective of their religious beliefs or sexual orientation." If CLS instead chose to operate outside the RSO program, Hastings stated, the school "would be pleased to provide [CLS] the use of Hastings facilities for its meetings and activities." CLS would also have access to chalkboards and generally available campus bulletin boards to announce its events. In other words, Hastings would do nothing to suppress CLS's endeavors, but neither would it lend RSO-level support for them.

Refusing to alter its bylaws, CLS did not obtain RSO status. It did, however, operate independently during the 2004-2005 academic year. CLS held weekly Bible-study meetings and invited Hastings students to Good Friday and Easter Sunday church services. It also hosted a beach barbeque, Thanksgiving dinner, campus lecture on the Christian faith and the legal practice, several fellowship dinners, an end-of-year banquet, and other informal social activities.

II

Before considering the merits of CLS's constitutional arguments, we must resolve a preliminary issue: CLS urges us to review the Nondiscrimination Policy as written—prohibiting discrimination on several enumerated bases, including religion and sexual orientation—and not as a requirement that all RSOs accept all comers. The written terms of the Nondiscrimination Policy, CLS contends, "targe[t] solely those groups whose beliefs are based on religion or that disapprove of a particular kind of sexual behavior," and leave other associations free to limit membership and leadership to individuals committed to the group's ideology. For example, "[a] political . . . group can insist that its leaders support its purposes and beliefs," CLS alleges, but "a religious group cannot."

CLS's assertion runs headlong into the stipulation of facts it jointly submitted with Hastings at the summary-judgment stage. In that filing, the parties specified: "Hastings requires that registered student organizations allow *any* student to participate, become a member, or seek leadership positions in the organization, regardless of [her] status or beliefs. Thus, for example, the Hastings Democratic Caucus cannot bar students holding Republican political beliefs from becoming members or seeking leadership positions in the organization."

"[Factual stipulations are] binding and conclusive . . . , and the facts stated are not subject to subsequent variation. So, the parties will not be permitted to deny the truth of the facts stated, . . . or to maintain a contention contrary to the agreed statement, . . . or to suggest, on appeal, that the facts were other than as stipulated or that any material fact was omitted." This Court has accordingly refused to consider a party's argument that contradicted a joint "stipulation [entered] at the outset of th[e] litigation." Time and again, the dissent races away from the facts to which CLS stipulated. But factual stipulations are "formal concessions . . . that have the effect of withdrawing a fact from issue and dispensing wholly with the need for proof of the fact. Thus, a judicial admission . . . is conclusive in the case."

In light of the joint stipulation, both the District Court and the Ninth Circuit trained their attention on the constitutionality of the all-comers requirement,

A. Government Properties and Speech

as described in the parties' accord. We reject CLS's unseemly attempt to escape from the stipulation and shift its target to Hastings' policy as written. This opinion, therefore, considers only whether conditioning access to a student-organization forum on compliance with an all-comers policy violates the Constitution.

III

A

In support of the argument that Hastings' all-comers policy treads on its First Amendment rights to free speech and expressive association, CLS draws on two lines of decisions. First, in a progression of cases, this Court has employed forum analysis to determine when a governmental entity, in regulating property in its charge, may place limitations on speech. Recognizing a State's right "to preserve the property under its control for the use to which it is lawfully dedicated," the Court has permitted restrictions on access to a limited public forum, like the RSO program here, with this key caveat: Any access barrier must be reasonable and viewpoint neutral. Second, as evidenced by another set of decisions, this Court has rigorously reviewed laws and regulations that constrain associational freedom. In the context of public accommodations, we have subjected restrictions on that freedom to close scrutiny; such restrictions are permitted only if they serve "compelling state interests" that are "unrelated to the suppression of ideas"—interests that cannot be advanced "through . . . significantly less restrictive [means]." "Freedom of association," we have recognized, "plainly presupposes a freedom not to associate." Insisting that an organization embrace unwelcome members, we have therefore concluded, "directly and immediately affects associational rights."

CLS would have us engage each line of cases independently, but its expressive-association and free-speech arguments merge: *Who* speaks on its behalf, CLS reasons, colors *what* concept is conveyed. It therefore makes little sense to treat CLS's speech and association claims as discrete. Instead, three observations lead us to conclude that our limited-public-forum precedents supply the appropriate framework for assessing both CLS's speech and association rights.

First, the same considerations that have led us to apply a less restrictive level of scrutiny to speech in limited public forums as compared to other environments, apply with equal force to expressive association occurring in limited public forums. As just noted, speech and expressive-association rights are closely linked.

Second, and closely related, the strict scrutiny we have applied in some settings to laws that burden expressive association would, in practical effect, invalidate a defining characteristic of limited public forums-the State may "reserv[e] [them] for certain groups."

Third, this case fits comfortably within the limited-public-forum category, for CLS, in seeking what is effectively a state subsidy, faces only indirect pressure to modify its membership policies; CLS may exclude any person for any reason if it forgoes the benefits of official recognition. The expressive-association precedents on which CLS relies, in contrast, involved regulations that *compelled* a group to include unwanted members, with no choice to opt out. In diverse contexts, our decisions have distinguished between policies that require action and those that withhold benefits.

In sum, we are persuaded that our limited-public-forum precedents adequately respect both CLS's speech and expressive-association rights, and fairly balance those rights against Hastings' interests as property owner and educational institution. We turn to the merits of the instant dispute, therefore, with the limited-public-forum decisions as our guide.

[B]

We first consider whether Hastings' policy is reasonable taking into account the RSO forum's function and "all the surrounding circumstances."

Our inquiry is shaped by the educational context in which it arises: "First Amendment rights," we have observed, "must be analyzed in light of the special characteristics of the school environment." This Court is the final arbiter of the question whether a public university has exceeded constitutional constraints, and we owe no deference to universities when we consider that question. Cognizant that judges lack the on-the-ground expertise and experience of school administrators, however, we have cautioned courts in various contexts to resist "substitut[ing] their own notions of sound educational policy for those of the school authorities which they review."

A college's commission—and its concomitant license to choose among pedagogical approaches—is not confined to the classroom, for extracurricular programs are, today, essential parts of the educational process. Schools, we have emphasized, enjoy "a significant measure of authority over the type of officially recognized activities in which their students participate." We therefore "approach our task with special caution," mindful that Hastings' decisions about the character of its student-group program are due decent respect.

With appropriate regard for school administrators' judgment, we review the justifications Hastings offers in defense of its all-comers requirement. First, the open-access policy "ensures that the leadership, educational, and social opportunities afforded by [RSOs] are available to all students." Just as "Hastings does not allow its professors to host classes open only to those students with a certain status or belief," so the Law School may decide, reasonably in our view, "that the . . . educational experience is best promoted when all participants in the forum must provide equal access to all students." RSOs, we count it significant, are eligible for financial assistance drawn from mandatory student-activity fees; the all-comers policy ensures that no Hastings student is forced to fund a group that would reject her as a member.

Second, the all-comers requirement helps Hastings police the written terms of its Nondiscrimination Policy without inquiring into an RSO's motivation for membership restrictions. To bring the RSO program within CLS's view of the Constitution's limits, CLS proposes that Hastings permit exclusion because of *belief* but forbid discrimination due to *status*. But that proposal would impose on Hastings a daunting labor. How should the Law School go about determining whether a student organization cloaked prohibited status exclusion in belief-based garb? If a hypothetical Male-Superiority Club barred a female student from running for its presidency, for example, how could the Law School tell whether the group rejected her bid because of her sex or because, by seeking to lead the club, she manifested a lack of belief in its fundamental philosophy?

A. Government Properties and Speech

Third, the Law School reasonably adheres to the view that an all-comers policy, to the extent it brings together individuals with diverse backgrounds and beliefs, "encourages tolerance, cooperation, and learning among students." And if the policy sometimes produces discord, Hastings can rationally rank among RSO-program goals development of conflict-resolution skills, toleration, and readiness to find common ground.

Fourth, Hastings' policy, which incorporates—in fact, subsumes—state-law proscriptions on discrimination, conveys the Law School's decision "to decline to subsidize with public monies and benefits conduct of which the people of California disapprove."

In sum, the several justifications Hastings asserts in support of its all-comers requirement are surely reasonable in light of the RSO forum's purposes.

The Law School's policy is all the more creditworthy in view of the "substantial alternative channels that remain open for [CLS-student] communication to take place." If restrictions on access to a limited public forum are viewpoint discriminatory, the ability of a group to exist outside the forum would not cure the constitutional shortcoming. But when access barriers are viewpoint neutral, our decisions have counted it significant that other available avenues for the group to exercise its First Amendment rights lessen the burden created by those barriers.

In this case, Hastings offered CLS access to school facilities to conduct meetings and the use of chalkboards and generally available bulletin boards to advertise events. Although CLS could not take advantage of RSO-specific methods of communication, the advent of electronic media and social-networking sites reduces the importance of those channels.

Private groups, from fraternities and sororities to social clubs and secret societies, commonly maintain a presence at universities without official school affiliation. Based on the record before us, CLS was similarly situated: It hosted a variety of activities the year after Hastings denied it recognition, and the number of students attending those meetings and events doubled. "The variety and type of alternative modes of access present here," in short, "compare favorably with those in other [limited public] forum cases where we have upheld restrictions on access."

CLS also assails the reasonableness of the all-comers policy in light of the RSO forum's function by forecasting that the policy will facilitate hostile takeovers; if organizations must open their arms to all, CLS contends, saboteurs will infiltrate groups to subvert their mission and message. This supposition strikes us as more hypothetical than real. CLS points to no history or prospect of RSO-hijackings at Hastings. Students tend to self-sort and presumably will not endeavor en masse to join—let alone seek leadership positions in—groups pursuing missions wholly at odds with their personal beliefs. And if a rogue student intent on sabotaging an organization's objectives nevertheless attempted a takeover, the members of that group would not likely elect her as an officer. RSOs, moreover, in harmony with the all-comers policy, may condition eligibility for membership and leadership on attendance, the payment of dues, or other neutral requirements designed to ensure that students join because of their commitment to a group's vitality, not its demise.

Hastings, furthermore, could reasonably expect more from its law students than the disruptive behavior CLS hypothesizes—and to build this expectation into its educational approach. A reasonable policy need not anticipate and preemptively close off every opportunity for avoidance or manipulation. If students begin to exploit an all-comers policy by hijacking organizations to distort or destroy their missions, Hastings presumably would revisit and revise its policy.

[c]
We next consider whether Hastings' all-comers policy is viewpoint neutral. Although this aspect of limited-public-forum analysis has been the constitutional sticking point in our prior decisions, as earlier recounted, we need not dwell on it here. It is, after all, hard to imagine a more viewpoint-neutral policy than one requiring *all* student groups to accept *all* comers.

Conceding that Hastings' all-comers policy is "nominally neutral," CLS attacks the regulation by pointing to its effect: The policy is vulnerable to constitutional assault, CLS contends, because "it systematically and predictably burdens most heavily those groups whose viewpoints are out of favor with the campus mainstream." Even if a regulation has a differential impact on groups wishing to enforce exclusionary membership policies, "[w]here the [State] does not target conduct on the basis of its expressive content, acts are not shielded from regulation merely because they express a discriminatory idea or philosophy."

Hastings' requirement that student groups accept all comers, we are satisfied, "is justified without reference to the content [or viewpoint] of the regulated speech." The Law School's policy aims at the *act* of rejecting would-be group members without reference to the reasons motivating that behavior: Hastings' "desire to redress th[e] perceived harms" of exclusionary membership policies "provides an adequate explanation for its [all-comers condition] over and above mere disagreement with [any student group's] beliefs or biases." CLS's conduct—not its Christian perspective—is, from Hastings' vantage point, what stands between the group and RSO status.

Finding Hastings' open-access condition on RSO status reasonable and viewpoint neutral, we reject CLS' free-speech and expressive-association claims.

Justice KENNEDY, concurring.

An objection might be that the all-comers policy, even if not so designed or intended, in fact makes it difficult for certain groups to express their views in a manner essential to their message. A group that can limit membership to those who agree in full with its aims and purposes may be more effective in delivering its message or furthering its expressive objectives; and the Court has recognized that this interest can be protected against governmental interference or regulation. By allowing like-minded students to form groups around shared identities, a school creates room for self-expression and personal development.

In the instant case, however, if the membership qualification were enforced, it would contradict a legitimate purpose for having created the limited forum in the first place. Many educational institutions, including respondent Hastings College of Law, have recognized that the process of learning occurs both formally in a classroom setting and informally outside of it. Students may be shaped as profoundly by their peers as by their teachers. Extracurricular activities, such as those in the Hastings "Registered Student Organization"

A. Government Properties and Speech

program, facilitate interactions between students, enabling them to explore new points of view, to develop interests and talents, and to nurture a growing sense of self. The Hastings program is designed to allow all students to interact with their colleagues across a broad, seemingly unlimited range of ideas, views, and activities.

In addition to a circumstance, already noted, in which it could be demonstrated that a school has adopted or enforced its policy with the intent or purpose of discriminating or disadvantaging a group on account of its views, petitioner also would have a substantial case on the merits if it were shown that the all-comers policy was either designed or used to infiltrate the group or challenge its leadership in order to stifle its views. But that has not been shown to be so likely or self-evident as a matter of group dynamics in this setting that the Court can declare the school policy void without more facts; and if there were a showing that in a particular case the purpose or effect of the policy was to stifle speech or make it ineffective, that, too, would present a case different from the one before us.

Justice ALITO, with whom The CHIEF JUSTICE, Justice SCALIA, and Justice THOMAS join, dissenting.

The proudest boast of our free speech jurisprudence is that we protect the freedom to express "the thought that we hate." Today's decision rests on a very different principle: no freedom for expression that offends prevailing standards of political correctness in our country's institutions of higher learning.

The Hastings College of the Law, a state institution, permits student organizations to register with the law school and severely burdens speech by unregistered groups. Hastings currently has more than 60 registered groups and, in all its history, has denied registration to exactly one: the Christian Legal Society (CLS). CLS claims that Hastings refused to register the group because the law school administration disapproves of the group's viewpoint and thus violated the group's free speech rights.

The Court's treatment of this case is deeply disappointing. The Court does not address the constitutionality of the very different policy that Hastings invoked when it denied CLS's application for registration. Nor does the Court address the constitutionality of the policy that Hastings now purports to follow. And the Court ignores strong evidence that the accept-all-comers policy is not viewpoint neutral because it was announced as a pretext to justify viewpoint discrimination. Brushing aside inconvenient precedent, the Court arms public educational institutions with a handy weapon for suppressing the speech of unpopular groups-groups to which, as Hastings candidly puts it, these institutions "do not wish to . . . lend their name[s]."

I

The Court provides a misleading portrayal of this case. I begin by correcting the picture.

The Court bases all of its analysis on the proposition that the relevant Hastings' policy is the so-called accept-all-comers policy. This frees the Court from the difficult task of defending the constitutionality of either the policy that Hastings actually—and repeatedly—invoked when it denied registration, *i.e.*, the school's written Nondiscrimination Policy, or the policy that Hastings belatedly unveiled when it filed its brief in this Court. Overwhelming evidence, however, shows that Hastings denied CLS's application pursuant to the Nondiscrimination Policy and that the accept-all-comers policy was nowhere to be found until it was mentioned by a former dean in a deposition taken well after this case began.

During the 2004-2005 school year, Hastings had more than 60 registered groups, including political groups (*e.g.*, the Hastings Democratic Caucus and the Hastings Republicans), religious groups (*e.g.*, the Hastings Jewish Law Students Association and the Hastings Association of Muslim Law Students), groups that promote social causes (*e.g.*, both pro-choice and pro-life groups), groups organized around racial or ethnic identity (*e.g.*, the Black Law Students Association, the Korean American Law Society, La Raza Law Students Association, and the Middle Eastern Law Students Association), and groups that focus on gender or sexuality (*e.g.*, the Clara Foltz Feminist Association and Students Raising Consciousness at Hastings).

Not surprisingly many of these registered groups were and are dedicated to expressing a message. For example, Silenced Right, a pro-life group, taught that "all human life from the moment of conception until natural death is sacred and has inherent dignity," while Law Students for Choice aimed to "defend and expand reproductive rights."

Hastings claims that this accept-all-comers policy has existed since 1990 but points to no evidence that the policy was ever put in writing or brought to the attention of members of the law school community prior to the dean's deposition. Indeed, Hastings has adduced no evidence of the policy's existence before that date.

[T]he record is replete with evidence that, at least until Dean Kane unveiled the accept-all-comers policy in July 2005, Hastings routinely registered student groups with bylaws limiting membership and leadership positions to those who agreed with the groups' viewpoints. For example, the bylaws of the Hastings Democratic Caucus provided that "any full-time student at Hastings may become a member of HDC *so long as they do not exhibit a consistent disregard and lack of respect for the objective of the organization* as stated in Article 3, Section 1." The constitution of the Association of Trial Lawyers of America at Hastings provided that every member must "adhere to the objectives of the Student Chapter as well as the mission of ATLA." A student could become a member of the Vietnamese American Law Society so long as the student did not "exhibit a consistent disregard and lack of respect for the objective of the organization," which centers on a "celebrat[ion] [of] Vietnamese culture." Silenced Right limited voting membership to students who "are committed" to the group's "mission" of "spread[ing] the pro-life message." La Raza limited voting membership to "students of Raza background." Since Hastings requires any student group applying for registration to submit a copy of its bylaws, Hastings cannot claim that it was unaware of such provisions.

Like the majority of this Court, the Ninth Circuit relied on the following Joint Stipulation. I agree that the parties must be held to their Joint Stipulation, but the terms of the stipulation should be respected. What was admitted in the Joint Stipulation filed in December 2005 is that Hastings had an accept-all-comers policy. CLS did not stipulate that its application had been denied more than a year earlier pursuant to such a policy. On the contrary, the Joint Stipulation notes that the reason repeatedly given by Hasting at that time was that the CLS bylaws did not comply with *the Nondiscrimination Policy.* Indeed, the parties did not even stipulate that the accept-all-comers policy existed in the fall of 2004. In addition, Hastings itself is now attempting to walk away from this stipulation by disclosing that its real policy is an accept-some-comers policy.

The Court also distorts the record with respect to the effect on CLS of Hastings' decision to deny registration. The Court quotes a letter written by Hastings' general counsel in which she stated that Hastings "would be pleased to provide [CLS] the use of Hastings facilities for its meetings and activities." Later in its opinion, the Court reiterates that "Hastings offered CLS access to school facilities to conduct meetings," but the majority does not mention that this offer was subject to important qualifications. As Hastings' attorney put it in the District Court, Hastings told CLS: "'Hastings allows community groups to some degree to use its facilities, sometimes on a pay basis, I understand, if they're available after priority is given to registered organizations.' We offered that."

Other statements in the majority opinion make it seem as if the denial of registration did not hurt CLS at all. The Court notes that CLS was able to hold Bible-study meetings and other events. And "[a]lthough CLS could not take advantage of RSO-specific methods of communication," the Court states, "the advent of electronic media and social-networking sites reduces the importance of those channels." At the beginning of the 2005 school year, the Hastings CLS group had seven members, so there can be no suggestion that the group flourished. And since one of CLS's principal claims is that it was subjected to discrimination based on its viewpoint, the majority's emphasis on CLS's ability to endure that discrimination—by using private facilities and means of communication—is quite amazing.

This Court does not customarily brush aside a claim of unlawful discrimination with the observation that the effects of the discrimination were really not so bad. We have never before taken the view that a little viewpoint discrimination is acceptable. Nor have we taken this approach in other discrimination cases.

[II]

In this case, the forum consists of the RSO program. Once a public university opens a limited public forum, it "must respect the lawful boundaries it has itself set." The university "may not exclude speech where its distinction is not 'reasonable in light of the purpose served by the forum.'" And the university must maintain strict viewpoint neutrality.

This requirement of viewpoint neutrality extends to the expression of religious viewpoints. In an unbroken line of decisions analyzing private religious speech in limited public forums, we have made it perfectly clear that "[r]eligion is [a] viewpoint from which ideas are conveyed."

Analyzed under this framework, Hastings' refusal to register CLS pursuant to its Nondiscrimination Policy plainly fails. As previously noted, when Hastings refused to register CLS, it claimed that the CLS bylaws impermissibly discriminated on the basis of religion and sexual orientation. As interpreted by Hastings and applied to CLS, both of these grounds constituted viewpoint discrimination.

As Hastings stated in its answer, the Nondiscrimination Policy "permit[ted] political, social, and cultural student organizations to select officers and members who are dedicated to a particular set of ideals or beliefs." But the policy singled out one category of expressive associations for disfavored treatment: groups formed to express a religious message. Only religious groups were required to admit students who did not share their views. An environmentalist group was not required to admit students who rejected global warming. An animal rights group was not obligated to accept students who supported the use of animals to test cosmetics. But CLS was required to admit avowed atheists. This was patent viewpoint discrimination. "By the very terms of the [Nondiscrimination Policy], the University . . . select[ed] for disfavored treatment those student [groups] with religious . . . viewpoints." It is no wonder that the Court makes no attempt to defend the constitutionality of the Nondiscrimination Policy.

The Court is also wrong in holding that the accept-all-comers policy is viewpoint neutral. The Court proclaims that it would be "hard to imagine a more viewpoint-neutral policy," but I would not be so quick to jump to this conclusion. Even if it is assumed that the policy is viewpoint neutral on its face, there is strong evidence in the record that the policy was announced as a pretext.

Here, CLS has made a strong showing that Hastings' sudden adoption and selective application of its accept-all-comers policy was a pretext for the law school's unlawful denial of CLS's registration application under the Nondiscrimination Policy. Here, Hastings claims that it has had an accept-all-comers policy since 1990, but it has not produced a single written document memorializing that policy.

[III]

One final aspect of the Court's decision warrants comment. In response to the argument that the accept-all-comers-policy would permit a small and unpopular group to be taken over by students who wish to silence its message, the Court states that the policy would permit a registered group to impose membership requirements "designed to ensure that students join because of their commitment to a group's vitality, not its demise." With this concession, the Court tacitly recognizes that Hastings does not really have an accept-all-comers policy—it has an accept-some-dissident-comers policy—and the line between members who merely seek to change a group's message (who apparently must be admitted) and those who seek a group's "demise" (who may be kept out) is hopelessly vague.

Justice Kennedy takes a similarly mistaken tack. He contends that CLS "would have a substantial case on the merits if it were shown that the all-comers policy was . . . used to infiltrate the group or challenge its leadership in order to stifle its views," but he does not explain on what ground such a claim could succeed. The Court holds that the accept-all-comers policy is viewpoint neutral and reasonable in light of the purposes of the RSO forum. How could those characteristics be altered by a change in the membership of one of the forum's registered groups? No explanation is apparent.

In the end, the Court refuses to acknowledge the consequences of its holding. A true accept-all-comers policy permits small unpopular groups to be taken over by students who wish to change the views that the group expresses. Rules requiring that members attend meetings, pay dues, and behave politely, would not eliminate this threat.

The possibility of such takeovers, however, is by no means the most important effect of the Court's holding. There are religious groups that cannot in good conscience agree in their bylaws that they will admit persons who do not share their faith, and for these groups, the consequence of an accept-all-comers policy is marginalization. This is where the Court's decision leads.

I do not think it is an exaggeration to say that today's decision is a serious setback for freedom of expression in this country. Our First Amendment reflects a "profound national commitment to the principle that debate on public issues should be uninhibited, robust, and wide-open." Even if the United States is the only Nation that shares this commitment to the same extent, I would not change our law to conform to the international norm. I fear that the Court's decision marks a turn in that direction. Even those who find CLS's views objectionable should be concerned about the way the group has been treated—by Hastings, the Court of Appeals, and now this Court. I can only hope that this decision will turn out to be an aberration.

d. *Nonpublic Forums*

Nonpublic forums are government properties that the government can close to all speech activities. The government may prohibit or restrict speech in nonpublic forums as long as the regulation is reasonable and viewpoint neutral. The Court has found many different types of government property to be nonpublic forums.

For example, in Adderley v. Florida, 385 U.S. 39 (1966), the Court held that the government could prohibit speech in the areas outside prisons and jails. Civil rights demonstrators held a rally outside a jail after a group of their colleagues had been arrested for engaging in a civil rights protest. The Court, in an opinion by Justice Black, upheld the convictions of those protesting at the jail who did not disperse in response to an order from the sheriff. Although the Court emphasized the government's security interests, it also spoke very broadly about the government's ability to restrict speech in public places. Justice Black declared, "The State, no less than a private owner of property, has the power to preserve the property under its control for the use to which it is lawfully dedicated. . . . The United States Constitution does not forbid a State to control the use of its own property for its own lawful nondiscriminatory purpose."

Justice Douglas wrote for the four dissenters and stressed the importance of the jail as a place for protest. He said, "The jailhouse, like an executive mansion, a legislative chamber, a courthouse, or the statehouse itself is one of the seats of government, whether it be the Tower of London, the Bastille, or a small county jail. And when it houses political prisoners or those who many think are unjustly held, it is an obvious center for protest."

In Greer v. Spock, 424 U.S. 828 (1976), the Court held that military bases, even parts of bases usually open to the public, are a nonpublic forum. Although civilians were allowed free access to nonrestricted areas of Fort Dix, a regulation prohibited "demonstrations, picketing, sit-ins, protest marches, [and] political speeches." The Supreme Court upheld this regulation and said that it is the business of a military installation like Fort Dix to train soldiers, not to provide a public forum. The Court said that the government could exclude such speech to insulate the military from political activities.

In United States v. Kokinda, 497 U.S. 720 (1990), the Court upheld a restriction on solicitations on post office properties. Sidewalks, of course, are the paradigm public forum. But the plurality opinion of Justice O'Connor said that sidewalks on post office property were a nonpublic forum. The plurality of four justices concluded that a postal sidewalk does not "have the characteristics of public sidewalks traditionally open to expressive activity." Justice O'Connor said that the "postal sidewalk was constructed solely to provide for the passage of individuals engaged in postal business." Although others had been allowed to use the postal property for speaking, leafleting, and picketing, the plurality concluded that this was not enough to transform it into a designated public forum because it did not add up to the dedication of postal property to speech activities.

Justice Kennedy, the fifth vote for upholding the regulation, wrote an opinion concurring in the judgment and said that there were strong grounds for applying the standards for public forums because of the wide array of activities allowed on the sidewalks. Justice Kennedy, however, said that the issue of how to characterize the forum did not need be resolved because the regulation was a reasonable time, place, and manner restriction.

In International Society for Krishna Consciousness, Inc. v. Lee, 505 U.S. 672 (1992), the Court ruled that airports are a nonpublic forum. Chief Justice Rehnquist, writing for the Court, said that "precedents foreclose the conclusion that airport terminals are public fora. Reflecting the general growth of the air travel industry, airport terminals have only recently achieved their contemporary size and character. But given the lateness with which the modern air terminal has made its appearance, it hardly qualifies for the description of having 'immemorially . . . time out of mind' been held in the public trust and used for purposes of expressive activity." The Court rejected the argument that the appropriate inquiry was the general openness of transportation facilities for speech; the issue, according to the Court, was solely about how airports should be characterized.

The Court also emphasized that airports are a commercial venture and that they obviously do not have as a "principal purpose promoting 'the free exchange of ideas.'" Thus, the Court concluded that airports are a nonpublic forum, and regulations would be upheld so long as they are reasonable. The Court, by a 5-to-4 margin, decided that the prohibition of solicitation of funds in airports is reasonable. The Court said that the government has an important interest in preventing fraud, but because travelers are frequently on a tight schedule, "the airport faces considerable difficulty in achieving its legitimate interest in monitoring solicitation activity to assure that travelers are not interfered with unduly."

But the Court also ruled by a 5-to-4 margin that the prohibition of the distribution of literature in airports was unconstitutional. Justice O'Connor, who voted with the majority in finding that airports are nonpublic forums and in upholding the ban on solicitation, joined with the four dissenters on those issues to create a majority to overturn the ban on distribution of literature. She concluded that the ban on leafleting was not reasonable and thus was impermissible even though the airport was a nonpublic forum.

Subsequent to International Society for Krishna Consciousness v. Lee, in Arkansas Educational Television Commission v. Forbes, 523 U.S. 666 (1998),

A. Government Properties and Speech

the Court held that a candidate debate sponsored by a government-owned television station is a nonpublic forum and that the exclusion of minor party candidates is not viewpoint discrimination. The state of Arkansas owns and operates a public television station that held a debate among candidates for a congressional seat. Only the Democratic and Republican candidates, and not the third-party candidates, were invited. A challenge was brought arguing that by holding the debate, the government created a limited public forum, and at the very least, excluding minor-party candidates was a form of viewpoint discrimination that is impermissible even in nonpublic forums.

In an opinion by Justice Kennedy, the Court rejected both of these contentions and ruled in favor of the public television station. Justice Kennedy said that "[h]aving first arisen in the context of streets and parks, the public forum doctrine should not be extended in a mechanical way to the very different context of public television broadcasting. . . . In the case of television broadcasting, however, broad rights of access for outside speakers would be antithetical, as a general rule, to the discretion that stations and their editorial staff must exercise to fulfill their journalistic purpose and statutory obligations." Indeed, the Court said that a broadcaster's choice of content and selection of speakers is itself expressive activity protected by the First Amendment.

Nor was the Court persuaded that the government, by holding the debate, had created a limited public forum. Justice Kennedy explained, "[The] debate was not a designated public forum. To create a forum of this type, the government must intend to make the property 'generally available.' A designated public forum is not created when the government allows selective access for individual speakers rather than general access for a class of speakers. . . . [The] cases illustrate the distinction between 'general access,' which indicates the property is a designated public forum, and 'selective access,' which indicates the property is a nonpublic forum." The Court was concerned that forcing the station to allow all candidates to participate could result in its choosing not to hold the debate at all.

The Court also rejected the claim that selecting major-party candidates and rejecting those from third parties was viewpoint discrimination. Justice Kennedy said that the selection was based on the level of popular support and thus the likely viability of the candidacy and not the viewpoint expressed. He concluded, "There is no substance to Forbes' suggestion that he was excluded because his views were unpopular or out of the mainstream. His own objective lack of support, not his platform, was the criterion. . . . The broadcaster's decision to exclude Forbes was a reasonable, viewpoint-neutral exercise of journalistic discretion consistent with the First Amendment."

Justice Stevens, in a dissenting opinion joined by Justices Souter and Ginsburg, expressed concern over the lack of standards in the government's decision-making process. The most troubling aspect of *Forbes* is whether the choice to include the Democratic and Republican candidates, while excluding third-party candidates, is viewpoint neutral. The Court said that the difference is in their degree of support, not their viewpoint. But the problem with this argument is that the less popular viewpoint is exactly the reason they are third-party candidates. Perhaps the case can be best understood as reflecting the majority's expressed judgment that candidate debates are extremely important and its concern that they will decrease if government-owned stations have to include every minor candidate.

The Supreme Court never has articulated clear criteria for deciding whether a place is a public forum, a designated public forum, or a nonpublic forum. Several criteria are implicit in the cases. Unfortunately, especially as applied in recent cases like *Kokinda*, *Lee*, and *Forbes*, it will be very difficult to find that any government property is a public or limited public forum.

One factor the Court considers is the tradition of availability of the place for speech. Sidewalks and parks, the classic public forums, are regarded as having been long available for speech purposes. But in recent cases, the Court's analysis has focused on whether the particular place has been open to speech. In *Kokinda*, for instance, the Court focused not on sidewalks generally, but on sidewalks on post office property; in *Lee*, the Court refused to consider places of transportation generally, but looked just at airports. Even as to airports, the Court said that because they are relatively new in American history, albeit decades old, they could not be regarded as places traditionally open to speech. This narrow focus makes it difficult to find that a place is a public forum based on a tradition of openness to speech.

Second, the Court considers the extent to which speech is incompatible with the usual functioning of the place. The greater the incompatibility, the more likely that the Court will find the place to be a nonpublic forum. For instance, in *Adderley*, the Court relied on security concerns to justify deeming areas outside prisons and jails to be a nonpublic forum. However, the cases indicate that the Court requires little proof that speech actually will interfere with the functioning of the place. For instance, in *Adderley*, there was no evidence that the peaceful protest on a grassy area outside the jail was a security threat. In *Greer*, there was no proof that speech on the military base would interfere with its functioning or cause the appearance of political entanglement with the military.

Third, the Court considers whether the primary purpose of the place is for speech. In *Lee*, the Court observed that this obviously is not the primary purpose of airports. In *Kokinda*, the plurality said that sidewalks on post office property were not even limited public forums because they had not been dedicated to speech activities. By this criteria, virtually no property ever would be a public forum or a limited public forum. Except for speakers corner in Hyde Park in London, virtually no government property was created for the purpose of speech or has been dedicated to speech activities. Sidewalks are constructed primarily for pedestrian traffic, and parks are built for recreation.

Although these recent cases indicate a strong presumption for finding government property to be a nonpublic forum, the criteria can be applied in a more speech-protective manner to safeguard expression in public property. Courts can find a tradition of availability to speech based on the general availability of that type of property for expressive purposes. Even some incompatibility with the usual functioning of a place can be tolerated so as to accommodate First Amendment values. For example, in *Schneider*, the Court held that the government could not prohibit leafletting even though it had an important interest in preventing litter and in preserving aesthetics. Although a place's primary purpose may not be for speech, it should be found to be a limited public forum if the government has opened it to some speech. A place should be found to be a public forum, even though it obviously has other uses, if it is an important place for the communication of messages.

A. Government Properties and Speech

3. Private Property and Speech

The cases described above all involve claims of a right to use *government* property for speech purposes. There is not a right to use private property owned by others for speech. Because it is private property, the Constitution does not apply.

Most of the cases involving a right to use private property for speech have concerned claims of a right to use privately owned shopping centers for expression. Initially, the Supreme Court recognized such a right and then later limited it and ultimately overruled it. In Amalgamated Food Employees Union v. Logan Valley Plaza, 391 U.S. 308 (1968), the Supreme Court held that a privately owned shopping center could not exclude striking laborers from picketing a store within it. The Court relied on an earlier decision, Marsh v. Alabama, 326 U.S. 501 (1946), which held that a company-owned town could not exclude Jehovah's Witnesses that wished to distribute literature. The Court in *Logan Valley* expressly analogized to *Marsh* and said that "[t]he similarities between the business block in *Marsh* and the shopping center . . . are striking. . . . The shopping center here is clearly the functional equivalent of the business district of Chickasaw involved in *Marsh*." The Court stressed that the shopping center was an important gathering place that served as the commercial center of town.

Four years later, in Lloyd Corp. v. Tanner, 407 U.S. 551 (1972), the Supreme Court held that a privately owned shopping center could exclude anti-Vietnam War protestors from distributing literature on its premises. The Court explained that *Logan Valley* involved a labor protest related to the functioning of a store in the shopping center, whereas the speech in *Lloyd* was an antiwar protest unrelated to the conduct of the business. The problem with this distinction is that it is a content-based distinction among speech. Under *Lloyd*, speech in shopping centers is constitutionally protected and cannot be the basis for a trespassing conviction only if its content concerns the functioning of the shopping centers. This runs afoul of the basic principle described in Chapter 2 that speech cannot be regulated based on its content.

In Hudgens v. National Labor Relations Board, 424 U.S. 507 (1976), the Court recognized these problems and expressly overruled *Logan Valley*. The Court said that "the reasoning of the Court's opinion in *Lloyd* cannot be squared with the reasoning of the Court's opinion in *Logan Valley*." The Court explained that if the First Amendment applies to privately owned shopping centers, then the law cannot permit a distinction based on the content of the speech. The Court concluded that the First Amendment does not create a right to use privately owned shopping centers for speech.

Subsequent to *Hudgens*, in PruneYard Shopping Center v. Robins, 447 U.S. 74 (1980), the Supreme Court held that a state could create a state constitutional right of access to shopping centers for speech purposes. The shopping center appealed to the Supreme Court and contended that forcing it to allow speakers violated its First Amendment rights and constituted a taking of its property without just compensation. The United States Supreme Court rejected both of these arguments and held that states could recognize a state constitutional right of access to shopping centers.

4. Speech in Authoritarian Environments: Military, Prisons, and Schools

The place where speech occurs is relevant in another sense: The Court has held that some government-operated places are environments where great deference is required to regulations of speech. Specifically, the Court generally has sided with the government when regulating expression in the military, in prisons, and in schools. Although there are obvious differences between these contexts, there also are similarities. All involve places where people often are involuntarily present. All are authoritarian environments that do not operate internally in a democratic fashion. In each, the Court has proclaimed a need for deference to authority and to the expertise of those managing the place.

The underlying issue as to each is whether the restrictions on speech upheld by the Court are appropriate or show excessive deference. The Court has presumed that aggressive judicial review and significant protection of speech is inconsistent with the functioning of such authoritarian environments. But, on the other hand, there is a strong argument that court protection of rights such as freedom of speech is essential in such places precisely because of the lack of political oversight and responsiveness to those in these places. The Court's decisions, described below, can be criticized as overly deferential in that they allowed restrictions of speech without any proof that the expression actually would interfere with the functioning of the institution.

a. Military

The Supreme Court generally has been extremely deferential to the military in its ability to restrict constitutional rights; this also has been true for First Amendment freedoms. Parker v. Levy is illustrative.

PARKER v. LEVY

417 U.S. 733 (1974)

Justice REHNQUIST delivered the opinion of the Court.

Appellee Howard Levy, a physician, was a captain in the Army stationed at Fort Jackson, South Carolina. From the time he entered on active duty in July 1965 until his trial by court-martial, he was assigned as Chief of the Dermatological Service of the United States Army Hospital at Fort Jackson. On June 2, 1967, appellee was convicted by a general court-martial of violations of Arts. 90, 133, and 134 of the Uniform Code of Military Justice, and sentenced to dismissal from the service, forfeiture of all pay and allowances, and confinement for three years at hard labor.

The facts upon which his conviction rests are virtually undisputed. [A]ppellee made several public statements to enlisted personnel at the post, of which the following is representative: "The United States is wrong in being involved in the Viet Nam War. I would refuse to go to Viet Nam if ordered to do so. I don't see why any colored soldier would go to Viet Nam: they should refuse to go to Viet Nam and if sent should refuse to fight because they are discriminated against and denied their freedom in the United States, and they are sacrificed and discriminated against in Viet Nam by being given all the hazardous duty and they are suffering the majority of casualties. If I were a colored soldier I would refuse to go to Viet Nam and if I were a colored soldier and were sent I would refuse to fight. Special Forces personnel are liars and thieves and killers of peasants and murderers of women and children." Appellee's military superiors originally contemplated nonjudicial proceedings against him under Art. 15 of the Uniform Code of Military Justice, 10 U.S.C. §815, but later determined that court-martial proceedings were appropriate.

This Court has long recognized that the military is, by necessity, a specialized society separate from civilian society. We have also recognized that the military has, again by necessity, developed laws and traditions of its own during its long history. The differences between the military and civilian communities result from the fact that "it is the primary business of armies and navies to fight or [be] ready to fight wars should the occasion arise."

While the members of the military are not excluded from the protection granted by the First Amendment, the different character of the military community and of the military mission requires a different application of those protections. The fundamental necessity for obedience, and the consequent necessity for imposition of discipline, may render permissible within the military that which would be constitutionally impermissible outside it. Doctrines of First Amendment overbreadth asserted in support of challenges to imprecise language like that contained in Arts. 133 and 134 are not exempt from the operation of these principles.

The Uniform Code of Military Justice applies a series of sanctions, varying from severe criminal penalties to administratively imposed minor sanctions, upon members of the military. However, for the reasons dictating a different application of First Amendment principles in the military context described above, we think that the "weighty countervailing policies," which permit the extension of standing in First Amendment cases involving civilian society, must be accorded a good deal less weight in the military context.

There is a wide range of the conduct of military personnel to which Arts. 133 and 134 may be applied without infringement of the First Amendment. While there may lurk at the fringes of the articles, even in the light of their narrowing construction by the United States Court of Military Appeals, some possibility that conduct which would be ultimately held to be protected by the First Amendment could be included within their prohibition, we deem this insufficient to invalidate either of them at the behest of appellee. His conduct, that of a commissioned officer publicly urging enlisted personnel to refuse to obey orders which might send them into combat, was unprotected under the most expansive notions of the First Amendment.

Justice DOUGLAS, dissenting.

This is the first case that presents to us a question of what protection, if any, the First Amendment gives people in the Armed Services. On its face there are no exceptions—no preferred classes for whose benefit the First Amendment extends, no exempt classes. The military by tradition and by necessity demands discipline; and those necessities require obedience in training and in action. A command is speech brigaded with action, and permissible commands may not be disobeyed. There may be a borderland or penumbra that in time can be established by litigated cases.

I cannot imagine, however, that Congress would think it had the power to authorize the military to curtail the reading list of books, plays, poems, periodicals, papers, and the like which a person in the Armed Services may read. Nor can I believe Congress would assume authority to empower the military to suppress conversations at a bar, ban discussions of public affairs, prevent enlisted men or women or draftees from meeting in discussion groups at times and places and for such periods of time that do not interfere with the performance of military duties.

Justice STEWART, with whom Justice DOUGLAS and Justice BRENNAN join, dissenting.

I cannot conclude that the statutory language clearly warned the appellee that his speech was illegal. It may have been, of course, that Dr. Levy had a subjective feeling that his conduct violated some military law. But that is not enough. [T]he general articles are unconstitutionally vague under the standards normally and repeatedly applied by this Court. It may be that military necessity justifies the promulgation of substantive rules of law that are wholly foreign to civilian life, but I fail to perceive how any legitimate military goal is served by enshrouding these rules in language so vague and uncertain as to be incomprehensible to the servicemen who are to be governed by them. Indeed, I should suppose that vague laws, with their serious capacity for arbitrary and discriminatory enforcement, can in the end only hamper the military's objectives of high morale and esprit de corps.

In Brown v. Glines, 444 U.S. 348 (1980), the Court went even further in exempting the military from the application of the First Amendment. *Brown* involved an Air Force regulation prohibiting members of the Air Force from posting or distributing printed materials at an Air Force installation without the permission of the commander. This, of course, is the most blatant form of prior restraint: a government licensing system for speech. Unlike Parker v. Levy, this was not punishment for specific speech that threatened the military's operation. Yet the Court upheld the prior restraint and concluded that "since a commander is charged with maintaining morale, discipline, and readiness, he must have authority over the distribution of materials that could affect adversely these essential attributes of an effective military." Again, the underlying issue is whether this is necessary deference to military authority or excessive deference by allowing a system of prior restraint that would be permitted in virtually no other situation.

b. Prisons

The Court has held that the general test is that the government may restrict and punish the speech of prisoners if the action is reasonably related to a legitimate penological interest.[8] The Court has said that "[i]n a prison context, an inmate does not retain those First Amendment rights that are inconsistent

---

8. Turner v. Safley, 482 U.S. 78 (1987).

A. Government Properties and Speech

with his status as a prisoner or with the legitimate penological objectives of the corrections system."[9] Thornburgh v. Abbott is illustrative.

THORNBURGH v. ABBOTT
490 U.S. 401 (1989)

Justice BLACKMUN delivered the opinion of the Court.

Regulations promulgated by the Federal Bureau of Prisons broadly permit federal prisoners to receive publications from the "outside," but authorize prison officials to reject incoming publications found to be detrimental to institutional security. The warden may reject it "only if it is determined detrimental to the security, good order, or discipline of the institution or if it might facilitate criminal activity." The warden, however, may not reject a publication "solely because its content is religious, philosophical, political, social or sexual, or because its content is unpopular or repugnant."

There is little doubt that the kind of censorship just described would raise grave First Amendment concerns outside the prison context. It is equally certain that "[p]rison walls do not form a barrier separating prison inmates from the protections of the Constitution," nor do they bar free citizens from exercising their own constitutional rights by reaching out to those on the "inside." We have recognized, however, that these rights must be exercised with due regard for the "inordinately difficult undertaking" that is modern prison administration. Acknowledging the expertise of these officials and that the judiciary is "ill equipped" to deal with the difficult and delicate problems of prison management, this Court has afforded considerable deference to the determinations of prison administrators who, in the interest of security, regulate the relations between prisoners and the outside world.

We deal here with incoming publications, material requested by an individual inmate but targeted to a general audience. Once in the prison, material of this kind reasonably may be expected to circulate among prisoners, with the concomitant potential for coordinated disruptive conduct. Furthermore, prisoners may observe particular material in the possession of a fellow prisoner, draw inferences about their fellow's beliefs, sexual orientation, or gang affiliations from that material, and cause disorder by acting accordingly.

The Court in Turner v. Safley identified several factors that are relevant to, and that serve to channel, the reasonableness inquiry. [W]e must determine whether the governmental objective underlying the regulations at issue is legitimate and neutral, and that the regulations are rationally related to that objective. We agree with the District Court that this requirement has been met.

The legitimacy of the Government's purpose in promulgating these regulations is beyond question. The regulations are expressly aimed at protecting prison security, a purpose this Court has said is "central to all other corrections goals." We also conclude that the broad discretion accorded prison wardens by the regulations here at issue is rationally related to security interests. We reach this conclusion for two reasons. The first has to do with the kind

---

9. Jones v. North Carolina Prisoners' Union, 433 U.S. 119 (1977).

of security risk presented by incoming publications. Second, we are comforted by the individualized nature of the determinations required by the regulation. Under the regulations, no publication may be excluded unless the warden himself makes the determination that it is "detrimental to the security, good order, or discipline of the institution or . . . might facilitate criminal activity."

In sum, we hold that *Turner*'s reasonableness standard is to be applied to the regulations at issue in this case, and that those regulations are facially valid under that standard.

Justice STEVENS, with whom Justice BRENNAN and Justice MARSHALL join, concurring in part and dissenting in part.

An article in Labyrinth, a magazine published by the Committee for Prisoner Humanity & Justice, began as follows:

> In January 1975, William Lowe, a black prisoner at the United States Penitentiary at Terre Haute, Indiana died of asthma. . . . In August 1975, Joseph (Yusef) Jones, Jr., a black prisoner at the U.S. Penitentiary, Terre Haute, IN died of asthma.
>
> . . . The prison infirmary at that time had only one respirator[,] known to be inoperative in January 1975 when William Lowe died. It was still broken in August 1975 when Joseph Jones needed it.
>
> On the day of his death Jones was suffering an acute asthma attack; he was gasping for breath in the stale, hot, humid air in the cell. He requested medical aid of the guards. After several hours of unheeded pleading, accompanied by complaints to the guards from fellow prisoners in the cell block, Jones became frantic. Each breath was painful; each breath brought him closer to suffocation. Finally, guards called the PA (physician's assistant) . . . , who brought with him the broken respirator. Finding the equipment unusable, the PA gave Jones an injection of the tranquilizer, thorazine, to calm him. Treatment with a tranquilizer was unquestionably contraindicated by Jones' medical condition. Twenty minutes later, Jones was dead.
>
> Conclusion: Jones, who was convicted of bank robbery and sentenced to 10 years in prison, was in fact, sentenced to death and was murdered by neglect.

Labyrinth's efforts to disseminate the article to its subscribers at Marion Federal Penitentiary met Government resistance. Marion officials, acting within Federal Bureau of Prisons (Bureau) regulations, returned the magazine on the ground that "the article entitled 'Medical Murder' would be detrimental to the good order and discipline of this institution. . . . [T]his type of philosophy could guide inmates in this institution into situations which could cause themselves and other inmates problems with the Medical Staff." Two years after publication a Marion official testified that he believed the article had posed no threat. Nonetheless, the District Court below found the suppression of this and 45 other publications "reasonable," and thus sustained the rejections wholesale.

I cannot agree with either [the majority's] holding that another finding of "reasonableness" will justify censorship or its premature approval of the Bureau's regulations. These latter determinations upset precedent in a headlong rush to strip inmates of all but a vestige of free communication with the world beyond the prison gate.

A. Government Properties and Speech

Most regulations of prisoner speech have been upheld under the reasonableness test. Procunier v. Martinez, 416 U.S. 396 (1974), is the exception; the Court declared unconstitutional a prison regulation that restricted the types of letters that prisoners can write. The regulation said that prisoners could not write letters that would "magnify grievances" or that were "lewd, obscene, defamatory, or otherwise inappropriate." The Court held that this restriction on the ability of prisoners to communicate with those outside the prison was unnecessary for the maintenance of order and discipline among prisoners. The prison had no legitimate interest in stopping prisoners from expressing their grievances to those outside the prison or in censoring the content of prisoner correspondence.

Yet Procunier v. Martinez is exceptional, even in the area of prisoner speech to those outside the prison. In other cases, the Court has allowed restrictions on prisoner correspondence and expression to others outside the prison. In Turner v. Safley, 482 U.S. 78 (1987), the Court upheld a prison regulation that prohibited correspondence between inmates at other prisons. The Court accepted the government's claim that correspondence among prisoners could lead to comparisons that could provoke dissatisfaction and unrest. The Court also accepted the government's concern that unrest could spread among institutions through such correspondence.

In several cases, the Court upheld the ability of prisons to restrict the ability of the press to interview prisoners or have access to prisons. In Pell v. Procunier, 417 U.S. 817 (1974), and Saxbe v. Washington Post Co., 417 U.S. 843 (1974), the Court upheld prison regulations that prevented the media from interviewing particular prisoners. The Court said that the regulations were justified because "press attention concentrated on a relatively small number of inmates who, as a result, became virtual 'public figures' within the prison society and gained a disproportionate degree of notoriety and influence among their fellow inmates . . . and became the source of severe disciplinary problems."

In Houchins v. KQED, 438 U.S. 1 (1978), the Court, in a plurality opinion, held that the press did not have a right of access to prisons to observe conditions. The media was allowed only monthly tours, without cameras or tape recorders, of the Greystone portion of the Santa Rita jail. The Court upheld the restriction, in part, based on the lack of any special First Amendment rights for the press to gather information and, in part, based on the need for government control over prisons.

The Court not only has restricted the ability of prisoners to communicate with those outside, but also has limited the ability of prisoners to receive information. In Bell v. Wolfish, 441 U.S. 520 (1979), the Court upheld a regulation that prevented jail inmates from receiving hardcover books except when mailed from publishers or bookstores. The Court accepted the prison's concern that books could contain contraband and that the need for security required limiting the source for such books. The Court rejected the argument that searching the books prior to delivery to the inmates could satisfy the security concern.

In Beard v. Banks, 548 U.S. 521 (2006), the Court upheld a Pennsylvania law denying newspapers, magazines, and photographs to certain prison inmates. The Court again stressed the need for deference to prison officials.

Finally, in addition to restricting speech from and to prisoners, the Court also has limited speech among inmates in a prison. In Jones v. North Carolina Prisoners' Union, 433 U.S. 119 (1977), the Court upheld a prison regulation that prohibited prisoners from forming a union and that specifically forbade inmates from soliciting others to join the union and outlawed union meetings. The Court expressed the need for great deference to prison authorities: "Because the realities of running a penal institution are complex and difficult, we have long recognized the wide-ranging deference to be accorded the decisions of prison administrators." The Court upheld the prohibition of the prison union because of the prison's claim that it threatened discipline and order within the institution. The Court said that the "prison officials concluded that the presence, perhaps even the objectives, of a prisoners' labor union would be detrimental to order and security; it is enough to say that they have not been conclusively shown to be wrong in this view."

In Shaw v. Murphy, 532 U.S. 223 (2001), a prisoner sent a letter containing legal advice to an inmate at another institution. Prison authorities intercepted it and did not deliver it. A suit was brought under the First Amendment.

The Supreme Court, in an opinion by Justice Thomas, unanimously held that there was no violation of the First Amendment rights of the prisoners. Justice Thomas reaffirmed that Turner v. Safley states the appropriate test: Prisoner speech may be regulated if it is rationally related to a legitimate penological interest. Justice Thomas stressed that this test is to be applied with great deference to prison authorities. He stated, "[U]nder *Turner* and its predecessors, prison officials are to remain the primary arbiters of the problems that arise in prison management. If courts were permitted to enhance constitutional protection based on their assessments of the content of the particular communications, courts would be in a position to assume a greater role in decisions affecting prison administration."

Although the letter contained legal advice, the *Court* accepted the claim that such speech has sufficient risks to justify the prison's refusal to deliver it. Justice Thomas wrote, "Although supervised inmate legal assistance programs may serve valuable ends, it is 'indisputable' that inmate law clerks 'are sometimes a menace to prison discipline' and that prisoners have an 'acknowledged propensity . . . to abuse both the giving and the seeking of [legal] assistance.' Prisoners have used legal correspondence as a means for passing contraband and communicating instructions on how to manufacture drugs or weapons."

In Overton v. Bazzetta, 539 U.S. 126 (2003), the Supreme Court, in an opinion by Justice Kennedy, upheld a law that regulated visits to prisoners. Michigan's prison regulations prevented inmates from having noncontact family visits with minor nieces, nephews, and children to whom parental rights had been terminated; prohibited inmates from visiting with former inmates; required children to be accompanied by a family member or legal guardian; and subjected inmates with two substance-abuse violations to a ban of at least two years on future visitation. The Court held that these restrictions were constitutional because they were rationally related to legitimate penological objectives and did not violate the substantive due process or free association guarantees of the First Amendment. Also, the Court held that a two-year ban on visitation for inmates with two substance-abuse violations did not violate the constitutional prohibition against cruel and unusual punishment. The Court emphasized the need for judicial deference to prison officials and that prison regulations should be upheld as long as they are rationally related to legitimate interests.

A. Government Properties and Speech

In Beard v. Banks, 548 U.S. 521 (2006), the Court upheld a Pennsylvania prison regulation that prevented some prison inmates from having access to newspapers, magazines, or photographs. The Court used the Turner v. Safley test, allowing regulations that are reasonably related to a legitimate penological interest, and found that it was met. Justice Breyer, writing for the Court in a six-to-three decision, said, "The Secretary in his motion set forth several justifications for the prison's policy, including the need to motivate better behavior on the part of particularly difficult prisoners, the need to minimize the amount of property they control in their cells, and the need to ensure prison safety, by, for example, diminishing the amount of material a prisoner might use to start a cell fire. We need go no further than the first justification, that of providing increased incentives for better prison behavior. Applying the well-established substantive and procedural standards . . . we find, on the basis of the record before us, that the Secretary's justification is adequate."

c. Schools

Schools, of course, are in many ways different from prisons and the military. An important function of schools is in teaching constitutional principles, such as the importance of freedom of speech. Restrictions of expression within schools is counter to that teaching. Also, although there is a need for discipline and order in schools, it is quite different in this regard from prisons or the military. On the other hand, courts tend to defer to the expertise of school officials and their need to make decisions about education and how to preserve discipline and order within the schools.

Some Supreme Court decisions have been very protective of student speech. In West Virginia Board of Education v. Barnette, 319 U.S. 624 (1943), discussed above in Chapter 2, the Court declared unconstitutional a state law that required that students salute the flag at the beginning of the school day. Although the Court focused on the First Amendment's prohibition against compelled expression, the decision obviously accepted the protection of First Amendment rights in schools.

Tinker v. Des Moines School District is the most important Supreme Court decision finding First Amendment protection for student speech.

TINKER v. DES MOINES INDEPENDENT COMMUNITY SCHOOL DISTRICT
393 U.S. 503 (1969)

Justice FORTAS delivered the opinion of the Court.

Petitioner John F. Tinker, 15 years old, and petitioner Christopher Eckhardt, 16 years old, attended high schools in Des Moines, Iowa. Petitioner Mary Beth Tinker, John's sister, was a 13-year-old student in junior high school. In December 1965, a group of adults and students in Des Moines held a meeting at the Eckhardt home. The group determined to publicize their objections to the hostilities in Vietnam and their support for a truce by wearing black armbands during the holiday season and by fasting on December 16 and New Year's Eve.

On December 16, Mary Beth and Christopher wore black armbands to their schools. John Tinker wore his armband the next day. They were all sent home and suspended from school until they would come back without their armbands. They did not return to school until after the planned period for wearing armbands had expired — that is, until after New Year's Day.

I

First Amendment rights, applied in light of the special characteristics of the school environment, are available to teachers and students. It can hardly be argued that either students or teachers shed their constitutional rights to freedom of speech or expression at the schoolhouse gate. This has been the unmistakable holding of this Court for almost 50 years. On the other hand, the Court has repeatedly emphasized the need for affirming the comprehensive authority of the States and of school officials, consistent with fundamental constitutional safeguards, to prescribe and control conduct in the schools.

II

The problem posed by the present case does not relate to regulation of the length of skirts or the type of clothing, to hair style, or deportment. It does not concern aggressive, disruptive action or even group demonstrations. Our problem involves direct, primary First Amendment rights akin to "pure speech." The school officials banned and sought to punish petitioners for a silent, passive expression of opinion, unaccompanied by any disorder or disturbance on the part of petitioners. There is here no evidence whatever of petitioners' interference, actual or nascent, with the schools' work or of collision with the rights of other students to be secure and to be let alone. Accordingly, this case does not concern speech or action that intrudes upon the work of the schools or the rights of other students. Only a few of the 18,000 students in the school system wore the black armbands. Only five students were suspended for wearing them. There is no indication that the work of the schools or any class was disrupted. Outside the classrooms, a few students made hostile remarks to the children wearing armbands, but there were no threats or acts of violence on school premises.

The District Court concluded that the action of the school authorities was reasonable because it was based upon their fear of a disturbance from the wearing of the armbands. But, in our system, undifferentiated fear or apprehension of disturbance is not enough to overcome the right to freedom of expression. Any departure from absolute regimentation may cause trouble. Any variation from the majority's opinion may inspire fear. Any word spoken, in class, in the lunchroom, or on the campus, that deviates from the views of another person may start an argument or cause a disturbance. But our Constitution says we must take this risk, and our history says that it is this sort of hazardous freedom — this kind of openness — that is the basis of our national strength and of the independence and vigor of Americans who grow up and live in this relatively permissive, often disputatious, society.

A. Government Properties and Speech

In order for the State in the person of school officials to justify prohibition of a particular expression of opinion, it must be able to show that its action was caused by something more than a mere desire to avoid the discomfort and unpleasantness that always accompany an unpopular viewpoint. Certainly where there is no finding and no showing that engaging in the forbidden conduct would "materially and substantially interfere with the requirements of appropriate discipline in the operation of the school," the prohibition cannot be sustained.

In the present case, the District Court made no such finding, and our independent examination of the record fails to yield evidence that the school authorities had reason to anticipate that the wearing of the armbands would substantially interfere with the work of the school or impinge upon the rights of other students. Even an official memorandum prepared after the suspension that listed the reasons for the ban on wearing the armbands made no reference to the anticipation of such disruption.

It is also relevant that the school authorities did not purport to prohibit the wearing of all symbols of political or controversial significance. The record shows that students in some of the schools wore buttons relating to national political campaigns, and some even wore the Iron Cross, traditionally a symbol of Nazism. The order prohibiting the wearing of armbands did not extend to these. Instead, a particular symbol—black armbands worn to exhibit opposition to this Nation's involvement in Vietnam—was singled out for prohibition. Clearly, the prohibition of expression of one particular opinion, at least without evidence that it is necessary to avoid material and substantial interference with schoolwork or discipline, is not constitutionally permissible.

In our system, state-operated schools may not be enclaves of totalitarianism. School officials do not possess absolute authority over their students. Students in school as well as out of school are "persons" under our Constitution. They are possessed of fundamental rights which the State must respect, just as they themselves must respect their obligations to the State. In our system, students may not be regarded as closed-circuit recipients of only that which the State chooses to communicate. They may not be confined to the expression of those sentiments that are officially approved. In the absence of a specific showing of constitutionally valid reasons to regulate their speech, students are entitled to freedom of expression of their views.

Justice BLACK, dissenting.

The Court's holding in this case ushers in what I deem to be an entirely new era in which the power to control pupils by the elected "officials of state supported public schools" in the United States is in ultimate effect transferred to the Supreme Court.

While the record does not show that any of these armband students shouted, used profane language, or were violent in any manner, detailed testimony by some of them shows their armbands caused comments, warnings by other students, the poking of fun at them, and a warning by an older football player that other, nonprotesting students had better let them alone. There is also evidence that a teacher of mathematics had his lesson period practically "wrecked" chiefly by disputes with Mary Beth Tinker, who wore her armband for her "demonstration."

Even a causal reading of the record shows that this armband did divert students' minds from their regular lessons, and that talk, comments, etc., made John Tinker "self-conscious" in attending school with his armband. While the absence of obscene remarks or boisterous and loud disorder perhaps justifies the Court's statement that the few armband students did not actually "disrupt" the classwork, I think the record overwhelmingly shows that the armbands did exactly what the elected school officials and principals foresaw they would, that is, took the students' minds off their classwork and diverted them to thoughts about the highly emotional subject of the Vietnam war. And I repeat that if the time has come when pupils of state-supported schools, kindergartens, grammar schools, or high schools, can defy and flout orders of school officials to keep their minds on their own schoolwork, it is the beginning of a new revolutionary era of permissiveness in this country fostered by the judiciary. The next logical step, it appears to me, would be to hold unconstitutional laws that bar pupils under 21 or 18 from voting, or from being elected members of the boards of education.

Nor are public school students sent to the schools at public expense to broadcast political or any other views to educate and inform the public. The original idea of schools, which I do not believe is yet abandoned as worthless or not of date, was that children had not yet reached the point of experience and wisdom which enabled them to teach all of their elders. It may be that the Nation has outworn the old-fashioned slogan that "children are to be seen not heard," but one may, I hope, be permitted to harbor the thought that taxpayers send children to school on the premise that at their age they need to learn, not teach.

This case, therefore, wholly without constitutional reasons in my judgment, subjects all the public schools in the country to the whims and caprices of their loudest-mouthed, but maybe not their brightest, students. I, for one, am not fully persuaded that school pupils are wise enough, even with this Court's expert help from Washington, to run the 23,390 public school systems in our 50 States. I wish, therefore, wholly to disclaim any purpose on my part to hold that the Federal Constitution compels the teachers, parents, and elected school officials to surrender control of the American public school system to public school students. I dissent.

The Court applied *Tinker* to the college context in Papish v. Board of Curators of the University of Missouri, 410 U.S. 667 (1973), where it held that a student could not be expelled for a political cartoon in a newspaper. A student drew a cartoon for publication in an off-campus underground newspaper, which depicted a police officer raping the Statue of Liberty. Also, the student wrote an article that used the word "motherfucker." The Court held that expelling the student for this speech violated the First Amendment: It was political speech; it appeared in an off-campus newspaper; it occurred at a university; and there was no showing of any disruption of the school's activities.

In more recent years, however, the Court has been much less protective of speech in school environments and much more deferential to school authorities. In Bethel School District No. 403 v. Fraser, Hazelwood School District v. Kuhlmeier, and Morse v. Frederick, the Court rejected student speech

A. Government Properties and Speech

claims and sided with school authorities. While reading these cases, consider whether they are a significant departure from *Tinker* or whether they can be distinguished from *Tinker*.

BETHEL SCHOOL DISTRICT NO. 403 v. FRASER
478 U.S. 675 (1986)

Chief Justice BURGER delivered the opinion of the Court.

We granted certiorari to decide whether the First Amendment prevents a school district from disciplining a high school student for giving a lewd speech at a school assembly.

I

On April 26, 1983, respondent Matthew N. Fraser, a student at Bethel High School in Pierce County, Washington, delivered a speech nominating a fellow student for student elective office. Approximately 600 high school students, many of whom were 14-year-olds, attended the assembly. Students were required to attend the assembly or to report to the study hall. The assembly was part of a school-sponsored educational program in self-government. Students who elected not to attend the assembly were required to report to study hall.

During the entire speech, Fraser referred to his candidate in terms of an elaborate, graphic, and explicit sexual metaphor. Two of Fraser's teachers, with whom he discussed the contents of his speech in advance, informed him that the speech was "inappropriate and that he probably should not deliver it," and that his delivery of the speech might have "severe consequences." A Bethel High School disciplinary rule prohibits the use of obscene language in the school.

During Fraser's delivery of the speech, a school counselor observed the reaction of students to the speech. Some students hooted and yelled; some by gestures graphically simulated the sexual activities pointedly alluded to in respondent's speech. Other students appeared to be bewildered and embarrassed by the speech. One teacher reported that on the day following the speech, she found it necessary to forgo a portion of the scheduled class lesson in order to discuss the speech with the class.

The morning after the assembly, the Assistant Principal called Fraser into her office and notified him that the school considered his speech to have been a violation of this rule. Fraser was then informed that he would be suspended for three days, and that his name would be removed from the list of candidates for graduation speaker at the school's commencement exercises.

II

This Court acknowledged in Tinker v. Des Moines Independent Community School Dist., that students do not "shed their constitutional rights to freedom of speech or expression at the schoolhouse gate." The marked distinction between the political "message" of the armbands in *Tinker* and the sexual content of respondent's speech in this case seems to have been given little weight by the Court of Appeals. In upholding the students' right to engage in a nondisruptive, passive expression of a political viewpoint in *Tinker*, this Court was careful to note that the case did "not concern speech or action that intrudes upon the work of the schools or the rights of other students."

Surely it is a highly appropriate function of public school education to prohibit the use of vulgar and offensive terms in public discourse. Indeed, the "fundamental values necessary to the maintenance of a democratic political system" disfavor the use of terms of debate highly offensive or highly threatening to others. Nothing in the Constitution prohibits the states from insisting that certain modes of expression are inappropriate and subject to sanctions. The inculcation of these values is truly the "work of the schools." The determination of what manner of speech in the classroom or in school assembly is inappropriate properly rests with the school board.

The process of educating our youth for citizenship in public schools is not confined to books, the curriculum, and the civics class; schools must teach by example the shared values of a civilized social order. Consciously or otherwise, teachers—and indeed the older students—demonstrate the appropriate form of civil discourse and political expression by their conduct and deportment in and out of class. Inescapably, like parents, they are role models. The schools, as instruments of the state, may determine that the essential lessons of civil, mature conduct cannot be conveyed in a school that tolerates lewd, indecent, or offensive speech and conduct such as that indulged in by this confused boy.

The pervasive sexual innuendo in Fraser's speech was plainly offensive to both teachers and students—indeed to any mature person. By glorifying male sexuality, and in its verbal content, the speech was acutely insulting to teenage girl students. The speech could well be seriously damaging to its less mature audience, many of whom were only 14 years old and on the threshold of awareness of human sexuality. Some students were reported as bewildered by the speech and the reaction of mimicry it provoked.

We hold that petitioner School District acted entirely within its permissible authority in imposing sanctions upon Fraser in response to his offensively lewd and indecent speech. Unlike the sanctions imposed on the students wearing armbands in *Tinker*, the penalties imposed in this case were unrelated to any political viewpoint. The First Amendment does not prevent the school officials from determining that to permit a vulgar and lewd speech such as respondent's would undermine the school's basic educational mission. A high school assembly or classroom is no place for a sexually explicit monologue directed towards an unsuspecting audience of teenage students.

Justice BRENNAN, concurring in the judgment.

Respondent gave the following speech at a high school assembly in support of a candidate for student government office: "I know a man who is firm—he's firm in his pants, he's firm in his shirt, his character is firm—but most . . . of all, his belief in you, the students of Bethel, is firm. Jeff Kuhlman is a man who takes his point and pounds it in. If necessary, he'll take an issue and nail it to the wall. He doesn't attack things in spurts—he drives hard, pushing and pushing until finally—he succeeds. Jeff is a man who will go to the very end—even the climax, for each and every one of you. So vote for Jeff for A.S.B. vice-president—he'll never come between you and the best our high school can be."

The Court, referring to these remarks as "obscene," "vulgar," "lewd," and "offensively lewd," concludes that school officials properly punished respondent for uttering the speech. Having read the full text of respondent's remarks, I find it difficult to believe that it is the same speech the Court describes. To my mind, the most that can be said about respondent's speech—and all that need be said—is that in light of the discretion school officials have to teach high school students how to conduct civil and effective public discourse, and to prevent disruption of school educational activities, it was not unconstitutional for school officials to conclude, under the circumstances of this case, that respondent's remarks exceeded permissible limits.

Justice MARSHALL, dissenting.

I dissent from the Court's decision, however, because in my view the School District failed to demonstrate that respondent's remarks were indeed disruptive. The District Court and Court of Appeals conscientiously applied Tinker v. Des Moines Independent Community School Dist. (1969), and concluded that the School District had not demonstrated any disruption of the educational process. I recognize that the school administration must be given wide latitude to determine what forms of conduct are inconsistent with the school's educational mission; nevertheless, where speech is involved, we may not unquestioningly accept a teacher's or administrator's assertion that certain pure speech interfered with education. Here the School District, despite a clear opportunity to do so, failed to bring in evidence sufficient to convince either of the two lower courts that education at Bethel School was disrupted by respondent's speech. I therefore see no reason to disturb the Court of Appeals' judgment.

The Court went even further in its deference to school authorities in *Hazelwood School District v. Kuhlmeier*, 484 U.S. 260 (1988). A school newspaper produced as part of a journalism class was going to publish, with the approval of its faculty advisor, stories about three students' experience with pregnancy and about the impact of divorce on students. No students' names were included in the article on pregnancy, and one was mentioned in the article on divorce (although the name had been deleted after the paper had been forwarded to the principal for review). The principal decided to publish the paper without these articles by deleting the two pages on which they appeared. The principal expressed the view that the articles on pregnancy discussed sexual activity and birth control in a manner that was inappropriate for some of the younger students at the school, that the three students in the article on pregnancy might be identified from other aspects of the article, and that the parents of the student identified in the article about divorce should have the opportunity to respond.

The Supreme Court upheld the principal's decision and rejected the First Amendment challenge. At the outset, Justice White, writing for the

Court, quoted *Tinker*, that "[s]tudents in public schools do not 'shed their constitutional rights to freedom of speech or expression at the schoolhouse gate.'" But he then added, quoting *Bethel*, that "the First Amendment rights of students in the public schools 'are not automatically coextensive with the rights of adults in other settings.'" Justice White concluded that the school newspaper was a nonpublic forum and that as a result "school officials were entitled to regulate the content of [the school newspaper] in any reasonable manner."

The Court emphasized the ability of schools to control curricular decisions, such as what appears in school newspapers published as part of journalism classes. Justice White wrote: "The question whether the First Amendment requires a school to tolerate particular student speech—the question that we addressed in *Tinker*—is different from the question whether the First Amendment requires a school affirmatively to promote particular student speech. The former question addresses educators' ability to silence a student's personal expression that happens to occur on the school premises. The latter question concerns educators' authority over school-sponsored publications, theatrical productions, and other expressive activities that students, parents, and members of the public might reasonably perceive to bear the imprimatur of the school." The Court said in this context schools have broad authority to regulate student speech.

The Court's most recent decision—albeit more than a decade ago on student speech—was Morse v. Frederick.

MORSE v. FREDERICK
551 U.S. 393 (2007)

Chief Justice ROBERTS delivered the opinion of the Court.

At a school-sanctioned and school-supervised event, a high school principal saw some of her students unfurl a large banner conveying a message she reasonably regarded as promoting illegal drug use. Consistent with established school policy prohibiting such messages at school events, the principal directed the students to take down the banner. One student—among those who had brought the banner to the event—refused to do so. The principal confiscated the banner and later suspended the student.

Our cases make clear that students do not "shed their constitutional rights to freedom of speech or expression at the schoolhouse gate." Tinker v. Des Moines Independent Community School Dist. (1969). At the same time, we have held that "the constitutional rights of students in public school are not automatically coextensive with the rights of adults in other settings," Bethel School Dist. No. 403 v. Fraser (1986), and that the rights of students "must be 'applied in light of the special characteristics of the school environment.'" Hazelwood School Dist. v. Kuhlmeier (1988). Consistent with these principles, we hold that schools may take steps to safeguard those entrusted to their care from speech that can reasonably be regarded as encouraging illegal drug use. We conclude that the school officials in this case did not violate the First Amendment by confiscating the pro-drug banner and suspending the student responsible for it.

A. Government Properties and Speech

I

On January 24, 2002, the Olympic Torch Relay passed through Juneau, Alaska, on its way to the winter games in Salt Lake City, Utah. The torchbearers were to proceed along a street in front of Juneau-Douglas High School (JDHS) while school was in session. Petitioner Deborah Morse, the school principal, decided to permit staff and students to participate in the Torch Relay as an approved social event or class trip. Students were allowed to leave class to observe the relay from either side of the street. Teachers and administrative officials monitored the students' actions.

Respondent Joseph Frederick, a JDHS senior, was late to school that day. When he arrived, he joined his friends (all but one of whom were JDHS students) across the street from the school to watch the event. Not all the students waited patiently. Some became rambunctious, throwing plastic cola bottles and snowballs and scuffling with their classmates. As the torchbearers and camera crews passed by, Frederick and his friends unfurled a 14-foot banner bearing the phrase: "BONG HiTS 4 JESUS." The large banner was easily readable by the students on the other side of the street.

Principal Morse immediately crossed the street and demanded that the banner be taken down. Everyone but Frederick complied. Morse confiscated the banner and told Frederick to report to her office, where she suspended him for 10 days. Morse later explained that she told Frederick to take the banner down because she thought it encouraged illegal drug use, in violation of established school policy. Juneau School Board Policy No. 5520 states: "The Board specifically prohibits any assembly or public expression that . . . advocates the use of substances that are illegal to minors. . . ." In addition, Juneau School Board Policy No. 5850 subjects "[p]upils who participate in approved social events and class trips" to the same student conduct rules that apply during the regular school program.

Frederick administratively appealed his suspension, but the Juneau School District Superintendent upheld it, limiting it to time served (8 days). In a memorandum setting forth his reasons, the superintendent determined that Frederick had displayed his banner "in the midst of his fellow students, during school hours, at a school-sanctioned activity." He further explained that Frederick "was not disciplined because the principal of the school 'disagreed' with his message, but because his speech appeared to advocate the use of illegal drugs."

The superintendent continued:

> The common-sense understanding of the phrase "bong hits" is that it is a reference to a means of smoking marijuana. Given [Frederick's] inability or unwillingness to express any other credible meaning for the phrase, I can only agree with the principal and countless others who saw the banner as advocating the use of illegal drugs. [Frederick's] speech was not political. He was not advocating the legalization of marijuana or promoting a religious belief. He was displaying a fairly silly message promoting illegal drug usage in the midst of a school activity, for the benefit of television cameras covering the Torch Relay. [Frederick's] speech was potentially disruptive to the event and clearly disruptive of and inconsistent with the school's educational mission to educate students about the dangers of illegal drugs and to discourage their use.

Frederick then filed suit under 42 U.S.C. §1983, alleging that the school board and Morse had violated his First Amendment rights.

II

At the outset, we reject Frederick's argument that this is not a school speech case. The event occurred during normal school hours. It was sanctioned by Principal Morse "as an approved social event or class trip," and the school district's rules expressly provide that pupils in "approved social events and class trips are subject to district rules for student conduct." Teachers and administrators were interspersed among the students and charged with supervising them. The high school band and cheerleaders performed. Frederick, standing among other JDHS students across the street from the school, directed his banner toward the school, making it plainly visible to most students. Under these circumstances, we agree with the superintendent that Frederick cannot "stand in the midst of his fellow students, during school hours, at a school-sanctioned activity and claim he is not at school."

III

The message on Frederick's banner is cryptic. It is no doubt offensive to some, perhaps amusing to others. To still others, it probably means nothing at all. Frederick himself claimed "that the words were just nonsense meant to attract television cameras." But Principal Morse thought the banner would be interpreted by those viewing it as promoting illegal drug use, and that interpretation is plainly a reasonable one.

As Morse later explained in a declaration, when she saw the sign, she thought that "the reference to a 'bong hit' would be widely understood by high school students and others as referring to smoking marijuana." She further believed that "display of the banner would be construed by students, District personnel, parents and others witnessing the display of the banner, as advocating or promoting illegal drug use"—in violation of school policy.

We agree with Morse. At least two interpretations of the words on the banner demonstrate that the sign advocated the use of illegal drugs. First, the phrase could be interpreted as an imperative: "[Take] bong hits . . ."—a message equivalent, as Morse explained in her declaration, to "smoke marijuana" or "use an illegal drug." Alternatively, the phrase could be viewed as celebrating drug use—"bong hits [are a good thing]," or "[we take] bong hits"—and we discern no meaningful distinction between celebrating illegal drug use in the midst of fellow students and outright advocacy or promotion.

Elsewhere in its opinion, the dissent emphasizes the importance of political speech and the need to foster "national debate about a serious issue," as if to suggest that the banner is political speech. But not even Frederick argues that the banner conveys any sort of political or religious message. Contrary to the dissent's suggestion, this is plainly not a case about political debate over the criminalization of drug use or possession.

IV

The question thus becomes whether a principal may, consistent with the First Amendment, restrict student speech at a school event, when that speech is reasonably viewed as promoting illegal drug use. We hold that she may.

A. Government Properties and Speech

In *Tinker*, this Court made clear that "First Amendment rights, applied in light of the special characteristics of the school environment, are available to teachers and students." *Tinker* involved a group of high school students who decided to wear black armbands to protest the Vietnam War. School officials learned of the plan and then adopted a policy prohibiting students from wearing armbands. When several students nonetheless wore armbands to school, they were suspended. The students sued, claiming that their First Amendment rights had been violated, and this Court agreed.

Tinker held that student expression may not be suppressed unless school officials reasonably conclude that it will "materially and substantially disrupt the work and discipline of the school."

This Court's next student speech case was *Fraser*. Matthew Fraser was suspended for delivering a speech before a high school assembly in which he employed what this Court called "an elaborate, graphic, and explicit sexual metaphor." The mode of analysis employed in *Fraser* is not entirely clear. The Court was plainly attuned to the content of Fraser's speech, citing the "marked distinction between the political 'message' of the armbands in *Tinker* and the sexual content of [Fraser's] speech." But the Court also reasoned that school boards have the authority to determine "what manner of speech in the classroom or in school assembly is inappropriate."

We need not resolve this debate to decide this case. For present purposes, it is enough to distill from *Fraser* two basic principles. First, *Fraser*'s holding demonstrates that "the constitutional rights of students in public school are not automatically coextensive with the rights of adults in other settings." Had Fraser delivered the same speech in a public forum outside the school context, it would have been protected. In school, however, Fraser's First Amendment rights were circumscribed "in light of the special characteristics of the school environment." Second, *Fraser* established that the mode of analysis set forth in *Tinker* is not absolute. Whatever approach *Fraser* employed, it certainly did not conduct the "substantial disruption" analysis prescribed by *Tinker*.

Drawing on the principles applied in our student speech cases, we have held in the Fourth Amendment context that "while children assuredly do not 'shed their constitutional rights . . . at the schoolhouse gate,' . . . the nature of those rights is what is appropriate for children in school."

Even more to the point, these cases also recognize that deterring drug use by schoolchildren is an "important—indeed, perhaps compelling" interest. Drug abuse can cause severe and permanent damage to the health and well-being of young people. The problem remains serious today. About half of American 12th graders have used an illicit drug, as have more than a third of 10th graders and about one-fifth of 8th graders. Nearly one in four 12th graders has used an illicit drug in the past month. Some 25% of high schoolers say that they have been offered, sold, or given an illegal drug on school property within the past year.

The "special characteristics of the school environment," and the governmental interest in stopping student drug abuse—reflected in the policies of Congress and myriad school boards[]—allow schools to restrict student expression that they reasonably regard as promoting illegal drug use. Tinker warned that schools may not prohibit student speech because of "undifferentiated fear or apprehension of disturbance" or "a mere desire to avoid the discomfort and unpleasantness that always accompany an unpopular viewpoint." The danger here is far more serious and palpable. The particular concern to prevent student drug abuse at issue here, embodied in established school policy, extends well beyond an abstract desire to avoid controversy.

School principals have a difficult job, and a vitally important one. When Frederick suddenly and unexpectedly unfurled his banner, Morse had to decide to act—or not act—on the spot. It was reasonable for her to conclude that the banner promoted illegal drug use—in violation of established school policy—and that failing to act would send a powerful message to the students in her charge, including Frederick, about how serious the school was about the dangers of illegal drug use. The First Amendment does not require schools to tolerate at school events student expression that contributes to those dangers.

Justice THOMAS, concurring.

The Court today decides that a public school may prohibit speech advocating illegal drug use. I agree and therefore join its opinion in full. I write separately to state my view that the standard set forth in Tinker v. Des Moines Independent Community School Dist. (1969) is without basis in the Constitution.

In my view, the history of public education suggests that the First Amendment, as originally understood, does not protect student speech in public schools. Although colonial schools were exclusively private, public education proliferated in the early 1800's. By the time the States ratified the Fourteenth Amendment, public schools had become relatively common. If students in public schools were originally understood as having free-speech rights, one would have expected 19th-century public schools to have respected those rights and courts to have enforced them. They did not.

Teachers instilled these values not only by presenting ideas but also through strict discipline. Schools punished students for behavior the school considered disrespectful or wrong. Rules of etiquette were enforced, and courteous behavior was demanded. To meet their educational objectives, schools required absolute obedience. In short, in the earliest public schools, teachers taught, and students listened. Teachers commanded, and students obeyed. Teachers did not rely solely on the power of ideas to persuade; they relied on discipline to maintain order.

Through the legal doctrine of in loco parentis, courts upheld the right of schools to discipline students, to enforce rules, and to maintain order. Applying in loco parentis, the judiciary was reluctant to interfere in the routine business of school administration, allowing schools and teachers to set and enforce rules and to maintain order. Thus, in the early years of public schooling, schools and teachers had considerable discretion in disciplinary matters.

Tinker effected a sea change in students' speech rights, extending them well beyond traditional bounds. *Tinker*'s reasoning conflicted with the traditional understanding of the judiciary's role in relation to public schooling, a role limited by in loco parentis.

Today, the Court creates another exception. In doing so, we continue to distance ourselves from *Tinker*, but we neither overrule it nor offer an explanation of when it operates and when it does not. I am afraid that our jurisprudence now says that students have a right to speak in schools except when they don't—a standard continuously developed through litigation against local schools and their administrators. In my view, petitioners could prevail for a much simpler reason: As originally understood, the Constitution does not afford students a right to free speech in public schools.

I join the Court's opinion because it erodes *Tinker*'s hold in the realm of student speech, even though it does so by adding to the patchwork of exceptions to the *Tinker* standard. I think the better approach is to dispense with *Tinker* altogether, and given the opportunity, I would do so.

Justice ALITO, with whom Justice KENNEDY joins, concurring.

I join the opinion of the Court on the understanding that (a) it goes no further than to hold that a public school may restrict speech that a reasonable observer would interpret as advocating illegal drug use and (b) it provides no support for any restriction of speech that can plausibly be interpreted as commenting on any political or social issue, including speech on issues such as "the wisdom of the war on drugs or of legalizing marijuana for medicinal use."

In most settings, the First Amendment strongly limits the government's ability to suppress speech on the ground that it presents a threat of violence. But due to the special features of the school environment, school officials must have greater authority to intervene before speech leads to violence. And, in most cases, *Tinker*'s "substantial disruption" standard permits school officials to step in before actual violence erupts.

Speech advocating illegal drug use poses a threat to student safety that is just as serious, if not always as immediately obvious. As we have recognized in the past and as the opinion of the Court today details, illegal drug use presents a grave and in many ways unique threat to the physical safety of students. I therefore conclude that the public schools may ban speech advocating illegal drug use. But I regard such regulation as standing at the far reaches of what the First Amendment permits. I join the opinion of the Court with the understanding that the opinion does not endorse any further extension.

Justice STEVENS, with whom Justice SOUTER and Justice GINSBURG join, dissenting.

A significant fact barely mentioned by the Court sheds a revelatory light on the motives of both the students and the principal of Juneau-Douglas High School (JDHS). On January 24, 2002, the Olympic Torch Relay gave those Alaska residents a rare chance to appear on national television. As Joseph Frederick repeatedly explained, he did not address the curious message — "BONG HiTS 4 JESUS" — to his fellow students. He just wanted to get the camera crews' attention. Moreover, concern about a nationwide evaluation of the conduct of the JDHS student body would have justified the principal's decision to remove an attention-grabbing 14-foot banner, even if it had merely proclaimed "Glaciers Melt!"

I agree with the Court that the principal should not be held liable for pulling down Frederick's banner [because of qualified immunity]. I would hold, however, that the school's interest in protecting its students from exposure to speech "reasonably regarded as promoting illegal drug use[]" cannot justify disciplining Frederick for his attempt to make an ambiguous statement to a television audience simply because it contained an oblique reference to drugs. The First Amendment demands more, indeed, much more.

The Court holds otherwise only after laboring to establish two uncontroversial propositions: first, that the constitutional rights of students in school settings are not coextensive with the rights of adults; and second, that deterring drug use by schoolchildren is a valid and terribly important interest. As to the first, I take the

Court's point that the message on Frederick's banner is not necessarily protected speech, even though it unquestionably would have been had the banner been unfurled elsewhere. As to the second, I am willing to assume that the Court is correct that the pressing need to deter drug use supports JDHS's rule prohibiting willful conduct that expressly "advocates the use of substances that are illegal to minors." But it is a gross non sequitur to draw from these two unremarkable propositions the remarkable conclusion that the school may suppress student speech that was never meant to persuade anyone to do anything.

In my judgment, the First Amendment protects student speech if the message itself neither violates a permissible rule nor expressly advocates conduct that is illegal and harmful to students. This nonsense banner does neither, and the Court does serious violence to the First Amendment in upholding—indeed, lauding—a school's decision to punish Frederick for expressing a view with which it disagreed.

I

In December 1965, we were engaged in a controversial war, a war that "divided this country as few other issues ever have." Tinker v. Des Moines Independent Community School Dist. (1969) (Black, J., dissenting). Two cardinal First Amendment principles animate both the Court's opinion in *Tinker* and Justice Harlan's dissent. First, censorship based on the content of speech, particularly censorship that depends on the viewpoint of the speaker, is subject to the most rigorous burden of justification. Second, punishing someone for advocating illegal conduct is constitutional only when the advocacy is likely to provoke the harm that the government seeks to avoid. See Brandenburg v. Ohio (1969) (per curiam).

Yet today the Court fashions a test that trivializes the two cardinal principles upon which *Tinker* rests. The Court's test invites stark viewpoint discrimination. In this case, for example, the principal has unabashedly acknowledged that she disciplined Frederick because she disagreed with the pro-drug viewpoint she ascribed to the message on the banner. It is also perfectly clear that "promoting illegal drug use[]" comes nowhere close to proscribable "incitement to imminent lawless action." Encouraging drug use might well increase the likelihood that a listener will try an illegal drug, but that hardly justifies censorship[.]

No one seriously maintains that drug advocacy (much less Frederick's ridiculous sign) comes within the vanishingly small category of speech that can be prohibited because of its feared consequences. Such advocacy, to borrow from Justice Holmes, "ha[s] no chance of starting a present conflagration."

II

The Court rejects outright these twin foundations of *Tinker* because, in its view, the unusual importance of protecting children from the scourge of drugs supports a ban on all speech in the school environment that promotes drug use. Whether or not such a rule is sensible as a matter of policy, carving out pro-drug speech for uniquely harsh treatment finds no support in our case law and is inimical to the values protected by the First Amendment.

I will nevertheless assume for the sake of argument that the school's concededly powerful interest in protecting its students adequately supports its restriction

A. Government Properties and Speech

on "any assembly or public expression that . . . advocates the use of substances that are illegal to minors. . . ." But it is one thing to restrict speech that advocates drug use. It is another thing entirely to prohibit an obscure message with a drug theme that a third party subjectively—and not very reasonably—thinks is tantamount to express advocacy.

There is absolutely no evidence that Frederick's banner's reference to drug paraphernalia "willful[ly]" infringed on anyone's rights or interfered with any of the school's educational programs. Therefore, just as we insisted in *Tinker* that the school establish some likely connection between the armbands and their feared consequences, so too JDHS must show that Frederick's supposed advocacy stands a meaningful chance of making otherwise-abstemious students try marijuana.

But instead of demanding that the school make such a showing, the Court punts. To the extent the Court independently finds that "BONG HiTS 4 JESUS" objectively amounts to the advocacy of illegal drug use—in other words, that it can most reasonably be interpreted as such—that conclusion practically refutes itself. This is a nonsense message, not advocacy. The Court's feeble effort to divine its hidden meaning is strong evidence of that (positing that the banner might mean, alternatively, "'[Take] bong hits,'" "'bong hits [are a good thing],'" or "'[we take] bong hits'"). Admittedly, some high school students (including those who use drugs) are dumb. Most students, however, do not shed their brains at the schoolhouse gate, and most students know dumb advocacy when they see it. The notion that the message on this banner would actually persuade either the average student or even the dumbest one to change his or her behavior is most implausible. That the Court believes such a silly message can be proscribed as advocacy underscores the novelty of its position, and suggests that the principle it articulates has no stopping point.

Among other things, the Court's ham-handed, categorical approach is deaf to the constitutional imperative to permit unfettered debate, even among high-school students, about the wisdom of the war on drugs or of legalizing marijuana for medicinal use. If Frederick's stupid reference to marijuana can in the Court's view justify censorship, then high school students everywhere could be forgiven for zipping their mouths about drugs at school lest some "reasonable" observer censor and then punish them for promoting drugs.

Although this case began with a silly, nonsensical banner, it ends with the Court inventing out of whole cloth a special First Amendment rule permitting the censorship of any student speech that mentions drugs, at least so long as someone could perceive that speech to contain a latent pro-drug message.

Even in high school, a rule that permits only one point of view to be expressed is less likely to produce correct answers than the open discussion of countervailing views. In the national debate about a serious issue, it is the expression of the minority's viewpoint that most demands the protection of the First Amendment. Whatever the better policy may be, a full and frank discussion of the costs and benefits of the attempt to prohibit the use of marijuana is far wiser than suppression of speech because it is unpopular.

Although *Barnette, Tinker, Papish, Bethel, Hazelwood,* and *Morse* all focused on student speech, other First Amendment issues arise in schools as well. For example, in Board of Education, Island Trees Union Free School District No. 26 v. Pico, 457 U.S. 853 (1982), the Court considered the ability of a school library to remove books because they were deemed "objectionable." The books included writings of authors such as Kurt Vonnegut, Desmond Morris, Langston Hughes, and Eldridge Cleaver. The Court said that the "First Amendment rights of students may be directly and sharply implicated by the removal of the books from a school library." The Court explained that the First Amendment protects a right to receive information and that the "special characteristics of the school *library* make that environment especially appropriate for the recognition of the First Amendment rights of students."

The Court observed that it would clearly violate the First Amendment if a Republican school board removed all books by Democratic authors or if the government removed all books written by blacks or arguing for racial equality. The Court said that "[o]ur Constitution does not permit the official suppression of ideas." The Court concluded that whether the "removal of the books from their school libraries [violated the] First Amendment depends upon the motivation behind [the government's] action. If petitioners *intended* by their removal decision to deny respondents access to ideas with which petitioners disagreed, and if this intent was the decisive factor in petitioners' decision, then petitioners exercised their discretion in violation of the Constitution. On the other hand, an unconstitutional motivation would *not* be demonstrated if it were shown that petitioners had decided to remove the books at issue because those books were pervasively vulgar." The Court remanded the case for a determination of this issue.

No school library can buy every book, and obtaining new volumes often means discarding old ones. Inherently, these choices are made based on the content of the books. Yet the Court also is obviously correct that a school board could not make these choices based on the political party affiliation or ideology of the authors. The problem is in courts striking the balance between deferring to the schools' inevitable choices and preventing school censorship of ideas or forms of expression that are unpopular, especially with some school board members. *Pico* attempts to do this by focusing on the motivation behind the decisions. Inevitably, this will turn on the content of the speech. It is difficult to imagine any permissible justification for a school library to remove from its shelves books by authors such as Kurt Vonnegut, Desmond Morris, Langston Hughes, or Eldridge Cleaver. On the other hand, no court would require that an elementary school library purchase *Hustler* magazine. As much as the prohibition of content-based discrimination is at the core of the First Amendment, this is an area where content-based choices are inevitable.

d. The Speech Rights of Government Employees

The Supreme Court has held that the government may not punish the speech of public employees if it involves matters of public concern unless the state can prove that the needs of the government outweigh the speech rights of the employee. In other words, speech by public employees is clearly less

A. Government Properties and Speech

protected than other speech; First Amendment protection does not exist unless the expression is about public concern, and even then, the employee can be disciplined or fired if the government can show, on balance, that the efficient operation of the office justified the action.

Pickering v. Board of Education, 391 U.S. 563 (1968), is a key case in holding that other speech by government employees is protected by the First Amendment. A teacher was fired for sending a letter to a local newspaper that was critical of the way school officials had raised money for the schools. The Supreme Court held that the firing violated the First Amendment. Justice Marshall, writing for the Court, said that its task was to balance the free speech rights of government employees with the government's need for efficient operation. Justice Marshall wrote: "[T]he State has interests as an employer in regulating the speech of its employees that differ significantly from those it possesses in connection with regulation of the speech of the citizenry in general. The problem in any case is to arrive at a balance between the interests of the teacher, as a citizen, in commenting upon matters of public concern and the interest of the State, as an employer, in promoting the efficiency of the public services it performs through its employees."

The Court emphasized that there was no indication that Pickering's statements in any way interfered with the teacher's ability to perform or the operation of the school district. The Court also stressed that the speech concerned a matter of public concern: the operation of the school district. Indeed, the Court said that a teacher is likely to have unique and important insights as to the adequacy of educational funding. Although there were some factual inaccuracies in the statement, the Court held that "absent proof of false statements knowingly or recklessly made by him, a teacher's exercise of his right to speak on issues of public importance may not furnish the basis for his dismissal from public employment."

In *Mt. Healthy City School District Board of Education v. Doyle*, 429 U.S. 274 (1977), the Court articulated a test to be used in applying *Pickering*. An untenured teacher was not rehired after several speech-related incidents, including arguing with another teacher, making an obscene gesture to students, and informing a local radio station about the principal's memorandum on teacher dress and appearance. The Court reiterated that speech by public employees is protected by the First Amendment. The Court said, however, that a public employee who otherwise would have been fired does not deserve special protection because of the speech.

Thus, the Court said that a public employee challenging an adverse employment action must initially meet the burden of showing that "his conduct was constitutionally protected, and that this conduct was a 'substantial factor' or, to put it in other words, that it was a 'motivating factor' for the government's action." If this is done, the burden shifts to the government to show "by a preponderance of the evidence that it would have reached the same decision . . . even in the absence of the protected conduct."

But in Garcetti v. Ceballos, the Court imposed a significant new limit on constitutional protection for the speech of government employees. The Court held that such speech is not protected if it is by a government employee while on the job and as part of his or her duties.

GARCETTI v. CEBALLOS
547 U.S. 410 (2006)

Justice KENNEDY delivered the opinion of the Court.

It is well settled that "a State cannot condition public employment on a basis that infringes the employee's constitutionally protected interest in freedom of expression." Connick v. Myers (1983). The question presented by the instant case is whether the First Amendment protects a government employee from discipline based on speech made pursuant to the employee's official duties.

I

Respondent Richard Ceballos has been employed since 1989 as a deputy district attorney for the Los Angeles County District Attorney's Office. During the period relevant to this case, Ceballos was a calendar deputy in the office's Pomona branch, and in this capacity he exercised certain supervisory responsibilities over other lawyers. In February 2000, a defense attorney contacted Ceballos about a pending criminal case. The defense attorney said there were inaccuracies in an affidavit used to obtain a critical search warrant. The attorney informed Ceballos that he had filed a motion to traverse, or challenge, the warrant, but he also wanted Ceballos to review the case. According to Ceballos, it was not unusual for defense attorneys to ask calendar deputies to investigate aspects of pending cases. After examining the affidavit and visiting the location it described, Ceballos determined the affidavit contained serious misrepresentations. The affidavit called a long driveway what Ceballos thought should have been referred to as a separate roadway. Ceballos also questioned the affidavit's statement that tire tracks led from a stripped-down truck to the premises covered by the warrant. His doubts arose from his conclusion that the roadway's composition in some places made it difficult or impossible to leave visible tire tracks.

Ceballos spoke on the telephone to the warrant affiant, a deputy sheriff from the Los Angeles County Sheriff's Department, but he did not receive a satisfactory explanation for the perceived inaccuracies. He relayed his findings to his supervisors, petitioners Carol Najera and Frank Sundstedt, and followed up by preparing a disposition memorandum. The memo explained Ceballos' concerns and recommended dismissal of the case.

Despite Ceballos' concerns, Sundstedt decided to proceed with the prosecution, pending disposition of the defense motion to traverse. The trial court held a hearing on the motion. Ceballos was called by the defense and recounted his observations about the affidavit, but the trial court rejected the challenge to the warrant.

Ceballos claims that in the aftermath of these events he was subjected to a series of retaliatory employment actions. The actions included reassignment from his calendar deputy position to a trial deputy position, transfer to another courthouse, and denial of a promotion.

II

As the Court's decisions have noted, for many years "the unchallenged dogma was that a public employee had no right to object to conditions placed upon

A. Government Properties and Speech

the terms of employment—including those which restricted the exercise of constitutional rights." That dogma has been qualified in important respects. The Court has made clear that public employees do not surrender all their First Amendment rights by reason of their employment. Rather, the First Amendment protects a public employee's right, in certain circumstances, to speak as a citizen addressing matters of public concern.

Pickering and the cases decided in its wake identify two inquiries to guide interpretation of the constitutional protections accorded to public employee speech. The first requires determining whether the employee spoke as a citizen on a matter of public concern. If the answer is no, the employee has no First Amendment cause of action based on his or her employer's reaction to the speech. If the answer is yes, then the possibility of a First Amendment claim arises. The question becomes whether the relevant government entity had an adequate justification for treating the employee differently from any other member of the general public. This consideration reflects the importance of the relationship between the speaker's expressions and employment. A government entity has broader discretion to restrict speech when it acts in its role as employer, but the restrictions it imposes must be directed at speech that has some potential to affect the entity's operations.

When a citizen enters government service, the citizen by necessity must accept certain limitations on his or her freedom. Government employers, like private employers, need a significant degree of control over their employees' words and actions; without it, there would be little chance for the efficient provision of public services. Public employees, moreover, often occupy trusted positions in society. When they speak out, they can express views that contravene governmental policies or impair the proper performance of governmental functions.

At the same time, the Court has recognized that a citizen who works for the government is nonetheless a citizen. The First Amendment limits the ability of a public employer to leverage the employment relationship to restrict, incidentally or intentionally, the liberties employees enjoy in their capacities as private citizens. So long as employees are speaking as citizens about matters of public concern, they must face only those speech restrictions that are necessary for their employers to operate efficiently and effectively.

III

With these principles in mind we turn to the instant case. Respondent Ceballos believed the affidavit used to obtain a search warrant contained serious misrepresentations. He conveyed his opinion and recommendation in a memo to his supervisor. That Ceballos expressed his views inside his office, rather than publicly, is not dispositive. Employees in some cases may receive First Amendment protection for expressions made at work. Many citizens do much of their talking inside their respective workplaces, and it would not serve the goal of treating public employees like "any member of the general public[]" to hold that all speech within the office is automatically exposed to restriction.

The memo concerned the subject matter of Ceballos' employment, but this, too, is nondispositive. The First Amendment protects some expressions related to the speaker's job.

The controlling factor in Ceballos' case is that his expressions were made pursuant to his duties as a calendar deputy. That consideration—the fact that Ceballos spoke as a prosecutor fulfilling a responsibility to advise his supervisor about how best to proceed with a pending case—distinguishes Ceballos' case from those in which the First Amendment provides protection against discipline. We hold that when public employees make statements pursuant to their official duties, the employees are not speaking as citizens for First Amendment purposes, and the Constitution does not insulate their communications from employer discipline. Ceballos wrote his disposition memo because that is part of what he, as a calendar deputy, was employed to do. It is immaterial whether he experienced some personal gratification from writing the memo; his First Amendment rights do not depend on his job satisfaction. The significant point is that the memo was written pursuant to Ceballos' official duties. Restricting speech that owes its existence to a public employee's professional responsibilities does not infringe any liberties the employee might have enjoyed as a private citizen. It simply reflects the exercise of employer control over what the employer itself has commissioned or created.

Ceballos did not act as a citizen when he went about conducting his daily professional activities, such as supervising attorneys, investigating charges, and preparing filings. In the same way he did not speak as a citizen by writing a memo that addressed the proper disposition of a pending criminal case. When he went to work and performed the tasks he was paid to perform, Ceballos acted as a government employee. The fact that his duties sometimes required him to speak or write does not mean his supervisors were prohibited from evaluating his performance.

This result is consistent with our precedents' attention to the potential societal value of employee speech. Our holding likewise is supported by the emphasis of our precedents on affording government employers sufficient discretion to manage their operations. Employers have heightened interests in controlling speech made by an employee in his or her professional capacity. Official communications have official consequences, creating a need for substantive consistency and clarity. Supervisors must ensure that their employees' official communications are accurate, demonstrate sound judgment, and promote the employer's mission. Ceballos' memo is illustrative. It demanded the attention of his supervisors and led to a heated meeting with employees from the sheriff's department. If Ceballos' superiors thought his memo was inflammatory or misguided, they had the authority to take proper corrective action.

Ceballos' proposed contrary rule, adopted by the Court of Appeals, would commit state and federal courts to a new, permanent, and intrusive role, mandating judicial oversight of communications between and among government employees and their superiors in the course of official business. This displacement of managerial discretion by judicial supervision finds no support in our precedents. When an employee speaks as a citizen addressing a matter of public concern, the First Amendment requires a delicate balancing of the competing interests surrounding the speech and its consequences. When, however, the employee is simply performing his or her job duties, there is no warrant for a similar degree of scrutiny. To hold otherwise would be to demand permanent judicial intervention in the conduct of governmental operations to a degree inconsistent with sound principles of federalism and the separation of powers.

A. Government Properties and Speech

Exposing governmental inefficiency and misconduct is a matter of considerable significance. As the Court noted in *Connick*, public employers should, "as a matter of good judgment," be "receptive to constructive criticism offered by their employees." The dictates of sound judgment are reinforced by the powerful network of legislative enactments—such as whistle-blower protection laws and labor codes—available to those who seek to expose wrongdoing. Cases involving government attorneys implicate additional safeguards in the form of, for example, rules of conduct and constitutional obligations apart from the First Amendment. These imperatives, as well as obligations arising from any other applicable constitutional provisions and mandates of the criminal and civil laws, protect employees and provide checks on supervisors who would order unlawful or otherwise inappropriate actions.

We reject, however, the notion that the First Amendment shields from discipline the expressions employees make pursuant to their professional duties. Our precedents do not support the existence of a constitutional cause of action behind every statement a public employee makes in the course of doing his or her job.

Justice STEVENS, dissenting.

The proper answer to the question "whether the First Amendment protects a government employee from discipline based on speech made pursuant to the employee's official duties[]," is "Sometimes," not "Never." Of course a supervisor may take corrective action when such speech is "inflammatory or misguided." But what if it is just unwelcome speech because it reveals facts that the supervisor would rather not have anyone else discover?

As Justice Souter explains, public employees are still citizens while they are in the office. The notion that there is a categorical difference between speaking as a citizen and speaking in the course of one's employment is quite wrong. Over a quarter of a century has passed since then-Justice Rehnquist, writing for a unanimous Court, rejected "the conclusion that a public employee forfeits his protection against governmental abridgment of freedom of speech if he decides to express his views privately rather than publicly." Givhan v. Western Line Consol. School Dist. (1979). We had no difficulty recognizing that the First Amendment applied when Bessie Givhan, an English teacher, raised concerns about the school's racist employment practices to the principal. Our silence as to whether or not her speech was made pursuant to her job duties demonstrates that the point was immaterial. That is equally true today, for it is senseless to let constitutional protection for exactly the same words hinge on whether they fall within a job description. Moreover, it seems perverse to fashion a new rule that provides employees with an incentive to voice their concerns publicly before talking frankly to their superiors.

Justice SOUTER, with whom Justice STEVENS and Justice GINSBURG join, dissenting.

The Court holds that "when public employees make statements pursuant to their official duties, the employees are not speaking as citizens for First Amendment purposes, and the Constitution does not insulate their communications from employer discipline." I respectfully dissent. I agree with the majority that a government employer has substantial interests in effectuating its chosen policy and objectives, and in demanding competence, honesty, and judgment from employees who speak for it in doing their work. But I would hold that private and public interests in addressing official wrongdoing and threats to health and safety can outweigh the government's stake in the efficient implementation of policy, and when they do public employees who speak on these matters in the course of their duties should be eligible to claim First Amendment protection.

Open speech by a private citizen on a matter of public importance lies at the heart of expression subject to protection by the First Amendment. At the other extreme, a statement by a government employee complaining about nothing beyond treatment under personnel rules raises no greater claim to constitutional protection against retaliatory response than the remarks of a private employee. In between these points lies a public employee's speech unwelcome to the government but on a significant public issue. Such an employee speaking as a citizen, that is, with a citizen's interest, is protected from reprisal unless the statements are too damaging to the government's capacity to conduct public business to be justified by any individual or public benefit thought to flow from the statements. Pickering v. Board of Ed. of Township High School Dist. 205, Will Cty. (1968). Entitlement to protection is thus not absolute.

This significant, albeit qualified, protection of public employees who irritate the government is understood to flow from the First Amendment, in part, because a government paycheck does nothing to eliminate the value to an individual of speaking on public matters, and there is no good reason for categorically discounting a speaker's interest in commenting on a matter of public concern just because the government employs him. Still, the First Amendment safeguard rests on something more, being the value to the public of receiving the opinions and information that a public employee may disclose. "Government employees are often in the best position to know what ails the agencies for which they work." The reason that protection of employee speech is qualified is that it can distract co-workers and supervisors from their tasks at hand and thwart the implementation of legitimate policy, the risks of which grow greater the closer the employee's speech gets to commenting on his own workplace and responsibilities. It is one thing for an office clerk to say there is waste in government and quite another to charge that his own department pays full-time salaries to part-time workers. Even so, we have regarded eligibility for protection by *Pickering* balancing as the proper approach when an employee speaks critically about the administration of his own government employer.

Nothing, then, accountable on the individual and public side of the *Pickering* balance changes when an employee speaks "pursuant" to public duties. On the side of the government employer, however, something is different, and to this extent, I agree with the majority of the Court. The majority is rightly concerned that the employee who speaks out on matters subject to comment in doing his own work has the greater leverage to create office uproars and fracture the government's authority to set policy to be carried out coherently through the ranks. "Official communications have official consequences, creating a need for substantive consistency and clarity. Supervisors must ensure that their employees' official communications are accurate, demonstrate sound judgment, and promote the employer's mission." Up to a point, then, the majority makes good points: government needs civility in the workplace, consistency in policy, and honesty and competence in public service.

But why do the majority's concerns, which we all share, require categorical exclusion of First Amendment protection against any official retaliation for things said on the job? Is it not possible to respect the unchallenged individual and public interests in the speech through a *Pickering* balance without drawing the strange line I mentioned before? This is, to be sure, a matter of judgment, but the judgment has to account for the undoubted value of speech to those, and by those, whose specific public job responsibilities bring them face to face with wrongdoing and incompetence in government, who refuse to avert their eyes and shut their mouths. And it has to account for the need actually to disrupt government if its officials are corrupt or dangerously incompetent. It is thus no adequate justification for the suppression of potentially valuable information simply to recognize that the government has a huge interest in managing its employees and preventing the occasionally irresponsible one from turning his job into a bully pulpit. Even there, the lesson of *Pickering* (and the object of most constitutional adjudication) is still to the point: when constitutionally significant interests clash, resist the demand for winner-take-all; try to make adjustments that serve all of the values at stake.

Justice BREYER, dissenting.

This case asks whether the First Amendment protects public employees when they engage in speech that both (1) involves matters of public concern and (2) takes place in the ordinary course of performing the duties of a government job. The majority answers the question by holding that "when public employees make statements pursuant to their official duties, the employees are not speaking as citizens for First Amendment purposes, and the Constitution does not insulate their communications from employer discipline." In a word, the majority says, "never." That word, in my view, is too absolute.

Like the majority, I understand the need to "affor[d] government employers sufficient discretion to manage their operations." And I agree that the Constitution does not seek to "displac[e] . . . managerial discretion by judicial supervision." Nonetheless, there may well be circumstances with special demand for constitutional protection of the speech at issue, where governmental justifications may be limited, and where administrable standards seem readily available — to the point where the majority's fears of department management by lawsuit are misplaced. In such an instance, I believe that courts should apply the *Pickering* standard, even though the government employee speaks upon matters of public concern in the course of his ordinary duties.

This is such a case. The respondent, a government lawyer, complained of retaliation, in part, on the basis of speech contained in his disposition memorandum that he says fell within the scope of his obligations under Brady v. Maryland (1963). The facts present two special circumstances that together justify First Amendment review.

First, the speech at issue is professional speech — the speech of a lawyer. Such speech is subject to independent regulation by canons of the profession. Those canons provide an obligation to speak in certain instances. And where that is so, the government's own interest in forbidding that speech is diminished.

Second, the Constitution itself here imposes speech obligations upon the government's professional employee. A prosecutor has a constitutional obligation to learn of, to preserve, and to communicate with the defense about exculpatory and impeachment evidence in the government's possession. Hence, I would find that the Constitution mandates special protection of employee speech in such circumstances. Thus I would apply the *Pickering* balancing test here.

I conclude that the First Amendment sometimes does authorize judicial actions based upon a government employee's speech that both (1) involves a matter of public concern and also (2) takes place in the course of ordinary job-related duties. But it does so only in the presence of augmented need for constitutional protection and diminished risk of undue judicial interference with governmental management of the public's affairs. In my view, these conditions are met in this case and *Pickering* balancing is consequently appropriate.

In Lane v. Franks, 573 U.S. 228 (2014), the Court said that Garcetti v. Ceballos does not apply to a situation where a government employee testifies truthfully pursuant to a subpoena.

Edward Lane worked for the community college system in Alabama. He conducted an audit of the program's expenses and discovered that Suzanne Schmitz, an Alabama State Representative on his payroll, had not been reporting for work. Lane eventually terminated Schmitz's employment. Shortly thereafter, federal authorities indicted Schmitz on charges of mail fraud and theft concerning a program receiving federal funds.

Lane testified before the grand jury and twice at trial under subpoena regarding the events that led to his terminating Schmitz. Schmitz was convicted and sentenced to 30 months in prison. Steve Franks then terminated Lane. Lane sued, claiming a violation of his First Amendment rights.

Justice Sotomayor, writing for a unanimous Court, found that Lane's speech was protected by the First Amendment. The Court said that it was citizen speech on a matter of public concern, as opposed to the speech of a government employee on the job. Sworn testimony in judicial proceedings is a quintessential example of citizen speech. Under *Garcetti*, the Court found, the speech must be within the duties of the employee and not just concern them. The Court said that the speech involved a matter of public concern and on balance protecting truthful testimony is desirable.

CHAPTER 5

FREEDOM OF ASSOCIATION

The Supreme Court has expressly held that freedom of association is a fundamental right protected by the First Amendment. Although "association" is not listed among those freedoms enumerated in the Amendment, the Court has nonetheless declared that "freedom to engage in association for the advancement of beliefs and ideas is an inseparable aspect of the 'liberty' assured by the Due Process Clause of the Fourteenth Amendment, which embraces freedom of speech."[1]

Freedom of association is regarded as integral to the speech and assembly protected by the First Amendment. The Supreme Court explained that "[e]ffective advocacy of both public and private points of view, particularly controversial ones, is undeniably enhanced by group association."[2] Groups have resources—in human capital and money—that a single person lacks. The Court has observed that an "individual's freedom to speak and to petition the Government for the redress of grievances could not be vigorously protected unless a correlative freedom to engage in group effort for those ends were not also guaranteed."[3] Additionally, the very existence of group support for an idea conveys a message. Association is also important as people benefit from being with others in many ways.[4]

This chapter considers four issues concerning freedom of association. Section A considers when the government may prohibit or punish membership in a group. Section B focuses on when the government may require disclosure of membership, particularly where disclosure will chill association. Section C focuses on when the government may "force" association, such as by requiring contributions. Finally, Section D looks at when freedom of association protects a right of groups to discriminate.

---

1. NAACP v. Alabama ex rel. Patterson, 357 U.S. 449 (1958).
2. *Id.* at 460.
3. Roberts v. Jaycees, 468 U.S. 609, 622 (1984).
4. The Court, however, generally has been unwilling to extend protection of freedom of association outside situations where it relates to First Amendment purpose. For instance, in City of Dallas v. Stanglin, 490 U.S. 19 (1989), the Court upheld a city ordinance that limited the ability of adults to gain access to teenage dance halls. The Court rejected a challenge based on freedom of association and emphasized that the restriction did not limit association for expressive purposes.

A. LAWS PROHIBITING AND PUNISHING MEMBERSHIP

Obviously, freedom of association is most directly infringed if the government outlaws and punishes membership in a group. The Court has held that the government may punish membership only if it proves that a person actively affiliated with a group, knowing of its illegal objectives, and with the specific intent to further those objectives. For example, in Scales v. United States, 367 U.S. 203 (1961), the Court affirmed the conviction of the chairman of the North Carolina and South Carolina Districts of the Communist Party under the "membership clause" of the Smith Act that made a felony "the acquisition or holding of knowing membership in any organization which advocates the overthrow of the Government by force or violence." The Court said that earlier precedents had established that "the advocacy with which we are here concerned is not constitutionally protected speech, and it was further established that a combination to promote such advocacy, albeit under the aegis of what purports to be a political party, is not such association as is protected by the First Amendment."

Justice Harlan, writing for the Court, said that the government's ability to prohibit such speech meant that it also had the authority to forbid associations to further these ideas and activities. Justice Harlan wrote, "We can discern no reason why membership, when it constitutes a purposeful form of complicity in a group engaging in this same forbidden advocacy, should receive any greater degree of protection from the guarantees of that Amendment." The Court emphasized that Scales was being punished for his active affiliation with the Communist Party, with knowledge of its illegal objectives and with proof that he "specifically intends to accomplish the aims of the party by resort to violence."

In contrast, in Noto v. United States, 367 U.S. 290 (1961), decided the same day, the Court reversed a conviction for membership in the Communist Party because of the absence of "illegal advocacy." The Court stressed that the speech was advocacy of abstract ideas and that there was not proof that the individual had the specific intent to further any illegal activities.

The court has applied this test for punishing association in many contexts.[5] For example, the Court has held that the government may deny public employment to an individual based on group affiliation, or require that an individual take an oath concerning group affiliation, only if it is limited to situations where the individual actively affiliated with the group, knowing of its illegal activities, and with the specific intent to further those illegal goals.

In Elfbrandt v. Russell, 384 U.S. 11 (1966), the Court declared unconstitutional a state's loyalty oath and law that prohibited anyone from holding office who was a member of a group such as the Communist Party. The Court explained that "[n]othing in the oath, the statutory gloss, or the construction of the oath and statutes given by the Arizona Supreme Court, purports to exclude association by one who does not subscribe to the organization's unlawful ends." The Court applied the Scales test and said that it was impermissible for the government to punish

---

5. See, e.g., Communist Party of Indiana v. Whitcomb, 414 U.S. 441 (1974) (declaring unconstitutional a state law that said that political parties could not be listed on the ballot unless they filed an affidavit that they did not advocate the overthrow of the government by force or violence); Aptheker v. Secretary of State, 378 U.S. 500 (1964) (declaring unconstitutional the law barring the use of a passport by a member of the Communist organization).

individuals for being members of a group without proof that the individual joined the organization knowing of its illegal objectives and with the specific intent to further them. The Court said that the law was unconstitutional because it "threatens the cherished freedom of association protected by the First Amendment."

Similarly, in Keyishian v. Board of Regents, 385 U.S. 589 (1967), the Court declared unconstitutional a state law that denied employment as teachers to those who were part of organizations that advocated the overthrow of the government. The Court emphasized that the law punished mere membership in a "subversive" group, without any requirement for proof that the individual knew of the illegal objectives or intended to further them.

The same standards have been applied with regard to the ability of states to deny bar membership to individuals based on their group affiliations. In Konigsberg v. State Bar, 366 U.S. 36 (1961), the Court held that the government could deny bar membership to an individual who refused to answer questions concerning membership in the Communist Party.[6] But a decade later, the Court said that the government may require individuals to answer such questions only if they are narrowly focused on whether the individual actively affiliated with a group, knowing of its illegal objectives, and with the specific intent to further those goals.

In Baird v. State Bar, 401 U.S. 1 (1971), and In re Stollar, 401 U.S. 23 (1971), the Court invalidated bar questions that asked whether a person was or had ever been a member of the Communist Party or any organization that advocated the overthrow of the government by force or violence. In contrast, in a companion case, Law Students Civil Rights Research Council v. Wadmond, 401 U.S. 154 (1971), the Court upheld a bar question that asked whether a person ever had joined a group knowing that its objective was the overthrow of the government by force or violence, and if so, whether the individual had the specific intent to advance those goals. The difference among these cases is obviously the specificity of the questions; the inquiry is allowed only if it is narrowly focused on whether a person actively affiliated with a group that advocated the overthrow of the government, knowing of its goals, and with the specific intent to further them.

B. LAWS REQUIRING DISCLOSURE OF MEMBERSHIP

The Supreme Court has held that the government may require disclosure of membership, where disclosure will chill association, only if it meets strict scrutiny. NAACP v. Alabama ex rel. Patterson articulates this principle.

NAACP v. STATE OF ALABAMA EX REL. PATTERSON
357 U.S. 449 (1958)

Justice HARLAN delivered the opinion of the Court.

We review from the standpoint of its validity under the Federal Constitution a judgment of civil contempt entered against petitioner, the National Association

---

6. *See also* In re Anastaplo, 366 U.S. 82 (1961).

for the Advancement of Colored People, in the courts of Alabama. The question presented is whether Alabama, consistently with the Due Process Clause of the Fourteenth Amendment, can compel petitioner to reveal to the State's Attorney General the names and addresses of all its Alabama members and agents, without regard to their positions or functions in the Association. The judgment of contempt was based upon petitioner's refusal to comply fully with a court order requiring in part the production of membership lists. Petitioner's claim is that the order, in the circumstances shown by this record, violated rights assured to petitioner and its members under the Constitution.

The Association both urges that it is constitutionally entitled to resist official inquiry into its membership lists, and that it may assert, on behalf of its members, a right personal to them to be protected from compelled disclosure by the State of their affiliation with the Association as revealed by the membership lists. Petitioner argues that in view of the facts and circumstances shown in the record, the effect of compelled disclosure of the membership lists will be to abridge the rights of its rank-and-file members to engage in lawful association in support of their common beliefs. It contends that governmental action which, although not directly suppressing association, nevertheless carries this consequence, can be justified only upon some overriding valid interest of the State.

Effective advocacy of both public and private points of view, particularly controversial ones, is undeniably enhanced by group association, as this Court has more than once recognized by remarking upon the close nexus between the freedoms of speech and assembly. It is beyond debate that freedom to engage in association for the advancement of beliefs and ideas is an inseparable aspect of the "liberty" assured by the Due Process Clause of the Fourteenth Amendment, which embraces freedom of speech.

Of course, it is immaterial whether the beliefs sought to be advanced by association pertain to political, economic, religious or cultural matters, and state action which may have the effect of curtailing the freedom to associate is subject to the closest scrutiny. It is hardly a novel perception that compelled disclosure of affiliation with groups engaged in advocacy may constitute as effective a restraint on freedom of association as the forms of governmental action in the cases above were thought likely to produce upon the particular constitutional rights there involved. This Court has recognized the vital relationship between freedom to associate and privacy in one's associations. Inviolability of privacy in group association may in many circumstances be indispensable to preservation of freedom of association, particularly where a group espouses dissident beliefs.

We think that the production order, in the respects here drawn in question, must be regarded as entailing the likelihood of a substantial restraint upon the exercise by petitioner's members of their right to freedom of association. Petitioner has made an uncontroverted showing that on past occasions revelation of the identity of its rank-and-file members has exposed these members to economic reprisal, loss of employment, threat of physical coercion, and other manifestations of public hostility. Under these circumstances, we think it apparent that compelled disclosure of petitioner's Alabama membership is likely to affect adversely the ability of petitioner and its members to pursue their collective effort to foster beliefs which they admittedly have the right to advocate, in that it may induce members to withdraw from the Association and dissuade others from joining it because of fear of exposure of their beliefs shown through their associations and of the consequences of this exposure.

B. Laws Requiring Disclosure of Membership

We turn to the final question whether Alabama has demonstrated an interest in obtaining the disclosures it seeks from petitioner which is sufficient to justify the deterrent effect which we have concluded these disclosures may well have on the free exercise by petitioner's members of their constitutionally protected right of association. It is important to bear in mind that petitioner asserts no right to absolute immunity from state investigation, and no right to disregard Alabama's laws. As shown by its substantial compliance with the production order, petitioner does not deny Alabama's right to obtain from it such information as the State desires concerning the purposes of the Association and its activities within the State. Petitioner has not objected to divulging the identity of its members who are employed by or hold official positions with it. It has urged the rights solely of its ordinary rank-and-file members. This is therefore not analogous to a case involving the interest of a State in protecting its citizens in their dealings with paid solicitors or agents of foreign corporations by requiring identifications.

We hold that the immunity from state scrutiny of membership lists which the Association claims on behalf of its members is here so related to the right of the members to pursue their lawful private interests privately and to associate freely with others in so doing as to come within the protection of the Fourteenth Amendment. And we conclude that Alabama has fallen short of showing a controlling justification for the deterrent effect on the free enjoyment of the right to associate which disclosure of membership lists is likely to have.

Similarly, in Shelton v. Tucker, 364 U.S. 479 (1960), the Court declared unconstitutional a state law that required that all teachers disclose their group memberships on an annual basis. The Court again stressed the impact of such disclosures in chilling constitutionally protected association. The Court explained, "[To] compel a teacher to disclose his every associational tie is to impair that teacher's right of free association. [The] statute does not provide that the information it requires be kept confidential. Even if there were no disclosure to the general public, the pressure upon a teacher to avoid any ties which might displease those who control his professional destiny would be constant and heavy." Although the Court recognized the government's important interest in having competent teachers, it concluded that the state cannot pursue the goal "by means that broadly stifle fundamental personal liberties when the end can be more narrowly achieved."

CAMPAIGN FINANCE DISCLOSURE

A crucial aspect of many campaign finance laws is a requirement that candidates disclose their contributors. Such disclosures may chill contributions. Nonetheless, the Court generally has upheld such requirements because of the government's compelling interest in stopping corruption, except where there is reason to believe that the disclosure will chill contributions to a minor party or candidate.

In Buckley v. Valeo, 424 U.S. 1 (1976), the Court upheld a provision in the Federal Election Campaign Act of 1971 that required that every political candidate and political committee keep records of the names and addresses of all who contributed more than $10. These records were required to be available to the Federal Election Commission and for public inspection and copying.

There is no doubt that in some contexts people might be chilled from making a contribution because of the disclosure requirement. But the Court found that the requirement served significant government interests. The Court said that "disclosure provides the electorate with information as to where political campaign money comes from in order to aid the voters in evaluating those who seek federal office." The Court also observed that the disclosure requirements discourage corruption and the appearance of corruption because of the "light of publicity." Finally, the Court explained that such "requirements are an essential means of gathering the data necessary to detect violations of the contribution limits."

The Court in *Buckley* recognized that disclosure might have a particularly harmful to the point where the movement cannot survive. The Court said that for a minor party there was much less need for disclosure to prevent corruption "for it is far less likely that the candidate will be victorious."

Although no such parties were involved in *Buckley*, in Brown v. Socialist Workers '74 Campaign Committee, 459 U.S. 87 (1982), the Court held that it was unconstitutional to require the Socialist Workers Party to comply with a state campaign disclosure law. The Court applied its dicta from *Buckley* and concluded that the Socialist Workers Party was a minor party that was historically unpopular so that disclosure requirements would serve little purpose and would likely chill contributions and associational activity.

In its most recent campaign finance case concerning disclosure requirements, Citizens United v. Federal Election Commission, 558 U.S. 310 (2010), the Court invalidated restrictions on independent expenditures by corporations and unions (the opinion can be found in Chapter 3), but once more upheld disclosure requirements. The Court explained "that disclosure is a less restrictive alternative to more comprehensive regulations of speech. . . . The First Amendment protects political speech; and disclosure permits citizens and shareholders to react to the speech of corporate entities in a proper way. This transparency enables the electorate to make informed decisions and give proper weight to different speakers and messages."

C. COMPELLED ASSOCIATION

In Abood v. Detroit Board of Education, 431 U.S. 209 (1977), the Court considered a state law that required all local government employees to pay a union service charge. Union members paid this amount as their dues; nonmembers were required to pay a charge of the same amount. The Court said that the nonmembers could be forced to pay a charge to subsidize the collective bargaining activities of the union. The Court explained that nonmembers would benefit from the gains of collective bargaining and would be "free riders" if not required to pay for these activities. Although nonmembers may disagree with the union's labor-related activities, or even to the existence of the union, the Court found no violation of the First Amendment in forcing nonmembers to pay for the union's collective bargaining conduct. But the Court said that it violated the First Amendment to force the nonmembers to pay for ideological causes with which they disagreed.

C. Compelled Association

JANUS v. AMERICAN FEDERATION OF STATE, COUNTY, AND MUNICIPAL EMPLOYEES, COUNCIL 31
138 S. Ct. 2448 (2018)

Justice ALITO delivered the opinion of the Court.

Under Illinois law, public employees are forced to subsidize a union, even if they choose not to join and strongly object to the positions the union takes in collective bargaining and related activities. We conclude that this arrangement violates the free speech rights of nonmembers by compelling them to subsidize private speech on matters of substantial public concern.

We upheld a similar law in Abood v. Detroit Bd. of Ed. (1977), and we recognize the importance of following precedent unless there are strong reasons for not doing so. But there are very strong reasons in this case. Fundamental free speech rights are at stake. *Abood* was poorly reasoned. It has led to practical problems and abuse. It is inconsistent with other First Amendment cases and has been undermined by more recent decisions. Developments since *Abood* was handed down have shed new light on the issue of agency fees, and no reliance interests on the part of public-sector unions are sufficient to justify the perpetuation of the free speech violations that *Abood* has countenanced for the past 41 years. *Abood* is therefore overruled.

I

Under the Illinois Public Labor Relations Act (IPLRA), employees of the State and its political subdivisions are permitted to unionize. If a majority of the employees in a bargaining unit vote to be represented by a union, that union is designated as the exclusive representative of all the employees. Employees in the unit are not obligated to join the union selected by their co-workers, but whether they join or not, that union is deemed to be their sole permitted representative.

Once a union is so designated, it is vested with broad authority. Only the union may negotiate with the employer on matters relating to "pay, wages, hours[,] and other conditions of employment." And this authority extends to the negotiation of what the IPLRA calls "policy matters," such as merit pay, the size of the work force, layoffs, privatization, promotion methods, and nondiscrimination policies.

Designating a union as the employees' exclusive representative substantially restricts the rights of individual employees. Among other things, this designation means that individual employees may not be represented by any agent other than the designated union; nor may individual employees negotiate directly with their employer. Protection of the employees' interests is placed in the hands of the union, and therefore the union is required by law to provide fair representation for all employees in the unit, members and nonmembers alike.

Employees who decline to join the union are not assessed full union dues but must instead pay what is generally called an "agency fee," which amounts to a percentage of the union dues. Under *Abood*, nonmembers may be charged for the portion of union dues attributable to activities that are "germane to [the union's] duties as collective-bargaining representative," but nonmembers may not be required to fund the union's political and ideological projects. In labor-law parlance, the outlays in the first category are known as "chargeable" expenditures, while those in the latter are labeled "nonchargeable."

Illinois law does not specify in detail which expenditures are chargeable and which are not. The IPLRA provides that an agency fee may compensate a union for the costs incurred in "the collective bargaining process, contract administration[,] and pursuing matters affecting wages, hours[,] and conditions of employment." Excluded from the agency-fee calculation are union expenditures "related to the election or support of any candidate for political office."

As illustrated by the record in this case, unions charge nonmembers, not just for the cost of collective bargaining *per se*, but also for many other supposedly connected activities. Here, the nonmembers were told that they had to pay for "[l]obbying," "[s]ocial and recreational activities," "advertising," "[m]embership meetings and conventions," and "litigation," as well as other unspecified "[s]ervices" that "may ultimately inure to the benefit of the members of the local bargaining unit." The total chargeable amount for nonmembers was 78.06% of full union dues.

Petitioner Mark Janus is employed by the Illinois Department of Healthcare and Family Services as a child support specialist. The employees in his unit are among the 35,000 public employees in Illinois who are represented by respondent American Federation of State, County, and Municipal Employees, Council 31 (Union). Janus refused to join the Union because he opposes "many of the public policy positions that [it] advocates," including the positions it takes in collective bargaining. Janus believes that the Union's "behavior in bargaining does not appreciate the current fiscal crises in Illinois and does not reflect his best interests or the interests of Illinois citizens." Therefore, if he had the choice, he "would not pay any fees or otherwise subsidize [the Union]." Under his unit's collective-bargaining agreement, however, he was required to pay an agency fee of $44.58 per month—which would amount to about $535 per year.

[II]

We first consider whether *Abood*'s holding is consistent with standard First Amendment principles. We have held time and again that freedom of speech "includes both the right to speak freely and the right to refrain from speaking at all." The right to eschew association for expressive purposes is likewise protected. As Justice Jackson memorably put it: "If there is any fixed star in our constitutional constellation, it is that no official, high or petty, can prescribe what shall be orthodox in politics, nationalism, religion, or other matters of opinion or *force citizens to confess by word or act their faith therein.*"

Compelling individuals to mouth support for views they find objectionable violates that cardinal constitutional command, and in most contexts, any such effort would be universally condemned. Suppose, for example, that the State of Illinois required all residents to sign a document expressing support for a particular set of positions on controversial public issues — say, the platform of one of the major political parties. No one, we trust, would seriously argue that the First Amendment permits this.

Perhaps because such compulsion so plainly violates the Constitution, most of our free speech cases have involved restrictions on what can be said, rather than laws compelling speech. But measures compelling speech are at least as threatening.

C. Compelled Association

Whenever the Federal Government or a State prevents individuals from saying what they think on important matters or compels them to voice ideas with which they disagree, it undermines these ends. When speech is compelled, however, additional damage is done. In that situation, individuals are coerced into betraying their convictions. Forcing free and independent individuals to endorse ideas they find objectionable is always demeaning, and for this reason, one of our landmark free speech cases said that a law commanding "involuntary affirmation" of objected-to beliefs would require "even more immediate and urgent grounds" than a law demanding silence.

Compelling a person to *subsidize* the speech of other private speakers raises similar First Amendment concerns. As Jefferson famously put it, "to compel a man to furnish contributions of money for the propagation of opinions which he disbelieves and abhor[s] is sinful and tyrannical." We have therefore recognized that a "'significant impingement on First Amendment rights'" occurs when public employees are required to provide financial support for a union that "takes many positions during collective bargaining that have powerful political and civic consequences."

Because the compelled subsidization of private speech seriously impinges on First Amendment rights, it cannot be casually allowed.

[P]etitioner in the present case contends that the Illinois law at issue should be subjected to "strict scrutiny." The dissent, on the other hand, proposes that we apply what amounts to rational-basis review, that is, that we ask only whether a government employer could reasonably believe that the exaction of agency fees serves its interests. This form of minimal scrutiny is foreign to our free-speech jurisprudence, and we reject it here. At the same time, we again find it unnecessary to decide the issue of strict scrutiny because the Illinois scheme cannot survive under even the more permissive standard.

In *Abood*, the main defense of the agency-fee arrangement was that it served the State's interest in "labor peace." By "labor peace," the *Abood* Court meant avoidance of the conflict and disruption that it envisioned would occur if the employees in a unit were represented by more than one union. In such a situation, the Court predicted, "inter-union rivalries" would foster "dissension within the work force," and the employer could face "conflicting demands from different unions." Confusion would ensue if the employer entered into and attempted to "enforce two or more agreements specifying different terms and conditions of employment." And a settlement with one union would be "subject to attack from [a] rival labor organizatio[n]."

We assume that "labor peace," in this sense of the term, is a compelling state interest, but *Abood* cited no evidence that the pandemonium it imagined would result if agency fees were not allowed, and it is now clear that *Abood*'s fears were unfounded. The *Abood* Court assumed that designation of a union as the exclusive representative of all the employees in a unit and the exaction of agency fees are inextricably linked, but that is simply not true.

Whatever may have been the case 41 years ago when *Abood* was handed down, it is now undeniable that "labor peace" can readily be achieved "through means significantly less restrictive of associational freedoms" than the assessment of agency fees.

In addition to the promotion of "labor peace," *Abood* cited "the risk of 'free riders'" as justification for agency fees. Respondents and some of their *amici* endorse this reasoning, contending that agency fees are needed to prevent nonmembers from enjoying the benefits of union representation without shouldering the costs.

Petitioner strenuously objects to this free-rider label. He argues that he is not a free rider on a bus headed for a destination that he wishes to reach but is more like a person shanghaied for an unwanted voyage.

Whichever description fits the majority of public employees who would not subsidize a union if given the option, avoiding free riders is not a compelling interest. As we have noted, "free-rider arguments . . . are generally insufficient to overcome First Amendment objections." To hold otherwise across the board would have startling consequences. Many private groups speak out with the objective of obtaining government action that will have the effect of benefiting nonmembers. May all those who are thought to benefit from such efforts be compelled to subsidize this speech?

Suppose that a particular group lobbies or speaks out on behalf of what it thinks are the needs of senior citizens or veterans or physicians, to take just a few examples. Could the government require that all seniors, veterans, or doctors pay for that service even if they object? It has never been thought that this is permissible. "[P]rivate speech often furthers the interests of nonspeakers," but "that does not alone empower the state to compel the speech to be paid for." In simple terms, the First Amendment does not permit the government to compel a person to pay for another party's speech just because the government thinks that the speech furthers the interests of the person who does not want to pay.

In any event, whatever unwanted burden is imposed by the representation of nonmembers in disciplinary matters can be eliminated "through means significantly less restrictive of associational freedoms" than the imposition of agency fees. Individual nonmembers could be required to pay for that service or could be denied union representation altogether. Thus, agency fees cannot be sustained on the ground that unions would otherwise be unwilling to represent nonmembers.

In sum, we do not see any reason to treat the free-rider interest any differently in the agency-fee context than in any other First Amendment context. We therefore hold that agency fees cannot be upheld on free-rider grounds.

[III]

Implicitly acknowledging the weakness of *Abood*'s own reasoning, proponents of agency fees have come forward with alternative justifications for the decision, and we now address these arguments.

The most surprising of these new arguments is the Union respondent's originalist defense of *Abood*. According to this argument, *Abood* was correctly decided because the First Amendment was not originally understood to provide *any* protection for the free speech rights of public employees.

The principal defense of *Abood* advanced by respondents and the dissent is based on our decision in Pickering [v. Board of Education (1968)], which held that a school district violated the First Amendment by firing a teacher for writing a letter critical of the school administration. Under *Pickering* and later cases in the same line, employee speech is largely unprotected if it is part of what the employee is paid to do, see Garcetti v. Ceballos (2006), or if it involved a matter of only private concern. On the other hand, when a public employee speaks as a citizen on a matter of public concern, the employee's speech is protected unless

C. Compelled Association

"'the interest of the state, as an employer, in promoting the efficiency of the public services it performs through its employees' outweighs 'the interests of the [employee], as a citizen, in commenting upon matters of public concern.'" *Abood* was not based on *Pickering*. The *Abood* majority cited the case exactly once—in a footnote—and then merely to acknowledge that "there may be limits on the extent to which an employee in a sensitive or policymaking position may freely criticize his superiors and the policies they espouse." We see no good reason, at this late date, to try to shoehorn *Abood* into the *Pickering* framework.

Even if we were to apply some form of *Pickering*, Illinois' agency-fee arrangement would not survive. Respondents begin by suggesting that union speech in collective-bargaining and grievance proceedings should be treated like the employee speech in *Garcetti*, *i.e.*, as speech "pursuant to [an employee's] official duties." Many employees, in both the public and private sectors, are paid to write or speak for the purpose of furthering the interests of their employers. There are laws that protect public employees from being compelled to say things that they reasonably believe to be untrue or improper, but in general when public employees are performing their job duties, their speech may be controlled by their employer. Trying to fit union speech into this framework, respondents now suggest that the union speech funded by agency fees forms part of the official duties of the union officers who engage in the speech.

This argument distorts collective bargaining and grievance adjustment beyond recognition. When an employee engages in speech that is part of the employee's job duties, the employee's words are really the words of the employer. The employee is effectively the employer's spokesperson. But when a union negotiates with the employer or represents employees in disciplinary proceedings, the union speaks for the *employees*, not the employer. Otherwise, the employer would be negotiating with itself and disputing its own actions. That is not what anybody understands to be happening.

What is more, if the union's speech is really the employer's speech, then the employer could dictate what the union says. Unions, we trust, would be appalled by such a suggestion. For these reasons, *Garcetti* is totally inapposite here.

Although the dissent would accept without any serious independent evaluation the State's assertion that the absence of agency fees would cripple public-sector unions and thus impair the efficiency of government operations, ample experience, as we have noted, shows that this is questionable. It is also not disputed that the State may require that a union serve as exclusive bargaining agent for its employees—itself a significant impingement on associational freedoms that would not be tolerated in other contexts. We simply draw the line at allowing the government to go further still and require all employees to support the union irrespective of whether they share its views. Nothing in the *Pickering* line of cases requires us to uphold every speech restriction the government imposes as an employer.

[V]

For the reasons given above, we conclude that public-sector agency-shop arrangements violate the First Amendment, and *Abood* erred in concluding otherwise. There remains the question whether *stare decisis* nonetheless counsels against overruling *Abood*. It does not.

The doctrine "is at its weakest when we interpret the Constitution because our interpretation can be altered only by constitutional amendment or by overruling our prior decisions." And *stare decisis* applies with perhaps least force of all to decisions that wrongly denied First Amendment rights: "This Court has not hesitated to overrule decisions offensive to the First Amendment (a fixed star in our constitutional constellation, if there is one)."

Our cases identify factors that should be taken into account in deciding whether to overrule a past decision. Five of these are most important here: the quality of *Abood*'s reasoning, the workability of the rule it established, its consistency with other related decisions, developments since the decision was handed down, and reliance on the decision.

An important factor in determining whether a precedent should be overruled is the quality of its reasoning. "*Abood* failed to appreciate the conceptual difficulty of distinguishing in public-sector cases between union expenditures that are made for collective-bargaining purposes and those that are made to achieve political ends." Likewise, "*Abood* does not seem to have anticipated the magnitude of the practical administrative problems that would result in attempting to classify public-sector union expenditures as either 'chargeable' . . . or nonchargeable." Nor did *Abood* "foresee the practical problems that would face objecting nonmembers." In sum, *Abood* was not well reasoned.

Another relevant consideration in the *stare decisis* calculus is the workability of the precedent in question, and that factor also weighs against *Abood*. *Abood*'s line between chargeable and nonchargeable union expenditures has proved to be impossible to draw with precision.

Developments since *Abood*, both factual and legal, have also "eroded" the decision's "underpinnings" and left it an outlier among our First Amendment cases. *Abood* is also an "anomaly" in our First Amendment jurisprudence. *Abood* particularly sticks out when viewed against our cases holding that public employees generally may not be required to support a political party. It is an odd feature of our First Amendment cases that political patronage has been deemed largely unconstitutional, while forced subsidization of union speech (which has no such pedigree) has been largely permitted.

In some cases, reliance provides a strong reason for adhering to established law, and this is the factor that is stressed most strongly by respondents, their *amici,* and the dissent. They contend that collective-bargaining agreements now in effect were negotiated with agency fees in mind and that unions may have given up other benefits in exchange for provisions granting them such fees. In this case, however, reliance does not carry decisive weight.

For one thing, it would be unconscionable to permit free speech rights to be abridged in perpetuity in order to preserve contract provisions that will expire on their own in a few years' time. "The fact that [public-sector unions] may view [agency fees] as an entitlement does not establish the sort of reliance interest that could outweigh the countervailing interest that [nonmembers] share in having their constitutional rights fully protected." For another, *Abood* does not provide "a clear or easily applicable standard, so arguments for reliance based on its clarity are misplaced." This is especially so because public-sector unions have been on notice for years regarding this Court's misgivings about *Abood*.

In short, the uncertain status of *Abood*, the lack of clarity it provides, the short-term nature of collective-bargaining agreements, and the ability of unions to

C. Compelled Association

protect themselves if an agency-fee provision was crucial to its bargain all work to undermine the force of reliance as a factor supporting *Abood*.

We recognize that the loss of payments from nonmembers may cause unions to experience unpleasant transition costs in the short term, and may require unions to make adjustments in order to attract and retain members. But we must weigh these disadvantages against the considerable windfall that unions have received under *Abood* for the past 41 years. It is hard to estimate how many billions of dollars have been taken from nonmembers and transferred to public-sector unions in violation of the First Amendment. Those unconstitutional exactions cannot be allowed to continue indefinitely.

[VI]

For these reasons, States and public-sector unions may no longer extract agency fees from nonconsenting employees. Neither an agency fee nor any other payment to the union may be deducted from a nonmember's wages, nor may any other attempt be made to collect such a payment, unless the employee affirmatively consents to pay. By agreeing to pay, nonmembers are waiving their First Amendment rights, and such a waiver cannot be presumed. Rather, to be effective, the waiver must be freely given and shown by "clear and compelling" evidence. Unless employees clearly and affirmatively consent before any money is taken from them, this standard cannot be met.

Abood was wrongly decided and is now overruled.

Justice KAGAN, with whom Justice GINSBURG, Justice BREYER, and Justice SOTOMAYOR join, dissenting.

For over 40 years, Abood v. Detroit Bd. of Ed. (1977), struck a stable balance between public employees' First Amendment rights and government entities' interests in running their workforces as they thought proper. Under that decision, a government entity could require public employees to pay a fair share of the cost that a union incurs when negotiating on their behalf over terms of employment. But no part of that fair-share payment could go to any of the union's political or ideological activities.

That holding fit comfortably with this Court's general framework for evaluating claims that a condition of public employment violates the First Amendment. The Court's decisions have long made plain that government entities have substantial latitude to regulate their employees' speech—especially about terms of employment—in the interest of operating their workplaces effectively. *Abood* allowed governments to do just that. While protecting public employees' expression about non-workplace matters, the decision enabled a government to advance important managerial interests—by ensuring the presence of an exclusive employee representative to bargain with. Far from an "anomaly," the *Abood* regime was a paradigmatic example of how the government can regulate speech in its capacity as an employer.

Not any longer. Its decision will have large-scale consequences. Public employee unions will lose a secure source of financial support. State and local governments that thought fair-share provisions furthered their interests will need to find new ways of managing their workforces. Across the country, the relationships of public employees and employers will alter in both predictable and wholly unexpected ways.

Rarely if ever has the Court overruled a decision—let alone one of this import—with so little regard for the usual principles of *stare decisis*. There are no special justifications for reversing *Abood*. It has proved workable. No recent developments have eroded its underpinnings. And it is deeply entrenched, in both the law and the real world. More than 20 States have statutory schemes built on the decision. Those laws underpin thousands of ongoing contracts involving millions of employees. Reliance interests do not come any stronger than those surrounding *Abood*. And likewise, judicial disruption does not get any greater than what the Court does today. I respectfully dissent.

[I]

Unlike the majority, I see nothing "questionable" about *Abood*'s analysis. The decision's account of why some government entities have a strong interest in agency fees (now often called fair-share fees) is fundamentally sound. And the balance *Abood* struck between public employers' interests and public employees' expression is right at home in First Amendment doctrine.

In many cases over many decades, this Court has addressed how the First Amendment applies when the government, acting not as sovereign but as employer, limits its workers' speech. Those decisions have granted substantial latitude to the government, in recognition of its significant interests in managing its workforce so as to best serve the public. *Abood* fit neatly with that caselaw, in both reasoning and result. Indeed, its reversal today creates a significant anomaly—an exception, applying to union fees alone, from the usual rules governing public employees' speech.

In striking the proper balance between employee speech rights and managerial interests, the Court has long applied a test originating in Pickering v. Board of Ed. of Township High School Dist. 205, Will Cty. (1968). *Abood* coheres with that framework. *Abood* and *Pickering* raised variants of the same basic issue: the extent of the government's authority to make employment decisions affecting expression. And in both, the Court struck the same basic balance, enabling the government to curb speech when—but only when—the regulation was designed to protect its managerial interests.

The key point about *Abood* is that it fit naturally with this Court's consistent teaching about the permissibility of regulating public employees, speech. The Court allows a government entity to regulate that expression in aid of managing its workforce to effectively provide public services. That is just what a government aims to do when it enforces a fair-share agreement. And so, the key point about today's decision is that it creates an unjustified hole in the law, applicable to union fees alone. This case is *sui generis* among those addressing public employee speech—and will almost surely remain so.

[II]

But the worse part of today's opinion is where the majority subverts all known principles of *stare decisis*. The majority makes plain, in the first 33 pages of its

C. Compelled Association

decision, that it believes *Abood* was wrong. But even if that were true (which it is not), it is not enough. "Respecting *stare decisis* means sticking to some wrong decisions." Any departure from settled precedent (so the Court has often stated) demands a "special justification—over and above the belief that the precedent was wrongly decided." And the majority does not have anything close. To the contrary: all that is "special" in this case—especially the massive reliance interests at stake—demands retaining *Abood*, beyond even the normal precedent.

And *Abood* is not just any precedent: It is embedded in the law (not to mention, as I'll later address, in the world) in a way not many decisions are. Over four decades, this Court has cited *Abood* favorably many times, and has affirmed and applied its central distinction between the costs of collective bargaining (which the government can charge to all employees) and those of political activities (which it cannot).

The majority is likewise wrong to invoke "workability" as a reason for overruling *Abood*. Does *Abood* require drawing a line? Yes, between a union's collective-bargaining activities and its political activities. Is that line perfectly and pristinely "precis[e]," as the majority demands? Well, not quite that—but as exercises of constitutional linedrawing go, *Abood* stands well above average. In the 40 years since *Abood*, this Court has had to resolve only a handful of cases raising questions about the distinction. To my knowledge, the circuit courts are not divided on any classification issue; neither are they issuing distress signals of the kind that sometimes prompt the Court to reverse a decision. And that tranquility is unsurprising: There may be some gray areas (there always are), but in the mine run of cases, everyone knows the difference between politicking and collective bargaining.

And in any event, one *stare decisis* factor—reliance—dominates all others here and demands keeping *Abood*. *Stare decisis*, this Court has held, "has added force when the legislature, in the public sphere, and citizens, in the private realm, have acted in reliance on a previous decision." That is because overruling a decision would then "require an extensive legislative response" or "dislodge settled rights and expectations." Both will happen here: The Court today wreaks havoc on entrenched legislative and contractual arrangements.

Over 20 States have by now enacted statutes authorizing fair-share provisions. To be precise, 22 States, the District of Columbia, and Puerto Rico—plus another two States for police and firefighter unions. Every one of them will now need to come up with new ways—elaborated in new statutes—to structure relations between government employers and their workers. Still more, thousands of current contracts covering millions of workers provide for agency fees. Usually, this Court recognizes that "[c]onsiderations in favor of *stare decisis* are at their acme in cases involving property and contract rights." Not today. The majority undoes bargains reached all over the country. It prevents the parties from fulfilling other commitments they have made based on those agreements. It forces the parties—immediately—to renegotiate once-settled terms and create new tradeoffs. It does so knowing that many of the parties will have to revise (or redo) multiple contracts simultaneously. It does so knowing that those renegotiations will occur in an environment of legal uncertainty, as state governments scramble to enact new labor legislation. It does so with no real clue of what will happen next—of how its action will alter public-sector labor relations. It does so even though the government services affected—policing, firefighting, teaching, transportation, sanitation (and more)—affect the quality of life of tens of millions of Americans.

[III]

There is no sugarcoating today's opinion. The majority overthrows a decision entrenched in this Nation's law—and in its economic life—for over 40 years. As a result, it prevents the American people, acting through their state and local officials, from making important choices about workplace governance. And it does so by weaponizing the First Amendment, in a way that unleashes judges, now and in the future, to intervene in economic and regulatory policy.

The majority has overruled *Abood* for no exceptional or special reason, but because it never liked the decision. It has overruled *Abood* because it wanted to.

Because, that is, it wanted to pick the winning side in what should be—and until now, has been—an energetic policy debate. Some state and local governments (and the constituents they serve) think that stable unions promote healthy labor relations and thereby improve the provision of services to the public. Other state and local governments (and their constituents) think, to the contrary, that strong unions impose excessive costs and impair those services. Americans have debated the pros and cons for many decades—in large part, by deciding whether to use fair-share arrangements. Yesterday, 22 States were on one side, 28 on the other (ignoring a couple of in-betweeners). Today, that healthy—that democratic—debate ends. The majority has adjudged who should prevail.

And maybe most alarming, the majority has chosen the winners by turning the First Amendment into a sword, and using it against workaday economic and regulatory policy. And it threatens not to be the last. Speech is everywhere—a part of every human activity (employment, health care, securities trading, you name it). For that reason, almost all economic and regulatory policy affects or touches speech. So the majority's road runs long. And at every stop are black-robed rulers overriding citizens' choices. The First Amendment was meant for better things. It was meant not to undermine but to protect democratic governance—including over the role of public-sector unions.

What will be the effect of *Janus* on other mandatory dues? For example, the Court reaffirmed and applied *Abood* in Keller v. State Bar of California, 496 U.S. 1 (1990). The Court said that compulsory bar dues could be used only if "reasonably incurred for the purpose of regulating the legal profession or improving the quality of the legal service available to the people of the State." The Court explained that bar dues could be collected from all members to pay for bar-related activities. But the Court said that "[c]ompulsory dues may not be expended to endorse or advance a gun control or nuclear weapons freeze initiative; at the other end of the spectrum petitioners have no valid constitutional objection to their compulsory dues being spent for activities connected with disciplining members of the bar or proposing ethical codes for the profession." After *Janus*, there are challenges to mandatory bar dues in a number of states.

Also, what about mandatory student fees that were approved in the following case?

C. Compelled Association

BOARD OF REGENTS OF THE UNIVERSITY OF WISCONSIN SYSTEM v. SOUTHWORTH
529 U.S. 217 (2000)

Justice KENNEDY delivered the opinion of the Court.

Respondents are a group of students at the University of Wisconsin. They brought a First Amendment challenge to a mandatory student activity fee imposed by petitioner Board of Regents of the University of Wisconsin and used in part by the University to support student organizations engaging in political or ideological speech. Respondents object to the speech and expression of some of the student organizations. Relying upon our precedents which protect members of unions and bar associations from being required to pay fees used for speech the members find objectionable, both the District Court and the Court of Appeals invalidated the University's student fee program. The University contends that its mandatory student activity fee and the speech which it supports are appropriate to further its educational mission.

We reverse. The First Amendment permits a public university to charge its students an activity fee used to fund a program to facilitate extracurricular student speech if the program is viewpoint neutral. We do not sustain, however, the student referendum mechanism of the University's program, which appears to permit the exaction of fees in violation of the viewpoint neutrality principle. As to that aspect of the program, we remand for further proceedings.

I

It seems that since its founding the University has required full-time students enrolled at its Madison campus to pay a nonrefundable activity fee. For the 1995-1996 academic year, when this suit was commenced, the activity fee amounted to $331.50 per year. The fee is segregated from the University's tuition charge. Once collected, the activity fees are deposited by the University into the accounts of the State of Wisconsin. The fees are drawn upon by the University to support various campus services and extracurricular student activities. In the University's view, the activity fees "enhance the educational experience" of its students by "promot[ing] extracurricular activities," "stimulating advocacy and debate on diverse points of view," enabling "participa[tion] in political activity," "promot[ing] student participa[tion] in campus administrative activity," and providing "opportunities to develop social skills," all consistent with the University's mission.

The board of regents classifies the segregated fee into allocable and nonallocable portions. The nonallocable portion approximates 80% of the total fee and covers expenses such as student health services, intramural sports, debt service, and the upkeep and operations of the student union facilities. Respondents did not challenge the purposes to which the University commits the nonallocable portion of the segregated fee.

The allocable portion of the fee supports extracurricular endeavors pursued by the University's registered student organizations or RSOs. To qualify for RSO status students must organize as a not-for-profit group, limit membership primarily to students, and agree to undertake activities related to student life on campus. During the 1995-1996 school year, 623 groups had RSO status on the Madison campus. To name but a few, RSOs included the Future Financial Gurus of America; the International Socialist Organization; the College Democrats; the College Republicans; and the American Civil Liberties Union Campus Chapter. As one would expect, the expressive activities undertaken by RSOs are diverse in range and content, from displaying posters and circulating newsletters throughout the campus, to hosting campus debates and guest speakers, and to what can best be described as political lobbying.

RSOs may obtain a portion of the allocable fees in one of three ways. Most do so by seeking funding from the Student Government Activity Fund (SGAF), administered by the ASM. SGAF moneys may be issued to support an RSO's operations and events, as well as travel expenses "central to the purpose of the organization." As an alternative, an RSO can apply for funding from the General Student Services Fund (GSSF), administered through the ASM's finance committee. A student referendum provides a third means for an RSO to obtain funding. While the record is sparse on this feature of the University's program, the parties inform us that the student body can vote either to approve or to disapprove an assessment for a particular RSO. One referendum resulted in an allocation of $45,000 to WISPIRG during the 1995-1996 academic year.

II

It is inevitable that government will adopt and pursue programs and policies within its constitutional powers but which nevertheless are contrary to the profound beliefs and sincere convictions of some of its citizens. The government, as a general rule, may support valid programs and policies by taxes or other exactions binding on protesting parties. Within this broader principle it seems inevitable that funds raised by the government will be spent for speech and other expression to advocate and defend its own policies. The case we decide here, however, does not raise the issue of the government's right, or, to be more specific, the state-controlled University's right, to use its own funds to advance a particular message. The University's whole justification for fostering the challenged expression is that it springs from the initiative of the students, who alone give it purpose and content in the course of their extracurricular endeavors.

The University of Wisconsin exacts the fee at issue for the sole purpose of facilitating the free and open exchange of ideas by, and among, its students. We conclude the objecting students may insist upon certain safeguards with respect to the expressive activities which they are required to support. Our public forum cases are instructive here by close analogy. This is true even though the student activities fund is not a public forum in the traditional sense of the term and despite the circumstance that those cases most often involve a demand for access, not a claim to be exempt from supporting speech. The standard of viewpoint neutrality found in the public forum cases provides the standard we find controlling. We decide that the viewpoint neutrality requirement of the University program is in general sufficient to protect the rights of the objecting students. The student referendum aspect of the program for funding speech and expressive activities, however, appears to be inconsistent with the viewpoint neutrality requirement.

We must begin by recognizing that the complaining students are being required to pay fees which are subsidies for speech they find objectionable, even offensive. The *Abood* and *Keller* cases, then, provide the beginning point for our analysis. While those precedents identify the interests of the protesting students,

C. Compelled Association

the means of implementing First Amendment protections adopted in those decisions are neither applicable nor workable in the context of extracurricular student speech at a university.

The proposition that students who attend the University cannot be required to pay subsidies for the speech of other students without some First Amendment protection follows from the *Abood* and *Keller* cases. Students enroll in public universities to seek fulfillment of their personal aspirations and of their own potential. If the University conditions the opportunity to receive a college education, an opportunity comparable in importance to joining a labor union or bar association, on an agreement to support objectionable, extracurricular expression by other students, the rights acknowledged in *Abood* and *Keller* become implicated. It infringes on the speech and beliefs of the individual to be required, by this mandatory student activity fee program, to pay subsidies for the objectionable speech of others without any recognition of the State's corresponding duty to him or her. Yet recognition must be given as well to the important and substantial purposes of the University, which seeks to facilitate a wide range of speech.

In *Abood* and *Keller* the constitutional rule took the form of limiting the required subsidy to speech germane to the purposes of the union or bar association. The standard of germane speech as applied to student speech at a university is unworkable, however, and gives insufficient protection both to the objecting students and to the University program itself. Even in the context of a labor union, whose functions are, or so we might have thought, well known and understood by the law and the courts after a long history of government regulation and judicial involvement, we have encountered difficulties in deciding what is germane and what is not.

The speech the University seeks to encourage in the program before us is distinguished not by discernible limits but by its vast, unexplored bounds. To insist upon asking what speech is germane would be contrary to the very goal the University seeks to pursue. It is not for the Court to say what is or is not germane to the ideas to be pursued in an institution of higher learning.

Just as the vast extent of permitted expression makes the test of germane speech inappropriate for intervention, so too does it underscore the high potential for intrusion on the First Amendment rights of the objecting students. It is all but inevitable that the fees will result in subsidies to speech which some students find objectionable and offensive to their personal beliefs. If the standard of germane speech is inapplicable, then, it might be argued the remedy is to allow each student to list those causes which he or she will or will not support. If a university decided that its students' First Amendment interests were better protected by some type of optional or refund system it would be free to do so. We decline to impose a system of that sort as a constitutional requirement, however. The restriction could be so disruptive and expensive that the program to support extracurricular speech would be ineffective. The First Amendment does not require the University to put the program at risk.

The University may determine that its mission is well served if students have the means to engage in dynamic discussions of philosophical, religious, scientific, social, and political subjects in their extracurricular campus life outside the lecture hall. If the University reaches this conclusion, it is entitled to impose a mandatory fee to sustain an open dialogue to these ends.

The University must provide some protection to its students' First Amendment interests, however. The proper measure, and the principal standard of protection for objecting students, we conclude, is the requirement of viewpoint neutrality in the allocation of funding support. The parties have stipulated that the program the University has developed to stimulate extracurricular student expression respects the principle of viewpoint neutrality. If the stipulation is to continue to control the case, the University's program in its basic structure must be found consistent with the First Amendment.

It remains to discuss the referendum aspect of the University's program. While the record is not well developed on the point, it appears that by majority vote of the student body a given RSO may be funded or defunded. It is unclear to us what protection, if any, there is for viewpoint neutrality in this part of the process. To the extent the referendum substitutes majority determinations for viewpoint neutrality it would undermine the constitutional protection the program requires. The whole theory of viewpoint neutrality is that minority views are treated with the same respect as are majority views. Access to a public forum, for instance, does not depend upon majoritarian consent. That principle is controlling here. A remand is necessary and appropriate to resolve this point; and the case in all events must be reexamined in light of the principles we have discussed.

D. LAWS PROHIBITING DISCRIMINATION

Many state and local governments have adopted laws that prohibit discrimination by private groups and clubs. Frequently, those wishing to discriminate bring challenges to these laws; the claim is that freedom of association protects their right to discriminate and exclude whomever they want from their group. The Supreme Court has held that the compelling interest in stopping discrimination justifies interfering with such associational freedoms. The Court has indicated that freedom of association would protect a right to discriminate only if it is intimate association or where the discrimination is integral to express activity. Roberts v. United States Jaycees is the leading case articulating this test.

ROBERTS v. UNITED STATES JAYCEES
468 U.S. 609 (1984)

Justice BRENNAN delivered the opinion of the Court.

This case requires us to address a conflict between a State's efforts to eliminate gender-based discrimination against its citizens and the constitutional freedom of association asserted by members of a private organization. In the decision under review, the Court of Appeals for the Eighth Circuit concluded that, by requiring the United States Jaycees to admit women as full voting members, the Minnesota Human Rights Act violates the First and Fourteenth Amendment rights of the organization's members. We now reverse.

D. Laws Prohibiting Discrimination

I

The United States Jaycees (Jaycees), founded in 1920 as the Junior Chamber of Commerce, is a nonprofit membership corporation, incorporated in Missouri with national headquarters in Tulsa, Okla. The objective of the Jaycees, as set out in its bylaws, is to pursue "such educational and charitable purposes as will promote and foster the growth and development of young men's civic organizations in the United States, designed to inculcate in the individual membership of such organization a spirit of genuine Americanism and civic interest, and as a supplementary education institution to provide them with opportunity for personal development and achievement and an avenue for intelligent participation by young men in the affairs of their community, state and nation, and to develop true friendship and understanding among young men of all nations." Regular membership is limited to young men between the ages of 18 and 35, while associate membership is available to individuals or groups ineligible for regular membership, principally women and older men. An associate member, whose dues are somewhat lower than those charged regular members, may not vote, hold local or national office, or participate in certain leadership training and awards programs.

The bylaws define a local chapter as "[a]ny young men's organization of good repute existing in any community within the United States, organized for purposes similar to and consistent with those" of the national organization. The ultimate policymaking authority of the Jaycees rests with an annual national convention, consisting of delegates from each local chapter, with a national president and board of directors. At the time of trial in August 1981, the Jaycees had approximately 295,000 members in 7,400 local chapters affiliated with 51 state organizations. There were at that time about 11,915 associate members. The national organization's executive vice president estimated at trial that women associate members make up about two percent of the Jaycees' total membership.

In 1974 and 1975, respectively, the Minneapolis and St. Paul chapters of the Jaycees began admitting women as regular members. Currently, the memberships and boards of directors of both chapters include a substantial proportion of women. As a result, the two chapters have been in violation of the national organization's bylaws for about 10 years. The national organization has imposed a number of sanctions on the Minneapolis and St. Paul chapters for violating the bylaws, including denying their members eligibility for state or national office or awards programs, and refusing to count their membership in computing votes at national conventions.

In December 1978, the president of the national organization advised both chapters that a motion to revoke their charters would be considered at a forthcoming meeting of the national board of directors in Tulsa. Shortly after receiving this notification, members of both chapters filed charges of discrimination with the Minnesota Department of Human Rights. The complaints alleged that the exclusion of women from full membership required by the national organization's bylaws violated the Minnesota Human Rights Act (Act), which provides in part: "It is an unfair discriminatory practice: To deny any person the full and equal enjoyment of the goods, services, facilities, privileges, advantages, and accommodations of a place of public accommodation because of race, color, creed, religion, disability, national origin or sex." The term "place of public accommodation" is defined in the Act as "a business, accommodation, refreshment, entertainment, recreation, or transportation facility of any kind, whether licensed or not, whose goods, services, facilities, privileges, advantages or accommodations are extended, offered, sold, or otherwise made available to the public."

II

Our decisions have referred to constitutionally protected "freedom of association" in two distinct senses. In one line of decisions, the Court has concluded that choices to enter into and maintain certain intimate human relationships must be secured against undue intrusion by the State because of the role of such relationships in safeguarding the individual freedom that is central to our constitutional scheme. In this respect, freedom of association receives protection as a fundamental element of personal liberty. In another set of decisions, the Court has recognized a right to associate for the purpose of engaging in those activities protected by the First Amendment—speech, assembly, petition for the redress of grievances, and the exercise of religion. The Constitution guarantees freedom of association of this kind as an indispensable means of preserving other individual liberties.

The intrinsic and instrumental features of constitutionally protected association may, of course, coincide. In particular, when the State interferes with individuals' selection of those with whom they wish to join in a common endeavor, freedom of association in both of its forms may be implicated. The Jaycees contend that this is such a case. Still, the nature and degree of constitutional protection afforded freedom of association may vary depending on the extent to which one or the other aspect of the constitutionally protected liberty is at stake in a given case. We therefore find it useful to consider separately the effect of applying the Minnesota statute to the Jaycees on what could be called its members' freedom of intimate association and their freedom of expressive association.

A

The Court has long recognized that, because the Bill of Rights is designed to secure individual liberty, it must afford the formation and preservation of certain kinds of highly personal relationships a substantial measure of sanctuary from unjustified interference by the State. The personal affiliations that exemplify these considerations, and that therefore suggest some relevant limitations on the relationships that might be entitled to this sort of constitutional protection, are those that attend the creation and sustenance of a family—marriage, childbirth, the raising and education of children, and cohabitation with one's relatives. Among other things, therefore, they are distinguished by such attributes as relative smallness, a high degree of selectivity in decisions to begin and maintain the affiliation, and seclusion from others in critical aspects of the relationship. As a general matter, only relationships with these sorts of qualities are likely to reflect the considerations that have led to an understanding of freedom of association as an intrinsic element of personal liberty. Conversely, an association lacking these qualities—such as a large business enterprise—seems remote from the concerns giving rise to this constitutional protection. Accordingly, the

D. Laws Prohibiting Discrimination

Constitution undoubtedly imposes constraints on the State's power to control the selection of one's spouse that would not apply to regulations affecting the choice of one's fellow employees.

Between these poles, of course, lies a broad range of human relationships that may make greater or lesser claims to constitutional protection from particular incursions by the State. Determining the limits of state authority over an individual's freedom to enter into a particular association therefore unavoidably entails a careful assessment of where that relationship's objective characteristics locate it on a spectrum from the most intimate to the most attenuated of personal attachments. We need not mark the potentially significant points on this terrain with any precision. We note only that factors that may be relevant include size, purpose, policies, selectivity, congeniality, and other characteristics that in a particular case may be pertinent. In this case, however, several features of the Jaycees clearly place the organization outside of the category of relationships worthy of this kind of constitutional protection.

The undisputed facts reveal that the local chapters of the Jaycees are large and basically unselective groups. At the time of the state administrative hearing, the Minneapolis chapter had approximately 430 members, while the St. Paul chapter had about 400. Apart from age and sex, neither the national organization nor the local chapters employ any criteria for judging applicants for membership, and new members are routinely recruited and admitted with no inquiry into their backgrounds. In fact, a local officer testified that he could recall no instance in which an applicant had been denied membership on any basis other than age or sex. In short, the local chapters of the Jaycees are neither small nor selective. Moreover, much of the activity central to the formation and maintenance of the association involves the participation of strangers to that relationship. Accordingly, we conclude that the Jaycees chapters lack the distinctive characteristics that might afford constitutional protection to the decision of its members to exclude women.

B

An individual's freedom to speak, to worship, and to petition the government for the redress of grievances could not be vigorously protected from interference by the State unless a correlative freedom to engage in group effort toward those ends were not also guaranteed. According protection to collective effort on behalf of shared goals is especially important in preserving political and cultural diversity and in shielding dissident expression from suppression by the majority. Consequently, we have long understood as implicit in the right to engage in activities protected by the First Amendment a corresponding right to associate with others in pursuit of a wide variety of political, social, economic, educational, religious, and cultural ends.

Government actions that may unconstitutionally infringe upon this freedom can take a number of forms. Among other things, government may seek to impose penalties or withhold benefits from individuals because of their membership in a disfavored group; it may attempt to require disclosure of the fact of membership in a group seeking anonymity; and it may try to interfere with the internal organization or affairs of the group. By requiring the Jaycees to admit women as full voting members, the Minnesota Act works an infringement of the last type. There can be no clearer example of an intrusion into the internal structure or affairs of an association than a regulation that forces the group to accept members it does not desire. Such a regulation may impair the ability of the original members to express only those views that brought them together. Freedom of association therefore plainly presupposes a freedom not to associate.

The right to associate for expressive purposes is not, however, absolute. Infringements on that right may be justified by regulations adopted to serve compelling state interests, unrelated to the suppression of ideas, that cannot be achieved through means significantly less restrictive of associational freedoms.

We are persuaded that Minnesota's compelling interest in eradicating discrimination against its female citizens justifies the impact that application of the statute to the Jaycees may have on the male members' associational freedoms. On its face, the Minnesota Act does not aim at the suppression of speech, does not distinguish between prohibited and permitted activity on the basis of viewpoint, and does not license enforcement authorities to administer the statute on the basis of such constitutionally impermissible criteria. Instead, as the Minnesota Supreme Court explained, the Act reflects the State's strong historical commitment to eliminating discrimination and assuring its citizens equal access to publicly available goods and services. That goal, which is unrelated to the suppression of expression, plainly serves compelling state interests of the highest order.

In applying the Act to the Jaycees, the State has advanced those interests through the least restrictive means of achieving its ends. Indeed, the Jaycees has failed to demonstrate that the Act imposes any serious burdens on the male members' freedom of expressive association.

There is, however, no basis in the record for concluding that admission of women as full voting members will impede the organization's ability to engage in these protected activities or to disseminate its preferred views. The Act requires no change in the Jaycees' creed of promoting the interests of young men, and it imposes no restrictions on the organization's ability to exclude individuals with ideologies or philosophies different from those of its existing members. Moreover, the Jaycees already invites women to share the group's views and philosophy and to participate in much of its training and community activities. Accordingly, any claim that admission of women as full voting members will impair a symbolic message conveyed by the very fact that women are not permitted to vote is attenuated at best.

It is similarly arguable that, insofar as the Jaycees is organized to promote the views of young men whatever those views happen to be, admission of women as voting members will change the message communicated by the group's speech because of the gender-based assumptions of the audience. Neither supposition, however, is supported by the record. In claiming that women might have a different attitude about such issues as the federal budget, school prayer, voting rights, and foreign relations, or that the organization's public positions would have a different effect if the group were not "a purely young men's association," the Jaycees relies solely on unsupported generalizations about the relative interests and perspectives of men and women. Although such generalizations may or may not have a statistical basis in fact with respect to particular positions adopted by the Jaycees, we have repeatedly condemned legal decisionmaking that relies uncritically on such assumptions. In the absence of a showing far

D. Laws Prohibiting Discrimination

more substantial than that attempted by the Jaycees, we decline to indulge in the sexual stereotyping that underlies appellee's contention that, by allowing women to vote, application of the Minnesota Act will change the content or impact of the organization's speech. In any event, even if enforcement of the Act causes some incidental abridgment of the Jaycees' protected speech, that effect is no greater than is necessary to accomplish the State's legitimate purposes.

Similarly, in Board of Directors of Rotary International v. Rotary Club of Duarte, 481 U.S. 537 (1987), the Court held that it did not violate the First Amendment rights of the Rotary Club to force them to admit women in compliance with a California law that prohibited private business establishments from discriminating based on characteristics such as gender.

In *Roberts* and *Rotary Club*, the Court recognized that freedom of association would protect a right to discriminate in limited circumstances. For instance, if the activity is "intimate association"—a small private gathering—freedom of association would protect a right to discriminate. Also, freedom of association would protect a right to discriminate where discrimination is integral to expressive activity. For example, the Klan likely could exclude African Americans or the Nazi party could exclude Jews because discrimination is a key aspect of their message.

In Hurley v. Irish-American Gay, Lesbian, and Bisexual Group of Boston, 515 U.S. 557 (1995), the Court found that freedom of association and freedom of speech allowed a group to discriminate. Every St. Patrick's Day, the Veterans Council, a private group, organizes a parade in Boston. The Veterans Council refused to allow the Irish-American Gay, Lesbian, and Bisexual Group of Boston to participate in its parade. The Irish-American Gay, Lesbian, and Bisexual Group sued in Massachusetts state court based on the state's public accommodations law that prohibited discrimination by business establishments based on sexual orientation. The Massachusetts Supreme Judicial Court sided with the Irish-American Gay, Lesbian, and Bisexual Group.

The U.S. Supreme Court unanimously reversed. The Court, in an opinion by Justice Souter, said that organizing a parade is inherently expressive activity and that it violated the First Amendment to force the organizers to include messages that they find inimical. Justice Souter explained that compelling the Veterans Council to include the Irish-American Gay, Lesbian, and Bisexual Group "violates the fundamental rule . . . under the First Amendment, that a speaker has the autonomy to choose the content of his own message."

The Court expressly invoked the principle that there is a First Amendment right not to speak. Justice Souter wrote that "the Council clearly decided to exclude a message it did not like from the communication it chose to make, and that is enough to invoke its right as a private speaker to shape its expression by speaking on one subject while remaining silent on another."

The most important Supreme Court case concerning a right to exclude based on freedom of association is Boy Scouts of America v. Dale.

BOY SCOUTS OF AMERICA v. DALE
530 U.S. 640 (2000)

Chief Justice REHNQUIST delivered the opinion of the Court.

Petitioners are the Boy Scouts of America and the Monmouth Council, a division of the Boy Scouts of America (collectively, Boy Scouts). The Boy Scouts is a private, not-for-profit organization engaged in instilling its system of values in young people. The Boy Scouts asserts that homosexual conduct is inconsistent with the values it seeks to instill. Respondent is James Dale, a former Eagle Scout whose adult membership in the Boy Scouts was revoked when the Boy Scouts learned that he is an avowed homosexual and gay rights activist. The New Jersey Supreme Court held that New Jersey's public accommodations law requires that the Boy Scouts admit Dale. This case presents the question whether applying New Jersey's public accommodations law in this way violates the Boy Scouts' First Amendment right of expressive association. We hold that it does.

I

James Dale entered scouting in 1978 at the age of eight by joining Monmouth Council's Cub Scout Pack 142. Dale became a Boy Scout in 1981 and remained a Scout until he turned 18. By all accounts, Dale was an exemplary Scout. In 1988, he achieved the rank of Eagle Scout, one of Scouting's highest honors. Dale applied for adult membership in the Boy Scouts in 1989. The Boy Scouts approved his application for the position of assistant scoutmaster of Troop 73. Around the same time, Dale left home to attend Rutgers University. After arriving at Rutgers, Dale first acknowledged to himself and others that he is gay. He quickly became involved with, and eventually became the copresident of, the Rutgers University Lesbian/Gay Alliance. In 1990, Dale attended a seminar addressing the psychological and health needs of lesbian and gay teenagers. A newspaper covering the event interviewed Dale about his advocacy of homosexual teenagers' need for gay role models. In early July 1990, the newspaper published the interview and Dale's photograph over a caption identifying him as the copresident of the Lesbian/Gay Alliance.

Later that month, Dale received a letter from Monmouth Council Executive James Kay revoking his adult membership. Dale wrote to Kay requesting the reason for Monmouth Council's decision. Kay responded by letter that the Boy Scouts "specifically forbid membership to homosexuals." In 1992, Dale filed a complaint against the Boy Scouts in the New Jersey Superior Court. The complaint alleged that the Boy Scouts had violated New Jersey's public accommodations statute and its common law by revoking Dale's membership based solely on his sexual orientation. New Jersey's public accommodations statute prohibits, among other things, discrimination on the basis of sexual orientation in places of public accommodation. The New Jersey Supreme Court held that the Boy Scouts was a place of public accommodation subject to the public accommodations law, that the organization was not exempt from the law under any of its express exceptions, and that the Boy Scouts violated the law by revoking Dale's membership based on his avowed homosexuality.

D. Laws Prohibiting Discrimination

II

The forced inclusion of an unwanted person in a group infringes the group's freedom of expressive association if the presence of that person affects in a significant way the group's ability to advocate public or private viewpoints. But the freedom of expressive association, like many freedoms, is not absolute. We have held that the freedom could be overridden "by regulations adopted to serve compelling state interests, unrelated to the suppression of ideas, that cannot be achieved through means significantly less restrictive of associational freedoms."

To determine whether a group is protected by the First Amendment's expressive associational right, we must determine whether the group engages in "expressive association." The First Amendment's protection of expressive association is not reserved for advocacy groups. But to come within its ambit, a group must engage in some form of expression, whether it be public or private.

The Boy Scouts is a private, nonprofit organization. According to its mission statement: "It is the mission of the Boy Scouts of America to serve others by helping to instill values in young people and, in other ways, to prepare them to make ethical choices over their lifetime in achieving their full potential. The values we strive to instill are based on those found in the Scout Oath and Law: On my honor I will do my best to do my duty to God and my country and to obey the Scout Law; To help other people at all times; To keep myself physically strong, mentally awake, and morally straight."

Thus, the general mission of the Boy Scouts is clear: "[T]o instill values in young people." The Boy Scouts seeks to instill these values by having its adult leaders spend time with the youth members, instructing and engaging them in activities like camping, archery, and fishing. During the time spent with the youth members, the scoutmasters and assistant scoutmasters inculcate them with the Boy Scouts' values—both expressly and by example. It seems indisputable that an association that seeks to transmit such a system of values engages in expressive activity. Given that the Boy Scouts engages in expressive activity, we must determine whether the forced inclusion of Dale as an assistant scoutmaster would significantly affect the Boy Scouts' ability to advocate public or private viewpoints. This inquiry necessarily requires us first to explore, to a limited extent, the nature of the Boy Scouts' view of homosexuality.

The values the Boy Scouts seeks to instill are "based on" those listed in the Scout Oath and Law. The Boy Scouts explains that the Scout Oath and Law provide "a positive moral code for living; they are a list of 'do's' rather than 'don'ts.'" The Boy Scouts asserts that homosexual conduct is inconsistent with the values embodied in the Scout Oath and Law, particularly with the values represented by the terms "morally straight" and "clean."

Obviously, the Scout Oath and Law do not expressly mention sexuality or sexual orientation. And the terms "morally straight" and "clean" are by no means self-defining. Different people would attribute to those terms very different meanings. For example, some people may believe that engaging in homosexual conduct is not at odds with being "morally straight" and "clean." And others may believe that engaging in homosexual conduct is contrary to being "morally straight" and "clean." The Boy Scouts says it falls within the latter category.

The Boy Scouts publicly expressed its views with respect to homosexual conduct by its assertions in prior litigation. For example, throughout a California case with similar facts filed in the early 1980's, the Boy Scouts consistently asserted the same position with respect to homosexuality that it asserts today. We cannot doubt that the Boy Scouts sincerely holds this view.

We must then determine whether Dale's presence as an assistant scoutmaster would significantly burden the Boy Scouts' desire to not "promote homosexual conduct as a legitimate form of behavior." As we give deference to an association's assertions regarding the nature of its expression, we must also give deference to an association's view of what would impair its expression. That is not to say that an expressive association can erect a shield against antidiscrimination laws simply by asserting that mere acceptance of a member from a particular group would impair its message. But here Dale, by his own admission, is one of a group of gay Scouts who have "become leaders in their community and are open and honest about their sexual orientation." Dale was the copresident of a gay and lesbian organization at college and remains a gay rights activist. Dale's presence in the Boy Scouts would, at the very least, force the organization to send a message, both to the youth members and the world, that the Boy Scouts accepts homosexual conduct as a legitimate form of behavior.

Having determined that the Boy Scouts is an expressive association and that the forced inclusion of Dale would significantly affect its expression, we inquire whether the application of New Jersey's public accommodations law to require that the Boy Scouts accept Dale as an assistant scoutmaster runs afoul of the Scouts' freedom of expressive association. We conclude that it does. We are not, as we must not be, guided by our views of whether the Boy Scouts' teachings with respect to homosexual conduct are right or wrong; public or judicial disapproval of a tenet of an organization's expression does not justify the State's effort to compel the organization to accept members where such acceptance would derogate from the organization's expressive message. "While the law is free to promote all sorts of conduct in place of harmful behavior, it is not free to interfere with speech for no better reason than promoting an approved message or discouraging a disfavored one, however enlightened either purpose may strike the government."

Justice STEVENS, with whom Justice SOUTER, Justice GINSBURG and Justice BREYER join, dissenting.

New Jersey "prides itself on judging each individual by his or her merits" and on being "in the vanguard in the fight to eradicate the cancer of unlawful discrimination of all types from our society." The New Jersey Supreme Court's construction of the statutory definition of a "place of public accommodation" has given its statute a more expansive coverage than most similar state statutes. The question in this case is whether that expansive construction trenches on the federal constitutional rights of the Boy Scouts of America (BSA).

In this case, Boy Scouts of America contends that it teaches the young boys who are Scouts that homosexuality is immoral. Consequently, it argues, it would violate its right to associate to force it to admit homosexuals as members, as doing so would be at odds with its own shared goals and values. This contention, quite plainly, requires us to look at what, exactly, are the values that BSA actually teaches.

BSA's mission statement reads as follows: "It is the mission of the Boy Scouts of America to serve others by helping to instill values in young people and, in other ways, to prepare them to make ethical choices over their lifetime in achieving their full potential." Its federal charter declares its purpose is "to promote, through organization, and cooperation with other agencies, the ability of boys to do things for themselves and others, to train them in scoutcraft,

D. Laws Prohibiting Discrimination

and to teach them patriotism, courage, self-reliance, and kindred values." BSA describes itself as having a "representative membership," which it defines as "boy membership [that] reflects proportionately the characteristics of the boy population of its service area." In particular, the group emphasizes that "[n]either the charter nor the bylaws of the Boy Scouts of America permits the exclusion of any boy. . . . To meet these responsibilities we have made a commitment that our membership shall be representative of all the population in every community, district, and council."

To bolster its claim that its shared goals include teaching that homosexuality is wrong, BSA directs our attention to two terms appearing in the Scout Oath and Law. The first is the phrase "morally straight," which appears in the Oath ("On my honor I will do my best . . . To keep myself . . . morally straight"); the second term is the word "clean," which appears in a list of 12 characteristics together comprising the Scout Law.

The Boy Scout Handbook defines "morally straight," as such: "To be a person of strong character, guide your life with honesty, purity, and justice. Respect and defend the rights of all people. Your relationships with others should be honest and open. Be clean in your speech and actions, and faithful in your religious beliefs. The values you follow as a Scout will help you become virtuous and self-reliant." As for the term "clean," the Boy Scout Handbook offers the following: "A Scout is CLEAN. A Scout keeps his body and mind fit and clean. He chooses the company of those who live by these same ideals. He helps keep his home and community clean." "You never need to be ashamed of dirt that will wash off. If you play hard and work hard you can't help getting dirty. But when the game is over or the work is done, that kind of dirt disappears with soap and water. There's another kind of dirt that won't come off by washing. It is the kind that shows up in foul language and harmful thoughts. Swear words, profanity, and dirty stories are weapons that ridicule other people and hurt their feelings. The same is true of racial slurs and jokes making fun of ethnic groups or people with physical or mental limitations. A Scout knows there is no kindness or honor in such mean-spirited behavior. He avoids it in his own words and deeds. He defends those who are targets of insults."

It is plain as the light of day that neither one of these principles — "morally straight" and "clean" — says the slightest thing about homosexuality. Indeed, neither term in the Boy Scouts' Law and Oath expresses any position whatsoever on sexual matters.

BSA's published guidance on that topic underscores this point. Scouts, for example, are directed to receive their sex education at home or in school, but not from the organization: "Your parents or guardian or a sex education teacher should give you the facts about sex that you must know." Boy Scout Handbook (1992). Moreover, Scoutmasters are specifically directed to steer curious adolescents to other sources of information: "If Scouts ask for information regarding . . . sexual activity, answer honestly and factually, but stay within your realm of expertise and comfort. If a Scout has serious concerns that you cannot answer, refer him to his family, religious leader, doctor, or other professional."

In light of BSA's self-proclaimed ecumenism, furthermore, it is even more difficult to discern any shared goals or common moral stance on homosexuality. Insofar as religious matters are concerned, BSA's bylaws state that it is "absolutely nonsectarian in its attitude toward . . . religious training." Because a number of religious groups do not view homosexuality as immoral or wrong and reject discrimination against homosexuals, it is exceedingly difficult to believe that BSA nonetheless adopts a single particular religious or moral philosophy when it comes to sexual orientation. BSA surely is aware that some religions do not teach that homosexuality is wrong.

[I]n *Jaycees*, we asked whether Minnesota's Human Rights Law requiring the admission of women "impose[d] any serious burdens" on the group's "collective effort on behalf of [its] shared goals." Notwithstanding the group's obvious publicly stated exclusionary policy, we did not view the inclusion of women as a "serious burden" on the Jaycees' ability to engage in the protected speech of its choice. Similarly, in *Rotary Club*, we asked whether California's law would "affect in any significant way the existing members' ability" to engage in their protected speech, or whether the law would require the clubs "to abandon their basic goals." The relevant question is whether the mere inclusion of the person at issue would "impose any serious burden," "affect in any significant way," or be "a substantial restraint upon" the organization's "shared goals," "basic goals," or "collective effort to foster beliefs."

The evidence before this Court makes it exceptionally clear that BSA has, at most, simply adopted an exclusionary membership policy and has no shared goal of disapproving of homosexuality. BSA's mission statement and federal charter say nothing on the matter; its official membership policy is silent; its Scout Oath and Law—and accompanying definitions—are devoid of any view on the topic; its guidance for Scouts and Scoutmasters on sexuality declare that such matters are "not construed to be Scouting's proper area," but are the province of a Scout's parents and pastor; and BSA's posture respecting religion tolerates a wide variety of views on the issue of homosexuality. Moreover, there is simply no evidence that BSA otherwise teaches anything in this area, or that it instructs Scouts on matters involving homosexuality in ways not conveyed in the Boy Scout or Scoutmaster Handbooks. In short, Boy Scouts of America is simply silent on homosexuality. There is no shared goal or collective effort to foster a belief about homosexuality at all—let alone one that is significantly burdened by admitting homosexuals. As in *Jaycees*, there is "no basis in the record for concluding that admission of [homosexuals] will impede the [Boy Scouts'] ability to engage in [its] protected activities or to disseminate its preferred views" and New Jersey's law "requires no change in [BSA's] creed." It is entirely clear that BSA in fact expresses no clear, unequivocal message burdened by New Jersey's law.

Unfavorable opinions about homosexuals "have ancient roots." Like equally atavistic opinions about certain racial groups, those roots have been nourished by sectarian doctrine. That such prejudices are still prevalent and that they have caused serious and tangible harm to countless members of the class New Jersey seeks to protect are established matters of fact that neither the Boy Scouts nor the Court disputes. That harm can only be aggravated by the creation of a constitutional shield for a policy that is itself the product of a habitual way of thinking about strangers. As Justice Brandeis so wisely advised, "we must be ever on our guard, lest we erect our prejudices into legal principles." If we would guide by the light of reason, we must let our minds be bold.

CHAPTER 6

FREEDOM OF THE PRESS

A. INTRODUCTION: ARE THERE SPECIAL RIGHTS FOR THE PRESS?

Although the First Amendment expressly protects "freedom of the press," most of the issues concerning press freedom have been covered in earlier chapters. For example, the basic methodological issues concerning the First Amendment—such as the distinction between content-based and content-neutral laws, the requirement that laws not be vague or overbroad, and especially the prohibition of prior restraints—all apply to the press. Indeed, many of these cases, particularly those concerning prior restraints, arose in the context of actions against newspapers. Similarly, the categories of unprotected and less protected speech apply to all speakers, including the press.

This chapter focuses on issues that uniquely apply to the press. The underlying question is whether the press is entitled to any protections greater than others under the First Amendment. For example, does freedom of the press provide the media with an exemption from general government laws? Does it protect a right to news gathering and thus give the media special access to government places and papers?

On the one hand, freedom of the press is enumerated as a distinct right from freedom of speech. This arguably reflects the important and unique role of informing the public and thereby checking government. Sometimes the failure to protect the press as an institution will mean that the people will be denied significant information. For instance, arguably the failure to allow reporters to keep their sources confidential will mean the loss of information that might have been available if secrecy could have been promised.

But others argue that the press is entitled to no special protections under the First Amendment. In part, the argument against special status for the press is based on the framers' intent and the view that they used the words "speech" and "press" synonymously. Also, those who oppose special protections for the press argue that defining the press poses insurmountable obstacles. For example, if reporters can keep their sources confidential, is anyone who purports to be writing a story entitled to the privilege? Any distinctions could raise serious First Amendment and equal protection issues. Opposition to special protections for the press also reflects a long-standing hostility to the media in American society. Some fear that special protection would unduly enlarge the power of the press.

The Supreme Court generally has taken the latter view that the press is not entitled to any special rights or protections under the First Amendment. The issue remains, though, as to whether this is a desirable interpretation of the First Amendment and whether it adequately protects the need of the people to be informed.

Two major types of issues arise concerning freedom of the press. First, does freedom of the press provide the media a shield that it can use to immunize itself from government regulation? Section B focuses on this issue and considers many specific issues. When do taxes on the press violate the First Amendment? Does freedom of the press exempt it from the application of general regulatory laws? Does the press have a constitutional right to keep its sources secret? Does the First Amendment protect the press from laws that create a right to use it to reply to attacks?

A second major set of issues concerns whether freedom of the press can be used as a "sword" to gain access to government places and papers. There are two interrelated issues here: Does the First Amendment create a right of access for anyone to government places and papers; and does the press have a preferred right of access or any rights greater than the general population? As discussed in section C, the Court has found a First Amendment right for people to attend judicial proceedings but otherwise has refused to find such a First Amendment right of access and has thus far failed to create greater rights for the press than for others in society.

B. FREEDOM OF THE PRESS AS A SHIELD TO PROTECT THE PRESS FROM THE GOVERNMENT

1. *Taxes on the Press*

The Supreme Court consistently has held that taxes that single out the press are unconstitutional, but the press can be required to pay general taxes applicable to all businesses. The obvious concern is that the government could use taxes to punish the press for aggressive reporting or pointed criticism. The fear of such taxes could chill the press. For example, in Grosjean v. American Press Co., 297 U.S. 233 (1936), the Court declared unconstitutional a state statute imposing a license tax on advertisements in publications having a circulation of more than 20,000 copies a week. The Court reviewed the history of the First Amendment and concluded that the framers clearly intended to prohibit taxes directed at the press because of fear that they could cripple or at least chill the press. The Court said that although the First Amendment did not exempt the press from ordinary taxation, it did provide immunity from taxes directed solely at them. Although the Court did not discuss the circumstances that caused Louisiana to adopt its tax on the press, it likely was influenced by the fact that Governor Huey Long initiated the tax as retaliation against newspapers that had opposed him.

B. Freedom of the Press as a Shield to Protect the Press from the Government

More recently, the Court applied *Grosjean* in Minneapolis Star & Tribune Co. v. Minnesota Commissioner of Revenue and declared unconstitutional a print and ink tax.

MINNEAPOLIS STAR & TRIBUNE CO. v. MINNESOTA COMMISSIONER OF REVENUE
460 U.S. 575 (1983)

Justice O'CONNOR delivered the opinion of the Court.

This case presents the question of a State's power to impose a special tax on the press and, by enacting exemptions, to limit its effect to only a few newspapers.

I

Since 1967, Minnesota has imposed a sales tax on most sales of goods for a price in excess of a nominal sum. The appellant, Minneapolis Star and Tribune Company ("Star Tribune") is the publisher of a morning newspaper and an evening newspaper in Minneapolis. From 1967 until 1971, it enjoyed an exemption from the sales and use tax provided by Minnesota for periodic publications. In 1971, however, while leaving the exemption from the sales tax in place, the legislature amended the scheme to impose a "use tax" on the cost of paper and ink products consumed in the production of a publication. In 1974, the legislature again amended the statute, this time to exempt the first $100,000 worth of ink and paper consumed by a publication in any calendar year, in effect giving each publication an annual tax credit of $4,000. After the enactment of the $100,000 exemption, 11 publishers, producing 14 of the 388 paid circulation newspapers in the State, incurred a tax liability in 1974. Star Tribune was one of the 11, and, of the $893,355 collected, it paid $608,634, or roughly two-thirds of the total revenue raised by the tax. In 1975, 13 publishers, producing 16 out of 374 paid circulation papers, paid a tax. That year, Star Tribune again bore roughly two-thirds of the total receipts from the use tax on ink and paper.

II

Star Tribune argues that we must strike this tax on the authority of Grosjean v. American Press Co., Inc. (1936). Although there are similarities between the two cases, we agree with the State that *Grosjean* is not controlling. We think that the result in *Grosjean* may have been attributable in part to the perception on the part of the Court that the state imposed the tax with an intent to penalize a selected group of newspapers. In the case currently before us, however, there is no legislative history and no indication, apart from the structure of the tax itself, of any impermissible or censorial motive on the part of the legislature. We cannot resolve the case by simple citation to *Grosjean*. Instead, we must analyze the problem anew under the general principles of the First Amendment.

III

Clearly, the First Amendment does not prohibit all regulation of the press. It is beyond dispute that the States and the Federal Government can subject newspapers to generally applicable economic regulations without creating constitutional problems. Minnesota, however, has not chosen to apply its general sales and use tax to newspapers. Instead, it has created a special tax that applies only to certain publications protected by the First Amendment. Although the State argues now that the tax on paper and ink is part of the general scheme of taxation, the use tax provision is facially discriminatory, singling out publications for treatment that is, to our knowledge, unique in Minnesota tax law.

By creating this special use tax, which, to our knowledge, is without parallel in the State's tax scheme, Minnesota has singled out the press for special treatment. We then must determine whether the First Amendment permits such special taxation. A tax that burdens rights protected by the First Amendment cannot stand unless the burden is necessary to achieve an overriding governmental interest.

There is substantial evidence that differential taxation of the press would have troubled the framers of the First Amendment. A power to tax differentially, as opposed to a power to tax generally, gives a government a powerful weapon against the taxpayer selected. When the State singles out the press, though, the political constraints that prevent a legislature from passing crippling taxes of general applicability are weakened, and the threat of burdensome taxes becomes acute. That threat can operate as effectively as a censor to check critical comment by the press, undercutting the basic assumption of our political system that the press will often serve as an important restraint on government.

Further, differential treatment, unless justified by some special characteristic of the press, suggests that the goal of the regulation is not unrelated to suppression of expression, and such a goal is presumptively unconstitutional. Differential taxation of the press, then, places such a burden on the interests protected by the First Amendment that we cannot countenance such treatment unless the State asserts a counterbalancing interest of compelling importance that it cannot achieve without differential taxation.

The main interest asserted by Minnesota in this case is the raising of revenue. Of course that interest is critical to any government. Standing alone, however, it cannot justify the special treatment of the press, for an alternative means of achieving the same interest without raising concerns under the First Amendment is clearly available: the State could raise the revenue by taxing businesses generally, avoiding the censorial threat implicit in a tax that singles out the press.

Addressing the concern with differential treatment, Minnesota invites us to look beyond the form of the tax to its substance. The tax is, according to the State, merely a substitute for the sales tax, which, as a generally applicable tax, would be constitutional as applied to the press. There are two fatal flaws in this reasoning. First, the State has offered no explanation of why it chose to use a substitute for the sales tax rather than the sales tax itself. Further, even assuming that the legislature did have valid reasons for substituting another tax for the sales tax, we are not persuaded that this tax does serve as a substitute. The State asserts that this scheme actually favors the press over other businesses, because the same rate of tax is applied, but, for the press, the rate applies to

B. Freedom of the Press as a Shield to Protect the Press from the Government

the cost of components rather than to the sales price. We would be hesitant to fashion a rule that automatically allowed the State to single out the press for a different method of taxation as long as the effective burden was no different from that on other taxpayers or the burden on the press was lighter than that on other businesses. One reason for this reluctance is that the very selection of the press for special treatment threatens the press not only with the current differential treatment, but with the possibility of subsequent differentially more burdensome treatment. Thus, even without actually imposing an extra burden on the press, the government might be able to achieve censorial effects, for "[t]he threat of sanctions may deter [the] exercise of [First Amendment] rights almost as potently as the actual application of sanctions." [C]ourts as institutions are poorly equipped to evaluate with precision the relative burdens of various methods of taxation.

Minnesota's ink and paper tax violates the First Amendment not only because it singles out the press, but also because it targets a small group of newspapers. The effect of the $100,000 exemption enacted in 1974 is that only a handful of publishers pay any tax at all, and even fewer pay any significant amount of tax. [W]hen the exemption selects such a narrowly defined group to bear the full burden of the tax, the tax begins to resemble more a penalty for a few of the largest newspapers than an attempt to favor struggling smaller enterprises. Since Minnesota has offered no satisfactory justification for its tax on the use of ink and paper, the tax violates the First Amendment.

Justice REHNQUIST, dissenting.

Today we learn from the Court that a State runs afoul of the First Amendment proscription of laws "abridging the freedom of speech, or of the press" where the State structures its taxing system to the advantage of newspapers. This seems very much akin to protecting something so overzealously that in the end it is smothered. While the Court purports to rely on the intent of the "framers of the First Amendment," I believe it safe to assume that in 1791 "abridge" meant the same thing it means today: to diminish or curtail. Not until the Court's decision in this case, nearly two centuries after adoption of the First Amendment has it been read to prohibit activities which in no way diminish or curtail the freedoms it protects.

The Court recognizes in several parts of its opinion that the State of Minnesota could avoid constitutional problems by imposing on newspapers the 4% sales tax that it imposes on other retailers. Rather than impose such a tax, however, the Minnesota legislature decided to provide newspapers with an exemption from the sales tax and impose a 4% use tax on ink and paper; thus, while both taxes are part of one "system of sales and use taxes," newspapers are classified differently within that system. The problem the Court finds too difficult to deal with is whether this difference in treatment results in a significant burden on newspapers.

The record reveals that in 1974 the Minneapolis Star & Tribune had an average daily circulation of 489,345 copies. Using the price we were informed of at argument of 25 cents per copy, gross sales revenue for the year would be $38,168,910. The Sunday circulation for 1974 was 640,756; even assuming that it did not sell for more than the daily paper, gross sales revenue for the year would be at least $8,329,828. Thus, total sales revenues in 1974 would be $46,498,738. Had a 4% sales tax been imposed, the Minneapolis Star & Tribune would have been liable for $1,859,950 in 1974. The same "complexities of factual economic proof" can be analyzed for 1975. Daily circulation was 481,789; at 25 cents per copy, gross sales revenue for the year would be $37,579,542. The Sunday circulation for 1975 was 619,154; at 25 cents per copy, gross sales revenue for the year would be $8,049,002. Total sales revenues in 1975 would be $45,628,544; at a 4% rate, the sales tax for 1975 would be $1,825,142. Therefore, had the sales tax been imposed, as the Court agrees would have been permissible, the Minneapolis Star & Tribune's liability for 1974 and 1975 would have been $3,685,092.

The record further indicates that the Minneapolis Star & Tribune paid $608,634 in use taxes in 1974 and $636,113 in 1975—a total liability of $1,244,747. We need no expert testimony from modern day Euclids or Einsteins to determine that the $1,224,747 paid in use taxes is significantly less burdensome than the $3,685,092 that could have been levied by a sales tax. A fortiori, the Minnesota taxing scheme which singles out newspapers for "differential treatment" has benefited, not burdened, the "freedom of speech, [and] of the press."

Where the State devises classifications that infringe on the fundamental guaranties protected by the Constitution the Court has demanded more of the State in justifying its action. But there is no infringement, and thus the Court has never required more, unless the State's classifications significantly burden these specially protected rights.

In *Grosjean* and *Minneapolis Star*, the tax both singled out the press and had a discriminatory effect among newspapers; larger papers would be taxed much more than small ones. In Arkansas Writers' Project, Inc. v. Ragland, 481 U.S. 221 (1987), the Court ruled that the government cannot discriminate among types of publications. A state exempted from its sales tax special interest publications such as religious, professional, trade, and sports journals, but did not exempt general interest magazines. The Court emphasized that any differential taxation of the press—either at the press as opposed to others in society or at particular parts of the press—risked chilling reporting. The Arkansas law also was found unconstitutional on more basic grounds: It was content-based. The application of the tax turned entirely on the content of the publication and thus ran afoul of the fundamental prohibition against content-based discrimination except where necessary to serve a compelling purpose.

However, in Leathers v. Medlock, 499 U.S. 439 (1991), the Court did uphold a tax that treated media differently from each other. *Leathers* involved a state law that exempted newspapers and magazines from a state gross receipts tax, but did not exempt cable television. Although the tax singled out a particular branch of the media, the Court found it constitutional. The Court said that unlike *Grosjean* and *Minneapolis Star*, the tax did not single out the press and unlike the tax in *Ragland* it was not content-based. The Court said that because the tax was not discriminatory on either of these grounds, it was constitutional. Justice O'Connor, who also wrote the opinion for the Court in *Minneapolis Star*, stated for the majority that the "extension of [a state's] generally applicable sales tax to cable television, while exempting the print media, does not violate the First Amendment."

The cases can be reconciled by seeing the earlier decisions only as prohibiting the government from having a tax that is directed solely at the press or that

B. Freedom of the Press as a Shield to Protect the Press from the Government

distinguishes among branches of the press. *Leathers* does not involve either of these features and thus the tax was upheld. But if the earlier cases are seen as establishing the broader principle that the government should not be able to discriminate among parts of the press, then *Leathers* cannot be reconciled with the earlier precedents. The concern is that the government could retaliate against a particular branch of the press by a tax directed at it or by denying it an exemption granted to other parts of the press.

2. Application of General Regulatory Laws

The Supreme Court consistently has refused to find that the protection of freedom of the press entitles it to exemptions from general regulatory laws. For example, attempts by the press to receive constitutionally based exemptions to antitrust statutes, labor laws, and liability under state contract law have been expressly rejected.

In Associated Press v. United States, 326 U.S. 1 (1945), the Court expressly rejected the claim that the First Amendment entitled the press to an exemption from federal antitrust laws. An action was brought against an alleged monopoly in the dissemination of news through an association of member newspapers where nonmembers were denied access to the association's news and membership was restricted. Justice Black, writing for the Court, flatly rejected the claim that the First Amendment protected the press from antitrust liability. He said, "Freedom to publish is guaranteed by the Constitution, but freedom to combine to keep others from publishing is not. Freedom of the press from governmental interference under the First Amendment does not sanction repression of that freedom by private interests. The First Amendment offers not the slightest support for the contention that a combination to restrain trade in news and views has any constitutional immunity." Indeed, the Court said that First Amendment values were served by the application of antitrust laws so as to ensure the widest possible dissemination of news.

The Court followed *Associated Press* in Citizens Publishing Co. v. United States, 394 U.S. 131 (1969), which again rejected the claim of a First Amendment exemption to antitrust laws. *Citizens Publishing* involved an antitrust action against two newspapers in Tucson, Arizona, that formed a joint operating agreement that involved price fixing, profit pooling, and market controls. The Court upheld a finding of antitrust violations by the papers and noted that "[n]either news gathering nor news dissemination is being regulated by the present decree." The Court invoked *Associated Press* for the proposition that antitrust laws enhance, not hinder, First Amendment values by encouraging diverse sources of information and news.

Likewise, the Court has rejected claims by the press that the First Amendment entitles it to exemptions from federal labor laws. In Associated Press v. NLRB, 301 U.S. 103 (1937), the Court rejected the argument that freedom of the press provided it an exemption from the National Labor Relations Act, which secures for employees the right to organize and bargain collectively. The Court explained, "The business of the Associated Press is not immune from regulation because it is an agency of the press. The publisher of a newspaper has no special immunity from the application of general laws. He has no special privilege to invade the rights and liberties of others. He must answer for libel. He may be punished for contempt of court. He is subject to anti-trust laws. Like others he must pay equitable and nondiscriminatory taxes. The regulation here in question has no relation whatsoever to the impartial distribution of news."

In Oklahoma Press Publishing Co. v. Walling, 327 U.S. 186 (1946), the Court held that the First Amendment does not exempt the press from the Fair Labor Standards Act, which requires payment of the minimum wage and sets maximum hours limits for employees. The Court said that *Associated Press* established that there was no merit to the claim that it violated the First Amendment to apply labor laws to the press. The Court said, "If Congress can remove obstructions to commerce by requiring publishers to bargain collectively with employees and refrain from interfering with their rights of self-organization, matters closely related to eliminating low wages and long hours, Congress likewise may strike directly at those evils when they adversely affect commerce."

The strongest statement that the press is not exempt from general laws was in Cohen v. Cowles Media Co.

COHEN v. COWLES MEDIA CO.
501 U.S. 663 (1991)

Justice WHITE delivered the opinion of the Court.

The question before us is whether the First Amendment prohibits a plaintiff from recovering damages, under state promissory estoppel law, for a newspaper's breach of a promise of confidentiality given to the plaintiff in exchange for information. We hold that it does not.

During the closing days of the 1982 Minnesota gubernatorial race, Dan Cohen, an active Republican associated with Wheelock Whitney's Independent-Republican gubernatorial campaign, approached reporters from the St. Paul Pioneer Press Dispatch (Pioneer Press) and the Minneapolis Star and Tribune (Star Tribune) and offered to provide documents relating to a candidate in the upcoming election. Cohen made clear to the reporters that he would provide the information only if he was given a promise of confidentiality. Reporters from both papers promised to keep Cohen's identity anonymous and Cohen turned over copies of two public court records concerning Marlene Johnson, the Democratic-Farmer-Labor candidate for Lieutenant Governor. The first record indicated that Johnson had been charged in 1969 with three counts of unlawful assembly, and the second that she had been convicted in 1970 of petit theft. Both newspapers interviewed Johnson for her explanation and one reporter tracked down the person who had found the records for Cohen. As it turned out, the unlawful assembly charges arose out of Johnson's participation in a protest of an alleged failure to hire minority workers on municipal construction projects, and the charges were eventually dismissed. The petit theft conviction was for leaving a store without paying for $6 worth of sewing materials. The incident apparently occurred at a time during which Johnson was emotionally distraught, and the conviction was later vacated.

After consultation and debate, the editorial staffs of the two newspapers independently decided to publish Cohen's name as part of their stories concerning Johnson. In their stories, both papers identified Cohen as the source of the court records, indicated his connection to the Whitney campaign,

B. Freedom of the Press as a Shield to Protect the Press from the Government

and included denials by Whitney campaign officials of any role in the matter. The same day the stories appeared, Cohen was fired by his employer.

Respondents rely on the proposition that "if a newspaper lawfully obtains truthful information about a matter of public significance then state officials may not constitutionally punish publication of the information, absent a need to further a state interest of the highest order." This case, however, is not controlled by this line of cases but, rather, by the equally well-established line of decisions holding that generally applicable laws do not offend the First Amendment simply because their enforcement against the press has incidental effects on its ability to gather and report the news. As the cases relied on by respondents recognize, the truthful information sought to be published must have been lawfully acquired. The press may not with impunity break and enter an office or dwelling to gather news. Neither does the First Amendment relieve a newspaper reporter of the obligation shared by all citizens to respond to a grand jury subpoena and answer questions relevant to a criminal investigation, even though the reporter might be required to reveal a confidential source. [E]nforcement of such general laws against the press is not subject to stricter scrutiny than would be applied to enforcement against other persons or organizations.

There can be little doubt that the Minnesota doctrine of promissory estoppel is a law of general applicability. It does not target or single out the press. Rather, insofar as we are advised, the doctrine is generally applicable to the daily transactions of all the citizens of Minnesota. The First Amendment does not forbid its application to the press.

Respondents and amici argue that permitting Cohen to maintain a cause of action for promissory estoppel will inhibit truthful reporting because news organizations will have legal incentives not to disclose a confidential source's identity even when that person's identity is itself newsworthy. But if this is the case, it is no more than the incidental, and constitutionally insignificant, consequence of applying to the press a generally applicable law that requires those who make certain kinds of promises to keep them.

Justice SOUTER, with whom Justice MARSHALL, Justice BLACKMUN, and Justice O'CONNOR join, dissenting.

"[T]here is nothing talismanic about neutral laws of general applicability," for such laws may restrict First Amendment rights just as effectively as those directed specifically at speech itself. Because I do not believe the fact of general applicability to be dispositive, I find it necessary to articulate, measure, and compare the competing interests involved in any given case to determine the legitimacy of burdening constitutional interests, and such has been the Court's recent practice in publication cases. Nor can I accept the majority's position that we may dispense with balancing because the burden on publication is in a sense "self-imposed" by the newspaper's voluntary promise of confidentiality.

[F]reedom of the press is ultimately founded on the value of enhancing such discourse for the sake of a citizenry better informed and thus more prudently self-governed. The importance of this public interest is integral to the balance that should be struck in this case. There can be no doubt that the fact of Cohen's identity expanded the universe of information relevant to the choice faced by Minnesota voters in that State's 1982 gubernatorial election, the publication of which was thus of the sort quintessentially subject to strict First Amendment protection. The propriety of his leak to respondents could be taken to reflect on his character, which in turn could be taken to reflect on the character of the candidate who had retained him as an adviser. An election could turn on just such a factor; if it should, I am ready to assume that it would be to the greater public good, at least over the long run.

This is not to say that the breach of such a promise of confidentiality could never give rise to liability. One can conceive of situations in which the injured party is a private individual, whose identity is of less public concern than that of petitioner; liability there might not be constitutionally prohibited. Nor do I mean to imply that the circumstances of acquisition are irrelevant to the balance, although they may go only to what balances against, and not to diminish, the First Amendment value of any particular piece of information.

Because I believe the State's interest in enforcing a newspaper's promise of confidentiality insufficient to outweigh the interest in unfettered publication of the information revealed in this case, I respectfully dissent.

3. Keeping Reporters' Sources and Secrets Confidential

Confidential sources are often crucial to the media's gathering of information and being able to inform the public. Individuals may be willing to disclose important information to reporters only with a promise that their identity will be kept confidential. "Deep Throat"—the confidential source who provided the basis for many of the key stories by *Washington Post* reporters Carl Bernstein and Bob Woodward—was instrumental in helping to expose the criminal acts surrounding the Watergate cover-up and actions of the Campaign to Reelect President Nixon.

Thus, the press has claimed that the First Amendment gives it a right to resist subpoenas that require it to disclose the identity of sources. The Supreme Court, however, rejected this position in Branzburg v. Hayes, in a 5-4 decision.

<u>BRANZBURG v. HAYES</u>
408 U.S. 665 (1972)

Opinion of the Court by Mr. Justice WHITE.

The issue in these cases is whether requiring newsmen to appear and testify before state or federal grand juries abridges the freedom of speech and press guaranteed by the First Amendment. We hold that it does not.

I

The writ of certiorari in Branzburg v. Hayes and *Meigs*, brings before us two judgments of the Kentucky Court of Appeals, both involving petitioner Branzburg, a staff reporter for the Courier-Journal, a daily newspaper published in Louisville, Kentucky. On November 15, 1969, the Courier-Journal carried a story under petitioner's byline describing in detail his observations of two young residents of Jefferson County synthesizing hashish from marihuana, an activity which, they asserted, earned them about $5,000 in three weeks. The

B. Freedom of the Press as a Shield to Protect the Press from the Government

article included a photograph of a pair of hands working above a laboratory table on which was a substance identified by the caption as hashish. The article stated that petitioner had promised not to reveal the identity of the two hashish makers. Petitioner was shortly subpoenaed by the Jefferson County grand jury; he appeared, but refused to identify the individuals he had seen possessing marihuana or the persons he had seen making hashish from marihuana. A state trial court judge ordered petitioner to answer these questions and rejected his contention that the Kentucky reporters' privilege statute, the First Amendment of the United States Constitution, or the Kentucky Constitution authorized his refusal to answer.

In re Pappas originated when petitioner Pappas, a television newsman-photographer working out of the Providence, Rhode Island, office of a New Bedford, Massachusetts, television station, was called to New Bedford on July 30, 1970, to report on civil disorders there which involved fires and other turmoil. He intended to cover a Black Panther news conference at that group's headquarters in a boarded-up store. Petitioner found the streets around the store barricaded, but he ultimately gained entrance to the area and recorded and photographed a prepared statement read by one of the Black Panther leaders at about 3 P.M. He then asked for and received permission to re-enter the area. Returning at about 9 o'clock, he was allowed to enter and remain inside Panther headquarters. As a condition of entry, Pappas agreed not to disclose anything he saw or heard inside the store except an anticipated police raid, which Pappas, "on his own," was free to photograph and report as he wished. Pappas stayed inside the headquarters for about three hours, but there was no police raid, and petitioner wrote no story and did not otherwise reveal what had occurred in the store while he was there. Two months later, petitioner was summoned before the Bristol County Grand Jury and appeared, answered questions as to his name, address, employment, and what he had seen and heard outside Panther headquarters, but refused to answer any questions about what had taken place inside headquarters while he was there, claiming that the First Amendment afforded him a privilege to protect confidential informants and their information.

United States v. Caldwell arose from subpoenas issued by a federal grand jury in the Northern District of California to respondent Earl Caldwell, a reporter for the New York Times assigned to cover the Black Panther Party and other black militant groups. A subpoena duces tecum was served on respondent on February 2, 1970, ordering him to appear before the grand jury to testify and to bring with him notes and tape recordings of interviews given him for publication by officers and spokesmen of the Black Panther Party concerning the aims, purposes, and activities of that organization.

II

Petitioners Branzburg and Pappas and respondent Caldwell press First Amendment claims that may be simply put: that to gather news it is often necessary to agree either not to identify the source of information published or to publish only part of the facts revealed, or both; that if the reporter is nevertheless forced to reveal these confidences to a grand jury, the source so identified and other confidential sources of other reporters will be measurably deterred from furnishing publishable information, all to the detriment of the free flow of information protected by the First Amendment. Although the newsmen in these cases do not claim an absolute privilege against official interrogation in all circumstances, they assert that the reporter should not be forced either to appear or to testify before a grand jury or at trial until and unless sufficient grounds are shown for believing that the reporter possesses information relevant to a crime the grand jury is investigating, that the information the reporter has is unavailable from other sources, and that the need for the information is sufficiently compelling to override the claimed invasion of First Amendment interests occasioned by the disclosure.

We do not question the significance of free speech, press, or assembly to the country's welfare. Nor is it suggested that news gathering does not qualify for First Amendment protection; without some protection for seeking out the news, freedom of the press could be eviscerated. But these cases involve no intrusions upon speech or assembly, no prior restraint or restriction on what the press may publish, and no express or implied command that the press publish what it prefers to withhold. No exaction or tax for the privilege of publishing, and no penalty, civil or criminal, related to the content of published material is at issue here. The use of confidential sources by the press is not forbidden or restricted; reporters remain free to seek news from any source by means within the law. No attempt is made to require the press to publish its sources of information or indiscriminately to disclose them on request.

The sole issue before us is the obligation of reporters to respond to grand jury subpoenas as other citizens do and to answer questions relevant to an investigation into the commission of crime. Citizens generally are not constitutionally immune from grand jury subpoenas; and neither the First Amendment nor any other constitutional provision protects the average citizen from disclosing to a grand jury information that he has received in confidence. The claim is, however, that reporters are exempt from these obligations because if forced to respond to subpoenas and identify their sources or disclose other confidences, their informants will refuse or be reluctant to furnish newsworthy information in the future. This asserted burden on news gathering is said to make compelled testimony from newsmen constitutionally suspect and to require a privileged position for them.

It is clear that the First Amendment does not invalidate every incidental burdening of the press that may result from the enforcement of civil or criminal statutes of general applicability. Under prior cases, otherwise valid laws serving substantial public interests may be enforced against the press as against others, despite the possible burden that may be imposed. The Court has emphasized that "[t]he publisher of a newspaper has no special immunity from the application of general laws. He has no special privilege to invade the rights and liberties of others." Associated Press v. NLRB (1937).

It has generally been held that the First Amendment does not guarantee the press a constitutional right of special access to information not available to the public generally. Despite the fact that news gathering may be hampered, the press is regularly excluded from grand jury proceedings, our own conferences, the meetings of other official bodies gathered in executive session, and the meetings of private organizations. Newsmen have no constitutional right of access to the scenes of crime or disaster when the general public is excluded, and they may be prohibited from attending or publishing information about trials if such

B. Freedom of the Press as a Shield to Protect the Press from the Government

restrictions are necessary to assure a defendant a fair trial before an impartial tribunal.

It is thus not surprising that the great weight of authority is that newsmen are not exempt from the normal duty of appearing before a grand jury and answering questions relevant to a criminal investigation. At common law, courts consistently refused to recognize the existence of any privilege authorizing a newsman to refuse to reveal confidential information to a grand jury.

A number of States have provided newsmen a statutory privilege of varying breadth, but the majority have not done so, and none has been provided by federal statute. Until now the only testimonial privilege for unofficial witnesses that is rooted in the Federal Constitution is the Fifth Amendment privilege against compelled self-incrimination. We are asked to create another by interpreting the First Amendment to grant newsmen a testimonial privilege that other citizens do not enjoy. This we decline to do.

On the records now before us, we perceive no basis for holding that the public interest in law enforcement and in ensuring effective grand jury proceedings is insufficient to override the consequential, but uncertain, burden on news gathering that is said to result from insisting that reporters, like other citizens, respond to relevant questions put to them in the course of a valid grand jury investigation or criminal trial.

This conclusion itself involves no restraint on what newspapers may publish or on the type or quality of information reporters may seek to acquire, nor does it threaten the vast bulk of confidential relationships between reporters and their sources. Grand juries address themselves to the issues of whether crimes have been committed and who committed them. Only where news sources themselves are implicated in crime or possess information relevant to the grand jury's task need they or the reporter be concerned about grand jury subpoenas. Nothing before us indicates that a large number or percentage of all confidential news sources falls into either category and would in any way be deterred by our holding that the Constitution does not, as it never has, exempt the newsman from performing the citizen's normal duty of appearing and furnishing information relevant to the grand jury's task.

Thus, we cannot seriously entertain the notion that the First Amendment protects a newsman's agreement to conceal the criminal conduct of his source, or evidence thereof, on the theory that it is better to write about crime than to do something about it. Insofar as any reporter in these cases undertook not to reveal or testify about the crime he witnessed, his claim of privilege under the First Amendment presents no substantial question. The crimes of news sources are no less reprehensible and threatening to the public interest when witnessed by a reporter than when they are not.

There remain those situations where a source is not engaged in criminal conduct but has information suggesting illegal conduct by others. Newsmen frequently receive information from such sources pursuant to a tacit or express agreement to withhold the source's name and suppress any information that the source wishes not published. Such informants presumably desire anonymity in order to avoid being entangled as a witness in a criminal trial or grand jury investigation. They may fear that disclosure will threaten their job security or personal safety or that it will simply result in dishonor or embarrassment.

The argument that the flow of news will be diminished by compelling reporters to aid the grand jury in a criminal investigation is not irrational, nor are the records before us silent on the matter. But we remain unclear how often and to what extent informers are actually deterred from furnishing information when newsmen are forced to testify before a grand jury.

Moreover, grand juries characteristically conduct secret proceedings, and law enforcement officers are themselves experienced in dealing with informers, and have their own methods for protecting them without interference with the effective administration of justice. There is little before us indicating that informants whose interest in avoiding exposure is that it may threaten job security, personal safety, or peace of mind, would in fact be in a worse position, or would think they would be, if they risked placing their trust in public officials as well as reporters. We doubt if the informer who prefers anonymity but is sincerely interested in furnishing evidence of crime will always or very often be deterred by the prospect of dealing with those public authorities characteristically charged with the duty to protect the public interest as well as his.

Neither are we now convinced that a virtually impenetrable constitutional shield, beyond legislative or judicial control, should be forged to protect a private system of informers operated by the press to report on criminal conduct, a system that would be unaccountable to the public, would pose a threat to the citizen's justifiable expectations of privacy, and would equally protect well-intentioned informants and those who for pay or otherwise betray their trust to their employer or associates.

We are unwilling to embark the judiciary on a long and difficult journey to such an uncertain destination. The administration of a constitutional newsman's privilege would present practical and conceptual difficulties of a high order. Sooner or later, it would be necessary to define those categories of newsmen who qualified for the privilege, a questionable procedure in light of the traditional doctrine that liberty of the press is the right of the lonely pamphleteer who uses carbon paper or a mimeograph just as much as of the large metropolitan publisher who utilizes the latest photocomposition methods. The informative function asserted by representatives of the organized press in the present cases is also performed by lecturers, political pollsters, novelists, academic researchers, and dramatists. Almost any author may quite accurately assert that he is contributing to the flow of information to the public, that he relies on confidential sources of information, and that these sources will be silenced if he is forced to make disclosures before a grand jury.

At the federal level, Congress has freedom to determine whether a statutory newsman's privilege is necessary and desirable and to fashion standards and rules as narrow or broad as deemed necessary to deal with the evil discerned and, equally important, to refashion those rules as experience from time to time may dictate. There is also merit in leaving state legislatures free, within First Amendment limits, to fashion their own standards in light of the conditions and problems with respect to the relations between law enforcement officials and press in their own areas. It goes without saying, of course, that we are powerless to bar state courts from responding in their own way and construing their own constitutions so as to recognize a newsman's privilege, either qualified or absolute.

Justice POWELL, concurring.

I add this brief statement to emphasize what seems to me to be the limited nature of the Court's holding. The Court does not hold that newsmen, subpoenaed

B. Freedom of the Press as a Shield to Protect the Press from the Government

to testify before a grand jury, are without constitutional rights with respect to the gathering of news or in safeguarding their sources. [T]he Court states that no harassment of newsmen will be tolerated. If a newsman believes that the grand jury investigation is not being conducted in good faith he is not without remedy. Indeed, if the newsman is called upon to give information bearing only a remote and tenuous relationship to the subject of the investigation, or if he has some other reason to believe that his testimony implicates confidential source relationship without a legitimate need of law enforcement, he will have access to the court on a motion to quash and an appropriate protective order may be entered. The asserted claim to privilege should be judged on its facts by the striking of a proper balance between freedom of the press and the obligation of all citizens to give relevant testimony with respect to criminal conduct. The balance of these vital constitutional and societal interests on a case-by-case basis accords with the tried and traditional way of adjudicating such questions. In short, the courts will be available to newsmen under circumstances where legitimate First Amendment interests require protection.

Justice STEWART, with whom Justice BRENNAN and Justice MARSHALL join, dissenting.

The Court's crabbed view of the First Amendment reflects a disturbing insensitivity to the critical role of an independent press in our society. The question whether a reporter has a constitutional right to a confidential relationship with his source is of first impression here, but the principles that should guide our decision are as basic as any to be found in the Constitution. While Mr. Justice Powell's enigmatic concurring opinion gives some hope of a more flexible view in the future, the Court in these cases holds that a newsman has no First Amendment right to protect his sources when called before a grand jury. The Court thus invites state and federal authorities to undermine the historic independence of the press by attempting to annex the journalistic profession as an investigative arm of government. Not only will this decision impair performance of the press' constitutionally protected functions, but it will, I am convinced, in the long run, harm rather than help the administration of justice. I respectfully dissent.

The reporter's constitutional right to a confidential relationship with his source stems from the broad societal interest in a full and free flow of information to the public. It is this basic concern that underlies the Constitution's protection of a free press. Enlightened choice by an informed citizenry is the basic ideal upon which an open society is premised, and a free press is thus indispensable to a free society.

A corollary of the right to publish must be the right to gather news. The full flow of information to the public protected by the free-press guarantee would be severely curtailed if no protection whatever were afforded to the process by which news is assembled and disseminated. No less important to the news dissemination process is the gathering of information. News must not be unnecessarily cut off at its source, for without freedom to acquire information the right to publish would be impermissibly compromised.

The right to gather news implies, in turn, a right to a confidential relationship between a reporter and his source. This proposition follows as a matter of simple logic once three factual predicates are recognized: (1) newsmen require informants to gather news; (2) confidentiality—the promise or understanding that names or certain aspects of communications will be kept off the record—is essential to the creation and maintenance of a news-gathering relationship with informants; and (3) an unbridled subpoena power—the absence of a constitutional right protecting, in *any* way, a confidential relationship from compulsory process—will either deter sources from divulging information or deter reporters from gathering and publishing information.

After today's decision, the potential informant can never be sure that his identity or off-the-record communications will not subsequently be revealed through the compelled testimony of a newsman. A public-spirited person inside government, who is not implicated in any crime, will now be fearful of revealing corruption or other governmental wrongdoing, because he will now know he can subsequently be identified by use of compulsory process. The potential source must, therefore, choose between risking exposure by giving information or avoiding the risk by remaining silent.

The impairment of the flow of news cannot, of course, be proved with scientific precision, as the Court seems to demand. Obviously, not every news-gathering relationship requires confidentiality. And it is difficult to pinpoint precisely how many relationship[s] do require a promise or understanding of nondisclosure. But we have never before demanded that First Amendment rights rest on elaborate empirical studies demonstrating beyond any conceivable doubt that deterrent effects exist; we have never before required proof of the exact number of people potentially affected by governmental action, who would actually be dissuaded from engaging in First Amendment activity.

To require any greater burden of proof is to shirk our duty to protect values securely embedded in the Constitution. We cannot await an unequivocal—and therefore unattainable—imprimatur from empirical studies. We can and must accept the evidence developed in the record, and elsewhere, that overwhelmingly supports the premise that deterrence will occur with regularity in important types of news-gathering relationships.

Thus, we cannot escape the conclusion that when neither the reporter nor his source can rely on the shield of confidentiality against unrestrained use of the grand jury's subpoena power, valuable information will not be published and the public dialogue will inevitably be impoverished.

The Supreme Court has followed *Branzburg* in other cases in refusing to find First Amendment exemption for the press in court proceedings and law enforcement actions. In Zurcher v. Stanford Daily, 436 U.S. 547 (1978), the Court upheld the ability of the police to search press newsrooms to gather information to aid criminal investigations. A student newspaper published stories about a violent confrontation between students and the police at a demonstration. The police then obtained a warrant to search the newspaper's offices for negatives, films, and pictures that would help to identify the demonstrators. The search was conducted, though it did not yield any information that had not already been punished.

The newspaper then sued the police for violating the First Amendment. The Court held that the First Amendment did not protect the press from valid searches pursuant to valid warrants. Justice White again wrote the opinion for the Court and once more rejected the claim of any special protection for the press

B. Freedom of the Press as a Shield to Protect the Press from the Government

under the First Amendment. He said, "Properly administered the preconditions for a warrant—probable cause, specificity with respect to the place to be searched and the things to be seized, and overall reasonableness—should afford sufficient protection against the harms that are assertedly threatened by warrants for searching newspaper offices. . . . [Nor] are we convinced, any more than we were in *Branzburg* that confidential sources will disappear."

Almost immediately after *Zurcher*, Congress enacted the Privacy Protection Act of 1980 to protect the press from searches of newsrooms.[1] The law prohibits law enforcement from searches of those reasonably believed to be engaged in disseminating information to the public unless there is probable cause to believe that the person committed a crime or that giving notice by subpoena likely would result in the loss of evidence.

4. Laws Requiring That the Media Make Access Available

The issues described above focus on the application of general laws and law enforcement procedures to the press. A distinct issue arises concerning laws that attempt to regulate the press and require that it allow others to use it. Can the government require that the media make newspaper space or broadcast time available to respond to personal attacks? Arguably, such access laws enhance First Amendment values; they expand the voices that the public can hear. But the laws also infringe the First Amendment value of press autonomy; the ability of the media to control what it publishes or broadcasts is compromised when the government mandates access.

Interestingly, the Court has found that the First Amendment is not violated by such requirements as applied to the broadcast media, but has invalidated these laws when applied to the print media. In Red Lion Broadcasting Co. v. FCC, 395 U.S. 367 (1969), the Court unanimously upheld the constitutionality of the fairness doctrine that required that broadcast stations present balanced discussion on public issues. The law also provided that when the honesty or character of a person is attacked, he or she must be given notice, a transcript, and an opportunity to reply. Additionally, a station that endorsed a candidate in an election was required to provide notice to the opponent and provide a reasonable opportunity to respond.

The Court upheld these requirements and emphasized that "[i]t is the right of the viewers and listeners, not the right of broadcasters, which is paramount." The Court concluded that the fairness doctrine enhanced this right by expanding the views and voices that the public could hear. Justice White, writing for the Court, said that "[t]here is no sanctuary in the First Amendment for unlimited private censorship operating in a medium not open to all." The Court stressed that broadcast frequencies are inherently scarce and that therefore the government was justified in regulating their use to increase the voices that the public could hear. Justice White declared: "In view of the scarcity of broadcast frequencies, the Government's role in allocating those frequencies, and the legitimate claims of those unable without governmental

---

1. 42 U.S.C. §2000a.

assistance to gain access to those frequencies for expression of their views, we hold the regulations . . . constitutional."

However, just five years later, in Miami Herald v. Tornillo, 418 U.S. 241 (1974), the Court unanimously declared unconstitutional a right-to-reply law as applied to newspapers. A Florida law required that a newspaper print a reply from any candidate for office whose character or official record had been attacked in its pages. The reply had to be printed free of charge in as conspicuous a place as the initial story. Without mentioning *Red Lion*, the Court struck down the Florida law as violating the First Amendment. The Court, in an opinion by Chief Justice Burger, said that "the Florida statute exacts a penalty on the basis of the content of a newspaper. The first phase of the penalty . . . is exacted in terms of the cost in printing and . . . in taking up space that could be devoted to other material the newspaper may have preferred to print. . . . Faced with [such a penalty], editors might well conclude that the safe course is to avoid controversy." The Court stressed that forcing newspapers to publish a reply intrudes on editorial discretion that is protected by the First Amendment.

There is an obvious tension between *Red Lion* and *Tornillo*. Right-to-reply laws are allowed as to the broadcast media, but not the print media. In *Tornillo*, the Court emphasized the danger that such laws will chill coverage; yet in *Red Lion* the Court rejected exactly this argument as unsupported conjecture. The distinction between *Red Lion* and *Tornillo* seems to be based on the inherent scarcity of the broadcast media. Broadcast frequencies are inherently limited. But the economics of publishing are such that the number of newspapers is also likely to be scarce, and it is unclear why technological scarcity deserves more weight in First Amendment analysis than economically induced scarcity. In every city, there are far more television and radio stations than newspapers. Indeed, the development of cable television and direct broadcast satellites undermines the claim that broadcast space is scarcer than print space, even if that was ever true. In fact, in 1987, the Federal Communications Commission repealed the fairness doctrine, although there have been repeated attempts to have it reinstituted by statute.

If the distinction between the print and broadcast media is rejected, the issue then becomes whether it would be better to apply the *Red Lion* or the *Tornillo* approach to both media. Allowing right-to-reply laws has the benefit of enhancing the viewpoints that are heard. But such laws also intrude on a crucial First Amendment value: press autonomy to decide what to publish.

C. FREEDOM OF THE PRESS AS A SWORD: A FIRST AMENDMENT RIGHT OF ACCESS TO GOVERNMENT PLACES AND PAPERS?

The previous section considered the extent to which the First Amendment provides the press with a shield that protects it from government regulation. A distinct issue is whether the First Amendment provides the press a "sword" that it can use to gain access to government proceedings and papers. Actually, there are two interrelated subquestions here: First, does the First Amendment provide anyone such a right of access, and second, if so, does the press have a preferred right of access?

C. Freedom of the Press as a Sword

Thus far, the Supreme Court has not answered either question in general terms, but rather, has dealt with the issues in two specific contexts. The Court has held that the public has a right of access to court proceedings, but has not recognized a preferred right of access for the press. In contrast, the Court has ruled that the public does not have a right of access to prison inmates and facilities, and the Court expressly has rejected any special right of access for the press.

On the one hand, without a right of access to government papers and places, the people will be denied information that is crucial in monitoring government and holding it accountable. The press obviously plays a crucial role in this regard. While it is not realistic to open a prison to all observers, the press can be the eyes and ears of the public. On the other hand, creating a right of access to government places and papers may be better accomplished through statutes, such as freedom of information acts and open meeting laws, which can be drawn with specificity and can balance competing interests. Additionally, any special rights for the press will raise the issues, described earlier, of defining who is entitled to the privileges.

1. Access to Judicial Proceedings

The Court has recognized a broad First Amendment right for people to attend judicial proceedings. Initially, the Court rejected such a right, at least for pretrial proceedings. In Gannett v. DePasquale, 443 U.S. 368 (1979), the Court held that the press could be excluded from a pretrial proceeding that considered the suppression of a confession. The prosecution and defense both consented to closing the courtroom for the hearing, and the trial judge had found a "reasonable probability of prejudice" to the defendant if the confession was deemed inadmissible but reported on in the press. The Court also emphasized that no one, including the press, had initially objected to the closure and that a transcript was made available once the proceedings were completed.

Yet it is questionable whether *Gannett* remains good law because the Court subsequently has consistently recognized a First Amendment right of access to court proceedings. Richmond Newspapers v. Virginia is the key case in the area.

RICHMOND NEWSPAPERS v. VIRGINIA
448 U.S. 555 (1980)

Chief Justice BURGER announced the judgment of the Court and delivered an opinion, in which Justice WHITE and Justice STEVENS joined.

The narrow question presented in this case is whether the right of the public and press to attend criminal trials is guaranteed under the United States Constitution.

I

In March 1976, one Stevenson was indicted for the murder of a hotel manager who had been found stabbed to death on December 2, 1975. Tried promptly in July 1976, Stevenson was convicted of second-degree murder in the Circuit

Court of Hanover County, Va. The Virginia Supreme Court reversed the conviction in October 1977, holding that a bloodstained shirt purportedly belonging to Stevenson had been improperly admitted into evidence. Stevenson was retried in the same court. This second trial ended in a mistrial on May 30, 1978, when a juror asked to be excused after trial had begun and no alternate was available. A third trial, which began in the same court on June 6, 1978, also ended in a mistrial. It appears that the mistrial may have been declared because a prospective juror had read about Stevenson's previous trials in a newspaper and had told other prospective jurors about the case before the retrial began.

Stevenson was tried in the same court for a fourth time beginning on September 11, 1978. Present in the courtroom when the case was called were appellants Wheeler and McCarthy, reporters for appellant Richmond Newspapers, Inc. Before the trial began, counsel for the defendant moved that it be closed to the public. The trial judge, who had presided over two of the three previous trials, asked if the prosecution had any objection to clearing the courtroom. The prosecutor stated he had no objection and would leave it to the discretion of the court.

II

We begin consideration of this case by noting that the precise issue presented here has not previously been before this Court for decision. In Gannett Co. v. DePasquale, the Court was not required to decide whether a right of access to trials, as distinguished from hearings on pretrial motions, was constitutionally guaranteed. The Court held that the Sixth Amendment's guarantee to the accused of a public trial gave neither the public nor the press an enforceable right of access to a pretrial suppression hearing.

In prior cases the Court has treated questions involving conflicts between publicity and a defendant's right to a fair trial; as we observed in Nebraska Press Assn. v. Stuart, "[t]he problems presented by this [conflict] are almost as old as the Republic." But here for the first time the Court is asked to decide whether a criminal trial itself may be closed to the public upon the unopposed request of a defendant, without any demonstration that closure is required to protect the defendant's superior right to a fair trial, or that some other overriding consideration requires closure.

The origins of the proceeding which has become the modern criminal trial in Anglo-American justice can be traced back beyond reliable historical records. We need not here review all details of its development, but a summary of that history is instructive. What is significant for present purposes is that throughout its evolution, the trial has been open to all who care to observe. From these early times, although great changes in courts and procedures took place, one thing remained constant: the public character of the trial at which guilt or innocence was decided. We have found nothing to suggest that the presumptive openness of the trial, which English courts were later to call "one of the essential qualities of a court of justice," was not also an attribute of the judicial systems of colonial America.

[T]he historical evidence demonstrates conclusively that at the time when our organic laws were adopted, criminal trials both here and in England had long been presumptively open. This is no quirk of history; rather, it has long been

C. Freedom of the Press as a Sword

recognized as an indispensable attribute of an Anglo-American trial. Both Hale in the 17th century and Blackstone in the 18th saw the importance of openness to the proper functioning of a trial; it gave assurance that the proceedings were conducted fairly to all concerned, and it discouraged perjury, the misconduct of participants, and decisions based on secret bias or partiality.

The early history of open trials in part reflects the widespread acknowledgment, long before there were behavioral scientists, that public trials had significant community therapeutic value. Even without such experts to frame the concept in words, people sensed from experience and observation that, especially in the administration of criminal justice, the means used to achieve justice must have the support derived from public acceptance of both the process and its results.

When a shocking crime occurs, a community reaction of outrage and public protest often follows. Thereafter the open processes of justice serve an important prophylactic purpose, providing an outlet for community concern, hostility, and emotion. Without an awareness that society's responses to criminal conduct are underway, natural human reactions of outrage and protest are frustrated and may manifest themselves in some form of vengeful "self-help," as indeed they did regularly in the activities of vigilante "committees" on our frontiers.

Civilized societies withdraw both from the victim and the vigilante the enforcement of criminal laws, but they cannot erase from people's consciousness the fundamental, natural yearning to see justice done—or even the urge for retribution. The crucial prophylactic aspects of the administration of justice cannot function in the dark; no community catharsis can occur if justice is "done in a corner [or] in any covert manner." A result considered untoward may undermine public confidence, and where the trial has been concealed from public view an unexpected outcome can cause a reaction that the system at best has failed and at worst has been corrupted. To work effectively, it is important that society's criminal process "satisfy the appearance of justice," and the appearance of justice can best be provided by allowing people to observe it.

Looking back, we see that when the ancient "town meeting" form of trial became too cumbersome, 12 members of the community were delegated to act as its surrogates, but the community did not surrender its right to observe the conduct of trials. The people retained a "right of visitation" which enabled them to satisfy themselves that justice was in fact being done.

People in an open society do not demand infallibility from their institutions, but it is difficult for them to accept what they are prohibited from observing. When a criminal trial is conducted in the open, there is at least an opportunity both for understanding the system in general and its workings in a particular case.

From this unbroken, uncontradicted history, supported by reasons as valid today as in centuries past, we are bound to conclude that a presumption of openness inheres in the very nature of a criminal trial under our system of justice. This conclusion is hardly novel; without a direct holding on the issue, the Court has voiced its recognition of it in a variety of contexts over the years.

III

The Bill of Rights was enacted against the backdrop of the long history of trials being presumptively open. Public access to trials was then regarded as an important aspect of the process itself; the conduct of trials "before as many of the people as chuse to attend" was regarded as one of "the inestimable advantages of a free English constitution of government." In guaranteeing freedoms such as those of speech and press, the First Amendment can be read as protecting the right of everyone to attend trials so as to give meaning to those explicit guarantees. "[T]he First Amendment goes beyond protection of the press and the self-expression of individuals to prohibit government from limiting the stock of information from which members of the public may draw." Free speech carries with it some freedom to listen. "In a variety of contexts this Court has referred to a First Amendment right to 'receive information and ideas.'" What this means in the context of trials is that the First Amendment guarantees of speech and press, standing alone, prohibit government from summarily closing courtroom doors which had long been open to the public at the time that Amendment was adopted. "For the First Amendment does not speak equivocally.... It must be taken as a command of the broadest scope that explicit language, read in the context of a liberty-loving society, will allow."

It is not crucial whether we describe this right to attend criminal trials to hear, see, and communicate observations concerning them as a "right of access," or a "right to gather information," for we have recognized that "without some protection for seeking out the news, freedom of the press could be eviscerated." The explicit, guaranteed rights to speak and to publish concerning what takes place at a trial would lose much meaning if access to observe the trial could, as it was here, be foreclosed arbitrarily.

The right of access to places traditionally open to the public, as criminal trials have long been, may be seen as assured by the amalgam of the First Amendment guarantees of speech and press; and their affinity to the right of assembly is not without relevance. From the outset, the right of assembly was regarded not only as an independent right but also as a catalyst to augment the free exercise of the other First Amendment rights with which it was deliberately linked by the draftsmen.

The State argues that the Constitution nowhere spells out a guarantee for the right of the public to attend trials, and that accordingly no such right is protected. But arguments such as the State makes have not precluded recognition of important rights not enumerated. Notwithstanding the appropriate caution against reading into the Constitution rights not explicitly defined, the Court has acknowledged that certain unarticulated rights are implicit in enumerated guarantees. For example, the rights of association and of privacy, the right to be presumed innocent, and the right to be judged by a standard of proof beyond a reasonable doubt in a criminal trial, as well as the right to travel, appear nowhere in the Constitution or Bill of Rights. Yet these important but unarticulated rights have nonetheless been found to share constitutional protection in common with explicit guarantees.

We hold that the right to attend criminal trials is implicit in the guarantees of the First Amendment; without the freedom to attend such trials, which people have exercised for centuries, important aspects of freedom of speech and "of the press could be eviscerated."[2] Absent an overriding interest articulated in findings, the trial of a criminal case must be open to the public.

---

2. Whether the public has a right to attend trials of civil cases is a question not raised by this case, but we note that historically both civil and criminal trials have been presumptively open. [Footnote by the Court.]

C. Freedom of the Press as a Sword

Justice BRENNAN, with whom Justice MARSHALL joins, concurring in the judgment.

Gannett Co. v. DePasquale (1979) held that the Sixth Amendment right to a public trial was personal to the accused, conferring no right of access to pretrial proceedings that is separately enforceable by the public or the press. The instant case raises the question whether the First Amendment, of its own force and as applied to the States through the Fourteenth Amendment, secures the public an independent right of access to trial proceedings. Because I believe that the First Amendment—of itself and as applied to the States through the Fourteenth Amendment—secures such a public right of access, I agree with those of my Brethren who hold that, without more, agreement of the trial judge and the parties cannot constitutionally close a trial to the public.

First, the case for a right of access has special force when drawn from an enduring and vital tradition of public entree to particular proceedings or information. Such a tradition commands respect in part because the Constitution carries the gloss of history. More importantly, a tradition of accessibility implies the favorable judgment of experience. Second, the value of access must be measured in specifics. Analysis is not advanced by rhetorical statements that all information bears upon public issues; what is crucial in individual cases is whether access to a particular government process is important in terms of that very process.

Tradition, contemporaneous state practice, and this Court's own decisions manifest a common understanding that "[a] trial is a public event. What transpires in the court room is public property." Craig v. Harney (1947). As a matter of law and virtually immemorial custom, public trials have been the essentially unwavering rule in ancestral England and in our own Nation.

Publicity serves to advance several of the particular purposes of the trial (and, indeed, the judicial) process. Open trials play a fundamental role in furthering the efforts of our judicial system to assure the criminal defendant a fair and accurate adjudication of guilt or innocence. But, as a feature of our governing system of justice, the trial process serves other, broadly political, interests, and public access advances these objectives as well. To that extent, trial access possesses specific structural significance.

The trial is a means of meeting "the notion, deeply rooted in the common law, that 'justice must satisfy the appearance of justice.'" Secrecy is profoundly inimical to this demonstrative purpose of the trial process. Open trials assure the public that procedural rights are respected, and that justice is afforded equally. Closed trials breed suspicion of prejudice and arbitrariness, which in turn spawns disrespect for law. Public access is essential, therefore, if trial adjudication is to achieve the objective of maintaining public confidence in the administration of justice.

But the trial is more than a demonstrably just method of adjudicating disputes and protecting rights. It plays a pivotal role in the entire judicial process, and, by extension, in our form of government. Under our system, judges are not mere umpires, but, in their own sphere, lawmakers—a coordinate branch of government. It follows that the conduct of the trial is pre-eminently a matter of public interest.

As previously noted, resolution of First Amendment public access claims in individual cases must be strongly influenced by the weight of historical practice and by an assessment of the specific structural value of public access in the circumstances. With regard to the case at hand, our ingrained tradition of public trials and the importance of public access to the broader purposes of the trial process, tip the balance strongly toward the rule that trials be open. What countervailing interests might be sufficiently compelling to reverse this presumption of openness need not concern us now, for the statute at stake here authorizes trial closures at the unfettered discretion of the judge and parties.

Justice REHNQUIST, dissenting.

In the Gilbert and Sullivan operetta "Iolanthe," the Lord Chancellor recites: "The Law is the true embodiment of everything that's excellent, It has no kind of fault or flaw, And I, my Lords, embody the Law."

It is difficult not to derive more than a little of this flavor from the various opinions supporting the judgment in this case. I do not believe that either the First or Sixth Amendment, as made applicable to the States by the Fourteenth, requires that a State's reasons for denying public access to a trial, where both the prosecuting attorney and the defendant have consented to an order of closure approved by the judge, are subject to any additional constitutional review at our hands.

We have at present 50 state judicial systems and one federal judicial system in the United States, and our authority to reverse a decision by the highest court of the State is limited to only those occasions when the state decision violates some provision of the United States Constitution. And that authority should be exercised with a full sense that the judges whose decisions we review are making the same effort as we to uphold the Constitution.

The issue here is not whether the "right" to freedom of the press conferred by the First Amendment to the Constitution overrides the defendant's "right" to a fair trial conferred by other Amendments to the Constitution; it is instead whether any provision in the Constitution may fairly be read to prohibit what the trial judge in the Virginia state-court system did in this case. Being unable to find any such prohibition in the First, Sixth, Ninth, or any other Amendment to the United States Constitution, or in the Constitution itself, I dissent.

In several subsequent cases, the Court applied *Richmond Newspapers* and declared unconstitutional the closure of judicial proceedings. In Globe Newspaper Co. v. Superior Court, 457 U.S. 596 (1982), the Court declared unconstitutional a Massachusetts law that allowed trial courts to exclude the press and the public from hearing the testimony of witnesses under age 18 who allegedly were the victims of sex crimes. The Court said that *Richmond Newspapers* "firmly established . . . that the press and general public have a constitutional right of access to criminal trials." The Court said, therefore, that closing court proceedings would be allowed only if it was demonstrated to be "necessitated by a compelling governmental interest, and is narrowly tailored to serve that interest." The Court accepted that protecting minor victims was a compelling interest, but concluded that the state law that required closure in all cases was not sufficiently narrowly tailored; a case-by-case approach would adequately serve the state's interests.

In Press-Enterprise Co. v. Superior Court, 464 U.S. 501 (1984), the Court held that it violated the First Amendment for a court to close voir dire proceedings to the public and the press. The Court explained that voir dire proceedings

C. Freedom of the Press as a Sword

are a key phase of the trial. The Court said that the "presumption of openness may be overcome only by an overriding interest based on findings that closure is essential to preserve the higher values and narrowly tailored to serve that interest." The Court acknowledged that in some instances closure might be justified, where questioning of prospective jurors would pertain to "deeply personal matters." But even then closure should be regarded as a last resort because of the importance of the public monitoring what occurs during the crucial phase of jury selection. For example, during the O.J. Simpson murder case, there were claims that the prosecution was treating prospective African American jurors differently from white jurors during voir dire. This raised an important issue concerning the conduct of a government officer and required that the press and public be present to observe and report on what occurred.

Although these cases emphatically recognize a First Amendment right of access to court proceedings, they leave many questions unanswered. Is *Gannett* still good law; can a court close pretrial proceedings involving the suppression of evidence? Arguably, press reporting on suppressed evidence could jeopardize the defendant's right to a fair trial. But suppression hearings are of great interest to the public: They concern the conduct of police and decisions by judges as to what evidence will be admitted.[3]

Another unanswered question is whether the press has a preferred right of access to judicial proceedings. If there are only a limited number of seats in a courtroom, must some of them be reserved for reporters? The values underlying the First Amendment would seem to require this because the public only can learn about what occurred in court if the press is present to observe and report. But the Court has not yet recognized a preferred right for the press and, as discussed throughout this chapter, has generally rejected any special rights for the press.

In fact, in Seattle Times Co. v. Rhinehart, 467 U.S. 20 (1984), the Court held that the press did not have a right of access to information produced in discovery in a civil suit that was covered by a protective order. Specifically, the press wanted to obtain a list of contributors to a controversial religious organization. The Court unanimously ruled against the newspaper and said that the press was not entitled to the information because the public would not have had a right to it. The Court concluded that "where a protective order is entered on a showing of good cause as required by Rule 26(c), is limited to the context of pretrial civil discovery, and does not restrict the dissemination of information if gained from other sources, it does not offend the First Amendment."

2. Prisons

The other context where the Supreme Court has considered a First Amendment right of access is with regard to prisons. Here the Court has expressly rejected such a right and has specifically ruled that the press is not entitled to any greater rights than the general public. In several cases, the Court upheld the ability of prisons to restrict the ability of the press to interview prisoners or have access

---

3. *See also* Press-Enterprise Co. v. Superior Court, 478 U.S. 1 (1986) (recognizing a First Amendment right to transcripts of a preliminary hearing).

to prisons. In Pell v. Procunier, 417 U.S. 817 (1974), and Saxbe v. Washington Post Co., 417 U.S. 843 (1974), the Court sustained prison regulations that prevented the media from interviewing particular prisoners. The Court said that the regulations were justified because "press attention . . . concentrated on a relatively small number of inmates who, as a result, became virtual 'public figures' within the prison society and gained a disproportionate degree of notoriety and influence among their fellow inmates . . . and became the source of severe disciplinary problems."

The Court followed this reasoning in Houchins v. KQED, in which the press sought access to the Greystone facility in the Santa Rita jail.

HOUCHINS v. KQED
438 U.S. 1 (1978)

Chief Justice BURGER announced the judgment of the Court and delivered an opinion, in which Justice WHITE and Justice REHNQUIST joined.

The question presented is whether the news media have a constitutional right of access to a county jail, over and above that of other persons, to interview inmates and make sound recordings, films, and photographs for publication and broadcasting by newspapers, radio, and television.

I

Petitioner Houchins, as Sheriff of Alameda County, Cal., controls all access to the Alameda County Jail at Santa Rita. Respondent KQED operates licensed television and radio broadcasting stations which have frequently reported newsworthy events relating to penal institutions in the San Francisco Bay Area. On March 31, 1975, KQED reported the suicide of a prisoner in the Greystone portion of the Santa Rita jail. The report included a statement by a psychiatrist that the conditions at the Greystone facility were responsible for the illnesses of his patient-prisoners there, and a statement from petitioner denying that prison conditions were responsible for the prisoners' illnesses.

KQED requested permission to inspect and take pictures within the Greystone facility. After permission was refused, KQED and the Alameda and Oakland branches of the National Association for the Advancement of Colored People (NAACP) filed suit. They alleged that petitioner had violated the First Amendment by refusing to permit media access and failing to provide any effective means by which the public could be informed of conditions prevailing in the Greystone facility or learn of the prisoners' grievances. Public access to such information was essential, they asserted, in order for NAACP members to participate in the public debate on jail conditions in Alameda County. They further asserted that television coverage of the conditions in the cells and facilities was the most effective way of informing the public of prison conditions.

On June 17, 1975, when the complaint was filed, there appears to have been no formal policy regarding public access to the Santa Rita jail. However, according to petitioner, he had been in the process of planning a program of regular monthly tours since he took office six months earlier. On July 8, 1975, he announced the program and invited all interested persons to make

C. Freedom of the Press as a Sword

arrangements for the regular public tours. News media were given notice in advance of the public and presumably could have made early reservations. Six monthly tours were planned and funded by the county at an estimated cost of $1,800. Each tour was limited to 25 persons and permitted only limited access to the jail. The tours did not include the disciplinary cells or the portions of the jail known as "Little Greystone," the scene of alleged rapes, beatings, and adverse physical conditions. Photographs of some parts of the jail were made available, but no cameras or tape recorders were allowed on the tours. Those on the tours were not permitted to interview inmates, and inmates were generally removed from view.

II

Notwithstanding our holding in Pell v. Procunier, respondents assert that the right recognized by the Court of Appeals flows logically from our decisions construing the First Amendment. They argue that there is a constitutionally guaranteed right to gather news. From the right to gather news and the right to receive information, they argue for an implied special right of access to government-controlled sources of information.

We can agree with many of the respondents' generalized assertions; conditions in jails and prisons are clearly matters "of great public importance." Penal facilities are public institutions which require large amounts of public funds, and their mission is crucial in our criminal justice system. It is equally true that with greater information, the public can more intelligently form opinions about prison conditions. Beyond question, the role of the media is important; acting as the "eyes and ears" of the public, they can be a powerful and constructive force, contributing to remedial action in the conduct of public business. They have served that function since the beginning of the Republic, but like all other components of our society media representatives are subject to limits.

The media are not a substitute for or an adjunct of government and, like the courts, they are "ill equipped" to deal with problems of prison administration. The public importance of conditions in penal facilities and the media's role of providing information afford no basis for reading into the Constitution a right of the public or the media to enter these institutions, with camera equipment, and take moving and still pictures of inmates for broadcast purposes. This Court has never intimated a First Amendment guarantee of a right of access to all sources of information within government control.

The right to receive ideas and information is not the issue in this case. The issue is a claimed special privilege of access which the Court rejected in *Pell* and *Saxbe*, a right which is not essential to guarantee the freedom to communicate or publish.

The respondents' argument is flawed, not only because it lacks precedential support and is contrary to statements in this Court's opinions, but also because it invites the Court to involve itself in what is clearly a legislative task which the Constitution has left to the political processes. Whether the government should open penal institutions in the manner sought by respondents is a question of policy which a legislative body might appropriately resolve one way or the other.

A number of alternatives are available to prevent problems in penal facilities from escaping public attention. The early penal reform movements in this country and England gained impetus as a result of reports from citizens and visiting committees who volunteered or received commissions to visit penal institutions and make reports. Petitioner cannot prevent respondents from learning about jail conditions in a variety of ways, albeit not as conveniently as they might prefer. Respondents have a First Amendment right to receive letters from inmates criticizing jail officials and reporting on conditions. Respondents are free to interview those who render the legal assistance to which inmates are entitled. They are also free to seek out former inmates, visitors to the prison, public officials, and institutional personnel, as they sought out the complaining psychiatrist here.

Neither the First Amendment nor the Fourteenth Amendment mandates a right of access to government information or sources of information within the government's control. [U]ntil the political branches decree otherwise, as they are free to do, the media have no special right of access to the Alameda County Jail different from or greater than that accorded the public generally.

Justice STEWART, concurring in the judgment.

In my view, however, KQED was entitled to injunctive relief of more limited scope. The First and Fourteenth Amendments do not guarantee the public a right of access to information generated or controlled by government, nor do they guarantee the press any basic right of access superior to that of the public generally. The Constitution does no more than assure the public and the press equal access once government has opened its doors. Accordingly, I agree substantially with what the opinion of The Chief Justice has to say on that score.

We part company, however, in applying these abstractions to the facts of this case. Whereas he appears to view "equal access" as meaning access that is identical in all respects, I believe that the concept of equal access must be accorded more flexibility in order to accommodate the practical distinctions between the press and the general public. When on assignment, a journalist does not tour a jail simply for his own edification. He is there to gather information to be passed on to others, and his mission is protected by the Constitution for very specific reasons.

That the First Amendment speaks separately of freedom of speech and freedom of the press is no constitutional accident, but an acknowledgment of the critical role played by the press in American society. The Constitution requires sensitivity to that role, and to the special needs of the press in performing it effectively. A person touring Santa Rita jail can grasp its reality with his own eyes and ears. But if a television reporter is to convey the jail's sights and sounds to those who cannot personally visit the place, he must use cameras and sound equipment. In short, terms of access that are reasonably imposed on individual members of the public may, if they impede effective reporting without sufficient justification, be unreasonable as applied to journalists who are there to convey to the general public what the visitors see.

Under these principles, KQED was clearly entitled to some form of preliminary injunctive relief. At the time of the District Court's decision, members of the public were permitted to visit most parts of the Santa Rita jail, and the First and Fourteenth Amendments required the Sheriff to give members of the press effective access to the same areas. The Sheriff evidently assumed that he could fulfill this obligation simply by allowing reporters to sign up for tours on the same terms as the public. I think he was mistaken in this assumption, as a matter of constitutional law.

C. Freedom of the Press as a Sword

Justice STEVENS, with whom Justice BRENNAN and Justice POWELL join, dissenting.

Respondent KQED, Inc., has televised a number of programs about prison conditions and prison inmates, and its reporters have been granted access to various correctional facilities in the San Francisco Bay area, including San Quentin State Prison, Soledad Prison, and the San Francisco County Jails at San Bruno and San Francisco, to prepare program material. They have taken their cameras and recording equipment inside the walls of those institutions and interviewed inmates. No disturbances or other problems have occurred on those occasions.

Here, the broad restraints on access to information regarding operation of the jail that prevailed on the date this suit was instituted are plainly disclosed by the record. The public and the press had consistently been denied any access to those portions of the Santa Rita facility where inmates were confined and there had been excessive censorship of inmate correspondence. Petitioner's no-access policy, modified only in the wake of respondents' resort to the courts, could survive constitutional scrutiny only if the Constitution affords no protection to the public's right to be informed about conditions within those public institutions where some of its members are confined because they have been charged with or found guilty of criminal offenses.

The preservation of a full and free flow of information to the general public has long been recognized as a core objective of the First Amendment to the Constitution. It is for this reason that the First Amendment protects not only the dissemination but also the receipt of information and ideas. In addition to safeguarding the right of one individual to receive what another elects to communicate, the First Amendment serves an essential societal function. Our system of self-government assumes the existence of an informed citizenry.

It is not sufficient, therefore, that the channels of communication be free of governmental restraints. Without some protection for the acquisition of information about the operation of public institutions such as prisons by the public at large, the process of self-governance contemplated by the framers would be stripped of its substance.

For that reason information gathering is entitled to some measure of constitutional protection. As this Court's decisions clearly indicate, however, this protection is not for the private benefit of those who might qualify as representatives of the "press" but to insure that the citizens are fully informed regarding matters of public interest and importance.

In this case, "[r]espondents do not assert a right to force disclosure of confidential information or to invade in any way the decisionmaking processes of governmental officials." They simply seek an end to petitioner's policy of concealing prison conditions from the public. Those conditions are wholly without claim to confidentiality. While prison officials have an interest in the time and manner of public acquisition of information about the institutions they administer, there is no legitimate penological justification for concealing from citizens the conditions in which their fellow citizens are being confined.

The reasons which militate in favor of providing special protection to the flow of information to the public about prisons relate to the unique function they perform in a democratic society. Not only are they public institutions, financed with public funds and administered by public servants, they are an integral component of the criminal justice system.

In this case, the record demonstrates that both the public and the press had been consistently denied any access to the inner portions of the Santa Rita jail, that there had been excessive censorship of inmate correspondence, and that there was no valid justification for these broad restraints on the flow of information. An affirmative answer to the question whether respondents established a likelihood of prevailing on the merits did not depend, in final analysis, on any right of the press to special treatment beyond that accorded the public at large. Rather, the probable existence of a constitutional violation rested upon the special importance of allowing a democratic community access to knowledge about how its servants were treating some of its members who have been committed to their custody. An official prison policy of concealing such knowledge from the public by arbitrarily cutting off the flow of information at its source abridges the freedom of speech and of the press protected by the First and Fourteenth Amendments to the Constitution.

PART II

FIRST AMENDMENT: RELIGION

CHAPTER 7

INTRODUCTION TO THE RELIGION CLAUSES

A. CONSTITUTIONAL PROVISIONS CONCERNING RELIGION AND THE TENSION BETWEEN THEM

The First Amendment begins with the words "Congress shall make no law respecting an establishment of religion, or prohibiting the free exercise thereof." These two clauses are commonly referred to, respectively, as the "Establishment Clause" and the "Free Exercise Clause." The Free Exercise Clause was first applied to the states through its incorporation into the Due Process Clause of the Fourteenth Amendment in Cantwell v. Connecticut, 310 U.S. 296 (1940). The Establishment Clause was first found to be incorporated and applied to the states in Everson v. Board of Education, 330 U.S. 1 (1947).[1] The incorporation of the Establishment Clause is more controversial than the incorporation of the Free Exercise Clause because the latter clearly safeguards individual liberty while the former seems directed at the government. The Supreme Court, however, has explained that the Establishment Clause, too, protects liberty. Justice Brennan, concurring in Abington School District v. Schempp, 374 U.S. 203 (1963), explained that "the Establishment Clause [is] a co-guarantor, with the Free Exercise Clause, of religious liberty. The framers did not entrust the liberty of religious beliefs to either clause alone." As the Court declared in Lee v. Weisman, 505 U.S. 577 (1992), "A state-created orthodoxy puts at grave risk that freedom of belief and conscience which are the sole assurance that religious faith is real, not imposed."

---

1. In addition to the provisions of the First Amendment, the text of the Constitution contains one other provision concerning religion. Article VI, Clause 3, says, "The Senators and Representatives before mentioned, and the Members of the several State Legislatures, and all executive and judicial Officers, both of the United States and of the several States, shall be bound by Oath or Affirmation, to support this Constitution; but no religious Test shall ever be required as a Qualification to any Office or public Trust under the United States." Although the provision did not protect religious freedom for the general public, it did assure that the government could not establish a religion as a condition for holding federal office or infringe free exercise of religion for these individuals. This provision was applied to the states in Torcaso v. Watkins, 367 U.S. 488 (1961).

To a large extent, the Establishment and Free Exercise Clauses are complementary. Both protect freedom of religious belief and actions. Many government actions would simultaneously violate both of these provisions. For example, if the state were to create a religion and compel participation, it obviously would be establishing religion and, at the same time, denying free exercise to those who did not want to participate in religion or who wished to choose a different faith. Mandatory school prayers likewise involve both the government establishing religion and interfering with free exercise of religious beliefs for those who do not believe in the prayers. In a recent case, presented below, Hosanna-Tabor Evangelical Lutheran Church and School v. EEOC, 565 U.S. 171 (2012), the Court held that it violated both the Establishment and the Free Exercise Clauses to hold a religious institution liable for discrimination in the choices it makes as to who will be its ministers. The case involved a religious elementary school where many of the teachers were designated as ministers. A teacher who lost her job after an illness and then was fired sued under the Americans with Disabilities Act. The Court unanimously ruled that it would infringe both the Establishment Clause and the Free Exercise Clause to hold a religious institution liable for the choices it makes as to who will be its ministers.

Yet there also is often tension between the Establishment and Free Exercise Clauses. Government actions to facilitate free exercise might be challenged as impermissible establishments, and government efforts to refrain from establishing religion might be objected to as denying the free exercise of religion. For instance, if the government pays for and provides ministers for those in the armed services, it arguably is establishing religion, but if the government refuses to do so on these grounds, it arguably is denying free exercise of religion.

Indeed, the primary test used for the Establishment Clause—articulated in Lemon v. Kurtzman, 403 U.S. 602 (1971), and reviewed in detail below in Chapter 9—makes this tension inevitable. Under the *Lemon* test, the government violates the Establishment Clause if the government's primary purpose is to advance religion, or if the principal effect is to aid or inhibit religion, or if there is excessive government entanglement with religion. Yet any time the government acts to protect free exercise of religion, its primary purpose is to advance religion; any time the principal effect is to facilitate free exercise, the government is aiding religion. For example, if the government creates an exemption to a law solely for religion, it arguably violates the Establishment Clause; if the government fails to create such an exemption for religion, it arguably infringes free exercise.

The Court has recognized that this tension is inherent in the First Amendment and has noted the difficulty of finding "a neutral course between the two Religion Clauses, both of which are cast in absolute terms, and either of which, if expanded to a logical extreme, would tend to clash with the other."[2] Additionally, there is a tension between the First Amendment's protection of speech and its prohibition against establishment of religion. For example, allowing government financial aid to student religious groups[3] or permitting

---

2. Walz v. Tax Commission, 397 U.S. 664, 668-669 (1970).
3. *See* Rosenberger v. Rector & Visitors of the University of Virginia, 515 U.S. 819 (1995), discussed in Chapter 9 below.

religious groups to use school facilities[4] arguably violates the Establishment Clause; but denying funds or facilities because of the religious content of the expression seems to infringe the First Amendment's protection of freedom of speech. This tension between the Establishment Clause and freedom of speech is discussed below.

B. HISTORY IN INTERPRETING THE RELIGION CLAUSES

As with all constitutional provisions, some look to history as a guide to the meaning of the Religion Clauses. This is particularly difficult for these provisions because there is no apparent agreement among the framers as to what they meant. Justice Brennan expressed this well when he stated: "A too literal quest for the advice of the Founding Fathers upon the issues of these cases seems to me futile and misdirected for several reasons. . . . [T]he historical record is at best ambiguous, and statements can readily be found to support either side of the proposition."[5] Yet justices on all sides of the issue continue to invoke history and the original understanding of that text to support their position. Chief Justice Rehnquist has remarked that "[t]he true meaning of Establishment Clause can only be seen in its history."[6] In Rosenberger v. Rector & Visitors of the University of Virginia, 515 U.S. 819 (1995), which concerned whether a public university could deny student activity funds to a religious group, both Justice Thomas, in a concurring opinion, and Justice Souter, dissenting, focused at length on James Madison's views of religious freedom.[7]

As Professor Laurence Tribe has cogently summarized, there were at least three main views of religion among key framers.[8]

> [A]t least three distinct schools of thought . . . influenced the drafters of the Bill of Rights: first, the evangelical view (associated primarily with Roger Williams) that "worldly corruptions . . . might consume the churches if sturdy fences against the wilderness were not maintained"; second, the Jeffersonian view that the church should be walled off from the state in order to safeguard secular interests (public and private) "against ecclesiastical depredations and incursions"; and, third, the Madisonian view that religious and secular interests alike would be advanced best by diffusing and decentralizing power so as to assure competition among sects rather than dominance by any one.[9]

These are quite distinct views of the proper relationship between religion and the government. Roger Williams was primarily concerned that government

---

4. *See, e.g.*, Lamb's Chapel v. Center Moriches Union Free School District, 508 U.S. 384 (1993), discussed below in Chapter 9.
5. Abington School Dist. v. Schempp, 374 U.S. at 237.
6. Wallace v. Jaffree, 472 U.S. 38, 113 (1985) (Rehnquist, J., dissenting).
7. James Madison issued his famous *Remonstrance* in arguing against a Virginia decision to renew a tax to support the church. This is reviewed in detail in Everson v. Board of Education, 330 U.S. 1, 12 (1947); *id.* at 31-34 (Rutledge, J., dissenting).
8. Laurence H. Tribe, *American Constitutional Law* 1158-1160 (2d ed. 1988).
9. *Id.* at 1158-1159 (citations omitted).

involvement with religion would corrupt and undermine religion, whereas Thomas Jefferson had the opposite fear that religion would corrupt and undermine the government. James Madison saw religion as one among many types of factions that existed. He wrote that "[i]n a free government the security for civil rights must be the same as that for religious rights. It consists in the one case in the multiplicity of interests, and the other in the multiplicity of sects. The degree of security in both cases will depend on the number of interests and sects."[10]

The problem of using history in interpreting the Religion Clauses is compounded by the enormous changes in the country since the First Amendment was adopted. The country is much more religiously diverse today than it was in 1791. Justice Brennan observed that "our religious composition makes us a vastly more diverse people than were our forefathers. They knew differences chiefly among Protestant sects. Today the nation is far more heterogeneous religiously, including as it does substantial minorities not only of Catholics and Jews but as well of those who worship according to no version of the Bible and those who worship no God at all."[11]

Also, as discussed below, a significant number of cases involving the Establishment Clause have arisen in the context of religious activities in connection with schools. But public education, as it exists now, did not exist when the Bill of Rights was ratified, and it is inherently difficult to apply the framers' views to situations that they could not have imagined. Justice Brennan remarked that "the structure of American education has greatly changed since the First Amendment was adopted. In the context of our modern emphasis upon public education available to all citizens, any views of the eighteenth century as to whether the exercises at bar are an 'establishment' offer little aid to decision."[12]

Nonetheless, debates about history and the framers' intent are likely to remain a key aspect of decisions concerning the Religion Clauses. Members of the Supreme Court who follow an originalist philosophy of constitutional interpretation believe that the Constitution's meaning is to be ascertained solely from its text and from its framers' intent. Also, the divergence of views among the framers, and the abstractness with which they are stated, makes it possible for those on all sides of the debate to invoke history in support of their positions.

C. WHAT IS RELIGION?

Under both the Establishment and the Free Exercise Clauses, the issue can arise as to what is "religion." Yet, not surprisingly, the Court has avoided trying to formulate a definition. It seems impossible to formulate a definition of religion that encompasses the vast array of spiritual beliefs and practices that

---

10. James Madison, Federalist No. 51, *The Federalist Papers* 322 (C. Rossiter ed. 1961).
11. Abington School Dist. v. Schempp, 374 U.S. at 240 (Brennan, J., concurring).
12. *Id.* at 238.

C. What Is Religion?

are present in the United States. As one commentator noted, "[T]here is no single characteristic or set of characteristics that all religions have in common that makes them religions."[13] Moreover, any attempt to define religion raises concern that choosing a single definition is itself an establishment of religion.

Additionally, there is a desire for a broad definition of religion for purposes of the Free Exercise Clause so as to maximize protection for religious conduct but a narrow definition of religion for Establishment Clause analysis so as to limit the constraints on government.

Although some commentators have argued for separate definitions of religion for the Establishment and the Free Exercise Clauses, the Supreme Court never has accepted this position. In fact, Justice Rutledge expressly rejected this approach in his opinion in Everson v. Board of Education: "'Religion' appears only once in the Amendment. But the word governs two prohibitions and governs them alike. It does not have two meanings, one narrow to forbid 'an establishment' and another, much broader, for 'securing' the free exercise thereof."

While the Supreme Court never has formulated a definition of religion, it has considered the issue in three contexts. First, in cases under the Selective Service Act, the Court struggled to define religion for purposes of the conscientious objector exemption. Second, the Court has said that a court can inquire as to whether a religious belief is sincerely held in deciding whether it is protected under the Constitution. Finally, the Court has made it clear that an individual's sincerely held religious belief is protected by the First Amendment even if it is not the dogma or dominant view within the religion. Each of these concepts is discussed in turn.

THE ATTEMPT TO DEFINE RELIGION UNDER THE SELECTIVE SERVICE ACT

The primary effort by the Supreme Court to define religion has not been in First Amendment cases, but rather in decisions concerning the scope of a religious exemption to the Selective Service Act, which authorized the military draft. In other words, these cases involved statutory construction, rather than constitutional interpretation. Yet these cases are important as the only decisions to attempt to define religion.

UNITED STATES v. SEEGER
380 U.S. 163 (1965)

Justice CLARK delivered the opinion of the court.

These cases involve claims of conscientious objectors under §6(j) of the Universal Military Training and Service Act, which exempts from combatant training and service in the armed forces of the United States those persons

---

13. George C. Freeman, *The Misguided Search for the Constitutional Definition of "Religion,"* 71 Geo. L.J. 1519, 1548 (1983).

who by reason of their religious training and belief are conscientiously opposed to participation in war in any form. The parties raise the basic question of the constitutionality of the section which defines the term "religious training and belief," as used in the Act, as "an individual's belief in a relation to a Supreme Being involving duties superior to those arising from any human relation, but (not including) essentially political, sociological, or philosophical views or a merely personal moral code."

Seeger was convicted in the District Court for the Southern District of New York of having refused to submit to induction in the armed forces. He was originally classified 1-A in 1953 by his local board, but this classification was changed in 1955 to 2-S (student) and he remained in this status until 1958 when he was reclassified 1-A. He first claimed exemption as a conscientious objector in 1957 after successive annual renewals of his student classification. Although he did not adopt verbatim the printed Selective Service System form, he declared that he was conscientiously opposed to participation in war in any form by reason of his "religious" belief; that he preferred to leave the question as to his belief in a Supreme Being open, "rather than answer 'yes' or 'no' "; that his "skepticism or disbelief in the existence of God" did "not necessarily mean lack of faith in anything whatsoever"; that his was a "belief in and devotion to goodness and virtue for their own sakes, and a religious faith in a purely ethical creed." He cited such personages as Plato, Aristotle and Spinoza for support of his ethical belief in intellectual and moral integrity "without belief in God, except in the remotest sense."

His belief was found to be sincere, honest, and made in good faith; and his conscientious objection to be based upon individual training and belief, both of which included research in religious and cultural fields. Seeger's claim, however, was denied solely because it was not based upon a "belief in a relation to a Supreme Being" as required by §6(j) of the Act.

Few would quarrel, we think, with the proposition that in no field of human endeavor has the tool of language proved so inadequate in the communication of ideas as it has in dealing with the fundamental questions of man's predicament in life, in death or in final judgment and retribution. This fact makes the task of discerning the intent of Congress in using the phrase "Supreme Being" a complex one. Nor is it made the easier by the richness and variety of spiritual life in our country. Over 250 sects inhabit our land. Some believe in a purely personal God, some in a supernatural deity; others think of religion as a way of life envisioning as its ultimate goal the day when all men can live together in perfect understanding and peace. There are those who think of God as the depth of our being; others, such as the Buddhists, strive for a state of lasting rest through self-denial and inner purification; in Hindu philosophy, the Supreme Being is the transcendental reality which is truth, knowledge and bliss. Even those religious groups which have traditionally opposed war in every form have splintered into various denominations. This vast panoply of beliefs reveals the magnitude of the problem which faced the Congress when it set about providing an exemption from armed service. It also emphasizes the care that Congress realized was necessary in the fashioning of an exemption which would be in keeping with its long-established policy of not picking and choosing among religious beliefs.

We have concluded that Congress, in using the expression "Supreme Being" rather than the designation "God," was merely clarifying the meaning of religious training and belief so as to embrace all religions and to exclude essentially political, sociological, or philosophical views. We believe that under this construction, the test of belief "in a relation to a Supreme Being" is whether a given belief that is sincere and meaningful occupies a place in the life of its possessor parallel to that filled by the orthodox belief in God of one who clearly qualifies for the exemption. Where such beliefs have parallel positions in the lives of their respective holders we cannot say that one is "in a relation to Supreme Being" and the other is not. We have concluded that the beliefs of the objectors in these cases meet these criteria.

The Court in *Seeger*, however, offered no criteria for assessing whether a particular view is religious under this definition. Nor did the Court do so in the subsequent case of Welsh v. United States, 398 U.S. 333 (1970). *Welsh*, like *Seeger*, involved a person seeking an exemption from the draft on religious grounds. Welsh actually crossed out the words "religious training" on his form. The plurality opinion by Justice Black said that his situation was indistinguishable from Seeger's: "[B]oth Seeger and Welsh affirmed on those applications that they held deep conscientious scruples against taking part in wars where people were killed. Both strongly believed that killing in war was wrong, unethical, and immoral, and their consciences forbade them to take part in such an evil practice." Again, the Court said that the crucial inquiry "in determining whether the registrant's beliefs are religious is whether these beliefs play the role of a religion and function as a religion in the registrant's life."

The plurality explained that belief in God is characteristic of most religions, but not a prerequisite for religion. Justice Black wrote, "Most of the great religions of today and of the past have embodied the idea of a Supreme Being or a Supreme Reality—a God—who communicates to man in some way a consciousness of what is right and should be done, of what is wrong and therefore should be shunned. If an individual deeply and sincerely holds beliefs that are purely ethical or moral in source and content but that nevertheless impose upon him a duty of conscience to refrain from participating in any war at any time, those beliefs certainly occupy in the life of that individual 'a place parallel to that filled by . . . God' in traditionally religious persons." The Court concluded that the statute "exempts from military service all those whose consciences, spurred by deeply held moral, ethical, or religious beliefs, would give them no rest or peace if they allowed themselves to become a part of an instrument of war." The Court concluded that Welsh's moral opposition to war fit within this definition of religion.

Although *Seeger* and *Welsh* involved the Court's interpreting a statutory provision and not the First Amendment, they likely would be the starting points for any cases that required the Court to define religion under the Establishment and Free Exercise Clauses. On the one hand, these cases can be praised for broadening the definition of religion to include nontheistic views. Many religions reject the idea of a Supreme Being, and *Seeger* and *Welsh* adopt an approach that allows these faiths to be protected by the First Amendment. Moreover, the broad definitions employed allow moral judgments to be protected whether they are based on religion or philosophy. This is desirable because it does not give special status to religious moral judgments over secular ones and thereby avoids an Establishment Clause problem.[14]

---

14. However, the Court also has said that "[t]here is no doubt that 'only beliefs rooted in religion are protected by the Free Exercise Clause.' Purely secular views do not suffice." Frazee v. Illinois Employment Security Department, 489 U.S. 829, 833 (1989) (citation omitted).

On other hand, these cases can be criticized because of the lack of guidance they provide in defining what is a religious belief. A judge in a future case has little guidance in deciding what is a belief that is "sincere and meaningful [and] occupies a place in the life of its possessor parallel to that filled by the orthodox belief in God of one who clearly qualifies for the exemption."

REQUIREMENT FOR SINCERELY HELD BELIEFS

The need to define "religion" might arise in the context of an individual who is seeking an exemption from a law because of views that he or she terms religious. How is a court to decide if they are "religious" beliefs? The Supreme Court has indicated that the judiciary can determine only whether they are sincerely held views, not whether they are true or false. The court drew this distinction in United States v. Ballard.

UNITED STATES v. BALLARD
322 U.S. 78 (1944)

Mr. Justice DOUGLAS delivered the opinion of the Court.

Respondents were indicted and convicted for using, and conspiring to use, the mails to defraud. The indictment was in twelve counts. It charged a scheme to defraud by organizing and promoting the I Am movement through the use of the mails. The charge was that certain designated corporations were formed, literature distributed and sold, funds solicited, and memberships in the I Am movement sought "by means of false and fraudulent representations, pretenses and promises." It is sufficient at this point to say that they covered respondents' alleged religious doctrines or beliefs. [The indictment charged] "that Guy W. Ballard, during his lifetime, and Edna W. Ballard and Donald Ballard had, by reason of supernatural attainments, the power to heal persons of ailments and diseases and to make well persons afflicted with any diseases, injuries, or ailments, and did falsely represent to persons intended to be defrauded that the three designated persons had the ability and power to cure persons of those diseases normally classified as curable and also of diseases which are ordinarily classified by the medical profession as being incurable diseases; and did further represent that the three designated persons had in fact cured either by the activity of one, either, or all of said persons, hundreds of persons afflicted with diseases and ailments." Each of the representations enumerated in the indictment was followed by the charge that respondents "well knew" it was false.

[W]e do not agree that the truth or verity of respondents' religious doctrines or beliefs should have been submitted to the jury. Whatever this particular indictment might require, the First Amendment precludes such a course, as the United States seems to concede. "The law knows no heresy, and is committed to the support of no dogma, the establishment of no sect." The First Amendment has a dual aspect. It not only "forestalls compulsion by law of the acceptance of any creed or the practice of any form of worship" but also "safeguards the free exercise of the chosen form of religion."

Thus the Amendment embraces two concepts — freedom to believe and freedom to act. The first is absolute but, in the nature of things, the second

C. What Is Religion?

cannot be. Freedom of thought, which includes freedom of religious belief, is basic in a society of free men. It embraces the right to maintain theories of life and of death and of the hereafter which are rank heresy to followers of the orthodox faiths. Heresy trials are foreign to our Constitution. Men may believe what they cannot prove. They may not be put to the proof of their religious doctrines or beliefs. Religious experiences which are as real as life to some may be incomprehensible to others. Yet the fact that they may be beyond the ken of mortals does not mean that they can be made suspect before the law.

Many take their gospel from the New Testament. But it would hardly be supposed that they could be tried before a jury charged with the duty of determining whether those teachings contained false representations. The miracles of the New Testament, the Divinity of Christ, life after death, the power of prayer are deep in the religious convictions of many. If one could be sent to jail because a jury in a hostile environment found those teachings false, little indeed would be left of religious freedom. The Fathers of the Constitution were not unaware of the varied and extreme views of religious sects, of the violence of disagreement among them, and of the lack of any one religious creed on which all men would agree. They fashioned a charter of government which envisaged the widest possible toleration of conflicting views. Man's relation to his God was made no concern of the state. He was granted the right to worship as he pleased and to answer to no man for the verity of his religious views.

The religious views espoused by respondents might seem incredible, if not preposterous, to most people. But if those doctrines are subject to trial before a jury charged with finding their truth or falsity, then the same can be done with the religious beliefs of any sect. When the triers of fact undertake that task, they enter a forbidden domain. The First Amendment does not select any one group or any one type of religion for preferred treatment. It puts them all in that position. So we conclude that the District Court ruled properly when it withheld from the jury all questions concerning the truth or falsity of the religious beliefs or doctrines of respondents.

Justice JACKSON, dissenting.

I should say the defendants have done just that for which they are indicted. If I might agree to their conviction without creating a precedent, I cheerfully would do so. I can see in their teachings nothing but humbug, untainted by any trace of truth. But that does not dispose of the constitutional question whether misrepresentation of religious experience or belief is prosecutable; it rather emphasizes the danger of such prosecutions.

The Ballard family claimed miraculous communication with the spirit world and supernatural power to heal the sick. They were brought to trial for mail fraud on an indictment which charged that their representations were false and that they "well knew" they were false. The trial judge, obviously troubled, ruled that the court could not try whether the statements were untrue, but could inquire whether the defendants knew them to be untrue; and, if so, they could be convicted.

I find it difficult to reconcile this conclusion with our traditional religious freedoms. In the first place, as a matter of either practice or philosophy I do not see how we can separate an issue as to what is believed from considerations as to what is believable. The most convincing proof that one believes his statements is to show that they have been true in his experience.

Likewise, that one knowingly falsified is best proved by showing that what he said happened never did happen. How can the Government prove these persons knew something to be false which it cannot prove to be false? If we try religious sincerity severed from religious verity, we isolate the dispute from the very considerations which in common experience provide its most reliable answer.

In the second place, any inquiry into intellectual honesty in religion raises profound psychological problems. William James, who wrote on these matters as a scientist, reminds us that it is not theology and ceremonies which keep religion going. Its vitality is in the religious experiences of many people. "If you ask what these experiences are, they are conversations with the unseen, voices and visions, responses to prayer, changes of heart, deliverances from fear, inflowings of help, assurances of support, whenever certain persons set their own internal attitude in certain appropriate ways." If religious liberty includes, as it must, the right to communicate such experiences to others, it seems to me an impossible task for juries to separate fancied ones from real ones, dreams from happenings, and hallucinations from true clairvoyance. Such experiences, like some tones and colors, have existence for one, but none at all for another. They cannot be verified to the minds of those whose field of consciousness does not include religious insight. When one comes to trial which turns on any aspect of religious belief or representation, unbelievers among his judges are likely not to understand and are almost certain not to believe him.

There appear to be persons — let us hope not many — who find refreshment and courage in the teachings of the "I Am" cult. If the members of the sect get comfort from the celestial guidance of their "Saint Germain," however doubtful it seems to me, it is hard to say that they do not get what they pay for. Scores of sects flourish in this country by teaching what to me are queer notions. It is plain that there is wide variety in American religious taste. The Ballards are not alone in catering to it with a pretty dubious product.

Prosecutions of this character easily could degenerate into religious persecution. I do not doubt that religious leaders may be convicted of fraud for making false representations on matters other than faith or experience, as for example if one represents that funds are being used to construct a church when in fact they are being used for personal purposes. But that is not this case, which reaches into wholly dangerous ground. When does less than full belief in a professed credo become actionable fraud if one is soliciting gifts or legacies? Such inquiries may discomfort orthodox as well as unconventional religious teachers, for even the most regular of them are sometimes accused of taking their orthodoxy with a grain of salt.

I would dismiss the indictment and have done with this business of judicial examining other people's faiths.

THE RELEVANCE OF RELIGIOUS DOGMA AND SHARED BELIEFS

One way to assess the sincerity of a religious belief is with reference to the prevailing doctrines, if any, of that religion. In other words, what do others of that faith think with regard to the particular question? The problem, however, is that religion is inherently personal, as well as often group-based, and an individual may have a sincere religious belief that departs from the dogma of

C. What Is Religion?

his or her religion. In fact, for this reason, the Court has said that the dominant views in a faith are not determinative in assessing whether a particular belief is religious.

In Thomas v. Review Board of the Indiana Employment Security Division, 450 U.S. 707 (1981), the Court ruled that an individual could claim a religious belief even though it was inconsistent with the doctrines of his or her religion. A person who was a member of Jehovah's Witnesses quit his job rather than be transferred to a department that produced turrets for military tanks. He claimed that producing armaments was contrary to his religious beliefs. The state denied him unemployment benefits because he had voluntarily left his job, but he sued under a line of cases holding that a state may not deny benefits to people who quit their jobs for religious reasons.

The state argued that the Jehovah's Witnesses' faith did not prevent an individual from working in the armaments plant. The state pointed to others from that religion who worked on tank turrets and to testimony that such work was "scripturally" acceptable. The Court said, however, that this was irrelevant and declared, "[T]he guarantee of free exercise is not limited to beliefs which are shared by all of the members of a religious sect. Particularly in this sensitive area, it is not within the judicial function and judicial competence to inquire whether the petitioner or his fellow worker more correctly perceived the commands of their common faith. Courts are not arbiters of scriptural interpretation."

Similarly, in Frazee v. Illinois Employment Security Department, 489 U.S. 829 (1989), the Court allowed an individual to claim a religious basis for refusing to work on Sundays even though others of his and similar religions did not have such a proscription. The Court said, "Undoubtedly, membership in an organized religious denomination, especially one with a specific tenet forbidding members to work on Sunday, would simplify the problem of identifying sincerely held religious beliefs, but we reject the notion that to claim the protection of the Free Exercise Clause, one must be responding to the commands of a particular religious organization." Thus, the inquiry must be whether a particular individual holds a sincere religious belief.

CHAPTER 8

THE FREE EXERCISE CLAUSE

A. INTRODUCTION: FREE EXERCISE CLAUSE ISSUES

The Supreme Court repeatedly has stated that the government may not compel or punish religious beliefs; people may think and believe anything that they want. In Reynolds v. United States, 98 U.S. 145, 164 (1878), the first case to construe the Free Exercise Clause, Chief Justice Waite wrote that "Congress was deprived of all legislative power over mere opinion, but was left free to reach actions." Likewise, in Braunfeld v. Brown, 366 U.S. 599, 603 (1961), Chief Justice Warren declared that "[t]he freedom to hold religious beliefs and opinions is absolute."

The Free Exercise Clause, however, obviously does not provide absolute protection for religiously motivated conduct. The Court has thus said that the Free Exercise Clause "embraces two concepts—freedom to believe and freedom to act. The first is absolute but, in the nature of things, the second cannot be."[1] Similarly, the Court spoke of the "distinction between the absolute constitutional protection against governmental regulation of religious beliefs on the one hand, and the qualified protection against the regulation of religiously motivated conduct."[2]

Governments, though, do not adopt laws prohibiting or requiring thoughts; statutes invariably regulate conduct. Thus, the Free Exercise Clause is invoked in several situations. One is when the government prohibits behavior that a person's religion requires. For example, in Reynolds v. United States, the Supreme Court upheld the constitutionality of a law forbidding polygamy even though Mormons said that it was required by their religion.

The Free Exercise Clause also is invoked when the government requires conduct that a person's religion prohibits. For instance, the Court rejected a challenge by Amish individuals who said that the requirement that they obtain Social Security numbers and pay Social Security taxes violated their religious beliefs.[3]

---

1. Cantwell v. Connecticut, 310 U.S. 296, 303-304 (1940).
2. Employment Division v. Smith, 485 U.S. 660, 670 n.13 (1988).
3. United States v. Lee, 455 U.S. 252 (1982).

Additionally, the Free Exercise Clause is invoked when individuals claim that laws burden or make more difficult religious observances. An illustration of this is the many cases where the Court held that the government impermissibly burdens religion if it denies benefits to individuals who quit their jobs for religious reasons.[4]

The current test for the Free Exercise Clause is found in Employment Division v. Smith (1990), below, where the Court very narrowly interpreted its scope. The law before *Smith* is initially presented, followed by *Smith*, then the Supreme Court cases about the Free Exercise Clause since *Smith*, and finally the law under two federal laws that were adopted to effectively overrule Smith: The Religious Freedom Restoration Act and the Religious Land Use and Institutionalized Persons Act.

B. THE LAW BEFORE EMPLOYMENT DIVISION v. SMITH

The Supreme Court's earliest treatment of free exercise of religion was in Reynolds v. United States, 98 U.S. (8 Otto) 145 (1878). A federal law prohibited polygamy in the territories and a defendant argued that his Mormon religion required that he have multiple wives. The Supreme Court rejected the Free Exercise Clause argument and the claim that the constitutional provision required an exemption from otherwise valid criminal laws. Chief Justice Waite wrote, "[A]s a law of the organization of society under the exclusive dominion of the United States, it is provided that plural marriages shall not be allowed. Can a man excuse his practices to the contrary because of his religious belief? To permit this would be to make the professed doctrines of religious belief superior to the law of the land, and in effect to permit every citizen to become a law unto himself. Government could exist only in name under such circumstances."

The Court thus drew a distinction between beliefs and action; the Free Exercise Clause limited government regulation of the former, but not the latter. Chief Justice Waite said, "Congress was deprived of all legislative power over mere opinion, but was left free to reach actions which were in violation of social duties or subversive of good order."

The Supreme Court's initial explicit protection of free exercise of religion occurred in a series of cases that involved laws restricting religious groups from soliciting funds. For example, Cantwell v. Connecticut, 310 U.S. 296 (1940), overturned the convictions of several Jehovah's Witnesses who were convicted of soliciting money without a license. Although the Court recognized that freedom of religious conduct was not absolute, it said that "[i]n every case the power to regulate must be so exercised as not, in attaining a permissible end, unduly to infringe the protected freedom." The Court said that a licensing system for

---

4. *See, e.g.*, Thomas v. Review Board, 450 U.S. 707 (1981); Sherbert v. Verner, 374 U.S. 398 (1963).

B. The Law Before Employment Division v. Smith

religious solicitations violated both the Free Exercise and Free Speech Clauses of the First Amendment.

In Sherbert v. Verner, 374 U.S. 398 (1963), the Court expressly held that strict scrutiny should be used in evaluating laws burdening free exercise of religion and declared unconstitutional the denial of unemployment benefits to a woman who was discharged from her job rather than work on her Saturday Sabbath. The Court described the facts: "Appellant, a member of the Seventh-day Adventist Church was discharged by her South Carolina employer because she would not work on Saturday, the Sabbath Day of her faith. When she was unable to obtain other employment because from conscientious scruples she would not take Saturday work, she filed a claim for unemployment compensation benefits under the South Carolina Unemployment Compensation Act. The appellee Employment Security Commission, in administrative proceedings under the statute, found that appellant's restriction upon her availability for Saturday work brought her within the provision disqualifying for benefits insured workers who fail, without good cause, to accept "suitable work when offered . . . by the employment office or the employer. . . .'"

The Court then explained why this was unconstitutional: "If, therefore, the decision of the South Carolina Supreme Court is to withstand appellant's constitutional challenge, it must be either because her disqualification as a beneficiary represents no infringement by the State of her constitutional rights of free exercise, or because any incidental burden on the free exercise of appellant's religion may be justified by a 'compelling state interest in the regulation of a subject within the State's constitutional power to regulate.'"

Here not only is it apparent that appellant's declared ineligibility for benefits derives solely from the practice of her religion, but the pressure upon her to forego that practice is unmistakable. The ruling forces her to choose between following the precepts of her religion and forfeiting benefits, on the one hand, and abandoning one of the precepts of her religion in order to accept work, on the other hand. Governmental imposition of such a choice puts the same kind of burden upon the free exercise of religion as would a fine imposed against appellant for her Saturday worship.

We must next consider whether some compelling state interest enforced in the eligibility provisions of the South Carolina statute justifies the substantial infringement of appellant's First Amendment right. It is basic that no showing merely of a rational relationship to some colorable state interest would suffice; in this highly sensitive constitutional area, even if the possibility of spurious claims did threaten to dilute the fund and disrupt the scheduling of work, it would plainly be incumbent upon the appellees to demonstrate that no alternative forms of regulation would combat such abuses without infringing First Amendment rights."

Although *Sherbert* clearly stated that strict scrutiny was to be used in evaluating laws infringing free exercise of religion, following *Sherbert* the Court rarely struck down laws on this basis. In fact, there were only two areas where the Court invalidated laws for violating free exercise: laws, like the statute in *Sherbert*, that denied benefits to those who quit their jobs for religious reasons; and the application of a compulsory school law to the Amish. In all other Free Exercise Clause cases between 1960 and 1990, the Court upheld the laws.

1. Government Benefit Cases

In several later cases, the Court reaffirmed its holding in Sherbert v. Verner that the government could not deny benefits to individuals who left their jobs because of religious reasons. For example, in Thomas v. Review Board, 450 U.S. 707 (1981), the Court held that the government could not deny unemployment benefits to an individual who quit his job rather than accept a transfer to work in the armaments section of a factory. The individual said that he was quitting for religious reasons, and the Court said it accepted this explanation even though others of his faith saw no problem in working in that part of the factory. The Court said that it was not for the judiciary to evaluate the proper content of religious doctrines and said it was "clear that Thomas terminated his employment for religious reasons."

In Hobbie v. Unemployment Appeals Commission of Florida, 480 U.S. 136 (1987), the Court applied *Sherbert* and *Thomas* and held that the state was required to provide unemployment benefits to a woman who was fired when she refused to work on her Saturday Sabbath. Similarly, in Frazee v. Illinois Department of Employment Security, 489 U.S. 829 (1989), the Court found that a state law that required unemployed individuals to be available for work seven days a week infringed free exercise when it was applied to deny benefits to an individual who refused to work on his Sunday Sabbath. The Court said it was immaterial that the individual was not a member of an organized church, sect, or denomination. His sincere religious belief was impermissibly burdened by the denial of benefits.

2. Compulsory Schooling

The only other case where the Court found a violation of the Free Exercise Clause during this time was in Wisconsin v. Yoder, 406 U.S. 205 (1972), where the Court held that free exercise of religion required that Amish parents be granted an exemption from compulsory school laws for their 14- and 15-year-old children. The Court noted that the "Amish objection to formal education beyond the eighth grade is firmly grounded in these central religious concepts. They object to the high school, and higher education generally, because the values they teach are in marked variance with Amish values and the Amish way of life; they view secondary school education as an impermissible exposure of their children to a 'worldly' influence in conflict with their beliefs." The Court said that "[a] regulation neutral on its face may, in its application, nonetheless offend the constitutional requirement for governmental neutrality if it unduly burdens the free exercise of religion."

The Court accepted this argument and found that requiring 14- and 15-year-old Amish children to attend school violated the Free Exercise Clause and also infringed the right of parents to control the upbringing of their children. Chief Justice Burger, writing for the Court, said that "the record in this case abundantly supports the claim that the traditional way of life of the Amish is not merely a matter of personal preference, but one of deep religious conviction, shared by an organized group, and intimately related to daily living." The Court concluded that "[t]he impact of the compulsory-attendance law on respondents' practice of the Amish religion is not only severe, but inescapable, for the Wisconsin

B. The Law Before Employment Division v. Smith

law affirmatively compels them, under threat of criminal sanction, to perform acts undeniably at odds with . . . their religious beliefs. . . . [E]nforcement of the State's requirement of compulsory formal education after the eighth grade would gravely endanger if not destroy the free exercise of respondents' religious beliefs."

The Court concluded that the "self-sufficient" nature of Amish society made education for 14- and 15-year-old children unnecessary. The Court said that the lack of "two additional years of compulsory education will not impair the physical or mental health of the child, or result in an inability to be self-supporting or to discharge the duties and responsibilities of citizenship, or in any other way materially detract from the welfare of society." In *Smith*, the Court distinguished *Yoder* as involving "hybrid" rights, specifically the right of parents to control the upbringing of their children.

3. Cases Rejecting Exemptions Based on the Free Exercise Clause

Other than the employment compensation cases and *Yoder*, the Court during this period found no other law to violate the Free Exercise Clause. The Court was asked in many cases to allow an exemption to a law based on free exercise. In each the Court rejected the constitutional claim.

The cases rejecting free exercise challenges occurred in a wide variety of contexts. For example, two years before *Sherbert*, in Braunfeld v. Brown, 366 U.S. 599 (1961), the Supreme Court rejected a Free Exercise Clause challenge to Sunday closing laws. Orthodox Jews argued that their religion required that their businesses be closed on Saturdays and that it was difficult for them to adhere to their religion if they also had to be closed Sundays. Chief Justice Warren, writing for the plurality, rejected this argument and said, "[T]he statute before us does not make criminal the holding of any religious belief or opinion, nor does it force anyone to embrace any religious belief. . . . To strike down legislation which imposes only an indirect burden on the exercise of religion would radically restrict the operating latitude of the legislature." The Court accepted the state's argument that Sunday closing laws served the important government interest of providing a uniform day of rest.

In many cases during this time period, the Court rejected challenges to tax laws based on free exercise of religion. In United States v. Lee, 455 U.S. 252 (1982), the Court rejected a claim by an Amish individual that the requirement for paying Social Security taxes violated the Free Exercise Clause. The argument was that "the Amish believe it sinful not to provide for their own elderly and therefore are religiously opposed to the national social security system." The Court found, however, that this restriction on religious freedom was "essential to accomplish an overriding governmental interest." The Court concluded that mandatory participation in the Social Security system was "indispensable to [its] fiscal vitality."

In Bob Jones University v. United States, 461 U.S. 574 (1983), where the Court held that the denial of tax exempt status to private schools that racially discriminated because of sincere religious beliefs did not violate the Free Exercise Clause. The Court, in an opinion by Chief Justice Burger, explained, "[T]he Government has a fundamental, overriding interest in eradicating racial discrimination in education [which] substantially outweighs whatever burden denial of tax benefits places on petitioners' exercise of their religious beliefs." The Court found that eliminating discrimination was a compelling government interest and that "no less restrictive means are available to achieve the government interest."

In Bowen v. Roy, 476 U.S. 693 (1986), the Court rejected the claim for a religious exemption to the requirement that individuals provide Social Security numbers in order to receive welfare benefits. Individuals argued that their religion was violated by the requirement for Social Security numbers. The Court denied this claim and declared, "Never to our knowledge has the Court interpreted the First Amendment to require the Government *itself* to behave in ways that the individual believes will further his or her spiritual development. . . . [The] Free Exercise Clause affords an individual protection from certain forms of governmental compulsion; it does not afford an individual a right to dictate the conduct of the Government's internal procedures."

The Court rejected a free exercise challenge to the military in Goldman v. Weinberger, 475 U.S. 503 (1986), where the Court, by a five-to-four margin, denied the claim of an Orthodox Jewish doctor in the Air Force who said that his religion required that he wear a yarmulke in violation of the dress code. Simcha Goldman, a clinical psychologist in the Air Force, was an Orthodox Jew and an ordained rabbi. He was ordered not to wear his yarmulke on duty because it was inconsistent with the Air Force dress code.

The Court proclaimed the need for deference to the military and said that "[o]ur review of military regulations challenged on First Amendment grounds is far more deferential than constitutional review of similar laws or regulations designed for civilian society." The Court said that "to accomplish its mission the military must foster instinctive obedience, unity, commitment and espirit de corps. The essence of military service is the subordination of the desires and interests of the individual to the needs of the service." The Court concluded that it accepted the "considered professional judgment of the Air Force . . . that the traditional outfitting of personnel in standardized uniforms encourages the subordination of personal preferences and identities in favor of the overall group mission." Justice Rehnquist, writing for the Court, concluded that the "First Amendment does not require the military to accommodate such practices in the face of its view that they would detract from the uniformity sought by the dress regulations."

In these cases, the Courts refused to uphold free exercise challenges to specific laws. In Lyng v. Northwest Indian Cemetery Protective Association, 485 U.S. 439 (1988), the Court made this even more explicit and rejected a Free Exercise Clause challenge to the federal government's building a road and allowing timber harvesting in a national forest that contained sacred Indian burial grounds. The Court recognized that the construction would "virtually . . . destroy the Indians' ability to practice their religion" because it would irreparably damage "sacred areas which are an integral and necessary part of their belief systems." Nonetheless, the Court said that "[t]he Free Exercise Clause simply cannot be understood to require the Government to conduct its own internal affairs in ways that comport with the religious beliefs of particular citizens. . . . [The] Free Exercise Clause affords an individual protection from certain forms of government compulsion; it does not afford an individual a right to dictate the conduct of the Government's internal procedures."

C. THE CURRENT TEST

In Employment Division v. Smith, in 1990, the Court substantially changed the law regarding the Free Exercise Clause and articulated the test that is used today.

EMPLOYMENT DIVISION, DEPARTMENT OF HUMAN RESOURCES OF OREGON v. SMITH
494 U.S. 872 (1990)

Justice SCALIA delivered the opinion of the Court.

This case requires us to decide whether the Free Exercise Clause of the First Amendment permits the State of Oregon to include religiously inspired peyote use within the reach of its general criminal prohibition on use of that drug, and thus permits the State to deny unemployment benefits to persons dismissed from their jobs because of such religiously inspired use.

I

Oregon law prohibits the knowing or intentional possession of a "controlled substance" unless the substance has been prescribed by a medical practitioner. Persons who violate this provision by possessing a controlled substance listed on Schedule I are "guilty of a Class B felony." As compiled by the State Board of Pharmacy under its statutory authority, Schedule I contains the drug peyote, a hallucinogen.

Respondents Alfred Smith and Galen Black (hereinafter respondents) were fired from their jobs with a private drug rehabilitation organization because they ingested peyote for sacramental purposes at a ceremony of the Native American Church, of which both are members. When respondents applied to petitioner Employment Division (hereinafter petitioner) for unemployment compensation, they were determined to be ineligible for benefits because they had been discharged for work-related "misconduct." The Oregon Supreme Court held that respondents' religiously inspired use of peyote [was protected by the] Free Exercise Clause.

II

The free exercise of religion means, first and foremost, the right to believe and profess whatever religious doctrine one desires. Thus, the First Amendment obviously excludes all "governmental regulation of religious beliefs as such." The government may not compel affirmation of religious belief, punish the expression of religious doctrines it believes to be false, impose special disabilities on the basis of religious views or religious status, or lend its power to one or the other side in controversies over religious authority or dogma.

But the "exercise of religion" often involves not only belief and profession but the performance of (or abstention from) physical acts: assembling with others for a worship service, participating in sacramental use of bread and wine, proselytizing, abstaining from certain foods or certain modes of transportation. It would be true, we think (though no case of ours has involved the point), that a State would be "prohibiting the free exercise [of religion]" if it sought to ban such acts or abstentions only when they are engaged in for religious reasons, or only because of the religious belief that they display. It would doubtless be unconstitutional, for example, to ban the casting of "statues that are to be used for worship purposes," or to prohibit bowing down before a golden calf.

Respondents in the present case, however, seek to carry the meaning of "prohibiting the free exercise [of religion]" one large step further. They contend that their religious motivation for using peyote places them beyond the reach of a criminal law that is not specifically directed at their religious practice, and that is concededly constitutional as applied to those who use the drug for other reasons. They assert, in other words, that "prohibiting the free exercise [of religion]" includes requiring any individual to observe a generally applicable law that requires (or forbids) the performance of an act that his religious belief forbids (or requires). As a textual matter, we do not think the words must be given that meaning.

We have never held that an individual's religious beliefs excuse him from compliance with an otherwise valid law prohibiting conduct that the State is free to regulate. On the contrary, the record of more than a century of our free exercise jurisprudence contradicts that proposition. [D]ecisions have consistently held that the right of free exercise does not relieve an individual of the obligation to comply with a "valid and neutral law of general applicability on the ground that the law proscribes (or prescribes) conduct that his religion prescribes (or proscribes)."

Our most recent decision involving a neutral, generally applicable regulatory law that compelled activity forbidden by an individual's religion was United States v. Lee. There an Amish employer, on behalf of himself and his employees, sought exemption from collection and payment of Social Security taxes on the ground that the Amish faith prohibited participation in governmental support programs. We rejected the claim that an exemption was constitutionally required. There would be no way, we observed, to distinguish the Amish believer's objection to Social Security taxes from the religious objections that others might have to the collection or use of other taxes. "If, for example, a religious adherent believes war is a sin, and if a certain percentage of the federal budget can be identified as devoted to war-related activities, such individuals would have a similarly valid claim to be exempt from paying that percentage of the income tax. The tax system could not function if denominations were allowed to challenge the tax system because tax payments were spent in a manner that violates their religious belief."

The only decisions in which we have held that the First Amendment bars application of a neutral, generally applicable law to religiously motivated action have involved not the Free Exercise Clause alone, but the Free Exercise Clause in conjunction with other constitutional protections, such as freedom of speech and of the press, see Cantwell v. Connecticut [1940] (invalidating a licensing system for religious and charitable solicitations under which the administrator had discretion to deny a license to any cause he deemed nonreligious); Murdock v. Pennsylvania (1943) (invalidating a flat tax on solicitation as applied to the dissemination of religious ideas); or the right of parents, acknowledged in

C. The Current Test

Pierce v. Society of Sisters (1925), to direct the education of their children, see Wisconsin v. Yoder (1972) (invalidating compulsory school-attendance laws as applied to Amish parents who refused on religious grounds to send their children to school).

The present case does not present such a hybrid situation, but a free exercise claim unconnected with any communicative activity or parental right. Respondents urge us to hold, quite simply, that when otherwise prohibitable conduct is accompanied by religious convictions, not only the convictions but the conduct itself must be free from governmental regulation. We have never held that, and decline to do so now. There being no contention that Oregon's drug law represents an attempt to regulate religious beliefs, the communication of religious beliefs, or the raising of one's children in those beliefs, the rule to which we have adhered ever since *Reynolds* plainly controls.

Respondents argue that even though exemption from generally applicable criminal laws need not automatically be extended to religiously motivated actors, at least the claim for a religious exemption must be evaluated under the balancing test set forth in Sherbert v. Verner (1963). Under the *Sherbert* test, governmental actions that substantially burden a religious practice must be justified by a compelling governmental interest. Applying that test we have, on three occasions, invalidated state unemployment compensation rules that conditioned the availability of benefits upon an applicant's willingness to work under conditions forbidden by his religion. We have never invalidated any governmental action on the basis of the *Sherbert* test except the denial of unemployment compensation. Although we have sometimes purported to apply the *Sherbert* test in contexts other than that, we have always found the test satisfied.

In recent years we have abstained from applying the *Sherbert* test (outside the unemployment compensation field) at all. In Bowen v. Roy (1986), we declined to apply *Sherbert* analysis to a federal statutory scheme that required benefit applicants and recipients to provide their Social Security numbers. The plaintiffs in that case asserted that it would violate their religious beliefs to obtain and provide a Social Security number for their daughter. We held the statute's application to the plaintiffs valid regardless of whether it was necessary to effectuate a compelling interest.

In Lyng v. Northwest Indian Cemetery Protective Assn. (1988), we declined to apply *Sherbert* analysis to the Government's logging and road construction activities on lands used for religious purposes by several Native American Tribes, even though it was undisputed that the activities "could have devastating effects on traditional Indian religious practices." In Goldman v. Weinberger (1986), we rejected application of the *Sherbert* test to military dress regulations that forbade the wearing of yarmulkes.

Even if we were inclined to breathe into *Sherbert* some life beyond the unemployment compensation field, we would not apply it to require exemptions from a generally applicable criminal law. The *Sherbert* test, it must be recalled, was developed in a context that lent itself to individualized governmental assessment of the reasons for the relevant conduct. As a plurality of the Court noted in *Roy*, a distinctive feature of unemployment compensation programs is that their eligibility criteria invite consideration of the particular circumstances behind an applicant's unemployment. Whether or not the decisions are that limited, they at least have nothing to do with an across-the-board criminal prohibition on a particular form of conduct.

The government's ability to enforce generally applicable prohibitions of socially harmful conduct, like its ability to carry out other aspects of public policy, "cannot depend on measuring the effects of a governmental action on a religious objector's spiritual development." To make an individual's obligation to obey such a law contingent upon the law's coincidence with his religious beliefs, except where the State's interest is "compelling"—permitting him, by virtue of his beliefs, "to become a law unto himself"—contradicts both constitutional tradition and common sense.

The "compelling government interest" requirement seems benign, because it is familiar from other fields. But using it as the standard that must be met before the government may accord different treatment on the basis of race, or before the government may regulate the content of speech, is not remotely comparable to using it for the purpose asserted here. What it produces in those other fields—equality of treatment and an unrestricted flow of contending speech—are constitutional norms; what it would produce here—a private right to ignore generally applicable laws—is a constitutional anomaly.

Nor is it possible to limit the impact of respondents' proposal by requiring a "compelling state interest" only when the conduct prohibited is "central" to the individual's religion. It is no more appropriate for judges to determine the "centrality" of religious beliefs before applying a "compelling interest" test in the free exercise field, than it would be for them to determine the "importance" of ideas before applying the "compelling interest" test in the free speech field. What principle of law or logic can be brought to bear to contradict a believer's assertion that a particular act is "central" to his personal faith? Judging the centrality of different religious practices is akin to the unacceptable "business of evaluating the relative merits of differing religious claims."

If the "compelling interest" test is to be applied at all, then, it must be applied across the board, to all actions thought to be religiously commanded. Moreover, if "compelling interest" really means what it says (and watering it down here would subvert its rigor in the other fields where it is applied), many laws will not meet the test. Any society adopting such a system would be courting anarchy, but that danger increases in direct proportion to the society's diversity of religious beliefs, and its determination to coerce or suppress none of them. Precisely because "we are a cosmopolitan nation made up of people of almost every conceivable religious preference," and precisely because we value and protect that religious divergence, we cannot afford the luxury of deeming presumptively invalid, as applied to the religious objector, every regulation of conduct that does not protect an interest of the highest order. The rule respondents favor would open the prospect of constitutionally required religious exemptions from civic obligations of almost every conceivable kind—ranging from compulsory military service to the payment of taxes, to health and safety regulation such as manslaughter and child neglect laws, compulsory vaccination laws, drug laws, and traffic laws, to social welfare legislation such as minimum wage laws, child labor laws, animal cruelty laws, environmental protection laws, and laws providing for equality of opportunity for the races. The First Amendment's protection of religious liberty does not require this.

Values that are protected against government interference through enshrinement in the Bill of Rights are not thereby banished from the political process. Just as a society that believes in the negative protection accorded to the press by the First Amendment is likely to enact laws that affirmatively foster the

C. The Current Test

dissemination of the printed word, so also a society that believes in the negative protection accorded to religious belief can be expected to be solicitous of that value in its legislation as well. It is therefore not surprising that a number of States have made an exception to their drug laws for sacramental peyote use.

But to say that a nondiscriminatory religious-practice exemption is permitted, or even that it is desirable, is not to say that it is constitutionally required, and that the appropriate occasions for its creation can be discerned by the courts. It may fairly be said that leaving accommodation to the political process will place at a relative disadvantage those religious practices that are not widely engaged in; but that unavoidable consequence of democratic government must be preferred to a system in which each conscience is a law unto itself or in which judges weigh the social importance of all laws against the centrality of all religious beliefs.

Because respondents' ingestion of peyote was prohibited under Oregon law, and because that prohibition is constitutional, Oregon may, consistent with the Free Exercise Clause, deny respondents unemployment compensation when their dismissal results from use of the drug.

Justice O'CONNOR, with whom Justice BRENNAN, Justice MARSHALL, and Justice BLACKMUN join as to Parts I and II, concurring in the judgment.

Although I agree with the result the Court reaches in this case, I cannot join its opinion. In my view, today's holding dramatically departs from well-settled First Amendment jurisprudence, appears unnecessary to resolve the question presented, and is incompatible with our Nation's fundamental commitment to individual religious liberty.

The Court today extracts from our long history of free exercise precedents the single categorical rule that "if prohibiting the exercise of religion . . . is . . . merely the incidental effect of a generally applicable and otherwise valid provision, the First Amendment has not been offended." Indeed, the Court holds that where the law is a generally applicable criminal prohibition, our usual free exercise jurisprudence does not even apply. To reach this sweeping result, however, the Court must not only give a strained reading of the First Amendment but must also disregard our consistent application of free exercise doctrine to cases involving generally applicable regulations that burden religious conduct.

The Court today interprets the Clause to permit the government to prohibit, without justification, conduct mandated by an individual's religious beliefs, so long as that prohibition is generally applicable. But a law that prohibits certain conduct—conduct that happens to be an act of worship for someone—manifestly does prohibit that person's free exercise of his religion. A person who is barred from engaging in religiously motivated conduct is barred from freely exercising his religion. Moreover, that person is barred from freely exercising his religion regardless of whether the law prohibits the conduct only when engaged in for religious reasons, only by members of that religion, or by all persons. It is difficult to deny that a law that prohibits religiously motivated conduct, even if the law is generally applicable, does not at least implicate First Amendment concerns.

The Court responds that generally applicable laws are "one large step" removed from laws aimed at specific religious practices. The First Amendment, however, does not distinguish between laws that are generally applicable and laws that target particular religious practices. Indeed, few States would be so naïve as to enact a law directly prohibiting or burdening a religious practice as such. Our free exercise cases have all concerned generally applicable laws that had the effect of significantly burdening a religious practice. If the First Amendment is to have any vitality, it ought not be construed to cover only the extreme and hypothetical situation in which a State directly targets a religious practice. As we have noted in a slightly different context, "[s]uch a test has no basis in precedent and relegates a serious First Amendment value to the barest level of minimum scrutiny that the Equal Protection Clause already provides."

To say that a person's right to free excise has been burdened, of course, does not mean that he has an absolute right to engage in the conduct. Under our established First Amendment jurisprudence, we have recognized that the freedom to act, unlike the freedom to believe, cannot be absolute. Instead, we have respected both the First Amendment's express textual mandate and the governmental interest in regulation of conduct by requiring the government to justify any substantial burden on religiously motivated conduct by a compelling state interest and by means narrowly tailored to achieve that interest.

The compelling interest test effectuates the First Amendment's command that religious liberty is an independent liberty, that it occupies a preferred position, and that the Court will not permit encroachments upon this liberty, whether direct or indirect, unless required by clear and compelling governmental interests "of the highest order." "Only an especially important governmental interest pursued by narrowly tailored means can justify exacting a sacrifice of First Amendments freedoms as the price for an equal share of the rights, benefits, and privileges enjoyed by other citizens."

The Court attempts to support its narrow reading of the Clause by claiming that "[w]e have never held that an individual's religious beliefs excuse him from compliance with an otherwise valid law prohibiting conduct that the State is free to regulate." But as the Court later notes, as it must, in cases such as *Cantwell* and *Yoder* we have in fact interpreted the Free Exercise Clause to forbid application of a generally applicable prohibition to religiously motivated conduct.

Moreover, in each of the other cases cited by the Court to support its categorical rule, we rejected the particular constitutional claims before us only after carefully weighing the competing interests. That we rejected the free exercise claims in those cases hardly calls into question the applicability of First Amendment doctrine in the first place. Indeed, it is surely unusual to judge the vitality of a constitutional doctrine by looking to the win-loss record of the plaintiffs who happen to come before us.

In my view, however, the essence of a free exercise claim is relief from a burden imposed by government on religious practices or beliefs, whether the burden is imposed directly through laws that prohibit or compel specific religious practices, or indirectly through laws that, in effect, make abandonment of one's own religion or conformity to the religious beliefs of others the price of an equal place in the civil community.

Once it has been shown that a government regulation or criminal prohibition burdens the free exercise of religion, we have consistently asked the government to demonstrate that unbending application of its regulation to the religious objector "is essential to accomplish an overriding governmental interest," or represents "the least restrictive means of achieving some compelling state interest."

C. The Current Test

To me, the sounder approach—the approach more consistent with our role as judges to decide each case on its individual merits—is to apply this test in each case to determine whether the burden on the specific plaintiffs before us is constitutionally significant and whether the particular criminal interest asserted by the State before us is compelling. Even if, as an empirical matter, a government's criminal laws might usually serve a compelling interest in health, safety, or public order, the First Amendment at least requires a case-by-case determination of the question, sensitive to the facts of each particular claim. Given the range of conduct that a State might legitimately make criminal, we cannot assume, merely because a law carries criminal sanctions and is generally applicable, that the First Amendment never requires the State to grant a limited exemption for religiously motivated conduct.

The Court today gives no convincing reason to depart from settled First Amendment jurisprudence. There is nothing talismanic about neutral law of general applicability or general criminal prohibitions, for laws neutral toward religion can coerce a person to violate his religious conscience or intrude upon his religious duties just as effectively as laws aimed at religion. Although the Court suggests that the compelling interest test, as applied to generally applicable laws, would result in a "constitutional anomaly," the First Amendment unequivocally makes freedom of religion, like freedom from race discrimination and freedom of speech a "constitutional nor[m]," not an "anomaly." Nor would application of our established free exercise doctrine to this case necessarily be incompatible with our equal protection cases. As the language of the Clauses itself makes clear, an individual's free exercise of religion is a preferred constitutional activity. A law that makes criminal such an activity therefore triggers constitutional concern—and heightened judicial scrutiny—even if it does not target the particular religious conduct at issue. Our free speech cases similarly recognize that neutral regulations that affect free speech values are subject to a balancing, rather than categorical, approach. The Court's parade of horribles not only fails as a reason for discarding the compelling interest test, it instead demonstrates just the opposite: that courts have been quite capable of applying our free exercise jurisprudence to strike sensible balances between religious liberty and competing state interests.

Finally, the Court today suggests that the disfavoring of minority religions is an "unavoidable consequence" under our system of government and that accommodation of such religions must be left to the political process. In my view, however, the First Amendment was enacted precisely to protect the rights of those whose religious practices are not shared by the majority and may be viewed with hostility. The history of our free exercise doctrine amply demonstrates the harsh impact majoritarian rule has had on unpopular or emerging religious groups such as the Jehovah's Witnesses and the Amish. Indeed, the words of Justice Jackson in West Virginia State Bd. of Ed. v. Barnette (1940) are apt:

> The very purpose of a Bill of Rights was to withdraw certain subjects from the vicissitudes of political controversy, to place them beyond the reach of majorities and officials and to establish them as legal principles to be applied by the courts. One's right to life, liberty, and property, to free speech, a free press, freedom of worship and assembly, and other fundamental rights may not be submitted to vote; they depend on the outcome of no elections.

The compelling interest test reflects the First Amendment's mandate of preserving religious liberty to the fullest extent possible in a pluralistic society. For the Court to deem this command a "luxury[]," is to denigrate "[t]he very purpose of a Bill of Rights."

The Court's holding today not only misreads settled First Amendment precedent; it appears to be unnecessary to this case. I would reach the same result applying our established free exercise jurisprudence. There is no dispute that Oregon's criminal prohibition of peyote places a severe burden on the ability of respondents to freely exercise their religion. Peyote is a sacrament of the Native American Church and is regarded as vital to respondents' ability to practice their religion. There is also no dispute that Oregon has a significant interest in enforcing laws that control the possession and use of controlled substances by its citizens. As we recently noted, drug abuse is "one of the greatest problems affecting the health and welfare of our population" and thus "one of the most serious problems confronting our society today." Oregon has a compelling interest in prohibiting the possession of peyote by its citizens. Although the question is close, I would conclude that uniform application of Oregon's criminal prohibition is "essential to accomplish[]," its overriding interest in preventing the physical harm caused by the use of a Schedule I controlled substance. Oregon's criminal prohibition represents that State's judgment that the possession and use of controlled substances, even by only one person, is inherently harmful and dangerous. Because the health effects caused by the use of controlled substances exist regardless of the motivation of the user, the use of such substances, even for religious purposes, violates the very purpose of the laws that prohibit them. Moreover, in view of the societal interest in preventing trafficking in controlled substances, uniform application of the criminal prohibition at issue is essential to the effectiveness of Oregon's stated interest in preventing any possession of peyote.

For these reasons, I believe that granting a selective exemption in this case would seriously impair Oregon's compelling interest in prohibiting possession of peyote by its citizens. Under such circumstances, the Free Exercise Clause does not require the State to accommodate respondents' religiously motivated conduct. I would therefore adhere to our established free exercise jurisprudence and hold that the State in this case has a compelling interest in regulating peyote use by its citizens and that accommodating respondents' religiously motivated conduct "will unduly interfere with fulfillment of the government interest."

Justice BLACKMUN, with whom Justice BRENNAN and Justice MARSHALL join, dissenting.

This Court over the years painstakingly has developed a consistent and exacting standard to test the constitutionality of a state statute that burdens the free exercise of religion. Such a statute may stand only if the law in general, and the State's refusal to allow a religious exemption in particular, are justified by a compelling interest that cannot be served by less restrictive means. Until today, I thought this was a settled and inviolate principle of this Court's First Amendment jurisprudence. The majority, however, perfunctorily dismisses it as a "constitutional anomaly." In short, it effectuates a wholesale overturning of settled law concerning the Religion Clauses of our Constitution.

The State proclaims an interest in protecting the health and safety of its citizens from the dangers of unlawful drugs. It offers, however, no evidence that the religious use of peyote has ever harmed anyone. The carefully circumscribed ritual context in which respondents used peyote is far removed from the irresponsible and unrestricted recreational use of unlawful drugs. The Native American Church's internal restrictions on, and supervision of, its members' use of peyote substantially obviate the State's health and safety concerns.

For these reasons, I conclude that Oregon's interest in enforcing its drug laws against religious use of peyote is not sufficiently compelling to outweigh respondents' right to the free exercise of their religion. The State could not constitutionally enforce its criminal prohibition against respondents, the interests underlying the State's drug laws cannot justify its denial of unemployment benefits.

D. SUPREME COURT DECISIONS SINCE EMPLOYMENT DIVISION v. SMITH

Since Employment Division v. Smith, the Court has invalidated laws under the free exercise clause in three contexts: where there is "animus" against religion; where the government has interfered with the ability of religions to choose their ministers; and where the government has discriminated against religions in receiving benefits.

1. *Animus Against Religion*

In Church of the Lukumi Babalu Aye, Inc. v. Hialeah, 508 U.S. 520 (1993), the Court struck down a law that prohibited ritual sacrifice of animals on the ground that it was not a neutral law of general applicability. The Santeria religion uses animal sacrifice as one of its principal forms of worship. Animals are killed and then cooked and eaten in accord with Santeria rituals. After practitioners of Santeria announced plans to establish a house of worship, a school, a cultural center, and a museum in Hialeah, Florida, the city adopted an ordinance prohibiting ritual sacrifice of animals. The law defined "sacrifice" as killing animals "not for the primary purpose of food consumption." The law applied only to an individual or group that "kills, slaughters, or sacrifices animals for any type of ritual, regardless of whether or not the flesh or blood of the animal is to be consumed."

All of the justices agreed the law was unconstitutional, with Justice Kennedy writing the opinion for the Court. At the outset, Justice Kennedy reaffirmed the *Smith* test and declared that "our cases establish the general proposition that a law that is neutral and of general applicability need not be justified by a compelling governmental interest even if the law has the incidental effect of burdening a particular religious practice." Kennedy said, however, that "[a] law failing to satisfy these requirements must be justified by a compelling interest and must be narrowly tailored to advance that interest."

The Court decided that the Hialeah law was not neutral because its clear object was to prohibit a religious practice. Justice Kennedy's majority opinion noted that the text of the law spoke of "sacrifice" and "ritual" and that its purpose was clearly to prohibit the practice of the Santeria religion. The Court also focused on the exceptions to the law that allowed killing of animals by other religions, such as in kosher slaughtering of animals, and that allowed killing of animals for nonreligious purposes. The Court said that this further indicated the lack of neutrality of the law. The Court concluded that "the neutrality inquiry leads to one conclusion: The ordinances had as their object the suppression of religion."

The Court also said that the law was not one of "general applicability." The Court again noted that "[d]espite the city's proffered interest in preventing cruelty to animals, the ordinances are drafted with care to forbid few killings but those occasioned by religious sacrifice. Many types of animal deaths or kills are either not prohibited or approved by express provision."

Because it concluded that the ordinance was neither neutral nor of general applicability, the Court applied strict scrutiny. The Court found the law unconstitutional because the government could achieve the goals of safe and sanitary disposal of animal remains without targeting the Santeria religion.

Justice Scalia, in an opinion concurring in part and concurring in the judgment and joined by Chief Justice Rehnquist, wrote separately to argue that the purpose behind a law should not be relevant in determining whether it is neutral and of general applicability. Justice Souter also wrote an opinion concurring in part and concurring in the judgment. He argued that the Court should reconsider and overrule *Smith*. Justice Blackmun concurred in the judgment, in an opinion joined by Justice O'Connor, and "emphasize[d] that the First Amendment's protection of religion extends beyond those rare occasions on which the government explicitly targets religion (or a particular religion) for disfavored treatment."

More recently, the Court found animus against religion when a state civil rights commission deemed a bakery to have violated its state civil rights law by refusing to design and bake a cake for the celebration of a same-sex wedding.

MASTERPIECE CAKE SHOP, LTD. v. COLORADO CIVIL RIGHTS COMMISSION
138 S. Ct. 1719 (2018)

Justice KENNEDY delivered the opinion of the Court.

In 2012 a same-sex couple visited Masterpiece Cakeshop, a bakery in Colorado, to make inquiries about ordering a cake for their wedding reception. The shop's owner told the couple that he would not create a cake for their wedding because of his religious opposition to same-sex marriages—marriages the State of Colorado itself did not recognize at that time. The couple filed a charge with the Colorado Civil Rights Commission alleging discrimination on the basis of sexual orientation in violation of the Colorado Anti-Discrimination Act.

The Commission determined that the shop's actions violated the Act and ruled in the couple's favor. The Colorado state courts affirmed the ruling and its enforcement order, and this Court now must decide whether the Commission's order violated the Constitution.

The case presents difficult questions as to the proper reconciliation of at least two principles. The first is the authority of a State and its governmental entities to protect the rights and dignity of gay persons who are, or wish to be, married but who face discrimination when they seek goods or services. The second is the right of all persons to exercise fundamental freedoms under the First Amendment, as applied to the States through the Fourteenth Amendment.

The freedoms asserted here are both the freedom of speech and the free exercise of religion. The free speech aspect of this case is difficult, for few persons who have seen a beautiful wedding cake might have thought of its creation as an exercise of protected speech. This is an instructive example, however, of the proposition that the application of constitutional freedoms in new contexts can deepen our understanding of their meaning.

One of the difficulties in this case is that the parties disagree as to the extent of the baker's refusal to provide service. If a baker refused to design a special cake with words or images celebrating the marriage—for instance, a cake showing words with religious meaning—that might be different from a refusal to sell any cake at all. In defining whether a baker's creation can be protected, these details might make a difference.

The same difficulties arise in determining whether a baker has a valid free exercise claim. A baker's refusal to attend the wedding to ensure that the cake is cut the right way, or a refusal to put certain religious words or decorations on the cake, or even a refusal to sell a cake that has been baked for the public generally but includes certain religious words or symbols on it are just three examples of possibilities that seem all but endless.

Whatever the confluence of speech and free exercise principles might be in some cases, the Colorado Civil Rights Commission's consideration of this case was inconsistent with the State's obligation of religious neutrality. The reason and motive for the baker's refusal were based on his sincere religious beliefs and convictions. The Court's precedents make clear that the baker, in his capacity as the owner of a business serving the public, might have his right to the free exercise of religion limited by generally applicable laws. Still, the delicate question of when the free exercise of his religion must yield to an otherwise valid exercise of state power needed to be determined in an adjudication in which religious hostility on the part of the State itself would not be a factor in the balance the State sought to reach. That requirement, however, was not met here. When the Colorado Civil Rights Commission considered this case, it did not do so with the religious neutrality that the Constitution requires.

Given all these considerations, it is proper to hold that whatever the outcome of some future controversy involving facts similar to these, the Commission's actions here violated the Free Exercise Clause; and its order must be set aside.

I

Masterpiece Cakeshop, Ltd., is a bakery in Lakewood, Colorado, a suburb of Denver. The shop offers a variety of baked goods, ranging from everyday cookies and brownies to elaborate custom-designed cakes for birthday parties, weddings, and other events.

Jack Phillips is an expert baker who has owned and operated the shop for 24 years. Phillips is a devout Christian. He has explained that his "main goal in life is to be obedient to" Jesus Christ and Christ's "teachings in all aspects of his life." And he seeks to "honor God through his work at Masterpiece Cakeshop." One of Phillips' religious beliefs is that "God's intention for marriage from the beginning of history is that it is and should be the union of one man and one woman." To Phillips, creating a wedding cake for a same-sex wedding would be equivalent to participating in a celebration that is contrary to his own most deeply held beliefs.

Phillips met Charlie Craig and Dave Mullins when they entered his shop in the summer of 2012. Craig and Mullins were planning to marry. At that time, Colorado did not recognize same-sex marriages, so the couple planned to wed legally in Massachusetts and afterwards to host a reception for their family and friends in Denver. To prepare for their celebration, Craig and Mullins visited the shop and told Phillips that they were interested in ordering a cake for "our wedding." They did not mention the design of the cake they envisioned.

Phillips informed the couple that he does not "create" wedding cakes for same-sex weddings. He explained, "I'll make your birthday cakes, shower cakes, sell you cookies and brownies, I just don't make cakes for same sex weddings." The couple left the shop without further discussion.

The following day, Craig's mother, who had accompanied the couple to the cakeshop and been present for their interaction with Phillips, telephoned to ask Phillips why he had declined to serve her son. Phillips explained that he does not create wedding cakes for same-sex weddings because of his religious opposition to same-sex marriage, and also because Colorado (at that time) did not recognize same-sex marriages. He later explained his belief that "to create a wedding cake for an event that celebrates something that directly goes against the teachings of the Bible, would have been a personal endorsement and participation in the ceremony and relationship that they were entering into."

Today, the Colorado Anti-Discrimination Act (CADA) carries forward the state's tradition of prohibiting discrimination in places of public accommodation. Amended in 2007 and 2008 to prohibit discrimination on the basis of sexual orientation as well as other protected characteristics, CADA in relevant part provides as follows:

"It is a discriminatory practice and unlawful for a person, directly or indirectly, to refuse, withhold from, or deny to an individual or a group, because of disability, race, creed, color, sex, sexual orientation, marital status, national origin, or ancestry, the full and equal enjoyment of the goods, services, facilities, privileges, advantages, or accommodations of a place of public accommodation."

The Act defines "public accommodation" broadly to include any "place of business engaged in any sales to the public and any place offering services . . . to the public," but excludes "a church, synagogue, mosque, or other place that is principally used for religious purposes."

Craig and Mullins filed a discrimination complaint against Masterpiece Cakeshop and Phillips in September 2012, shortly after the couple's visit to the shop. App. 31. The complaint alleged that Craig and Mullins had been denied "full and equal service" at the bakery because of their sexual orientation, and that it was Phillips' "standard business practice" not to provide cakes for same-sex weddings.

The Civil Rights Division opened an investigation. The investigator found that "on multiple occasions," Phillips "turned away potential customers on the basis of their sexual orientation, stating that he could not create a cake for a same-sex wedding ceremony or reception" because his religious beliefs prohibited it and because the potential customers "were doing something illegal" at that time. The investigation found that Phillips had declined to sell custom wedding cakes to about six other same-sex couples on this basis. The investigator also recounted that, according to affidavits submitted by Craig and Mullins, Phillips' shop had refused to sell cupcakes to a lesbian couple for their commitment celebration because the shop "had a policy of not selling baked goods to same-sex couples for this type of event." Based on these findings, the Division found probable cause that Phillips violated CADA and referred the case to the Civil Rights Commission.

The Commission found it proper to conduct a formal hearing, and it sent the case to a State ALJ. Finding no dispute as to material facts, the ALJ entertained cross-motions for summary judgment and ruled in the couple's favor. The ALJ first rejected Phillips' argument that declining to make or create a wedding cake for Craig and Mullins did not violate Colorado law. It was undisputed that the shop is subject to state public accommodations laws. And the ALJ determined that Phillips' actions constituted prohibited discrimination on the basis of sexual orientation, not simply opposition to same-sex marriage as Phillips contended.

The Commission affirmed the ALJ's decision in full. The Commission ordered Phillips to "cease and desist from discriminating against . . . same-sex couples by refusing to sell them wedding cakes or any product [they] would sell to heterosexual couples." It also ordered additional remedial measures, including "comprehensive staff training on the Public Accommodations section" of CADA "and changes to any and all company policies to comply with . . . this Order." The Commission additionally required Phillips to prepare "quarterly compliance reports" for a period of two years documenting "the number of patrons denied service" and why, along with "a statement describing the remedial actions taken." Phillips appealed to the Colorado Court of Appeals, which affirmed the Commission's legal determinations and remedial order.

II

Our society has come to the recognition that gay persons and gay couples cannot be treated as social outcasts or as inferior in dignity and worth. For that reason the laws and the Constitution can, and in some instances must, protect them in the exercise of their civil rights. The exercise of their freedom on terms equal to others must be given great weight and respect by the courts. At the same time, the religious and philosophical objections to gay marriage are protected views and in some instances protected forms of expression. As this Court observed in Obergefell v. Hodges (2015), "[t]he First Amendment ensures that religious organizations and persons are given proper protection as they seek to teach the principles that are so fulfilling and so central to their lives and faiths." Nevertheless, while those religious and philosophical objections are protected, it is a general rule that such objections do not allow business owners and other actors in the economy and in society to deny protected persons equal access to goods and services under a neutral and generally applicable public accommodations law.

When it comes to weddings, it can be assumed that a member of the clergy who objects to gay marriage on moral and religious grounds could not be compelled to perform the ceremony without denial of his or her right to the free exercise of religion. This refusal would be well understood in our constitutional order as an exercise of religion, an exercise that gay persons could recognize and accept without serious diminishment to their own dignity and worth. Yet if that exception were not confined, then a long list of persons who provide goods and services for marriages and weddings might refuse to do so for gay persons, thus resulting in a community-wide stigma inconsistent with the history and dynamics of civil rights laws that ensure equal access to goods, services, and public accommodations.

It is unexceptional that Colorado law can protect gay persons, just as it can protect other classes of individuals, in acquiring whatever products and services they choose on the same terms and conditions as are offered to other members of the public. And there are no doubt innumerable goods and services that no one could argue implicate the First Amendment. Petitioners conceded, moreover, that if a baker refused to sell any goods or any cakes for gay weddings, that would be a different matter and the State would have a strong case under this Court's precedents that this would be a denial of goods and services that went beyond any protected rights of a baker who offers goods and services to the general public and is subject to a neutrally applied and generally applicable public accommodations law.

Phillips claims, however, that a narrower issue is presented. He argues that he had to use his artistic skills to make an expressive statement, a wedding endorsement in his own voice and of his own creation. As Phillips would see the case, this contention has a significant First Amendment speech component and implicates his deep and sincere religious beliefs. In this context the baker likely found it difficult to find a line where the customers' rights to goods and services became a demand for him to exercise the right of his own personal expression for their message, a message he could not express in a way consistent with his religious beliefs. Phillips' dilemma was particularly understandable given the background of legal principles and administration of the law in Colorado at that time. His decision and his actions leading to the refusal of service all occurred in the year 2012. At that point, Colorado did not recognize the validity of gay marriages performed in its own State. Since the State itself did not allow those marriages to be performed in Colorado, there is some force to the argument that the baker was not unreasonable in deeming it lawful to decline to take an action that he understood to be an expression of support for their validity when that expression was contrary to his sincerely held religious beliefs, at least insofar as his refusal was limited to refusing to create and express a message in support of gay marriage, even one planned to take place in another State.

At the time, state law also afforded storekeepers some latitude to decline to create specific messages the storekeeper considered offensive. Indeed, while enforcement proceedings against Phillips were ongoing, the Colorado Civil Rights Division itself endorsed this proposition in cases involving other bakers' creation of cakes, concluding on at least three occasions that a baker acted lawfully in declining to create cakes with decorations that demeaned gay persons or gay marriages.

[A]ny decision in favor of the baker would have to be sufficiently constrained, lest all purveyors of goods and services who object to gay marriages for moral and religious reasons in effect be allowed to put up signs saying "no goods or services will be sold if they will be used for gay marriages," something that would impose a serious stigma on gay persons. But, nonetheless, Phillips was entitled to the neutral and respectful consideration of his claims in all the circumstances of the case.

D. Supreme Court Decisions Since Employment Division v. Smith

The neutral and respectful consideration to which Phillips was entitled was compromised here, however. The Civil Rights Commission's treatment of his case has some elements of a clear and impermissible hostility toward the sincere religious beliefs that motivated his objection.

That hostility surfaced at the Commission's formal, public hearings, as shown by the record. On May 30, 2014, the seven-member Commission convened publicly to consider Phillips' case. At several points during its meeting, commissioners endorsed the view that religious beliefs cannot legitimately be carried into the public sphere or commercial domain, implying that religious beliefs and persons are less than fully welcome in Colorado's business community. One commissioner suggested that Phillips can believe "what he wants to believe," but cannot act on his religious beliefs "if he decides to do business in the state." A few moments later, the commissioner restated the same position: "[I]f a businessman wants to do business in the state and he's got an issue with the—the law's impacting his personal belief system, he needs to look at being able to compromise." Standing alone, these statements are susceptible of different interpretations. On the one hand, they might mean simply that a business cannot refuse to provide services based on sexual orientation, regardless of the proprietor's personal views. On the other hand, they might be seen as inappropriate and dismissive comments showing lack of due consideration for Phillips' free exercise rights and the dilemma he faced. In view of the comments that followed, the latter seems the more likely.

On July 25, 2014, the Commission met again. This meeting, too, was conducted in public and on the record. On this occasion another commissioner made specific reference to the previous meeting's discussion but said far more to disparage Phillips' beliefs. The commissioner stated:

> "I would also like to reiterate what we said in the hearing or the last meeting. Freedom of religion and religion has been used to justify all kinds of discrimination throughout history, whether it be slavery, whether it be the holocaust, whether it be—I mean, we—we can list hundreds of situations where freedom of religion has been used to justify discrimination. And to me it is one of the most despicable pieces of rhetoric that people can use to—to use their religion to hurt others."

To describe a man's faith as "one of the most despicable pieces of rhetoric that people can use" is to disparage his religion in at least two distinct ways: by describing it as despicable, and also by characterizing it as merely rhetorical—something insubstantial and even insincere. The commissioner even went so far as to compare Phillips' invocation of his sincerely held religious beliefs to defenses of slavery and the Holocaust. This sentiment is inappropriate for a Commission charged with the solemn responsibility of fair and neutral enforcement of Colorado's antidiscrimination law—a law that protects against discrimination on the basis of religion as well as sexual orientation.

The record shows no objection to these comments from other commissioners. And the later state-court ruling reviewing the Commission's decision did not mention those comments, much less express concern with their content. Nor were the comments by the commissioners disavowed in the briefs filed in this Court. For these reasons, the Court cannot avoid the conclusion that these statements cast doubt on the fairness and impartiality of the Commission's adjudication of Phillips' case. Members of the Court have disagreed on the question whether statements made by lawmakers may properly be taken into account in determining whether a law intentionally discriminates on the basis of religion. In this case, however, the remarks were made in a very different context—by an adjudicatory body deciding a particular case.

Another indication of hostility is the difference in treatment between Phillips' case and the cases of other bakers who objected to a requested cake on the basis of conscience and prevailed before the Commission. As noted above, on at least three other occasions the Civil Rights Division considered the refusal of bakers to create cakes with images that conveyed disapproval of same-sex marriage, along with religious text. Each time, the Division found that the baker acted lawfully in refusing service. It made these determinations because, in the words of the Division, the requested cake included "wording and images [the baker] deemed derogatory," featured "language and images [the baker] deemed hateful," or displayed a message the baker "deemed as discriminatory[.]"

The treatment of the conscience-based objections at issue in these three cases contrasts with the Commission's treatment of Phillips' objection. The Commission ruled against Phillips in part on the theory that any message the requested wedding cake would carry would be attributed to the customer, not to the baker. Yet the Division did not address this point in any of the other cases with respect to the cakes depicting anti-gay marriage symbolism. Additionally, the Division found no violation of CADA in the other cases in part because each bakery was willing to sell other products, including those depicting Christian themes, to the prospective customers. But the Commission dismissed Phillips' willingness to sell "birthday cakes, shower cakes, [and] cookies and brownies," to gay and lesbian customers as irrelevant. The treatment of the other cases and Phillips' case could reasonably be interpreted as being inconsistent as to the question of whether speech is involved, quite apart from whether the cases should ultimately be distinguished. In short, the Commission's consideration of Phillips' religious objection did not accord with its treatment of these other objections.

For the reasons just described, the Commission's treatment of Phillips' case violated the State's duty under the First Amendment not to base laws or regulations on hostility to a religion or religious viewpoint. In view of these factors the record here demonstrates that the Commission's consideration of Phillips' case was neither tolerant nor respectful of Phillips' religious beliefs. The Commission gave "every appearance," of adjudicating Phillips' religious objection based on a negative normative "evaluation of the particular justification" for his objection and the religious grounds for it. It hardly requires restating that government has no role in deciding or even suggesting whether the religious ground for Phillips' conscience-based objection is legitimate or illegitimate. On these facts, the Court must draw the inference that Phillips' religious objection was not considered with the neutrality that the Free Exercise Clause requires.

While the issues here are difficult to resolve, it must be concluded that the State's interest could have been weighed against Phillips' sincere religious objections in a way consistent with the requisite religious neutrality that must be strictly observed. The official expressions of hostility to religion in some of the commissioners' comments—comments that were not disavowed at the Commission or by the State at any point in the proceedings that led to affirmance of the order—were inconsistent with what the Free Exercise Clause requires. The Commission's disparate consideration of Phillips' case compared to the cases of the other bakers suggests the same. For these reasons, the order must be set aside.

III

The Commission's hostility was inconsistent with the First Amendment's guarantee that our laws be applied in a manner that is neutral toward religion. Phillips was entitled to a neutral decisionmaker who would give full and fair consideration to his religious objection as he sought to assert it in all of the circumstances in which this case was presented, considered, and decided. However later cases raising these or similar concerns are resolved in the future, for these reasons the rulings of the Commission and of the state court that enforced the Commission's order must be invalidated.

The outcome of cases like this in other circumstances must await further elaboration in the courts, all in the context of recognizing that these disputes must be resolved with tolerance, without undue disrespect to sincere religious beliefs, and without subjecting gay persons to indignities when they seek goods and services in an open market.

Justice GORSUCH, with whom Justice ALITO joins, concurring.

In Employment Div., Dept. of Human Resources of Ore. v. Smith, this Court held that a neutral and generally applicable law will usually survive a constitutional free exercise challenge. *Smith* remains controversial in many quarters. But we know this with certainty: when the government fails to act neutrally toward the free exercise of religion, it tends to run into trouble. Then the government can prevail only if it satisfies strict scrutiny, showing that its restrictions on religion both serve a compelling interest and are narrowly tailored.

Today's decision respects these principles. As the Court explains, the Colorado Civil Rights Commission failed to act neutrally toward Jack Phillips's religious faith. Maybe most notably, the Commission allowed three other bakers to refuse a customer's request that would have required them to violate their secular commitments. Yet it denied the same accommodation to Mr. Phillips when he refused a customer's request that would have required him to violate his religious beliefs. As the Court also explains, the only reason the Commission seemed to supply for its discrimination was that it found Mr. Phillips's religious beliefs "offensive." That kind of judgmental dismissal of a sincerely held religious belief is, of course, antithetical to the First Amendment and cannot begin to satisfy strict scrutiny. The Constitution protects not just popular religious exercises from the condemnation of civil authorities. It protects them all.

Justice THOMAS, with whom Justice GORSUCH joins, concurring in part and concurring in the judgment.

I agree that the Colorado Civil Rights Commission (Commission) violated Jack Phillips' right to freely exercise his religion. While Phillips rightly prevails on his free-exercise claim, I write separately to address his free-speech claim. The Court does not address this claim because it has some uncertainties about the record.

The conduct that the Colorado Court of Appeals ascribed to Phillips—creating and designing custom wedding cakes—is expressive. Phillips considers himself an artist. The logo for Masterpiece Cakeshop is an artist's paint palette with a paintbrush and baker's whisk. Behind the counter Phillips has a picture that depicts him as an artist painting on a canvas. Phillips takes exceptional care with each cake that he creates—sketching the design out on paper, choosing the color scheme, creating the frosting and decorations, baking and sculpting the cake, decorating it, and delivering it to the wedding. Examples of his creations can be seen on Masterpiece's website.

Phillips is an active participant in the wedding celebration. He sits down with each couple for a consultation before he creates their custom wedding cake. He discusses their preferences, their personalities, and the details of their wedding to ensure that each cake reflects the couple who ordered it. In addition to creating and delivering the cake—a focal point of the wedding celebration—Phillips sometimes stays and interacts with the guests at the wedding. And the guests often recognize his creations and seek his bakery out afterward. Phillips also sees the inherent symbolism in wedding cakes. To him, a wedding cake inherently communicates that "a wedding has occurred, a marriage has begun, and the couple should be celebrated."

Wedding cakes do, in fact, communicate this message. A tradition from Victorian England that made its way to America after the Civil War, "[w]edding cakes are so packed with symbolism that it is hard to know where to begin." If an average person walked into a room and saw a white, multi-tiered cake, he would immediately know that he had stumbled upon a wedding. The cake is "so standardised and inevitable a part of getting married that few ever think to question it." Almost no wedding, no matter how spartan, is missing the cake.

Accordingly, Phillips' creation of custom wedding cakes is expressive. The use of his artistic talents to create a well-recognized symbol that celebrates the beginning of a marriage clearly communicates a message—certainly more so than nude dancing, or flying a plain red flag. By forcing Phillips to create custom wedding cakes for same-sex weddings, Colorado's public-accommodations law "alter[s] the expressive content" of his message. Forcing Phillips to make custom wedding cakes for same-sex marriages requires him to, at the very least, acknowledge that same-sex weddings are "weddings" and suggest that they should be celebrated—the precise message he believes his faith forbids. The First Amendment prohibits Colorado from requiring Phillips to "bear witness to [these] fact[s]," or to "affir[m] . . . a belief with which [he] disagrees."

Justice GINSBURG, with whom Justice SOTOMAYOR joins, dissenting.

There is much in the Court's opinion with which I agree. "[I]t is a general rule that [religious and philosophical] objections do not allow business owners and other actors in the economy and in society to deny protected persons equal access to goods and services under a neutral and generally applicable public accommodations law." "Colorado law can protect gay persons, just as it can protect other classes of individuals, in acquiring whatever products and services they choose on the same terms and conditions as are offered to other members of the public." "[P]urveyors of goods and services who object to gay marriages for moral and religious reasons [may not] put up signs saying 'no goods or services will be sold if they will be used for gay marriages.'" Gay persons may be spared from "indignities when they seek goods and services in an open market."

D. Supreme Court Decisions Since Employment Division v. Smith

I strongly disagree, however, with the Court's conclusion that Craig and Mullins should lose this case. All of the above-quoted statements point in the opposite direction.

The Court concludes that "Phillips' religious objection was not considered with the neutrality that the Free Exercise Clause requires." This conclusion rests on evidence said to show the Colorado Civil Rights Commission's (Commission) hostility to religion. Hostility is discernible, the Court maintains, from the asserted "disparate consideration of Phillips' case compared to the cases of" three other bakers who refused to make cakes requested by William Jack. The Court also finds hostility in statements made at two public hearings on Phillips' appeal to the Commission. The different outcomes the Court features do not evidence hostility to religion of the kind we have previously held to signal a free-exercise violation, nor do the comments by one or two members of one of the four decisionmaking entities considering this case justify reversing the judgment below.

The Court concludes that "the Commission's consideration of Phillips' religious objection did not accord with its treatment of [the other bakers'] objections." But the cases the Court aligns are hardly comparable. The bakers would have refused to make a cake with Jack's requested message for any customer, regardless of his or her religion. And the bakers visited by Jack would have sold him any baked goods they would have sold anyone else. The bakeries' refusal to make Jack cakes of a kind they would not make for any customer scarcely resembles Phillips' refusal to serve Craig and Mullins: Phillips would *not* sell to Craig and Mullins, for no reason other than their sexual orientation, a cake of the kind he regularly sold to others. When a couple contacts a bakery for a wedding cake, the product they are seeking is a cake celebrating *their* wedding—not a cake celebrating heterosexual weddings or same-sex weddings—and that is the service Craig and Mullins were denied. Colorado, the Court does not gainsay, prohibits precisely the discrimination Craig and Mullins encountered. Jack, on the other hand, suffered no service refusal on the basis of his religion or any other protected characteristic. He was treated as any other customer would have been treated—no better, no worse.

The fact that Phillips might sell other cakes and cookies to gay and lesbian customers was irrelevant to the issue Craig and Mullins' case presented. What matters is that Phillips would not provide a good or service to a same-sex couple that he would provide to a heterosexual couple. In contrast, the other bakeries' sale of other goods to Christian customers was relevant: It shows that there were no goods the bakeries would sell to a non-Christian customer that they would refuse to sell to a Christian customer.

Statements made at the Commission's public hearings on Phillips' case provide no firmer support for the Court's holding today. Whatever one may think of the statements in historical context, I see no reason why the comments of one or two Commissioners should be taken to overcome Phillips' refusal to sell a wedding cake to Craig and Mullins. The proceedings involved several layers of independent decisionmaking, of which the Commission was but one. First, the Division had to find probable cause that Phillips violated CADA. Second, the ALJ entertained the parties' cross-motions for summary judgment. Third, the Commission heard Phillips' appeal. Fourth, after the Commission's ruling, the Colorado Court of Appeals considered the case *de novo*. What prejudice infected the determinations of the adjudicators in the case before and after the Commission? The Court does not say. Phillips' case is thus far removed from the only precedent upon which the Court relies, Church of Lukumi Babalu Aye, Inc. v. Hialeah (1993), where the government action that violated a principle of religious neutrality implicated a sole decisionmaking body, the city council.

The Court in *Masterpiece Cakeshop* left open the underlying question: Does it violate free exercise of religion or freedom of speech to hold a business liable when it refuses to serve a same-sex couple because of the business owner's religious beliefs? Lower courts have considered this in the context of photographers, florists, bakeries, and stationery stores. One of these cases is likely to be soon taken by the Supreme Court.

2. Interfering with Choices as to Clergy and Teachers

Another instance where the Court found a violation of free exercise of religion was Hosanna-Tabor Evangelical Lutheran Church and School v. EEOC, 565 U.S. 171 (2012). The Court held that it would violate the Free Exercise Clause, as well as the Establishment Clause, to hold a religious institution liable under an antidiscrimination law for the choices it makes as to who will be its ministers. The case involved a teacher at a religious elementary school who was fired for insubordination when the school thought she might sue them under the Americans with Disability Act after she lost her job when she developed a serious illness.

The Court found that holding the religious institution liable for choices it makes as to who will be its ministers infringes the Free Exercise Clause. Chief Justice Roberts, writing for a unanimous Court, distinguished Employment Division v. Smith:

> By imposing an unwanted minister, the state infringes the Free Exercise Clause, which protects a religious group's right to shape its own faith and mission through its appointments.
>
> The [Equal Employment Opportunity Commission and the teacher] also contend that our decision in Employment Div., Dept. of Human Resources of Ore. v. Smith (1990), precludes recognition of a ministerial exception. It is true that the ADA's prohibition on retaliation, like Oregon's prohibition on peyote use, is a valid and neutral law of general applicability. But a church's selection of its ministers is unlike an individual's ingestion of peyote. *Smith* involved government regulation of only outward physical acts. The present case, in contrast, concerns government interference with an internal church decision that affects the faith and mission of the church itself. The contention that *Smith* forecloses recognition of a ministerial exception rooted in the Religion Clauses has no merit.

In 2020, the Court went further and held that it violated free exercise of religion to hold a religious school liable for the choices it makes as to its teachers, at least when they have some involvement in teaching religion.

OUR LADY OF GUADALUPE SCHOOL v. MORRISSEY-BERRU
140 S. Ct. 2049 (2020)

Justice ALITO delivered the opinion of the Court.

These cases require us to decide whether the First Amendment permits courts to intervene in employment disputes involving teachers at religious schools who are entrusted with the responsibility of instructing their students in the faith. The First Amendment protects the right of religious institutions "to decide for themselves, free from state interference, matters of church government as well as those of faith and doctrine."

Applying this principle, we held in *Hosanna-Tabor Evangelical Lutheran Church and School v. EEOC* (2012), that the First Amendment barred a court from entertaining an employment discrimination claim brought by an elementary school teacher, Cheryl Perich, against the religious school where she taught. Our decision built on a line of lower court cases adopting what was dubbed the "ministerial exception" to laws governing the employment relationship between a religious institution and certain key employees. We did not announce "a rigid formula" for determining whether an employee falls within this exception, but we identified circumstances that we found relevant in that case, including Perich's title as a "Minister of Religion, Commissioned," her educational training, and her responsibility to teach religion and participate with students in religious activities.

In the cases now before us, we consider employment discrimination claims brought by two elementary school teachers at Catholic schools whose teaching responsibilities are similar to Perich's. Although these teachers were not given the title of "minister" and have less religious training than Perich, we hold that their cases fall within the same rule that dictated our decision in *Hosanna-Tabor*. The religious education and formation of students is the very reason for the existence of most private religious schools, and therefore the selection and supervision of the teachers upon whom the schools rely to do this work lie at the core of their mission. Judicial review of the way in which religious schools discharge those responsibilities would undermine the independence of religious institutions in a way that the First Amendment does not tolerate.

I

The first of the two cases we now decide involves Agnes Morrissey-Berru, who was employed at Our Lady of Guadalupe School (OLG), a Roman Catholic primary school in the Archdiocese of Los Angeles. For many years, Morrissey-Berru was employed at OLG as a lay fifth or sixth grade teacher. Like most elementary school teachers, she taught all subjects, and since OLG is a Catholic school, the curriculum included religion. As a result, she was her students' religion teacher.

Morrissey-Berru earned a B.A. in English Language Arts, with a minor in secondary education, and she holds a California teaching credential. While on the faculty at OLG, she took religious education courses at the school's request, and was expected to attend faculty prayer services.

Each year, Morrissey-Berru and OLG entered into an employment agreement that set out the school's "mission" and Morrissey-Berru's duties. The agreement stated that the school's mission was "to develop and promote a Catholic School Faith Community," and it informed Morrissey-Berru that "[a]ll [her] duties and responsibilities as a Teache[r were to] be performed within this overriding commitment." The agreement explained that the school's hiring and retention decisions would be guided by its Catholic mission, and the agreement made clear that teachers were expected to "model and promote" Catholic "faith and morals." Under the agreement, Morrissey-Berru was required to participate in "[s]chool liturgical activities, as requested," and the agreement specified that she could be terminated "for 'cause'" for failing to carry out these duties or for "conduct that brings discredit upon the School or the Roman Catholic Church." The agreement required compliance with the faculty handbook, which sets out similar expectations. The pastor of the parish, a Catholic priest, had to approve Morrissey-Berru's hiring each year.

Like all teachers in the Archdiocese of Los Angeles, Morrissey-Berru was "considered a catechist," *i.e.*, "a teacher of religio[n]." Catechists are "responsible for the faith formation of the students in their charge each day." Morrissey-Berru provided religious instruction every day using a textbook designed for use in teaching religion to young Catholic students. Under the prescribed curriculum, she was expected to teach students, among other things, "to learn and express belief that Jesus is the son of God and the Word made flesh"; to "identify the ways" the church "carries on the mission of Jesus"; to "locate, read and understand stories from the Bible"; to "know the names, meanings, signs and symbols of each of the seven sacraments"; and to be able to "explain the communion of saints." She tested her students on that curriculum in a yearly exam. *Id.*, at 87a. She also directed and produced an annual passion play.

Morrissey-Berru prepared her students for participation in the Mass and for communion and confession. She also occasionally selected and prepared students to read at Mass. And she was expected to take her students to Mass once a week and on certain feast days, and to take them to confession and to pray the Stations of the Cross. Each year, she brought them to the Catholic Cathedral in Los Angeles, where they participated as altar servers.

Morrissey-Berru also prayed with her students. Her class began or ended every day with a Hail Mary. She led the students in prayer at other times, such as when a family member was ill. And she taught them to recite the Apostle's Creed and the Nicene Creed, as well as prayers for specific purposes, such as in connection with the sacrament of confession. The school reviewed Morrissey-Berru's performance under religious standards. The "Classroom Observation Report" evaluated whether Catholic values were "infused through all subject areas" and whether there were religious signs and displays in the classroom.

In 2014, OLG asked Morrissey-Berru to move from a full-time to a part-time position, and the next year, the school declined to renew her contract. She filed a claim with the Equal Employment Opportunity Commission (EEOC), received a right-to-sue letter, and then filed suit under the Age Discrimination in Employment Act of 1967, claiming that the school had demoted her and had failed to renew her contract so that it could replace her with a younger teacher. The school maintains that it based its decisions on classroom performance—specifically, Morrissey-Berru's difficulty in administering a new reading and writing program, which had been introduced by the school's new principal as part of an effort to maintain accreditation and improve the school's academic program.

D. Supreme Court Decisions Since Employment Division v. Smith

The second case concerns the late Kristen Biel, who worked for about a year and a half as a lay teacher at St. James School, another Catholic primary school in Los Angeles. For part of one academic year, Biel served as a long-term substitute teacher for a first grade class, and for one full year she was a full-time fifth grade teacher. Like Morrissey-Berru, she taught all subjects, including religion.

During her time at St. James, she attended a religious conference that imparted "[d]ifferent techniques on teaching and incorporating God" into the classroom. Biel was Catholic. Biel's employment agreement was in pertinent part nearly identical to Morrissey-Berru's.

St. James declined to renew Biel's contract after one full year at the school. She filed charges with the EEOC, and after receiving a right-to-sue letter, brought this suit, alleging that she was discharged because she had requested a leave of absence to obtain treatment for breast cancer. The school maintains that the decision was based on poor performance—namely, a failure to observe the planned curriculum and keep an orderly classroom.

II

The First Amendment provides that "Congress shall make no law respecting an establishment of religion, or prohibiting the free exercise thereof." Among other things, the Religion Clauses protect the right of churches and other religious institutions to decide matters "of faith and doctrine" without government intrusion. State interference in that sphere would obviously violate the free exercise of religion, and any attempt by government to dictate or even to influence such matters would constitute one of the central attributes of an establishment of religion. The First Amendment outlaws such intrusion.

The independence of religious institutions in matters of "faith and doctrine" is closely linked to independence in what we have termed "'matters of church government.'" This does not mean that religious institutions enjoy a general immunity from secular laws, but it does protect their autonomy with respect to internal management decisions that are essential to the institution's central mission. And a component of this autonomy is the selection of the individuals who play certain key roles.

The "ministerial exception" was based on this insight. Under this rule, courts are bound to stay out of employment disputes involving those holding certain important positions with churches and other religious institutions. The rule appears to have acquired the label "ministerial exception" because the individuals involved in pioneering cases were described as "ministers." But it is instructive to consider why a church's independence on matters "of faith and doctrine" requires the authority to select, supervise, and if necessary, remove a minister without interference by secular authorities. Without that power, a wayward minister's preaching, teaching, and counseling could contradict the church's tenets and lead the congregation away from the faith. The ministerial exception was recognized to preserve a church's independent authority in such matters.

When the so-called ministerial exception finally reached this Court in *Hosanna-Tabor*, we unanimously recognized that the Religion Clauses foreclose certain employment discrimination claims brought against religious organizations. The constitutional foundation for our holding was the general principle of church autonomy to which we have already referred: independence in matters of faith and doctrine and in closely linked matters of internal government. Because Cheryl Perich, the teacher in *Hosanna-Tabor*, had a title that included the word "minister," we naturally concentrated on historical events involving clerical offices, but the abuses we identified were not limited to the control of appointments.

In determining whether a particular position falls within the *Hosanna-Tabor* exception, a variety of factors may be important. The circumstances that informed our decision in *Hosanna-Tabor* were relevant because of their relationship to Perich's "role in conveying the Church's message and carrying out its mission," but the other noted circumstances also shed light on that connection. In a denomination that uses the term "minister," conferring that title naturally suggests that the recipient has been given an important position of trust. In Perich's case, the title that she was awarded and used demanded satisfaction of significant academic requirements and was conferred only after a formal approval process, and those circumstances also evidenced the importance attached to her role. But our recognition of the significance of those factors in Perich's case did not mean that they must be met—or even that they are necessarily important—in all other cases.

Take the question of the title "minister." Simply giving an employee the title of "minister" is not enough to justify the exception. And by the same token, since many religious traditions do not use the title "minister," it cannot be a necessary requirement. Requiring the use of the title would constitute impermissible discrimination, and this problem cannot be solved simply by including positions that are thought to be the counterparts of a "minister," such as priests, nuns, rabbis, and imams. Nuns are not the same as Protestant ministers. A brief submitted by Jewish organizations makes the point that "Judaism has many 'ministers,'" that is, "the term 'minister' encompasses an extensive breadth of religious functionaries in Judaism." For Muslims, "an inquiry into whether imams or other leaders bear a title equivalent to 'minister' can present a troubling choice between denying a central pillar of Islam—*i.e.*, the equality of all believers—and risking loss of ministerial exception protections."

If titles were all-important, courts would have to decide which titles count and which do not, and it is hard to see how that could be done without looking behind the titles to what the positions actually entail. Moreover, attaching too much significance to titles would risk privileging religious traditions with formal organizational structures over those that are less formal.

For related reasons, the academic requirements of a position may show that the church in question regards the position as having an important responsibility in elucidating or teaching the tenets of the faith. Presumably the purpose of such requirements is to make sure that the person holding the position understands the faith and can explain it accurately and effectively. But insisting in every case on rigid academic requirements could have a distorting effect. This is certainly true with respect to teachers. Teaching children in an elementary school does not demand the same formal religious education as teaching theology to divinity students. Elementary school teachers often teach secular subjects in which they have little if any special training. In addition, religious traditions may differ in the degree of formal religious training thought to be needed in order to teach. In short, these circumstances, while instructive in *Hosanna-Tabor*, are not inflexible requirements and may have far less significance in some cases.

D. Supreme Court Decisions Since Employment Division v. Smith

What matters, at bottom, is what an employee does. And implicit in our decision in *Hosanna-Tabor* was a recognition that educating young people in their faith, inculcating its teachings, and training them to live their faith are responsibilities that lie at the very core of the mission of a private religious school. As we put it, Perich had been entrusted with the responsibility of "transmitting the Lutheran faith to the next generation."

When we apply this understanding of the Religion Clauses to the cases now before us, it is apparent that Morrissey-Berru and Biel qualify for the exemption we recognized in *Hosanna-Tabor*. There is abundant record evidence that they both performed vital religious duties. Educating and forming students in the Catholic faith lay at the core of the mission of the schools where they taught, and their employment agreements and faculty handbooks specified in no uncertain terms that they were expected to help the schools carry out this mission and that their work would be evaluated to ensure that they were fulfilling that responsibility. As elementary school teachers responsible for providing instruction in all subjects, including religion, they were the members of the school staff who were entrusted most directly with the responsibility of educating their students in the faith. And not only were they obligated to provide instruction about the Catholic faith, but they were also expected to guide their students, by word and deed, toward the goal of living their lives in accordance with the faith. They prayed with their students, attended Mass with the students, and prepared the children for their participation in other religious activities. Their positions did not have all the attributes of Perich's. Their titles did not include the term "minister," and they had less formal religious training, but their core responsibilities as teachers of religion were essentially the same. And both their schools expressly saw them as playing a vital part in carrying out the mission of the church, and the schools' definition and explanation of their roles is important. In a country with the religious diversity of the United States, judges cannot be expected to have a complete understanding and appreciation of the role played by every person who performs a particular role in every religious tradition. A religious institution's explanation of the role of such employees in the life of the religion in question is important.

Respondents argue that the *Hosanna-Tabor* exception is not workable unless it is given a rigid structure, but we declined to adopt a "rigid formula" in *Hosanna-Tabor*, and the lower courts have been applying the exception for many years without such a formula. Here, as in *Hosanna-Tabor*, it is sufficient to decide the cases before us. When a school with a religious mission entrusts a teacher with the responsibility of educating and forming students in the faith, judicial intervention into disputes between the school and the teacher threatens the school's independence in a way that the First Amendment does not allow.

Justice THOMAS, with whom Justice GORSUCH joins, concurring.

I agree with the Court that Morrissey-Berru's and Biel's positions fall within the "ministerial exception," because, as Catholic school teachers, they are charged with "carry[ing] out [the religious] mission" of the parish schools. The Court properly notes that "judges have no warrant to second-guess [the schools'] judgment" of who should hold such a position "or to impose their own credentialing requirements." Accordingly, I join the Court's opinion in full. I write separately, however, to reiterate my view that the Religion Clauses require civil courts to defer to religious organizations' good-faith claims that a certain employee's position is "ministerial."

This deference is necessary because, as the Court rightly observes, judges lack the requisite "understanding and appreciation of the role played by every person who performs a particular role in every religious tradition." What qualifies as "ministerial" is an inherently theological question, and thus one that cannot be resolved by civil courts through legal analysis. Contrary to the dissent's claim, judges do not shirk their judicial duty or provide a mere "rubber stamp" when they defer to a religious organization's sincere beliefs. Rather, they heed the First Amendment, which "commands civil courts to decide [legal] disputes without resolving underlying controversies over religious doctrine."

Justice SOTOMAYOR, with whom Justice GINSBURG joins, dissenting.

Two employers fired their employees allegedly because one had breast cancer and the other was elderly. Purporting to rely on this Court's decision in *Hosanna-Tabor Evangelical Lutheran Church and School v. EEOC* (2012), the majority shields those employers from disability and age-discrimination claims. In the Court's view, because the employees taught short religion modules at Catholic elementary schools, they were "ministers" of the Catholic faith and thus could be fired for any reason, whether religious or nonreligious, benign or bigoted, without legal recourse. The Court reaches this result even though the teachers taught primarily secular subjects, lacked substantial religious titles and training, and were not even required to be Catholic. In foreclosing the teachers' claims, the Court skews the facts, ignores the applicable standard of review, and collapses *Hosanna-Tabor*'s careful analysis into a single consideration: whether a church thinks its employees play an important religious role. Because that simplistic approach has no basis in law and strips thousands of schoolteachers of their legal protections, I respectfully dissent.

I

Our pluralistic society requires religious entities to abide by generally applicable laws. *E.g., Employment Div., Dept. of Human Resources of Ore. v. Smith* (1990). Consistent with the First Amendment (and over sincerely held religious objections), the Government may compel religious institutions to pay Social Security taxes for their employees, deny nonprofit status to entities that discriminate because of race, require applicants for certain public benefits to register with Social Security numbers, enforce child-labor protections, and impose minimum-wage laws.

Congress, however, has crafted exceptions to protect religious autonomy. Some antidiscrimination laws, like the Americans with Disabilities Act, permit a religious institution to consider religion when making employment decisions. Under that Act, a religious organization may also "require that all applicants and employees conform" to the entity's "religious tenets." Title VII further permits a school to prefer "hir[ing] and employ[ing]" people "of a particular religion" if its curriculum "propagat[es]" that religion. These statutory exceptions protect a religious entity's ability to make employment decisions—hiring or firing—for religious reasons.

D. Supreme Court Decisions Since Employment Division v. Smith

The "ministerial exception," by contrast, is a judge-made doctrine. This Court first recognized it eight years ago in *Hosanna-Tabor*, concluding that the First Amendment categorically bars certain antidiscrimination suits by religious leaders against their religious employers. When it applies, the exception is extraordinarily potent: It gives an employer free rein to discriminate because of race, sex, pregnancy, age, disability, or other traits protected by law when selecting or firing their "ministers," even when the discrimination is wholly unrelated to the employer's religious beliefs or practices. That is, an employer need not cite or possess a religious reason at all; the ministerial exception even condones animus.

This analysis is context-specific. It necessarily turns on, among other things, the structure of the religious organization at issue. Put another way (and as the Court repeats throughout today's opinion), *Hosanna-Tabor* declined to adopt a "rigid formula for deciding when an employee qualifies as a minister." Rather, *Hosanna-Tabor* focused on four "circumstances" to determine whether a fourth-grade teacher, Cheryl Perich, was employed at a Lutheran school as a "minister": (1) "the formal title given [her] by the Church," (2) "the substance reflected in that title," (3) "her own use of that title," and (4) "the important religious functions she performed for the Church." Confirming that the ministerial exception applies to a circumscribed sub-category of faith leaders, the Court analyzed those four "factors," to situate Perich as a minister within the Lutheran Church's structure. Those considerations showed that Perich had a unique leadership role within her church.

II

Until today, no court had held that the ministerial exception applies with disputed facts like these and lay teachers like respondents, let alone at the summary-judgment stage.

Only by rewriting *Hosanna-Tabor* does the Court reach a different result. Today's Court yields to the concurrence's view with identical rhetoric. "What matters," the Court echoes, "is what an employee does."

But this vague statement is no easier to comprehend today than it was when the Court declined to adopt it eight years ago. It certainly does not sound like a legal framework. Rather, the Court insists that a "religious institution's explanation of the role of [its] employees in the life of the religion in question is important." But because the Court's new standard prizes a functional importance that it appears to deem churches in the best position to explain, one cannot help but conclude that the Court has just traded legal analysis for a rubber stamp.

Indeed, the Court reasons that "judges cannot be expected to have a complete understanding and appreciation" of the law and facts in ministerial-exception cases, and all but abandons judicial review. Although today's decision is limited to certain "teachers of religion," its reasoning risks rendering almost every Catholic parishioner and parent in the Archdiocese of Los Angeles a Catholic minister. That is, the Court's apparent deference here threatens to make nearly anyone whom the schools might hire "ministers" unprotected from discrimination in the hiring process. That cannot be right. Although certain religious functions may be important to a church, a person's performance of some of those functions does not mechanically trigger a categorical exemption from generally applicable antidiscrimination laws.

Today's decision thus invites the "potential for abuse" against which circuit courts have long warned. Nevermind that the Court renders almost all of the Court's opinion in *Hosanna-Tabor* irrelevant. It risks allowing employers to decide for themselves whether discrimination is actionable. Indeed, today's decision reframes the ministerial exception as broadly as it can, without regard to the statutory exceptions tailored to protect religious practice. As a result, the Court absolves religious institutions of any animus completely irrelevant to their religious beliefs or practices and all but forbids courts to inquire further about whether the employee is in fact a leader of the religion. Nothing in *Hosanna-Tabor* (or at least its majority opinion) condones such judicial abdication.

III

The Court's conclusion portends grave consequences. As the Government (arguing for Biel at the time) explained to the Ninth Circuit, "thousands of Catholic teachers" may lose employment-law protections because of today's outcome. Other sources tally over a hundred thousand secular teachers whose rights are at risk. And that says nothing of the rights of countless coaches, camp counselors, nurses, social-service workers, in-house lawyers, media-relations personnel, and many others who work for religious institutions. All these employees could be subject to discrimination for reasons completely irrelevant to their employers' religious tenets.

In expanding the ministerial exception far beyond its historic narrowness, the Court overrides Congress' carefully tailored exceptions for religious employers. Little if nothing appears left of the statutory exemptions after today's constitutional broadside. So long as the employer determines that an employee's "duties" are "vital" to "carrying out the mission of the church," then today's laissez-faire analysis appears to allow that employer to make employment decisions because of a person's skin color, age, disability, sex, or any other protected trait for reasons having nothing to do with religion.

This sweeping result is profoundly unfair. The Court is not only wrong on the facts, but its error also risks upending antidiscrimination protections for many employees of religious entities. Recently, this Court has lamented a perceived "discrimination against religion." Yet here it swings the pendulum in the extreme opposite direction, permitting religious entities to discriminate widely and with impunity for reasons wholly divorced from religious beliefs. The inherent injustice in the Court's conclusion will be impossible to ignore for long, particularly in a pluralistic society like ours. One must hope that a decision deft enough to remold *Hosanna-Tabor* to fit the result reached today reflects the Court's capacity to cabin the consequences tomorrow.

3. *Denial of Funding to Religious Entities*

Does it violate free exercise of religion for the government to deny funding to a religious entity that it provides to a private secular entity? Initially, in Locke v. Davey, the Court rejected a free exercise challenge. Subsequently, in Trinity

D. Supreme Court Decisions Since Employment Division v. Smith

Lutheran v. Comer, the Court found a free exercise violation. Most recently, in Espinoza v. Montana Department of Revenue, the Court expanded on this and the government's duty to fund religious schools when it funds secular private schools.

LOCKE v. DAVEY
540 U.S. 714 (2004)

Chief Justice REHNQUIST delivered the opinion of the Court.

The State of Washington established the Promise Scholarship Program to assist academically gifted students with postsecondary education expenses. In accordance with the State Constitution, students may not use the scholarship at an institution where they are pursuing a degree in devotional theology. We hold that such an exclusion from an otherwise inclusive aid program does not violate the Free Exercise Clause of the First Amendment.

To be eligible for the scholarship, a student must meet academic, income, and enrollment requirements. The student must enroll "at least half time in an eligible postsecondary institution in the state of Washington," and may not pursue a degree in theology at that institution while receiving the scholarship. Private institutions, including those religiously affiliated, qualify as "eligible postsecondary institution[s]" if they are accredited by a nationally recognized accrediting body. A "degree in theology" is not defined in the statute, but, as both parties concede, the statute simply codifies the State's constitutional prohibition on providing funds to students to pursue degrees that are "devotional in nature or designed to induce religious faith."

Respondent, Joshua Davey, was awarded a Promise Scholarship, and chose to attend Northwest College. Northwest is a private, Christian college affiliated with the Assemblies of God denomination, and is an eligible institution under the Promise Scholarship Program. Davey had "planned for many years to attend a Bible college and to prepare [himself] through that college training for a lifetime of ministry, specifically as a church pastor." To that end, when he enrolled in Northwest College, he decided to pursue a double major in pastoral ministries and business management/administration. There is no dispute that the pastoral ministries degree is devotional and therefore excluded under the Promise Scholarship Program.

At the beginning of the 1999-2000 academic year, Davey met with Northwest's director of financial aid. He learned for the first time at this meeting that he could not use his scholarship to pursue a devotional theology degree. He was informed that to receive the funds appropriated for his use, he must certify in writing that he was not pursuing such a degree at Northwest. He refused to sign the form and did not receive any scholarship funds.

The Religion Clauses of the First Amendment provide: "Congress shall make no law respecting an establishment of religion, or prohibiting the free exercise thereof." These two Clauses, the Establishment Clause and the Free Exercise Clause, are frequently in tension. Yet we have long said that "there is room for play in the joints" between them. Walz v. Tax Comm'n of City of New York (1970). In other words, there are some state actions permitted by the Establishment Clause but not required by the Free Exercise Clause.

This case involves that "play in the joints" described above. Under our Establishment Clause precedent, the link between government funds and religious training is broken by the independent and private choice of recipients. See Zelman v. Simmons-Harris (2002). As such, there is no doubt that the State could, consistent with the Federal Constitution, permit Promise Scholars to pursue a degree in devotional theology, and the State does not contend otherwise. The question before us, however, is whether Washington, pursuant to its own constitutions,[5] which has been authoritatively interpreted as prohibiting even indirectly funding religious instruction that will prepare students for the ministry, can deny them such funding without violating the Free Exercise Clause.

Even though the differently worded Washington Constitution draws a more stringent line than that drawn by the United States Constitution, the interest it seeks to further is scarcely novel. In fact, we can think of few areas in which a State's antiestablishment interests come more into play. Since the founding of our country, there have been popular uprisings against procuring taxpayer funds to support church leaders, which was one of the hallmarks of an "established" religion. Most States that sought to avoid an establishment of religion around the time of the founding placed in their constitutions formal prohibitions against using tax funds to support the ministry.

Far from evincing the hostility toward religion which was manifest in *Lukumi*, we believe that the entirety of the Promise Scholarship Program goes a long way toward including religion in its benefits. The program permits students to attend pervasively religious schools, so long as they are accredited. And under the Promise Scholarship Program's current guidelines, students are still eligible to take devotional theology courses. Davey notes all students at Northwest are required to take at least four devotional courses, and some students may have additional religious requirements as part of their majors.

In short, we find neither in the history or text of Article I, §11 of the Washington Constitution, nor in the operation of the Promise Scholarship Program, anything that suggests animus towards religion. Given the historic and substantial state interest at issue, we therefore cannot conclude that the denial of funding for vocational religious instruction alone is inherently constitutionally suspect.

Without a presumption of unconstitutionality, Davey's claim must fail. The State's interest in not funding the pursuit of devotional degrees is substantial and the exclusion of such funding places a relatively minor burden on Promise Scholars. If any room exists between the two Religion Clauses, it must be here. We need not venture further into this difficult area in order to uphold the Promise Scholarship Program as currently operated by the State of Washington.

Justice SCALIA, with whom Justice THOMAS joins, dissenting.

When the State makes a public benefit generally available, that benefit becomes part of the baseline against which burdens on religion are measured; and when the State withholds that benefit from some individuals solely on the

---

5. The relevant provision of the Washington Constitution, Art. I, §11, states: "Religious Freedom, Absolute freedom of conscience in all matters of religious sentiment, belief and worship, shall be guaranteed to every individual, and no one shall be molested or disturbed in person or property on account of religion; but the liberty of conscience hereby secured shall not be so construed as to excuse acts of licentiousness or justify practices inconsistent with the peace and safety of the state. No public money or property shall be appropriated for or applied to any religious worship, exercise or instruction, or the support of any religious establishment." [Footnote by the Court.]

D. Supreme Court Decisions Since Employment Division v. Smith

basis of religion, it violates the Free Exercise Clause no less than if it had imposed a special tax. That is precisely what the State of Washington has done here. It has created a generally available public benefit, whose receipt is conditioned only on academic performance, income, and attendance at an accredited school. It has then carved out a solitary course of study for exclusion: theology. No field of study but religion is singled out for disfavor in this fashion. Davey is not asking for a special benefit to which others are not entitled. He seeks only equal treatment—the right to direct his scholarship to his chosen course of study, a right every other Promise Scholar enjoys.

The Court does not dispute that the Free Exercise Clause places some constraints on public benefits programs, but finds none here, based on a principle of "play in the joints." I use the term "principle" loosely, for that is not so much a legal principle as a refusal to apply any principle when faced with competing constitutional directives. There is nothing anomalous about constitutional commands that abut. A municipality hiring public contractors may not discriminate against blacks or in favor of them; it cannot discriminate a little bit each way and then plead "play in the joints" when haled into court. If the Religion Clauses demand neutrality, we must enforce them, in hard cases as well as easy ones.

Even if "play in the joints" were a valid legal principle, surely it would apply only when it was a close call whether complying with one of the Religion Clauses would violate the other. But that is not the case here.

In any case, the State already has all the play in the joints it needs. There are any number of ways it could respect both its unusually sensitive concern for the conscience of its taxpayers and the Federal Free Exercise Clause. It could make the scholarships redeemable only at public universities (where it sets the curriculum), or only for select courses of study. Either option would replace a program that facially discriminates against religion with one that just happens not to subsidize it. The State could also simply abandon the scholarship program altogether. If that seems a dear price to pay for freedom of conscience, it is only because the State has defined that freedom so broadly that it would be offended by a program with such an incidental, indirect religious effect.

What is the nature of the State's asserted interest here? It cannot be protecting the pocketbooks of its citizens; given the tiny fraction of Promise Scholars who would pursue theology degrees, the amount of any citizen's tax bill at stake is de minimis. It cannot be preventing mistaken appearance of endorsement; where a State merely declines to penalize students for selecting a religious major, "[n]o reasonable observer is likely to draw . . . an inference that the State itself is endorsing a religious practice or belief." Nor can Washington's exclusion be defended as a means of assuring that the State will neither favor nor disfavor Davey in his religious calling. Davey will throughout his life contribute to the public fisc through sales taxes on personal purchases, property taxes on his home, and so on; and nothing in the Court's opinion turns on whether Davey winds up a net winner or loser in the State's tax-and-spend scheme.

No, the interest to which the Court defers is not fear of a conceivable Establishment Clause violation, budget constraints, avoidance of endorsement, or substantive neutrality—none of these. It is a pure philosophical preference: the State's opinion that it would violate taxpayers' freedom of conscience not to discriminate against candidates for the ministry. This sort of protection of "freedom of conscience" has no logical limit and can justify the singling out of religion for exclusion from public programs in virtually any context. The Court never says whether it deems this interest compelling (the opinion is devoid of any mention of standard of review) but, self-evidently, it is not.

TRINITY LUTHERAN CHURCH OF COLUMBIA, INC. v. COMER
137 S. Ct. 2012 (2017)

Chief Justice ROBERTS delivered the opinion of the Court, except as to footnote 3.

The Missouri Department of Natural Resources offers state grants to help public and private schools, nonprofit daycare centers, and other nonprofit entities purchase rubber playground surfaces made from recycled tires. Trinity Lutheran Church applied for such a grant for its preschool and daycare center and would have received one, but for the fact that Trinity Lutheran is a church. The Department had a policy of categorically disqualifying churches and other religious organizations from receiving grants under its playground resurfacing program. The question presented is whether the Department's policy violated the rights of Trinity Lutheran under the Free Exercise Clause of the First Amendment.

I

A

The Trinity Lutheran Church Child Learning Center is a preschool and daycare center open throughout the year to serve working families in Boone County, Missouri, and the surrounding area. Established as a nonprofit organization in 1980, the Center merged with Trinity Lutheran Church in 1985 and operates under its auspices on church property. The Center admits students of any religion, and enrollment stands at about 90 children ranging from age two to five.

The Center includes a playground that is equipped with the basic playground essentials: slides, swings, jungle gyms, monkey bars, and sandboxes. Almost the entire surface beneath and surrounding the play equipment is coarse pea gravel. Youngsters, of course, often fall on the playground or tumble from the equipment. And when they do, the gravel can be unforgiving.

In 2012, the Center sought to replace a large portion of the pea gravel with a pour-in-place rubber surface by participating in Missouri's Scrap Tire Program. Run by the State's Department of Natural Resources to reduce the number of used tires destined for landfills and dump sites, the program offers reimbursement grants to qualifying nonprofit organizations that purchase playground surfaces made from recycled tires. It is funded through a fee imposed on the sale of new tires in the State.

Due to limited resources, the Department cannot offer grants to all applicants and so awards them on a competitive basis to those scoring highest based on several criteria, such as the poverty level of the population in the surrounding area and the applicant's plan to promote recycling. When the Center applied, the Department had a strict and express policy of denying grants to any applicant owned or controlled by a church, sect, or other religious entity. That policy, in

D. Supreme Court Decisions Since Employment Division v. Smith

the Department's view, was compelled by Article I, Section 7 of the Missouri Constitution, which provides: "That no money shall ever be taken from the public treasury, directly or indirectly, in aid of any church, sect or denomination of religion, or in aid of any priest, preacher, minister or teacher thereof, as such; and that no preference shall be given to nor any discrimination made against any church, sect or creed of religion, or any form of religious faith or worship."

The Center ranked fifth among the 44 applicants in the 2012 Scrap Tire Program. But despite its high score, the Center was deemed categorically ineligible to receive a grant. In a letter rejecting the Center's application, the program director explained that, under Article I, Section 7 of the Missouri Constitution, the Department could not provide financial assistance directly to a church.

The Department ultimately awarded 14 grants as part of the 2012 program. Because the Center was operated by Trinity Lutheran Church, it did not receive a grant.

B

Trinity Lutheran sued the Director of the Department in Federal District Court. The Church alleged that the Department's failure to approve the Center's application, pursuant to its policy of denying grants to religiously affiliated applicants, violates the Free Exercise Clause of the First Amendment. Trinity Lutheran sought declaratory and injunctive relief prohibiting the Department from discriminating against the Church on that basis in future grant applications.

The District Court granted the Department's motion to dismiss. The Free Exercise Clause, the District Court stated, prohibits the government from outlawing or restricting the exercise of a religious practice; it generally does not prohibit withholding an affirmative benefit on account of religion. The District Court likened the Department's denial of the scrap tire grant to the situation this Court encountered in Locke v. Davey (2004). In that case, we upheld against a free exercise challenge the State of Washington's decision not to fund degrees in devotional theology as part of a state scholarship program. Finding the present case "nearly indistinguishable from *Locke*," the District Court held that the Free Exercise Clause did not require the State to make funds available under the Scrap Tire Program to religious institutions like Trinity Lutheran. The Court of Appeals for the Eighth Circuit affirmed.

II

The First Amendment provides, in part, that "Congress shall make no law respecting an establishment of religion, or prohibiting the free exercise thereof." The parties agree that the Establishment Clause of that Amendment does not prevent Missouri from including Trinity Lutheran in the Scrap Tire Program. That does not, however, answer the question under the Free Exercise Clause, because we have recognized that there is "play in the joints" between what the Establishment Clause permits and the Free Exercise Clause compels.

The Free Exercise Clause "protect[s] religious observers against unequal treatment" and subjects to the strictest scrutiny laws that target the religious for "special disabilities" based on their "religious status." Applying that basic principle, this Court has repeatedly confirmed that denying a generally available benefit solely on account of religious identity imposes a penalty on the free exercise of religion that can be justified only by a state interest "of the highest order."

In Everson v. Board of Education of Ewing, 330 U.S. 1, 67 S. Ct. 504, 91 L. Ed. 711 (1947), for example, we upheld against an Establishment Clause challenge a New Jersey law enabling a local school district to reimburse parents for the public transportation costs of sending their children to public and private schools, including parochial schools. In the course of ruling that the Establishment Clause allowed New Jersey to extend that public benefit to all its citizens regardless of their religious belief, we explained that a State "cannot hamper its citizens in the free exercise of their own religion. Consequently, it cannot exclude individual Catholics, Lutherans, Mohammedans, Baptists, Jews, Methodists, Non-believers, Presbyterians, or the members of any other faith, *because of their faith, or lack of it,* from receiving the benefits of public welfare legislation."

III

A

The Department's policy expressly discriminates against otherwise eligible recipients by disqualifying them from a public benefit solely because of their religious character. If the cases just described make one thing clear, it is that such a policy imposes a penalty on the free exercise of religion that triggers the most exacting scrutiny. This conclusion is unremarkable in light of our prior decisions.

The Department contends that merely declining to extend funds to Trinity Lutheran does not *prohibit* the Church from engaging in any religious conduct or otherwise exercising its religious rights. Here the Department has simply declined to allocate to Trinity Lutheran a subsidy the State had no obligation to provide in the first place. That decision does not meaningfully burden the Church's free exercise rights. And absent any such burden, the argument continues, the Department is free to heed the State's antiestablishment objection to providing funds directly to a church.

It is true the Department has not criminalized the way Trinity Lutheran worships or told the Church that it cannot subscribe to a certain view of the Gospel. But, as the Department itself acknowledges, the Free Exercise Clause protects against "indirect coercion or penalties on the free exercise of religion, not just outright prohibitions." As the Court put it more than 50 years ago, "[i]t is too late in the day to doubt that the liberties of religion and expression may be infringed by the denial of or placing of conditions upon a benefit or privilege."

Trinity Lutheran is not claiming any entitlement to a subsidy. It instead asserts a right to participate in a government benefit program without having to disavow its religious character. The "imposition of such a condition upon even a gratuitous benefit inevitably deter[s] or discourage[s] the exercise of First Amendment rights." The express discrimination against religious exercise here is not the denial of a grant, but rather the refusal to allow the Church—solely because it is a church—to compete with secular organizations for a grant. Trinity Lutheran is a member of the community too, and the State's decision to exclude it for purposes of this public program must withstand the strictest scrutiny.

D. Supreme Court Decisions Since Employment Division v. Smith

B

The Department attempts to get out from under the weight of our precedents by arguing that the free exercise question in this case is instead controlled by our decision in Locke v. Davey. It is not. In *Locke,* the State of Washington created a scholarship program to assist high-achieving students with the costs of postsecondary education. The scholarships were paid out of the State's general fund, and eligibility was based on criteria such as an applicant's score on college admission tests and family income. While scholarship recipients were free to use the money at accredited religious and non-religious schools alike, they were not permitted to use the funds to pursue a devotional theology degree—one "devotional in nature or designed to induce religious faith." Davey was selected for a scholarship but was denied the funds when he refused to certify that he would not use them toward a devotional degree. He sued, arguing that the State's refusal to allow its scholarship money to go toward such degrees violated his free exercise rights.

At the outset the Court made clear that *Locke* was not like the case now before us.

Washington's restriction on the use of its scholarship funds was different. According to the Court, the State had "merely chosen not to fund a distinct category of instruction." Davey was not denied a scholarship because of who he *was*; he was denied a scholarship because of what he proposed *to do*—use the funds to prepare for the ministry. Here there is no question that Trinity Lutheran was denied a grant simply because of what it is—a church.

The Court in *Locke* also stated that Washington's choice was in keeping with the State's antiestablishment interest in not using taxpayer funds to pay for the training of clergy; in fact, the Court could "think of few areas in which a State's antiestablishment interests come more into play." The claimant in *Locke* sought funding for an "essentially religious endeavor . . . akin to a religious calling as well as an academic pursuit," and opposition to such funding "to support church leaders" lay at the historic core of the Religion Clauses. Here nothing of the sort can be said about a program to use recycled tires to resurface playgrounds.

Relying on *Locke*, the Department nonetheless emphasizes Missouri's similar constitutional tradition of not furnishing taxpayer money directly to churches. But *Locke* took account of Washington's antiestablishment interest only after determining, as noted, that the scholarship program did not "require students to choose between their religious beliefs and receiving a government benefit." As the Court put it, Washington's scholarship program went "a long way toward including religion in its benefits." Students in the program were free to use their scholarships at "pervasively religious schools." Davey could use his scholarship to pursue a secular degree at one institution while studying devotional theology at another. He could also use his scholarship money to attend a religious college and take devotional theology courses there. The only thing he could not do was use the scholarship to pursue a degree in that subject.

In this case, there is no dispute that Trinity Lutheran *is* put to the choice between being a church and receiving a government benefit. The rule is simple: No churches need apply.[6]

---

6. This case involves express discrimination based on religious identity with respect to playground resurfacing. We do not address religious uses of funding or other forms of discrimination. [Footnote by the Court.]

C

The State in this case expressly requires Trinity Lutheran to renounce its religious character in order to participate in an otherwise generally available public benefit program, for which it is fully qualified. Our cases make clear that such a condition imposes a penalty on the free exercise of religion that must be subjected to the "most rigorous" scrutiny.

Under that stringent standard, only a state interest "of the highest order" can justify the Department's discriminatory policy. Yet the Department offers nothing more than Missouri's policy preference for skating as far as possible from religious establishment concerns. In the face of the clear infringement on free exercise before us, that interest cannot qualify as compelling. As we said when considering Missouri's same policy preference on a prior occasion, "the state interest asserted here — in achieving greater separation of church and State than is already ensured under the Establishment Clause of the Federal Constitution — is limited by the Free Exercise Clause."

The State has pursued its preferred policy to the point of expressly denying a qualified religious entity a public benefit solely because of its religious character. Under our precedents, that goes too far. The Department's policy violates the Free Exercise Clause.

Nearly 200 years ago, a legislator urged the Maryland Assembly to adopt a bill that would end the State's disqualification of Jews from public office: "If, on account of my religious faith, I am subjected to disqualifications, from which others are free, . . . I cannot but consider myself a persecuted man. . . . An odious exclusion from any of the benefits common to the rest of my fellow-citizens, is a persecution, differing only in degree, but of a nature equally unjustifiable with that, whose instruments are chains and torture."

The Missouri Department of Natural Resources has not subjected anyone to chains or torture on account of religion. And the result of the State's policy is nothing so dramatic as the denial of political office. The consequence is, in all likelihood, a few extra scraped knees. But the exclusion of Trinity Lutheran from a public benefit for which it is otherwise qualified, solely because it is a church, is odious to our Constitution all the same, and cannot stand.

Justice THOMAS, with whom Justice GORSUCH joins, concurring in part.

This Court's endorsement in *Locke* of even a "mil[d] kind," id., at 720, 124 S. Ct. 1307 of discrimination against religion remains troubling. But because the Court today appropriately construes *Locke* narrowly, and because no party has asked us to reconsider it, I join nearly all of the Court's opinion. I do not, however, join footnote 3, for the reasons expressed by Justice Gorsuch.

Justice GORSUCH, with whom Justice THOMAS joins, concurring in part.

Missouri's law bars Trinity Lutheran from participating in a public benefits program only because it is a church. I agree this violates the First Amendment and I am pleased to join nearly all of the Court's opinion. I offer only two modest qualifications.

First, the Court leaves open the possibility a useful distinction might be drawn between laws that discriminate on the basis of religious *status* and religious *use*. Respectfully, I harbor doubts about the stability of such a line. Does a religious man say grace before dinner? Or does a man begin his meal in a religious manner? Is it a religious group that built the playground? Or did a group

D. Supreme Court Decisions Since Employment Division v. Smith

build the playground so it might be used to advance a religious mission? The distinction blurs in much the same way the line between acts and omissions can blur when stared at too long, leaving us to ask (for example) whether the man who drowns by awaiting the incoming tide does so by act (coming upon the sea) or omission (allowing the sea to come upon him). Often enough the same facts can be described both ways.

Neither do I see why the First Amendment's Free Exercise Clause should care. After all, that Clause guarantees the free *exercise* of religion, not just the right to inward belief (or status). And this Court has long explained that government may not "devise mechanisms, overt or disguised, designed to persecute or oppress a religion or its practices." Generally the government may not force people to choose between participation in a public program and their right to free exercise of religion. I don't see why it should matter whether we describe that benefit, say, as closed to Lutherans (status) or closed to people who do Lutheran things (use). It is free exercise either way. For these reasons, reliance on the status-use distinction does not suffice for me to distinguish Locke v. Davey.

Second and for similar reasons, I am unable to join the footnoted observation that "[t]his case involves express discrimination based on religious identity with respect to playground resurfacing." Of course the footnote is entirely correct, but I worry that some might mistakenly read it to suggest that only "playground resurfacing" cases, or only those with some association with children's safety or health, or perhaps some other social good we find sufficiently worthy, are governed by the legal rules recounted in and faithfully applied by the Court's opinion. Such a reading would be unreasonable for our cases are "governed by general principles, rather than ad hoc improvisations." And the general principles here do not permit discrimination against religious exercise—whether on the playground or anywhere else.

Justice BREYER concurring in the judgment.

I agree with much of what the Court says and with its result. But I find relevant, and would emphasize, the particular nature of the "public benefit" here at issue. The Court stated in *Everson* that "cutting off church schools from" such "general government services as ordinary police and fire protection . . . is obviously not the purpose of the First Amendment." Here, the State would cut Trinity Lutheran off from participation in a general program designed to secure or to improve the health and safety of children. I see no significant difference. The fact that the program at issue ultimately funds only a limited number of projects cannot itself justify a religious distinction. Nor is there any administrative or other reason to treat church schools differently. The sole reason advanced that explains the difference is faith. And it is that last-mentioned fact that calls the Free Exercise Clause into play. We need not go further. Public benefits come in many shapes and sizes. I would leave the application of the Free Exercise Clause to other kinds of public benefits for another day.

Justice SOTOMAYOR, with whom Justice GINSBURG joins, dissenting.

To hear the Court tell it, this is a simple case about recycling tires to resurface a playground. The stakes are higher. This case is about nothing less than the relationship between religious institutions and the civil government—that is, between church and state. The Court today profoundly changes that relationship by holding, for the first time, that the Constitution requires the government to provide public funds directly to a church. Its decision slights both our precedents and our history, and its reasoning weakens this country's longstanding commitment to a separation of church and state beneficial to both.

I

Founded in 1922, Trinity Lutheran Church (Church) "operates . . . for the express purpose of carrying out the commission of . . . Jesus Christ as directed to His church on earth." The Church uses "preaching, teaching, worship, witness, service, and fellowship according to the Word of God" to carry out its mission "to 'make disciples.'" The Church's religious beliefs include its desire to "associat[e] with the [Trinity Church Child] Learning Center." The Learning Center serves as "a ministry of the Church and incorporates daily religion and developmentally appropriate activities into . . . [its] program." In this way, "[t]hrough the Learning Center, the Church teaches a Christian world view to children of members of the Church, as well as children of non-member residents" of the area. These activities represent the Church's "sincere religious belief . . . to use [the Learning Center] to teach the Gospel to children of its members, as well to bring the Gospel message to non-members."

II

Properly understood then, this is a case about whether Missouri can decline to fund improvements to the facilities the Church uses to practice and spread its religious views. This Court has repeatedly warned that funding of exactly this kind—payments from the government to a house of worship—would cross the line drawn by the Establishment Clause. So it is surprising that the Court mentions the Establishment Clause only to note the parties' agreement that it "does not prevent Missouri from including Trinity Lutheran in the Scrap Tire Program." Constitutional questions are decided by this Court, not the parties' concessions. The Establishment Clause does not allow Missouri to grant the Church's funding request because the Church uses the Learning Center, including its playground, in conjunction with its religious mission. The Court's silence on this front signals either its misunderstanding of the facts of this case or a startling departure from our precedents.

The government may not directly fund religious exercise. Nowhere is this rule more clearly implicated than when funds flow directly from the public treasury to a house of worship. A house of worship exists to foster and further religious exercise. When a government funds a house of worship, it underwrites this religious exercise.

This case is no different. The Church seeks state funds to improve the Learning Center's facilities, which, by the Church's own avowed description, are used to assist the spiritual growth of the children of its members and to spread the Church's faith to the children of nonmembers. The Church's playground surface—like a Sunday School room's walls or the sanctuary's pews—are integrated with and integral to its religious mission. The conclusion that the funding the Church seeks would impermissibly advance religion is inescapable.

D. Supreme Court Decisions Since Employment Division v. Smith

True, this Court has found some direct government funding of religious institutions to be consistent with the Establishment Clause. But the funding in those cases came with assurances that public funds would not be used for religious activity, despite the religious nature of the institution. The Church has not and cannot provide such assurances here. The Church has a religious mission, one that it pursues through the Learning Center. The playground surface cannot be confined to secular use any more than lumber used to frame the Church's walls, glass stained and used to form its windows, or nails used to build its altar.

The Court may simply disagree with this account of the facts and think that the Church does not put its playground to religious use. If so, its mistake is limited to this case. But if it agrees that the State's funding would further religious activity and sees no Establishment Clause problem, then it must be implicitly applying a rule other than the one agreed to in our precedents.

When the Court last addressed direct funding of religious institutions, in *Mitchell*, it adhered to the rule that the Establishment Clause prohibits the direct funding of religious activities.

Today's opinion suggests the Court has made the leap the *Mitchell* plurality could not. For if it agrees that the funding here will finance religious activities, then only a rule that considers that fact irrelevant could support a conclusion of constitutionality. It has no basis in the history to which the Court has repeatedly turned to inform its understanding of the Establishment Clause. It permits direct subsidies for religious indoctrination, with all the attendant concerns that led to the Establishment Clause. And it favors certain religious groups, those with a belief system that allows them to compete for public dollars and those well-organized and well-funded enough to do so successfully.

Such a break with precedent would mark a radical mistake. The Establishment Clause protects both religion and government from the dangers that result when the two become entwined, "*not* by providing every religion with an *equal opportunity* (say, to secure state funding or to pray in the public schools), but by drawing fairly clear lines of *separation* between church and state—at least where the heartland of religious belief, such as primary religious [worship], is at issue."

III

Even assuming the absence of an Establishment Clause violation and proceeding on the Court's preferred front—the Free Exercise Clause—the Court errs. It claims that the government may not draw lines based on an entity's religious "status." But we have repeatedly said that it can. When confronted with government action that draws such a line, we have carefully considered whether the interests embodied in the Religion Clauses justify that line. The question here is thus whether those interests support the line drawn in Missouri's Article I, §7, separating the State's treasury from those of houses of worship. They unquestionably do.

The Establishment Clause prohibits laws "respecting an establishment of religion" and the Free Exercise Clause prohibits laws "prohibiting the free exercise thereof." "[I]f expanded to a logical extreme," these prohibitions "would tend to clash with the other." Even in the absence of a violation of one of the Religion Clauses, the interaction of government and religion can raise concerns that sound in both Clauses. For that reason, the government may sometimes act to accommodate those concerns, even when not required to do so by the Free Exercise Clause, without violating the Establishment Clause. And the government may sometimes act to accommodate those concerns, even when not required to do so by the Establishment Clause, without violating the Free Exercise Clause. "[T]here is room for play in the joints productive of a benevolent neutrality which will permit religious exercise to exist without sponsorship and without interference." This space between the two Clauses gives government some room to recognize the unique status of religious entities and to single them out on that basis for exclusion from otherwise generally applicable laws.

Invoking this principle, this Court has held that the government may sometimes relieve religious entities from the requirements of government programs. A State need not, for example, require nonprofit houses of worship to pay property taxes. Nor must a State require nonprofit religious entities to abstain from making employment decisions on the basis of religion. But the government may not invoke the space between the Religion Clauses in a manner that "devolve[s] into an unlawful fostering of religion."

Missouri has decided that the unique status of houses of worship requires a special rule when it comes to public funds. Its Constitution reflects that choice and provides:

> "That no money shall ever be taken from the public treasury, directly or indirectly, in aid of any church, sect, or denomination of religion, or in aid of any priest, preacher, minister or teacher thereof, as such; and that no preference shall be given to nor any discrimination made against any church, sect or creed of religion, or any form of religious faith or worship." Art. I, §7.

Missouri's decision, which has deep roots in our Nation's history, reflects a reasonable and constitutional judgment.

This Court has consistently looked to history for guidance when applying the Constitution's Religion Clauses. Those Clauses guard against a return to the past, and so that past properly informs their meaning. This case is no different.

Those who fought to end the public funding of religion based their opposition on a powerful set of arguments, all stemming from the basic premise that the practice harmed both civil government and religion. The civil government, they maintained, could claim no authority over religious belief. For them, support for religion compelled by the State marked an overstep of authority that would only lead to more. Equally troubling, it risked divisiveness by giving religions reason to compete for the State's beneficence. Faith, they believed, was a personal matter, entirely between an individual and his god. Religion was best served when sects reached out on the basis of their tenets alone, unsullied by outside forces, allowing adherents to come to their faith voluntarily. Over and over, these arguments gained acceptance and led to the end of state laws exacting payment for the support of religion.

In *Locke*, this Court expressed an understanding of, and respect for, this history.

The same is true of this case, about directing taxpayer funds to houses of worship. Like the use of public dollars for ministers at issue in *Locke*, turning over public funds to houses of worship implicates serious antiestablishment and free exercise interests. The history just discussed fully supports this conclusion. As states disestablished, they repealed laws allowing taxation to support religion because the practice threatened other forms of government support for, involved some government control over, and weakened supporters' control of religion. Common sense also supports this conclusion. Recall that a state may not fund religious activities without violating the Establishment Clause. A state can reasonably use status as a "house of worship" as a stand-in for "religious activities." Inside a house of worship, dividing the religious from the secular would require intrusive line-drawing by government, and monitoring those lines would entangle government with the house of worship's activities. And so while not every activity a house of worship undertakes will be inseparably linked to religious activity, "the likelihood that many are makes a categorical rule a suitable means to avoid chilling the exercise of religion." Finally, and of course, such funding implicates the free exercise rights of taxpayers by denying them the chance to decide for themselves whether and how to fund religion. If there is any "'room for play in the joints' between" the Religion Clauses, it is here.

As was true in *Locke*, a prophylactic rule against the use of public funds for houses of worship is a permissible accommodation of these weighty interests. The rule has a historical pedigree identical to that of the provision in *Locke*. Today, thirty-eight States have a counterpart to Missouri's Article I, §7. The provisions, as a general matter, date back to or before these States' original Constitutions. That so many States have for so long drawn a line that prohibits public funding for houses of worship, based on principles rooted in this Nation's understanding of how best to foster religious liberty, supports the conclusion that public funding of houses of worship "is of a different ilk."

Missouri has recognized the simple truth that, even absent an Establishment Clause violation, the transfer of public funds to houses of worship raises concerns that sit exactly between the Religion Clauses. To avoid those concerns, and only those concerns, it has prohibited such funding. In doing so, it made the same choice made by the earliest States centuries ago and many other States in the years since. The Constitution permits this choice.

In the Court's view, none of this matters. It focuses on one aspect of Missouri's Article I, §7, to the exclusion of all else: that it denies funding to a house of worship, here the Church, "simply because of what it [i]s—a church."

Start where the Court stays silent. Its opinion does not acknowledge that our precedents have expressly approved of a government's choice to draw lines based on an entity's religious status. Those cases did not deploy strict scrutiny to create a presumption of unconstitutionality, as the Court does today. Instead, they asked whether the government had offered a strong enough reason to justify drawing a line based on that status.

The Court takes two steps to avoid these precedents. First, it recasts *Locke* as a case about a restriction that prohibited the would-be minister from "us[ing] the funds to prepare for the ministry." A faithful reading of *Locke* gives it a broader reach. *Locke* stands for the reasonable proposition that the government may, but need not, choose not to fund certain religious entities (there, ministers) where doing so raises "historic and substantial" establishment and free exercise concerns.

Second, it suggests that this case is different because it involves "discrimination" in the form of the denial of access to a possible benefit. But in this area of law, a decision to treat entities differently based on distinctions that the Religion

Clauses make relevant does not amount to discrimination. To understand why, keep in mind that "the Court has unambiguously concluded that the individual freedom of conscience protected by the First Amendment embraces the right to select any religious faith or none at all." If the denial of a benefit others may receive is discrimination that violates the Free Exercise Clause, then the accommodations of religious entities we have approved would violate the free exercise rights of nonreligious entities. We have, with good reason, rejected that idea and instead focused on whether the government has provided a good enough reason, based in the values the Religion Clauses protect, for its decision.

The Court offers no real reason for rejecting the balancing approach in our precedents in favor of strict scrutiny, beyond its references to discrimination. The Court's desire to avoid what it views as discrimination is understandable. But in this context, the description is particularly inappropriate. A State's decision not to fund houses of worship does not disfavor religion; rather, it represents a valid choice to remain secular in the face of serious establishment and free exercise concerns. That does not make the State "atheistic or antireligious." The Court's conclusion "that the only alternative to governmental support of religion is governmental hostility to it represents a giant step backward in our Religion Clause jurisprudence."

At bottom, the Court creates the following rule today: The government may draw lines on the basis of religious status to grant a benefit to religious persons or entities but it may not draw lines on that basis when doing so would further the interests the Religion Clauses protect in other ways. Nothing supports this lopsided outcome. Not the Religion Clauses, as they protect establishment and free exercise interests in the same constitutional breath, neither privileged over the other. Not precedent, since we have repeatedly explained that the Clauses protect not religion but "the individual's freedom of conscience,"—that which allows him to choose religion, reject it, or remain undecided. And not reason, because as this case shows, the same interests served by lifting government-imposed burdens on certain religious entities may sometimes be equally served by denying government-provided benefits to certain religious entities.[7] Today's decision discounts centuries of history and jeopardizes the government's ability to remain secular.

IV

The Court today dismantles a core protection for religious freedom provided in these Clauses. It holds not just that a government may support houses of worship with taxpayer funds, but that—at least in this case and perhaps in others, it must do so whenever it decides to create a funding program. History shows that the Religion Clauses separate the public treasury from religious coffers as one measure to secure the kind of freedom of conscience that benefits both

---

7. In the end, the soundness of today's decision may matter less than what it might enable tomorrow. The principle it establishes can be manipulated to call for a similar fate for lines drawn on the basis of religious use. It is enough for today to explain why the Court's decision is wrong. The error of the concurrences' hoped-for decisions can be left for tomorrow. [Footnote by Justice Sotomayor.]

religion and government. If this separation means anything, it means that the government cannot, or at the very least need not, tax its citizens and turn that money over to houses of worship. The Court today blinds itself to the outcome this history requires and leads us instead to a place where separation of church and state is a constitutional slogan, not a constitutional commitment.

The question after *Trinity Lutheran* is when, if at all, can the government provide benefits to secular private institutions, but not religious institutions? Chief Justice Roberts' majority opinion emphasizes that the holding in *Trinity Lutheran* is just about surfaces for playgrounds. But he also says that the denial of benefits to religious institutions that are provided to secular ones must meet strict scrutiny. The Court provided clarification, and made clear that *Trinity Lutheran* extends far beyond aid for playgrounds in Espinoza v. Montana Department of Revenue.

ESPINOZA v. MONTANA DEPARTMENT OF REVENUE
140 S. Ct. 2246 (2020)

Chief Justice ROBERTS delivered the opinion of the Court.

The Montana Legislature established a program to provide tuition assistance to parents who send their children to private schools. The program grants a tax credit to anyone who donates to certain organizations that in turn award scholarships to selected students attending such schools. When petitioners sought to use the scholarships at a religious school, the Montana Supreme Court struck down the program. The Court relied on the "no-aid" provision of the State Constitution, which prohibits any aid to a school controlled by a "church, sect, or denomination." The question presented is whether the Free Exercise Clause of the United States Constitution barred that application of the no-aid provision.

I

In 2015, the Montana Legislature sought "to provide parental and student choice in education" by enacting a scholarship program for students attending private schools. The program grants a tax credit of up to $150 to any taxpayer who donates to a participating "student scholarship organization." The scholarship organizations then use the donations to award scholarships to children for tuition at a private school.

A family whose child is awarded a scholarship under the program may use it at any "qualified education provider"—that is, any private school that meets certain accreditation, testing, and safety requirements. Virtually every private school in Montana qualifies. Upon receiving a scholarship, the family designates its school of choice, and the scholarship organization sends the scholarship funds directly to the school. Neither the scholarship organization nor its donors can restrict awards to particular types of schools.

The Montana Legislature allotted $3 million annually to fund the tax credits, beginning in 2016. If the annual allotment is exhausted, it increases by 10% the following year. The program is slated to expire in 2023.

The Montana Legislature also directed that the program be administered in accordance with Article X, section 6, of the Montana Constitution, which contains a "no-aid" provision barring government aid to sectarian schools.

This suit was brought by three mothers whose children attend Stillwater Christian School in northwestern Montana. Stillwater is a private Christian school that meets the statutory criteria for "qualified education providers." It serves students in prekindergarten through 12th grade, and petitioners chose the school in large part because it "teaches the same Christian values that [they] teach at home." The child of one petitioner has already received scholarships from Big Sky, and the other petitioners' children are eligible for scholarships and planned to apply. While in effect, however, Rule 1 blocked petitioners from using scholarship funds for tuition at Stillwater. To overcome that obstacle, petitioners sued the Department of Revenue in Montana state court.

In December 2018, the Montana Supreme Court [held] that the program aided religious schools in violation of the no-aid provision of the Montana Constitution. In the Court's view, the no-aid provision "broadly and strictly prohibits aid to sectarian schools." The scholarship program provided such aid by using tax credits to "subsidize tuition payments" at private schools that are "religiously affiliated" or "controlled in whole or in part by churches." In that way, the scholarship program flouted the State Constitution's "guarantee to all Montanans that their government will not use state funds to aid religious schools."

The Montana Supreme Court went on to hold that the violation of the no-aid provision required invalidating the entire scholarship program. The Court explained that the program provided "no mechanism" for preventing aid from flowing to religious schools, and therefore the scholarship program could not "under *any* circumstance" be construed as consistent with the no-aid provision. As a result, the tax credit is no longer available to support scholarships at either religious or secular private schools.

II

A

The Religion Clauses of the First Amendment provide that "Congress shall make no law respecting an establishment of religion, or prohibiting the free exercise thereof." Here, the parties do not dispute that the scholarship program is permissible under the Establishment Clause. Nor could they. We have repeatedly held that the Establishment Clause is not offended when religious observers and organizations benefit from neutral government programs. Any Establishment Clause objection to the scholarship program here is particularly unavailing because the government support makes its way to religious schools only as a result of Montanans independently choosing to spend their scholarships at such schools. The Montana Supreme Court, however, held as a matter of state law that even such indirect government support qualified as "aid" prohibited under the Montana Constitution.

D. Supreme Court Decisions Since Employment Division v. Smith

The question for this Court is whether the Free Exercise Clause precluded the Montana Supreme Court from applying Montana's no-aid provision to bar religious schools from the scholarship program.

The Free Exercise Clause, which applies to the States under the Fourteenth Amendment, "protects religious observers against unequal treatment" and against "laws that impose special disabilities on the basis of religious status." Those "basic principle[s]" have long guided this Court.

Most recently, *Trinity Lutheran* [*Church of Columbia, Inc. v. Comer* (2017)], distilled these and other decisions to the same effect into the "unremarkable" conclusion that disqualifying otherwise eligible recipients from a public benefit "solely because of their religious character" imposes "a penalty on the free exercise of religion that triggers the most exacting scrutiny."

Here too Montana's no-aid provision bars religious schools from public benefits solely because of the religious character of the schools. The provision also bars parents who wish to send their children to a religious school from those same benefits, again solely because of the religious character of the school. This is apparent from the plain text. The provision bars aid to any school "controlled in whole or in part by any church, sect, or denomination." The provision's title—"Aid prohibited to sectarian schools"—confirms that the provision singles out schools based on their religious character. And the Montana Supreme Court explained that the provision forbids aid to any school that is "sectarian," "religiously affiliated," or "controlled in whole or in part by churches." The provision plainly excludes schools from government aid solely because of religious status.

To be eligible for government aid under the Montana Constitution, a school must divorce itself from any religious control or affiliation. Placing such a condition on benefits or privileges "inevitably deters or discourages the exercise of First Amendment rights." The Free Exercise Clause protects against even "indirect coercion," and a State "punishe[s] the free exercise of religion" by disqualifying the religious from government aid as Montana did here. Such status-based discrimination is subject to "the strictest scrutiny." It is enough in this case to conclude that strict scrutiny applies under *Trinity Lutheran* because Montana's no-aid provision discriminates based on religious status.

B

Seeking to avoid *Trinity Lutheran*, the Department contends that this case is instead governed by *Locke v. Davey* (2004). *Locke* also involved a scholarship program. The State of Washington provided scholarships paid out of the State's general fund to help students pursuing postsecondary education. The scholarships could be used at accredited religious and nonreligious schools alike, but Washington prohibited students from using the scholarships to pursue devotional theology degrees, which prepared students for a calling as clergy. This prohibition prevented Davey from using his scholarship to obtain a degree that would have enabled him to become a pastor. We held that Washington had not violated the Free Exercise Clause.

Locke differs from this case in two critical ways. First, *Locke* explained that Washington had "merely chosen not to fund a distinct category of instruction": the "essentially religious endeavor" of training a minister "to lead a congregation." Thus, Davey "was denied a scholarship because of what he proposed *to do*—use the funds to prepare for the ministry." Apart from that narrow restriction,

Washington's program allowed scholarships to be used at "pervasively religious schools" that incorporated religious instruction throughout their classes. By contrast, Montana's Constitution does not zero in on any particular "essentially religious" course of instruction at a religious school. Rather, as we have explained, the no-aid provision bars all aid to a religious school "simply because of what it is," putting the school to a choice between being religious or receiving government benefits. At the same time, the provision puts families to a choice between sending their children to a religious school or receiving such benefits.

Second, *Locke* invoked a "historic and substantial" state interest in not funding the training of clergy, explaining that "opposition to . . . funding 'to support church leaders' lay at the historic core of the Religion Clauses." As evidence of that tradition, the Court in *Locke* emphasized that the propriety of state-supported clergy was a central subject of founding-era debates, and that most state constitutions from that era prohibited the expenditure of tax dollars to support the clergy.

But no comparable "historic and substantial" tradition supports Montana's decision to disqualify religious schools from government aid. In the founding era and the early 19th century, governments provided financial support to private schools, including denominational ones. "Far from prohibiting such support, the early state constitutions and statutes actively encouraged this policy." Local governments provided grants to private schools, including religious ones, for the education of the poor. Even States with bans on government-supported clergy, such as New Jersey, Pennsylvania, and Georgia, provided various forms of aid to religious schools. Early federal aid (often land grants) went to religious schools. Congress provided support to denominational schools in the District of Columbia until 1848, and Congress paid churches to run schools for American Indians through the end of the 19th century. After the Civil War, Congress spent large sums on education for emancipated freedmen, often by supporting denominational schools in the South through the Freedmen's Bureau.

The Department argues that a tradition *against* state support for religious schools arose in the second half of the 19th century, as more than 30 States—including Montana—adopted no-aid provisions. Such a development, of course, cannot by itself establish an early American tradition. In addition, many of the no-aid provisions belong to a more checkered tradition shared with the Blaine Amendment of the 1870s. That proposal—which Congress nearly passed—would have added to the Federal Constitution a provision similar to the state no-aid provisions, prohibiting States from aiding "sectarian" schools. "[I]t was an open secret that 'sectarian' was code for 'Catholic.'" The Blaine Amendment was "born of bigotry" and "arose at a time of pervasive hostility to the Catholic Church and to Catholics in general"; many of its state counterparts have a similarly "shameful pedigree." The no-aid provisions of the 19th century hardly evince a tradition that should inform our understanding of the Free Exercise Clause.

c

Two dissenters would chart new courses. Justice Sotomayor would grant the government "some room" to "single . . . out" religious entities "for exclusion," based on what she views as "the interests embodied in the Religion Clauses." Justice Breyer, building on his solo opinion in *Trinity Lutheran*, would adopt a "flexible, context-specific approach" that "may well vary" from case to case. As best we can tell, courts applying this approach would contemplate the particular benefit and restriction at issue and discern their relationship to religion and society, taking into account "context and consequences measured in light of [the] purposes" of the Religion Clauses. What is clear is that Justice Breyer would afford much freer rein to judges than our current regime, arguing that "there is 'no test-related substitute for the exercise of legal judgment.'"

The simplest response is that these dissents follow from prior separate writings, not from the Court's decision in *Trinity Lutheran* or the decades of precedent on which it relied. These precedents have "repeatedly confirmed" the straightforward rule that we apply today: When otherwise eligible recipients are disqualified from a public benefit "solely because of their religious character," we must apply strict scrutiny. This rule against express religious discrimination is no "doctrinal innovation." Far from it. As *Trinity Lutheran* explained, the rule is "unremarkable in light of our prior decisions."

For innovation, one must look to the dissents. Their "room[y]" or "flexible" approaches to discrimination against religious organizations and observers would mark a significant departure from our free exercise precedents. The protections of the Free Exercise Clause do not depend on a "judgment-by-judgment analysis" regarding whether discrimination against religious adherents would somehow serve ill-defined interests.

D

Because the Montana Supreme Court applied the no-aid provision to discriminate against schools and parents based on the religious character of the school, the "strictest scrutiny" is required. That "stringent standard" is not "watered down but really means what it says," To satisfy it, government action "must advance 'interests of the highest order' and must be narrowly tailored in pursuit of those interests."

The Montana Supreme Court asserted that the no-aid provision serves Montana's interest in separating church and State "more fiercely" than the Federal Constitution. But "that interest cannot qualify as compelling" in the face of the infringement of free exercise here. A State's interest "in achieving greater separation of church and State than is already ensured under the Establishment Clause . . . is limited by the Free Exercise Clause."

The Department also suggests that the no-aid provision advances Montana's interests in public education. According to the Department, the no-aid provision safeguards the public school system by ensuring that government support is not diverted to private schools. But, under that framing, the no-aid provision is fatally underinclusive because its "proffered objectives are not pursued with respect to analogous nonreligious conduct." On the Department's view, an interest in public education is undermined by diverting government support to *any* private school, yet the no-aid provision bars aid only to *religious* ones. A law does not advance "an interest of the highest order when it leaves appreciable damage to that supposedly vital interest unprohibited."

State need not subsidize private education. But once a State decides to do so, it cannot disqualify some private schools solely because they are religious.

III

The Department argues that, at the end of the day, there is no free exercise violation here because the Montana Supreme Court ultimately eliminated the scholarship program altogether. According to the Department, now that there is no program, religious schools and adherents cannot complain that they are excluded from any generally available benefit. Two dissenters agree.

The descriptions are not accurate. The Montana Legislature created the scholarship program; the Legislature never chose to end it, for policy or other reasons. The program was eliminated by a court, and not based on some innocuous principle of state law. Rather, the Montana Supreme Court invalidated the program pursuant to a state law provision that expressly discriminates on the basis of religious status. The Court applied that provision to hold that religious schools were barred from participating in the program. Then, seeing no other "mechanism" to make absolutely sure that religious schools received no aid, the court chose to invalidate the entire program. The final step in this line of reasoning eliminated the program, to the detriment of religious and non-religious schools alike. But the Court's error of federal law occurred at the beginning. When the Court was called upon to apply a state law no-aid provision to exclude religious schools from the program, it was obligated by the Federal Constitution to reject the invitation. Had the Court recognized that this was, indeed, "one of those cases" in which application of the no-aid provision "would violate the Free Exercise Clause," the Court would not have proceeded to find a violation of that provision. And, in the absence of such a state law violation, the Court would have had no basis for terminating the program. Because the elimination of the program flowed directly from the Montana Supreme Court's failure to follow the dictates of federal law, it cannot be defended as a neutral policy decision, or as resting on adequate and independent state law grounds.

Justice THOMAS, with whom Justice GORSUCH joins, concurring.

The Court correctly concludes that Montana's no-aid provision expressly discriminates against religion in violation of the Free Exercise Clause. And it properly provides relief to Montana religious schools and the petitioners who wish to use Montana's scholarship program to send their children to such schools. I write separately to explain how this Court's interpretation of the Establishment Clause continues to hamper free exercise rights. Until we correct course on that interpretation, individuals will continue to face needless obstacles in their attempts to vindicate their religious freedom.

I

This case involves the Free Exercise Clause, not the Establishment Clause. But as in all cases involving a state actor, the modern understanding of the Establishment Clause is a "brooding omnipresence," ever ready to be used to justify the government's infringement on religious freedom. Under the modern, but erroneous, view of the Establishment Clause, the government must treat all religions equally and treat religion equally to nonreligion. As this Court stated in its first case applying the Establishment Clause to the States, the government cannot "pass laws which aid one religion, aid all religions, or prefer one religion over another." This "equality principle," the theory goes, prohibits the government from expressing any preference for religion—or even permitting any signs of religion in the governmental realm. Thus, when a plaintiff brings a free exercise claim, the government may defend its law, as Montana did here, on the ground that the law's restrictions are *required* to prevent it from "establishing" religion.

D. Supreme Court Decisions Since Employment Division v. Smith

This understanding of the Establishment Clause is unmoored from the original meaning of the First Amendment. As I have explained in previous cases, at the founding, the Clause served only to "protec[t] States, and by extension their citizens, from the imposition of an established religion by the *Federal* Government." Under this view, the Clause resists incorporation against the States.

II

The Court's current understanding of the Establishment Clause actually thwarts, rather than promotes, equal treatment of religion. Under a proper understanding of the Establishment Clause, robust and lively debate about the role of religion in government is permitted, even encouraged, at the state and local level. The Court's distorted view of the Establishment Clause, however, removes the entire subject of religion from the realm of permissible governmental activity, instead mandating strict separation.

This interpretation of the Establishment Clause operates as a type of content-based restriction on the government. The Court has interpreted the Free Speech Clause to prohibit content-based restrictions because they "value some forms of speech over others," thus tending to "tilt public debate in a preferred direction." The content-based restriction imposed by this Court's Establishment Clause jurisprudence operates no differently. It communicates a message that religion is dangerous and in need of policing, which in turn has the effect of tilting society in favor of devaluing religion.

Historical evidence suggests that many advocates for this separationist view were originally motivated by hostility toward certain disfavored religions. And this Court's adoption of a separationist interpretation has itself sometimes bordered on religious hostility.

As I have recently explained, this Court has an unfortunate tendency to prefer certain constitutional rights over others. The Free Exercise Clause, although enshrined explicitly in the Constitution, rests on the lowest rung of the Court's ladder of rights, and precariously so at that. Returning the Establishment Clause to its proper scope will not completely rectify the Court's disparate treatment of constitutional rights, but it will go a long way toward allowing free exercise of religion to flourish as the Framers intended. I look forward to the day when the Court takes up this task in earnest.

Justice ALITO, concurring.

I join the opinion of the Court in full. The basis of the decision below was a Montana constitutional provision that, according to the Montana Supreme Court, forbids parents from participating in a publicly funded scholarship program simply because they send their children to religious schools. Regardless of the motivation for this provision or its predecessor, its application here violates the Free Exercise Clause.

Nevertheless, the provision's origin is relevant under the decision we issued earlier this Term in *Ramos v. Louisiana* (2020). The question in *Ramos* was whether Louisiana and Oregon laws allowing non-unanimous jury verdicts in criminal trials violated the Sixth Amendment. The Court held that they did, emphasizing that the States originally adopted those laws for racially discriminatory reasons. The role of the Ku Klux Klan was highlighted.

I argued in dissent that this original motivation, though deplorable, had no bearing on the laws' constitutionality because such laws can be adopted for non-discriminatory reasons, and "both States readopted their rules under different circumstances in later years." But I lost, and *Ramos* is now precedent. If the original motivation for the laws mattered there, it certainly matters here.

The origin of Montana's "no-aid" provision, is emphasized in petitioners' brief and in the briefs of numerous supporting *amici*. These briefs, most of which were not filed by organizations affiliated with the Catholic Church, point out that Montana's provision was modeled on the failed Blaine Amendment to the Constitution of the United States. Named after House Speaker James Blaine, the Congressman who introduced it in 1875, the amendment was prompted by virulent prejudice against immigrants, particularly Catholic immigrants. In effect, the amendment would have "bar[red] any aid" to Catholic and other "sectarian" schools. As noted in a publication from the United States Commission on Civil Rights, a prominent supporter of this ban was the Ku Klux Klan.

The Blaine Amendment was narrowly defeated, passing in the House but falling just short of the two-thirds majority needed in the Senate to refer the amendment to the States. fterwards, most States adopted provisions like Montana's to achieve the same objective at the state level, often as a condition of entering the Union. Thirty-eight States still have these "little Blaine Amendments" today.

The resulting wave of state laws withholding public aid from "sectarian" schools cannot be understood outside this context. Indeed, there are stronger reasons for considering original motivations here than in *Ramos* because, unlike the neutral language of Louisiana's and Oregon's nonunanimity rules, Montana's no-aid provision retains the bigoted code language used throughout state Blaine Amendments.

The tax-credit program adopted by the Montana Legislature but overturned by the Montana Supreme Court provided necessary aid for parents who pay taxes to support the public schools but who disagree with the teaching there. The program helped parents of modest means do what more affluent parents can do: send their children to a school of their choice. The argument that the decision below treats everyone the same is reminiscent of Anatole France's sardonic remark that "'[t]he law, in its majestic equality, forbids the rich as well as the poor to sleep under bridges, to beg in the streets, and to steal bread.'"

Justice GINSBURG, with whom Justice KAGAN joins, dissenting.

The Montana Legislature enacted a scholarship program to fund tuition for students attending private secondary schools. In the decision below, the Montana Supreme Court struck down that program in its entirety. The program, the state court ruled, conflicted with the State Constitution's no-aid provision, which forbids government appropriations to religious schools. Parents who sought to use the program's scholarships to fund their children's religious education challenged the state court's ruling. They argue in this Court that the Montana court's application of the no-aid provision violated the Free Exercise Clause of the Federal Constitution. Importantly, the parents, petitioners here, disclaim any challenge to the no-aid provision on its face. They instead argue—and this Court's majority accepts—that the provision is unconstitutional as applied because the First Amendment prohibits discrimination in tuition-benefit programs based on a school's religious status. Because the state court's decision does not so discriminate, I would reject petitioners' free exercise claim.

Petitioners argue that the Montana Supreme Court's decision fails when measured against *Trinity Lutheran*. I do not see how. Past decisions in this area have entailed *differential treatment* occasioning a burden on a plaintiff's religious exercise. This case is missing that essential component. Recall that the Montana court remedied the state constitutional violation by striking the scholarship program in its entirety. Under that decree, secular and sectarian schools alike are ineligible for benefits, so the decision cannot be said to entail differential treatment based on petitioners' religion. Put somewhat differently, petitioners argue that the Free Exercise Clause requires a State to treat institutions and people neutrally when doling out a benefit—and neutrally is how Montana treats them in the wake of the state court's decision.

Accordingly, the Montana Supreme Court's decision does not place a burden on petitioners' religious exercise. Petitioners may still send their children to a religious school. And the Montana Supreme Court's decision does not pressure them to do otherwise. Unlike the law in *Trinity Lutheran*, the decision below puts petitioners to no "choice": Neither giving up their faith, nor declining to send their children to sectarian schools, would affect their entitlement to scholarship funding. There simply are no scholarship funds to be had.

Nearing the end of its opinion, the Court writes: "A State need not subsidize private education. But once a State decides to do so, it cannot disqualify some private schools solely because they are religious." Because Montana's Supreme Court did not make such a decision—its judgment put all private school parents in the same boat—this Court had no occasion to address the matter. On that sole ground, and reaching no other issue, I dissent from the Court's judgment.

Justice BREYER, with whom Justice KAGAN joins as to Part I, dissenting.

The majority holds that the Free Exercise Clause forbids a State to draw any distinction between secular and religious uses of government aid to private schools that is not required by the Establishment Clause. The majority's approach and its conclusion in this case, I fear, risk the kind of entanglement and conflict that the Religion Clauses are intended to prevent. I consequently dissent.

I

We all recognize that the First Amendment prohibits discrimination against religion. At the same time, our history and federal constitutional precedent reflect a deep concern that state funding for religious teaching, by stirring fears of preference or in other ways, might fuel religious discord and division and thereby threaten religious freedom itself. The Court has consequently made it clear that the Constitution commits the government to a "position of neutrality" in respect to religion.

The inherent tension between the Establishment and Free Exercise Clauses means, however, that the "course of constitutional neutrality in this area cannot be an absolutely straight line." Indeed, "rigidity could well defeat the basic purpose of these provisions, which is to insure that no religion be sponsored or favored, none commanded, and none inhibited.

That, in significant part, is why the Court has held that "there is room for play in the joints" between the Clauses' express prohibitions that is "productive of a benevolent neutrality," allowing "religious exercise to exist without sponsorship and without interference." It has held that there "are some state actions permitted by the Establishment Clause but not required by the Free Exercise Clause." And that "play in the joints" should, in my view, play a determinative role here.

It may be that, under our precedents, the Establishment Clause does not *forbid* Montana to subsidize the education of petitioners' children. But, the question here is whether the Free Exercise Clause *requires* it to do so. The majority believes that the answer to that question is "yes." It writes that "once a State decides" to support nonpublic education, "it cannot disqualify some private schools solely because they are religious." I shall explain why I disagree.

The majority finds that the school-playground case, *Trinity Lutheran*, and not the religious-studies case, *Locke*, controls here. I disagree. In my view, the program at issue here is strikingly similar to the program we upheld in *Locke* and importantly different from the program we found unconstitutional in *Trinity Lutheran*. Like the State of Washington in *Locke*, Montana has chosen not to fund (at a distance) "an essentially religious endeavor"—an education designed to "'induce religious faith.'" That kind of program simply cannot be likened to Missouri's decision to exclude a church school from applying for a grant to resurface its playground.

The Court in *Locke* recognized that the study of devotional theology can be "akin to a religious calling as well as an academic pursuit." Indeed, "the shaping, through primary education, of the next generation's minds and spirits" may be as critical as training for the ministry, which itself, after all, is but one of the activities necessary to help assure a religion's survival. That is why many faith leaders emphasize the central role of schools in their religious missions. It is why at least some teachers at religious schools see their work as a form of ministry. And petitioners have testified that it is a "major reason" why they chose religious schools for their children.

Nothing in the Constitution discourages this type of instruction. To the contrary, the Free Exercise Clause draws upon a history that places great value upon the freedom of parents to teach their children the tenets of their faith.

What, then, is the difference between *Locke* and the present case? And what is it that leads the majority to conclude that funding the study of religion is more like paying to fix up a playground (*Trinity Lutheran*) than paying for a degree in theology (*Locke*)? The majority's principal argument appears to be that, as in *Trinity Lutheran*, Montana has excluded religious schools from its program "solely because of the religious character of the schools." The majority seeks to contrast this *status*-based discrimination with the program at issue in *Locke*, which it says denied scholarships to divinity students based on the religious *use* to which they put the funds—*i.e.*, training for the ministry, as opposed to secular professions.

It is true that Montana's no-aid provision broadly bars state aid to schools based on their religious affiliation. But this case does not involve a claim of status-based discrimination. The schools do not apply or compete for scholarships, they are not parties to this litigation, and no one here purports to represent their interests. We are instead faced with a suit by *parents* who assert that *their* free exercise rights are violated by the application of the no-aid provision to

D. Supreme Court Decisions Since Employment Division v. Smith

prevent them from *using* taxpayer-supported scholarships to attend the schools of their choosing. In other words, the problem, as in *Locke*, is what petitioners "'propos[e] *to do*—use the funds to'" obtain a religious education.

Even if the schools' status were relevant, I do not see what bearing the majority's distinction could have here. There is no dispute that religious schools seek generally to inspire religious faith and values in their students. How else could petitioners claim that barring them from using state aid to attend these schools violates their free exercise rights? Thus, the question in this case—unlike in *Trinity Lutheran*—boils down to what the schools would *do* with state support. And the upshot is that here, as in *Locke*, we confront a State's decision not to fund the inculcation of religious truths.

If, for 250 years, we have drawn a line at forcing taxpayers to pay the salaries of those who teach their faith from the pulpit, I do not see how we can today require Montana to adopt a different view respecting those who teach it in the classroom.

II

In reaching its conclusion that the Free Exercise Clause requires Montana to allow petitioners to use taxpayer-supported scholarships to pay for their children's religious education, the majority makes several doctrinal innovations that, in my view, are misguided and threaten adverse consequences. I disagree, then, with what I see as the majority's doctrinal omission, its misplaced application of a legal presumption, and its suggestion that this presumption is appropriate in many, if not all, cases involving government benefits. As I see the matter, our differences run deeper than a simple disagreement about the application of prior case law.

For one thing, government benefits come in many shapes and sizes. The appropriate way to approach a State's benefit-related decision may well vary depending upon the relation between the Religion Clauses and the specific benefit and restriction at issue. For another, disagreements that concern religion and its relation to a particular benefit may prove unusually difficult to resolve. They may involve small but important details of a particular benefit program. Does one detail affect one religion negatively and another positively? What about a religion that objects to the particular way in which the government seeks to enforce mandatory (say, qualification-related) provisions of a particular benefit program? Or the religious group that for religious reasons cannot accept government support? And what happens when qualification requirements mean that government money flows to one religion rather than another? Courts are ill equipped to deal with such conflicts. Yet, in a Nation with scores of different religions, many such disagreements are possible. And I have only scratched the surface.

The majority claims that giving weight to these considerations would be a departure from our precedent and give courts too much discretion to interpret the Religion Clauses. But we have long understood that the "application" of the First Amendment's mandate of neutrality "requires interpretation of a delicate sort." "Each value judgment under the Religion Clauses," we have explained, must "turn on whether particular acts in question are intended to establish or interfere with religious beliefs and practices or have the effect of doing so."

Nor does the majority's approach avoid judicial entanglement in difficult and sensitive questions. To the contrary, as I have just explained, it burdens courts with the still more complex task of untangling disputes between religious organizations and state governments, instead of giving deference to state legislators' choices to avoid such issues altogether. At the same time, it puts States in a legislative dilemma, caught between the demands of the Free Exercise and Establishment Clauses, without "breathing room" to help ameliorate the problem.

And what are the limits of the Court's holding? The majority asserts that States "need not subsidize private education." But it does not explain why that is so. If making scholarships available to only secular nonpublic schools exerts "coercive" pressure on parents whose faith impels them to enroll their children in religious schools, then how is a State's decision to fund only secular *public* schools any less coercive? Under the majority's reasoning, the parents in both cases are put to a choice between their beliefs and a taxpayer-sponsored education.

Accepting the majority's distinction between public and nonpublic schools does little to address the uncertainty that its holding introduces. What about charter schools? States vary widely in how they permit charter schools to be structured, funded, and controlled. How would the majority's rule distinguish between those States in which support for charter schools is akin to public school funding and those in which it triggers a constitutional obligation to fund private religious schools? The majority's rule provides no guidance, even as it sharply limits the ability of courts and legislatures to balance the potentially competing interests that underlie the Free Exercise and Antiestablishment Clauses.

Justice SOTOMAYOR, dissenting.

The majority holds that a Montana scholarship program unlawfully discriminated against religious schools by excluding them from a tax benefit. The threshold problem, however, is that such tax benefits no longer exist for anyone in the State. The Montana Supreme Court invalidated the program on state-law grounds, thereby foreclosing the as-applied challenge petitioners raise here. Indeed, nothing required the state court to uphold the program or the state legislature to maintain it. The Court nevertheless reframes the case and appears to ask whether a longstanding Montana constitutional provision is facially invalid under the Free Exercise Clause, even though petitioners disavowed bringing such a claim. But by resolving a constitutional question not presented, the Court fails to heed Article III principles older than the Religion Clause it expounds.

Not only is the Court wrong to decide this case at all, it decides it wrongly. In *Trinity Lutheran Church of Columbia, Inc. v. Comer* (2017), this Court held, "for the first time, that the Constitution requires the government to provide public funds directly to a church." Here, the Court invokes that precedent to require a State to subsidize religious schools if it enacts an education tax credit. Because this decision further "slights both our precedents and our history" and "weakens this country's longstanding commitment to a separation of church and state beneficial to both," I respectfully dissent.

I

The Montana Supreme Court invalidated a state tax-credit program because it was inconsistent with the Montana Constitution's "no-aid provision," which forbids government appropriations for sectarian purposes, including funding religious schools. In so doing, the court expressly declined to resolve federal constitutional issues. The court also remedied the only potential harm of discriminatory treatment by striking down the program altogether. After the state court's decision, neither secular nor sectarian schools receive the program's tax benefits.

Petitioners' free exercise claim is not cognizable. The Free Exercise Clause, the Court has said, protects against "indirect coercion or penalties on the free exercise of religion." Accordingly, this Court's cases have required not only differential treatment, cf. *ante*, at ___ – ___, but also a resulting burden on religious exercise.

Neither differential treatment nor coercion exists here because the Montana Supreme Court invalidated the tax-credit program entirely. Because no secondary school (secular or sectarian) is eligible for benefits, the state court's ruling neither treats petitioners differently based on religion nor burdens their religious exercise. Petitioners remain free to send their children to the religious school of their choosing and to exercise their faith.

To be sure, petitioners may want to apply for scholarships and would prefer that Montana subsidize their children's religious education. But this Court had never before held unconstitutional government action that merely failed to benefit religious exercise.

II

The Court's analysis of Montana's defunct tax program reprises the error in *Trinity Lutheran*. Contra the Court's current approach, our free exercise precedents had long granted the government "some room to recognize the unique status of religious entities and to single them out on that basis for exclusion from otherwise generally applicable laws."

Until *Trinity Lutheran*, the right to exercise one's religion did not include a right to have the State pay for that religious practice. That is because a contrary rule risks reading the Establishment Clause out of the Constitution. Although the Establishment Clause "permit[s] some government funding of secular functions performed by sectarian organizations," the Court's decisions "provide[d] no precedent for the use of public funds to finance religious activities." After all, the government must avoid "an unlawful fostering of religion."

Here, a State may refuse to extend certain aid programs to religious entities when doing so avoids "historic and substantial" antiestablishment concerns. Properly understood, this case is no different from *Locke* because petitioners seek to procure what the plaintiffs in *Locke* could not: taxpayer funds to support religious schooling.

The Court further suggests that by abstaining from funding religious activity, the State is "suppress[ing]" and "penaliz[ing]" religious activity. But a State's decision not to fund religious activity does not "disfavor religion; rather, it represents a valid choice to remain secular in the face of serious establishment and free exercise concerns." That is, a "legislature's decision not to subsidize the exercise of a fundamental right does not infringe the right." Finally, it is no answer to say that this case involves "discrimination." A "decision to treat entities differently based on distinctions that the Religion Clauses make relevant does not amount to discrimination."

Today's ruling is perverse. Without any need or power to do so, the Court appears to require a State to reinstate a tax-credit program that the Constitution did not demand in the first place. We once recognized that "[w]hile the Free Exercise Clause clearly prohibits the use of state action to deny the rights of free exercise to anyone, it has never meant that a majority could use the machinery of the State to practice its beliefs." Today's Court, by contrast, rejects the Religion Clauses' balanced values in favor of a new theory of free exercise, and it does so only by setting aside well-established judicial constraints.

E. STATUTORY PROTECTION OF RELIGIOUS FREEDOM

The Religious Freedom Restoration Act (RFRA) of 1993, 42 U.S.C. §2000bb, was adopted to negate the *Smith* test and require strict scrutiny for Free Exercise Clause claims. The act declares that its purpose is "to restore the compelling interest test as set forth in Sherbert v. Verner and Wisconsin v. Yoder, and to guarantee its application in all cases where free exercise of religion is substantially burdened; and to provide a claim or defense to persons whose religious exercise is substantially burdened by government." In City of Boerne v. Flores, 521 U.S. 507 (1997), the Supreme Court declared the law unconstitutional as applied to state and local governments. *City of Boerne* held that Congress lacked the authority under §5 of the Fourteenth Amendment to expand the scope of rights and that RFRA was thus unconstitutional as applied to state and local governments.

The Supreme Court has never expressly upheld the constitutionality of RFRA as applied to the federal government. However, in Gonzales v. O Centro Espirita Beneficente Unia Do, 546 U.S. 418 (2006), the Supreme Court applied the Religious Freedom Restoration Act to the federal government. Although the Court did not expressly address the issue of whether the statute is constitutional as applied to the federal government, the Court did use the act to rule in favor of a religion and against the federal government. The case involved a small religion, with relatively few adherents in the United States, whose members receive communion by drinking hoasca, a tea brewed from plants unique to the Amazon rainforest that contains a hallucinogen regulated under Schedule I of the Controlled Substances Act. Members of the religion brought a suit seeking a declaratory judgment that their use of the tea was protected by the Religious Freedom Restoration Act.

Chief Justice Roberts wrote for a unanimous Court and ruled in favor of the religion. In response to the government's claim of a need to stop the availability of hallucinogenic drugs, the Court stated, "RFRA requires the Government to demonstrate that the compelling interest test is satisfied through application of the challenged law 'to the person'—the particular claimant whose sincere exercise of religion is being substantially burdened. RFRA expressly adopted the compelling interest test 'as set forth in Sherbert v. Verner (1963) and Wisconsin v. Yoder (1972).' In each of those cases, this Court looked beyond broadly formulated interests justifying the general applicability of government mandates and scrutinized the asserted harm of granting specific exemptions to particular religious claimants."

E. Statutory Protection of Religious Freedom

Applying this test, the Court concluded, "Under the more focused inquiry required by RFRA and the compelling interest test, the Government's mere invocation of the general characteristics of Schedule I substances, as set forth in the Controlled Substances Act, cannot carry the day. It is true, of course, that Schedule I substances are exceptionally dangerous. Nevertheless, there is no indication that Congress considered the harms posed by the particular use at issue here—the circumscribed, sacramental use of hoasca by [this religion]."

The case indicates that RFRA is applicable to the federal government and that the Court approves a rigorous application of strict scrutiny under the statute.

This also was clear from the Supreme Court's subsequent, and undoubtedly most important, decision concerning RFRA: Burwell v. Hobby Lobby, 573 U.S. 682 (2014). The Court held that it violates the Religious Freedom Restoration Act to require that a closely held corporation provide insurance coverage for contraceptives that violates its owners' religious beliefs. A federal law required that the Department of Health and Human Services promulgate regulations requiring that health insurance provided by employers include preventative health care coverage for women. These regulations mandate that employer-provided insurance include contraceptive coverage for women. Although religious institutions and nonprofit corporations affiliated with religious institutions may exempt themselves from this requirement, for-profit companies must comply.

In a 5-4 decision, the Supreme Court held that it violated the federal Religious Freedom Restoration Act to require a closely held for-profit corporation to provide coverage for contraceptives that it says violate the religious beliefs of its owners. Justice Alito wrote the majority opinion. The Court said that Congress "included corporations within RFRA's definition of 'persons.'" The Court held that corporations can claim to have religious beliefs and religious free exercise. It stated: "A corporation is simply a form of organization used by human beings to achieve desired ends. . . . When rights, whether constitutional or statutory, are extended to corporations, the purpose is to protect the rights of these people."

The Court said that it had "little trouble concluding" that the contraceptive mandate substantially burdened the religious beliefs of owners of closely held corporations who opposed certain contraceptives. The Court said that it would assume that the government has a compelling interest in ensuring the availability of contraceptives for women, but that there were less restrictive alternatives: Congress could directly pay for these contraceptives or Congress could allow for-profit companies the same ability to opt out that it had given to not-for-profit companies that are affiliated with religions that oppose contraception. The Court thus concluded that "[t]he contraceptive mandate, as applied to closely held corporations, violates RFRA."

Justice Ginsburg wrote a vigorous dissent, joined by Justices Breyer, Sotomayor, and Kagan, and disagreed with every aspect of the majority's opinion. The dissent disagreed that for-profit corporations can have religious beliefs or religious free exercise and stated that "until today, religious exemptions had never been extended to any entity operating in the commercial, profit-making world." The dissent also disagreed that there is a substantial burdening of religious belief from requiring employers to provide insurance that includes coverage for contraceptives. Justice Ginsburg wrote: "The requirement carries no command that Hobby Lobby or Conestoga purchase or provide the contraceptives they find objectionable. Instead, it calls on the companies covered by the requirement to direct money into undifferentiated funds that finance a wide variety of benefits under comprehensive health plans. . . . Any decision to use contraceptives made by a woman covered under Hobby Lobby's or Conestoga's plan will not be propelled by the Government, it will be the woman's autonomous choice, informed by the physician she consults."

The dissent also disagreed with the majority's conclusion that there are less restrictive alternatives. Justice Ginsburg's dissenting opinion stressed that this will open the door to other claims under RFRA for an exemption to providing health insurance coverage. She wrote: "Would the exemption the Court holds RFRA demands for employers with religiously grounded objections to the use of certain contraceptives extend to employers with religiously grounded objections to blood transfusions (Jehovah's Witnesses); antidepressants (Scientologists); medications derived from pigs, including anesthesia, intravenous fluids, and pills coated with gelatin (certain Muslims, Jews, and Hindus); and vaccinations (Christian Scientists, among others)?"

The dissent was concerned, too, that this could lead to claims for religious exemptions to other federal laws, such as antidiscrimination statutes. The majority opinion responded to this by denying this possibility because "[t]he Government has a compelling interest in providing an equal opportunity to participate in the workforce without regard to race, and prohibitions on racial discrimination are precisely tailored to achieve that critical goal. . . ."

After RFRA was declared unconstitutional as applied to state and local governments, Congress enacted the Religious Land Use and Institutionalized Persons Act (RLUIPA), 42 U.S.C. §2001cc-1, which says the government land use decisions and treatment of prisoners that significantly burden religion must meet strict scrutiny.

In *Cutter v. Wilkinson*, 544 U.S. 709 (2005), the Court rejected a constitutional challenge that the law violated the establishment clause by impermissibly favoring religion. In a unanimous opinion written by Justice Ginsburg, the Court concluded that the government's accommodation of religion and protection of free exercise of religion did not impermissibly establish religion. The Court concluded:

> Our decisions recognize that "there is room for play in the joints" between the Clauses, some space for legislative action neither compelled by the Free Exercise Clause nor prohibited by the Establishment Clause. In accord with the majority of Courts of Appeals that have ruled on the question, we hold that §3 of RLUIPA fits within the corridor between the Religion Clauses: On its face, the Act qualifies as a permissible legislative accommodation of religion that is not barred by the Establishment Clause.
>
> Foremost, we find RLUIPA's institutionalized-persons provision compatible with the Establishment Clause because it alleviates exceptional government-created burdens on private religious exercise. Furthermore, the Act on its face does not founder on shoals our prior decisions have identified: Properly applying RLUIPA, courts must take adequate account of the burdens a requested accommodation may impose on nonbeneficiaries, and they must be satisfied that the Act's prescriptions are and will be administered neutrally among different faiths.

CHAPTER 9

THE ESTABLISHMENT CLAUSE

A. COMPETING THEORIES OF THE ESTABLISHMENT CLAUSE

There are three major competing approaches to the Establishment Clause.[1] Each has adherents on the Court, and each is supported by a body of scholarly literature. The theory chosen determines the approach used and often the result.

1. Strict Separation

The first theory often is termed "strict separation." This approach says that to the greatest extent possible, government and religion should be separated. The government should be, as much as possible, secular; religion should be entirely in the private realm of society. This theory is perhaps best described by Thomas Jefferson's metaphor that there should be a wall separating church and state.[2] As the Supreme Court declared in Everson v. Board of Education, 330 U.S. 1 (1947), "The First Amendment has erected a wall between church and state. That wall must be kept high and impregnable."

Jefferson's famous words were uttered, as was Madison's Remonstrance, as part of a campaign against Virginia's renewing its tax to support the church. In *Everson,* Justice Rutledge reviewed this history in describing the philosophy underlying the Establishment Clause: "The Amendment's purpose was not to strike merely at the official establishment of a single sect, creed or religion, outlawing only a formal relation such as had prevailed in England and some of the colonies. Necessarily it was to uproot all such relationships. But the object

---

[1]. Although these theories have been presented and discussed most by the justices and commentators in the context of the Establishment Clause, they also can be used in Free Exercise Clause analysis. Also, these three theories are not exhaustive of all views, and there are variants of each.

[2]. Thomas Jefferson, Letter to Messrs. Nehemiah Dodge and Others, a Committee of the Danbury Baptist Assoc., *Writings* 510 (1984).

was broader than separating church and state in this narrow sense. It was to create a complete and permanent separation of the spheres of religious activity and civil authority by comprehensively forbidding every form of public aid or support for religion."

A strict separation of church and state is seen as necessary to protect religious liberty.[3] When religion becomes a part of government, separationists argue, there is inevitable coercion to participate in that faith. Those of different faiths and those who profess no religious beliefs are made to feel excluded and unwelcome when government and religion become intertwined. Moreover, government involvement with religion is inherently divisive in a country with so many different religions and many people who claim no religion at all.[4]

There are problems with the strict separation approach, as there are with all of the theories. A complete prohibition of all government assistance to religion would threaten the free exercise of religion. For example, a refusal by the government to provide police, fire, or sanitation services obviously would seemingly infringe free exercise. Thus, a total wall separating church and state is impossible, and the issue becomes how to draw the appropriate line. Moreover, religion has traditionally been a part of many government activities, from the phrase "In God We Trust" on coins to the invocation before Supreme Court session, "God save this honorable Court."

2. *Neutrality Theory*

A second major approach to the Establishment Clause says that the government must be neutral on religion; that is, the government cannot favor religion over secularism or one religion over others. Professor Philip Kurland, a key exponent of this approach to the Religion Clauses, wrote that "the clauses should be read as stating a single precept: that government cannot utilize religion as a standard for action or inaction because these clauses, read together as they should be, prohibit classification in terms of religion either to confer a benefit or to impose a burden."[5] Professor Douglas Laycock has said that substantive neutrality means that "the religion clauses require government to minimize the extent to

---

3. *See* Alan Schwarz, *No Imposition of Religion: The Establishment Clause Value*, 77 Yale L.J. 692, 708 (1968).

4. Justice Brennan has articulated these purposes behind the Establishment Clause:

> The first, which is most closely related to the more general conceptions of liberty found in the remainder of the First Amendment, is to guarantee the individual right to conscience. . . . The second purpose of separation and neutrality is to keep the state from interfering in the essential autonomy of religious life, either by taking upon itself the decision of religious issues, or by unduly involving itself in the supervision of religious institutions or officials. The third purpose of separation and neutrality is to prevent the trivialization and degradation of religion by too close an attachment to the organs of government. . . . Finally, the principles of separation and neutrality help assure that essentially religious issues, precisely because of their importance and sensitivity, not become the occasion for battle in the political arena.

Marsh v. Chambers, 463 U.S. 783, 803-805 (1983) (Brennan, J., dissenting) (citations omitted).

5. Philip Kurland, *Of Church and State and the Supreme Court*, 29 U. Chi. L. Rev. 1, 96 (1961).

A. Competing Theories of the Establishment Clause

which it either encourages or discourages religious belief or disbelief, practice or nonpractice, observance or nonobservance."[6]

Several Supreme Court justices have advanced an "endorsement" test in evaluating the neutrality of a government's action. Under this approach, the government violates the Establishment Clause if it symbolically endorses a particular religion or if it generally endorses either religion or secularism. For example, Justice O'Connor has written that "[e]very government practice must be judged in its unique circumstances to determine whether it constitutes an endorsement or disapproval of religion."[7]

Justice O'Connor explained the importance of such government neutrality: "As a theoretical matter, the endorsement test captures the essential command of the Establishment Clause, namely, that government must not make a person's religious beliefs relevant to his or her standing in the political community by conveying a message 'that religion or a particular religious belief is favored or preferred.' . . . If government is to be neutral in matters of religion, rather than showing either favoritism or disapproval towards citizens based on their personal religious choices, government cannot endorse the religious practices and beliefs of some citizens without sending a clear message to nonadherents that they are outsiders or less than full members of the political community."[8]

The difficulty is in determining what government actions constitute an "endorsement" of religion. Several justices discussed this in Capitol Square Review & Advisory Board v. Pinette, 515 U.S. 753 (1995). The issue in *Pinette* was whether it was unconstitutional for the government to preclude the Ku Klux Klan from erecting a large Latin cross in the park across from the Ohio Statehouse. Although there was no majority opinion for the Court, seven justices voted that excluding the cross violated the Klan's free speech rights and that allowing it to be present would not violate the Establishment Clause. In the course of the Establishment Clause discussion, several of the justices addressed what constitutes a symbolic endorsement.

Justice O'Connor, in an opinion concurring in the judgment joined by Justices Souter and Breyer, concluded that the cross should be allowed because the reasonable observer would not perceive it as an endorsement of religion. O'Connor said that "[w]here the government's operation of a public forum has the effect of endorsing religion, even if the governmental actor neither intends nor actively encourages that result, the Establishment Clause is violated." Justice O'Connor said that a reasonable observer would not likely perceive the cross as being endorsed by the government because there was "a sign disclaiming government sponsorship or endorsement" and this would "remove doubt about State approval of [the] religious message."

O'Connor said that the endorsement test is applied "from the perspective of a hypothetical observer who is presumed to possess a certain level of information that all citizens might not share." She said that the reasonable observer "must be deemed aware of the history and content of the community and forum in which

---

6. Douglas Laycock, *Formal, Substantive and Disaggregated Neutrality Toward Religion*, 39 DePaul L. Rev. 993, 1001 (1990).
7. Lynch v. Donnelly, 465 U.S. 668, 694 (1984).
8. County of Allegheny v. Greater Pittsburgh ACLU, 492 U.S. 573, 627 (1989) (O'Connor, J., concurring in part and concurring in the judgment) (citations omitted).

the religious display appears [and] the general history of the place in which the cross is displayed. [An] informed observer will know how the public space in question has been used in the past."

Justices Stevens and Ginsburg dissented and argued that endorsement exists if a reasonable person passing by would perceive government support for religion. Justice Stevens wrote, "If a reasonable person could perceive a government endorsement of religion from a private display, then the State may not allow its property to be used as a forum for that display. No less stringent rule can adequately protect non-adherents from a well-grounded perception that their sovereign supports a faith to which they do not subscribe." Justice Stevens argued that Justice O'Connor's "'reasonable person' comes off as a well-schooled jurist, a being finer than the tort-law model. . . . [T]his enhanced tort-law standard is singularly out of place in the Establishment Clause context. It strips of constitutional protection every person whose knowledge happens to fall below some 'ideal' standard."

Thus, three different approaches to the endorsement test were expressed in *Pinette*. Justice Scalia, writing for the plurality, rejected using the test at all where the issue is private speech on government property. Justice O'Connor, writing for herself and Justices Souter and Breyer, said that the symbolic endorsement test should be applied from the perspective of the perceptions of a well-educated and well-informed observer. Justice Stevens, dissenting and joined by Justice Ginsburg, said that the symbolic endorsement test should look to the perceptions of the reasonable passerby.

The endorsement test is defended as a desirable approach to the Establishment Clause because it is a way of determining whether the government is neutral or whether it is favoring religion. A key purpose of the Establishment Clause is to prevent the government from making those who are not a part of the favored religion from feeling unwelcome. The symbolic endorsement test is seen as a way of assessing the likely perceptions of and reactions to government conduct.[9]

Those who criticize the endorsement test often focus on its ambiguity and indeterminancy.[10] People will perceive symbols in widely varying ways. The Court inevitably is left to make a subjective choice as to how people will perceive a particular symbol. Moreover, judges who are part of the dominant religion may be insensitive to how those of minority religions perceive particular symbols. At the same time, some argue that the endorsement test is too restrictive of government involvement with religion. Justice Kennedy, for example, said, "Either the endorsement test must invalidate scores of traditional practices recognizing the place religion holds in our culture, or it must be twisted and stretched to avoid inconsistency with practices we know to have been permitted in the past, while condemning similar practices with no greater endorsement

---

9. For a defense of the symbolic endorsement test, *see* Jesse Choper, *Securing Religious Liberty: Principles for Judicial Interpretation of the Religion Clauses* 28-29 (1995); Arnold H. Loewy, *Rethinking Government Neutrality Towards Religion Under the Establishment Clause: The Untapped Potential of Justice O'Connor's Insight*, 64 N.C. L. Rev. 1049 (1986).

10. *See, e.g.*, William Marshall, *"We Know It When We See It," the Supreme Court and the Establishment Clause*, 59 So. Cal. L. Rev. 495, 537 (1986); Steven D. Smith, *Symbols, Perceptions, and Doctrinal Illusions: Establishment Neutrality and the "No Endorsement" Test*, 86 Mich. L. Rev. 266, 283 (1987) (identifying this and other problems with the symbolic endorsement test).

A. Competing Theories of the Establishment Clause

effect simply by reason of their lack of historical antecedent. Neither result is acceptable."[11]

3. Accommodation

A third major theory is termed an "accommodation" approach. Under this view, the Court should interpret the Establishment Clause to recognize the importance of religion in society and accommodate its presence in government. Specifically, under the accommodation approach the government violates the Establishment Clause only if it literally establishes a church or coerces religious participation. Justice Kennedy, for example, has said that "the Establishment Clause . . . guarantees at a minimum that a government may not coerce anyone to support or participate in religion or its exercise, or otherwise act in a way which establishes a [state] religion or religious faith, or tends to do so."[12] In fact, wrote Justice Kennedy, "[b]arring all attempts to aid religion through government coercion goes far toward the attainment of [the] object [of the Establishment Clause]."[13]

The key question under this approach concerns what constitutes government "coercion." Several justices discussed this in Lee v. Weisman, 505 U.S. 577 (1992), presented below, where the Court declared unconstitutional clergy-delivered prayers at public school graduations. Justice Kennedy, writing for the Court, found that such prayers are inherently coercive because there is great pressure on students to attend their graduation ceremonies and to not leave during the prayers.

Justice Blackmun, in an opinion joined by Justices Stevens and O'Connor, wrote to emphasize that the Establishment Clause can be violated even without coercion. He remarked that it "is not enough that the government refrain from compelling religious practices; it must not engage in them either." Likewise, Justice Souter, joined by Justices Stevens and O'Connor, wrote separately to stress that coercion is sufficient for a finding of Establishment Clause violation, but it is not necessary; Establishment Clause violations exist without coercion if there is symbolic government endorsement of religion.

The dissenting opinion by Justice Scalia, joined by Chief Justice Rehnquist and Justices White and Thomas, advocated the accommodation approach, but defined coercion much more narrowly than Justice Kennedy. Justice Scalia said that "[t]he coercion that was a hallmark of historical establishments of religion was coercion of religious orthodoxy and of financial support by force of law and threat of penalty." In other words, for the dissenters in *Lee*, coercion exists only if the law requires and punishes the failure to engage in religious practices.

In a subsequent case, presented below, Town of Greece v. Galloway, 572 U.S. 565 (2014), Justice Thomas in a concurring opinion joined in relevant part by Justice Scalia, said that coercion must be legal coercion enforced by penalty of law: "'The coercion that was a hallmark of historical establishments of religion was coercion of religious orthodoxy and of financial support *by force of law and*

---

11. County of Allegheny v. Greater Pittsburgh ACLU, 492 U.S. at 674.
12. Lee v. Weisman, 505 U.S. 577 (1992).
13. County of Allegheny v. Greater Pittsburgh ACLU, 492 U.S. at 660 (Kennedy, J., concurring in the judgment in part and dissenting in part).

threat of penalty.' Thus, to the extent coercion is relevant to the Establishment Clause analysis, it is actual legal coercion that counts—not the 'subtle coercive pressures.' [I]n light of the foregoing history of the Establishment Clause, '[p]eer pressure, unpleasant as it may be, is not coercion' either."

Those who defend the accommodation approach argue that it best reflects the importance and prevalence of religion in American society. Professor Michael McConnell, an advocate of this view, said that it is desirable because it makes "religion . . . a welcome element in the mix of beliefs and associations present in the community. Under this view, the emphasis is placed on freedom of choice and diversity among religious opinion. The nation is understood not as secular but as pluralistic. Religion is under no special disability in public life; indeed, it is at least as protected and encouraged as any other form of belief and association—in some ways more so."[14] Anything less than accommodation, it is argued, is unacceptable hostility to religion.

Opponents of the accommodation approach argue that, especially as defined by Justice Scalia, little ever will violate the Establishment Clause.[15] Nothing except the government creating its own church or by force of law requiring religious practices or discriminating among religions will offend the provision. Those disagreeing with this theory argue that the Establishment Clause also should serve to prevent the government from making those of other religions feel unwelcome and to keep the government from using its power and influence to advance religion or a particular religion. Justice O'Connor expressed this view when she wrote, "An Establishment Clause standard that prohibits only 'coercive' practices or overt efforts at government proselytization, but fails to take account of the numerous more subtle ways that government can show favoritism to particular beliefs or convey a message of disapproval to others, would not, in my view, adequately protect the religious liberty or respect the religious diversity of the members of our pluralistic political community. Thus, this Court has never relied on coercion alone as the touchstone of Establishment Clause analysis."

4. The Theories Applied: An Example

The importance of these three theories in determining the inquiry and the results in Establishment Clause cases is reflected in Allegheny County v. Greater Pittsburgh ACLU.

COUNTY OF ALLEGHENY v. AMERICAN CIVIL LIBERTIES UNION, GREATER PITTSBURGH CHAPTER
492 U.S. 573 (1989)

Justice BLACKMUN announced the judgment of the Court.

This litigation concerns the constitutionality of two recurring holiday displays located on public property in downtown Pittsburgh. The first is a

---

14. Michael W. McConnell, *Accommodation of Religion*, 1985 Sup. Ct. Rev. 1, 14.
15. Professor Sherry argues that the coercion test "makes the Establishment Clause redundant. Any government action that coerces religious belief violates the Free Exercise Clause." Suzanna Sherry, *Lee v. Weisman: Paradox Redux*, 1992 Sup. Ct. Rev. 123, 134.

A. Competing Theories of the Establishment Clause

creche placed on the Grand Staircase of the Allegheny County Courthouse. The second is a Chanukah menorah placed just outside the City-County Building, next to a Christmas tree and a sign saluting liberty. The Court of Appeals for the Third Circuit ruled that each display violates the Establishment Clause of the First Amendment because each has the impermissible effect of endorsing religion. We agree that the creche display has that unconstitutional effect but reverse the Court of Appeals' judgment regarding the menorah display.

In the course of adjudicating specific cases, this Court has come to understand the Establishment Clause to mean that government may not promote or affiliate itself with any religious doctrine or organization, may not discriminate among persons on the basis of their religious beliefs and practices, may not delegate a governmental power to a religious institution, and may not involve itself too deeply in such an institution's affairs. Our subsequent decisions further have refined the definition of governmental action that unconstitutionally advances religion. In recent years, we have paid particularly close attention to whether the challenged governmental practice either has the purpose or effect of "endorsing" religion, a concern that has long had a place in our Establishment Clause jurisprudence. Of course, the word "endorsement" is not self-defining. Rather, it derives its meaning from other words that this Court has found useful over the years in interpreting the Establishment Clause. Thus, it has been noted that the prohibition against governmental endorsement of religion "preclude[s] government from conveying or attempting to convey a message that religion or a particular religious belief is favored or preferred." Whether the key word is "endorsement," "favoritism," or "promotion," the essential principle remains the same.

We have had occasion in the past to apply Establishment Clause principles to the government's display of objects with religious significance. In Lynch v. Donnelly, we considered whether the city of Pawtucket, R.I., had violated the Establishment Clause by including a creche in its annual Christmas display, located in a private park within the downtown shopping district. By a 5-to-4 decision in that difficult case, the Court upheld inclusion of the creche in the Pawtucket display, holding that the inclusion of the creche did not have the impermissible effect of advancing or promoting religion. The five Justices in concurrence and dissent in *Lynch* agreed upon the relevant constitutional principles: the government's use of religious symbolism is unconstitutional if it has the effect of endorsing religious beliefs, and the effect of the government's use of religious symbolism depends upon its context. These general principles are sound, and have been adopted by the Court in subsequent cases. Since *Lynch*, the Court has made clear that, when evaluating the effect of government conduct under the Establishment Clause, we must ascertain whether "the challenged governmental action is sufficiently likely to be perceived by adherents of the controlling denominations as an endorsement, and by the nonadherents as a disapproval, of their individual religious choices."

We turn first to the county's creche display. There is no doubt, of course, that the creche itself is capable of communicating a religious message. Under the Court's holding in *Lynch*, the effect of a creche display turns on its setting. Here, unlike in *Lynch*, nothing in the context of the display detracts from the creche's religious message. The *Lynch* display composed a series of figures and objects, each group of which had its own focal point. Santa's house and his reindeer were objects of attention separate from the creche, and had their specific visual story to tell. Similarly, whatever a "talking" wishing well may be, it obviously was a center of attention separate from the creche. Here, in contrast, the creche stands alone: it is the single element of the display on the Grand Staircase.

The display of the Chanukah menorah in front of the City-County Building may well present a closer constitutional question. The menorah, one must recognize, is a religious symbol: it serves to commemorate the miracle of the oil as described in the Talmud. But the menorah's message is not exclusively religious. The menorah is the primary visual symbol for a holiday that, like Christmas, has both religious and secular dimensions.

[T]he menorah here stands next to a Christmas tree and a sign saluting liberty. While no challenge has been made here to the display of the tree and the sign, their presence is obviously relevant in determining the effect of the menorah's display. The necessary result of placing a menorah next to a Christmas tree is to create an "overall holiday setting" that represents both Christmas and Chanukah — two holidays, not one. The mere fact that Pittsburgh displays symbols of both Christmas and Chanukah does not end the constitutional inquiry. If the city celebrates both Christmas and Chanukah as religious holidays, then it violates the Establishment Clause. The simultaneous endorsement of Judaism and Christianity is no less constitutionally infirm than the endorsement of Christianity alone.

Accordingly, the relevant question for Establishment Clause purposes is whether the combined display of the tree, the sign, and the menorah has the effect of endorsing both Christian and Jewish faiths, or rather simply recognizes that both Christmas and Chanukah are part of the same winter-holiday season, which has attained a secular status in our society. Of the two interpretations of this particular display, the latter seems far more plausible and is also in line with *Lynch*.

Justice O'CONNOR concurring in part and concurring in the judgment.

I agree that the creche displayed on the Grand Staircase of the Allegheny County Courthouse, the seat of county government, conveys a message to nonadherents of Christianity that they are not full members of the political community, and a corresponding message to Christians that they are favored members of the political community. In contrast to the creche in *Lynch*, which was displayed in a private park in the city's commercial district as part of a broader display of traditional secular symbols of the holiday season, this creche stands alone in the county courthouse. The display of religious symbols in public areas of core government buildings runs a special risk of "mak[ing] religion relevant, in reality or public perception, to status in the political community." The Court correctly concludes that placement of the central religious symbol of the Christmas holiday season at the Allegheny County Courthouse has the unconstitutional effect of conveying a government endorsement of Christianity.

For reasons which differ somewhat from those set forth in Justice Blackmun's opinion, I also conclude that the city of Pittsburgh's combined holiday display of a Chanukah menorah, a Christmas tree, and a sign saluting liberty does not have the effect of conveying an endorsement of religion. In my view, the relevant question for Establishment Clause purposes is whether the city of Pittsburgh's display of the menorah, the religious symbol of a religious holiday, next to a Christmas tree and a sign saluting liberty sends a message of government endorsement of Judaism or whether it sends a message of pluralism

A. Competing Theories of the Establishment Clause

and freedom to choose one's own beliefs. The message of pluralism conveyed by the city's combined holiday display is not a message that endorses religion over nonreligion.

Justice BRENNAN, with whom Justice MARSHALL and Justice STEVENS join, concurring in part and dissenting in part.

I continue to believe that the display of an object that "retains a specifically Christian [or other] religious meaning" is incompatible with the separation of church and state demanded by our Constitution. I therefore agree with the Court that Allegheny County's display of a creche at the county courthouse signals an endorsement of the Christian faith in violation of the Establishment Clause. Court's opinion. I cannot agree, however, that the city's display of a 45-foot Christmas tree and an 18-foot Chanukah menorah at the entrance to the building housing the mayor's office shows no favoritism towards Christianity, Judaism, or both. Indeed, I should have thought that the answer as to the first display supplied the answer to the second.

Justice STEVENS, with whom Justice BRENNAN and Justice MARSHALL join, concurring in part and dissenting in part.

In my opinion the Establishment Clause should be construed to create a strong presumption against the display of religious symbols on public property. There is always a risk that such symbols will offend nonmembers of the faith being advertised as well as adherents who consider the particular advertisement disrespectful. Some devout Christians believe that the creche should be placed only in reverential settings, such as a church or perhaps a private home; they do not countenance its use as an aid to commercialization of Christ's birthday. In this very suit, members of the Jewish faith firmly opposed the use to which the menorah was put by the particular sect that sponsored the display at Pittsburgh's City-County Building. Even though "[p]assersby who disagree with the message conveyed by these displays are free to ignore them, or even to turn their backs," displays of this kind inevitably have a greater tendency to emphasize sincere and deeply felt differences among individuals than to achieve an ecumenical goal. The Establishment Clause does not allow public bodies to foment such disagreement.

Justice KENNEDY, with whom THE CHIEF JUSTICE, Justice WHITE, and Justice SCALIA join, concurring in the judgment in part and dissenting in part.

The majority holds that the County of Allegheny violated the Establishment Clause by displaying a creche in the county courthouse, because the "principal or primary effect" of the display is to advance religion. This view of the Establishment Clause reflects an unjustified hostility toward religion, a hostility inconsistent with our history and our precedents, and I dissent from this holding. The creche display is constitutional, and, for the same reasons, the display of a menorah by the city of Pittsburgh is permissible as well. On this latter point, I concur in the result, but not the reasoning, of Justice Blackmun's opinion.

Rather than requiring government to avoid any action that acknowledges or aids religion, the Establishment Clause permits government some latitude in recognizing and accommodating the central role religion plays in our society. Any approach less sensitive to our heritage would border on latent hostility toward religion, as it would require government in all its multifaceted roles to acknowledge only the secular, to the exclusion and so to the detriment of the religious. A categorical approach would install federal courts as jealous guardians of an absolute "wall of separation," sending a clear message of disapproval. In this century, as the modern administrative state expands to touch the lives of its citizens in such diverse ways and redirects their financial choices through programs of its own, it is difficult to maintain the fiction that requiring government to avoid all assistance to religion can in fairness be viewed as serving the goal of neutrality.

The ability of the organized community to recognize and accommodate religion in a society with a pervasive public sector requires diligent observance of the border between accommodation and establishment. Our cases disclose two limiting principles: government may not coerce anyone to support or participate in any religion or its exercise; and it may not, in the guise of avoiding hostility or callous indifference, give direct benefits to religion in such a degree that it in fact "establishes a [state] religion or religious faith, or tends to do so."

These principles are not difficult to apply to the facts of the cases before us. In permitting the displays on government property of the menorah and the creche, the city and county sought to do no more than "celebrate the season," and to acknowledge, along with many of their citizens, the historical background and the religious, as well as secular, nature of the Chanukah and Christmas holidays. This interest falls well within the tradition of government accommodation and acknowledgment of religion that has marked our history from the beginning. It cannot be disputed that government, if it chooses, may participate in sharing with its citizens the joy of the holiday season, by declaring public holidays, installing or permitting festive displays, sponsoring celebrations and parades, and providing holiday vacations for its employees. All levels of our government do precisely that. As we said in *Lynch*, "Government has long recognized—indeed it has subsidized—holidays with religious significance."

If government is to participate in its citizens' celebration of a holiday that contains both a secular and a religious component, enforced recognition of only the secular aspect would signify the callous indifference toward religious faith that our cases and traditions do not require; for by commemorating the holiday only as it is celebrated by nonadherents, the government would be refusing to acknowledge the plain fact, and the historical reality, that many of its citizens celebrate its religious aspects as well. Judicial invalidation of government's attempts to recognize the religious underpinnings of the holiday would signal not neutrality but a pervasive intent to insulate government from all things religious. The Religion Clauses do not require government to acknowledge these holidays or their religious component; but our strong tradition of government accommodation and acknowledgment permits government to do so.

There is no suggestion here that the government's power to coerce has been used to further the interests of Christianity or Judaism in any way. No one was compelled to observe or participate in any religious ceremony or activity. Neither the city nor the county contributed significant amounts of tax money to serve the cause of one religious faith. The creche and the menorah are purely passive symbols of religious holidays. Passersby who disagree with the message conveyed by these displays are free to ignore them, or even to turn their backs, just as they are free to do when they disagree with any other form of government speech.

B. GOVERNMENT DISCRIMINATION AMONG RELIGIONS

It is firmly established that the government violates the Establishment Clause if it discriminates among religious groups. Such discrimination will be allowed only if strict scrutiny is met. If there is not discrimination, the case is discussed under the *Lemon* test described in the next subsection. In Hernandez v. Commissioner, 490 U.S. 680 (1989), the Court explained, "[W]hen it is claimed that a denominational preference exists, the initial inquiry is whether the law facially differentiates among religions. If no such facial preference exists, we proceed to apply the customary three-pronged Establishment Clause inquiry derived from Lemon v. Kurtzman."

Larson v. Valente, 456 U.S. 228 (1982), applied this principle to declare unconstitutional a Minnesota law that imposed registration and reporting requirements on charitable organizations but exempted religious institutions that received more than half of their financial support from members' contributions.

The Court said that the "history and logic of the Establishment Clause [mean] that no State can 'pass laws which aid one religion' or that 'prefer one religion over another.'" The Court concluded that the 50 percent requirement "clearly grants denominational preferences of the sort consistently and firmly deprecated in our precedents" and thus could not be allowed unless strict scrutiny was met. Religions that met the requirement, such as the Catholic Church, had the great benefit of being exempt from the burdens of the statute; religions that did not meet the requirement, such as the "Moonies," would have to comply with the law. The Court found that there was no compelling interest to justify the discrimination and thus concluded that the "fifty percent rule sets up precisely the sort of official denominational preference that the Framers of the First Amendment forbade."

The Court also applied this neutrality principle in Board of Education of Kiryas Joel Village School District v. Grumet, 512 U.S. 687 (1994), to declare unconstitutional a state law that created a separate school district for a small village that was inhabited by Hasidic Jews. The Village of Kiryas Joel was created by a sect known as Satmar Hasidim. They maintained two parochial schools, one for boys and one for girls. However, they did not have any services available for children with disabilities. Until the Supreme Court declared it unconstitutional in 1985, the government provided special education for such children within the parochial schools.[16] In response to these Supreme Court decisions, the State of New York adopted a law that created a public school district with boundaries identical to those of the Village of Kiryas Joel. The school board for the village was like all other school boards, except that all of its elected members were part of the Satmar Hasidic sect.

Justice Souter, writing for the Court, declared the New York law unconstitutional as impermissible preference for one religion over others. The government created a school district specifically to help one religion so that it could provide special education without its children having to attend school

---

16. Grand Rapids School District v. Ball, 473 U.S. 373 (1985); Aguilar v. Felton, 473 U.S. 402 (1985). As indicated below, *Aguilar* was overruled in Agostini v. Felton, 521 U.S. 203 (1997).

with those outside the faith. Justice Souter explained that "the fundamental source of constitutional concern here is that the legislature itself may fail to exercise governmental authority in a religiously neutral way."

In a part of the opinion that was joined only by a plurality, Justice Souter also said that the law violated the Establishment Clause because the government was impermissibly delegating government authority to a religious entity. He said that creating a government entity contiguous with a religious community and thereby allowing the religion to control its political process was an impermissible "fusion of governmental and religious functions."

Thus, cases such as *Larson* and *Kiryas Joel* establish that a government action violates the Establishment Clause if it prefers one religion or sect over others. In such instances, the Court invalidates the law without reaching the *Lemon* test, discussed below. Yet the neutrality approach taken in cases such as *Larson* and *Kiryas Joel* is remarkably similar to the analysis under the first two prongs of the *Lemon* test: If the government is favoring one religion, it is acting with the purpose, and there is the effect of fostering that religion.

C. THE *LEMON* TEST FOR THE ESTABLISHMENT CLAUSE

If a law is not discriminatory, the Supreme Court says that a court should apply the three-part test articulated in Lemon v. Kurtzman.

LEMON v. KURTZMAN
403 U.S. 602 (1971)

Chief Justice BURGER delivered the opinion of the Court.

These two appeals raise questions as to Pennsylvania and Rhode Island statutes providing state aid to church-related elementary and secondary schools. Pennsylvania has adopted a statutory program that provides financial support to nonpublic elementary and secondary schools by way of reimbursement for the cost of teachers' salaries, textbooks, and instructional materials in specified secular subjects. Rhode Island has adopted a statute under which the State pays directly to teachers in nonpublic elementary schools a supplement of 15% of their annual salary. Under each statute state aid has been given to church-related educational institutions. We hold that both statutes are unconstitutional.

The language of the Religion Clauses of the First Amendment is at best opaque, particularly when compared with other portions of the Amendment. Its authors did not simply prohibit the establishment of a state church or a state religion, an area history shows they regarded as very important and fraught with great dangers. Instead they commanded that there should be "no law respecting an establishment of religion." A law may be one "respecting" the forbidden objective while falling short of its total realization. A law "respecting" the proscribed result, that is, the establishment of religion, is not always easily identifiable as one violative of the Clause. A given law might not establish a state religion but

C. The *Lemon* Test for the Establishment Clause

nevertheless be one "respecting" that end in the sense of being a step that could lead to such establishment and hence offend the First Amendment.

In the absence of precisely stated constitutional prohibitions. we must draw lines with reference to the three main evils against which the Establishment Clause was intended to afford protection: "sponsorship, financial support, and active involvement of the sovereign in religious activity."

Every analysis in this area must begin with consideration of the cumulative criteria developed by the Court over many years. Three such tests may be gleaned from our cases. First, the statute must have a secular legislative purpose; second, its principal or primary effect must be one that neither advances nor inhibits religion; finally, the statute must not foster "an excessive government entanglement with religion."

Inquiry into the legislative purposes of the Pennsylvania and Rhode Island statutes affords no basis for a conclusion that the legislative intent was to advance religion. On the contrary, the statutes themselves clearly state that they are intended to enhance the quality of the secular education in all schools covered by the compulsory attendance laws. There is no reason to believe the legislatures meant anything else. [However,] we conclude that the cumulative impact of the entire relationship arising under the statutes in each State involves excessive entanglement between government and religion. In order to determine whether the government entanglement with religion is excessive, we must examine the character and purposes of the institutions that are benefited, the nature of the aid that the State provides, and the resulting relationship between the government and the religious authority. Mr. Justice Harlan echoed the classic warning as to "programs whose very nature is apt to entangle the state in details of administration." Here we find that both statutes foster an impermissible degree of entanglement.

Although there have been many cases where the Court decided Establishment Clause cases without applying the *Lemon* test,[17] it has been frequently used. While several justices have criticized the test and called for it to be overruled, this has not occurred.[18] Indeed, Justice Scalia, the primary advocate for overruling the *Lemon* test, colorfully lamented its survival and analogized it to "a ghoul in a late-night horror movie that repeatedly sits up in its grave and shuffles abroad, after being repeatedly killed and buried. [It] is there to scare us [when] we wish it to do so, but we can command it to return to the tomb at will. When we wish to strike down a practice it forbids, we invoke it, when we wish to uphold a practice it forbids, we ignore it entirely."[19]

The *Lemon* test is favored and used by justices taking the strict separationist approach to the Establishment Clause. It also is used by justices taking the

---

17. *See, e.g.*, Board of Education of Kiryas Joel Village School Dist. v. Grumet, 512 U.S. 687 (1994) (finding favoritism for one religion by creating a school district contiguous with a religious community violates the Establishment Clause); Lynch v. Donnelly, 465 U.S. 668 (1984) (allowing nativity scene on government property); Marsh v. Chambers, 463 U.S. 783 (1983) (allowing government payment of a legislative chaplain because of history of the practice).

18. *See* Lamb's Chapel v. Center Moriches Union Free School District, 508 U.S. 384 (1993) (applying the *Lemon* test and concluding that the Establishment Clause was not violated by allowing religious groups to use school facilities during evenings and weekends).

19. Lamb's Chapel v. Center Moriches Union Free School Dist., 508 U.S, at 398-399 (Scalia, J., dissenting).

neutrality approach, although they emphasize whether the purpose or effect is to symbolically endorse religion.[20] Justices favoring the accommodationist approach urge the overruling of the *Lemon* test.

The current and future role of the *Lemon* test is uncertain. The test has not been expressly overruled or discarded, and it has been invoked in recent years. For example, in McCreary County v. American Civil Liberties Union of Kentucky, 545 U.S. 844 (2005), below, the Court used the *Lemon* test in invalidating a county's requirement that the court post the Ten Commandments. In its most recent case, American Legion v. American Humanist Association, 139 S. Ct. 2067 (2019), presented below, Justice Alito's majority opinion rejected use of the *Lemon* test in evaluating religious symbols on government property, but did not overrule *Lemon* or use of the test with regard to other Establishment Clause issues.

THE REQUIREMENT FOR A SECULAR PURPOSE

The first prong of the *Lemon* test is the requirement that there be a secular purpose for a law. For example, in Stone v. Graham, 449 U.S. 39 (1980), the Supreme Court declared unconstitutional a state law that required the Ten Commandments to be posted on the walls of every public school classroom. The Court concluded that the law "has no secular legislative purpose" and therefore violated the Establishment Clause. Similarly, in Wallace v. Jaffree, 472 U.S. 38 (1985), the Court invalidated a state law that authorized public school teachers to hold a one-minute period of silence for meditation or voluntary prayer. The Court found that the purpose behind the law was to reintroduce prayer into public schools and deemed the law unconstitutional because it "was not motivated by any clearly secular purpose—indeed, the statute had *no* secular purpose."

In Edwards v. Aguillard, 482 U.S. 578 (1987), the Court followed this reasoning and ruled unconstitutional a state law that required that public schools that teach evolution also teach "creation science." Since "creation science" is a religious theory explaining the origin of human life, the Court concluded, "Because the primary purpose of the Creationism Act is to endorse a particular religious doctrine, the Act furthers religion in violation of the establishment clause."

In contrast, in McGowan v. Maryland, 366 U.S. 420 (1961), the Supreme Court upheld the constitutionality of state laws requiring businesses to be closed on Sunday. The Court acknowledged "the strongly religious origin of these laws." Nonetheless, the Court found the laws permissible because "[t]he present purpose and effect of most of them is to provide a uniform day of rest for all citizens; the fact that this day is Sunday, a day of particular significance for the dominant Christian sects, does not bar the State from achieving its secular goals."

---

20. *See, e.g.*, Lynch v. Donnelly, 465 U.S. at 690 (O'Connor, J., concurring) ("The purpose prong of the *Lemon* test asks whether government's actual purpose is to endorse or disapprove of religion. The effect prong asks whether, irrespective of government's actual purpose, the practice under review in fact conveys a message of endorsement or disapproval. An affirmative answer to either question should render the challenged practice invalid.").

Several of the justices—especially Chief Justice Rehnquist and Justice Scalia—have criticized the first prong of the *Lemon* test. Rehnquist has argued that the requirement for a secular purpose "is a constitutional theory [that] has no basis in the history of the amendment it seeks to interpret, is difficult to apply and yields unprincipled results."[21] Scalia contended, "[D]iscerning the subjective motivation of those enacting the statue is, to be honest, almost always an impossible task. The number of possible motivations . . . is not binary, or indeed even finite. . . . To look for *the sole purpose* of even a single legislator is probably to look for something that does not exist."[22]

On the other hand, the Court considers legislative purpose, despite the difficulty in ascertaining it, in other areas of constitutional law, such as in the requirement for proof of a discriminatory purpose to prove a race or gender classification when there is a facially neutral law.[23] The rationale for the first prong of the *Lemon* test is that the very essence of the Establishment Clause is to keep the government from acting to advance religion.

THE REQUIREMENT FOR A SECULAR EFFECT

The second prong of the *Lemon* test requires that the principal or primary effect of a law must be one that neither advances nor inhibits religion. In recent years, this often has been expressed in terms of symbolic endorsement: The government's action must not symbolically endorse religion or a particular religion.[24]

Estate of Thornton v. Caldor, 472 U.S. 703 (1985), is an example where the Court used the second part of the *Lemon* test to invalidate a law. A Connecticut statute provided that no person may be required by an employer to work on his or her Sabbath. The Supreme Court declared the law unconstitutional and emphasized that the law created an absolute and unqualified right for individuals to not work for religious reasons and thus favored religion over all other interests. The Court concluded that "the statute goes beyond having an incidental or remote effect of advancing religion. The statute has a primary effect that impermissibly advances a particular religious practice."

However, in other cases, the Court has upheld exemptions from laws for religion. In Corporation of the Presiding Bishop of the Church of Jesus Christ of Latter-Day Saints v. Amos, 483 U.S. 327 (1987), the Court found constitutional an exemption for religious organizations from Title VII's prohibition against discrimination in employment based on religion. The Court concluded that the exemption met the first prong of the *Lemon* test because it was a permissible purpose "to alleviate significant government interference with the ability of religious organizations to define and carry out their religious missions."

---

21. Wallace v. Jaffree, 472 U.S. at 112 (Rehnquist, J., dissenting).
22. Edwards v. Aguillard, 482 U.S. at 636-637 (Scalia, J., dissenting).
23. *See, e.g.,* Washington v. Davis, 426 U.S. 229 (1976).
24. *See, e.g.,* Board of Education of Westside Community Schools v. Mergens, 496 U.S. 226, 249-253 (1990) (plurality opinion) (using the symbolic endorsement test to determine whether the effect of a government action was to advance religion impermissibly).

More significantly, the Court found that the exemption was not inconsistent with the second part of the *Lemon* test. Justice White, writing for the majority, said that "[a] law is not unconstitutional simply because it *allows* churches to advance religion, which is their very purpose. For a law to have forbidden 'effects' under *Lemon*, it must be fair to say that the *government itself* has advanced religion through its own activities and influence."

The difference between *Thornton* and *Amos* is that the latter involved an exemption in a statute for religion, whereas the former concerned a law that provided a benefit solely for religion. The Court found that the latter was permissible, but that the former was the government advancing religion through its own activities and influence. Yet the distinction is difficult because both laws provided a preference for religion alone.

THE PROHIBITION OF EXCESSIVE ENTANGLEMENT

The final prong of the *Lemon* test forbids government actions that cause excessive entanglement with religion. The Court has said that a law violates the Establishment Clause when it requires a "comprehensive, discriminating, and continuing state surveillance."[25] The Court also has said that "apart from any specific entanglement of the State in particular religious programs, assistance . . . [violates the Establishment Clause if it] carries the [grave] potential for entanglement in the broader sense of continuing political strife over aid to religion."[26]

For example, the Supreme Court has held that the government cannot pay teacher salaries in parochial schools, even for teachers of secular subjects.[27] If the government paid such salaries, it would need to monitor whether the teachers were teaching secular or religious material. Any such monitoring would be excessive government entanglement with religion.

In Agostini v. Felton, 521 U.S. 203 (1997), however, the Court held that it was permissible for public schoolteachers to provide remedial education in parochial schools. In doing so, the Court cast doubt as to whether the "entanglement prong" remains a separate prong of the analysis. The Court said, "Thus, it is simplest to recognize why entanglement is significant and treat it as an aspect of the inquiry into a statute's effect." But the Court also reiterated that "excessive entanglement" violates the Establishment Clause: "Not all entanglements, of course, have the effect of advancing or inhibiting religion. Interaction between church and state is inevitable, and we have always tolerated some level of involvement between the two. Entanglement must be 'excessive' before it runs afoul of the Establishment Clause." Subsequently, Justice O'Connor observed, "In Agostini v. Felton (1997), we folded the entanglement inquiry into the primary effect inquiry."[28]

---

25. Lemon v. Kurtzman, 403 U.S. at 619.
26. Committee for Public Education v. Nyquist, 413 U.S. 756, 794 (1973).
27. *See, e.g.*, Grand Rapids v. Ball, 473 U.S. 373 (1985).
28. Zelman v. Simmons-Harris, 536 U.S. 639 (2002).

D. RELIGIOUS SPEECH AND THE FIRST AMENDMENT

A number of cases concerning the Establishment Clause have involved free speech claims. Specifically, these cases concern situations where the government chooses to restrict private religious speech on government property or with government funds because of a desire to avoid violating the Establishment Clause. The Supreme Court consistently has held that excluding such religious speech violates the First Amendment's protection of freedom of speech because it is an impermissible content-based restriction of expression.

These cases mark a significant development in Establishment Clause jurisprudence that changes the way many cases will be litigated and decided. If a government action can be characterized as a restriction of private religious speech, it can be challenged as violating the First Amendment's protection of freedom of speech, and the challenger has a strong likelihood of prevailing; no longer will such cases be seen as exclusively or even predominantly involving the Establishment Clause.

1. *Religious Group Access to School Facilities*

The initial Supreme Court cases in this area concerned efforts by the government to restrict religious groups from using school facilities so as to avoid violating the Establishment Clause. In Widmar v. Vincent, 454 U.S. 263 (1981), the Supreme Court declared unconstitutional a state university's policy of preventing student groups from using school facilities for religious worship or religious discussion. The University of Missouri at Kansas City allowed registered student groups to use its facilities, but forbade their use "for purposes of religious worship or religious teaching."

The Court said that the university "discriminated against student groups and speakers based on their desire to use a generally open forum to engage in religious worship and discussion. These are forms of speech and association protected by the First Amendment." The Court expressly rejected the dissent's argument that religious worship is not speech protected by the free speech guarantee of the First Amendment. The Court said that the university had created a public forum by opening these places to speech and said that "[i]n order to justify discriminatory exclusion from a public forum based on the religious content of a group's intended speech, the University must therefore satisfy the standard of review appropriate to content-based exclusions. It must show that its regulation is necessary to serve a compelling state interest and that it is narrowly drawn to achieve that end."

The Court then concluded that excluding religious speech was not necessary in order to be consistent with the Establishment Clause. The Court applied the *Lemon* test and said that opening school facilities to all groups served the secular purpose of providing a forum for student meetings. The Court said that any effect in advancing religion would be "incidental." The Court concluded that allowing religious groups to use school facilities was not excessive entanglement with religion; no state monitoring would be necessary if the university allowed secular and religious groups to use the facilities.

The Court followed similar reasoning in Board of Education of Westside Community Schools v. Mergens, 496 U.S. 226 (1990). *Mergens* involved a constitutional challenge to the federal Equal Access Act, which applies to any public school that receives federal financial assistance. The Equal Access Act says that any such school that opens its facilities to noncurricular student groups may not deny equal access to any students who wish to conduct meetings on similar terms because of the religious, political, philosophical, or other content of their speech.

Justice O'Connor, writing for the plurality, said that "the logic of *Widmar* applies." Justice O'Connor used the *Lemon* test and concluded that preventing discrimination against speech because of its religious, political, or philosophical content was a legitimate secular purpose. She said that the effect was not to advance religion because allowing religious groups to use school facilities was not likely to be perceived as a symbolic government endorsement of religion. Justice O'Connor wrote that "secondary school students are mature enough and are likely to understand that a school does not endorse or support student speech that it merely permits on a nondiscriminatory basis." She said that "there is a crucial difference between government speech endorsing religion, which the Establishment Clause forbids, and private speech endorsing religion, which the Free Speech and Free Exercise Clauses protect." Finally, Justice O'Conner concluded that there was not excessive entanglement with religion because faculty sponsors were not allowed to participate actively in religious groups' meetings.

Justices Brennan and Marshall concurred in the judgment and emphasized that schools had the consitutional duty to make it clear that the government was not endorsing the views or activities of the religious groups. Justices Kennedy and Scalia also concurred in the judgment, though they used an accommodationist approach rather than the *Lemon* test. They said that the only relevant inquiries were whether the government aid was so extensive as to have a clear tendency to establish a state religion or whether the government was coercing student religious participation. They concluded that the Establishment Clause was not violated because there was neither the establishment of a state religion nor coercion of religious activities.

In Lamb's Chapel v. Center Moriches Union Free School District, 508 U.S. 384 (1993), the Court followed this reasoning and declared unconstitutional a school district's policy of excluding religious groups from using school facilities during evenings and weekends. Pursuant to state law, a school district opened its facilities to community and civic groups during evenings and weekends, but said that "school premises shall not be used by any group for religious purposes."

The Court expressly followed the reasoning in *Widmar* and said that once the government chose to open its facilities to community groups it could not discriminate against those engaging in religious speech unless strict scrutiny was met. The Court again rejected the claim that avoiding violation of the Establishment Clause provided such a compelling interest. The Court said: "We have no more trouble than did the *Widmar* Court in disposing of the claimed defense on the ground that the posited fears of an Establishment Clause violation are unfounded. The showing of this film series would not have been during school hours, would not have been sponsored by the school, and would have been open to the public, not just to church members." The Court concluded that "[a]s in *Widmar*, permitting District property to be used . . . would not have

D. Religious Speech and the First Amendment

been an establishment of religion under the three-part test articulated in Lemon v. Kurtzman. The challenged governmental action has a secular purpose, does not have the principal or primary effect of advancing or inhibiting religion, and does not foster an excessive entanglement with religion."

In Good News Club v. Milford Central School, 533 U.S. 98 (2001), the Supreme Court declared unconstitutional a school policy that allowed community groups to conduct after-school programs for students, but excluded a religious group that was essentially conducting workshop sessions, including Bible study. The Court, in an opinion by Justice Thomas, found that excluding the group was an impermissible content-based restriction on speech because it was denied access solely because of the religious content of its speech. The Court also found that allowing the group use of the facilities did not violate the Establishment Clause as long as religious and nonreligious groups were treated equally.

2. Student Religious Groups' Receipt of Government Funds

The Court applied these cases in Rosenberger v. Rector and Visitors of the University of Virginia, 515 U.S. 819 (1995), to declare unconstitutional a state university's refusal to give student activity funds to a Christian group that published an expressly religious magazine.

Kennedy reasoned in two steps. First, he said that denying funds to the religious student group was impermissible content-based discrimination against religious speech. Kennedy expressly relied on *Widmar, Mergens,* and *Lamb's Chapel* to conclude that the government unconstitutionally was discriminating against the Christian group because of the religious content of its speech. He said that although the government has wide discretion when it chooses to allocate scarce financial resources, "[i]t does not follow . . . that viewpoint-based restrictions are proper when the University does not itself speak or subsidize transmittal of a message it favors but instead expends funds to encourage a diversity of views from private speakers." Kennedy said that "[v]ital First Amendment speech principles are at stake here. The first danger to liberty lies in granting the State the power to examine publications to determine whether or not they are based on some ultimate idea and if so for the State to classify them. The second, and corollary, danger is to speech from the chilling of individual thought and expression."

Second, Justice Kennedy concluded that providing funds to the religious group would not violate the Establishment Clause. He emphasized that "[t]he governmental program here is neutral toward religion." The government was acting with the purpose and effect of helping student groups and fostering a wide array of activities and viewpoints on campus. Justice Kennedy cited to *Widmar, Mergens,* and *Lamb's Chapel* and said that "[t]here is no difference in logic or principle, and no difference of constitutional significance, between a school using its funds to operate a facility to which students have access, and a school paying a third-party contractor to operate the facility on its behalf." Justice Kennedy's majority opinion concluded: "There is no Establishment Clause violation in the University's honoring its duties under the Free Speech Clause."

Justice Souter dissented and was joined by Justices Stevens, Ginsburg, and Breyer. He emphasized that this was the first time that the Court ever had allowed, let alone required, direct government financial subsidies to a religious group. Souter stated that "[u]sing public funds for the direct subsidization of preaching the word is categorically forbidden under the Establishment Clause, and if the Clause was meant to accomplish nothing else, it was meant to bar this use of public money." He concluded that "[t]he principle against direct funding with public money is patently violated by the contested use of today's student activity fee."

E. WHEN CAN RELIGION BECOME A PART OF GOVERNMENT ACTIVITIES?

Many cases under the Establishment Clause have involved issues of when, if at all, religion can become a part of government activities. For example, a large number of decisions have concerned the question of when religion impermissibly becomes a part of public school education. The Court has considered this topic in evaluating laws that allow children to be released from school for religious education, in considering prayers in public schools, and in evaluating curricular decisions made for religious reasons. In contrast to this area in which the Court has been very restrictive of religious presence in government activities, the Court has upheld the constitutionality of the government's employment of a chaplain for the legislature. These cases are discussed in turn.

1. Religion as a Part of Government Activities: Schools

RELEASE TIME

The first Supreme Court cases to consider religion as a part of public school activities concerned policies that allowed students to be released from classes to receive religious instruction. The Court said that this was impermissible if the religious teaching occurred on school premises, but allowed if the students were released to receive religious training elsewhere.

In McCollum v. Board of Education, 333 U.S. 203 (1948), the Court declared unconstitutional a school's policy of allowing students to be released, with parental permission, to religious instruction classes conducted during regular school hours in the school building by outside teachers. The superintendent of schools approved the religious teachers, and attendance records were kept and reported to school authorities in the same way as for other classes. Students not attending the religion classes were left in a study hall; Justice Jackson referred to turning the school into a temporary jail for those who did not go to church.

The Court, in an opinion by Justice Black, found the law unconstitutional as violating the "wall of separation between church and state." Justice Black explained, "Here not only are the state's tax-supported public school buildings used for the dissemination of religious doctrines. The State also affords sectarian groups an invaluable aid in that it helps to provide pupils for their religious classes through use of the State's compulsory public school machinery. This is not separation of Church and State."

E. When Can Religion Become a Part of Government Activities?

A few years later, in Zorach v. Clauson, 343 U.S. 306 (1952), the Supreme Court upheld a school board policy that allowed students to be released, during the school day, for religious instruction outside the school. Although Justice Douglas, writing for the Court, said that "[t]here cannot be the slightest doubt that the First Amendment reflects the philosophy that Church and State should be separated." He also said, "We are a religious people whose institutions presuppose a Supreme Being." The Court concluded that allowing students to receive religious instruction during school hours was simply accommodating religion and not a violation of the Establishment Clause since government funds and facilities were not used. Douglas wrote, "We would have to press the concept of separation of Church and State to these extremes to condemn the present law on constitutional grounds. . . . When the state encourages religious instruction or cooperates with religious authorities by adjusting the schedule of public events to sectarian needs, it follows the best of our traditions. For it then respects the religious nature of our people and accommodates the public service to their spiritual needs."

The Court distinguished *McCollum* because there "the classrooms were used for religious instruction and the force of the public school was used to promote that instruction." In contrast, in *Zorach*, all of the religious education occurred off school premises.

SCHOOL PRAYERS AND BIBLE READING

Few Supreme Court decisions have been as controversial as those that declared unconstitutional prayers and Bible readings in public schools. The Supreme Court has invalidated prayer in public schools, including voluntary prayers led by instructors and a government-mandated moment of "silent prayer." The Court also has followed this reasoning to invalidate clergy-delivered prayers at public school graduations. The Court, however, has not yet ruled as to whether a government-mandated moment of silent reflection would be allowed; nor has it decided the constitutionality of student-delivered prayers at public school graduations.

Engel v. Vitale was the initial Supreme Court case holding prayers in public schools to be unconstitutional.

<u>ENGEL v. VITALE</u>
370 U.S. 421 (1962)

Justice BLACK delivered the opinion of the Court.

The respondent Board of Education of Union Free School District No. 9, New Hyde Park, New York, acting in its official capacity under state law, directed the School District's principal to cause the following prayer to be said aloud by each class in the presence of a teacher at the beginning of each school day: "Almighty God, we acknowledge our dependence upon Thee, and we beg Thy blessings upon us, our parents, our teachers and our Country."

This daily procedure was adopted on the recommendation of the State Board of Regents, a governmental agency created by the State Constitution to which the New York Legislature has granted broad supervisory, executive, and legislative powers over the State's public school system. These state officials composed the prayer which they recommended and published as a part of their "Statement on Moral and Spiritual Training in the Schools," saying: "We believe that this Statement will be subscribed to by all men and women of good will, and we call upon all of them to aid in giving life to our program."

We think that by using its public school system to encourage recitation of the Regents' prayer, the State of New York has adopted a practice wholly inconsistent with the Establishment Clause. There can, of course, be no doubt that New York's program of daily classroom invocation of God's blessings as prescribed in the Regents' prayer is a religious activity. It is a solemn avowal of divine faith and supplication for the blessings of the Almighty. The nature of such a prayer has always been religious, none of the respondents has denied this and the trial court expressly so found.

The petitioners contend among other things that the state laws requiring or permitting use of the Regents' prayer must be struck down as a violation of the Establishment Clause because that prayer was composed by governmental officials as a part of a governmental program to further religious beliefs. For this reason, petitioners argue, the State's use of the Regents' prayer in its public school system breaches the constitutional wall of separation between Church and State. We agree with that contention since we think that the constitutional prohibition against laws respecting an establishment of religion must at least mean that in this country it is no part of the business of government to compose official prayers for any group of the American people to recite as a part of a religious program carried on by government.

It is a matter of history that this very practice of establishing governmentally composed prayers for religious services was one of the reasons which caused many of our early colonists to leave England and seek religious freedom in America. The Book of Common Prayer, which was created under governmental direction and which was approved by Acts of Parliament in 1548 and 1549, set out in minute detail the accepted form and content of prayer and other religious ceremonies to be used in the established, tax-supported Church of England. The controversies over the Book and what should be its content repeatedly threatened to disrupt the peace of that country as the accepted forms of prayer in the established church changed with the views of the particular ruler that happened to be in control at the time. Powerful groups representing some of the varying religious views of the people struggled among themselves to impress their particular views upon the Government and obtain amendments of the Book more suitable to their respective notions of how religious services should be conducted in order that the official religious establishment would advance their particular religious beliefs. Other groups, lacking the necessary political power to influence the Government on the matter, decided to leave England and its established church and seek freedom in America from England's governmentally ordained and supported religion.

There can be no doubt that New York's state prayer program officially establishes the religious beliefs embodied in the Regents' prayer. The respondents' argument to the contrary, which is largely based upon the contention that the Regents' prayer is "nondenominational" and the fact that the program, as modified and approved by state courts, does not require all pupils to recite the prayer but permits those who wish to do so to remain silent or be excused from the room, ignores the essential nature of the program's constitutional defects. Neither the fact that the prayer may be denominationally neutral nor the fact that its observance on the part of the students is voluntary can serve to free it from the limitations of the Establishment Clause.

It has been argued that to apply the Constitution in such a way as to prohibit state laws respecting an establishment of religious services in public schools is to indicate a hostility toward religion or toward prayer. Nothing, of course, could be more wrong. It is neither sacrilegious nor antireligious to say that each separate government in this country should stay out of the business of writing or sanctioning official prayers and leave that purely religious function to the people themselves and to those the people choose to look to for religious guidance.

Justice STEWART, dissenting.

A local school board in New York has provided that those pupils who wish to do so may join in a brief prayer at the beginning of each school day, acknowledging their dependence upon God and asking His blessing upon them and upon their parents, their teachers, and their country. The Court today decides that in permitting this brief non-denominational prayer the school board has violated the Constitution of the United States. I think this decision is wrong.

With all respect, I think the Court has misapplied a great constitutional principle. I cannot see how an "official religion" is established by letting those who want to say a prayer say it. On the contrary, I think that to deny the wish of these school children to join in reciting this prayer is to deny them the opportunity of sharing in the spiritual heritage of our Nation.

At the opening of each day's Session of this Court we stand, while one of our officials invokes the protection of God. Since the days of John Marshall our Crier has said, "God save the United States and this Honorable Court." Both the Senate and the House of Representatives open their daily Sessions with prayer. Each of our Presidents, from George Washington to John F. Kennedy, has upon assuming his Office asked the protection and help of God.

Countless similar examples could be listed, but there is no need to belabor the obvious. It was all summed up by this Court just ten years ago in a single sentence: "We are a religious people whose institutions presuppose a Supreme Being." Zorach v. Clauson. I do not believe that this Court, or the Congress, or the President has by the actions and practices I have mentioned established an "official religion" in violation of the Constitution. And I do not believe the State of New York has done so in this case. What each has done has been to recognize and to follow the deeply entrenched and highly cherished spiritual traditions of our Nation — traditions which come down to us from those who almost two hundred years ago avowed their "firm Reliance on the Protection of divine Providence" when they proclaimed the freedom and independence of this brave new world.

A year later, in Abington School District v. Schempp, 374 U.S. 203 (1963), the Court declared unconstitutional a state's law and a city's rule that required the reading, without comment, at the beginning of each school day of verses from the Bible and the recitation of the Lord's Prayer by students in unison. Although *Schempp*, unlike *Engel*, did not involve a state-composed prayer, the laws requiring Bible reading and reciting of the Lord's Prayer were deemed to violate the Establishment Clause. The Court emphasized that these religious exercises were prescribed as part of the curricular activities of students, conducted in school buildings, and supervised by teachers.

The Court distinguished studying the Bible in a literature or comparative religion course, which would be permissible. The Court said that "the exercises here do not fall into those categories. They are religious exercises, required by the States in violation of the command of the First Amendment that the Government maintain strict neutrality, neither aiding nor opposing religion."

In Wallace v. Jaffree, 472 U.S. 38 (1985), the Court followed *Engel* and *Schempp* and declared unconstitutional an Alabama law that authorized a moment of silence in public schools for "meditation or voluntary prayer." The legislative history of the law was clear that its purpose was to reintroduce prayer into the public schools. The Court said that the record was "unambiguous" that the law "was not motivated by any clearly secular purpose — indeed, the statute had *no* secular purpose."

The Court did not resolve the question of whether a moment of "silent reflection" would be permissible absent legislative history that indicated that its purpose was to reintroduce prayer into public schools. For some people, there seems little objectionable about teachers asking students to be silent for a moment at the beginning of the school day to collect their thoughts and mentally prepare for learning. But for others, government-mandated moments of silent reflection and prayer seem unnecessary; students surely have been saying silent prayers as long as teachers have been giving tests.

In Lee v. Weisman, the Court declared unconstitutional clergy-delivered prayers at public school graduations. The competing theories of the Establishment Clause, discussed earlier in this chapter, are very much in evidence in the opinions in *Lee*.

LEE v. WEISMAN
505 U.S. 577 (1992)

Justice KENNEDY delivered the opinion of the Court.

School principals in the public school system of the city of Providence, Rhode Island, are permitted to invite members of the clergy to offer invocation and benediction prayers as part of the formal graduation ceremonies for middle schools and for high schools. The question before us is whether including clerical members who offer prayers as part of the official school graduation ceremony is consistent with the Religion Clauses of the First Amendment, provisions the Fourteenth Amendment makes applicable with full force to the States and their school districts.

I

Deborah Weisman graduated from Nathan Bishop Middle School, a public school in Providence, at a formal ceremony in June 1989. She was about 14 years old. For many years it has been the policy of the Providence School

E. When Can Religion Become a Part of Government Activities?

Committee and the Superintendent of Schools to permit principals to invite members of the clergy to give invocations and benedictions at middle school and high school graduations. Many, but not all, of the principals elected to include prayers as part of the graduation ceremonies. Acting for himself and his daughter, Deborah's father, Daniel Weisman, objected to any prayers at Deborah's middle school graduation, but to no avail. The school principal, petitioner Robert E. Lee, invited a rabbi to deliver prayers at the graduation exercise for Deborah's class. Rabbi Leslie Gutterman, of the Temple Beth El in Providence, accepted.

It has been the custom of Providence school officials to provide invited clergy with a pamphlet entitled "Guidelines for Civic Occasions," prepared by the National Conference of Christians and Jews. The guidelines recommend that public prayers at nonsectarian civic ceremonies be composed with "inclusiveness and sensitivity," though they acknowledge that "[p]rayer of any kind may be inappropriate on some civic occasions." The principal gave Rabbi Gutterman the pamphlet before the graduation and advised him the invocation and benediction should be nonsectarian.

Rabbi Gutterman's prayers were as follows:

INVOCATION

God of the Free, Hope of the Brave:

For the legacy of America where diversity is celebrated and the rights of minorities are protected, we thank You. May these young men and women grow up to enrich it.

For the liberty of America, we thank You. May these new graduates grow up to guard it.

For the political process of America in which all its citizens may participate, for its court system where all may seek justice we thank You. May those we honor this morning always turn to it in trust.

For the destiny of America we thank You. May the graduates of Nathan Bishop Middle School so live that they might help to share it.

May our aspirations for our country and for these young people, who are our hope for the future, be richly fulfilled.

AMEN

BENEDICTION

O God, we are grateful to You for having endowed us with the capacity for learning which we have celebrated on this joyous commencement.

Happy families give thanks for seeing their children achieve an important milestone. Send Your blessings upon the teachers and administrators who helped prepare them.

The graduates now need strength and guidance for the future, help them to understand that we are not complete with academic knowledge alone. We must each strive to fulfill what You require of us all: To do justly, to love mercy, to walk humbly.

We give thanks to You, Lord, for keeping us alive, sustaining us and allowing us to reach this special, happy occasion.

AMEN

II

These dominant facts mark and control the confines of our decision. State officials direct the performance of a formal religious exercise at promotional and graduation ceremonies for secondary schools. Even for those students who object to the religious exercise, their attendance and participation in the state-sponsored religious activity are in a fair and real sense obligatory, though the school district does not require attendance as a condition for receipt of the diploma.

[T]he controlling precedents as they relate to prayer and religious exercise in primary and secondary public schools compel the holding here that the policy of the city of Providence is an unconstitutional one. We can decide the case without reconsidering the general constitutional framework by which public schools' efforts to accommodate religion are measured. Thus we do not accept the invitation of petitioners and amicus the United States to reconsider our decision in Lemon v. Kurtzman.

The government involvement with religious activity in this case is pervasive, to the point of creating a state-sponsored and state-directed religious exercise in a public school. Conducting this formal religious observance conflicts with settled rules pertaining to prayer exercise for students, and that suffices to determine the question before us.

The principle that government may accommodate the free exercise of religion does not supersede the fundamental limitations imposed by the Establishment Clause. It is beyond dispute that, at a minimum, the Constitution guarantees that government may not coerce anyone to support or participate in religion or its exercise, or otherwise act in a way which "establishes a [state] religion or religious faith, or tends to do so." The State's involvement in the school prayers challenged today violates these central principles.

That involvement is as troubling as it is undenied. A school official, the principal, decided that an invocation and a benediction should be given; this is a choice attributable to the State, and from a constitutional perspective it is as if a state statute decreed that the prayers must occur. The principal chose the religious participant, here a rabbi, and that choice is also attributable to the State.

The State's role did not end with the decision to include a prayer and with the choice of a clergyman. Principal Lee provided Rabbi Gutterman with a copy of the "Guidelines for Civic Occasion," and advised him that his prayers should be nonsectarian. Through these means the principal directed and controlled the content of the prayers. Even if the only sanction for ignoring the instructions were that the rabbi would not be invited back, we think no religious representative who valued his or her continued reputation and effectiveness in the community would incur the State's displeasure in this regard. It is a cornerstone principle of our Establishment Clause jurisprudence that "it is no part of the business of government to compose official prayers for any group of the Amercian people to recite as a part of a religious program carried on by government," Engel v. Vitale (1962), and that is what the school officials attempted to do.

The First Amendment's Religion Clauses mean that religious beliefs and religious expression are too precious to be either proscribed or prescribed by the State. The design of the Constitution is that preservation and transmission

E. When Can Religion Become a Part of Government Activities?

of religious beliefs and worship is a responsibility and a choice committed to the private sphere, which itself is promised freedom to pursue that mission.

We turn our attention now to consider the position of the students, both those who desired the prayer and she who did not. As we have observed before, there are heightened concerns with protecting freedom of conscience from subtle coercive pressure in the elementary and secondary public schools. What to most believers may seem nothing more than a reasonable request that the nonbeliever respect their religious practices, in a school context may appear to the nonbeliever or dissenter to be an attempt to employ the machinery of the State of enforce a religious orthodoxy.

We need not look beyond the circumstances of this case to see the phenomenon at work. The undeniable fact is that the school district's supervision and control of a high school graduation ceremony places public pressure, as well as peer pressure, on attending students to stand as a group or, at least, maintain respectful silence during the invocation and benediction. This pressure, though subtle and indirect, can be as real as any overt compulsion. Of course, in our culture standing or remaining silent can signify adherence to a view or simple respect for the views of others. And no doubt some persons who have no desire to join a prayer have little objection to standing as a sign of respect for those who do. But for the dissenter of high school age, who has a reasonable perception that she is being forced by the State to pray in a manner her conscience will not allow, the injury is no less real. There can be no doubt that for many, if not most, of the students at the graduation, the act of standing or remaining silent was an expression of participation in the rabbi's prayer. That was the very point of the religious exercise. It is of little comfort to a dissenter, then, to be told that for her the act of standing or remaining in silence signifies mere respect, rather than participation. What matters is that, given our social conventions, a reasonable dissenter in this milieu could believe that the group exercise signified her own participation or approval of it.

The injury caused by the government's action, and the reason why Daniel and Deborah Weisman object to it, is that the State, in a school setting, in effect required participation in a religious exercise. There was a stipulation in the District Court that attendance at graduation and promotional ceremonies is voluntary. Petitioners and the United States, as amicus, made this a center point of the case, arguing that the option of not attending the graduation excuses any inducement or coercion in the ceremony itself. The argument lacks all persuasion. Law reaches past formalism. And to say a teenage student has a real choice not to attend her high school graduation is formalistic in the extreme. True, Deborah could elect not to attend commencement without renouncing her diploma; but we shall not allow the case to turn on this point. Everyone knows that in our society and in our culture high school graduation is one of life's most significant occasions. A school rule which excuses attendance is beside the point. Attendance may not be required by official decree, yet it is apparent that a student is not free to absent herself from the graduation exercise in any real sense of the term "voluntary," for absence would require forfeiture of those intangible benefits which have motivated the student through youth and all her high school years. Graduation is a time for family and those closest to the student to celebrate success and express mutual wishes of gratitude and respect, all to the end of impressing upon the young person the role that it is his or her right and duty to assume in the community and all of its diverse parts.

The Government's argument gives insufficient recognition to the real conflict of conscience faced by the young student. The essence of the Government's position is that with regard to a civic, social occasion of this importance it is the objector, not the majority, who must take unilateral and private action to avoid compromising religious scruples, hereby electing to miss the graduation exercise. This turns conventional First Amendment analysis on its head. It is a tenet of the First Amendment that the State cannot require one of its citizens to forfeit his or her rights and benefits as the price of resisting conformance to state-sponsored religious practice. To say that a student must remain apart from the ceremony at the opening invocation and closing benediction is to risk compelling conformity in an environment analogous to the classroom setting, where we have said the risk of compulsion is especially high.

The sole question presented is whether a religious exercise may be conducted at a graduation ceremony in circumstances where, as we have found, young graduates who object are induced to conform. No holding by this Court suggests that a school can persuade or compel a student to participate in a religious exercise. That is being done here, and it is forbidden by the Establishment Clause of the First Amendment.

Justice BLACKMUN, with whom Justice STEVENS and Justice O'CONNOR join, concurring.

Nearly half a century of review and refinement of Establishment Clause jurisprudence has distilled one clear understanding: Government may neither promote not affiliate itself with any religious doctrine or organization, nor may it obtrude itself in the internal affairs of any religious institution. The application of these principles to the present case mandates the decision reached today by the Court.

I join the Court's opinion today because I find nothing in it inconsistent with the essential precepts of the Establishment Clause developed in our precedents. The Court holds that the graduation prayer is unconstitutional because the State "in effect required participation in a religious exercise." Although our precedents make clear that proof of government coercion is not necessary to prove an Establishment Clause violation, it is sufficient. Government pressure to participate in a religious activity is an obvious indication that the government is endorsing or promoting religion.

But it is not enough that the government restrain from compelling religious practices: It must not engage in them either. The Court repeatedly has recognized that a violation of the Establishment Clause is not predicated on coercion. The Establishment Clause proscribes public schools from "conveying or attempting to convey a message that religion or a particular religious belief is favored or preferred," even if the schools do not actually "impos[e] pressure upon a student to participate in a religious activity."

We have believed that religious freedom cannot exist in the absence of a free democratic government, and that such a government cannot endure when there is fusion between religion and the political regime. We have believed that religious freedom cannot thrive in the absence of a vibrant religious community and that such a community cannot prosper when it is bound to the secular. And we have believed that these were the animating principles behind the adoption of the Establishment Clause. To that end, our cases have prohibited government

E. When Can Religion Become a Part of Government Activities?

endorsement of religion, its sponsorship, and active involvement in religion, whether or not citizens were coerced to conform.

[Justice Souter also concurred, saying that coercion is sufficient, though not necessary, for a violation of the Establishment Clause.]

Justice SCALIA, with whom THE CHIEF JUSTICE, Justice WHITE, and Justice THOMAS join, dissenting.

Three Terms ago, I joined an opinion recognizing that the Establishment Clause must be construed in light of the "[g]overnment policies of accommodation, acknowledgement, and support for religion [that] are an accepted part of our political and cultural heritage." That opinion affirmed that "the meaning of the Clause is to be determined by reference to historical practices and understandings." County of Allegheny v. American Civil Liberties Union, Greater Pittsburgh Chapter (1989) (Kennedy, J., concurring in judgment in part and dissenting in part).

These views of course prevent me from joining today's opinion, which is conspicuously bereft of any reference to history. In holding that the Establishment Clause prohibits invocations and benedictions at public-school graduation ceremonies, the Court—with nary a mention that it is doing so—lays waste a tradition that is as old as public-school graduation ceremonies themselves, and that is a component of an even more longstanding American tradition of nonsectarian prayer to God at public celebrations generally. As its instrument of destruction, the bulldozer of its social engineering, the Court invents a boundless, and boundlessly manipulable, test of psychological coercion.

Justice Holmes' aphorism that "a page of history is worth a volume of logic," applies with particular force to our Establishment Clause jurisprudence. The history and tradition of our Nation are replete with public ceremonies featuring prayers of thanksgiving and petition. From our Nation's origin, prayer has been a prominent part of governmental ceremonies and proclamations. The Declaration of Independence, the document marking our birth as a separate people, "appeal[ed] to the Supreme Judge of the world for the rectitude of our intentions" and avowed "a firm reliance on the protection of divine providence." In his first inaugural address, after swearing his oath of office on a Bible, George Washington deliberately made a prayer a part of his first official act as President.

The Court presumably would separate graduation invocations and benedictions from other instances of public "preservation and transmission of religious beliefs" on the ground that they involve "psychological coercion." I find it a sufficient embarrassment that our Establishment Clause jurisprudence regarding holiday displays, see County of Allegheny v. American Civil Liberties Union, Greater Pittsburgh Chapter (1989), has come to "requir[e] scrutiny more commonly associated with interior decorators than with the judiciary." But interior decorating is a rock-hard science compared to psychology practiced by amateurs. A few citations of "[r]esearch in psychology" that have no particular bearing upon the precise issue here, cannot disguise that fact that the Court has gone beyond the realm where judges know what they are doing. The Court's argument that state officials have "coerced" students to take part in the invocation and benediction at graduation ceremonies is, not to put too fine a point on it, incoherent.

The Court declares that students' "attendance and participation in the [invocation and benediction] are in a fair and real sense obligatory." But what exactly is this "fair and real sense"? According to the Court, students at graduation who want "to avoid the fact or appearance of participation," in the invocation and benediction are psychologically obligated by "public pressure, as well as peer pressure, . . . to stand as a group or, at least, maintain respectful silence" during those prayers. This assertion—the very linchpin of the Court's opinion—is almost as intriguing for what it does not say as for what it says. It does not say, for example, that students are psychologically coerced to bow their heads, place their hands in a Durer-like prayer position, pay attention to the prayers, utter "Amen," or in fact pray. (Perhaps further intensive psychological research remains to be done on these matters.) It claims only that students are psychologically coerced "to stand . . . or, at least, maintain respectful silence."

To begin with the latter: The Court's notion that a student who simply sits in "respectful silence" during the invocations and benediction (when all others are standing) has somehow joined—or would somehow be perceived as having joined—in the prayers is nothing short of ludicrous. We indeed live in a vulgar age. But surely "our social conventions," have not coarsened to the point that anyone who does not stand on his chair and shout obscenities can reasonably be deemed to have assented to everything said in his presence. Since the Court does not dispute that students exposed to prayer at graduation ceremonies retain (despite "subtle coercive pressures") the free will to sit, there is absolutely no basis for the Court's decision. It is fanciful enough to say that "a reasonable dissenter," standing head erect in a class of bowed heads, "could believe that the group exercise signified her own participation or approval of it." It is beyond the absurd to say that she could entertain such a belief while pointedly declining to rise.

But let us assume the very worst, that the nonparticipating graduate is "subtly coerced" . . . to stand! Even that half of the disjunctive does not remotely establish a "participation" (or an "appearance of participation") in a religious exercise. I may add, moreover, that maintaining respect for the religious observances of others is a fundamental civic virtue that government (including the public schools) can and should cultivate—so that even if it were the case that the displaying of such respect might be mistaken for taking part in the prayer, I would deny that the dissenter's interest in avoiding even the false appearance of participation constitutionally trumps the government's interest in fostering respect for religion generally.

The opinion manifests that the Court itself has not given careful consideration to its test of psychological coercion. For if it had, how could it observe, with no hint of concern or disapproval, that students stood for the Pledge of Allegiance, which immediately preceded Rabbi Gutterman's invocation? The government can, of course, no more coerce political orthodoxy than religious orthodoxy.

I also find it odd that the Court concludes that high school graduates may not be subject to this supposed psychological coercion, yet refrains from addressing whether "mature adults" may. I had though that the reason graduation from high school is regarded as so significant an event is that it is generally associated with transition from adolescence to young adulthood. Many graduating seniors, of course, are old enough to vote. Why then, does the Court treat them as though they were first-graders? Will we soon have a jurisprudence that distinguishes between mature and immature adults?

E. When Can Religion Become a Part of Government Activities?

The deeper flaw in the Court's opinion does not lie in its wrong answer to the question whether there was state-induced "peer-pressure" coercion; it lies, rather, in the Court's making violation of the Establishment Clause hinge on such a precious question. The coercion that was a hallmark of historical establishments of religion was coercion of religious orthodoxy and of financial support by force of law and threat of penalty. The Establishment Clause was adopted to prohibit such an establishment of religion at the federal level (and to protect state establishments of religion from federal interference).

Thus, while I have no quarrel with the Court's general proposition that the Establishment Clause "guarantees that government may not coerce anyone to support or participate in religion or its exercise," I see no warrant for expanding the concept of coercion beyond acts backed by threat of penalty—a brand of coercion that, happily, is readily discernible to those of us who have made a career of reading the disciples of Blackstone rather than of Freud. The framers were indeed opposed to coercion of religious worship by the National Government; but, as their own sponsorship of nonsectarian prayer in public events demonstrates, they understood that "[s]peech is not coercive; the listener may do as he likes."

The reader has been told much in this case about the personal interest of Mr. Weisman and his daughter, and very little about the personal interests on the other side. They are not inconsequential. Church and state would not be such a difficult subject if religion were, as the Court apparently thinks it to be, some purely personal avocation that can be indulged entirely in secret, like pornography, in the privacy of one's room. For most believers it is not that, and has never been. Religious men and women of almost all denominations have felt it necessary to acknowledge and beseech the blessing of God as a people, and not just as individuals, because they believe in the "protection of divine Providence," as the Declaration of Independence put it, not just for individuals but for societies; because they believe God to be, as Washington's first Thanksgiving Proclamation put it, the "Great Lord and Ruler of Nations." One can believe in the effectiveness of such public worship, or one can deprecate and deride it. But the longstanding Amercian tradition of prayer at official ceremonies displays with unmistakable clarity that the Establishment Clause does not forbid the government to accommodate it.

I must add one final observation: The Founders of our Republic knew the fearsome potential of sectarian religious belief to generate civil dissension and civil strife. And they also knew that nothing, absolutely nothing, is so inclined to foster among religious believers of various faith a toleration—no, an affection—for one another than voluntarily joining in prayer together, to the God whom they all worship and seek. Needless to say, no one should be compelled to do that, but it is a shame to deprive our public culture of the opportunity, and indeed the encouragement, for people to do it voluntarily. The Baptist or Catholic who heard and joined in the simple and inspiring prayers of Rabbi Gutterman on this official and patriotic occasion was inoculated from religious bigotry and prejudice in a manner that cannot be replicated. To deprive our society of that important unifying mechanism, in order to spare the nonbeliever what seems to me the minimal inconvenience of standing or even sitting in respectful nonparticipation, is as senseless in policy as it in unsupported in law.

The Court's subsequent decision concerning prayer in public schools, Santa Fe Independent School District v. Doe, declared unconstitutional student-delivered prayers at public school football games.

SANTA FE INDEPENDENT SCHOOL DISTRICT v. DOE
530 U.S. 290 (2000)

Justice STEVENS delivered the opinion of the Court.

Prior to 1995, the Santa Fe High School student who occupied the school's elective office of student council chaplain delivered a prayer over the public address system before each varsity football game for the entire season. This practice, along with others, was challenged in District Court as a violation of the Establishment Clause of the First Amendment. While these proceedings were pending in the District Court, the school district adopted a different policy that permits, but does not require, prayer initiated and led by a student at all home games. The District Court entered an order modifying that policy to permit only nonsectarian, nonproselytizing prayer. The Court of Appeals held that, even as modified by the District Court, the football prayer policy was invalid.

I

The Santa Fe Independent School District (District) is a political subdivision of the State of Texas, responsible for the education of more than 4,000 students in a small community in the southern part of the State. The District includes the Santa Fe High School, two primary schools, an intermediate school and the junior high school. Respondents are two sets of current or former students and their respective mothers. One family is Mormon and the other is Catholic. The District Court permitted respondents (Does) to litigate anonymously to protect them from intimidation or harassment.

[The school's policy evolved over time.] The August policy was titled "Prayer at Football Games." It authorized two student elections, the first to determine whether "invocations" should be delivered, and the second to select the spokesperson to deliver them. Like the July policy, it contained two parts, an initial statement that omitted any requirement that the content of the invocation be "nonsectarian and nonproselytising," and a fallback provision that automatically added that limitation if the preferred policy should be enjoined. On August 31, 1995, according to the parties' stipulation, "the district's high school students voted to determine whether a student would deliver prayer at varsity football games. . . . The students chose to allow a student to say a prayer at football games." A week later, in a separate election, they selected a student "to deliver the prayer at varsity football games."

The final policy (October policy) is essentially the same as the August policy, though it omits the word "prayer" from its title, and refers to "messages" and "statements" as well as "invocations." It is the validity of that policy that is before us.

We granted the District's petition for certiorari, limited to the following question: "Whether petitioner's policy permitting student-led, student-initiated

E. When Can Religion Become a Part of Government Activities?

prayer at football games violates the Establishment Clause." We conclude, as did the Court of Appeals, that it does.

II

In Lee v. Weisman (1992), we held that a prayer delivered by a rabbi at a middle school graduation ceremony violated that Clause. Although this case involves student prayer at a different type of school function, our analysis is properly guided by the principles that we endorsed in *Lee.*

In this case the District first argues that this principle is inapplicable to its October policy because the messages are private student speech, not public speech. It reminds us that there is a crucial difference between *government* speech endorsing religion, which the Establishment Clause forbids, and *private* speech endorsing religion, which the Free Speech and Free Exercise Clauses protect.

We certainly agree with that distinction, but we are not persuaded that the pregame invocations should be regarded as "private speech." These invocations are authorized by a government policy and take place on government property at government-sponsored school-related events. Of course, not every message delivered under such circumstances is the government's own. We have held, for example, that an individual's contribution to a government-created forum was not government speech. See Rosenberger v. Rector and Visitors of Univ. of Va. (1995). Although the District relies heavily on *Rosenberger* and similar cases involving such forums, it is clear that the pregame ceremony is not the type of forum discussed in those cases. The Santa Fe school officials simply do not "evince either 'by policy or by practice,' any intent to open the [pregame ceremony] to 'indiscriminate use,' . . . by the student body generally." Rather, the school allows only one student, the same student for the entire season, to give the invocation. The statement or invocation, moreover, is subject to particular regulations that confine the content and topic of the student's message.

Granting only one student access to the stage at a time does not, of course, necessarily preclude a finding that a school has created a limited public forum. Here, however, Santa Fe's student election system ensures that only those messages deemed "appropriate" under the District's policy may be delivered. That is, the majoritarian process implemented by the District guarantees, by definition, that minority candidates will never prevail and that their views will be effectively silenced.

In *Lee,* the school district made the related argument that its policy of endorsing only "civic or nonsectarian" prayer was acceptable because it minimized the intrusion on the audience as a whole. We rejected that claim by explaining that such a majoritarian policy "does not lessen the offense or isolation to the objectors. At best it narrows their number, at worst increases their sense of isolation and affront." Similarly, while Santa Fe's majoritarian election might ensure that most of the students are represented, it does nothing to protect the minority; indeed, it likely serves to intensify their offense.

Moreover, the District has failed to divorce itself from the religious content in the invocations. It has not succeeded in doing so, either by claiming that its policy is "'one of neutrality rather than endorsement'" or by characterizing the individual student as the "circuit-breaker" in the process. Contrary to the District's repeated assertions that it has adopted a "hands-off" approach to the pregame invocation, the realities of the situation plainly reveal that its policy involves both perceived and actual endorsement of religion. In this case, as we found in *Lee*, the "degree of school involvement" makes it clear that the pregame prayers bear "the imprint of the State and thus put school-age children who objected in an untenable position."

In addition to involving the school in the selection of the speaker, the policy, by its terms, invites and encourages religious messages. The policy itself states that the purpose of the message is "to solemnize the event." A religious message is the most obvious method of solemnizing an event. Moreover, the requirements that the message "promote good citizenship" and "establish the appropriate environment for competition" further narrow the types of message deemed appropriate, suggesting that a solemn, yet nonreligious, message, such as commentary on United States foreign policy, would be prohibited. Indeed, the only type of message that is expressly endorsed in the text is an "invocation"—a term that primarily described an appeal for divine assistance. In fact, as used in the past at Santa Fe High School, an "invocation" has always entailed a focused religious message. Thus, the expressed purposes of the policy encourage the selection of a religious message, and that is precisely how the students understand the policy. The results of the elections described in the parties' stipulation make it clear that the students understood that the central question before them was whether prayer should be a part of the pregame ceremony. We recognize the important role that public worship plays in many communities, as well as the sincere desire to include public prayer as a part of various occasions so as to mark those occasions' significance. But such religious activity in public schools, as elsewhere, must comport with the First Amendment.

The actual or perceived endorsement of the message, moreover, is established by factors beyond just the text of the policy. Once the student speaker is selected and the message composed, the invocation is then delivered to a large audience assembled as part of a regularly scheduled, school-sponsored function conducted on school property. The message is broadcast over the school's public address system, which remains subject to the control of school officials. It is fair to assume that the pregame ceremony is clothed in the traditional indicia of school sporting events, which generally include not just the team, but also cheerleaders and band members dressed in uniforms sporting the school name and mascot. The school's name is likely written in large print across the field and on banners and flags. The crowd will certainly include many who display the school colors and insignia on their school T-shirts, jackets, or hats and who may also be waving signs displaying the school name. It is in a setting such as this that "[t]he board has chosen to permit" the elected student to rise and give the "statement or invocation."

In this context the members of the listening audience must perceive the pregame message as a public expression of the views of the majority of the student body delivered with the approval of the school administration. In cases involving state participation in a religious activity, one of the relevant questions is "whether an objective observer, acquainted with the text, legislative history, and implementation of the statute, would perceive it as a state endorsement of prayer in public schools." Regardless of the listener's support for, or objection to, the message, an objective Santa Fe High School student will unquestionably

E. When Can Religion Become a Part of Government Activities?

perceive the inevitable pregame prayer as stamped with her school's seal of approval.

School sponsorship of religious message is impermissible because it sends the ancillary message to members of the audience who are nonadherents "that they are outsiders, not full members of the political community, and an accompanying message to adherents that they are insiders, favored members of the political community." The delivery of such a message—over the school's public address system, by a speaker representing the student body, under the supervision of school faculty, and pursuant to a school policy that explicitly and implicitly encourages public prayer—is not properly characterized as "private" speech.

The District next argues that its football policy is distinguishable from the graduation prayer in *Lee* because it does not coerce students to participate in religious observances. Attendance at a high school football game, unlike showing up for class, is certainly not required in order to receive a diploma. Moreover, we may assume that the District is correct in arguing that the informal pressure to attend an athletic event is not as strong as a senior's desire to attend her own graduation ceremony. There are some students, however, such as cheerleaders, members of the band, and, of course, the team members themselves, for whom seasonal commitments mandate their attendance, sometimes for class credit. The District also minimizes the importance to many students of attending and participating in extracurricular activities as part of a complete educational experience.

High school home football games are traditional gatherings of a school community; they bring together students and faculty as well as friends and family from years present and past to root for a common cause. Undoubtedly, the games are not important to some students, and they voluntarily choose not to attend. For many others, however, the choice between whether to attend these games or to risk facing a personally offensive religious ritual is in no practical sense an easy one. The Constitution, moreover, demands that the school may not force this difficult choice upon these students for "[i]t is a tenet of the First Amendment that the State cannot require one of its citizens to forfeit his or her rights and benefits as the price of resisting conformance to state-sponsored religious practice."

Even if we regard every high school student's decision to attend a home football game as purely voluntary, we are nevertheless persuaded that the delivery of a pregame prayer has the improper effect of coercing those present to participate in an act of religious worship. For "the government may no more use social pressure to enforce orthodoxy than it may use more direct means."

Chief Justice REHNQUIST, with whom Justice SCALIA and Justice THOMAS join, dissenting.

The Court distorts existing precedent to conclude that the school district's student-message program is invalid on its face under the Establishment Clause. But even more disturbing than its holding is the tone of the Court's opinion; it bristles with hostility to all things religious in public life. Neither the holding nor the tone of the opinion is faithful to the meaning of the Establishment Clause, when it is recalled that George Washington himself, at the request of the very Congress which passed the Bill of Rights, proclaimed a day of "public thanksgiving and prayer, to be observed by acknowledging with grateful hearts the many and signal favors of Almighty God."

The Court, venturing into the realm of prophesy, decides that it "need not wait for the inevitable" and invalidates the district's policy on its face. To do so, it applies the most rigid version of the oft-criticized test of Lemon v. Kurtzman (1971). Even if it were appropriate to apply the *Lemon* test here, the district's student-message policy should not be invalidated on its face.

[W]ith respect to the policy's purpose, the Court holds that "the simple enactment of this policy, with the purpose and perception of school endorsement of student prayer, was a constitutional violation." But the policy itself has plausible secular purposes: "[T]o solemnize the event, to promote good sportsmanship and student safety, and to establish the appropriate environment for the competition." Where a governmental body "expresses a plausible secular purpose" for an enactment, "courts should generally defer to that stated intent." Under the Court's logic, a public school that sponsors the singing of the national anthem before football games violates the Establishment Clause. Although the Court apparently believes that solemnizing football games is an illegitimate purpose, the voters in the school district seem to disagree. Nothing in the Establishment Clause prevents them from making this choice.

CURRICULAR DECISIONS

The Supreme Court has declared unconstitutional government decisions concerning the curriculum that were motivated by religious purpose. These cases primarily have concerned state law prohibiting the teaching of evolution or requiring the teaching of "creationism" when evolution is taught.

In Epperson v. Arkansas, 393 U.S. 97 (1968), the Court declared unconstitutional an Arkansas law that made it unlawful for a teacher in a state-supported school or university "to teach the theory or doctrine that mankind ascended or descended from a lower order of animals" or "to adopt or use in any such institution a textbook that teaches" this theory. The Court held that the law prohibiting teaching of evolution was motivated by a religious purpose and thus violated the Establishment Clause. The Court explained, "The overriding fact is that Arkansas' law selects from the body of knowledge a particular segment which it proscribes for the sole reason that it is deemed to conflict with a particular religious doctrine; that is, with a particular interpretation of the Book of Genesis by a particular religious group." The Court observed that "[t]here is and can be no doubt that the First Amendment does not permit the State to require that teaching and learning must be tailored to the principles or prohibitions of any religious sect or dogma." The Arkansas law did exactly that: preclude teaching of evolution because it was a theory opposed by some religions.

In Edwards v. Aguillard, 482 U.S. 578 (1987), the Court followed this same reasoning and declared unconstitutional a Louisiana law that prohibited the teaching of the theory of evolution in public schools unless accompanied by instruction in "creation science." The Court noted that, as in *Epperson*, the "same historic and contemporaneous antagonisms between the teachings of certain religious denominations and the teaching of evolution are present in this case." The Court said that the law's "primary purpose was to change the science curriculum of public schools in order to provide persuasive advantage to a particular religious doctrine that rejects the factual basis of evolution in

E. When Can Religion Become a Part of Government Activities?

its entirety." The Court thus concluded, "Because the primary purpose of the Creationism Act is to advance a particular religious belief, the Act endorses religion in violation of the First Amendment."

2. *Religion as a Part of Government Activities: Legislative Chaplains*

In contrast to the prohibition of religion in public school activities, in two cases, Marsh v. Chambers (1983) and Town of Greece v. Galloway (2014), the Court upheld the constitutionality of the state's employment of a minister to begin legislative sessions with a prayer.

In Marsh v. Chambers, 463 U.S. 783 (1983), the issue was the constitutionality of a state legislature employing a Presbyterian minister for 18 years to begin each session with a prayer. The Nebraska legislature had employed Robert E. Palmer, a Presbyterian minister, since 1965 to open each legislative day with a prayer. The Court rejected the argument that this violated the Establishment Clause:

> The opening of sessions of legislative and other deliberative public bodies with prayer is deeply embedded in the history and tradition of this country. From colonial times through the founding of the Republic and ever since, the practice of legislative prayer has coexisted with the principles of disestablishment and religious freedom. This unique history leads us to accept the interpretation of the First Amendment draftsmen who saw no real threat to the Establishment Clause arising from a practice of prayer similar to that now challenged.
>
> In light of the unambiguous and unbroken history of more than 200 years, there can be no doubt that the practice of opening legislative sessions with prayer has become part of the fabric of our society. Nor is the compensation of the chaplain from public funds a reason to invalidate the Nebraska Legislature's chaplaincy: remuneration is grounded in historic practice initiated by the same Congress that drafted the Establishment Clause of the First Amendment.

TOWN OF GREECE v. GALLOWAY
572 U.S. 565 (2014)

Justice KENNEDY delivered the opinion of the Court, except as to Part II-B.

The Court must decide whether the town of Greece, New York, imposes an impermissible establishment of religion by opening its monthly board meetings with a prayer. It must be concluded, consistent with the Court's opinion in Marsh v. Chambers, that no violation of the Constitution has been shown.

I

Greece, a town with a population of 94,000, is in upstate New York. For some years, it began its monthly town board meetings with a moment of silence. In 1999, the newly elected town supervisor, John Auberger, decided to replicate the prayer practice he had found meaningful while serving in the county legislature. Following the roll call and recitation of the Pledge of Allegiance, Auberger would invite a local clergyman to the front of the room to deliver an invocation. After the prayer, Auberger would thank the minister for serving as the board's "chaplain for the month" and present him with a commemorative plaque. The prayer was intended to place town board members in a solemn and deliberative frame of mind, invoke divine guidance in town affairs, and follow a tradition practiced by Congress and dozens of state legislatures.

The town followed an informal method for selecting prayer givers, all of whom were unpaid volunteers. A town employee would call the congregations listed in a local directory until she found a minister available for that month's meeting. The town eventually compiled a list of willing "board chaplains" who had accepted invitations and agreed to return in the future. The town at no point excluded or denied an opportunity to a would-be prayer giver. Its leaders maintained that a minister or layperson of any persuasion, including an atheist, could give the invocation. But nearly all of the congregations in town were Christian; and from 1999 to 2007, all of the participating ministers were too.

Greece neither reviewed the prayers in advance of the meetings nor provided guidance as to their tone or content, in the belief that exercising any degree of control over the prayers would infringe both the free exercise and speech rights of the ministers. The town instead left the guest clergy free to compose their own devotions. The resulting prayers often sounded both civic and religious themes. Typical were invocations that asked the divinity to abide at the meeting and bestow blessings on the community. Some of the ministers spoke in a distinctly Christian idiom; and a minority invoked religious holidays, scripture, or doctrine.

Respondents Susan Galloway and Linda Stephens attended town board meetings to speak about issues of local concern, and they objected that the prayers violated their religious or philosophical views. At one meeting, Galloway admonished board members that she found the prayers "offensive," "intolerable," and an affront to a "diverse community." After respondents complained that Christian themes pervaded the prayers, to the exclusion of citizens who did not share those beliefs, the town invited a Jewish layman and the chairman of the local Baha'i temple to deliver prayers. A Wiccan priestess who had read press reports about the prayer controversy requested, and was granted, an opportunity to give the invocation.

Galloway and Stephens brought suit in the United States District Court for the Western District of New York. They alleged that the town violated the First Amendment's Establishment Clause by preferring Christians over other prayer givers and by sponsoring sectarian prayers, such as those given "in Jesus' name."

II

In Marsh v. Chambers, the Court found no First Amendment violation in the Nebraska Legislature's practice of opening its sessions with a prayer delivered by a chaplain paid from state funds. The decision concluded that legislative prayer, while religious in nature, has long been understood as compatible with the Establishment Clause. As practiced by Congress since the framing of the Constitution, legislative prayer lends gravity to public business, reminds lawmakers to transcend petty differences in pursuit of a higher purpose, and expresses a common aspiration to a just and peaceful society. The Court has considered this symbolic expression to be a "tolerable acknowledgement of

E. When Can Religion Become a Part of Government Activities?

beliefs widely held," rather than a first, treacherous step towards establishment of a state church.

Marsh is sometimes described as "carving out an exception" to the Court's Establishment Clause jurisprudence, because it sustained legislative prayer without subjecting the practice to "any of the formal 'tests' that have traditionally structured" this inquiry. The Court in *Marsh* found those tests unnecessary because history supported the conclusion that legislative invocations are compatible with the Establishment Clause. The First Congress made it an early item of business to appoint and pay official chaplains, and both the House and Senate have maintained the office virtually uninterrupted since that time.

Marsh must not be understood as permitting a practice that would amount to a constitutional violation if not for its historical foundation. The case teaches instead that the Establishment Clause must be interpreted "by reference to historical practices and understandings." That the First Congress provided for the appointment of chaplains only days after approving language for the First Amendment demonstrates that the Framers considered legislative prayer a benign acknowledgment of religion's role in society. In the 1850's, the judiciary committees in both the House and Senate reevaluated the practice of official chaplaincies after receiving petitions to abolish the office. The committees concluded that the office posed no threat of an establishment because lawmakers were not compelled to attend the daily prayer, no faith was excluded by law, nor any favored, and the cost of the chaplain's salary imposed a vanishingly small burden on taxpayers. *Marsh* stands for the proposition that it is not necessary to define the precise boundary of the Establishment Clause where history shows that the specific practice is permitted. Any test the Court adopts must acknowledge a practice that was accepted by the Framers and has withstood the critical scrutiny of time and political change. A test that would sweep away what has so long been settled would create new controversy and begin anew the very divisions along religious lines that the Establishment Clause seeks to prevent.

The Court's inquiry, then, must be to determine whether the prayer practice in the town of Greece fits within the tradition long followed in Congress and the state legislatures.

A

Respondents maintain that prayer must be nonsectarian, or not identifiable with any one religion; and they fault the town for permitting guest chaplains to deliver prayers that "use overtly Christian terms" or "invoke specifics of Christian theology." A prayer is fitting for the public sphere, in their view, only if it contains "the most general, nonsectarian reference to God," and eschews mention of doctrines associated with any one faith.

An insistence on nonsectarian or ecumenical prayer as a single, fixed standard is not consistent with the tradition of legislative prayer outlined in the Court's cases. The Court found the prayers in *Marsh* consistent with the First Amendment not because they espoused only a generic theism but because our history and tradition have shown that prayer in this limited context could "coexis[t] with the principles of disestablishment and religious freedom." The Congress that drafted the First Amendment would have been accustomed to invocations containing explicitly religious themes of the sort respondents find objectionable. One of the Senate's first chaplains, the Rev. William White, gave prayers in a series that included the Lord's Prayer, the Collect for Ash Wednesday, prayers for peace and grace, a general thanksgiving, St. Chrysostom's Prayer, and a prayer seeking "the grace of our Lord Jesus Christ, &c."

To hold that invocations must be nonsectarian would force the legislatures that sponsor prayers and the courts that are asked to decide these cases to act as supervisors and censors of religious speech, a rule that would involve government in religious matters to a far greater degree than is the case under the town's current practice of neither editing or approving prayers in advance nor criticizing their content after the fact. Our Government is prohibited from prescribing prayers to be recited in our public institutions in order to promote a preferred system of belief or code of moral behavior. It would be but a few steps removed from that prohibition for legislatures to require chaplains to redact the religious content from their message in order to make it acceptable for the public sphere. Government may not mandate a civic religion that stifles any but the most generic reference to the sacred any more than it may prescribe a religious orthodoxy.

Respondents argue, in effect, that legislative prayer may be addressed only to a generic God. The law and the Court could not draw this line for each specific prayer or seek to require ministers to set aside their nuanced and deeply personal beliefs for vague and artificial ones. There is doubt, in any event, that consensus might be reached as to what qualifies as generic or nonsectarian. Honorifics like "Lord of Lords" or "King of Kings" might strike a Christian audience as ecumenical, yet these titles may have no place in the vocabulary of other faith traditions.

In rejecting the suggestion that legislative prayer must be nonsectarian, the Court does not imply that no constraints remain on its content. The relevant constraint derives from its place at the opening of legislative sessions, where it is meant to lend gravity to the occasion and reflect values long part of the Nation's heritage. Prayer that is solemn and respectful in tone, that invites lawmakers to reflect upon shared ideals and common ends before they embark on the fractious business of governing, serves that legitimate function. If the course and practice over time shows that the invocations denigrate nonbelievers or religious minorities, threaten damnation, or preach conversion, many present may consider the prayer to fall short of the desire to elevate the purpose of the occasion and to unite lawmakers in their common effort. That circumstance would present a different case than the one presently before the Court.

The prayers delivered in the town of Greece do not fall outside the tradition this Court has recognized. A number of the prayers did invoke the name of Jesus, the Heavenly Father, or the Holy Spirit, but they also invoked universal themes, as by celebrating the changing of the seasons or calling for a "spirit of cooperation" among town leaders.

Absent a pattern of prayers that over time denigrate, proselytize, or betray an impermissible government purpose, a challenge based solely on the content of a prayer will not likely establish a constitutional violation. *Marsh*, indeed, requires an inquiry into the prayer opportunity as a whole, rather than into the contents of a single prayer.

Finally, the Court disagrees with the view taken by the Court of Appeals that the town of Greece contravened the Establishment Clause by inviting a predominantly Christian set of ministers to lead the prayer. The town made reasonable efforts to identify all of the congregations located within its borders and represented that it would welcome a prayer by any minister or layman who

E. When Can Religion Become a Part of Government Activities?

wished to give one. That nearly all of the congregations in town turned out to be Christian does not reflect an aversion or bias on the part of town leaders against minority faiths. So long as the town maintains a policy of nondiscrimination, the Constitution does not require it to search beyond its borders for non-Christian prayer givers in an effort to achieve religious balancing. The quest to promote "a 'diversity' of religious views" would require the town "to make wholly inappropriate judgments about the number of religions [it] should sponsor and the relative frequency with which it should sponsor each," a form of government entanglement with religion that is far more troublesome than the current approach.

B

Respondents further seek to distinguish the town's prayer practice from the tradition upheld in *Marsh* on the ground that it coerces participation by nonadherents. They and some *amici* contend that prayer conducted in the intimate setting of a town board meeting differs in fundamental ways from the invocations delivered in Congress and state legislatures, where the public remains segregated from legislative activity and may not address the body except by occasional invitation. Citizens attend town meetings, on the other hand, to accept awards; speak on matters of local importance; and petition the board for action that may affect their economic interests, such as the granting of permits, business licenses, and zoning variances. Respondents argue that the public may feel subtle pressure to participate in prayers that violate their beliefs in order to please the board members from whom they are about to seek a favorable ruling. In their view the fact that board members in small towns know many of their constituents by name only increases the pressure to conform.

It is an elemental First Amendment principle that government may not coerce its citizens "to support or participate in any religion or its exercise." On the record in this case the Court is not persuaded that the town of Greece, through the act of offering a brief, solemn, and respectful prayer to open its monthly meetings, compelled its citizens to engage in a religious observance. The inquiry remains a fact-sensitive one that considers both the setting in which the prayer arises and the audience to whom it is directed.

The prayer opportunity in this case must be evaluated against the backdrop of historical practice. As a practice that has long endured, legislative prayer has become part of our heritage and tradition, part of our expressive idiom, similar to the Pledge of Allegiance, inaugural prayer, or the recitation of "God save the United States and this honorable Court" at the opening of this Court's sessions. It is presumed that the reasonable observer is acquainted with this tradition and understands that its purposes are to lend gravity to public proceedings and to acknowledge the place religion holds in the lives of many private citizens, not to afford government an opportunity to proselytize or force truant constituents into the pews.

The principal audience for these invocations is not, indeed, the public but lawmakers themselves, who may find that a moment of prayer or quiet reflection sets the mind to a higher purpose and thereby eases the task of governing. For members of town boards and commissions, who often serve part-time and as volunteers, ceremonial prayer may also reflect the values they hold as private citizens. The prayer is an opportunity for them to show who and what they are without denying the right to dissent by those who disagree.

The analysis would be different if town board members directed the public to participate in the prayers, singled out dissidents for opprobrium, or indicated that their decisions might be influenced by a person's acquiescence in the prayer opportunity. No such thing occurred in the town of Greece.

In their declarations in the trial court, respondents stated that the prayers gave them offense and made them feel excluded and disrespected. Offense, however, does not equate to coercion. Adults often encounter speech they find disagreeable; and an Establishment Clause violation is not made out any time a person experiences a sense of affront from the expression of contrary religious views in a legislative forum, especially where, as here, any member of the public is welcome in turn to offer an invocation reflecting his or her own convictions.

Ceremonial prayer is but a recognition that, since this Nation was founded and until the present day, many Americans deem that their own existence must be understood by precepts far beyond the authority of government to alter or define and that willing participation in civic affairs can be consistent with a brief acknowledgment of their belief in a higher power, always with due respect for those who adhere to other beliefs. The prayer in this case has a permissible ceremonial purpose. It is not an unconstitutional establishment of religion.

The town of Greece does not violate the First Amendment by opening its meetings with prayer that comports with our tradition and does not coerce participation by nonadherents.

Justice THOMAS, with whom Justice SCALIA joins as to Part II, concurring in part and concurring in the judgment.

I write separately to reiterate my view that the Establishment Clause is "best understood as a federalism provision," and to state my understanding of the proper "coercion" analysis.

I

As I have explained before, the text and history of the [Establishment] Clause "resis[t] incorporation" against the States. If the Establishment Clause is not incorporated, then it has no application here, where only municipal action is at issue.

As an initial matter, the Clause probably prohibits Congress from establishing a national religion. The text of the Clause also suggests that Congress "could not interfere with state establishments, notwithstanding any argument that could be made based on Congress' power under the Necessary and Proper Clause." That choice of language—"Congress shall make no law"—effectively denied Congress any power to regulate state establishments.

II

Even if the Establishment Clause were properly incorporated against the States, the municipal prayers at issue in this case bear no resemblance to the coercive state establishments that existed at the founding. "The coercion that was a hallmark of historical establishments of religion was coercion of religious orthodoxy and of financial support *by force of law and threat of penalty.*"

E. When Can Religion Become a Part of Government Activities?

Thus, to the extent coercion is relevant to the Establishment Clause analysis, it is actual legal coercion that counts—not the "subtle coercive pressures" allegedly felt by respondents in this case. The majority properly concludes that "[o]ffense . . . does not equate to coercion," since "[a]dults often encounter speech they find disagreeable[,] and an Establishment Clause violation is not made out any time a person experiences a sense of affront from the expression of contrary religious views in a legislative forum." I would simply add, in light of the foregoing history of the Establishment Clause, that "[p]eer pressure, unpleasant as it may be, is not coercion" either.

Justice KAGAN, with whom Justice GINSBURG, Justice BREYER, and Justice SOTOMAYOR join, dissenting.

For centuries now, people have come to this country from every corner of the world to share in the blessing of religious freedom. Our Constitution promises that they may worship in their own way, without fear of penalty or danger, and that in itself is a momentous offering. Yet our Constitution makes a commitment still more remarkable—that however those individuals worship, they will count as full and equal American citizens. A Christian, a Jew, a Muslim (and so forth)—each stands in the same relationship with her country, with her state and local communities, and with every level and body of government. So that when each person performs the duties or seeks the benefits of citizenship, she does so not as an adherent to one or another religion, but simply as an American.

I respectfully dissent from the Court's opinion because I think the Town of Greece's prayer practices violate that norm of religious equality—the breathtakingly generous constitutional idea that our public institutions belong no less to the Buddhist or Hindu than to the Methodist or Episcopalian. I do not contend that principle translates here into a bright separationist line. To the contrary, I agree with the Court's decision in Marsh v. Chambers (1983), upholding the Nebraska Legislature's tradition of beginning each session with a chaplain's prayer. And I believe that pluralism and inclusion in a town hall can satisfy the constitutional requirement of neutrality; such a forum need not become a religion-free zone. But still, the Town of Greece should lose this case. The practice at issue here differs from the one sustained in *Marsh* because Greece's town meetings involve participation by ordinary citizens, and the invocations given—directly to those citizens—were predominantly sectarian in content. Still more, Greece's Board did nothing to recognize religious diversity: In arranging for clergy members to open each meeting, the Town never sought (except briefly when this suit was filed) to involve, accommodate, or in any way reach out to adherents of non-Christian religions. So month in and month out for over a decade, prayers steeped in only one faith, addressed toward members of the public, commenced meetings to discuss local affairs and distribute government benefits. In my view, that practice does not square with the First Amendment's promise that every citizen, irrespective of her religion, owns an equal share in her government.

I

To begin to see what has gone wrong in the Town of Greece, consider several hypothetical scenarios in which sectarian prayer—taken straight from this case's record—infuses governmental activities. None involves, as this case does, a proceeding that could be characterized as a legislative session, but they are useful to elaborate some general principles. In each instance, assume (as was true in Greece) that the invocation is given pursuant to government policy and is representative of the prayers generally offered in the designated setting:

You are a party in a case going to trial; let's say you have filed suit against the government for violating one of your legal rights. The judge bangs his gavel to call the court to order, asks a minister to come to the front of the room, and instructs the 10 or so individuals present to rise for an opening prayer. The clergyman faces those in attendance and says: "Lord, God of all creation. . . . We acknowledge the saving sacrifice of Jesus Christ on the cross. We draw strength . . . from his resurrection at Easter. Jesus Christ, who took away the sins of the world, destroyed our death, through his dying and in his rising, he has restored our life. Blessed are you, who has raised up the Lord Jesus, you who will raise us, in our turn, and put us by His side. . . . Amen." The judge then asks your lawyer to begin the trial.

It's election day, and you head over to your local polling place to vote. As you and others wait to give your names and receive your ballots, an election official asks everyone there to join him in prayer. He says: "We pray this [day] for the guidance of the Holy Spirit as [we vote]. . . . Let's just say the Our Father together. 'Our Father, who art in Heaven, hallowed be thy name; thy Kingdom come, thy will be done, on earth as it is in Heaven. . . .'" And after he concludes, he makes the sign of the cross, and appears to wait expectantly for you and the other prospective voters to do so too.

You are an immigrant attending a naturalization ceremony to finally become a citizen. The presiding official tells you and your fellow applicants that before administering the oath of allegiance, he would like a minister to pray for you and with you. The pastor steps to the front of the room, asks everyone to bow their heads, and recites: "[F]ather, son, and Holy Spirit—it is with a due sense of reverence and awe that we come before you [today] seeking your blessing. . . . You are . . . a wise God, oh Lord, . . . as evidenced even in the plan of redemption that is fulfilled in Jesus Christ. We ask that you would give freely and abundantly wisdom to one and to all . . . in the name of the Lord and Savior Jesus Christ, who lives with you and the Holy Spirit, one God for ever and ever. Amen."

I would hold that the government officials responsible for the above practices—that is, for prayer repeatedly invoking a single religion's beliefs in these settings—crossed a constitutional line. I have every confidence the Court would agree.

Why? The reason, of course, has nothing to do with Christianity as such. This opinion is full of Christian prayers, because those were the only invocations offered in the Town of Greece. But if my hypotheticals involved the prayer of some other religion, the outcome would be exactly the same. Suppose, for example, that government officials in a predominantly Jewish community asked a rabbi to begin all public functions with a chanting of the Sh'ma and V'ahavta. ("Hear O Israel! The Lord our God, the Lord is One. . . . Bind [these words] as a sign upon your hand; let them be a symbol before your eyes; inscribe them on the doorposts of your house, and on your gates.") Or assume officials in a mostly Muslim town requested a muezzin to commence such functions, over and over again, with a recitation of the Adhan. ("God is greatest, God

E. When Can Religion Become a Part of Government Activities?

is greatest. I bear witness that there is no deity but God. I bear witness that Muhammad is the Messenger of God.") In any instance, the question would be why such government-sponsored prayer of a single religion goes beyond the constitutional pale.

One glaring problem is that the government in all these hypotheticals has aligned itself with, and placed its imprimatur on, a particular religious creed. "The clearest command of the Establishment Clause," this Court has held, "is that one religious denomination cannot be officially preferred over another."

By authorizing and overseeing prayers associated with a single religion—to the exclusion of all others—the government officials in my hypothetical cases (whether federal, state, or local does not matter) have violated that foundational principle. They have embarked on a course of religious favoritism anathema to the First Amendment. And making matters still worse: They have done so in a place where individuals come to interact with, and participate in, the institutions and processes of their government. And so a civic function of some kind brings religious differences to the fore: That public proceeding becomes (whether intentionally or not) an instrument for dividing her from adherents to the community's majority religion, and for altering the very nature of her relationship with her government.

That is not the country we are, because that is not what our Constitution permits. Here, when a citizen stands before her government, whether to perform a service or request a benefit, her religious beliefs do not enter into the picture.

II

In both Greece's and the majority's view, everything I have discussed is irrelevant here because this case involves "the tradition of legislative prayer outlined" in Marsh v. Chambers. And before I dispute the Town and Court, I want to give them their due: They are right that, under *Marsh*, legislative prayer has a distinctive constitutional warrant by virtue of tradition. As the Court today describes, a long history, stretching back to the first session of Congress (when chaplains began to give prayers in both Chambers). And so I agree with the majority that the issue here is "whether the prayer practice in the Town of Greece fits within the tradition long followed in Congress and the state legislatures."

Where I depart from the majority is in my reply to that question. Instead, the prayers given in Greece, addressed directly to the Town's citizenry, were *more* sectarian, and *less* inclusive, than anything this Court sustained in *Marsh*. For those reasons, the prayer in Greece departs from the legislative tradition that the majority takes as its benchmark.

Marsh upheld prayer addressed to legislators alone, in a proceeding in which citizens had no role—and even then, only when it did not "proselytize or advance" any single religion. It was that legislative prayer practice (not every prayer in a body exercising any legislative function) that the Court found constitutional given its "unambiguous and unbroken history." But that approved practice, as I have shown, is not Greece's. None of the history *Marsh* cited—and none the majority details today—supports calling on citizens to pray, in a manner consonant with only a single religion's beliefs, at a participatory public proceeding, having both legislative and adjudicative components. Or to use the majority's phrase, no "history shows that th[is] specific practice is permitted."

And so, contra the majority, Greece's prayers cannot simply ride on the constitutional coattails of the legislative tradition *Marsh* described. The Board's practice must, in its own particulars, meet constitutional requirements.

And the guideposts for addressing that inquiry include the principles of religious neutrality I discussed earlier. The government (whether federal, state, or local) may not favor, or align itself with, any particular creed. And that is nowhere more true than when officials and citizens come face to face in their shared institutions of governance. In performing civic functions and seeking civic benefits, each person of this nation must experience a government that belongs to one and all, irrespective of belief. And for its part, each government must ensure that its participatory processes will not classify those citizens by faith, or make relevant their religious differences.

But Greece could not do what it did: infuse a participatory government body with one (and only one) faith, so that month in and month out, the citizens appearing before it become partly defined by their creed—as those who share, and those who do not, the community's majority religious belief. In this country, when citizens go before the government, they go not as Christians or Muslims or Jews (or what have you), but just as Americans (or here, as Grecians). That is what it means to be an equal citizen, irrespective of religion. And that is what the Town of Greece precluded by so identifying

When the citizens of this country approach their government, they do so only as Americans, not as members of one faith or another. And that means that even in a partly legislative body, they should not confront government-sponsored worship that divides them along religious lines. I believe, for all the reasons I have given, that the Town of Greece betrayed that promise. I therefore respectfully dissent from the Court's decision.

3. *Religion as a Part of Government Activities: Religious Symbols on Government Property*

In *Allegheny County*, above, the Court considered the constitutionality of a nativity scene and a menorah on government property. In two cases decided on the same day in 2005, the Court considered the constitutionality of Ten Commandments displays on government property.

The court declared the display in *McCreary County* unconstitutional, but upheld the display in *Van Orden*. In reading the decisions, consider whether there is a meaningful distinction between these cases. Following these cases is the Court's most recent decision about religious symbols on government property, American Legion v. American Humanist Association.

McCREARY COUNTY v. AMERICAN CIVIL
LIBERTIES UNION OF KENTUCKY

545 U.S. 844 (2005)

Justice SOUTER delivered the opinion of the Court.

Executives of two counties posted a version of the Ten Commandments on the walls of their courthouses. After suits were filed charging violations of the Establishment Clause, the legislative body of each county adopted a resolution

E. When Can Religion Become a Part of Government Activities?

calling for a more extensive exhibit meant to show that the Commandments are Kentucky's "precedent legal code." The result in each instance was a modified display of the Commandments surrounded by texts containing religious references as their sole common element. After changing counsel, the counties revised the exhibits again by eliminating some documents, expanding the text set out in another, and adding some new ones.

The issues are whether a determination of the counties' purpose is a sound basis for ruling on the Establishment Clause complaints, and whether evaluation of the counties' claim of secular purpose for the ultimate displays may take their evolution into account. We hold that the counties' manifest objective may be dispositive of the constitutional enquiry, and that the development of the presentation should be considered when determining its purpose.

I

In the summer of 1999, petitioners McCreary County and Pulaski County, Kentucky (hereinafter Counties), put up in their respective courthouses large, gold-framed copies of an abridged text of the King James version of the Ten Commandments, including a citation to the Book of Exodus. In McCreary County, the placement of the Commandments responded to an order of the county legislative body requiring "the display [to] be posted in 'a very high traffic area' of the courthouse." In Pulaski County, amidst reported controversy over the propriety of the display, the Commandments were hung in a ceremony presided over by the county Judge-Executive, who called them "good rules to live by" and who recounted the story of an astronaut who became convinced "there must be a divine God" after viewing the Earth from the moon.

In November 1999, respondents American Civil Liberties Union of Kentucky et al. sued the Counties in Federal District Court and sought a preliminary injunction against maintaining the displays, which the ACLU charged were violations of the prohibition of religious establishment included in the First Amendment of the Constitution. Within a month, and before the District Court had responded to the request for injunction, the legislative body of each County authorized a second, expanded display, by nearly identical resolutions reciting that the Ten Commandments are "the precedent legal code upon which the civil and criminal codes of . . . Kentucky are founded," and stating several grounds for taking that position: that "the Ten Commandments are codified in Kentucky's civil and criminal laws"; that the Kentucky House of Representatives had in 1993 "voted unanimously . . . to adjourn . . . 'in remembrance and honor of Jesus Christ, the Prince of Ethics'"; that the "County Judge and . . . magistrates agree with the arguments set out by Judge [Roy] Moore" in defense of his "display [of] the Ten Commandments in his courtroom"; and that the "Founding Father[s] [had an] explicit understanding of the duty of elected officials to publicly acknowledge God as the source of America's strength and direction."

As directed by the resolutions, the Counties expanded the displays of the Ten Commandments in their locations, presumably along with copies of the resolution, which instructed that it, too, be posted. In addition to the first display's large framed copy of the edited King James version of the Commandments, the second included eight other documents in smaller frames, each either having a religious theme or excerpted to highlight a religious element. The documents were the "endowed by their Creator" passage from the Declaration of Independence; the Preamble to the Constitution of Kentucky; the national motto, "In God We Trust"; a page from the Congressional Record of February 2, 1983, proclaiming the Year of the Bible and including a statement of the Ten Commandments; a proclamation by President Abraham Lincoln designating April 30, 1863, a National Day of Prayer and Humiliation; an excerpt from President Lincoln's "Reply to Loyal Colored People of Baltimore upon Presentation of a Bible," reading that "[t]he Bible is the best gift God has ever given to man"; a proclamation by President Reagan marking 1983 the Year of the Bible; and the Mayflower Compact.

II

Twenty-five years ago in a case prompted by posting the Ten Commandments in Kentucky's public schools, this Court recognized that the Commandments "are undeniably a sacred text in the Jewish and Christian faiths" and held that their display in public classrooms violated the First Amendment's bar against establishment of religion. Stone v. Graham (1980). *Stone* found a predominantly religious purpose in the government's posting of the Commandments, given their prominence as "'an instrument of religion.'" The Counties ask for a different approach here by arguing that official purpose is unknowable and the search for it inherently vain.

A

Ever since Lemon v. Kurtzman (1971) summarized the three familiar considerations for evaluating Establishment Clause claims, looking to whether government action has "a secular legislative purpose" has been a common, albeit seldom dispositive, element of our cases. Though we have found government action motivated by an illegitimate purpose only four times since *Lemon*, and "the secular purpose requirement alone may rarely be determinative . . . , it nevertheless serves an important function."

The touchstone for our analysis is the principle that the "First Amendment mandates governmental neutrality between religion and religion, and between religion and nonreligion." When the government acts with the ostensible and predominant purpose of advancing religion, it violates that central Establishment Clause value of official religious neutrality, there being no neutrality when the government's ostensible object is to take sides. Manifesting a purpose to favor one faith over another, or adherence to religion generally, clashes with the "understanding, reached . . . after decades of religious war, that liberty and social stability demand a religious tolerance that respects the religious views of all citizens. . . ." By showing a purpose to favor religion, the government "sends the . . . message to . . . nonadherents 'that they are outsiders, not full members of the political community, and an accompanying message to adherents that they are insiders, favored members. . . .'"

B

Despite the intuitive importance of official purpose to the realization of Establishment Clause values, the Counties ask us to abandon *Lemon*'s purpose test, or at least to truncate any enquiry into purpose here. Their first argument is that the very consideration of purpose is deceptive: according to them, true "purpose" is unknowable, and its search merely an excuse for courts to act selectively and unpredictably in picking out evidence of subjective intent. The assertions are as seismic as they are unconvincing.

Examination of purpose is a staple of statutory interpretation that makes up the daily fare of every appellate court in the country, and governmental purpose is a key element of a good deal of constitutional doctrine, e.g., Washington v. Davis (1976) (discriminatory purpose required for Equal Protection violation); Hunt v. Washington State Apple Advertising Comm'n (1977) (discriminatory purpose relevant to dormant Commerce Clause claim); Church of Lukumi Babalu Aye, Inc. v. Hialeah (1993) (discriminatory purpose raises level of scrutiny required by free exercise claim). With enquiries into purpose this common, if they were nothing but hunts for mares' nests deflecting attention from bare judicial will, the whole notion of purpose in law would have dropped into disrepute long ago.

But scrutinizing purpose does make practical sense, as in Establishment Clause analysis, where an understanding of official objective emerges from readily discoverable fact, without any judicial psychoanalysis of a drafter's heart of hearts. The eyes that look to purpose belong to an "objective observer," one who takes account of the traditional external signs that show up in the "text, legislative history, and implementation of the statute," or comparable official act. There is, then, nothing hinting at an unpredictable or disingenuous exercise when a court enquires into purpose after a claim is raised under the Establishment Clause.

Nor is there any indication that the enquiry is rigged in practice to finding a religious purpose dominant every time a case is filed. In the past, the test has not been fatal very often, presumably because government does not generally act unconstitutionally, with the predominant purpose of advancing religion.

Lemon said that government action must have "a secular . . . purpose," and after a host of cases it is fair to add that although a legislature's stated reasons will generally get deference, the secular purpose required has to be genuine, not a sham, and not merely secondary to a religious objective.

III

We take *Stone* as the initial legal benchmark, our only case dealing with the constitutionality of displaying the Commandments. *Stone* recognized that the Commandments are an "instrument of religion" and that, at least on the facts before it, the display of their text could presumptively be understood as meant to advance religion: although state law specifically required their posting in public school classrooms, their isolated exhibition did not leave room even for an argument that secular education explained their being there.

This is not to deny that the Commandments have had influence on civil or secular law; a major text of a majority religion is bound to be felt. The point is simply that the original text viewed in its entirety is an unmistakably religious statement dealing with religious obligations and with morality subject to religious sanction. When the government initiates an effort to place this statement alone in public view, a religious object is unmistakable.

We hold only that purpose needs to be taken seriously under the Establishment Clause and needs to be understood in light of context; an implausible claim that governmental purpose has changed should not carry the day in a court of law any more than in a head with common sense. It is enough to say here that district courts are fully capable of adjusting preliminary relief to take account of genuine changes in constitutionally significant conditions.

Nor do we have occasion here to hold that a sacred text can never be integrated constitutionally into a governmental display on the subject of law, or American history. We do not forget, and in this litigation have frequently been reminded, that our own courtroom frieze was deliberately designed in the exercise of governmental authority so as to include the figure of Moses holding tablets exhibiting a portion of the Hebrew text of the later, secularly phrased Commandments; in the company of 17 other lawgivers, most of them secular figures, there is no risk that Moses would strike an observer as evidence that the National Government was violating neutrality in religion.

IV

The dissent, however, puts forward a limitation on the application of the neutrality principle, with citations to historical evidence said to show that the Framers understood the ban on establishment of religion as sufficiently narrow to allow the government to espouse submission to the divine will. The dissent identifies God as the God of monotheism, all of whose three principal strains (Jewish, Christian, and Muslim) acknowledge the religious importance of the Ten Commandments. On the dissent's view, it apparently follows that even rigorous espousal of a common element of this common monotheism is consistent with the establishment ban.

But the dissent's argument for the original understanding is flawed from the outset by its failure to consider the full range of evidence showing what the Framers believed. The dissent is certainly correct in putting forward evidence that some of the Framers thought some endorsement of religion was compatible with the establishment ban.

But the fact is that we do have more to go on, for there is also evidence supporting the proposition that the Framers intended the Establishment Clause to require governmental neutrality in matters of religion, including neutrality in statements acknowledging religion. The very language of the Establishment Clause represented a significant departure from early drafts that merely prohibited a single national religion, and the final language instead "extended [the] prohibition to state support for 'religion' in general."

The historical record, moreover, is complicated beyond the dissent's account by the writings and practices of figures no less influential than Thomas Jefferson and James Madison. Jefferson, for example, refused to issue Thanksgiving Proclamations because he believed that they violated the Constitution. And Madison, whom the dissent claims as supporting its thesis, criticized Virginia's general assessment tax not just because it required people to donate "three pence" to religion, but because "it is itself a signal of persecution. It degrades from the equal rank of Citizens all those whose opinions in Religion do not bend to those of the Legislative authority."

The fair inference is that there was no common understanding about the limits of the establishment prohibition, and the dissent's conclusion that its narrower view was the original understanding stretches the evidence beyond tensile capacity. What the evidence does show is a group of statesmen, like others before and after them, who proposed a guarantee with contours not wholly worked out, leaving the Establishment Clause with edges still to be determined. And none the worse for that. Indeterminate edges are the kind to have in a constitution meant to endure, and to meet "exigencies which, if foreseen at all, must have been seen dimly, and which can be best provided for as they occur."

While the dissent fails to show a consistent original understanding from which to argue that the neutrality principle should be rejected, it does manage to deliver a surprise. As mentioned, the dissent says that the deity the Framers had in mind was the God of monotheism, with the consequence that government may espouse a tenet of traditional monotheism. This is truly a remarkable view. Today's dissent, however, apparently means that government should be free to approve the core beliefs of a favored religion over the tenets of others, a view that should trouble anyone who prizes religious liberty. Certainly history cannot justify it; on the contrary, history shows that the religion of concern to the Framers was not that of the monotheistic faiths generally, but Christianity in particular, a fact that no member of this Court takes as a premise for construing the Religion Clauses.

Historical evidence thus supports no solid argument for changing course (whatever force the argument might have when directed at the existing precedent), whereas public discourse at the present time certainly raises no doubt about the value of the interpretative approach invoked for 60 years now. We are centuries away from the St. Bartholomew's Day massacre and the treatment of heretics in early Massachusetts, but the divisiveness of religion in current public life is inescapable. This is no time to deny the prudence of understanding the Establishment Clause to require the Government to stay neutral on religious belief, which is reserved for the conscience of the individual.

Justice O'CONNOR, concurring.

I join in the Court's opinion. The First Amendment expresses our Nation's fundamental commitment to religious liberty by means of two provisions—one protecting the free exercise of religion, the other barring establishment of religion. They were written by the descendents of people who had come to this land precisely so that they could practice their religion freely. Together with the other First Amendment guarantees—of free speech, a free press, and the rights to assemble and petition—the Religion Clauses were designed to safeguard the freedom of conscience and belief that those immigrants had sought. They embody an idea that was once considered radical: Free people are entitled to free and diverse thoughts, which government ought neither to constrain nor to direct.

Reasonable minds can disagree about how to apply the Religion Clauses in a given case. But the goal of the Clauses is clear: to carry out the Founders' plan of preserving religious liberty to the fullest extent possible in a pluralistic society.

By enforcing the Clauses, we have kept religion a matter for the individual conscience, not for the prosecutor or bureaucrat. At a time when we see around the world the violent consequences of the assumption of religious authority by government, Americans may count themselves fortunate: Our regard for constitutional boundaries has protected us from similar travails, while allowing private religious exercise to flourish. The well-known statement that "[w]e are a religious people" has proved true. Americans attend their places of worship more often than do citizens of other developed nations, and describe religion as playing an especially important role in their lives. Those who would renegotiate the boundaries between church and state must therefore answer a difficult question: Why would we trade a system that has served us so well for one that has served others so poorly?

When we enforce these restrictions, we do so for the same reason that guided the Framers—respect for religion's special role in society. Our Founders conceived of a Republic receptive to voluntary religious expression, and provided for the possibility of judicial intervention when government action threatens or impedes such expression. Voluntary religious belief and expression may be as threatened when government takes the mantle of religion upon itself as when government directly interferes with private religious practices. When the government associates one set of religious beliefs with the state and identifies nonadherents as outsiders, it encroaches upon the individual's decision about whether and how to worship. In the marketplace of ideas, the government has vast resources and special status. Government religious expression therefore risks crowding out private observance and distorting the natural interplay between competing beliefs. Allowing government to be a potential mouthpiece for competing religious ideas risks the sort of division that might easily spill over into suppression of rival beliefs. Tying secular and religious authority together poses risks to both.

Given the history of this particular display of the Ten Commandments, the Court correctly finds an Establishment Clause violation. The purpose behind the counties' display is relevant because it conveys an unmistakable message of endorsement to the reasonable observer. It is true that many Americans find the Commandments in accord with their personal beliefs. But we do not count heads before enforcing the First Amendment. Nor can we accept the theory that Americans who do not accept the Commandments' validity are outside the First Amendment's protections. There is no list of approved and disapproved beliefs appended to the First Amendment—and the Amendment's broad terms do not admit of such a cramped reading.

We owe our First Amendment to a generation with a profound commitment to religion and a profound commitment to religious liberty—visionaries who held their faith "with enough confidence to believe that what should be rendered to God does not need to be decided and collected by Caesar." In my opinion, the display at issue was an establishment of religion in violation of our Constitution.

Justice SCALIA, with whom THE CHIEF JUSTICE and Justice THOMAS join, and with whom Justice KENNEDY joins as to Parts II and III, dissenting.

I would uphold McCreary County and Pulaski County, Kentucky's (hereinafter Counties) displays of the Ten Commandments. I shall discuss, first, why the Court's oft repeated assertion that the government cannot favor religious practice is false; second, why today's opinion extends the scope of that falsehood even beyond prior cases; and third, why even on the basis of the Court's false assumptions the judgment here is wrong.

I

That is one model of the relationship between church and state—a model spread across Europe by the armies of Napoleon, and reflected in the Constitution of

E. When Can Religion Become a Part of Government Activities?

France, which begins "France is [a] . . . secular . . . Republic." France Const., Art. 1. Religion is to be strictly excluded from the public forum. This is not, and never was, the model adopted by America. George Washington added to the form of Presidential oath prescribed by Art. II, §1, cl. 8, of the Constitution, the concluding words "so help me God." The Supreme Court under John Marshall opened its sessions with the prayer, "God save the United States and this Honorable Court." The First Congress instituted the practice of beginning its legislative sessions with a prayer. The same week that Congress submitted the Establishment Clause as part of the Bill of Rights for ratification by the States, it enacted legislation providing for paid chaplains in the House and Senate. The day after the First Amendment was proposed, the same Congress that had proposed it requested the President to proclaim "a day of public thanksgiving and prayer, to be observed, by acknowledging, with grateful hearts, the many and signal favours of Almighty God." President Washington offered the first Thanksgiving Proclamation shortly thereafter, devoting November 26, 1789, on behalf of the American people "'to the service of that great and glorious Being who is the beneficent author of all the good that is, that was, or that will be,'" thus beginning a tradition of offering gratitude to God that continues today. The same Congress also reenacted the Northwest Territory Ordinance of 1787, Article III of which provided: "Religion, morality, and knowledge, being necessary to good government and the happiness of mankind, schools and the means of education shall forever be encouraged." And of course the First Amendment itself accords religion (and no other manner of belief) special constitutional protection.

These actions of our First President and Congress and the Marshall Court were not idiosyncratic; they reflected the beliefs of the period. Those who wrote the Constitution believed that morality was essential to the well-being of society and that encouragement of religion was the best way to foster morality. The "fact that the Founding Fathers believed devoutly that there was a God and that the unalienable rights of man were rooted in Him is clearly evidenced in their writings, from the Mayflower Compact to the Constitution itself."

Nor have the views of our people on this matter significantly changed. Presidents continue to conclude the Presidential oath with the words "so help me God." Our legislatures, state and national, continue to open their sessions with prayer led by official chaplains. The sessions of this Court continue to open with the prayer "God save the United States and this Honorable Court." Invocation of the Almighty by our public figures, at all levels of government, remains commonplace. Our coinage bears the motto "IN GOD WE TRUST." And our Pledge of Allegiance contains the acknowledgment that we are a Nation "under God." As one of our Supreme Court opinions rightly observed, "We are a religious people whose institutions presuppose a Supreme Being." Zorach v. Clauson (1952).

With all of this reality (and much more) staring it in the face, how can the Court possibly assert that "the First Amendment mandates governmental neutrality between . . . religion and nonreligion," and that "[m]anifesting a purpose to favor . . . adherence to religion generally," is unconstitutional? Who says so? Surely not the words of the Constitution. Surely not the history and traditions that reflect our society's constant understanding of those words. Surely not even the current sense of our society, recently reflected in an Act of Congress adopted unanimously by the Senate and with only 5 nays in the House of Representatives, criticizing a Court of Appeals opinion that had held "under God" in the Pledge of Allegiance unconstitutional. Nothing stands behind the Court's assertion that governmental affirmation of the society's belief in God is unconstitutional except the Court's own say-so, citing as support only the unsubstantiated say-so of earlier Courts going back no farther than the mid-20th century. And it is, moreover, a thoroughly discredited say-so. It is discredited, to begin with, because a majority of the Justices on the current Court (including at least one Member of today's majority) have, in separate opinions, repudiated the brain-spun "*Lemon* test" that embodies the supposed principle of neutrality between religion and irreligion. And it is discredited because the Court has not had the courage (or the foolhardiness) to apply the neutrality principle consistently.

Besides appealing to the demonstrably false principle that the government cannot favor religion over irreligion, today's opinion suggests that the posting of the Ten Commandments violates the principle that the government cannot favor one religion over another. That is indeed a valid principle where public aid or assistance to religion is concerned, or where the free exercise of religion is at issue, but it necessarily applies in a more limited sense to public acknowledgment of the Creator. If religion in the public forum had to be entirely nondenominational, there could be no religion in the public forum at all. One cannot say the word "God," or "the Almighty," one cannot offer public supplication or thanksgiving, without contradicting the beliefs of some people that there are many gods, or that God or the gods pay no attention to human affairs. With respect to public acknowledgment of religious belief, it is entirely clear from our Nation's historical practices that the Establishment Clause permits this disregard of polytheists and believers in unconcerned deities, just as it permits the disregard of devout atheists. The Thanksgiving Proclamation issued by George Washington at the instance of the First Congress was scrupulously nondenominational—but it was monotheistic. In Marsh v. Chambers (1983), we said that the fact the particular prayers offered in the Nebraska Legislature were "in the Judeo-Christian tradition" posed no additional problem, because "there is no indication that the prayer opportunity has been exploited to proselytize or advance any one, or to disparage any other, faith or belief."

Historical practices thus demonstrate that there is a distance between the acknowledgment of a single Creator and the establishment of a religion. The former is, as Marsh v. Chambers put it, "a tolerable acknowledgment of beliefs widely held among the people of this country." The three most popular religions in the United States, Christianity, Judaism, and Islam—which combined account for 97.7% of all believers—are monotheistic. All of them, moreover (Islam included), believe that the Ten Commandments were given by God to Moses, and are divine prescriptions for a virtuous life. Publicly honoring the Ten Commandments is thus indistinguishable, insofar as discriminating against other religions is concerned, from publicly honoring God. Both practices are recognized across such a broad and diverse range of the population—from Christians to Muslims—that they cannot be reasonably understood as a government endorsement of a particular religious viewpoint.

I must respond to Justice Stevens' assertion that I would "marginaliz[e] the belief systems of more than 7 million Americans" who adhere to religions that are not monotheistic. Surely that is a gross exaggeration. The beliefs of those citizens are entirely protected by the Free Exercise Clause, and by those aspects of the Establishment Clause that do not relate to government acknowledgment of the Creator. Invocation of God despite their beliefs is permitted not because nonmonotheistic religions cease to be religions recognized by the religion clauses of the First Amendment, but because governmental invocation of God is not an establishment. Justice Stevens fails to recognize that in the context of public acknowledgments of God there are legitimate competing interests: On the one hand, the interest of that minority in not feeling "excluded"; but on the other, the interest of the overwhelming majority of religious believers in being able to give God thanks and supplication as a people, and with respect to our national endeavors. Our national tradition has resolved that conflict in favor of the majority.

II

As bad as the *Lemon* test is, it is worse for the fact that, since its inception, its seemingly simple mandates have been manipulated to fit whatever result the Court aimed to achieve. Today's opinion is no different. In two respects it modifies *Lemon* to ratchet up the Court's hostility to religion. First, the Court justifies inquiry into legislative purpose, not as an end itself, but as a means to ascertain the appearance of the government action to an "'objective observer.'" Because in the Court's view the true danger to be guarded against is that the objective observer would feel like an "outside[r]" or "not [a] full membe[r] of the political community," its inquiry focuses not on the actual purpose of government action, but the "purpose apparent from government action." Under this approach, even if a government could show that its actual purpose was not to advance religion, it would presumably violate the Constitution as long as the Court's objective observer would think otherwise.

I have remarked before that it is an odd jurisprudence that bases the unconstitutionality of a government practice that does not actually advance religion on the hopes of the government that it would do so. But that oddity pales in comparison to the one invited by today's analysis: the legitimacy of a government action with a wholly secular effect would turn on the misperception of an imaginary observer that the government officials behind the action had the intent to advance religion.

Second, the Court replaces *Lemon*'s requirement that the government have "a secular . . . purpose" with the heightened requirement that the secular purpose "predominate" over any purpose to advance religion. The Court treats this extension as a natural outgrowth of the longstanding requirement that the government's secular purpose not be a sham, but simple logic shows the two to be unrelated. If the government's proffered secular purpose is not genuine, then the government has no secular purpose at all. The new demand that secular purpose predominate contradicts *Lemon*'s more limited requirement, and finds no support in our cases.

I have urged that *Lemon*'s purpose prong be abandoned, because (as I have discussed in Part I) even an exclusive purpose to foster or assist religious practice is not necessarily invalidating. But today's extension makes things even worse. By shifting the focus of *Lemon*'s purpose prong from the search for a genuine, secular motivation to the hunt for a predominantly religious purpose, the Court converts what has in the past been a fairly limited inquiry into a rigorous review of the full record. Those responsible for the adoption of the Religion Clauses would surely regard it as a bitter irony that the religious values they designed those Clauses to protect have now become so distasteful to this Court that if they constitute anything more than a subordinate motive for government action they will invalidate it.

III

Even accepting the Court's *Lemon*-based premises, the displays at issue here were constitutional. To any person who happened to walk down the hallway of the McCreary or Pulaski County Courthouse during the roughly nine months when the Foundations Displays were exhibited, the displays must have seemed unremarkable — if indeed they were noticed at all. The walls of both courthouses were already lined with historical documents and other assorted portraits; each Foundations Display was exhibited in the same format as these other displays and nothing in the record suggests that either County took steps to give it greater prominence. On its face, the Foundations Displays manifested the purely secular purpose that the Counties asserted before the District Court: "to display documents that played a significant role in the foundation of our system of law and government." That the Displays included the Ten Commandments did not transform their apparent secular purpose into one of impermissible advocacy for Judeo-Christian beliefs.

Acknowledgment of the contribution that religion has made to our Nation's legal and governmental heritage partakes of a centuries-old tradition. Display of the Ten Commandments is well within the mainstream of this practice of acknowledgment. Federal, State, and local governments across the Nation have engaged in such display. The Supreme Court Building itself includes depictions of Moses with the Ten Commandments in the Courtroom and on the east pediment of the building, and symbols of the Ten Commandments "adorn the metal gates lining the north and south sides of the Courtroom as well as the doors leading into the Courtroom." Similar depictions of the Decalogue appear on public buildings and monuments throughout our Nation's Capital. The frequency of these displays testifies to the popular understanding that the Ten Commandments are a foundation of the rule of law, and a symbol of the role that religion played, and continues to play, in our system of government.

VAN ORDEN v. PERRY
545 U.S. 677 (2005)

Chief Justice REHNQUIST announced the judgment of the Court and delivered an opinion, in which Justice SCALIA, Justice KENNEDY, and Justice THOMAS join.

The question here is whether the Establishment Clause of the First Amendment allows the display of a monument inscribed with the Ten Commandments on the Texas State Capitol grounds. We hold that it does.

The 22 acres surrounding the Texas State Capitol contain 17 monuments and 21 historical markers commemorating the "people, ideals, and events that compose Texan identity." The monolith challenged here stands 6-feet high and 3 1/2 feet wide. It is located to the north of the Capitol building, between the

E. When Can Religion Become a Part of Government Activities? 635

Capitol and the Supreme Court building. Its primary content is the text of the Ten Commandments. An eagle grasping the American flag, an eye inside of a pyramid, and two small tablets with what appears to be an ancient script are carved above the text of the Ten Commandments. Below the text are two Stars of David and the superimposed Greek letters Chi and Rho, which represent Christ. The bottom of the monument bears the inscription "PRESENTED TO THE PEOPLE AND YOUTH OF TEXAS BY THE FRATERNAL ORDER OF EAGLES OF TEXAS 1961."

The legislative record surrounding the State's acceptance of the monument from the Eagles—a national social, civic, and patriotic organization—is limited to legislative journal entries. After the monument was accepted, the State selected a site for the monument based on the recommendation of the state organization responsible for maintaining the Capitol grounds. The Eagles paid the cost of erecting the monument, the dedication of which was presided over by two state legislators.

Petitioner Thomas Van Orden is a native Texan and a resident of Austin. At one time he was a licensed lawyer, having graduated from Southern Methodist Law School. Van Orden testified that, since 1995, he has encountered the Ten Commandments monument during his frequent visits to the Capitol grounds. Forty years after the monument's erection and six years after Van Orden began to encounter the monument frequently, he sued numerous state officials in their official capacities seeking both a declaration that the monument's placement violates the Establishment Clause and an injunction requiring its removal.

Our cases, Januslike, point in two directions in applying the Establishment Clause. One face looks toward the strong role played by religion and religious traditions throughout our Nation's history. The other face looks toward the principle that governmental intervention in religious matters can itself endanger religious freedom.

This case, like all Establishment Clause challenges, presents us with the difficulty of respecting both faces. Our institutions presuppose a Supreme Being, yet these institutions must not press religious observances upon their citizens. One face looks to the past in acknowledgment of our Nation's heritage, while the other looks to the present in demanding a separation between church and state. Reconciling these two faces requires that we neither abdicate our responsibility to maintain a division between church and state nor evince a hostility to religion by disabling the government from in some ways recognizing our religious heritage.

In this case we are faced with a display of the Ten Commandments on government property outside the Texas State Capitol. Such acknowledgments of the role played by the Ten Commandments in our Nation's heritage are common throughout America. We need only look within our own Courtroom. Since 1935, Moses has stood, holding two tablets that reveal portions of the Ten Commandments written in Hebrew, among other lawgivers in the south frieze. Representations of the Ten Commandments adorn the metal gates lining the north and south sides of the Courtroom as well as the doors leading into the Courtroom. Moses also sits on the exterior east facade of the building holding the Ten Commandments tablets.

Similar acknowledgments can be seen throughout a visitor's tour of our Nation's Capital. For example, a large statue of Moses holding the Ten Commandments, alongside a statue of the Apostle Paul, has overlooked the rotunda of the Library of Congress' Jefferson Building since 1897. And the Jefferson Building's Great Reading Room contains a sculpture of a woman beside the Ten Commandments with a quote above her from the Old Testament (Micah 6:8). A medallion with two tablets depicting the Ten Commandments decorates the floor of the National Archives. Inside the Department of Justice, a statue entitled "The Spirit of Law" has two tablets representing the Ten Commandments lying at its feet. In front of the Ronald Reagan Building is another sculpture that includes a depiction of the Ten Commandments. So too a 24-foot-tall sculpture, depicting, among other things, the Ten Commandments and a cross, stands outside the federal courthouse that houses both the Court of Appeals and the District Court for the District of Columbia. Moses is also prominently featured in the Chamber of the United States House of Representatives.

Of course, the Ten Commandments are religious—they were so viewed at their inception and so remain. The monument, therefore, has religious significance. According to Judeo-Christian belief, the Ten Commandments were given to Moses by God on Mt. Sinai. But Moses was a lawgiver as well as a religious leader. And the Ten Commandments have an undeniable historical meaning, as the foregoing examples demonstrate. Simply having religious content or promoting a message consistent with a religious doctrine does not run afoul of the Establishment Clause.

There are, of course, limits to the display of religious messages or symbols. For example, we held unconstitutional a Kentucky statute requiring the posting of the Ten Commandments in every public schoolroom. Stone v. Graham (1980) (per curiam). In the classroom context, we found that the Kentucky statute had an improper and plainly religious purpose.

The placement of the Ten Commandments monument on the Texas State Capitol grounds is a far more passive use of those texts than was the case in *Stone*, where the text confronted elementary school students every day. Indeed, Van Orden, the petitioner here, apparently walked by the monument for a number of years before bringing this lawsuit. Texas has treated her Capitol grounds monuments as representing the several strands in the State's political and legal history. The inclusion of the Ten Commandments monument in this group has a dual significance, partaking of both religion and government. We cannot say that Texas' display of this monument violates the Establishment Clause of the First Amendment.

Justice THOMAS, concurring.

This case would be easy if the Court were willing to abandon the inconsistent guideposts it has adopted for addressing Establishment Clause challenges, and return to the original meaning of the Clause. I have previously suggested that the Clause's text and history "resis[t] incorporation" against the States. If the Establishment Clause does not restrain the States, then it has no application here, where only state action is at issue.

Even if the Clause is incorporated, or if the Free Exercise Clause limits the power of States to establish religions, our task would be far simpler if we returned to the original meaning of the word "establishment" than it is under the various approaches this Court now uses. The Framers understood an establishment "necessarily [to] involve actual legal coercion." "In other words, establishment at the founding involved, for example, mandatory observance or mandatory payment of taxes supporting ministers." And "government practices that have nothing to do with creating or maintaining . . . coercive state establishments" simply do not "implicate the possible liberty interest of being free from coercive state establishments."

There is no question that, based on the original meaning of the Establishment Clause, the Ten Commandments display at issue here is constitutional. In no sense does Texas compel petitioner Van Orden to do anything. The only injury to him is that he takes offense at seeing the monument as he passes it on his way to the Texas Supreme Court Library. He need not stop to read it or even to look at it, let alone to express support for it or adopt the Commandments as guides for his life. The mere presence of the monument along his path involves no coercion and thus does not violate the Establishment Clause.

Finally, the very "flexibility" of this Court's Establishment Clause precedent leaves it incapable of consistent application. The inconsistency between the decisions the Court reaches today in this case and in McCreary County v. American Civil Liberties Union of Ky. (2005) only compounds the confusion.

Much, if not all, of this would be avoided if the Court would return to the views of the Framers and adopt coercion as the touchstone for our Establishment Clause inquiry. Every acknowledgment of religion would not give rise to an Establishment Clause claim. Courts would not act as theological commissions, judging the meaning of religious matters. Most important, our precedent would be capable of consistent and coherent application. While the Court correctly rejects the challenge to the Ten Commandments monument on the Texas Capitol grounds, a more fundamental rethinking of our Establishment Clause jurisprudence remains in order.

Justice BREYER, concurring in the judgment.

In School Dist. of Abington Township v. Schempp (1963), Justice Goldberg, joined by Justice Harlan, wrote, in respect to the First Amendment's Religion Clauses, that there is "no simple and clear measure which by precise application can readily and invariably demark the permissible from the impermissible." One must refer instead to the basic purposes of those Clauses. They seek to "assure the fullest possible scope of religious liberty and tolerance for all." They seek to avoid that divisiveness based upon religion that promotes social conflict, sapping the strength of government and religion alike. They seek to maintain that "separation of church and state" that has long been critical to the "peaceful dominion that religion exercises in [this] country," where the "spirit of religion" and the "spirit of freedom" are productively "united," "reign[ing] together" but in separate spheres "on the same soil."

The Court has made clear, as Justices Goldberg and Harlan noted, that the realization of these goals means that government must "neither engage in nor compel religious practices," that it must "effect no favoritism among sects or between religion and nonreligion," and that it must "work deterrence of no religious belief." The government must avoid excessive interference with, or promotion of, religion. But the Establishment Clause does not compel the government to purge from the public sphere all that in any way partakes of the religious. Such absolutism is not only inconsistent with our national traditions, but would also tend to promote the kind of social conflict the Establishment Clause seeks to avoid.

The case before us is a borderline case. It concerns a large granite monument bearing the text of the Ten Commandments located on the grounds of the

Texas State Capitol. On the one hand, the Commandments' text undeniably has a religious message, invoking, indeed emphasizing, the Deity. On the other hand, focusing on the text of the Commandments alone cannot conclusively resolve this case. Rather, to determine the message that the text here conveys, we must examine how the text is used. And that inquiry requires us to consider the context of the display.

In certain contexts, a display of the tablets of the Ten Commandments can convey not simply a religious message but also a secular moral message (about proper standards of social conduct). And in certain contexts, a display of the tablets can also convey a historical message (about a historic relation between those standards and the law) — a fact that helps to explain the display of those tablets in dozens of courthouses throughout the Nation, including the Supreme Court of the United States.

Here the tablets have been used as part of a display that communicates not simply a religious message, but a secular message as well. The circumstances surrounding the display's placement on the capitol grounds and its physical setting suggest that the State itself intended the latter, nonreligious aspects of the tablets' message to predominate. And the monument's 40-year history on the Texas state grounds indicates that that has been its effect.

The group that donated the monument, the Fraternal Order of Eagles, a private civic (and primarily secular) organization, while interested in the religious aspect of the Ten Commandments, sought to highlight the Commandments' role in shaping civic morality as part of that organization's efforts to combat juvenile delinquency. The Eagles' consultation with a committee composed of members of several faiths in order to find a nonsectarian text underscores the group's ethics-based motives. The tablets, as displayed on the monument, prominently acknowledge that the Eagles donated the display, a factor which, though not sufficient, thereby further distances the State itself from the religious aspect of the Commandments' message.

The physical setting of the monument, moreover, suggests little or nothing of the sacred. The monument sits in a large park containing 17 monuments and 21 historical markers, all designed to illustrate the "ideals" of those who settled in Texas and of those who have lived there since that time. The setting does not readily lend itself to meditation or any other religious activity. But it does provide a context of history and moral ideals. It (together with the display's inscription about its origin) communicates to visitors that the State sought to reflect moral principles, illustrating a relation between ethics and law that the State's citizens, historically speaking, have endorsed.

If these factors provide a strong, but not conclusive, indication that the Commandments' text on this monument conveys a predominantly secular message, a further factor is determinative here. As far as I can tell, 40 years passed in which the presence of this monument, legally speaking, went unchallenged (until the single legal objection raised by petitioner). And I am not aware of any evidence suggesting that this was due to a climate of intimidation. Those 40 years suggest that the public visiting the capitol grounds has considered the religious aspect of the tablets' message as part of what is a broader moral and historical message reflective of a cultural heritage.

This case, moreover, is distinguishable from instances where the Court has found Ten Commandments displays impermissible. The display is not on the grounds of a public school, where, given the impressionability of the young, government must exercise particular care in separating church and state. This case also differs from *McCreary County*, where the short (and stormy) history of the courthouse Commandments' displays demonstrates the substantially religious objectives of those who mounted them, and the effect of this readily apparent objective upon those who view them. That history there indicates a governmental effort substantially to promote religion, not simply an effort primarily to reflect, historically, the secular impact of a religiously inspired document. And, in today's world, in a Nation of so many different religious and comparable nonreligious fundamental beliefs, a more contemporary state effort to focus attention upon a religious text is certainly likely to prove divisive in a way that this longstanding, pre-existing monument has not.

For these reasons, I believe that the Texas display—serving a mixed but primarily nonreligious purpose, not primarily "advanc[ing]" or "inhibit[ing] religion," and not creating an "excessive government entanglement with religion"—might satisfy this Court's more formal Establishment Clause tests. But, as I have said, in reaching the conclusion that the Texas display falls on the permissible side of the constitutional line, I rely less upon a literal application of any particular test than upon consideration of the basic purposes of the First Amendment's Religion Clauses themselves. This display has stood apparently uncontested for nearly two generations. That experience helps us understand that as a practical matter of degree this display is unlikely to prove divisive. And this matter of degree is, I believe, critical in a borderline case such as this one.

At the same time, to reach a contrary conclusion here, based primarily on the religious nature of the tablets' text would, I fear, lead the law to exhibit a hostility toward religion that has no place in our Establishment Clause traditions. Such a holding might well encourage disputes concerning the removal of longstanding depictions of the Ten Commandments from public buildings across the Nation. And it could thereby create the very kind of religiously based divisiveness that the Establishment Clause seeks to avoid.

Justice STEVENS, with whom Justice GINSBURG joins, dissenting.

The sole function of the monument on the grounds of Texas' State Capitol is to display the full text of one version of the Ten Commandments. The monument is not a work of art and does not refer to any event in the history of the State. Viewed on its face, Texas' display has no purported connection to God's role in the formation of Texas or the founding of our Nation; nor does it provide the reasonable observer with any basis to guess that it was erected to honor any individual or organization. The message transmitted by Texas' chosen display is quite plain: This State endorses the divine code of the "Judeo-Christian" God.

For those of us who learned to recite the King James version of the text long before we understood the meaning of some of its words, God's Commandments may seem like wise counsel. The question before this Court, however, is whether it is counsel that the State of Texas may proclaim without violating the Establishment Clause of the Constitution. If any fragment of Jefferson's metaphorical "wall of separation between church and State" is to be preserved—if there remains any meaning to the "wholesome 'neutrality' of which this Court's [Establishment Clause] cases speak"—a negative answer to that question is mandatory.

In my judgment, at the very least, the Establishment Clause has created a strong presumption against the display of religious symbols on public property. The adornment of our public spaces with displays of religious symbols and messages undoubtedly provides comfort, even inspiration, to many individuals who subscribe to particular faiths. Unfortunately, the practice also runs the risk of "offend[ing] nonmembers of the faith being advertised as well as adherents who consider the particular advertisement disrespectful." Government's obligation to avoid divisiveness and exclusion in the religious sphere is compelled by the Establishment and Free Exercise Clauses, which together erect a wall of separation between church and state.

The monolith displayed on Texas Capitol grounds cannot be discounted as a passive acknowledgment of religion, nor can the State's refusal to remove it upon objection be explained as a simple desire to preserve a historic relic. This Nation's resolute commitment to neutrality with respect to religion is flatly inconsistent with the plurality's wholehearted validation of an official state endorsement of the message that there is one, and only one, God.

The reason this message stands apart is that the Decalogue is a venerable religious text. As we held 25 years ago, it is beyond dispute that "[t]he Ten Commandments are undeniably a sacred text in the Jewish and Christian faiths." For many followers, the Commandments represent the literal word of God as spoken to Moses and repeated to his followers after descending from Mount Sinai. Attempts to secularize what is unquestionably a sacred text defy credibility and disserve people of faith.

The profoundly sacred message embodied by the text inscribed on the Texas monument is emphasized by the especially large letters that identify its author: "I AM the LORD thy God." It commands present worship of Him and no other deity. It directs us to be guided by His teaching in the current and future conduct of all of our affairs. It instructs us to follow a code of divine law, some of which has informed and been integrated into our secular legal code ("Thou shalt not kill"), but much of which has not ("Thou shalt not make to thyself any graven images. . . . Thou shalt not covet").

Moreover, despite the Eagles' best efforts to choose a benign nondenominational text, the Ten Commandments display projects not just a religious, but an inherently sectarian message. There are many distinctive versions of the Decalogue, ascribed to by different religions and even different denominations within a particular faith; to a pious and learned observer, these differences may be of enormous religious significance. In choosing to display this version of the Commandments, Texas tells the observer that the State supports this side of the doctrinal religious debate.

Even if, however, the message of the monument, despite the inscribed text, fairly could be said to represent the belief system of all Judeo-Christians, it would still run afoul of the Establishment Clause by prescribing a compelled code of conduct from one God, namely a Judeo-Christian God, that is rejected by prominent polytheistic sects, such as Hinduism, as well as nontheistic religions, such as Buddhism. And, at the very least, the text of the Ten Commandments impermissibly commands a preference for religion over irreligion. Any of those bases, in my judgment, would be sufficient to conclude that the message should not be proclaimed by the State of Texas on a permanent monument at the seat of its government.

The plurality relies heavily on the fact that our Republic was founded, and has been governed since its nascence, by leaders who spoke then (and speak still) in plainly religious rhetoric. The speeches and rhetoric characteristic of the founding era, however, do not answer the question before us. I have already

E. When Can Religion Become a Part of Government Activities?

explained why Texas' display of the full text of the Ten Commandments, given the content of the actual display and the context in which it is situated, sets this case apart from the countless examples of benign government recognitions of religion. But there is another crucial difference. Our leaders, when delivering public addresses, often express their blessings simultaneously in the service of God and their constituents. Thus, when public officials deliver public speeches, we recognize that their words are not exclusively a transmission from the government because those oratories have embedded within them the inherently personal views of the speaker as an individual member of the polity. The permanent placement of a textual religious display on state property is different in kind; it amalgamates otherwise discordant individual views into a collective statement of government approval. Moreover, the message never ceases to transmit itself to objecting viewers whose only choices are to accept the message or to ignore the offense by averting their gaze. In this sense, although Thanksgiving Day proclamations and inaugural speeches undoubtedly seem official, in most circumstances they will not constitute the sort of governmental endorsement of religion at which the separation of church and state is aimed.

The plurality's reliance on early religious statements and proclamations made by the Founders is also problematic because those views were not espoused at the Constitutional Convention in 1787 nor enshrined in the Constitution's text. The original understanding of the type of "religion" that qualified for constitutional protection under the Establishment Clause likely did not include those followers of Judaism and Islam who are among the preferred "monotheistic" religions Justice Scalia has embraced in his *McCreary County* opinion. Given the original understanding of the men who championed our "Christian nation"—men who had no cause to view anti-Semitism or contempt for atheists as problems worthy of civic concern—one must ask whether Justice Scalia "has not had the courage (or the foolhardiness) to apply [his originalism] principle consistently."

Indeed, to constrict narrowly the reach of the Establishment Clause to the views of the Founders would lead to more than this unpalatable result; it would also leave us with an unincorporated constitutional provision—in other words, one that limits only the federal establishment of "a national religion." Under this view, not only could a State constitutionally adorn all of its public spaces with crucifixes or passages from the New Testament, it would also have full authority to prescribe the teachings of Martin Luther or Joseph Smith as the official state religion. Only the Federal Government would be prohibited from taking sides (and only then as between Christian sects).

A reading of the First Amendment dependent on either of the purported original meanings expressed above would eviscerate the heart of the Establishment Clause. It would replace Jefferson's "wall of separation" with a perverse wall of exclusion—Christians inside, non-Christians out. It would permit States to construct walls of their own choosing—Baptists inside, Mormons out; Jewish Orthodox inside, Jewish Reform out. A Clause so understood might be faithful to the expectations of some of our Founders, but it is plainly not worthy of a society whose enviable hallmark over the course of two centuries has been the continuing expansion of religious pluralism and tolerance.

It is our duty, therefore, to interpret the First Amendment's command that "Congress shall make no law respecting an establishment of religion" not by merely asking what those words meant to observers at the time of the founding, but instead by deriving from the Clause's text and history the broad principles that remain valid today. The principle that guides my analysis is neutrality. The basis for that principle is firmly rooted in our Nation's history and our Constitution's text. I recognize that the requirement that government must remain neutral between religion and irreligion would have seemed foreign to some of the Framers; so too would a requirement of neutrality between Jews and Christians. The evil of discriminating today against atheists, "polytheists[,] and believers in unconcerned deities," is in my view a direct descendent of the evil of discriminating among Christian sects. The Establishment Clause thus forbids it and, in turn, forbids Texas from displaying the Ten Commandments monument the plurality so casually affirms.

The judgment of the Court in this case stands for the proposition that the Constitution permits governmental displays of sacred religious texts. This makes a mockery of the constitutional ideal that government must remain neutral between religion and irreligion. If a State may endorse a particular deity's command to "have no other gods before me," it is difficult to conceive of any textual display that would run afoul of the Establishment Clause.

Justice SOUTER, with whom Justice STEVENS and Justice GINSBURG join, dissenting.

Although the First Amendment's Religion Clauses have not been read to mandate absolute governmental neutrality toward religion, the Establishment Clause requires neutrality as a general rule, and thus expresses Madison's condemnation of "employ[ing] Religion as an engine of Civil policy." A governmental display of an obviously religious text cannot be squared with neutrality, except in a setting that plausibly indicates that the statement is not placed in view with a predominant purpose on the part of government either to adopt the religious message or to urge its acceptance by others.

Until today, only one of our cases addressed the constitutionality of posting the Ten Commandments, Stone v. Graham (1980). A Kentucky statute required posting the Commandments on the walls of public school classrooms. [The Court stated:]

> "The pre-eminent purpose for posting the Ten Commandments on schoolroom walls is plainly religious in nature. The Ten Commandments are undeniably a sacred text in the Jewish and Christian faiths, and no legislative recitation of a supposed secular purpose can blind us to that fact. The Commandments do not confine themselves to arguably secular matters, such as honoring one's parents, killing or murder, adultery, stealing, false witness, and covetousness. Rather, the first part of the Commandments concerns the religious duties of believers: worshipping the Lord God alone, avoiding idolatry, not using the Lord's name in vain, and observing the Sabbath Day."

What these observations underscore are the simple realities that the Ten Commandments constitute a religious statement, that their message is inherently religious, and that the purpose of singling them out in a display is clearly the same.

To drive the religious point home, and identify the message as religious to any viewer who failed to read the text, the engraved quotation is framed by religious symbols: two tablets with what appears to be ancient script on them, two Stars of David, and the superimposed Greek letters Chi and Rho as the familiar monogram of Christ. Nothing on the monument, in fact, detracts from its

E. When Can Religion Become a Part of Government Activities? 643

religious nature, and the plurality does not suggest otherwise. It would therefore be difficult to miss the point that the government of Texas is telling everyone who sees the monument to live up to a moral code because God requires it, with both code and conception of God being rightly understood as the inheritances specifically of Jews and Christians. And it is likewise unsurprising that the District Court expressly rejected Texas's argument that the State's purpose in placing the monument on the capitol grounds was related to the Commandments' role as "part of the foundation of modern secular law in Texas and elsewhere."

The monument's presentation of the Commandments with religious text emphasized and enhanced stands in contrast to any number of perfectly constitutional depictions of them, the frieze of our own Courtroom providing a good example, where the figure of Moses stands among history's great lawgivers. While Moses holds the tablets of the Commandments showing some Hebrew text, no one looking at the lines of figures in marble relief is likely to see a religious purpose behind the assemblage or take away a religious message from it. Only one other depiction represents a religious leader, and the historical personages are mixed with symbols of moral and intellectual abstractions like Equity and Authority. Since Moses enjoys no especial prominence on the frieze, viewers can readily take him to be there as a lawgiver in the company of other lawgivers; and the viewers may just as naturally see the tablets of the Commandments (showing the later ones, forbidding things like killing and theft, but without the divine preface) as background from which the concept of law emerged, ultimately having a secular influence in the history of the Nation. Government may, of course, constitutionally call attention to this influence, and may post displays or erect monuments recounting this aspect of our history no less than any other, so long as there is a context and that context is historical. Hence, a display of the Commandments accompanied by an exposition of how they have influenced modern law would most likely be constitutionally unobjectionable. And the Decalogue could, as *Stone* suggested, be integrated constitutionally into a course of study in public schools.

Texas seeks to take advantage of the recognition that visual symbol and written text can manifest a secular purpose in secular company, when it argues that its monument (like Moses in the frieze) is not alone and ought to be viewed as only 1 among 17 placed on the 22 acres surrounding the state capitol. Texas, indeed, says that the Capitol grounds are like a museum for a collection of exhibits, the kind of setting that several Members of the Court have said can render the exhibition of religious artifacts permissible, even though in other circumstances their display would be seen as meant to convey a religious message forbidden to the State.

But 17 monuments with no common appearance, history, or esthetic role scattered over 22 acres is not a museum, and anyone strolling around the lawn would surely take each memorial on its own terms without any dawning sense that some purpose held the miscellany together more coherently than fortuity and the edge of the grass. One monument expresses admiration for pioneer women. One pays respect to the fighters of World War II. In like circumstances, we rejected an argument similar to the State's, noting in *County of Allegheny* that "[t]he presence of Santas or other Christmas decorations elsewhere in the . . . [c]ourthouse, and of the nearby gallery forum, fail to negate the [crèche's] endorsement effect. . . . The record demonstrates . . . that the crèche, with its floral frame, was its own display distinct from any other decorations or exhibitions in the building."

Nor can the plurality deflect *Stone* by calling the Texas monument "a far more passive use of [the Decalogue] than was the case in *Stone*, where the text confronted elementary school students every day." Placing a monument on the ground is not more "passive" than hanging a sheet of paper on a wall when both contain the same text to be read by anyone who looks at it. The problem in *Stone* was simply that the State was putting the Commandments there to be seen, just as the monument's inscription is there for those who walk by it.

The monument in this case sits on the grounds of the Texas State Capitol. There is something significant in the common term "statehouse" to refer to a state capitol building: it is the civic home of every one of the State's citizens. If neutrality in religion means something, any citizen should be able to visit that civic home without having to confront religious expressions clearly meant to convey an official religious position that may be at odds with his own religion, or with rejection of religion.

AMERICAN LEGION v. AMERICAN HUMANIST ASSOCIATION
139 S. Ct. 2067 (2019)

Justice ALITO announced the judgment of the Court and delivered the opinion of the Court with respect to Parts I, II-B, II-C, III, and IV, and an opinion with respect to Parts II-A and II-D, in which THE CHIEF JUSTICE, Justice BREYER, and Justice KAVANAUGH join.

Since 1925, the Bladensburg Peace Cross (Cross) has stood as a tribute to 49 area soldiers who gave their lives in the First World War. Eighty-nine years after the dedication of the Cross, respondents filed this lawsuit, claiming that they are offended by the sight of the memorial on public land and that its presence there and the expenditure of public funds to maintain it violate the Establishment Clause of the First Amendment. To remedy this violation, they asked a federal court to order the relocation or demolition of the Cross or at least the removal of its arms. The Court of Appeals for the Fourth Circuit agreed that the memorial is unconstitutional and remanded for a determination of the proper remedy. We now reverse.

Although the cross has long been a preeminent Christian symbol, its use in the Bladensburg memorial has a special significance. After the First World War, the picture of row after row of plain white crosses marking the overseas graves of soldiers who had lost their lives in that horrible conflict was emblazoned on the minds of Americans at home, and the adoption of the cross as the Bladensburg memorial must be viewed in that historical context. For nearly a century, the Bladensburg Cross has expressed the community's grief at the loss of the young men who perished, its thanks for their sacrifice, and its dedication to the ideals for which they fought. It has become a prominent community landmark, and its removal or radical alteration at this date would be seen by many not as a neutral act but as the manifestation of "a hostility toward religion that has no place in our Establishment Clause traditions." And contrary to respondents' intimations, there is no evidence of discriminatory intent in the selection of the design of the memorial or the decision of a Maryland commission to maintain it. The Religion Clauses of the Constitution aim to foster a society in which

E. When Can Religion Become a Part of Government Activities?

people of all beliefs can live together harmoniously, and the presence of the Bladensburg Cross on the land where it has stood for so many years is fully consistent with that aim.

I

The cross came into widespread use as a symbol of Christianity by the fourth century, and it retains that meaning today. But there are many contexts in which the symbol has also taken on a secular meaning. Indeed, there are instances in which its message is now almost entirely secular.

A cross appears as part of many registered trademarks held by businesses and secular organizations, including Blue Cross Blue Shield, the Bayer Group, and some Johnson & Johnson products. Many of these marks relate to health care, and it is likely that the association of the cross with healing had a religious origin. But the current use of these marks is indisputably secular.

The familiar symbol of the Red Cross—a red cross on a white background—shows how the meaning of a symbol that was originally religious can be transformed. The International Committee of the Red Cross (ICRC) selected that symbol in 1863 because it was thought to call to mind the flag of Switzerland, a country widely known for its neutrality. The Swiss flag consists of a white cross on a red background. In an effort to invoke the message associated with that flag, the ICRC copied its design with the colors inverted. Thus, the ICRC selected this symbol for an essentially secular reason, and the current secular message of the symbol is shown by its use today in nations with only tiny Christian populations. But the cross was originally chosen for the Swiss flag for religious reasons. So an image that began as an expression of faith was transformed.

The image used in the Bladensburg memorial—a plain Latin cross—also took on new meaning after World War I. "During and immediately after the war, the army marked soldiers' graves with temporary wooden crosses or Stars of David"—a departure from the prior practice of marking graves in American military cemeteries with uniform rectangular slabs. The vast majority of these grave markers consisted of crosses, and thus when Americans saw photographs of these cemeteries, what struck them were rows and rows of plain white crosses. As a result, the image of a simple white cross "developed into a 'central symbol'" of the conflict. Contemporary literature, poetry, and art reflected this powerful imagery. Perhaps most famously, John McCrae's poem, In Flanders Fields, began with these memorable lines:

> "In Flanders fields the poppies blow
>   Between the crosses, row on row."

Recognition of the cross's symbolism extended to local communities across the country. In late 1918, residents of Prince George's County, Maryland, formed a committee for the purpose of erecting a memorial for the county's fallen soldiers. Among the committee's members were the mothers of 10 deceased soldiers. The committee decided that the memorial should be a cross and hired sculptor and architect John Joseph Earley to design it.

The Cross was to stand at the terminus of another World War I memorial—the National Defense Highway, which connects Washington to Annapolis. The community gathered for a joint groundbreaking ceremony for both memorials on September 28, 1919; the mother of the first Prince George's County resident killed in France broke ground for the Cross.

The completed monument is a 32-foot tall Latin cross that sits on a large pedestal. The American Legion's emblem is displayed at its center, and the words "Valor," "Endurance," "Courage," and "Devotion" are inscribed at its base, one on each of the four faces. The pedestal also features a 9- by 2.5-foot bronze plaque explaining that the monument is "Dedicated to the heroes of Prince George's County, Maryland who lost their lives in the Great War for the liberty of the world."

In 2012, nearly 90 years after the Cross was dedicated and more than 50 years after the Commission acquired it, the American Humanist Association (AHA) lodged a complaint with the Commission. The complaint alleged that the Cross's presence on public land and the Commission's maintenance of the memorial violate the Establishment Clause of the First Amendment.

II

The Establishment Clause of the First Amendment provides that "Congress shall make no law respecting an establishment of religion." While the concept of a formally established church is straightforward, pinning down the meaning of a "law respecting an establishment of religion" has proved to be a vexing problem. After grappling with such cases for more than 20 years, *Lemon* ambitiously attempted to distill from the Court's existing case law a test that would bring order and predictability to Establishment Clause decisionmaking. That test, as noted, called on courts to examine the purposes and effects of a challenged government action, as well as any entanglement with religion that it might entail. The Court later elaborated that the "effect[s]" of a challenged action should be assessed by asking whether a "reasonable observer" would conclude that the action constituted an "endorsement" of religion.

For at least four reasons, the *Lemon* test presents particularly daunting problems in cases, including the one now before us, that involve the use, for ceremonial, celebratory, or commemorative purposes, of words or symbols with religious associations. Together, these considerations counsel against efforts to evaluate such cases under *Lemon* and toward application of a presumption of constitutionality for longstanding monuments, symbols, and practices.

First, these cases often concern monuments, symbols, or practices that were first established long ago, and in such cases, identifying their original purpose or purposes may be especially difficult.

Second, as time goes by, the purposes associated with an established monument, symbol, or practice often multiply.

Third, just as the purpose for maintaining a monument, symbol, or practice may evolve, "[t]he 'message' conveyed . . . may change over time." Consider, for example, the message of the Statue of Liberty, which began as a monument to the solidarity and friendship between France and the United States and only decades later came to be seen "as a beacon welcoming immigrants to a land of freedom." With sufficient time, religiously expressive monuments, symbols, and practices can become embedded features of a community's landscape and identity.

E. When Can Religion Become a Part of Government Activities?

In the same way, consider the many cities and towns across the United States that bear religious names. Religion undoubtedly motivated those who named Bethlehem, Pennsylvania; Las Cruces, New Mexico; Providence, Rhode Island; Corpus Christi, Texas; Nephi, Utah, and the countless other places in our country with names that are rooted in religion. Yet few would argue that this history requires that these names be erased from the map.

Fourth, when time's passage imbues a religiously expressive monument, symbol, or practice with this kind of familiarity and historical significance, removing it may no longer appear neutral, especially to the local community for which it has taken on particular meaning. A government that roams the land, tearing down monuments with religious symbolism and scrubbing away any reference to the divine will strike many as aggressively hostile to religion. Militantly secular regimes have carried out such projects in the past, and for those with a knowledge of history, the image of monuments being taken down will be evocative, disturbing, and divisive.

These four considerations show that retaining established, religiously expressive monuments, symbols, and practices is quite different from erecting or adopting new ones. The passage of time gives rise to a strong presumption of constitutionality.

The role of the cross in World War I memorials is illustrative of each of the four preceding considerations. Immediately following the war, "[c]ommunities across America built memorials to commemorate those who had served the nation in the struggle to make the world safe for democracy." "[T]he First World War witnessed a dramatic change in . . . the symbols used to commemorate th[e] service" of the fallen soldiers. In the wake of the war, the United States adopted the cross as part of its military honors, establishing the Distinguished Service Cross and the Navy Cross in 1918 and 1919, respectively. And as already noted, the fallen soldiers' final resting places abroad were marked by white crosses or Stars of David. The solemn image of endless rows of white crosses became inextricably linked with and symbolic of the ultimate price paid by 116,000 soldiers. And this relationship between the cross and the war undoubtedly influenced the design of the many war memorials that sprang up across the Nation.

This is not to say that the cross's association with the war was the sole or dominant motivation for the inclusion of the symbol in every World War I memorial that features it. But today, it is all but impossible to tell whether that was so. The passage of time means that testimony from those actually involved in the decisionmaking process is generally unavailable, and attempting to uncover their motivations invites rampant speculation. And no matter what the original purposes for the erection of a monument, a community may wish to preserve it for very different reasons, such as the historic preservation and traffic-safety concerns the Commission has pressed here.

In addition, the passage of time may have altered the area surrounding a monument in ways that change its meaning and provide new reasons for its preservation. Such changes are relevant here, since the Bladensburg Cross now sits at a busy traffic intersection, and numerous additional monuments are located nearby.

Finally, as World War I monuments have endured through the years and become a familiar part of the physical and cultural landscape, requiring their removal would not be viewed by many as a neutral act. A monument may express many purposes and convey many different messages, both secular and religious. Thus, a campaign to obliterate items with religious associations may evidence hostility to religion even if those religious associations are no longer in the forefront.

While the *Lemon* Court ambitiously attempted to find a grand unified theory of the Establishment Clause, in later cases, we have taken a more modest approach that focuses on the particular issue at hand and looks to history for guidance. Our cases involving prayer before a legislative session are an example.

The prevalence of this philosophy at the time of the founding is reflected in other prominent actions taken by the First Congress. It requested — and President Washington proclaimed — a national day of prayer and it reenacted the Northwest Territory Ordinance, which provided that "[r]eligion, morality, and knowledge, being necessary to good government and the happiness of mankind, schools and the means of education shall forever be encouraged." President Washington echoed this sentiment in his Farewell Address, calling religion and morality "indispensable supports" to "political prosperity."

III

Applying these principles, we conclude that the Bladensburg Cross does not violate the Establishment Clause. As we have explained, the Bladensburg Cross carries special significance in commemorating World War I. Due in large part to the image of the simple wooden crosses that originally marked the graves of American soldiers killed in the war, the cross became a symbol of their sacrifice, and the design of the Bladensburg Cross must be understood in light of that background. That the cross originated as a Christian symbol and retains that meaning in many contexts does not change the fact that the symbol took on an added secular meaning when used in World War I memorials.

Not only did the Bladensburg Cross begin with this meaning, but with the passage of time, it has acquired historical importance. It reminds the people of Bladensburg and surrounding areas of the deeds of their predecessors and of the sacrifices they made in a war fought in the name of democracy. As long as it is retained in its original place and form, it speaks as well of the community that erected the monument nearly a century ago and has maintained it ever since. The memorial represents what the relatives, friends, and neighbors of the fallen soldiers felt at the time and how they chose to express their sentiments. And the monument has acquired additional layers of historical meaning in subsequent years. The Cross now stands among memorials to veterans of later wars. It has become part of the community.

The monument would not serve that role if its design had deliberately disrespected area soldiers who perished in World War I. More than 3,500 Jewish soldiers gave their lives for the United States in that conflict, and some have wondered whether the names of any Jewish soldiers from the area were deliberately left off the list on the memorial or whether the names of any Jewish soldiers were included on the Cross against the wishes of their families.

Finally, it is surely relevant that the monument commemorates the death of particular individuals. It is natural and appropriate for those seeking to honor the deceased to invoke the symbols that signify what death meant for those who are memorialized. And this is why the memorial for soldiers from the

Bladensburg community features the cross—the same symbol that marks the graves of so many of their comrades near the battlefields where they fell.

IV

The cross is undoubtedly a Christian symbol, but that fact should not blind us to everything else that the Bladensburg Cross has come to represent. For some, that monument is a symbolic resting place for ancestors who never returned home. For others, it is a place for the community to gather and honor all veterans and their sacrifices for our Nation. For others still, it is a historical landmark. For many of these people, destroying or defacing the Cross that has stood undisturbed for nearly a century would not be neutral and would not further the ideals of respect and tolerance embodied in the First Amendment.

Justice BREYER, with whom Justice KAGAN joins, concurring.

I have long maintained that there is no single formula for resolving Establishment Clause challenges. The Court must instead consider each case in light of the basic purposes that the Religion Clauses were meant to serve: assuring religious liberty and tolerance for all, avoiding religiously based social conflict, and maintaining that separation of church and state that allows each to flourish in its "separate spher[e]."

I agree with the Court that allowing the State of Maryland to display and maintain the Peace Cross poses no threat to those ends. The Court's opinion eloquently explains why that is so: The Latin cross is uniquely associated with the fallen soldiers of World War I; the organizers of the Peace Cross acted with the undeniably secular motive of commemorating local soldiers; no evidence suggests that they sought to disparage or exclude any religious group; the secular values inscribed on the Cross and its place among other memorials strengthen its message of patriotism and commemoration; and, finally, the Cross has stood on the same land for 94 years, generating no controversy in the community until this lawsuit was filed. Nothing in the record suggests that the lack of public outcry "was due to a climate of intimidation." In light of all these circumstances, the Peace Cross cannot reasonably be understood as "a government effort to favor a particular religious sect" or to "promote religion over nonreligion." And, as the Court explains, ordering its removal or alteration at this late date would signal "a hostility toward religion that has no place in our Establishment Clause traditions."

The case would be different, in my view, if there were evidence that the organizers had "deliberately disrespected" members of minority faiths or if the Cross had been erected only recently, rather than in the aftermath of World War I. But those are not the circumstances presented to us here, and I see no reason to order *this* cross torn down simply because *other* crosses would raise constitutional concerns.

Nor do I understand the Court's opinion today to adopt a "history and tradition test" that would permit any newly constructed religious memorial on public land. The Court appropriately "looks to history for guidance," but it upholds the constitutionality of the Peace Cross only after considering its particular historical context and its long-held place in the community. A newer memorial, erected under different circumstances, would not necessarily be permissible under this approach.

Justice KAVANAUGH, concurring.

I join the Court's eloquent and persuasive opinion in full. I write separately to emphasize two points.

Consistent with the Court's case law, the Court today applies a history and tradition test in examining and upholding the constitutionality of the Bladensburg Cross. As this case again demonstrates, this Court no longer applies the old test articulated in Lemon v. Kurtzman (1971).

The opinion identifies five relevant categories of Establishment Clause cases: (1) religious symbols on government property and religious speech at government events; (2) religious accommodations and exemptions from generally applicable laws; (3) government benefits and tax exemptions for religious organizations; (4) religious expression in public schools; and (5) regulation of private religious speech in public forums. The *Lemon* test does not explain the Court's decisions in any of those five categories.

The practice of displaying religious memorials, particularly religious war memorials, on public land is not coercive and is rooted in history and tradition. The Bladensburg Cross does not violate the Establishment Clause.

II

The Bladensburg Cross commemorates soldiers who gave their lives for America in World War I. I agree with the Court that the Bladensburg Cross is constitutional. At the same time, I have deep respect for the plaintiffs' sincere objections to seeing the cross on public land. I have great respect for the Jewish war veterans who in an *amicus* brief say that the cross on public land sends a message of exclusion. I recognize their sense of distress and alienation. Moreover, I fully understand the deeply religious nature of the cross. It would demean both believers and nonbelievers to say that the cross is not religious, or not all that religious. A case like this is difficult because it represents a clash of genuine and important interests. Applying our precedents, we uphold the constitutionality of the cross. In doing so, it is appropriate to also restate this bedrock constitutional principle: All citizens are equally American, no matter what religion they are, or if they have no religion at all.

The conclusion that the cross does not violate the Establishment Clause does not necessarily mean that those who object to it have no other recourse. The Court's ruling *allows* the State to maintain the cross on public land. The Court's ruling does not *require* the State to maintain the cross on public land. The Maryland Legislature could enact new laws requiring removal of the cross or transfer of the land. The Maryland Governor or other state or local executive officers may have authority to do so under current Maryland law. And if not, the legislature could enact new laws to authorize such executive action. The Maryland Constitution, as interpreted by the Maryland Court of Appeals, may speak to this question. And if not, the people of Maryland can amend the State Constitution.

Those alternative avenues of relief illustrate a fundamental feature of our constitutional structure: This Court is not the *only* guardian of individual rights in America. This Court fiercely protects the individual rights secured by the U.S. Constitution. But the Constitution sets a floor for the protection of individual

E. When Can Religion Become a Part of Government Activities?

rights. The constitutional floor is sturdy and often high, but it is a floor. Other federal, state, and local government entities generally possess authority to safeguard individual rights above and beyond the rights secured by the U. S. Constitution.

Justice THOMAS, concurring in the judgment.

The Establishment Clause states that "Congress shall make no law respecting an establishment of religion." The text and history of this Clause suggest that it should not be incorporated against the States. Even if the Clause expresses an individual right enforceable against the States, it is limited by its text to "law[s]" enacted by a legislature, so it is unclear whether the Bladensburg Cross would implicate any incorporated right. And even if it did, this religious display does not involve the type of actual legal coercion that was a hallmark of historical establishments of religion. Therefore, the Cross is clearly constitutional.

Justice GORSUCH, with whom Justice THOMAS joins, concurring in the judgment.

The American Humanist Association wants a federal court to order the destruction of a 94-year-old war memorial because its members are offended. Today, the Court explains that the plaintiffs are not entitled to demand the destruction of longstanding monuments, and I find much of its opinion compelling. In my judgment, however, it follows from the Court's analysis that suits like this one should be dismissed for lack of standing. Accordingly, while I concur in the judgment to reverse and remand the court of appeals' decision, I would do so with additional instructions to dismiss the case.

The Association claims that its members "regularly" come into "unwelcome direct contact" with a World War I memorial cross in Bladensburg, Maryland "while driving in the area." And this, the Association suggests, is enough to allow it to insist on a federal judicial decree ordering the memorial's removal. Maybe, the Association concedes, others who are less offended lack standing to sue. Maybe others still who are equally affected but who come into contact with the memorial too infrequently lack standing as well. But, the Association assures us, its members are offended enough—and with sufficient frequency—that they may sue.

This "offended observer" theory of standing has no basis in law. Federal courts may decide only those cases and controversies that the Constitution and Congress have authorized them to hear. Unsurprisingly, this Court has already rejected the notion that offense alone qualifies as a "concrete and particularized" injury sufficient to confer standing. Offended observer standing cannot be squared with this Court's longstanding teachings about the limits of Article III.

In a large and diverse country, offense can be easily found. Really, most every governmental action probably offends *somebody*. No doubt, too, that offense can be sincere, sometimes well taken, even wise. But recourse for disagreement and offense does not lie in federal litigation. Instead, in a society that holds among its most cherished ambitions mutual respect, tolerance, self-rule, and democratic responsibility, an "offended viewer" may "avert his eyes," or pursue a political solution. Today's decision represents a welcome step toward restoring this Court's recognition of these truths, and I respectfully concur in the judgment.

Justice GINSBURG, with whom Justice SOTOMAYOR joins, dissenting.

An immense Latin cross stands on a traffic island at the center of a busy three-way intersection in Bladensburg, Maryland. "[M]onumental, clear, and bold" by day, the cross looms even larger illuminated against the night-time sky.

Decades ago, this Court recognized that the Establishment Clause of the First Amendment to the Constitution demands governmental neutrality among religious faiths, and between religion and nonreligion. Numerous times since, the Court has reaffirmed the Constitution's commitment to neutrality. Today the Court erodes that neutrality commitment, diminishing precedent designed to preserve individual liberty and civic harmony in favor of a "presumption of constitutionality for longstanding monuments, symbols, and practices."

The Latin cross is the foremost symbol of the Christian faith, embodying the "central theological claim of Christianity: that the son of God died on the cross, that he rose from the dead, and that his death and resurrection offer the possibility of eternal life." Precisely because the cross symbolizes these sectarian beliefs, it is a common marker for the graves of Christian soldiers. For the same reason, using the cross as a war memorial does not transform it into a secular symbol. Just as a Star of David is not suitable to honor Christians who died serving their country, so a cross is not suitable to honor those of other faiths who died defending their nation. Soldiers of all faiths "are united by their love of country, but they are not united by the cross."

By maintaining the Peace Cross on a public highway, the Commission elevates Christianity over other faiths, and religion over nonreligion. Memorializing the service of American soldiers is an "admirable and unquestionably secular" objective. But the Commission does not serve that objective by displaying a symbol that bears "a starkly sectarian message."

Holding the Commission's display of the Peace Cross unconstitutional would not, as the Commission fears, "inevitably require the destruction of other cross-shaped memorials throughout the country." When a religious symbol appears in a public cemetery—on a headstone, or as the headstone itself, or perhaps integrated into a larger memorial—the setting counters the inference that the government seeks "either to adopt the religious message or to urge its acceptance by others." In a cemetery, the "privately selected religious symbols on individual graves are best understood as the private speech of each veteran." Such displays are "linked to, and sho[w] respect for, the individual honoree's faith and beliefs." They do not suggest governmental endorsement of those faith and beliefs.

Recognizing that a Latin cross does not belong on a public highway or building does not mean the monument must be "torn down." "[L]ike the determination of the violation itself," the "proper remedy . . . is necessarily context specific." In some instances, the violation may be cured by relocating the monument to private land or by transferring ownership of the land and monument to a private party.

F. WHEN CAN GOVERNMENT GIVE AID TO RELIGION?

Many Establishment Clause cases have involved the issue of government assistance to religion. Decisions in this area are numerous but often difficult to reconcile. The Court inevitably is involved in line drawing. Total government subsidy of churches or parochial schools undoubtedly would violate the Establishment

F. When Can Government Give Aid to Religion?

Clause. Indeed, James Madison's *Memorial and Remonstrance Against Religious Assessments* was made in the context of opposing a state tax to aid the church.[29] But it also would be clearly unconstitutional if the government provided no public services—no police or fire protection, no sanitation services—to religious institutions. Such discrimination surely would violate equal protection and infringe free exercise of religion.[30]

Therefore, the Court must draw a line between aid that is permissible and that which is forbidden. No bright line test exists or likely ever will be developed. Any aid provided to a religious institution or a parochial school frees resources that can be used to further its religious mission.[31] The dominant approach for the past quarter of a century has been to apply the test from Lemon v. Kurtzman, presented above, and to ask whether there is a secular purpose for the assistance, whether the aid has the effect of advancing religion, and whether the particular form of assistance causes excessive government entanglement with religion. But not every case has used the *Lemon* test.

There have been four major areas where the Court has considered government aid to religion: assistance to parochial elementary and secondary schools; tax exemptions for religious institutions; aid to religious colleges and universities; and assistance to religious institutions other than schools. Each of these is considered below in turn. By far, most cases have concerned aid to religious elementary and secondary schools, and it thus receives the most attention.

AID TO PAROCHIAL ELEMENTARY AND SECONDARY SCHOOLS

The Court has considered the constitutionality of a vast array of different types of assistance, ranging from tuition tax credits to textbooks to audiovisual equipment to medical diagnostic tests to many other kinds of aid. The decisions often seem difficult to reconcile. For example, the Court has upheld the government providing buses to take children to and from parochial schools,[32] but not buses to take parochial school students on field trips.[33] The Court has forbidden the government from paying teacher salaries in parochial schools, even for teachers of secular subjects;[34] but the Court allowed the government to provide a sign language interpreter for hearing-impaired students in parochial schools.[35] The Court has permitted the government to pay for administering

---

29. Madison's *Remonstrance* is reprinted in Everson v. Board of Education, 330 U.S. 1, 63 (1947).
30. *See, e.g.*, Lemon v. Kurtzman, 403 U.S. at 614 ("Fire inspections, building and zoning regulations, and state requirements under compulsory school attendance laws are examples of necessary and permissible contacts.").
31. In the initial case concerning government aid to parochial schools, Everson v. Board of Education, 330 U.S. 1 (1947), the Court upheld the constitutionality of the government reimbursing parents for the costs of bus transportation to and from parochial school. The Court recognized that "[t]here is even a possibility that some of the children might not be sent to the church schools if the parents were compelled . . . to pay their children's bus fares out of their own pockets . . . when transportation to a public school would have been paid for by the State."
32. Everson v. Board of Education, 330 U.S. 1 (1947).
33. Wolman v. Walter, 433 U.S. 229 (1977).
34. Grand Rapids School Dist. v. Ball, 473 U.S. 373 (1985); Aguilar v. Felton, 473 U.S. 402 (1985); Lemon v. Kurtzman, 403 U.S. 602 (1971).
35. Zobrest v. Catalina Foothills School Dist., 509 U.S. 1 (1993).

standardized tests in parochial schools,[36] but not for essay exams assessing writing achievement.[37]

In 1997, the Court signaled a likely shift to its approach to the Establishment Clause. In Agostini v. Felton, 521 U.S. 203 (1997), the Court held that public school remedial education teachers may provide instruction in private schools. In doing so, the Court overruled a decision from a decade earlier, Aguilar v. Felton, 473 U.S. 402 (1985), which held that such instruction violates the Establishment Clause. *Agostini* was a five-to-four decision, and the majority opinion was written by Justice O'Connor and joined by Chief Justice Rehnquist and Justices Scalia, Kennedy, and Thomas.

At the end of the majority opinion, Justice O'Connor appeared to state a new test for the Establishment Clause: "To summarize, New York City's Title I program does not run afoul of any of the three primary criteria we currently use to evaluate whether government aid has the effect of advancing religion: it does not result in government indoctrination; define its recipient by reference to religion; or create an excessive entanglement." Justice O'Connor presents this as if it is restating existing law, and yet this seems to articulate a new approach that aid to parochial schools is unconstitutional only if the government participates in indoctrinating religion, or if the government discriminates among religions, or if there is excessive government entanglement with religion.

In Mitchell v. Helms, several of the opinions discuss this aspect of Justice O'Connor's opinion in *Agostini*. In *Mitchell*, the Supreme Court reconsidered whether the government violates the Establishment Clause when it provides instructional equipment to parochial schools. Earlier, in Meek v. Pittenger, 421 U.S. 349 (1975), the Court declared unconstitutional a state law that provided instructional materials, including audiovisual equipment, to parochial schools. In reconsidering this issue, the justices expressed their views as to the more general issue: What aid to parochial school violates the Establishment Clause? There is no majority opinion, but instead several different answers to this question.

MITCHELL v. HELMS
530 U.S. 793 (2000)

Justice THOMAS announced the judgment of the Court and delivered an opinion, in which THE CHIEF JUSTICE, Justice SCALIA, and Justice KENNEDY join.

As part of a longstanding school aid program known as Chapter 2, the Federal Government distributes funds to state and local governmental agencies, which in turn lend educational materials and equipment to public and private schools, with the enrollment of each participating school determining the amount of aid that it receives. The question is whether Chapter 2, as applied in Jefferson Parish, Louisiana, is a law respecting an establishment of religion, because many of the private schools receiving Chapter 2 aid in that parish are religiously affiliated. We hold that Chapter 2 is not such a law.

---

36. Committee for Public Education & Religious Liberty v. Regan, 444 U.S. 646 (1980).
37. Levitt v. Community for Public Education, 413 U.S. 472 (1973).

F. When Can Government Give Aid to Religion?

I

Chapter 2 of the Education Consolidation and Improvement Act of 1981, has its origins in the Elementary and Secondary Education Act of 1965 (ESEA), and is a close cousin of the provision of the ESEA that we recently considered in Agostini v. Felton (1997). Like the provision at issue in *Agostini*, Chapter 2 channels federal funds to local educational agencies (LEA's), which are usually public school districts, via state educational agencies (SEA's), to implement programs to assist children in elementary and secondary schools. Among other things, Chapter 2 provides aid "for the acquisition and use of instructional and educational materials, including library services and materials (including media materials), assessments, reference materials, computer software and hardware for instructional use, and other curricular materials."

Several restrictions apply to aid to private schools. Most significantly, the "services, materials, and equipment" provided to private schools must be "secular, neutral, and nonideological." In addition, private schools may not acquire control of Chapter 2 funds or title to Chapter 2 materials, equipment, or property. A private school receives the materials and equipment by submitting to the LEA an application detailing which items the school seeks and how it will use them; the LEA, if it approves the application, purchases those items from the school's allocation of funds, and then lends them to that school.

In Jefferson Parish (the Louisiana governmental unit at issue in this case), as in Louisiana as a whole, private schools have primarily used their allocations for nonrecurring expenses, usually materials and equipment. In the 1986-1987 fiscal year, for example, 44% of the money budgeted for private schools in Jefferson Parish was spent by LEA's for acquiring library and media materials, and 48% for instructional equipment. Among the materials and equipment provided have been library books, computers, and computer software, and also slide and movie projectors, overhead projectors, television sets, tape recorders, VCR's, projection screens, laboratory equipment, maps, globes, filmstrips, slides, and cassette recordings.

It appears that, in an average year, about 30% of Chapter 2 funds spent in Jefferson Parish are allocated for private schools. For the 1985-1986 fiscal year, 41 private schools participated in Chapter 2. For the following year, 46 participated, and the participation level has remained relatively constant since then. Of these 46, 34 were Roman Catholic; 7 were otherwise religiously affiliated; and 5 were not religiously affiliated.

II

The Establishment Clause of the First Amendment dictates that "Congress shall make no law respecting an establishment of religion." In the over 50 years since *Everson*, we have consistently struggled to apply these simple words in the context of governmental aid to religious schools.

In *Agostini*, however, we brought some clarity to our case law, by overruling two anomalous precedents and by consolidating some of our previously disparate considerations under a revised test. Whereas in *Lemon* we had considered whether a statute (1) has a secular purpose, (2) has a primary effect of advancing or inhibiting religion, or (3) creates an excessive entanglement between government and religion, in *Agostini* we modified *Lemon* for purposes of evaluating aid to schools and examined only the first and second factors. We acknowledged that our cases discussing excessive entanglement had applied many of the same considerations as had our cases discussing primary effect, and we therefore recast *Lemon*'s entanglement inquiry as simply one criterion relevant to determining a statute's effect. We also acknowledged that our cases had pared somewhat the factors that could justify a finding of excessive entanglement.

We then set out revised criteria for determining the effect of a statute: "To summarize, New York City's Title I program does not run afoul of any of three primary criteria we currently use to evaluate whether government aid has the effect of advancing religion: It does not result in governmental indoctrination; define its recipients by reference to religion; or create an excessive entanglement."

In this case, our inquiry under *Agostini*'s purpose and effect test is a narrow one. Because respondents do not challenge the District Court's holding that Chapter 2 has a secular purpose, and because the Fifth Circuit also did not question that holding, we will consider only Chapter 2's effect. Further, in determining that effect, we will consider only the first two *Agostini* criteria, since neither respondents nor the Fifth Circuit has questioned the District Court's holding, that Chapter 2 does not create an excessive entanglement. Considering Chapter 2 in light of our more recent case law, we conclude that it neither results in religious indoctrination by the government nor defines its recipients by reference to religion. We therefore hold that Chapter 2 is not a "law respecting an establishment of religion." In so holding, we acknowledge what both the Ninth and Fifth Circuits saw was inescapable — *Meek* and *Wolman* are anomalies in our case law. We therefore conclude that they are no longer good law.

A

As we indicated in *Agostini*, and have indicated elsewhere, the question whether governmental aid to religious schools results in governmental indoctrination is ultimately a question whether any religious indoctrination that occurs in those schools could reasonably be attributed to governmental action. We have also indicated that the answer to the question of indoctrination will resolve the question whether a program of educational aid "subsidizes" religion, as our religion cases use that term.

In distinguishing between indoctrination that is attributable to the State and indoctrination that is not, we have consistently turned to the principle of neutrality, upholding aid that is offered to a broad range of groups or persons without regard to their religion. If the religious, irreligious, and areligious are all alike eligible for governmental aid, no one would conclude that any indoctrination that any particular recipient conducts has been done at the behest of the government. For attribution of indoctrination is a relative question. If the government is offering assistance to recipients who provide, so to speak, a broad range of indoctrination, the government itself is not thought responsible for any particular indoctrination. To put the point differently, if the government, seeking to further some legitimate secular purpose, offers aid on the same terms, without regard to religion, to all who adequately further that purpose, then it is fair to say that any aid going to a religious recipient only has the effect of furthering that secular purpose. The government, in crafting such

F. When Can Government Give Aid to Religion?

an aid program, has had to conclude that a given level of aid is necessary to further that purpose among secular recipients and has provided no more than that same level to religious recipients.

As a way of assuring neutrality, we have repeatedly considered whether any governmental aid that goes to a religious institution does so "only as a result of the genuinely independent and private choices of individuals." We have viewed as significant whether the "private choices of individual parents," as opposed to the "unmediated" will of government, determine what schools ultimately benefit from the governmental aid, and how much. For if numerous private choices, rather than the single choice of a government, determine the distribution of aid pursuant to neutral eligibility criteria, then a government cannot, or at least cannot easily, grant special favors that might lead to a religious establishment. Private choice also helps guarantee neutrality by mitigating the preference for pre-existing recipients that is arguably inherent in any governmental aid program, and that could lead to a program inadvertently favoring one religion or favoring religious private schools in general over nonreligious ones.

Witters and *Mueller* employed similar reasoning. In *Witters*, we held that the Establishment Clause did not bar a State from including within a neutral program providing tuition payments for vocational rehabilitation a blind person studying at a Christian college to become a pastor, missionary, or youth director.

The tax deduction for educational expenses that we upheld in *Mueller* was, in these respects, the same as the tuition grant in *Witters*. We upheld it chiefly because it "neutrally provides state assistance to a broad spectrum of citizens," and because "numerous, private choices of individual parents of school-age children," determined which schools would benefit from the deductions. We explained that "[w]here, as here, aid to parochial schools is available only as a result of decisions of individual parents no 'imprimatur of state approval' can be deemed to have been conferred on any particular religion, or on religion generally."

We hasten to add, what should be obvious from the rule itself, that simply because an aid program offers private schools, and thus religious schools, a benefit that they did not previously receive does not mean that the program, by reducing the cost of securing a religious education, creates, under *Agostini*'s second criterion, an "incentive" for parents to choose such an education for their children. For any aid will have some such effect.

B

Respondents offer two rules that they contend should govern our determination of whether Chapter 2 has the effect of advancing religion. They argue first, and chiefly, that "direct, nonincidental" aid to the primary educational mission of religious schools is always impermissible. Second, they argue that provision to religious schools of aid that is divertible to religious use is similarly impermissible. Respondents' arguments are inconsistent with our more recent case law and we therefore reject them.

Although some of our earlier cases did emphasize the distinction between direct and indirect aid, the purpose of this distinction was merely to prevent "subsidization" of religion. As even the dissent all but admits, our more recent cases address this purpose not through the direct/indirect distinction but rather through the principle of private choice, as incorporated in the first *Agostini* criterion (i.e., whether any indoctrination could be attributed to the government). If aid to schools, even "direct aid," is neutrally available and, before reaching or benefiting any religious school, first passes through the hands (literally or figuratively) of numerous private citizens who are free to direct the aid elsewhere, the government has not provided any "support of religion." Although the presence of private choice is easier to see when aid literally passes through the hands of individuals—which is why we have mentioned directness in the same breath with private choice, there is no reason why the Establishment Clause requires such a form.

Further, respondents' formalistic line breaks down in the application to real-world programs. In Board of Education v. Allen, for example, although we did recognize that students themselves received and owned the textbooks, we also noted that the books provided were those that the private schools required for courses, that the schools could collect students' requests for books and submit them to the board of education, that the schools could store the textbooks, and that the textbooks were essential to the schools' teaching of secular subjects.

Of course, we have seen "special Establishment Clause dangers," when money is given to religious schools or entities directly rather than, as in *Witters* and *Mueller*, indirectly. But direct payments of money are not at issue in this case, and we refuse to allow a "special" case to create a rule for all cases.

Respondents also contend that the Establishment Clause requires that aid to religious schools not be impermissibly religious in nature or be divertible to religious use. We agree with the first part of this argument but not the second. Respondents' "no divertibility" rule is inconsistent with our more recent case law and is unworkable. So long as the governmental aid is not itself "unsuitable for use in the public schools because of religious content," and eligibility for aid is determined in a constitutionally permissible manner, any use of that aid to indoctrinate cannot be attributed to the government and is thus not of constitutional concern. And, of course, the use to which the aid is put does not affect the criteria governing the aid's allocation and thus does not create any impermissible incentive under *Agostini*'s second criterion.

The issue is not divertibility of aid but rather whether the aid itself has an impermissible content. Where the aid would be suitable for use in a public school, it is also suitable for use in any private school. Similarly, the prohibition against the government providing impermissible content resolves the Establishment Clause concerns that exist if aid is actually diverted to religious uses.

A concern for divertibility, as opposed to improper content, is misplaced not only because it fails to explain why the sort of aid that we have allowed is permissible, but also because it is boundless—enveloping all aid, no matter how trivial—and thus has only the most attenuated (if any) link to any realistic concern for preventing an "establishment of religion." Presumably, for example, government-provided lecterns, chalk, crayons, pens, paper, and paintbrushes would have to be excluded from religious schools under respondents' proposed rule. But we fail to see how indoctrination by means of (i.e., diversion of) such aid could be attributed to the government. In fact, the risk of improper attribution is less when the aid lacks content, for there is no risk (as there is with books), of the government inadvertently providing improper content. Finally, any aid, with or without content, is "divertible" in the sense that it allows schools to "divert" resources. Yet we have "not accepted the recurrent argument that all aid is forbidden because aid to one aspect of an institution frees it to spend its other resources on religious ends."

F. When Can Government Give Aid to Religion?

It is perhaps conceivable that courts could take upon themselves the task of distinguishing among the myriad kinds of possible aid based on the ease of diverting each kind. But it escapes us how a court might coherently draw any such line. It not only is far more workable, but also is actually related to real concerns about preventing advancement of religion by government, simply to require that a program of aid to schools not provide improper content and that it determine eligibility and allocate the aid on a permissible basis.

One of the dissent's factors deserves special mention: whether a school that receives aid (or whose students receive aid) is pervasively sectarian. The dissent is correct that there was a period when this factor mattered, particularly if the pervasively sectarian school was a primary or secondary school. But that period is one that the Court should regret, and it is thankfully long past.

There are numerous reasons to formally dispense with this factor. First, its relevance in our precedents is in sharp decline. Although our case law has consistently mentioned it even in recent years, we have not struck down an aid program in reliance on this factor since 1985.

Second, the religious nature of a recipient should not matter to the constitutional analysis, so long as the recipient adequately furthers the government's secular purpose. If a program offers permissible aid to the religious (including the pervasively sectarian), the areligious, and the irreligious, it is a mystery which view of religion the government has established, and thus a mystery what the constitutional violation would be. The pervasively sectarian recipient has not received any special favor, and it is most bizarre that the Court would, as the dissent seemingly does, reserve special hostility for those who take their religion seriously, who think that their religion should affect the whole of their lives, or who make the mistake of being effective in transmitting their views to children.

Third, the inquiry into the recipient's religious views required by a focus on whether a school is pervasively sectarian is not only unnecessary but also offensive. It is well established, in numerous other contexts, that courts should refrain from trolling through a person's or institution's religious beliefs.

Finally, hostility to aid to pervasively sectarian schools has a shameful pedigree that we do not hesitate to disavow. Although the dissent professes concern for "the implied exclusion of the less favored," the exclusion of pervasively sectarian schools from government-aid programs is just that, particularly given the history of such exclusion. Opposition to aid to "sectarian" schools acquired prominence in the 1870's with Congress's consideration (and near passage) of the Blaine Amendment, which would have amended the Constitution to bar any aid to sectarian institutions. Consideration of the amendment arose at a time of pervasive hostility to the Catholic Church and to Catholics in general, and it was an open secret that "sectarian" was code for "Catholic." Notwithstanding its history, of course, "sectarian" could, on its face, describe the school of any religious sect, but the Court eliminated this possibility of confusion when it coined the term "pervasively sectarian"—a term which, at that time, could be applied almost exclusively to Catholic parochial schools and which even today's dissent exemplifies chiefly by reference to such schools.

In short, nothing in the Establishment Clause requires the exclusion of pervasively sectarian schools from otherwise permissible aid programs, and other doctrines of this Court bar it. This doctrine, born of bigotry should be buried now.

Applying the two relevant *Agostini* criteria, we see no basis for concluding that Jefferson Parish's Chapter 2 program "has the effect of advancing religion." Chapter 2 does not result in governmental indoctrination, because it determines eligibility for aid neutrally, allocates that aid based on the private choices of the parents of schoolchildren, and does not provide aid that has an impermissible content. Nor does Chapter 2 define its recipients by reference to religion.

Justice O'CONNOR, with whom Justice BREYER joins, concurring in the judgment.

In 1965, Congress passed the Elementary and Secondary Education Act. Under Title I, Congress provided monetary grants to States to address the needs of educationally deprived children of low-income families. Under Title II, Congress provided further monetary grants to States for the acquisition of library resources, textbooks, and other instructional materials for use by children and teachers in public and private elementary and secondary schools. Since 1965, Congress has reauthorized the Title I and Title II programs several times. I believe that *Agostini* likewise controls the constitutional inquiry respecting Title II presented here, and requires the reversal of the Court of Appeals' judgment that the program is unconstitutional as applied in Jefferson Parish, Louisiana. To the extent our decisions in Meek v. Pittenger (1975), and Wolman v. Walter (1977), are inconsistent with the Courts judgment today, I agree that those decisions should be overruled. I therefore concur in the judgment.

I write separately because, in my view, the plurality announces a rule of unprecedented breadth for the evaluation of Establishment Clause challenges to government school-aid programs. Reduced to its essentials, the plurality's rule states that government aid to religious schools does not have the effect of advancing religion so long as the aid is offered on a neutral basis and the aid is secular in content. The plurality also rejects the distinction between direct and indirect aid, and holds that the actual diversion of secular aid by a religious school to the advancement of its religious mission is permissible. Although the expansive scope of the plurality's rule is troubling, two specific aspects of the opinion compel me to write separately. First, the plurality's treatment of neutrality comes close to assigning that factor singular importance in the future adjudication of Establishment Clause challenges to government school-aid programs. Second, the plurality's approval of actual diversion of government aid to religious indoctrination is in tension with our precedents and, in any event, unnecessary to decide the instant case.

I agree with Justice Souter that the plurality, by taking such a stance, "appears to take evenhanded neutrality and in practical terms promote it to a single and sufficient test for the establishment of the constitutionality of school aid." I do not quarrel with the plurality's recognition that neutrality is an important reason for upholding government-aid programs against Establishment Clause challenges. Nevertheless, we have never held that a government-aid program passes constitutional muster solely because of the neutral criteria it employs as a basis for distributing aid. I also disagree with the plurality's conclusion that actual diversion of government aid to religious indoctrination is consistent with the Establishment Clause.

I believe the distinction between a per-capita school-aid program and a true private-choice program is significant for purposes of endorsement. In terms of public perception, a government program of direct aid to religious schools based on the number of students attending each school differs meaningfully from the government distributing aid directly to individual students who, in turn, decide to use the aid at the same religious schools.

In the former example, if the religious school uses the aid to inculcate religion in its students, it is reasonable to say that the government has communicated a message of endorsement. Because the religious indoctrination is supported by government assistance, the reasonable observer would naturally perceive the aid program as government support for the advancement of religion. That the amount of aid received by the school is based on the school's enrollment does not separate the government from the endorsement of the religious message. The aid formula does not—and could not—indicate to a reasonable observer that the inculcation of religion is endorsed only by the individuals attending the religious school, who each affirmatively choose to direct the secular government aid to the school and its religious mission. No such choices have been made. In contrast, when government aid supports a school's religious mission only because of independent decisions made by numerous individuals to guide their secular aid to that school, "[n]o reasonable observer is likely to draw from the facts . . . an inference that the State itself is endorsing a religious practice or belief."

Finally, the distinction between a per-capita-aid program and a true private-choice program is important when considering aid that consists of direct monetary subsidies. This Court has "recognized special Establishment Clause dangers where the government makes direct money payments to sectarian institutions." If, as the plurality contends, a per-capita-aid program is identical in relevant constitutional respects to a true private-choice program, then there is no reason that, under the plurality's reasoning, the government should be precluded from providing direct money payments to religious organizations (including churches) based on the number of persons belonging to each organization. And, because actual diversion is permissible under the plurality's holding, the participating religious organizations (including churches) could use that aid to support religious indoctrination. To be sure, the plurality does not actually hold that its theory extends to direct money payments. That omission, however, is of little comfort. In its logic—as well as its specific advisory language—the plurality opinion foreshadows the approval of direct monetary subsidies to religious organizations, even when they use the money to advance their religious objectives.

Because divertibility fails to explain the distinction our cases have drawn between textbooks and instructional materials and equipment, there remains the question of which of the two irreconcilable strands of our Establishment Clause jurisprudence we should now follow. Between the two, I would adhere to the rule that we have applied in the context of textbook lending programs: To establish a First Amendment violation, plaintiffs must prove that the aid in question actually is, or has been, used for religious purposes.

Because I believe that the Court should abandon the presumption adopted in *Meek* and *Wolman* respecting the use of instructional materials and equipment by religious-school teachers, I see no constitutional need for pervasive monitoring under the Chapter 2 program. The safeguards employed by the program are constitutionally sufficient. At the federal level, the statute limits aid to "secular, neutral, and nonideological services, materials; and equipment"; requires that the aid only supplement and not supplant funds from non-Federal sources; and prohibits "any payment . . . for religious worship or instruction." At the state level, the Louisiana Department of Education (the relevant SEA for Louisiana) requires all nonpublic schools to submit signed assurances that they will use Chapter 2 aid only to supplement and not to supplant non-Federal funds, and that the instructional materials and equipment "will only be used for secular, neutral and nonideological purposes." The evidence proffered by respondents concerning actual diversion of Chapter 2 aid in Jefferson Parish is de minimis.

Justice SOUTER, with whom Justice STEVENS and Justice GINSBURG join, dissenting.

The First Amendment's Establishment Clause prohibits Congress (and, by incorporation, the States) from making any law respecting an establishment of religion. It has been held to prohibit not only the institution of an official church, but any government act favoring religion, a particular religion, or for that matter irreligion. Thus it bars the use of public funds for religious aid.

The establishment prohibition of government religious funding serves more than one end. It is meant to guarantee the right of individual conscience against compulsion, to protect the integrity of religion against the corrosion of secular support, and to preserve the unity of political society against the implied exclusion of the less favored and the antagonism of controversy over public support for religious causes.

These objectives are always in some jeopardy since the substantive principle of no aid to religion is not the only limitation on government action toward religion. Because the First Amendment also bars any prohibition of individual free exercise of religion, and because religious organizations cannot be isolated from the basic government functions that create the civil environment, it is as much necessary as it is difficult to draw lines between forbidden aid and lawful benefit. For more than 50 years, this Court has been attempting to draw these lines. Owing to the variety of factual circumstances in which the lines must be drawn, not all of the points creating the boundary have enjoyed self-evidence.

So far as the line drawn has addressed government aid to education, a few fundamental generalizations are nonetheless possible. There may be no aid supporting a sectarian school's religious exercise or the discharge of its religious mission, while aid of a secular character with no discernible benefit to such a sectarian objective is allowable. Because the religious and secular spheres largely overlap in the life of many such schools, the Court has tried to identify some facts likely to reveal the relative religious or secular intent or effect of the government benefits in particular circumstances. We have asked whether the government is acting neutrally in distributing its money, and about the form of the aid itself, its path from government to religious institution, its divertibility to religious nurture, its potential for reducing traditional expenditures of religious institutions, and its relative importance to the recipient, among other things.

In all the years of its effort, the Court has isolated no single test of constitutional sufficiency, and the question in every case addresses the substantive principle of no aid: what reasons are there to characterize this benefit as aid to the sectarian school in discharging its religious mission? Particular factual circumstances control, and the answer is a matter of judgment.

At least three concerns have been expressed since the founding and run throughout our First Amendment jurisprudence. First, compelling an individual to support religion violates the fundamental principle of freedom of conscience. Madison's and Jefferson's now familiar words establish clearly that liberty of personal conviction requires freedom from coercion to support religion, and

F. When Can Government Give Aid to Religion?

this means that the government can compel no aid to fund it. Madison put it simply: "[T]he same authority which can force a citizen to contribute three pence only of his property for the support of any one establishment, may force him to conform to any other establishment."

Second, government aid corrupts religion. Madison argued that establishment of religion weakened the beliefs of adherents so favored, strengthened their opponents, and generated "pride and indolence in the Clergy; ignorance and servility in the laity; [and] in both, superstition, bigotry and persecution." In a variant of Madison's concern, we have repeatedly noted that a government's favor to a particular religion or sect threatens to taint it with "corrosive secularism."

Third, government establishment of religion is inextricably linked with conflict. In our own history, the turmoil thus produced has led to a rejection of the idea that government should subsidize religious education, a position that illustrates the Court's understanding that any implicit endorsement of religion is unconstitutional.

The insufficiency of evenhandedness neutrality as a stand-alone criterion of constitutional intent or effect has been clear from the beginning of our interpretative efforts, for an obvious reason. Evenhandedness in distributing a benefit approaches the equivalence of constitutionality in this area only when the term refers to such universality of distribution that it makes no sense to think of the benefit as going to any discrete group. Conversely, when evenhandedness refers to distribution to limited groups within society, like groups of schools or schoolchildren, it does make sense to regard the benefit as aid to the recipients. Hence, if we looked no further than evenhandedness, and failed to ask what activities the aid might support, or in fact did support, religious schools could be blessed with government funding as massive as expenditures made for the benefit of their public school counterparts, and religious missions would thrive on public money. This is why the consideration of less than universal neutrality has never been recognized as dispositive and has always been teamed with attention to other facts bearing on the substantive prohibition of support for a school's religious objective.

[O]ne point [is] clear beyond peradventure: together with James Madison we have consistently understood the Establishment Clause to impose a substantive prohibition against public aid to religion and, hence, to the religious mission of sectarian schools. Evenhandedness neutrality is one, nondispositive pointer toward an intent and (to a lesser degree) probable effect on the permissible side of the line between forbidden aid and general public welfare benefit. Other pointers are facts about the religious mission and education level of benefited schools and their pupils, the pathway by which a benefit travels from public treasury to educational effect, the form and content of the aid, its adaptability to religious ends, and its effects on school budgets. The object of all enquiries into such matters is the same whatever the particular circumstances: is the benefit intended to aid in providing the religious element of the education and is it likely to do so?

The facts most obviously relevant to the Chapter 2 scheme in Jefferson Parish are those showing divertibility and actual diversion in the circumstance of pervasively sectarian religious schools. The type of aid, the structure of the program, and the lack of effective safeguards clearly demonstrate the divertibility of the aid. While little is known about its use, owing to the anemic enforcement system in the parish, even the thin record before us reveals that actual diversion occurred.

The aid that the government provided was highly susceptible to unconstitutional use. Much of the equipment provided under Chapter 2 was not of the type provided for individual students, but included "slide projectors, movie projectors, overhead projectors, television sets, tape recorders, projection screens, maps, globes, filmstrips, cassettes, computers," and computer software and peripherals, as well as library books and materials. The videocassette players, overhead projectors, and other instructional aids were of the sort that we have found can easily be used by religious teachers for religious purposes. The same was true of the computers, which were as readily employable for religious teaching as the other equipment, and presumably as immune to any countervailing safeguard.

The divertibility thus inherent in the forms of Chapter 2 aid was enhanced by the structure of the program in Jefferson Parish. Requests for specific items under Chapter 2 came not from secular officials, but from officials of the religious schools (and even parents of religious school pupils). The sectarian schools decided what they wanted and often ordered the supplies, to be forwarded directly to themselves. It was easy to select whatever instructional materials and library books the schools wanted, just as it was easy to employ computers for the support of the religious content of the curriculum infused with religious instruction.

The plurality nonetheless condemns any enquiry into the pervasiveness of doctrinal content as a remnant of anti-Catholic bigotry (as if evangelical Protestant schools and Orthodox Jewish yeshivas were never pervasively sectarian), and it equates a refusal to aid religious schools with hostility to religion (as if aid to religious teaching were not opposed in this very case by at least one religious respondent and numerous religious amici curiae in a tradition claiming descent from Roger Williams). My concern with these arguments goes not so much to their details as it does to the fact that the plurality's choice to employ imputations of bigotry and irreligion as terms in the Court's debate makes one point clear: that in rejecting the principle of no aid to a school's religious mission the plurality is attacking the most fundamental assumption underlying the Establishment Clause, that government can in fact operate with neutrality in its relation to religion. I believe that it can, and so respectfully dissent.

Prior to Mitchell v. Helms, it was possible to explain most of the cases by seeing them as applying three criteria. First, the aid must be available to all students enrolled in public and parochial schools; aid that is available only to parochial school students is sure to be invalidated. Second, the aid is more likely to be allowed if it is provided directly to the students than if it is provided to the schools. Third, the aid will be permitted if it is a type that likely cannot be used for religions instruction, but it will be invalidated if it can be easily used for religious education. After *Mitchell*, the first two criteria still seem to be followed by a majority of the justices, but the third criterion seems no longer used.

The first factor is whether the aid is available to all students. Aid that is available only to parochial school students is sure to be invalidated, but that same assistance is likely to be allowed if it is given to public school students as well and meets the other criteria. For example, in Committee for Public Education v.

F. When Can Government Give Aid to Religion?

Nyquist, 413 U.S. 756 (1973), and Sloan v. Lemon, 413 U.S. 825 (1973), the Court declared unconstitutional state laws that provided reimbursement and tax credits to students attending nonpublic schools. In *Nyquist*, a New York statute provided for reimbursement and tax credits for costs of nonpublic school elementary and secondary education for up to one-half of the costs of tuition for low- and middle-income students. Specifically, the law provided for reimbursement payments to families with incomes below $15,000 and tax credits for families with incomes below $25,000. *Sloan* involved a Pennsylvania law that provided funds to reimburse parents for a portion of tuition expenses incurred in sending their children to nonpublic schools. Unlike the New York law in *Nyquist*, the Pennsylvania statute allowed families of all incomes to receive funds.

The Supreme Court declared both of these laws unconstitutional even though the aid went directly to the families rather than the schools. The Court emphasized that the aid was available only to nonpublic school students. The Court concluded that the aid "has a 'primary effect that advances religion' and offends the constitutional prohibition 'respecting an establishment of religion.'"

In contrast, in Mueller v. Allen, 463 U.S. 388 (1983), discussed by all of the justices in *Mitchell*, the Court upheld a program of tax credits that were available to all students at both public and parochial schools. A Minnesota law allowed taxpayers to deduct certain expenses incurred in providing education to their children from their state income taxes. The deduction was limited to actual expenses for tuition, textbooks, and transportation and could not exceed $500 per dependent for grades kindergarten through six and $700 per student in grades seven through twelve.

By a five-to-four decision, the Court applied the *Lemon* test and upheld the income tax credits as constitutional. As to the first part of the *Lemon* test, the Court said that "[a] State's decision to defray the cost of educational expenses incurred by parents—regardless of the type of schools their children attend—evidences a purpose that is both secular and understandable. An educated populace is essential to the political and economic health of any community, and a State's efforts to assist parents in meeting the rising cost of educational expenses plainly serves this secular purpose of ensuring that the State's citizenry is well educated."

In applying the second prong of the *Lemon* test, the Court emphasized that the tax credits were one of many deductions available and were limited in size. The Court said that the "[l]egislature's judgment that a deduction for educational expenses fairly equalizes the tax burden of its citizens and encourages desirable expenditures for educational purposes is entitled to substantial deference." Most importantly, the Court stressed that the "deduction is available for educational expenses incurred by *all* parents, including those whose children attend public schools and those whose children attend nonsectarian private schools or sectarian private schools." The Court saw this as the key distinction with *Nyquist* where the aid was available only to students attending nonpublic schools.

Finally, the Court concluded that allowing the tax credits did not entail government entanglement with religion. No government monitoring was involved in the program; the government was not required by the law to oversee any aspect of the parochial schools.

Justice Marshall dissented and was joined by Justices Brennan, Blackmun, and Stevens. Justice Marshall contended that the Establishment Clause prohibits the government from subsidizing parochial schools, even if it is providing the same assistance to public schools students. Justice Marshall said, "The Establishment Clause of the First Amendment prohibits a State from subsidizing religious education, whether it does so directly or indirectly. In my view, this principle of neutrality forbids not only the tax benefits struck down in Committee for Public Education v. Nyquist, but any tax benefit, including the tax deduction at issue here, which subsidizes tuition payments to sectarian schools."

The Court appeared to resolve this tension in Zelman v. Simmons-Harris, where the Court, by a five-to-four margin, upheld a voucher program through which aid could be used for parochial schools.

ZELMAN v. SIMMONS-HARRIS
536 U.S. 639 (2002)

Chief Justice Rehnquist delivered the opinion of the Court.

The State of Ohio has established a pilot program designed to provide educational choices to families with children who reside in the Cleveland City School District. The question presented is whether this program offends the Establishment Clause of the United States Constitution. We hold that it does not.

There are more than 75,000 children enrolled in the Cleveland City School District. The majority of these children are from low-income and minority families. Few of these families enjoy the means to send their children to any school other than an inner-city public school. For more than a generation, however, Cleveland's public schools have been among the worst performing public schools in the Nation. In 1995, a Federal District Court declared a "crisis of magnitude" and placed the entire Cleveland school district under state control. Shortly thereafter, the state auditor found that Cleveland's public schools were in the midst of a "crisis that is perhaps unprecedented in the history of American education." The district had failed to meet any of the 18 state standards for minimal acceptable performance. Only 1 in 10 ninth graders could pass a basic proficiency examination, and students at all levels performed at a dismal rate compared with students in other Ohio public schools. More than two-thirds of high school students either dropped or failed out before graduation. Of those students who managed to reach their senior year, one of every four still failed to graduate. Of those students who did graduate, few could read, write, or compute at levels comparable to their counterparts in other cities.

It is against this backdrop that Ohio enacted, among other initiatives, its Pilot Project Scholarship Program. The program provides financial assistance to families in any Ohio school district that is or has been "under federal court order requiring supervision and operational management of the district by the state superintendent." Cleveland is the only Ohio school district to fall within that category.

The program provides two basic kinds of assistance to parents of children in a covered district. First, the program provides tuition aid for students in kindergarten through third grade, expanding each year through eighth grade, to attend a participating public or private school of their parent's choosing. Second, the program provides tutorial aid for students who choose to remain enrolled in public school.

F. When Can Government Give Aid to Religion?

The tuition aid portion of the program is designed to provide educational choices to parents who reside in a covered district. Any private school, whether religious or nonreligious, may participate in the program and accept program students so long as the school is located within the boundaries of a covered district and meets statewide educational standards. Participating private schools must agree not to discriminate on the basis of race, religion, or ethnic background, or to "advocate or foster unlawful behavior or teach hatred of any person or group on the basis of race, ethnicity, national origin, or religion." Any public school located in a school district adjacent to the covered district may also participate in the program. Adjacent public schools are eligible to receive a $2,250 tuition grant for each program student accepted in addition to the full amount of per-pupil state funding attributable to each additional student. All participating schools, whether public or private, are required to accept students in accordance with rules and procedures established by the state superintendent.

Tuition aid is distributed to parents according to financial need. Families with incomes below 200% of the poverty line are given priority and are eligible to receive 90% of private school tuition up to $2,250. For these lowest-income families, participating private schools may not charge a parental co-payment greater than $250. For all other families, the program pays 75% of tuition costs, up to $1,875, with no co-payment cap. These families receive tuition aid only if the number of available scholarships exceeds the number of low-income children who choose to participate. Where tuition aid is spent depends solely upon where parents who receive tuition aid choose to enroll their child. If parents choose a private school, checks are made payable to the parents who then endorse the checks over to the chosen school.

The tutorial aid portion of the program provides tutorial assistance through grants to any student in a covered district who chooses to remain in public school. Parents arrange for registered tutors to provide assistance to their children and then submit bills for those services to the State for payment. Students from low-income families receive 90% of the amount charged for such assistance up to $360. All other students receive 75% of that amount. The number of tutorial assistance grants offered to students in a covered district must equal the number of tuition aid scholarships provided to students enrolled at participating private or adjacent public schools.

The program has been in operation within the Cleveland City School District since the 1996-1997 school year. In the 1999-2000 school year, 56 private schools participated in the program, 46 (or 82%) of which had a religious affiliation. None of the public schools in districts adjacent to Cleveland have elected to participate. More than 3,700 students participated in the scholarship program, most of whom (96%) enrolled in religiously affiliated schools. Sixty percent of these students were from families at or below the poverty line. In the 1998-1999 school year, approximately 1,400 Cleveland public school students received tutorial aid. This number was expected to double during the 1999-2000 school year.

The program is part of a broader undertaking by the State to enhance the educational options of Cleveland's schoolchildren in response to the 1995 takeover. That undertaking includes programs governing community and magnet schools. Community schools are funded under state law but are run by their own school boards, not by local school districts. These schools enjoy academic independence to hire their own teachers and to determine their own curriculum. They can have no religious affiliation and are required to accept students by lottery. During the 1999-2000 school year, there were 10 start-up community schools in the Cleveland City School District with more than 1,900 students enrolled. For each child enrolled in a community school, the school receives state funding of $4,518, twice the funding a participating program school may receive.

Magnet schools are public schools operated by a local school board that emphasize a particular subject area, teaching method, or service to students. For each student enrolled in a magnet school, the school district receives $7,746, including state funding of $4,167, the same amount received per student enrolled at a traditional public school. As of 1999, parents in Cleveland were able to choose from among 23 magnet schools, which together enrolled more than 13,000 students in kindergarten through eighth grade. These schools provide specialized teaching methods, such as Montessori, or a particularized curriculum focus, such as foreign language, computers, or the arts.

The Establishment Clause of the First Amendment, applied to the States through the Fourteenth Amendment, prevents a State from enacting laws that have the "purpose" or "effect" of advancing or inhibiting religion. There is no dispute that the program challenged here was enacted for the valid secular purpose of providing educational assistance to poor children in a demonstrably failing public school system. Thus, the question presented is whether the Ohio program nonetheless has the forbidden "effect" of advancing or inhibiting religion.

To answer that question, our decisions have drawn a consistent distinction between government programs that provide aid directly to religious schools, Mitchell v. Helms (2000), and programs of true private choice, in which government aid reaches religious schools only as a result of the genuine and independent choices of private individuals, Mueller v. Allen (1983); Witters v. Washington Dept. of Servs. for Blind (1986); Zobrest v. Catalina Foothills School Dist. (1993). While our jurisprudence with respect to the constitutionality of direct aid programs has "changed significantly" over the past two decades, our jurisprudence with respect to true private choice programs has remained consistent and unbroken. Three times we have confronted Establishment Clause challenges to neutral government programs that provide aid directly to a broad class of individuals, who, in turn, direct the aid to religious schools or institutions of their own choosing. Three times we have rejected such challenges.

In *Mueller*, we rejected an Establishment Clause challenge to a Minnesota program authorizing tax deductions for various educational expenses, including private school tuition costs, even though the great majority of the program's beneficiaries (96%) were parents of children in religious schools. We began by focusing on the class of beneficiaries, finding that because the class included "all parents," including parents with "children [who] attend nonsectarian private schools or sectarian private schools," the program was "not readily subject to challenge under the Establishment Clause." Then, viewing the program as a whole, we emphasized the principle of private choice, noting that public funds were made available to religious schools "only as a result of numerous, private choices of individual parents of school-age children." This, we said, ensured that "'no imprimatur of state approval' can be deemed to

F. When Can Government Give Aid to Religion? 669

have been conferred on any particular religion, or on religion generally." We thus found it irrelevant to the constitutional inquiry that the vast majority of beneficiaries were parents of children in religious schools, saying: "We would be loath to adopt a rule grounding the constitutionality of a facially neutral law on annual reports reciting the extent to which various classes of private citizens claimed benefits under the law." That the program was one of true private choice, with no evidence that the State deliberately skewed incentives toward religious schools, was sufficient for the program to survive scrutiny under the Establishment Clause.

In *Witters*, we used identical reasoning to reject an Establishment Clause challenge to a vocational scholarship program that provided tuition aid to a student studying at a religious institution to become a pastor. Looking at the program as a whole, we observed that "[a]ny aid . . . that ultimately flows to religious institutions does so only as a result of the genuinely independent and private choices of aid recipients." We further remarked that, as in *Mueller*, "[the] program is made available generally without regard to the sectarian-nonsectarian, or public-nonpublic nature of the institution benefited." In light of these factors, we held that the program was not inconsistent with the Establishment Clause. Five Members of the Court, in separate opinions, emphasized the general rule from *Mueller* that the amount of government aid channeled to religious institutions by individual aid recipients was not relevant to the constitutional inquiry. Our holding thus rested not on whether few or many recipients chose to expend government aid at a religious school but, rather, on whether recipients generally were empowered to direct the aid to schools or institutions of their own choosing.

Finally, in *Zobrest*, we applied *Mueller* and *Witters* to reject an Establishment Clause challenge to a federal program that permitted sign-language interpreters to assist deaf children enrolled in religious schools. Reviewing our earlier decisions, we stated that "government programs that neutrally provide benefits to a broad class of citizens defined without reference to religion are not readily subject to an Establishment Clause challenge." Looking once again to the challenged program as a whole, we observed that the program "distributes benefits neutrally to any child qualifying as 'disabled.'" Its "primary beneficiaries," we said, were "disabled children, not sectarian schools." We further observed that "[b]y according parents freedom to select a school of their choice, the statute ensures that a government-paid interpreter will be present in a sectarian school only as a result of the private decision of individual parents." Our focus again was on neutrality and the principle of private choice, not on the number of program beneficiaries attending religious schools. Because the program ensured that parents were the ones to select a religious school as the best learning environment for their handicapped child, the circuit between government and religion was broken, and the Establishment Clause was not implicated.

Mueller, Witters, and *Zobrest* thus make clear that where a government aid program is neutral with respect to religion, and provides assistance directly to a broad class of citizens who, in turn, direct government aid to religious schools wholly as a result of their own genuine and independent private choice, the program is not readily subject to challenge under the Establishment Clause. A program that shares these features permits government aid to reach religious institutions only by way of the deliberate choices of numerous individual recipients. The incidental advancement of a religious mission, or the perceived endorsement of a religious message, is reasonably attributable to the individual recipient, not to the government, whose role ends with the disbursement of benefits. As a plurality of this Court recently observed: "[I]f numerous private choices, rather than the single choice of a government, determine the distribution of aid, pursuant to neutral eligibility criteria, then a government cannot, or at least cannot easily, grant special favors that might lead to a religious establishment." Mitchell v. Helms (2000).

We believe that the program challenged here is a program of true private choice, consistent with *Mueller*, *Witters*, and *Zobrest*, and thus constitutional. As was true in those cases, the Ohio program is neutral in all respects toward religion. It is part of a general and multifaceted undertaking by the State of Ohio to provide educational opportunities to the children of a failed school district. It confers educational assistance directly to a broad class of individuals defined without reference to religion, i.e., any parent of a school-age child who resides in the Cleveland City School District. The program permits the participation of all schools within the district, religious or nonreligious. Adjacent public schools also may participate and have a financial incentive to do so. Program benefits are available to participating families on neutral terms, with no reference to religion. The only preference stated anywhere in the program is a preference for low-income families, who receive greater assistance and are given priority for admission at participating schools.

There are no "financial incentive[s]" that "ske[w]" the program toward religious schools. Such incentives "[are] not present . . . where the aid is allocated on the basis of neutral, secular criteria that neither favor nor disfavor religion, and is made available to both religious and secular beneficiaries on a nondiscriminatory basis." The program here in fact creates financial disincentives for religious schools, with private schools receiving only half the government assistance given to community schools and one-third the assistance given to magnet schools. Adjacent public schools, should any choose to accept program students, are also eligible to receive two to three times the state funding of a private religious school. Families too have a financial disincentive to choose a private religious school over other schools. Parents that choose to participate in the scholarship program and then to enroll their children in a private school (religious or nonreligious) must copay a portion of the school's tuition. Families that choose a community school, magnet school, or traditional public school pay nothing. Although such features of the program are not necessary to its constitutionality, they clearly dispel the claim that the program "creates . . . financial incentive[s] for parents to choose a sectarian school."

Respondents suggest that even without a financial incentive for parents to choose a religious school, the program creates a "public perception that the State is endorsing religious practices and beliefs." But we have repeatedly recognized that no reasonable observer would think a neutral program of private choice, where state aid reaches religious schools solely as a result of the numerous independent decisions of private individuals, carries with it the imprimatur of government endorsement. The argument is particularly misplaced here since "the reasonable observer in the endorsement inquiry must be deemed aware" of the "history and context" underlying a challenged program.

There also is no evidence that the program fails to provide genuine opportunities for Cleveland parents to select secular educational options for

F. When Can Government Give Aid to Religion?

their school-age children. Cleveland schoolchildren enjoy a range of educational choices: They may remain in public school as before, remain in public school with publicly funded tutoring aid, obtain a scholarship and choose a religious school, obtain a scholarship and choose a nonreligious private school, enroll in a community school, or enroll in a magnet school. That 46 of the 56 private schools now participating in the program are religious schools does not condemn it as a violation of the Establishment Clause. The Establishment Clause question is whether Ohio is coercing parents into sending their children to religious schools, and that question must be answered by evaluating all options Ohio provides Cleveland schoolchildren, only one of which is to obtain a program scholarship and then choose a religious school.

Justice Souter speculates that because more private religious schools currently participate in the program, the program itself must somehow discourage the participation of private nonreligious schools. But Cleveland's preponderance of religiously affiliated private schools certainly did not arise as a result of the program; it is a phenomenon common to many American cities. Indeed, by all accounts the program has captured a remarkable cross-section of private schools, religious and nonreligious. It is true that 82% of Cleveland's participating private schools are religious schools, but it is also true that 81% of private schools in Ohio are religious schools. To attribute constitutional significance to this figure, moreover, would lead to the absurd result that a neutral school-choice program might be permissible in some parts of Ohio, such as Columbus, where a lower percentage of private schools are religious schools, but not in inner-city Cleveland, where Ohio has deemed such programs most sorely needed, but where the preponderance of religious schools happens to be greater. Likewise, an identical private choice program might be constitutional in some States, such as Maine or Utah, where less that 45% of private schools are religious schools, but not in other States, such as Nebraska or Kansas, where over 90% of private schools are religious schools.

Respondents and Justice Souter claim that even if we do not focus on the number of participating schools that are religious schools, we should attach constitutional significance to the fact that 96% of scholarship recipients have enrolled in religious schools. They claim that this alone proves parents lack genuine choice, even if one parent has ever said so. We need not consider this argument in detail, since it was flatly rejected in *Mueller*, where we found it irrelevant that 96% of parents taking deductions for tuition expenses paid tuition at religious schools. Indeed, we have recently found it irrelevant even to the constitutionality of a direct aid program that a vast majority of program benefits went to religious schools. The constitutionality of a neutral educational aid program simply does not turn on whether and why, in a particular area, at a particular time, most private schools are run by religious organizations, or most recipients choose to use the aid at a religious school. As we said in *Mueller*, "[s]uch an approach would scarcely provide the certainty that this field stands in need of, nor can we perceive principled standards by which such statistical evidence might be evaluated."

This point is aptly illustrated here. The 96% figure upon which respondents and Justice Souter rely discounts entirely (1) the more than 1,900 Cleveland children enrolled in alternative community schools, (2) the more than 13,000 children enrolled in alternative magnet schools, and (3) the more than 1,400 children enrolled in traditional public schools with tutorial assistance.

Including some or all of these children in the denominator of children enrolled in nontraditional schools during the 1999-2000 school year drops the percentage enrolled in religious schools from 96% to under 20%. The 96% figure also represents but a snapshot of one particular school year. In the 1997-1998 school year, by contrast, only 78% of scholarship recipients attended religious schools.

In sum, the Ohio program is entirely neutral with respect to religion. It provides benefits directly to a wide spectrum of individuals, defined only by financial need and residence in a particular school district. It permits such individuals to exercise genuine choice among options public and private, secular and religious. The program is therefore a program of true private choice. In keeping with an unbroken line of decisions rejecting challenges to similar programs, we hold that the program does not offend the Establishment Clause.

Justice O'CONNOR, concurring.

There is little question in my mind that the Cleveland voucher program is neutral as between religious schools and nonreligious schools. Justice Souter rejects the Court's notion of neutrality, proposing that the neutrality of a program should be gauged not by the opportunities it presents but rather by its effects. But Justice Souter's notion of neutrality is inconsistent with that in our case law. As we put it in *Agostini*, government aid must be "made available to both religious and secular beneficiaries on a nondiscriminatory basis."

I do not agree that the nonreligious schools have failed to provide Cleveland parents reasonable alternatives to religious schools in the voucher program. For nonreligious schools to qualify as genuine options for parents, they need not be superior to religious schools in every respect. They need only be adequate substitutes for religious schools in the eyes of parents. The District Court record demonstrates that nonreligious schools were able to compete effectively with Catholic and other religious schools in the Cleveland voucher program. The best evidence of this is that many parents with vouchers selected nonreligious private schools over religious alternatives and an even larger number of parents send their children to community and magnet schools rather than seeking vouchers at all. Moreover, there is no record evidence that any voucher-eligible student was turned away from a nonreligious private school in the voucher program, let alone a community or magnet school.

I find the Court's answer to the question whether parents of students eligible for vouchers have a genuine choice between religious and nonreligious schools persuasive. In looking at the voucher program, all the choices available to potential beneficiaries of the government program should be considered.

Considering all the educational options available to parents whose children are eligible for vouchers, including community and magnet schools, the Court finds that parents in the Cleveland schools have an array of nonreligious options.

Based on the reasoning in the Court's opinion, which is consistent with the realities of the Cleveland educational system, I am persuaded that the Cleveland voucher program affords parents of eligible children genuine nonreligious options and is consistent with the Establishment Clause.

Justice THOMAS, concurring.

Frederick Douglass once said that "[e]ducation . . . means emancipation. It means light and liberty. It means the uplifting of the soul of man into the

F. When Can Government Give Aid to Religion?

glorious light of truth, the light by which men can only be made free." Today many of our inner-city public schools deny emancipation to urban minority students. Despite this Court's observation nearly 50 years ago in Brown v. Board of Education, that "it is doubtful that any child may reasonably be expected to succeed in life if he is denied the opportunity of an education," urban children have been forced into a system that continually fails them. These cases present an example of such failures. Besieged by escalating financial problems and declining academic achievement, the Cleveland City School District was in the midst of an academic emergency when Ohio enacted its scholarship program.

The dissents and respondents wish to invoke the Establishment Clause of the First Amendment, as incorporated through the Fourteenth, to constrain a State's neutral efforts to provide greater educational opportunity for underprivileged minority students. Today's decision properly upholds the program as constitutional, and I join it in full.

Whatever the textual and historical merits of incorporating the Establishment Clause, I can accept that the Fourteenth Amendment protects religious liberty rights. But I cannot accept its use to oppose neutral programs of school choice through the incorporation of the Establishment Clause. There would be a tragic irony in converting the Fourteenth Amendment's guarantee of individual liberty into a prohibition on the exercise of educational choice.

The wisdom of allowing States greater latitude in dealing with matters of religion and education can be easily appreciated in this context. Respondents advocate using the Fourteenth Amendment to handcuff the State's ability to experiment with education. But without education one can hardly exercise the civic, political, and personal freedoms conferred by the Fourteenth Amendment. Faced with a severe educational crisis, the State of Ohio enacted wide-ranging educational reform that allows voluntary participation of private and religious schools in educating poor urban children otherwise condemned to failing public schools. The program does not force any individual to submit to religious indoctrination or education. It simply gives parents a greater choice as to where and in what manner to educate their children. This is a choice that those with greater means have routinely exercised.

In addition to expanding the reach of the scholarship program, the inclusion of religious schools makes sense given Ohio's purpose of increasing educational performance and opportunities. Religious schools, like other private schools, achieve far better educational results than their public counterparts. For example, the students at Cleveland's Catholic schools score significantly higher on Ohio proficiency tests than students at Cleveland public schools. Of Cleveland eighth graders taking the 1999 Ohio proficiency test, 95 percent in Catholic schools passed the reading test, whereas only 57 percent in public schools passed. And 75 percent of Catholic school students passed the math proficiency test, compared to only 22 percent of public school students. But the success of religious and private schools is in the end beside the point, because the State has a constitutional right to experiment with a variety of different programs to promote educational opportunity. That Ohio's program includes successful schools simply indicates that such reform can in fact provide improved education to underprivileged urban children.

Although one of the purposes of public schools was to promote democracy and a more egalitarian culture, failing urban public schools disproportionately affect minority children most in need of educational opportunity. At the time of Reconstruction, blacks considered public education "a matter of personal liberation and a necessary function of a free society." Today, however, the promise of public school education has failed poor inner-city blacks. While in theory providing education to everyone, the quality of public schools varies significantly across districts. Just as blacks supported public education during Reconstruction, many blacks and other minorities now support school choice programs because they provide the greatest educational opportunities for their children in struggling communities. Opponents of the program raise formalistic concerns about the Establishment Clause but ignore the core purposes of the Fourteenth Amendment.[38]

While the romanticized ideal of universal public education resonates with the cognoscenti who oppose vouchers, poor urban families just want the best education for their children, who will certainly need it to function in our high-tech and advanced society. As Thomas Sowell noted 30 years ago: "Most black people have faced too many grim, concrete problems to be romantics. They want and need certain tangible results, which can be achieved only by developing certain specific abilities." The same is true today. An individual's life prospects increase dramatically with each successfully completed phase of education. For instance, a black high school dropout earns just over $13,500, but with a high school degree the average income is almost $21,000. Blacks with a bachelor's degree have an average annual income of about $37,500, and $75,500 with a professional degree. Staying in school and earning a degree generates real and tangible financial benefits, whereas failure to obtain even a high school degree essentially relegates students to a life of poverty and, all too often, of crime. The failure to provide education to poor urban children perpetuates a vicious cycle of poverty, dependence, criminality, and alienation that continues for the remainder of their lives. If society cannot end racial discrimination, at least it can arm minorities with the education to defend themselves from some of discrimination's effects.

Ten States have enacted some form of publicly funded private school choice as one means of raising the quality of education provided to underprivileged urban children. These programs address the root of the problem with failing urban public schools that disproportionately affect minority students. Converting the Fourteenth Amendment from a guarantee of opportunity to an obstacle against education reform distorts our constitutional values and disserves those in the greatest need. As Frederick Douglass poignantly noted "no greater benefit can be bestowed upon a long benighted people, than giving to them, as we are here earnestly this day endeavoring to do, the means of an education."

---

38. Minority and low-income parents express the greatest support for parental choice and are most interested in placing their children in private schools. "[T]he appeal of private schools is especially strong among parents who are low in income, minority, and live in low-performing districts: precisely the parents who are the most disadvantaged under the current system." T. Moe, Schools, Special Vouchers, and the American Public 164 (2001). Nearly three-fourths of all public school parents with an annual income less than $20,000 support vouchers, compared to 57 percent of public school parents with an annual income of over $60,000. In addition, 75 percent of black public school parents support vouchers, as do 71 percent of Hispanic public school parents. [Footnote by the Court.]

F. When Can Government Give Aid to Religion?

Justice SOUTER with whom Justice STEVENS, Justice GINSBURG, and Justice BREYER join, dissenting.

The Court's majority holds that the Establishment Clause is no bar to Ohio's payment of tuition at private religious elementary and middle schools under a scheme that systematically provides tax money to support the schools' religious missions. The occasion for the legislation thus upheld is the condition of public education in the city of Cleveland. The record indicates that the schools are failing to serve their objective, and the vouchers in issue here are said to be needed to provide adequate alternatives to them. If there were an excuse for giving short shrift to the Establishment Clause, it would probably apply here. But there is no excuse. Constitutional limitations are placed on government to preserve constitutional values in hard cases, like these.

Today, however, the majority holds that the Establishment Clause is not offended by Ohio's Pilot Project Scholarship Program, under which students may be eligible to receive as much as $2,250 in the form of tuition vouchers transferable to religious schools. In the city of Cleveland the overwhelming proportion of large appropriations for voucher money must be spent on religious schools if it is to be spent at all, and will be spent in amounts that cover almost all of tuition. The money will thus pay for eligible students' instruction not only in secular subjects but in religion as well, in schools that can fairly be characterized as founded to teach religious doctrine and to imbue teaching in all subjects with a religious dimension. Public tax money will pay at a systemic level for teaching the covenant with Israel and Mosaic law in Jewish schools, the primacy of the Apostle Peter and the Papacy in Catholic schools, the truth of reformed Christianity in Protestant schools, and the revelation to the Prophet in Muslim schools, to speak only of major religious groupings in the Republic.

II

Although it has taken half a century since *Everson* to reach the majority's twin standards of neutrality and free choice, the facts show that, in the majority's hands, even these criteria cannot convincingly legitimize the Ohio scheme.

A

Consider first the criterion of neutrality. As recently as two Terms ago, a majority of the Court recognized that neutrality conceived of as evenhandedness toward aid recipients had never been treated as alone sufficient to satisfy the Establishment Clause. Today, however, the majority employs the neutrality criterion in a way that renders it impossible to understand.

In order to apply the neutrality test, then, it makes sense to focus on a category of aid that may be directed to religious as well as secular schools, and ask whether the scheme favors a religious direction. Here, one would ask whether the voucher provisions, allowing for as much as $2,250 toward private school tuition (or a grant to a public school in an adjacent district), were written in a way that skewed the scheme toward benefiting religious schools. This, however, is not what the majority asks. The majority looks not to the provisions for tuition vouchers, but to every provision for educational opportunity.

The illogic is patent. If regular, public schools (which can get no voucher payments) "participate" in a voucher scheme with schools that can, and public expenditure is still predominantly on public schools, then the majority's reasoning would find neutrality in a scheme of vouchers available for private tuition in districts with no secular private schools at all. "Neutrality" as the majority employs the term is, literally, verbal and nothing more. This, indeed, is the only way the majority can gloss over the very nonneutral feature of the total scheme covering "all schools": public tutors may receive from the State no more than $324 per child to support extra tutoring (that is, the State's 90% of a total amount of $360), whereas the tuition voucher schools (which turn out to be mostly religious) can receive up to $2,250.

Why the majority does not simply accept the fact that the challenge here is to the more generous voucher scheme and judge its neutrality in relation to religious use of voucher money seems very odd. It seems odd, that is, until one recognizes that comparable schools for applying the criterion of neutrality are also the comparable schools for applying the other majority criterion, whether the immediate recipients of voucher aid have a genuinely free choice of religious and secular schools to receive the voucher money. And in applying this second criterion, the consideration of "all schools" is ostensibly helpful to the majority position.

B

The majority addresses the issue of choice the same way it addresses neutrality, by asking whether recipients or potential recipients of voucher aid have a choice of public schools among secular alternatives to religious schools. Again, however, the majority asks the wrong question and misapplies the criterion. The majority has confused choice in spending scholarships with choice from the entire menu of possible educational placements, most of them open to anyone willing to attend a public school. I say "confused" because the majority's new use of the choice criterion, which it frames negatively as "whether Ohio is coercing parents into sending their children to religious schools," ignores the reason for having a private choice enquiry in the first place. Cases since *Mueller* have found private choice relevant under a rule that aid to religious schools can be permissible so long as it first passes through the hands of students or parents. The majority's view that all educational choices are comparable for purposes of choice thus ignores the whole point of the choice test: it is a criterion for deciding whether indirect aid to a religious school is legitimate because it passes through private hands that can spend or use the aid in a secular school. The question is whether the private hand is genuinely free to send the money in either a secular direction or a religious one. The majority now has transformed this question about private choice in channeling aid into a question about selecting from examples of state spending (on education) including direct spending on magnet and community public schools that goes through no private hands and could never reach a religious school under any circumstance. When the choice test is transformed from where to spend the money to where to go to school, it is cut loose from its very purpose.

If, contrary to the majority, we ask the right question about genuine choice to use the vouchers, the answer shows that something is influencing choices in a way that aims the money in a religious direction: of 56 private schools in the district participating in the voucher program (only 53 of which accepted voucher students in 1999-2000); 46 of them are religious; 96.6% of all voucher recipients go to religious schools, only 3.4% to nonreligious ones. Unfortunately

F. When Can Government Give Aid to Religion?

for the majority position, there is no explanation for this that suggests the religious direction results simply from free choices by parents. One answer to these statistics, for example, which would be consistent with the genuine choice claimed to be operating, might be that 96.6% of families choosing to avail themselves of vouchers choose to educate their children in schools of their own religion. This would not, in my view, render the scheme constitutional, but it would speak to the majority's choice criterion. Evidence shows, however, that almost two out of three families using vouchers to send their children to religious schools did not embrace the religion of those schools. The families made it clear they had not chosen the schools because they wished their children to be proselytized in a religion not their own, or in any religion, but because of educational opportunity.

Even so, the fact that some 2,270 students chose to apply their vouchers to schools of other religions, might be consistent with true choice if the students "chose" their religious schools over a wide array of private nonreligious options, or if it could be shown generally that Ohio's program had no effect on educational choices and thus no impermissible effect of advancing religious education. But both possibilities are contrary to fact. First, even if all existing nonreligious private schools in Cleveland were willing to accept large numbers of voucher students, only a few more than the 129 currently enrolled in such schools would be able to attend, as the total enrollment at all nonreligious private schools in Cleveland for kindergarten through eighth grade is only 510 children, and there is no indication that these schools have many open seats. Second, the $2,500 cap that the program places on tuition for participating low-income pupils has the effect of curtailing the participation of nonreligious schools: "nonreligious schools with higher tuition (about $4,000) stated that they could afford to accommodate just a few voucher students." By comparison, the average tuition at participating Catholic schools in Cleveland in 1999-2000 was $1,592, almost $1,000 below the cap.

There is, in any case, no way to interpret the 96.6% of current voucher money going to religious schools as reflecting a free and genuine choice by the families that apply for vouchers. The 96.6% reflects, instead, the fact that too few nonreligious school desks are available and few but religious schools can afford to accept more than a handful of voucher students. And contrary to the majority's assertion, public schools in adjacent districts hardly have a financial incentive to participate in the Ohio voucher program, and none has. For the overwhelming number of children in the voucher scheme, the only alternative to the public schools is religious. And it is entirely irrelevant that the State did not deliberately design the network of private schools for the sake of channeling money into religious institutions. The criterion is one of genuinely free choice on the part of the private individuals who choose, and a Hobson's choice is not a choice, whatever the reason for being Hobsonian.

III

I do not dissent merely because the majority has misapplied its own law, for even if I assumed arguendo that the majority's formal criteria were satisfied on the facts, today's conclusion would be profoundly at odds with the Constitution. Proof of this is clear on two levels.

The scale of the aid to religious schools approved today is unprecedented, both in the number of dollars and in the proportion of systemic school expenditure supported. As we said in *Meek*, "it would simply ignore reality to attempt to separate secular educational functions from the predominantly religious role" as the object of aid that comes in "substantial amounts."

It is virtually superfluous to point out that every objective underlying the prohibition of religious establishment is betrayed by this scheme, but something has to be said about the enormity of the violation. I anticipated these objectives earlier, the first being respect for freedom of conscience. Jefferson described it as the idea that no one "shall be compelled to . . . support any religious worship, place, or ministry whatsoever," even a "teacher of his own religious persuasion," and Madison thought it violated by any "'authority which can force a citizen to contribute three pence . . . of his property for the support of any . . . establishment.'" Memorial and Remonstrance ¶3. "Any tax to establish religion is antithetical to the command that the minds of men always be wholly free." Madison's objection to three pence has simply been lost in the majority's formalism.

As for the second objective, to save religion from its own corruption, Madison wrote of the "'experience . . . that ecclesiastical establishments, instead of maintaining the purity and efficacy of Religion, have had a contrary operation.'" Memorial and Remonstrance ¶7. In Madison's time, the manifestations were "pride and indolence in the Clergy; ignorance and servility in the laity[,] in both, superstition, bigotry and persecution"; in the 21st century, the risk is one of "corrosive secularism" to religious schools, and the specific threat is to the primacy of the schools' mission to educate the children of the faithful according to the unaltered precepts of their faith. Even "[t]he favored religion may be compromised as political figures reshape the religion's beliefs for their own purposes; it may be reformed as government largesse brings government regulation." The risk is already being realized. In Ohio, for example, a condition of receiving government money under the program is that participating religious schools may not "discriminate on the basis of . . . religion," which means the school may not give admission preferences to children who are members of the patron faith; children of a parish are generally consigned to the same admission lotteries as non-believers. For perspective on this foot-in-the-door of religious regulation, it is well to remember that the money had barely begun to flow.

If the divisiveness permitted by today's majority is to be avoided in the short term, it will be avoided only by action of the political branches at the state and national levels. Legislatures not driven to desperation by the problems of public education may be able to see the threat in vouchers negotiable in sectarian schools. Perhaps even cities with problems like Cleveland's will perceive the danger, now that they know a federal court will not save them from it.

My own course as judge on the Court cannot, however, simply be to hope that the political branches will save us from the consequences of the majority's decision. *Everson*'s statement is still the touchstone of sound law, even though the reality is that in the matter of educational aid the Establishment Clause has largely been read away. True, the majority has not approved vouchers for religious schools alone, or aid earmarked for religious instruction. But no scheme so clumsy will ever get before us, and in the cases that we may see, like these, the Establishment Clause is largely silenced. I do not have the option to

F. When Can Government Give Aid to Religion?

leave it silent, and I hope that a future Court will reconsider today's dramatic departure from basic Establishment Clause principle.

Justice BREYER, with whom Justice STEVENS and Justice SOUTER join, dissenting.

I write separately, however, to emphasize the risk that publicly financed voucher programs pose in terms of religiously based social conflict. I do so because I believe that the Establishment Clause concern for protecting the Nation's social fabric from religious conflict poses an overriding obstacle to the implementation of this well-intentioned school voucher program. And by explaining the nature of the concern, I hope to demonstrate why, in my view, "parental choice" cannot significantly alleviate the constitutional problem.

With respect to government aid to private education, did not history show that efforts to obtain equivalent funding for the private education of children whose parents did not hold popular religious beliefs only exacerbated religious strife? As Justice Rutledge recognized: "Public money devoted to payment of religious costs, educational or other, brings the quest for more. It brings too the struggle of sect against sect for the larger share or for any. Here one [religious sect] by numbers [of adherents] alone will benefit most, there another. This is precisely the history of societies which have had an established religion and dissident groups." Everson v. Board of Ed. of Ewing (1947) (dissenting opinion).

The upshot is the development of constitutional doctrine that reads the Establishment Clause as avoiding religious strife, not by providing every religion with an equal opportunity (say, to secure state funding or to pray in the public schools), but by drawing fairly clear lines of separation between church and state—at least where the heartland of religious belief, such as primary religious education, is at issue.

The principle underlying these cases—avoiding religiously based social conflict—remains of great concern. As religiously diverse as America had become when the Court decided its major 20th century Establishment Clause cases, we are exponentially more diverse today. America boasts more than 55 different religious groups and subgroups with a significant number of members.

Under these modern-day circumstances, how is the "equal opportunity" principle to work—without risking the "struggle of sect against sect" against which Justice Rutledge warned? School voucher programs finance the religious education of the young. And, if widely adopted, they may well provide billions of dollars that will do so. Why will different religions not become concerned about, and seek to influence, the criteria used to channel this money to religious schools? Why will they not want to examine the implementation of the programs that provide this money—to determine, for example, whether implementation has biased a program toward or against particular sects, or whether recipient religious schools are adequately fulfilling a program's criteria? If so, just how is the State to resolve the resulting controversies without provoking legitimate fears of the kinds of religious controversies without provoking legitimate fears of the kinds of religious favoritism that, in so religiously diverse a Nation, threaten social dissension?

Consider the voucher program here at issue. That program insists that the religious school accept students of all religions. Does that criterion treat fairly groups whose religion forbids them to do so? The program also insists that no participating school "advocate or foster unlawful behavior or teach hatred of any person or group on the basis of race, ethnicity, national origin, or religion." And it requires the State to "revoke the registration of any school if, after a hearing, the superintendent determines that the school is in violation" of the program's rules. As one amicus argues, "it is difficult to imagine a more divisive activity" than the appointment of state officials as referees to determine whether a particular religious doctrine "teaches hatred or advocates lawlessness."

How are state officials to adjudicate claims that one religion or another is advocating, for example, civil disobedience in response to unjust laws, the use of illegal drugs in a religious ceremony, or resort to force to call attention to what it views as an immoral social practice? What kind of public hearing will there be in response to claims that one religion or another is continuing to teach a view of history that casts members of other religions in the worst possible light? How will the public react to government funding for schools that take controversial religious positions on topics that are of current popular interest—say, the conflict in the Middle East or the war on terrorism? Yet any major funding program for primary religious education will require criteria. And the selection of those criteria, as well as their application, inevitably pose problems that are divisive. Efforts to respond to these problems not only will seriously entangle church and state, but also will promote division among religious groups, as one group or another fears (often legitimately) that it will receive unfair treatment at the hands of the government.

I recognize that other nations, for example Great Britain and France, have in the past reconciled religious school funding and religious freedom without creating serious strife. Yet British and French societies are religiously more homogeneous—and it bears noting that recent waves of immigration have begun to create problems of social division there as well. See, e.g., The Muslims of France, 75 Foreign Affairs 78 (1996) (describing increased religious strife in France, as exemplified by expulsion of teenage girls from school for wearing traditional Muslim scarves); Ahmed, Extreme Prejudice; Muslims in Britain, The Times of London, May 2, 1992, p. 10 (describing religious strife in connection with increased Muslim immigration in Great Britain).

In a society as religiously diverse as ours, the Court has recognized that we must rely on the Religion Clauses of the First Amendment to protect against religious strife, particularly when what is at issue is an area as central to religious belief as the shaping, through primary education, of the next generation's minds and spirits.

The Court, in effect, turns the clock back. It adopts, under the name of "neutrality," an interpretation of the Establishment Clause that this Court rejected more than half a century ago. In its view, the parental choice that offers each religious group a kind of equal opportunity to secure government funding overcomes the Establishment Clause concern for social concord. An earlier Court found that "equal opportunity" principle insufficient; it read the Clause as insisting upon greater separation of church and state, at least in respect to primary education. In a society composed of many different religious creeds, I fear that this present departure from the Court's earlier understanding risks creating a form of religiously based conflict potentially harmful to the Nation's social fabric. Because I believe the Establishment Clause was written in part to avoid this kind of conflict, I respectfully dissent.

F. When Can Government Give Aid to Religion?

TAX EXEMPTIONS FOR RELIGIOUS ORGANIZATIONS

Tax exemptions that benefit only religion are unconstitutional, but those that benefit other groups along with religion, such as charitable and educational institutions, are permissible. In Walz v. Tax Commission, 397 U.S. 664 (1970), the Court upheld a state law that provided property tax exemptions for real or personal property used exclusively for religious, educational, or charitable purposes. The plaintiffs argued that the Establishment Clause was violated by the tax exemption for religious property that was used solely for religious worship. The Supreme Court disagreed and emphasized that the government "granted exemption to all houses of religious worship within a broad class of property owned by nonprofit, quasi-public corporations which include hospitals, libraries, playgrounds, scientific, professional, historical, and patriotic groups."

The Court said that "[t]he legislative purpose of a property tax exemption is neither the advancement nor the inhibition of religion; it is neither sponsorship nor hostility." Rather, the goal is to help nonprofit institutions that the government regards as important to the community. The Court also concluded that granting the tax exemption did not entail excessive government involvement with religion. In fact, the Court said that "[e]limination of exemption would tend to expand the involvement of government by giving rise to tax valuation of church property, tax liens, tax foreclosures, and the direct confrontations and conflicts that follow in the train of those legal processes."

In contrast, in Texas Monthly, Inc. v. Bullock, 489 U.S. 1 (1989), the Court declared unconstitutional a tax exemption that was available only for religious organizations. A Texas law provided an exemption from the state sales and use tax for periodicals that were published or distributed by a religious faith and that consisted solely of writings promulgating the teaching of the faith and for books that consisted wholly of writings sacred to a religions faith. The plurality opinion by Justice Brennan, and joined by Justices Marshall and Stevens, emphasized that *Walz* was distinguishable because there "the benefits derived by religious organizations flowed to a large number of nonreligious groups as well." Justice Brennan explained, "Insofar as that subsidy is conferred upon a wide array of nonsectarian groups as well as religious organizations . . . , the fact that religious groups benefit incidentally does not deprive the subsidy of the secular purpose and primary effect mandated by the Establishment Clause. However, when government directs a subsidy exclusively to religious organizations that is not required by the Free Exercise Clause . . . , it provide[s] unjustifiable awards of assistance to religious organizations and cannot but 'convey a message of endorsement' to slighted members of the community."

Justice Scalia dissented and was joined by Chief Justice Rehnquist and Justice Kennedy. Scalia objected in strong language claiming that "[a]s a judicial demolition project today's decision is impressive," and that the "decision introduces a new strain of irrationality in our Religion Clause jurisprudence." Scalia lamented that laws, like Texas's, that existed in 15 states were declared unconstitutional. For the dissent, the tax exemption for religious publications was a permissible accommodation of religion and did not have the purpose or effect of advancing religion or entail excessive government entanglement with religion.

Thus, *Walz* and *Texas Monthly* together indicate that states may give tax exemptions to religious groups only if nonreligious charitable organizations also are beneficiaries. A tax exemption solely for religious groups violates the Establishment Clause.[39]

AID TO RELIGIOUS COLLEGES AND UNIVERSITIES

The Court has been more lenient in allowing government assistance to religious colleges and universities. The Court has distinguished colleges and universities on the grounds that they are not likely to be as permeated with religious doctrine and dogma as are elementary and secondary schools. Also, the Court has emphasized the difference in the age of the students and their ability to understand that government assistance is not endorsement of religion. Additionally, the Court has stressed that aid to colleges and universities is much less likely to produce the political divisiveness that seems inherent to assistance to parochial elementary and secondary schools.

In Tilton v. Richardson, 403 U.S. 672 (1971), the Court upheld the constitutionality of religious colleges and universities receiving federal money for the construction of facilities that would not be used for religious instruction. *Tilton* concerned Title I of the Higher Education Facilities Act of 1963, which provided construction grants for buildings and facilities used exclusively for secular purposes. The Court applied the *Lemon* test and concluded that it was permissible for religious schools to receive the assistance. The Court concluded that the purpose of the aid was to expand facilities in colleges and universities to "accommodate rapidly growing numbers of youth who aspire to a higher education." The Court said that this is a "legitimate secular objective entirely appropriate for governmental action."

Moreover, the Court found that the aid did not have the effect of advancing religion because the law "was carefully drafted to ensure that the federally subsidized facilities would be devoted to the secular and not the religious function of the recipient institutions. It authorizes grants and loans only for academic facilities that will be used for defined secular purposes and expressly prohibits their use for religious instruction, training or worship." The Court, however, invalidated a part of the act that allowed the facilities to be used for religious purposes after 20 years. The Court said that allowing the building to be converted to religious use at that time would impermissibly have the "effect of advancing religion."

Finally, the Court concluded that allowing the aid would not cause excessive government entanglement with religion. The Court said that "[t]here are generally significant differences between the religious aspects of church-related institutions of higher learning and parochial elementary and secondary schools. . . . [C]ollege students are less impressionable and less susceptible to religious indoctrination. . . . Since religious indoctrination is not a substantial

---

39. However, the Court upheld an exemption solely for religious groups from Title VII's prohibition of employment discrimination based on religion. *See* Corporation of the Presiding Bishop of the Church of Jesus Christ of Latter-Day Saints v. Amos, 483 U.S. 327 (1987).

F. When Can Government Give Aid to Religion?

purpose or activity of these church-related colleges and universities, there is less likelihood than in primary and secondary schools that religion will permeate the area of secular education."

Justices Douglas, Black, Marshall, and Brennan dissented. They argued that direct government financial aid to religious institutions, including at the college and university level, violates the Establishment Clause. Justice Douglas said that "even a small amount coming out of the pocket of taxpayers and going into the coffers of a church was not in keeping with our constitutional ideal."

In Hunt v. McNair, 413 U.S. 734 (1973), the Court followed the same reasoning as in *Tilton* and allowed the use of state revenue bonds for religious colleges and universities. A state's Educational Facilities Authority issued bonds to finance the construction of facilities in colleges and universities in the state. Beneficiaries included religious schools, but they were not allowed to use the funds for the construction of facilities to be used for religious activities and the bonds had to be repaid by the schools. The Court relied on *Tilton* to uphold the aid, again emphasizing that the use of the funds was restricted, that the money was available to secular and religious schools, and that the institution was not permeated with religious instruction in the same way as an elementary or secondary school.

In Roemer v. Board of Public Works, 426 U.S. 736 (1976), the distinction between colleges and universities as compared to elementary and secondary schools was even clearer as the Court upheld a program of direct state financial aid to religious colleges and universities. Maryland created a program whereby it provided for grants to private colleges and universities for students and universities. The aid was calculated at 15 percent of the amount per student that the state spent in the public college system. Religious schools, except for seminaries, were allowed to receive the aid. The Court, by a five-to-four margin, but without a majority opinion, upheld the program.

Justice Blackmun's plurality opinion invoked *Tilton* and *Hunt* and found that the requirements of the *Lemon* test were met. Justice Blackmun said that the "purpose of Maryland's aid program is the secular one of supporting private higher education generally, as an economic alternative to a wholly public system." Moreover, he said that the "institutions are not so permeated by religion that the secular side cannot be separated from the sectarian."[40] Therefore, the effect was not to advance religion because the state law required that "state funds not be used to support specifically religious activity."[41] Finally, the plurality opinion concluded that there was not excessive entanglement because there was minimal state oversight required and because "the danger of political divisiveness is substantially less when the aided institution is not an elementary or secondary school, but a college, whose student constituency is not local but diverse and widely dispersed." Justices White and Rehnquist concurred in the judgment and criticized the *Lemon* test but agreed that this aid was not motivated by a religious purpose and did not have a primary effect of advancing religion.

---

40. *Roemer*, 426 U.S. at 759 (citation omitted).
41. *Id.*

AID TO RELIGIOUS INSTITUTIONS OTHER THAN SCHOOLS

Relatively few cases have involved attempts by the government to give assistance to religious institutions other than schools. The decisions thus far indicate that the Court is more likely to be deferential to the government—as in reviewing aid to colleges and universities—than it is to be more vigilant in its review—as it is concerning aid to elementary and secondary schools.

In Bradfield v. Roberts, 175 U.S. 291 (1899), the Court upheld the constitutionality of the government building a new facility for a church-affiliated hospital. The Court allowed the government aid to a hospital operated by members of the Roman Catholic Church under the auspices of the Church. The Court noted that the hospital did not discriminate based on religion and said that it was "wholly immaterial" that a religious group ran the hospital.

More recently, in Bowen v. Kendrick, 487 U.S. 549 (1988), the Court deemed constitutional the Adolescent Family Life Act, which provided for grants to organizations to provide counseling and care to pregnant adolescents and their parents, and also to provide counseling to prevent adolescent sexual activity. The law specifically authorized receipt of grants by religious, as well as nonreligious, organizations. The law prohibited the use of any federal funds for family planning services, for abortion counseling, or for abortions.

Chief Justice Rehnquist wrote for the majority in the five-to-four decision and applied the *Lemon* test to uphold the law. Rehnquist said that the law "was motivated primarily, if not entirely, by a legitimate secular purpose—the elimination or reduction of social and economic problems caused by teenage sexuality, pregnancy, and parenthood."

The Court also said that the law did not have an impermissible effect of advancing religion, even though it specifically encouraged organizations to allow religious groups to play a role. The Court concluded that the law did not favor or disfavor religious groups compared to secular ones and thus was permissible. Rehnquist stressed that the statute was successful in its "maintenance of a course of neutrality among religions and between religion and nonreligion." The Court said that it was "important that the aid is made available regardless of whether it will ultimately flow to a secular or sectarian institution." In fact, the Court invoked Bradfield v. Roberts as establishing the proposition that "religious institutions are [not] disabled by the First Amendment from participating in publicly sponsored social welfare programs."

Finally, the Court said that there was not excessive entanglement with religion. Although the law did not require monitoring by the government, the Court said that most of the cases that had applied the entanglement test had involved elementary and secondary schools that "were pervasively sectarian and had as a substantial purpose the inculcation of religious values." The Court said that "[h]ere, by contrast, there is no reason to assume that the religious organizations which may receive grants are pervasively sectarian in the same sense as the Court has held parochial schools to be."

Justice Blackmun wrote a dissenting opinion joined by Justices Brennan, Marshall, and Stevens. Blackmun focused on the act's subsidizing religious teaching. He said that the "statute encouraged the use of public funds for such instruction, by giving religious groups a central pedagogical and counseling role without imposing any restraints on the sectarian quality of the participation." Blackmun particularly objected to the Court's claim that the groups were not

F. When Can Government Give Aid to Religion?

pervasively sectarian; he questioned both the relevance of this factor and the characterization of the particular groups that would receive funds. Blackmun argued that the law clearly had the effect of advancing religion: "Government funds are paying for religious organizations to teach and counsel impressionable adolescents on a highly sensitive subject of considerable religious significance, often on the premises of a church or parochial school and without any effort to remove religious symbols from the sites."

Bowen is a relatively narrow decision. What types of aid the government can provide to religious institutions and under what circumstance remain to be resolved.

TABLE OF CASES

Italics indicate principal cases. Alphabetization is letter-by-letter (e.g., "Nationalist Socialist Party" precedes "National Right to Work Comm.").

Abington Sch. Dist. v. Schempp. *See* School Dist. of Abington Twp. v. Schempp
Abood v. Detroit Bd. of Educ., 431 U.S. 209 (1977), 446-456, 458-459
Abrams v. United States, 250 U.S. 616 (1919), 7, *145*
Adderley v. Florida, 385 U.S. 39 (1966), 366, 405, 408
Agency for Int'l Dev. v. Alliance for Open Soc'y Int'l, 140 S. Ct. 2082 (2020), 136
Agency for Int'l Dev. v. Alliance for Open Soc'y Int'l, Inc., 570 U.S. 205 (2013), 135-136
Agostini v. Felton, 521 U.S. 203 (1997), 589, 594, 654, 655, 656, 657, 658, 660, 672
Aguilar v. Felton, 473 U.S. 402 (1985), 589, 653, 654
Alabama; NAACP v., 357 U.S. 449 (1958), 11
Alabama ex rel. Patterson; NAACP v., 357 U.S. 449 (1958), 441, *443*
Alexander v. United States, 509 U.S. 444 (1993), 66, *83*
Allegheny, County of, v. American Civil Liberties Union, Greater Pittsburgh Chapter, 492 U.S. 573 (1989), 581, 583, *584*, 607, 624, 643
Alvarez; United States v., 567 U.S. 709 (2012), 20
Amalgamated Food Emps. Union Local 590 v. Logan Valley Plaza, Inc., 391 U.S. 308 (1968), 409
American Booksellers Ass'n, Inc. v. Hudnut, 771 F.2d 323 (7th Cir. 1985), 187, 206, 207
American Legion v. American Humanist Association, 139 S. Ct. 2067 (2019), 592, 624, *644*
American Library Ass'n; United States v., 539 U.S. 194 (2003), 46
Anastaplo, In re, 366 U.S. 82 (1961), 443
Aptheker v. Secretary of State, 378 U.S. 500 (1964), 442
Arizona Free Enterprise Club's Freedom Club PAC v. Bennett, 564 U.S. 721 (2011), *357*
Arkansas Educ. Television Comm'n v. Forbes, 523 U.S. 666 (1998), 352, 406-407, 408
Arkansas Writers' Project, Inc. v. Ragland, 481 U.S. 221 (1987), 476
Ashcroft v. ACLU, 542 U.S. 656 (2004), 220, 234
Ashcroft v. Free Speech Coalition, 535 U.S. 234 (2002), 207, 210-211
Associated Press v. NLRB, 301 U.S. 103 (1937), 477-478, 482
Associated Press v. United States, 326 U.S. 1 (1945), 477, 478
Associated Press v. Walker, 388 U.S. 130 (1967), 294
Austin v. Michigan State Chamber of Commerce, 494 U.S. 652 (1990), 339, 340, 343-346, 350-351, 353-356

Baggett v. Bullitt, 377 U.S. 360 (1964), 59
Baird v. State Bar, 401 U.S. 1 (1971), 443
Ballard; United States v., 322 U.S. 78 (1944), *510*
Bantam Books, Inc. v. Sullivan, 372 U.S. 58 (1963), 66, 136-137
Barnes v. Glen Theatre, Inc., 501 U.S. 560 (1991), 215-216, 217-219, 220
Bartnicki v. Vopper, 532 U.S. 514 (2001), 312
Bates v. State Bar of Ariz., 433 U.S. 350 (1977), 268, 273, 285, 286
Beard v. Banks, 548 U.S. 521 (2006), 415, 417
Beauharnais v. Illinois, 343 U.S. 250 (1952), 187-188
Bell v. Wolfish, 441 U.S. 520 (1979), 415
Bethel School District No. 403 v. Fraser, 478 U.S. 675 (1986), 420, *421*, 424, 427, 431
Bigelow v. Virginia, 421 U.S. 809 (1975), 252, 253
Blount v. Rizzi, 400 U.S. 410 (1971), 94
Board of Airport Comm'rs of L.A. v. Jews for Jesus, Inc., 482 U.S. 569 (1987), 60, 64, 65
Board of Dirs. of Rotary Int'l v. Rotary Club of Duarte, 481 U.S. 537 (1987), 465, 470
Board of Educ., Island Trees Union Free Sch. Dist. No. 26 v. Pico, 457 U.S. 853 (1982), 432
Board of Educ. of Cent. Sch. Dist. No. 1 v. Allen, 392 U.S. 236 (1968), 658
Board of Educ. of Kiryas Joel Vill. Sch. Dist. v. Grumet, 512 U.S. 687 (1994), 589-590, 591
Board of Educ. of Westside Cmty. Schs. v. Mergens, 496 U.S. 226 (1990), 593, 596, 597
Board of Regents of the University of Wisconsin System v. Southworth, 529 U.S. 217 (2000), 131, *457*
Board of Trs. of State Univ. of N.Y. v. Fox, 492 U.S. 469 (1989), 269, 271, 278
Bob Jones Univ. v. United States, 461 U.S. 574 (1983), 519
Boerne, City of, v. Flores, 521 U.S. 507 (1997), 576
Bolger v. Youngs Drug Products Corp., 463 U.S. 60 (1983), *258*, 259, 269
Bond v. Floyd, 385 U.S. 116 (1966), 160
Boos v. Barry, 485 U.S. 312 (1988), 41
Bose Corp. v. Consumers Union of United States, Inc., 466 U.S. 485 (1984), 292
Bowen v. Kendrick, 487 U.S. 549 (1988), 684-685
Bowen v. Roy, 476 U.S. 693 (1986), 520, 523
Boy Scouts of America v. Dale, 530 U.S. 640 (2000), 465, *466*
Bradfield v. Roberts, 175 U.S. 291 (1899), 684
Brady v. Maryland, 373 U.S. 83 (1963), 439
Brandenburg v. Ohio, 395 U.S. 444 (1969), 154, *161*, 162-163, 192, 430
Branzburg v. Hayes, 408 U.S. 665 (1972), *480*, 486-487

Branzburg v. Meigs (unreported), 480
Braunfeld v. Brown, 366 U.S. 599 (1961), 515, 519
Bridges v. California, 314 U.S. 252 (1941), 154
Briggs v. Elliott. *See* Brown v. Board of Educ. (1954)
Broadrick v. Oklahoma, 413 U.S. 601 (1973), 60, 61
Brown v. Board of Education, 347 U.S. 483 (1954), 673
Brown v. Entertainment Merchants Association, 564 U.S. 786 (2011), *244*
Brown v. Glines, 444 U.S. 348 (1980), 412
Brown v. Louisiana, 383 U.S. 131 (1966), 389
Brown v. Oklahoma, 408 U.S. 914 (1972), 177
Brown v. Socialist Workers '74 Campaign Comm. (Ohio), 459 U.S. 87 (1982), 446
Buckley v. American Constitutional Law Found., Inc., 525 U.S. 182 (1999), 122
Buckley v. Valeo, 424 U.S. 1 (1976), *325*, 332-335, 339, 342, 343, 345-346, 357, 363-364, 445-446
Burson v. Freeman, 504 U.S. 191 (1992), 352, 373
Burwell v. Hobby Lobby Stores, Inc., 573 U.S. 682 (2014), 577
Butchers' Benevolent Ass'n of New Orleans v. Crescent City Live-Stock Landing & Slaughter-House Co. *See* Slaughter-House Cases
Button; NAACP v., 371 U.S. 415 (1963), 58

Cable News Network, Inc. v. Noriega, 498 U.S. 976 (1990), 82
Caldwell; United States v., 434 F.2d 1081 (9th Cir. 1970), 481
California Med. Ass'n v. FEC, 453 U.S. 182 (1981), 333
Cantwell v. Connecticut, 310 U.S. 296 (1940), 154, 185, 503, 515, 516, 522, 526
Capitol Square Review & Advisory Bd. v. Pinette, 515 U.S. 753 (1995), 581-582
Carey v. Brown, 447 U.S. 455 (1980), 29, 373, 377
Carroll v. President & Comm'rs of Princess Anne Cnty., 393 U.S. 175 (1968), 94
Central Hudson Gas & Electric Corp. v. Public Service Commission of New York, 447 U.S. 557 (1980), 257, 258, 264, 265, *266*, 269, 271, 272, 278, 279-282, 285
Chaplinsky v. New Hampshire, 315 U.S. 568 (1942), *173*, 174, 176, 177, 179, 180, 182, 226, 229
Christian Legal Society Chapter of the University of California, Hastings College of the Law v. Martinez, 561 U.S. 661 (2010), 370, 392, 393, *394*
Church of the Lukumi Babalu Aye, Inc. v. Hialeah, 508 U.S. 520 (1993), 529, 540, 627
Cincinnati, City of, v. Discovery Network, Inc., 507 U.S. 410 (1993), 42
Citizens Publ'g Co. v. United States, 394 U.S. 131 (1969), 477
Citizens United v. Federal Election Commission, 558 U.S. 310 (2010), 335, *340*, 446
City Council of. *See name of city*
City of. *See name of city*
Claiborne Hardware Co.; NAACP v., 458 U.S. 886 (1982), 163
Clark v. Community for Creative Non-Violence, 468 U.S. 288 (1984), 388, 389
Coates v. City of Cincinnati, 402 U.S. 611 (1971), 58, 65
Cohen v. California, 403 U.S. 15 (1971), 175, *223*, 226, 227
Cohen v. Cowles Media Co., 501 U.S. 664 (1991), 216, *478*
Collin v. Smith, 578 F.2d 1197 (7th Cir. 1978), 187, 188
Committee for Pub. Educ. & Religious Liberty v. Regan, 444 U.S. 646 (1980), 654
Committee for Pub. Educ. v. Nyquist, 413 U.S. 756 (1973), 594, 665-666
Communist Party of Ind. v. Whitcomb, 414 U.S. 441 (1974), 442
Connally v. General Constr. Co., 269 U.S. 385 (1926), 57
Connick v. Myers, 461 U.S. 138 (1983), 434, 437
Consolidated Edison Co. of N.Y., Inc. v. Public Serv. Comm'n of N.Y., 447 U.S. 530 (1980), 21, 40
Corporation of the Presiding Bishop of the Church of Jesus Christ of Latter-Day Saints v. Amos, 483 U.S. 327 (1987), 593-594, 682
County of. *See name of county*
Cox Broadcasting Corp. v. Cohn, 420 U.S. 469 (1975), *309*, 311
Cox v. Louisiana, 379 U.S. 536 (1965), 186, 389
Cox v. New Hampshire, 312 U.S. 569 (1941), 92, 389, 390
Craig v. Harney, 331 U.S. 367 (1947), 493
Crane v. Arizona Republic, 972 F.2d 1511 (9th Cir. 1992), 292
Curtis Publ'g Co. v. Butts, 388 U.S. 130 (1967), 294
Cutter v. Wilkinson, 544 U.S. 709 (2005), 578

Dallas, City of, v. Stanglin, 490 U.S. 19 (1989), 314, 441
Davis v. Federal Election Comm'n, 554 U.S. 724 (2008), 359-360
Davis v. Massachusetts, 167 U.S. 43 (1897), 365, 367
Dawson v. Delaware, 503 U.S. 159 (1992), 188
Debs v. United States, 249 U.S. 211 (1919), 142, *144*, 145, 147
DeJonge v. Oregon, 299 U.S. 353 (1937), 154
Dennis v. United States, 341 U.S. 494 (1951), *155*, 160, 162, 163
Denver Area Educ. Telecomms. Consortium, Inc. v. FCC, 518 U.S. 727 (1996), 234, 236
Dun & Bradstreet, Inc. v. Greenmoss Builders, Inc., 472 U.S. 749 (1985), 300, 301-302

Edenfield v. Fane, 507 U.S. 761 (1993), 269, 274, 275
Edge Broad. Co.; United States v., 509 U.S. 418 (1993), 275, 285
Edwards v. Aguillard, 482 U.S. 578 (1987), 592, 593, 614
Edwards v. South Carolina, 372 U.S. 229 (1963), 186
Eichman; United States v., 496 U.S. 310 (1990), 325
Elfbrandt v. Russell, 384 U.S. 11 (1966), 442

Table of Cases

Employment Division, Department of Human Resources of Oregon v. Smith, 494 U.S. 872 (1990), 216, 515, 516, 519, *521*, 529-530, 537, 540, 546, 576
Engel v. Vitale, 370 U.S. 421 (1962), *599*, 601, 602, 604
Epperson v. Arkansas, 393 U.S. 97 (1968), 614
Erie, City of, v. Pap's A.M., 529 U.S. 277 (2000), 42, *216*, 220
Erznoznik v. City of Jacksonville, 422 U.S. 205 (1975), 220-221
Espinoza v. Montana Department of Revenue, 140 S. Ct. 2246 (2020), 549, *563*
Estes v. Texas, 381 U.S. 532 (1965), 79
Euclid, Village of, v. Ambler Realty Co., 272 U.S. 365 (1926), 229
Everson v. Board of Educ., 330 U.S. 1 (1947), 503, 505, 507, 554, 557, 579, 653, 655, 675, 678, 679

FCC v. *See name of opposing party*
FEC v. *See name of opposing party*
Feiner v. New York, 340 U.S. 315 (1951), 185-186
First National Bank of Boston v. Bellotti, 435 U.S. 765 (1978), *336*, 339, 343, 345-346, 348, 352
Fish v. State, 124 Ga. 416 (1905), 177
Fiske v. Kansas, 274 U.S. 380 (1927), 154
Florida Bar v. Went for It, Inc., 515 U.S. 618 (1995), 269, 274, 280
Florida Star v. B.J.F., 491 U.S. 524 (1989), 96, 311
Forsyth Cnty., Ga. v. Nationalist Movement, 505 U.S. 123 (1992), 94, 390
44 Liquormart, Inc. v. Rhode Island, 517 U.S. 484 (1996), 270, 275, *276*
Fox Television Stations, Inc.; FCC v., 567 U.S. 239 (2012), 230
Frazee v. Illinois Emp't Sec. Dep't, 489 U.S. 829 (1989), 509, 513, 518
Freedman v. Maryland, 380 U.S. 51 (1965), 94, 95
Friedman v. Rogers, 440 U.S. 1 (1979), 272-273
Frisby v. Schultz, 487 U.S. 474 (1988), 373, 375
Frohwerk v. United States, 249 U.S. 204 (1919), 142, *143*, 145, 146, 147
FW/PBS, Inc. v. City of Dallas, 493 U.S. 215 (1990), 94

Gannett v. DePasquale, 443 U.S. 368 (1979), 489, 490, 493, 495
Garcetti v. Ceballos, 547 U.S. 410 (2006), 433, *434*, 440, 450, 451
Garrison v. Louisiana, 379 U.S. 64 (1964), 291, 293
Gentile v. State Bar of Nev., 501 U.S. 1030 (1991), 83
Gertz v. Welch, 418 U.S. 323 (1974), 292, 293, 294, *295*, 300
Ginsberg v. New York, 390 U.S. 629 (1968), 234, 245, 249, 251
Ginzburg v. United States, 383 U.S. 463 (1966), 199
Gitlow v. New York, 268 U.S. 652 (1925), *148*, 154, 160, 163
Givhan v. Western Line Consol. Sch. Dist., 439 U.S. 410 (1979), 437
Globe Newspaper Co. v. Superior Court, 457 U.S. 596 (1982), 494

Goldman v. Weinberger, 475 U.S. 503 (1986), 520, 523
Gonzales v. O Centro Espirita Beneficente Unia Do, 546 U.S. 418 (2006), 576
Gooding v. Wilson, 405 U.S. 518 (1972), 62, 63, *176*, 177
Good News Club v. Milford Cent. Sch., 533 U.S. 98 (2001), 393, 597
Grace; United States v., 461 U.S. 171 (1983), 389
Grand Rapids Sch. Dist. v. Ball, 473 U.S. 373 (1985), 589, 594, 653
Grayned v. Rockford, 408 U.S. 104 (1972), 388, 389
Greater New Orleans Broad. Ass'n, Inc. v. United States, 527 U.S. 173 (1999), 271, 285
Greece, Town of, v. Galloway, 572 U.S. 565 (2014), 583, *615*
Greer v. Spock, 424 U.S. 828 (1976), 405, 408
Gregory v. City of Chi., 394 U.S. 111 (1969), 186
Grosjean v. American Press Co., 297 U.S. 233 (1936), 472, 473, 476

Hague v. Committee for Industrial Organization, 307 U.S. 496 (1939), *366*, 369
Hamling v. United States, 418 U.S. 87 (1974), 204
Hazelwood School District v. Kuhlmeier, 484 U.S. 260 (1988), 420, 423, 424, 431
Heffron v. International Soc'y for Krishna Consciousness, 452 U.S. 640 (1981), 374, 389
Hernandez v. Commissioner, 490 U.S. 680 (1989), 589
Hess v. Indiana, 414 U.S. 105 (1973), 163
Hill v. Colorado, 530 U.S. 703 (2000), *374*, 380, 385, 389
Hobbie v. Unemployment Appeals Comm'n of Fla., 480 U.S. 136 (1987), 518
Hoffman Estates, Village of, v. Flipside, Hoffman Estates, Inc., 455 U.S. 489 (1982), 62
Holder v. Humanitarian Law Project, 561 U.S. 1 (2010), *163*
Hosanna-Tabor Evangelical Lutheran Church & Sch. v. EEOC, 565 U.S. 171 (2012), 504, 540, 541, 543-548
Houchins v. KQED, 438 U.S. 1 (1978), 415, *496*
Houston, Tex., City of, v. Hill, 482 U.S. 451 (1987), 61, 178
Hudgens v. National Labor Relations Bd., 424 U.S. 507 (1976), 409
Hunt v. McNair, 413 U.S. 734 (1973), 683
Hunt v. Washington State Apple Adver. Comm'n, 432 U.S. 333 (1977), 627
Hurley v. Irish-Am. Gay, Lesbian, & Bisexual Grp. of Bos., Inc., 515 U.S. 557 (1995), 115, 116, 465
Hustler Magazine v. Falwell, 485 U.S. 46 (1988), 96, *302*
Hutchinson v. Proxmire, 443 U.S. 111 (1979), 300

Iancu v. Brunetti, 139 S. Ct. 2294 (2019), 28
Ibanez v. Florida Dep't of Bus. & Prof'l Regulation, 512 U.S. 136 (1994), 287
In re. *See name of party*
International Soc'y for Krishna Consciousness, Inc. v. Lee, 505 U.S. 672 (1992), 406, 408

Jacobellis v. Ohio, 378 U.S. 184 (1964), 199, 201
Janus v. American Federation of State, County, and Municipal Employees, Council 31, 138 S. Ct. 2448 (2018), 112, *447*, 456
Jenkins v. Georgia, 418 U.S. 153 (1974), 204
Johannes v. Livestock Mktg. Ass'n, 544 U.S. 550 (2005), 112
John Doe No. 1 v. Reed, 561 U.S. 186 (2010), 122
Jones v. North Carolina Prisoners' Union, 433 U.S. 119 (1977), 413, 415

Keller v. State Bar of Cal., 496 U.S. 1 (1990), 456, 458-459
Keyishian v. Board of Regents, 385 U.S. 589 (1967), 443
Kingsley Int'l Pictures Corp. v. Regents, 360 U.S. 684 (1959), 205
Kokinda; United States v., 497 U.S. 720 (1990), 406, 408
Kolender v. Lawson, 461 U.S. 352 (1983), 57
Konigsberg v. State Bar of Cal., 366 U.S. 36 (1961), 5, 443
Kovacs v. Cooper, 336 U.S. 77 (1949), 388, 389
Kunz v. New York, 340 U.S. 290 (1951), 93

Lakewood, City of, v. Plain Dealer Publ'g Co., 486 U.S. 750 (1988), 92
Lamb's Chapel v. Center Moriches Union Free Sch. Dist., 508 U.S. 384 (1993), 393, 505, 591, 596, 597
Landmark Commc'ns, Inc. v. Virginia, 435 U.S. 829 (1978), 312
Lane v. Franks, 573 U.S. 228 (2014), 440
Larson v. Valente, 456 U.S. 228 (1982), 589-590
Law Students Civil Rights Research Council v. Wadmond, 401 U.S. 154 (1971), 443
League of Women Voters of Cal.; FCC v., 468 U.S. 364 (1984), 124, 127
Leathers v. Medlock, 499 U.S. 439 (1991), 476-477
Lee; United States v., 455 U.S. 252 (1982), 515, 519, 522
Lee v. Weisman, 505 U.S. 577 (1992), 503, 583, 584, *602*, 611, 612, 613
Legal Services Corp. v. Velazquez, 531 U.S. 533 (2001), 124, *129*
Lehman v. Shaker Heights, 418 U.S. 298 (1974), 393
Lemon v. Kurtzman, 403 U.S. 602 (1971), 504, 589, *590*, 591-597, 604, 614, 626-627, 632, 633, 634, 646, 648, 650, 653, 655, 656, 665, 682, 683, 684
Levitt v. Community for Pub. Educ., 413 U.S. 472 (1973), 654
Lewis v. City of New Orleans, 408 U.S. 913 (1972), 177
Linmark Assocs. v. Township of Willingboro, 431 U.S. 85 (1977), 276
Littleton, Colo., City of, v. Z.J. Gifts D-4, L.L.C., 541 U.S. 774 (2004), 95
Lloyd Corp. v. Tanner, 407 U.S. 551 (1972), 409
Lochner v. New York, 198 U.S. 45 (1905), 109, 264, 266
Locke v. Davey, 540 U.S. 714 (2004), 548, *549*, 553, 555-557, 560-561, 565-566, 572-573, 575
Lorillard Tobacco Co. v. Reilly, 533 U.S. 525 (2001), *278*

Los Angeles, City of, v. Alameda Books, Inc., 535 U.S. 425 (2002), 215
Los Angeles, Members of the City Council of, v. Taxpayers for Vincent, 466 U.S. 789 (1984), 38, 60-61
Lovell v. City of Griffin, Ga., 303 U.S. 444 (1938), 85, 390
Lynch v. Donnelly, 465 U.S. 668 (1984), 581, 585-586, 588, 591, 592
Lyng v. Northwest Indian Cemetery Protective Ass'n, 485 U.S. 439 (1988), 520, 523
Lyons v. State, 94 Ga. App. 570 (1956), 177

Madsen v. Women's Health Ctr., Inc., 512 U.S. 753 (1994), 375, 385
Maher v. Roe, 432 U.S. 464 (1977), 126, 134
Marbury v. Madison, 5 U.S. (1 Cranch) 137 (1803), 132
Marsh v. Alabama, 326 U.S. 501 (1946), 409
Marsh v. Chambers, 463 U.S. 783 (1983), 580, 591, 615, 616-619, 621, 623-624, 632
Martin v. City of Struthers, 319 U.S. 141 (1943), 88, 90
Masses Publ'g Co. v. Patten, 244 F. 535 (S.D.N.Y.), *rev'd*, 246 F. 24 (2d Cir. 1917) 142
Masson v. New Yorker Magazine, Inc., 501 U.S. 496 (1991), 293
Masterpiece Cake Shop, Ltd. v. Colorado Civil Rights Commission, 138 S. Ct. 1719 (2018), *530*, 540
Matal v. Tam, 137 S. Ct. 1744 (2017), *22*
McCollum v. Board of Educ., 333 U.S. 203 (1948), 598-599
McConnell v. Federal Election Comm'n, 540 U.S. 93 (2003), 340, 346, 350-351, 353-354
McCreary County v. American Civil Liberties Union of Kentucky, 545 U.S. 844 (2005), 592, *624*, 637, 639, 641
McCullen v. Coakley, 573 U.S. 464 (2014), 374, *379*
McCutcheon v. Federal Election Comm'n, 572 U.S. 185 (2014), 335
McGowan v. Maryland, 366 U.S. 420 (1961), 592
McIntyre v. Ohio Elections Commission, 514 U.S. 334 (1995), 89, *118*, 122
McKinley v. Baden, 777 F.2d 1017 (5th Cir. 1985), 292
Meek v. Pittenger, 421 U.S. 349 (1975), 654, 656, 660, 661, 678
Meese v. Keene, 481 U.S. 465 (1987), 136-137
Members of the City Council of L.A. v. Taxpayers for Vincent, 466 U.S. 789 (1984), 38, 60
Memoirs v. Massachusetts, 383 U.S. 413 (1966), 199, 203
Miami Herald Publ'g Co. v. Tornillo, 418 U.S. 241 (1974), 116, 488
Milkovich v. Lorain Journal Co., 497 U.S. 1 (1990), 293
Miller v. California, 413 U.S. 15 (1973), 182, 199, 201, *202*, 203, 204, 208-210, 241, 249
Mills v. Alabama, 384 U.S. 214 (1966), 337
Minneapolis Star & Tribune Co. v. Minnesota Commissioner of Revenue, 460 U.S. 575 (1983), *473*, 476
Minnesota Voters Alliance v. Mansky, 138 S. Ct. 1876 (2018), 370, 373
Mishkin v. New York, 383 U.S. 502 (1966), 199

Mitchell v. Helms, 530 U.S. 793 (2000), 559, *654*, 664-665, 668, 670
Monitor Patriot Co. v. Roy, 401 U.S. 265 (1971), 291
Morse v. Frederick, 551 U.S. 393 (2007), 420, *424*, 431
Mt. Healthy City Sch. Dist. Bd. of Educ. v. Doyle, 429 U.S. 274 (1977), 433
Mueller v. Allen, 463 U.S. 388 (1983), 657, 658, 665, 668-670, 671, 676
Murdock v. Pennsylvania, 319 U.S. 105 (1943), 88, 522

NAACP v. *See name of opposing party*
National Conservative PAC; FEC v., 470 U.S. 480 (1985), 333
National Endowment for the Arts v. Finley, 524 U.S. 569 (1998), *43*, 134
National Federation of Family and Life Advocates v. Becerra, 138 S. Ct. 2361 (2018), *101*
National Socialist Party of Am. v. Village of Skokie, 432 U.S. 43 (1977), 94, 188
National Right to Work Comm.; FEC v., 459 U.S. 197 (1982), 349
National Treasury Employees Union; United States v., 513 U.S. 454 (1995), *97*
NCAA v. *See name of opposing party*
Near v. State of Minnesota ex rel. Olson, 283 U.S. 697 (1931), *68*, 72, 73, 80, 83, 84
Nebraska Press Association v. Stuart, 427 U.S. 539 (1976), 65, *78*, 82, 83, 490
New York Times Co. v. Sullivan, 376 U.S. 254 (1964), 5, 7, 41, 96, 188, 258, 272, 287, *288*, 291-292, 294, 295, 296, 297, 298, 302, 304, 305
New York Times Co. v. United States, 403 U.S. 713 (1971), 65, *71*, 77, 83
New York v. Ferber, 458 U.S. 747 (1982), 60, 61, 182, *207*, 210-211, 223, 239, 243
Niemotko v. Maryland, 340 U.S. 268 (1951), 371
Nixon v. Shrink Mo. Gov't PAC, 528 U.S. 377 (2000), 334
Noriega; United States v., 752 F. Supp. 1032 (S.D. Fla.), aff'd, 917 F.2d 1543 (11th Cir.), cert. denied sub nom. Cable News Network, Inc. v. Noriega, 498 U.S. 976 (1990) 82
Noto v. United States, 367 U.S. 290 (1961), 160, 162, 442

Obergefell v. Hodges, 576 U.S. 644 (2015), 533
O'Brien; United States v., 391 U.S. 367 (1968), 218, 315, *316*, 319, 321, 326, 333
Ohralik v. Ohio State Bar Ass'n, 436 U.S. 447 (1978), 273, 274, 275
Oklahoma Press Publ'g Co. v. Walling, 327 U.S. 186 (1946), 478
Oklahoma Publ'g Co. v. District Court, 430 U.S. 308 (1977), 82
Olmstead v. United States, 277 U.S. 438 (1928), 375
Osborne v. Ohio, 495 U.S. 103 (1990), 62, 222
Our Lady of Guadalupe School v. Morrissey-Berru, 140 S. Ct. 2049 (2020), *541*
Overton v. Bazzetta, 539 U.S. 126 (2003), 416

Pacifica Foundation; FCC v., 438 U.S. 726 (1978), 227, 230, 232, 234, 235
Pacific Gas & Elec. Co. v. Public Util. Comm'n of Cal., 475 U.S. 1 (1986), 116
Packingham v. North Carolina, 137 S. Ct. 1730 (2017), 63
Papachristou v. Jacksonville, 405 U.S. 156 (1972), 57
Papish v. Board of Curators of the Univ. of Mo., 410 U.S. 667 (1973), 420, 431
Pappas, In re, 402 U.S. 942 (1971), 481
Paris Adult Theatre I v. Slaton, 413 U.S. 49 (1973), *199*, 204, 205, 221
Parker v. Levy, 417 U.S. 733 (1974), *410*, 412
Peel v. Attorney Registration & Disciplinary Comm'n of Ill., 496 U.S. 91 (1990), 287
Pell v. Procunier, 417 U.S. 817 (1974), 415, 496, 497
Penthouse Int'l, Ltd. v. Meese, 939 F.2d 1011 (D.C. Cir. 1991), 137
Perry Educ. Ass'n v. Perry Local Educators' Ass'n, 460 U.S. 37 (1983), 22, 369-370, 371
Perry v. Sindermann, 408 U.S. 593 (1972), 123
Philadelphia Newspapers, Inc. v. Hepps, 475 U.S. 767 (1986), 301
Pickering v. Board of Educ. of Twp. High Sch. Dist. 205, Will Cnty., Ill., 391 U.S. 563 (1968), 433, 435, 438-440, 450, 451, 454
Pierce v. Society of Sisters of the Holy Names of Jesus & Mary, 268 U.S. 510 (1925), 523
Pittsburgh Press Co. v. Pittsburgh Comm'n on Human Relations, 413 U.S. 376 (1973), 271-272
Planned Parenthood of Se. Pa. v. Casey, 505 U.S. 833 (1992), 105, 110, 350
Playboy Entm't Grp.; United States v., 529 U.S. 803 (2000), 220, 236
Pleasant Grove City, Utah v. Summum, 555 U.S. 460 (2009), *47*, 52, 53, 54
Police Department of the City of Chicago v. Mosley, 408 U.S. 92 (1972), 13, *371*, 373
Pope v. Illinois, 481 U.S. 497 (1987), 204
Posadas de P.R. Assocs. v. Tourism Co. of P.R., 478 U.S. 328 (1986), 275, 284
Poulos v. New Hampshire, 345 U.S. 395 (1953), 67-68
Press-Enterprise Co. v. Superior Court, 464 U.S. 501 (1984), 494-495
Press-Enterprise Co. v. Superior Court, 478 U.S. 1 (1986), 495
Primus, In re, 436 U.S. 412 (1978), 273, 274
Prince v. Massachusetts, 321 U.S. 158 (1944), 208
Procunier v. Martinez, 416 U.S. 396 (1974), 9, 415
Progressive, Inc.; United States v., 467 F. Supp. 990 (W.D. Wis. 1979), 77
PruneYard Shopping Ctr. v. Robins, 447 U.S. 74 (1980), 116, 409

Ramos v. Louisiana, 140 S. Ct. 1390 (2020), 569-570
Randall v. Sorrell, 548 U.S. 230 (2006), 334
R.A.V. v. City of St. Paul, Minnesota, 505 U.S. 377 (1992), 13, 21, 139, *178*, 184, 188, 193
Red Lion Broad. Co. v. FCC, 395 U.S. 367 (1969), 487-488

Redrup v. New York, 386 U.S. 767 (1967), 199
Reed v. Town of Gilbert, 576 U.S. 155 (2015), *14*
Regan v. Taxation with Representation of Wash., 461 U.S. 540 (1983), 123, 124, 127
Reidel; United States v., 402 U.S. 351 (1971), 222
Reno v. American Civil Liberties Union, 521 U.S. 844 (1997), 230, *231*, 281
Renton, City of, v. Playtime Theatres, Inc., 475 U.S. 41 (1986), *39*, 41-42, 180, 214, 216, 218, 220, 386
Republican Party of Minn. v. White, 536 U.S. 765 (2002), 29, 31-32, 36
Reynolds v. United States, 98 U.S. (8 Otto) 145 (1878), 515, 516, 523
Rhode Island v. Massachusetts, 37 U.S. 657 (1838), 121
Richmond Newspapers v. Virginia, 448 U.S. 555 (1980), *489*, 494
R.M.J., In re, 455 U.S. 191 (1982), 286
Roberts v. United States Jaycees, 468 U.S. 609 (1984), 441, *460*, 465, 470
Roemer v. Board of Pub. Works, 426 U.S. 736 (1976), 683
Rosenberger v. Rector & Visitors of the Univ. of Va., 515 U.S. 819 (1995), 131, 134, 504, 505, 597, 611
Rosenblatt v. Baer, 383 U.S. 75 (1966), 292
Rosenbloom v. Metromedia, Inc., 403 U.S. 29 (1971), 294, 298, 300
Rosenfeld v. New Jersey, 408 U.S. 901 (1972), 177
Roth v. United States, 354 U.S. 476 (1957), 139, *197*, 199, 201-202, 204, 221-222
Rubin v. Coors Brewing Co., 514 U.S. 476 (1995), 269, 270, 276
Rumsfeld v. Forum for Academic & Institutional Rights, Inc., 547 U.S. 47 (2006), *113*
Rust v. Sullivan, 500 U.S. 173 (1991), 124, *125*, 130-131, 133, 134-135

Sable Commc'ns v. FCC, 492 U.S. 115 (1989), 230
Saia v. New York, 334 U.S. 558 (1948), 93
Santa Fe Independent School District v. Doe, 530 U.S. 290 (2000), *610*
Saxbe v. Washington Post Co., 417 U.S. 843 (1974), 415, 496, 497
Scales v. United States, 367 U.S. 203 (1961), 160, 442
Schacht v. United States, 398 U.S. 58 (1970), 315
Schad v. Borough of Mount Ephraim, 452 U.S. 61 (1981), 59
Schenck v. United States, 249 U.S. 47 (1919), 65, 70, 73, *142*, 145, 147, 150, 163, 182
Schneider v. New Jersey, 308 U.S. 147 (1939), 366, *367*, 369, 408
School Dist. of Abington Twp. v. Schempp, 374 U.S. 203 (1963), 503, 505-506, 601, 602, 637
Seattle Times Co. v. Rhinehart, 467 U.S. 20 (1984), 495
Secretary of State v. J.H. Munson Co., 467 U.S. 947 (1984), 61
Seeger; United States v., 380 U.S. 163 (1965), *507*, 509
Shaffer v. United States, 255 F. 886 (9th Cir. 1919), 142

Shapero v. Kentucky Bar Ass'n, 486 U.S. 466 (1988), 274
Shaw v. Murphy, 532 U.S. 223 (2001), 416
Shelley v. Kraemer, 334 U.S. 1 (1948), 96
Shelton v. Tucker, 364 U.S. 479 (1960), 445
Sheppard v. Maxwell, 384 U.S. 333 (1966), 79
Sherbert v. Verner, 374 U.S. 398 (1963), 516, 517-518, 519, 523, 576
Shuttlesworth v. City of Birmingham, 394 U.S. 147 (1969), 68
Simon & Schuster, Inc. v. Members of the N.Y. State Crime Victims Bd., 502 U.S. 105 (1991), 21, 29, 97
Sloan v. Lemon, 413 U.S. 825 (1973), 665
Smith v. Collin, 436 U.S. 953 (1978), 188
Smith v. Daily Mail Publ'g Co., 443 U.S. 97 (1979), 311
Smith v. Goguen, 415 U.S. 566 (1974), 319
Snyder v. Phelps, 562 U.S. 443 (2011), 302, *304*
Sorrell v. IMS Health Inc., 564 U.S. 552 (2011), *259*
South Carolina v. United States, 199 U.S. 437 (1905), 121
Southeastern Promotions, Ltd. v. Conrad, 420 U.S. 546 (1975), 67, 232
Speiser v. Randall, 357 U.S. 513 (1958), 123-124, 134
Spence v. Washington, 418 U.S. 405 (1974), 314-315, 319, 320
St. Amant v. Thompson, 390 U.S. 727 (1968), 293
Stanley v. Georgia, 394 U.S. 557 (1969), *221*, 222-223
Stevens; United States v., 559 U.S. 460 (2010), *237*, 243, 244
Stevens v. Tillman, 855 F.2d 394 (7th Cir. 1988), 292
Stollar, In re, 401 U.S. 23 (1971), 443
Stone v. Graham, 449 U.S. 39 (1980), 592, 626, 627, 636, 642, 643-644
Street v. New York, 394 U.S. 576 (1969), 175, 319
Stromberg v. California, 283 U.S. 359 (1931), 314

Talley v. California, 362 U.S. 60 (1960), 118, 119
Teitel Film Corp. v. Cusack, 390 U.S. 139 (1968), 94
Terminiello v. Chicago, 337 U.S. 1 (1949), 185
Texas Monthly, Inc. v. Bullock, 489 U.S. 1 (1989), 681-682
Texas v. Johnson, 491 U.S. 397 (1989), 46, 116, 175, *320*, 325
Thirty-Seven Photographs; United States v., 402 U.S. 363 (1971), 94
Thomas & Windy City Hemp Dev. Bd. v. Chicago Park Dist., 534 U.S. 316 (2002), 95
Thomas v. Review Bd. of the Ind. Emp't Sec. Div., 450 U.S. 707 (1981), 513, 516, 518
Thornburgh v. Abbott, 490 U.S. 401 (1989), *413*
Thornton, Estate of, v. Caldor, 472 U.S. 703 (1985), 593-594
Tilton v. Richardson, 403 U.S. 672 (1971), 682-683
Time, Inc. v. Firestone, 424 U.S. 448 (1976), 299, 300
Time, Inc. v. Hill, 385 U.S. 374 (1967), 7, 96

Tinker v. Des Moines Independent Community School District, 393 U.S. 503 (1969), 315, *417*, 420, 421-423, 424, 427-431
Torcaso v. Watkins, 367 U.S. 488 (1961), 503
Town of. *See name of town*
Trinity Lutheran Church of Columbia, Inc. v. Comer, 137 S. Ct. 2012 (2017), 548-549, *552*, 563, 565-567, 571-575
Turner Broad. Sys., Inc. v. FCC, 512 U.S. 622 (1994), 14, 21, 38, 39
Turner v. Safley, 482 U.S. 78 (1987), 412-413, 414, 415, 416, 417

United States v. *See name of opposing party*

Valentine v. Christensen, 316 U.S. 52 (1942), 251, 252
Van Orden v. Perry, 545 U.S. 677 (2005), 624, *634*
Village of. *See name of village*
Virginia State Board of Pharmacy v. Virginia Citizens Consumer Council, Inc., 425 U.S. 748 (1976), *252*, 256, 258, 268, 286
Virginia v. Black, 538 U.S. 343 (2003), *189*

Walker v. City of Birmingham, 388 U.S. 307 (1967), 67
Walker v. Texas Division, Sons of Confederate Veterans, 576 U.S. 200 (2015), *51*
Wallace v. Jaffree, 472 U.S. 38 (1985), 505, 592-593, 602
Walz v. Tax Comm'n, 397 U.S. 664 (1970), 504, 549, 681-682
Ward v. Illinois, 431 U.S. 767 (1977), 204
Ward v. Rock Against Racism, 491 U.S. 781 (1989), 386, *391*
Washington v. Davis, 426 U.S. 229 (1976), 593, 627
Watchtower Bible & Tract Society of New York, Inc. v. Village of Stratton, 536 U.S. 150 (2002), 86, *87*

Watts v. United States, 394 U.S. 705 (1969), 161, 192
Welsh v. United States, 398 U.S. 333 (1970), 509
West Virginia Board of Education v. Barnette, 319 U.S. 624 (1943), *99*, 115, 314, 417, 431, 527
Whitney v. California, 274 U.S. 357 (1927), 6, 8, 140, *151*, 154, 161-162, 163
Widmar v. Vincent, 454 U.S. 263 (1981), 393, 595, 596, 597
Williams; United States v., 553 U.S. 285 (2008), 211
Williams-Yulee v. Florida Bar, 575 U.S. 433 (2015), 29, *30*
Wisconsin v. Yoder, 406 U.S. 205 (1972), 518, 519, 523, 526, 576
Witters v. Washington Dep't of Servs. for the Blind, 474 U.S. 481 (1986), 657, 658, 668-670
Wolman v. Walter, 433 U.S. 229 (1977), 653, 656, 660, 661
Wolston v. Reader's Digest Ass'n, 443 U.S. 157 (1979), 299
Wooley v. Maynard, 430 U.S. 705 (1977), 54, 101, 115

Yates v. United States, 354 U.S. 298 (1957), 160
Young v. American Mini Theatres, Inc., 427 U.S. 50 (1976), 40, *212*, 214, 218, 220

Zacchini v. Scripps-Howard Broad. Co., 433 U.S. 562 (1977), 313-314
Zauderer v. Office of Disciplinary Counsel of the Supreme Court of Ohio, 471 U.S. 626 (1985), 286
Zelman v. Simmons-Harris, 536 U.S. 639 (2002), 550, 594, *666*
Zobrest v. Catalina Foothills Sch. Dist., 509 U.S. 1 (1993), 653, 668-670
Zorach v. Clauson, 343 U.S. 306 (1952), 599, 601, 631
Zurcher v. Stanford Daily, 436 U.S. 547 (1978), 486-487

INDEX

Abortion
  advertising, 252
  buffer zones outside facilities, 379-388
  commercial speech, 252
  government property, freedom of expression on, 374-379, 379-388
  notice requirement, freedom of expression and, 101-112
  unconstitutional condition doctrine, 124-129
Accommodation of religion, 583-584
Accountants, solicitation by, 274-275
Actual malice and defamation, 291, 293-294
ADA. *See* Americans with Disabilities Act of 1990 (ADA)
Adult entertainment
  content-based vs. content-neutral laws, 39-41
  obscenity, 199-202
  overbreadth, 59-60
  prior restraints, 66, 83
  zoning ordinances, 212-215
Advertising. *See also* Commercial speech
  abortion, 252
  alcohol sales, 270, 276-278
  attorneys, 285-286
  contraception, 258-259
  false advertising, 269, 272
  gambling, 271, 284-285
  housing and "for sale" signs, 276
  illegal activities, 269, 271-272
  "image advertisements," 259
  inherent risk of deception in, 272-275
  optometrists, 272-273
  pharmaceuticals, 252-256
  tobacco sales, 278-284
  trade names, 272-273
  utilities, 266-269
Airport terminals and freedom of expression on government property, 64-65, 406
Alcohol sales
  advertising, 270, 276-278
  commercial speech, 270, 276-278
Alien and Sedition Acts of 1978, 4-5
Americans with Disabilities Act of 1990 (ADA)
  Establishment Clause, 504
  Free Exercise Clause, 504
Animal cruelty and freedom of expression, 237-243
Animal sacrifice and Free Exercise Clause, 529-530
Animus against religion, 529-540
Antitrust law and freedom of press, 477-478
Arizona Citizens Clean Elections Act, 357-364
Armed forces. *See* Military affairs
Arts, public funding for, 43-46
Association, freedom of, 441-470
  attorneys and bar dues, 456
  campaign finance disclosure, 445-446
  colleges and universities, student activity fees at, 457-460
  Communist Party membership, 442-443
  compelled association, 446-460
  disclosure of membership, requiring, 443-446
  discrimination laws, 460-470
  Due Process Clause compared, 441
  gender discrimination, 460-465
  intimate association, 465
  labor unions, 446-456
  liberty interests compared, 441
  membership, prohibiting and punishing, 442-443
  overview, 441
  redress of grievances, 441
  sexual orientation, 465-470
Atomic Energy Act of 1954, 77
Attorneys
  advertising by, 285-286
  bar dues and freedom of association, 456
  defamation, 295-299
  solicitation by, 273-274

Bar associations. *See* Attorneys
Bible reading in public schools, 599, 601-602
Bipartisan Campaign Finance Reform Act, 335
Blue laws
  Free Exercise Clause, 519
  Lemon test, 592
Brandenburg test, 160-172
Broadcast media. *See also* Press, freedom of
  cable television regulation
    press, freedom of, 476
    profanity, 234-236
  fairness doctrine, 487
  profanity in, 227-230
  public television
    government property, freedom of expression on, 406-407
    unconstitutional condition doctrine, 124
  right-to-reply laws, 487

Cable television regulation
  press, freedom of, 476
  profanity, 234-236
California Criminal Syndicalism Act, 151-154
California Reproductive Freedom, Accountability, Comprehensive Care, and Transparency Act (FACT Act), 101-112

Campaign finance, 325-364
   contributions vs. expenditures, 333-334
   corporate expenditures as speech, 336-357
   criticisms of Buckley v. Valeo, 332-333
   disclosure requirements, 325-332, 445-446
   electioneering communication, 340-357
   independent expenditures, 340-357
   limits on contributions, 334-336
   public financing of elections, 357-364
   referendum elections, 336-339
   spending as political speech, 325-332
Captive audiences, 230, 373
Casinos. *See* Gambling
Central Hudson test, 266-269
Certified public accountants, solicitation by, 274-275
Charitable organizations and Establishment Clause, 589
Child On-Line Protection Act of 1998, 234
Child pornography, 207-211
   mere possession, 222-223
   sexual performances by children, 207-210
   virtual images, 210-211
Child Pornography Prevention Act of 1996, 210-211
Cigarettes. *See* Tobacco sales
Clear and convincing evidence of defamation, 291, 292
"Clear and present danger" test, 141-148
Collateral bar rule, 67-68
Colleges and universities
   government aid to religious colleges and universities and Establishment Clause, 682-683
   hate speech, 187
   law schools
      military recruiters as compelled speech, 113-117
      student groups and freedom of expression, 394-405
   religious group access to school facilities, 393, 595-597
   student activity fees and freedom of association, 456-460
   student religious groups, funding of, 597-598
Commercial speech, 251-287
   abortion, 252
   accountants, solicitation by, 274-275
   advertising. *See* Advertising
   alcohol sales, 270, 276-278
   attorneys
      advertising by, 285-287
      solicitation by, 273-274
   Central Hudson test, 266-269
   commercial transactions, regulation of, 259-266
   constitutional protections, 251-257
   contraception, 258-259
   deference to regulation, 256
   defined, 258-266
   false advertising, 269, 272
   gambling, 271, 284-285
   gender discrimination, 271-272
   housing and "for sale" signs, 276
   illegal activities, advertising of, 269, 271-272
   inherent risk of deception in advertising, 272-275
   least restrictive alternative analysis, 269-271
   optometrists, 272-273
   overbreadth, 62
   pharmaceuticals, 252-256, 259-266
   political speech compared, 256-257
   regulation for other purposes, 275-287
   solicitation, 273-275
   substantial government interest, 269
   tests, 266-271
   tobacco sales, 278-284
   trade names, 272-273
   utilities, 266-269
Commission on Obscenity and Pornography, 205
Communicative conduct, 314-364. *See also* Symbolic speech
Communist Party membership and freedom of association, 442-443
Community standards regarding obscenity, 203-204
Compelled speech, 99-123
   campaign literature disclosure requirement as, 118-122
   flag salute requirements as, 99-101
   license plates, 101
   military recruiters as, 113-117
   notice requirement, 101-112
   petition disclosure requirement as, 122-123
   taxation, 112-113
   union dues payment by non-union members, 112, 446-456
Conduct as speech, 314-364. *See also* Symbolic speech
Confidentiality of press sources and secrets, 480-486
Conscientious objectors and freedom of religion, 507-510
Content-based vs. content-neutral laws, 13-57
   adult entertainment, 39-41
   arts, public funding for, 43-46
   determining distinction, 22-38
   embassies, political speech in proximity to, 41-42
   fighting words, 178-184
   government making content-based choices, 43, 47-57
   government property, freedom of expression on, 371-373
   government speech vs. private speech, 51-57
   handbilling, 42
   importance of distinction, 14-21
   judicial candidates, speech by, 29-38
   license plate design, 51-57
   military affairs, 20-21
   permissible purposes and content-neutrality, 39-43
   picketing, 29
   problems in applying distinction, 38-57
   religious symbols on government property, 47-51
   sign ordinances, 14-20
   "Son of Sam" laws, 20
   Stolen Valor Act of 2005, 20-21
   subject-matter restrictions, 21, 22, 29
   temporary directional signs, 14-20
   viewpoint neutrality, requirement for, 22-29

Index

Contraception
   advertising, 258-259
   commercial speech, 258-259
   religious objection to mandated provision of, 577-578
Corporations' campaign expenditures as speech, 336-357
Court orders as prior restraints, 68-85
   fair trials, protection of, 78-83
   national security, protection of, 71-77
   seizure of assets of businesses convicted of obscenity violations, 83-85
Creation science, teaching of, 592
Creches on government property, 584-588
Credit reporting agencies and defamation, 300-301
Crime victims and public disclosure of private facts, 309-312
Criminal anarchy and incitement of illegal activity, 148-151
Criminal law and procedure
   incitement of illegal activity, 140-172. *See also* Incitement of illegal activity
   obscenity, effect of, 205-206
   press, freedom of, 78-83, 486-487, 489-495
   prisoners. *See* Prisoners
Criminal syndicalism and incitement of illegal activity, 151-154, 161-162
Cross burnings
   fighting words, 178-184
   hate speech, 189-196
Crosses on government property, 581-583

Defamation, 287, 288-302
   actual malice, 291, 293-294
   attorneys, 295-299
   civil liability for speech, 96
   clear and convincing evidence, 291, 292
   credit reporting agencies, 300-301
   falsity of statement, 291, 292-293
   overview, 301-302
   prior restraints, 68-71
   private figures
      matters not of public concern, 301
      matters of public concern, 300-301
   public figures, 294-300
   public officials, 288-294
Designated public forums, 370, 392-393
Disability discrimination and Free Exercise Clause, 540
Discovery and freedom of press, 495
Discrimination. *See* Disability discrimination; Gender discrimination
Door-to-door advocacy and prior restraints, 87-92
Draft card burning as symbolic speech, 315-319
Drug use
   Free Exercise Clause, 521-529, 576-577
   pharmaceuticals. *See* Pharmaceuticals
   public school and speech advocating, 424-431
Due Process Clause and freedom of association compared, 441

Education
   colleges and universities. *See* Colleges and universities
   compulsory schooling and Free Exercise Clause, 518-519
   creation science, teaching of, 592
   delegation of governmental authority to religious entity, 590
   evolution, teaching of, 592
   funding of religious education, 548-552
   law schools
      military recruiters as compelled speech, 113-117
      student groups and freedom of expression, 394-405
   parochial schools, government aid to, 653-680. *See also* Parochial schools, government aid to
   public schools. *See* Public schools
Education Consolidation and Improvement Act of 1981, 654-664
Electioneering communication, 340-357
Election law
   campaign finance, 325-364. *See also* Campaign finance
   campaign literature disclosure requirement as compelled speech, 118-122
   petition disclosure requirement as compelled speech, 122-123
   public financing of elections, 357-364
Embassies, political speech in proximity to, 41-42
Emotional distress, intentional infliction of, 302-309
   picketing, 304-309
   print media, 302-304
Espionage Act of 1917, 141-148
Establishment Clause, 579-685
   accommodation, 583-584
   Americans with Disabilities Act of 1990, 504
   Bible reading in public schools, 599, 601-602
   charitable organizations, 589
   coercion, 583
   colleges and universities, government aid to, 682-683
   competing theories, 579-588
   creches on government property, 584-588
   crosses on government property, 581-583
   curricular decisions, 614-615
   delegation of governmental authority to religious entity, 590
   discrimination among religions, 589-590
   Free Exercise Clause, tension with, 503-505
   government aid to religion, 652-685
   historical background, 505-506
   holiday displays on government property, 584-588
   incorporation doctrine, 503
   interpretation of, 505-506
   legislative chaplains, 615-624
   Lemon test, 590-594
   menorahs on government property, 584-588
   moments of silence in public schools, 602
   neutrality theory, 580-583
   parochial schools, government aid to, 653-680. *See also* Parochial schools, government aid to

Establishment Clause (*cont'd*)
  prayer in public schools, 599-614. *See also* Prayer in public schools
  public schools, religion in, 598-615
  release time, 598-599
  religious group access to school facilities, 393, 595-597
  religious institutions other than schools, government aid to, 684-685
  religious speech, 595-598. *See also* Religious speech
  religious symbols on government property, 584-588, 624-652. *See also* Religious symbols on government property
  strict separation, 579-580
  student-delivered prayers, 610-614
  student religious groups, funding of, 597-598
  symbolic endorsement test, 581-583
  tax exemptions for religious organizations, 681-682
  Ten Commandments on government property, 592, 624-644
Evolution, teaching of, 592
Expression, freedom of, 1-440
  absolutist position, 5
  Alien and Sedition Acts of 1978, 4-5
  animal cruelty, depiction of, 237-243
  autonomy advancement as justification for protecting, 9-10
  captive audiences, 230, 373
  child pornography, 207-211. *See also* Child pornography
  citizen speech, 440
  civil liability for speech, 96
  commercial speech, 251-287. *See also* Commercial speech
  compelled speech, 99-123. *See also* Compelled speech
  compensation prohibitions for speech, 97-98
  conduct as speech, 314-364. *See also* Symbolic speech
  content-based vs. content-neutral laws, 13-57. *See also* Content-based vs. content-neutral laws
  defamation, 288-302. *See also* Defamation
  emotional distress, intentional infliction of, 302-309. *See also* Emotional distress, intentional infliction of
  false light, 287
  fighting words, 172-184. *See also* Fighting words
  fleeting expletives, 230
  foreign affiliates of U.S. entities, 136
  freedom of press compared, 471
  fundamental rights, protection of, 5-10
  government employee testimony pursuant to subpoena, 440
  government employment, 432-440
  government pressures regarding, 136-137
  government property, 365-408. *See also* Government property, freedom of expression on
  government speech vs. private speech, 51-57
  handbilling
    content-based vs. content-neutral laws, 42
    government property, freedom of expression on, 367-369
    hate speech, 187-188
    prior restraints, 85-86
  hate speech, 187-196
    colleges and universities, 187
    cross burnings as, 189-196
    handbilling, 187-188
    injunctions, 188
  historical background, 3-5
  hostile audiences, provoking, 184-196. *See also* Hostile audiences, provoking
  incitement of illegal activity, 140-172. *See also* Incitement of illegal activity
  infringement of, 95-137
  intent of framers, 4-5
  issues regarding, 11-12
  judicial office candidates, 29-38
  less protected speech, 139-140. *See also specific types of speech*
  locations available for speech, 365-440. *See also specific locations*
  low-value sexual speech, 211-221
    adult entertainment, 212-215
    arguments for protecting, 220-221
    nude dancing, 215-220
    zoning ordinances, 212-215
  "marketplace of ideas" metaphor, 7-9, 145
  methodology, 13-137
  military affairs, 410-412. *See also* Military affairs
  notice requirement, 101-112
  nude dancing, 215-220
  obscenity, 196, 197-207. *See also* Obscenity
  overbreadth, 57, 59-65. *See also* Overbreadth
  overview, 3-12
  picketing
    content-based vs. content-neutral laws, 29
    emotional distress, intentional infliction of, 304-309
    government property, freedom of expression on, 371-373
    vagueness, 58-59
  places available for speech, 365-440
  political speech. *See* Political speech
  pornography, 206-207
  prior restraints, 65-95. *See also* Prior restraints
  prisoners, 412-417. *See also* Prisoners
  private property, 409
  profanity, 223-236. *See also* Profanity
  professional speech, 101-112
  public disclosure of private facts, 309-313. *See also* Public disclosure of private facts
  public forums
    content neutrality, 371-373
    least restrictive alternative analysis, 391-392
    licensing systems, 389-391
    tests, 408
    time, place, and manner restrictions, 373-389
  publicity, right of, 313-314
  public schools, 417-432. *See also* Public schools
  refraining from speaking, 62, 64, 99-101, 124, 360, 448
  religious speech, 595-598. *See also* Religious speech
  seditious libel, 3-5
  self-governance as justification for protecting, 6-7
  shopping centers, 409

Index

subpoena, testimony pursuant to, 440
symbolic speech, 314-364. *See also* Symbolic speech
theories regarding, 5-10
tolerance promotion as justification for protecting, 10
truth discovery as justification for protecting, 7-9
unconstitutional condition doctrine, 123-136
    abortion, 124-129
    legal aid, 129-135
    opposition to prostitution and human trafficking, policy of, 135-136
    public television, 124
    veterans and property tax exemption, 123-124
unprotected speech, 139-140. *See also specific types of speech*
vagueness, 57-59, 64-65. *See also* Vagueness
video games, 244-251
violent speech, 236-251
    animal cruelty, depiction of, 237-243
    video games, 244-251

FACT Act (California), 101-112
Fairness doctrine, 487-488
    broadcast media, 487-488
    print media, 487-488
Fair trial protection court orders as prior restraints, 78-83
False advertising, 269, 272
False light, 287
Falsity of statement, defamation, 291, 292-293
Federal Alcohol Administration Act, 270
Federal Cigarette Labeling and Advertising Act of 1965, 278-284
Federal Communications Commission (FCC)
    fairness doctrine, 487, 488
    press, freedom of, 488
Federal Election Campaign Act of 1971
    association, freedom of, 445-446
    campaign finance, 325-332
Fees and freedom of expression on government property, 389-391
Fighting words, 172-184
    content-based vs. content-neutral laws, 178-184
    cross burnings as, 178-184
    flag desecration as, 175
    immediate emotional harm, likelihood of, 174
    narrowing scope of doctrine, 175
    overbreadth, 176-178
    overview, 172-173
    profanity as, 175, 177-178
    religious speech, 173-174
    threats as, 176-177
    vagueness, 176-178
    violent response, likelihood of, 174-175
First Amendment
    association, freedom of, 441-470. *See also* Association, freedom of
    citizen speech, 440
    Establishment Clause, 579-685. *See also* Establishment Clause
    expression, freedom of, 1-440. *See also* Expression, freedom of
    foreign affiliates of U.S. entities, 136

Free Exercise Clause, 515-578. *See also* Free Exercise Clause
    government speech vs. private speech, 51-57
    press, freedom of, 471-500. *See also* Press, freedom of
    religion, freedom of, 501-685. *See also* Religion, freedom of
Flag desecration
    fighting words, 175
    symbolic speech, 319-325
Flag Protection Act of 1989, 325
Flag salute requirements as compelled speech, 99-101
Foreign affiliates of U.S. entities
    non-applicability of First Amendment to, 136
Foreign Agents Registration Act of 1938, 136
Framers, intent of. *See* Intent of framers regarding freedom of expression
Freedom of association, 441-470. *See also* Association, freedom of
Freedom of expression, 1-440. *See also* Expression, freedom of
Freedom of press, 471-500. *See also* Press, freedom of
Freedom of religion, 501-685. *See also* Religion, freedom of
Free Exercise Clause, 515-578
    action vs. belief, 515-516
    aid to secular private versus religious schools, 549, 552-576
    Americans with Disabilities Act of 1990, 504
    animal sacrifice, 529-530
    animus against religion, 529-540
    case law rejecting exemptions, 519-520
    clergy, choice of, 504, 540-548
    compulsory schooling, 518-519
    disability discrimination, 540
    drug use, 521-529, 576-577
    Establishment Clause, tension with, 503-505
    funding of religious education, 548-552
    funding to religious entities, denial of, 548-576
    grant for playground resurfacing, denial of, 552-563
    government benefits, 518
    historical background, 505-506
    incorporation doctrine, 503
    interpretation of, 505-506
    issues regarding, 515-516
    military affairs, 520
    ministers, choice of, 504, 540-548
    no-aid provision in state constitution, 563-576
    overview, 515-516
    polygamy, 516
    prisoners, 578
    Sabbath observance, 517
    same-sex couple, business owner's refusal to serve, 529-540
    Smith test, 521-529
    Sunday closing laws, 529
    taxation, 519-520
    teachers, choice of, 540-548
    tests, 516-517, 521-529
    unemployment compensation, 518
    welfare, 520

Fundamental rights, protection of
contraception
advertising, 258-259
commercial speech, 258-259
expression, freedom of, 5-10. *See also*
Expression, freedom of

Gambling
advertising, 271, 284-285
commercial speech, 271, 284-285
Gays. *See* Sexual orientation and freedom of association
Gender discrimination
association, freedom of, 460-465
commercial speech, 271-272
pornography as, 205
Government benefits
Free Exercise Clause, 518
welfare. *See* Welfare and Free Exercise Clause
Government employment
compensation prohibitions for speech, 97-98
expression, freedom of, 432-440
Government property, freedom of expression on, 365-411
abortion protesters, 374-379
airport terminals, 64-65, 406
content neutrality, 371-373
designated public forums, 370, 392-393
fees, 389-391
handbilling, 367-369
historical background, 365-369
homeless persons, 388-389
labor unions, 366-367, 369-370
law school student groups, 394-405
least restrictive alternative analysis, 391-392
licensing systems, 389-391
limited public forums, 370, 393-405
musical performances, 391-392
nonpublic forums, 370, 405-411
picketing, 371-373
political speech, 393
public forums, 370, 371-405
public television, 406-407
sidewalks, 374-379, 406, 408
sound amplification devices, 388
time, place, and manner restrictions, 373-389
types of property and circumstances, 369-371
Grand juries and freedom of press, 480-486

Handbilling
content-based vs. content-neutral laws, 42
government property, freedom of expression on, 367-369
hate speech, 187-188
prior restraints, 85-86
Hate speech, 187-196
colleges and universities, 187
cross burnings as, 189-196
handbilling, 187-188
injunctions, 188
Higher Education Facilities Act of 1963, 682
Holiday displays on government property, 584-588

Homeless persons and freedom of expression on government property, 388-389
Homosexuals. *See* Sexual orientation and freedom of association
Hostile audiences, provoking, 184-196
hate speech, 187-196
colleges and universities, 187
cross burnings as, 189-196
handbilling, 187-188
injunctions, 188
overview, 172-173, 184-186
political speech, 185-186
religious speech, 185
Housing "for sale" signs, 276

Incitement of illegal activity, 140-172
Brandenburg test, 160-172
"clear and present danger" test, 141-148
criminal anarchy, 148-151
criminal syndicalism, 148, 151-154, 161-162
imminence of harm, 162-163
intent to cause imminent illegality, 162-163
likelihood of producing illegal action, 162-163
overview, 140-141
reasonableness test, 148-154
risk formula, 155-160
subversive organizations, 155-160
terrorism, 163-172
war protesters, 141-148, 160
Incorporation doctrine
Free Exercise Clause, 503
Indecency. *See* Profanity
Injunctions
hate speech, 188
profanity, 234
Intentional infliction of emotional distress. *See* Emotional distress, intentional infliction of
Intent of framers regarding freedom of expression, 4-6
Internet
child pornography and virtual images, 210-211
expression, freedom of, 63
profanity on, 230-234

Judicial candidates, restrictions on speech by, 29-38
Judicial proceedings, access of press to, 489-495
Jury trials, voir dire and freedom of press in, 494-495

Labor unions
compelled association, 112, 446-456
compelled speech, 112, 446-456
government property, freedom of expression on, 365-367, 369-370
mandatory dues, 112, 446-456
press, freedom of, 477-478
Lanham Act, 22-29
Law enforcement officers and freedom of press, 486-487
Law schools
military recruiters as compelled speech, 113-117
student groups, freedom of expression, 394-405
Lawyers. *See* Attorneys

Index

Leadership Act (United States Leadership Against HIV/AIDS, Tuberculosis, and Malaria Act of 2003), 135-136
Least restrictive alternative analysis
   commercial speech, 269-271
   government property, freedom of expression on, 391-392
Legal aid and unconstitutional condition doctrine, 129-135
Legal Services Corporation Act of 1974, 129-135
Legislative chaplains, 615-624
Lemon test, 590-594
Lesbians. *See* Sexual orientation and freedom of association
Libel. *See* Defamation
Liberty interests
   freedom of association compared, 441
Licensing systems
   clear standards for, 92-94
   door-to-door advocacy, 87-92
   government property, freedom of expression on, 389-391
   handbilling, 85-86
   motion pictures, 94
   obscenity, 94
   print media, 92-93
   prior restraints, 68, 85-95
   procedural safeguards regarding, 94-95
   reason for, 92
   sound amplification systems, 93
Limited public forums, 370, 393-405
Liquor. *See* Alcohol sales
Low-value sexual speech, 211-221
   adult entertainment, 212-215
   arguments for protecting, 220-221
   nude dancing, 215-220
   zoning ordinances, 212-215

Magazines. *See* Print media
Mail, obscenity in, 197-199
Mandatory dues, 112, 446-456
"Marketplace of ideas" metaphor, 7-9, 145
Marriage, polygamous, and Free Exercise Clause, 516
Massachusetts Reproductive Health Care Facilities Act, 379-388
Media. *See also* Press, freedom of
   broadcast media
      cable television regulation. *See* Cable television regulation
      fairness doctrine, 487-488
      profanity in, 227-230
      public television. *See* Public television
      right-to-reply laws, 487-488
   print media. *See* Print media
Medicine. *See* Pharmaceuticals
Membership in private organizations. *See* Association, freedom of
Menorahs on government property, 584-588
Military affairs
   content-based vs. content-neutral laws, 20-21
   expression, freedom of, 410-412
   Free Exercise Clause, 520
   law schools and military recruiters as compelled speech, 113-117
   nonpublic forums, 405-406
   Stolen Valor Act, 20-21
   veterans' property tax exemption and unconstitutional condition doctrine, 123-124
Moments of silence in public schools, 602
Motion pictures and prior restraints, 94
Musical performances and freedom of expression on government property, 391-392

National Foundation on the Arts and Humanities Act of 1965, 43-47
National Labor Relations Act of 1935, 477
National security and prior restraints, 71-78
Neutrality theory, 580-583
Newspapers. *See* Print media
Nonpublic forums, 370, 405-411

O'Brien test, 315-319
Obscenity, 196, 197-207
   adult entertainment as, 199-202
   arguments for protecting, 204
   artistic, literary, political, or scientific value, 204
   case law, 197-204
   community standards, 203-204
   criminal law and procedure, 95
   defined, 199
   mail, 197-199
   mere possession, 221-222
   patently offensive material, 204
   prior restraints, 94
   unprotected speech, 197-204
   unwilling recipients, 202-203
Ohio Criminal Syndicalism Statute, 161-162
Optometrists
   advertising, 272-273
   commercial speech, 272-273
Overbreadth, 57, 59-63
   adult entertainment, 59-60
   commercial speech, 62
   defined, 59
   fighting words, 176-178
   substantial overbreadth, 60-61
   unconstitutional as applied to others, 59, 61
   vagueness, relationship to, 64-65

Parochial schools, government aid to, 653-680
   direct assistance, 654-664
   educational choice, 666-680
   Education Consolidation and Improvement Act of 1981, 654-664
   Lemon test, 594
   tax credits, 665-666
   test for, 664-665
   vouchers, 666-680
Patient Protection and Affordable Care Act of 2010
   contraceptive mandate, 577-578
   preventive care, 577-578
Pentagon Papers, 71-78
Permit systems. *See* Licensing systems

Pharmaceuticals
  advertising, 252-256
  commercial speech, 252-256, 259-266
  detailing, 259-266
  marketing, 259-266
Picketing
  content-based vs. content-neutral laws, 29
  emotional distress, intentional infliction of, 304-309
  government property, freedom of expression on, 371-373
  vagueness, 58-59
Police. *See* Law enforcement officers and freedom of press
Political contributions and expenditures. *See* Campaign finance
Political speech
  campaign spending as, 325-332
  commercial speech compared, 256-257
  embassies in proximity to, 41-42
  government property, freedom of expression on, 393
  hostile audiences, provoking, 185-186
  judicial candidates, 29-38
  profanity as, 223-226
  public schools, 417-421
Polygamy and Free Exercise Clause, 516
Pornography, 206-207. *See also* Child pornography
Prayer in public schools, 599-614
  athletic events, 610-614
  beginning of school day, 599-601
  curricular decisions, 614-615
  graduation ceremonies, 602-609
  Lemon test, 592
  moments of silence, 602
  student-delivered prayer, 610-614
Prescription drugs. *See* Pharmaceuticals
Presidential Election Campaign Fund Act of 1966, 333-334
Press, freedom of, 471-500
  antitrust law, 477-478
  availability of access, requiring, 487-488
  cable television regulation, 476
  confidentiality of sources and secrets, 480-487
  criminal law and procedure, 78-82, 486-487, 489-495
  defamation. *See* Defamation
  discovery, 495
  discrimination among types of media, 476-477
  Fair Labor Standards Act of 1938, 478
  fairness doctrine, 487-488
    broadcast media, 487-488
    print media, 487-488
  freedom of expression compared, 471
  general regulatory laws, 477-480
  grand juries, 480-486
  judicial proceedings, access to, 489-495
  labor law, 477-478
  law enforcement officers, 486-487
  overview, 471-472
  prior restraints, 65-95. *See also* Prior restraints
  prisoners, access to, 415, 495-500
  promissory estoppel, 478-480
  right-to-reply laws, 487-488
  "shield" from government regulation, 472-488
  special rights, 471-472
  "sword" for access to government, 488-500
  taxation of press, 472-477
  voir dire, 494-495
Print media. *See also* Press, freedom of
  defamation. *See* Defamation
  discrimination among types of media, 476-477
  emotional distress, intentional infliction of, 302-304
  fairness doctrine, 487-488
  prior restraints, 92-93
  prisoners, access by, 412-415, 417
  public schools and newspapers, 423-424
  right-to-reply laws, 487-488
Prior restraints, 65-95
  adult entertainment, 83-85
  clear standards for licensing systems, 92-94
  collateral bar rule, 67-68
  court orders, 68-85
    fair trials, protection of, 78-83
    national security, protection of, 71-78
    seizure of assets of businesses convicted of obscenity violations, 83-85
  dangers of, 66-68
  defamation, 68-71
  defined, 65-66
  door-to-door advocacy, 87-92
  fair trials, protection of, 78-83
  handbilling, 85-86
  licensing systems, 68, 85-95
    clear standards leaving almost no discretion to government, 92-94
    procedural safeguards, 94-95
    reason for licensing systems, 92
  motion pictures, 94
  national security, 71-78
  obscenity, 83-85, 94
  overview, 11-12, 65-66
  Pentagon Papers, 71-78
  print media, 92-93
  procedural safeguards regarding licensing systems, 94-95
  reason for licensing systems, 92
  sound amplification systems, 93
  types, 68-95
    court orders, 68-85
    licensing systems, 85-95
Prisoners
  correspondence, access to, 416
  expression, freedom of, 412-417
  Free Exercise Clause, 578
  legal advice, access to, 416
  nonpublic forums, 405
  press access to, 415, 495-500
  print media, access to, 413-415, 417
  visitation, right to, 416
Privacy Protection Act of 1980, 487
Privacy rights and public disclosure of private facts, 309-313
  nongovernment sources, 312-313
  rape victims, 309-312
Private figures, defamation
  matters not of public concern, 301
  matters of public concern, 300-301
Private organizations. *See* Association, freedom of
Private property, freedom of expression on, 409
Profanity, 223-236

Index

broadcast media, 227-230
cable television, 234-236
fighting words, 175, 177-178
injunctions, 234
Internet, 230-234
overview, 223
political speech, 223-226
telephones, 230
war protesters, 223-226
Professional speech, 101-112
Promissory estoppel and freedom of press, 478-480
Property tax exemption for veterans and unconstitutional condition doctrine, 123-124
Prosecutorial Remedies and Other Tools to End the Exploitation of Children Today Act of 2003, 211
PROTECT Act of 2003, 211
Public benefits. *See* Government benefits
Public disclosure of private facts, 309-313
nongovernment sources, 312-313
rape victims, 309-312
Public employment
compensation prohibitions for speech, 97-98
expression, freedom of, 432-440
Public figures and defamation, 294-300
Public forums, 371-405
content neutrality, 371-373
least restrictive alternative analysis, 391-392
licensing systems, 389-391
tests, 408
time, place, and manner restrictions, 373-389
Publicity, right of, 313-314
Public officials and defamation, 288-294
Public property, freedom of expression on. *See* Government property, freedom of expression on
Public schools
Bible reading in, 599, 601-602
compulsory schooling and Free Exercise Clause, 518-519
creation science, teaching of, 592
drug use, speech advocating, 424-431
evolution, teaching of, 592
expression, freedom of, 417-432
freedom of association of teachers, 445
libraries, freedom of expression in, 432
moments of silence in, 602
newspapers, 423-424
obscenity by students, 421-423
political speech by students, 417-421
prayer in, 599-614. *See also* Prayer in public schools
release time, 598-599
religion in, 598-615
student-delivered prayers, 610-614
student religious groups, funding of, 597-598
teachers
association, freedom of, 445
public school teachers in parochial schools, 654
Ten Commandments, 592
Public television
government property, freedom of expression on, 406-407
unconstitutional condition doctrine, 124

Public utilities
advertising, 266-269
commercial speech, 266-269

Racist speech, 187-196. *See also* Hate speech
Radio. *See* Broadcast media
Reasonableness test and incitement of illegal activity, 148-154
Release time, 598-599
Religion, freedom of, 501-685
animus against religion, 529-540
clergy, choice of, 504, 540-548
conscientious objectors, 507-510
dogma, relevance of, 512-513
Establishment Clause, 579-685. *See also* Establishment Clause
Free Exercise Clause, 515-578. *See also* Free Exercise Clause
funding to religious entities, denial of, 548-576
historical background, 505-506
Lemon test, 590-594
ministers, choice of, 504, 540-548
parochial schools, government aid to, 653-680. *See also* Parochial schools, government aid to
prayer in public schools, 599-614. *See also* Prayer in public schools
"religion" defined, 506-513
Religious Freedom Restoration Act of 1993, 576-578
Religious Land Use and Institutionalized Persons Act of 2000, 578
religious speech, 595-598. *See also* Religious speech
religious symbols on government property, 624-652. *See also* Religious symbols on government property
Sabbath observance
Free Exercise Clause, 517
Lemon test, 592
same-sex couple, business owner's refusal to serve, 529-540
Selective Service Act of 1948, 507-510
shared beliefs, relevance of, 512-513
sincerely held belief requirement, 510-512
statutory protection, 576-578
teachers, choice of, 540-548
tension between constitutional provisions, 503-505
Religious Freedom Restoration Act of 1993 (RFRA), 576-578
Religious institutions other than schools, government aid to, 684-685
Religious Land Use and Institutionalized Persons Act of 2000 (RLUIPA), 578
Religious speech, 595-598
access to school facilities, 393, 595-597
fighting words, 173-174
hostile audiences, provoking, 185
student-delivered prayers, 610-614
student religious groups, funding of, 597-598
symbols on government property, 624-652
Religious symbols on government property
content-based vs. content-neutral laws, 47-51
crosses, 581-583, 644-652
holiday displays, 584-588

Religious symbols on government property (cont'd)
   monument on public land, 644-652
   Ten Commandments, 592, 624-644
     display on government property, 592, 624-644
     Lemon test, 592
Reproductive autonomy regarding contraception
   advertising, 258-259
   commercial speech, 258-259
RFRA. *See* Religious Freedom Restoration Act of 1993 (RFRA)
Right-to-reply laws
   broadcast media, 487-488
   print media, 487-488
Risk formula and incitement of illegal activity, 155-160

RLUIPA. *See* Religious Land Use and Institutionalized Persons Act of 2000 (RLUIPA)
Sabbath observance
   Free Exercise Clause, 517
   Lemon test, 592
Same-sex couple, business owner's refusal to serve, 529-540
Schools. *See* Colleges and universities; Education; Public schools
Sedition Act of 1918, 142, 145-148
Seditious libel, 3-5
Selective Service Act of 1948, 507-510
Separation of church and state. *See* Establishment Clause
Sex discrimination. *See* Gender discrimination
Sex offenders, 63
Sexually oriented speech, 196-236
   child pornography, 207-211
     mere possession, 222-223
     sexual performances by children, 207-210
     virtual images, 210-211
   control of, 221-223
   low-value sexual speech, 211-221
     adult entertainment, 212-215
     arguments for protecting, 220-221
     nude dancing, 215-220
     zoning ordinances, 212-215
   nude dancing, 215-220
   obscenity, 196, 197-206. *See also* Obscenity
   overview, 196-197
   pornography, 206-207
   profanity, 223-236. *See also* Profanity
Sexual orientation and freedom of association, 465-470
Shopping centers, freedom of expression in, 409
Sidewalks and freedom of expression on government property, 374-379, 406, 408
Sign ordinances, 14-20
Slander. *See* Defamation
Smith Act of 1940
   association, freedom of, 442
   incitement of illegal activity, 155-160
Social media, 63
Solicitation. *See also* Commercial speech
   accountants, 274-275
   attorneys, 273-274

"Son of Sam" laws, 29
Sound amplification devices
   government property, freedom of expression on, 388
   prior restraints, 93
Speech, freedom of. *See* Expression, freedom of
Speech or Debate Clause, 300
States
   incorporation doctrine. *See* Incorporation doctrine
   legislative chaplains, 615-624
Stolen Valor Act of 2005, 20-21
Strict separation, 579-580
Subject-matter restrictions
   content-based versus content-neutral laws, 21, 22, 29
   limited public forums, 393
Substance abuse. *See* Drug use
Subversive organizations
   incitement of illegal activity, 155-160
   vagueness, 59
Sunday closing laws
   Free Exercise Clause, 519
   Lemon test, 592
Symbolic endorsement test, 581-583
Symbolic speech, 314-364
   campaign finance, 325-364. *See also* Campaign finance
   conduct as communicative, 314-315
   draft card burning, 315-319
   flag desecration, 319-325
   government regulation of, 315-364
   intent to communicate, 315
   O'Brien test, 315-319
   overview, 314
   "speech" construed, 314
   substantial likelihood of understanding conduct, 315

Taxation
   Free Exercise Clause, 519-520
   parochial schools, tax credits for, 665-666
   press, freedom of, 472-477
   religious organizations, tax exemptions for, 681-682
   veterans' tax exemption and unconstitutional condition doctrine, 123-124
Teachers
   association, freedom of, 445
   free exercise of religion, and choice of teachers, 540-548
   public school teachers in parochial schools, 654
Telephones, profanity on, 230
Television. *See* Broadcast media; Cable television regulation
Ten Commandments
   display on government property, 592, 624-644
   Lemon test, 592
Terrorism and incitement of illegal activity, 163-172
Texas license plate design, 51-57
Threats as fighting words, 176-177
Time, place, and manner restrictions and freedom of expression on government property, 373-389

Index

Tobacco sales
   advertising, 278-284
   commercial speech, 278-284
Tort actions
   defamation, 288-302. *See also* Defamation
   emotional distress, intentional infliction of, 302-309
     picketing, 304-309
     print media, 302-304
   public disclosure of private facts, 309-313
     nongovernment sources, 312-313
     rape victims, 309-312
   publicity, right of, 313-314
Trademarks, 22-29
Trade names
   advertising, 272-273
   commercial speech, 272-273

Unconstitutional condition doctrine, 123-136
   abortion, 124-129
   legal aid, 129-135
   opposition to prostitution and human trafficking, policy of, 135-136
   public television, 124
   veterans and property tax exemption, 123-124
Unemployment compensation and Free Exercise Clause, 518
Unions. *See* Labor unions
United States Leadership Against HIV/AIDS, Tuberculosis, and Malaria Act of 2003, 135
Universities. *See* Colleges and universities
Utilities
   advertising, 266-269
   commercial speech, 266-269

Vagueness, 57-59, 373
   defined, 57
   fighting words, 176-178
   overbreadth, relationship to, 64-65
   overview, 57
   picketing, 58-59
   subversive organizations, 59
Vermont
   contribution and expenditure limits, 334-335
   Prescription Confidentiality Law, 259-266
Veterans' property tax exemption and unconstitutional condition doctrine, 123-124
Victims of crime and public disclosure of private facts, 309-312
Video games and freedom of expression, 244-251
Viewpoint neutrality
   compelled association, 457-460
   conduct that communicates, 352
   content-based versus content-neutral laws, 22-29, 43, 50
   government property, speech on, 370, 407
   limited public forums, 393-405
   when government must make content-based choices, 43
Violent speech, 236-251
   animal cruelty, depiction of, 237-243
   video games, 244-251
Voir dire and freedom of press, 494-495
Vouchers for parochial schools, 666-680

War protesters
   incitement of illegal activity, 141-148, 160
   profanity, 223-226
Watergate affair and freedom of press, 480
Welfare and Free Exercise Clause, 520

Zoning ordinances
   adult entertainment, 212-215
   low-value sexual speech, 211-215